THE
AMERICAN
PEOPLES

ENCYCLOPEDIA
YEAR BOOK
1976

Grolier
INCORPORATED
NEW YORK

EDITORIAL STAFF

CONTENTS

FEATURE ARTICLES OF THE YEAR

THE UNITED STATES BICENTENNIAL   Page 17

Contributor—**Warren Stanton Woodward.** The executive secretary of the National Society of the Sons of the American Revolution reviews what has been done and what is planned for the Bicentennial, discusses the background and meaning of the celebration, and describes the Freedom Train. A list of major Bicentennial events in 1976 is also included.

SOUTHEAST ASIA: THE END OF THE WAR   Page 22

Contributors—**Richard Butwell, Andrew H. Malcolm,** and **Elmer Plischke.** With the end of the Indochina War in 1975, a new cultural and political era began in Southeast Asia. The feature includes a review of the year's events, a special report on the refugees, and an analysis of the impact of the Vietnam experience on U. S. foreign policy. There is also a chronology of the political and military events in 1940–75.

THE LEGACY OF MICHELANGELO   Page 32

Contributor—**Charles Seymour, Jr.** The year 1975 marked the 500th anniversary of the Italian artist's birth. The feature discusses Michelangelo's work and life and appraises his extraordinary influence on the arts. There is also a list of significant celebrations in 1975.

THE NEW POWER IN THE MIDDLE EAST: IRAN TODAY   Page 36

Contributors—**Arthur Campbell Turner, John R. Matthews, Jr.,** and **Roger M. Savory.** A political scientist examines the domestic and foreign policy of Iran, the emerging power of the Middle East, and the nation's influence on the rest of the world. A profile of the Shah and his family, a special report on the Iranian petroleum industry, and a review of Iran's historical and cultural traditions are also included.

HOCKEY FEVER   Page 46

Contributors—**Hal Trumble** and **Gerald Eskenazi.** There has been a tremendous increase in player participation and spectator interest in hockey during the 1970's, and more and more children are making hockey their sport. An amateur hockey official describes the boom in the amateur game. A sports reporter and author outlines the expansion in professional hockey.

HOUSEPLANTS   Page 54

Contributor—**James Fanning.** A landscape architect and gardening editor examines the increasing interest in houseplants and indoor gardening. In addition to a discussion of home and office horticulture, there is a section describing the selection and care of popular houseplants.

PREVENTIVE HEALTH CARE   Page 60

Contributors—**Jane F. Jackson** and **Irwin J. Polk, M. D.** Millions of people in the United States are utilizing medical screening to diagnose diseases in their early stages. The feature describes the trends and various techniques in preventive health care, including cancer diagnosis, prenatal diagnosis, modern X ray, ultrasonic monitoring, and thermography.

THE ALPHABETICAL SECTION

Articles listed below are in the *Review of the Year* section, which begins on page 66, and are grouped in broad subject categories for the aid of the reader. In addition, separate entries on the continents, the major nations of the world, U. S. states, and Canadian provinces will be found under their own alphabetically arranged headings.

ECONOMICS, BUSINESS, AND INDUSTRY

ENTERTAINMENT AND HOBBIES

GOVERNMENT, LAW, AND POLITICS

HUMAN WELFARE

HUMANITIES AND THE ARTS

SCIENCE AND MEDICINE

MISCELLANEOUS

CHRONOLOGY 1975

JANUARY

S	M	T	W	T	F	S
			1	2	3	4
5	6	7	8	9	10	11
12	13	14	15	16	17	18
19	20	21	22	23	24	25
26	27	28	29	30	31	

TOP NIXON AIDES CONVICTED
STEELERS CAPTURE NFL TITLE
FRAUNCES TAVERN BOMBED

JANUARY

1 H. R. Haldeman, John N. Mitchell, John D. Erlichman, and Robert C. Mardian, former top aides of President Richard Nixon, are convicted of conspiracy to obstruct justice in the Watergate case.

2 U. S. Secretary of State Henry Kissinger warns that the United States would consider using military force in the Middle East if "the strangulation of the industrialized world" is threatened.

5 President Gerald R. Ford names an eight-member commission, headed by Vice President Nelson A. Rockefeller, to investigate charges against the Central Intelligence Agency.

8 John W. Dean III, Herbert W. Kalmbach and Jeb Stuart Magruder, three former Nixon aides, are released from prison.

12 The Pittsburgh Steelers capture their first National Football League title by defeating the Minnesota Vikings 16–6 at the ninth annual Super Bowl.

15 President Ford outlines a shift in economic policy to combat recession in his State of the Union Message to Democratic 94th Congress.

17 The People's Republic of China adopts a new constitution.

22 In a challenge to the seniority system House Democrats remove three committee chairmen: Wright Patman, W. P. Poage, and F. Edward Hébert.

23 Canadian External Affairs Minister MacEachen announces that the end of a "special relationship" between the United States and Canada was in Canada's best economic interests.

24 A bomb explosion in Fraunces Tavern, a New York City landmark, kills 4 and injures 53.

31 Charles W. Colson, President Nixon's former special counsel, is released from prison.

President Ford delivers his State of the Union message on January 15 as Vice President Rockefeller (*left*) and House Speaker Albert applaud.

UPI

MENOMINEES END OCCUPATION
THATCHER NAMED TORY HEAD
KING CROWNED IN NEPAL

FEBRUARY

S	M	T	W	T	F	S
						1
2	3	4	5	6	7	8
9	10	11	12	13	14	15
16	17	18	19	20	21	22
23	24	25	26	27	28	

FEBRUARY

2 To conserve energy, the Canadian government imposes a 55-mile (88-km) speed limit for federal vehicles.

3 President Ford submits a $349.44 billion budget, with a projected deficit of $51.9 billion, to Congress.

4 A group of Menominee Indians voluntarily end their 35-day occupation of a Roman Catholic novitiate in Gresham, Wis., in return for an agreement for the deed to the property.

5 The Senate confirms the nomination of Edward H. Levi as U. S. attorney general.

7 The U. S. Labor Department announces that the January unemployment rate reached 8.2%, the highest in 33 years.

9 Two Soviet cosmonauts land in central Asia after spending a period of 30 days in an orbiting space station, completing the Soviet Union's longest manned space flight.

11 Margaret Thatcher is elected leader of the Conservative party, becoming the first woman to head a British political party.

12 A national referendum in South Korea approves President Park Chung Hee's government and the new constitution that followed Park's imposition of martial law in 1972.

13 Turkish Cypriots announce the formation of a separate state in the northern section of the island, a move denounced by Greek Cypriots.

14 A pact between the United States and representatives of the Mariana Islands establishes the Commonwealth of the Northern Mariana Islands and paves the way for the first U. S. territorial acquisition since 1917.

24 Birendra Biv Bikram Shah Dev is crowned king of Nepal in ceremonies held in Katmandu.

25 Greece reports the arrest of 37 officers charged with plotting against the government.

27 A national referendum in the Philippines expresses strong support for the martial law of President Ferdinand E. Marcos. ● Attorney General Levi confirms the existence of secret Federal Bureau of Investigation files kept on the private lives of presidents, congressmen, and other prominent people by order of J. Edgar Hoover.

28 The European Economic Community and 46 developing nations in Africa, the Pacific, and the Caribbean sign a comprehensive, five-year trade aid pact in Lomé, Togo.

UPI

Margaret Thatcher, first woman to head a political party in Great Britain, was selected as the Conservative leader on February 11. She visited the United States later in the year.

MARCH

S	M	T	W	T	F	S
						1
2	3	4	5	6	7	8
9	10	11	12	13	14	15
16	17	18	19	20	21	22
23 30	24 31	25	26	27	28	29

U.S. BICENTENNIAL BEGINS
N.Y.C. DOCTORS' STRIKE ENDS
KING FAISAL ASSASSINATED

MARCH

1 The American Revolution Bicentennial celebration officially begins.

2 Iran's two-party system is dissolved by Shah Mohammed Reza Pahlavi, making Iran a one party state "for at least the next two years."

3 A congressional fact-finding delegation studying President Ford's request for $522 million in supplemental aid to South Vietnam and Cambodia returns from Indochina.

4 President Ford vetoes a bill suspending the president's power to raise imported oil tariffs by $3 a barrel, but he agrees to 60-day delay in increase. ● Ethiopia's provisional military government nationalizes all rural land. ● For the first time, regular proceedings of Canadian parliament are televised.

5 In a clash that takes 18 lives, Israeli soldiers storm a Tel Aviv hotel captured by Palestinian guerrillas.

6 John T. Dunlop is confirmed by Congress as U. S. secretary of labor.

11 Followers of Gen. António de Spinola attempt a military coup against Portugal's leftist provisional government but are defeated by loyal troops.

12 Maurice H. Stans, former Nixon cabinet member and chief fund raiser, enters a guilty plea to violating federal campaign finance laws.

17 In a unanimous ruling, the U. S. Supreme Court awards to the federal government exclusive rights to oil and natural gas reserves under the Atlantic Ocean's continental shelf.

18 Details of a $250 million CIA operation in 1974 to salvage a Soviet submarine that sank in 1968 in the Pacific Ocean are disclosed.

20 President Nguyen Van Thieu acknowledges a worsening military situation in South Vietnam as northern and highland provinces are abandoned by government forces as the Communists advance. ● A strike by interns and resident physicians at 21 New York City hospitals ends.

24 The beaver is adopted as the official symbol of Canada.

25 Faisal, king of Saudi Arabia since 1964, is assassinated by a nephew and is succeeded by his half-brother Khalid.

29 President Ford signs a compromise bill providing for a $22.8 billion tax cut.

31 UCLA defeats the University of Kentucky, 92–85, to win the NCAA basketball championship. ● The clemency program for Vietnam War deserters and draft evaders ends, with 22,500 of a possible 124,-400 participating.

UPI

(*Below*) Representatives John Flynt (*center*) and Paul McClosky (*right*) confer with President Ford on March 5, following their return on March 3 from a fact-finding trip to Southeast Asia. (*Right*) New York City doctors picket Mount Sinai Hospital during strike that threatened medical care before it ended on March 20.

UPI

DALEY REELECTED TO 6TH TERM

CHIANG KAI-SHEK DIES AT 87

WAR ENDS IN SOUTHEAST ASIA

			APRIL			
S	M	T	W	T	F	S
		1	2	3	4	5
6	7	8	9	10	11	12
13	14	15	16	17	18	19
20	21	22	23	24	25	26
27	28	29	30			

UPI

Chicago's Mayor Richard Daley (*above*) won an unprecedented sixth 4-year term in April 1 election. (*Below*) After South Vietnam's surrender on April 30, soldiers of the Communist forces, protected by tanks, enter the presidential palace in the center of Saigon.

UPI

APRIL

1 President Lon Nol leaves Cambodia in an attempt to facilitate attempts at peace negotiations between the government and Khmer Rouge rebels. ● Chicago Mayor Richard J. Daley is reelected to a sixth 4-year term, defeating the opposing candidate by 5–1 margin. ● Canada begins a gradual conversion to the metric system.

4 A U.S. Air Force cargo jet carrying 319 passengers, mostly Vietnam orphans bound for the United States, crashes near Saigon, killing over 200 people.

5 The leader of Nationalist China, President Chiang Kai-shek, dies in Taipei at the age of 87. His son, Chiang Ching-kuo, remains premier; C. K. Yen becomes president.

8 The Canadian government announces that March unemployment reached a 14-year high.

13 President Ngarta Tombalbaye of Chad dies in a military coup that overthrows his government.

14 In a referendum voters in Sikkim approve the abolition of the monarchy and a merger with India.

16 The Cambodian government surrenders to the Khmer Rouge rebels, ending the bitterly contested, 5-year civil war in Cambodia.

17 John B. Connally, Jr., former secretary of the treasury, is acquitted of bribery charges.

21 President Nguyen Van Thieu of South Vietnam resigns and is succeeded by Vice President Tran Van Huong.

22 A bloodless coup in Honduras results in the replacement of president Gen. Oswaldo López Arellano with Col. Juan Alberto Melgar Castro, the commander of the armed forces.

23 In an address at Tulane University in New Orleans, President Ford announces the end of American involvement in the Vietnam War.

24 The U.S. Congress approves emergency evacuation and humanitarian relief to South Vietnam, including the use of U.S. troops for protection.

25 The Khmer Rouge government in Cambodia names Prince Norodom Sihanouk, in exile in China, as chief of state for life.

30 The South Vietnamese government surrenders to the Communists, ending the war in Vietnam. The U.S. evacuation airlift from South Vietnam is completed. Many flee South Vietnam in small boats and are eventually rescued at sea by U.S. ships.

MAY

S	M	T	W	T	F	S
				1	2	3
4	5	6	7	8	9	10
11	12	13	14	15	16	17
18	19	20	21	22	23	24
25	26	27	28	29	30	31

U.S. JOBLESS AT RECORD HIGH
MAYAGUEZ CREW RESCUED
WARRIORS CAPTURE NBA TITLE

MAY

2 An unemployment rate of 8.9% in April, the highest since 1941, is announced by the U. S. Labor Department.

5 Canada raises the export price of its natural gas and lowers the export tax on crude oil to bring prices in line with world market conditions.

8 Members of Canadian parliament receive controversial 33⅓% pay increase retroactive to July 8, 1974.

11 A trade and cooperation pact between the European Economic Community and Israel is signed in Brussels.

14 U. S. forces rescue 39 crewmen of the U. S. merchant ship *Mayaguez,* seized by Cambodia on May 12 in the Gulf of Siam.

15 Rashid Solh, premier of Lebanon, resigns over criticism of the government's handling of April clashes with Palestinian guerrillas. ● Portugal declares martial law in Angola following weeks of violence.

16 Britain announces that the country's rate of inflation rose a record 3.9% in April.

20 President Ford vetoes strip mining bill.

21 Britain announces that the British Solomon Islands will be granted independence by mid-1977.

22 The American Basketball Association crown goes to the Kentucky Colonels, victors over the Indiana Pacers.

25 The Golden State Warriors defeat the Washington Bullets to capture the National Basketball Association championship.

27 In an 8–1 vote, the U. S. Supreme Court upholds congressional subpoena power. ● Hockey's Philadelphia Flyers repeat as Stanley Cup champions, defeating the Buffalo Sabres.

28 Officials of 15 West African nations sign a treaty in Lagos, Nigeria, forming the Economic Community of West African States (ECOWAS).

29 President Ford vetoes a $5.3 billion job bill, calling its provisions of "questionable value" to economic recovery. ● NATO summit meeting convenes in Brussels.

U.S. NAVY

UPI

(Above) U. S. Marines guard the *Mayaguez* following its recapture on May 14. Cambodian Communists had captured the ship on May 12. *(Right)* Golden State Warriors' Keith Wilkes tries to shoot over Elvin Hayes of Washington Bullets in NBA championship won by Warriors.

SUEZ CANAL IS REOPENED
ROCKEFELLER REPORTS ON CIA
CRASH AT JFK KILLS 113

JUNE

S	M	T	W	T	F	S
1	2	3	4	5	6	7
8	9	10	11	12	13	14
15	16	17	18	19	20	21
22	23	24	25	26	27	28
29	30					

JUNE

5 Egyptian president Anwar el-Sadat formally opens the Suez Canal, closed since the 1967 Israeli-Arab War. ● In Britain's first national referendum, 67.2% of the voters endorse continued British membership in the European Economic Community.

7 UN-sponsored discussions in Vienna between Greek Cypriot and Turkish Cypriot leaders end without agreement on the future of the divided island.

9 Greek President Michael Stassinopoulos signs a new republican constitution approved by parliament two days earlier.

10 The report issued by the Rockefeller Commission finds that the Central Intelligence Agency engaged in unlawful acts and makes recommendations to prevent the recurrence of such illegal operations. ● The New York state legislature establishes the Municipal Assistance Corporation, to direct the financial practices of New York City.

12 Prime Minister Indira Gandhi of India is convicted of illegal election practices in her campaign for her seat in parliament in 1971.

13 The World Bank plans establishment of a facility to provide low-cost loans totaling $1 billion to developing countries. ● A treaty of "reconciliation" between Iran and Iraq, fixing the border and ending Iran's long-standing support of Kurdish rebels, is signed in Baghdad, Iraq.

16 The U. S. Supreme Court rules unanimously that setting uniform legal fees is price fixing and a violation of antitrust laws.

17 Results in regional elections throughout Italy show substantial gains for the Communist party, which polled 33.4% of the vote. ● In a plebiscite, the people of the Mariana Islands vote to accept U. S. commonwealth status and to become U. S. citizens.

23 A record budget of nearly $36 billion is presented to the Canadian House of Commons.

24 An Eastern Airlines jet crashes while landing at Kennedy Airport in New York City, killing 113 people.

25 After 500 years of colonial rule by Portugal and a bitter guerrilla war, the People's Republic of Mozambique becomes independent.

26 India's Prime Minister Gandhi declares a state of emergency and arrests of her political foes begin. ● Responding to pressure from the Pathet Lao government, the United States ends its program of economic assistance in Laos. ● The U. S. Supreme Court declares that mentally ill persons cannot be held in institutions against their will if they present no danger to the public and can live in society. ● The United States terminates its economic aid program in Laos.

30 President Ford signs a bill extending unemployment compensation to a maximum of 65 weeks through 1975. On June 25 the Labor Department had announced that 6,073,400 people were receiving unemployment benefits.

UPI

Egyptian destroyer (*left*) reopens Suez Canal on June 5. (*Below*) Vice President Rockefeller discusses report on CIA with President Ford.

UPI

JULY

S	M	T	W	T	F	S
		1	2	3	4	5
6	7	8	9	10	11	12
13	14	15	16	17	18	19
20	21	22	23	24	25	26
27	28	29	30	31		

WATERGATE JURY DISMISSED
APOLLO/SOYUZ MEET IN SPACE
OAS VOTES TO END BAN ON CUBA

JULY

2 The UN-sponsored International Women's Year Conference, meeting in Mexico City, ends with the adoption of a 10-year plan to promote equality between the sexes and participation of women in national development.

3 The third and last Watergate grand jury, which had served since January 1974, is dismissed in Washington.

5 Portuguese rule in the Cape Verde Islands ends with the islands' independence; the new nation retains close ties with Guinea-Bissau. ● Arthur Ashe defeats Jimmy Connors at Wimbledon to win the coveted tennis title for the first time.

9 British trade unions agree to limited pay raises and salary freezes in an effort to curb Britain's high inflation rate and to restore economic confidence.

10 British citizen Denis Hills is released following his pardon by President Idi Amin in Uganda, where he had been condemned to death for criticism of Amin.

12 The islands of São Tomé and Príncipe, off the west coast of Africa, gain independence as five centuries of Portuguese domination end.

15 The Apollo/Soyuz space mission begins, marking the first time that manned spacecraft built and launched by two different nations, the United States and the USSR, will rendezvous in space.

16 Canadian government officials announce plans to reduce exports of natural gas to the United States, citing a threatened domestic shortage.

19 Constantine Tsatsos is elected first president of the Greek republic under the new constitution.

25 After only six weeks in office as secretary of the interior, Stanley K. Hathaway resigns for health reasons.

26 U. S. military bases in Turkey are taken over by Turkish military forces following the refusal of Congress to permit arms sales to Turkey.

29 Fifteen Latin American nations and the United States vote to end the ban of the Organization of American States (OAS) on diplomatic and commercial relations with Cuba. ● The 12th annual Organization of African Unity (OAU) summit conference in Kampala, Uganda, is interrupted by reports of a Nigerian coup that ends the rule of Gen. Yakubu Gowon.

30 In Helsinki, 35 nations are represented at the opening of the Conference on Security and Cooperation in Europe, the largest summit conference ever held in Europe.

31 Former teamster president James R. Hoffa is reported missing in Detroit.

UPI

(*Above*) Mexican Foreign Minister Rabaza discusses sanctions against Cuba, which were ended on July 29. (*Below*) Cosmonaut Valery Kubasov autographs the Soyuz capsule following space mission that began on July 15.

UPI

TERRORISTS SEIZE U.S. CONSUL
SAMUEL BRONFMAN KIDNAPPED
PRESIDENT OF PERU OUSTED

AUGUST

S	M	T	W	T	F	S
					1	2
3	4	5	6	7	8	9
10	11	12	13	14	15	16
17	18	19	20	21	22	23
24 31	25	26	27	28	29	30

AUGUST

4 Portugal begins emergency airlift to evacuate Portuguese refugees from Angola before the oil-rich, west African territory becomes independent on November 11.

6 The Indian Parliament votes retroactive changes in the election law under which Prime Minister Indira Gandhi was convicted of campaign violations. ● President Ford signs a seven-year extension of the Voting Rights Act, which is broadened to include linguistic minorities.

8 The U. S. consul and 52 hostages, seized when the U. S. Consulate in Kuala Lumpur, Malaysia, was raided by armed terrorists of the Japanese Red Army on August 4, are released in exchange for freedom for the terrorists and 5 comrades imprisoned in Japan.

10 On the fourth anniversary of the introduction of the British government's internment policy, Belfast, Northern Ireland, is hit by the worst violence in two years.

11 The announcement is made of the return by Cuba to the United States of nearly $2 million in ransom money taken from three airline hijackers who landed on the island in 1972.

15 Sheik Mujibur Rahman, president of Bangladesh, is assassinated in a coup led by dissident military officers; Commerce Minister Khandakar Mushtaque Ahmed takes over the presidency.

17 Samuel Bronfman 2nd, 21-year-old heir to the Seagram distilling fortune, is released unharmed after being kidnapped eight days earlier.

18 Maritime unions of the AFL-CIO boycott the loading of grain sold to the Soviet Union, to protest the sale's effects on domestic consumer prices and to try to force an agreement to carry the grain in U. S. ships. ● China and Cambodia sign an agreement on economic and technical cooperation in Peking.

20 Former President Richard M. Nixon asserts his right to decide on the public release of his White House tapes and documents in a deposition made public for the first time.

21 The U. S. trade embargo, in force since the 1960's, against Cuba is eased.

25 Death sentences of former Greek President George Papadopoulos and two fellow officers, who participated in a military coup in 1967, are commuted by the Greek cabinet.

27 Ohio Gov. James A. Rhodes and 27 other defendants in the Kent State trial are exonerated of responsibility in connection with the shooting of students in 1970.

29 Juan Velasco Alvarado, president of Peru, is overthrown by his military commanders and is replaced by Gen. Francisco Morales Bermúdez.

31 The House Select Committee on Intelligence Activities learns that almost all overseas telephone calls from and to the United States are being monitored by the National Security Agency.

(Below) Rioters are dispersed after violence broke out in Northern Ireland on August 10. **(Right)** Malaysian Prime Minister Razak enters terrorist-occupied U. S. Embassy.

UPI

UPI

SEPTEMBER

S	M	T	W	T	F	S
	1	2	3	4	5	6
7	8	9	10	11	12	13
14	15	16	17	18	19	20
21	22	23	24	25	26	27
28	29	30				

ISRAEL AND EGYPT OK PACT
EARTHQUAKE HITS TURKEY
PATTY HEARST APPREHENDED

SEPTEMBER

1 In Ecuador, a revolt led by the armed forces chief of staff, Gen. Raul Alvéar, and supported by conservative civilian politicians, is crushed by troops loyal to President Guillermo Rodríguez Lara.

2 Canada, with the world's fourth largest foreign aid budget, announces a policy that would concentrate its assistance on the 40 poorest nations.

4 Israel and Egypt sign an interim agreement on the Sinai, with Israel giving up territory and receiving access to the Suez Canal; the United States will help finance peace-keeping costs and will provide civilian advisors to monitor the accord.

5 The 30th annual joint meeting of the International Monetary Fund and the World Bank ends its sessions in Washington, D. C., with a spirit of compromise and cooperation among the participating nations. ● Lynette Fromme, a member of convicted murderer Charles Manson's "family," is apprehended in Sacramento after she points a gun at President Ford. ● Sudanese rebel army officers seize a state radio station and announce the overthrow of the government of President Jaafar al-Numeiry, but the revolt is crushed by loyal troops within hours.

6 Gen. Vasco Gonçalves resigns as head of Portugal's caretaker government. ● An earthquake levels an area of eastern Turkey and causes 2,312 deaths.

8 Boston public schools begin city-wide busing to achieve integration in an atmosphere of tension, but violence is avoided. ● The Republican party selects Kansas City as the site of its 1976 national convention.

9 Prince Norodom Sihanouk returns to Cambodia after five years of exile in Peking.

13 President Isabel Perón of Argentina begins a month-long leave of absence as criticism of her rule mounts but cites health reasons for the decision.

14 Elizabeth Ann Bayley Seton, the first native American to become a saint, is canonized by Pope Paul VI in ceremonies in Rome.

16 A special election in New Hampshire ends the dispute over New Hampshire's vacant U. S. Senate seat, with Democrat John Durkin defeating Republican Louis Wyman. ● Papua New Guinea achieves independence as a member of the British Commonwealth of Nations.

18 Patricia Hearst is arrested by the Federal Bureau of Investigation after a nationwide search of 19 months.

22 A shot is fired at President Gerald Ford by Sara Jane Moore in San Francisco, but for the second time in a month he escapes harm.

27 Canada's Prime Minister Pierre Elliott Trudeau announces cabinet changes in the wake of the resignation of Finance Minister John Turner two weeks earlier. ● The Organization of Petroleum Exporting Countries agrees in Vienna to a 10% increase in the price of crude oil, effective October 1.

Patricia Hearst, arrested by agents of the Federal Bureau of Investigation on September 18, leaves jail for a court appearance.

UPI

HIROHITO VISITS U.S.

MAIL STRIKE STUNS CANADA

REDS WIN WORLD SERIES

OCTOBER

S	M	T	W	T	F	S
			1	2	3	4
5	6	7	8	9	10	11
12	13	14	15	16	17	18
19	20	21	22	23	24	25
26	27	28	29	30	31	

UPI

(*Above*) Controversy erupted in the World Series when the Cincinnati Reds' Ed Armbrister collided with Boston Red Sox catcher Carlton Fisk. (*Below*) Emperor Hirohito (*left*) and Empress Nagako of Japan see the sights of San Francisco with Mayor Joseph Alioto.

UPI

OCTOBER

1 Italian Premier Aldo Moro anounces the settlement of the dispute between his country and Yugoslavia over Trieste, with Italy surrendering claim to the Istrian coast area. ● In Manila, Muhammad Ali defeats Joe Frazier in the 15th round to retain the world heavyweight boxing title.

4 Canada's Mirabel International Airport, said to be the world's largest, opens near Montreal.

9 Thomas S. Kleppe, formerly administrator of the Small Business Administration, is confirmed by the U. S. Senate as secretary of the interior.

10 Israel signs the protocol of the Sinai disengagement pact, which had been signed September 23 by Egypt. ● I. K. Acheampong, Ghana's head of state, creates a seven-member Supreme Military Council as the country's highest legislative and administrative body in an effort to enhance the role of the military.

13 King Khalid of Saudi Arabia forms a new cabinet, distributing power evenly between two factions of the royal family. ● Japanese Emperor Hirohito ends his goodwill tour of the United States, the first reigning Japanese monarch to make such a visit.

16 Argentine President Isabel Perón returns to office after rejecting advice by top military and political aides that she prolong her leave of absence or resign in view of the nation's political and economic crisis.

17 The New York City teachers union agrees to purchase $150 million of Municipal Assistance Corporation bonds from pension funds, rescuing New York City from default.

20 The United States and the Soviet Union reach a 5-year agreement whereby the Soviets will purchase 6–8 million tons of U. S. grain annually.

21 A nationwide mail strike begins in Canada after negotiations with the Canadian Union of Postal Workers breaks down.

22 The Cincinnati Reds defeat the Boston Red Sox in 7 games to win their first World Series in 35 years. Cincinnati's Pete Rose is selected as the series' most valuable player:

24 Turkey's ambassador to France Ismail Erez is shot to death in Paris, two days after Danis Tunaligil, ambassador to Austria, was assassinated in Vienna.

30 Prince Juan Carlos assumes power as Spain's chief of state during the critical illness of Generalissimo Francisco Franco.

NOVEMBER

S	M	T	W	T	F	S
						1
2	3	4	5	6	7	8
9	10	11	12	13	14	15
16	17	18	19	20	21	22
23 30	24	25	26	27	28	29

SCHLESINGER LEAVES POST
ANGOLA GETS INDEPENDENCE
FRANCISCO FRANCO DIES

NOVEMBER

3 Vice President Nelson A. Rockefeller announces that he has withdrawn his name from consideration as vice president in 1976. ● President Gerald Ford reorganizes his cabinet. Donald H. Rumsfeld replaces James R. Schlesinger as secretary of defense; George Bush is named to succeed William E. Colby as CIA director; Brent Scowcroft replaces Henry Kissinger as National Security Council director; and Eliott Richardson replaces Rogers Morton as secretary of commerce.

6 Thousands of Moroccans begin a march into Spanish Sahara, upon which Algeria and Mauritania have also made claims. ● Bangladesh President Khandakar Mushtaque Ahmed is replaced by former Supreme Court Chief Justice A. S. Sayem.

7 India's Supreme Court reverses the conviction of Prime Minister Indira Gandhi for election fraud, citing the retroactive changes in the election code by Parliament.

10 The UN approves 72–35 a resolution that terms Zionism as "a form of racism." ● New Jersey Superior Court Judge Robert Muir, Jr., refuses to authorize removal of life-sustaining devices from Karen Ann Quinlan, whose parents had instituted a suit asking that the brain-damaged girl be permitted to die.

11 For the first time in Australia's history a governor general, Sir John Kerr, removed a prime minister, Gough Whitlam, and dissolved Parliament. ● Angola becomes independent as Portuguese rule ends, with distinct governments proclaimed by rival liberation groups.

12 Supreme Court Justice William O. Douglas retires from the court after 36 years, citing poor health.

13 Finance Minister Donald Macdonald predicts that Canada will end its current fiscal year March 31 with a $5 billion deficit.

14 President Ford signs into law an increase of $18 billion in the temporary debt ceiling, effective through March 15, that raises the total debt ceiling to $595 billion.

20 Generalissimo Francisco Franco, Spain's dictator since 1939, dies after a prolonged illness. ● The Senate select committee investigating the Central Intelligence Agency reports that U. S. officials participated in plots to kill foreign leaders.

22 Juan Carlos, acting chief of state since October 30, is proclaimed King Juan Carlos I of Spain.

25 Surinam is granted independence from the Netherlands after 300 years of colonial rule.

UPI

(*Above*) Juan Carlos, who became king of Spain on November 22, meets with tribesmen in the Spanish Sahara. (*Below*) At his departure ceremony, Secretary of Defense James Schlesinger, replaced in November 3 cabinet reshuffle, reviews the troops for the last time.

UPI

ISRAELI JETS RAID LEBANON
FORD VISITS PEKING
OPEC MINISTERS KIDNAPPED

DECEMBER

S	M	T	W	T	F	S
1	2	3	4	5	6	7
8	9	10	11	12	13	14
15	16	17	18	19	20	21
22	23	24	25	26	27	28
29	30	31				

DECEMBER

2 Israeli jets raid Palestinian refugee camps in Lebanon, with heavy death toll reported.

3 The Pathet Lao announce the end of the monarchy in Laos, the abolition of the coalition government, and the establishment of a republic.

5 President Ford leaves China after conferences with Chinese leaders. ● Britain ends the detention without trial of suspected Northern Ireland terrorists, a practice begun in 1971.

9 South Boston High School is placed in federal receivership by federal Judge Arthur Garrity, Jr., for stalling on desegregation.

12 In London four Irish Republican Army terrorists surrender and release their hostages after a 6-day siege. ● Three years of Socialist government ends in British Columbia as voters restore the conservative Social Credit party to power.

14 After being held hostage for 12 days, 23 captives are released in Beilin, the Netherlands, by terrorists demanding the independence of South Moluccas from Indonesia.

17 Lynette Fromme is sentenced to life imprisonment for attempting to assassinate President Gerald Ford on September 5.

18 The Canadian government announces a $1.5 billion cut in government expenditures.

19 John Paul Stevens is sworn in by Chief Justice Warren Burger as the 101st Supreme Court justice. ● The U. S. Congress passes a compromise tax bill that includes a commitment to control government spending and extends the tax cut for six months.

21 An attempted coup against the government of Argentine President Isabel Perón by members of the air force ends in a peace agreement.

27 An explosion, followed by flooding, traps hundreds of Indian coal miners 160 miles (255 km) northwest of Calcutta; at least 400 are feared dead.

29 A bomb explodes at New York City's LaGuardia Airport, killing 11 and injuring at least 75.

31 Higher U. S. postal rates take effect.

UPI

Chinese Deputy Premier Teng Hsiao-p'ing and President Gerald Ford dine on December 4 at the final banquet during the President's state visit to China.

Bicentennial marchers in Concord, Mass., recreate on April 19, 1975, the conflict of which, poet Ralph Waldo Emerson said, "embattled farmers . . . fired the shot heard round the world." Over 150,000 people attended the reenactment of the Battle of Lexington and Concord.

THE UNITED STATES
BICENTENNIAL

By Warren Stanton Woodward
Executive Secretary, National Society of the
Sons of the American Revolution

On July 4, 1976, the United States of America will observe its 200th birthday. The year 1975 saw the acceleration of Bicentennial events, especially in the East. As the nation stands on the threshold of its third century of independence, a re-dedication to those principles established by the Founding Fathers and a renewed pride in heritage are emerging prominently. The Bicentennial is being celebrated by Americans and the friends of America throughout the world.

Although the Bicentennial will not lose its identity as an American event, it will underline the critical importance of mutual international understanding and respect among all men. In a similar vein, it stresses that, while the past is important, the United States must concentrate on the future of the nation, so it can provide an even better life for future generations.

Background. Plans for the Bicentennial celebration officially commenced on July 4, 1966, with the establishment of the American Revolution Bicentennial Commission by Congress. The Commission was replaced by the American Revolution Bicentennial Administration (ARBA) on Dec. 11, 1973. The mission of the ARBA, as defined by Congress, is "to coordinate, to facilitate, and to aid in the scheduling of events, activities, and projects of local, state, national, and international significance sponsored by both governmental and nongovernmental entities in commemoration of the Bicentennial." The agency also develops criteria for the observance and evaluates the feasibility, relevance, status, and desirability of the various programs.

In 1972 an initial Bicentennial invitation was extended to all who would visit the nation during the celebration. Early in 1973, the American Revolution Bicentennial Commission inaugurated a program of compiling, publishing, and distributing material on pertinent activities. These suggestions and guidelines were designed to generate the interest of citizens at the local, state, and national levels. The American public had been quite apathetic toward the Bicentennial until the beginning of 1975, at which time a sudden and enthusiastic awareness of the approaching anniversary emerged almost overnight.

Originally, the centerpiece of the 200th anniversary was to be a gigantic exposition, similar to an international world's fair, but this plan was abandoned to ensure the unrestricted participation of the American people. By not concentrating the celebration at one geographic point, the opportunities and effectiveness of local, state, and national themes will result in a more successful Bicentennial.

Bicentennial Themes. The Federal program established three basic themes: Horizons '76, Heritage '76, and Festival USA. Horizons '76 promotes the adoption of goals that hold promise for a better life in America. Conservation, education, ecology, transportation, health, and communications are but a few of the subjects within the category of Horizons '76.

Heritage '76 encourages Americans to recognize and honor their heritage, placing it in historical perspective. This program might be termed the philosophical

Cannon smoke swirls over Great Barrington, Mass., field (*below*) at restaging of 1744 resistance to British rule. New York's Fort Ticonderoga (*right*) was recaptured by modern Ethan Allen (*left on stairs*) and Green Mountain Boys in May 10 Bicentennial celebration.

The Freedom Train began its tour of the United States in Delaware in April 1975. The train's exhibits have drawn enthusiastic crowds.

THE FREEDOM TRAIN

The Freedom Train is a prominent attraction of the Bicentennial and has captured the heart of America. The red, white, and blue train is visiting 80 cities along its 17,000-mile (27,000-km) route and attracting record crowds. Even between actual stops, crowds line the tracks.

Its 12 display cars contain magnificent examples of Americana and highlight local Bicentennial programs. A U.S. Army honor guard is on board the train and is participating in many ceremonies. The 700 items that are displayed include historical documents, artifacts, and memorabilia relevant to two centuries of American progress and accomplishment. By meticulous planning, the train will be on display within a one-hour driving distance of 90% of the nation's population, thus bringing the Bicentennial close to almost everyone's home town.

It is anticipated that 50 million people will visit the train.

Exhibits. The viewers are within inches c George Washington's copy of the Constitutic the Freedom Bell, the first Bible printed in United States, Benjamin Franklin's draft of Articles of Confederation, a Moon rock, ex' of exploration, patent drawings and mod important American inventions, a panor' American sports, a montage of the per arts, a gallery of American paintings a' ture, and much more. A moving wa' sures equal viewing opportunity. / country's many thousands of projec' dom Train seems destined to be most successful and effective in Bicentennial to the people of the

WARREN STANT

phase of the Bicentennial, with concentration upon the Declaration of I dence, the Bill of Rights, the Constitution, the preservation and restor historical sites, and reenactments of significant events of the Revolutiona'

Festival USA includes the actual expression of hospitality and we' consists of exhibits, pageants, tours, fairs, cultural performances, cc festivals. These events not only offer the opportunity of actual par visitors in many cases, but exhibit American handicrafts, culture, an

Programs. The Bicentennial Communities Program is a focal poi anniversary program. It began in 1973 with the endorsement of

An old Ben Franklin chats with a younger, smaller one during a Philadelphia kite-flying program (*above*). The Statue of Liberty (*right*) in New York City received Bicentennial repairs and cleaning.

Cities and the U. S. Conference of Mayors. Most of the country's 156 cities with a population over 100,000, as well as thousands of smaller communities, qualified for official designation. By the end of 1975, about 10,000 projects and 5,000 events had been reported at the local, state, and national levels. In addition, 26 federal agencies were involved with about 2,000 projects. Since its founding, the program has also expanded to include approximately 600 university campuses and several military facilities.

American youth is deeply involved in such programs as the Spirit Of '76 And Beyond and the National Youth Debates. The Future Farmers of America, Boy and Girl Scouts of America, Order of DeMolay, Four-H, and countless other groups are implementing programs that include community beautification, development of recreational areas, and general assistance in local Bicentennial projects.

National women's organizations have joined together in a tremendous Bicentennial program to accentuate the role and achievements of American women in society and their contributions to the nation during the past 200 years. Patriotic societies have also developed programs designed to utilize their educational, historical, and patriotic aims.

At the international level, 27 foreign countries have established American Revolution Bicentennial committees to join in the celebration. Several of these nations are sending art treasures, performing groups, and even sailing vessels to the United States to represent them. Such representation is both justified and traditional because volunteers from many nations assisted in the Revolutionary War. Further, the U. S. population, except for American Indians, has its roots in other lands.

Bicentennial Events. The first conflicts of the Revolutionary War occurred along the eastern seaboard in 1775, and the major Bicentennial programs of 1975 celebrated these landmark events. On April 19 the battles of Lexington and Concord were reenacted in those Massachusetts towns, with a crowd of over 150,000 attending the festivities, at which President Ford spoke. The restaging on June 14 of the Battle of Bunker Hill in Boston also drew huge crowds.

In New York, Fort Ticonderoga was again captured from the British on May 10, this time by descendants of Ethan Allen's original Green Mountain Boys. New

MAJOR BICENTENNIAL EVENTS
1976

Bicentennial wagon train moves east from Washington state in June on journey to Valley Forge, Pa.

Jan. 1, 1976—Nation of Nations Exhibit opens, Smithsonian Institution, Washington, D. C.

Jan. 1, 1976—Science Conference on American Future, U. S. Air Force Academy, Colorado Springs

Feb. 22, 1976—George Washington Birthday Celebration at his birthplace, Fredericksburg, Va.

March 19–21, 1976—Pioneer Crafts Festival, Rison, Ark.

April 3, 1976—Pony Express Anniversary Celebration, Sacramento, Cal.

April 23, 1976—Holiday in Dixie '76 Festival opens, Shreveport, La.

April 30, 1976—Philadelphia Festival opens with major museum exhibits

May 4, 1976—Rhode Island Independence Day Celebration, Providence

May 11, 1976—Second Continental Congress Program begins, Philadelphia

June 3, 1976—The Eye of Thomas Jefferson Exhibit opens, National Gallery of Art, Washington, D. C.

June 18–24, 1976—Hudson River Sloop Festival, Beacon and Poughkeepsie, N. Y.

June 19, 1976—Pacific Nations Festival opens, Los Angeles

June 28–July 17, 1976—George Rogers Clark Trek, Cahokia, Ill.

July 1, 1976—The World of Franklin and Jefferson Exhibit opens, The Art Institute, Chicago

July 3–4, 1976—Operation Sail, New York Harbor

July 4, 1976—Bicentennial Wagon Trains arrive in Valley Forge, Pa.

July 4, 1976—Independence Day Celebration at Washington Monument, Washington, D. C.

July 4, 1976—Formal Opening of the National Air and Space Museum, Washington, D. C.

August 14–19, 1976—Whiskey Rebellion Pageant, Washington, Pa.

August 22, 1976—Reenactment of the Battle of Long Island, Brooklyn, N. Y.

Sept. 11–12, 1976—Reenactment of 1776 Peace Conference, Staten Island, N. Y.

Sept. 13, 1976—Farmfest '76, Lake Crystal, Minn.

Dec. 25, 1976—Reenactment of Washington crossing the Delaware, Washington Crossing, Pa.

York City kicked off the Bicentennial on May 22, the 200th anniversary of the meeting of New York representatives to discuss Lexington and Concord. Philadelphia, the city with perhaps the most ambitious Bicentennial programs, marked the opening of the Second Continental Congress with a giant street festival on May 11. On July 24, Detroit celebrated the landing of its founder, Antoine de la Mothe Cadillac, in 1701.

An exotic and impressive feature of the 1976 events is Operation Sail, which involves approximately 30 tall-masted sailing ships, of which very few remain in the world. The fleet's host ship is the U. S. Coast Guard bark *Eagle*. The ships will assemble in Europe and then race to Bermuda, where they will be joined by additional vessels from the Americas and the Far East for a race to historic Newport, R. I. From there, the ships will proceed to New York Harbor for a parade in review up the Hudson River to the George Washington Bridge on July 4.

Fleeing from the advancing North Vietnamese, people from Pleiku region jam the highway leading south in March 1975.

SOUTHEAST ASIA:

The End of the War

This article consists of three parts. Richard Butwell outlines the regional changes in 1975, while Andrew H. Malcolm describes the plight of the refugees. Elmer Plischke considers the implications for American foreign policy.

THE NEW ERA

By RICHARD BUTWELL
*State University of New York
College at Fredonia*

More than the third quarter of the twentieth century ended for Southeast Asia in 1975. One era came to an end, and a new one began. The end of the old era completed the lengthy process of decolonization that began in 1946, when the United States became the first of the colonial powers to relinquish territory it ruled (the Philippines) in Southeast Asia.

Ironically, the Americans played a prominent part in the concluding chapter of decolonization in the region in 1975. The unrepresentative regimes they supported in South Vietnam and Cambodia collapsed in April and were followed by a bloodless Communist takeover of Laos in May, which ended a year of ineffective coalition government in that country.

On Sept. 2, 1945, in the wake of World War II, Ho Chi Minh declared the independence of all of Vietnam, but more than 25 years were to pass before

UPI

April and May were tumultuous in South Vietnam as the Thieu regime collapsed and the Communists consolidated their rule. In April the outskirts of Saigon burn (*left*) as the North Vietnamese attack, while east of Saigon soldiers and civilians pile aboard a Chinook helicopter (*above*) to escape from Xuan Loc. In May a giant rally in Saigon (*below*) celebrated the Communist victory.

SYGMA

RAPHO GUILLUMETTE—LEROY

Crowded Vietnamese refugee boats approach a U. S. Navy cargo ship in the South China Sea during the exodus from Vietnam. Refugees took to the water without knowing whether they would be saved.

Ho's successors were to realize his dream—the liquidation of a determining foreign presence on Vietnamese soil. The United States had prevented the extension of Communist rule over the whole of Vietnam in the 1960's and early 1970's. However, the U. S.-Communist Vietnamese "cease-fire" agreement of January 1973, followed by a cutback in American military assistance to the Saigon government of President Nguyen Van Thieu, left the South Vietnamese leader to stand increasingly by himself both militarily and politically. He could not do so, and Saigon fell to the Communists on April 30, 1975. The even less representative Lon Nol regime in neighboring Cambodia had been toppled from power two weeks earlier, on April 16.

New Balance of Power. The new Southeast Asia that existed as a consequence of these changes of political control in Indochina dramatically shifted the balance of power in the area. The strongest military presence in Southeast Asia was no longer that of the United States but the victorious Communist Vietnamese who, with aid and equipment from the Soviet Union and China, had successfully held out against the powerful Americans. The Communist Vietnamese, moreover, had fallen heir to millions of dollars worth of U. S.-provided military equipment and ammunition, abandoned by fleeing South Vietnamese soldiers. The implications of this formidable military force with its surplus weapons were frightening for all the countries in Southeast Asia where Communist insurgencies could be intensified by smuggled arms from Communist Vietnam. This danger was especially alarming to Thailand, the Americans' closest ally in the Indochina War.

There was no true military counterweight to the Communist Vietnamese in all Southeast Asia in the aftermath of the war. Indonesia was the second most important military power in the area, although far inferior to the Communist Vietnamese, as well as a leading force in the fledgling Association of Southeast Asian Nations (ASEAN). ASEAN came into being in 1967 after an anti-Communist counter-revolution in Indonesia had brought to power a military rul-

THE WAR REFUGEES

By Andrew H. Malcolm
"The New York Times"

They were fishermen, farmers, doctors, lawyers, secretaries, and soldiers. They came from towns, from huts, and from cities. They used bicycles, buses, boats, and planes. Their names were Nguyen, Pran, and Ngon. And they had one thing in common. They were the refugees of 1975—at least 2 million of them. Men, women, and children were seizing a few possessions, a little food, and a couple of pans and fleeing for their lives in the face of fierce fighting throughout Southeast Asia in the first four months of 1975.

Through more than 30 years of war they had run at times. Many had run so often it was a routine. When the bullets—anybody's bullets—started flying locally, it had become far easier to run down that familiar road to what might be security than it was to stay and face the potentially lethal realities of the battle zone—or of a new regime and its policies.

Flight and Escape. And so they ran. What started with a few people on a dirt road became a stream in a town and a flood further along and a mass exodus in the larger cities. Hysteria and panic flourished, bringing out the worst in many and ending the lives of others.

For the advancing Communists in Vietnam the refugees became an invaluable weapon. They clogged roads. And the simple sight of them panicked many others—civilian and military alike. By running, the refugees fanned the flames of fear further.

Months later, evidence in Vietnam indicated that many refugees eventually returned to their homes. In Cambodia, however, the new regime created hundreds of thousands of new refugees *after* the fighting ended. By uprooting the populations of entire cities and sending them into the countryside, the government apparently hoped to start a new national life from scratch.

But eventually, despite the chaotic end to U. S. involvement in Vietnam and Cambodia, more than 130,000 refugees, almost all Vietnamese, reached the United States to begin their own new lives. Many had escaped in cargo planes, fishing boats, or helicopters lifting off from the roofs of buildings in downtown Saigon. Many crammed aboard U. S. ships standing offshore. And from there they began the long journey of 10,000 miles (16,000 km) across land and water and a cultural gap whose width no one could measure.

ing group desirous of cooperating with the area's other non-Communist states. Thailand, the Philippines, Malaysia, and Singapore were Indonesia's partners in ASEAN, and, while none of these countries could truly be called *the* leader of the grouping, Indonesia clearly was bidding for such a role and came closest to filling it.

The impact of the fall of Vietnam, Cambodia, and Laos was great upon the ASEAN lands, which are the rest of Southeast Asia except for isolationist Burma. In the eyes of the leaders of the anti-Communist countries, the United States was seen as incapable of sustaining in power beseiged regimes that relied on it for their survival. It was not only that these regimes had fallen but that this had allegedly happened because the United States had withdrawn support from them.

Diplomatic Reactions. The defeat of the anti-Communists in Saigon, Phnom Penh, and Vientiane had been widely expected throughout the region, but there had still been hope that the worst would not come to pass. Malaysia, chief advocate of an ASEAN proposal to "neutralize" Southeast Asia, recognized the People's Republic of China in 1974, and both Thailand and the Philippines had taken steps in this direction. But they actually agreed to exchange diplomatic representatives with Peking only after the fall of the Indochinese countries—the developments in Vietnam and Cambodia clearly hastening the process. The same two governments, the only Asian allies of the Americans in the Southeast Asia Treaty Organization (SEATO), also called in July for that anti-Communist alliance's abandonment.

The Malaysian proposal to make Southeast Asia "a zone of peace and neutrality"—endorsed in principle by the other ASEAN lands—envisaged an end to all foreign military bases in the area. And, consistent with their support of this proposal, the president of the Philippines and the prime minister of Thailand called U. S. base arrangements in the region "temporary" in a communiqué issued after their July meeting. The Philippines moved to change the conditions under

Safety on Guam. Some traveled via the Philippines or Wake Island. For most, however, life in U. S. territory began on Guam, a long tropical strip of sand, naval installations, and a squad of resort hotels catering principally to Japanese honeymooners. Ironically, the refugees landed on the same runway the giant B-52's used for so many years to lumber off for high-altitude bombing runs over Southeast Asia.

On Guam the refugees got new clothes, plentiful food, and the first inklings of life in their new land: the strange game involving a stick, a bat, and four dusty bases and the strange Easter custom that features a giant, mythological rabbit who hides eggs in people's homes. Other new features included the strange restaurant where diners eat in their cars, the strange coins that carry no numbers to indicate their value, and the strange telephones that actually work.

It was a humbling and bewildering experience, and a few hundred decided to return to Vietnam. But most patiently waited in countless lines to complete the immigration process.

They lived in Quonset huts and tent cities erected virtually overnight by soldiers and sailors who worked 18 and 19 hours straight and then volunteered to help serve breakfast to the newest arrivals. For some time Orote Point, Guam's largest refugee center, had 39,000 residents in over 3,200 tents. It also had 2 newspapers, an orphanage, 2 hospitals, 19 doctors, 8 dining halls, 5 movies, 300 showers, and a bank buying the thin sheets of gold called *taels* into which the Vietnamese traditionally convert their wealth in times of uncertainty. The camp, once an airfield for Japanese fighter planes, even had its own zip code.

There were funny scenes in Guam—Army enlisted men trying to convince skeptical Vietnamese mothers to put disposable diapers on their infants. There were pleasant scenes—hundreds of Vietnamese unable to speak English laughing and clapping at Walt Disney cartoons. There were bizarre scenes—children playing with massive bundles of worthless South Vietnamese currency. And there were sad scenes —the immigration officer asking the young woman where her husband was, and the woman responding, "He is die five years."

There were also tales of terror. Some people woke screaming in the night, recalling the time near Hue when the land-mine blast cut their neighbor in half. Or the days awaiting evacuation from the beach at Danang when mutinous South Vietnamese soldiers roamed the sand stealing and raping. Or the night they scrambled aboard the departing ship only to realize other family members were left behind.

U. S. Marines storm aboard the *Mayaguez* on May 14 to recapture the American merchant ship taken by Cambodian Communists.

U. S. NAVY

Or the moment on that crowded roadside when they realized their baby was no longer breathing.

The Future. Slowly, however, the fears of the past gave way to the hopes of the future. Plane after plane carried the chattering family groups —very large by American standards—to camps in the United States where security checks were completed and the families assigned to American "sponsors," individuals, organizations, or families who took responsibility for shepherding the new arrivals through the apartment hunt, the school registration, and the job search.

Many soon had work. Many studied English. Many received public assistance, at least initially. Some had met resentment and hostility. Some succeeded or would succeed, and some would fail. They were much like the millions of other refugees who had preceded them to the United States during its preceding 199 years.

For some, life in the new environment was an unhappy experience. Some wanted to rejoin families from which they had been separated in Vietnam, and some others declared that they had left Vietnam against their wills. A shipload of 1,600 refugees who wanted to return home left Guam for Vietnam on October 16.

But some of the fragile young Indochinese never had much of a new life due to events far beyond their control. In the Naval Cemetery on Guam now the grass has grown back over the piles of dirt by the simple white crosses with inscriptions like: "Tran Kien Thaun. Born Jan. 7, 1975. Died May 2, 1975."

WIDE WORLD

Vietnamese evacuees on Guam wait patiently in broiling sun during processing. Orote Point, the island's largest center, had over 39,000 refugees in its "Tent City."

which the Americans continued to use giant Clark Air Force Base and strategically important Subic Bay Naval Base.

Thailand called in July for the departure of all American forces from their soil by March 1976. The leaders of Thailand had come to power as a result of January 1975 elections made possible by the overthrow of a strongly pro-U. S. military government in October 1973. They clearly were trying to break away from the close partnership with the Americans that had existed since 1950 and throughout the Indochina War. Besides recognizing Peking and necessarily breaking relations with the Chinese Nationalist government, Thailand also held talks with both the North and South Vietnamese Communists following the fall of Saigon. Thailand also responded favorably in July to a preliminary overture from Cambodia's new Communist rulers for resumed relations.

Philippines and Indonesia. In the case of the Philippines, however, there was greater doubt as to the intentions of President Ferdinand Marcos' government. U. S. bases in the country had been a political irritant for years, and Manila—no less than the other Southeast Asian governments—was shaken by American abandonment of the Thieu regime in Saigon. At the same time, the Marcos government seemed aware of Subic Bay's importance to an American naval presence in the Western Pacific. To the Filipinos, Clark Air Force Base seemed less essential to a U. S. air capability in the area because of alternate American facilities. The fall of Indochina, however, raised new questions about the reliability of the United States as an ally and placed American bases in greater jeopardy than at any time since Philippine independence.

Indonesia clearly hoped that the United States would not abandon the area militarily altogether. The Jakarta government appeared to be reconciled to the early withdrawal of U. S. military aircraft from Thailand, but it very much desired that the Americans retain a naval presence in the region—for which the Subic Bay facility might well be necessary. In July, President Suharto visited

1940—Japanese invasion drives out French.

1941—Ho Chi Minh forms Viet Minh resisters.

1945—Vietnam declares independence; Emperor Bao Dai abdicates.

1946—French return, restore control in Cambodia and Laos, attack Ho's government in Vietnam.

1949—French restore Bao Dai in South Vietnam.

1954—French defeated at Dien Bien Phu. Geneva Conference recognizes independent Cambodia and Laos and an independent, but temporarily divided, Vietnam. Ho retains control in North; Ngo Dinh Diem gains control in South.

1955—South Vietnam declares itself a republic.

1960—2,000 U. S. military advisers in South Vietnam. National Liberation Front formed. Civil war breaks out in Laos.

1962—Prince Souvanna Phouma forms neutralist government in Laos. Second Geneva Accord guarantees Laotian independence and neutrality.

1963—Diem killed in military coup; Gen. Duong Van Minh seizes power in South Vietnam.

1964—Gen. Nguyen Khanh seizes South Vietnam government.

1965—Air Vice Marshal Nguyen Cao Ky becomes prime minister in South Vietnam. United States commits ground combat troops in South Vietnam and launches air attacks on North.

1967—Buddhist and U. S. pressure lead to South Vietnam elections. Gen. Nguyen Van Thieu is elected president; Marshall Ky, vice-president.

1968—Tet Offensive. My Lai Massacre. Paris Peace Talks convene.

1969—U. S. troop commitment in Vietnam peaks at 543,000; withdrawals begin. Ho Chi Minh dies.

1970—Sihanouk is overthrown in Cambodia and replaced by pro-American Gen. Lon Nol. U. S. and South Vietnamese troops invade Cambodia.

1971—South Vietnamese troops, with U. S. support, invade Laos and Cambodia. U. S. air strikes continue, but land forces are greatly reduced.

1972—North Vietnam "Easter" offensive stopped by South Vietnam, backed by massive U. S. bombing. United States mines Haiphong harbor and bombs major North Vietnam cities.

1973—Vietnam cease-fire agreement is signed in Paris; last U. S. troops withdrawn; prisoners of war exchanged. Cease-fire in Laos. U. S. Congress orders bombing halt in Cambodia.

1974—U. S. Congress blocks increased Vietnam aid. Last U. S. troops withdrawn from Laos.

1975—Lon Nol leaves Cambodia; Communist Khmer Rouge enter Phnom Penh. Thieu resigns in South Vietnam; government surrenders. Thousands of U. S. civilians and Vietnamese nationals are evacuated. Khmer Rouge orders all Cambodians out of the cities and all foreigners expelled. Cambodians seize U. S. merchant ship *Mayaguez*, recaptured by U. S. troops. Pathet Lao take over Laotian government to end civil war. Sihanouk returns to Cambodia as ceremonial head of state.

Washington, for talks with President Ford, as Singapore's Lee Kuan Yew had done earlier. The Indonesian leader told the American chief executive that the United States should not completely quit the area militarily, and President Ford assured him that the United States remained very much a Pacific power. Suharto was the most opposed of Southeast Asia's non-Communist leaders to exchanging diplomatic representatives with China. He was finding himself increasingly isolated, however, in an area where most other political leaders were trying, almost desperately, to mend fences with former enemies.

Roles of USSR and China. There were now so many different Communists in power in Southeast Asia, however, and their postures toward the Chinese and the Soviets differed so much, that the process of redefining relations was difficult. The victorious Communist Vietnamese seemed to lean toward the USSR, still very much involved in a continuing political conflict with China, while Cambodia's Communists clearly favored Peking—partly to keep the Vietnamese, their traditional enemy, from interfering in Cambodian affairs. Moscow moved promptly to assist the Vietnamese with rehabilitation aid.

China, for its part, seemed to play down its hostility to the United States—not apparently even asking for an end to American bases in the Philippines as a price for Peking-Manila ties. At the same time, the Chinese Communists expanded their political contacts with the area's countries at a faster rate in 1975 than at any time since they came to power in 1949. Peking, besides having national interests of its own, was clearly seeking to prevent the USSR from moving into the vacuum created by the defeat of American allies in Indochina.

But the leaders of Southeast Asia, including the new Communist ones of Indochina, did not want to see the former U. S.–Communist confrontation, fought at the expense of the countries of the area, replaced by a new Sino-Soviet struggle for regional ascendancy. The efforts by the Communist rulers of Vietnam and Cambodia to regularize relations with other states of the region seemed to suggest that even the ideological sympathizers of the major Marxist powers wanted to minimize great-power intervention in Southeast Asian affairs in the years ahead. This had also been the main goal of the non–Communist ASEAN states' proposal to "neutralize" the area.

AMERICAN FOREIGN POLICY AND THE FAR EAST

By Elmer Plischke
Professor of Government and Politics
University of Maryland

The wholesale victories of Communist forces in Indochina in 1975 could be regarded as the culmination of a traumatic crisis for the United States. They came after the experiences of Watergate, impeachment proceedings, and the resignation of the vice president and president, plus the controversy over the war powers resolution and the Central Intelligence Agency investigation. In addition, the United States had suffered diplomatic setbacks in Portugal, Turkey, and Cyprus. Certainly the Communist triumphs required rethinking of American policies, interests, and power alignments, not only in Southeast Asia but in other areas as well.

Secretary of State Henry Kissinger called it a time of testing—reassessment of conditions, perceptions (both American and those of others), resolution, and commitments. Attention needed to be paid to reviewing U. S. containment and joint defense arrangements, to considering changes in geopolitical relations, and to revival of American credibility and leadership.

First Repercussions. Two decades of intense, at times dominant, U. S. involvement in Indochina came to an end. The immediate impact of the Communist military victory in Vietnam and Cambodia forced the complete withdrawal of the United States, and the political victory of the Communist Pathet Lao forces in Laos resulted in the reduction of the American presence and influence in that country.

Political reaction in Cambodia was rapid and ruthless. The Khmer Rouge ejected not only American but all (including North Vietnamese) foreign influence and instituted a zealous, self-imposed isolation. Political realignment in Vietnam involved the broader issues of reunification and solidification of Communist leadership. Changes were effected more slowly in Laos. While the United States was reduced to formal diplomatic relations, the Communist-dominated Laotian government appeared amenable to continued U. S. aid, but without the United States' previous influence. American policy options in Indochina were virtually reduced to matters of recognition, exchange of diplomatic missions, and, in the case of Laos, continuing economic assistance.

Thailand, having a 1,000-mile (1,600-km) border with Laos and Cambodia, found itself virtually surrounded by hostile forces and regarded itself particularly vulnerable. Although an ally of the United States for two decades, it shifted rapidly toward a more independent posture and normalizing diplomatic relations with Communist countries, while keeping its options flexible. Thailand's nervousness flowed from both the insurgency of native rebel forces and its fear of the Vietnamese, with whom it had warred over the centuries. Its future relations with the United States depend, in part, on what happens when SEATO is disbanded, but the reduction of the American role commenced immediately. Other Southeast Asian states—Burma, Malaysia, Singapore, Indonesia, and the Philippines—were less immediately affected. Except for the Philippines, which had sent troops, they had not been directly involved in the Indochina War.

Geopolitical Realignment. With the decline of American influence in continental Southeast

Representatives Paul McCloskey (*left*) and Bella Abzug (*center*) talk to newsmen in Phnom Penh, Cambodia, in March during Congressional fact-finding tour of Southeast Asia.

President Ford announces the end of the Indochina War for the United States to a Tulane University audience in New Orleans on April 23.

Asia, geopolitical realignment became a primary concern of both Communist and non-Communist states. A unified Vietnam of some 40 million people, combining the massive arsenals of North and South Vietnam, would constitute the pre-eminent military power in Southeast Asia. The future of the area hinged on whether the Communists would be content with victory and concentrate on internal development or would turn to territorial expansion and support of Communist subversion and insurgency in peripheral countries.

Future developments also involve the policies of the Soviet Union and Communist China. Fearing Soviet influence in Hanoi, Peking may oppose North Vietnamese domination of Cambodia, Laos, and other territories—which could provide Moscow with a powerful base on China's southern flank. Peking may prefer a continued American presence in the area as a counterweight to the Soviet Union. Following the fall of South Vietnam, Moscow appeared

restrained, prepared to await events. Its rivalry with Peking for Communist leadership, its border warfare with China, and its interest in détente with the West may also induce the Kremlin to accept a continuing American role. For the time being, the relations among Washington, Peking, and Moscow are likely to remain fluid, and the status of the area will depend primarily on the policy of Hanoi.

Reactions in the Western Pacific. Other American allies in the Western Pacific were also affected by the fall of Vietnam. The Philippines, Australia, and New Zealand, which supported the United States in South Vietnam, have been shifting their positions. Australia and New Zealand, partners in SEATO and ANZUS, adopted a more independent role. The Philippines, located closer to China and Vietnam, appeared to be more nervous, reviewed its security position, and proceeded to establish normal diplomatic relations with Peking and Moscow. Manila questioned U. S. reliability, not so much in the context of foreign attack as in the event of internal Communist guerrilla warfare.

Nationalist China (Taiwan)—its international political position deteriorating for some time —is convinced that it needs to defend itself, but that continued U. S. assistance under the defense pact of 1954 is vital. Although Nationalist China is the country most exposed to mainland China, at the time of the fall of Vietnam it seemed calm and unaffected. Its status quo appears to be accepted internally. Its future depends less on what happens in Southeast Asia than on the normalization of U. S.–Communist Chinese relations and its effect on the U. S.–Nationalist alliance, the possibility of accommodation with Peking, and, to a lesser extent, the restiveness of ethnic Taiwanese.

Korean Problem. In certain respects Korea posed the most critical immediate problem following the Communist victories in Indochina. The United States maintained some 40,000 troops in an exposed position in South Korea and reaffirmed its commitments under the treaty of 1953, but the North Koreans showed an inclination to take advantage of the situation. Communist China, the Soviet Union, and the United States all feared independent military aggression by North Korea. China may not wish a diminished American presence in Korea (in order to preserve a counterforce to the Kremlin), and the Soviets may fear that a unified Communist Korea would upset the existing posture of Japan. Both Moscow and Peking realize that a new Korean outbreak would destroy existing relations with Washington.

Korea, therefore, became a critical focal point of Peking, Moscow, and Washington interests. In the wake of Vietnam, crucial in the situation were the perceptions of the certainty and rapidity of American military response, of the practical constraint of the war powers resolution, of the reaction of Congress, and of the

dependability of American popular will to support another war in Korea. South Korea questioned whether the United States would really commit its forces in time to back up the South and therefore sought concrete rather than spoken reassurances of American support.

Position of Japan. Perhaps the most important aspects of averting an outbreak in Korea were the effect it would have on Japan and resulting geopolitical changes in the area. In the event of a U. S. failure in Korea, Japan could no longer depend on the United States for its security. If American forces were withdrawn from Japanese bases, Tokyo would have little alternative but to arm itself and assume a major politico-military—and presumably a nuclear—role in the Western Pacific. Policymakers needed to consider the possible consequences of such developments, including the apprehensions of other states in the area, the internal political crisis that could ensue in Japan (undermining its democratic government), and further decline or possible withdrawal of the United States from the Far East.

Future Policy. Although U. S. leaders have repeatedly reasserted the American intent to back up existing commitments, it is to be expected that they will be reinterpreted or renegotiated. The question remains as to whether, in time of crisis, Congress and the American people will support the President in fulfilling them.

Among the principal issues are whether the crisis involves foreign aggression (or internal war of liberation) and whether military action is likely to involve traditional or guerrilla warfare. These issues also include whether an ally is not only willing but also able to defend itself, whether other allies are prepared to help, and whether American action enjoys substantial expectancy of success.

It is clear that the loss of Vietnam did not produce a massive resurgence of isolationism in the United States. Questions of the effect of the war powers resolution on security commitments, the quality of leadership and strength of the presidency, and the stability of public opinion complicate projections respecting future U. S. policy. However, the American venture in Indochina is over, and it did not seriously undermine the American posture in other areas. In addition, arrangements of an earlier generation are likely to be revised in the light of changed conditions, and the United States consequently gained greater policy flexibility. Since the status of the powers in the Far East will take some time to restabilize, U. S. policy will remain fluid for the foreseeable future.

BLACK STAR—DENNIS BRACK

Arrival in the United States meant a new life for Vietnamese children. *Below*, field-jacketed youngsters stand in line at Travis Air Force Base, California. Many orphans were adopted when they arrived in their new homeland (*right*).

MAGNUM—PAUL FUSCO

The Legacy of MICHELANGELO

By CHARLES SEYMOUR, JR.
Professor of the History of Art, Yale University

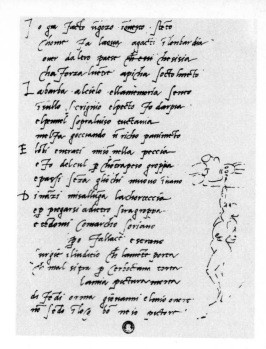

In the margin of his Sonnet to Giovanni da Pistoia, *Michelangelo drew himself at work on the ceiling of the Sistine Chapel.*

The year 1975 marked the 500th anniversary of the birth of the Italian artist Michelangelo Buonarroti (1475–1564). His genius and the universality of his art were commemorated in celebrations throughout the Western world. At his birthplace in Caprese, there was a Mass and polyphonic singing of 15th-century music. In Florence, which houses many of his masterpieces, there were exhibits, popular events, and historical tours. In London, the British Museum exhibited 183 of Michelangelo's drawings, and at the Royal Academy *The Doni Tondo,* the circular painting showing the Madonna and St. John, was shown outside Italy for the first time.

Canada marked the event with an international birthday party, a symposium held at McMaster University, Hamilton, Ont. In the Soviet Union, the poet Andrei Voznesensky read his translation of Michelangelo's poems at the Pushkin Museum.

The Message of Michelangelo. Today, we turn less to the outer expressions of Michelangelo's creativity and look more intently into the mystery of his private thoughts. In the concluding lines of an exuberant, semi-burlesque poem addressed to an acquaintance in Florence, Michelangelo appealed: *John, come to the rescue of my dead painting now, and of my honor; I'm not in a good place. And I'm not a painter.*

In these words he reveals the tremendous pressures under which he worked in Rome between 1508 and 1512 while painting the Sistine Chapel ceiling. That he intended to be ironic may be seen in the manuscript of the poem (*above*). In the margin Michelangelo sketched himself as an heroic nude at work on a goblin-like caricature of the titanic images that we admire today in the Sistine Chapel.

His bitter struggle to find a universal statement of the indestructible worth of the individual and the enduring aspects of man's fate remains significant today. The vehicle for this message was the human figure re-created in epic proportions as, for example, in the tombs of the Medici dukes in Florence (*opposite, top*). The subject may be interpreted as the triumph of Fame over Death, and then as the triumph of Eternity over Time.

A related theme, the coming of salvation and the future triumph of God's eternity in Christian theology, is developed in the hundreds of interlocking figures and pictorial themes of the ceiling of the Sistine Chapel (*opposite*). This is certainly the most ambitious program in all of Western painting.

At the right is one wall of the tomb of the Medici dukes in Florence. Here the male and female allegories of the Times of Day, *twisting in restless energy, contrast with the brooding seated figure of Lorenzo de' Medici in the niche above.*

The architectural setting for this sculpture is Michelangelo's own design. It obviously owes much to classical precedent, but the expression and spirit are altogether different. Shapes move aggressively into space, while the niches for statuary, except for one in each tomb, are paradoxically left blank. The scale of the architecture is subtly reduced so that the sculpture appears the more assertive and monumental.

SCALA NEW YORK/FLORENCE

One of the central frescoes of the vault of the Sistine Chapel is the Creation of Man. *The Almighty is enveloped by swirling drapery and a cluster of lesser figures as he rushes toward Adam to endow the languid giant with the gift of the Holy Spirit.*

SCALA NEW YORK/FLORENCE

*The dome of St. Peter's in Rome, finished several decades after
Michelangelo's death in 1564, became in time the model for a widespread
architectural symbolism. This is reflected, for one familiar example,
in the Capitol in Washington.*

As Michelangelo grew old, the problem of expressing the nature of spiritual
forces through visible images, and therefore to some extent material images, became both an obsession and a source of despair. His earlier delight in physical
beauty began to fade. Painting and sculpture he came to call "idols." More ex-
pressive drawings, more difficult poetry, and more grandiose architecture appear to
have absorbed him.

Thus in his last three decades, still in Rome, we find the final great religious
sonnets, the plan and the basic design of the huge dome of St. Peter's, and, almost
as afterthoughts, two unfinished marble *Pietàs,* more profound than the better
known youthful *Pietà* of 1498–99 in St. Peter's. The magnificent dome (*above*)
expresses power and glory. The reverse is found in one of the unfinished *Pietà*
groups (*opposite*), now in Florence, intended to be Michelangelo's own funeral
monument. The features of Nicodemus, who supports the dead Christ, are believed
to be Michelangelo's own. It is a face of indescribable weariness and yet of
courage and hope. All irony has vanished. Time has been overcome. In the
presence of this late, very personal legacy of his spirit in stone, the span of 500
years celebrated in this anniversary of his birth does not seem so long.

This unfinished Pietà, *in the cathedral in Florence, was intended by Michelangelo to be his own funeral monument. The dominant figure of Nicodemus, supporting Christ, is believed to be a self-portrait.*

MICHELANGELO—A CHRONOLOGY

1475—Born in Caprese, Tuscany
1488—Apprenticed to the painter Domenico Ghirlandajo in Florence
1489—Entered art school in the Medici gardens under Bertoldo, a student of Donatello
1490–92—Lived in the household of his patron Lorenzo de' Medici
1498–99—Carved the notable marble *Pietà* in St. Peter's, the Vatican, Rome
1501–04—Returned to Florence and executed *The Doni Tondo* and sculpted the huge marble *David*
1505—Began his commission of the monumental tomb of Pope Julius II, which was to occupy him for 40 years

1508–12—Painted the Sistine ceiling
1513–21—Completed the sculptures *Moses* and the *Bound Slaves* (now in the Louvre, Paris) for the tomb of Pope Julius II
1529—Assisted as engineer in the defense of Florence to preserve Medici power
1534–41—Painted the *Last Judgment* on the altar wall of the Sistine Chapel
1541–50—Executed frescoes for the Pauline Chapel in the Vatican, Rome
1546—Appointed chief architect of St. Peter's; the dome was completed by others on his design
1555–64—Michelangelo's last work, the Rondanini *Pietà,* unfinished at his death

Iran today

By Arthur Campbell Turner
Professor of Political Science
University of California, Riverside

Iran is the emerging giant of the Middle East. Islamic, but of the Shiite sect, and non-Arab, it is unique in a number of ways. One exceptional aspect is in the nature of the changes it is experiencing. There is a common pattern of change that has been observed in many countries in recent years. A traditional monarchy is suddenly overthrown and its place taken by some dictatorial leader or group. The new leadership is radical, loudly critical of the West, and it proceeds to attempt a hasty modernization of the country along leftward lines.

Change Decreed from Above. Nothing of this kind, however, has happened in Iran. There, change is being created, directed, and enforced by the traditional monarchy itself, in the person of Shah Mohammed Reza Pahlavi. Clearly he made a decision early in his reign to avert revolution not by blind obstruction but by a creative policy of guided change, directed from above, that would deflate the potential causes of revolution by a visible improvement of the condition of the nation.

A Family Tradition of Reform. To some extent the Shah can be said to be continuing and intensifying a policy of reform initiated by his father. Iran, known

The stunning Shahyad Tower, built to commemorate Iran's 2,500th anniversary, soars over Teheran.

MAGNUM—BRUNO BARBEY

SYGMA—DE RAEMY

Shah Mohammed Reza Pahlavi

THE SHAH AND HIS FAMILY

His Imperial Majesty, Mohammed Reza Pahlavi, Shah of Iran, is an unusually energetic monarch in his mid-fifties who rules as well as reigns. Reports of the Shah's illness in 1975 were denied. He works long hours and participates enthusiastically in skiing and other sports. Like his wife, the beautiful Empress Farah Diba, he speaks excellent English and has given several lengthy U. S. television interviews. Not everyone likes his views, but no one has any excuse for not knowing them. He expresses his clearly-formed judgments about his country and the world with a pungency and precision unusual at any level of society and almost unheard-of in a crowned head.

Earlier Life. The Shah was born in Teheran, Iran, on Oct. 26, 1919, the son of Shah Reza Khan Pahlavi, the first of the dynasty to occupy the Iranian throne, and Tajomolouk Pahlavi. He was educated in Switzerland, which he continues to visit frequently on vacation, and at the Teheran Military Academy. He succeeded to the throne on Sept. 16, 1941, when his father, who had shown pro-German tendencies, was compelled to abdicate by British and Russian pressure. The Shah's for-

mal coronation, intended to underline the stability of his regime, took place in October 1967.

The Shah's Marriages. The Shah has been married three times; the first two marriages were dissolved because they did not lead to the male heir regarded as essential for the dynasty's continuance and the country's stability. In 1939, while still Crown Prince, he married Princess Fawzia, sister of King Farouk of Egypt. There was one daughter, Princess Shahnaz. The marriage was dissolved in 1948. In 1951 he married Soraya Esfandiari, a member of a wealthy Iranian family; this marriage ended in divorce in 1958.

On Dec. 21, 1959, he married his present consort, Empress Farah Diba, who was born in 1938. Belonging to an eminent Iranian family, she had been educated at the Jeanne d'Arc and Razi Schools in Teheran. She went on to the Ecole Spéciale d'Architecture in Paris and was a student there when the Shah met her. Her Majesty has broad social and cultural interests and is active on the governing bodies of a number of educational, health, and cultural organizations in Iran, France, and the United States.

The Family. The royal couple has four children, two boys and two girls. Crown Prince Reza was born in 1960; Princess Farahnaz in 1963; Prince Ali Reza in 1966; and Princess Leila in 1970. The Shah's confidence in his consort's judgment is shown by his having named her to be Regent, though he has four brothers, in the event of his own absence, incapacity, or death during the Crown Prince's minority. Her influence is credited with having contributed to raising the status of Iranian women, who have had the vote since 1963.

ARTHUR CAMPBELL TURNER

The Shah, Empress Farah Diba, and their family vacation at St. Moritz. Crown Prince Reza is at left.

GAMMA—BERTRAND LAFORET

until 1935 in the West as Persia, is a proud and ancient empire. But the present Pahlavi dynasty is a new, half-century old holder of an ancient throne that has existed for 2,500 years. The Kajar dynasty had fallen into decadence by the early 20th century and the country into a disorder that invited foreign occupation. Reza Khan Pahlavi emerged as leader of the growing nationalist movement in the period of near anarchy after World War I. War minister in 1920, prime minister in 1922, he accepted the crown from the *majlis* (parliament) in 1925. He reorganized the military forces, restored internal peace and order, broke the power of the reactionary Shiite clergy, developed new industries, and revised the legal system. His reforms were facilitated by the growing wealth from the oil fields. On all these counts the reign of Reza Shah provided a kind of first sketch for his son's.

The Present Shah. Iran had declared its neutrality in World War II, but Reza Shah allowed Germany to use Iran as a base for subversive activities in the Middle East. To prevent this, and to open a supply route to the USSR, Britain and the Soviet Union jointly occupied Iran in August 1941, forced the abdication of Reza Shah (who died three years later in South Africa), and replaced him with his son, Mohammed Reza. The Russians treated their zone as a colonial area, and it took major international pressure to persuade them finally in December 1946 to give up their hold on the northern province of Azerbaijan and return it to Iranian rule.

Economically, Iran was dominated by the Anglo-Iranian Oil Company. In the early 1950's, Mohammed Mossadegh spearheaded the nationalist attack on the company and at the same time was very nearly able to substitute himself for the Shah as the ruler of Iran. The prolonged crisis in oil and politics, 1950–55, was resolved in a surprisingly smooth fashion. An international embargo on Iranian oil led to the resumption of Western operation of oil industry in 1955 through a new consortium in which the United States had a larger share and Britain a smaller one. Mossadegh, ousted in 1953, faded away into obscurity.

In subsequent years the Shah consolidated his position and became, in effect, his country's chief executive, which he remains. Until 1957 no political parties were allowed. The armed forces were purged of disloyal elements. Land reform —involving the partial breakup of the great estates—which had been frustrated by landowners' opposition in 1950–51, began to be enforced in the early 1960's.

The White Revolution. The great watershed in the present Shah's reign was 1963, when the Shah announced under the name of the White Revolution his far-reaching plans for social and economic reforms and secured near unanimous approval for them from the people in a plebiscite. The program envisaged such measures as land reform, nationalization of forests, worker profit-sharing in state-owned industries, woman suffrage, and the formation of a Literacy Corps to train teachers. Opposition to the reforms led to extensive riots in 1963, but these were suppressed, as were later disorders in 1965, in which year the prime minister was assassinated. This was the end of large-scale opposition to the Shah's plans.

The Iranian elite began to participate profitably in the new industrial developments. A. A. Hoveida became prime minister in 1965 and completed ten years in office in 1975, years for Iran of increasing prosperity and success. In 1967 the reform program was broadened in various ways, Hoveida's *Iran Novin* party won a general election, and the solemn coronation of the Shah took place. A further occasion of great pomp with world visibility was the celebration at Persepolis in 1971 of Iran's 2,500 years of monarchy.

Economic Development. The social and economic advance of Iran in these years of the White Revolution has been enormously impressive. From 1963 to 1973 there was a steady rise in gross national product of about 10% per year. But the whole process underwent a stupendous acceleration when the fourfold increase in the price of petroleum at the beginning of 1974 provided an enormous reservoir of capital for every conceivable kind of expansion. In 1973 and 1974 the growth rate more than tripled in real—not merely nominal—terms.

Oil revenues skyrocketed from some $2.5 billion in 1972 to close to $20 billion in 1974. In import-export terms, 1974 provided a spendable surplus of about $6 billion. Prior to the rise in oil prices, much of Iran's development was being financed by borrowing abroad, and debt service was absorbing the disquietingly high figure of 20% of the budget. But all that is, for the present at least, transformed. The Shah has become a lender instead of a borrower and is an extensive giver of foreign aid.

Iran combines the modern and the traditional. Cosmopolitan Teheran (*right*) has become a focus of international trade and finance, but skilled craftsmen still follow their trades. An artisan polishes a turquoise (*above*), while villagers wash the renowned Persian carpets (*below*).

ALL PHOTOS: IRAN TOURIST

IRANIAN PETROLEUM INDUSTRY

By John R. Matthews, Jr.
Professor of Economics,
College of William and Mary

Iran is the world's fourth largest producer (about 10% of world output) and second largest exporter (15% of global exports) of petroleum. Reserves are estimated at 6.6 billion barrels. Production has grown at about 15% annually over the past decade and reached 6.1 million barrels a day in 1974. Potential production is estimated at 10 million barrels a day by 1985. Oil has been the mainstay of Iran's economic development plans and is of particular importance in the fifth five-year plan, the country's economic blueprint for 1973–78.

The primary oil producing area in Iran is the province of Khuzistan at the head of the Persian Gulf. The key events in the development of the petroleum industry were:

1872   First concession granted.
1908   Oil found in commercial quantities.
1909   Anglo-Persian Oil Company founded. Name later changed to Anglo-Iranian.
1914   British government purchased conditional control of Anglo-Persian.
1916   Pipeline from oil fields to Abadan refinery completed.
1951   Anglo-Iranian Oil Company nationalized and properties transferred to National Iranian Oil Company (NIOC). British withdrew operating personnel and Iranian oil was boycotted by major oil companies.
1954   Agreement reached between Iran and consortium of foreign companies for exploration and production.
1960   Iran helped establish Organization of Petroleum Exporting Countries (OPEC).

Role of NIOC. The 1954 consortium agreement gave foreign companies the right to operate within a 100,000 square mile (260,000 sq km) area in southern Iran for a maximum period of 40 years with 50% of the profits going to Iran. NIOC would function outside the agreement area, handle internal distribution of petroleum products, and provide overall administration. NIOC also made contractual agree-

SYGMA—ALAIN NOGUES

Worker monitoring machinery in a petroleum refinery characterizes Iran's increased industrial emphasis.

ments providing for service and joint ventures with other companies. These have enabled it to enter foreign markets on its own or through partners and to carry out offshore exploration.

To diversify operations NIOC formed the National Iranian Gas Company, National Petrochemical Company, and National Iranian Tanker Company as wholly owned subsidiaries and in 1972 set up a company to explore for oil in the North Sea in partnership with British Petroleum. The old consortium agreement was superseded in 1973 by a new 20-year contract. NIOC now sets production targets and other oil policies with consortium companies performing services and buying crude oil from it.

Revenues and Development. Iran's oil revenue stems from a 12.5% royalty plus a 55% income tax imposed on petroleum companies. Both the

The leading families of Iran, in their enthusiastic pursuit of industrial expansion, are aided and assisted by government. Expansion has covered a wide spectrum of products including vehicle assembly, textiles, steel rolling mills, and television sets. The auto industry, to take one example, began in Iran only in 1967. In 1974, 70,000 cars were produced; in 1975, output was about 120,000, and production is expected to reach 750,000 units annually by 1980.

Foreign business executives crowd into the hotels of Teheran, attracted by the honey pot of new affluence. Many spectacular deals have been concluded. In 1974 a $5 billion deal was announced between Iran and France, and in March 1975 the United States and Iran signed an economic agreement of unprecedented size, committing Iran to spend $15 billion by 1980 on American goods and services. Iran has bought a one-quarter interest in the German firm, Krupp Steel.

royalty and tax are based on posted prices, which rose 360% between January 1973 and January 1974 with a further 11% increase during 1974. Consortium payments during the period increased government revenues more than 500%. Iran's foreign exchange receipts have more than quadrupled since 1968. These receipts were about $20.5 billion in 1975, with estimated receipts exceeding payments by nearly $12 billion.

In 1973 oil revenues provided 64% of total public revenues in Iran; the ratio in 1975 was about 85%. Oil exports accounted for 74% of foreign earnings during the five-year period ending in 1972. The ratio was 81% in 1973, and it is still increasing.

Hence, petroleum revenues provide the bulk of financing for development in Iran, allow it to participate in aid programs, and provide funds for trade and development deals with de-veloped nations. For example, oil revenue has been used to buy military equipment. Iran placed $3.8 billion in orders with the United States in fiscal 1974 and $1.7 billion through early fiscal 1975.

Yet by summer 1975, Iran was reviewing its major financial transactions in a comprehensive reappraisal of its financial commitments. Oil production and revenues were running below earlier expectations as Iran and other OPEC members made deliberate cutbacks to maintain high petroleum prices in the face of weak world demand. During 1975, Iran's production dropped 15% below the January level. A longer view suggests that Iran's reserves of oil will last only about 20 years. The Shah, therefore, decreed that in 10 years non-oil income should be on a par with petroleum generated income and that current oil revenues are to be used to achieve that goal.

Massive oil pipes lead to the jetty on Kharg Island, a deepwater shipping terminal in the Persian Gulf.

Potential Problems. However, Iranian revenues in 1975 from oil fell from the $20 billion of 1974 to about $16 or $17 billion. The Shah's government is taking a hard look at many commitments made since early 1974. Some projects have been quietly dropped without announcement. Ailing Pan American World Airways will not, after all, be bailed out by Iran, although the deal was first announced in 1974 and confirmed in the spring of 1975.

What shadows exist in the bright Iranian picture? Inflation runs about 25%, though government measures protect the poorest from its effects. There is a pronounced shortage of trained personnel. Agricultural development lags behind that of industry. And the price of modernization is, inevitably, some loss of the traditional culture of Iran. The danger is recognized; as the Shah said in an interview, "We will keep the Iranian soul as intact as possible." The guidelines for

the vast new architectural project of a city center for Teheran, announced early in 1975, stress that Iranian architectural motifs should be incorporated in the designs. However, some traditional industries decay. Caviar from the partly-polluted Caspian is becoming scarcer. Fewer and fewer of the exquisite Persian carpets are being produced; the young people who labored on them now work for higher wages in factories.

Also, it is quite clear that the government has little patience with those who dissent from the premises of Iran's monarchical society. The activities of *Savak*—the secret police—are paradoxically far from secret, and some 200 terrorists and guerrillas were executed or killed in various incidents in 1973–75. Terrorism persists, however; in May 1975 two senior U. S. military officers were shot to death in Teheran. Iran became a single-party state in March 1975. Student radical dissent is widespread. Many who go abroad for subsidized study never come home.

There are other doubts concerning the long-term future of the Iranian boom. Iran's oil reserves may be exhausted in 15 to 20 years. Hence the Shah's enthusiasm for higher and higher prices. However, there are other vast resources. Gas reserves are second only to the Soviet Union's, and within the next few years Iran will probably become one of the world's largest copper producers. The official forecast that by the mid-1980's Iran will have a gross national product as large as that of France (with two-thirds of the population)—and far larger than Britain's—may well prove justified.

Iranian Foreign Policy. The Shah is the realistic son of a very tough father. He has been rightly described as "one of the last great believers in undiluted *Realpolitik*." The rich are always a tempting prey. The USSR has ambitions to break into the Indian Ocean—and now has a fleet presence there. Twice in the 20th century, in 1914 and 1941, Iran found itself crushed in a pincer—Russian power from the north, British from the south. The fact that British power has gone does not imply that the Russian has.

With such considerations in mind, within the last few years the Shah has made Iran into the greatest military power in the Persian Gulf area. The potential was always there: Iran is between two and three times the size of Texas, and its population of 32 million is by far the largest in the area. Oil revenues have made possible a great military buildup. Since 1973, Iran has received or contracted for some $8 billion in advanced weaponry from the United States to add to its already formidable armament. The armed forces total some 300,000 men. There are

Soldier on a hovercraft in the Persian Gulf mans a forward gun. Increased Gulf forces have made Iran the dominant military power in this strategic area.

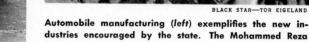

Automobile manufacturing (*left*) exemplifies the new industries encouraged by the state. The Mohammed Reza Shah Dam (*above*) is a source of hydroelectric power.

1,000 tanks, a modern air force, and naval forces in the Gulf that include the largest armed hovercraft squadron in the world. The Gulf forces and bases are to secure safe passage through the narrow Strait of Hormuz for the all-important tankers and their cargoes. This is the jugular vein not only of Iran, but of Western Europe and Japan.

Ambitions of Power. The withdrawal of British power from the Gulf, announced in 1968, took place in 1971. It is quite clear that the Shah's intention is for Iran to replace Britain as the major power in the region. By the end of 1975 it could be said that this policy was largely successful. Occupation of disputed islands on the south side of the Gulf and military aid to the ruler of Oman against rebels backed by the radical People's Democratic Republic of Yemen and using Soviet equipment have made the policy very clear. Now Iranian ambitions seem to be expanding to aim at ensuring stability and freedom of traffic throughout the Indian Ocean. Iran would rather have all Great Power presence removed from the area. Opposed to Russian penetration, it is also against the U. S. base in Bahrein and U. S. plans for a naval base on the island of Diego Garcia.

An Active Diplomacy. The foreign policy of Iran combines military strength with conciliatory policies and has been generally successful. Iran cooperates economically with the Soviet Union to offset its major partnership with the United States. Since 1974, Iranian diplomacy has been particularly active and rewarding. In September 1974 the Shah made a tour of India, Singapore, New Zealand, Australia, and Indonesia to lay groundwork for future regional cooperation. His visit to Washington in May 1975 was a triumph. In July 1975 a visit from the President of Mexico led to the creation of a joint investment fund by the two fast-developing countries.

In March 1975 the long hostility with the radical Baathist regime in Iraq was defused by an agreement that terminated Iranian support for the long rebellion of the Kurds and settled boundary problems. Poor relations with Egypt have ended, and the imperial family was represented at the Suez Canal reopening. Arab potentates are given red-carpet treatment as part of the policy of rapprochement with the Arab world. Iran continues to sell oil to Israel, but now calls for an Israeli return of Arab lands as a necessary step to a definitive Mideast settlement, which Iran wants for reasons of general stability.

PHOTO RESEARCHERS—GEORGE HOLTON

Persepolis, now well-preserved ruins near Shiraz, was the ancient summer capital of Iran's rulers.

The Heritage of Iran

By Roger M. Savory
Professor of Islamic Studies
University of Toronto

In 1971, Iran celebrated the 2,500th anniversary of the founding of the first Persian empire by Cyrus the Great in 550 B. C. This event, in a dramatic way, drew the attention of the rest of the world, not only to the fact that Iran has an ancient civilization and a long historical and cultural tradition but also to the fact that Iran now plays an important role both in the Middle East and in world affairs.

The Monarchy. At the heart of this historical and cultural tradition lies the institution of the monarchy. The king of Iran still bears the title Shahanshah, the "king of kings," which dates from the Achaemenid era, when the king of Iran was the paramount ruler who had made neighboring kings his vassals. As Darius the Great, who reigned 521–486 B. C., states in the Behistun (Bisutun) inscriptions: "I am Darius, the great king, the king of kings, the king of Persia . . . from antiquity are we descended; from antiquity hath our race been kings."

The authority of the ancient kings of Iran was based on the theory of the divine right of kings. Inherent, too, in the concept of kingship was the messianic role of the king as the savior of his people. This concept was enshrined in the Iranian national epic, the *Shah Nameh* of Firdausi, completed about 1000 A. D., which still has a potent influence on the Iranian ethos.

The present Shahanshah of Iran, Mohammed Reza Pahlavi, sees himself as being, in a very real sense, the heir of the tradition of Cyrus the Great, although the dynastic succession has by no means been unbroken since that time.

National Identity. Closely linked with the Iranian reverence for the monarchical tradition is the sense of identity as an Iranian. The Iranians have always called their land "Iran" rather than "Persia," a name made popular in the West by the Greeks. The name "Iran" means "land of the Aryans," and it reflects their sense of being different from both their Arab and their Turkish neighbors in race, language, and tradition. Iranians have managed to preserve their distinctive cultural tradition despite endless waves of foreign invasion and conquest. Two of these invasions in particular had far-reaching effects on the history and cultural development of Iran: the Arab conquest in the 7th century and the Mongol invasions of the 13th century.

The Arab Conquest. The conquest by the Arabs not only meant the political eclipse of Iran for centuries, but it also meant that Islam, the religion of the conquerors, superseded Zoroastrianism, the ancient religion of Iran, which had under the Sassanian empire produced a closely-knit alliance between church and state. The egalitarian spirit of Islam was at variance with the Iranian tradition. Iranians soon adopted the Shiite form of Islam, which, with its more authoritarian dogmas and its strongly messianic emphasis, was more congenial to the Iranian spirit than the more orthodox Sunni Islam. Today, Iranians still constitute the largest group of Shiite Muslims.

The Arab conquest not only caused the submergence of the Iranian religion but also of the Iranian language. For several centuries Arabic replaced Persian as the administrative and cultural language of Iran. When Persian reappeared as a literary language in the 10th century, it was written in the Arabic script and is still so written today. In addition, many Arabic words had become permanently incorporated into this "New Persian" language.

Thus, as a result of the Arab conquest Iranians suffered a loss of identity in a religious, linguistic, political, and ethnic sense. However, the strength and flexibility of the Iranian tradition were demonstrated by the rapidity with which it reasserted itself. Under the influence

of Iranian bureaucrats, the Arab caliphs began to look more and more like Iranian kings. By adopting the Shiite form of Islam and linking it to their own historical tradition, Iranians were able to avoid total absorption by Sunni Islam.

On the cultural level, Iranians, though frequently writing in Arabic, immeasurably enriched Islamic culture. Their contributions to branches of learning not considered suitable for study by Arabs (for example, philosophy, medicine, mathematics, astronomy, astrology, music, and alchemy) were especially notable, but they also made significant contributions to the development of Islamic thought and theology itself.

The subtle, speculative Iranian mind refused to be confined by the arguments of Islamic theologians and jurists, and Iranians took the lead in Sufism, the mystical interpretation of the Islamic faith. Before long, Sufism had become the "popular" or "folk" form of Islam as opposed to the "high" Islam of the religious seminaries and schools of law. Iranian preoccupation with mystical themes produced in the 11th to 14th centuries an unbelievably rich outpouring of literature, particularly poetry, by such men of genius as Nizami, Rumi, Attar, and Hafiz, who have made an imperishable contribution to world literature.

The Mongols. Another watershed in the history of Iran was the Mongol invasions of the 13th century. Once again, the country was occupied by alien forces, but the situation was fundamentally different from that of the 7th century. The Mongols, by destroying the historic caliphate, removed the symbol that, however ineffectively from the 10th century onward, had unified the Islamic world. Shiism was given greater freedom to develop and acquired political power at the beginning of the 16th century when it became the official state religion in Iran (as it still is today).

At the same time, the Mongols, by establishing in Iran and Mesopotamia a state whose boundaries were approximately those of the ancient Iranian empires, created the conditions for the eventual emergence of an Iranian national state.

The Safavids. The Safavid shahs, who ruled Iran from 1501 to 1722, restored to Iran not only political strength after eight and a half centuries of alien rule but also economic prosperity after the period of decline caused by the devastations of the Mongols and of Timur (Tamerlane). The court of Shah Abbas I (1588–1629) was thronged with the ambassadors of European powers, merchants, and Catholic missionaries. At the same time, the patronage of the Safavid shahs resulted in a remarkable flowering of the arts and crafts. Building on the very considerable achievements of their Timurid predecessors, Safavid artists and craftsmen produced masterpieces in the fields of painting, the illumination of manuscripts, textiles, metalwork, and, above all, carpet-weaving. In 1598, Shah Abbas

The Royal Mosque, built in the early 17th century, is one of the architectural jewels of Isfahan.

transferred his capital from Qazvin to Isfahan and made the Maydan-i-Shah (Royal Piazza), with its architectural masterpieces the Shaykh Lutfullah Mosque and the Royal Mosque, the showpiece of his superbly-planned city, leading its inhabitants to boast: "Isfahan is half the world."

Modern Times. After the collapse of the Safavids, Iran was rent by 50 years of civil war. This was followed by 150 years of Anglo-Russian political and economic rivalry in the Middle East that reduced Iran, ruled by a succession of weak shahs, to quasi-colonial status.

With the establishment of the Pahlavi dynasty in 1925, Iran began to rid itself of foreign control and to regain its national identity, a process brought to fruition by the present Shah. The modern capital, Teheran, is, like Safavid Isfahan, a center of diplomatic and commercial activity, as foreign entrepreneurs vie with one another to obtain a share in Iran's industrial and technological development. The pace of modernization is rapid, and social attitudes have, inevitably, not changed as quickly, but Iran's relative stability in an area notorious for its instability stems in no small measure from the durability of its political and social institutions.

A capacity crowd in New York City's Madison Square Garden watches the New York Rangers sweep down the ice. Amateur play has been spurred by interest in the professional sport.

hockey fever
THE BOOM ON ICE

BY HAL TRUMBLE, *Executive Director,*
Amateur Hockey Association of the United States

The phenomenal growth in player participation and spectator interest in ice hockey in the United States has had an immense effect on the amateur and the professional sides of the sport. The expansion of professional hockey is described in the second section of this article.

Amateur hockey includes kids on ponds and backyard rinks, community and other formal amateur leagues, clubs, secondary school teams, and intercollegiate competition—any type of nonprofessional play. The amateur sport has snowballed: more players has meant more fans, which has led to new teams and rinks, which has spurred the development of new players. The sport is not limited to the young or to men; there are leagues for older players and teams for girls and women. Soon, there will be 500,000 amateur players, who will be watched by millions of fans each year.

Although hockey has had to compete for attention with basketball in the United States, ice hockey has always been the preeminent winter sport in Canada. Young Canadians often learn to skate when they learn to walk, and Canadians long dominated the highest levels of the amateur game and the professional leagues. The best U. S. college teams were stocked almost entirely by Canadian players, and it was rare for a U. S. player to advance to the National Hockey League. Now, with vastly increased participation in the United States, U. S. play-

ers are much more visible in the collegiate game and are found with increasing frequency in the professional ranks. The acceleration in hockey interest is recent, but the sport's heritage in the United States stretches back to the 19th century.

Early History. Although it has not been definitely established where and when the first formal game of ice hockey was played in the United States, records are available indicating that it was played on an organized basis in Baltimore, Minneapolis, and St. Paul's School of Concord, N. H., in the winter of 1894–95. The game may have been played earlier, but records attesting to this are incomplete.

Hockey was played on an organized basis in Canada about 20 years before it was formally played in the United States. Students at Montreal's McGill University drafted a set of rules in 1875, and the first league was formed about 1885. In the 1893–94 season, Lord Stanley, Canada's governor-general, donated a cup to be awarded to the best amateur hockey team. Intense competition for the cup stimulated professionalism over the years, and since 1913 the Stanley Cup has been the symbol of supremacy in professional hockey rather than amateur.

Canadians have always had a significant role in popularizing the sport in the United States. The University of Minnesota organized a team in 1895, mainly through the efforts of H. A. Parkyn, a native of Toronto and quarterback on the Minnesota football team. This team played the Winnipeg Victorias in Minneapolis on Feb. 18, 1895. St. Paul's School, a private preparatory school that had been playing ice polo in the 1880's and early 1890's, changed to ice hockey rules for the season of 1894–95. On Jan. 23, 1896, teams from St. Paul, Minneapolis, and Winnipeg held a four-team international tournament in St. Paul. This may have been the first international tournament ever played in the United States.

NHL

Notre Dame defenseman bursts between two Boston College skaters in pursuit of the puck. College hockey was first played in 1895.

Before the 1890's a game similar to ice hockey and known as ice polo had been played on a formal basis in New England and the upper Midwest areas as early as 1883. Minnesota held statewide tournaments in ice polo as early as 1887.

The New York Hockey Club, composed entirely of Canadian residents, introduced the game to New York City during the winter of 1895–96 and during the season met the Montclair Athletic Club (N. J.), two teams from Montreal, and the Baltimore Athletic Club.

The Amateur Hockey League, composed of four teams from New York City, was formed in November 1896 and played its first league schedule in 1896–97. Many of the games were played at the famous St. Nicholas Arena, which opened in March 1896. During the period from 1900 to 1917, the St. Nicholas Arena was a mecca for the high society of New York as they gathered to cheer for Yale, Harvard, Dartmouth, Princeton, and St. Paul's teams. The Amateur Hockey League flourished through the years, adding teams from Boston, and continued to operate through the 1917 season. Baltimore also had a league functioning in the late 1890's.

Following the University of Minnesota's lead, other colleges soon formed teams. Yale became interested in the sport after some of their students visited Canada in 1895 and came back to organize a team that played in the winter of 1896. Besides Yale, Cornell, Johns Hopkins, and the University of Maryland started hockey in 1896, and within a few years Brown, Columbia, Dartmouth, Harvard, and Princeton were competing. For the 1899–1900 season the Intercollegiate Hockey League was formed with Yale, Harvard, Brown, Princeton, and Columbia as members. This was the first U. S. college league to operate.

By the early 1900's amateur hockey was being played in Boston, Duluth, Philadelphia, Pittsburgh, St. Louis, and many small communities in northern Michigan and Minnesota. Within the next decade the amateur game spread to Buffalo, Chicago, Cleveland, Detroit, New Haven, and San Francisco. High school and prep school hockey was played as early as 1902 in Minneapolis, St. Paul, and New York City and within a decade had spread to many cities in New England and the Midwest.

During the period immediately preceding World War I, interest in ice hockey showed tremendous growth, especially in the upper Midwest and Boston areas,

BLACK STAR—EIJI MIYAZAWA

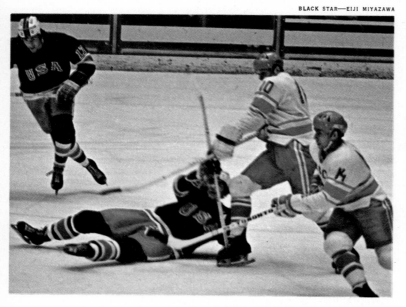

Red-helmeted Russians skate around a sprawled American in 1972 Olympic Games contest in Sapporo, Japan.

Kids on Skates

Youngsters mill around the goalie as he protects the puck. Play in amateur leagues has almost tripled since 1970.

As the hockey boom has intensified, more and more youngsters have made hockey their sport. Rinks are being built at a rapid pace, and eager young players flock to the competitive amateur leagues. Hockey camps and clinics are crowded with skaters—from beginners trying out new equipment to experienced players honing individual skills. Although most players are still boys, girls' participation has increased rapidly.

Only a few years ago, hockey rinks were primarily in large buildings, and these rinks were inaccessible to 10, 12, or 14 year-old players. Spurred by public demand, small public and private rinks with limited or no seating have been constructed for comparatively modest amounts and have proved a great success.

The expansion of facilities throughout the country has been accompanied by a phenomenal increase in amateur players. In 1949 the AHAUS sponsored its first national championship for youth teams. By the 1959–60 season there were slightly over 1,000 teams; by 1969–70, there were 4,255. Only five years later the number had jumped almost 250% to about 10,300 teams. Kids can begin playing in AHAUS registered leagues as Mites (7–8), or in community and informal leagues throughout the United States.

HAL TRUMBLE

the regions that have produced the best American players. During this period Boston, Calumet, Cleveland, Duluth, Pittsburgh, St. Paul, and Sault Ste. Marie had strong amateur teams. These cities and others formed the United States Amateur Hockey Association (USAHA) at a meeting in Philadelphia on Oct. 25, 1920. The newly organized USAHA affiliated with the Amateur Athletic Union (AAU) and the Canadian Amateur Hockey Association.

Organization of the Amateurs. Ice hockey during World War I and through the season of 1919–20 was under the control of the International Skating Union. It was under the auspices of this group that the first Olympic team was organized and sent to Antwerp, Belgium, to compete in the 1920 games.

The USAHA governed U. S. amateur hockey through the 1925–26 season, after which it disbanded. Until the AAU assumed control for the season of 1930–31, the sport was not under the control of a national body. This led to

problems of selecting and organizing a team for the 1928 Winter Olympic Games held in Amsterdam, with the result that the United States did not send a hockey squad to the games.

In the mid-1930's hockey enthusiasts in the United States realized that the AAU could not give its customary efficiency to an alien sport such as ice hockey and that a group wholly devoted to ice hockey should govern the sport on a nationwide basis. Thus, at a meeting in New York on Oct. 29, 1937, the Amateur Hockey Association of the United States was formed. Thomas F. Lockhart of New York was elected president, and a working agreement with the Canadian amateur association was effected. The charter league members of the AHAUS were the Eastern Amateur Hockey League, International Hockey League (Minnesota and Michigan teams), New York Metropolitan League, and the Michigan-Ontario League.

In February 1947 at a meeting held in Prague, Czechoslovakia, the AHAUS was elected to membership in the International Ice Hockey Federation and sent the first team under its sponsorship to the 1948 Winter Olympic Games in St. Moritz, Switzerland. Since 1947 the AHAUS has been the governing body of amateur hockey in the United States.

Modern History. During the 1920's amateur ice hockey, especially in the high school and college area showed a tremendous growth as many educational institutions in the East, upper Midwest, and, to a limited extent, California added hockey to their athletic programs.

The sport continued to flourish during the 1930's, and in the late 1940's and early 1950's many colleges added hockey to their program. Since then the sport has continued to show a steady growth and to exhibit a high caliber of play. Currently, there are about 120 colleges playing hockey on a varsity basis and another 60 playing club hockey. High and prep school hockey is played on a varsity basis in over 500 schools, with about 60% of these located in Massachusetts and Minnesota.

The present surge in hockey interest was generated by two main factors: professional expansion and increased facilities. In 1967 the National Hockey League expanded from 6 teams primarily located in the eastern United States and Canada to 12 teams. New additions included cities from the central United States and the West Coast. Because of this added interest, communities and private investors began building more and more indoor ice rinks that were designed for use by the amateur program.

The Minnesota and Michigan areas always had the advantage of having ice available because of their winter climate, but the indoor facilities meant as much to the growth of hockey there as it did to the southern states. The extreme cold, while providing ice, had a tendency to discourage both players and coaches from getting involved in an outdoor sport.

The AHAUS sponsors national championships in four age classifications: Junior (17–19), Midget (15–16), Bantam (13–14), and Pee Wee (11–12).

Each year the teams in each classification begin a series of play-offs in seven regions throughout the United States. The regional winners are then invited to participate in the National Championships, held the first full weekend in April at various sites throughout the country.

It is estimated that there are more than 350,000 youngsters now participating in amateur hockey throughout the country. This includes the AHAUS, college, high school, and the local recreational programs where most of the players get their start. Although the rate of growth has slowed down somewhat since the early 1970's, there continues to be a tremendous interest in the sport, which is expected to have more than 500,000 participants by the 1980's.

PROFESSIONAL HOCKEY

By GERALD ESKENAZI
"The New York Times"

All-Star Game face-off pits Chicago's Stan Mikita (*left*) against Boston's Phil Esposito. Bobby Orr, Esposito's teammate, watches intently.

When major league hockey was a six-city sport in North America, the owner of the Chicago Black Hawks roared when someone suggested that the National Hockey League (NHL) might expand and take in Buffalo.

"I don't want a town named Buffalo playing in my building!" snorted James Norris.

The statement was not made in the 1920's or the 1930's. It was made in 1965. The NHL had been content since 1942 to limit itself to only six teams, four in the United States and two in Canada.

Expansion. But look at the explosion in recent years as hockey has burst upon the American consciousness with teams not only in the familiar surroundings of New England but, yes, in sunny California, deep in the heart of Texas, and Atlanta, where the only ice had been in glasses.

In 1975 there were 18 National Hockey League teams and 14 in the World Hockey Association. They were not all healthy, and they were not all good. In fact, the NHL suffered its first bankruptcy in 1975 with the Pittsburgh Penguins. But the teams existed. Just eight years before, in 1967, the NHL had taken what it considered its most drastic step by expanding from 6 teams to 12.

Hockey's rise in the 1960's and 1970's paralleled the rise of a burgeoning middle class in the United States. It was a middle class affluent enough to spend money on season tickets (the secret to getting good hockey seats in the seller's market) and to spend a few hundred dollars to outfit each child who wanted to play.

Salaries. In 1967 the six NHL cities were New York, Montreal, Boston, Chicago, Detroit, and Toronto. The average salary per man was about $15,000. The average education of each player was about three years of high school. Three-quarters of the major league players had not graduated from high school.

Soon the NHL Players Association was formed, and then, in 1972, the World Hockey Association (WHA) was founded. The bidding by the rival leagues for players changed the face of the game. Salaries did not simply double or triple; often, they quintupled. The New York Rangers' Brad Park, for example, who had been earning $14,000 in 1970, leaped to $175,000 in 1972 when New York convinced him not to jump to the rival WHA.

By 1975, with 32 major-league hockey teams, the average player's salary jumped to about $45,000, a figure exceeded only by pro basketball's $70,000 average per man. Not only were virtually all the new players high school graduates, but about 10% had attended college.

Ken Dryden of the Montreal Canadiens blocks the goal as he waits for a shot. A Canadian, Dryden was a U. S. collegiate star.

NHL—LEWIS PORTNOY

Fan Enthusiasm. The additional teams, added games, and obvious extra exposure did not diminish fan enthusiasm. It only whetted the crowd's appetite for more. In the NHL, 15 of the 18 teams played to more than 90% capacity. The WHA meanwhile, in its third year, saw its attendance increase 70% over its first season.

Player Violence. While hockey rose to prominence, tempers flared. The sport for the first time came under the scrutiny of a sizable percentage of sports fans in the United States, fans who had been nurtured on basketball, baseball, and football. In those sports, fighting was unacceptable. Even football, in which players talk of the "pit," where there is elbowing and kneeing, did not condone all-out fighting. If you fought in football, you could be ejected. Hockey? It appeared to many fans that fighting was encouraged. The worst that happened was that your hero was sent off the ice for a few minutes. Soon, he'd be back, as belligerent as ever.

This aspect of hockey—violence—was analyzed. It was discussed in the Canadian Parliament. It was discussed by American psychiatrists. New rules were formed, and it became, for example, "illegal" to jump into a fight in progress. Whoever did would automatically be ejected. And the instigator of a fight was to be given a more severe penalty than the poor soul who had to defend himself by fighting.

These new regulations halted fighting to a significant degree. Still, they did not prevent Dave (The Hammer) Schultz of the Philadelphia Flyers from amassing a record 472 penalty minutes for the 1974–75 season. That is the equivalent of eight games in the penalty box. The total was 124 minutes more than the league record—set by Schultz himself the season before. Public opinion was aroused by the arrest of Boston's Dave Forbes after he injured Minnesota's Henry Boucha in a game. Forbes was prosecuted for aggravated assault with a deadly weapon (his hockey stick), but the case ended

in a hung jury. The possibility remained, however, that violence on the ice would be followed in the future by court action.

Gordie Howe and Bobby Hull. Players like Dave Schultz often overshadowed the more gracious aspects of the game. Perhaps the finest story of hockey's explosive decade was the saga of the Howe family, Gordie and his two young sons.

Rick MacLeish fires a shot at the goal. His aggressive play helped the Philadelphia Flyers take the Stanley Cup in 1975.

NHL—LEWIS PORTNOY

When Howe retired from hockey in 1971, he had amassed career NHL records for goals, assists, total points, games played, seasons performed, scoring titles, and most-valuable-player trophies. He stopped after a remarkable 25 seasons. No other major-league athlete had ever played as a regular so long.

His dream had not been realized, though. He had always wanted to play on the same team with his two boys. That became a reality in 1973 when, at the age of 45, he was coaxed out of retirement by the Houston Aeros of the WHA. They had courted Gordie and his sons, Mark and Marty. Finally, all three signed a package worth about $1.5 million for four years. Half of that belonged to Gordie, which was more money than he made his first 20 seasons with the Detroit Red Wings of the NHL.

In fact, he reflected, somewhat wistfully, "the interest on my sons' money each year is more than I earned after 10 years in the NHL." The elder Howe finally called it a career in 1975—after finishing second in scoring in his league's play-offs—and after leading the Aeros to their second straight WHA championship.

Another former NHL star at home in the WHA was Bobby Hull, once the NHL's top goal-scorer with the Chicago Black Hawks. For the Winnipeg Jets to land Hull, it took a $1 million cash bonus. The financial deal was so complicated it was signed in two countries.

Bobby Orr and Other Stars. Money often overshadowed skill. Until the era of the million-dollar player, most of hockey's followers talked mostly about Bobby Orr of the Boston Bruins. He is probably the most dominant factor the game has known. In the charged atmosphere at ice level, where players approach 30 miles an hour on lethal skates, and the puck zooms goalward at better than 100 miles per hour, it often is impossible for one man to dominate the action.

But Orr has. He has changed the face of the game. He is a defenseman who scores goals, sets up forward drives, blasts shots—yet who still is skillful enough to play defense. He was the first defenseman to score more than 20 goals in a season, and if that did not seem like such a big deal to purists who believed modern hockey was nothing much, he went ahead and scored 30 goals. He became the first defenseman to lead the league in scoring, the first to capture the league's top defenseman's award more than four years' running. When he amassed 139 points in the 1970–71 season, he more than doubled the point output of any defenseman before him for one season. In that campaign he set a record for all players of 102 assists. That was 26 assists more than any player in league history had accomplished. In 1975, Orr turned down a $4 million package from the WHA in order to remain in Boston.

It appeared for a while that Orr's club, the Bruins, would be the dynasty to supplant the

Rangers and Flyers scramble for the puck as Flyers' goalie Bernie Parent falls to the ice.

fabled Montreal Canadiens as Stanley Cup champions. The Bruins also had Phil Esposito, the burly center who had established a record of 76 goals in a season along with 152 total points. But expansion had helped spread talent around hockey. And the rule on drafting players—the teams with the poorest records had the pick of the top young skaters—enabled these poor clubs to establish themselves quickly.

Thus, the young Buffalo Sabres were able to draft superstars such as Gil Perreault and Richard Martin. The New York Islanders, after finishing with the worst record in NHL history, drafted Denis Potvin. He quickly became a star on defense and led the Islanders into contention.

New players and new coaches helped change some of the sport's older ideas. They were not afraid to borrow some techniques from the Russians, who embarrassed the NHL in 1972 by almost taking an eight-game series and who defeated the WHA all-stars in 1974, losing only once in eight games. One student of the Russians was the Flyers' coach, Fred Shero, whose club won the Stanley Cup in 1974 and 1975. And Buffalo? They became good enough to play in anyone's building.

HOUSEPLANTS:

a growing interest

By James Fanning
Landscape Architect and Contributing
Editor to Gardening Magazines

The year 1975 saw a spectacular growth of interest in indoor gardening. No city apartment was really furnished unless it had a collection of plants, and every windowsill displayed an abundance of greenery. This enthusiasm for plants was attributable, mainly, to a surge of concern for environmental quality and conservation, as well as the desire for living green as an element of interior decoration. To most people the interest in plants was a newfound one, and suppliers of

A modern home lavishly decorated with plants.

Plant shops now place their major emphasis on greenery, rather than on flowering plants. Old reliables such as aspidistra and rubber plant are much in demand, and there is great interest in tree-like plants such as the various types of ficus, orange trees, and schefflera. Flowering plants being offered are mostly those requiring little care, notably the bromeliads.

houseplants found themselves swamped by demands for information and advice. This led to the publication of a great number of books and periodicals about indoor plants. Associations devoted to particular kinds of plants experienced a surge in membership, and demand for all kinds of equipment, from watering cans to greenhouses, saw a sharp increase.

Naturally, increasing numbers of people are able to earn a living growing and selling houseplants. And, because more and more of them are genuinely interested in the plants they handle, they have been able to sell others on the idea of growing houseplants and of taking proper care of them. Fortunately, there are very few plants that cannot be grown successfully indoors. People interested primarily in decoration may concentrate on the relatively trouble-free foliage plants that dominate indoor collections. For the serious grower or hobbyist there are literally thousands of species from which to choose, whether of the foliage or flowering type.

It was inevitable, of course, that a mystique should grow up around houseplants. Many people love their plants in much the same way that dog or cat owners love their pets and are convinced that some kind of spiritual rapport exists between them. Although there is no scientifically acceptable evidence that plants respond to the emotions of people, they do certainly respond to the care given them by emotionally involved people, so the end result is the same.

Types of Plants. The easiest to care for houseplants are those whose main attraction is their foliage. The selection is very large, and plants of this type are also more suitable for indoor decoration than the more spectacular flowering ones. Philodendrons, schefflera, ficus, and ferns are the most commonly grown foliage houseplants. They are reliable enough to be treated as permanent parts of a room's decoration. They need little direct sunlight, can stand drying out for brief periods without harm, and are fairly pest-free. Misting of the leaves with

JANCO GREENHOUSES

HOME GREENHOUSES

Many people who began with a few green plants in the living room have found their interest developing to such an extent that additional space had to be made for a constantly increasing collection of growing things. This has often led to the conversion of living room or cellar space into plant-growing setups, usually with elaborate lighting arrangements. Mostly, though, home greenhouses are being built to fill this need for additional growing space. A much-used type is the lean-to, such as that shown above. One wall is the side of the house to which it is attached. This kind of greenhouse may be completely open to the adjoining room, requires little or no additional heating, and brings light and a sense of openness into the room. More spacious is the ridge-roof greenhouse, built to extend outward from the house at a right angle, with a simple doorway into the room adjoining. A structure of this type may be of any length, and, since the roof slopes two ways, has much more light than the lean-to.

A completely free-standing greenhouse needs its own system of plumbing, heating, and electrical connections. Therefore, it is relatively costly to build. Greenhouses of all three types are available in a variety of sizes, usually as prefabricated modules with extruded aluminum framework. A wide variety of equipment is also available: automatic ventilation, watering, and light-control systems, as well as automatic heat and humidity regulators.

a sprayer goes a long way toward keeping them in good condition, and light applications of fertilizer help produce new growth.

Hanging plants are the second most popular category. Any plant that will trail over the edge of a pot is suitable for this purpose. Quite satisfactory are members of the spiderwort family. These include zebrina, commelina, and all of the many plants called "wandering Jew." Vines of the grape family, such as cissus, or grape ivy, also make good hanging plants and will climb on any handy support as well.

Flowering plants are not overlooked, of course, although they usually call for more care. Begonias, most particularly, have a high popularity rating. They flower almost constantly, with a great variety of form and color. Most of them also have attractive leaves—some are grown only for their leaves—although these need more care and attention than the tougher foliage plants.

Choosing and Caring for Plants. A few basic rules should be kept in mind when buying houseplants or looking after the ones you already have:

A plant loaded with bright flowers when you buy it cannot be expected to last indefinitely in prime condition. Most plants have a relatively brief flowering period, so be prepared to nurse them through a long flowerless period before their

EZRA STOLLER

OFFICE HORTICULTURE

In keeping with the general feeling of a need for living green, business offices also make plants an integral part of their decor. Plants decorate lobbies and serve as dividers between sections of open-floor office space. Since Friday-to-Monday closing is the usual rule, these plants must be able to survive a regimen that includes two days a week of decreased light and lowered heat. This makes the ficus, philodendron, and schef-

flera popular for city apartments also ideal as office plants. These are usually available in the large sizes demanded by open office space. It is generally more difficult in commercial buildings to avoid hot or cold blasts of air than in the home, but commercial heating and cooling units are usually louvered so that air currents may be redirected. Watering and the general care of office plants are too exacting to be left to the office staff. It is best to have these chores done by an outside professional. Usually, the horticultural contractor who provides the plants can arrange a regular maintenance program.

next display. Professional growers usually discard plants after they have finished flowering. Even plants grown only for their foliage flower at one time or another. Consider these flowers a bonus, since they are not a prime reason for growing the plant.

In a plant shop or commercial greenhouse, foliage plants should have lots of bright, healthy-looking leaves. They should not be coated with any preparation to make them look glossy. Coatings of this sort block plant pores and eventually become discolored and coated with dust.

When buying plants in winter, make sure they are well wrapped before taking them outdoors and make the trip home as brief as possible. In summer, do not leave any plant sitting in a sun-baked automobile. Tell the florist where you intend to place your plant in its new home and get his opinion on the suitability of the location. Also, find out about any special requirements the plant may have and decide whether you can meet them. Study the watering and feeding requirements of your plants. Needs vary from plant to plant, so ask your florist or consult one of the many houseplant reference books.

The following two pages provide specific suggestions for the selection and care of houseplants.

Selected Houseplants

The majority of houseplants do best in bright light, but with partial shade to avoid scorching by direct, hot sunshine. Some of the most popular ones also need to be kept evenly moist, never dry. Ferns (Boston fern, *left*), certain philodendrons (*Philodendron selloum*, *center*), palms (date palm, *right*), African violets, and zebra plants all demand constant moisture, but not soggy conditions.

Another group of plants does best with partial shade and a watering regimen that allows them to dry completely between waterings. Peperomia (*left*), begonia (*center*), grape ivy (*right*), Swedish ivy, philodendron, and sansevieria all belong in this category. Apply water until it runs through the pot; water again when it is bone dry.

A few houseplants need full, direct sunlight for the greater part of the day. Geraniums and bougainvillea are two of these that also do best if kept quite dry. Asparagus fern (*left*), caladium (*center*), prayer plant (*right*), hibiscus, and coleus also need as much light as they can get, but need a constant supply of moisture as well.

Succulent plants store water in their leaves and stems, which makes it possible for them to go through long periods without water at the roots. Most of these—Christmas, Thanksgiving, and Easter cactuses, for example—actually need a month or two of complete dryness before they produce flower buds. Succulents shown (*left to right*): Hoodia cactus, crassula, nidularium, jade plant.

ALL PHOTOS:
RICHARD CHAPMAN, COURTESY OF
WHITE HOUSE FLORISTS, GUILFORD. CT.

Selected Houseplants

BASKET PLANT

Hanging plants, like this wandering Jew, may be attached to window frames or wall brackets, or hung from ceiling beams or from the edges of shelves. A long-spouted watering can and lightweight stepladder make watering easier. Insert a swivel between the hook and the hanger so the plant can be rotated. When they are moved outdoors in summer they can hang from tree branches or a porch overhang.

TERRARIUM

Terrariums make it possible to grow small, delicate plants that must be kept out of drafts and in an atmosphere of constant high humidity. Once planted, watered, and closed, they may be left without attention for weeks. It is usually necessary to let air into the container only when excess moisture collects on the glass. Since the terrarium serves primarily a decorative function, an attractive container, such as this lighted one, is essential.

AVOCADO

An easy way to arouse children's interest in growing things is by letting them start a plant from an avocado pit. Put four toothpicks around the middle of the pit and suspend it in a glass of water so that only the lower third is covered. When the shoot produces two or three leaves it should be transferred to a pot of soil. In time the tree will become quite large and should be pruned to keep it manageable.

TREES

Houseplant trees, such as this Norfolk Island pine, may be an important part of the decor. The size of the pot or tub depends on the size of the plant itself, and this, in turn, depends on room size and furniture arrangement. Containers should be on a movable platform, so that the trees may be taken outdoors in summer or into an enclosed area for spraying or other special treatment as necessary.

HOUSEPLANTS OUTDOORS

All houseplants benefit from an outdoor vacation during the warm months. Most, such as this coleus, do best in the dappled shade of trees or trellis. Some plants, such as geraniums and hibiscus, do best in full sun. Outdoors, plants generally need a great deal more water than they do inside, particularly during hot, dry weather. Outdoors, the plants need to be watched for attack by insect pests.

Preventive Health Care:

EARLY DIAGNOSIS

By Jane F. Jackson
Medical Editor and Contributor
to Professional Journals

Across the United States, millions of people are taking advantage of free screening for many diseases. The screening tests, designed to detect a wide variety of diseases, are conveniently provided in trailers or vans, in neighborhood health clinics, or in hospitals or medical centers. Any person in whom an abnormality is found is referred to physicians for further evaluation, diagnosis, and treatment. People are encouraged to have these screenings even though they may have no physical complaints, because discovering that a disease is present before noticeable symptoms appear is often the key to successful treatment.

Sometimes these screenings are concentrated on one disease, such as tuberculosis, breast cancer, or hypertension (high blood pressure). In "Operation Hi-Blood" in Kansas City, Mo., for example, technicians took the blood pressures of thousands of persons in the lobby of the Federal Building. About 20% of the persons screened had high blood pressure on the first reading and returned for a second reading or were referred to their own physicians or a clinic.

Screening Techniques. More often, however, such projects are multiphasic; that is, they screen for a variety of diseases. Multiphasic screening in a Washington, D. C., program has been carried on for years in both a neighborhood health

A staff member of a community hypertension evaluation clinic takes a blood-pressure reading of a shopper at a busy mall, using a sphygmomanometer. More than 23 million Americans are known to have high blood pressure.

CIBA

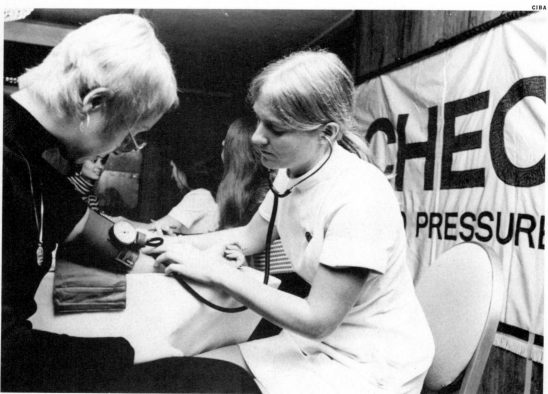

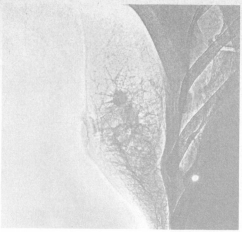

Modern X-ray Techniques

Various methods have been developed to improve X-ray pictures. Xeroradiography is an adaptation that produces more distinct images. In xeroradiography the X-ray beam deposits an electric charge on a metal plate proportional to the amount of radiation that penetrates the plate. By coating the plate with a charged powder, or toner, a high-quality picture, characteristically blue, is produced on paper rather than on film. This sharper, more distinct image is particularly useful in mammography, the examination of the breast for cancer (*right*). The thistle-like pattern in the xeroradiograph (*above*) is an indication of cancer.

Computerized X-ray tomography is a system that allows the examination of body tissues as a series of thin slices. Each computer-produced scan appears as a shadowless cross-section, as if one were looking through the body from the feet to the head. For examination, the patient lies on a motorized couch that extends through a circular opening in the scanner. As the X-ray beam is traversed across the patient, thousands of intensity readings are taken, processed by a minicomputer, displayed on a TV monitor, and recorded photographically. The patient at right is undergoing a brain scan. The body scan (*below*) is a section of the chest, showing the spinal column and the tip of the heart.

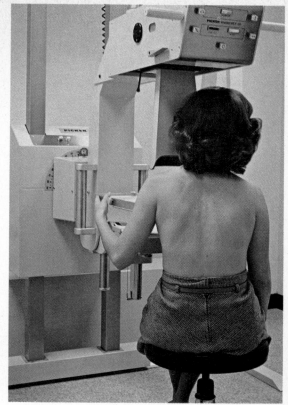

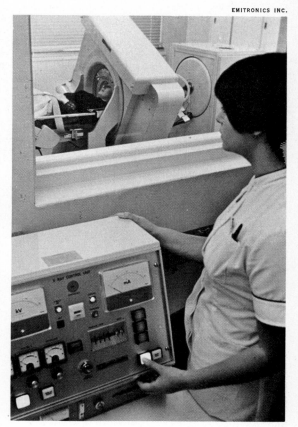

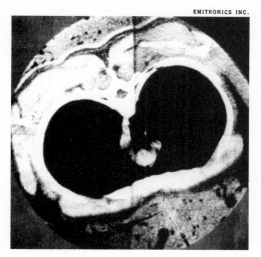

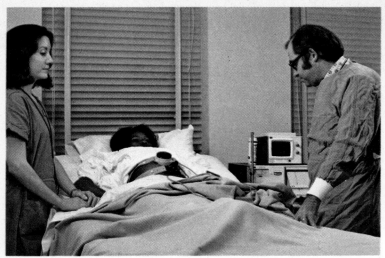

One method of fetal monitoring employs a small, lightweight sensor called an ultrasonic transducer. The device is placed low on the abdomen of a mother in labor. It uses sound waves to detect the baby's heartbeats, which are recorded continuously. At the same time, another sensor monitors labor contractions. From the two records, the attending physician receives continuous information on the baby's reaction to the stress of labor.

NATIONAL FOUNDATION/MARCH OF DIMES

PRENATAL DIAGNOSIS

BY IRWIN J. POLK, M. D.
Saint Luke's Hospital, New York City

Many of the new techniques for early diagnosis have been designed or adapted to the investigation of the pregnant woman and her developing fetus.

Ultrasound. Examination by ultrasound permits exact measurement of the size of the fetus throughout pregnancy. Ultrasound employs high-frequency sound waves to provide description of parts of the body as small as 0.1 milli-

meter in size. The technique distinguishes differences in tissue density, but, unlike X ray, which requires special precautions to prevent damage to healthy tissue, there is no danger in the use of ultrasound. The small, portable units can be used in a doctor's office or at the bedside.

Knowing the size of the developing fetus is especially valuable toward the time of delivery, when the relationship of the size of the baby's head to the pelvic outlet is important. The hazard of delivery when there is a disproportionately large baby or small pelvic outlet can be predicted and steps taken to prevent difficulty in the delivery that in turn might cause damage to the infant. Ultrasound is useful, too, in lo-

center and in a mobile trailer taken to various locations where the needs for health care are greatest. In a two-year period some 20,000 persons were screened in this program, and 52% were referred for further medical evaluation and treatment. Almost all of the abnormalities detected were not known to the persons who were tested.

The Washington program was advertised through newspapers, television, and radio, but only a quarter of those screened came on their own initiative. Direct personal activities of community health workers brought in half of those who came to the clinics, and health and welfare departments and neighborhood health centers brought in the rest. In a program in Buffalo, N. Y., it was found that trained health-care aides who visit people in their homes, discuss their health problems with them, and recommend suitable services greatly increase the use of the health centers and clinics in the community.

Specialized Screening. Some screening programs are highly specialized, focusing not on the general public but on population groups that are particularly susceptible to a certain disease. Thus, checks for bone porosity are made in elderly persons, blood tests for sickle-cell anemia in blacks, pregnancy tests in adolescent girls, and lead-poisoning tests in children living in impoverished neighborhoods. For young children who have chewed lead-based paint the only screening procedure has been to obtain a whole-blood sample from a vein. Both children and

cating the site of the placenta on the uterine wall and also in monitoring the baby's heart when the mother is in labor, like a continuously applied stethoscope.

In the procedure, a small transducer, a device that changes electrical energy into sound energy, is placed over the area to be examined. The sound energy is reflected by the tissues underneath and reconverted into an electrical signal. Amplified electronically, the sound-energy pattern (echogram) is displayed on a cathode-ray tube, like a television image. It may be recorded photographically.

Amniocentesis. Knowing the location of the placenta is also important for the use of another technique of fetal monitoring—amniocentesis. Sometimes it is helpful to sample the amniotic fluid, in which the baby is bathed in the uterus. The fluid, which reflects the general health of the fetus, is obtained by entering the amniotic sac with a sterile needle. The site for this puncture can be selected by first locating the position of the baby and the placenta through ultrasound techniques. The fluid obtained can be analyzed for cellular content and chemistry.

For example, increase in the bilirubin—the principal bile pigment—contained in the amniotic fluid is suggestive of Rh-disease, or erythroblastosis fetalis. In this illness fetal red blood cells are destroyed by maternal antibodies transmitted across the placenta. Also, by examining the fetal cells that are shed into the amniotic fluid, certain genetic disorders, such as Mongolism, can be predicted. A chemical determination of the amount of a particular protein in the amniotic fluid can indicate the presence of defects in the central nervous system.

These disorders are often genetic in origin and require prompt attention after birth. It is particularly helpful for mothers who have given birth to one baby with a birth defect to have these studies done during pregnancy.

Fiber-Optic Endoscopy. An endoscope is any instrument that permits the operator to examine areas within the body. Fiber-optics are very thin, glass or plastic filaments whose refractive index permits transmission of light around corners. Fiber-optic endoscopes have been used for examining many organs in the body, and it is now also possible with similar fiber-optic instruments to examine visually a developing fetus in the uterus.

Other Fetal Monitoring Devices. Monitoring of the fetus just before and during delivery is also possible. The heart rate of the infant during delivery is an indication of its well-being; a high rate suggests danger to the infant. Recently, it has been proved useful to attach a small electrode to the infant either in the uterus or as soon as the head is visible so that the heart rate during labor can be monitored continuously by a fetal electrocardiograph. The instrument also simultaneously records the strength and rate of uterine contractions for comparison with the status of the infant. Alternatively, this monitoring of mother and child may be done with ultrasonic equipment. In addition, in some hospitals, blood is sampled continually from the scalp of the infant during delivery so that chemical determinations can be made. All of this is aimed at advising the doctor about the condition of the infant during delivery, so that measures needed to assure the health of the infant and the mother may be taken promptly.

parents often strongly resist this technique. However, a new finger-prick blood test is now available that makes mass screening of children a simple matter.

Most states now require screening at birth for the genetic disease of phenylketonuria (PKU), a condition that leads to arrested brain development by four months of age and eventually to mental retardation. The PKU test is widely used to detect abnormal levels of the protein phenylalanine in the blood of newborn infants. When the condition is diagnosed, infants are put on a diet to prevent or minimize brain damage from this disease.

Cancer Diagnosis. One of the tests often used in multiphasic screening is the Papanicolaou (Pap) test to detect cancer or precancerous conditions. Cells are taken from the organ to be checked, smeared across a glass slide, and examined under the microscope for abnormalities that signal the development of cancer. Pap tests have been found reliable for early detection of cancer of the uterine cervix, from which specimens are readily and painlessly obtained, and such tests have saved the lives of many women. The technique can also be used for finding cancer of the kidneys, bladder, colon, lungs, or breast from specimens of the secretions of these organs.

Can mass screening of women reduce the incidence of breast cancer? The death rate for women from all causes decreased by 42% from 1935 to 1967, going down from 15.2 to 8.8 per 1,000 annually. However, their death rate from

breast cancer did not change during this period, remaining close to 40 per 100,000 women annually.

This gloomy picture prompted the development of a periodic breast-cancer screening program by the Health Insurance Plan of Greater New York (HIP) to determine whether or not periodic screening and early detection could affect the death rate from this serious disease. The HIP study found that the proportion of breast cancers that had spread into the underarm lymph glands of women in the study group was substantially lower than in a control group of unscreened women. Furthermore, there were only 31 breast cancer deaths among screened women as compared with 52 among women in the control group. These findings indicate that screening for breast cancer substantially improves early detection and successful treatment. In recent years, interest in such screening has greatly increased, especially with the wide publicity given the experiences of Betty Ford and Margaretta (Happy) Rockefeller with this disease.

Results and Reactions. Multiphasic screening has proved very effective in bringing people into the health-care system and evaluating their conditions rapidly and comprehensively. Those who are screened almost unanimously praise such programs. They do not complain of feeling that they are on a medicine assembly line. Rather, they appreciate the efficiency of a program that gives them such extensive testing so quickly. Many of those who have used such programs remark that it makes it easier for them to get a yearly health checkup. This in turn makes them more conscious of their state of health and more likely to take care of it. With proper organization and quality controls, screening programs can be provided that use a minimum of patient and physician time and reliably detect the presence of a host of crippling or potentially fatal diseases.

Thermography is a technique in which a scanning device measures the amount of heat energy given off by the surface of the body and converts the temperature information to color. The energy (infrared) measured is produced by the body itself, and the warmer the body is, the more intense the radiated energy. Thermography is particularly useful in finding breast tumors, which show up as warmer zones than the surrounding tissue. Thermograms are also used in finding areas of increased or decreased circulation and are helpful for diagnosing lesions in the skin surface.

BARNES ENGINEERING COMPANY

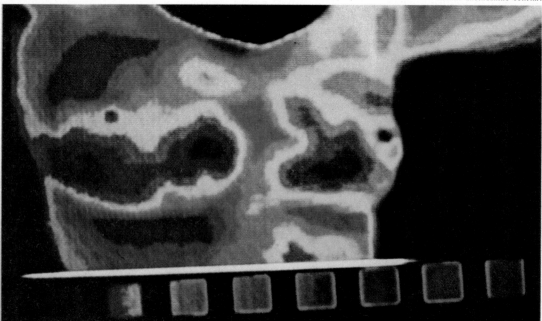

President Ford received enthusiastic welcomes around the United States during his first year in office. He waves to crowd in Concord, N. H., in April.

REVIEW OF THE YEAR
1975

Soldiers survey the wreckage of U.S.-bound jet carrying Vietnamese orphans that crashed on April 4 near Saigon.

UPI

ACCIDENTS AND DISASTERS

Accidents and disasters claimed a high toll in 1975. The worst air disaster in the United States in over a decade occurred on June 24 when an Eastern Airlines jet crashed at Kennedy Airport during heavy turbulence, killing 113 persons. The weather was also responsible for heavy losses, as were earthquakes, of which one in Turkey claimed the lives of over 2,000 people. A list of the year's major disasters follows.

AVIATION

Jan. 30—Turkish jetliner crashes into the Sea of Marmara, killing all 37 persons aboard.

Feb. 3—Philippine airplane makes crash landing in Manila when engine catches fire, killing 31 of 32 passengers.

Feb. 9—West German military transport plane crashes during a storm over Crete, killing all 42 persons aboard.

March 16—Argentine air force jet carrying civilians crashes into Andes, killing all 47 passengers.

March 20—U. S. military jet crashes into Olympic Mountains in Washington, killing 16 servicemen.

April 4—U. S. Air Force jet carrying Vietnam refugees crashes shortly after takeoff from Saigon, killing over 200 persons, at least 100 of them children.

June 24—Eastern Airlines 727 jetliner crashes during attempt to land at Kennedy Airport in New York, killing 113 of 124 persons aboard.

July 5—Soviet airliner crashes near Black Sea, killing 28 passengers.

July 31—Taiwan domestic airliner crashes during landing attempt in Taipei, killing 26 of 75 passengers.

Aug. 3—Jordanian jetliner carrying Moroccan workers from France crashes into mountainside in Morocco during heavy fog, killing all 188 persons aboard.

Aug. 20—Czechoslovak jetliner crashes while attempting to land in Damascus, killing 126 of 128 persons aboard.

Sept. 30—Hungarian airliner crashes in Mediterranean Sea, killing 60 persons.

Oct. 25—Bolivian air force transport crashes in Andes near La Paz, killing all 70 persons aboard.

Oct. 30—Yugoslav charter jetliner crashes during heavy fog in attempt to land at Prague, Czechoslovakia, killing 68 of 120 people aboard.

LAND AND SEA TRANSPORTATION

Jan. 1—Bus carrying holiday skiers plunges off road in Japan Alps and into a lake killing 23 persons. The other 36 passengers swam to shore.

Jan. 30—Bus crash in Ecuador kills 30.

Feb. 17—Train collision in Cape Town, South Africa, kills 27.

Feb. 22—Head-on crash of two trains 80 miles north of Oslo, Norway, leaves 27 dead.

Feb. 24—Bus plunges down steep mountain in Medellin, Colombia, killing 20 persons.

Feb. 28—Worst subway crash in London history leaves 41 dead when train crashes in dead-end tunnel.

May 19—Truck carrying wedding party collides with train, killing 66 persons in New Delhi, India.

May 27—Bus plunges off bridge in North Yorkshire, England, after brakes fail, killing 32 people.

June 29—Indian passenger boat capsizes in monsoon-swollen Ganges River near Patna, killing 80 of 100 persons aboard.

July 5—Bus-truck collision kills 21 persons in southern Iran.

Aug. 3—Two Chinese river ferries collide and sink in Hsi Kiang River, 50 miles (80 km) west of Canton, leaving 500 persons dead.

Oct. 20—Subway collision in Mexico City kills 27 people.

STORMS AND FLOODS

Jan. 11—Tornadoes whip through southern Mississippi, killing 12 people; heavy flooding due to unseasonal rain in southern Thailand leaves 131 dead.

Jan. 14—Blizzard with 90 m. p. h. winds whips across U. S. Middle West, killing 50 people.

Jan. 27—Tropical storm hits Manila, Philippines, killing 30 people.

March 24—Atlanta tornado kills three people.

May 11—Cyclones hit delta region of Burma, killing 187 people.

FIRES, EXPLOSIONS, AND BUILDING CAVE-INS

Jan. 22—Five-story commercial building in Manila, engulfed in flames, leaves 51 dead.

March 9—Cement embankment collapses and crushes dormitory housing employees of Seoul, Korea, wig factory, leaving 17 women dead.

March 28—Yugoslavian hospital maternity-ward fire takes the lives of 25 infants.

Dec. 12—Fire sweeps through tent camp of Muslim pilgrims, near Mecca, killing at least 138.

Dec. 27—Explosion, followed by flooding, in coal mine northwest of Calcutta, India, causes death of approximately 400 miners.

Dec. 29—A bomb detonates in New York City's LaGuardia Airport, killing 11.

EARTHQUAKES

Feb. 4—A major earthquake hits southern Manchuria, but Chinese make no casualty or damage reports.

Sept. 6—Earthquake strikes town of Lice and surrounding areas in eastern Turkey, killing 2,312 people and injuring 3,372.

ADVERTISING

The year 1975 was another difficult one for the U. S. advertising industry. The recession curtailed consumer buying and forced many advertisers to hold down spending. By year's end, slowly rising consumer confidence began to be felt, and U. S. advertising budgets reflected this. Total ad expenditure, however, again failed to keep pace with inflation, rising only 6% from 1974 to $26.8 billion, with local advertising growing faster than national advertising. The industry increased its self-regulatory efforts in the face of continuing government intervention in advertising matters.

Regulation. Advertising continued to face regulatory threats from the Federal Trade Commission, including proposed nutritional disclosure rules for food advertising, new restrictions on the use of warranties and guarantees, and tougher scrutiny of proprietary drug ingredients and claims. On state and local levels, the industry fought back against the imposition of special taxes on advertising. It also stepped up self-policing programs in sensitive areas such as advertising to children, product safety claims, and more realistic portrayal of women and minorities in advertising.

Copy. Matching the buying public's sober mood, advertising stressed product information presented in factual, serious tones. Promotional use of high-priced spokesmen from the worlds of sport, fashion, and entertainment showed a significant increase. Amid growing public disenchantment with big business and government, advertising increasingly strove to personalize industries and products from cars to fast foods. The government relied heavily on advertising to educate the public about social issues, including energy conservation and drunk driving.

Media. Television networks, responding to viewer criticism about sex and violence, created a "family" entertainment hour in the early evening. Magazines, hit by escalating postal rates, raised copy and subscription prices, while maintaining or dropping advertising rates. Newspapers, continuing to automate, were plagued by labor problems. Direct-response advertising, selling direct by mail or telephone, boomed. FM radio grew rapidly by broadening from classical and rock-only formats to all-news and others.

USING SUGAR CAN SAVE YOU MONEY.

Mixing your sugar with our Kool-Aid® Brand Unsweetened Soft Drink Mix is still a great way to save money. Because even with adding your own sugar, Unsweetened Kool-Aid® is just about the least expensive soft drink you can buy. Only 15¢ for a whole delicious quart.

So do something sweet for yourself. Save yourself some money. Mix your sugar with our Unsweetened Kool-Aid®.

OUR KOOL-AID AND YOUR SUGAR. IT'S SMARTER THAN YOU THINK.

SOFT DRINK	PER QT.	8-OZ. SERVING
Unsweetened 2 qt. env. **KOOL-AID** with 1 cup of sugar	15¢	4¢
Six 12 fl. oz. cans **COCA-COLA**	67¢	17¢
1 qt. env. **WYLER'S** sugar-sweetened	27¢	7¢
46 fl. oz. can **HI-C**	40¢	10¢

And kids really love Kool-Aid®. So, if you can give them something they love without spending too much money, why not? Besides, Kool-Aid® has Vitamin C.

GREY ADVERTISING
CHRYSLER CORPORATION

Advertising Volume. Total spending for advertising increased to $28.4 billion, 6% over 1974's $26.8 billion. Local advertising's growth of 6.7% to $12.8 billion outpaced national spending, up 5.4% to $15.6 billion. The fastest-growing media area was local television, where retailers helped boost advertising dollars by 11.2%. The dominant medium remained newspapers, up by 5.3% to $8.4 billion, while television continued to close the gap, growing 8.8% to $5.3 billion. Direct mail totaled $4.3 billion, up 7%. Radio rose 7.8% to just under $2 billion. Magazines were down 0.9% to $1.5 billion, while business publications grew 1.7% to $915 million, and outdoor publications 4.4% to $235 million. All other media, from car cards to counter displays, gained 5.9% to $5.7 billion.

Canada. All provinces introduced or passed legislation on consumer protection, labeling, advertising to children, misleading copy, or credit disclosure. Canada's broadcast regulatory body proposed that by 1976 television content be 70% Canadian and that all commercials be produced nationally.

A bill was introduced to disallow business deductions for advertising in Canadian editions of U. S. magazines. Total advertising dollars rose 13% to $476 million. Television increased 18% to $230 million and totaled 48% of spending. Consumer magazines gained 22% to $46 million, and newspapers were up 9% to $114 million. Weekend papers held steady at $29 million, while radio grew 7% to $51 million and farm books 13% to $6 million.

EDWARD H. MEYER
Chairman of the Board and President,
Grey Advertising, Inc.

AFGHANISTAN

The Republic of Afghanistan, which supplanted the monarchy in 1973, survived in 1975. The economy showed weakness, and relations with Pakistan were tense.

Politics. President Mohammed Daud dominated all segments of government. Assumptions that he was a figurehead for young army and leftist intellectual radicals dissipated as Daud emerged in full command.

In domestic and foreign policy Daud maintained a right-of-center stance, balancing elements at both ends of the political spectrum. His policy of *bi-tarafi* (balancing two sides) disappointed extremists who thought that a republican regime would automatically bring radical policy departures. They remained resentful, but Daud's firm control of the security apparatus kept dissent mute.

Political activists eagerly awaited the new constitution, which Daud promised in 1973. Drafting committees were reportedly working on it but little surfaced publicly. Daud publicly announced that it will be submitted to public ratification, probably through a *loya jirgah,* a traditional Afghan tribal institution. He also said that Afghanistan will eventually have a two-party system.

Economy. Official policy is to establish a mixed, guided economy with government domination over major economic sectors and with merchandising and minor projects left to private enterprise. A private investment law, promulgated by executive decree, offered new incentives to small industries, but their role in national development remained modest. The government was the principal recipient of foreign aid and the major source of capital.

Daud nationalized the Bank-e-Milli, the only major source of private capital in the country. The bank pioneered in capital formation and founded the first large industrial (textiles) and agricultural (cotton) enterprises in Afghanistan.

In spite of vigorous economic initiatives, the Afghan economy remained lethargic during 1975. Long-term economic weaknesses overshadowed serious short-term problems such as marketing agricultural commodities in a depressed world market. Afghanistan's food-to-population ratio remained fragile; a recurrence of the 1971 famine remained a menacing possibility. Long-term debt-service obligations piled up despite partial moratoria by creditor nations. More than 40% of exports went to external debt repayment in 1975. Economic bright spots included $150 million in gold reserves; adequate energy supplies because of low consumption, and exchange of natural gas for Soviet petroleum products; and the emergence of new major foreign aid donors, such as Iran, India, Saudi Arabia and Kuwait. The USSR remained the largest donor.

Foreign Affairs. Relations between Pakistan and Afghanistan continued to deteriorate during 1975, as Daud championed the Pushtun tribes, which live on both sides of the border. In world politics Afghanistan continued in 1975 its traditional policy of delicate nonalignment. It also usually supported the policies of moderate members of the Third World bloc.

LEON B. POULLADA
Northern Arizona University

―――― **AFGHANISTAN • Information Highlights** ――――

Official Name: Republic of Afghanistan.
Location: Central Asia.
Area: 250,000 square miles (647,497 sq km).
Population (1975 est.): 19,300,000.
Chief Cities (1972 est.): Kabul, the capital, 500,000; Kandahar, 200,000; Herat, 100,000.
Government: *Head of state,* Mohammed Daud Khan, president (took office July 1973). *Head of government,* Mohammed Daud Khan, prime minister (took office July 1973). *Legislature*—Shura (dissolved July 1973).
Monetary Unit: Afghani (45 Afghanis equal U. S.$1, July 1975).
Gross National Product (1973 est.): $1,500,000,000.
Manufacturing (major products): Textiles, cement, processed fruit, carpets, furniture.
Major Agricultural Products: Wheat, cotton, fruit and nuts, karakul pelts.
Foreign Trade (1972): *Exports,* $99,000,000; *imports,* $166,000,000.

A military parade in Luanda celebrates Angolan independence, which came on November 11. Fierce fighting among rival factions continued after independence.

AFRICA

Africa in 1975 saw Portugal grant independence to Angola, Cape Verde, Mozambique, and São Tomé and Príncipe. Angola was strifetorn by competing nationalist groups. Ethiopia's military rulers continued to fight an Eritrean separatist movement and underground opposition. Emperor Haile Selassie's death on August 27 was little noticed. Uganda's mercurial President Idi Amin continued to irritate both African and Western leaders, particularly in a clash at the United Nations with the U. S. ambassador. A USSR buildup in Somalia led the United States to consider enlarging its base in the Indian Ocean. Military coups occurred in Nigeria, Chad, and the Malagasy Republic, and a political death caused controversy in Kenya. Thousands of Moroccans marching into Spanish Sahara were halted in time to prevent bloodshed. The Organization of African Unity (OAU) leaders approved working with white South Africa in the drive for black rule in Rhodesia and South West Africa (Namibia).

PORTUGUESE AFRICA

Angola Independence. Beset with internal problems, Portugal gave Angola its promised independence on November 11. Angola's three rival nationalist groups continued their fierce fighting. Seeking to oust the dominant pro-Marxist and USSR-supported Popular Movement for the Liberation of Angola (MPLA) was the Chinese and Zaire-backed anti-Communist Nationalist Front for the Liberation of Angola (FNLA). The third group was the previously neutral but later pro-FNLA National Union for the Total Independence of Angola (UNITA). Besides the Russian-Chinese rivalry and the struggle for personal power, Angola's near an-

archy reflected explosive tribal differences. The MPLA's leader, Agostinho Neto, is a Mbundu, a group that is part of the Kimbundu tribe. The FNLA's leader, Holden Roberto, brother-in-law of Zaire's President Mobutu Sese Seko, was supported by the Kibongo tribe, which consisted of 20% of Angola's blacks plus 1 million living in Zaire. The UNITA's leader, Jonas Savimbi, was supported by the Ovimbundu tribe, comprising 33% of Angola's blacks. Since the MPLA held the capital of Luanda, Agostinho Neto was named president on November 10. Observers believed he would continue to be militarily challenged by the FNLA and UNITA.

The power struggle left Angola with public services halted, food and gasoline nearly depleted, and deaths mounting from combat and starvation. Portuguese troops could not keep order nor fully protect the approximately 350,000 Portuguese settlers who sought to escape to Portugal at the rate of over 1,000 a day from July, when fighting raged around Luanda. Since 1961, about 1.5 million blacks reportedly have also fled into South West Africa.

Besides internal political problems and a dismal economy, Angola also faced a separatist threat from the tiny 2,800-square-mile (7,250-sq-km) enclave of oil-rich Cabinda.

Mozambique Independence. Mozambique became independent from Portugal on June 25, after a 10-year struggle by the Mozambique Liberation Front (FRELIMO). As president, FRELIMO leader Samora M. Machel returned from exile in Tanzania to the capital of Lourenço Marques to build a Maoist-Marxist state. While providing a sanctuary for guerrilla raids into neighboring white-ruled Rhodesia, Mozambique also expanded relations with Tanzania, its socialist neighbor.

Other New Nations. Two other former Portuguese colonies achieved independence in 1975. The Cape Verde Islands became a sovereign na-

INFORMATION HIGHLIGHTS ON THE COUNTRIES OF AFRICA

Nation	Population (in millions)	Capital	Area (in sq mi)	Head of State and/or Government (as of Dec. 1, 1975)
Algeria	16.8	Algiers	919,593	Houari Boumédienne, president
Angola	6.4	Luanda	481,351	(disputed)
Benin (Dahomey)	3.1	Porto-Novo	43,483	Mathieu Kerekou, president
Botswana	.7	Gaborone	231,804	Sir Seretse Khama, president
Burundi	3.8	Bujumbura	10,747	Michel Micombero, president
Cameroon	6.4	Yaoundé	183,569	Ahmadou Ahidjo, president
Cape Verde	.3	Praia	1,557	Aristides Pereira, president
Central African Republic	1.6	Bangui	240,535	Jean Bedel Bokassa, president
Chad	4.0	N'Djemena	495,754	Felix Malloum, chief of state
Comoro Islands	.3	Moroni	838	Ali Soilih, head of triumvirate
Congo	1.3	Brazzaville	132,047	Marien Ngouabi, president
Egypt	37.5	Cairo	386,660	Anwar el-Sadat, president
Equatorial Guinea	.3	Malabo	10,831	Francisco Macias Nguema, president
Ethiopia	28.0	Addis Ababa	471,777	Teferi Banti, chairman, Provisional Military Administrative Committee
Gabon	.5	Libreville	103,346	Omar Bongo, president
Gambia, The	.5	Banjul	4,361	Sir Dauda K Jawara, president
Ghana	9.9	Accra	92,099	Ignatius K. Acheampong, Supreme Military Council
Guinea	4.4	Conakry	94,926	Ahmed Sékou Touré, president
Guinea-Bissau	.5	Bissau	13,948	Luiz de Almeida Cabral, president
Ivory Coast	4.9	Abidjan	124,503	Félix Houphouët-Boigny, president
Kenya	13.3	Nairobi	224,959	Jomo Kenyatta, president
Lesotho	1.1	Maseru	11,720	Moshoeshoe II, king Leabua Jonathan, prime minister
Liberia	1.7	Monrovia	43,000	William R. Tolbert, president
Libya	2.3	Tripoli and Benghazi	679,360	Muammar el Qaddafi, president Revolutionary Command Council
Malagasy Republic	8.0	Tananarive	226,657	Didier Ratsiraka, president
Malawi	4.9	Zomba	45,757	H. Kamuzu Banda, president
Mali	5.7	Bamako	478,765	Moussa Traoré, president
Mauritania	1.3	Nouakchott	397,954	Mokhtar Ould Daddah, president
Mauritius	.9	Port Louis	720	Sir Rawan Osman, governor-general Sir Seewoosagur Ramgoolam, prime minister
Morocco	17.5	Rabat	172,413	Hassan II, king
Mozambique	9.2	Lourenço-Marques	302,328	Samora M. Machel, president
Niger	4.6	Niamey	489,190	Seyni Kountche, head of military government
Nigeria	62.9	Lagos	356,668	Murtala Rufai Mohammed, head of military government
Rhodesia	6.3	Salisbury	150,803	Clifford W. Dupont, president Ian D. Smith, prime minister
Rwanda	4.2	Kigali	10,169	Juvenal Habyalimana, president
São Tomé and Príncipe	.076	São Tomé	372	Mañuel Pinto da Costa, president Miguel Trovoada, prime minister
Senegal	4.4	Dakar	75,750	Léopold S. Senghor, president Abdou Diouf, premier
Sierra Leone	3.0	Freetown	27,700	Siaka P. Stevens, president Sorie I. Koroma, prime minister
Somalia	3.2	Mogadishu	246,200	Mohammed Siad Barre, president Supreme Revolutionary Council
South Africa, Rep. of	24.7	Pretoria and Cape Town	471,444	J. J. Fouché, president Balthazar J. Vorster, prime minister
Sudan	18.3	Khartoum	967,497	Jaafar al-Numeiry, president
Swaziland	.5	Mbabane	6,704	Sobhuza II, king Makhosini Dlamini, prime minister
Tanzania	15.4	Dar es Salaam	364,899	Julius K. Nyerere, president
Togo	2.2	Lomé	21,622	Gnassingbe Eyadema, president
Tunisia	5.7	Tunis	63,170	Habib Bourguiba, president Hedi Nouira, premier
Uganda	11.4	Kampala	91,134	Idi Amin, president
Upper Volta	6.0	Ouagadougou	105,869	Sangoulé Lamizana, president
Zaire	24.5	Kinshasa	905,565	Mobuto Sese Seko, president
Zambia	5.0	Lusaka	290,585	Kenneth W. Kuanda, president Mainza Chona, prime minister

tion on June 5, but the country's relationship with Guinea-Bissau remained undecided. Many of Guinea-Bissau's leaders are natives of the Cape Verdes. São Tomé and Príncipe, two islands off the west coast of Africa, became a sovereign nation on July 12.

EAST AFRICA

Ethiopia. A year after he was deposed, Emperor Haile Selassie was found dead in his bed on August 27 at the age of 83. Lack of witnesses or an autopsy and hasty burial the same day evoked speculation about the nature of his death. With his long rule ended, Ethiopia's 3,000-year-old monarchy seemed unlikely to regain power. (See also OBITUARIES.)

Ethiopia's governing socialist military council, the Dergue, faced drought and virtual civil war in 1975. Half its forces were fighting the separatist Eritrean Liberation Front (ELF), which stepped up its 13-year war to remove Eritrea from Ethiopia. Around the capital of Addis Ababa the government was also fighting a "counterrevolutionary" group, the dissident Ethiopian Democratic Union, which wanted to topple the Dergue because of its increasingly arbitrary rule. One report cited over 200 executions by the government. On September 25, to halt distribution of antigovernment handbills, security forces killed 7 and wounded 19 at Addis Ababa airport. A general strike followed on September 30.

The ELF captured two U. S. citizens on July 14 and two more on September 13 from the U. S. communications relay station near Asmara, capital of Eritrea province, and held them hostage in an effort to force the United States to stop financial aid and weapons shipments to Ethiopia's government.

Uganda. On July 10, after two postponed execution dates, British teacher Denis Cecil Hills was freed. He had been arrested on April 1 after referring to President Amin as "a village tyrant" in an unpublished book. That Hills and other imprisoned British subjects were political pawns became clear when Amin demanded that Britain cease criticizing him and sell him parts for military equipment. He clashed with two British military representatives who carried a letter from Queen Elizabeth requesting clemency. Amin's release of Hills during the visit of British Foreign Secretary James Callaghan was prompted by the need to avoid bad publicity prior to the meeting of the OAU in Kampala in late July.

In January, Finance Minister Emmanuel Wakhweya fled to London and resigned, saying that Amin had brought Uganda to economic ruin. On March 25, Amin set the sentence for the "economic crimes" of smuggling and hoarding at death. Ordinary home and industrial items were in short supply. However, Amin did secure Arab funds to overcome shortages temporarily and to complete hotel facilities for the OAU meeting.

In August, Amin vowed to crush a secret opposition group. Since ousting President Milton Obote in 1971, Amin has expelled over 30,000 Asian residents and allegedly killed up to 90,000 Ugandans opposing him. He has had strained relations with Tanzania (where Obote is in exile), Zambia, and other countries, including Israel. At the United Nations on October 1, he denounced Zionism as racism. Critics have called Amin a despot who seeks scapegoats to hide internal troubles; nevertheless, his military grip on Uganda seems firm.

Tanzania. On October 30, Dr. Mary D. Leakey, widow of archaeologist Louis Leakey, reported finding the oldest known fossil remains of man in Laetolil, 25 miles (40 km) south of Olduvai Gorge. The remains were dated as 3.75 million years old, 1 million years older than man's previously established age.

UPI

Uganda's President Idi Amin (*center*) meets with British lecturer Denis Hills (*right*) and British Foreign Secretary James Callaghan. Hills, condemned to death for criticizing Amin, was pardoned by the Ugandan president.

Ready for its official opening on October 24, the Chinese-built and financed Tanzam railway will carry passengers and freight, including Zambia's copper, to Tanzania's Indian Ocean port of Dar es Salaam. It goes through black-governed countries, where Zambia had previously been dependent on rail lines through white-governed Rhodesia and South Africa. Begun in 1970, the 1,200-mile (1,920-km) rail line is China's most ambitious and successful aid project in Africa.

On October 26, Julius K. Nyerere was re-elected president for five years. The only candidate on the ballot, he won 92% of the vote. In 1970 he won 95% of the vote.

Kenya. Joshia Mwangi Kariuka, popular critic of President Jomo Kenyatta, was murdered on March 2. A June 3 report on the murder, which Kenyatta first tried to squelch and then to alter, implicated Kenyatta's colleagues. The parliamentary vote on June 11 accepting the report seriously challenged Kenyatta's 12-year leadership. Corruption charges were leveled at Kenyatta, his relatives and friends in high government posts. The belief was that the murdered Kariuka not only seriously rivaled Kenyatta for the presidency but, knowing of the administration's corruption, was about to reveal it in a book. On October 16, Kenyatta, after jailing two members of Parliament, told that body that he would not tolerate dissidents.

Comoro Islands. The Comoro Islands, four islands about 300 miles (480 km) off the coast of the Malagasy Republic, became independent on July 6. In a December 1974 referendum 94% of the electorate voted for independence from France. France delayed the formal granting of independence because one of the islands, Mayotte, voted to retain ties to France. Leaders of the other three islands then unilaterally declared their independence and declared that Mayotte was within the new country. The Comoro Islands have a largely-Muslim population of 400,000. The UN Security Council in October and the General Assembly in November voted to admit the new nation as the 143rd member of the United Nations.

SPANISH SAHARA

Morocco, Algeria, and Mauritania competed for control of phosphate-rich Spanish Sahara in Northwest Africa. On November 6, Morocco's King Hassan II massed 350,000 volunteer citizens for a march toward El Aiun, capital of neighboring Spanish Sahara. Opposing Spanish and Algerian troops massed nearby. Mine fields and trenches temporarily halted over 100,000 Moroccan marchers 6 miles (10 km) inside the territory on November 8. The next day King Hassan called off the march.

Hassan's motives supposedly were to protect Morocco's phosphate exports from competition and to strengthen his own power. Algeria's left-wing government wanted to curb expansion of Morocco's conservative monarchy, with which it has historically clashed. Both the United Nations and Spain, which is giving up the Spanish Sahara, want the territory's population of 88,000 nomads to decide their own fate by referendum. In late December, Mauritanian forces took the southern port city of La Guera.

COUPS

Nigeria. On July 29, while attending the OAU meeting in Kampala, Uganda, Gen. Yakubu Gowon was deposed as Nigeria's head of state and commander of the armed forces. His successor, Brig. Gen. Muritala Rufai Mohammed, who had helped to bring Gowon to power nine years before, assured Gowon that he could safely return to Nigeria. Gowon, who pledged support to the new government, left for Britain August 11 for an indefinite stay. Observers felt that the coup resulted from Gowon's failure to resolve political and economic problems, his intent to return Nigeria to civilian rule, inflation, continued government and military corruption, and his failure to increase the number of Nigerian states as promised.

Chad. President Ngarta Tombalbaye, Chad's president since independence in 1960, was killed April 13 in a miltary coup. The new chief of state was Brig. Gen. Felix Malloum, who had been imprisoned as a political threat in July 1973. He headed a nine-member military government in the former French central African country of 4 million people.

Marxist opponents of General Malloum held several French citizens as hostages, including Françoise Claustre, an archaeologist captured in mid-1972, and her husband Pierre, who flew from France to find her. The French government at first refused to pay the requested $2.2 million ransom plus military supplies, but French journalist Thierry Desjardins' interviews with the hostages, published in the newspaper *Le*

At King Hassan's urging, 350,000 Moroccans began a "peace march" into Spanish Sahara on November 6.

UPI

Figaro, embarrassed the French government. France then wanted to ransom its nationals, but Chad objected to France's dealing directly with the rebels.

Malagasy Republic. On Dec. 31, 1974, a coup attempt failed on this Texas-size island in the Indian Ocean, 250 miles (400 km) east of Mozambique. However, President Gabriel Ramanantsoa dissolved his government on Jan. 25, 1975, to placate the opposition. He turned over the presidency to Col. Richard Ratsimandrava, who was assassinated on Feb. 11. A trial convicted three minor figures for involvement in the assassination. On June 15 the ruling military group appointed as new president Didier Ratsiraka, who was said to be responsible for the Malagasy Republic's pro-Soviet and anti-French attitude. Underlying the political upheaval is a long rivalry between the coastal people and the population of the interior, which is mountainous.

INTRA-AFRICAN RELATIONS

OAU. Meeting in Addis Ababa, Ethiopia, February 13–21, the OAU Council of Ministers criticized the nomination on January 16 of Nathaniel Davis as U. S. assistant secretary of state for African affairs. Davis, who was believed by Africans to favor white South Africa and who was linked to alleged U. S. involvement in the overthrow of Chile's President Salvador Allende, later resigned. The ministers also criticized the Arab bloc for increasing oil prices without compensating African nations. Meeting in Tanzania in April, OAU ministers issued the Dar es Salaam Declaration, which approved negotiating with white South Africa to achieve black rule in Rhodesia and independence for Namibia (South West Africa).

When African heads of state gathered in Kampala, Uganda, on July 28–August 1, they approved the Dar es Salaam Declaration and a variety of other measures. Rather than support an Arab-backed resolution to expel Israel from the United Nations, they voted to exert pressure on Israel to return Arab lands. They also decided to send a mission to mediate among Angola's three rival liberation groups. After hearing of the overthrow of Nigerian leader Yakubu Gowon, who was attending the Kampala meeting, four of the 19 heads of state left immediately for their countries. During the OAU meetings in Kampala, four bombs attributed to an underground Uganda Liberation Movement opposed to President Amin went off. Despite efforts by some African leaders to find a substitute, Amin, as head of state of the host country, became the new OAU chairman.

AFRICA IN WORLD AFFAIRS

Amin-Moynihan UN Clash. In a UN General Assembly speech on October 1, Amin, speaking as OAU chairman and as Uganda's president, criticized France, Britain, the United States, and Israel. He called for the expulsion of Israel from the United Nations and the extinction of Israel as a state. French and British representatives walked out on Amin's talk. Israel officially protested to the United Nations. Jewish-American groups pressed U. S. Ambassador to the United Nations Daniel P. Moynihan to reply to Amin's slander of the United States and of Jewish people.

Addressing an AFL-CIO convention in San Francisco on October 3, Moynihan quoted a New York *Times* characterization of Amin as a "racist murderer." He angered African leaders by implying that Amin's anti-Israel statement as OAU head reflected African opinion. While many African leaders agreed privately that Amin was a brutal ruler and regretted his automatic election to the OAU presidency, they felt that to insult Amin as OAU head was to insult all Africans. Moynihan, known for speaking bluntly to Third World nations critical of the United States, said he hoped the OAU would disavow Amin. President Gerald Ford supported Moynihan during the incident. When a UN body passed a resolution equating Zionism with racism, Moynihan attacked the resolution.

UNITED STATES AND AFRICA

State Department Africa Appointments. In the face of opposition by the OAU and the U. S. Congressional Black Caucus, Secretary of State Henry Kissinger accepted Nathaniel Davis' resignation as assistant secretary of state for Africa. In October, Kissinger replaced Davis with William E. Schaufele, Jr., a 25-year veteran diplomat who had worked with the Africa bloc at the United Nations for four years and who had previously served in Morocco, Zaire, Upper Volta, and as Africa desk officer at the State Department. He is said to be liked by key African leaders.

U. S. Students Kidnapped. On May 19, 40 members of Zaire's antigovernment People's Revolutionary party (PRP) crossed Lake Tanganyika and kidnapped three Americans and a Dutch national from Gombe animal research station in western Tanzania. The four were Stanford University student researchers at the animal behavior study center directed by Dr. Jane Goodall, British primatologist and Stanford University visiting lecturer. She was the target of the raiders but escaped capture by hiding.

The captors released one U. S. student on May 25 to convey their ransom demands for $460,000, weapons, and the release of two PRP rebels held in Tanzania. Two more student hostages were returned from Zaire to Tanzania on June 28, and the last was freed on July 25.

Release of the students was hampered by Zaire's President Mobutu. On June 17 he charged the U. S. Central Intelligence Agency with directing an abortive coup against him. He expelled U. S. Ambassador Deane R. Hinton, who was replaced by the more acceptable Am-

Nomad refugees from famine-stricken northern Somalia eat their first meal in southern resettlement camps.

bassador Sheldon Vance. Observers believed the coup charge was fabricated so that Mobutu could remove threatening army officers and ingratiate himself with anti-U. S. African nations.

Somalia: Soviet Base. In June, Defense Secretary James Schlesinger showed photos to the Senate Armed Services Committee of a USSR military buildup at the coastal city of Berbera, Somalia, on Africa's eastern horn, a location strategic to the Suez Canal, the Red Sea, and the Gulf of Aden. Denying the charge, Somali leaders invited reporters and congressmen to visit. One group was kept from crucial sites, but Sen. Dewey Bartlett, heading a congressional group in July, confirmed the installation of a USSR missile handling, refueling, and storage facility rather than an offensive launching site. Asked why Somalia invited inspection, Bartlett and others surmised that Somali leaders themselves did not know the extent of the USSR buildup but, hoping to get U. S. aid, did want to publicize their severe refugee problem caused by long drought. Bartlett approved giving aid to Somalia.

Diego Garcia: U. S. Base. Observers said that Secretary of Defense Schlesinger stressed the USSR buildup in Somalia to strengthen his request for $13.6 million to enlarge a U. S. base on Diego Garcia, a tiny island in the Indian Ocean about 1,000 miles (1,600 km) south of India. Critics maintained that Diego Garcia's remoteness limits its value and that a base there might lead the USSR to escalate activity at its Somalia base or to seek other nearby bases. The U. S.-USSR naval rivalry in the Indian Ocean along strategic sea lanes intensified since Britain's withdrawal from the area.

SOUTHERN AFRICA

Détente. The April 1974 coup in Portugal shook white southern Africa because Portugal would no longer be fighting black guerrillas in Angola and Mozambique. Whites feared that the guerrillas were bent on their massacre. To head off world hostility toward white rule and the threat of black guerrilla invasion, the Republic of South Africa's Prime Minister John Vorster moved quickly toward peaceful coexistence with black-ruled Africa. On August 1, in line with his new détente policy, Vorster withdrew South African police who were aiding white Rhodesians in their fight against guerrilla attacks from Mozambique. In talks in Pretoria with Rhodesia's Prime Minister Ian D. Smith on August 8–9, he urged Smith to meet Rhodesian black nationalist leaders for constitution talks aimed at some measure of black rule in Rhodesia. Although Vorster and Zambia's President Kenneth D. Kaunda attended the Victoria Falls talks on August 25–26 between Smith and black Rhodesian leaders, the talks broke down. Still, with Vorster's urging, Smith continued to meet with black Rhodesian leader Joshua Nkomo.

Rhodesia. Rhodesia became the focal point of détente. The black leadership was divided, with the September 28 election of moderate Nkomo as head of the African National Council (ANC) disputed by militant black leaders, self-exiled in Zambia and urging increased guerrilla warfare. A divided black leadership worked to the temporary advantage of Smith, who must persuade the 275,000 whites, including white extremists ready for prolonged war, to allow Rhodesia's 5.7 million blacks quicker progress toward ruling the country.

Republic of South Africa. Critics reported that, while South Africa's public policy was for negotiations with other black-ruled countries, inside South Africa detentions without trial and little noticed executions of blacks continued. One account cited 47 political arrests in the first nine months of 1975, while another reported 36 executions during the first six months of the same year. The Vorster government proceeded to carry out its apartheid policy by separating the 18 million black Africans from the 4 million whites. Blacks were being resettled into eight homelands, only one of which, the Transkei homeland for the Xhosa tribe, has been promised self-government in 1976. Since jobs were scarce in these black areas, males were forced to migrate for work, and the breakup of black family life continued. Some observers who witnessed the South African blacks' misery and anger believed that, next to the Middle East, South Africa was the most dangerous threat to world peace.

It was reported in October that documents stolen from South Africa's embassy in Bonn, West Germany, contained information about secret West German help in creating a nuclear capability for South Africa. The documents were published with commentary by the outlawed ANC of South Africa, headquartered in exile in Zambia. The ANC said that South Africa, while publicly pursuing détente, was secretly building up a nuclear-weapon capability to make it an impregnable white stronghold in Africa.

FRANKLIN PARKER
West Virginia University

Chinese growers bring their cotton crop to a purchasing station. World consumption exceeded production in 1975.

UPI

agriculture

In 1975 world food production rose slightly, particularly in the developing countries. In the United States record harvests were made, despite adverse weather and climbing production costs. This overview of 1975 agricultural developments is divided into three sections: (1) World Agriculture; (2) U. S. Agriculture; and (3) U. S. Agricultural Research.

World Agriculture

Preliminary reports indicate that a modest increase in world food production occurred in 1975. Late in the year, the U. S. Department of Agriculture in a report entitled "The World Agricultural Situation" concluded: "The world agricultural outlook continues to be more favorable than a year ago, although reductions in the estimates for the USSR, European and U. S. grain crops since midsummer indicate tighter food supplies than thought earlier. . . ."

FOOD PRODUCTION

Food supply prospects in the developing countries improved in 1975, the U. S. Department of Agriculture (USDA) said, particularly in Asia where good monsoon rainfall contributed to record grain crops in India. China had record harvests. Despite plentiful plantings of grains, oilseeds, and other food crops in Latin America, growth in farm output was restricted by adverse weather, which reduced per-acre yields. Agricultural prospects were bright in most of Africa and West Asia, except for below-average grain production in parts of North Africa.

In the developed lands, European grain production was hurt by poor weather early in 1975. The continuing hot, dry weather brought successive reductions in Soviet grain production estimates. The result was increased demand for food imports, met largely by the U. S. food and feed-grain harvests that reached record levels in 1975.

Grain. World grain crops had yields well above 1974's output, although below the 1960–74 trend. The deterioration in world wheat and coarse-grain crop prospects from the early summer was concentrated in countries that feed large amounts of grain to livestock. Prospects for the world rice harvest, much of which took place late in 1975, were for a crop above both 1974's levels and trends.

The disappointing output in many major grain-feeding countries, especially the USSR and Europe, forced adjustments such as using grain reserves, reducing feeding, or increasing imports. The anticipated increase in world grain stocks failed to materialize because of smaller grain production and decreased supplies available from stocks in the United States.

Crop and Livestock Production. Reduced demand for livestock and dairy products resulting from slack economic activity around the world dampened demand for oilseed meal. Oilseed stocks were then built up, and prices softened despite smaller production in 1974. The 1975 oilseed crop was larger, and utilization in 1976 could rise if economic growth accelerates in the developed countries and leads to more feeding of cattle, hogs, and poultry.

World stocks of nonfat dry milk have been building up, particularly in the European Economic Community where production was up and exports and animal feeding were down. Preliminary sugar production estimates indicated world output was above 1974 levels and in line with the 1960–74 trend. Cotton consumption exceeded production for the first time in five years.

Late in 1975 the USDA said, "the world economy appears poised for recovery. . . . The economies of the principal developed countries have either begun expanding or have halted the sharp decline in business activity. Most coun-

tries are looking to the United States, Japan, and West Germany to act as pacesetters."

World agricultural output increased about 3% in 1975, most experts estimated. This was slightly above the 2.8% annual increase that occurred on average over the past 20 years. World grain production totaled about 1.2 billion metric tons, about 4% more than in 1974, but about 20 million tons less than suggested by the trend of increases that occurred in the 15 years ending in 1975. Nevertheless, worldwide alarm about the possibility of massive starvation in lands such as India, Bangladesh, and sub-Saharan Africa tapered off as production improved in these regions.

United Nations Programs. The Food and Agriculture Organization (FAO) of the UN noted that the low level of world grain stocks continued to make grain prices volatile and to keep the world dependent upon current harvests for meeting current food needs. The FAO announced that the governing body of its affiliated World Food Program had set a $750 million target for pledges in food, cash, and services, such as shipping, to assist developing countries in the 1977–78 biennium. The FAO's intergovernmental committee also approved $165 million in food aid for 18 economic and social development projects in 15 countries. This aid is mainly used in food-for-work projects, special feeding programs, and as incentive to voluntary work.

For the 1975–76 biennium, pledges of food aid exceeded the original target of $440 million, according to Dr. Francisco Aquino, executive director of the World Food Program. Total resources were about $598 million. In October the UN General Assembly called for at least 500,000 tons of grains to be placed at the disposal of the World Food Program to strengthen its ability to deal with any crises.

WORLD FARM OUTPUT

U. S. livestock and grain production slightly exceeded the record output of 1973. Bad weather hampered what otherwise would have been a far more impressive record outpouring of U. S. food and fiber.

Western Europe's grain crop also fell short of expectations, mainly because of too much rain at planting time and drought later in the season, especially in the northern and northwestern regions of Europe. Total wheat production was placed at 50 million tons, down from about 56 million tons in 1974. At 83 million tons, coarse-grain production was down slightly from 1974. In Canada wheat and coarse-grain output was up 22% and 12%, respectively, from 1974. Australia's wheat crop of 11.3 million tons was somewhat smaller than 1974's. Livestock and poultry production did not change substantially in 1975 in these developed countries. Supplies of nonfat dry milk became excessive, especially in Western Europe.

USSR. Soviet agricultural prospects gradually deteriorated during most of the 1975 growing season, particularly for grains. Hot, dry weather prevailed during most of the season over much of the major spring grain region from the Volga River eastward. Also, soil moisture over much of European USSR was significantly below average during the season.

Total Soviet grain output was about 150 million tons, 30 million tons less than expected and 57 million tons less than in 1974. The 1975 wheat harvest was about 75 million tons, down from 84 million in 1974 and smaller than the others in the past five years. Coarsegrain production fell about 24 million tons short of 1974's levels. Russian farmers planted about 317.5 million acres (128.5 million hectares) in grain, about 3.2 million acres (1.3 million hectares)

UPI

Machine sprayer stores raw sugar in a Florida warehouse. Sugar prices declined during 1975 but still remained high.

more than in 1974 but somewhat less than estimated earlier in the year.

Production of livestock products on collective and state farms exceeded 1974 totals. Meat and eggs were up 7% and 9%, respectively, but milk was up only 2%. Mutton and goat meat output was up 16%, probably due to increased slaughter because of drought. The drought also held down growth in livestock herds.

Eastern Europe. Increases in livestock numbers slowed in this region in 1975. There were a few declines. Cattle were up 6% in Bulgaria and 3% in Yugoslavia. Czechoslovakia reported a slight decline. In Hungary hog numbers declined nearly 10%. Farmers in Poland reduced private stock, more than offsetting stock increases in the socialist sector. Bulgaria, East Germany, and Poland had a 4% to 5% increase in the number of sheep. Poultry declined more than 5% in Czechoslovakia and 3% in Bulgaria. In Rumania a flood in July destroyed many animals and poultry.

The harvest outlook, at first considered very promising in every country in Eastern Europe, deteriorated severely in July. Floods inundated 1.97 million acres (800,000 hectares) of farm land in Rumania. Heavy rain caused serious harvest losses in Hungary and Yugoslavia. Warm, dry weather in East Germany and Poland caused below average yields.

People's Republic of China. The spring-summer harvest of 1975 in China was hailed by officials as the best ever. Grain increases of as much as 20% were reported in some provinces. Dry weather in the north and northeast affected production, but timely rain saved these crops. Total wheat production totaled a record high over 1974's 31.2 million tons. Rice output was also said to be a record. China's total grain crop, therefore, was assumed to have exceeded the 260 million tons officially estimated in 1974.

Production of other crops—including cotton, sugar, tobacco, and other industrial crops—equaled or exceeded the record harvests in 1974. Because of this, China's imports of farm stuffs, particularly grain, were expected to continue to decline. The United States did not export any major farm commodities to China in 1975.

Asia. Elsewhere in Asia, harvests were well above average in 1975. One of the most spectacular commodities providing a boost to Asian farm exports was sugar, produced by India, the Philippines, Thailand, and Nationalist China. The best markets for this sugar were in the Middle East, partly because these lands no longer bought much sugar from the USSR or Eastern Europe.

India's food output rebounded from the poor results of 1974. Nevertheless, grain import needs were strong because stocks fell to low levels in 1974, and some rebuilding of stocks was planned. Food-grain production was about 10 million tons larger than the 102 million tons harvested in 1974.

Pakistan's wheat crop totaled 7.5 million tons, well below the record 1974 crop. Indonesia's rice output topped the 1974 harvest of 14.8 million tons. Bangladesh's rice output at 12.3 million tons was 8% larger than in 1974. Nevertheless, Bangladesh's grain imports continued to make up differences between demand and supply. Burma's rice production was up 2% from 1974. Thailand had record grain harvests. South Korea's rice production rose slightly, and Malaysia's 1975 rice crop was also up.

Latin America. High 1974 prices and increased emphasis on farm expansion in most lands encouraged record 1975 plantings of grains, oilseeds, and other food crops in Latin America. Gains in livestock products, however, were limited. Low prices led to cutbacks in cotton plantings to the lowest level in recent years. Adverse weather reduced yields of major crops, especially in Argentina, Brazil, the Caribbean, and Central America.

Dry weather delayed plantings of feed grains and oilseeds in Argentina, and wet weather reduced yields. Severe cold in Brazil damaged pastures, coffee trees, sugarcane, wheat, fruits, and vegetables. Midyear rains and flooding also damaged crops in northeastern Brazil. Mexico's 1975 farm output recovered significantly from the previous year.

Africa. Angola, torn by civil disorders, suffered sharp declines in farm production, particularly of coffee. The crop, fourth largest in the world, was largely unpicked in 1975. The Republic of South Africa's corn crop declined to 9.8 million tons, 12% smaller than the previous year's record crop; wheat output declined 14% from 1974.

Wheat and barley production in Morocco and Algeria were below average. Tunisia had a good harvest. Coffee growers in Africa expected to be able to supply large demands that may be triggered by frost damage to the Brazilian crop. The Ivory Coast, Uganda, Angola, and Ethiopia were the largest coffee producers in Africa in 1975, but Cameroon, Kenya, Malagasy Republic, Zaire, Tanzania, Burundi, Rwanda, Togo, and Central African Republic also produced significant quantities.

West Asia. Wheat production in Turkey and Iran was bountiful. Poorer weather visited such other countries in this area as Israel, Syria, and Jordan and held grain output down to below average levels.

JOE WESTERN
Senior Editor, "The National Observer"

U. S. Agriculture

Despite unsatisfactory weather and soaring costs, the United States' superb agricultural sector set new production records in 1975. With the number of people engaged in commercial agriculture continuing to decline in 1975 to about 5% of the population, never have so few produced so much for so many.

UPI

Sheyenne River floodwaters cover the fields of a farm near Kindred, N. Dak., in July. Midsummer floods damaged millions of dollars of crops.

The largest increase was in grain production, especially the food grains of wheat, rye, and rice. Production of meat and poultry actually lagged behind earlier levels.

Farm exports rose to a record high in the fiscal year that ended June 30, 1975, resulting in an overall trade surplus for the United States. "Imported petroleum cost over $25 billion in fiscal 1975," said Secretary of Agriculture Earl L. Butz, "and in a very real sense these imports were paid for by U. S. grains, soybeans, and other farm product exports."

Production. In 1975, U. S. farm output of crops and livestock reached an index number of 113 (1967=100), up from 106 in 1974, and up slightly from the previous record of 112 in 1973. Plantings for harvest expanded a bit from 1974's total of about 329 million acres (133 million hectares). Yields per acre were generally higher than 1974's disappointingly low figures.

With better weather farm output probably would have leaped farther ahead of the previous record in 1973, but serious flooding occurred in the key production areas of central and lower Red River Valley areas of North Dakota and Minnesota in midsummer. The floods were followed by searing heat and drought in the upper Midwest, which held down maturation of the corn crop, the largest of all U. S. crops. The official July forecast of more than 6 billion bushels had to be revised downward. Nevertheless, the U. S. Department of Agriculture reported corn production of more than 5.7 billion bushels, still a record high and 23% more than in 1974. Total output of feed grains—corn, grain sorghums, oats, and barley—totaled 202 million tons, 23% more than in 1974 but slightly less than 1973's record.

Wheat output of more than 2.1 billion bushels was 19% larger than the previous year's record. Combined production of wheat, rye, and rice was 71 million tons, 18% more than the previous record in 1974.

Peanut production was high at nearly 4 billion pounds (1.8 billion kg), 9% more than the previous high in 1974. Total production of oilseeds—soybeans, cottonseed, peanuts, and flaxseed—was about 50 million tons, 15% more than in 1974 but somewhat below the record output of 1973.

Exports. The most important development of 1975 was the prospect of unusually heavy export demands for the year's huge farm production, particularly from the USSR. Adverse weather in the USSR caused several declines of grain output down to 150 million tons, 30 million tons short of target and about 57 million tons less than in 1974.

As it did in 1972, the Soviet Union turned to the United States to buy grain, especially wheat, to offset disappointing production. News of large Soviet purchases caused commodity prices to rise and touched off a political furor in the United States over whether Soviet buying would cause U. S. food prices to rise substantially.

When Soviet purchases of U. S. grains rose to a total of about 10.2 million tons by September 1, President Gerald R. Ford suspended further sales and began negotiating with the USSR for a long-term grain-buying agreement that would provide for certain minimum buying annually, rather than subject U. S. markets to erratic buying patterns as occurred in the past. On October 20 a U. S.-USSR agreement was concluded. Under its terms, the USSR would purchase 6–8 million tons of grain annually, beginning in October 1976.

The expected sales to the USSR and other foreign markets were forecast to be at least as large in the fiscal year ending June 30, 1976, as the record $21.6 billion in the preceding fiscal year. As a result, commodity prices, which had been trending downward because of expectations of record U. S. output, turned up. Export volume totaled nearly 100 million tons, 12 million tons more than in fiscal 1975 and near the record of fiscal 1974.

Stronger commodity prices cheered policymakers in Washington. The Ford administration has committed itself to relying more on market prices to bolster or maintain farm income and less on government regulation and subsidies. President Ford vetoed farm legislation aimed at increasing farm subsidies and government controls.

Livestock and Poultry. In 1975 livestock and livestock products fell to a production index number of 104, down from 106 in 1974. The high cost of grain for feed beginning in 1973 led U. S. livestock and poultry producers to cull herds and flocks of all marginal stock. Even so, the ensuing two years dealt severe financial losses to cattle feeders, who bought the grain at high prices and sold the fattened animals on a declining livestock market. Meat prices declined because consumers reduced per capita meat eating.

UPI

UPI

(*Right*) Sec. of Agriculture Earl Butz (*right*) discusses record U.S. wheat (*left*) and corn crops.

In 1975, U. S. consumers ate about 180 pounds (81.5 kg) of beef, veal, and pork, down from about 188 pounds (85.2 kg) in 1974.

Livestock prices improved, however, in mid-year, and there were signs that production was beginning to rise again. The U. S. spring pig crop was the smallest in 40 years, and total pork output in 1975 was expected to be 20% smaller than the 81.8 million head slaughtered in 1974. Cattle and calves on hand on July 1 totaled 140.1 million head, 1% more than 1974 and 7% above 1973. Milk production nearly matched the 115.4 billion pounds (52.3 billion kg) of 1974.

Income and Consumption. Realized farm net income in 1975 was about $23 billion, down from $27.2 billion in 1974 and well below the record $32.2 billion in 1973. Per capita consumption declined a bit in 1975 to an index number of 101, down from 102.4 in the previous year and also below record 103.8 in 1972. A sharp reduction in consumption of livestock-related food products accounted for almost all of the decline.

Assets and Land Values. Farm real estate values rose 14% in the year ending March 1, 1975. Total value of farm real estate reached $370.1 billion. The average value per acre on farm land was $354, up $44 from a year earlier. The average farm operating unit was valued at $143,900. Total farm assets were $520 billion, up $44 billion from a year earlier. Outstanding farm debt was $82 billion, up $8 billion from 1974. The equity position of farmers of $438 billion was a record high, up $36 billion from 1974.

JOE WESTERN
Senior Editor, "The National Observer"

U. S. Agricultural Research

The Agricultural Research Service (ARS) of the U. S. Department of Agriculture is the principal agricultural research agency of the federal government. Its chief objectives are to increase farm production efficiency, reduce costs of marketing agricultural products, and develop new products and processes; to protect and improve the environment; and to make effective use of natural resources. Other major objectives are to reduce food-related health hazards, provide new knowledge of human nutrient requirements, develop knowledge and technology about new plants and ornamentals, develop foreign markets for U. S. farm products, and help other countries accelerate their agricultural development process.

New crop varieties that are pest resistant reduce the need for pesticides, an important consideration in environmental and energy conservation. One such newly developed variety is ARC alfalfa, which is resistant to four major disease and insect pests. In a two-year test, ARC averaged 1 to 2 tons more hay per acre each year than other varieties, thus providing more protein for less energy.

A protein-enriched bread made with a new formula without sugar is highly nutritious and as attractive in appearance as bread currently marketed. The bread, enriched with soy protein, eliminates excessive browning and thickness of crust. As much as 1,500 pounds (680 kg) of sugar might be saved in making 10,000 1-pound (.45-kg) loaves of white bread with the no-sugar ARS formula.

More efficient livestock production and greater use of forage crops will increase beef and milk supplies to consumers and will divert

UPI   UPI

USDA

Agricultural research developments aided U.S. farmers in 1975. (*Above, left*) New alfalfa strain resists weevils, while a tiny wasp (*above*) imported from India kills the Mexican bean beetle larva. (*Left*) Drip irrigation, feeding water directly to the roots, promotes faster growth with less water and fertilizer. The drip-irrigated tree at right is the same age and was grown in same soil as tree at left.

grain to human use or export. A new grazing management system developed by the Agricultural Research Service has improved production on the range by 68%. In another study, ARS scientists developed an all-season grazing system in the southern cornbelt region.

A tiny wasp imported from India may spell doom for the Mexican bean beetle, which ravages soybeans in the Middle Atlantic states. The wasp, which does not sting, is smaller than a gnat and will not harm any beneficial U.S. insect. In controlled tests, the wasp parasitized 70% to 90% of the Mexican bean beetle larvae and dramatically reduced the beetle populations. The wasps are currently being tested in five states and may reduce or eliminate the need for expensive chemical controls for Mexican bean beetles.

Plastics that are biodegradable may make for a cleaner, healthier environment. ARS scientists have added cornstarch to the formulas for polyvinyl chloride and polyvinyl alcohol, both widely used synthetics, and developed a plastic that is degradable. Most plastics currently on the market do not decompose easily, and some even release toxic compounds when burned. The new plastics are more degradable than plastics made entirely of petroleum-based resins.

A new ARS process for flameproofing wool could reduce the 3,000 to 5,000 fatalities caused yearly by flammable fabrics. The wool process, which works equally well with wool blends and nylon, is economical, easy to apply, and non-irritating.

MARCELLA M. MEMOLO
U. S. Agricultural Research Service

Gov. George Wallace and Britain's Conservative party leader Margaret Thatcher met in London in October during Wallace's European tour.

UPI

ALABAMA

In January 1975, George C. Wallace was inaugurated for an unprecedented third term as governor. The 1975 legislature was composed entirely of Democrats, including 15 blacks and 1 woman. The legislature was in session for most of the year, with the result that the noteworthy events occurring in 1975 related mainly to that branch of the state government. In the fall Governor Wallace made a tour of Western Europe and then announced that he would seek the presidency in 1976.

Legislative Actions. The legislature met in organizational session in January and immediately thereafter was called by Governor Wallace into three separate special sessions. None of the special sessions was particularly productive, but the third was perhaps the most important of them. That session was called to consider a set of regulatory measures proposed by the governor to check rising utility rates, but all of these failed to be enacted. One important bill was passed at the second special session, however. This measure was a proposed constitutional amendment to establish annual, rather than biennial, legislative sessions beginning in 1976. The proposal was submitted to the electorate on June 10, 1975, and was adopted by a vote of 95,330 to 75,966.

ALABAMA · Information Highlights

Area: 51,609 square miles (133,667 sq km).
Population (1974 est.): 3,577,000. *Density:* 69 per sq mi.
Chief Cities (1970 census): Montgomery, the capital, 133,386; Birmingham, 300,910; Mobile, 190,026.
Government (1975): *Chief Officers*—governor, George C. Wallace (D); lt. gov., Jere L. Beasley (D); *Legislature*—Senate, 35 members; House of Representatives, 105 members.
Education (1974–75): *Enrollment*—public elementary schools, 390,685 pupils; public secondary, 373,656; nonpublic, 49,900; colleges and universities, 143,-188. *Public school expenditures*, $529,175,000 ($719 per pupil).
State Finances (fiscal year 1974): *Revenues*, $2,073,445,-000; *expenditures*, $1,994,183,000.
Personal Income (1974): $15,016,000,000; per capita, $4,198.
Labor Force (Aug. 1975): *Nonagricultural wage and salary earners*, 1,162,400; *insured unemployed*, 48,-500.

The regular legislative session extended from May 6 through October 9 and was highlighted by a controversial administration proposal to divert some funds earmarked for education to other state programs such as highways, prisons, and mental health. Partially because of this controversy, the legislature did not enact a general appropriation measure until the last day of the session and failed altogether to pass a measure to fund education, even though the fiscal year 1975–76 had already begun on October 1. On the basis of the state attorney general's opinion, Governor Wallace authorized the release of funds to finance education until the legislature could enact the necessary appropriations. A legislator later brought suit to settle the important constitutional question of whether the governor had authority to make appropriations of state funds by executive order.

Meanwhile, however, the governor had already called a fourth special legislative session to convene in November to enact the education appropriation measure. Important new laws passed during the regular session included legislation reinstating the death penalty and implementing the new constitutional article to establish a unified system of state courts, adopted in December 1973.

Other Developments. Other events that received national attention included the appointment in August of F. David Mathews, president of The University of Alabama, as secretary of the U. S. Department of Health, Education, and Welfare. Also, in September, Hurricane Eloise caused extensive damage in southern and eastern Alabama. Exploration and development drilling for oil and gas continued at a high rate in 1975, and Alabama's ranking as an energy producing state was expected to rise substantially from its 1974 levels.

Federal court judges ordered state officials to relieve severe overcrowding in the prisons. A federal court also ordered revision of the welfare system, which would have the effect of increasing aid to children. At the same time Alabama was praised for reform of its state court system.

JAMES D. THOMAS
The University of Alabama

UPI

A crew on the Alaska pipeline uses vibrating compactors to pack fill around a buried section of the pipe.

ALASKA

During 1975, pipeline construction and its impact dominated Alaskan life. An emergency was declared in Anchorage, Fairbanks, and Valdez because of severe housing shortages and soaring rents generated by pipeline construction. Pipeline workers' wages were not matched by nonpipeline salaries, causing many Alaskans to view inflation along with the dislocations caused by boom-growth as the greatest problems of 1975.

Pipeline Construction. The first and only bridge over the Yukon River was officially opened on Oct. 14, 1975, two months ahead of schedule. Nearly one-half-mile (.8-km) long, it will carry a 48-inch (121-cm) pipe on each side of a 30-foot (9-meter) roadway.

By early October, 245 miles (392 km) of pipe were in place, and by December 31 more than 50% of the pipe had been laid. The work force on the project was reduced from its peak of 21,600 to between 8,100 and 9,900.

Gas Line. The lieutenant governor traveled throughout the Middle West and New England to promote construction of a natural gas pipeline through Alaska rather than through Canada. Private groups stressed a fear that Canadian provincial governments would place excessive taxes on a trans-Canada line, thus raising the price to U. S. customers.

Other Industries. With current high world market prices justifying the expense, gold dredges were reactivated near Nome. Estimated reserves in the area run to 1.2 million ounces, enough for 30 years of mining. At Ester, near Fairbanks, a major mine reopened. Here $30,000 a day can be extracted with a potential reserve of $27 million.

In southeast Alaska, salmon fishing produced the lowest catch in five years, though Bristol Bay catches were up sharply. Alaskan fishermen welcomed presidential support of a 200-mile (320-km) offshore limit to protect fishing rights on the high seas. The state traded land with Cook Inlet Region, Inc., a native corporation, for control over the Lake Iliamna watershed, the world's largest red salmon fishery, upon which the Bristol Bay fishing industry depends.

Hundreds of Alaskans were idled during the summer because of closure of pulp mills, due to environmental protection requirements, rising costs of production, and a depressed international market. Japanese firms are heavily involved in Alaska's timber industry, with an investment of about $142 million.

Legal Affairs. The legislature passed a number of controversial bills. Smoking in public places was banned. Possession of marihuana for personal use was decriminalized. Concurrently, the state supreme court ruled that a right to privacy protects possession of any amount of marihuana in the home. Gov. Jay Hammond ordered an end to plea-bargaining, believing that police investigations would improve and only well-constructed prosecutions would come to the courts.

North Slope Resupply. Food, fuel, and equipment resupply of Barrow and Prudhoe Bay camps before winter was hampered by Arctic Ocean ice. Some supplies had to be flown in. A few barges were able to get close enough to use lighters.

A severe spring storm destroyed Nome's generators and many homes. Barges capsized, and a generator and nearly one-third of the supplies for Nome, Kotzebue, and St. Michael sank. The ship delivering food to Little Diomede Island was delayed, and inhabitants were forced to use school lunches and to kill a walrus.

ANDREA R. C. HELMS
University of Alaska

————— ALASKA • Information Highlights —————

Area: 586,412 square miles (1,518,807 sq km).
Population (1974 est.): 337,000.
Chief Cities (1970 census): Juneau, the capital, 6,050; Anchorage, 48,081; Fairbanks, 14,771.
Government (1975): *Chief Officers*—governor, Jay S. Hammond (R); lt. gov., Lowell Thomas, Jr. (R); *Legislature*—Senate, 20 members; House of Representatives, 40 members.
Education (1974–75): *Enrollment*—public elementary schools, 48,306 pupils; public secondary schools, 38,270; nonpublic schools, 500; colleges and universities, 14,043. *Public school expenditures*, $138,-937,000 ($1,780 per pupil).
State Finances (fiscal year 1974): *Revenues*, $527,045,-000; *expenditures*, $697,584,000.
Personal Income (1974): $2,367,000,000; per capita, $7,023.
Labor Force (July 1975): *Nonagricultural wage and salary earners*, 142,700.

ALBANIA

During 1975 there were a number of significant changes within the ranks of the Albanian military and economic elites.

Political Developments. The ouster of Defense Minister Beqir Balluku in July 1974 marked the beginning of a thorough purge of the Albanian military leadership. By early 1975, Petrit Dume, chief of staff of the armed forces and second ranking member of the military hierarchy, had also been deposed. In addition, all four deputy defense ministers were replaced. The purge of the military establishment apparently stemmed from differences that had arisen between this group and the party leadership over both domestic and foreign policy issues.

Following the May 26–29 meeting of the Central Committee of the Albanian Party of Labor (APL), Deputy Prime Minister and Chairman of the State Planning Commission Abdyl Kellezi, Minister of Heavy Industry and Mining Koco Theodosi, and Minister of Trade Kico Ngjela were relieved of their duties. Their dismissals were attributable to the regime's unhappiness with the performance of those sectors of the economy for which they were responsible. Petro Dode succeeded Kellezi, Pali Miska replaced Theodosi, and Nedin Hoxha supplanted Ngjela. It was announced in October that the APL central committee had approved the draft of a new constitution for the nation.

The Ideological and Cultural Revolution. During 1975 a campaign against "bureaucratism" was launched. The APL leadership seemed determined to make the bureaucracy more responsive to the party by reducing the size of the state and economic administrations and by transferring hundreds of bureaucrats from the cities to the countryside.

The Economy. During 1974 industrial production increased by 7.3% and agricultural output rose by 11%. According to the 1975 economic plan, industrial output was expected to be 4.4% greater and agricultural production 15.9% higher than in 1974.

NICHOLAS C. PANO
Western Illinois University

------------ **ALBANIA · Information Highlights** ------------

Official Name: People's Republic of Albania.
Location: Southern Europe, Balkan peninsula.
Area: 11,100 square miles (28,748 sq km).
Population (1973 est.): 2,500,000.
Chief Cities (1970 est.): Tiranë, the capital, 171,300; Shkodër, 55,300; Dürres, 53,800.
Government: *Head of state*, Haxhi Lleshi, president of the Presidium (took office 1953). *Head of government*, Maj. Gen. Mehmet Shehu, premier (took office 1954). *First secretary of the Albanian Party of Labor*, Gen. Enver Hoxha (took office 1941). *Legislature* (unicameral)—People's Assembly.
Monetary Unit: Lek (4.10 leks equal U. S.$1, 1975).
Gross National Product (1974 est.): $1,100,000,000.
Manufacturing (major products): Processed foods, textiles, cement, tobacco products.
Major Agricultural Products: Corn, sugar beets, wheat, cotton, tobacco, potatoes.

ALBERTA

During 1975, a buoyant economy insulated Alberta from recession, keeping unemployment under 4%. Euphoria was reflected in Calgary's celebration of its 1875 founding as a Mounted Police post.

Government. Following their complete sweep of Alberta in the 1974 federal election, the Progressive Conservatives under Peter Lougheed almost annihilated the once powerful Social Credit (SC) opposition, winning 69 of 75 seats in the provincial legislature in 1975. Even the Social Credit leader was defeated. One New Democratic party member, one Independent, and four SC members completed the legislative roster. The failure of the Liberals to win in a single constituency reflected continued controversy over federal taxation of provincially owned oil resources. Albertans regard such action as subsidization at their expense of oil prices elsewhere in Canada.

A windfall profit estimated at $1.5 billion from oil revenues resulted in establishment of a heritage fund for development of secondary industry against the foreseeable exhaustion of the province's nonrenewable resources.

Ralph Steinhauer, Canada's first Indian lieutenant governor, completed his first year in office in 1975.

Industry. The increases in world oil prices since 1973 have led to further development of oil sand industry in northeastern Alberta. This was jeopardized by withdrawal of one partner from the $2 billion Syncrude consortium. Its commitments to the extent of $600 million were assumed by the federal, Alberta, and Ontario

Calgary celebrated its centennial in 1975. Sergeant True Heart and Whiskey Willy perform in recreating the city's frontier days.

ALBERTA GOVERNMENT PHOTOGRAPHIC SERVICES

ALBERTA GOVERNMENT PHOTOGRAPHIC SERVICES

Calgary, the second largest city in Alberta, has benefited from the province's oil boom.

Framed by the city's modern skyline, old-West chuck-wagons race for the finish during the Calgary Stampede, a reminder of frontier days.

ALBERTA GOVERNMENT PHOTOGRAPHIC SERVICES

governments. Because Alberta produces 85% of Canada's oil, Premier Lougheed was able to cut income taxes 28% while increasing social services. Other provinces wanted either to share the profits or have the price kept artificially low and the supply regulated as a national resource.

Despite work stoppages, the construction industry appeared headed for new records. Edmonton area projects included a major oil refinery and rapid-transit system; Calgary rebuilt its airport and constructed a major convention center. Both cities added extensive commercial and housing developments. However, housing still fell far short of demand, with resultant sharp rises in rentals. Developments elsewhere followed the government's announced policy of encouraging the decentralization of industry.

Agriculture. Good harvest weather in 1974 and 1975, eager markets, and satisfactory yields ensured prosperity for grain farmers, despite numerous difficulties in moving crops to overseas buyers. High production costs and a below average hay yield adversely affected beef and pork producers.

Education. Falling enrollments (elementary), insistent teacher demands for higher salaries, other inflationary pressures, and firm limits on governmental grants combined to place school systems in tight financial straits. Threatened or actual strikes by teachers and other employees and developing teacher shortages led to brief closing of some classrooms. Rapid expansion of publicly funded kindergartens also created problems.

Similar difficulties appeared at post-secondary levels, where the trend toward stationary or falling enrollments has been reversed. Imminent government action to replace individual educational institution acts with a comprehensive advanced education statute caused unease among academics, who feared erosion of their institutions' autonomy.

JOHN W. CHALMERS
University of Alberta

ALBERTA · Information Highlights

Area: 255,285 square miles (661,189 sq km).
Population (1975 est.): 1,772,000.
Chief Cities (1974): Edmonton, the capital, 529,000; Calgary, 444,000.
Government (1975): *Chief Officers*—lt. gov., Ralph Steinhauer; premier, Peter Lougheed (Progressive Conservative); chief justice, Sidney Bruce Smith. *Legislature*—Legislative Assembly, 75 members.
Education (1975–76): *Enrollment:* public elementary and secondary schools, 437,080 pupils; private, 5,050; Indian (federal) schools, 3,230; colleges and universities, 28,440. *Public school expenditures,* $438,074,000.
Public Finance (fiscal year 1973): *Revenues,* $1,310,900,000; *expenditures,* $1,479,200,000.
Personal Income (1972): $6,217,000,000; average annual income per person, $3,349.
(All monetary figures are in Canadian dollars.)

UPI

Algerian President Houari Boumédienne addresses the opening of the oil nations summit conference on March 4.

ALGERIA

Sagging oil prices and sales through most of 1975 caused many of Algeria's economic dreams to sour momentarily. However, the nation continued on its cautious path to industrialization and planned national elections.

Economy. Despite the depressed world demand for oil, Algeria maintained a 1975 price of $11.75 per barrel—down from 1974's $14 a barrel—and on October 1 raised the charge by

$1, in accordance with an Organization of Petroleum Exporting Countries (OPEC) decision.

Earlier in the year, the North African nation had chastised three other members of OPEC—Libya, Nigeria, and Iraq—for lowering the prices of their oil. Algeria's position on the subject was explained in part by the feeling of President Houari Boumédienne that raw-material-producing countries should get a fair return on diminishing resources and in part by the fact that Algeria's own oil resources are being depleted rapidly. Algeria will have to receive top prices for its crude oil for the next 20 years if oil is to finance the nation's industrialization.

Algeria's economic woes were further compounded by a $1 billion trade deficit projected for 1975. In addition, the nation's agricultural production declined to the point where Algeria, previously a net food exporter, had become a net importer.

Many observers retained hope for the long-term success of the Algerian economic strategy, and the Boumédienne government succeeded in obtaining its largest loan ever, $400 million, from a consortium of 46 North American, European, Soviet, and Arab banks. The money was earmarked for industrial development projects. Part of the lenders' confidence may have been based not on oil but on natural gas. Algeria is known to have what is probably the world's greatest reserve of natural gas, and 1975 saw large increases in lucrative export contracts with U. S. firms.

Politics. Algeria's confidence in itself and in its revolution was demonstrated in a June announcement by Boumédienne that there would be elections within a year and a vote for a head of state. The balloting would be the first since Boumédienne's Revolutionary Council seized power in 1965.

Seemingly more important to Algerians was a July 5 announcement that French law was no longer in effect in the former French colony. Following independence, French legislation had continued in use wherever it did not abrogate national sovereignty. In 1971, however, Boumédienne set up a commission to establish an Algerian code of law. The July announcement did not mean that all new Algerian laws were in effect, but it did make official the Algerianization of the legal system. A commission to establish a national code that will define the Algerian path toward socialism was created.

Foreign Relations. During the fall Algeria came into conflict with its neighbor Morocco over the phosphate-rich Spanish Sahara. By backing the claims for independence by some groups of native inhabitants, Algeria had hopes of establishing a dominant position in the territory and possibly of obtaining a direct outlet to the Atlantic Ocean. The situation in the Spanish Sahara remained unresolved at year's end.

NANCY McKEON
The African-American Institute

ALGERIA · Information Highlights

Official Name: Democratic and Popular Republic of Algeria.

Location: North Africa.

Area: 919,590 square miles (2,381,741 sq km).

Population (1975 est.): 16,800,000.

Chief Cities (1974): Algiers, the capital, 1,000,000; Oran, 330,000; Constantine, 254,000.

Government: *Head of state,* Houari Boumédienne, president (took office June 1965). *Head of government,* Houari Boumédienne.

Monetary Unit: Dinar (4.049 dinars equal U. S.$1, July 1975).

Gross National Product (1974 est.): $8,800,000,000.

Manufacturing (major products): Processed foods, textiles, leather goods, liquefied natural gas, cement, petroleum products.

Major Agricultural Products: Wheat, citrus fruits, wine grapes, cork, olives, dates, figs, tobacco, fish, livestock.

Foreign Trade (1973): *Exports,* $1,900,000,000; *imports,* $2,236,900,000.

ANGOLA

As it approached its official independence date of Nov. 11, 1975, the Portuguese territory of Angola sank ever more deeply into a welter of civil strife and international rivalries that threatened total destruction for the country. Angola is a potentially prosperous nation of 6.4 million people on Africa's west coast.

Bitter fighting continued after independence with rival claims to the control of the government unresolved. Portugal's disengagement in Angola merely exacerbated the rivalry that had been raging for a decade among the three major African nationalist groups: the MPLA (Movimento Popular de Libertação de Angola), the FNLA (Frente Nacional de Libertação de Angola) and UNITA (União para a Independência Total de Angola). The international tensions generated by the Angolan war became more evident in December as the United States spoke against Soviet and Cuban involvement in Angola.

Alvor Agreement. After a formal cease-fire between Portugal and the independence movements was reached on Oct. 7, 1974, Portugal recognized Angola's right to its independence. The date and terms of independence were to be settled as soon as possible with the three nationalist movements. On Jan. 5, 1975, the three factions agreed on a common political platform, the only firm plank of which was their unanimous determination to retain the oil-rich enclave of Cabinda as part of Angola. Yet, the independence agreement, known as the Alvor Agreement, signed on Jan. 15, 1975, with Portugal reflected above all the continuing suspicion among the three African groups. The agreement selected the date of Angola's independence and set up a transitional government in which every position was meticulously apportioned among Portugal, the MPLA, FNLA, and UNITA.

Internecine Fighting. Virtually from the moment it was signed, the Alvor Agreement was ignored by all three movements. On March 23, FNLA commandos attacked MPLA offices in two Luanda townships, and three days later they massacred 51 MPLA recruits. Fighting continued sporadically through the first part of April and included a misguided attempt by the FNLA against MPLA leader Agostinho Neto's life, which left a South African jet riddled with bullets.

At the end of April, a new round of fighting reportedly left 700 killed and over 1,000 wounded. By the middle of May, fighting had spread to all major centers despite efforts to arrange a cease-fire between the warring factions. At the end of May, the MPLA counterattacked and initiated a third round of fighting. In the course of these skirmishes the FNLA was driven out of the Cabinda enclave. Jonas Savimbi, leader of UNITA, arranged for yet another conciliation meeting on June 21 at Nakuru, Kenya.

Under the Nakuru Agreement, the nationalist groups vowed to proceed with the long-overdue implementation of the Alvor Agreement's clauses, and a hastily drafted constitution was published on July 6. Three days later major fighting resumed between the MPLA and FNLA, which was driven out of Luanda.

From that moment, the conflict assumed the dimensions of a major military campaign in which all non-MPLA forces increasingly coordinated their action in an attempt to control a wide swath of territory extending from Zaire to Namibia/South West Africa. The FNLA leader, Holden Roberto, an Angolan who had spent virtually his entire life in Zaire, led the FNLA advance on Luanda and Malanje. In its drive, the FNLA used Western military equipment technically supplied by Zaire, as well as smaller amounts supplied by China and Rumania. With this force, the FNLA captured Caxito, some 50 miles (80 km) northeast of Luanda, and took over the Portuguese air force base of Negage. UNITA claimed the central section of Angola and reportedly controlled an extensive section of the Benguela railway.

International Ramifications. The international ramifications of the conflict reinforced the threat of major foreign intervention. On September 23, U. S. Secretary of State Henry Kissinger expressed his concern over "the interference of extracontinental powers who do not wish Africa well and whose involvement is inconsistent with the promise of true independence." This was interpreted as a reference to the support extended to the MPLA by the USSR, other Eastern European countries, and Cuba, but the United States itself had been involved for years in Angola. Ever since the outbreak of nationalist insurgency against Portuguese rule in 1961, the United States offered material and diplomatic backing for Portugal's attempt to retain control of its African possessions, while at the same time extending covert support to Holden Roberto's FNLA.

Support for the FNLA by China and Rumania appeared to be motivated by their anti-Soviet preoccupations. South Africa's backing of anti-MPLA forces revealed that country's desire to prevent the emergence of a radical African nationalist government on Namibia's frontier.

EDOUARD BUSTIN, *Boston University*

ANGOLA · Information Highlights

Official Name: Angola.
Location: Southwestern Africa.
Area: 481,351 square miles (1,246,700 sq km).
Population (1975 est.): 6,400,000.
Chief Cities (1973): Luanda, the capital, 540,000; Nova Lisboa, 89,000; Lobito, 74,000.
Government: Transitional government.
Monetary Unit: Escudo (27.25 escudos equal U. S.$1, Sept. 1973).
Gross National Product (1972): $1,240,000,000.
Manufacturing: Chemicals, foodstuffs, tobacco products, cotton textiles, petroleum products.
Major Agricultural Products: Coffee, cotton, sisal, corn, sugar, palm oil.
Foreign Trade (1973): *Exports,* $709,000,000; *imports,* $491,000,000.

Dr. Donald C. Johanson examines the skeleton of "Lucy," the fossil woman he discovered in Ethiopia in the fall of 1974. Between 3.0 and 3.5 million years old, it is the most complete skeleton of such age ever found.

ANTHROPOLOGY

Analysis of the hominid fossils found in the Afar region of Ethiopia in 1974 and in Kenya in 1973 continued to elicit considerable response in anthropological circles in 1975. Ethnicity, medical anthropology, and the origin and evolution of language were also of concern to anthropologists.

Hominid Reevaluation. A reevaluation of the genus *Homo* developed in 1973 with the announcement by Richard Leakey, a Kenyan paleoanthropologist, of the discovery of a hominid skull, approximately 2.9 million years old. It had a brain cavity considerably larger than expected for its antiquity. The form came to be known as "1470" from its catalog number in the expedition's records. Late in 1974, Dr. Donald C. Johanson of Case Western Reserve University and curator of physical anthropology at the Cleveland Museum of Natural History announced the recovery of a partial skeleton from the Afar region of Ethiopia. Originally thought to be perhaps as old as 4.4 million years, it is now dated at between 3.0 and 3.5 million years. This skeleton, about 40% complete, is the most complete hominid fossil ever found.

The reevaluation made by Dr. Richard Leakey, which was supported by Dr. Johanson's data, is an echo of a long-standing contention of Dr. Louis Leakey. He stated that the genus *Homo* developed as a separate lineage 3 to 4 million years ago and diverged from the Australopithecine hominids. According to this view, there were two lineages of early hominids, the Australopithecines and a lineage representing the genus *Homo,* characterized by a much larger brain, bipedal motion, and with cheek teeth quite small in relation to the skeleton's size. The "1470" would then be a direct descendant of modern *Homo sapiens,* surviving because of a superior competitive ability and of an enlarged brain that was still enlarging.

Language Data. An important event of 1975 was the Conference on the Origins of Language and Speech, sponsored by the New York Academy of Sciences and held September 21–25 in New York City. The conference was a result of current concerns with the nature and evolution of language and speech, stimulated by reports of chimpanzees learning sign language and in one case communicating by symbols through a specially built computer.

Drs. Allan and Beatrice Gardner, psychologists at the University of Nevada and trainers of the famous chimp "Washoe," are training two chimps they acquired almost at birth. The chimps are being raised with sign language for communication. Early reports indicated that the chimps began making recognizable signs when they were about three months old and by the age of six months had learned 13 to 15 signs. The significance of these experiments seems to be that signs are easier for chimps to make than words, perhaps promising further development in understanding the acquisition of sign language. However, Dr. Duane Rumbaugh, professor of psychology at Georgia State University, reported that language is a continuum ranging through various degrees of sophistication, and it is useless to attempt to define language in terms of any precise set of factors.

Deaths. A prominent anthropologist, Leslie A. White, died March 31, 1975, at the age of 75. At his death he was research anthropologist at the University of California, Santa Barbara. Professor White taught at the University of Michigan from 1930 to 1970 and was visiting professor at San Francisco State University, 1970–71. A Viking Medalist in 1959, he was also president of the American Anthropological Association in 1964. He was known for his many articles and books: *Pueblo of Santa Ana, New Mexico* (1942), *The Science of Culture* (1949), *The Evolution of Culture* (1959), and *The Concept of Culture* (1975), and his theory on the relationship between energy and culture.

Anthropologist Dorothy Lee, known for her work in existential anthropology, also died in 1975. Her major works were *Freedom and Culture* (1959) and "Being and Value in Primitive Culture" (*Journal of Philosophy,* 1949).

HERMAN J. JAFFE
Brooklyn College, City University of New York

Dr. John C. Brandt points to rock etching believed to show the supernova that created the Crab Nebula in 1504. Found near Zuni, N. M., the pictographs are similar to Chinese interpretations of the event.

archaeology

Significant work in archaeology continued in both the Western Hemisphere and the Eastern in 1975. In the Western, finds in Alaska, Pennsylvania, Ohio, Indiana, and Illinois made the news. In the Eastern, there were new finds in both Asia and Europe. A new process, thermoluminescence (TL), helped to authenticate the dates of artifacts.

Western Hemisphere

Archaeologists throughout the Western Hemisphere are expressing growing concern over increasing incidents of archaeological vandalism. National Forest officials in Arizona feel the situation in their state has reached "epidemic" proportions. Burial grounds, some of a relatively recent nature, are prime objectives of the vandals. The presence of intact art objects and contemporary fashion trends featuring American Indian jewelry, may be strongly influencing the looting of Indian graves.

In Oregon, vandals are employing extreme measures, including dynamite to remove stone pictographs and petroglyphs. While some are taken with personal or commercial purposes in mind, others have been intentionally defaced. A particularly famous series of pictographs was sprayed with blue paint near Bend, Ore. Authorities in Mexico have also expressed concern over the use of helicopters to remove large stone carvings from Mayan and other ruins.

Some archaeologists now feel that discretion must be used when discussing archaeological site locations in a publication since potential vandals can easily have access to such sources.

Alaska. Archaeologists from Washington State University spent the summer months excavating a former Eskimo winter village located between the Yukon and Kuskokwim Rivers in southwestern Alaska. Scientists have determined that this region underwent a major climatic change between 1000–1300 A. D., during which time a warmer climate may have caused significant cultural adaptation among the resident Eskimo population.

Located in a permafrost region, the site may produce artifacts such as clothing and plant remains not preserved in other areas. Earliest occupation of the site began about 800 A. D. and continued until the 19th century. From the latter period, examples of ironstone china, rifle cartridges, grass mats, knives, and glass beads have been found.

Pennsylvania. Recent findings at the Meadowcroft Rockshelter, 25 miles (40 km) southwest of Pittsburgh, have confirmed theories that early man crossed the Bering Strait from Siberia between 20,000 and 30,000 B. C. This year Carbon-14 dating of the rockshelter has established proof of human occupation in Pennsylvania by 14,225 B. C.

The charcoal used in dating the site and artifacts came from a fire pit near the base of the deeply stratified midden. Newest discoveries include more than 50 blade-like tools that, together with 100 other stone tools, constitute the earliest and best documented tool assemblage in the Western Hemisphere prior to 10,000 B. C. Scientists from the University of Pittsburgh are hopeful that continued excavations may reveal even earlier evidence of human occupation.

Elsewhere in Pennsylvania, excavations at the Shawnee-Minisink site uncovered a fluted projectile point associated with two fire pits. Charcoal from the pits has been dated to 8640–8800 B. C., confirming the Paleo-Indian nature of deposits at the 11-foot (3.5-meter) level.

Ohio. Graduate students from the University of Cincinnati working in cooperation with an Ohio utilities company recently excavated a prehistoric village site near the Ohio River. The site contains evidence of prehistoric structures, as demonstrated by numerous post molds as well as storage and trash pits and burials. Among the burials excavated, one skeleton had a large projectile point imbedded in the pelvis region, quite probably the cause of death.

Other artifacts excavated include a marble atlatl weight, good evidence of trade with other areas where marble formations exist. Axes, pestles, sinkers, gorgets, flint knives, awls, needles, fishhooks, and various ornaments have been recovered. Earliest occupation of the site is placed at 2000 B. C., the late Archaic Period.

Indiana. Archaeologists from Indiana State University are continuing their efforts to salvage data from a section of the Daughtery-Monroe site in Sullivan County in advance of levee construction. Excavation has revealed a domestic center in the Middle Woodland site where numerous storage and refuse features contain identifiable food remains, such as squash. Mammal remains include evidence of beaver, porcupine, and elk, animals no longer present in Sullivan County.

Two types of house structures have been identified and together suggest year-round occupation. Some feature a permanent style of construction with sunken floors and thick walls. Others are of lighter construction.

A salvage project at Columbus, Ind., succeeded in recovering a significant number of Late Woodland human skeletal remains with associated artifacts from a burial mound 140 feet (43 meters) in diameter and 6 feet (2 meters) high. Burials were varied in type from individual flexed burials to secondary deposits and cremations. Among the artifacts found were shell gorgets, copper and shell beads, red ochre, bone pins, and pottery vessels.

Illinois. Excavations continued at the Koster site along the central Mississippi River Valley. The artifacts recovered revealed that these people living in 6500 B. C. were not primitive savages. They lived as nuclear families in a central village, hunted deer, caught birds and fish, and preserved food.

GEORGE E. PHEBUS
Smithsonian Institution

Eastern Hemisphere

Although the most remarkable archaeological discoveries in the Eastern Hemisphere in 1975 came to light in Asia, laboratories in the West authenticated finds almost too startling to be credible through the newly-established technique of thermoluminescence (TL) analysis.

Hunter's Concerns. Much of west European Upper Palaeolithic cave art was related to fertility and reproduction, such as the recently discovered wall paintings at Tito Bastillo Cave

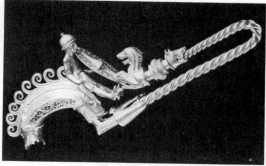

COURTESY UNIVERSITY OF MISSOURI—COLUMBIA

A gold Celtic fibula, or safety pin, was dated to 200 B. C. through the process of thermoluminescence.

in northern Spain. At Gonnersdorf, in the German Rhineland, Upper Palaeolithic hunters engraved, along with numerous drawings of animals, a somewhat schematic scene dealing with reproduction, representing either humans or horses.

The virtual absence of Mesolithic graves in Denmark had always hampered an understanding of the development of northern populations, but at Vedbaek Station near Copenhagen, 21 Ertebølle graves dating to about 4000 B. C. were dug by Sven E. Ulbrechtsen. Most of the graves are single burials, but one double grave contained an adult woman with a child about nine months old. The baby boy wore, at the position of the belly-band, a flint dagger like those found with adult males. The infant was laid to rest on the wings of a swan, while the apparent mother had at her head over 100 beads made from animal teeth.

Early Food Producers. The site at Vlasac, in Yugoslavia's Dinaric Alps, contains evidence of early agricultural times. The flintwork is like that of ostensibly non-food producing Lepenski Vir, but the houses are not trapezoidal. Riverine resources and red deer were hunted, with many fish bones and elaborate bone and antler tools found. Carbon-14 dates the center around 6000 B. C.

In a Yangshao neolithic village of north China, archaeologists have uncovered an effigy vessel in the form of an owl, almost 9 inches (22 cm) high, along with painted pottery and flint harvesting implements.

An entirely new food producing neolithic culture has been recognized in east-central China. The Ching-lien-kiang Culture, dated to about 5000 B. C., is characterized by painted pottery adorned with rosettes and star patterns, and perforated harvesting knives. The stepped adz, a Southeast Asian tool, reflects the role this culture played in transmitting the considerable neolithic developments of Southeast Asia, such as rice agriculture and domesticated water buffalo, to north China.

More Southeast Asian Inventions. Previous evidence that the world's first metallurgy was in

Southeast Asia was confirmed by Chester Gorman's excavation at Ban Chiang, Thailand. Bronze implements have been dated to 3500 B.C. by thermoluminescence (TL) analysis of the accompanying pots painted in red curvilinear scrollwork. These people carefully buried their dead with bracelets and bangles of bronze and elephant ivory.

Hunting was an esteemed profession, judging from the burial of a man over 70-inches (180-cm) tall with bronze spear and deer antler. A bronze bracelet adorned his wrist; he had a bone pin in his hair and a necklace of tiger claws.

Asiatic Urban Civilization. Soviet archaeologists have identified in Uzbekistan the lost city Nautakaa, known to the historian of Alexander the Great. Finds include potsherds, coins, turquoise and bronze jewelry, and other metal objects proving the city actually dates back to the Bronze Age.

China, which already had produced the best preserved of ancient bodies, has yielded in Hupeh Province an even better specimen. Thanks to inhumation in three nested "Chinese box" coffins and a red fluid surrounding the body in the innermost one, the skin was perfectly intact and the limbs still bend easily at the joints. The former official of the Han Empire, who was about 66-inches (167-cm) tall and weighed

about 115 pounds (52 kg), was buried about 167 B.C. at age 50. His name was carved on a jade seal inserted in his mouth. Surrounding him in the burial chambers were over 500 artifacts, furniture, and three chests of food. Small wooden hand-carved horses and cattle with wagons and boats and other equipment lay by his pen and ink case, along with lacquer boxes and pottery.

Offshore of Fukien Province, China, a well-preserved wooden sailing junk dating to the Sung Dynasty (960–1279 A.D.) was found. The ship sank with a full cargo of Indonesian incense at the entrance to a harbor. The absence of bodies on board suggests that the crew escaped.

TL Analyses. Thermoluminescence, aided by neutron activation analysis, and a computerized analysis of style have verified that a golden safety pin, ostensibly dating from about 200 B.C. in the Iron Age, is authentic. The pin carries the delicately made figure of a Celtic warrior, nude except for belt and helmet, warding off an attacking canine with his sword, now broken away, and shield. This informative piece is one of the finest examples of Celtic art recognized since World War II.

Perhaps the most sensational contribution yet made by TL, however, was the verification of the site of Glozel, near Vichy, France. Long cited as a blatant hoax, the mysterious script on clay tablets, glassworks, and owlish and phallic figurines have been dated to the late Iron Age by this technique in analyses performed at laboratories in France, Scotland, and Denmark.

Imperial Art. An amateur archaeologist found in Israel, near the Jordan River, the bronze head of a statue of the Roman Emperor Hadrian. Israeli government archaeologists, continuing the exploration, recovered the rest of the statue of the armored ruler, as well as a second statue thought to be the Emperor's wife, Sabina. The high quality of the artistry indicates an official Roman product and represents one of the finest pieces of classical art unearthed in this century.

Barbarian Splendor. The gold-adorned queen of the Silla Kingdom, which in essence founded Korea, was unearthed at Kyongju, South Korea. The 3rd century tomb, the first found intact, enclosed an eastward oriented body adorned in gold. A solid gold crown at the head, gold bangles at the arms, and canine-tooth jade pieces were still in position. A golden belt was at the waist, and at the feet were annular ankle ornaments. The tomb of King Chijung of the 6th century also contained a gold crown, earrings, belt, bracelets, and finger rings, plus four horse saddles and a pair of birchbark mudguards in a chest preserved by the conditions of the grave.

In England a Durham University crew digging at Jarrow, Northumbria, found 6th century Anglo-Saxon stained glass, the oldest in Europe. It was underneath a clay deposit, which seemed like subsoil.

RALPH M. ROWLETT
University of Missouri

Chinese archaeologists made two important finds in 1975. Life-sized clay figures (*below*), 2,200 years old, are from the northwest; Hupeh man was found in central China.

UPI

architecture

In 1975 architecture in the United States may well have gone beyond its long fascination with opulent modernism as it sought to meet new concerns for conservation of the environment and of energy.

The Economy and Architecture. When the economy slows, the building industry is generally the first to feel the pinch, and often one of the last to recover. Architects, much of whose work precedes the building, are therefore prone to long and severe famines. One of them was underway during 1975. Architecture schools were jammed with students, more across the United States than the total of architects already in practice. The unemployment rate among architects, however, was said to be over 40% in some large cities, and the attendant mood of reflection was the most intense since the 1930's.

Modern Architecture Now Historic. That the 1930's were already remote was dramatized by an act that may be the most important historical milestone of the year. The modest but enormously important house that architect Walter Gropius designed for himself in Lincoln, Mass., when he came from the Bauhaus to Harvard in 1937, was acquired by the Society for the Preservation of New England Antiquities. Thus, modern architecture has become "historic."

A study of skyscrapers in the "other" modern style of the 1930's, now called Art Deco, produced a book, *Skyscraper Style: Art Deco New York,* by Rosemarie Haag Bletter and Cervin Robinson and inspired a series of enthusiastically acclaimed exhibitions. Terms such as "moderne" and "zig zag modernistic," once developed as put-downs, have hastened along the same route to respectable nomenclature trod earlier by "gothic" and "baroque," both of which had been coined as derisive terms.

Skyscraper Grandeur. A rather limited number of grand projects embodying the more opulent possibilities of the previous era were in the news. A 70-story, cylindrical hotel tower designed by John Portman was underway in Atlanta, and for Los Angeles the same firm had made a hotel of a cluster of five high cylinders.

The Hirshhorn Museum and Sculpture Garden, designed by Gordon Bunshaft of SOM, brought to the Mall in Washington a kind of spartan opulence, a richly detailed but brutally blank cylinder hovering above a sculpture garden. This structure drew the fire of critics ("neo-penitentiary modern" in *The New York Times*), who made clear how different the mood of the country had become from the one that had enjoyed the simple heroic gestures of the 1950's.

Architect Philip Johnson's I. D. S. Center in Minneapolis, much more opulent than the aspirations of a recession year seemed to allow, has a crystalline wonder. It consists of a 51-story office tower connected to an 8-story office annex, a 19-story hotel and a 2-story commercial struc-

UPI

The South's tallest building, the Peachtree Plaza Hotel in Atlanta, Ga., was topped out on October 2.

ture, all surrounding a skylight-covered plaza called the "crystal court." This is connected to all adjacent blocks by "skyways" at the second floor level, with four more floors underground including parking. The plaza is a sort of crystalline lean-to and reaches the breathtaking height of 121 feet (37 meters). It makes an almost-outdoor openness possible throughout the winter.

In Tune with the Environment. An unusually handsome group of dwellings on Hilton Head Island, S. C., by architects Stoller/Glasser and Marquis Associates, served to represent the possibilities of inventive housing. On a densely forested site, 300 units were inserted into the forest atmosphere by stacking two- and three-story dwellings to make five-story buildings. Access from a perimeter parking area was provided via an elevated walkway through the treetops.

The complexities that mark the end of a confident era emerged in 1975's most interesting design competition, which was a scheme for 1,000 units on Roosevelt Island, in New York City's East River. There, over the past few years, under Edward Logue's New York State Urban Devel-

HEDRICH-BLESSING

The Crystal Court, a skylight-covered plaza, is the heart of the I. D. S. Center in Minneapolis, Minn.

opment Corp. (UDC), a master plan by Philip Johnson, had begun to make the former prison island a desirable New York address. It included housing by Jose Luis Sert and Johansen-Bhavhani. It was clear by the time the competition was underway that Logue's visions for UDC were ending (he resigned just afterward), and that the scheme would not be built. However, 268 architects submitted designs, and 4 received awards.

Kyu Sung Woo stressed choices and options for the residents between four high-rise towers, gallery-accessed middle rises, and family clusters, scaled like a New York street of brownstones. Robert Amico and Robert Brandon continued the configurations of Jose Luis Sert's already-standing housing. Sam Davis and the ELS Design Group broke the site into a series of smaller and more intimate spaces, and Stern and Hagmann put the tallest buildings next to the river and focused on a pedestrian way cutting through the middle of the site. Although they evidenced it in differing ways, the winning schemes had in common a deep concern for the context, both social and physical, in which they were to fit.

The firm of Hardy Holzman Pfeiffer Associates was very much in evidence in 1975 with a series of buildings, many of them theaters, which manipulated the structural context as well in a set of ebullient fabrications. In the Fisher Theater at Phillips Exeter Academy in New Hampshire, the architects used standard parts from a preengineered building to save money and to exploit the drama that resulted when familiar building components collided in unfamiliar ways. The same firm's Olmsted Theater for Adelphi University in New York used concrete block and a conventional speculative building system to house an extraordinarily flexible theater that provides a maximum number of ways for players and audience to relate to one another.

Energy Conservation and Design. The recession helped provide the leisure to consider concerns other than the completion of new buildings. Even as interest in new buildings centered more and more in their connections with their physical, social, and even historical contexts, so interest mounted in the conservation of energy and the development of alternative energy sources, especially the sun. The conservation and recycling of old buildings and the design of new buildings to intensify a connection with the old were also a prime concern.

The American Institute of Architects Research Corporation mounted a major project, to commission designs for Solar Energy Utilization. The results published first surveyed the state of the art, which exhibits houses from the 1938 solar houses by George Fred Keck, near Chicago, to the Copper Development Association's 1975 "Decade 80" house in Tucson, Ariz. The study then described designs for houses suitable for various American climates that cut the nonrenewable energy consumed to less than 25% of the conventional amount. A frequent discovery in the pursuit of this goal has been that careful design and extensive insulation can come very close to making the requisite saving without even the need for solar collectors. On the other hand, the solar collectors and especially the vats for storing the warmed medium have excited designers by providing dramatic new forms.

Possibly the country's most serendipitous collection of energy-conserving devices and ideas has been assembled in the Rhode Island Energy Conservation Station. It is an old foundry building in Providence reconstituted by REDE, the Research and Development Institute of Providence. REDE has gathered sponsors to test energy-conserving devices from a wind-driven power generator atop a rebuilt brick chimney to a recycling toilet.

A particularly impressive full-scale cut in energy costs can be seen in the Children's Hospital of Philadelphia, for which Harbeson, Hough, Livingston, and Larson were the architects. This enormous but remarkably humane building is shaped into a solid square to minimize heat loss, with a high atrium that serves to exhaust the heat from the interior of the building. Even in the coldest weather, people and

equipment in the interior produce more heat than they use and some of the excess is returned to the perimeter to help heat that. Even the clear glass skylight over the atrium is placed at angles that reflect the rays of the summer sun.

Historic Conservation and Design. Conservation has taken other forms, too, and from across the country came dramatic stories of fine old buildings recycled. The St. Louis Symphony, for instance, is now installed in a flamboyant old movie theater with excellent (and tested) acoustics, very simply remodeled by architect Angelo Corrubia. The alternative was to build a new $15–20 million concert hall. In Princeton, N. J., architect William Short saved a fine mid-19th century mansion slated for demolition by converting it to five condominium apartments with minimum damage to the elegant old building.

In Boston, where an unusually extensive supply of old masonry buildings exists and a continuing sense of the importance of the past has persisted, a series of dramatic reconstitutions of the city's wharves has revivified the waterfront. Architects Anderson Notter Associates rebuilt the four-story granite Custom House Block on Long Wharf into luxury apartments and turned a smaller adjacent brick building into a spacious restaurant, stripped back to the brick walls and rafters.

Conservation and Urban Design. In the urban design field, too, most of the news was made by efforts to preserve old places, rather than by the emergence of any new ones. Controversy raged in Georgetown, D. C., among proponents of dense new development along that town's formerly industrial waterfront, proponents of no growth (whose power across the country seemed to be on a very rapid rise), and those who favored limited and careful development, who may be winning.

The San Antonio River, which flows through a little canyon in a bend below the level of downtown San Antonio, Tex., was saved from being filled in 40 years ago, and in the years since it has been developed into a beautiful verdant pleasure garden. Although it has been greatly extended from its beginnings, no special events pushed it into the news media. Yet it was frequently being rediscovered in the press, since its special qualities, its greenery, its romance, and its redolence of the past, are now so highly valued.

The value of the past was demonstrated in many ways. In Florence, Italy, architect Richard Meier was designing a sparkling new museum of art behind a preserved façade of a stable building at the Villa Strozzi. In Biloxi, Miss., a design festival brought six architects from across the country to work for a week with students from nearby architecture schools to design a library and museum for the center of the hurricane-devastated town. All the teams recommended the abandonment of a blockbusting 1960's style urban-renewal scheme the city had

COPPER DEVELOPMENT ASSOCIATION INC.

The "Decade 80" solar house in Tucson, Ariz., is one of the innovative models designed to make maximum use of solar energy for cooling and heating.

intended, with huge parking garage and covered shopping mall, and a return to a more humane fabric for this quiet Gulf Coast city. William Turnbull won the commission for a library building with a romantic design that curves gracefully around a square facing the old city hall. Stern and Hagmann's Lang house in Washington, Conn., was extensively discussed for its pointed use of specific historical precedents, with details indebted to sources from two continents over the last three centuries.

Contrasts with the past, but sensitive and gentle ones, are evident in Architect Arthur Erickson's 51–61–71 project in Vancouver, B. C. Part conservation and part new development, it unites old buildings and new ones and features a park on the roof of new low buildings adjacent to the old in what becomes a three-block-long park.

CHARLES W. MOORE
University of California at Los Angeles

Argentine President Isabel Perón resumed her official duties in October after a month's leave of absence. Acting president Italo Luder (*center*) fulfilled the presidential duties during her absence.

UPI

ARGENTINA

Political turmoil surrounded the regime of President Perón in 1975, a year in which economic problems increased dramatically.

Crisis Politics. The political vacuum created by the death in 1974 of President Juan Perón appeared, early in 1975, to have been filled by Perón's widow María Estela ("Isabel") Martínez de Perón. Her chief aide was Social Welfare Minister José López Rega, who, in January, added the key post of secretary to the presidency to his many duties.

Of major concern to the regime was the suppression of guerrilla units, which were spreading subversion in rural and urban industrial areas. President Perón ordered federal troops into mountainous Tucumán in February to eradicate leftists. Even though the state of siege declared in 1974 remained in effect, the dissidents continued to kidnap for ransom and assassination. Victims included businessmen, politicians, bureaucrats, and uniformed officers. Jorge and Juan Born, grain exporters, were ransomed by the Montoneros in June for $60 million. John P. Egan, U. S. honorary consul in Córdoba, had been murdered by the same group in February. Other than the Montoneros, the principal irregular force was the People's Revolutionary Army (ERP). Both bands wanted to convert Argentina into a socialist state.

In addition to soldiers and police, the Perón government's anti-subversion plan could rely on a deadly right-wing assassination squad, the Argentine Anti-Communist Alliance (AAA), whose activists allegedly included off-duty policemen. The AAA sought guerrilla suspects, left-wing Peronist politicians, and journalists. By June, unofficial estimates of 1975 political murders, often victims of the AAA, reached 1,200.

Because the tenure of President Perón was increasingly questioned by most political elements, except the Radicals and the right wing of organized labor, López Rega obtained the resignation of the Senate president, who was first in line to succeed Isabel Perón. The Senate vacancy made the presiding officer of the Chamber of Deputies the presidential successor. López Rega easily maneuvered his son-in-law, Raúl Lastiri, into the leadership of that chamber.

Resentment over the growing political power of López Rega and generalized discontent with the regime's failure to surmount urgent economic problems brought down the López Rega "dictatorship" on July 11. López Rega was exiled, and President Perón named a series of his protégés to important posts in her administration, only to find her appointments rejected by rightist unions, the armed forces, and the Radical party. Unable to stabilize either the political or the economic situation, President Perón took a month-long sick-leave at an air force retreat, leaving Italo A. Luder, president of the Argentine Senate, in charge of the executive branch.

Seeking a democratic solution to the crisis, Luder replaced those remaining in the cabinet who had been close to López Rega and entered into dialogue, as the military had suggested, with powerful groups overlooked by President Perón. Luder also tried to improve relations with the press.

President Perón returned in time for the Peronist Loyalty Day celebration on October 17, even though political insiders and military leaders had suggested that she extend her leave or resign. Almost immediately she was thrust into a new controversy. President Perón called it all a "mistake." She had transferred $700,000 in welfare funds into her late husband's estate. Payment on the check was stopped, but the

damage had been done. Mrs. Perón named Aníbal Demarco, a follower of López Rega, to head the social welfare ministry, and checked into a local clinic on November 3, complaining of a gall bladder condition.

President Perón's opportune illness may have prolonged her mandate, but the funding scandal cost her valuable support. Radical party congressmen called for the impeachment of Perón if she blocked an investigation of alleged corruption in the social welfare ministry, which controls 30%–40% of the federal budget. Rightwing labor leader Lorenzo Miguel deserted her, as did Ricardo Balbín, leader of the Radical party. A revolt by air force units was quelled in December through military intervention, underlining the military's political role. On December 17 the government announced that general elections would be held in October 1976. The announcement was interpreted as a government attempt to hold off opposition pressures.

Economy. While political forces fought, economic conditions deteriorated rapidly. By August, the cost-of-living index was 240% above that of a year earlier. Automobile purchases at midyear had plummeted by 45%–80%, depending on the model. Sales in July were so bad that business spokesmen claimed there were no funds to pay employees. With 300,000 workers laid off in Buenos Aires in July and August, the national unemployment rate reached 7%.

Imports had to be curtailed; payments of $500 million for auto industry imports were deferred. Exports of grain were down because of a reduction in acreage planted for the 1974–75 growing season. The corn harvest was 20% below normal. Export duties were lifted on numerous items—including wool, leather, and rice—to increase foreign exchange holdings, which amounted to only $900 million in April. Venezuela agreed to a $600 million loan to alleviate the balance-of-payments problem.

Even so, the foreign debt grew by $1 billion in 1975, reaching $10 billion by August. Economy Minister Antonio Cafiero traveled to the United States to obtain new loans and to renegotiate the foreign debt. The peso was devalued

periodically throughout the year. A 50% devaluation, against the dollar, in March was the most severe adjustment.

Efforts by successive economy ministers to revive a 1974 "social pact," encompassing both wage and price restraints, failed. Strikes became commonplace. The most devastating was a March–May stoppage in the auto industry that cost $800 million. Farmers struck in March and again in October for higher agricultural prices and lower taxes. Both cattle and grain were withheld from the market to underscore the farmers' demands. By midyear many of the unions had accepted officially-authorized 45% wage increases. However, strikes spread among the holdouts until a 48-hour general strike, unprecedented in a Peronist administration, was called. President Perón capitulated to labor pressure and granted strikers wage increases of 100% to 135% in July.

Fabricaciones Militares announced plans in March for the construction of an integrated steel mill, with a projected output of 2.5–3 million tons annually. It will be partially financed by private capital.

Foreign Affairs. A meeting between presidents Perón and Pinochet of Chile finally took place at Morón air force base, near the capital. Dominating discussions between the two leaders was the subject of international subversion. The Argentine ERP had been supporting clandestine activities in Chile, while Chilean exiles were found in guerrilla activities being suppressed in Argentina.

LARRY L. PIPPIN, *Elbert Covell College University of the Pacific*

ARIZONA

The year 1975 saw an intensification of Arizona's problem of dealing with a rapidly-growing population at a time of national economic recession. Controversies reflecting aspects of this problem dominated municipal elections in Phoenix and Tucson, and a record-length state legislative session.

Population and Economy. Since the 1970 census, the Arizona population has increased approximately five times faster than the national population, and a 1975 projection predicted a further 18% increase by 1980. Jobs for this increasing population continued to be in short supply throughout 1975, especially in the Phoenix area, where the unemployment rate was substantially above 10% for most of the year.

State Politics. In January, Democratic Gov. Raul Castro called for strict government economy in view of revenue losses caused by the recession. There was bitter partisan controversy in the legislature, where Democrats controlled the Senate and Republicans the House. The 1975 session lasted 152 days, an all-time record for Arizona, but the number of bills passed, 171, was the smallest in years.

------ **ARGENTINA · Information Highlights** ------

Official Name: Argentine Republic.
Location: Southern South America.
Area: 1,072,158 square miles (2,776,889 sq km).
Population (1975 est.): 25,400,000.
Chief Cities (1970 census, met. areas): Buenos Aires, the capital, 8,352,900; Rosario, 810,840; Córdoba, 798,663.
Government: *Head of state,* Isabel Perón, president (took office July 1974). *Head of government,* Isabel Perón. *Legislature*—Congress: Senate and Chamber of Deputies.
Monetary Unit: Peso (34 pesos equal U. S.$1, Aug. 1975).
Gross National Product (1973 est.): $27,750,000,000.
Manufacturing (major products): Iron and steel, automobiles, machinery, processed foods, chemicals, petroleum products, meat.
Major Agricultural Products: Wheat, corn, grapes, sugarcane, oats, sunflower seeds, sorghum.
Foreign Trade (1973): *Exports,* $3,266,000,000; *imports,* $2,235,000,000.

ARIZONA BICENTENNIAL COMMISSION

An Arizona Bicentennial celebration featured a reenactment of the Juan Bautista de Anza Expedition of 1775.

The proposed Equal Rights Amendment (ERA) to the federal constitution received another setback in Arizona in 1975. Senate Democrats split on the issue, and with Republicans heavily opposed, the amendment was defeated. Since this effectively killed ERA for the 1975 session, it was not brought to a vote in the House.

As an economy measure, the legislature delayed the introduction of a Medicaid program until 1976, and Arizona thus remained the only state without such a program. Another legislative casualty was a bill to repeal Arizona's "fair trade" law, which fixes retail prices. Both parties claimed to favor the repeal, but the Republican House insisted on exempting liquor stores. When Senate Democrats would not agree to the House amendment, the resulting stalemate killed the bill.

The legislature did succeed in passing several important anti-crime bills. Largely as a result of massive frauds in the nationwide sale of Arizona land, a new law allows the state attorney general to convene a statewide grand jury to investigate any of 21 named crimes. In addition, the scandal-ridden state real estate department was reorganized and enlarged to include public members. Criminal penalties for drug-trafficking conspiracies were increased, and a "drug strike force" was created in four counties on the Mexican border.

Municipal Elections. In Phoenix, the Charter Government Committee, which had controlled city government since 1949, met its first major defeat. Its candidate for mayor, political newcomer Lyman Davidson, was challenged by incumbent charter councilman Margaret Hance and by six minor candidates. Two other incumbent charter councilmen ran for reelection as in-

dependents, and the six charter candidates faced a record field of 22 opponents in the November election. Mrs. Hance, a 52-year-old Republican, won a surprisingly easy victory over Lyman Davidson in the November election and became the first woman mayor of Phoenix. However, no council candidates received a majority in the council elections, necessitating a December 9 runoff election in which two Charter candidates and four Independents gained places on the council.

Charter opponents also sponsored a proposal to enlarge the council and to provide for a modified ward system, but this was rejected by the voters. Environmentalists received a setback when Phoenix voters reversed a 1973 referendum and approved the construction of a controversial east-west freeway across Phoenix.

In Tucson, the major issue in the municipal campaign was a police-firefighter strike in September. The strike had been tentatively settled when a divided city council approved a measure to grant major pay increases and to drop legal action against the strikers. The settlement was opposed by Republican Mayor Lewis C. Murphy, who denounced the strike as illegal and the settlement as one the city could not afford. His Democratic opponent, former mayor James Corbett, was generally sympathetic to the strikers. In the race for three, of six, council seats, the strike issue cut across party lines, and although Democrats swept all three races, it appeared that the elections had produced an anti-strike majority. The possibility was raised of a renewal of the strike in the event of a rejection of the earlier agreement.

The other major issue in the Tucson election was the "controlled growth" policy advocated by most Democratic candidates. The issue was between those who favored increasing restriction on industrial development and urban sprawl, and those pointing to the need to attract new business and industry. Though the issue was not entirely partisan, the results of the 1975 election appeared to favor the "controlled growth" forces.

JOHN P. WHITE
Arizona State University

--------- **ARIZONA · Information Highlights** ---------

Area: 113,909 square miles (295,024 sq km).
Population (1974 est.): 2,153,000. *Density:* 17 per sq mi.
Chief Cities (1970 census): Phoenix, the capital, 581,-562; Tucson, 262,933; Scottsdale, 67,823.
Government (1975): *Chief Officers*—governor, Raul H. Castro (D); secy. of state, Wesley Bolin (D). *Legislature*—Senate, 30 members; House of Representatives, 60 members.
Education (1974–75): *Enrollment*—public elementary schools, 346,599 pupils; public secondary, 140,441; nonpublic, 27,400; colleges and universities, 152,299 students. *Public school expenditures,* $401,147,000 ($908 per pupil).
State Finances (fiscal year 1974): *Revenues,* $1,339,553,-000; *expenditures,* $1,237,830,000.
Personal Income (1974): $10,742,000,000; per capita, $4,989.
Labor Force (Aug. 1975): *Nonagricultural wage and salary earners,* 719,300; *insured unemployed,* 36,900.

ARKANSAS

Uncertainty characterized Arkansas government, economy, and politics during 1975. Inflation and an unemployment rate of 10%, a 25-year record, made doubtful the adequacy of revenues to finance all state and local government activities. Legislative factions and supporters of George C. Wallace of Alabama jockeyed for a 1976 election advantage by passing a presidential primary act. A new governor, David H. Pryor, labored to control state administration and to influence the veteran lawmakers.

The Governor. Despite some legislative-gubernatorial controversy, 21 full vetoes, and 13 item vetoes, Governor Pryor's legislative leadership was considered generally successful. The governor fixed his image upon state administration by such actions as passing over higher ranking police officers to appoint a new state police director; by selecting Dr. John C. Pickett, who testified against utility rate increases, to fill a vacancy on the Public Service Commission; and by appointing the state's first woman supreme court justice, Elsijane Trimble Roy. His pro-labor and reform image was tarnished when Pryor directed the National Guard to replace striking Pine Bluff firemen. In addition, the state Soil and Water Commission allegedly falsified its minutes to indicate approval of a $166,-000 water and sewer grant, endorsed by the governor, to the city of Mena.

The General Assembly. Among the record 1,009 bills passed during the regular biennial session were laws increasing appropriations for teachers' salaries and pensions, education, county and city roads and streets, and social services. There were also acts calling an appointed constitutional convention, limiting campaign expenditures, and creating a state building service council to supervise construction and operation of the buildings of the capitol.

The Equal Rights Amendment was defeated again, as were attempts to authorize collective bargaining and to require loyalty oaths for teachers and state employees. Legislation set procedures for replacing the cumbersome county-quorum courts, which had almost 400 members in one county, with small county councils that could create county-manager governments.

The Courts. The judiciary continued to restrain the legislature and administrative officials. The state supreme court invalidated the act calling the constitutional convention, all of whose members were appointed by the governor or legislature, because it exempted from change without popular approval certain sections of the 1874 charter. The court also upheld taxpayers' suits voiding salary increases in the form of expense reimbursements for legislators and county officials. It reversed the conviction of the controversial editor of the *Sharp Citizen*, Joseph H. Weston. He had been convicted of criticizing county officials under an 1868 criminal libel law.

STATE OF ARKANSAS

Gov. David H. Pryor, shown at the opening of a new plant, had a generally successful year of legislative leadership.

Federal courts set aside the 30-day residency requirement for voting and the law requiring women to register as "Miss" or "Mrs."

Public Utilities. Consumer and industrial groups, assisted by Attorney General Jim Guy Tucker, opposed in hearings before the Public Service Commission the request for electrical power rate increases by the Arkansas Power and Light Company.

WILLIAM C. NOLAN
Southern State College

--------- **ARKANSAS · Information Highlights** ---------

Area: 53,104 square miles (137,539 sq km).
Population (1974 est.): 2,035,000. *Density:* 38 per sq mi.
Chief Cities (1970 census): Little Rock, the capital, 132,483; Fort Smith, 62,802.
Government (1975): *Chief Officers*—governor, David H. Pryor (D); lt. gov., Joe Purcell (D). *General Assembly*—Senate, 35 members; House of Representatives, 100 members.
Education (1974–75): *Enrollment*—public elementary schools, 243,758 pupils; public secondary, 210,648; nonpublic, 11,100; colleges and universities, 56,688 students. *Public school expenditures,* $292,542,000 ($712 per pupil).
State Finances (fiscal year 1974): *Revenues,* $1,079,787,-000; *expenditures,* $997,543,000.
Personal Income (1974): $8,826,000,000; per capita, $4,-280.
Labor Force (July 1975): *Nonagricultural wage and salary earners,* 615,300; *insured unemployed* (Aug. 1975), 33,500.

The center painting in this room in the new Lehman Pavilion at New York City's Metropolitan Museum is "Adoration of the Magi" by Sienese artist Bartolo Di Fredi. As part of the gift stipulation, the new wing reproduces intact seven rooms from the Lehman mansion.

art

During 1975 the art market provided a faithful reflection of the world's economic condition, a relationship first noted by economists 25 years ago. The worldwide erosion of financial stability unsettled dealers and collectors on both sides of the Atlantic, and the once-bold Japanese collectors disappeared.

The London market, most important for its auction sales, held up amazingly well considering the serious state of the British economy. It was noted, however, that private dealers, particularly those dealing in Old Masters, were holding back prime works, realizing that important art must eventually increase in value. Continental art capitals—Paris, Cologne, Munich, and Milan—were less affected by the depressed art market, mostly because the general public by tradition is not as involved with the contemporary art scene.

New York City, the world's capital of contemporary art, suffered the greatest change because a broad base of buyers had a strong grip on the city's 200 professional galleries. The old and well-established houses were able to survive, but most avant-garde establishments experienced difficulty, and several important, newer galleries failed.

This market lull was not due only to the recession. It appeared that collectors were influenced by the public's skeptical view of new directions. The excitement for the "new" and "way-out" had been fading for two years. The art world sobered a great deal, with renewed interest in realism and more traditional media. Many felt that the New York City attitude, important to the international art mind, was becoming more balanced than it has been in several decades. And many were relieved to note that the random purchase of art for investment, without concern for aesthetic values, had largely disappeared.

U. S. Events in the Bicentennial Year. The first museum to open officially in the U. S. Bicentennial Year was the Palm Spring Desert (Calif.) Museum. The exhibition of works by traditional, established artists was balanced by a large display of Agam, the abstract modernist.

In April, Boston's Institute of Contemporary Art inaugurated the city's Bicentennial art fare with "Boston Celebrations: Jubilee Projects for the Bicentennial." The projects included scale-model building constructions that could be worn as costumes, not to mention wooden T-shirts, glass coats, and sugar-tablet boots. The show was climaxed when all churches in the city rang their bells simultaneously, augmented by the clang and clamor of bands, on Patriots' Day, April 19.

San Francisco was outstanding as far as unique exhibitions and activity were concerned. The Palace of the Legion of Honor with the De Young Gallery mounted a "Rainbow Show," a multimedia extravaganza that included painting, sculpture, holography, light shows, color demonstrations, theatrical presentations, mime, lectures, a magic circus, a self-healing energy show, and religious participations. The celebration was inspired by the Legion of Honor's acquisition of a major rainbow painting by Frederick E. Church.

Not to be outdone, the San Francisco Museum of Art staged a benefit on the theme of an artists' soapbox derby. This show featured everything from four-wheeled live nudes to a moving bush and a pumpernickel sports car.

In Nebraska a project to line Interstate Highway 80 with 10 large-scale abstract sculptures drew derisive laughter from many local citizens, who called the works "incomprehensible junk." They were told they did not have to look at it since it would be seen primarily by passing drivers. It cost more than $500,000 and was funded by $100,000 from the state's Bicentennial Commission, three-quarters of which was provided by the federal government; $20,000 from the National Endowment for the Arts, and $420,000 from various other sources.

Naturally, the Bicentennial shows from coast to coast made the public more aware of traditional art forms and inspiration. Most artists who have been commissioned to create Bicentennial-oriented paintings, graphics, and sculpture have chosen traditional media and subject matter. Even Alexander Calder's latest airplane revealed his appreciation for the conventional: he chose red and blue stripes.

Museum Survival and Box Office Mentality. Critics of New York's Metropolitan Museum of Art insist that the institution has become a circus, a place where the public is shown only the best, biggest, and most opulent. The criticism may be justified, but in 1975 the Metropolitan had a number of exciting surprises. The "Impressionist Epoch" brought 1,500 persons per hour through the museum's doors before the painting show closed in February. "From the Lands of the Scythians," an exhibition that was shown at the Metropolitan from April through June, attracted the largest first-day attendance ever at a Metropolitan show. In September, the Museum opened ten galleries devoted to Islamic art. *The New York Times* reported that the museum earned $200,000 in royalties in 1975 by allowing Springs Mills to copy fabric patterns for sheets and pillowcases.

The museum also opened the new Lehman Pavilion, which displays, intact, the collection and actual environment of one of America's last art moguls. The modern wing, designed by Kevin Roche, John Dinkeloo & Associates, overpowers the older art exhibited within because of its imaginative, unorthodox construction.

Director Thomas P. F. Hoving expressed delight with the change in the museum's image. He said of the Metropolitan's main entrance, "It's becoming the place where people congregate, a real street fair with vendors and jugglers and musicians. It's begun to change the nature of our audience, bringing many more kids into the Museum."

Whether the direction taken by the Metropolitan deserves strong criticism or praise, the fact remains that museums were faced with more trouble in 1975 than ever in the past. The

UPI
Braniff Airline's new flagship, designed by Alexander Calder in red, white and blue, salutes the Bicentennial.

prestigious Philadelphia Museum closed for 10 months, although installation of air conditioning was the excuse. The New York Cultural Center and the Finch College Museum closed permanently. Growing exhibition costs, salary increases, loss of the traditional philanthropists, and expanding general operating expenses mean that U. S. museums must seek out new sources of revenue. Even municipal, state, and federal funds are going to be granted more and more on the expedient grounds of public interest. The day of the isolated art scholar is rapidly disappearing.

The National Endowment for the Arts has helped hundreds of U. S. institutions organize exhibitions and research programs, but it cannot finance the cultural fabric of the nation. U. S. museums are benefiting increasingly from private industry, encouraged by such groups as the Business Committee for the Arts, but this is only a pebble in the sea. Substantial support must come from the private sector, but in 1975 this support was hard to find.

One indication of the seriousness of the recession and its effect on public institutions was the dearth of museum expansions. Besides the expansions at the Metropolitan in New York, only one major museum wing was inaugurated in 1975—at the Milwaukee Art Center in September.

Exhibitions of Special Merit. Although the economic climate affected the number of major museum exhibitions, several were of high quality. "French Painting 1774–1830: The Age of Revolution," composed of master works on loan from the Louvre Museum in Paris, opened in Detroit in March. The show went on to New York's Metropolitan Museum, where it showed in June. This was possibly the most stunning general exhibition of the year.

Another major event was the simply-mounted but comprehensive Monet show at the Chicago Art Institute, which opened in March. Chicago's

UPI

An admirer views Caravaggio's "Lute Player" at the National Gallery of Art, part of a large exhibition on loan from the USSR to the United States.

Museum of Contemporary Art organized a unique exhibition titled "Made in Chicago," which included everything from "Hairy Who" to oddments, including toys and boxes, billed as clarifying more than refining the vernacular.

Two major retrospective sculpture shows opened at the Whitney Museum in New York in the fall. In "The Sculpture of Elie Nadelman" nearly 150 highly-stylized and often humorous works by the Polish-born immigrant who died in the United States in 1946 were exhibited. The Whitney also exhibited smaller pieces by the contemporary sculptor Mark di Suvero. His larger pieces—giant-scale, open, linear steel sculptures—were placed on outdoor sites around the city.

Detente. Détente with the Soviet Union and China was significant in 1975 not only politically but artistically. Unfortunately, the thaw did not extend to relations between Washington's National Gallery of Art and the Metropolitan Museum of Art in New York City.

The rivalry between these institutions has far more subtlety and excitement than any national sport. Once again Washington's museum on the Mall outwitted the palace on New York's Fifth Avenue by forming an alliance with Russian-born oil tycoon Armand Hammer in presenting "Master Paintings from the Hermitage and the State Russian Museum." The only kindness between the two nationally-important institutions

is that the National, which won the long battle for the prestige of exhibiting King Tutankhamen's treasures, agreed to let the Metropolitan show them in late 1978, just before their return to Egypt. The Metropolitan exhibition will follow the National Gallery opening in November 1976 and viewings in Chicago, New Orleans, Los Angeles, and Seattle.

The National also won "The Archaeological Finds of the People's Republic of China" exhibition, which, after opening in Toronto at the Royal Ontario Museum, was seen in Washington, D. C., through March 30, 1975. It was also on view at the Nelson Gallery-Atkins Museum in Kansas City, Mo., and the Asian Art Museum in San Francisco before returning to Peking in September.

As détente is a two-way street, New York's Metropolitan Museum sent 100 19th- and 20th-century realist paintings to the USSR, where they were seen at the Hermitage in Leningrad in May before the show moved to Moscow's Pushkin Museum in August. Remembering the Moscow exhibition that was literally plowed under by tractors because of official opposition to "decadent" avant-gardism, it is not surprising that the Metropolitan sent traditional figurative paintings. U. S. art professionals who have been watching the Soviet Union for many years still give great support to exchange programs. They are certain there will be an eventual break-

"Great Folds in the Wind," a sculpture by Giacomo Manzu was exhibited in June in Rome's Borghese Garden.

comic strips and cartoons waxed even hotter. The art market slump may have been a contributing factor in the phenomenal rise in the number of galleries specializing in old and contemporary photographs and, to a lesser extent, in comic strips. Whatever the eventual decision as to their aesthetic merit, both were bringing high prices in 1975. In relation to their past significance, the 1975 change in artistic and financial valuation was no less than astounding.

Archaeological Finds. The most exciting archaeological find of the year was the group of 3rd-century, life-sized pottery figures of warriors and horses unearthed in China in July.

The most interesting archaeological theory promulgated was that of Kurt Mendelssohn of Oxford University. He theorized that all of Egypt's pyramids were built within one century, not by forced labor but by paid, positively-motivated citizens. His sound argument may revolutionize a great part of Egyptology.

Conclusion. In summation, the art year was perhaps a little less happy than most, and certainly it did not have the great variety of activity of the recent past. Yet many of the incidents and directions set during 1975 augured well for a brighter picture, particularly with the stimulation of the Bicentennial in the United States in 1976. Also, the art world can hope to be stimulated by the new-found wealth and artistic influence of oil-rich collectors and governments.

WILLIAM C. BENDIG
Publisher and Editor-in-Chief,
"The Art Gallery Magazine"

through culminating in freedom of expression for all artists concerned.

International Events. Exhibitions of international significance were held in many countries. London's Tate Gallery's anniversary exhibition of Joseph Turner's work was one of the most significant.

Paris was blessed with the complete exhibition of the uncut "Age of Revolution," the show that later went to Detroit and New York. The Louvre hosted the Pierre-Albert Marquet show, and the Grand Palais originated the opulent Scythian show that New Yorkers saw later at the Metropolitan. A Jacques Villon exhibition that opened in Paris will travel to the United States in 1976.

The National Gallery of Canada in Ottawa exhibited a notable Francisco Goya show, "The Changing Image." The Montreal Museum of Fine Arts was closed for the year, to be opened before the Olympics, completely remodeled and with a new wing doubling its exhibition area.

The most important international museum opening of the year was the semi-official unveiling in Barcelona of the Miro Foundation's Center for the Study of Contemporary Art. The unusual building was designed by architect Josep Luis Sert.

Controversy: Photographs and Comic Strips. Philosophical arguments continued as to whether the photographic image should be considered art. Arguments over the aesthetic merit of

A bed designed by surrealist artist Max Ernst was sold to Vice President Rockefeller for $35,000.

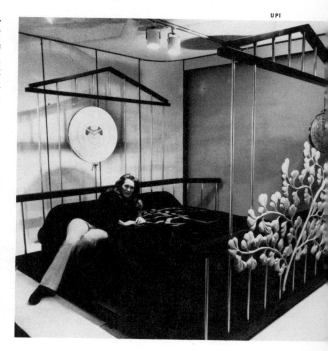

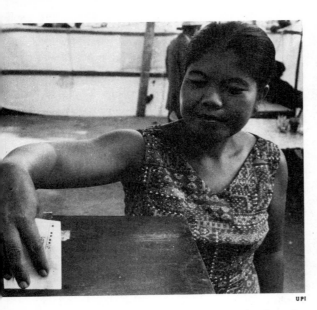

In November election, the first since the Pathet Lao take-over, Vientiane voters elected district councils.

ASIA

For hundreds of millions of Asians, 1975 was a year of unusual political significance. The political changes were more remarkable than in any one single year for many decades, possibly centuries. The decolonialization period of the late 1940's was more revolutionary, but that process took several years. See also the special feature on Southeast Asia, pages 22–31.

The Power Shift. Events in 1975 established that a U. S. military presence on mainland Asia was untenable. The United States withdrew its troops from Southeast Asia in haste while Secretary of State Kissinger tried to reassure other nations that the United States would still be a major Asian power and uphold other commitments. The words were not very convincing. The leaders of Thailand and the Philippines rushed to Peking to exchange diplomatic relations. With considerable bravado, South Korea's President Park Chung Hee announced that U. S. troops would no longer be needed after 1980, an indication that U. S. withdrawal from mainland Asia may be inevitable.

Thailand's newly elected government, although dominated by pro-Western middle class interests, asked the United States, barring an emergency, to withdraw all armed personnel within a year. All aircraft were withdrawn. U. S. troops were leaving Japan, and they were also withdrawing from Nationalist China in accordance with the 1972 agreement made with Communist China.

Political Trends. Whether U. S. power among Asia's island republics would continue was not resolved. Singapore's Lee Kwan Yew urged the United States not to withdraw from the area. Support came also from other countries connected with the Association of Southeast Asian Nations (ASEAN), such as Indonesia, which refused to invite Communist states to become its members. President Marcos of the Philippines at first questioned the need for U. S. bases at Subic Bay and at Clark Air Force Base, but this seemed to be a diplomatic ploy. Such statements allowed him to drive a tougher bargain for permitting their continuance.

It was doubtful that any outside power would again influence Asian politics as much as the United States. Power was left divided among the Asians. Vietnam was left with 1,000 fixed wing U. S.-made aircraft. Some intelligence estimates indicated that China had developed the third largest navy in the world, the consequence of a 10-year crash program. However, the U. S. Central Intelligence Agency (CIA) reported that China had reduced military spending by 25% since 1970–71, with the sharpest curtailment in aircraft acquisition. China nevertheless retained the world's largest army, 3 million troops. The Soviet Union seemed to receive considerable deference in some nations, particularly in North Vietnam, Laos, and India, all of which share a border with China. The Soviet Union, with all of its resources—economic, military, and diplomatic—was probably the greatest beneficiary of the U. S. withdrawal from Asia, but competition from Communist China, Japan, and others was significant.

Japan tried to normalize relations with the new leftist states in order to expand its own economic interests, and Indonesia and India also expanded their regional economic trade. Nationalist China, even as other Asian nations were withdrawing recognition, was increasing its trade with the very same nations. In three years, its trade with other Asian nations had increased more than threefold, from over $3 billion to over $10 billion.

Iran. In South Asia, Iran continued its rise as a major regional power. Three submarines and six destroyers were ordered to match Pakistan's and India's naval prowess. Plans were made to manufacture Iranian tanks, trucks, and other military hardware. Iran also sent substantial aid to India, Pakistan, and other nations bordering the Indian Ocean. With former CIA chief Richard Helms as its U. S. ambassador, Iran took the first steps toward creating a major $500 million intelligence facility involving air- and ground-based radio and telephone monitoring equipment. Such capability would be of value in monitoring not only the activities of its traditional enemies, Iraq and the Soviet Union, but also those of its more friendly neighbors to the East. There was hope in 1975 that the long-standing enmity between Iran and Iraq had come to an end with the signing of a treaty of reconciliation between the two nations. Iraq ceded frontier rights, while Iran promised to stop aiding the Kurdish rebel-

Cambodian refugees gather at a temporary refugee camp near the Mekong River town of Neak Luong in April.

lion in Iraq. Although falling oil revenues curtailed some spending, Iran was still in a position to be the primary power on the Indian Ocean.

Vietnam and Cambodia. The biggest political change in Southeast Asia came for the people of Cambodia and South Vietnam. During January the Vietcong forces continued their buildup, while the South Vietnamese forces had difficulty getting soldiers. By mid-March the highlands were abandoned by government forces. North Vietnamese and Vietcong troops wasted little time in exploiting their initial successes. After the highlands, they took over the northern cities of Hue and Danang and then drove toward Saigon. By the end of April, the Saigon government had surrendered. The life styles of many Vietnamese were disrupted, and others lost their lives, but for the first time in years most Vietnamese experienced peace.

A few days before the fall of Vietnam, the Cambodian government had capitulated. President Lon Nol had been promised $1 million to leave by those wishing accommodation with the enemy, but he left too late to prevent widespread bloodshed. Hundreds of thousands of people in Phnom Penh were ordered to the countryside to plant rice.

Laos. A radical change in government was also underway in Laos. The Pathet Lao took over slowly, initially allowing Premier Souvanna Phouma to hold his office as they gradually took over more government posts and disbanded the opposing forces. On December 2, the Pathet Lao took full command, abolishing the country's ancient monarchy, ending the coalition govern-

ment, and announcing the creation of a people's democratic republic. Most Laotians had a sense of stability even as the revolutionaries took over, but thousands of Meo tribesmen fled in fear to Thailand, which was also a haven for Cambodians and Vietnamese. The Thai government tried to keep them out, as it was most interested in establishing amicable relations with its Marxist neighbors.

Thailand. Even before this problem arose, the Thai people experienced a new political event when the first general election in over 25 years was held. It was a result of the repercussions that followed from the student uprising against military rule in 1973. There were 42 parties involved in the election, and the results were indecisive. The middle-of-the-road Thai Democratic party got the largest proportion of seats, 30%, but the government put together by its leader, Seni Pramoj, lasted only a few days. A new coalition led by his brother, Kukrit Pramoj, head of the military-backed Thai Nation party, took over, to the disappointment of the students and labor reformers. Some of the parties in the new coalition were more leftist in orientation, but the old guard seemed to be in control. At least the Thai people again enjoyed political freedom.

Other Countries. Political freedom was on the decline nearly everywhere else in Asia. More repression occurred in South Korea, the Philippines, Singapore, Bangladesh, and Iran.

India. Most significant was what happened to India's 600 million people. A series of events led to a crisis in June. Economic problems had followed higher oil and fertilizer prices, and there were food riots. Prime Minister Indira Gandhi was embarrassed by the rise of a formidable anti-corruption protest movement led by Jayaprakash Narayan and by an attempt by the Socialist party leader, Raj Narayan, to unseat her in the courts on charges of improper election procedures. Her Congress party was defeated in Gujarat, and there was new Naxalite terrorist activity. On June 26 Prime Minister Gandhi declared a state of emergency in which she arrested thousands of opposition political leaders. Press censorship followed.

Her party gave her full support. The homes of the rich were raided for gold, and the universities started the school year on time, without their usual several-month delay. Most civil servants put in full hours. Inflation stopped; hoarders were arrested; and laws were passed to lessen rural debt and redistribute land. Later in the year press censorship was lightened, and some prisoners were released, but Gandhi warned that discipline must become a permanent feature of Indian life. She stated that the emergency would last only a few months, but in December her Congress party called for the indefinite extension of the emergency and the postponement of the general elections scheduled for March 1976.

Bangladesh. Neighboring Bangladesh had its own political turmoil. Early in the year Sheikh

Following the Indian Supreme Court's ruling June 24th that Prime Minister Indira Gandhi could remain in office while appealing her conviction, university students and professors demanded her resignation.

UPI

Mujibur Rahman proclaimed his country a one-party state, but in mid-August he was killed in an army revolt. A cabinet member, Khondakar Moshtaque Ahmad, temporarily got control of the revolution, but by November a group of generals led by Maj. Gen. Zaiur Rahman seemed to be in control. Ahmad was replaced as president by former Chief Justice Abu Sadat Mohammed Sayem. The domestic consequences of this change were unclear, but it appeared likely that Bangladesh-Indian relations would be less cordial than they had been.

Change in China. Significant political developments took place in China. Moderate political leadership seemed to reestablish itself. With Chou En-lai and Mao Tse-tung ill, senior Deputy Premier Teng Hsiao-ping became the functional leader. Leftist leaders were verbally attacked, and those like Teng who had been targets of the 1960's cultural revolution consolidated their positions. Teng had himself declared the army chief of staff. Several thousand troops were sent to cities to quiet labor unrest, and later in the year the army high command again appeared publicly. It was not clear whether the moderates had the army under complete control.

Transition. Economically, Asia seemed to be on the upswing. Some nations such as Burma continued to wallow in stagnation, but Pakistan, India, China, Japan, South Korea, and Indonesia appeared to be making small to moderate economic gains. Even with less oil revenue, Iran again led Asia economically. The government planned to build a spectacular $3 billion plaza in Teheran and to rebuild the Persepolis columns originally built by Xerxes.

Other notable events in 1975 included the charge by President Tsedenbal of Mongolia that China was herding infected cattle into Mongolia. China made some spectacular archaeological finds including a 3,400-year-old tomb with models of life-sized men and horses. King Birendra Bir Bikram Shah Deva was crowned emperor of Nepal at the age of 29. Sikkim became a part of India.

End of an Era. Asia faced many problems as it turned into the last quarter of the 20th century. It seemed clear that its population size would continue to dwarf that of the rest of the world. China, for example, claimed about 800 million people. The CIA said it was over 900 million. No Asian nation except Japan clearly had population growth under control. Although China and several Southeast Asian nations invested more of their resources into agricultural production, it remained doubtful that famine could be averted in the future.

With the demise of democracy in India, Asia was left with only two free multi-party states, Thailand and Japan. In Thailand the students, who were the original proponents of liberal principles, were in the streets actively protesting the actions of the newly-elected government.

Even in Japan, Prime Minister Miki publicly questioned the ability of democracy to solve Japan's problems. The ruling Liberal-Democrats were split with factionalism, and the other parties were unable to form a formidable opposition. Yet the consensus traditions of the culture allowed minorities to veto action, and, in Miki's view, keep the cabinet from fulfilling its administrative duties. The prime minister's comments that "parliamentary politics is in a crisis" and that "parliamentary democracy is on trial" suggested a lessening of commitment to liberal governing principles. Before long, there could be a uniformly autocratic Asia along with mass starvation.

RALPH C. MEYER
Fordham University at Lincoln Center

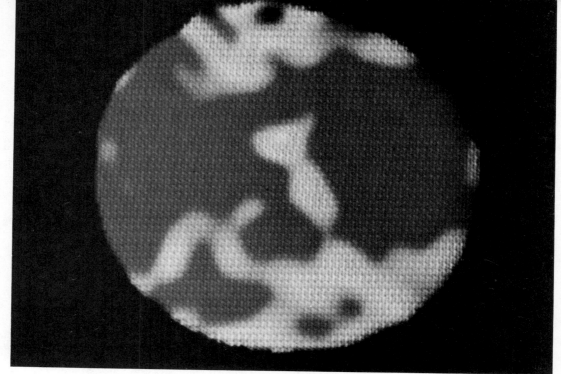

KITT PEAK NATIONAL OBSERVATORY

Astronomers at Arizona's Kitt Peak National Observatory used computer technology to obtain new photographs of the star Betelgeuse. Called speckle interferometry, the new process combines separate shots into a single image.

astronomy

Striking developments took place in 1975 in the instruments used by astronomers, as well as in the understanding of the solar system, stars, external galaxies, and cosmology.

Instrumentation. An important "window" in the earth's atmosphere permits the passage of radiation of infrared wavelengths in the electromagnetic spectrum. An "upconverter" is a sensational new development that is based on the principle of heterodyne radio receivers. Essentially, it adds the short wavelengths of a laser beam to the longer wavelengths of incoming radiation to produce a signal of short enough wavelengths to be photographed by ordinary techniques.

An 84-inch (2.13-meter) telescope will be built in Wyoming at a 9,480-foot (3,000-meter) elevation for the study of infrared stellar and galactic sources, while a 118-inch (3-meter) telescope is to be built near the summit of Mauna Kea (13,792 feet, or 4,205 meters) in Hawaii primarily for planetary studies. The telescope will have a pointing accuracy to within a second of arc, a resolution of two arc seconds, and the capacity for quick pointing adjustments. Since the first mirror cracked, the project will be delayed. Several other large telescopes are proposed for this site, including a British 150-inch (3.8-meter) and a French-Canadian 142-inch (3.6-meter) telescope.

Even at the highest mountain elevations, important segments of the infrared spectral region are cut out by water vapor in the earth's atmosphere. This difficulty is being overcome by flying infrared telescopes in a jet plane at elevations of 8–9 miles (14–15 km). Important advances are also being made in the optical range. Theoretically, the aperture of a telescope determines its resolution; however, a limit of about two arc seconds is fixed by atmospheric turbulence. For bright stars, it is possible to take a series of very short exposures and process them by the method of "speckle interferometry" to obtain images from which the effects of turbulence on seeing are essentially removed. In this way, surface details of the red-giant star Betelgeuse were resolved, the first time the surface of a star other than the sun has been photographed. Another way to compensate for the distortion of the incoming wave by bad seeing conditions is to use rapid real-time corrections of the shape of the mirror by piezoelectric or other effects.

In August, the European space agency launched a satellite to measure gamma-ray fluxes and time variations in the energy range of 30 MeV (million electron volts) to 3 BeV (billion electron volts) in supernova remnants, X-ray sources, and quasars. The joint American–Russian Apollo–Soyuz Test Project secured a number of interesting astronomical observations, including the measurement of a strong radiation source in the extreme ultraviolet wavelengths, which supposedly would have been absorbed completely by particles in interstellar space.

The two spacecrafts of the Viking mission to Mars were successfully launched in 1975. An attempt will be made in 1976 to land vehicles on Mars from these spacecraft in orbit of the planet in order to study Martian chemistry and weather and to search for evidence of life.

Solar System. Measurements by H. Hill and R. T. Stebbins show the shape of the sun to be indistinguishable from a sphere, contrary to the earlier suggestion of R. H. Dicke that the sun is squashed down, or oblate, in shape. Lunar seismic data, electrical conductivity studies, and heat-flow data all indicate that the interior of the moon is hot. Its origin still remains obscure.

The processing of data from Mariner 10 indicated that Mercury has an internal magnetic field about 1% as strong as that of the earth. The origin of Mercury's field is perplexing, as the planet's temperature lies above the Curie point, at which materials lose their ferromagnetism. Dynamo theories seem inapplicable, since the planet rotates slowly and apparently has no liquid core.

This view of Jupiter, taken by the Pioneer 11 spacecraft, shows the planet's north temperate and polar regions and what appear to be huge, hurricane-like storms.

UPI

Russian probes indicated a surface temperature of 890° F (750° K) for Venus. Contrary to expectations, the surface seems to be at least partly covered with sharp rocks, according to data from Russian landers.

Jupiter and Saturn appear to differ basically from Uranus and Neptune. Jupiter (and possibly Saturn) have internal magnetic fields and heat sources, and both apparently have a chemical composition similar to the sun's. Uranus and probably also Neptune have no internal heat sources. They probably consist of ices of oxygen, carbon, and nitrogen, with small amounts of hydrogen. Jupiter's atmosphere, in which water vapor and acetylene were recently found, was shown by Pioneer 10 and 11 probe data to be in violent agitation, probably involving severe thunderstorms. The thirteenth moon of Jupiter, JXIII, discovered in 1974, is probably a captured asteroid. Pioneer photographs suggested surface features for JIII (Ganymede) of frost, snow, and rock, and radar measurements showed that Titan (Saturn's largest moon) has a rough surface. Studies indicated that the Martian atmosphere may contain argon as well as carbon dioxide.

Detailed studies of the reflected and infrared spectra and polarization properties of asteroids demonstrate that, in most, the optical properties resemble those of carbonaceous chondrites, a type of stony meteorites. This lends further support to the theory that most meteorites originate from asteroids.

Stars. Nova Cygni, discovered August 29, brightened from its pre-outburst state by a factor of 40 million, greater than that of any previously observed nova. The star then faded rapidly.

Galaxies. Centaurus A is a radio source consisting of a visible galaxy, NGC 5128, surrounded by lobes that emit radio waves. Photographs made by the Cerro Tololo Observatory in Chile showed filaments extending outward from the galaxy into the lobes that are presumably associated with the radio emission.

At Lick Observatory, a distance of 8 billion light years was calculated for the strong radio source 3C123, which makes it the most distant known galaxy. From a careful reevaluation of the distance scale for galaxies, a revised value of the Hubble constant of 55 kilometers per second per megaparsec (million parsecs) was found. In particular, the distance of the giant spiral galaxy M101 is now estimated at 7.2 megaparsecs, about 10 times more distant than Hubble estimated in his pioneering work.

Cosmology. By allowing mass (and physical "constants") to change with time, F. Hoyle suggested that the question of the origin of the universe can be evaded. Essentially, this substitutes one type of singularity (the change of mass) for another singularity, the origin of the universe in a big bang. This interesting hypothesis remained to be explored as 1975 ended.

LAWRENCE H. ALLER
University of California, Los Angeles

UPI

Australia's caretaker Prime Minister Malcolm Fraser won an easy victory in December election.

AUSTRALIA

After one of Australia's most bitter political campaigns, the Liberal-National Country party (L-NCP) coalition led by Malcolm Fraser won a landslide victory in the general elections held on December 13. The election returns showed an extremely large majority for Fraser's coalition in the House of Representatives and a similar majority in the Senate. Fraser immediately began revising the nation's administration.

Elections. Political affairs dominated the news throughout the year, with Gough Whitlam's Australian Labor party (ALP) administration showing what a formerly pro-labor newspaper called "arrogance and incompetence" in handling the nation's affairs. A major criticism was that "Labor does not have the measure of business." Rampant inflation, a 40-year record level of unemployment, and a rash of business failures robbed the nation of its former confidence in Whitlam's administration.

The end came for the ALP government after a long series of administrative blunders and Whitlam's declared unwillingness to call an election despite the absence of parliamentary approval for major expenditures. Earlier, two senior ministers had been dismissed by Whitlam when an investigation showed that their answers to parliamentary questions about government loan-raising were misleading. A major cabinet reshuffle was carried out in the hope of reviving the party's flagging fortunes. However, a series of personality clashes within the caucus room and in public did much to destroy the ALP's earlier luster. In September public opinion polls credited the party with only 36% popular support, the lowest level recorded in a generation.

The election was precipitated when the L-NCP opposition, under the new leadership of Malcolm Fraser, pressed its point of view in the Senate and postponed consideration of appropriation bills. In spite of the deepening constitutional crisis, Whitlam played for time in the hope that an economic upturn would revive the ALP's fortunes. He refused to call a general election, saying that the term of the House of Representatives still had 18 months to run. Gov.-Gen. Sir John Kerr's action on November 11 in dismissing Whitlam and appointing Fraser to head a "caretaker" administration able to secure appropriations and "willing to let the issue go to the people," was unprecedented in 75 years of federal history.

The move touched off a furor concerning its legitimacy, with the ALP stressing its right to govern as long as it held a majority in the House of Representatives.

The governor-general explained his responsibilities in the dismissal statement. "The decisions I have made were made after I was satisfied that Mr. Whitlam could not obtain (appropriations)," Kerr said. "No other decision open to me would enable the Australian people to decide for themselves what should be done."

Reacting sharply, Whitlam said, "Clearly the great issue, almost the sole issue of this campaign, will be whether the government, which the people elect in the House of Representatives, will be allowed to govern from now on. The whole system is under challenge, as we see."

A few newspapers ran editorials questioning the wisdom of Kerr's move, but most considered it the only course. The Melbourne *Age* commented that from the beginning the parliamentary crisis "derived from the deep division of opinion among Australians about the larger crisis —our deteriorating economy."

As the election campaign developed, Whitlam did his best to direct the attack against a Kerr-Fraser "conspiracy," but economic issues and the ALP government's record in office moved increasingly into the spotlight. The *Age* concluded that in trying to frighten the electorate into believing that democracy would die unless he was reelected, Whitlam "took overstatement to the point of misrepresentation." Newspapers generally considered that Whitlam's campaign relied too heavily on condemnation without offering positive measures for correction of economic failure.

Political Crises. The year's political crises began with revelations that Minerals and Energy Minister Rex Connor had been authorized to secure U.S. $5.2 billion in foreign loans to be spent on government purchases of mining assets and on development of resources and facilities. The unorthodox methods proposed for loan-raising through intermediaries were widely criticized. Newspaper revelations soon showed that Treasurer Jim Cairns had also been encouraging businessmen to seek loans for the government. The

In Port Moresby Sir John Guise, after his installation as governor-general of newly independent Papua New Guinea, addresses a gathering that includes Sir John Kerr (left) and Britain's Prince Charles.

UPI

matter grew into a volatile political issue when answers by Cairns and Connor about negotiations were found to have misled Parliament, and both ministers were forced to resign from the cabinet.

Other political moves that precipitated unforeseen reactions were the elevation to the High Court of Sen. Lionel Murphy, whose seat was filled by the New South Wales Parliament with a non-party nominee rather than an ALP man, and the resignation of Defense Minister Lance Barnard, whose House of Representatives seat was won by a Liberal candidate. The death of a Labor senator from Queensland resulted in a further loss of ALP strength when he was replaced by a long-time ALP member who proved sharply critical of the government.

As Labor's prospects declined, the stock market—especially mining and energy stocks—rose. By late November the market level was about 40% above the year's low point. Meanwhile, Connor's resignation resulted in a revamping of policy. With the easing of restrictions on foreign investment and an end to the embargo on development of coal and uranium, Australia appeared to move toward a mining upsurge.

Economy. Economic drift was in evidence throughout 1975, and there was fading confidence among businessmen, who complained of decreased profit margins, reduced sales, and

higher capital requirements. Whitlam admitted that a stable and profitable private sector was essential to the community well-being, but businessmen considered there was "little action to support such words."

Over the year, rates of increase in consumer price indices indicated an inflation of about 16%. Average weekly earnings rose by about 20%, and the rate of the money-supply increase, which was in excess of 20% in the early months of the year, eased somewhat after July. By the third quarter, unemployment had reached a record high of 4.8% of the work force.

Labor's budget, presented by Treasurer Bill Hayden in August, reported a domestic deficit in the fiscal year ending June 30 of U. S. $2.5 billion, and proposed deficit spending of over U. S. $2.7 billion for 1975–76. The budget promised some minor and delayed income-tax reductions, but it also imposed some higher consumer taxes and approved sharply-increased charges for postal and telephone services. Overall, the budget provided for personal income tax receipts to rise by 43% as a result of wage escalations of 22%. By year's end, expenditures and receipts were running at levels foreshadowing a deficit of about U. S. $5.2 billion.

Deposits in banks and other savings institutions continued to rise, reflecting a lack of consumer confidence. There was a decline of about 2% in the gross national product, attributable to under-utilization of capacity and unemployment. Commercial building slowed, but housing starts were up from previous depressed levels.

Exports continued to run at record levels, and imports showed some easing from 1974 peaks. In August a strong outflow of capital was noted, but the effect was countered by a favorable trade balance. Many rural industries and mining enterprises, confronted with sharp cost increases, were experiencing difficulty, with the rural sector generally facing its greatest crisis since the 1930's.

Social Welfare. A committee of inquiry into poverty reported that about 7% of Australian households, including single people and families, was living below the poverty level. The September report suggested that a guaranteed income

---

——— AUSTRALIA · Information Highlights ———

Location: Southwestern Pacific Ocean.
Area: 2,967,900 square miles (7,686,848 sq km).
Population (1975 est.): 13,800,000.
Chief Cities (1971 census, met. areas): Canberra, the capital, 156,298; Sydney, 2,725,064; Melbourne, 2,394,117.
Government: *Head of state,* Elizabeth II, queen; represented by Sir John Kerr, governor-general (took office July 1974). *Head of government,* Malcolm Fraser, prime minister (took office Dec. 1975). *Legislature*—Parliament: Senate and House of Representatives.
Monetary Unit: Australian dollar (0.7816 A. dollar equals U. S.$1, Aug. 1975).
Gross National Product (1974 est.): $73,500,000,000.
Manufacturing (major products): Petroleum products, steel, machinery, chemicals, automobiles, meat.
Major Agricultural Products: Wool, sugarcane, barley, fruit, tobacco, dairy products, sheep.
Foreign Trade (1973): *Exports,* $9,389,000,000; *imports,* $6,802,000,000.

plan should be introduced, financed by a flat-rate proportional tax on income, as part of a reform of welfare payments and services. Evidence of a continued decline in the birthrate toward zero population growth was seen in a 1% natural increase for the year.

Foreign Affairs. In foreign affairs, concern over the collapse of Vietnam died down quickly. Australians accepted the new situation with minimal comment and found homes for refugees. An unexpected development was North Korea's sudden withdrawal of diplomatic representation from Canberra in October following Australia's UN vote to admit South Korea.

An important L-NCP policy statement on foreign policy indicated that Australia's alliance with the United States under the ANZUS treaty remained the cornerstone of the country's foreign policy, and that there would be closer ties with regional powers. The statement called for additional emphasis on old friendships and less attention to Labor's Third World relationships.

R. M. YOUNGER
Author, "Australia and the Australians"

AUSTRIA

The celebration on May 15 of the 20th anniversary of the signing of the Austrian State Treaty and the parliamentary elections on October 5 highlighted the year's events.

Political Events. Karl Schleinzer, leader of the opposition conservative People's party, was killed on July 19 in an automobile accident. The party elected Josef Taus, director of the Gironzentrale, Austria's second largest bank, as his successor. At the same time Dr. Erhard Busek was chosen to succeed Hermann Kohlmaier as general secretary of the party. The People's party under Schleinzer's leadership had made slight gains in the provincial elections in Carinthia on March 2 and in Tirol on June 9. As chairman of the party, Taus became the People's party candidate for chancellor in the parliamentary elections held on October 5.

The electoral campaign lacked luster and centered on economic issues. In the balloting the Socialists, led by Chancellor Bruno Kreisky, won 94 (93 in 1971) seats; the People's party won 78 (80) seats; and the Liberal party under the leadership of Friedrich Peter took 11 (10) seats. Chancellor Kreisky, having a clear majority, still headed an all-Socialist government.

Economic Developments. The industrial output for the first quarter of 1975 was down 10% over the same period of 1974. Whereas the growth rate was 4.5% overall in 1974, the rate for 1975 was about 2.5%. Wages rose about 13% in 1975 with inflation running at around 10%. To stimulate the economy, the government on April 7 announced plans to inject 12.7 billion schillings ($762 million) into industry, with 1 billion schillings to be used as export guarantees. On April 24 the Austrian National

Bank lowered its discount rate from 6.5% (in effect since May 15, 1974) to 6%. Unemployment averaged around 1.5% to 2% of the population. As a result of a 1972 agreement with the European Economic Community, tariffs on most industrial products traded with these countries were again reduced by 20% as of Jan. 1, 1975. They stand at 60% of their 1972 level and are to be eliminated in 1977.

Foreign Affairs. A dispute with Yugoslavia, stemming from an October 1974 charge by Yugoslavia that Austria was not granting Slovenian and Croatian minorities cultural and linguistic rights guaranteed them in the State Treaty of 1955, flared up again in May. Austria's celebration of the 20th anniversary of the signing of the State Treaty triggered the reopening of the controversy, which remains unsettled.

An agreement with Czechoslovakia had been signed on Dec. 19, 1974, settling the problem of Czech compensation for property confiscated when Austrians were expelled from Czechoslovakia after World War II. This led both countries in January 1975 to raise their legations to the rank of embassies.

An Austrian consular agreement with the German Democratic Republic, signed on March 26, recognized a separate East German nationality. It brought sharp protests from the Federal Republic of Germany, which both Austria and East Germany rejected.

On March 21, Wiley T. Buchanan Jr. was confirmed as U. S. ambassador to Austria. Austria continued to serve as neutral ground for important international negotiations. Among them were discussions in May between U. S. Secretary of State Henry Kissinger and Soviet Foreign Minister Andrei Gromyko. There was a meeting between President Gerald R. Ford and Egyptian President Anwar el-Sadat on June 1–2 and a conference of the Organization of Petroleum Exporting Countries (OPEC) in September. OPEC headquarters in Vienna were raided on December 22 by terrorists, who kidnapped 10 oil ministers, later released unharmed.

ERNST C. HELMREICH, *Bowdoin College*

AUSTRIA · Information Highlights

Official Name: Republic of Austria.
Location: Central Europe.
Area: 32,374 square miles (83,849 sq km).
Population (1975 est.): 7,500,000.
Chief Cities (1971 census): Vienna, the capital, 1,614,-841; Graz, 248,500; Linz, 202,874; Salzburg, 128,845.
Government: *Head of state,* Rudolf Kirchschläger, president (took office July 1974). *Head of government,* Bruno Kreisky, chancellor (took office April 1970). *Legislature*—Federal Assembly: Federal Council and National Council.
Monetary Unit: Schilling (18.24 schillings equal U. S.$1, Aug. 1975).
Gross National Product (1973): $27,887,000,000.
Manufacturing (major products): Processed foods, chemicals, textiles, iron, steel, electrical goods, machinery, paper, wood products.
Major Agricultural Products: Rye, wheat, barley, potatoes, sugar beets, oats, forest products.
Foreign Trade (1974 est.): *Exports,* $7,060,000,000; *imports,* $8,000,000,000.

New Models for 1976

AMC's wide-bodied Pacer (*right*) offered new options and faster acceleration for 1976. Introduced in 1975, the Pacer's innovative design proved successful.

AMERICAN MOTORS CORPORATION

GENERAL MOTORS CORPORATION

The Chevette (*left*), a new car from General Motors' Chevrolet Division, is the lightest U. S.-built car and is designed to compete with popular imports.

The Bobcat "MPG" from Ford's Lincoln-Mercury Division (*right*) is a subcompact that combines fuel economy and a convenient size with luxury and quality.

FORD MOTOR COMPANY

CHRYSLER MOTOR CORPORATION

Chrysler Corporation's Plymouth Volare (*left*) is a new six-cylinder compact for 1976, designed to offer big-car comfort and convenience in a small car.

automobiles

Consumer resistance to higher prices sharply reduced U. S. car production for the second consecutive year during 1975. Canadian production, which had bucked the trend and increased in 1974, fell about 5% in 1975.

Imported car sales in the United States benefited in 1975 as sales of domestic units slumped, despite price increases resulting from the worldwide inflationary trend. Mileage per gallon became a paramount buying consideration, and American car shoppers were impressed by official Environmental Protection Agency fuel-economy data showing that 1975 models from abroad outperformed competitive domestic subcompacts. Imported new-car sales in the United States for the first eight months of 1975 jumped 20.3% from the comparable 1974 period and were taking upward of 20% of U. S. retail new-car sales. In the top market, California, the import share was close to 50%. The 23 imported makes accounted for 1,137,343 sales in the January-August period of 1975, compared with 945,518 for the same period of 1974.

1975 MODEL PRODUCTION

Output of 1975 new-car models through August 1975 declined 24.5% from the comparable 1974-model production total, which itself had tumbled 22% from the record 1973-model volume. The 1975 model run reached 6,481,892

cars through August, compared with 8,067,303 the previous model year and the all-time peak of 9,915,803 in 1973. Detroit-headquartered car builders had not suffered as low a model production run since 1961, when 5,407,256 cars were produced.

General Motors. General Motors' share of the 1975-model run increased to 53.5% from 49.8% in 1974, despite a substantial numerical decline of nearly 600,000 cars. GM's main loser was Chevrolet, which nevertheless held the number 1 sales position over Ford Motor Company's Ford division, 1,604,240 to 1,319,475. Chevrolet's loss from 1974 model output was nearly 500,000, the main victims of price resistance being at the opposite ends of Chevrolet's lineup—the full-sized "standard" series and the subcompact Vega. Only 66,622 Chevrolet Monzas were built in 1975 as the new sporty subcompact entry ran head-on into a pricing "boycott" in the fall of 1974 and had to be trimmed in price.

Value-minded car buyers turned to such offerings as the Oldsmobile Cutlass in the intermediate bracket and the compact Buick Apollo. Oldsmobile's production loss was less than 30,000 for 1975, with the division finishing at 593,954. Pontiac dropped more than 35,000 to 522,224, despite the introduction of the Astre, a subcompact derived from the Vega. Buick fell less than 14,000 to 482,006. Cadillac, whose buyers were less affected by the recession, showed a 1975-model gain of more than 22,000. More than 264,000 Cadillacs were built, including 16,355 of the newly-introduced "compact" Sevilles, priced at $13,000-plus.

Ford Production. EPA's fuel-economy data for 1975 models were lowest on Ford Motor Co. models, and the company blamed this for a loss of close to 500,000 units from 1974. The Ford division star was the new Granada compact, which reached 302, 649 units in its first year and outsold all other Ford series substantially. The Granada, with its twin Mercury Monarch compact, underlined the economy-car vogue but also demonstrated that a fresh, appealing design still would attract sales. The Granada and Monarch, the latter of which topped 103,000 units for Mercury, were priced at $4,000 and up. Mercury also built 38,650 Bobcats, a new, Pinto-related subcompact. Ford's top-of-the-line Lincoln Continental matched Cadillac in showing a production gain to nearly 55,000, compared with 36,000 in 1974.

Chrysler and AMC. Chrysler Corp.'s production volume shrank nearly 400,000 cars to 948,-773. Its newest entry, the intermediate-sized Chrysler Cordoba, surpassed 60,000 in sales. Likewise, at American Motors, a new subcompact, the Pacer, stood out with 66,574 first-year production as declines among other AMC entries decreased the company's total more than 170,000 cars to 240,574. Ford Motor's final total for 1975-model production was 1,825, 310 and GM's was 3,467,235.

THE 1976 MODELS

Except for three new models, U. S. automakers concentrated their model-change efforts on mileage-per-gallon refinements, which they felt would restore sales momentum more than sheer "sheet-metal" revisions alone. But the trio of new models was designed to exert dramatic impact on the sluggish market. These included Chevrolet's Chevette, the first domestic subcompact minicar, and a pair of redesigned compacts from Chrysler Corp., the Plymouth Volare and the Dodge Aspen.

The Chevette was targeted at popular imported 2-door cars such as Volkswagen's Rabbit and Beetle, Toyota's Corolla, and Datsun's B-210. The Chevette weighed less than 2,000 lbs, was only 158 inches (401 cm) long and 52 inches (132 cm) high. At a suggested retail price of below $3,000, it commenced the U. S. car industry's major thrust to compete in the worldwide economy-car segment. But major American competition for the Chevette was not due until 1977.

Chrysler's Volare and Aspen were aimed at the successful Ford Granada and Monarch, though they retained Chrysler styling touches. For 1977, GM planned to reduce the size of larger models toward the new compact mode of Granada and Volare. Few important new emissions or safety standards were launched with the 1976 models. The year-old catalytic converters, controlling exhaust emissions, equipped nearly all 1976's despite criticism over alleged sulphate emissions and fire hazards.

MAYNARD M. GORDON
Editor, "Motor News Analysis"

WORLD MOTOR VEHICLE DATA, 1974

Country	Passenger car production	Truck and bus production	Motor vehicle registrations
Argentina	212,088	74,224	2,934,547
Australia	400,287	89,052	5,583,115
Austria	1,469	3,173	1,711,062
Belgium	148,917	34,211	2,670,028
Brazil	515,680	342,799	5,391,479
Canada	1,165,635	359,239	9,709,391
Czechoslovakia	164,000	31,000	1,345,950
France	3,045,283	417,564	16,800,000
Germany, East	160,000	32,000	2,031,988
Germany, West	2,839,596	260,181	18,383,527
Hungary	...	12,000	518,000
India	36,009	51,880	1,289,101
Italy	1,630,686	141,829	14,507,777
Japan	3,931,842	2,609,998	24,999,281
Mexico	248,574	102,181	2,448,870
Netherlands	69,234	12,847	3,579,900
Poland	142,900	85,500	1,172,400
Portugal	...	316	941,990
Rumania	54,000	46,000	130,000
Spain	704,574	132,840	4,736,965
Sweden	326,743	41,616	2,666,784
Switzerland	132	1,272	1,822,096
USSR	1,119,000	727,000	7,000,000
United Kingdom	1,534,119	402,566	15,483,562
United States	7,324,504	2,746,538	125,420,876[1]
Yugoslavia	171,283	18,445	1,353,997
Other Countries			23,323,003
Total	25,946,555[2]	8,786,271	297,955,689[3]

[1] U. S. total includes 101,762,477 cars and 23,658,399 trucks and buses, excluding Puerto Rico (610,000 and 125,000, respectively); Canal Zone (18,157 and 492); and Virgin Islands (30,000 and 5,000). [2] Excludes approximately 1,400,000 assembled in other countries, principally Belgium and South Africa. [3] Registration total includes all countries, of which non-producing countries exceeding 1 million registrations were: Denmark, 1,466,925; Finland, 1,028,122; Norway, 1,084,739; New Zealand, 1,258,334; Venezuela, 1,114,111; and South Africa, 2,429,347. Total includes 235,997,543 cars and 61,958,146 trucks and buses. Source: Motor Vehicle Manufacturers Association of the United States, Inc.

BANGLADESH

After 4 years of independence Bangladesh, formerly the eastern wing of Pakistan, remained in desperate straits, politically as well as economically. In 1975, Bangladesh abandoned parliamentary government, and this was followed by the overthrow and death of Sheikh Mujibur Rahman, the prime minister, and then by the overthrow of his successor.

Domestic Affairs. In December 1974, the government of Sheikh Mujib, as he was popularly known, proclaimed a state of national emergency in the effort to cope with what was termed the "state of lawlessness and internal subversion." In January his party, the Awami League, gave him a mandate to act as necessary. Sheikh Mujib chose to have the constitution amended to give him complete authority virtually to rule by decree, through the establishment of a presidential government independent of any representative assembly. Opposition political parties were banned, and Sheikh Mujib became president under the new arrangement.

He termed the change the start of a "second revolution," but he reinstalled his old cabinet, and the political feeling in Dacca was one of disappointment and distrust. Although Sheikh Mujib was thought of as the "Father of Bangladesh," his ability to deal with the country's chronic problems of overpopulation, famine, disease, poverty, and corruption were questioned more and more by even his most loyal supporters. Apparently the constitutional change in January was initiated by Sheikh Mujib as an unplanned move of desperation. Little changed in the months that followed, although in late June the national administration was reorganized into 60 new districts.

In mid-August the army mounted a bloody coup against Sheikh Mujib, who was killed in the uprising. Sheikh Mujib was accused of having permitted "corruption, nepotism, and attempts to concentrate power." The coup had been haphazardly planned, and the first few days after it occurred were chaotic. Out of it came a reinstallation of civilian rule, with Khondakar Mushtaque Ahmed becoming president and reappointing many of the old cabinet.

The new president promised a return to "democracy," but his first acts were in the authoritarian tradition. All political parties, including the Awami League, were banned. Ahmed claimed to rule without regard to the constitution and was supported by martial law. He promised trials for political offenders, and a number of politicians were arrested.

Although it quickly became evident that the coup leaders had been only lower-ranking field officers and that much of the army was unhappy over what had been done in its name, there were few immediate repercussions. The new president was generally considered pro-Western. He was a long-time friend of Sheikh Mujib and had impeccable credentials as a founder of the Awami League.

In November senior military officers forced the resignation of Mushtaque Ahmed and installed A. M. Sayen, chief justice of the supreme court, as president. The new upheaval followed the murders in jail of several political leaders who had been associated with Sheikh Mujib.

The tasks facing the new leaders were no less than those of their predecessors: the incredible problems of a makeshift economy, the nonending burdens of a population of 75 million continuing to grow beyond control, and periodic natural devastations. In addition they must placate the army, defuse the intense political atmosphere, permit the resumption of representative forms, and survive.

A major cholera epidemic broke out in Bangladesh during the year, but world public health authorities were encouraged by the fact that all the currently known cases of smallpox—some 16 in September—were quarantined in Bangladesh. Epidemiologists hope that for the first time in history a disease will have been eradicated when the cases in Bangladesh have been eliminated. The target date is 1976.

Foreign Affairs. The new government of Bangladesh was quickly recognized by other governments, including India, which had supported Sheikh Mujib. Indeed President Mushtaque Ahmed apologized to Prime Minister Gandhi for the death of Sheikh Mujib. The new government was a little more friendly to Pakistan, and in October the two countries announced that they had restored normal diplomatic relations. In May a long standing dispute with India over the water resources of the Ganges River was resolved, but some controversy over the boundaries in the Bay of Bengal remained.

At year's end Bangladesh had survived a year of unusual political trouble, in addition to its more typical economic difficulties, but it remained the world's neediest case. Despite some increases in foreign assistance, notably by Canada, there appeared to be little hope of averting periodic mass starvation.

CARL LEIDEN
The University of Texas at Austin

—— **BANGLADESH · Information Highlights** ——

Official Name: People's Republic of Bangladesh.
Location: South Asia.
Area: 55,126 square miles (142,776 sq km).
Population (1975 est.): 73,700,000.
Chief Cities (1974 census): Dacca, the capital, 1,310,976; Khulna, 436,000; Chittagong, 416,733.
Government: *Head of state,* A. M. Sayen, president (took office Nov. 1975).
Monetary Unit: Taka (7.873 takas equal U. S.$1, March 1975).
Gross National Product (1972 est.): $5,300,000,000.
Manufacturing (major products): Jute products, cotton textiles, processed foods, wood products.
Major Agricultural Products: Rice, jute, sugarcane, tea, oilseeds, pulses, fish, forest products.
Foreign Trade (1971): *Exports,* $263,000,000; *imports,* $331,000,000.

BANKING

The falling economy of the United States reached a low point in May 1975 with industrial production 28% below the high of 1973 and unemployment at 9.2%, while prices continued to rise. From that point business picked up, but sluggishly. President Ford and Congress agreed on an expansionary fiscal policy to keep down unemployment, but the resulting federal deficit ($44 billion for fiscal 1975 and an estimated $75 billion for fiscal 1976) threatened to push up both commodity prices and interest rates.

The international monetary system continued to move further away from gold, resulting in gold prices below $130 temporarily.

Money Markets and Interest Rates. As demand for funds shrank during the depression, interest rates dropped precipitously. From July 1974 to June 1975, the federal funds rate fell from 13.6% to 5.1%; the prime rate went from 12% to 7%; and other short-term rates showed similar changes. Long-term U. S. bonds dropped from 7.3% to 6.8%, and corporate bonds went from 9.8% to 9.4%. Mortgage rates dropped slightly, but banks were reluctant to grant mortgages, contributing to the weakness in construction.

With the business turnaround and the need for large Treasury borrowings in the second half, interest rates rose again. The severe financial crisis in New York City resulted in a threat of default on its sizable debt and upset the financial markets, which also pushed rates up.

Federal Reserve System. During the downswing the Federal Reserve dropped the discount rate from 8% to 6% and in February lowered reserve requirements against demand deposits by ½ %. In May, Arthur Burns, Chairman of the Federal Reserve Board, took the unprecedented step of announcing publicly that the Federal Reserve had set a target for the growth of the money supply of between 5% and 7.5% for the 12 months starting in March (later moved to the second quarter). The money supply, which had turned down in December, started up in February and by July had already increased 5.2% over the February low. At that time the Federal Reserve acted to slow down the increase to check any intensification of inflation. Short-term interest rates responded by rising. The prime rate was expected to reach 8.5% or 9%.

Banking Structure. In their competition for scarce funds many commercial banks lowered service charges, extended overdraft privileges to consumers, and introduced automatic teller machines that accept deposits and loan payments and dispense cash 24 hours a day.

Negotiable Order of Withdrawal (NOW) accounts, which permit savings depositors to make check-like payments to third parties, pioneered by savings banks (SB's) in Massachusetts and New Hampshire in 1972, have been extended to savings and loan associations (S&L's) as well as commercial bank savings accounts in those two

Federal Reserve Board Chairman Arthur Burns (*left*) testified before Senate Budget Committee in March on credit and monetary policies, which affect banking.

states. In Connecticut and Minnesota, SB's use a "pay-by-phone" system by which customers can make payments from savings accounts to third parties. A ruling by the Board of Governors in April permitted member banks of the Federal Reserve System to do likewise. In New York SB's began in 1975 to offer non-interest-bearing Payment Order Accounts, which essentially provide free checking service to clients who also maintain a savings account.

Although the practice is being tested legally, federal S&L's have been permitted by the Federal Home Loan Bank Board to issue non-transferable payment orders by which their customers may pay their bills. S&L's were also authorized to install remote teller stations in supermarkets and shopping centers so customers may withdraw cash at the store to pay for purchases. National banks were permitted by the Comptroller of the Currency to offer similar facilities.

The proposed Financial Institutions Act of 1975 would permit all thrift institutions to offer limited checking accounts and credit card services. At the same time, interest rate ceilings would be phased out, and uniform reserve requirements for commercial banks and thrift institutions would be provided.

Personal savings in the United States reached a very high 10.5% of national income in the second quarter. Much of this, however, apparently was going directly into the securities market, where high rates were more attractive than dividends paid by thrift institutions.

WALTER W. HAINES, *New York University*

BELGIUM

In 1975, Belgians were primarily concerned with a worsening economic recession, but even this worry failed to check the persistent linguistic conflict between the Flemings and the Walloons. On February 9 in Brussels some 50 people were injured in demonstrations against alleged anti-Flemish discriminations.

Economics. Like other industrialized countries, Belgium is experiencing a high rate of inflation and serious unemployment. The inflation rate was over 15% in 1974 and continued high during the first months of 1975, but declined to 5% in June. Unemployment increased continuously; in July it stood at 7% of the insured, full-time labor force. Fully 30% of the industrial productive capacity was not in use.

An important means of stabilizing the socio-economic life of the country is the cost-of-living compensation system. Whenever the cost-of-living index goes up by 2%, nearly all wages, salaries, and rents automatically increase by the same percentage. In 1974 there were eight cost-of-living increases, totaling 22%, and there were two more in 1975. A third increase in July was prevented by a government measure on May 7 freezing prices for two months and later extended beyond that date. Nevertheless the June–July index threatened to rise over 2%. A small crop, due to unfavorable weather conditions, caused the price of potatoes to soar. An automatic increase in wages would have placed industrial employers in a difficult position. Their labor costs would have gone up but the selling price of their products would have remained fixed. By a last minute emergency change, the government modified the index calculating system so that the rise in the cost-of-living index was slightly less than 2%, thus averting another round of wage increases for a time.

For a country like Belgium, exporting 60% of its industrial production, a system that guarantees automatic wage and salary increases with rising domestic prices may find itself in an unfavorable position in world competition. Suggestions for changes in the system are often met with hostility from the labor unions, which, in spite of division into language, religious, and secular groups, are capable of uniting for political purposes.

Defense and Foreign Policy. A political crisis was threatened by the tardy decision of the Belgian government on June 6 to join Denmark, Norway, and the Netherlands in purchasing 300 F-16 jet fighters from the United States. The four North Atlantic Treaty Organization (NATO) members had agreed in 1974 to replace their obsolescent fighters through a common purchasing agreement. The Belgian government favored the French Mirage F-1, as the large purchase of French planes would stimulate the development of a strong European aviation industry and promote European unity.

UPI

Prime Minister Leo Tindemans addresses parliament on June 10 to defend decision to purchase U. S. jets.

A more pressing reason was that the decision threatened Premier Leo Tindeman's coalition government. The Walloons have strong ties with France and wanted the French contract. The Belgian government made a gesture to European unity sentiment by reducing its component of the American order from 116 to 102 planes and by planning to use the amount saved for a joint European research and development fund. It was not until the last minutes of the parliamentary debate on the issue that the Walloon· Union, whose 13 members hold the balance of power in the chamber, withdrew its threat to join the opposition.

AMRY VANDENBOSCH
University of Kentucky

──────── BELGIUM · Information Highlights ────────

Official Name: Kingdom of Belgium.
Location: Northwestern Europe.
Area: 11,781 square miles (30,513 sq km).
Population (1975 est.): 9,800,000.
Chief Cities (1975 est.): Brussels, the capital, 1,100,000; Antwerp, 670,000; Liège, 440,000.
Government: *Head of state,* Baudouin I, king (acceded 1951). *Head of government,* Leo Tindemans, premier (took office 1974). *Legislature*—Parliament: Senate and Chamber of Representatives.
Monetary Unit: Franc (35.06 francs equal U. S.$1, May 1975).
Gross National Product (1974): $53,300,000,000.
Manufacturing (major products): Steel, metals, textiles, cut diamonds, chemicals, glass.
Major Agricultural Products: Sugar beets, potatoes, wheat, oats, barley, flax, hay.
Foreign Trade (1974): *Exports,* $28,100,000,000; *imports,* $29,600,000,000.

BIOCHEMISTRY

A major restructuring of biochemistry and molecular biology made 1975 relatively unproductive. A retooling of both thought and methods preoccupied some of the major laboratories as the application of molecular biology shifted toward more "human-related" research. Most agreed with this trend, but many feared that basic research would suffer, with science and society the losers. In any case, the individual biochemist faced myriad problems, ranging from the technical to the ethical.

The Moratorium and the Asilomar Conference. The growing concern over the ethics and hazards of "genetic engineering" led in the summer of 1975 to a voluntary moratorium by several leading scientists on certain kinds of experimentation until strict controls are established. A new technique of genetic manipulation allows the splicing together of the genetic material DNA into hybrid molecules derived from very different organisms. Such techniques could quickly lead to the production of custom-made "organisms" different from any present species and with unknown properties and potential for interaction with existing organisms, including man.

In an attempt to deal with this problem, an "International Conference on Recombinant DNA Molecules" was held in Asilomar, Calif., in February 1975. Two strategies evolved from the often heated exchanges among some 140 scientists, primarily from the United States, Great Britain, the USSR, and Western Europe. One essentially involved stricter application of long-used laboratory techniques to prevent the spread of infection. The other concerned the use of a "fail-safe" backup control in the event that containment fails. This involves the creation of a biological barrier, such as a fragile host organism that will die outside the laboratory. However, this would not guarantee that some combination of the "new DNA" and host would not manage to survive somewhere in some ecological niche.

The delegates made a not-too-successful attempt to rank types of experiments or experimental systems in order of hazard and recommended that certain high-risk experiments with known pathogens should not be performed now under any circumstances. Even though the ground rules for experimentation were approved by a large majority, and later by the National Academy of Sciences, it is clear that the question of hazards will continue to take precedence over far-ranging experimentation for some time.

Human Biochemical Genetics. The field of biochemical genetics arose as a result of G. W. Beadle and E. Tatum's efforts with the fungus *Neurospora*. The exact role of genes in enzyme control, and thus in biosynthesis, was gradually delineated, and the giant field of molecular genetics grew out of these studies. Workers have now turned full circle and are again focusing on biochemical genetics, particularly in human beings.

One result of the new focus is that human fibroblasts (connective tissue cells) can now be cultured in much the same way as are microorganisms, providing a powerful tool for the study of genetic diseases of metabolism. For example, in several genetic enzyme deficiencies affecting mucopolysaccharide metabolism and leading to malformations, sensory defects, and mental retardation (Hurler's, Hunter's, and Sanfilippo's syndromes), the missing enzyme can be supplied to fibroblasts.

The enzyme, which is obtained from normal human cells, is actually taken up by fibroblasts in which it is lacking, and the normal catabolic pathway is restored. This raises the hope that such knowledge can eventually be applied to humans with these presently untreatable genetic diseases.

Other genetic diseases under assault by biochemical and molecular geneticists include diabetes, for which a viral origin is now suggested, and hemophilia, the disease of "bleeders." Cystic fibrosis, the genetic mutation in children that is carried and transmitted by 1 of every 20 American adults, is being studied with the fibroblast cell-culture technique. These studies suggest that altered membrane function is the basic cause of the disease.

Biological aging is also being studied by biochemical techniques. The basis of senescence appears to be a loss of fidelity in the synthesis of large molecules such as DNA and protein, perhaps due to an altered cell-membrane function. The National Institutes of Health's new institute for the study of aging supports this research.

Cell-Membrane Phenomena. It is difficult to think of a biochemical study that has not implicated cell-membrane function. Relationships to membrane function or malfunction have been revealed in such diverse areas of investigation as cancer, vision, behavior, and nutrition.

The most important aspect of cell membranes aside from their containment of cell contents is their protein complement. The complex proteins directly involved in the movement of simple building-block molecules such as amino acids into cells are one example. During 1975, one such "transport molecule" was identified as a glycoprotein to which RNA is attached. The actual role of this protein in membrane function is likely to be far more profound than that of amino-acid transport alone.

Bead-String Concept of DNA. It has long been known that cell biochemistry is ultimately controlled by DNA, with the flow of information from DNA to RNA to protein, but the exact mechanism of the association was not clear. Now the "bead-string" concept has returned, the "beads" being DNA complexes with special proteins called histones and the "string" consisting of short stretches of DNA association that controls gene expression.

A. GIB DEBUSK
Florida State University

Biography

A selection of biographical sketches of persons prominent in the news during 1975 appears on this and the following pages. The subjects include men and women from many parts of the world, and representing a wide variety of pursuits. The list is confined to living persons; for biographical data on prominent people who died during the year, see OBITUARIES. Unless otherwise indicated, all articles in this section are by Henry S. Sloan, Associate Editor, Current Biography.

ASHE, Arthur

At the beginning of 1975, Arthur Ashe had two goals. He wanted to win the World Championship Tennis (WCT) tour final and the Wimbledon title. By July 5 he had reached those goals and in achieving the second one, he startled the tennis world by drubbing Jimmy Connors. Later, the Association of Tennis Professionals named him the player of the year.

Because of his record, especially in 1974, he was called the "world champion runner-up." He has been among the 10 top-ranked U. S. players since 1963. He gained the No. 1 spot in 1969 after winning the first United States Open at Forest Hills as an amateur as well as the amateur title at Brookline, Mass., in 1968.

Background. Arthur Robert Ashe, Jr., who was born in Richmond, Va., July 10, 1943, is the only black player on the professional tennis tour. He won the National Collegiate Championship in 1965 while attending UCLA. He helped the United States regain the Davis Cup from Australia in 1968 and to retain it the next two years. Overall in cup play he has won 25 matches and lost 3. He has also been involved in trying to break South Africa's apartheid barrier.

Ashe led his group in the WCT competition in 1975 and reached the eight-man finals for the fifth straight year. In the title round he defeated Bjorn Borg, 3–6, 6–4, 6–4, 6–0. For his triumph Ashe was awarded $50,-000 and a gold tennis ball. He led all the WCT players in 1975 earnings with $177,161.

In what may have been his finest hour, Ashe rebuffed a late surge by Connors on center court at Wimbledon. Playing what was described as one of the most intelligent games seen in the famous tourney, Ashe blunted the power of Connors. Careful, well-placed serves and excellent volleying kept the 22-year-old favorite off balance. Even after Connors had won the third set and taken a lead of 3–0 in the fourth, Ashe was able to regain control. He won, 6–1, 6–1, 5–7, 6–4. The first black to win at Wimbledon said of his victory: "I thought I would win because I was playing so well and was so confident. I played to a careful plan but I'm not going to tell what it was. I may play him again."

Asked if this was his greatest victory, Ashe said: "No, winning the Davis Cup in 1968 would be the first. And winning at Forest Hills in '68 was second until this one."

BILL BRADDOCK

BEAME, Abraham D.

Mayor Abraham D. Beame of New York City faced a financial crisis of major proportions during 1975. To avert the city's economic collapse, he was forced to take strict austerity measures, including dismissals of tens of thousands of city employees; the closing of some schools, hospitals, and other institutions; cutbacks in police, firefighting, and sanitation services; a freeze on wages and new construction projects; and increases in transit fares and tax revenues.

Beame lost some of his fiscal authority in June with the creation of the Municipal Assistance Corporation (commonly called Big MAC), a state agency designed to alleviate the city's fiscal crisis and to oversee its

UPI

Mayor Abraham Beame gestures to reporters during discussion on New York City's fiscal crisis.

long-range borrowing policies. His powers were further diminished by the state-mandated Emergency Financial Control Board, established in September to impose budgetary reform on the city. In October and November the city narrowly averted default.

On October 29, President Ford, charging New York City's administration with gross mismanagement, declared that he would veto any bill designed as a "federal bailout" for the city. In response, Beame sharply criticized the president for "subjecting America's largest city to humiliation and impoverishment" and asserted that "the innocent" and "the powerless" would be hurt most by a default. In late November and December the federal government became more conciliatory toward the city, and Beame was mollified.

Background. Abraham David Beame, the son of Polish Jews, was born in London on March 20, 1906 and grew up in New York City. After obtaining his degree cum laude from City College in 1928, he combined a career as an accountant with teaching and became active in Democratic politics. In 1946 he was named the city's assistant budget director, and in 1952 he became budget director. He was elected city comptroller in 1961 but lost the mayoral election in 1965 to John V. Lindsay. In 1969 he was again elected comptroller. Campaigning as a sound money manager, Beame won the 1973 mayoral election in a four-way race and was sworn in as New York's 104th mayor on Jan. 1, 1974.

BREZHNEV, Leonid Ilich

For Leonid Brezhnev, secretary-general of the Communist party of the USSR, 1975 was marked by persistent personal health difficulties, a long desired Conference on Security and Cooperation in Europe, the

uncertain development of détente with the West, and attempts to strengthen Moscow's role as the leader of international socialism.

Respiratory infections and extensive dental surgery caused Brezhnev to make infrequent public appearances. Those he did make were primarily devoted to détente. In February he met with Britain's Prime Minister Harold Wilson to announce that the USSR had been granted $2.4 billion worth of low interest credits. Later he met with two delegations of U. S. congressmen, the first headed by Sen. Hubert Humphrey and Sen. Hugh Scott, the second by House Speaker Carl Albert. Although two summit visits to the United States were postponed because U. S.-USSR negotiations could not reach agreement on methods of limiting weapons delivery, Brezhnev and Ford did meet twice in Helsinki during the Conference on Security and Cooperation in Europe with what was described as "encouraging progress." The conference also legitimized the Soviet Union's acquisition of territory occupied during World War II and its subsequent dominance over much of Eastern Europe.

Despite his persistent emphasis on détente Brezhnev, in a message to the Council of the Afro-Asian People's Solidarity Organization, urged Communist countries, developing nations, and colonial guerrillas to unite to help free the remaining Western colonies in Asia and Africa.

While Brezhnev was clearly not up to par in 1975, the "collective leadership" that he heads took pains to praise him lavishly. During the May celebration of the 30th anniversary of victory in World War II, Soviet newspapers glorified Brezhnev's wartime role as a political officer. In September the publication of two new volumes of his collected works were worshipfully reviewed by the Soviet press.

Background. Brezhnev, a Russian of worker parentage, was born in Dneprodzerzhinsk, Ukraine, on Dec. 19, 1906. A college graduate in metallurgical engineering, he worked his way up in the party hierarchy. He held a wide variety of positions, including agricultural administrator, regional Communist party chief, high-ranking army political officer, chief political commissar of the Soviet navy, and secretary of the party's central apparatus. From 1960 to 1964 he served as president of the USSR. After helping to oust Nikita Khrushchev from power in October 1964, he replaced him as head of the Communist party. Looking more like a capitalist businessman than a Communist politician, by 1975, Brezhnev had ruled Russia longer than either Lenin or Khrushchev.

ELLSWORTH RAYMOND

BROWN, Edmund G., Jr.

In January 1975, Edmund G. (Jerry) Brown, Jr., took office as governor of California. He is the son of Edmund G. (Pat) Brown, who served as attorney general and governor of the state (1959–67).

Since taking office, he appeared to be pleading for a more liberal, ascetic way of life for the United States, with less dependence upon big government, mass culture, and materialism. He expressed concern for impoverished minorities, but also for the ordinary taxpayer. He attacked bureaucracy, high taxes, "elitist" educational systems, and government waste. He dislikes pretentious official language, elaborate planning schemes, and the assumption that the answer to every program is to spend more money on it. He has urged people to "lower their expectations," to live more simply, to seek new nonmaterialistic meanings in life. Perhaps most politically unconventional of all, he freely admits that while he has some insight into what does not work, he does not necessarily have counterproposals that will work. Some observers thought that Brown was trying to modernize the meaning of liberalism, others that he was introducing his own radical concepts. Nearly all agree that he will bear close watching.

The policies of Gov. Edmund G. Brown, Jr., provoked controversy in California during the year.

Background. Edmund G. Brown, Jr., was born in San Francisco on April 7, 1938. He spent eight years as a Jesuit seminarian, but later abandoned his goal of the priesthood. He graduated from the University of California at Berkeley in 1961 and from Yale Law School in 1964 and then established his law practice in Los Angeles.

Brown began his political career as a trustee of the Los Angeles Community College District in 1969. The following year he won the Democratic primary and the general election for California secretary of state, the chief elections officer in the state. Brown took advantage of this situation, gaining favorable publicity through vigorous enforcement of the state elections laws.

Unlike the stereotypic politician, Brown is a very private person. An unapologetic intellectual, he is knowledgeable about serious music and fluent in Latin and Greek. During the 1974 primary campaign, an opponent, Mayor Joseph Alioto of San Francisco, irritably grumbled that Brown acted "as though he invented honesty."

During the 1974 gubernatorial campaign, he easily won the Democratic nomination. In the campaign, however, he contacted few of the politicans who had loved his father, Pat, and almost ignored the party machinery. He made relatively few public appearances. Instead, he ran a campaign via mass media, managed by a professional campaign management firm.

CHARLES R. ADRIAN

BURGER, Warren E.

U. S. Chief Justice Warren E. Burger continued during 1975 in his dual role as a conservative on the Supreme Court and as an activist and reformer in his public statements. Addressing the American Bar Association in February 1975, he urged Congress to authorize the appointment of new federal judges and to grant a 20% increase in federal judicial salaries. In June he endorsed proposals for a new national court of appeals to alleviate the Supreme Court's increasing work load, and he urged the elimination of all direct appeals to the Supreme Court. Other reforms advocated by Burger included the upgrading of U. S. attorneys through a screening process and the creation of an effective system for the removal of unfit federal judges.

Burger and the three other Nixon appointees—Harry A. Blackmun, Lewis F. Powell, and William H. Rehnquist—voted as a bloc 69% of the time. They dominated a majority of the 137 cases in the term that ended in June 1975 and generally adhered to a conservative and "strict constructionist" position. The Burger court declined to review several cases involving key legal questions, such as one dealing with prepublication censorship of the writings of a former Central Intelligence Agency employee, and it postponed other important cases, including one on the death penalty, until the 1975–76 term.

Burger voted with the majority in such decisions as those permitting Southern cities to change their racial composition by annexing predominantly white suburbs and denying black inter-city residents the right to challenge zoning restrictions in suburban areas. He dissented from rulings granting suspended public-school pupils the right to due process, striking down a local ordinance against nude scenes in drive-in movies, awarding back pay to victims of job discrimination, and permitting a defendant to reject a court-appointed lawyer. Burger also took part in the court's unanimous decisions holding that a non-dangerous mental patient could not be institutionalized against his will, and that the fixing of lawyers' fees by local bar associations violated antitrust laws.

Background. Warren Earl Burger, born in St. Paul, Minn., on Sept. 12, 1907, graduated from the University of Minnesota and obtained his LL. B. degree magna cum laude from St. Paul College of Law in 1931. Combining the practice of law with teaching, he also was active in the Republican party. He served as President Eisenhower's assistant attorney general in charge of the civil division in the Justice Department in 1953–56 and then as a judge of the district court of appeals for the District of Columbia, establishing a reputation as an "enlightened law-and-order man." Appointed by President Nixon to succeed Earl Warren, Burger was sworn in as the 15th chief justice on June 23, 1969.

BURSTYN, Ellen

In 1975 actress Ellen Burstyn attained the distinction of winning top honors in Hollywood motion pictures and on the Broadway stage. Her realistic and intelligent portrayal of a young widow in search of self-fulfillment in *Alice Doesn't Live Here Anymore* earned her the best actress award at Hollywood's Academy Award presentations in April. Later that month, she won an Antoinette Perry (Tony) Award for her performance in *Same Time, Next Year,* a two-character Broadway comedy hit about a couple engaged in a 24-year extramarital affair.

Earlier, Burstyn had won an Academy Award nomination and awards from the New York Film Critics and the National Society of Film Critics as best supporting actress for her performance as a small-town matron in *The Last Picture Show* (1971). She received her second Oscar nomination for her portrayal of the mother of a "possessed" teen-ager in *The Exorcist* (1973) and won acclaim as Art Carney's disenchanted daughter in *Harry and Tonto* (1974). According to film critic Vincent Canby, Burstyn is "one of the few actresses . . . who is able to seem appealing, tough, intelligent, funny, and bereft, all at approximately the same moment."

Background. Of Irish-American parentage, Ellen Burstyn was born Edna Rae Gillooly on Dec. 7, 1932, in Detroit, Mich. As a young woman, she worked as a model, soda jerk, short-order cook, sign painter, fashion coordinator, and nightclub dancer and educated herself by reading and working crossword puzzles. Minor television roles led to her regular appearance on the Jackie Gleason show in 1956–57. Taking the name Ellen McRae, she then appeared in the Broadway comedy *Fair Game* (1957–58) and later in such uninspired films as *For Those Who Think Young* (1964), *Goodby Charlie* (1964), and *Pit Stop* (1969), while ap-

pearing regularly in the NBC-TV soap opera *The Doctors.* She studied Method acting with Lee Strasberg and became a member of the Actors Studio in 1969. Burstyn's talents won recognition with her performances in the film version of Henry Miller's *Tropic of Cancer* (1970), *Alex in Wonderland* (1970), *The King of Marvin Gardens* (1972), and the ABC-TV comedy *Thursday's Game* (1974). She has also directed films as a member of a women's workshop.

Ellen Burstyn's third marriage, to Neil Burstyn, ended in divorce. She lives in Rockland county, N. Y., with her teen-age son Jefferson.

CHIANG Ching-kuo

After the death of Generalissimo Chiang Kai-shek on April 5, 1975, his son, Chiang Ching-kuo emerged as the dominant political personality of the Taiwan-based Republic of China. Vice President C. K. Yen formally succeeded the generalissimo as president. However, the real power in the government of Nationalist China resided in the younger Chiang, who as premier had been the country's actual ruler for three years. He was confirmed as head of the governing Kuomintang party on April 28.

While Chiang Ching-kuo still gave lip service to his father's goal of reestablishing Nationalist rule on the Chinese mainland, he concentrated his efforts on the economic and political development of the island. Chiang relaxed his father's authoritarian rule and permitted more of the native Taiwanese, who constitute 85% of the island's population, to move into government positions. He enjoyed meeting peasants and local dignitaries in the countryside, and devoted more resources to rural welfare. He eased the penalties for political offenders and allowed some opposition to emerge in the mass media.

Taiwan began to recover from the effects of the oil crisis and the worldwide economic slump, which slowed the island's economy. Chiang promoted the construction of highways, railroads, power plants, and ports. A large steel mill and a petrochemical complex were also planned. At the same time, he maintained the strength of the 500,000-man armed forces established by his father. Despite his precarious diplomatic position, Taiwan under Chiang Ching-kuo appeared in 1975 to be one of the most stable and one of the most prosperous countries in Asia.

Background. Chiang Ching-kuo, the son of Chiang Kai-shek and his first wife, was born in Chikou, Chekiang province, on March 18, 1910. As a student he became involved in radical activities, and in 1925 he was sent to the USSR to study in Moscow and at the military academy in Leningrad. Eventually he fell into disfavor with Soviet authorities because of his Trotskyite views. He returned to China in 1937, and during China's war with Japan he was a regional administrator in Kiangsi. From 1945 to 1947 he was a foreign affairs commissioner, and in 1948 he became deputy economic control supervisor for Shanghai. After the Nationalist regime moved to Taiwan in 1949 he was placed in charge of the security police apparatus and proceeded harshly against Communist agents. He became defense minister in 1965, vice-premier in 1969, and premier in May, 1972. Chiang Ching-kuo and his Russian-born wife have three sons, a daughter, and several grandchildren.

ECHEVERRIA ALVAREZ, Luis

President Luís Echeverría Álvarez of Mexico continued in 1975 as a leading spokesman for Latin America and the nations of the Third World. At the same time he asserted his country's independent but friendly policy toward the United States. He criticized the great-power politics of the United States and the Soviet Union and denounced the new U. S. trade reform act as discriminatory to Latin America, while defending the charter of economic rights and duties of states, en-

dorsed by the UN General Assembly in December 1974 and proposed by him in 1972.

In February he presided over a session of the International Commission to Investigate Crimes of the Chilean Junta. The following month, he and Venezuelan President Carlos Andrés Pérez proposed a Latin American economic system to promote development projects and establish financial institutions to stimulate Latin American economies. The two presidents also helped to create a new multinational coffee corporation in collaboration with the governments of Costa Rica and El Salvador.

In June, Echeverría delivered an address to the International Women's Year conference in Mexico City. Winding up a 42-day tour of 14 Third World nations in Asia, Africa, and Latin America, Echeverría visited Cuba for 4 days in August. There he called for solidarity of the world's developing nations in creating a "more just society."

Domestically, Echeverría tried to close the gap between the impoverished campesinos (farmers) and the more prosperous urban classes. He toured the country to learn its problems and to explain his reform policies. He also tried to placate the right by making economic concessions to business and by cracking down on leftist guerrillas.

Background. Luís Echeverría Álvarez was born on Jan. 17, 1922, in Mexico City, the son of a civil servant. He graduated from the University of Mexico with a law degree in 1945 and joined its law faculty in 1947. After becoming a member of Mexico's dominant Institutional Revolutionary party in 1946, he served in party administrative jobs and in subcabinet posts in the government. Appointed minister of the interior in 1964, he forcefully suppressed the 1968 student riots. After succeeding Gustavo Díaz Ordaz as president on Dec. 1, 1970, he adopted a conciliatory policy toward the left and instituted a program of major economic and social reforms. Echeverría, whose six-year term ends in 1976, chose Finance Minister José López Portillo as his successor.

EVERT, Chris

Late in October, Chris Evert reported that she was changing her tactics. "I am trying to play more aggressively. I am making myself go to the net and trying to make my opponents make the mistakes," said the 20-year-old tennis star. In the process, she defeated Evonne Goolagong Cawley, 6–3, 6–3, at Hilton Head, S. C., won her 19th clay-court tournament in a row, and collected $25,000.

In the past Evert preferred to stay on the backline and hammer away with accurate forehands and two-fisted backhands. With her superb ground strokes, she swept through the latter part of the big tournament season in 1975, winning the U. S. Open after taking the national clay court title for the fourth straight year. Billy Jean King, with two dazzling surges, beat her on the grass at Wimbledon in a 3-set semifinal battle. It was King's exploitation of the net game that again made her younger opponent aware of the one weakness in her game. Evert has also been alert to the criticism of her baseline game as "boring." It was, however, by playing that type of game that Chris wore down Miss Goolagong, after being on the verge of losing, and took the U. S. Open. The new champion called "winning my own country's title" her most satisfying victory. The triumph at Forest Hills ran her string of victories on clay courts to 84 in 25 months.

By the end of the U. S. Tennis Association's professional tour she had won a total of $320,227, in 1975, bettering the earnings records of King and Margaret Court. Her celebrated romance with fellow champion Jimmy Connors suffered a setback as Chris dissolved her engagement.

Christine Marie Evert was born in Ft. Lauderdale, Fla., on Dec. 21, 1954. Taught by her tennis teacher father, Jim, and chaperoned by her mother, Collette,

UPI

Chris Evert smashes a hard forehand while winning the Rome International championship in May.

Chris gained national prominence at the age of 16 when she won the decisive match against Britain for the Wightman Cup. In 1973 she turned professional and collected $32,000 as she reached the Italian, French, and Wimbledon finals. In 1974 she captured 10 straight tournaments, including Wimbledon, winning 52 straight matches and $261,460 before bowing to Evonne Goolagong in the U. S. Open semi-finals.

BILL BRADDOCK

FORD, Betty

First lady Betty Ford, despite her ordeal of breast-cancer surgery in September 1974, maintained a full schedule in 1975. She accompanied President Ford on his travels, entertained visitors, attended social and civic functions, expressed her candid opinions in interviews, and continued to take an active interest in aiding the handicapped and promoting the performing arts. In the spring she traveled with President Ford to Western Europe, and in the summer she joined him on a 10-day tour of Central and Eastern European capitals that was highlighted by the European Security Conference at Helsinki. In June she acted as honorary head of the 50th anniversary celebration committee of the Martha Graham Dance Company. Earlier, she received the Anti-Defamation League's Human Relations Award for "inspirational commitment to democratic principles and special dedication to securing equal rights for women." In December she joined President Ford on his trip to the People's Republic of China.

In August the first lady became a center of controversy when she answered a television interviewer's hypothetical question that she "wouldn't be surprised" if her 18-year-old daughter, Susan, were having an affair. She also suggested that premarital sex might lower divorce rates and praised the Supreme Court's legalization of abortion. Ford has indicated approval of her husband's decision to seek election in 1976.

Background. Betty Ford, whose maiden name was Elizabeth Anne Bloomer, was born on April 8, 1918, in Chicago, the daughter of a businessman. She grew up in Grand Rapids, Mich. After attending the school of dance at Vermont's Bennington College and studying with Martha Graham, in 1939 she joined the Martha Graham troupe in New York, working as a Powers model between dance engagements. Her marriage, in 1942, to William C. Warren, ended in divorce in 1947. From 1943 to 1948 she worked as fashion director of a Grand Rapids department store. On Oct. 15, 1948, she married Gerald R. Ford, who was elected to his first term as a Republican congressman from Michigan that November. Ford accompanied her husband on campaign tours and was active in civic affairs. Betty Ford became the first lady of the United States when Gerald Ford took office as the nation's 38th president on Aug. 9, 1974, after the resignation of Richard Nixon. President and Mrs. Ford have three sons, Michael, John, and Steven, and a daughter, Susan.

FORD, Gerald R.

The first year in office for President Gerald Ford was clouded by the bitter aftertaste of the Vietnam War and the Watergate scandals. His early pardon of former President Richard Nixon brought his "honeymoon" period to a rapid close and caused his popularity to drop sharply. After several months his popular standing improved and in July 1975 he announced his candidacy for a full term as president. Two separate alleged assassination attempts in September in California caused alarm about the president's safety. Two women were apprehended, one after a shot was fired, and the second while pointing a gun.

Ford's main attack on a deteriorating economy beset by both recessionary and inflationary factors was a substantial tax reduction as well as sizable cuts in federal spending. The president and the Democratic Congress were unable to agree on the proper approach to overcoming the energy shortage, but in late 1975 Ford proposed the creation of a $100 billion Federal Energy Corporation to stimulate commercial development of necessary energy sources.

Critics of President Ford contended that his was a negative administration based on inaction and veto. Ford, however, argued that the federal government had become overly-powerful and too bureaucratically complex and urged that many federal programs be abandoned, restricted, or returned to the states. His principal weapon in the controversy was the presidential veto, which he used more than 35 times during his first year in office. Congress was able to override fewer than 20% of the vetoes.

On November 3, Ford reshuffled key cabinet posts. Secretary of Defense James Schlesinger was fired with Ford nominating Donald Rumsfeld to succeed Schlesinger. Rumsfeld, until then Ford's White House chief of staff, was quickly confirmed. William Colby was dropped as director of the Central Intelligence Agency and replaced by George Bush, head of the U. S. liaison office in China. Secretary of State Henry Kissinger was relieved of his second hat as director of the National Security Council and replaced by his deputy, Lt. Gen. Brent Scowcroft. Vice President Nelson Rockefeller withdrew from consideration as Ford's running mate in 1976, giving the president numerous options. Ford's intent had been to demonstrate that he was in command of his presidency, but his moves were severely criticized both in terms of style and substance.

In foreign policy Ford followed the patterns established by President Nixon and Secretary of State Kissinger. After the collapse of U. S. efforts in Southeast Asia, the president concentrated his attention on furthering détente with the Soviet Union, opening new doors to the People's Republic of China, and attempting to mediate among the various parties in the Middle East. In September 1975, Israel and Egypt signed an interim Sinai accord negotiated by Kissinger.

Background. Gerald Rudolf Ford's rise to the presidency followed a long career in the House of Representatives, where he was chosen minority leader in 1965. Born on July 14, 1913, in Omaha, Neb., Ford was christened Leslie King, Jr., but after his parents' divorce his mother remarried, and he took the name of his stepfather. He grew up in Grand Rapids, Mich., and received a B. A. degree from the University of Michigan in 1935 and an LL. B. from Yale University Law School in 1941. After serving for four years in the Navy during World War II, Ford returned to Grand Rapids to practice law. He soon became interested in politics and was elected to Congress in 1948.

In 1963 he was elected chairman of the House Republican Conference and served as a member of the Warren Commission. Ford became president on Aug. 9, 1974, at a time of deep national crisis. He succeeded to the office upon the resignation of Richard M. Nixon, having been appointed vice president in 1973 under the terms of the 25th Amendment. He thus became the first person to serve in both of the nation's highest offices without having been elected to either.

In 1948 Ford married Elizabeth Bloomer, a former professional dancer and fashion coordinator. They have four children: Michael, John, Steven, and Susan.

ROBERT J. HUCKSHORN

President Gerald Ford had a strong impact on diplomatic affairs and traveled widely in 1975.

THE WHITE HOUSE

GANDHI, Indira

India's Prime Minister Indira Gandhi was faced in 1975 with a growing threat to her political position by opposition parties and movements, a court ruling that she had been guilty of election offenses in the 1971 general elections, and reverses in legislative elections involving her personal prestige. On June 26 she reacted to these difficulties by proclaiming, through the president of India, a state of national emergency.

She defended this action and the draconian measures that followed, which included the arrest of several thousand opposition leaders and strict censorship of the press, as a regrettable necessity. She also promised that the emergency would be lifted as soon as the internal situation ceased to be "abnormal." The majority of the Indian people seemed to approve of her actions, especially her call for self-discipline and order, her 20-point economic program, and the steps she ordered to reduce the prices of basic commodities and to improve bureaucratic procedures. She reacted indignantly to outside charges that she had proclaimed the emergency mainly to protect her own position and that her actions heralded "the end of democracy" in India.

In late July the Indian parliament, in which her party held more than two-thirds of the seats, approved the proclamation of emergency, and in early August it amended both the election law and the constitution to provide retroactively that Mrs. Gandhi could not be debarred from office for any past electoral offenses. In November the Supreme Court of India overturned her conviction and upheld her actions. The retroactive law prevented the court from reaching any other decision. By the end of the year she had silenced all significant opposition and was steadily increasing her extraordinary powers.

Background. The only child of Jawaharlal Nehru, Indira Gandhi was born in Allahabad on Nov. 19, 1917. With her grandfather, father, and mother heavily involved in the independence struggle and often in prison, she led a lonely childhood, an experience that made her "a very private person." She was educated in India and Switzerland and at Somerville College, Oxford. Her mother, Kamala Nehru, died in Switzerland in February 1935. On her return to India in March 1941, she took an active part in the independence movement, and in 1942–43 she was imprisoned by the British.

In March 1942, she married Feroze Gandhi (no relation to Mahatma Gandhi), a Parsi by whom she had two sons. Gradually she and her husband became estranged, especially after 1947 when she became virtually a full-time hostess for her father, the prime minister. Shortly before Feroze's sudden death in September 1960, however, according to Mrs. Gandhi, "we were somehow getting very close."

Mrs. Gandhi was president of the Congress party in 1959–60, and minister of information and broadcasting in 1964–66. In January 1966, she became prime minister. In the fall of 1969 the Congress party split, and her wing of the party gained increasing support. Her decisive victories in the fifth general elections in 1971 and in state assembly elections in 1972, and her firm handling of the crisis with Pakistan in 1971, culminating in the Indo-Pakistan war in December, gave her a commanding position on the Indian political scene. This position was considerably eroded after 1972, but it was reasserted after the proclamation of a national emergency in mid-1975.

NORMAN D. PALMER

GRASSO, Ella

Gov. Ella Grasso of Connecticut needed in 1975 all the resourcefulness, persuasion, and adroit patience of her mentor, the late Democratic chairman John M. Bailey, to hold the line in state spending. Over 150,000 people, more than 9% of the labor force, were unemployed in 1975. Buttressed by Democratic majorities of 118 to 33 in the House and 29 to 7 in the Senate, Governor Grasso pledged to sign only a balanced 1975–76 budget in spite of an inherited deficit. The $1.68 billion in expenditures were met, not by a state income tax, which she opposed, but by a 7% sales tax and a "laundry list" of taxes that exceeded the previous year's tax income by $125 million. Setting a personal example, Governor Grasso refused the 1974-approved, $7,000 raise of the governor's salary to $42,000.

Called a "tough conventional politician" and known as a product of the Hartford-based Democratic political machine, she made openness in government her cardinal principle. Press conferences were frequent. A log of her incoming and outgoing telephone calls was available. Budget meetings were held throughout the state, and the citizens could present their views to the governor during scheduled office hours in local town halls.

Grasso's election campaign criticized utility companies for overcharging consumers. As governor she approved an act creating a Public Utilities Authority with an expanded staff, which was expected to reduce electric bills. With her approval, the state Social Services Department denied payments for medically un-

necessary abortions, an action strongly opposed by civil rights and women groups. When 30,000 state employees were denied pay raises in May 1975, Governor Grasso pressured the legislature into a partial restoration of annual salary increments.

Background. Born in Windsor Locks, Conn., on May 10, 1919, the daughter of James and Maria Tambussi, she graduated cum laude from Mount Holyoke College. Ella Grasso was elected to the state House of Representatives in 1953 and 1955. In her second term she was the first woman to serve as floor leader. She was elected secretary of the state in 1958 and reelected in 1962 and 1966. Chairman of the Commission to Prepare for the Constitutional Convention of 1965, she was elected floor leader of the convention. In 1970 she was elected U. S. representative and was reelected in 1972. Ella Grasso won the governorship in a landslide in 1974 and became the first woman to be elected governor on her own merits rather than as a successor to her husband. Her husband, Dr. Thomas Grasso, is a retired East Hartford school principal. The Grassos have a daughter and a son. Ella Grasso has been named one of four persons to co-chair the 1976 Democratic National Convention.

GEORGE ADAMS

HILLS, Carla A.

On March 5 the U. S. Senate confirmed President Gerald Ford's appointment of 41-year-old Carla Anderson Hills as secretary of housing and urban development. She was the third woman in U. S. history to serve in the cabinet.

The president's spokesman said that her sex was not a factor in the appointment and praised Hills as "a highly competent lawyer and extremely competent administrator." Even some of the senators who voted against her confirmation on the ground that she lacked specialized experience in the field of housing acknowledged her legal brilliance and executive abilities.

Hills observed that in the cabinet she would be pledged to provide decent shelter for all. In hard times, she said, when the poor could not meet their mortgage payments, "HUD has the power to assume mortgages and forbear rather than foreclose." At her appointment, Hills had served a year and a day as an assistant attorney general in charge of the civil division of the Justice Department, directing the work of more than 200 lawyers.

Background. Hills, whose maiden name was Carla Anderson, was born in Los Angeles on Jan. 3, 1934. She studied at Oxford University in 1954 and graduated with honors from Stanford University in 1955. She won her law degree at Yale Law School in 1958, standing 20th in a class of 167.

She married Roderick M. Hills, a lawyer, in 1958 and has four children. She was an assistant U. S. attorney in Los Angeles from 1959 to 1961, when she joined her husband and three other lawyers in forming a firm. She is the co-author of *Federal Civil Practice* (1961) and the editor and co-author of *Anti-Trust Advisor* (1971). In April 1975 her husband was named a counsel to the President and in October was named Securities and Exchange Commission chairman.

RICHARD G. WEST

JUAN CARLOS I

Juan Carlos I of Spain was formally proclaimed king on November 22, following the death of Francisco Franco, the Spanish head of state, on November 20. The new monarch faced a host of problems, ranging from economic recession to political mistrust on both the left and the right.

Juan Carlos had been groomed as monarch by Franco. On July 22, 1969, Franco formally nominated Juan Carlos as future king and asked the Cortes (parliament) to ratify the choice. He insisted that the new monarchy owed nothing to the past, but dated from the

civil war of 1936, thus disposing of Juan Carlos' father's claim. The Cortes, though not unanimously, voted for the prince as future sovereign.

Juan Carlos remained under Franco's direction until 1974, when, during the latter's illness, he took his place for two months. On Oct. 30, 1975, with the 82-year-old dictator near death, power as head of state, though not yet as king, was transferred to him. This gave him command of the armed forces and authority to appoint and dismiss high military and civil officials, sign treaties, declare war, and make peace.

Background. Juan Carlos de Borbón y Borbón is the son of Prince Juan, Count of Barcelona, and grandson of King Alfonso XIII of Spain, who was overthrown in 1931. Juan Carlos was born in Rome on Jan. 5, 1938 during his family's exile. In 1947, Spain officially became a monarchy again, with Generalissimo Francisco Franco empowered to name as his successor a king of royal blood, Spanish nationality, Roman Catholic faith, aged at least 30, and pledged to uphold the Falangist framework of government.

Although the count of Barcelona was dynastic heir, Franco groomed Juan Carlos, holding that the senior prince's long absence from Spain disqualified him from understanding its contemporary problems. Juan Carlos was taken there at age 9 and educated privately and at the *Instituto San Isidro* in Madrid. Franco and Prince Juan agreed that the boy should receive a complete military training. He studied at the Zaragoza Military Academy, the Spanish Naval College, and the Spanish Air Academy, presumably qualifying as an officer in all three branches. He learned to speak several foreign languages, including English.

CHARLES E. NOWELL

KHALID, King

Khalid ibn Abd al-Azia al-Saud was chosen king of Saudi Arabia on March 25, 1975, within a few hours of the assassination of his older half-brother, King Faisal. Selected by the royal princes and by the religious leaders, Khalid had been crown prince since 1965 and first deputy prime minister since 1962. In Saudi Arabia he is known as "the quiet prince" and "the man of the desert," and he is popular with the people. Within the royal family he is known for honesty, loyalty, modesty, and wisdom.

Among his remaining brothers, two loose groups have formed. One is led by Prince Fahd, the eldest of seven full brothers—the so-called Sudairi Seven. Six of the seven hold important government positions. The other group is led by Prince Abdallah who is head of the 30,000-man National Guard. Prince Khalid did not belong to either group.

One of King Khalid's first acts was to name a new Council of Ministers. Prince Fahd was named crown prince, first vice president, and minister of interior. Prince Abdallah was named second vice president and head of the National Guard, while Prince Nayif (Fahd's brother) was named minister of state for interior affairs and deputy minister of the interior, and Prince Faisal (King Faisal's son) as minister of state for foreign affairs.

King Khalid remained prime minister and minister of foreign affairs. He announced that policies of Saudi Arabia would not be changed under his reign. It is assumed, however, that with younger men about him the pace of government will be quickened.

Background. King Khalid was born in 1912 in Riyadh, the son of famed Ibn Saud and Jauhara, Saud's first cousin on his mother's side. Her father belonged to the powerful and highly respected Jiluwi tribe. Thus, Khalid was doubly royal and had strong desert ties. Khalid was educated by a private tutor in the palace. He has shunned the glare of public life and visits the desert tribes whenever possible. A hunter of big game in Africa, he has the finest collection of falcons in Arabia. He has traveled widely, attending the charter meeting of the United Nations in San Francisco, visiting

most of the European states, and meeting with President Lyndon Johnson of the United States in 1968. The father of five sons and seven daughters, he has a history of heart trouble.

SYDNEY NETTLETON FISHER

KISSINGER, Henry Alfred

Kinetic diplomacy contined to characterize the activities of Secretary of State Henry A. Kissinger in 1975. Shuttle diplomacy between Cairo and Jerusalem culminated in an agreement in August by which Egypt and Israel created new truce lines in the Sinai Peninsula. Israel yielded some of the territory it had captured in the 1973 war while the Egyptian line was moved eastward from the Suez Canal. The resulting buffer zone was to be overseen by U. S. watch stations, and the entire cost to the United States over these years was estimated at $9 billion. The projected costs and potential dangers of stationing U. S. personnel in the Sinai caused some congressional opposition, but by mid-October the necessary legislation had been passed by Congress and signed by President Ford.

Repeatedly in 1975, Kissinger came into conflict with Congress. When Congress voted to ban further U. S. military sales to Turkey in an attempt to influence Turkey to negotiate on the Cyprus question, Turkey responded by asking the United States to leave its bases in Turkey. Kissinger tried unsuccessfully to persuade Congress to end the ban. As the United States sought to negotiate with Panama over the future status of the canal, bills were introduced in Congress that, if passed, would have cut off funds for the U. S. negotiator, Ellsworth Bunker. In November, Kissinger's difficulties with Congress reached their peak when the secretary was cited for contempt of Congress for refusing, at President Ford's request, to turn over State Department memoranda.

Détente with the Soviet Union was also a highly controversial policy. Kissinger drew praise and some criticism for his support of the accord reached at the Conference on Security and Cooperation in Europe, which 35 nations signed in August. Praise centered on provisions that gave promise of improved relations in Europe and of further progress in détente, especially in the Strategic Arms Limitation Talks. Criticism emphasized the continued mistreatment of Jews and dissidents inside the USSR, the abandonment of the policy of liberating Eastern Europe, and the lack of provisions on the free movement of ideas and information.

The increasingly heated debate between Kissinger and Defense Secretary Schlesinger over détente was one of the prime reasons that President Ford made the dramatic reshuffling of his cabinet in early November. Schlesinger was fired and Kissinger was relieved of his responsibilities as director of the National Security Council. Ford declared that Kissinger, as secretary of state, would continue to "have the dominant role in the formulation and the carrying out of foreign policy."

Background. Henry Alfred Kissinger was born in Fürth, Germany on May 27, 1923. He emigrated to New York City in 1938 and received a doctorate in political science in 1954 from Harvard University, where he later served on the faculty. In 1969 he joined the administration of President Nixon as special assistant for national security affairs. In 1974 he won the Nobel Prize for Peace for his efforts in ending the Vietnam War. He has a son and a daughter by his first marriage and is married to the former Nancy Maginnes.

WALTER DARNELL JACOBS

LEVI, Edward Hirsh

In February 1975 Edward Levi became the 71st attorney general of the United States. During the turbulent Watergate period the Department of Justice had been run by four different men—John Mitchell, Richard Kleindienst, Elliot Richardson, and John Saxbe. The conviction of Mitchell and Kleindienst for illegal activ-

ities while in office sensitized Levi's approach to his post. He viewed his new position as requiring "the necessity of restoring faith in the administration of justice" and sought to calm and stabilize the department.

Levi's appointment was approved by a voice vote of the Senate without debate after some opponents sought to suggest that his previous membership in the National Lawyers Guild indicated leftist sympathies. These charges were dismissed by his supporters, who included the conservative columnist William F. Buckley, Jr.

In office Levi has sought to be his own man in the handling of such issues as the role of the Federal Bureau of Investigation, crime, handguns, quotas in hiring, and other matters. He confirmed the existence of secret FBI files on legitimate politicians and the existence of counterintelligence harassment programs against supposed radical groups during the 1960–71 period, and he cooperated with FBI Director Clarence M. Kelley in controlling the activities of FBI agents. Levi also defended the President's constitutional right to conduct "electronic surveillance in the interests of national security . . . without obtaining a judicial warrant" and prepared a number of bills designed to control the rising crime rate and the sale of handguns.

Background. Born in Chicago in 1911, Levi's training and much of his adult life have been associated with the University of Chicago. He entered a university laboratory school when he was five. He later attended college and law school at the University. Levi joined the faculty of law at Chicago in 1936, leaving for a while to get a graduate law degree from Yale and, during World War II, to serve in the antitrust division of the Department of Justice. In 1955 he became dean of the Chicago Law School and gained a reputation as an expert on antitrust law. In 1962 he was appointed provost of the university, and in 1968 he became its president.

WALTER DARNELL JACOBS

MIKI, Takeo

On Dec. 9, 1974, Takeo Miki was designated premier of Japan by the Diet, after he had been chosen president of the majority Liberal-Democratic party (LDP) early in the month. Having served 14 consecutive terms in the Diet, he has earned the name, "Child of the Diet." He is the only postwar leader of Japan to have studied in the United States.

On Aug. 5–6, 1975, Premier Miki made his first visit to the United States since assuming office, and met President Ford in Washington. While in Washington he authorized the release of terrorists imprisoned in Japan in exchange for the release of terrorist-held hostages in the U. S. consulate in Malaysia. On August 29, U. S. Secretary of Defense Schlesinger visited Premier Miki to discuss security problems.

Background. Takeo Miki was born on March 17, 1907, in a family of farmers in Donari, Tokushima prefecture, Shikoku. In 1929 he completed the commercial course in Meiji University and then interrupted his studies for four years' travel and study in California. After returning to Japan and completing his law degree, he entered the Diet in 1937 at the minimum eligible age of 30. One of a few parliamentarians who opposed the drift to war with the United States, he organized the Japan-American Friendship Society in 1939. He stood for reelection without official support in 1942 and was returned to the Diet.

In 1947 he became the youngest member of the Katayama cabinet. In 1955 he helped engineer the merger of the Japan Liberal and Democratic parties to form the LDP, which has controlled the government for 20 years. He was appointed to 12 cabinet posts and to key positions in the LDP including two terms as its secretary general. His career has reflected a spirit of independence and devotion to democratic government. He was one of the first to call for the reversion of Okinawa to Japanese control and for normalization of relations with the People's Republic of China.

The former Foreign Affairs Minister succeeded Kakuei Tanaka, who announced his intention to resign in November 1974, shortly after the visit of U. S. President Gerald Ford. Shortly before that, Miki resigned from the cabinet in a protest of campaign finance irregularities, which eventually led to Tanaka's downfall.

Takeo Miki married Mutsuko Mori in 1940. Their two sons and a daughter followed in their father's footsteps by studying in the United States.

ARDATH W. BURKS

MOYNIHAN, Daniel Patrick

Daniel Patrick Moynihan was nominated by President Gerald Ford in May 1975 to succeed John A. Scali as U. S. permanent representative to the United Nations. He was sworn in on June 30 at a White House ceremony at which President Ford called him "an outstanding political, economic, and social philosopher" who "knows what America is all about and what it actually stands for."

Noted for his blunt, candid manner, he provoked controversy by stating in an article in *Commentary* in March, that the United States should drop its apologetic attitude toward Third World nations. Later, he recognized the "community of interest" between Western democracies and developing nations but asserted the USSR could move into any power vacuum left by the United States. Moynihan also suggested that expulsion of Israel from the United Nations by the Arabs might prompt the United States to walk out of the session and to cut off UN funds.

On August 11, Moynihan vetoed the admission of North and South Vietnam and asserted that the Security Council's earlier refusal to admit South Korea was "selective universality, a principle which in practice admits only new members acceptable to the totalitarian states." On September 1, Moynihan read a message to the United Nations by Secretary of State Henry Kissinger, outlining U. S. proposals for bridging the gap between rich and poor nations. Moynihan's outspoken manner created tension in Washington, and he nearly

UN Ambassador Daniel Moynihan often came into conflict with Third World nations in 1975.

UPI

resigned his post in November when he considered State Department support for him too weak.

Background. Daniel Patrick Moynihan was born in Tulsa, Okla., on March 16, 1927, and grew up in New York City slums. As a teen-ager he worked as a long-shoreman, studied at City College of New York, and served in the U. S. Navy. He earned his undergraduate degree cum laude from Tufts University in 1948 and later received masters and doctorate degrees. In the 1950's, Moynihan was on the staff of New York Gov. W. Averill Harriman, and in 1961 he was appointed special assistant in the Department of Labor by President Kennedy. As assistant secretary of labor from 1963 to 1965, he helped to draft President Johnson's antipoverty legislation and to prepare a controversial report on the black family. Concurrently, he served in various academic posts and was coauthor with Nathan Glazer of *Beyond the Melting Pot* (1963), a study of ethnic groups in New York City. In 1966 he became director of the Harvard-MIT Joint Center for Urban Studies. Appointed White House assistant for urban affairs in late 1968, Moynihan worked on drafting the Nixon administration's welfare reform proposals. In December 1972 President Nixon named him ambassador to India, where he served for two years.

PAUL VI, Pope

During 1975, proclaimed by the Vatican as Holy Year, Pope Paul VI continued in his efforts to maintain a balance between orthodoxy of faith and gradual institutional reform of the Roman Catholic Church. In February, in response to the challenges of the liberal Swiss theologian Hans Küng, the pope ordered Küng to desist from expounding his unorthodox views. Küng questioned the doctrine of papal infallibility and criticized the church for failing to implement Vatican II reforms. But the fact that no disciplinary action was taken against the theologian, who in earlier years might have been excommunicated, seemed to indicate Pope Paul's acceptance of some degree of pluralism. The pontiff also took steps early in the year to maintain the Church's control over the Society of Jesus.

Pope Paul was concerned with the Church's external as well as its internal affairs. Recently he called for improved relations betweeen Catholics and Jews, expressed concern for Roman Catholics in Indochina, and condemned the Spanish government's "harsh repressions" after it had executed five Basque separatists. In November he called on Christians and Muslims to "put an end to fratricidal combat" in Lebanon. The audiences granted by the pontiff also reflected the Church's diplomacy. In June he received U. S. President Gerald Ford, who ended a European tour with a ceremonial visit to Rome. The pontiff took steps to cement ties with Communists and Third World countries, receiving Bulgarian Communist party chief Todor Zhivkov and Ugandan President Idi Amin, among other chiefs of state.

Background. Pope Paul VI was born Giovanni Battista Montini in Concesio near Brescia, Italy, on Sept. 26, 1897. The son of a lawyer and newspaper editor, he was educated in the Arici Institute and the Arnaldo Lyceum in Brescia. He was ordained a priest in 1920 and later undertook graduate studies at Gregorian University and the University of Rome. After a brief stint as an apprentice foreign service officer in Poland in 1923 he served for the next three decades in various posts with the Vatican's secretariat of state. From 1954 to 1963 he served as archbishop of Milan, and in 1958 he was created a cardinal. After the death of Pope John XXIII in June 1963, Cardinal Montini was elected to succeed him, taking the name of Paul VI.

RABIN, Itzhak

For Itzhak Rabin the year 1975 was crucial in Israel's perennial search for peace with security. Like all other Israeli premiers, Rabin has had only fragile

coalition backing in parliament, yet he has had to deal with the aftermath of the Israeli-Arab war of 1973, an inflation rate approaching 30%, and the unceasing terrorism of the Palestine liberation forces. Most important, Rabin has been compelled (as no other Israeli government has been) to make continuing concessions to his Arab neighbors, particularly Egypt.

In January, Rabin opened the way for negotiations toward an interim peace agreement with Egypt by saying in an interview in the French newspaper *Le Figaro* that Israel was willing to return "most of the Sinai" as well as the strategic Mitla and Gidi passes and the Abu Rudeis oil fields. In March, however, U. S. Secretary of State Henry Kissinger's shuttle diplomacy failed to get Rabin's agreement in exchange for what the Israelis termed "minor Egyptian political concessions." Rabin acted in the face of enormous U. S. pressure, including President Ford's statement that the United States would now have to "reassess" its relations with Israel.

By late summer mounting U. S. diplomatic pressure, as well as U. S. financial inducements and the promise to station U. S. observers in the Sinai, had made an agreement with the Egyptians impossible to avoid. U. S. Secretary of State Kissinger's August 21–September 1 round of shuttle diplomacy between Jerusalem and Alexandria resulted in the signing of an interim agreement in Geneva on September 4. The accord meant another interim pullback in Sinai, abandonment of the Abu Rudeis oil fields on the Gulf of Suez, and yielding control of the Mitla and Gidi passes. Rabin, however, had made the agreement conditional on U. S. congressional approval, and he had succeeded in keeping his government in power despite a wave of protests in Israel.

In July, Rabin made the first official visit of any Israeli premier to West Germany. He expressed the wish that although the past should not be forgotten, Israelis were looking forward to "a more hopeful and better future" with Germany and Europe.

Background. Of Russian immigrant extraction, Rabin was born on March 1, 1922. A member of the Jewish Defense Force, Haganah, before World War II, he joined the British forces in the war. A brilliant military career followed. He was a brigade commander in the 1948 war, became chief of staff in 1963, and planned and led the stunning Israeli victory in the June War in 1967. He retired in 1968 to become ambassador to the United States, where he cultivated a close relationship with official Washington, particularly with Henry Kissinger. In 1973 he returned to Israel, was elected to parliament, and in 1974 entered the cabinet of Golda Meir as minister of labor. Upon the collapse of her government in April 1974, he became Israel's first native-born premier, assuming office in June 1974.

CARL LEIDEN

REAGAN, Ronald Wilson

On Nov. 20, 1975, Ronald Reagan announced that he would challenge President Gerald Ford for the 1976 Republican presidential nomination. A former sportscaster, actor, and governor of California (1967–75), Reagan had been a favorite of Republican conservatives since 1964 and was considered the only serious threat to Ford's renomination.

At the 1968 Republican convention Reagan was a formal candidate for nomination, but he was defeated by Richard Nixon on the first ballot. After leaving the California governorship in January 1975, although he delayed his decision on candidacy for the 1976 Republican nomination, Reagan acted very much like a candidate. His political exposure was maintained by frequent political tours, a daily radio program, "Viewpoints," aired on over 200 stations, a syndicated weekly column published in 130 daily newspapers, and the formation in July of a Citizens For Reagan Committee.

Background. Reagan was born in Tampico, Ill., on Feb. 6, 1911, and graduated from Eureka (Illinois) Col-

lege in 1932. As a Des Moines radio sportscaster and columnist, Reagan gained a national reputation and the attention of Warner Brothers. He made his film debut in 1937 and appeared in some 50 movies by 1964, usually acting as the "nice guy." From 1954 to 1965 his major interest was television, and he was host and performer with the weekly *General Electric Theater* and *Death Valley Days*.

He was president of the AFL-affiliated Screen Actors' Guild (1947–52, 1959) and supported President Truman in 1948 and liberal Helen Gahagan Douglas in her 1950 U. S. Senate race against Richard Nixon. Campaigning as a Democrat for Dwight Eisenhower in 1952 and 1956 and for Nixon in 1960, he became a Republican in 1962. He was California Republican co-chairman for Goldwater in 1964. Running as a conservative opposing high taxes, waste, bureaucracy, crime, welfare costs, and student unrest, he was elected California governor in 1966 and again in 1970. A decisive person, Reagan overhauled welfare and medicaid programs, vetoed spending measures, balanced the budget, and provided a $400 million surplus at the end of his term.

ORVILLE H. ZABEL

ROCKEFELLER, Nelson A.

Vice President Nelson Rockefeller completed his first full year as the nation's number two man with skill and dignity, despite the fact of his unacceptability to the Republican party's conservative wing. Conservative criticism caused him to announce in early November that he was removing his name from consideration as a possible running-mate for President Ford in 1976.

When he was nominated to be vice president in August 1974, some observers thought that Rockefeller might try to upstage President Ford. In office, however, Rockefeller made every effort to be a careful, discriminating, and faithful subordinate. In turn, President Ford assigned Rockefeller missions of significance, naming him head of the Domestic Council and chairman of a presidential commission on Central Intelligence Agency (CIA) activities in the United States.

President Anwar el-Sadat of Egypt played a prominent role in global affairs during the year.

UPI

Rockefeller used the Domestic Council to bring technocrats from his own network of experts into the government. As a fundraiser and campaigner, Rockefeller was an energetic supporter of Ford, although after his withdrawal as a possible running-mate there was speculation that Rockefeller might himself become a candidate for the Republican nomination.

The CIA commission was appointed by President Ford to investigate charges that the CIA had engaged in numerous illegal activities inside the country. The report, submitted in June, concluded that the CIA had committed some "deviations" from its assigned missions and recommended that the CIA's role as related to foreign intelligence be clarified and its role in domestic areas be strictly controlled. The Rockefeller report did not end the matter and investigations of the intelligence community by Congress continued.

Background. Nelson Aldrich Rockefeller was born in Bar Harbor, Me., on July 8, 1908. He attended Dartmouth College and worked with Rockefeller family interests before entering public service in 1940 and subsequently served every president from Franklin D. Roosevelt. Elected governor of New York in 1958, he was reelected in 1962, 1966, and 1970. He resigned in December 1973 and became vice president in 1974 by appointment under the 25th Amendment. Rockefeller tried for the Republican presidential nomination in 1960, 1964, and 1968. He has carried on and diversified the family tradition of philanthropy. Rockefeller has five children from his first marriage to Mary Todhunter Clark, which ended in divorce in 1962. His second marriage, to Margaretta (Happy) Murphy, produced two sons.

WALTER DARNELL JACOBS

SADAT, Anwar el-

In 1975 Egypt's President Anwar el-Sadat proved himself to be one of the world's most astute and bold international politicians. In the September 4 interim agreement between Egypt and Israel, Sadat regained control of crucial Sinai territory and oil while enhancing his reputation in the faction-torn Arab world and in the international community. Earlier, in January 1975. Sadat denounced the Soviet Union for failing to replace the arms Egypt had lost in the 1973 war with Israel and warned the United States that the Arabs would not hesitate to "blow up oil wells" should the United States ever employ force to gain Arab oil. In the same month he risked splitting the Arab world by hinting that an interim agreement over Sinai was possible and secured Mirage jets from France.

Sadat has been particularly successful in maintaining his ties with other Arab and Muslim states such as Iran. With the Palestinians his task has been more difficult. Yasir Arafat, leader of the Palestine Liberation Organization, viewed the latest agreement between Egypt and Israel as a betrayal of the Palestinians. Acting more violently, Palestinian guerrillas kidnapped the Egyptian ambassador to Spain in September and threatened his life. Sadat denounced such actions and pledged that regardless of the Palestinians his course would be maintained. The reopening of the Suez Canal by Sadat in June was not only a skillful ploy in the negotiations with Israel over Sinai, but a move that attracted international attention.

Background. Born in the Nile Delta on Dec. 25, 1918, Sadat early chose the army as a career. He also became a revolutionary and was among the young officers led by Col. Gamal Abdel Nasser, who staged the successful coup that overthrew King Farouk in 1952. Over the years his influence with Nasser waxed and waned, but in late 1969 he was appointed vice president. Upon Nasser's death in 1970, Sadat became president, then was elected in his own right. In 1971 he survived a serious coup attempt by Ali Sabry and other highly placed politicians. Since then he has enjoyed enormous popularity and, most important of all, prestige within the army.

His chief problem with Israel has been the recovery of Sinai. In 1972, Sadat expelled the Soviet military advisors because the Soviet Union apparently was unwilling to support renewed hostilities with Israel. His constant subsequent saber rattling was taken seriously by few, and because of this the Egyptian strike across the Suez Canal in October 1973 enjoyed considerable initial tactical success. Instrumental to this success and essential to the strategic victory that followed it was the support of oil-producing Arabs, primarily the Saudi Arabians.

Since the 1973 Arab oil embargo against the United States and others, Sadat has been extremely astute in exploiting U. S. support for Israel without alienating the United States. He has regularized relations with the United States, received President Nixon in Egypt in June 1974, met with President Ford in Austria in 1975, and maintained a close personal relationship with U. S. Secretary of State Henry Kissinger.

CARL LEIDEN

SILLS, Beverly

Bel canto soprano Beverly Sills made her long-awaited debut at the Metropolitan Opera on April 7, 1975, after 20 years as a distinguished member of the New York City Opera and a guest star with the world's leading opera companies. Appearing in the role of Pamira in Rossini's *The Siege of Corinth,* in which she had made her debut at Milan's La Scala in 1970, Sills won plaudits, not only for the richness and beauty of her voice, but for the total theater of her performance. Minimizing the importance of her debut at the Met, Sills told interviewers that "In a sense, I revolutionized the operatic scene, because I proved you can make a great international career without the Metropolitan." Her failure to sing there previously had been the result of a "clash of personalities" between herself and former Met director Sir Rudolf Bing.

A few days before her Met debut, she sang the role of Elvira in *I Puritani* at the City Opera, in her first New York appearance since undergoing successful cancer surgery in the fall of 1974. During 1975–76 she was to appear in *Daughter of the Regiment* and *Lucrezia Borgia* at the City Opera, in *La Traviata* at the Met, and with the San Francisco Opera. In 1975 she also portrayed Giulietta in *Capuletti e Montecchi* for the Opera Company of Boston in June, and was on television on Danny Kaye's *Look-In at the Metropolitan Opera* in April and in an interview with Mike Wallace on *60 Minutes* in July. She also performed at the Hollywood Bowl, at Saratoga Springs, N. Y., and at Wolf Trap, D. C., where she is program chairman.

Background. The daughter of an insurance broker, Beverly Sills was born Belle Silverman in Brooklyn, N. Y., on May 25, 1929. She began to sing regularly on radio shows at the age of three. After graduating from the Professional Children's School in New York in 1945, she toured with the Gilbert and Sullivan Opera Company and the Charles Wagner Opera Company. In 1955 she joined the New York City Opera, where she soon distinguished herself in such coloratura roles as *Lucia di Lammermoor, Anna Bolena,* and Donna Anna in *Don Giovanni* and won international recognition as Cleopatra in Handel's *Julius Caesar* in 1966. As a recording star, her *Manon* earned her an Edison award. Sills is married to newspaper executive Peter Greenough and has two children, Meredith and Peter, Jr.

SIMON, William E.

William E. Simon, U. S. secretary of the treasury and chairman of the Economic Policy Board, continued in 1975 to serve as the Ford administration's chief economic spokesman, as well as its most articulate champion of a free-market economy and fiscal restraint. He fought against anti-recession deficit spending proposals adopted by President Ford, asserting that the fight against inflation should have top priority. He also

CHRISTIAN STEINER

Opera star Beverly Sills made her first appearance at New York City's Metropolitan Opera in April.

spoke out against using federal aid to alleviate New York City's financial crisis.

In an address to the National Association for the Advancement of Colored People convention in July, Simon held out little hope for government action to improve employment opportunities for minority groups hit by the recession, arguing that such action would result in higher taxes and increased inflation. Later that month he offered the House Ways and Means Committee a plan to reduce taxes paid by corporations and by their shareholders, as a means of improving the long-term health of the economy. He also spoke against federal regulation of the energy and transportation industries.

Simon visited Moscow in April to discuss pending U. S. trade legislation with Soviet officials. In May he met with Israel's finance minister in Washington to sign a U. S.-Israeli economic pact and addressed a meeting of the Organization of Economic Development in Paris, arguing in favor of continued flexibility in international monetary arrangements. Unlike Secretary of State Henry Kissinger, who favored political-economic dialogue with Third World nations, Simon emphasized improving the climate for private investment in the underdeveloped countries. He again emphasized his support of flexible monetary policies at the 30th annual joint meeting of the International Monetary Fund and the World Bank, held in Washington in September. In November he accompanied President Ford to France for the economic summit of six major industrial nations.

Background. William Edward Simon, the son of an insurance broker, was born in Paterson, N. J., on Nov. 27, 1927. After graduating from Lafayette College, with a B. A., he joined in 1952 the Union Securities Co. in New York City, and in 1957 he became a vice president of Weeden & Co. In 1964 he joined the Wall Street investment firm of Salomon Brothers, where he acquired a senior partnership within a year. In December 1972 he was named deputy secretary of the treasury, and a year later succeeded John A. Love as director of the new Federal Energy Office, where he acted decisively to alleviate the fuel crisis. In April 1974 he was named secretary of the treasury by President Nixon, and in September he was also appointed chairman of the new Economic Policy Board by President Ford.

STEVENS, John Paul

On Dec. 19, 1975, John Paul Stevens was sworn in as an associate justice of the U. S. Supreme Court by

UPI

Justice John Paul Stevens took the U. S. Supreme Court seat of Justice Douglas in December.

Chief Justice Warren Burger. Justice Stevens filled the vacancy on the court created by the retirement of Justice William O. Douglas in November.

Stevens was considered a legal centrist, and most observers believed that he would have views similar to moderates on the court such as Justices Byron White and Potter Stewart. After his nomination Stevens said that he would "do everything in my power to render the best possible judicial service of which I am capable."

Background. He was born in Chicago on April 20, 1920, the son of a prominent and prosperous businessman. Stevens graduated from the University of Chicago in 1941 and then served in the U. S. Navy from 1942 to 1945. He was first in his law class at Northwestern University in 1947.

After law school Stevens had his first contact with the Supreme Court, serving as law clerk to Justice Wiley Rutledge for two years. He then returned to Chicago to enter private law practice. He specialized in antitrust and corporate law, interrupting his practice for occasional public-service assignments. In 1950 he was an associate counsel for a congressional committee studying monopoly practices, and in 1954–55 he served on a national committee studying antitrust laws. In 1969 he was general counsel on an Illinois commission investigating misconduct by two state supreme court justices who later resigned. He also lectured at the University of Chicago and Northwestern.

In 1970 he was appointed by President Nixon to serve as judge of the U. S. Court of Appeals for the Seventh Circuit in Chicago. In the five years he held that post he handed down more than 200 opinions and earned a reputation for thoughtfulness and for a solid and scholarly approach to the law. An observer of his actions on the Seventh Circuit said "he is highly regarded throughout this jurisdiction as just a superb judicial craftsman."

Justice Stevens married Elizabeth Jane Sheeren in 1942, and they have four children—John, Kathryn, Elizabeth, and Susan. Stevens flies his own airplane and likes to play bridge and golf.

THATCHER, Margaret

On Feb. 11, 1975, Margaret Thatcher succeeded Edward Heath as leader of Great Britain's Conservative party. Her second-ballot victory over four male opponents, including party chairman William Whitelaw, made her the first woman in British parliamentary history to head a major political party and the first to be eligible for the prime ministership.

As opposition spokesman on economic affairs since the fall of 1974, Thatcher clashed frequently with Harold Wilson's Labour government, attacking its efforts to increase taxes on inherited wealth and arguing that Britain's economic plight could best be alleviated by a balanced budget and sound monetary policies. She opposed government efforts to promote full employment and control prices. Although her views have been widely criticized as "elitist," Thatcher's outspoken defense of what she regards as traditional British values, and her assertion that "the workers, not the shirkers" should be encouraged, won her substantial public support.

Background. Thatcher, whose maiden name was Margaret Hilda Roberts, was born on Oct. 13, 1925, in Grantham, Lincolnshire. She was the daughter of a grocer who also served as mayor of the town. Educated in private schools, she won a scholarship to Somerville College, Oxford, and was elected president of the Oxford University Conservative Association. She graduated in 1947 with a chemistry degree and subsequently earned an advanced degree from Oxford. While working as a research chemist from 1947 to 1951 she made two unsuccessful bids for a seat in parliament. In 1951 she married businessman Denis Thatcher, and in 1953 she became the mother of twins.

Having qualified as a barrister in 1954, Thatcher entered law practice. In 1959 she won election to the House of Commons. From 1961 to 1964 she was joint parliamentary secretary to the ministry of pensions and national insurance, and from 1964 to 1970, while Labour was in power, she served as opposition spokesman on economic affairs and education. Named in 1970 to the cabinet post of secretary of state for education and science by Prime Minister Heath, Thatcher provoked controversy by eliminating free milk for some 3.5 million schoolchildren, but won praise for her effective school construction and improvement program. In March 1974, when Labour returned to power, she became opposition spokesman for the environment and then Tory spokesman on treasury matters and economic affairs.

TRUDEAU, Pierre Elliott

Leader of the Liberal party and Prime Minister of Canada, Pierre Elliott Trudeau faced serious problems in his government in 1975. He refused the resignations of Minister of Labour John Munro and Minister of Transportation Jean Marchand, but he did accept the resignation of Minister of Finance John Turner. Turner represented Ontario business interests and stood to the right in economic policy.

The consequent shift in the cabinet reflected shifts in public opinion that have been reflected in government policy and the public image assumed by the prime minister. When he first came to power, Trudeau faced the threat of separatism in Quebec. Accordingly, he assumed the stance of a young, innovative philosopher-statesman, bending his efforts to domesticating and reforming the constitution and to rendering the government bilingual. Since then, however, with the victory of the pro-confederationist Bourassa Liberals in Quebec, and with the apparent coming success of bilingualism, these issues have slipped in importance.

Following a near defeat in 1972, the prime minister changed his image to that of the chastened servant, openly reducing the authority of the prime minister's office. In the subsequent election Trudeau's party recovered some of its losses, but it did so with a do-nothing policy. Since then increasing federal-provincial tensions over oil policy, provincial royalties on resources and federal export taxes, and a grass roots demand for action on inflation and unemployment, have forced the prime minister's hand.

Shortly after he replaced Turner with Donald MacDonald as minister of finance and reshuffled the im-

portant cabinet posts, Trudeau announced his New Economic Proposals. They included commissions to monitor wage and price increases and to roll back prices if the increases are excessive. This means a new image for the prime minister, who now appears as a seasoned senior statesman taking a tough stand on economic issues.

Background. Born in Montreal on Oct. 18, 1919, he graduated from the University of Montreal Law School in 1943 and did postgraduate studies in economics and political science at Harvard and in London and Paris. He practiced law in Montreal, then became Liberal member of Parliament in 1965. He served as minister of justice and attorney general in 1967, and was elected prime minister in 1968. In 1971 he married Margaret Sinclair of Vancouver. The Trudeaus have three sons.

R. F. NEILL

WALLACE, George C.

Since becoming governor of Alabama in 1963, George C. Wallace has been a national figure both because of his position on racial integration of schools and because of his persistent interest in presidential politics. A conservative with charismatic appeal, he opposes federal intervention in local schools, high taxes, inflation, and foreign aid. He supports the free enterprise system, welfare reform, vigorous law and order measures, and improved national defense.

In 1968, Wallace was the presidential candidate of the new American Independent party and carried five states: Georgia, Alabama, Mississippi, Louisiana, and Arkansas. In 1972, Wallace campaigned for the presidential nomination of the Democratic party, winning primaries in Florida, Tennessee, and North Carolina before being shot by a would-be assassin, Arthur Bremer, on May 15. After the assault, although paralyzed below the waist, he won primaries in Maryland and Michigan and appeared in a wheel chair to address the Democratic convention.

By November 1975 Wallace announced his intention to run for the presidency in 1976, had qualified for federal matching funds under the new campaign reform law, and was shown by the Gallup Poll to be first choice of Democratic voters when Sen. Edward Kennedy was not included. In October, to prove he was physically fit to be president, Wallace made a two-week trip to Europe. He has refused to rule out running as a third party candidate.

Background. George Corley Wallace was born in Clio, Ala., Aug. 25, 1919. In 1942 he received a law degree from the University of Alabama. After World War II service (1942–45), he was assistant attorney general of Alabama (1946–47), a member of the state legislature (1947–53), and judge of the third judicial district (1953–58). He then practiced law until elected governor of Alabama in 1962. During his first term he gained national prominence by supporting the racial segregation policy of the University of Alabama. President John F. Kennedy used the Alabama National Guard to force integration at the university. Prohibited from succeeding himself as governor by the Alabama constitution, Wallace supported his wife, Lurleen, for the office. She was elected, but died of cancer in May 1968. Wallace was reelected governor in 1970 and, after a change in the constitution, in 1974.

ORVILLE H. ZABEL

WILSON, Harold

British Prime Minister Harold Wilson was faced in 1975 with a worsening economic situation and discords within his own Labour party and his cabinet. The "social contract" for voluntary restraint that he had negotiated with organized labor in 1974 was largely invalidated when some unions obtained wage increases of as much as 35% in early 1975, and by midyear, the inflation rate exceeded 25%.

During the early months of 1975, the Wilson government was preoccupied with the question of Britain's continued membership in the European Economic Community (EEC). In January, the prime minister announced that the first national referendum in British parliamentary history would be held on that issue. The Wilson government won a substantial victory when 67.2% of the British electorate voted for continued EEC membership in the June 6 referendum. A few days later, Wilson made several changes in his cabinet, including the demotion of leftist Anthony Wedgwood Benn, a leader of the anti-EEC campaign, from his key post as secretary of state for industry.

In view of the continuing economic crisis, Wilson introduced a program in July that included the limiting of wage increases to the equivalent of about $13 a week. The plan received support from key unions, including the militant National Union of Mineworkers, and it won endorsement in the House of Commons.

Wilson met with Ulster Protestant and Catholic church leaders in January in an effort to end continued sectarian strife in Northern Ireland. Later that month he had his first meeting with President Gerald Ford in Washington and visited Canadian Prime Minister Pierre Trudeau in Ottawa, and in February he met with Soviet officials in Moscow. At the Commonwealth Conference, held at Kingston, Jamaica, in May, Wilson called for a redress in the balance between rich and poor nations.

Background. James Harold Wilson, the son of an industrial chemist, was born in Huddersfield, Yorkshire, on March 11, 1916. He graduated from Oxford University with first-class honors in 1937, remaining there as a lecturer in economics. During World War II he held key civil service posts, and in 1945 he was elected to the House of Commons as a Labour party candidate. From 1947 to 1951 he served in the cabinet as president of the Board of Trade. In 1963 he succeeded the late Hugh Gaitskell as party leader. He served as prime minister from 1964 until 1970, when he was succeeded by Conservative Edward Heath. In March 1974, after elections had given Labour a plurality, Wilson returned to the prime ministership.

WILSON, Margaret Bush

Margaret Bush Wilson, a St. Louis, Mo., lawyer, public servant, and civil rights leader, was chosen on Jan. 13, 1975 as chairman of the national board of directors of the National Association for the Advancement of Colored People (NAACP). She was the first black woman to head the 450,000-member NAACP, oldest and largest civil rights organization in the United States. Once nicknamed "Mary Poppins—with a razor blade" by her colleagues, Wilson combined an optimistic zeal with a tough-minded pragmatism. She planned to continue the NAACP's tactics of promoting racial equality and integration by peaceful and legal means, while also modernizing and rejuvenating the organization to bring more young black people into its ranks. In her keynote address to the 66th national convention of the NAACP in June, Wilson asserted that the Ford administration was "indifferent and unresponsive to the humiliation and suffering" of minority groups hard hit by the economic recession.

Background. A member of a black middle-class family long associated with the NAACP, Wilson, whose maiden name was Margaret Berenice Bush, was born in St. Louis, Mo., on Jan. 30, 1919. Her father, a real estate broker, spearheaded the legal struggle resulting in the historic *Shelley* v. *Kraemer* (1947) decision of the U. S. Supreme Court, which declared restrictive housing covenants unenforceable by law. After graduating cum laude from Talladega College in 1940, she earned her law degree in 1943 from Lincoln University in St. Louis.

In the NAACP, Wilson served as the first woman chairman of the St. Louis branch from 1958 to 1962 and as president of the Missouri state conference of NAACP branches in 1962–63. Elected to the national board in 1963, she was chairman of the annual NAACP conventions in 1973 and 1974.

BOLIVIA

Bolivia in 1975 continued its attempt to achieve controlled economic growth by combining traditional Spanish forms of state control with modern corporate organizations in the public and private sectors. The military government, led by Gen. Hugo Banzer Suárez since 1971, remained strong militarily, but continued to lack popular support. President Banzer has evidently abandoned his effort to locate a stable power base in the political party system.

Politics. President Banzer announced in November 1974 that elections scheduled for October 1975 were indefinitely postponed and that the military would stay in control of the government until 1980. Key military leaders declared in a statement issued prior to Banzer's announcement that holding elections would weaken and divide Bolivia at a time when the neighboring countries of Brazil, Chile, and Peru were consolidating themselves internally under "strong and inflexible" military governments.

The decision to suspend elections caused considerable but ineffectual dissent. Former President Hernan Siles Zuazo secretly reentered Bolivia in January 1975 to mobilize opposition to the Banzer government over the election issue. The government deported Siles, charging him with plotting to replace the Banzer government with a leftist civilian regime. The government also implicated Siles, together with exiled former presidents Paz Estensorro and Juan José Torres, in a wave of strikes by miners.

The Bolivian Roman Catholic Church emerged as a vocal critic of the government. The government's alleged repression of civil and political rights, economic practices benefiting privileged groups, and systematic attacks on the Church were severely criticized.

Gulf Oil Issue. Gulf Oil Corporation disclosed that it had made $460,000 worth of political contributions to supporters of President René Barrientos. Gulf officials said they had given Barrientos a $100,000 helicopter for helping to forestall nationalization of Gulf holdings in Bolivia and obtaining profitable drilling rights for the corporation. Barrientos was killed in a helicopter crash in 1969.

Members of the military, which traces its "revolutionary" role in government back to the Barrientos years, were indignant over charges impugning the dead president. Opposition political party leaders tried to link the scandal to alleged current corruption in the Banzer government. President Banzer called on the Organization of American States to condemn Gulf's political activities in developing countries. The issue threatened to interrupt the payment to Gulf of $57.2 million still owed by the Bolivian government for exploration of oil installations in 1969.

Development Activity and Economy. The Bolivian population of 5.4 million has a per capita income of $222, one of the lowest in Latin America. One-half of the population lives in the central highlands, mainly on subsistence farming. Illiteracy runs high among the population over 15 years of age, although literacy campaigns have registered important gains and a pride of culture has increased among the rural Indian populations. Serious deficiencies in health and nutrition still exist.

The Banzer government achieved a base of strength in its balance-of-payments position from which to conduct development activity. Precedent setting gains in foreign exchange holdings were achieved as a result of spectacular increases in world prices for oil and natural gas, two of Bolivia's growing exports. The tin industry also gave a strong performance. Bolivia's international reserves at the end of the second quarter of 1975 were $192.3 million, compared with $151.2 million for the same period in 1974 and $72.8 million in 1973.

Through the National Economic Development Plan, 1975–79, Bolivia is committed to a strategy of export-led growth and market building in a framework of financial stability. However, inflation of the demand-pull, wage-push variety has dogged the development activity of the government. Price controls were being expanded and the government appeared to be developing an explicit wage-income policy in 1975.

International Affairs. Bolivia remained one of the least-developed countries of the Andean Group. It received preferential trading treatment from other countries, giving it access to wider markets. Investment loans from the Andean Development Corporation were also available. The Andean economic connection proved a counterweight to Bolivia's growing reliance on Brazilian loans and investments. Venezuela was a major capital exporter to its Latin American neighbors, and Bolivia became an active candidate for Venezuelan financial aid. Venezuela's President Andrés Pérez visited Bolivia in August, which symbolized this new relationship.

Thomas M. Millington
Hobart and William Smith Colleges

BOLIVIA • Information Highlights

Official Name: Republic of Bolivia.
Location: West-central South America.
Area: 424,163 square miles (1,098,581 sq km).
Population (1975 est.): 5,400,000.
Chief Cities (1970 est.): Sucre, the legal capital, 85,000; La Paz, the actual capital, 562,000; Cochabamba, 150,000.
Government: *Head of state,* Hugo Banzer Suárez, president (took office Aug. 1971). *Head of government,* Hugo Banzer Suárez. *Legislature*—Congress (suspended Sept. 1969): Senate and Chamber of Deputies.
Monetary Unit: Peso (20 pesos equal U.S.$1, May 1975).
Gross National Product (1974 est.): 1,700,000,000.
Manufacturing (major products): Processed foods, textiles, leather goods, cement.
Major Agricultural Products: Sugar, cotton, corn, potatoes, wheat, rice, coffee, bananas.
Foreign Trade (1973): Exports, $259,000,000; imports, $255,000,000.

Coffee trees in Parana state were pruned back after a freeze that may affect the 1976–77 coffee crop.

BRAZIL

The slowdown in Brazil's economic growth continued in 1975, as frost in the coffee region foreshadowed a meager 1975–76 harvest of this important export crop. Foreseeing difficult days ahead, the government cracked down on political dissent, reversing a recent trend toward liberalization, but also made the first significant move since 1964 to halt the decline in living standards of the masses.

Economy. The recession that hit the manufacturing sector in 1974 deepened in 1975. Brazilian industrialists, who must sell most of their products in the domestic market, were among the strongest advocates of increasing the purchasing power of the masses. In May 1975 the minimum legal wage, which had been in effect for 12 months, was increased by 41.4%. This was the first time in more than a decade that a minimum-wage increase surpassed the inflation rate. The difference, however, was not as great as the government claimed. While the government calculated the inflation rate for the 12 months prior to May 1975 to be 26%, independent sources put the figure at more than 30%.

Despite the recession in manufacturing, recent heavy investment in other sectors and the momentum of seven years of accelerated growth boosted Brazil's 1975 gross national product above that of 1974. The percentage increase for 1975, however, was believed to be the smallest since 1968, perhaps less than 4%. Finance Minister Mário Henrique Simonsen conceded that continued rapid economic growth was no certainty and could not be relied upon to solve Brazil's social problems. Simonsen became the first high official to suggest publicly that Brazil

limit its population growth, currently 2.7% a year, through birth control.

In 1975, Brazilian economists also worried that the expected drop in coffee exports in 1976 would aggravate Brazil's already serious balance-of-payments problem. The country's dwindling foreign exchange reserves, down to $4 billion by July 1975, were further depleted to pay for essential imports, principally petroleum. The government had hoped that domestic oil production would rise 14% during the year, but the actual increase was less than half that. The newly-discovered oil field off the southern coast could not be put into full production before 1979. In October, the government announced that foreign oil companies would be allowed to explore in Brazil.

Energy Policy. While self-sufficiency in petroleum at current rates of consumption seemed possible by the 1980's, alternate sources of energy had to be developed to allow for growth. Hydroelectric projects, like the mammoth Itaipú Dam on the Paraná River, were pushed by President Ernesto Geisel and his energy minister, Shigeaki Ueki, but the long-range solution to Brazil's energy problems, they decided, lay in nuclear power. With a nuclear power plant already under construction in Brazil by Westinghouse Corporation of the United States, the government in 1975 concluded a $3.8 billion deal to buy eight nuclear plants from West Germany, the last to be delivered by 1990.

An agreement with West Germany included the purchase of a plant for the production of nuclear fuel. Brazil has uranium, the raw material for nuclear fuel, in relative abundance. With the capability of enriching uranium, Brazil would be in a position to develop nuclear weapons. Some observers, noting that Brazil never signed the 1970 Nuclear Nonproliferation Treaty, saw the nuclear weapons capability as an ulterior motive for the deal with West Germany. Brazil's right-wing military regime disclaimed any intention of making Brazil a nuclear power.

Brazil continued to build up its arsenal of conventional weapons in 1975, taking delivery of 42 F-5 jet fighters purchased from the Northrop Corporation of the United States. The government was embarrassed when two of the planes crashed in Brazil and when it was revealed in the United States that Northrop had paid bribes to some Brazilian air force officers to smooth the way for the deal. Government censors forbade discussion of the bribes in the Brazilian press.

Politics. Press censorship, relaxed early in the year, was tightened toward the end of 1975. President Geisel, apparently bowing to hardliners in his government, declared in August that the country must have "four more years of order and tranquility" in which to solve its social and economic problems. Geisel termed thoughts of a return to democracy as it had existed prior to the 1964 coup as "only the result of imagination, if not intrigue." He called demands for the revision of the national security law, political am-

UPI

Fashions in São Paulo included antipollution masks after reports detailed the city's high pollution.

and to locate and win the release of "missing persons" believed held incommunicado by government security forces.

While Brazil remained relatively placid, civil disorder seemed to be on the rise in 1975. In June and July angry passengers, disgusted with poor train service, wrecked nine railroad stations on a Rio de Janeiro commuter line. In the Copacabana beach area of Rio in August, rioting broke out after police shot and killed a student. A decline in middle-class employment opportunities and the revolutionary example of Portugal were seen as factors in growing student militancy.

Some opposition politicians and journalists took up the issue of industrial pollution, which approached the crisis stage in parts of Brazil. The city of São Paulo in 1975 experienced the worst air pollution it had ever recorded. Industrial wastes dumped into the bay at Salvador virtually eliminated fishing in that area, once famous for its seafood. City and state officials pressed for pollution controls, but the federal government refused to authorize any measures that might "harm the economy." In August the federal government took away from the states all authority to set pollution standards or impose controls.

The Amazon. With population growth no longer regarded by the government as a positive good, less was heard about the need to populate Brazil's "vacant" spaces. Funds for the construction and maintenance of the Trans-Amazon highway were slashed, and some of the completed sections of the road became impassable. A project to build a parallel road north of the river was abandoned after a party of explorers was massacred by Indians. The Brazilian government, however, continued to search for mineral deposits in the area, using infrared aerial photography. Major deposits of iron and manganese were indicated in a fairly accessible location near the navigable Rio Negro, the major northern tributary of the Amazon.

NEILL MACAULAY
University of Florida

nesty, reductions of the president's and expansion of the Congress's powers "nostalgia for the past." He also said that Communist infiltration of "the mass media, trade unions, the public services—particularly the schools—as well as political parties" made democratization inappropriate.

Criticism of the regime in the press and in Congress, by the opposition Brazilian Democratic Movement (MDB), was suppressed, and hundreds of alleged "Communist agitators" were arrested. Many MDB congressmen and state officials were accused of accepting Communist support in the November 1974 elections and were threatened with removal from office. The Roman Catholic Church continued its efforts to stop the police from torturing political prisoners

---
BRAZIL • Information Highlights

Official Name: Federative Republic of Brazil.
Location: Eastern South America.
Area: 3,286,478 square miles (8,511,965 sq km).
Population (1975 est.): 109,700,000.
Chief Cities (1974 est.): Brasília, the capital, 545,000; São Paulo, 6,000,000; Rio de Janeiro, 4,400,000; Belo Horizonte, 1,300.
Government: *Head of state,* Ernesto Geisel, president (took office March 1974). *Head of government,* Ernesto Geisel. *Legislature*—National Congress: Federal Senate and Chamber of Deputies.
Monetary Unit: Cruzeiro (7.735 cruzeiros equal U. S.$1, March 1974).
Gross National Product (1974 est.): $70,000,000,000.
Manufacturing (major products): Processed foods, chemicals, textiles, automobiles, metals, petroleum products, paper, fertilizers.
Major Agricultural Products: Coffee, soybeans, rice, corn, sugarcane, wheat, oranges, cacao.
Foreign Trade (1974): *Exports,* $7,968,000,000; *imports,* $14,063,000,000.

Popular with tourists, the Royal Hudson Excursion Train runs between Vancouver and Squamish.

BRITISH COLUMBIA

On December 12 voters restored William H. Bennett's Social Credit party to power in the province, unseating Premier David Barrett's New Democratic party. Earlier in 1975, Premier Barrett presented the government's job security budget that, for the fiscal year ending March 31, 1975, developed revenues totaling $2,625,723,749.

The progressive fiscal policy measures brought forward provided jobs for British Columbians and moved the province toward a fairer tax structure. These policies were introduced within a budgetary framework of a small revenue surplus in 1976.

Fiscal Policies. Budgetary plans included the creation and expansion of jobs through special employment programs and through public works, ferry, hospital, housing, schools, and community and recreation construction programs. A historic revenue-sharing arrangement between the province and its municipalities based on natural gas revenues, should provide millions of dollars to assist the municipalities in providing services to their residents. The government continued its program of alleviating the burden of rising school taxes. A Renter Tax Credit Program provided relief to those in the middle and lower income brackets, as well as those on fixed incomes, such as senior citizens.

Beginning in July the province was hit by a series of strikes. The walkouts began in the forestry industry and spread to the rail, food, and propane gas industries. The provincial legislature passed a bill setting a 90-day cooling-off period, during which strikes and lockouts were prohibited, that took effect October 10. One of the province's worst periods of labor turmoil then ended.

Economic Development. The 1974 gross provincial product, representing the market value of all goods and services produced in the province, increased by an estimated $2.35 billion to $16.17 billion, or by 17% from 1973, equivalent to the rate of growth in the gross national product for Canada. The increase in provincial

product in 1965–74 was 176.8%. Personal income in 1974 totaled $12.4 billion, up 16.7% from 1973. Personal income per capita, at $5,170, was up 12.9% from 1973.

A reduced rate of economic growth in the province during the early months of 1975 reflected the impact of a worldwide recession on British Columbia's major trading partners, particularly the United States, the European Economic Community, and Japan.

Production gains in the early months of 1975 over the corresponding period in 1974 included coal, fish, net generation of electric power, and pulp production. Production declines were listed for copper, molybdenum, lead, and zinc shipments; lumber sawn; plywood production; and natural gas production.

The British Columbia labor force increased 5.7% to 1,164,000 people between August 1974 and August 1975, reflecting the continued influx of large numbers of people from other regions of Canada. Employment amounted to 1,074,000 in August 1975, compared with 1,044,000 in August 1974.

Labor income from salaries and wages in May 1975 totaled $788.1 million, a gain of 19% over the May 1974 value of $662.1 million. The provincial average weekly wages were $227.54 in May 1975, up $32.82 or 16.8%.

HERBERT W. KEE, *Executive Director*
Economic Plans and Statistics
Department of Economic Development

--- **BRITISH COLUMBIA · Information Highlights** ---

Area: 366,255 square miles (948,597 sq km).
Population (1975 est.): 2,462,000.
Chief Cities (1974 est.): Metro Victoria, the capital, 208,000; Metro Vancouver, 1,137,000.
Government (1975): *Chief Officers*—lt. gov., Walter S. Owen; premier, William H. Bennett (Social Credit party). *Legislature*—Legislative Assembly, 55 members.
Education (1975–76): *Enrollment*—public elementary and secondary schools, 547,730 pupils; private schools, 21,140; Indian (federal) schools, 3,510; colleges and universities, 28,900 full-time students. *Public school expenditures,* $479,846,000.
Public Finance (fiscal year 1974–75): *Revenues,* $2,459,-000,000; *expenditures,* $2,457,000,000.
Personal Income (1973 est.): $10,575,000,000; average annual income per person, $4,568.
(All monetary figures are in Canadian dollars.)

BULGARIA

While the Bulgarian Communist party called for "widening and deepening" relations with the Soviet Union, Bulgaria moved toward increased trade with the United States. Deputy Premier Ivan Popov, the highest-ranking Bulgarian Communist to visit the United States, toured the country for two weeks.

In other domestic developments, 33-year-old Lyudmila Zhivkova, daughter of President Todor Zhivkov, was formally installed as chairman of the nation's powerful arts and culture committee. In September, Bulgarian television offered a regular second channel of programing, from 38 major stations.

Economic Progress. According to the government data released in the spring of 1975, Bulgaria's economy made more than satisfactory progress in 1974. In comparison with 1973, the national income rose by 7.5%, and the real per capita income increased by 5%. Industrial production grew by 8.5%; engineering and metal working industries by 13.6%; chemical industry by 14.5%; production of building materials by 9%; and construction by 10%.

Foreign trade rose by 23.6% in 1974. Over 50% of all exports went to the Soviet Union, and over 30% was sent to other socialist countries. Machinery and equipment represented 40% of all Bulgarian exports.

According to the official data covering the first six months of 1975 the progress continued. In comparison with the same period of 1974, industrial production grew by 11.6%; electricity output by 11.5%; engineering and metalworking industries by 17.9%; chemical and rubber industries by 18.3%; ferrous metallurgy by 10%; and construction by 5.8%. Almost 13,000 family houses were built, an increase of 31.4%. Foreign trade rose by 26.7%. In the first half of 1975 about 57% of all exports went to the Soviet Union and 24% to other socialist countries.

Other economic developments included the extension to 80% of all workers of a 5-day work week with a maximum of 42.5 hours. About 75.7% of capital investments were used to in-crease economic productivity. The remaining 24.3% served science, education, health services, and housing construction.

Foreign Policy and Trade. Bulgaria's international activities intensified, and numerous exchange visits of government or party high officials took place with Rumania, Czechoslovakia, Algeria, Syria, Ethiopia, Turkey, Canada, Italy, and Greece. In April, David Rockefeller, chairman of the Chase Manhattan Bank, visited Sofia. Marshal Andrei Grechko, Soviet minister of defense, and Marshal Ivan Yakubovsky, commander-in-chief of the Warsaw Pact armed forces, paid official visits in late spring.

Plans for building a joint Bulgarian-Rumanian hydroelectric complex were completed with a projected electricity output for each country of 2,000 million kilowatt hours annually. Bulgaria's production and use of electricity have climbed sharply in recent years.

The 31st International Plovdiv Fair, held in September, led to over $1 billion in foreign-currency contracts. There were over 35,000 exhibits from more than 2,200 firms representing over 40 nations. Contracts for the purchase of Bulgarian wines reached record proportions, making the country the world's leader in bottled-wine exports, with export contracts for more than 200 million bottles.

JAN KARSKI
Georgetown University

BULGARIA · Information Highlights

Official Name: People's Republic of Bulgaria.
Location: Southeastern Europe.
Area: 42,823 square miles (110,912 sq km).
Population (1975 est.): 8,800,000.
Chief Cities (1973 est.): Sofia, the capital, 870,000; Plovdiv, 255,000; Varna, 235,000.
Government: *Head of state*, Todor Zhivkov, chairman of the State Council and first secretary of the Communist party (took office July 1971). *Head of government*, Stanko Todorov, chairman of the Council of Ministers (took office July 1971). *Legislature* (unicameral)—National Assembly.
Monetary Unit: Lev (0.94 lev equals U. S.$1, July 1974).
Gross National Product (1974 est.): $13,000,000,000.
Manufacturing (major products): Processed foods, machinery, chemicals, steel, tobacco products, petroleum products, clothing.
Major Agricultural Products: Corn, wheat, barley, fruits, tobacco, sugar beets.
Foreign Trade (1974): *Exports*, $3,721,000,000; *imports*, $4,195,000,000.

BURMA

Students, workers, and Buddhist monks took to the streets repeatedly in 1975 leading major demonstrations against President Ne Win. The increasing opposition of these groups to the military government added to the country's difficulties, which had resulted from crop-destroying rains and a sagging economy, plus chronic Communist and ethnic minority insurgencies. There was also an earthquake that destroyed or damaged more than 200 historic temples in Burma's 11th-century capital of Pagan.

Politics. The five-day demonstration that broke out in June was the least violent of the three nationwide protests that took place between June 1974 and June 1975. There were no deaths in the 1975 demonstrations, reportedly because soldiers were unwilling to fire upon unarmed civilians. Thirty persons were killed in a similar June 1974 uprising, which the 1975 demonstration was intended to commemorate. There were additional fatalities and casualties in a December 1974 outburst ostensibly over burial arrangements for former UN Secretary General U Thant.

Economic factors sparked all three protests as unemployment, low wages, and worsening inflation added to mounting political dissatisfaction with the Ne Win government.

Insurgencies. Communist rebel activity in lower and central Burma was completely ended.

The main body of the Communist insurgents, however, increased their military efforts along the Chinese border in the Wa and Kokang states east of the Salween River and the adjacent northeastern Shan States. Numbering less than 10,000 troops, compared with the 130,000-man Burmese army, the Communists crossed the Salween for the first time in a major military action. The insurgents were beaten back, but their increasing boldness was noticed by the Ne Win government, which is fearful of its increased vulnerability in light of Communist advances in the Indochina War.

Economy. Prices rose an average 30% in 1975, but wages did not increase. The government inaugurated a new rice procurement program, increasing the purchase price of the grain from the farmer by approximately 50%. Initial sales of the rice to the government increased 75% in volume, but violent May rains, in which 200 people lost their lives, severely damaged crops and offset the gain in government grain purchases.

The Earthquake. Ninety-four of the most important surviving 2,217 temples at Pagan, sacked by Kublai Khan's troops in the 13th century, were very seriously damaged in a July 8 earthquake that lasted only 35 seconds. Another 180 structures in the former holy city were also damaged but to a lesser extent.

Foreign Relations. Burma raised its consulates in Hanoi and Saigon to embassies after Vietnam's fall and sent congratulations to the new Communist governments of Cambodia and Laos. The government feared possible arms aid from across the Laotian border to its Communist insurgents from the arsenal left behind in Indochina by U. S. troops. Because of continued Chinese assistance to these rebels, relations with Peking were cool but correct. Ne Win, however, did pay a state visit to China in November. Secret talks were also held with both the United States and the Soviet Union concerning weapons for use against the insurrectionists.

RICHARD BUTWELL
*State University of New York College
at Fredonia*

BURMA · Information Highlights

Official Name: Socialist Republic of the Union of Burma.
Location: Southeast Asia.
Area: 261,789 square miles (678,033 sq km).
Population (1975 est.): 31,200,000.
Chief Cities (1975 est.): Rangoon, the capital, 2,100,000; Mandalay, 417,000; Moulmein, 202,000.
Government: *Head of state,* U Ne Win, president (took office March, 1974). *Head of government,* U Sein Win, prime minister (took office March 1974). *Legislature* (unicameral)—People's Assembly.
Monetary Unit: Kyat (6.265 kyats equal U. S.$1, March 1975).
Gross National Product (1974 est.): $2,800,000,000.
Manufacturing (major products): Processed foods, textiles, tobacco products, wood products.
Major Agricultural Products: Rice, groundnuts, sesame, tobacco, sugarcane, millet, cotton, forest products.
Foreign Trade (1974 est.): *Exports,* $190,000,000; *imports,* $100,700,000.

CALIFORNIA

In January 1975, Edmund G. (Jerry) Brown, Jr., was inaugurated as governor of California. Unconventional and enigmatic, Brown proved to be a puzzle to citizens, public employees, journalists, political scientists, and legislators alike. (See also BIOGRAPHY—*Brown, Edmund G., Jr.*) Despite coolness between the executive and legislative branches, much legislation was enacted. State leaders continued to try to find politically and economically feasible approaches to environmental problems, and higher education entered a new phase in the state. In San Francisco, Mayor Joseph Alioto was barred by the city charter from seeking a third term. Liberal Democratic State Sen. George Moscone was elected to succeed him.

Legislation. The legislature passed 1,433 bills during the 1975 session. Of these, Governor Brown allowed 102 to become law without his signature, and he vetoed 148 items, 10.3% of the total. California governors have always made extensive use of the veto. The previous year former Gov. Ronald Reagan vetoed 198 bills.

New laws included a much-heralded Agricultural Relations Act, designed to bring labor peace to the vineyards and other agricultural operations by establishing a secret ballot mechanism for settling disputes. Also, unemployment benefits were extended to farm workers. In the general area of increasing individual freedoms, a matter of special interest to the governor, new laws reduced the penalty for possession of small amounts of marihuana to a misdemeanor citation and legalized all sex acts between consenting adults in private. Other laws permitted school boards to establish student smoking areas on high school premises and to make physical education classes optional for the 11th and 12th grades.

Somewhat unexpectedly, the legislature refused to pass a bill, strongly opposed by local government organizations, to provide collective bargaining for all state and local government employees. The governor vetoed a bill that would have required state agencies to tell citizens what data are kept on them. He considered it too complex, requiring an elaborate bureaucracy for enforcement.

Environment. In the area of environmental issues, California imposed a moratorium through 1977, on laying pipelines across state tidelines, banned flip-top beverage cans, and eliminated the state's oil-depletion allowance. Strong public resistance forced the repeal of legislation requiring the installation of smog-control devices on all 1966–70 model automobiles registered within the South Coast Air Basin. In a further setback for the environmentalists, a federal court held void an order of the California Water Resources Board to limit artificially the capacity of the New Melones Dam being built by the U. S. Bureau of Reclamation on the Stanislaus River.

Edmund Brown, Jr. (*left*) and former governor Edmund G. Brown, Sr., arrive at a January social gathering prior to the younger Brown's inauguration as California's governor.

UPI

Government Expenses. A huge, multi-million dollar mansion to house the state's governors was completed during the year, but Governor Brown, preferring to live simply, refused to move in. Efforts were made to find some other use for it, or to rent it to some private person. The mansion had been urged by former Governor Reagan, who declared the old Victorian mansion a "fire trap." It is now a museum. About $43 million was appropriated to restore one wing of the State Capitol and make it earthquake-safe. Legislators voted themselves a 10% pay increase, to $23,232 annually. With various perquisites, their annual benefits equaled about $50,000.

Criminal Justice. In matters of criminal justice, prison sentences were made mandatory in certain crimes involving the use of firearms or the sale of heroin. Prisoners' rights were enumerated for the first time, and the long list of professional and other persons exempted from jury duty was abolished.

California experienced another year of bizarre criminal activities, causing social psychologists once again to attempt to explain why the state should be the site of so many unusual crimes. Patricia C. Hearst and Emily and William Harris, the last known at-large members of the so-called Symbionese Liberation Army, were captured in San Francisco and held for trial on a number of felony charges. Two other members of that group, Joseph Remiro and Russell Little, already convicted of the murder of Dr. Marcus Foster, Oakland superintendent of schools, underwent trial on additional attempted murder charges in Los Angeles due to a change of venue from northern California.

On September 5, Lynette Fromme drew a pistol and pointed it at President Gerald Ford,

who was on a visit to Sacramento. It did not discharge. Fromme, formerly associated with convicted murderer Charles Manson, was convicted of attempted assassination. Seventeen days later, while the president was in San Francisco, a shot was fired at him, again by a woman. A bystander deflected the gun and no one was hurt. In this case, Sara Jane Moore was charged with attempted assassination.

The University of California and, to a lesser extent, the state university and colleges system adopted new plans, adjusting to a new "steady state" condition for public higher education. University of California President Charles J. Hitch retired on June 30 and was replaced by David Saxon, a physicist and administrator on the Los Angeles campus. He was the first president of the university whose roots were not on the Berkeley campus.

CHARLES R. ADRIAN
University of California, Riverside

——— **CALIFORNIA** · **Information Highlights** ———

Area: 158,693 square miles (411,015 sq km).
Population (1974 est.): 20,907,000. *Density:* 132 per sq mi.
Chief Cities (1970 census): Sacramento, the capital, 257,105; Los Angeles, 2,809,596; San Francisco, 715,674.
Government (1975): *Chief Officer*—governor, Edmund G. Brown, Jr. (D); lt. gov., Mervyn M. Dymally (D). *Legislature*—Senate, 40 members; Assembly, 80 members.
Education (1974–75): *Enrollment*—public elementary schools, 2,674,385 pupils; public secondary schools, 1,753,058; nonpublic schools, 309,800; colleges and universities 1,597,179 students. *Public school expenditures,* $4,994,911,000 ($1,101 per pupil).
State Finances (fiscal year 1974): *Revenues,* $16,507,-414,000; *expenditures,* $15,519,227,000.
Personal Income (1974): $125,379,000,000; per capita, $5,997.
Labor Force (Aug. 1975): *Nonagricultural wage and salary earners,* 7,832,000; *insured unemployed,* 374,-900.

A stream of refugees moves toward Phnom Penh as the tempo of war quickens in Cambodia. Refugees swelled the capital's population, but the Communists evicted most of the people from the city after their takeover in April.

UPI

CAMBODIA

The five-year-old Cambodian civil war that erupted after the overthrow of Prince Norodom Sihanouk in March 1970 ended April 16, 1975, with the military victory of the Communist National United Front, better known as the Khmer Rouge. By the war's end, more than half the Cambodian population had become refugees, and 13% had been killed or wounded. In the first quarter of 1975, 25% of the soldiers in President Lon Nol's army lost their lives each month. Such staggering attrition was one of the reasons that the anti-Communist government gave in to the Khmer Rouge.

The War. When 1975 began, the Khmer Rouge controlled more than 90% of the nation's territory and 5 million of Cambodia's 8 million inhabitants. The rebels' strategy was to strangle the capital of Phnom Penh, which they partly did by blocking the vital Mekong River water link with South Vietnam. An expanded U. S. airlift brought in both ammunition and food, but a sharply reduced U. S. military-aid program and an increased rate of ammunition depletion doomed the Lon Nol regime to defeat. President Gerald Ford asked the U. S. Congress for $222 million in additional military aid for Cambodia in January, but Congress refused to endorse this request despite the claim that such rejection would lead to a Communist victory.

Whether negotiations would have ended the war earlier—and cost fewer lives—will never be known. But it was revealed in March that U. S. Secretary of State Henry Kissinger turned down a recommendation a year earlier from U. S. Ambassador John Gunther Dean to try to open talks with Communist leader Khieu Samphan. Kissinger apparently felt it was useless to negotiate as long as the Khmer Rouge had the upper hand militarily.

In early April, President Lon Nol fled the country. His leadership in the last year of the war had been indecisive and lacked a purposeful strategy. The refugee-swollen population of Phnom Penh, one of the few areas held by the government, was tired, apathetic, and increasingly opposed to his rule. The strangulation of Phnom Penh, corruption, and military bungling coupled with the persistence and high morale of the Khmer Rouge, all contributed to the regime's fall.

The Takeover. Lon Nol's chief lieutenants, who stayed behind when their leader fled the country, lost their lives almost immediately after the Communists' takeover. Lon Non, the unpopular younger brother of the departed chief of state, was killed by an angry mob, while Premier Long Boret, Prince Sirik Matak, and top military leaders were shot to death by firing squads.

The forced eviction of the population of Phnom Penh occurred immediately after the Khmer Rouge came to power. The city's size had grown from a prewar level of 500,000 to more than 2 million people in the last months of the war. Almost all of them were forced to march into the countryside in the wake of the Communists' takeover. Three months after the defeat of the Lon Nol government, there were reportedly only 50,000 inhabitants of Phnom Penh—mostly soldiers. External observers of the new leadership interpreted the evacuation as a Maoist-style return to an agrarian society. The regime, however, subsequently explained its action as a response to imminent famine in the capital and the greater possibilities for feeding such a large population by moving the people elsewhere in the country.

Politics. Within the collective leadership that took over the country in April, 44-year-old Khieu Samphan was apparently the dominant figure. Reportedly, he had once been ordered executed by Prince Sihanouk. Samphan's top aides, named after an August visit to Phnom Penh by North Vietnamese Communist Party Secretary Le Duan, were Ieng Sary, given primary responsibility for foreign affairs, and Son Sen. Both men were believed to be pro-Hanoi,

and clearly preferred to live abroad. After the visit, reports attributed to Sihanouk's aides claimed that he wept at the sight of the destruction to Phnom Penh and the changes made by the Khmer Rouge. It was also claimed that he believed that the Communists had betrayed him.

According to unconfirmed reports from some of the 8,000 refugees who escaped to neighboring Thailand, armed resistance to Communist rule was continuing late in the year in at least four regions. All reports indicated that life in the country was extremely harsh and that severe punishment, including execution, was meted out to those who refused to obey the Khmer Rouge.

Economy. The economy of Cambodia was ravaged by the war. On the eve of the Communist takeover, there was serious malnutrition in refugee-swollen Phnom Penh and even some deaths from starvation. The once rice-rich country's capital was spared greater hardship by the U. S. airlift of food, primarily rice, in the last months of the war.

The strained state of the economy, especially the dire food shortage, made more credible the new government's claim that it evacuated Phnom Penh to avoid a famine. Forced labor battalions of former urban residents and refugees were subsequently used in a crash effort to grow enough rice and other food.

Foreign Relations. The new Cambodian government proclaimed a foreign policy of "neutrality" and "nonalignment" but concentrated on domestic problems in its first months in power. A May 12 incident in which Cambodian gunboats seized the U. S. freighter *Mayaguez* appeared to have resulted from the initiative of a local command, but the incident was used by the Ford administration for a display of U. S. military power and resolve. The first trip abroad by Khieu Samphan was in August to China, where a joint statement indicated strong support of Peking in its quarrel with the USSR. In October, Ieng Sary visited Bangkok and agreed to establish diplomatic relations with anti-Communist Thailand. (See also feature pages 22–31.)

RICHARD BUTWELL
State University of New York
College at Fredonia

UPI

Soldiers of the Khmer Rouge celebrate the surrender of Phnom Penh to the Communist forces in April.

although Cambodia's foreign policy clearly inclined strongly toward the People's Republic of China.

In September, Prince Sihanouk, an exile in Peking for over five years, returned to the country but stayed only briefly. Khieu Samphan had to travel to North Korea to persuade the prince even to make such a symbolic return. Sihanouk was the titular head of government in the new regime and was given roving-ambassador duties, despite the fact that he was not a Communist

Cambodian President Lon Nol and his wife fled Cambodia in early April. His chief aides were later executed.

UPI

CAMBODIA · Information Highlights

Official Name: The Khmer Republic.
Location: Southeast Asia.
Area: 69,898 square miles (181,035 sq km).
Population (1975 est.): 8,100,000.
Chief Cities (1963 census): Phnom Penh, the capital, 393,995; Battambang, 38,780; Kempong Cham, 28,532.
Government: *Head of State,* Gen. Lon Nol, president (March 1972–April 1975). *Head of government,* Long Boret, premier (Dec. 1973–April 1975). From April 1975 the government was under a collective leadership.
Monetary Unit: Riel (650 riels equal U. S.$1, Feb. 1975).
Gross National Product (1972 est.): $680,000,000.
Manufacturing (major products): Paper, textiles, tobacco products, sawnwood.
Major Agricultural Products: Rice, corn, rubber, beans, sweet potatoes and yams.
Foreign Trade (1972): *Exports,* $15,000,000; *imports,* $98,000,000.

CANADA

Prime Minister Pierre Trudeau met with President Ford in Helsinki during a European security conference in July.

Three provincial elections, none of which indicated federal-provincial accord, and evident weakness in the federal Liberal cabinet reflected the general apprehension that marked Canada in 1975.

Continued labor unrest, the worst unemployment rate since 1959, and the highest rate of inflation since 1952 intensified the pervading sense of uncertainty. These factors led the government of Prime Minister Pierre Trudeau to offer "New Economic Proposals," which included wage and price controls. Internationally, Prime Minister Trudeau continued his efforts to find new markets for Canadian goods.

DOMESTIC AFFAIRS

The Provinces. Late in 1974, Premier Hatfield of New Brunswick led his Progressive Conservatives to a prosaic victory over the Liberals, winning a 33–25 margin in the provincial legislature. The election was marked only by some shift in the French-English vote split. The disturbing element in the election did not occur until two days after the count was completed, when Bricklin Canada Limited, a publicly supported automobile manufacturer, applied to the government for an additional $7 million. Hatfield had campaigned in a Bricklin, and the enterprise was his government's show piece. By October 1975, Bricklin was in receivership. New Brunswick had put $20 million into the venture, owning 64%. The federal government had advanced $3 million in loans.

In April, Premier Lougheed of Alberta led his Progressive Conservatives to a resounding victory over the Social Credit and the New Democrat parties (NDP). The final makeup in the legislature was Progressive Conservatives 69, Social Credit 4, and New Democrat 1. The disturbing element in this election was the strong support given the premier in his quarrels with Ottawa and its implications for interprovincial conflict over the price of oil and gas.

In his December 1974 budget John Turner, the federal minister of finance, denied to oil companies the right to deduct provincial royalties from their federal income taxes. Within the same week the minister of energy announced that an impending shortage of oil would require a reduction in exports. At that point Premier Lougheed of oil-rich Alberta announced that the federal government had voided the agreement of March 1974, and that a rise in the price of oil within Canada was warranted. Shortly thereafter he called the election in which he was strongly supported.

Within two weeks of the confrontation, Atlantic Richfield pulled out of Syncrude, a consortium formed to extract oil from tar sands in northern Alberta. Three of the four other interests involved threatened to follow. Inflating costs were making the project unprofitable in the face of fixed prices, export taxes, and higher royalties. Under this pressure the federal government agreed to an increase in the price of oil, from $6.50 to $8.00 per barrel. Nova

Prime Minister Trudeau announced major changes in his cabinet in September. The shuffle brought in two new ministers and changed the positions of six others.

Scotia, New Brunswick, British Columbia, and Manitoba rallied behind Premier Davis of Ontario to object, and before the increase went into effect in mid-August both Nova Scotia and Ontario had legislated a freeze on gasoline prices.

It was in this situation and in the midst of shock over a 27% hike in rents that Premier Davis called a fall election in Ontario. In the previous election Davis' Progressive Conservative (PC) party had won 74 of the 117 seats, and the Liberals were the official opposition. In the September election, the PC won 51 of the 125 seats in the new legislature, the New Democrats (NDP) 38, and the Liberals 36. The NDP members were the official opposition. The result confounded analysis and expectation.

While Ontario was surprising the nation with evidence of voter unrest, Newfoundland surprised no one with the same sort of evidence. Progressive Conservative (PC) Frank Moores called an election that virtually coincided with Ontario's. Inflation was running at 10.6% in St. John's, and unemployment was 15%. The federal government was hesitating over action to reduce foreign fishing on the Grand Banks, particularly by Russian trawlers.

The precise timing of the election, however, was determined by Joey Smallwood's reappearance in politics. Smallwood, who had guided Newfoundland into confederation in 1949, had retired when defeated by Moores' Conservatives in 1972. At a subsequent leadership convention he confounded his former colleagues by his attempt to regain the leadership. When he failed, he formed his own Liberal Reform party.

In 1972 the PC's had gained 32 seats to the Liberals' 8, but since then 9 additional seats had been added to the assembly. The count in August gave the PC's 30, the regular Liberals

16, and Smallwood's Liberals 4. Frank Moores took his victory as a basis for attack on federal policies with respect to inflation, offshore oil, and fishing. He suggested that if there was no action the province would consider secession.

In British Columbia the New Democratic government of David Barrett, by Barrett's own admission, had moved ahead of the voters into guaranteed incomes, free drugs, higher resource

THE CANADIAN MINISTRY
(According to precedence, December 1975)

Pierre Elliott Trudeau, Prime Minister
Mitchell W. Sharp, President of the Queen's Privy Council for Canada
Allan J. MacEachen, Secretary of State for External Affairs
Charles M. Drury, Minister of State for Science and Technology; Minister of Public Works
Jean Marchand, Minister without Portfolio
Jean Chrétien, President of the Treasury Board
Bryce S. Mackasey, Postmaster General
Donald S. Macdonald, Minister of Finance
John C. Munro, Minister of Labour
Stanley R. Basford, Minister of Justice; Attorney General of Canada
Donald C. Jamieson, Minister of Industry, Trade and Commerce
Robert K. Andras, Minister of Manpower and Immigration
James A. Richardson, Minister of National Defence
Otto E. Lang, Minister of Transport
Jean-Pierre Goyer, Minister of Supply and Services
Alastair W. Gillespie, Minister of Energy, Mines and Resources
Eugene F. Whelan, Minister of Agriculture
W. Warren Allmand, Solicitor General of Canada
James H. Faulkner, Secretary of State of Canada
André Ouellet, Minister of Consumer and Corporate Affairs
Daniel J. MacDonald, Minister of Veterans Affairs
Marc Lalonde, Minister of National Health and Welfare
Jeanne Sauvé, Minister of the Environment
Raymond J. Perrault, Leader of the Government in the Senate
Barnett J. Danson, Minister of State for Urban Affairs
J. Judd Buchanan, Minister of Indian Affairs and Northern Development
Roméo LeBlanc, Minister of State (Fisheries)
Jeanne Sauvé, Minister of Communications
Marcel Lessard, Minister of Regional Economic Expansion
Jack S. Cullen, Minister of National Revenue

royalties, and public ownership of pulpmills and realty companies. Increasing opposition began to crystallize in June when William Bennett, son of former Premier Bennett, once again tried to rally the support of PC's and Liberals under the Social Credit banner in an attempt to defeat the socialists. In September the province was hit by a number of serious strikes. Sugar refinery workers, meat cutters, and bakers in supermarkets in Vancouver; two pulp unions; workers in the government-owned insurance corporation; and the United Fishermen and Allied Workers all went out on strike. From September through December an additional 182 contracts had to be negotiated for 123,763 workers. Wage increases were averaging 18.9%.

In October, Premier Barrett legislated an end to all strikes and a return to bargaining, for a minimum of 90 days. The labor unions that had played an important role in electing the NDP declared that they had been betrayed. The election was announced November 2, but it had not been held by the end of the year.

National Politics. General unrest at the provincial level appeared at the federal level in an evident crumbling of the Liberal cabinet. Both in December 1974 and in April 1975 it appeared that Finance Minister John Turner was not getting his own way in the formation of the budget. Early in the spring he successfully insisted that a group of eminent economists who had been meeting with Prime Minister Trudeau cease their deliberations. It was a further attack on the once-burgeoning prime minister's office. Within the same month top aide Simon Reisman resigned, allegedly because the regular departments were being ignored in policy formation.

In March news broke of a multi-million dollar, bid-rigging scandal. Harbor dredging companies from Hamilton to Quebec were involved, and prominent families in Toronto and Montreal were implicated. John Munro, minister of labour and member of parliament for Hamilton, came under such severe attack that he was forced to offer his resignation. The prime minister refused to accept it. About this time there were mounting scandals surrounding the Liberal regime in Quebec and the controversy over Bill 22. The bill limits English education in Quebec to those who are fluent in English, and the controversy made the position of the leader of the Quebec caucus extremely difficult. The ailing minister of transport, Jean Marchand, was replaced by Marc Lalonde.

Cabinet changes did eventually come. In September, Gerard Pelletier, minister of communications, resigned. He was replaced by Pierre Juneau, former head of the Canadian Radio and Television Commission. The replacement reflected an intense conflict between Quebec and Ottawa over jurisdiction in the field of cable television. Pelletier became Canada's ambassador to France, while Juneau failed to get elected to the House of Commons. Early in November his cabinet post was given to Jeanne Sauvé, minister of the environment.

The major shift came when Minister of Finance Turner finally resigned in mid-September. By early October the most controversial position in the cabinet had changed hands. Alastair Gillespie was shifted to energy, mines, and resources, replacing Donald Macdonald, who became the new minister of finance. Donald Jamieson took industry, trade, and commerce, replacing Gillespie. This left the ministry of regional economic expansion open. It went to a newcomer, Marcel Lessard. Jean Marchand was taken out of transport, but he was kept in the cabinet without portfolio. Transport then went to Otto Lang, who left the justice portfolio open for Stanley R. Basford. Basford, in

UPI

Quebec Federation of Labour president Louis Laberge called a special meeting in May to force a settlement of a 17-month strike at the Pratt and Whitney Co. aircraft plant.

THE CANADIAN ECONOMY

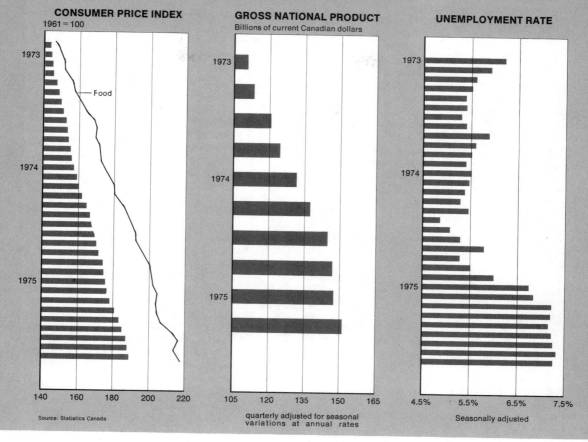

CONSUMER PRICE INDEX
1961 = 100

Food

Source: Statistics Canada

GROSS NATIONAL PRODUCT
Billions of current Canadian dollars

quarterly adjusted for seasonal
variations at annual rates

UNEMPLOYMENT RATE

Seasonally adjusted

turn, was replaced as minister of national revenue by Jack Cullen, another newcomer.

Trudeau, Marchand, and Pelletier, who had entered the Liberal government in the mid-1960's, when separatism was the most important issue, were clearly losing their reputations for wisdom as economic issues came to the fore. Otto Lang's removal from justice relieved some tensions related to the abortion issue; Lang opposed abortion. The removal of John Turner opened the door to new economic programs.

The Economy. Much of the difficulty leading to the restructuring of the cabinet was economic. Turner's late 1974 budget had been predicated on a greater fear of depression than of inflation. Taxes were cut, and a deficit of $1.5 billion was projected in the hope of keeping unemployment down and real growth up to 4%. Steps were taken to get a "wage-price consensus" to keep inflation below 10%. When December figures came in, however, overall unemployment was down to 5.5%, seasonally adjusted, but inflation was at 12%, and a weakness in exports existed.

In January, Parliament began debate on its own pay raise, which eventually went over 50%. Perhaps this encouraged inflation elsewhere, but inflation seemed to need no encouragement. In January unemployment ran at 6.7%, seasonally adjusted. About 817,000 were out of work,

more than at any time since the 1930's. Inflation continued at an annual rate of 12.1%, and textiles joined copper in suffering from a world glut. By April inflation had abated to a 7% annual rate, but unemployment was up to a seasonally-adjusted 7.2%. Worst of all, the economy was clearly heading for zero real growth in 1975.

In the face of clear proof that prices were outstripping wages, labor became aggressive. Wage settlements ran at 17.4% annually, in the first quarter of the year. Wage-rate increases were twice those in the United States, and exports were reduced as prices of Canadian goods rose in foreign markets. West coast grain handlers got a 61% wage increase, and by October postal workers were demanding 71%. Failure to satisfy the postal workers led to a crippling national postal strike in the late fall. In mid-June it was reported that real gross national product (GNP) was down 1.4% in the first quarter of the year. Housing starts were down 25%–45%. When Turner's second budget was finally passed in early summer, it included a record deficit of $3.7 billion. By September the rate of unemployment was still over 7%, and inflation was still over 10%. The trade-off had become intolerable. Real GNP was predicted to shrink 2% by the year's end.

Olympic Montreal

The games of the XXI Olympiad will be staged in Montreal, the Canadian metropolis, from July 17 to August 1, 1976. Montreal is the first Canadian, and only the fourth North American, city to host the Olympics.

Facilities. The focal point of the main competition site is Olympic Park. This 125-acre (50-hectare) park contains the stadium-pool-tower complex. The tower is 18 stories high and provides all the space required for systematic training activities in a variety of sports prior to the Games.

The stadium itself accommodates 70,000 spectators in stands constructed to guarantee unencumbered visibility of all events from any part of the stadium. Following the Olympics, the stadium will be reduced in size to hold 50,000 spectators and will be used by the Montreal Expos baseball team.

The Olympic program includes all 21 sports approved by the International Olympic Committee. Archery, athletics (track and field), basketball, boxing, canoeing, cycling, equestrian, fencing, gymnastics, judo, handball, field hockey, modern pentathlon, rowing, shooting, soccer, swimming, volleyball, weightlifting, wrestling, and yachting will be represented.

Because a large number of events are scheduled, additional facilities outside the main park will accommodate some activities. Yachting will be held at a new yacht basin in Kingston. There is a man-made rowing and canoeing course on an island in the St. Lawrence River and an archery field at Joliette. Construction costs for the main Games site and for the various Olympic facilities outside the park approached $1 billion in 1975.

An apartment complex, dubbed Olympic Village and located across the street from Olympic Park, has been erected to house some 9,000 participating athletes. Accommodations for the 125,000 additional guests expected to visit the city each day are also being built. The Olympic Committee has also arranged for guests to stay in private homes.

Problems. In addition to the massive construction expense, over $60 million will be spent on security during the Games. The high cost of security reflects one of the problems of the 1976 Olympics: the politicization of the Games and the growth of international terrorism. Officials are determined to prevent a repetition of the terrorism at the 1972 Olympic Games in Munich.

Despite rising inflation, which has more than doubled initial construction and administration costs, Mayor Jean Drapeau of Montreal has vowed the Olympics will eventually pay for themselves. Sources of revenue include a national lottery, admission tickets, television money, and Olympic postage stamps and coins. Estimated revenues rose beyond expectations, but the projected deficit was nearly $500 million. Mayor Drapeau's opponents complained loudly that the money spent on the Olympics should have been spent on housing the city's poor.

The City of Montreal remained optimistic that the construction on the complex would be completed ahead of schedule. However, labor strikes and work stoppages at the site continued to push construction costs upward. Fears that the Games were jeopardized led the province of Quebec to take over the main stadium's financing from the city on November 14.

For all its troubles the city remains physically clean and attractive in a sparkling sort of way that few others can match. The largest French-speaking city outside of France, and one of the oldest in North America, it has an irresistible, cosmopolitan charm. Like earlier international expositions in the city, however, the 1976 Olympics will probably be another great Montreal party with an inevitable economic and perhaps political hangover.

R. F. NEILL

The roof of the shield-shaped Olympic Velodrome is one of the striking features of the Olympic Games site in Montreal. Olympic competitions are scheduled to begin July 17, 1976.

The new Montreal International Airport at Mirabel is the largest in the world and is planned to accommodate expansion well into the 21st century.

Under these circumstances Minister of Finance Turner resigned. The cabinet was reshuffled and the government produced what was in substance a modified, two-year wage and price control program called the New Economic Proposals. By law, neither wages nor prices were to move much more than 10%.

Supreme Court Notes. The Supreme Court upheld Prince Edward Island's legislation controlling land sales to aliens. It overturned an inferior court jury decison in favor of abortionist Dr. Henry Morgentaller of Montreal. Quebec's Bill 22, limiting the rights of Quebec citizens, particularly non-English-speaking immigrants, to attend English schools, was challenged and appealed to the Supreme Court.

FOREIGN AFFAIRS

The problem of the Canadian economy was reflected in the nation's relations with the outside world. Prime Minister Trudeau continued his diplomatic tour of the European Economic Community in February and March 1975. His aim was to achieve a special relation with Europe in the hope of exporting more manufactured goods. One result of these efforts was a cessation in the reduction of Canadian forces in Europe, despite a January reduction in the military-manpower ceiling from 83,000 to 78,000. At the Law of the Sea conference held March 17–May 9, Canada continued to press for a 200-mile (320-km) economic zone in coastal waters. In line with this policy, the federal government closed Newfoundland ports to Russian shipping in late summer, pending assurances that certain types of fishing on the Grand Banks would cease.

U. S. Relations. Late in the fall U. S. Secretary of State Henry Kissinger made an official visit to Canada. He announced that a special relationship no longer existed between Canada and the United States. His statement meant that in discussions between Canada and the United States, there would be no prior commitment to agree on anything. Canada had been pressing for such a statement for more than a year.

R. F. NEILL, *Carleton University*

CANADA · Information·Highlights

Official Name: Canada.
Location: Northern North America.
Area: 3,851,809 square miles (9,976,185 sq km).
Population (1975 est.): 22,737,000,000.
Chief Cities (1971 census): Ottawa, the capital, 302,341; Montreal, 1,214,352; Toronto, 712,786; Edmonton, 438,152.
Government: *Head of state,* Elizabeth II, queen; represented by Jules Léger, governor general (took office Jan. 1974). *Head of government,* Pierre Elliott Trudeau, prime minister (took office April 1968). *Legislature*—Parliament: Senate and House of Commons.
Monetary Unit: Canadian dollar (1.0228 C. dollars equal U. S.$1, May 1975).
Gross National Product (2d quarter 1975 est.): $150,300,000,000.
Manufacturing (major products): Pulp and paper, petroleum products, iron and steel, motor vehicles, aircraft, machinery, aluminum, chemicals.
Major Agricultural Products: Wheat, barley, oats, rye, potatoes, fish, forest products, livestock, furs.
Foreign Trade (1974): *Exports,* $32,177,000,000; *imports,* $31,639,000,000.

CANADA: CULTURAL AFFAIRS

Either by accident or design International Women's Year illuminated the fact that women have been and are a fundamental factor in Canada's artistic growth and development. The evidence poured in throughout 1975. It came in books and magazine articles and newspaper features; in biographical studies and public awards and television broadcasts; in exhibitions and in concerts. It showed the influence of Canadian women in literature, drama, art, music, and dance, both as creators and as animators. The acknowledgment and tribute was seen in all media and in concert halls, theaters, and studios. In retrospect, it was a significant aspect in Canada's 1975 cultural year.

The Economy and the Arts. 1975 was also the year when the Canadian artistic community had to admit, reluctantly, that the country's inflationary spiral and economic recession had affected the arts. In the years following Canada's centennial celebrations of 1967, public and private support for the arts was very generous. The right to be subsidized substantially had become an article of faith with cultural creators, performers, and administrators. But throughout 1975 reports from every quarter made it clear that the combination of box-office income, government subsidies, and grants from the private sector could not keep pace with the rising costs of operation.

Many cultural leaders failed to get the message and demanded greater help from various levels of governments. In October the Canada Council, the official benefactor of the arts, took a firm position. The unequivocal message was, "Tighten your belts until further notice." A new trend set in. By year's end a revised, realistic attitude toward budgeting and management in the arts was a fact of life.

Cultural Exchange. In every part of Canada warm approval greeted an announcement that the federal government intended to send a two-week arts festival to Washington, D. C., in October, as a neighborly gesture to help the United States celebrate its Bicentennial. The program included presentations by the Shaw Festival Company, the Royal Winnipeg Ballet, the National Arts Centre orchestra, the Toronto Mendelssohn Choir, the Canadian Brass, and the Neptune Theatre. There were also concert appearances by jazz pianist Oscar Peterson and singers Monique Leyrac, Maureen Forrester, and Louis Quillico. Concerned Canadians were nervously interested in what the reactions might be. The U. S. critics were perceptive and objective, and the U. S. audiences loved the programs. Canadians were happy because their gift was enthusiastically received.

Music. It was another good year for Canadian music, with a surprising explosion of folk and country performances stealing the headlines. Canada's traditional devotion to all forms of music was evident in the country's wholehearted participation in International Music Week (September 26–October 5) in Calgary, Montreal, Ottawa, Quebec, and Toronto. The events were guided by Yehudi Menuhin, president of the world-based Music Council.

Symphony orchestras in Canada enjoyed a good artistic season, but the joys of musical success were largely offset by the pains of financial hardship. The Canadian Opera Company had the biggest and best season of its 25-year history, but still finished with a financial deficit. Smaller orchestras and opera companies with more elastic budgets were happier.

Visual Arts. Public interest in the visual arts slipped badly from its 1974 peak of enthusiasm. Probably the lapse was due to Canada's economic recession. Of great attraction was a federally sponsored exhibit of Canadian paintings,

ROBERT C. RAGSDALE

Caesar and Cleopatra was featured at the Shaw Festival in Ontario during the fall of 1975.

prints, and sculpture depicting athletic events and personalities. The aim of the exhibition, which visited 30 Canadian and 4 U. S. cities and drew about 10 million viewers, was to stimulate interest in the 1976 Olympic Games in Montreal.

One local show of exceptional merit was the First Visual Arts Survey Exhibition by artists working in the Ottawa River valley, an area that had often been overlooked. The National Art Gallery's retrospective exhibition of works by the Canadian Group-of-Seven painter Edwin Holgate was one of the few truly outstanding shows of the year.

It seems likely that 1975 will be remembered as the year when the Stratford Festival's well-established excellence was suddenly transformed from traditional to modern, through the skill

Director Robin Phillips' staging of *Measure For Measure* was a highlight of the 1975 Stratford Festival.

of a new artistic director, Robin Phillips. The young Englishman's fresh interpretations, great enthusiasm, stubborn methods, and boundless dedication amazed and delighted the critics and audiences. Nearly half the customers were visitors from the United States.

Theater. In many ways it was a vintage year for theater throughout Canada. Well-attended summer and winter seasons were enjoyed by Halifax's Neptune, Vancouver's Holiday, Winnipeg's Theatre Centre, Montreal's English-language Centaur, and Toronto's Workshop Productions. An interesting and newsworthy event was the 10,000-mile (16,000-km), 4-week tour of far-Arctic communities by the Canadian Puppet Festival Company. Voice production was presented both in Inuit and English.

Ballet. In addition to its prestigious appearance in the Washington, D. C., bicentennial program, the Royal Winnipeg Ballet enjoyed a 10-week tour of U. S. cities. Meanwhile, Toronto's National Ballet Company did a cross-country tour of Canada and a two week stint in New York City. The other major ballet company in Canada, Les Grands Ballets Canadiens, stayed close to home in Montreal and added a stunning new *Romeo and Juliet* to its repertoire.

The smaller companies, emphasizing contemporary dance concepts and techniques, continued to attract a growing share of the Canadian box-office receipts. These companies also attracted noteworthy financial support from both the public and private sectors, despite the general trend to reduce subsidies. An unusual event in the dance world was the commissioning by the Vancouver Art Gallery of *Klee Wyck,* a small modern ballet dedicated as an International Women's Year tribute to the memory of Emily Carr, British Columbia's great artist. The work was first performed in July by the Anna Wymen Dance Theatre.

Radio and Television. From the beginning of radio and television broadcasting activity in Canada, the federal government has exercised constitutional control. During 1975, however, the cultural aspects of broadcasting were only occasionally matters of public interest, while the national government's control of the use of the air channels was seriously challenged by provincial governments and commercial interests. The province of Quebec, engaged in an increasingly bitter promotion of French language rights, regarded control of broadcasting within its boundaries as essential to the province's "cultural sovereignty." Several bizarre incidents involving federal and Quebec police forces and related to cable television occurred during the year. It seemed likely that the situation would become worse in the near future and that the problems would have to be resolved by the Supreme Court of Canada.

WALTER B. HERBERT

CAPE VERDE

On June 5, 1975, Cape Verde became independent. The president of the republic, Aristides Pereira, and the prime minister, Pedro Pires, were both veterans of the liberation struggle in Guinea-Bissau. Although the new state was seated in the United Nations, it pledged to achieve unity between the two territories, possibly modeled on Tanzania, the union between Tanganyika and Zanzibar. Since both countries are ruled by the same party, PAIGC (African Party for the Independence of Guinea and Cape Verde), this should prove relatively easy. The new Cape Verde government pledged that it would never permit a foreign power to use Portugal's naval installations and air base on the islands, a declaration intended to reassure both the United States and the Soviet Union. Meanwhile, there was little hope for immediate improvement of the near-catastrophic economic situation on the drought-stricken islands.

Portugal had administered Cape Verde, a group of 12 islands, and Guinea-Bissau together. Cape Verdeans working in Guinea-Bissau organized PAIGC for the purpose of liberating both areas. Portugal recognized Guinea-Bissau's independence on Sept. 10, 1974, but the fate of Cape Verde remained undetermined. A transitional government consisting of three Portuguese and three PAIGC members was set up on Dec. 30, 1974, and ruled until independence.

EDOUARD BUSTIN, *Boston University*

CARIBBEAN

There is emerging in the Caribbean a series of changes that may have a lasting effect on the region. Some, like the change in the weather pattern, are beyond man's control, but others are man-made, like the changes brought about by the rising importance of oil-producing nations or the political changes from a colonial status to independence. These changes were all evident in 1975.

Weather. For the third straight year extensive drought conditions affected most of the Caribbean from January to September. A cloud of fine sand from the Sahara Desert covered an extensive part of the Caribbean on several occasions during 1975, repeating a phenomenon that was noticed by meteorologists in 1973 and 1974. The clouds, which vary in density and altitude, prevent the full effect of the rays of the sun from reaching the surface of the sea, and thus lessen the chances of rain for the islands of the Caribbean.

The drought, which caused a decline in the agricultural production of Puerto Rico, Jamaica, Cuba, and many of the other northern islands of the Caribbean, had a devastating effect on Haiti. There, some 350,000 rural inhabitants of the northern peninsula suffered severe famine. In mid-July the United Nations announced that $1.3 million in food would be sent to the starving Haitians.

As in previous years, when the rains finally came to the region, the torrential downpours caused extensive property destruction and even loss of life.

Although tropical storms still caused hundreds of millions of dollars of damage (as tropical storm Eloise did in Puerto Rico and the Dominican Republic), they no longer seem to be accompanied by winds of hurricane force. Only when the storms move from the Caribbean over the warmer waters of the Gulf of Mexico do the winds build up to hurricane strength. This is not to suggest that hurricanes will no longer occur in the Caribbean, but rather that a changing weather pattern is noticeable.

Regional Economic Activity. Two oil-producing nations, Mexico and Venezuela, turned their attention to the Caribbean region in 1975. In January, Mexico entered into an agreement with Jamaica for closer trade ties and joint economic ventures. This agreement was implemented specifically by the establishment in Mexico of a binational company to produce 90,000 tons of aluminum annually.

In April, after an exchange of visits between President Carlos Andrés Pérez of Venezuela and Prime Minister Michael Manley of Jamaica, an agreement was announced for the establishment of joint economic ventures. In exchange for oil, delivered on a cash-loan basis similar to the arrangement with some Central American states, Venezuela will receive bauxite for a new aluminum smelter located on the banks of the Orinoco River. Venezuela has already entered into joint agreements with Surinam and Guyana to secure bauxite. Venezuela will also invest 20% of the capital necessary for the construction of the 900,000-ton alumina plant in Jamaica that will supply part of its output to the Mexican-Jamaican aluminum plant.

In April, Mexico and Venezuela brought together in San Jose, Costa Rica, representatives from 17 Central American and Caribbean countries to work out an agreement for the establishment of a Caribbean merchant fleet. It would serve the internal transportation needs of the region. Representatives from Cuba, the Dominican Republic, Jamaica, Barbados, and Trinidad-Tobago signed the preliminary agreement.

Although much of this economic activity centers around agreements with Jamaica, Venezuela also explored joint economic and cultural ventures with Barbados, Antigua, and Grenada. In June, for example, Venezuela agreed to establish a cultural center in Bridgetown, Barbados.

The possible adverse effect of such economic activity on the regional economic institutions and on Caribbean economic cooperation was suggested by Prime Minister Eric Williams of Trinidad-Tobago. In June he warned the rest of the Caribbean that he feared that Venezuela was trying to "recolonize" the Caribbean. In the light of the new agreements with Mexico and Venezuela, he questioned the wisdom of proceeding with the previous agreement between Guyana, Jamaica, and Trinidad for the establishment of an alumina smelter plant on the southern coast of Trinidad. Plans for the plant, which was to have used Trinidad's supply of natural gas for power, presumably at reduced rates, may have been reconsidered for reasons other than those stated by Prime Minister Williams. At any rate, Venezuela strengthened the Caribbean Development Bank through the sizable assignment of $40 million.

In another area, Mexico took the initiative in April to bring together in Puerto Plata, Dominican Republic, the representatives of 22 sugar-producing nations in Latin America and the Caribbean. The objective of the meeting was to reach an agreement among the sugar-producing nations of the new world to stabilize and strengthen world sugar prices. The meeting met with only modest success in an agreement to work for a minimum price of 20 cents a pound for raw or unrefined sugar. No production limitations were established, but it was agreed that a central statistical bureau would be set up in Mexico City to facilitate the exchange of information concerning international sugar production and prices.

The Caribbean Common Market announced the formation of an $8.4 million food corporation designed to reduce the annual $525 million food import costs. The corporation will establish two multinational farms in the region, one in

TRINIDAD & TOBAGO INDUSTRIAL DEVELOPMENT CORP.

UNITED NATIONS—KING

Trinidad's gas and oil and Jamaica's bauxite figured in Caribbean joint ventures in 1975.
Left, refinery at Pointe-à-Pierre, Trinidad; *right,* bauxite plant at Spalding, Jamaica.

Guyana to be owned and operated jointly with Trinidad-Tobago and the other to be established in Belize and operated jointly with Jamaica. Both farms will concentrate on raising maize, soya, and red kidney beans.

As a result of an agreement by which the European Economic Community consented to give substantial financial support to the third world nations, the Caribbean Development Bank expected to receive approximately $360 million. Through the bank the members of the Caribbean Common Market would benefit.

The Lesser Antilles. Elections were held in two islands of the Lesser Antilles. In Dominica the Democratic Labour party, which had controlled the island government for the last 15 years, retained power by electing 16 of the 21 members of the legislature. On the island of St. Vincent, the Labor party turned out of office the People's Progressive party by winning 10 of the 13 seats in the legislature. The new premier, Milton Cato, promised to work for complete independence for the island.

The report of the Constitutional Commission of the West Indian Associated States recommended in March 1975 that "the Leeward and Windward Islands should proceed to independence and enter into a scheme of constitutional association for the purpose of functioning as a single entity in their relations with other states in international bodies."

Grenada, in its second year of independence in 1975, continued to face severe economic problems. British financial support of the new nation was suspended pending clarification of the use of some £250,000, which Great Britain claimed was misused.

Labor unrest disturbed an otherwise bright economic picture in Trinidad. About 8,000 oil workers striking for higher wages were joined by 15,000 sugar workers in a jurisdictional strike. To complicate matters, both water and light facilities were cut off, allegedly because of technical breakdowns, putting the island in a state of chaos for two weeks in March.

Press Freedom. At an October meeting in Brazil, the Inter-American Press Association (IAPA) singled out Antigua, Grenada, St. Kitts, St. Vincent, Trinidad-Tobago, and the Bahamas as countries in the Caribbean where freedom of the press was being threatened by government action. The IAPA recognized that freedom of the press was absent from the Caribbean countries of Cuba, Haiti, and Guyana.

Surinam. Although geographically part of the South American continent, Surinam is culturally an integral part of the Caribbean region. On November 25 the Netherlands granted full independence to this multiracial community of approximately 360,000 people.

THOMAS G. MATHEWS
University of Puerto Rico

UPI

William Maillaird (*left*), U. S. ambassador to the Organization of American States (OAS), talks with Mexican officials during the OAS meeting in Costa Rica in July.

CENTRAL AMERICA

In 1975 a planned invasion of the British Colony of Belize by Guatemala, bribery of Honduran government officials, which triggered a coup d'etat, and an outbreak of guerrilla warfare in Nicaragua highlighted a year of turbulence in Central America.

Guatemala-Belize. The most dangerous situation to develop in Central America in 1975 occurred in early November when Guatemalan troops massed on the border of Belize (formerly British Honduras), a small semi-independent British colony that Guatemala claims as its territory. Since World War II, the Guatemalan military has threatened Belize on a number of occasions, most recently in 1972. In early 1972 the Guatemalan army had planned to invade and capture the colony, which has a population of only 140,000, but British reinforcements poured into Belize and the Guatemalan army stopped.

A similar situation developed on November 5 when in London an official government spokesman announced that "because of increased Guatemalan military activity near the Belizian border, the British government has reluctantly decided that it has no alternative but to increase the small British garrison." The British response was triggered by intelligence reports that more than 1,000 Guatemalan troops, along with 10 armored personnel carriers, had been detected moving toward the border in northern Guatemala. The British response was prompt. To beef up the 650-man garrison maintained in

Belize, C-130 transports flew in additional troops and munitions. In addition, the British Navy frigate *Zulu* was deployed along the Belizian coast, and Royal Air Force jet fighters flew into Belize International Airport to provide air cover.

Authoritative sources in Central America said the Guatemalan invasion plan called for an airborne assault on Belize International Airport by an armored assault down the central highway that runs from the Guatemalan border past the new Belizian capital of Belmopan to Belize City, on the coast. By late November, the Guatemalan government, which apparently was testing the willingness of the British to continue defending the colony, had begun negotiations with British and Mexican diplomats.

Also in November, Belizian Premier George Price for the first time presented a budget to the colony's House of Assembly, which appropriated $1.5 million for "strengthening and improving" security. Apparently the funds were to be used to form a small Belizian army. At present Belize has a 400-man paramilitary group, the Police Special Force, and a 300-man national volunteer guard.

In the United Nations the Fourth Committee, or Committee on Trust and Non-Self-Governing Territories, approved a resolution sponsored by some 60 countries calling for the right of self-determination for Belize. By December, sources in Belize reported that some Guatemalan troops were being withdrawn from the tense border area.

Honduras. Political unrest marked the year

Col. Juan Melgar Castro succeeded Gen. Oswaldo López Arellano as chief of state in Honduras after a bloodless coup in April.

UPI

for this small nation, which was attempting to recover from the greatest natural disaster in its history, 1974's Hurricane Fifi. In April, the U. S. Securities and Exchange Commission accused a U. S. firm, United Brands, of paying a $1.25 million bribe to Honduran President Oswaldo López Arellano and former Economic Minister Abraham Bennaton. United Brands, one of the largest purchasers of Honduran bananas, reportedly paid the bribe in a successful effort to reduce the export tax.

Following the disclosure, the Honduran army in a bloodless coup d'etat deposed López Arellano (who was also chief of the armed forces) on April 22, with Col. Juan Melgar Castro replacing him as president. Two months later, 29 ranking Honduran army officers were forced to retire, in a drive to end corruption in the military. Compounding the situation was a series of clashes between landless peasants and wealthy landowners backed by the army. In June peasants fought with army units in eastern Honduras, and 15 persons were killed, including a U. S. priest.

Nicaragua. For four decades the Somoza family has ruled Nicaragua as a personal fiefdom with only occasional opposition, but the year 1975 dawned inauspiciously for the current chief executive, President Anastasio Somoza. On Dec. 27, 1974 guerrillas of the Frente Sandinista de Liberacional Nacional in a spectacular raid had invaded a Christmas party honoring U. S. Ambassador Turner B. Sheldon and seized 35 hostages. Three days later, in return for a $1 million ransom and the release of

14 political prisoners, the hostages, including Foreign Minister Alejandro Montiel Arguello, were released. The guerrillas were given free passage by air to Cuba. Subsequently, President Somoza declared a state of siege, suspending constitutional guarantees, and in January he ordered the creation of a special 8,000-man counterinsurgency unit.

Despite efforts by the Nicaraguan military to suppress the guerrillas, by August it was apparent to observers that the Sandinista guerrillas were growing numerically and that the clandestine group was receiving support from landowners in the mountainous areas where it was operating. The same month the government reported that 7 rebels had been killed in a clash with the National Guard; unofficial reports indicated that 15 government troops were casualties in the same encounter.

In late summer President Somoza announced that the state of siege would remain in effect indefinitely.

Costa Rica. The year 1975 began with shortages of basic foods such as powdered milk, sugar, and cooking oil, which created momentary panic among the citizenry in January. In addition, Costa Rica had entered the new year having recorded in 1974 the largest trade deficit in the nation's history, $385 million.

Public attention during much of 1975 was focused on the presence in Costa Rica of Robert L. Vesco, a U. S. businessman sought in the United States on criminal charges stemming from a large illegal campaign contribution to former President Richard Nixon and on civil

--- **CENTRAL AMERICA**—Information Highlights ---

Nation	Population (in millions)	Area (in sq mi)	Capital	Head of State and Government
Costa Rica	2.0	19,575	San José	Daniel Oduber Quirós, president
El Salvador	3.9	8,260	San Salvador	Arturo Armando Molina, president
Guatemala	5.6	42,042	Guatemala City	Gen. Kjell Laugerud García, president
Honduras	3.0	43,277	Tegucigalpa	Col. Juan Melgar Castro, president
Nicaragua	2.2	50,193	Managua	Anastasio Somoza, president

charges by the Securities and Exchange Commission, in which he was accused of diverting to himself $227 million in mutual funds. Despite widespread political opposition to Vesco's residence in the country, President Daniel Oduber Quirós stoutly insisted that there were no legal grounds to deport him. Vesco had reportedly invested millions of dollars in Costa Rican government bonds and real estate shortly after his arrival and had close financial ties with former Costa Rican President José "Pepe" Figueres.

El Salvador. Compared with its neighbors, El Salvador experienced a relatively quiet year. The Inter-American Press Association, which held a semiannual meeting of its board of directors in March in El Salvador, noted that the host country was "one of the few Latin nations that enjoys real freedom of expression and of the press."

In common with other Central American governments, El Salvador uncovered bribery in official ranks during 1975, but on a much smaller scale than other nations. The government learned in May that a U. S. grain company executive had distributed $15,500 in bribes to two Salvadorean government officials to obtain permission to illegally ship 14,000 tons of South African grain to El Salvador. Economically, El Salvador obtained a larger beef quota from United States, harvested a sugar crop about 10% larger than the 1974 crop, and signed commercial treaties with the Soviet Union, Bulgaria, South Korea, and the United States.

LOUIS R. SADLER
New Mexico State University

CEYLON. See SRI LANKA.

CHEMISTRY

By 1975 it was apparent that the problems created by chemicals in the environment would claim attention from all segments of society for years to come. The topic was sufficiently newsworthy for the Columbia Broadcasting System to present two hour-long telecasts on the topic, one on drinking water and the other on cancer-producing chemicals in the environment.

The Atmosphere. The National Academy of Sciences issued a report, "Atmospheric Chemistry—Problems and Scope," in which it was pointed out that only 10 to 20 qualified atmospheric chemists were working in this field and that few academic departments offer training courses in atmospheric chemistry. The academy noted further that insufficient knowledge of the chemistry of the atmosphere has led to erroneous conclusions, overreaction, and inefficient approaches to policy development. Therefore, the academy recommended that basic research should be expanded so that potential problems can be addressed before they reach crisis proportions.

In 1975 public controversy over fluorocarbons flared anew. These compounds, including CCl_2F_2 and CCl_3F, are used as refrigerants and as propellants for aerosol sprays. The stakes were high. On the one hand was the prosperity of the fluorcarbon and allied industries and the jobs they provided, together with consumer demand for refrigeration and aerosol sprays. On the other hand, according to some scientists, was the survival of life on Earth. It was proposed that because of the widespread use of fluorocarbons, they are reaching the stratosphere, where they liberate chlorine, a gas that converts ozone to oxygen. This means that the stratospheric ozone layer that filters out lethal ultraviolet rays from the sun is being depleted, according to this view.

Opponents countered that this was a hypothesis unsupported by hard experimental data. However, scientists at the National Oceanic and Atmospheric Administration sent balloons aloft to gather air samples, which, when analyzed with gas chromatography, showed concentrations and vertical distributions of fluorocarbons similar to those predicted. Also, the scientists could find no reactions that could prevent chlorine from decomposing ozone. Even before this study was reported, Oregon had banned the sale of fluorocarbon-propelled sprays, effective in 1977, and Nevada had announced that it would no longer purchase such sprays.

Atmospheric pollutants detected for the first time were nitrosoamines, known to cause cancer in laboratory animals. They were found in less than one part per billion over two industrial cities, but tests over three others were negative. Whether these concentrations represent high, low, or average values was not established, and the sources of the chemicals were unknown. They might stem from industrial processes or from reactions of nitrogen oxides with airborne amines from natural or industrial sources.

Toxic Substances. The National Institute of Occupational Safety and Health estimated that of 250,000 chemicals in use, 1,500 had been identified as having potential tumorigenic, neoplastic, or carcinogenic activity in laboratory animals. However, environmental health standards have been established for only 700.

Congressional action on three bills concerning control of toxic substances bogged down over the issue of premarket testing of new chemicals. In dispute were three bills. One proposed that all new chemicals should be tested; another that only those considered by the Environmental Protection Agency to pose unreasonable risks to health or environment should be tested; and a third, that only those that pose substantial danger should be tested. The American Chemical Society (ACS) supported the second measure, but the Manufacturing Chemists Association opposed it.

Polyvinyl Chloride. The Food and Drug Administration (FDA) proposed a ban on rigid and semirigid polyvinyl chloride as a packaging

The Gulf Oil chemicals plant in Baytown, Tex., receives a 600-ton fractionating column on March 24. It was the largest piece of equipment ever hauled by a U.S. railroad and covered six railroad cars.

UPI

material for luncheon meats, salad dressings, and vegetable oils. Residual vinyl chloride, a known carcinogen, from which such packaging material is made, can migrate into food. However, the FDA would permit the use of flexible polyvinyl chloride film, such as that used to package fresh meats and vegetables, as well as polyvinyl liners for bottle caps and beverage cans. However, a spokesman for the Ralph Nader group questioned such use on the grounds that even flexible film contains significant amounts of vinyl chloride. The spokesman also pointed out that consumers cannot determine whether or not the packaging of a particular food contains polyvinyl chloride.

Hydrogen. Work continued on inexpensive methods of producing hydrogen for use as a fossil-fuel substitute, but progress was slow. One experiment done at the Massachusetts Institute of Technology involved action of sunlight on water. A titanium dioxide crystal and a bit of platinum were placed in a beaker of water and connected by a wire carrying a low-voltage current (0.2 volt). When exposed to a laser beam of ultraviolet light, the titanium appeared to strip electrons from hydroxyl ions, which then combined to form hydrogen peroxide. The stripped electrons travel along the wire to the platinum, where they react with hydrogen ions to form molecular hydrogen. The main problem is that only about 1% of the light is converted to chemical energy by this technique.

Plastic Alarm. An interesting phenomenon potentially useful against burglars was announced at the 9th Great Lakes Meeting of the ACS. If a film of polyvinylidene fluoride, a plastic similar to that used for bread wrappings, is placed in a strong electric field and held to a near-boiling temperature, it subsequently produces a voltage on slight pressure. Thus, if the material were used as a floor covering and connected to

proper sensors and circuitry, the step of an intruder would activate an alarm.

A Metallic Polymer. A polymer $(SN)_n$ of sulfur nitride that behaves like a metal was synthesized at the University of Pennsylvania. It contains long chains of alternating nitrogen and sulfur atoms, stacked in parallel bundles. Like metals, it is malleable and conducts electricity, although it conducts better along the bundles than across them. Light reflection from the polymer's bundles, which creates a metallic sheen, is also better along the bundles. Near absolute zero, the material becomes superconducting. Studies indicate that the polymer might become the forerunner of an entirely new class of compounds that could replace metals for some uses just as synthetic fibers have replaced natural fibers.

Olfactory Depressants. At the year's end a class of compounds, called odor counteractants, was reaching final development at the Monsanto Chemical Co. Rather than masking unpleasant odors, these compounds temporarily block the ability to smell a certain odor. Their main advantage is that, unlike maskants that might be effective against bathroom odors but not tobacco or kitchen odors, counteractants can be effective against several odors.

Monsanto plans to sell counteractants only to manufacturers of such consumer products as shampoos, depilatories, or deodorant soaps having unpleasant odors. Another advantage of counteractants is that they do not block most pleasant scents, nor do they destroy the ability to smell delicate perfumes that enhance the attractiveness of such products to consumers. Another potential use is incorporation of slow-release forms into box board, plastic tile, and certain papers that might emit unpleasant odors.

EUGENIA KELLER
Managing Editor, "Chemistry" Magazine

Chilean President Augusto Pinochet was criticized for repression of basic civil liberties and the campaign against supporters of former President Allende.

CHILE

Chile entered its third year under Gen. Augusto Pinochet Ugarte in September. During 1975 the country was beset by economic problems and international criticism regarding violations of human rights.

Military to Stay in Power. In September, President Pinochet said that the country's existing political parties—either outlawed or placed in "indefinite recess"—would have no role to play in Chile in the foreseeable future. "I will die, and my successor will have to die, before elections are held," he declared. Pinochet was determined to "extract the cancer of Marxism . . . no matter how long the surgery takes." While Pinochet said some restrictions imposed under the state of siege, including the curfew, might be lifted, penalties for infractions of the internal security law were stiffened. This action was aimed at government opponents, who were

responsible for an occasional killing or explosion.

At a July meeting in Caracas, Venezuela, exiled leaders of the Christian Left, Radical, and Socialist parties along with Christian Democratic leaders Bernardo Leighton and Renán Fuenteabla met. They agreed to promote an "anti-fascist front which would work for the establishment of a socialist, democratic, and pluralist regime in Chile." Later, Christian Democratic President Patricio Aylwin publicly rejected any possibility of collaboration between his party and the "Marxist left."

Political Prisoners. Official figures released by the interior ministry in March stated that 41,359 persons had been arrested since the September 1973 coup ousting Socialist President Salvador Allende; 27,438 of the 36,605 released had remained in Chile, while 9,167 Chileans and foreigners were expelled from the country. On October 23, Justice Minister Miguel Schweitzer acknowledged that 4,027 persons were still held as political prisoners.

Growing evidence of torture of political prisoners appeared substantiated on July 4 when President Pinochet refused to allow the UN Human Rights Commission to study the situation. Because the U. S. government felt that it had assurances to the contrary, the State Department protested. In August the Pinochet regime announced it was conducting its own inquiry.

Among those exiled in 1975 were Clodomiro Almeyda, Socialist foreign minister under Allende; Laura Allende de Pascal, a former Socialist deputy and sister of the late president; and Anselmo Sule, Carlos Morales Abarzua, and Hugo Miranda, all former presidents of the middle class conservative Radical party. In October, Lutheran Bishop Helmut Frenz, who had been working with other religious leaders to improve the conditions of political prisoners and their families, was told he would not be allowed to return from Switzerland. Organizations critical of events in Chile included Amnesty International, the Interparliamentary Union, and the International Labor Organization.

Army and Cabinet Reorganization. Gen. Oscar Bonilla, one of President Pinochet's closest associates, died with six other persons March 3 in a helicopter crash near Curicó, south of Santiago. Bonilla's death led to a reorganization of the army that strengthened Pinochet's power. Gen. Hernán Brady Roche was sworn in as minister of defense and replaced as chief of the National Defense Staff by Gen. Sergio Arellano Stark, commander of the second division in Santiago province. Gen. Hector Bravo Muñoz, previously next to Pinochet and Bonilla in seniority, was retired prematurely and named ambassador to South Vietnam and Thailand.

To improve the government's image abroad, Pinochet increased the number of civilian members in the cabinet from 3 to 6 on April 14, while naming military men to the other 11 posts.

General Pinochet and his top aides review a parade on September 11 during the second anniversary celebration of the military's assumption of power in Chile.

SYGMA

Economic Affairs. The government remained unable to control the world's highest inflation rate. However, there were some hopeful signs in August when the consumer price index increased only 8.9%, down from 9.3% in July and 19.8% in June. Although the National Institute of Statistics said inflation was held to 351% in 1974, compared with an official 352.8% in 1973, the Inter-American Development Bank estimated 1974 inflation at 504.7%.

On April 25, Finance Minister Jorge Cauas announced a series of measures designed to curb inflation and to deal with increasing unemployment. Government spending was to be cut 15–25%, taxes on luxury goods increased 10%, and income taxes increased. The "social costs" of moving toward a "freer economy" remained high. Unemployment in greater Santiago crept up to 16.1% in June 1975 compared with 10.3% in June 1974.

Chile's balance of payments deficit was expected to reach $1 billion in 1975, due chiefly to the low international price of copper, which constitutes 70–80% of Chile's exports, and the high cost of oil imports. In an effort to force up world prices, Chile and other members of the Intergovernmental Council of Copper Exporting Countries agreed on April 14 to a further 5% reduction of output in addition to an earlier February cutback.

In August, the Statistics Institute announced increases in the 1974–75 production of rice, sugar beets, sunflower seeds, and wheat over 1973–74 yields, much of which was due to an increase of about 247,000 acres (100,000 hectares) in cultivation. Although there were slight drops in the harvests of maize, potatoes, and barley, officials predicted a drop in food imports from $554 million in 1974 to $303 million in 1975.

In January, Chile agreed to compensate International Telephone and Telegraph (ITT) $125 million, Kennecott $68 million, and Cerro de Pasco $59 million for properties nationalized during the Allende regime.

After the escudo had been devalued several times to keep it on a par with the U. S. dollar and to stimulate exports, it was abandoned in September. It was replaced by the peso, a new currency worth 1,000 old escudos.

Foreign Relations. The cool relations among Chile, Bolivia, and Peru were not greatly enhanced during 1975, although Chile's Press Secretary Federico Willoughby said in February that Chile wished to give Bolivia "its own sovereign access to the Pacific Ocean." On February 8, Bolivia resumed diplomatic relations with Chile, nearly 13 years after breaking them over a Chilean decision to divert the waters of the Lauca River, which flow into Bolivia. After Peruvian President Velasco Alvarado proposed a three-country solution to Bolivia's access problem, Venezuela's President Carlos Andrés Pérez offered to arrange a summit meeting. This offer was greeted by Santiago's *El Mercúrio* as an unacceptable "interference in the internal affairs of other countries."

NEALE J. PEARSON
Texas Tech University

CHILE • Information Highlights

Official Name: Republic of Chile.
Location: Southwestern coast of South America.
Area: 292,257 square miles (756,945 sq km).
Population (1975 est.): 9,910,000.
Chief Cities: Santiago, the capital, 2,661,920 (1970 census, met. area); Valparaiso, 292,850 (1970 est.).
Government: *Head of state and of government,* Gen. Augusto Pinochet Ugarte, president (took power Sept. 1973). *Legislature*—Congress (dissolved Sept. 1973).
Monetary Unit: Peso (6 pesos equal U. S.$1, Sept. 1975).
Gross National Product (1974 est.): $7,940,000,000.
Manufacturing (major products): Iron and steel, petroleum products, pulp and paper, chemicals.
Major Agricultural Products: Wheat, sugar beets, potatoes, corn, grapes, citrus fruits, rapeseed, fish.
Foreign Trade (1974): *Exports,* $2,000,000,000; *imports,* $2,250,000,000.

U. S. Secretary of State Henry A. Kissinger met with Chairman Mao Tse-tung in Peking, October 21, for what state-department spokesmen termed a "very useful" session.

CHINA

China, the world's most populous nation, remains divided into two opposing parts. The Chinese mainland is controlled by the Communist government of the People's Republic of China, and the island province of Taiwan is controlled by the Nationalist government of the Republic of China.

PEOPLE'S REPUBLIC OF CHINA

The People's Congress, convened in January 1975, revised the constitution and reorganized the governmental leadership. The new constitution emphasized party leadership and reaffirmed the power of the party's chairman to command the armed forces. With Chou En-lai reelected premier, the "moderates" achieved a dominant position in the administration, though not in the party.

The object of Chinese foreign policy was to curb Soviet influence, not only in Eastern Asia, but also in Western Europe. China was unhappy about U. S. policy toward Taiwan, but considered friendship with the United States necessary to check Soviet expansion. Reports from China indicated an industrial growth rate of 9%–11% for the first six months of 1975. Peking also expected a good harvest despite flood and famine in some areas.

The National Congress. The 4th National People's Congress, after a long delay for political reasons, held its first session at Peking on Jan. 13–18, 1975. Three major tasks faced the Congress: the revision of the constitution that had practically been suspended since the 1966 Cultural Revolution; the setting forth of basic policies, internal and external; and the reconstruction of the governmental leadership. The leadership had been badly decimated by the Cultural Revolution and the subsequent purges. All of these motions were first approved by the Central

Committee of the Chinese Communist party in a meeting held on January 8–10. The action by the Congress, although a mere formality, was necessary to put into effect the Central Committee's decisions that were concerned with the structure and policies of the government.

The New Constitution. The revised constitution abolished the post of the chief of the state, which had been left vacant since its last incumbent, Liu Shao-ch'i, was purged at an early stage of the Cultural Revolution. The functions of the chief of the state were to be assumed by the Standing Committee of the Congress, whose new chairman was Chu Teh, the former marshal who had led the Red Army to victory over the Nationalists in 1949. Although the Congress remained "the highest organ of state power," the constitution stipulated that it was to function under the leadership of the Communist party.

It was made clear by Chang Ch'un-ch'iao, the leftist leader who presented the constitution to the Congress, that the document aimed at "strengthening the party's centralized leadership of the structure of the state." He called attention to the provision that the chairman of the Central Committee of the Communist party "commands the country's armed forces." (Mao Tse-tung had been chairman of the Central Committee for 40 years.) In general the new constitution embodied the basic precepts of Chairman Mao. It held that "class contradictions" and "class struggle" must persist in a socialist society. It enjoined the state personnel to study earnestly the thought of Mao Tse-tung and "firmly put proletarian politics in command."

A significant feature of the new constitution is its enunciation on international politics. "China," the document said, "will never be a superpower." It would oppose "the imperialist and socialist imperialist policies of aggression and war and the hegemonism of the superpowers."

Report by Chou En-lai. It fell on Premier Chou En-lai to set forth the basic policies of the

government when he presented the political report to the Congress. Extensively citing Mao Tse-tung, the premier envisaged the economic development of China in two stages. The first stage was to build an independent and "relatively comprehensive industrial and economic system" before the year 1980. The second stage was to achieve the "comprehensive modernization" of agriculture, industry, national defense, and science and technology before the end of the century. The priorities for developing the national economy were agriculture, then light industry, and finally heavy industry.

In international affairs Premier Chou saw the contention for world hegemony between the two superpowers, the United States and the Soviet Union, growing more and more intense. Their struggle, said Chou, "has extended to every corner of the world" and "is bound to lead to world war some day." While describing Sino-American relations as having improved since 1972, he pointed out that the relations between China and the Soviet Union had worsened because of the hostile actions on the part of the Soviet leadership. He called for vigilance and preparedness against war.

The New Leadership. The new slate of governmental ministers, as approved by the People's Congress, was headed by Premier Chou En-lai. Under him were 12 deputy premiers, with Teng Hsiao-p'ing as the first deputy premier and Chang Ch'un-ch'iao as the second. Teng, the former secretary-general of the Communist party, had been purged during the Cultural Revolution. He was rehabilitated in 1973 and had since rapidly risen to a prominent position. In 1975, in addition to being the first deputy premier, he was named chief of the army staff, thus holding a key position in the political-military power structure.

Chang Ch'un-ch'iao, a leader of the "radical" faction that had played a powerful role in the Cultural Revolution, was the only one of the faction elected to the new administration. Besides the post of deputy premier, he was appointed chief political commissioner of the army. This gave the leftists an important connection with the armed forces that might prove crucial in a power struggle.

The post of minister of defense, which had been left vacant since Lin Piao's fall in 1971, was given to Yeh Chien-ying. Since he was 76, he was generally regarded as devoid of political ambitions.

If the "moderates" were dominant in the central government, the "radicals" led by Chiang Ch'ing, Chairman Mao's wife, and Chang Ch'un-ch'iao had a strong voice at the high levels of the party hierarchy, particularly the Standing Committee of the Politburo. The leadership alignment appeared to be based on a compromise between the moderates and the radicals. It was, in fact, a transitional arrangement pending the final successions to Chairman Mao and Premier

Wheat being harvested in Honan Province. China reported a record wheat crop for the summer of 1975.

Chou. Chou was reported to be very ill in October when he failed to attend the celebrations for the 20th anniversary of the People's Republic of China.

Economic Developments. In line with Premier Chou's program to transform China into a "powerful modern socialist country" in 20 years, workers throughout the country were urged to make the utmost effort to raise production. Not all workers cooperated, however. In July the government found it necessary to send 10,000 troops into 13 factories in the city of Hangchow, Chekiang province, to help with production, which was stalled because of "disturbances from bourgeois factionalism." The situation was soon brought under control.

Statistics from various provinces indicated an industrial growth of 9%–11% for the first half of 1975. China expected a good harvest for the year, as a record wheat crop was reported for the summer.

Foreign Trade and Oil. China had large trade deficits amounting to $1.3 billion in 1974. To improve the trade balance, Peking took vigorous steps to increase its oil production. It was expected that China's oil export would rise sharply in 1975. China was believed to have extensive deposits of oil, ranking it possibly with Saudi Arabia. Its 1975 production was estimated by western experts to be around 1.3 million barrels a day with expansion proceeding at an annual growth rate of 25% or more.

Peking used oil export not only to earn foreign exchange but also as an instrument to realize its diplomatic aims. A contract signed in March to export 58 million barrels of crude oil to Japan, with the hint that China could export

more to meet Japanese needs, was plainly intended to deter Japan from cooperating with the Soviet Union in the huge project to develop oil production in eastern Siberia. Peking's oil diplomacy was also extended to other parts of Asia, particularly Thailand, Hong Kong, North Korea, and the Philippines.

Foreign Relations—United States. Peking was displeased at the United States' continued maintenance of diplomatic relations with Taiwan and its repeated declarations to honor its mutual defense treaty with Nationalist China. However, Communist China considered U. S. friendship necessary in the face of its deteriorating relations with the Soviet Union. Chinese representatives had indicated to U. S. congressmen and reporters that Peking would like the United States to maintain armed forces in Asia as a deterrent to Soviet expansion.

Secretary of State Henry A. Kissinger arrived in Peking on October 19 for a four-day visit. He talked with Chairman Mao Tse-tung and held a series of conferences with Deputy Premier Teng Hsiao-p'ing. China opposed Washington's détente with Moscow, but Secretary Kissinger deemed it necessary to avoid "needless confrontation" with the Soviet Union. Peking was disappointed but did not abandon efforts to influence the United States.

China had become the United States' largest grain customer in 1974, buying 3 million tons of U. S. wheat. But the situation drastically changed in 1975 when Peking canceled two orders of wheat for a total of 983,000 tons. No official reasons were given for these cancellations, but economic observers found several reasons for the Chinese action. These included China's foreign exchange shortages; improved weather conditions early in the year; a decline in wheat prices

Oil refinery in Shantung Province. China increased oil production in 1975 to improve its balance of trade.

in the world market; and the traces of smut, a plant disease, found in the U. S. wheat imported in 1974. On the other hand, Peking showed a renewed interest in purchasing high-technology equipment from the United States. In December President Ford visited Peking for further negotiations.

The Soviet Union. The chief object of China's foreign policy was to contain and isolate the Soviet Union, which China considered as its main enemy. The Chinese saw a Soviet quest for global hegemony more dangerous than that of the United States. To curb Soviet influence, China made strenuous efforts to develop closer ties with Western European countries. The Chinese Communists sought to discredit Soviet attempts at a détente between Western and Eastern Europe fearing that if the Soviet Union felt relieved at its western flank, it would concentrate its forces against China in the east.

Western Europe. The Chinese supported a united Western Europe and formally recognized the European Economic Community on May 8, believing that it would help restrain the Soviet Union. On May 12, Chinese Deputy Premier Teng Hsiao-p'ing arrived in Paris for a six-day state visit. He had several meetings with French President Valéry Giscard d'Estaing and Premier Jacques Chirac and invited them both to visit China in 1976. The two nations agreed to hold regular political consultations and to set up a joint economic commission to promote commercial exchanges.

Asia. Peking brought heavy pressure to bear upon Japan to sign a treaty of peace and friendship that would pledge both countries to oppose attempts of any third nation to establish hegemony in Asia. The Japanese government under Premier Takeo Miki desired closer relations with Peking, for Japan saw no threat from China but was not so sure about the Soviet Union. Japan, however, did not deem it advisable to be dragged into the Sino-Soviet conflict, and therefore the treaty negotiations continued with no sign of immediate conclusion.

President Kim Il Sung of North Korea arrived in Peking for an official visit on April 18. The purpose of his visit was not made known, but if President Kim was seeking China's military support for a new Korean war, he may have been disappointed. It seemed that Peking had cautioned North Korea against military adventures. In any case, at a banquet given by President Kim in honor of the Chinese leaders on April 26, Chinese Deputy Premier Teng Hsiao-p'ing stressed China's support of a "peaceful unification" of Korea. Peking, however, backed the North Korean position that the United States should withdraw its troops from South Korea and negotiate directly with North Korea.

With the U. S. withdrawal from Indochina, Peking was faced not only with the danger of Soviet penetration, but also with the possibility of a Vietnamese hegemony over Southeast Asia.

Prince Norodom Sihanouk (left), who had Chinese support for his efforts to return to a post in Cambodia, is shown with Deputy Premier Teng Hsiao-p'ing.

UPI

A unified state from a consolidation of North and South Vietnam could first gain ascendency over Laos and Cambodia and then extend its political influence to the rest of Southeast Asia. Furthermore, North Vietnam leaned much closer to Moscow than to Peking.

China had maintained closer relations with the Cambodian insurgents, however. A delegation of Cambodian Communist leaders visiting Peking on August 15 was given a warm welcome by the Chinese. An agreement on economic and technical cooperation between the two countries was signed on August 18. The Cambodian Communists seemed responsive to the Chinese efforts at having Prince Norodom Sihanouk, the former Cambodian head of state who had lived in Peking since his overthrow in 1970, restored to some nominal position in the new government.

China established diplomatic relations with the Philippines on June 9 and with Thailand on July 1. The winning over of two formerly anti-Communist countries further extended China's influence in Southeast Asia.

— COMMUNIST CHINA • Information Highlights —

Official Name: People's Republic of China.
Location: Central part of eastern Asia.
Area: 3,705,396 square miles (9,596,961 sq km).
Population (1975 est.): 822,800,000.
Chief Cities (1974 est.): Peking, the capital, 7,600,000; Shanghai, 10,800,000; Tientsin, 4,000,000.
Government: *Chairman of the Chinese Communist Party,* Mao Tse-tung (took office 1935). *Head of government,* Chou En-lai, premier (took office 1949). *Legislature* (unicameral)—National People's Congress.
Monetary Unit: Yuan (1.80 yuan equal U. S.$1, 1975).
Gross National Product (1973): $172,000,000,000.
Manufacturing (major products): Iron and steel, machinery, cotton textiles, fertilizers, electronics, pharmaceuticals, instruments, transportation equipment.
Major Agricultural Products: Rice, wheat, sweet potatoes, sorghum, corn, cotton, tobacco, soybeans, barley, tea, fish.
Foreign Trade (1973): *Exports,* $4,000,000,000; *imports,* $4,500,000,000.

Chinese and Indian troops clashed on October 20 in the disputed territory of Arunachal Pradesh along the eastern border between the two countries. Four Indian soldiers were killed. India protested, but China claimed that it was the Indian troops that crossed the Chinese border.

REPUBLIC OF CHINA

The death of Chiang Kai-shek did not interrupt the continuity of Nationalist China's basic policies. Premier Chiang Ching-kuo held prime political authority in Taiwan; he had been the practical leader for the past three years.

The Communist takeover in Indochina and the U. S. withdrawal from the area worried the Nationalists, who were particularly concerned about Washington's further accommodation with Peking. Diplomatic isolation, however, did not prevent Taiwan from expanding its foreign trade with non-Communist nations.

The Death of Chiang Kai-shek. Chiang Kai-shek, the president of Nationalist China, died of a heart attack on April 5. The Chinese leader, who had led the Chinese movement of unification in the 1920's and the war of resistance against Japan in 1937–45, had been driven from the Chinese mainland by the Communists in 1949. (See also OBITUARIES.)

C. K. Yen, the vice president since 1966, was promptly inaugurated as president, in accordance with the provisions of the constitution. Premier Chiang Ching-kuo, the elder son of President Chiang, had been the practical leader of Taiwan since President Chiang was incapacitated by illness in May 1972. The premier continued to exercise prime political authority, with the new president confining himself largely to ceremonial functions.

No significant changes were indicated in foreign or domestic policies under the new administration. Premier Chiang was expected to continue the basic policies he had pursued since 1972. The Nationalists made it clear that they would adhere to the policy of opposing the Chinese Communists.

Foreign Relations. The Communist takeover in Indochina and the United States withdrawal from the area caused grave concern in Taiwan. Nationalist China was particularly worried about the U. S. position toward the mutual-defense treaty between the two countries. The Nationalists were somewhat assured by President Ford, who at a news conference on May 6 stated that the United States would maintain its commitments to Taiwan. They also found encouragement in the report that conservatives in Congress were advising President Ford not to make further concessions to Peking. John J. Rhodes, the House minority leader, told reporters that U. S. moves to loosen ties with Taiwan were unlikely "if President Ford wants to be renominated by the Republican party."

Despite these assurances, the Nationalists

Madame Chiang Kai-shek and Vice President Nelson Rockefeller attend the funeral of President Chiang Kai-shek, who died on April 5 after a long illness.

were wary that further U. S. conciliation with Peking might seriously affect the international status of Taiwan. The withdrawal in May of the last squadron of U. S. combat aircraft from Taiwan added to the uneasiness of the Nationalists. The withdrawal was in accordance with the agreement reached between Communist China and the United States during former President Nixon's visit to Peking in 1972.

Air service between Taiwan and Japan resumed on August 10 when a China Air Lines plane bearing the flag of Nationalist China landed in Tokyo. The air link was broken in April 1974, when Japan, under Peking's pressure, refused to consider Nationalist China's flag a national flag. The agreement on air traffic resumption was signed on July 9, after the Japanese foreign minister expressed regret over the misunderstanding about the Nationalist flag.

Nationalist China severed diplomatic relations with the Philippines on June 9, immediately after Manila recognized Peking. The Philippine government informed the Nationalist embassy that it would protect Chinese citizens living in the Philippines and that these overseas Chinese would not be required to change their Nationalist citizenship. Manila expressed interest in setting up a semi-official agency in Taiwan to handle trade, travel, and cultural relations. On July 1, Taiwan terminated diplomatic relations with Thailand after the Thai government announced its recognition of Peking.

With these two Southeast Asian nations turning away, Taiwan had diplomatic relations with only 25 countries, compared with 59 in 1971, when it was replaced at the United Nations by Communist China. The growing diplomatic isolation, however, did not stop Taiwan from expanding its trade relations. By establishing nonofficial trade offices in countries with which it had no diplomatic ties, Taiwan's foreign trade tripled between 1971 and 1974, from $4.1 billion to $12.6 billion.

The Economy. Speaking at the National Conference on March 24, Premier Chiang Ching-kuo called for a maximum development of the economy. In the industrial sector top priority would be given to developing energy resources and basic industries. Efforts would be made to exploit offshore oil prospects and to develop steel and aluminum industries. The government would continue to invest in capital-intensive and technology-intensive industries, with emphasis on machinery, electric appliances, electronics, and chemical industries.

In the agricultural sector the government

CHINESE INFORMATION SERVICE

UPI

Premier Chiang Ching-kuo (*left*), elder son of Chiang Kai-shek, is the prime political authority in the Republic of China. President C. K. Yen (*above*), the former vice president, was installed on April 6.

would improve irrigation, fisheries, livestock, forestry, and slopeland farming. Rural reconstruction was to be accelerated with attention to balanced development between agriculture and industry.

Because of the worldwide economic recession in 1974, Taiwan was cautious in setting its economic objectives. The economic target for 1975 was first set at 3.3%, but in June when orders from foreign buyers increased gradually, the growth rate for the year was expected to reach 4%–6%. In May the industrial production index showed an increase of 6.2% over April.

The target of the two-way foreign trade for 1975 was set at $15 billion. Total foreign trade in the first eight months, however, was slightly over $7 billion, with a trade deficit of $374.5 million. Efforts were made to narrow the trade gap by expanding exports, especially with Japan.

Asian markets, including Japan, South Korea, and countries in Southeast Asia, were seen in Taiwan as good opportunities for export expansion. The Nationalists also recognized the need to step up trade promotion with European Economic Community countries. To promote sales of Taiwan-made products abroad, the Nationalist government sent a number of trade missions to various areas in the second half of 1975,

including the United States, Canada, Latin America, Europe, the Middle East, New Zealand, and Australia.

Military Independence. Taiwan's industrial growth and its diplomatic isolation led to an emphasis on "self-reliance." In an enormous parade in October, Taiwan displayed locally-built military hardware such as jet fighters, helicopters, tanks, artillery, and rifles.

CHESTER C. TAN, *New York University*

— NATIONALIST CHINA • Information Highlights —

Official Name: Republic of China.
Location: Island off the southeastern coast of mainland China.
Area: 13,885 square miles (35,961 sq km).
Population (1975 est.): 16,000,000.
Chief Cities (1974 est.): Taipei, the capital, 1,900,000; Kaohsiung, 784,502; Taichung, 428,426.
Government: *Head of state,* C. K. Yen, president (installed April 1975). *Head of government,* Chiang Ching-kuo, premier (took office May 1972). *Legislature* (unicameral)—Legislative Yuan.
Monetary Unit: New Taiwan dollar (38.10 NT dollars equal U. S.$1, July 1974).
Gross National Product (1973): $9,400,000,000.
Manufacturing (major products): Petroleum products, processed foods, textiles, electrical machinery, electronics, chemicals, apparel.
Major Agricultural Products: Sugarcane, bananas, mushrooms, pineapples, rice, tea, vegetables, fish.
Foreign Trade (1973): *Exports,* $4,473,000,000; *imports,* $3,791,000,000.

UPI

Mayor Joseph Alioto (*second from right*) of San Francisco held a news conference in Boston after he arrived on July 5 for the 43rd annual meeting of the U. S. Mayors Conference, of which he was the president.

CITIES AND URBAN AFFAIRS

During the 1960's, particularly in light of widespread rioting in central cities, there was considerable discussion of a myriad of urban problems. All of these added up to something that experts referred to as the urban crisis. Most of the solutions to the problems proposed by the national study commissions and other groups involved the expenditure of funds. Subsequently, urbanologists began to conclude that the biggest problem—the essence of all the others— was urban finance. If cities could find ways to pay for solutions to problems, they would be all right. This message was carried to the federal government and led to growth in programs designed to aid urban areas.

In 1975, the idea that spending money could solve urban problems came under question. Spending more money had not necessarily solved problems or even curbed them. Indeed, there was at least one notable case where expenditure of funds had not only not diminished problems but had caused them. That case, of course, was New York City.

Crisis in New York City. By its physical size and the size of its problem, New York City set the tone for cities throughout the nation during 1975. The subject of cities could scarcely be brought up without New York being mentioned. The New York City government spent the year in the throes of a financial crisis that centered on its inability to make payments to its municipal bondholders.

In May, Mayor Abraham Beame proposed an austerity budget for the city that totaled $12.8 billion and called for layoffs of over 19,000 employees. He appealed to Gov. Hugh Carey and to President Ford for assistance, claiming that without their aid New York would default on its debts. The city weathered the formulation of a municipal assistance corporation in June, a sanitation strike in July, a teachers walkout in September.

No one had solid evidence of what a default would mean to the rest of the country. There was considerable disagreement among recognized experts. Economist Milton Friedman stated that "default by New York City would have no adverse consequence for the rest of us." Treasury Secretary William Simon told a congressional committee that a default would not make good municipal bonds bad but rather would make good bonds better. But, there was evidence that their conclusions might not be sound. Fluctuations in the stock market during the year were often attributed to news about New York's financial situation. The cost of borrowing money for state and local governments throughout the country rose. Many experts pointed to a "ripple effect" influencing the finances of urban governments trying to borrow.

There were those who questioned whether the federal government had a legitimate role in

the New York City crisis. They contended that the New York problem was, at most, a state problem that should be solved in that context.

During most of 1975, the state and the city scurried in search of a solution. On numerous occasions, Mayor Beame and Governor Carey journeyed to Washington to seek federal help. In June, the city attempted to avoid default by forming the Municipal Assistance Corporation ("Big" MAC). It was intended to issue bonds to assist the city in managing its debt. Because the situation was so serious, however, the bond market closed down to Big MAC. To avoid a default early in September, the state stepped in with an emergency assistance plan that included supervision of city finances and provided approximately $2.3 billion in short term credit. This action threatened to bring New York state down, too, since it also was operating at a deficit and needed to be in a position to borrow. Together, New York state and the city accounted for 15% of the state and local debt outstanding in the nation.

At that point, city and state officials took the position that they had done all that they could do and that without federal action the city would default. They carried this message to the U. S. Congress, which began to develop legislation providing loan guarantees to New York. In a widely publicized speech, President Ford promised to veto any legislation that provided assistance to New York. With this seemingly unequivocal refusal, city and state officials made a subsequent attempt to do something that would avoid default. What resulted was a substantial package of state and city taxes and financial control measures that, on the face of it, changed Ford's position about the need for federal involvement.

Prior to Thanksgiving, Ford announced support for $2.3 billion in seasonal loan guarantees to New York. Subsequently, a bill resembling the proposal that the President supported passed both houses of Congress, and it appeared that the corner had been turned in avoiding default for the nation's largest city. Late in December the city drew for the first time from the funds provided by the bill.

Economics. One problem concerning the possibility of a New York City default was that the existing federal municipal bankruptcy law, originally formulated in 1934, is too cumbersome to allow large cities to declare bankruptcy and make financial adjustments under the protection of a federal court. Again, Congress was asked to respond by revamping the law so that cities with large numbers of creditors could utilize it if the need arose.

Although the level of urban governmental spending was coming under intense scrutiny, it was still obvious that recessionary and inflationary trends had a strong impact on cities. It was no new trend, but demands for services continued to soar while revenues had fallen short of expectations. Many mayors admitted that New York was not the only city in financial trouble.

Urban Unions. During the year, numerous municipal strikes occurred because hard-pressed city governments could not come to terms with hard-pressed employees. Policemen struck in Albuquerque and San Francisco. The San Francisco officers demanded a 13% pay increase. To assure a return to work, Mayor Joseph Alioto agreed, without city board of supervisors approval, to their demands. San Francisco firemen walked out in sympathy with their police colleagues, and firemen in nearby Berkeley also left the stations. In Seattle, firemen struck when their chief was fired, and they attempted to recall Mayor Wes Uhlman. Local voters, however, supported the mayor by a nearly two-to-one margin.

Teachers walked out in Fort Wayne, Ind.; Atlanta; Boston; and New York City. Other urban services were also the victims of strikes—transit drivers in Omaha, Neb.; subway construction crews in Washington, D. C.; sanitation men in New York City; and hospital workers in Memphis, Tenn., walked out.

Revenue Sharing. The fight to renew the federal revenue sharing program, which had since 1972 returned billions of federal tax dollars to state and local governments, began to heat up in 1975. Recipient local governments were seeking reenactment in the program during 1975 so they could plan on receiving funds when they formulated their budgets in early 1976. In Septem-

New York City sanitation men held a wildcat strike in July in protest to layoffs within the department.

UPI

UPI

Chicago teachers cheer September decision to strike, which closed public schools for seven days. Teachers strikes hit several major cities in 1975.

ber, a House subcommittee began hearings on program renewal but, shortly afterward, the panel's chairman announced that there was no possibility for passage of a renewal bill before the end of the year. Local officials nevertheless continued lobbying for the earliest possible renewal. In November, more than 1,700 county officials made a one-day journey to Washington to convey to the Congress their feelings about the program's importance.

Experts agreed that the renewal in some form is likely. However, numerous issues need to be resolved. Civil rights groups allege that widespread discrimination in public employment and services is being financed with shared funds, and they urge that citizen participation in decisions about revenue sharing expenditures be required by law.

Because of the delay in early reenactment of general revenue sharing, it seemed likely that the program would become involved in the new congressional budget procedures, which became effective on Jan. 1, 1976. These new procedures, an overdue effort to get control of the federal budget, seemed to preclude the long-term financing provisions of the existing program. These provisions had allowed Congress to authorize a program and to appropriate funds for it at the same time.

Antirecessionary Legislation. Urban officials also spent considerable effort to achieve passage of an antirecessionary package of federal legis-

lation. A comprehensive bill seeking public works, job opportunities, and counter-cyclical assistance was developed in Congress but differences between House and Senate versions caused the legislation to bog down. At year's end, however, the impasse was broken, but the package still faced a presidential veto.

Crime and Violence. There was nothing new about the fact that crime increased again in 1975. The number of major offenses, compiled by the Federal Bureau of Investigation, rose 18%. Teenagers, who constitute only 10% of the population, were responsible for 31% of the crimes resulting in arrests. The murder rate continued to rise, and data indicated that 54% had been committed with handguns.

Before these figures were even revealed, however, the Congress, in response to demands by urban leaders, attempted to develop a gun-control amendment bill. Proposals ranged from a ban on manufacture, sale, and possession of handguns to milder measures. The controversy surrounding the issue, however, dimmed the likelihood of passage in 1975.

In Washington, D. C., in late May, 125,000 people assembled on the grounds of the Washington Monument for "Human Kindness Day." The opposite spirit prevailed—racial fights, robberies, and beatings by the dozens could not be stopped by law enforcement personnel who were present. The incident called into question the wisdom of sponsored mass gatherings and caused concern that 1976 Bicentennial celebrations would be marked by similar incidents.

In Boston, for the second straight year, court-ordered school busing was vehemently opposed, leading eventually to court jurisdiction over one high school. During the summer, prior to the opening of schools, numerous violent incidents took place at city beaches. Disturbances also marked the opening of schools in Louisville where school busing had been ordered.

Community Development. The first year of operation of the federal community-development, block-grant program revealed that larger cities were satisfied with the plan's automatic-funding mechanism. However, smaller jurisdictions in metropolitan areas were faced with little or no discretionary funds. Only a $54 million supplemental appropriation from Congress managed to satisfy the needs of these communities.

Substantial evidence of a practice known as "red lining" was revealed during the year. This involved the failure of lending institutions to make loans to persons seeking to buy or renovate property in sections of cities with concentrations of poor and minority persons. These neighborhoods had traditionally been the objects of programs of urban renewal. Yet, a nationwide study of the concept in practice concluded that urban renewal should continue to have a major role in community development programs.

ROBERT M. LLOYD, *South Carolina Appalachian Council of Governments*

CIVIL LIBERTIES AND CIVIL RIGHTS

The post-Watergate period of 1975 was a time for the United States to focus on the outdated acts dealing with civil liberties and civil rights. The American Civil Liberties Union was awarded $12 million in damages for the false arrest and infringement of rights of 1,200 antiwar demonstrators on the steps of the Capitol in 1971. It was thought to be one of the largest awards ever in a civil liberties suit. Despite the absence of Justice William O. Douglas from the U. S. Supreme Court for all but three weeks of the first six months of 1975, the conservatives did not overturn the record of the Warren Court. Two of the Nixon appointees, Justices Harry A. Blackmun and Lewis F. Powell, proved less conservative than had been expected in their decisions on sex, race, obscenity, and free speech.

Criminal Justice. Since 1972, 33 states have passed new capital punishment laws reinstating the death penalty for certain crimes. It had been expected that the Supreme Court in 1975 would reconsider capital punishment. However, with Justice Douglas incapacitated, the closely divided judges held over the *Fowler* v. *North Carolina* case until its 1975–76 sitting.

In North Carolina the murder trial of Joan Little received national attention. A 20-year-old black woman charged with the fatal stabbing of a jailer, she received support from women's and civil rights groups. She pleaded self-defense, alleging she had been subjected to sexual abuse. The jury found her not guilty.

Lower courts and lawmakers were moving toward more humane treatment and began to acknowledge prisoner complaints against overcrowding, brutality, and the invasion of privacy. Inmates gained access to reading materials and to news interviewers as well as having their voting rights restored after completing sentences. In addition, a number of states also modified occupational licensing restrictions and protected ex-offenders from discrimination in private employment.

Sex Equality. The drive for the Equal Rights Amendment made little progress, picking up only one state in 1975, four short of the number required for ratification. Sexual equality did make progress on other legal fronts. Feminists continued to lobby for changes in the rape laws to encourage more women to seek police help in arresting their attackers and to give prosecutors a better chance of getting them convicted. The groups are fighting to eliminate the type of cross-examination that tends to put the victim, rather than the rapist, on trial.

Regulations were issued in 1975 by the Department of Health, Education, and Welfare to implement Title IX of the Educational Amendments of 1972, which prohibited discrimination by sex in all federally-aided schools. There were exceptions guaranteeing the right to privacy: separate toilets, locker rooms, shower facilities, and classes on human sexuality, and permitting separate physical education classes or activities involving body-contact sports.

The gay activists won a suit in Suffolk County, N. Y., where a district judge ruled that homosexuals and other unmarried persons have the same sexual legal rights as married people. The ruling made it unconstitutional to differentiate between married and unmarried persons.

Racial Equality. Changing attitudes, competing forces, and a rapidly changing class structure made civil rights proponents more pessimistic than in the 1960's. Hostility to busing polarized Boston, as federal Judge W. Arthur Garrity, Jr., attempted to counteract a de facto dual school system. Bowing to pressure, the Philadelphia School Board voted to scrap a busing approach that it had been ordered to draft by a state court. In Detroit a federal district court judge declined to order widespread busing under plans devised by the Detroit Board of Education and the NAACP.

The Afro-American Patrolmen's Association went to court against the Chicago police department and got federal law enforcement assistance funds withheld until the city was in compliance with court-enforced equal employment opportunity programs. The U. S. Supreme Court ruled that awards of back pay should ordinarily be granted to persons who proved themselves the victims of employment discrimination.

In a time of recession, when industry was trying to reduce costs through employee layoffs, the Civil Rights Act of 1964 posed a tough problem. Customarily, the first employees laid off were the most recently hired. That approach, however, could erase most of the gains by women and minorities during the past 10 years. With cases already filed with the Supreme Court, the seniority system will no doubt be questioned in 1976.

The U. S. Congress acted to extend the Voting Rights Act of 1965 for 10 years and to broaden its protection to include Spanish-speaking citizens and other language minorities. The act was originally extended for five years in 1970, and its original purpose was to guarantee blacks in seven southern states the right to register and vote.

A decision of the Supreme Court barred the award of attorneys' fees to citizens' groups that win public-interest suits. The ruling threatened to cut off millions of dollars awarded in behalf of lower class minorities.

Age Discrimination. Congress drafted a bill making it easier for elderly people to obtain loans and credit. The measure prohibited lenders and credit officials from discriminating on the basis of age. The bill, however, did provide the lender the option of rejecting cases such as an 85-year-old person seeking a 30-year mortgage.

Church-State Relations. The court agreed to consider a Maryland case that challenged state aid to colleges with religious affiliations. Defiance of the court's ban on prayers and Bible reading in the public schools continued in some areas, primarily rural. New Hampshire in 1975 passed a law permitting school districts to decide whether to allow programs for the voluntary recitation of the Lord's Prayer in the public schools.

Other Issues. Attorney General Edward H. Levy, a vigilant Congress, and the press maneuvered in 1975 to control the way the Federal Bureau of Investigation, the Central Intelligence Agency, and other intelligence agencies collected, stored, and disseminated information on private individuals. Wiretapping, mail opening, burglaries, and infiltration were exposed and measures were taken to prevent recurrence.

A federal code of criminal law was proposed that would assure more uniformity in sentencing, compensate victims of crime for their injuries or losses, narrow the legal concept of insanity, and make civil-rights enforcement easier for the Justice Department, particularly in criminal prosecution or for sex discrimination. Critics attacked a provision on espionage and theft for amounting to an official secrets act, and sections making it more difficult for defendants and prisoners to obtain probation or parole. There were also objections to relaxing regulations against use of voluntary confessions by suspects who have not been informed of their rights.

MARTIN GRUBERG
University of Wisconsin, Oshkosh

COIN COLLECTING

The year 1975 was an exciting one for coin collecting. Emphasis was on old and rare coins —items of recognized numismatic value—rather than on silver and gold bullion, which characterized the market in 1974.

Gold Rush. Attention focused on gold. On Dec. 31, 1974, it became legal for U. S. citizens to hold gold in bullion form for the first time since 1933. While speculators anticipated a "gold rush," bullion gold soared to nearly $200 per ounce. When the "gold rush" did not occur, the price drifted downward, to a low of $135.50 per ounce in London on September 19.

Bicentennial Coins. In the collectors' spotlight in 1975 were the new 1776–1976 coin issues featuring bicentennial motifs: a colonial drummer on the quarter, Independence Hall on the half dollar, and the Liberty Bell and the moon on the silver dollar. The first bicentennial coin, the 1776–1976 half dollar, was released from the Federal Reserve Bank of Minneapolis on July 7. Shortly thereafter all three denominations were in circulation and were being actively sought by collectors.

In addition to pieces made for circulation in special "clad" metal, the mint prepared special collectors' sets containing 40% silver. Initially these were priced at $15 per set, but due to production economies the figure was reduced to $12, with refunds sent to those who ordered at the higher price earlier.

The three United States mints—Philadelphia, Denver, and San Francisco—were so busy producing new bicentennial quarters, half dollars, and dollars with the 1776–1976 date that no 1975-dated pieces of these denominations were made.

New Issues. During the year there was a movement for the production of a $2 bill, a denomination that is obsolete. Late in the year it was decided that the $2 bill would be issued in the spring of 1976. Secretary of the Treasury William Simon and mint director Mary Brooks announced in June that a two-cent piece was being discussed for possible production, but at years' end issuance of such a denomination appeared unlikely.

Rarities. The market for choice and rare U. S. coins continued strong throughout the year, with a number of record prices being realized for scarcities and rarities. Aluminum Lincoln cents bearing a 1973 date were reportedly valued at close to $30,000 by their owners. The coins were made to test the suitability of aluminum as a coinage metal; and after most were melted, 12

The obverse of the 1975 Bicentennial Medal carries a likeness of Paul Revere and the reverse shows the famous Minuteman statue.

or 14 were distributed to congressmen to show them the new format. Despite speculation, there were no plans to coin additional pieces.

International Collectors' Items. Many countries around the world issued coins and sets especially for collectors. Panama issued a 500 Balboa gold coin, the largest denomination numismatic issue of all time, convertible at face value into $500. Two international series of coins attracted great interest. The Conservation Collection of coins featured animals and bore the imprint of many different countries. These pieces were struck in gold and silver and were minted especially for collectors. Portions of the profits were earmarked to help save endangered animal species. The popular FAO (English translation: "Food For All") coins, produced under UN auspices and featuring various sizes and denominations, were struck in countries throughout the world. Profits went to feed hungry people around the globe.

Also important in the market for world coins were the 1976-dated silver pieces of $5 and $10 denominations produced to raise additional capital for the 1976 Olympics in Montreal. In order to maximize the number of designs and sustain collector interest over a long period of time, the Olympics sets were released in seven different series, five of which had reached the marketplace by the end of 1975.

Q. DAVID BOWERS
Author of "High Profits from Rare Coin Investment;" Columnist, "Coin World"

COLOMBIA

During 1975, the initial broad support for the government of Liberal President Alfonso López Michelsen gradually eroded as more and more particular interests were affected by government economic policies. Strikes in diverse areas demonstrated labor's growing disenchantment with the activities of the government. A military coup, led by army commander Álvaro Valencia Tovar, was narrowly averted in late May. Valencia Tovar and others were ultimately forced by the president to resign. In June widespread student riots led to the proclamation of a state of siege for the first time since December 1973. In spite of this measure, antigovernment terrorists succeeded in assassinating Gen. José Ramón Rincón Quiñones, inspector-general of the army and a noted counter-guerrilla expert, on the outskirts of Bogotá. Former dictator (1953–57) Gustavo Rojas Pinilla died on Jan. 17, 1975.

Faced with a situation in which his economic measures had alienated the establishment without creating a constituency among the poor, President López began ruling more in the "law and order" tradition of previous Colombian presidents. At the end of the year, it appeared the López's "Mandato claro" (clear mandate) for an attempt at social reform of the highly structured Colombian society was, temporarily at least, at an end.

Politics. Although presidential alternation under the National Front ended in 1974, the arrangement whereby cabinet posts would be divided between Conservatives and Liberals will continue until 1978. Much political maneuvering during the year centered around cabinet appointments, and as the year progressed it became increasingly apparent that the Conservative party was exerting increased influence within the government. During most of the year the strategic post of minister of interior, with responsibility for internal security, was held by Conservative Cornelio Reyes. A minor cabinet shuffle in July did little to counteract what many Liberals saw as increasing Conservative influence within the government.

During the year, the Conservatives appeared to be much more active than the Liberals in organizing for the forthcoming 1976 congressional elections. The Conservatives, traditionally strong in the countryside, spent most of their energies attempting to organize in the cities. The Liberal party still appeared to be suffering from the split caused the previous year by the refusal of former president Carlos Lleras Restrepo to endorse López's candidacy. The eight-man national directorate of the Liberal party contained three men who favored Lleras's presidential candidacy in 1978, while a majority of five favored that of the *Designado* (vice president), Julio César Turbay Ayala.

Economy. Beset by world inflationary problems over which it had no control, the Colombian economy ended 1974 on the downside, with real economic growth for the year at about 6%, down from the 7.5% figure for 1973. In 1975 there was a continued downward trend, caused by government austerity, a tightening of credit, and hesitancy in the private sector. Consumer prices, which increased at about 25% during 1974, increased slightly less during 1975, due to a significantly lower increase in the money supply and the austerity program.

ERNEST A. DUFF
Randolph-Macon Woman's College

COLOMBIA · Information Highlights

Official Name: Republic of Colombia.
Location: Northwest South America.
Area: 439,736 square miles (1,138,914 sq km).
Population (1975 est.): 25,900,000.
Chief Cities (1975 est.): Bogotá, the capital, 2,800,000; Medellín, 1,100,000; Cali, 920,000.
Government: *Head of state and of government,* Alfonso López Michelsen, president (took office Aug. 7, 1974). *Legislature*—Congress: Senate and Chamber of Representatives.
Monetary Unit: Peso (30.6 pesos equal U. S.$1, May 1975).
Gross National Product (1974 est.): $13,600,000,000.
Manufacturing (major products): Textiles, beverages, iron and steel, petroleum products.
Major Agricultural Products: Coffee, bananas, rice, cotton, sugarcane, tobacco, potatoes, corn.
Foreign Trade (1974): *Exports,* $1,369,000,000; *imports,* $876,000,000.

Sixth graders from Golden are directing the restoration of this 100-year-old school for the Bicentennial.

COLORADO

A faltering economy imposed a shaky truce on the long-standing war between environmentalists and developers in Colorado during 1975. The recession forced a slowdown in the rapid development in ecologically fragile Colorado, a move that environmentalists had sought for years.

Recession. By national standards the recession in Colorado was not severe. Unemployment in the Denver metropolitan area averaged 5.6%, less than the national average, for the first 8 months of 1975. That contrasted, however, with only 3.6% in the same period in 1974.

The economic dip was concentrated in construction, with both business and residential building dropping sharply. Partly as a result, the state's new, environmentally-minded governor, Richard Lamm, tentatively put aside his long-term goal of comprehensive land-use legislation during the 1975 legislature's session.

Legislature. The legislators studied strip mining, oil shale development, and mineral severance taxes after the session ended. The governor said he hoped state lawmakers could find a compromise on the issues in 1976.

Lamm, allied with a liberal House controlled 39–26 by Democrats, often clashed with conservative Republicans who controlled the Senate 19–16 by virtue of holdovers from the 1972 election. The Senate killed Lamm's tax reform proposal, which the governor said would have shifted more of the state's fiscal burdens to big corporations and affluent citizens. A bill granting collective bargaining rights to public employees, avidly backed by Colorado teachers, also died in the Senate.

The legislature did pass a bill reducing penalties for possession of less than 1 ounce (28 grams) of marihuana to a fine of up to $100 with no jail term and making it a petty offense. Stiff felony provisions remained, however, for those who grew or sold marihuana.

Chicano leaders spearheaded by House Speaker Ruben Valdez, a Democrat from Denver, struck an alliance with longtime Senate powerhouse Joseph Shoemaker, a Republican, to pass a milestone bilingual education bill. It provided bilingual instruction in kindergarten through third grade for students whose prime language is not English.

Lamm tried to veto construction of a controversial superhighway in the southwest Denver area, but the Colorado Supreme Court ruled that the highway commission, not the governor, had that authority. The Senate then refused even to vote on Lamm's nominees for the commission, leaving lame-duck Republicans in control even though their terms had expired. That sent the issue back to court.

Other Developments. The Army began phasing out its Pueblo Army Depot in southern Colorado. Citizens of that area were pleased when their college was upgraded to Southern Colorado State University. Gen. Daniel "Chappy" James became the first black to command the North American Air Defense Command headquarters in Colorado Springs.

A prompt hiring freeze by Lamm in the face of falling state revenues helped cut $25 million from the budget without forcing layoffs of state employees. Denver was neither as prompt nor as lucky, and 321 city workers were scheduled to be laid off.

Racial progress in the state was symbolized when the state had a white, a black, and a Chicano as governor in the same day. Lamm left the state early one day, leaving Lt. Gov. George Brown, a black, as acting governor. When Brown also left, the constitution provided for House Speaker Valdez, a Chicano, to be acting chief executive.

BOB EWEGEN
The Denver "Post"

COLORADO · Information Highlights

Area: 104,247 square miles (270,000 sq km).
Population (1974 est.): 2,496,000. *Density:* 24 per sq mi.
Chief Cities (1970 census): Denver, the capital, 514,678; Colorado Springs, 135,060; Pueblo, 97,453.
Government (1975): *Chief Officers*—governor, Richard D. Lamm (D); lt. gov., George L. Brown (D). *General Assembly*—Senate, 35 members; House of Representatives, 65 members.
Education (1974–75): *Enrollment*—public elementary schools, 304,705 pupils; public secondary, 263,355; nonpublic, 32,500; colleges and universities, 141,269 students. *Public school expenditures,* $529,048,000 ($991 per pupil).
State Finances (fiscal year 1974): *Revenues,* $1,641,788,000; *expenditures,* $1,409,801,000.
Personal Income (1974): $13,337,000,000; per capita, $5,343.
Labor Force (Aug. 1975): *Nonagricultural wage and salary earners,* 956,700; *insured unemployed,* 20,700.

of 4%. It was balanced by $163 million in increased taxes. Capital gains and sales taxes increased from 6% to 7% with business services included. A dividends tax was reinstated at 7% but limited to those with incomes of $20,000 or higher. Corporate tax rates were raised to 10% and motorists' registration fees were increased to $20. A Public Utilities Control Authority was established to give greater consumer protection. Under court order to equalize school aid, the legislature established a new "instant lottery" to increase school aid for poorer towns.

Other legislative actions included a Freedom of Information Act, stricter nursing-home regulations, legalized hitchhiking on all but limited access highways, and repeal of fair-trade law pricing. Pharmacies were required to post the prices of 100 prescription drugs, and food stores were forbidden to raise prices once goods were on the shelf. The sperm whale was designated the official state animal.

Transportation. The state completed a $4.5 million automated shuttle transit to parking lots at Bradley Field. Funds for the first year's operating expenses were in doubt. A Federal Aviation Administration proposal allowing Concorde supersonic aircraft landings at Bradley was opposed by Governor Grasso.

Elections. Only municipal elections were held in 1975. Frederick K. Biebel of Stratford was elected chairman of the Republican party. John M. Bailey, the Democrats' long-time leader, died in April. The Democrats will have a statewide presidential primary in May 1976 with the names of all recognized presidential candidates on the ballot.

Disasters. A fire bombing destroyed the Sponge Rubber Products Co. in Shelton, causing $10 million damage. Floods in the wake of Hurricane Eloise caused $9.3 million damage in Watertown, Danbury, and Torrington.

Education. The University of Connecticut at Storrs broke ground for construction of a new $18.5 million library. The Hartford Seminary Foundation sold 215,000 volumes to Emory University in Atlanta, for $1.75 million.

GEORGE ADAMS, *Connecticut State Library*

AMERICAN REVOLUTION BICENTENNIAL COMMISSION OF CONNECTICUT

Bicentennial commission administrator John Warner (left), presents Bicentennial flag to Sharon, Conn. officials on July 3. Connecticut was the first state to have all towns designated bicentennial communities.

CONNECTICUT

Increased living costs, layoffs, strikes, and school finances were Connecticut's major concerns in 1975. Former Gov. Thomas J. Meskill was sworn in as judge of the U. S. Second Court of Appeals. Serious attempts by activist Ned Coll and the Civil Liberties Union failed to open more than the six state-owned miles (9.6 km) of shoreline to nonresident bathers. President Ford's visit to Hartford on October 15 was marred by a motorist's collision with the presidential limousine, caused by the failure of police to block an intersection.

Economy. State tax revenue decreased by $33 million, and the fiscal year ended with a $70 million deficit. The unemployment rate of 11.5% was the highest in the state since the depression, but there were 1,476,000 employed in August. The per capita personal income of $6,455 was third highest among the states. The state and individual municipalities were hard pressed to meet school finance needs. Willimantic taxpayers revolted, forcing a 9% city budget cut. Democratic Gov. Ella Grasso forced the Democratic Assembly to reduce spending, continued a freeze on state hiring, pay, and promotions, and eliminated many publications. The total number of state employees dropped slightly during 1975.

Legislature. The legislature painfully arrived at a $1.6 billion budget, which was an increase

CONSUMERISM

Consumer concern in 1975 focused on the economy, the environment, and the growing reluctance of the federal government to impose regulations in the market place. Rebates on 1974 income taxes and a tax credit for the purchase of a new home were instituted as antirecession measures but consumers were cautious, and the rebate failed to stimulate the economy significantly. At the end of 1975 surveys indicated that consumers were more pessimistic than ever about the ability of either government or business to cope with the economic problems that confronted the United States.

Inflation. Inflation continued to be a major problem for consumers. From January 1973 to June 1975 fuel oil and coal costs rose 91.1%; food costs rose 35.6%; and gas and electricity costs rose 36.5%. From August 1974 to August 1975 the consumer price index increased 8.6%. These large increases, coupled with a high rate of unemployment, reduced the real income of many families.

Environment. The skyrocketing cost of foreign fuel oil and the dwindling supply of U. S. supplies of coal, oil, and natural gas led consumers to investigate seriously the development of new sources of energy. Environmentalists were not convinced that nuclear energy was a safe alternative, and many recommended the development of solar, hydroelectric, geothermal, or wind energy.

Government chemist inspects the results of a new flame retardant. The U. S. Consumer Product Safety Commission passed regulations in 1975 concerning the manufacture of flammable clothing.

USDA

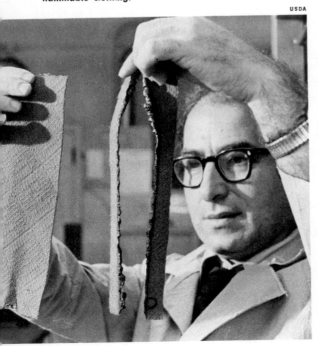

On another issue in 1975, consumers joined environmentalists in expressing concern that fluorocarbon emissions from aerosol cans were breaking down the ozone layer of the atmosphere. Although a petition to the Consumer Product Safety Commission was denied, there were several bills pending in Congress to ban the offending fluorocarbons. Among other bills pending were one that would reinstitute the returnable bottle, thereby reducing the national problem of solid waste disposal, and one to limit and identify artificial additives in food.

Legislation. A bill to establish an Agency for Consumer Advocacy was passed by Congress, but President Gerald Ford promised to veto it, and prospects for a congressional override were dim. The President favored regulatory reform by existing agencies, so as not to increase the size of federal government.

Consumer legislation that passed into law included the Real Estate Settlement Procedures Act, the Fair Credit Billing Act, the Equal Credit Opportunity Act, and the Magnuson-Moss Warranty Act. The assumption underlying these laws is the consumer's basic right to information and equity in transactions. Proposed legislation to further safeguard this right included a bill that would require unit and item price disclosure in conjunction with a universal product code. There were also Federal Trade Commission proposals to encourage availability of price information on drugs, eyeglasses, funerals, and attorneys' services; proposals to require energy-use information on home appliances; and a truth-in-savings law.

Government Controls. While Congress considered antitrust legislation against oil companies and other large firms, the administration proposed the reduction of federal regulations in the marketplace. For example, the administration favored the removal of constraints against competition first instituted by agencies such as the Civil Aeronautics Board and the Interstate Commerce Commission. There was danger, however, that the antiregulation movement might eliminate some vital and hard-won consumer protections.

The Consumer Product Safety Commission passed a regulation that forbade the manufacture of small children's sleepwear that had not been treated with flame retardant. Older children's sleepwear was not required to be treated in this way, but stores marketing the flammable clothing were required to display signs advising customers of this fact.

Finally, in a decision that will have a profound impact on consumer litigation, the U. S. Supreme Court ruled that the plaintiff in class action suits must notify every other member of the class of the action before it takes place. It was expected that this would have the effect of seriously limiting the possibility for filing class action suits.

EDWARD J. METZEN
University of Missouri

CRIME

Gun control remained a highly controversial subject in the United States during 1975, while reported crime rates continued to increase and many, including President Gerald Ford, proposed legislation to reduce them. At the year's end, the U. S. Supreme Court had not yet handed down a new ruling on capital punishment.

Gun Control. Gun control was the most hotly debated crime issue in the United States in 1975. Interest in the subject became particularly intense after two attempts were made to assassinate President Ford during the year, both of them involving handguns. At the end of the year, however, federal legislative drives to register gun ownership remained stalled in Congress. In Massachusetts, however, the Bartley-Fox law, effective April 1, made a one-year jail term mandatory for those found carrying a firearm without a license. The bill was the strictest gun control measure yet enacted in the United States.

Results of the Massachusetts approach are not as yet apparent. Police fear that attempts to enforce the statute might endanger officers, since suspects may try to shoot their way out rather than face a stiff prison term. On the other hand, gun penalties were expected to lead to the imprisonment of armed burglars, rapists, and other offenders in cases where there might be insufficient evidence to prove guilt for the more serious crimes.

National statistics indicated that about half of all gun-related crimes involved "Saturday night specials," which are small, short-barreled, readily-concealed weapons. They sell for less than $50 and are of .32 caliber or less. Although the Gun Control Act of 1958 banned importation of these weapons, its passage encouraged a thriving domestic production that now turns out about 200,000 "Saturday night specials" annually.

About 70% of the U. S. public favors strict gun control laws, according to the Gallup Poll. Congressmen, however, remain notoriously "gun-shy," an attitude stemming from awareness that opponents of gun-control measures tend to unite to vote against legislators sponsoring or favoring control laws. Proponents, on the other hand, tend to vote their feelings on a wider range of issues. Thus, a fear of political suicide appears to lie behind congressional reluctance to move forcefully into the gun-control legislation area, despite popular sentiment.

U.S.-Japanese Comparisons. About 10,000 people die each year from gun-related episodes in the United States, and half of the country's murders involve handguns. These figures contrast sharply with those in Japan, which maintains a rigid gun control policy. There, in 1974, only 0.4% of the country's 1,707 murders were committed with firearms, and only 1.5% of robberies involved guns. No one in Japan is permitted to own a pistol or revolver except law enforcement officials, members of self-defense forces, and a small number of sportsmen. Possession of toy and model pistols is also prohibited if they are too realistic.

Acts of violence directed at public officials have been about as common in Japan as in the United States. But in Japan, such attempts do not involve guns and therefore rarely succeed. Weapons such as firebombs, knives, and clubs make it much more difficult to move within effective range of assassination targets without alerting bystanders, police, and bodyguards. There has not been a successful political assassination in Japan since 1958, when the gun control law went into effect.

The President on Crime. President Ford announced during the year that he continued to be "unalterably opposed" to gun control laws. He looked to a number of other means to reduce escalating crime rates. On June 19, President Ford proposed legislation that would establish mandatory prison sentences for armed persons who commit violent crimes in areas under federal jurisdiction.

In a message to Congress, the President underlined the sense of failure in regard to crime control that pervades the United States. "America has been far from successful in dealing with the sort of crime that obsesses Americans day and night—street crime, crime that invades our neighborhoods and our homes—murders, robberies, rapes, muggings, holdups, break-ins—the kind of brutal violence that makes us fear strangers and afraid to go out at night," the President said. He called for a shift in emphasis from what he perceived to be undue concern with the rights of criminals and neglect of the rights of their victims. What the country longs for, the President said, was "domestic tranquility." He hoped that his proposed program would serve as a model for the states to duplicate.

In an April 25 speech at Yale University Law School, the President focused on white-collar crime. He noted that "crime in high places—whether in the federal government, state governments, or in business and organized labor—sets an example that makes it all the more difficult to foster a law-abiding spirit among ordinary citizens." The President pledged to restore to the executive branch of the government "decency, honesty, and adherence for law at all levels."

Crime Statistics. The President's concern grew out of statistics that indicated ominously soaring crime rates. A study by the National Center for Health Statistics showed that in 1975 people in the United States were killing one another in greater numbers than ever before in the 20th century. It was predicted that the record-setting murder rate will not decline until the 1980's, when children born in the "baby boom" following World War II will be over 30 years old. The present heavy concentration of people in the 18–29-year age bracket contributes dispropor-

Lynette Fromme (*below*) is led away by police after she was apprehended in Sacramento, Calif., on September 5 while aiming a gun at President Ford, then only a few feet away.

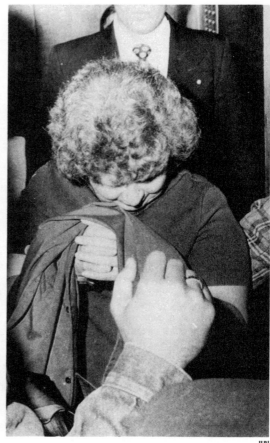

UPI

UPI

Sara Jane Moore (*above*) was apprehended on September 22 for allegedly trying to assassinate President Ford in San Francisco, Calif. At the sound of the shot, the President (*below*), visibly shaken, was hurried to his limousine.

UPI

tionately to the homicide statistics, since homicide shows a strong relationship with age. Also, men have a homicide rate 4 times higher than that of women, and blacks have a rate 11 times higher than that of whites. According to a calculation by Franklin E. Zimring, a University of Chicago law professor, black male children in the United States have about 1 chance in 10 of being murdered.

Another researcher, Donald T. Lunde, a Stanford University professor of law and psychiatry, maintained that permissive child rearing, a decline in self-reliance, and the diminishing influence of religion all have contributed to the current "murder epidemic." Lunde said that people in the United States increasingly blame their troubles on society instead of on themselves and take out their frustrations on others. Lunde's conclusions were based on a 5-year study of 40 murderers.

Kidnappings have also increased dramatically in the United States. There were 96 convictions in federal courts in fiscal 1974 for kidnapping, compared with 39 such convictions 7 years earlier. Other countries also report similar increases. In Latin America, particularly in Argentina, there were scores of kidnappings in 1975 by political extremists. A number netted ransoms of $1 million, and one resulted in the payment of $60 million to the kidnappers for the release of their victim. In Italy, Milan's police chief, Mario Massagrande, predicted that "kidnapping is the crime of the future."

Gerald M. Caplan, director of the National Institute of Law Enforcement and Criminal Justice, expressed his belief during the year that a certain level of crime is an inevitable part of a free society. In democratic countries, where social controls are not imposed by government, Caplan said, "We can expect greater degrees of deviation—more eccentricity, more spontaneity, and at the same time, more crime." Caplan noted that factors that have helped to reduce crime have largely been technological innovations, such as metal detectors at airports, which have deterred skyjacking, and mandatory steering-lock components on automobiles, which have brought about a decrease in auto theft.

Crime and Unemployment. Part of the growing crime wave during 1975 was traced to the prevailing U. S. economic recession. Property crimes tripled, while crimes against persons were doubling. Writing in *The New York Times,* columnist Tom Wicker noted that the crime increases were sharpest in the last months of 1974, when the economic recession was intensifying and producing large-scale layoffs and business failures. Wicker also pointed out that cities where unemployment was highest suffered the largest increases in crime. In Detroit, where the number of unemployed nearly doubled (from 7.9% to 14.9%), the crime rate rose by 17.9%. In Houston, where the growth in unemployment was only 0.9% (from 3.7% to 4.6%), crime increased by only 10%. Unemployment particularly affected former convicts, who have difficulty securing jobs even when jobs are plentiful. The recession, Wicker said, had contributed notably to repeat offenses by persons released from prison and unable to secure legitimate employment.

Capital Punishment. The constitutionality of capital punishment, often a controversial subject in periods of rapid increase in crime, continued to be unresolved in the United States in 1975. In late June the Supreme Court announced postponement of reexamination of its 1972 ruling that capital punishment as then administered was unconstitutional.

Meanwhile, more than 300 persons condemned to death remained uncertain about their fate. Death penalty statutes tailored to meet objections noted by the Supreme Court in 1972 have now been enacted in 33 states. The case before the court involved Jesse T. Fowler of North Carolina, who shot an acquaintance to death in a dispute over a dice game in Raleigh before several witnesses. The only issue before the court is whether or not he can be executed.

The death penalty controversy was intensified when proponents of capital punishment filed with the court the results of a study by Isaac Ehrlich, a University of Chicago professor, who used sophisticated mathematical techniques to analyze crime statistics. Ehrlich concluded that for the period 1935–69 "an additional execution per year may have resulted, on the average, in 7 or 8 fewer murders." The Legal Defense Fund, opposing capital punishment, strongly disputed Ehrlich's findings. Two Columbia University economists, Peter Passell and John B. Taylor, said in a counterstudy that Ehrlich's paper was "riddled with theoretical and technical errors that render its conclusions meaningless."

A UN survey indicated that 103 of the then-current 135 member nations of the organization retained capital punishment. The Economic and Social Council social committee reaffirmed the long-range UN principle of promoting progressive restriction on the number of offenses for which the death penalty may be imposed "with a view to the desirability of eliminating the punishment."

Crime in the News. Major criminal events of the year included the two assassination attempts in California against the life of President Ford. The first was made on September 5, allegedly by Lynette ("Squeaky") Fromme, a follower of Charles Manson, who has been in prison for involvement in a number of murders in the late 1960's. The second attempt, on September 22, allegedly was made by Sara Jane Moore. In mid-September, the capture of Patricia Hearst, who allegedly had figured prominently in the activities of the Symbionese Liberation Army after her kidnapping by the group, concluded a 19-month search.

GILBERT GEIS, *Professor*
University of California, Irvine

UPI

Sen. George McGovern visited Fidel Castro in Cuba in May to discuss U. S.-Cuban relations.

CUBA

The year 1975 was a bittersweet one for the Cuban government of Prime Minister Fidel Castro. In midsummer the Organization of American States (OAS) formally voted to end diplomatic and economic sanctions imposed against the island nation in 1964. But the United States, which earlier had taken several diplomatic steps toward an eventual rapprochement with Cuba, announced in December that the introduction of a brigade of Cuban army troops into the newly-independent African nation of Angola had ended efforts to resume U. S.-Cuban relations.

Sugar. The production of sugar, the island's largest export, was estimated at approximately 5.5 million tons or less, a decrease of about 8.5% from the previous year's crop. The decrease was attributed in part to drought conditions. The reduction in the crop, coupled with a precipitous decline in the world price of sugar (from 50 cents per pound in January to about 20 cents by December), will inevitably mean less revenue for the Cuban government.

Foreign Relations. The most significant development in 1975 was the abrupt shift in U. S.-Cuban relations, which throughout much of the year seemed to portend an eventual resumption of relations between the two nations. Beginning with the February release of three U. S. citizens imprisoned in Cuba for allegedly smuggling marihuana, a number of steps toward improved relations were taken by each nation. In March the U. S. State Department announced that Cuban diplomats accredited to the United Nations, who previously had been restricted to a 25-mile (40-km) radius of New York City, could now travel up to 250 miles (400 km) from the city. The same month Secretary of State

Henry Kissinger, in a speech at Houston, said "We see no virtue in a perpetual antagonism" between the United States and Cuba.

In May, Sen. George McGovern visited Cuba, met with Castro, and learned that the bearded prime minister had decided to return some $2 million seized by his government from hijackers who had forced a Southern Airways jet to fly to the island in 1972. In June, Castro deported to the United States four individuals accused of hijacking three U. S. commercial aircraft to Cuba in 1971–72.

The trend toward reconciliation between the two countries seemed to be accelerating when the OAS meeting in San José, Costa Rica, voted on July 29 to end economic and political sanctions imposed on Cuba by the OAS 11 years earlier. The United States was 1 of 16 nations that voted in favor of the resolution. Paraguay, Chile, and Uruguay opposed the move, with Brazil and Nicaragua abstaining.

At the same time the commission on Central Intelligence Agency (CIA) activities within the United States, chaired by Vice President Nelson Rockefeller, and the Senate Select Committee on Intelligence, headed by Sen. Frank Church, disclosed that the CIA had during the 1960's made several attempts to assassinate Castro. The net effect of the disclosures, which Castro confirmed in interviews with foreign newsmen, was to clear the air.

But by early fall the U. S. government learned that Cuba was sending combat troops to Angola. On November 24, Secretary of State Kissinger in a speech in Detroit, stated that the United States could not "ignore the thousands of Cubans sent into an African conflict." As the fighting escalated in Angola between the Soviet-backed popular movement for the liberation of Angola and the two other factions, supported by Zaire, China, South Africa, and the United States, Castro, presumably at the behest of the Soviet Union, began to send reinforcements. By late December an estimated 4–6,000 black Cuban army troops were reportedly fighting in Angola. On December 20, President Ford announced that the Cuban decision to send troops

---

CUBA · Information Highlights

Official Name: Republic of Cuba.
Location: Caribbean Sea.
Area: 44,218 square miles (114,524 sq km).
Population (1975 est.): 9,500,000.
Chief Cities (1970 census): Havana, the capital, 1,755,-400; Santiago de Cuba, 276,000; Camagüey, 196,900.
Government: *Head of state,* Osvaldo Dorticós Torrade, president (took office July 1959). *Head of government,* Fidel Castro Ruz, premier (took office Feb. 1959).
Monetary Unit: Peso (0.815 peso equals U. S.$1, 1975).
Gross National Product (1973 est.): $3,400,000,000.
Manufacturing (major products): Sugar products, tobacco products.
Major Agricultural Products: Sugarcane, tobacco, rice, oranges and tangerines, sweet potatoes and yams.
Foreign Trade (1972): *Exports,* $803,000,000; *imports,* $1,292,000,000.

to Angola ended any efforts at all to have friend-ly relations with the Cuban government.

Economy. Despite a decline in sugar produc-tion, the Cuban economy grew in 1975. A num-ber of nations, including France, Spain, Japan, Canada, and Mexico, extended credits totaling more than $1 billion to Cuba during the year. The credits were to be used for the purchase of industrial machinery, cargo and fishing vessels, and other capital goods. The island's largest trading partner, the Soviet Union, maintained its support of Cuba, apparently at an increased level.

New Constitution. Continuing efforts to in-stitutionalize his revolution, Castro convened in late December the First Congress of the Cuban Communist party and published a draft constitu-tion, which will undoubtedly be approved. Un-der the proposed constitution, a national People's Assembly will be established along with a 31-member State Council, which will include a pres-ident, a first vice president, and five other vice presidents.

LOUIS SADLER
New Mexico State University

CYPRUS

During 1975, Cyprus continued to feel the upheaval caused by the Turkish invasion that took place during the summer of 1974. Citing the need to protect the Turkish Cypriot minority, the Turkish government took over approximately 40% of the island, even though the Turkish Cypriots comprised only about 18% of the pop-ulation, while the Greek Cypriots made up about 80%. During the invasion 200,000 Greek Cyp-riots, or a third of the total population, fled the northern part of Cyprus. The well-being of the refugees was a particular problem to the Cypriot government, the more so since the economy was in total disarray because the territory lost to the Turks was previously the most prosperous part of Cyprus.

Negotiations. From time to time during the year negotiations were held between Glafkos Clerides, speaker of the Cyprus House of Rep-resentatives, and Rauf Denktaş, who spoke for the Turkish Cypriots. Clearly, however, Denktaş was subject to the wishes of the Turkish govern-ment. The talks broke down on February 13, when the Turkish Cypriots proclaimed that the Turkish-held part of the island was a separate state that could eventually join in a federation with the Greek Cypriots. Denktaş, who pre-viously had served as vice president of Cyprus, became head of the new Turkish administration. This unilateral action was strongly denounced by Archbishop Makarios III, president of Cy-prus, and by Premier Constantine Caramanlis of Greece. The Turkish government gave full ap-proval.

Under the auspices of UN Secretary-General Kurt Waldheim the talks between Clerides and Denktaş resumed at Vienna in late April. These lasted until May 3, with the two agreeing that Nicosia airport, closed since the Turkish inva-sion, ought to be reopened, and that a joint group would be set up to study proposals for a new central government. While the Greek Cypriot side seemed willing to compromise, the Turkish Cypriots were obviously unwilling to agree to any formula that would deprive them of the control they had secured through armed force. The Turkish Cypriots called for a bizonal federation—one zone Turkish, one zone Greek —with each community controlling its own af-fairs under a weak central government. The Greek Cypriots wanted a more powerful central government and a smaller territorial area for the Turks.

A second series of meetings at Vienna in June lasted for three unproductive days. A third round of talks at Vienna started on July 31. This time it was agreed that 9,000 Turkish Cypriots who were resident outside the Turkish area could move there, and that 10,000 Greek Cyp-riots remaining under Turkish rule could either

UPI

Trouble over Cyprus continued throughout 1975 with Greek and Turkish Cypriot leaders failing to come to an agree-ment at a meeting in Vienna in June.

Greek Cypriot national guardsmen were forced to use tear gas and warning shots to hold back students trying to storm the American Center in January 1975.

stay or leave for parts of the island under the Greek Cypriot jurisdiction. In September, Clerides and Denktaş met at the United Nations to start a fourth round of talks, but these broke down immediately without even the setting of a date for resumption. Clerides placed the blame on Denktaş, who, he said, had failed to keep a promise made at Vienna to submit a plan showing what the Turkish Cypriots envisaged as a new government for Cyprus. In November the UN General Assembly voted overwhelmingly for the removal of all foreign troops from Cyprus and for the voluntary return of the refugees to their homes. The assembly further urged the Greek and Turkish Cypriots to resume their talks under the auspices of Waldheim.

The Archbishop's Diplomacy. Archbishop Makarios undertook during 1975 to seek support for the Greek Cypriots. He conferred with Premier Caramanlis at Athens in April before attending a Commonwealth conference in Jamaica. From there he flew to the United States, where in May he met with Secretary of State Henry Kissinger. Then he went to Athens for another meeting with Caramanlis. In late spring Makarios toured Arab countries, including Egypt and Syria. During the summer he represented Cyprus at the Helsinki security conference, where he met with U. S. President Gerald Ford and Kissinger, among others.

The archbishop's presence at Helsinki prompted a protest by Turkish Premier Süleyman Demirel, who stormed out of a session when Makarios accused Turkey of violating (through its Cyprus policy) the conference's stated ideals on territorial integrity. When the archbishop ad-

dressed the UN General Assembly on October 7, the Turkish delegation was not present, and a message from the Turkish Cypriot administration affirmed he did not speak for them. In his address to the General Assembly, Makarios stressed that the negative attitude of the Turkish government was to blame for the lack of progress in a settlement, and he called for international guarantees of any Cyprus peace settlement. During this visit to the United States, the archbishop met again with Secretary Kissinger. On his way back to Nicosia, Makarios once again stopped at Athens where he and Premier Caramanlis announced that they had identical views about Cyprus.

The Issue of American Arms. The failure to reach a settlement on Cyprus had repercussions on U. S. domestic politics. As a means of pressuring the Turks to withdraw troops from the island and to allow the Greek Cypriot refugees

——— CYPRUS · Information Highlights ———

Official Name: Cyprus.
Location: Eastern Mediterranean.
Area: 3,572 square miles (9,251 sq km).
Population (1975 est.): 700,000.
Chief Cities (1973 est.): Nicosia, the capital, 112,000; Limassol, 48,000.
Government: *Head of state,* Archbishop Makarios III, president.
Monetary Unit: Pound (.3270 pound equals U. S.$1, July 1975).
Gross National Product (1971 est.): $608,000,000.
Manufacturing: Food and beverage processing, nonmetallic mineral products.
Major Agricultural Products: Potatoes, grapes, citrus fruits, wheat, barley, carobs, sheep, goats, pigs.
Foreign Trade (1974): *Exports,* $137,000,000; *imports,* $369,000,000.

to return to their homes, Congress enacted legislation cutting off arms aid to Turkey on February 5. President Ford and Secretary Kissinger then mounted an intense campaign to persuade Congress to modify its stand, citing the United States' need to maintain a strong Turkey as part of NATO. In May the Senate voted 41–40 to lift the ban; and it did so again in July by a vote of 47–46. A week before, the House of Representatives had already voted 223–206 to retain the cutoff. In retaliation the Turkish government moved to take over operations at U. S. bases in Turkey, after which President Ford put even greater pressure on the members of Congress. Finally, on October 2, the House reversed itself by a vote of 237–176, easing the embargo against Turkey.

Turkish Colonization of the North. Almost all of the approximately 110,000 Turkish Cypriots —once located about the island in various areas —were settled under the Turkish administration in the north, and persistent reports indicated that mainland Turks were also living there. Since the nearly 200,000 Greek Cypriot refugees were not allowed to return to their homes, the ethnic composition of northern Cyprus had been radically altered by the Turkish invasion. This situation further complicated the prospects for a lasting, peaceful solution to the island's problems.

GEORGE J. MARCOPOULOS
Tufts University

CZECHOSLOVAKIA

The major political event of the year was the change in the republic's presidency. After months of intense maneuvering, including consultations with Soviet party leader Leonid Brezhnev, the way was cleared for Gustav Husák, secretary general of the Czechoslovak Communist party, to replace ailing Ludvík Svoboda as president of Czechoslovakia. Thus the most prestigious party and government posts were once again entrusted to the same individual, even though this was reminiscent of the previously criticized "personality cult." Since the Czechoslovak constitution did not provide for the removal of a president for inability to fulfill his duty, and since Svoboda could not be persuaded to resign, the constitution was amended accordingly.

Troubles With Dissidents. Throughout the year the regime was plagued by continued resistance on the part of dissidents. An interview taped with the late Josef Smrkovský, the most outspoken personality of the 1968 reform movement, was published in serialized form in the Western press. There was also a letter denouncing the Husák regime that Alexandr Dubček, the deposed leader of the 1968 "Czechoslovak spring," had sent to the federal assembly and the Slovak national council. Its publication prompted a bitter anti-Dubček campaign in the communications media. Other letters that appeared in the Western press in 1975 were those of prominent writers Václav Havel and Ludvík Vaculík and the noted philosopher Karel Kosík. Even more frustrating for the regime was its failure to intercept a 250-page analysis of the 1968 events and the Soviet invasion prepared by another well-known reformist, Zdenek Mlynář. It was intended for presentation at the conference of the European Communist parties.

Economy. By mid-1975 numerous economic increases over the corresponding period of 1974 had been announced. Industrial production was up 7%; consumer goods output increased 7.5%; and construction jumped 9%. Foreign trade and retail trade increased 13.1% and 3.5% respectively, and personal income was up 4%. As usual, the performance of agriculture was less satisfactory. The number of hogs increased, but the number of cattle and poultry went down. Preliminary harvest reports indicated a decrease in potatoes, wheat, corn, and feed grains.

Foreign Affairs. While persisting in following the lead of the Soviet Union, Husák's regime continued its endeavors to improve relations with Western countries. A treaty with Austria was signed in December 1974 concerning compensation for confiscated Austrian property, and an agreement designed to step up economic relations with West Germany was concluded in January 1975. Cordial welcomes were extended to foreign ministers from Denmark, Austria, West Germany, and Belgium. The president of Chase Manhattan Bank, David Rockefeller, and UN Secretary General Kurt Waldheim also visited. During the Helsinki European Security Conference, Husák conferred with British Prime Minister Harold Wilson and the West German and Austrian chancellors. The Czechoslovak foreign ministry reached an agreement with U. S. Secretary of State Henry Kissinger to begin talks on scientific and cultural exchanges. However, Czechoslovak spokesmen remained critical of congressional disapproval of the U. S.-Czechoslovak agreement on mutual property claims initialed in 1974.

EDWARD TABORSKY
University of Texas at Austin

— CZECHOSLOVAKIA · Information Highlights —

Location: East central Europe.
Area: 49,370 square miles (127,869 sq km).
Population (1975 est.): 14,800,000.
Chief Cities (1974 est.): Prague, the capital, 1,078,096; Brno, 335,000; Bratislava, 281,000.
Government: *Head of state,* Gustav Husák, president, (took office 1975). *Head of government,* Lubomir Strougal, premier (took office 1970). *Communist party secretary general,* Gustav Husák (took office 1969). *Legislature*—Federal Assembly: Chamber of Nations and Chamber of the People.
Monetary Unit: Koruna (5.97 koruny equal U. S.$1, July 1975).
Gross National Product (1973 est.): $35,300,000,000.
Manufacturing (major products): Machinery, chemicals, petroleum products, glass, textiles, iron, steel.
Major Agricultural Products: Rye, oats, sugar beets.
Foreign Trade (1973): *Exports,* $8,606,000,000; *imports,* $8,799,000,000.

Erik Bruhn (*left*) dances with Cynthia Gregory and Rudolf Nureyev in Nureyev's re-staging of the Petipa-Glazunov ballet *Raymonda* for the American Ballet Theatre.

MARTHA SWOPE

dance

The year in dance was marked by a welcome return of the old and a continuing resurgence of the new. Despite the recession and a general shortage of funds, both private and public, dance in all its forms experienced in 1975 a new upswing in popularity throughout virtually the entire industrialized world.

For the United States the return of the old came in the form of a tour by the Bolshoi Ballet of Moscow, which made its first U. S. visit in nearly 10 years. The new was the ever-upward trend of interest in modern dance, including a major season by the oldest modern group of them all, the Martha Graham troupe.

Nureyev. Rudolf Nureyev, who danced in some 200 performances all over the world during the year, was the link between the old and the new. Still at the peak of his powers at 37, Nureyev spread his talents over a wide range of dance activities. He kept up his classical appearances with the American Ballet Theatre (ABT) and dozens of other companies but also created new modern roles for the Martha Graham Company and for Het Nationale Ballet of Holland. He also restaged the turn-of-the-century Petipa-Glazunov ballet *Raymonda* for the ABT and danced a new work created for him by modernist Murray Louis.

More significantly, perhaps, he proved that the attraction of his name, coupled with that of Dame Margot Fonteyn, could fill a theater for a two-week season even with tickets costing twice the usual rate. His success might encourage other well-known dancers to think of organizing similar star-studded evenings away from the established companies. Nureyev's persistence in the modern field, despite early criticism that his technique was too rigidly classical, ensured Russian domination of all aspects of the dance.

Other Notable Ballet Performances. Mikhail Baryshnikov, who, like Nureyev, had defected to the West from the Kirov Ballet in Leningrad, achieved superstar status with cover stories on him in both *Time* and *Newsweek* and led the galaxy of stars appearing regularly with the American Ballet Theatre. Another standout performer was Denmark's Erik Bruhn, who came out of a too-early retirement at the age of 40 to demonstrate he was still a great talent. Natalia Makarova, also a Kirov defector, danced with ABT and, in addition, made her debut with the Royal Ballet in London. ABT's major production of the year was the Nureyev *Raymonda*. The Royal Ballet welcomed Baryshnikov as a guest artist in a reworked Kenneth MacMillan choreography of *Romeo and Juliet* and showed new major talents in Wayne Sleep and Anthony Dowell. At the year's end the company, which was celebrating its 35th year, was presenting three new works and a revival of *Spectre de la Rose*, the ballet created by Nijinsky.

At the New York City Ballet (NYCB) the only avowed star remained George Balanchine, another Russian emigré who knew the Leningrad ballet companies of an earlier era. Balanchine proved his creative powers were undimmed with the creation of 16 works set to the music of French composer Maurice Ravel to mark the 100th anniversary of the composer's birth. Critical reception of the works varied but was generally favorable, and 10 of them, including *Gaspard de la Nuit*, *Daphnis and Chlöe*, *Ma Mère l'Oye*, and *Tzigane*, entered the NYCB's repertory. Another work brought back into the repertory was *Jewels*, revived by Balanchine to welcome the return of Suzanne Farrell, reputedly his favorite dancer and also the best interpreter of his deceptively simple-looking style. Farrell was newly-returned from Brussels, where she had danced since 1969 with Maurice Bejart's Ballet of the 20th Century. Just before return-

ing to New York, Farrell had danced Bejart's work based on the *Triumphs of Petrarch*.

Bolshoi Visit. The visit by the Bolshoi proved interesting if only in proving how far behind their Western colleagues the Russian choreographers have fallen. Two new productions, *Ivan the Terrible* and *Spartacus,* tried to give an air of modernity to the Bolshoi's repertoire but failed artistically, even while perhaps satisfying the stultifying demands of Soviet authorities for "socialist realism." In the classical productions of *Sleeping Beauty, Giselle,* and *Swan Lake,* the Bolshoi showed its real strength and depth. Ekaterina Maximova and Nina Timofeyeva headed up the female stars, while Vladimir Vasiliev and Alexander Bogatyrev were outstanding among the men. The Bolshoi managed to get back to Moscow without any of its personnel deciding to stay on in the West.

The Panovs. Valery Panov and his dancer-wife, Galina Ragozina, a Soviet couple who had emigrated in 1974, starred in a series of gala evenings. They presented *pas de deux* they had danced at the Kirov, including the *Lady and the Hooligan* and *The Corsaire.* Valery Panov had not danced for several years, barred from working because of his campaign to obtain a Soviet exit visa. The enforced layoff left him considerably below his former power, and the critical reception of his early appearances was mixed. The Panovs danced with the Festival Ballet in London, which was marking its 25th anniversary, but at year's end still had not found a permanent artistic home.

Modern Dance. The greatest upsurge in interest throughout 1975 was in modern dance. In 1974 some 15 million seats at dance performances of all kinds were sold in the United States. In 1975 the number increased substantially, and by far the greatest numbers were being bought by young persons attending modern dance performances.

Two companies set new records. The Martha Graham Company presented New York's first four-week season by a modern dance group and played to full houses. In London the Contemporary Dance Theatre set a similar record with a three-week run at Covent Garden, delighting and shocking audiences with their ballets that included nude male solos. Miss Graham, now 81, did not dance but made an introductory speech each night to explain some of her theories on the dance. She created two roles for Nureyev: Lucifer in a treatment of the angel's confusion on first being assigned to the stewardship of hell and the errant Rev. Arthur Dimmesdale in *The Scarlet Letter*.

One of Nureyev's other ventures into modern dance was in *Moments,* a work created for him by Murray Louis. Nureyev performed the witty, ironic piece in his short season with Fonteyn, but Louis took over the role when the Louis dance company itself presented the work. Louis also worked up a dance entitled *Catalogue,* which he said was inspired by a Sears Roebuck catalogue of the 1890's. Louis in 1976 would be creating for the Royal Danish Ballet a new full-evening work set to folk music collected on a trip to Iran.

Dance for the Bicentennial. Bicentennial tributes began early. The Alvin Ailey City Center Dance Theater began with five works danced to the music of the late jazz bandleader Duke Ellington. Ailey planned to choreograph 13 Ellington works to be presented in a 5-evening show accompanied by the Ellington orchestra in 1976. The early production presented in 1975 included *The Mooche* and *Night Creature,* both drawing heavily on ethnic sources to create an authentic interpretation of Ellington's music.

Another bicentennial salute came from the Joffrey Ballet Company. Gerald Arpino, the controversial main choreographer for the company, presented *Drums, Dreams and Banjos* to a collage of music by Stephen Foster. The work emphasized the Southern aspects of the music and evoked echoes of the Civil War and minstrel shows. Joffrey, which is ranked after the ABT and the NYCB among classic companies in the United States, also offered a tightened and improved version of Twyla Tharp's *Deuce Coupe,* set to the music of the Beach Boys.

At year's end Tharp was invited to create a new work for the American Ballet Theatre. Her own small company, representing the avant garde of the dance movement, was one of dozens that sprang up in lofts and small theaters all over the United States. Much interesting work

Natalia Makarova and Mikhail Baryshnikov combined their talents in a production of *Don Quixote.*

MARTHA SWOPE

Valery Panov and his wife, Galina Ragozina, perform a *pas de deux* from *The Nutcracker* during their February U. S. debut in Philadelphia.

came from these small groups, and a dozen of them, of which the best-known are probably Lar Lubovitch and Viola Farber, got together to form the Dance Umbrella. This new venture in cooperation, sharing the costs of a theatre, may be the beginning of another trend to keep small companies alive.

Ballet flourished throughout the United States, and many bicentennial committees decided to use the broad-based appeal of the dance as a way of signifying the unity of the people. Funds made available for the dance ensured that 1976 would be an even more significant year for the art than was 1975.

JOHN F. SIMS
United Press International

DELAWARE

During 1975, Delaware was confronted with financial problems and labor strife, particularly among unions of school teachers and other public employees. Sharp budget cuts, brought about by reduced public revenue, caused the state to make severe cutbacks in funds for welfare and education. Across-the-board reductions in appropriations to state agencies resulted in a series of strike threats by public employees, but compromise between officials and workers was effected with the latter accepting a lesser increase in salary than at first demanded.

Legislature. The legislature attempted to increase revenue by levying a one-cent-per-barrel tax on crude oil processed by the Getty Oil Company, the state's only crude oil refiner. Under severe pressure from both labor and industry, Gov. Sherman Tribbitt vetoed the tax, and the General Assembly had to look elsewhere for revenue. The legislature increased the civil jurisdiction of the court of common pleas from $3,000 to $5,000, the family court was given jurisdiction over divorce, and the pay of magistrates was increased. Attempts were made to repeal the state fair-trade act and to end restrictions concerning the retail price of liquor. Neither measure passed. The General Assembly authorized a state lottery, but due to inept administration the lottery did not go into effect until late in 1975. The custody of adult and juvenile offenders was placed in a newly created Department of Corrections.

Education. Beginning on the first day of school in September, Wilmington teachers went on a strike for better pay. The strike ended six weeks later after both sides agreed to a three-year package that would not necessitate a rise in taxes. The U. S. district court in Wilmington ordered the state board of education to present plans for rectifying the racial imbalance in the school districts of northern New Castle county and the city of Wilmington. The state appealed this ruling.

Economy. Unemployment peaked at 11% in March 1975, and was down to 9% by September. The auto and construction industries bore the brunt of unemployment. In spite of an economic downturn, personal income was up 5% in 1974 over 1973, with indications that it would continue to increase.

Redevelopment. In Wilmington, three blocks of the city's main street were developed into a downtown mall. Costs were met by public and private funds. In the central area of the city the old opera house was restored and refurbished, and new public housing was erected on the site of old slums.

PAUL DOLAN
University of Delaware

--------- **DELAWARE · Information Highlights** ---------

Area: 2,057 square miles (5,328 sq km).
Population (1974 est.): 573,000.
Chief Cities (1970 census): Dover, the capital, 17,488; Wilmington, 80,386; Newark, 21,078.
Government (1975): *Chief Officers*—governor, Sherman W. Tribbitt (D); lt. gov., Eugene D. Bookhammer (R). *General Assembly*—Senate, 21; House of Representatives, 41 members.
Education (1974–75): *Enrollment*—public elementary schools, 67,214; public secondary, 63,402; nonpublic schools, 17,000; colleges and universities, 30,357 students. *Public school expenditures,* $157,258,000 ($1,275 per pupil).
State Finances (fiscal year 1974): *Revenues,* $502,903,-000; *expenditures,* $496,142,000.
Personal Income (1974): $3,568,000,000; per capita, $6,-227.
Labor Force (Aug. 1975): *Nonagricultural wage and salary earners,* 227,500; *insured unemployed,* 10,900.

DENMARK

The year 1975 in Denmark was highlighted by a national election, followed shortly thereafter by a change in government. On Dec. 5, 1974, Prime Minister Poul Hartling, of the Moderate Liberal party, announced that elections for a new Folketing (parliament) would be held in January 1975. His dissolution of the Folketing in December and his call for new elections were brought on by a government economic plan that included such controversial measures as a freeze on wages and profits and price controls on foods and other consumer goods.

The election on January 9 turned out to be a hollow victory for the Liberals. They doubled their representation in the Folketing, winning 20 additional seats, but their gain was at the expense of parties that had supported them in the governing of the nation. Moreover, the Social Democrats, the largest party, increased its representation by seven seats. The election resulted in the representation of 10 parties in the Folketing.

The parties and seats held were as follows: Social Democrats (53), Moderate Liberals (42), Progress party (24), Radical Liberals (13), Conservatives (10), Christian People's party (9), People's Socialists (9), Communists (7), Center Democrats (4), and Left Socialists (4).

Hartling's cabinet was forced to resign on January 29, following a one-vote defeat on a motion to that effect supported by the Social Democrats. For two weeks, representatives of the 10 parties negotiated as to the makeup of the new cabinet. Agreement was finally reached to have former Premier Anker Jørgensen form a minority Social Democratic government. The important post of foreign minister was given to Knud Børge Andersen, an experienced negotiator in international affairs. It was clear that the selection of the cabinet members had been made with a view to cooperation with the parties on the right.

Economy. The sagging Danish economy, afflicted by an adverse balance-of-payments situation, increasing unemployment, and a high rate

DANISH INFORMATION OFFICE

Queen Margrethe II tours Moscow with Prince Henrik during her visit to the USSR in May.

of inflation, did not improve very much during the year. Industrial exports fell by 4% during the first quarter of 1975 compared to the same period in 1974. However, due to reduced imports, it seemed as if the trade balance deficit might be reduced by year's end.

Soviet Visit. Queen Margrethe II and her husband, Prince Henrik, visited the Soviet Union in late May, the first Danish royal couple to do so since the Russian Revolution. They visited Leningrad, Moscow, and Zagorsk, as well as Tbilisi in Georgia, and everywhere met with great shows of friendliness.

Personal Crisis. Prime Minister Anker Jørgensen suffered a personal setback during the year, being found guilty of slandering the editor of *Minut,* a small right-wing newspaper. Jørgensen had said that the paper's contents represented "the darkest fascism imaginable" and had also indicated that the paper was supported by foreign oil companies.

ERIK J. FRIIS
Editor, "The Scandinavian-American Bulletin"

DENMARK · Information Highlights

Official Name: Kingdom of Denmark.
Location: Northwest Europe.
Area: 16,629 square miles (43,069 sq km).
Population (1975 est.): 5,000,000.
Chief Cities (1974 est.): Copenhagen, the capital, 1,-400,000; Aarhus, 190,000; Odense, 136,000.
Government: *Head of state,* Margrethe II, queen (acceded Jan. 1972). *Head of government,* Anker Jørgensen, prime minister (took office Feb. 1975). *Legislature* (unicameral)—Folketing.
Monetary Unit: Krone (5.461 kroner equal U. S.$1, May 1975).
Gross National Product (1973): $26,800,000,000.
Manufacturing (major products): Beverages, processed foods, machinery, ships, chemicals, furniture.
Major Agricultural Products: Barley, oats, sugar beets, dairy products, cattle, hogs, fish.
Foreign Trade (1974 est.): *Exports,* $7,800,000,000; *imports,* $10,030,000,000.

DISARMAMENT AND ARMS CONTROL

The stalemate in nuclear arms control that characterized 1975 reflected the complexity of the problem, the disinclination of the Soviet Union to accept external controls, and the growing fear in the United States that Moscow was using détente diplomacy to disguise its massive arms buildup.

The SALT Stalemate. The Strategic Arms Limitation Talks (SALT) culminated in the Vladivostok Declaration by U. S. President Gerald Ford and Soviet Chairman Leonid Brezhnev on Nov. 25, 1974, with the expectation that it would be the basis of a formal SALT 2 agreement in 1975. The accord would limit each side to 2,400 strategic delivery vehicles (intercontinental ballistic missiles, submarine-launched missiles, and heavy bombers) of which 1,320 could be armed with multiple warheads (MIRVs).

For several reasons, the accord was not translated into an agreement. On the technical side, the two parties could not agree on whether two weapons systems should be considered strategic vehicles. Washington wanted to include Soviet Backfire bombers, which are capable of delivering large nuclear bombs to any target in the United States. Moscow objected and insisted that U. S. cruise missiles be included.

Cruise missiles are small winged devices that can carry nuclear or conventional warheads and can be launched from aircraft, ships, or submarines. The United States, considerably ahead of the Soviet Union in cruise missile development, objected to including these weapons in the delivery-vehicle limitation. On Sept. 21, 1975, Secretary of State Henry Kissinger presented a formula to Moscow to try to reconcile the differences, but the Soviet reply five weeks later rejected it.

Defense Secretary Dismissal. The abrupt firing of Secretary of Defense James R. Schlesinger by President Ford on November 9 brought to public attention the muted differences between Kissinger and Schlesinger on dealing with the Soviet Union in general and with the SALT negotiations in particular. Schlesinger had been the chief critic within the administration. He had expressed deep concern about mounting Soviet military might and advocated a strong U. S. defense. On November 23 he contended that "the Soviets have expanded in every conceivable area" and had over 4 million men under arms.

Schlesinger's dismissal alarmed North Atlantic Treaty Organization (NATO) allies and precipitated a defense-arms control debate in the United States, which virtually assured that SALT would be an issue in the 1976 presidential campaign.

The strategic arms control debate is further complicated by increasing criticism of the 1972 SALT 1 agreement, including charges that Moscow has violated the spirit if not the letter of the limits imposed by that pact. Within the numerical limits of SALT 1, the Soviet Union has deployed much larger missiles than has the United States, achieving a throw-weight advantage of about three to one. The United States has retained a qualitative advantage that, however, appears to be diminishing.

Proliferation. With the continuing world oil crisis, 1975 witnessed a giant step in plans to export nuclear technology and fuels from the developed to the developing world. This transfer is designed to create an alternative source of energy, but the technology for building a nuclear power plant is very similar to that for conducting a nuclear explosion or making a bomb, as the May 18, 1974, underground test in India demonstrated.

On March 4, the United States and Iran signed a $15-billion, five-year agreement under which Iran plans to acquire several large nuclear power plants and a fuel reprocessing facility. In October, South Korea agreed to purchase from France equipment capable of producing weapons-grade plutonium. Brazil negotiated a deal with West Germany for the purchase of nuclear reactors and a complete fuel cycle to support them. There were also other smaller and less dramatic developments in the proliferation of nuclear technology.

Confronted by this situation, the principal supplier states who are also signatories to the Nuclear Non-Proliferation Treaty (NPT) strengthened their efforts to deter the development of nuclear weapons in additional states. The United States, with the support of Britain and the Soviet Union, was most active. Three major courses were pursued: a drive to get more governments to ratify the NPT, which prohibits non-nuclear states from acquiring nuclear arms; efforts to deny the capability to produce nuclear explosions; and diplomatic efforts to persuade governments not to pursue the nuclear arms route.

The chief effort was to broaden adherence to the NPT. During 1975 the United States and Canada persuaded South Korea to ratify the NPT. Eleven other governments also ratified the treaty, making a total of 95. The NPT obligates the recipient government to accept technical safeguards, including the inspection of nuclear facilities, fuels, and processes, designed to prevent the diversion of fuels to weapons use. The safeguard system is operated by the International Atomic Energy Agency, with headquarters in Vienna, Austria.

Recognizing that a pledge of nuclear abstention is not enough, the United States has sought to deny a nuclear weapons capability to the countries now acquiring nuclear technology. To this end Washington is attempting to get other supplier states to follow its example and to refuse to sell fuel-cycle equipment that would make it possible for the recipient country to conduct a nuclear explosion.

ERNEST W. LEFEVER, *The Brookings Institution*

DRUG ADDICTION AND ABUSE

In 1975 drug addiction and abuse continued as major worldwide problems despite changing supply routes, relaxed attitudes toward the use of marihuana, and changing patterns of drug use. As one supply route was crippled, others quickly developed or expanded to fill the vacuum. At the same time that marihuana use became decriminalized, the use of cocaine increased dramatically.

The Heroin Supply Network. A major shift in the transportation pattern of heroin into the United States and Canada has taken place since 1972. Traditionally, gum opium and morphine base had moved from the poppy fields of Turkey and other Middle Eastern countries into southern France for processing into heroin. From France it was smuggled into the consumer markets of eastern North America. The southwestern United States was supplied with brown (Mexican grown and prepared) heroin. Western cities such as San Francisco, Seattle, and Vancouver received much of their heroin from Southeast Asia via Hong Kong or Macao.

The French-Corsican syndicates have sustained a series of reverses that has crippled their operations. Turkey's decision in 1973 to prohibit poppy production was a serious blow. Seizures of large amounts of morphine base and heroin by French and American officials interfered with the distribution capability of the syndicates. The established syndicates had been bringing large quantities of heroin in through Latin America; this channel was temporarily disrupted with the arrest of major traffickers. Thus, a "panic" developed along the Eastern seaboard in 1973. Heroin supplies were sharply reduced, and "bags" sold on the street contained less than 5% heroin.

Unfortunately, since 1973, Mexico has displaced the Mediterranean as the main supply route for heroin. Sixty percent of the heroin brought into the United States now originates in Mexican fields and laboratories. In New York as well as other parts of the country brown heroin was readily available in 1975. The amount of heroin in the "bag" increased, and the "panic" was over. New criminal networks dominated by Latin Americans controlled the major distribution chains. Mexico was the top priority country for Drug Enforcement Administration officials in cooperation with the Mexican authorities, who were concerned about the increasing heroin abuse in their large cities.

One important development that was being watched closely at year's end was Turkey's decision to allow 100,000 farmers to raise the Oriental poppy during 1975. The Turkish government declared that criminal diversion into illicit channels would not occur. They issued instructions to the farmers that the pods of the poppies were not to be cut, preventing the formation and collection of gum opium.

In 1975 no one claimed that the number of addicts was declining. Instead, available data indicated that treatment facilities were filled and that waiting lists for treatment were getting longer. Larger percentages of arrested juveniles had positive tests for opiates than ever before. It appeared that more effective preventive measures must be developed or a new wave of heroin addiction will occur.

Reduction in Marihuana Possession Penalties. A number of states, including Alaska, California, Colorado, and Maine in 1975, have reduced the penalty for possession of small amounts of marihuana from a felony or misdemeanor to a violation. A federal proposal, the Marihuana Control Act of 1975, recommended that possession of less than an ounce of marihuana be changed to a civil fine of $100 or less.

The decriminalization of marihuana possession initiated by Oregon had apparently not resulted in a marked increase in its use or in accidents or criminal activity associated with marihuana intoxication. The trend to reduce penalties for possession of small quantities of marihuana was expected to extend to other states. There was no inclination on state or federal levels to change the penalties for possession for sale, cultivation, or trafficking in marihuana.

Increased Use of Cocaine. With federal regulations on amphetamines tightened, many drug users turned to the use of cocaine, a potent, non-addictive drug. Cocaine was readily available from South American sources, and undercover agents in New York City increased their street purchases of it.

SIDNEY COHEN, M. D.
Executive Director, Council on Drug and Alcohol Abuse, University of California, Los Angeles

U. S. Customs agents sort through bags of marihuana, part of 40 tons accidentally spotted on a flight over Grand Bahamas Island, Bahamas, on August 16.

UPI

Rep. Al Ullman (*left*) and Sen. Russell Long took part in several House-Senate conferences aimed at drafting a tax-cut bill that would meet with President Ford's approval.

ECONOMY OF THE U. S.

The year 1975 was one of the worst for the U. S. economy since the great depression of the 1930's. Viewed in retrospect, however, it was not truly alarming because most measures of economic activity show that it was at its most depressed level in the early half of the year. The strength of the economic gains that followed also marked the year as one of recovery, and by December varied degrees of optimism were heard. Increasing orders, gains in production levels, and rising profits sustained the more optimistic outlook. But lagging housing construction, a fairly high rate of unemployment, sagging regional economies, and continuing inflation were causes of concern.

The year started from a low point, and low marks continued to be registered in various economic areas during the first half of the year. The stimulus of the federal income-tax cut and rebate achieved a substantial part of the goal that had been set for it, as basic demand began pushing up the economy after the first quarter. With the slowdown in economic activity came some relief from 1974's high inflation rates. Indications of this improvement heartened the outlook of consumers.

Gross National Product. The total gross national product (GNP) handily passed the $1.5 trillion mark early in the last quarter of the year, an achievement that reflected both rising levels of product output and a decelerating rate of inflation. In the first quarter, however, real GNP showed an absolute decline as production dipped and price inflation continued. Adjusted to a constant dollar level and excluding price changes, the GNP declined to $780 billion in the first quarter, the lowest seasonally-adjusted annual rate registered since early 1972. After the trough, however, there was a moderate upturn in the second quarter to a real GNP level of $783.6 billion. This accelerated in the third quarter to $808.3 billion, and there was a grad-

ual increase in the fourth quarter. The rate of increase in real GNP in the third quarter was the sharpest quarterly surge since 1950. Overall, however, 1975 was the second year in a row for a declining real GNP, with the total for the year dropping below the $800 billion mark.

Inflation Rate. Price inflation continued to attract attention, but the curtailment in the rate of its growth was universally greeted as one of the year's most favorable developments. In the third quarter of 1975 the inflation rate as measured by all prices included in GNP was down to 5% on a seasonally-adjusted annual basis. This was highly encouraging when put against the 10.3% rate for all of 1974 against 1973. Still, the rate of increase for all of 1975 was high, and fears that the earlier rampant inflation rate would return continued to influence policy decisions. Confirmation of a declining rate of price increases came from the consumer price index, which rose at moderate levels throughout 1975. Food prices even showed some declines during parts of the year.

Industrial Production. Industrial production, as measured by the Federal Reserve Board's index, dropped markedly in 1975, reaching a low of 109.9 in April (1967 = 100). Through much of 1974 the index held within a narrow range around 125, but in the last quarter of the year it dropped sharply. The decline continued to the low period in April, and then it turned slowly upward as 1975 progressed. A principal area of weakness was durable manufactures, which in May dropped below the 1965 average. The decline was led by drops in motor vehicle production, lumber and wood products, and furniture and fixtures. In nondurable manufactures textiles, apparel, and leather products were down in the early part of the year and showed even more weakness in recovery than other areas of the economy. Mining and utilities showed little deterioration during the year but these industries lacked the bursts of strength that they had shown in the past.

THE U. S. ECONOMY 1975
MOVEMENT TOWARD RECOVERY

GROSS NATIONAL PRODUCT

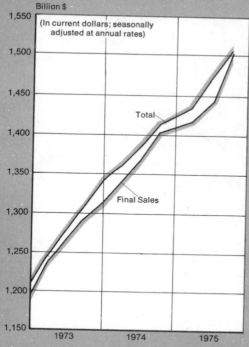

Billion $

(In current dollars; seasonally adjusted at annual rates)

Total

Final Sales

1973   1974   1975

Source: U.S. Department of Commerce

UNEMPLOYMENT RATE

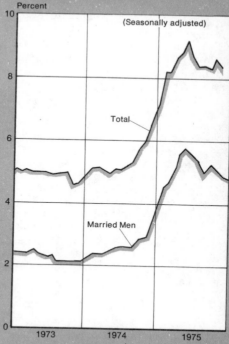

Percent

(Seasonally adjusted)

Total

Married Men

1973   1974   1975

Source: U.S. Department of Labor

INDUSTRIAL PRODUCTION

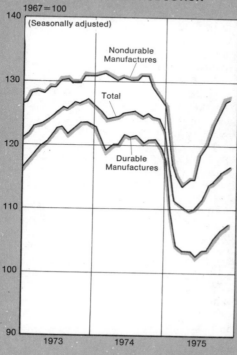

1967 = 100

(Seasonally adjusted)

Nondurable Manufactures

Total

Durable Manufactures

1973   1974   1975

Source: U.S. Federal Reserve System

CONSUMER PRICE INDEX

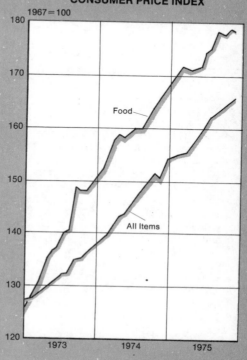

1967 = 100

Food

All Items

1973   1974   1975

Source: U.S. Department of Labor

SPECIAL REPORT:

UNEMPLOYMENT

A child of a laid-off auto worker joins pickets demanding strong union action to restore lost jobs.

Unemployment in the United States in 1975 was at its highest rate since the onset of World War II, averaging around 8.5% for the year. In May 1975 a midyear seasonally-adjusted unemployment rate of 9.2% was by far the worst showing for a single month in over three decades.

Occupations. Among occupation groups, patterns of unemployment were typical of most U. S. recessions in the postwar period. At the year's peak level of unemployment, the rate was over twice as high for blue collar workers (11.9%) as for white collar (4.8%), while service workers (7.5%) fell below the average level, and farm laborers (2.2%) felt only a minor effect. Construction workers were the hardest hit with a peak rate in excess of 25%, nearly double that for the month a year earlier. Unskilled blue collar workers also ranged above the average at a 15.3% rate of unemployment.

Industries. Industries hit by unemployment were construction and manufacturing, which ranged substantially above the averages for the economy as a whole. The rate of unemployment in all manufacturing in May 1975 was 11.7%, with durable manufactures registering 12.1% and nondurables 11.1%. In line with the severe problems of the auto industry and the poor condition of the housing industry, the unemployment rate among auto workers was 15.8%, electrical equipment workers 14.8%, and lumber and wood products workers 14.9%. Among the nondurable manufacturing workers, the highest rates of unemployment were registered by textile mill workers at 16.4%, apparel workers at 15.6%, and rubber and plastic product workers at 13.2%. While trade and service industries were below average, they showed increases over 1974. Only the mining industry showed an actual improvement, as unemployment dropped to 2.4% from 4% a year earlier.

Social Patterns. In social groupings, unemployment patterns were also similar to those shown in previous recessions. Among age groups, those in the 16-19 year-old category showed 21.8% unemployment in May, 20-24 years 14.8%, and 25-and-over 6.4%. Non-whites showed 14.7%, and females were at 10.2%. By contrast, the Bureau of Labor Statistics grouping designated "married men" showed a 5.8% unemployment rate.

States. Geographic unemployment rates reflect the percent of average insurance-covered workers seeking but unable to find work. On this basis, the national average rate was 6.5% in May 1975. The highest rates of unemployment were in Puerto Rico, 13.9%; Rhode Island, 9.3%; Michigan, 8.9%; New Jersey, 8.9%; South Carolina, 8.7%; Washington, 8.6%; and Arkansas, 8.5%. The lowest rates were in Wyoming, 2.4%; Texas, 2.5%; Colorado and South Dakota, 3.0%; Kansas and Nebraska, 3.4%; Iowa and North Dakota, 3.7%; and the District of Columbia, 3.8%. These patterns largely reflect the industrial and occupational structures of the states involved.

Labor Force. The civilian labor force in the United States continued to increase in 1975, although at a slower rate than had prevailed previously. By the end of the third quarter it numbered over 93.1 million, and of this total, unemployment on a seasonally adjusted basis was over 7.8 million. Clearly, however, unemployed workers were a reflection of structural weaknesses in the economy rather than of a diseased economy.

The inability of the nation to revive its housing industry contributed heavily to unemployment in the construction industry, as did the general malaise in the capital market sector. Failure to regain a pre-1974 energy equilibrium added stress to consumers' decision to purchase automobiles, and the slump in auto sales exerted a consequent upward push on unemployment rates. As has been true over the last few recessions, groups lacking skills and experience tended to suffer unemployment more heavily.

JACKSON PHILLIPS

After months of curtailed production due to a slumping economy, this crowded shipping area at the Chrysler works in Detroit was a welcome sight to automobile manufacturers in the spring of 1975.

UPI

Production declines in 1975 were significant in both the auto and steel industries, contributing to rises in unemployment and slackening in the entire economy. Steel output held up remarkably well in 1974, registering a drop of only a little over 3%, but with continued weakness in auto production and declines in heavy construction generally. In 1975 raw steel production dropped over 17% below 1974 totals.

In the domestic production of autos for 1975 there was a further decline of over 11% on top of the nearly 25% drop shown for 1974. While there was some cause for cheer that the rate of decline was slowing down, Detroit was nevertheless anxious about its future. The energy scare of 1973, confusion over safety standards, and controversy over environmental safeguards were clearly still affecting the consumer's decision to purchase automobiles, a product that occupies a central position in the U. S. economy.

Plummeting sales influenced the big declines in production of cars and durables in the first part of 1975, but even with the cutbacks in production, inventory accumulations mounted to record levels. After the first quarter, however, sales and shipments improved relative to inventories, and by the third quarter inventory adjustments had cleared the way for solid production gains.

Domestic Investment. Business outlays for private domestic investment followed business trends closely during the year. In 1974, this sector stayed even with the 1973 level, registering $209.4 billion. Considering price inflation, however, to stay even was really to decline, and in 1975 private domestic investment dropped markedly in both dollar and real terms, hitting a low of $148.1 billion at a seasonally-adjusted annual rate in the second quarter. Tied as they are to business expectations about the future course of the economy, purchases of capital goods rose in the last part of the year, and the outlook for 1976 was optimistic. An improved outlook for profits also foreshadowed growth in capital outlays.

Personal Income and Employment. Coming into 1975 consumers had perhaps the most pessimistic view of economic prospects since the 1930's. Because of inflation dollar figures continued to rise, reflecting only marginal advances in price increases. Total personal income in 1974 had increased 9% over 1973, and similar or better gains were registered quarterly in 1975. But in real terms, after accounting for price changes, personal charges, and personal tax and nontax payments, per capita disposable personal income declined to $2,845 in 1974 from $2,945 in 1973. In the first quarter of 1975 it fell farther to $2,775. As the year progressed there were improvements, but disposable personal income did not regain the 1973 level.

Consumers' loss of confidence was strongly influenced, of course, by what was happening in the job market. Steadily rising unemployment pushed the rate to the highest level since the 1930's great depression, although the rate did turn down after a monthly high of 9.2% in May. The rising feeling of insecurity, however, did cause the consumer to cut back his expenditures, and personal savings reached new high levels. Aided by the impact of the federal income tax reduction in the second quarter, consumers pushed personal savings for the quarter to a phenomenal level of $113.8 billions (computed on the basis of a seasonally-adjusted annual rate). Later, however, a delayed reaction set in and manifested itself throughout the economy. Sales picked up and the savings rate

dropped back to an above-average but sustainable rate.

Housing Starts. A lagging sector of the economy in recent years has been housing, and consumers' attitudes strongly affect decisions in this sphere. From the 1973 level of nearly 2.1 million new units started, there was a decline of 34% to about 1.3 million in 1974. On the basis of a seasonally-adjusted annual rate, new starts had dropped to 980,000 by April, and while it turned up after that, the level of activity had not reached the 1974 level by the fourth quarter of the year. Building permits, which usually foreshadow starts, indicated no quick recovery. There seemed to be general agreement that new housing starts were laboring under the high price structure for new houses that has emerged in recent years and discourages purchases by new families, for whom income has not risen as rapidly as the price of houses. There also seems to be agreement among economists that a strong recovery in housing will have to accompany any strong recovery by the economy.

Government Spending. Government expenditures continued to increase in 1975, although restraint was exercised in certain sectors. Federal outlays rose, reflecting pay increases and rises in the national defense budget. These increases were only slightly larger than those of recent years. The rise of the federal deficit continued to increase to an expected level of around $60 billion for the 1975–76 fiscal year, reflecting tax cuts and rebates as well as continued spending. While this added stimulus perked up the economy, others worried that it was adding inflationary fuel for the near future.

State and local government expenditures for goods and services also increased, but as the year continued the rate decelerated. There was fairly widespread budgetary difficulty as the recession reduced state and local tax revenues and inflation helped push up expenditures. New York City dramatized the situation for the nation when it allowed its debt difficulties to become entangled with its financial operations and had to seek federal financial assistance to extricate itself. (See also CITIES AND URBAN AFFAIRS.) On a wider scale there was a general rollback in state government outlays, which, together with tax increases, dampened the federal attempt to pull the economy out of the recession.

Stocks and Bonds. The financial sector was buffeted by the economic crosswinds during the year. Stock prices, moving in anticipation of production levels and general economic activity, were at 10-year-low marks as the year commenced, rose gradually at midyear, and then showed hesitation in the latter half. Bond prices declined and were weak during much of the year. Fear of default by New York City and anxiety that inflation was about to escalate anew raised serious questions of basic security in the bond market. This situation confronted financially-weaker business and governmental units

with cash flow and liquidity crises, and bankruptcies, business failures, and rising installment payment delinquency rates became front page news.

Geographic Inequalities. There were areas in which the economy continued to function with few or only minor signs of distress. Buoyed by world demand for food, the agriculture sector of the economy operated with an eye mainly to the weather, and favorable levels of activity dominated. The mining and energy-producing industries suffered with the low production rate of heavy durables, but otherwise functioned without trouble. Geographically, these trends meant that some states, particularly in the Southwest and Middle West, operated at normal levels or above, while in the Northeast and in areas dependent on heavy manufacturing, the recession was felt even more deeply than national averages indicated.

The Outlook. The year closed out on a generally optimistic note, and many of the significant economic indicators were rising sharply. Basic demand was returning in the strength needed to carry production trends upward through 1976. Business capital outlays were generally expected to rise in 1976 to fuel the recovery further. The size of the gains remained problematic, and two schools of thought developed. One based its prediction of a strong recovery on the potential revealed in the third quarter of 1975, but the other predicted a weaker, more drawn-out recovery because of the soft spots that still plagued the economy. It was generally held, however, that the economy could sustain a real growth rate, accounting for a price change of a little better than 4%, while total growth, including a price-increase factor of 8%, might push over 12% for the year.

The most persistent problem facing the economy at year's end was the combination of a high unemployment rate and a high inflation rate. Progress was encouraging in lowering both of these from prior peak levels, but the problem remained of how to push one down without causing a seemingly reflexive rise in the other. The economic dilemma is, of course, a political one as well; the goals of the people of the United States, given an unpalatable choice, are not clear enough that a consistent policy emerges. Other major problems that the economy faced included the failure of housing construction and construction generally to rise to add the spark that is needed for a really strong recovery. The strength of the recovery now under way depends on how these and other problems are addressed in 1976.

(See also INDUSTRIAL REVIEW; INTERNATIONAL FINANCE; INTERNATIONAL TRADE; LABOR; STOCKS AND BONDS; UNITED STATES. For economic developments in other nations, see articles on the individual countries.)

JACKSON PHILLIPS, *Senior Vice President Moody's Investors Service, Inc.*

ECUADOR

The military regime of President Guillermo Rodríguez Lara, in power since February 1972, remained in control in Ecuador throughout the year. However, it encountered growing political and economic difficulties, and faced a major revolt attempt on September 1. Inflation continued at a rapid rate, and relations with the United States were strained.

Opposition. Mounting civilian opposition was obvious throughout the year. Late in April the Conservative party announced that it was against the regime, and the government exiled Conservative party leader Julio Cesar Trujillo to a remote part of the Amazonian area of the republic.

In May the president reorganized his cabinet, a move widely interpreted as strengthening "hard-line" military men. In July, Asaad Bucaram, former mayor of Guayaquil and head of the majority party in the coastal region, the Concentracion de Fuerzas Populares, issued a call for new elections. Some other politicians echoed Bucaram's call, and there was extensive criticism of the government's economic policies in the press.

On August 29 the formation of a Civic Junta for Institutional Restoration was announced with the backing of all important parties except the Communist party, which backed the government. The junta demanded new elections.

On September 1 a military revolt, headed by Gen. Raúl González Alvear, head of the joint chiefs of staff, erupted in Quito. Although President Rodríguez Lara was forced to flee the capital, he was able to escape to Riobamba. Military and naval commanders in Guayaquil, as well as the head of the Peruvian frontier garrison in El Oro, backed the president. The revolt was over within 48 hours.

The principal civilian support for the September 1 uprising apparently came from the followers of former President José María Velasco Ibarra. His exhortation to support the revolt was broadcast while the rebels held the capital.

After the suppression of the revolt, President Rodríguez Lara again reorganized his cabinet. However, there was no clear indication of a change in government policy resulting from this change.

Economic Conditions. The country suffered some negative consequences of the sudden oil boom begun two years before. Inflation ran at 30% or higher. There were extensive complaints that few benefits from the new oil prosperity were trickling down to the masses.

In mid-year the government faced a crisis with the oil companies. In January it had substantially raised taxes on oil, over protests from the companies, and when the government did nothing about these protests, the companies virtually ceased production. On June 13 the ministry of natural resources announced a temporary suspension of oil exports.

UPI

Government troops attack the presidential palace on September 2 during brief, unsuccessful revolt.

Early in July the government capitulated to the oil companies. The tax rate on oil was reduced from 58.5% to 53.1%, resulting in a reduction in the international price of Ecuadorian petroleum by 43 cents to $10.84 a barrel.

Relationship with United States. Ecuador had several problems with the United States during the year. It protested against the new trade law that became effective at the beginning of the year. Foreign Minister Antonio Jose Lucio Paredes labeled the new law "coercive" and threatened to boycott the American Foreign Ministers Conference in Buenos Aires in May. He was officially congratulated by President Carlos Andrés Pérez of Venezuela.

In January and February seven U. S. fishing vessels were seized by the Ecuadorian Navy. As a result, the American Tunaboat Association demanded U. S. naval escorts for fishing boats in Ecuadorian waters, and California Congressman Lionel Van Deerlin demanded an end to all military aid to Ecuador. Neither request was acted on by Washington.

ROBERT J. ALEXANDER
Rutgers University

ECUADOR • Information Highlights

Official Name: Republic of Ecuador.
Location: Northwest South America.
Area: 109,483 square miles (283,561 sq km).
Population (1975 est.): 7,100,000.
Chief Cities (1973 est.): Quito, the capital, 570,000; Guayaquil, 870,000.
Government: *Head of state,* Guillermo Rodríguez Lara, president (took office Feb. 1972). *Head of government,* Guillermo Rodríguez Lara. *Legislature*—Congress (suspended June 1970).
Monetary Unit: Sucre (25 sucres equal U. S.$1, June 1975).
Gross National Product (1974 est.): $3,200,000,000.
Manufacturing (major products): Processed foods, textiles, petroleum products.
Major Agricultural Products: Bananas, coffee, cacao, rice, potatoes, sugarcane, cotton, fish, forest products.
Foreign Trade (1974): *Exports,* $1,062,000,000; *imports,* $958,000,000.

In Lexington, Ky., buses taking white children to predominantly black schools were often only partially filled in September. Busing to achieve racial balance remained a volatile issue in 1975.

UPI

education

During 1975, U. S. education was buffeted by serious social and economic problems as the effects of the economic recession began to pile up and as unresolved social issues remained the focus of bitter controversy. Busing, strikes, rising costs and falling resources, violence, and a back-to-basics movement were the most prominent concerns.

BUSING AND INTEGRATION

The controversy over busing to achieve racial balance in public schools intensified as new court orders to implement desegregation plans were put into effect when schools opened in September 1975.

Boston. School openings in Boston, postponed one week, again produced mass demonstrations as the number of students bused rose to 25,000 from last year's 18,000. School officials decided upon a massive show of force to prevent disorder. At least 1,500 city and state police and 100 U. S. marshals guarded bus routes and school areas. National guardsmen were called in and stationed in South Boston to assist police if needed.

Crowds were not allowed near the schools or along bus routes. Students were checked by police as they entered newly-integrated Charlestown High School. Buses carrying black pupils unloaded without incident, but few white students rode from Charlestown into predominantly black Roxbury.

As the first week wore on, school attendance slowly rose. Both black and white pupils began to ride the buses and attend classes. However, an undercurrent of resentment persisted among the parents of white children being bused into black neighborhood schools.

Louisville. Louisville, Ky., was faced with the largest new court-ordered racial busing program in the nation, as 22,600 pupils were transported between suburban Jefferson county, largely white, and Louisville schools, largely black.

Rioting flared at the end of the first week of busing as an estimated 10,000 demonstrators rioted at three locations. Buses were damaged and stores looted. By Saturday morning 800 national guardsmen had been called in to assist police.

On Monday morning, schools reopened with 2,500 police and guardsmen on duty. Each of the 470 school buses carried an armed guard. By the end of the week a white boycott had become largely ineffective as attendance in the 120,000-student city-county school district rose to 77.3%.

Detroit Decision. In a long-awaited decision in Detroit, U. S. District Court Judge Robert E. DeMascio rejected two divergent desegregation proposals, both involving extensive busing. A plan put forward by the National Association for the Advancement of Colored People called for elimination of all-black schools and for forced busing of more than 70,000 students. The board of education plan would have retained 112 of the 326 schools as all-black, but would have required the busing of more than 50,000 students. The judge ordered the school board to devise a less sweeping plan that would employ a variety of mixing techniques and involve less busing.

Attitudes toward Busing. Doubts about the wisdom and desirability of busing to achieve racial balance in schools were increasing. Anti-

busing groups have been unsuccessful in getting Congress to approve a constitutional amendment that would ban forced busing. However, Congress has repeatedly, through amendments to legislation, prohibited the use of federal funds to finance busing. Federal courts have ruled that this does not relieve cities of their obligation to use this method of integration.

Many black leaders regarded the opposition to busing as racist and comparable to resistance to desegregation in the Southern states in the 1950's. However, other leaders wondered whether busing is worth all the uproar.

There was some question about whether forced busing achieves its goals. Certainly it accelerated white flight to the suburbs, leaving the inner cities increasingly black and with a significantly diminished tax base. At the end of 1975, there were at least 19 major urban school systems in which half or more of the pupils were black.

President Ford has observed, "I don't think that forced busing to achieve racial balance is the proper way to get quality education." He called for better school facilities, lower teacher-pupil ratios, and the improvement of neighborhood schools.

One proposal attracting attention was the creation of schools with special programs that would attract students from all parts of the city. Known as "magnet schools," they proved successful in Detroit and Boston, and new ones were planned for Chicago and New York. The costs of these schools is a major problem.

PROBLEMS, ENROLLMENTS, AND COSTS

Teachers' strikes and student violence in the schools were major problems. Enrollments decreased slightly, while costs increased sharply.

Teachers' Strikes. The fall opening of public schools was delayed by strikes of teachers in widely scattered areas, including two of the nation's largest cities, New York and Chicago. In New York City, plagued by financial problems, the issue was not salaries (the median pay of teachers was $17,350), but a reduction in teaching positions, an increase in class size, and a longer work week, all economy measures.

After a week-long strike, the 65,000 teachers grudgingly accepted a compromise settlement that cut class time for teachers, maintained maximum class sizes, and reinstated 2,400 of the 4,000 eliminated positions. About 1.1 million pupils resumed classes.

Chicago's 600 schools were closed down when teachers demanded cost-of-living raises and additional fringe benefits. The 11-day strike ended when the 27,000-member union accepted a new contract that increased salaries, retained 1,525 teaching jobs, and decreased maximum

class size slightly. Estimates of the cost of the new contract ranged from the teachers' $39.3 million to the board of education's $79.6 million.

There were other strikes in nine states, mainly involving salary increases and class size. In Boston a one-week strike ended when teachers won a 6% raise and job security for tenured teachers.

Violence in Public Schools. There was growing concern over violence in the nation's schools. The National Association of School Security Directors reported 8,568 rapes and other sex offenses, 11,160 armed robberies, 256,000 burglaries, and 189,332 "major assaults" in schools in 1974. In Gallup Polls parents repeatedly ranked lack of discipline as the paramount problem in public schools. Parents, students, teachers, and administrators blamed each other for the situation.

While the problem was most critical in ghetto schools, the scholastic crime wave spread to upper-class suburban areas. Use of drugs and alcohol, defiance of teachers and administrators, wanton destruction of school property, and intimidation of younger pupils disrupted many schools. Parents demanded action.

Larger cities spent millions of dollars on school guards. Sophisticated security systems, including closed-circuit television, have been installed in thousands of schools. Laws specifically directed against violence in schools have been passed.

There was evidence of a long-awaited crackdown upon unruly pupils. Prompt and sure suspension or expulsion were the rule in many school systems. Pupils themselves organized to make halls and rest rooms safe and to turn in violators.

UPI

Albert Shanker (*center*), leader of New York City teachers' union, walks on the picket line during September strike.

Overt racial friction was the cause of some disorders, and charges of racial bias complicated the problem. It was claimed that blacks were suspended more often than whites. However, it was also charged that teachers were likely to be more lenient with students of the opposite race to avoid the appearance of bias.

In September 1975 the Department of Health, Education, and Welfare (HEW) ordered the nation's 16,000 public school systems to keep detailed disciplinary records as to type of offense, sex and race, and punishment, to show whether there was discrimination against minority students. Later, the order was modified.

Administrators, teachers, and parents sought solutions. Special programs involving a wide range of vocational skills seemed to be one answer. More individual attention to pupil needs was another. A third was stronger leadership on the part of the school principal.

Enrollments and Graduates. Overall school and college fall enrollments decreased 0.25% between 1974 and 1975, from 59,089,000 to 58,940,000, according to U. S. Office of Education estimates. The greatest decline, 2% or about 619,000 pupils, occurred at the elementary school level, where the declining birthrate of the late 1960's and early 1970's was being felt increasingly. Public and private elementary enrollment in fall 1975 was estimated at 34 million.

Enrollments in secondary schools increased about 1%, from 15.4 million to 15.6 million in fall 1975. High school graduates in 1975 totaled 3.1 million. Higher education enrollments continued to increase, mainly in public community colleges. Students in degree-credit courses in two- and four-year colleges, universities, and professional schools in fall 1975 totaled 9,330,-000, an increase of more than 3% over the 1974 figure. Approximately 1 million additional undergraduate students were enrolled in occupational programs not carrying degree credit.

Public institutions enrolled 7,120,000 degree-credit students; private, 2,210,000. Undergraduate enrollment in 1975–76 was estimated at 8,100,000; graduate, 1,230,000. During 1974–75 colleges and universities conferred 975,000 bachelor's degrees, 54,000 first professional degrees, 280,000 master's degrees, and 35,000 doctorates.

Expenditures for Education. The cost of education in the United States will total about $11 billion more in 1975–76 as compared with the previous school year, according to U. S. Office of Education statisticians. Expenditures for public and private education at all levels are estimated at $119 billion for the current school year, as compared with about $108 billion in 1974–75.

Federal support for education at all levels continued to grow. Federal grants increased from $3.4 billion in 1965 to approximately $16.2 billion in 1975. Educational expenditures, by source of funds, by public and private institutions for the session of 1974–75 were estimated as follows by HEW: State governments, $36.0 billion (33.4%); local governments, $32.7 billion (30.3%); federal government, $11.6 billion (10.8%); and all other sources of funds, $27.5 billion (25.5%).

Rising Costs. The cost of operating schools continued to rise. According to *Nation's Schools and Colleges,* a trade publication, it cost almost $1,170 to educate the average public school student in the 1974–75 academic session. This was 14.4% more than in 1973–74.

Salaries of teachers, the largest single item in school budgets, continued to go up. Fuel costs soared. Books and supplies went up in price. The cost of liability insurance, a must for school systems today, trebled. Elimination of some teaching and staff positions, increase in class size, and reduction in school services were the principal means taken to reduce costs.

Roman Catholic Schools. The Roman Catholic school system, which enrolled 3,492,000 children in elementary and secondary schools in 1974–75, faced serious problems. Enrollment has declined from an all-time high of 5,600,000 in 1964. Since 1964, 2,144 Catholic elementary and secondary schools have closed. Fewer nuns are available to teach. They constituted only about one-third of the teaching staff in 1975. The employment of lay teachers, even at low salaries, placed a serious burden on the schools.

The U. S. Supreme Court has declared unconstitutional various plans that might have aided Catholic schools. In May 1975 the court ruled that states may not lend them instructional materials, such as films, or pay for special services for pupils with learning difficulties. (See also LAW—*U. S. Supreme Court.*)

Tuition fees, the chief means of support, placed a heavy burden on parents who also pay taxes for public schools. In the Washington, D. C., metropolitan area, for example, tuition charges in 1975–76 ranged from $200 to $2,000 per student. Despite these problems, Catholic schools were still popular. Parents mentioned better discipline and educational excellence as reasons; Catholic leaders cited the teaching of the Gospel message and the formation of character as distinguishing characteristics of their schools.

SEX EQUALITY

The demand for sex equality in sports opportunities and the entrance of women into traditionally-male institutions were in the news in 1975. The trend toward coeducation in private secondary schools continued.

Federal Regulations. In June 1975 new federal rules barring sex discrimination in U. S. schools and colleges were issued by HEW after being approved by President Ford. Equal treatment for men and women was required in admission, financial aid, classrooms, and athletics.

Protest demonstration in Boston, Mass., in April condemned college budget cuts, a common action in a recession year.

The most controversial provisions dealt with sports. Schools and colleges were not required to spend the same amount of money on athletic programs for women as they did on those for men, but female students had to be given equal opportunities to participate in sports. Secondary schools and colleges were given three years in which to comply with the new regulations. However, some universities had already begun to implement the new rules. By a vote of 212–211 the House eliminated a proposed ban on separate physical education classes for boys and girls or on single-sex organizations such as honorary fraternities.

Service Academies. In October 1975, President Ford signed a Defense Department authorization bill that would allow women to enter the U. S. Military, Naval, and Air Force academies in 1976. They are already admitted to the Coast Guard Academy.

Rhodes Scholarships. American administrators of the Rhodes scholarships announced plans to make women eligible for the fellowships, beginning in 1976. Modification of the traditional all-male policy had to await action by the British House of Commons, but approval was regarded as a formality.

Coeducational Preparatory Schools. Many private boarding schools in the United States are now coeducational. According to F. Porter Sergent, publisher of the well-known *Sergent Handbook of Private Schools,* 61 private secondary schools have instituted coeducational boarding since 1970. Among them are such prestigious boys' preparatory schools as St. Paul's, Phillips Exeter, Phillips Andover, Taft, and Culver. Hotchkiss and Groton became coeducational in 1974.

Both financial exigencies and changing philosophies of education, as well as the attitudes of young people themselves, brought about the change. The limitation of enrollment to a single sex, once a distinguishing characteristic of private-school education, is no longer the prevailing practice.

A large number of the private preparatory schools are coeducational for day students. The vast majority of those that have elementary school departments for day students are coeducational in these grades.

Despite their considerable cost, private boarding and day prep school enrollments have risen in response to the increased competition for admission to the better colleges, concern about the quality of public education at the high school level, and, in some areas, in reaction to busing.

OTHER ISSUES

The climbing cost of a college education, falling test-score averages, and the back-to-basics movement in elementary and secondary education also received close attention in 1975.

College Costs. The College Entrance Examination Board (CEEB) estimated that the average total cost at a four-year public college in 1975–76 was $2,679, a 12% increase in one year. The average at a private college was $4,391, a 9% increase. The reason given for the high costs was that expenses are up and that income, because of the depressed economy, was down.

CEEB Test Scores. For the 12th consecutive year, scores on the CEEB verbal and mathematical tests administered to college-bound high school seniors dropped. The average verbal score declined by 10 points to 434; the mathematical score dropped 8 points to 472. Taken by approximately 1 million graduates annually, these standardized tests are used extensively by colleges in evaluating academic ability of applicants.

The sharp drop in scores from 1974 to 1975, the greatest in two decades, represented a continuation of an alarming and puzzling trend. Numerous explanations were offered: too much television watching, too little concern with basics among educators, and a change in the composition of the college-bound population. Since 1972 the CEEB has been conducting research into possible causes of the decline, but has not been able to reach a generally-accepted explanation.

In one research study, the board administered the test to students who did not plan to attend college. Analysis of these data revealed that the decline was characteristic of the general high school population, not just the college-bound segment.

Disappointing test results have intensified the back-to-basics movement in education, which stresses reading, writing, and math in the lower grades. At the high school level, the movement concentrates on basic-knowledge and vocationally-oriented courses.

EDWARD ALVEY, JR.
Mary Washington College

UPI

In early June, Presidents Ford and Sadat met in Salzburg for a second session of talks on Middle East problems.

EGYPT

The year 1975 was another crucial one for Egypt and its president, Anwar el-Sadat. A further interim agreement with the Israelis took place, and Sadat came to the United States for the first visit of an Egyptian president. Many political and economic problems remained, but it was a year of achievement.

Egyptian-Israeli Relations. In early January Shah Mohammed Reza Pahlavi of Iran visited Egypt and although he gave strong backing to Sadat, he urged a resumption of the Geneva talks in an effort to secure a more substantial agreement over the Sinai question. Another early visitor was Soviet Foreign Minister Andrei A. Gromyko, who promised limited arms support to Egypt. In late January the French sale to Egypt of Mirage jet fighters was announced. The Egyptians themselves felt that unless major withdrawals by the Israelis from the Sinai took place, war in some form would ensue.

Officially, Egypt promised the Israelis considerable demilitarization in the Sinai, but they were unwilling to offer the non-belligerency pledge the Israelis demanded. There was much jockeying about in the very early spring as both countries made offers and counter-offers. U. S. Secretary of State Henry Kissinger resumed his shuttle diplomacy in March, moving among Middle Eastern capitals with proposals and counter-proposals. Although Sadat expressed great optimism at first, the mission ended in failure, apparently because Prime Minister Rabin's weak political position in Israel prevented him from making further concessions.

The public postures of Egypt and Israel were aired once more as the behind-the-scenes negotiations resumed. Sadat urged U. S. pressure on Israel. He also stated that no Israeli cargoes would be permitted through the Suez Canal unless Israel agreed to some Sinai settlement. Sadat toured the Arab world in May, and in June he met with President Ford in Austria for what were termed "friendly talks."

By midsummer U. S. and world pressure on the Israelis became so great that it was apparent that concessions would be made. The United States continued all through the summer to act as the intermediary for the Egyptians and Israelis. In August, Kissinger returned once more to the Middle East, this time with strong assurances that an agreement would be forthcoming.

On September 4, Israeli and Egyptian representatives met in Geneva, Switzerland, and signed another interim peace agreement. The agreement called for a modest Israeli withdrawal in the Sinai, but this withdrawal was to include the vitally strategic Mitla and Gidi passes. Most importantly, Israel was to abandon the Abu Rudeis oil fields on the Gulf of Suez, which had been seized from the Egyptians in the 1967 war. These oil fields produced about 60% of Israeli petroleum needs. In return the Egyptians agreed to let Israeli cargoes through the Suez Canal and to renounce war as an instrument of policy with Israel for the duration of the agreement. The Egyptians also agreed to a larger UN zone in the Sinai between the two countries. The United States had not only contributed much to the mechanism through which this arrangement was effected but also engaged to contribute rather heavily to its implementation. The United States agreed to man an "early-warning" system in Sinai with about 200 U. S. observers and promised about $2.3 billion in aid (partly military) to Israel along with $800 million to Egypt. The agreement was a signal achievement but one that ran into some bitterness in both Egypt and Israel in the weeks that followed and caused unhappiness in the U. S. Congress over the observer provision.

The Suez Canal. In May the Egyptians announced that the Suez Canal would be opened to commercial traffic on June 5, although the canal had actually been traversed by various vessels for

---

EGYPT · Information Highlights

Official Name: Arab Republic of Egypt.
Location: Northeastern Africa.
Area: 386,660 square miles (1,001,449 sq km).
Population (1975 est.): 37,500,000.
Chief Cities (1975 est.): Cairo, the capital, 8,400,000; Alexandria, 2,500,000.
Government: *Head of state,* Anwar el-Sadat, president (took office Oct. 1970). *Head of government,* Abdul Aziz Hegazi, premier (took office Sept. 1974). *Legislature* (unicameral)—People's Assembly.
Monetary Unit: Pound (0.3913 pound equals U. S.$1, July 1975).
Gross National Product (1974 est.): $17,900,000,000.
Manufacturing (major products): Cotton textiles, processed foods, fertilizer, iron and steel.
Major Agricultural Products: Cotton, forage plants (berseem), rice, wheat, sugarcane, millet, corn, fish.
Foreign Trade (1974 est.): *Exports,* $1,400,000,000; *imports,* $2,100,000,000.

several months. The United States aided substantially in the clearing of the canal. The canal
had been closed because of the war with Israel
in 1967, when the annual revenues were about
$250 million. Although at the time that the
canal was reopened Egypt barred Israeli cargoes,
it began to permit the unimpeded flow of Israeli
cargo traffic later in the fall, in accordance with
the interim peace agreement. The Egyptians had
estimated that about $450 million in tolls would
be obtained in 1975 by the canal, but world
shipping interests expressed skepticism. In fact
about $41 million had been received by early
October. The canal is too narrow and shallow
for passage of the biggest of the world's tanker
fleets.

Foreign Relations. Relations with the Arab
world were generally good during the year but
not without flaws. Syria was unhappy with the
Egyptian-Israeli agreement, and relations with
Libya were at an all-time low. Although lip service was given as expected to the Palestinian
cause, in fact there was considerable enmity between Egypt and the various Palestine liberation
groups. This hostility was symbolized in September when Palestinian guerrillas seized the Egyptian embassy, along with the ambassador, in
Madrid. Relations with the Soviet Union were
cool throughout the year. Understandably,
Egyptian-U. S. relations were on the upswing,
and Sadat staked much on U. S. influence and
upon his own personal relationship with Kissinger.

At the end of October, Sadat visited the
United States and traveled widely throughout the
country. He was greeted warmly by President
Ford and addressed a joint meeting of Congress,
but Mayor Beame of New York City refused to
meet him when he came to address the United
Nations. Sadat explained his 10-day U. S. visit
as a quest for economic aid as well as arms.
Ford reiterated President Nixon's earlier pledge
to provide nuclear technology, fuel, and two reactors for Egypt and promised substantial aid,
although not enough for Sadat to term it even-
handed.

Domestic Affairs. The year was not without
its domestic troubles. Sadat pledged to continue
his policy of easing the political and social restrictions of the Nasser era. The year opened
with a major riot in Cairo over inflation, and
there were riots again in March. Economically,
Egypt was still struggling with incredible poverty
and overpopulation. In April the government
fell and Sadat, in appointing a new prime minister, conceded shortcomings in the past and
vowed to move strongly toward their solution.
Considerable debate occurred during the year
over the Aswan High Dam and the failure to
realize the expected benefits from it.

At year's end Sadat had achieved much for
Egypt's relations with Israel and had strengthened his ties with the United States. Domestically, many problems remained unsolved, yet life
in Egypt was more free politically than it had
been in a generation. A measure of this was revealed in the October statement by Mohammed
Hussanein Heykel, former President Nasser's
favorite newspaper editor, that Sadat's Sinai
agreement was a "tragic mistake" and that new
war was likely. In Nasser's day such public
criticism of the government would have been un-
thinkable. At the end of October, two political
groups were formed within the Arab Socialist
Union, Egypt's only political party, a further
sign of the easing of political restrictions.

CARL LEIDEN
University of Texas at Austin

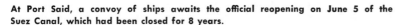

At Port Said, a convoy of ships awaits the official reopening on June 5 of the
Suez Canal, which had been closed for 8 years.

UPI

Ronald Reagan (*right*) and Alabama Gov. George Wallace share a speaker's platform in Alabama. Both men declared their presidential candidacy in 1975.

ELECTIONS AND POLITICAL PARTIES

In 1975 the House of Representatives Democratic majority of 291 to 144 Republicans changed to 290 to 145 when Rep. John Jarman, Oklahoma, switched his allegiance to the Republicans. In the Senate the Democrats had a majority of 61–38 which became 62–38 when the hotly-contested New Hampshire seat was decided. The U. S. Senate ordered a new election after it had been unable to decide the winner of the 1974 election. On Sept. 16, 1975, Democrat John Durkin, carrying 53.5% of the vote, defeated Republican Louis Wyman.

1975 Elections. Political alienation of voters remained a major concern of both the Republicans and Democrats. The Gallup Poll in the summer of 1975 showed that only 21% of U. S. adults considered themselves Republicans and 44% Democrats. Some 35% of those polled referred to themselves as independents.

Voting in state and local elections in November was rather light. Democratic gubernatorial incumbents enjoyed landslide victories in Louisiana and Kentucky. Louisiana operated under a new open-primary law, and Gov. Edwin W. Edwards garnered 62.3% of the vote against five Democratic opponents, thus avoiding a runoff election. In Kentucky, Gov. Julian Carroll defeated Republican Robert Gable, also with 62.3% of the vote. Although Republican Gil Carmichael of Mississippi made a strong bid against Democrat Cliff Finch, Mississippians gave Finch the governor's chair by a narrow 51.8% of the vote. With 3 Democrats winning their races, the Democrats held 36 governorships, including 8 of the 10 largest states. The Republicans held 13 governorships, and Maine had an independent.

Kentucky and Mississippi elected women to serve as lieutenant governors in 1975. Democrats Thelma Stovall of Kentucky and Evelyn Gandy of Mississippi became the second and third women elected to that position, joining Mary Ann Krupsak of New York, who had been elected in 1974.

In Arizona Margaret Hance was elected mayor of Phoenix in 1975, making Phoenix the nation's second largest city with a woman mayor, the other being San Antonio, Tex.

Important mayorships were decided in Philadelphia, where conservative-Democrat Frank L. Rizzo was reelected, and Boston. In Boston a school-busing issue had heated the campaign to a marked degree, but incumbent Democratic Mayor Kevin H. White managed to eke out a victory in a non-partisan race over state Sen. Joseph F. Timilty. In Salt Lake City, Utah, Democrat Ted Wilson ousted incumbent Republican Conrad Harrison.

Democrats also kept their control of the state legislatures in Mississippi, Kentucky, Louisiana, and New Jersey, although in the latter state Republicans did gain 17 seats in the state assembly. New York and New Jersey also held referendums on Equal Rights Amendments (ERA) to

their respective state constitutions. In both states the amendments were soundly defeated.

Apprehensive about increasing taxes and rising inflation, voters also rejected many bond issues for schools, housing, and highways in several states, including New York and Ohio. In trying to look ahead to the 1976 national elections, Democratic and Republican leaders could determine no discernible pattern in the 1975 elections. Voter turnouts were relatively light, no important governorships were contested, and no national issues seemed to have emerged in the elections. It was obvious, however, that the Republican party had not turned the corner from their heavy defeats in the 1974 elections.

Campaign Finance Law. The 93rd Congress, in part pressed by the Watergate disclosures, passed a campaign finance law in 1974, severely limiting the amount of money that could be contributed and spent on federal campaigns. Contributions were limited to $1,000 per individual for each primary, runoff, and general election and to an aggregate contribution of $25,000 for all federal candidates and $5,000 per organization,

political committee, and state party organization for each election. A candidate's and his family's contributions were limited to $50,000 for presidential elections; $35,000 for the senate seats; and $25,000 for the House. Cash contributions over $100 and all foreign contributions were specifically barred.

Spending limits for presidential primaries were set at $10 million total per candidate for all primaries. Presidential general elections were limited to $20 million per candidate. Senate primaries were limited to $100,000 in spending and the general election to $150,000. House primaries and general elections were limited to $70,000 in each case.

Another feature of the new law is full optional public funding for presidential general elections and matching public funds in presidential primaries up to $5 million per candidate. The law is to be enforced by an eight-member, bipartisan, full-time supervisory board controlled by six voting public members, two appointed by the Speaker of the House, two by the president of the Senate, and two by the president. All candidates must be congressionally confirmed.

Presidential Primaries and Candidates. By midsummer of 1975, 31 states had scheduled presidential primaries for 1976, the first traditionally being New Hampshire on February 24. There were 23 primaries held in 1972. There would be a total of 3,008 delegates to the Democratic convention and 2,259 to the Republican. No doubt the primary system would enable presidential candidates in both parties to attempt to capture a substantial portion of delegates even before the conventions met in the summer of 1976. President Gerald R. Ford announced in July 1975 that he was a candidate for reelection, and four months later former California Gov. Ronald Reagan announced his own candidacy for the top spot on the Republican ticket. On Nov. 3, 1975, Vice President Nelson A. Rockefeller stated that he would not be a candidate for vice president in 1976. The president's campaign for the nomination moved rather sluggishly in the fall and winter of 1975.

The announced Democratic hopefuls included Rep. Morris Udall of Arizona, former Gov. Jimmy Carter of Georgia, former Sen. Fred Harris of Oklahoma, Sen. Henry M. Jackson of Washington, Sen. Lloyd Bentsen of Texas, former Gov. Terry Sanford of North Carolina, and Sargent Shriver, the Democratic candidate for vice president in 1972. Other Democratic candidates were Gov. Milton Shapp of Pennsylvania, Sen. Birch Bayh of Indiana, and Gov. George C. Wallace of Alabama. Although Sen. Edward Kennedy of Massachusetts had ruled himself out of the race, the polls continued to show him to be a strong contender in the event he became a candidate.

UPI

Democratic presidential candidates in 1975 included Sen. Birch Bayh (*above*) and (*below*) Sen. Lloyd Bentsen (*left*) and Rep. Morris Udall.

UPI

ERWIN L. LEVINE
Skidmore College

The largest U.S. solar energy system, which provides 60% of an Atlanta elementary school's energy requirements, was dedicated in November.

energy

Energy developments in 1975 are reviewed in this article under the following headings: (1) Survey; (2) Coal; (3) Synthetic Fuels; (4) Natural Gas; (5) Petroleum; (6) Nuclear Energy; and (7) Solar Energy. Worldwide production details on coal, natural gas, and petroleum are discussed under MINING.

Survey

The world was fortunate in 1975 because two events expected by many did not materialize. First, there was no war in the Middle East and no accompanying oil embargo. Second, the Organization of Petroleum Exporting Countries (OPEC) did not increase the price of oil as much as was feared.

Although the worst did not happen, nations generally maintained their efforts to develop energy programs designed to sustain their individual economies. Many national energy programs were similar to that of the United States in their emphasis on three types of activity: efforts to find more traditional energy reserves, to develop new sources of energy through the use of advanced technology, and to use energy more prudently.

Energy Development Program. In the United States, the world's greatest consumer of energy, efforts continued, without complete success, to develop a comprehensive national energy policy. A major component of such a policy was created late in 1974, when several federal energy agencies were combined into the Energy Research and Development Administration (ERDA). In

1975, the new agency announced a research and development (R and D) strategy to implement the earlier Project Independence, whose objective is to reduce U. S. dependence on foreign energy.

The development program announced by ERDA in 1975 divides R and D efforts into three time periods: the near-term (1975–85); the mid-term (1985–2000); and the long-term (beyond 2000). The near-term effort will center on means to facilitate greater recovery of oil and natural gas from known fields, greater utilization of coal and light-water nuclear reactors, and the conservation of energy. The latter goal is to be obtained by stressing better insulation of homes and buildings and increasing the efficiency of energy-using machines.

ERDA's highest mid-term priorities are the development of synthetic fuels from coal and oil

Sheikh Yamani, Saudi Arabian oil minister, attends a Vienna meeting of the oil-producing nations. In October a 10% increase in oil prices became effective.

United States or the long term security of energy supplies for the United States." The funding would support projects that would not receive sufficient financing at reasonable terms from other sources to make the project commercially feasible.

The president's plan, which was not acted on by the Congress in 1975, called for the creation of an Energy Independence Authority that would be authorized to operate with $25 billion from the U. S. Treasury and $75 billion in debt securities. The proposal for such a massive infusion of capital into the energy companies suggested to some observers that the U. S. economic system was evolving toward socialism for the rich and capitalism for the middle class.

Another troublesome aspect of the attempt of the United States to develop a national energy policy was the growing insistence by certain energy-rich states that they be provided the opportunity to contribute to federal decision-making about energy development in their regions. The growing confrontation between some states and the federal government arose because much of the nation's remaining fossil fuel reserves, plus geothermal and uranium resources, are located in the western United States, with substantial amounts of energy deposits under federally owned land.

Coal

Coal, the most abundant fossil fuel found in the United States, ranks behind oil and natural gas in usage. Government policy in effect, or proposed, will gradually increase coal use as it replaces some oil and natural gas in electricity-producing plants. In the future it is expected that coal will be converted to synthetic fuels. Expanded use of coal is possible because the proven U. S. coal reserves are 723 times greater than current annual consumption.

A number of environmental problems resulting from the expanded use of coal remained partially unsolved in 1975. For example, when coal is burned in a power plant, sulfur dioxide and nitrogen oxide gases are produced along with particulate matter called fly ash. Much of the latter can be removed from stack emissions by means of mechanical and electrical devices, but the problem of the gases is not fully solved. A partial solution may be the increased use of low-sulfur western coal as a substitute for high-sulfur eastern coal, or the removal of sulfur from eastern coal prior to combustion. In addition to shipping western coal east by means of unit trains, proposals are under study to use pipelines to carry pulverized coal in a water slurry as far as 1,000 miles (1,600 km).

Because strip-mined coal is generally less costly than deep-mined coal, and because western coal beds are particularly suitable for stripping, a growing tendency to strip coal is clearly in evidence. This trend increases the problems of reclaiming strip-mine areas, which are partic-

shale. Long-term emphasis is on the development of new types of nuclear energy and electric energy produced from solar power. ERDA also supports, but at reduced levels of urgency, solar heating and cooling of structures, the tapping of geothermal energy sources, more effective utilization of waste heat, and the use of the energy found in the biomass (animal and human wastes, and plants) and in certain elements, such as hydrogen.

A major problem associated with the R and D effort and its subsequent application to commercial uses is how such activities should be funded. In 1975, there was general agreement in the U. S. Congress and between Congress and the Ford administration about the propriety and necessity for the federal government to fund basic research activity, with some cooperation from the private sector. A more controversial fiscal problem arose over the question of how funds should be obtained to move advanced technology into commercial energy production.

New Proposals. Late in the year, President Ford proposed to the Congress a program recommended by Vice President Rockefeller for providing $100 billion to be used for energy development over a 10-year period. This program would assist "business concerns" with projects that would "make a significant contribution to the achievement of energy independence by the

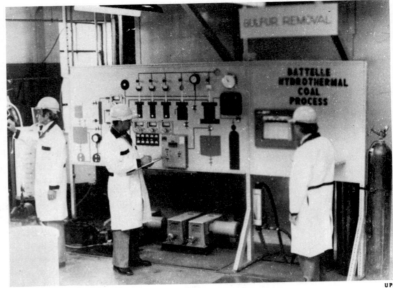

A new process for removing sulfur from coal was developed in 1975. It could make high-sulfur coal economically competitive and environmentally acceptable.

ularly troublesome in the west, where natural aridity hinders revegetative efforts.

Synthetic Fuels

In addition to abundant coal, the United States also has large reserves of oil shale. These reserves, plus the determination of the government to reduce U. S. dependence on imported fuels substantially, have increased interest in developing a synthetic-fuels industry. There are three general possibilities for synthetic fuels: synthetic gasoline and natural gas from coal, and synthetic gasoline from oil shale. Despite the attractive possibilities of converting coal and oil shale into synthetic fuels, such an industry would face serious problems before commercial production could start.

Problems. One problem is cost. It is cheaper to pump oil and natural gas from the ground than to convert coal and oil shale to synthetic fuels. Energy companies, lending institutions, and private investors are thus reluctant to involve themselves in such costly and risky ventures without protection for their investments. The federal government studied, but was unable to solve, the problem of making synthetic fuel investment sufficiently attractive financially to promote development by the private sector. Possible solutions that have been proposed are federal loan guarantees and price supports. The latter would protect companies against a sudden drop in world prices.

A second problem with synthetic fuel development is environmental. Increased use of coal in a synthetic-fuels industry would increase the environmental problems caused by coal production. Developing a new oil-shale industry would introduce entirely new kinds of environmental degradation to Colorado, Utah, and Wyoming, where the richest shale deposits are located.

Natural Gas

Natural gas is the second largest source of energy used in the United States. In 1975 gas continued to be an unusually attractive bargain because government restrictions on the price of natural gas sold in interstate commerce kept the cost artificially low. An effort made in the Congress, backed by the Ford administration, to deregulate interstate natural gas prices failed in 1975, but proponents of the proposition indicated that the effort would be made again. Those favoring deregulation of natural gas prices argued that a price increase would provide incentives to spur the search for new gas fields. In addition, it was suggested that letting gas prices rise would serve to encourage conservation of natural gas by consumers. Opponents of the measure were concerned about the effect of a natural-gas price increase upon poor and middle-income consumers.

As the production of natural gas from onshore wells in the United States continued to decline, considerable hope was expressed by government and industry officials that new fields under the outer continental shelf would prove exploitable. For the short term, however, government officials warned that cold winters could bring on localized natural gas shortages.

Petroleum

During 1975 work on the Alaskan oil pipeline moved ahead, and the United Kingdom began receiving its first natural gas from the North Sea oil fields it has divided with Norway. If work proceeds as planned, by 1980, Norway could be producing 1.8 million barrels of petroleum a day, more than six times its domestic production. By 1981, 1.5 million barrels a day could be flowing to the United Kingdom. This

would make it self-sufficient and one of the world's largest petroleum producers. By 1985, Britain could be producing 3 to 4 million barrels a day and exporting as much as 1 million barrels.

In September members of the Organization of Petroleum Exporting Countries (OPEC) met to discuss price increases for their oil. After considerable argument, OPEC announced a 10% price hike effective until July 1976, when the group will meet again. Saudi Arabia argued for a temporary freeze on prices, while Iran, at the other extreme, suggested a 20% increase.

U. S. Petroleum Policies. President Ford used the announcement of the oil price increase to berate the Congress for failing to pass his recommended energy plan. Ford noted that since Congress cannot control the price of OPEC oil, it must seek other ways to assist the U. S. consumer.

During much of 1975, the Republican administration of President Ford was at loggerheads with the Democratic Congress over the question of removing price controls from "old oil," the 60% of domestically-produced oil that is under a price ceiling of $5.25 a barrel. Ford's position was that decontrol of oil prices would accomplish two objectives. First, letting the controlled oil rise in price to somewhere near the $13 a barrel that uncontrolled oil is bringing would encourage individuals and industry to adopt oil-saving measures. This in turn would substantially reduce the dependence of the United States on foreign oil suppliers. Second, the administration believed that allowing the price of oil to increase would serve as an incentive to oil companies to shoulder the costs of a more extensive and vigorous search for new oil fields.

Many in Congress wanted to retain the price ceiling of $5.25 and reduce the price of uncontrolled oil. Domestic oil price controls, due to expire on Nov. 15, 1975, were extended for 30 days to provide time for Congress and the administration to work out a compromise. Its outlines included rolling back the price of domestic oil until 1977 (after the 1976 elections) and then permitting the price to increase by 10% or more annually for the remainder of a 40-month period after enactment of the bill.

A rather surprising aspect of the debate on oil policy was the nearly successful effort in the Senate to pass legislation designed to break apart the major oil companies. It would also have forced them to give up control of other energy enterprises in coal and uranium development.

Although the oil companies successfully opposed the divestiture proposals, they lost on another issue—the decision by Congress to eliminate the depletion allowance that oil companies had used in computing their federal taxes.

Nuclear Energy

The debate over the wisdom of constructing many more nuclear power plants increased in intensity during 1975. However, in spite of con-

The concrete deck section of the oil-drilling platform "Beryl A" is floated atop two tankers to its station in the North Sea.

UPI

WORLD CRUDE OIL PRODUCTION
(Thousands of barrels daily)

	1971	1972	1973	1974
North America				
Canada*.	1,347.5	1,531.9	1,974.0	1,729.3
United States*.	9,462.8	9,440.9	9,187.3	8,794.4
Totals.	10,810.3	10,972.8	11,161.3	10,523.7
Latin America				
Argentina.	423.3	433.0	418.1	416.6
Bolivia.	36.2	43.6	47.2	47.3
Brazil.	174.0	166.9	170.8	177.4
Chile.	35.3	34.2	30.5	27.7
Colombia.	214.0	195.8	184.7	168.1
Ecuador.	4.5	78.1	208.8	177.0
Mexico.	427.1	440.8	519.5	525.5
Peru.	61.9	64.6	68.2	72.1
Trinidad & Tobago.	129.2	141.3	166.0	163.0
Venezuela.	3,549.1	3,219.9	3,366.0	2,976.3
Others.	2.2	2.2	3.3	4.4
Totals.	5,056.8	4,820.4	5,183.1	4,755.4
Western Europe				
Austria.	48.3	47.4	47.2	43.9
France.	37.4	29.6	25.8	21.6
Germany, West.	146.8	140.2	132.7	124.7
Italy.	24.1	21.4	19.0	19.0
Netherlands.	32.1	29.8	29.0	29.9
Norway.	6.0	33.2	37.5	36.2
Spain.	2.4	2.9	20.6	37.9
Turkey.	65.8	64.5	58.9	68.7
United Kingdom.	4.1	7.2	8.0	1.8
Yugoslavia.	58.0	64.8	71.0	71.0
Others.	....	1.7	1.8	1.8
Totals.	425.0	442.7	451.5	456.5
Eastern Europe				
Albania.	27.0	28.7	30.0	43.9
Bulgaria.	6.3	4.9	5.0	3.0
Hungary.	41.0	41.8	42.0	41.8
Poland.	8.0	8.2	8.5	10.2
Rumania.	280.0	287.7	295.0	290.0
USSR.	7,400.0	7,912.6	8,450.0	9,202.6
Others.	6.0	9.8	10.0	7.0
Totals.	7,778.3	8,293.7	8,840.5	9,598.5

	1971	1972	1973	1974
Middle East				
Bahrain.	75.3	69.7	63.2	67.4
Iran.	4,539.5	5,023.1	5,860.9	6,021.6
Iraq.	1,694.1	1,465.5	2,018.1	1,974.6
Kuwait.	3,196.7	3,283.0	3,020.4	2,546.1
Oman.	294.3	281.8	295.0	290.3
Qatar.	430.7	482.4	570.3	518.4
Saudi Arabia.	4,769.1	6,012.5	7,601.2	8,479.8
Syria.	103.0	123.5	85.6	110.3
United Arab Emirates.	1,059.5	1,202.7	1,532.6	1,678.6
Others.	120.0	120.0	100.0	101.6
Totals.	16,282.2	18,064.2	21,147.3	21,788.4
Africa				
Algeria.	785.6	1,062.3	1,097.3	1,008.6
Angola.	113.1	139.1	154.5	167.8
Congo (Brazzaville).	0.8	6.4	33.8	61.5
Egypt.	293.9	202.6	165.7	142.4
Gabon.	114.6	125.2	150.2	201.5
Libya.	2,760.8	2,239.4	2,174.9	1,521.3
Nigeria.	1,531.2	1,815.7	2,054.3	2,255.0
Tunisia.	87.3	83.0	95.0	84.5
Others.	0.5	0.6	0.7	1.0
Totals.	5,687.6	5,674.3	5,892.6	5,443.6
Asia & Far East				
Brunei & Malaysia.	192.1	275.9	325.7	274.9
Burma.	19.0	20.3	20.0	20.4
China.	510.0	525.0	720.0	1,260.0
India.	142.7	155.6	161.0	148.8
Indonesia.	892.1	1,078.7	1,336.9	1,374.5
Japan.	15.1	14.6	14.2	14.1
Pakistan.	8.2	8.2	9.9	7.1
Others.	0.5	2.5	2.0	3.8
Totals.	1,779.7	2,080.8	2,589.7	3,103.6
Oceania.	311.6	393.9	390.5	391.4
World Totals.	45,556.4	48,131.5	50,742.8	56,061.4

* Does not include synthetic crude or natural gas liquids, but does include lease condensate. Source: Annual Statistical Bulletin, 1974, Organization of Petroleum Exporting Countries.

Note: Due to rounding, totals may not add exactly.

siderable concern expressed about the safety of nuclear reactors, the U. S. reactor industry continued to grow, although not at the rate some had previously predicted. In 1975, the United States had 55 operating reactors; 63 reactors were under construction, and 100 more were in the ordering phase. President Ford expressed the hope that by 1985 the United States would have 200 nuclear power plants in operation.

Opposition to Development. A high point in the activity of those opposed to further nuclear-reactor construction was reached late in the summer. Seeking to refute the nuclear industry's claims that no reputable scientists had doubts about nuclear reactor safety, the Union of Concerned Scientists presented a petition to the White House calling for drastic reduction in nuclear power plant construction in the United States and in the export of such plants.

The petition, which bore the signatures of some 2,000 scientists, called for a major study of hazards in nuclear-reactor operation, guarding of fissionable material from being used for unauthorized purposes, and the disposal of radioactive nuclear wastes.

Federal Policy. The director of ERDA, Robert C. Seamans, Jr., disagreed with the thrust of the petition. He stated, "We are fully aware of these questions and have good reason to believe they will be resolved in ways acceptable to all concerned. The potential of nuclear power is too great and our future energy needs too demanding to let our determination now flag because of the problems remaining to be overcome."

Although efforts were made in the Congress to cut off funding for the nation's primary nuclear development program—the liquid metal fast breeder reactor—ERDA was authorized to continue with the design of the Clinch River breeder reactor project. Located at Oak Ridge, Tenn., this small reactor is scheduled for operation in the early 1980's. Its purpose is to provide design and operating information that can be used in scaled-up commercial breeder reactors.

Further removed from realization than the breeder reactor is the development of a fusion reactor. ERDA is engaged in two alternative fusion research efforts. One is the confinement of fuel plasmas in magnetic "bottles." The other effort is the ignition and compression of fusion fuel by laser beams.

World Nuclear Development. The U. S. government was not alone in its support of nuclear power as an alternative to fossil fuels. Other industrialized states operate impressive and expanding civil nuclear programs. A number of the industrializing nations have either made substantial progress in nuclear power production, or

changing, with substantial increases in the cost of standard fuels and with additional rises expected.

In general, the use of solar energy involves collecting the sun's heat under glass panels over a black background. These collectors trap part of the solar heat, which is then stored by various means until it is needed. Alternatively, during the hot months, the solar heat may be used to provide the energy for an air conditioning system.

The possibility of converting solar energy by various means into electrical energy is feasible but still too costly. This option is being developed by private industry and by government scientists.

The federal government's interest in solar energy is indicated by passage of the Solar Energy Research Development and Demonstration Act. Following the mandate of this legislation, ERDA announced in 1975 the creation of a Solar Energy Research Institute (SERI), which will function as a national center for solar energy investigations. The site for SERI had not been determined by year's end, but there is speculation that it will be located in one of the sun-rich states, such as Arizona, Colorado, Florida, New Mexico, or Texas.

R. M. LAWRENCE
Colorado State University

A new nuclear generating station, under construction in LaSalle county, Ill., is expected to be operating by 1979.

This space-age windmill, an experiment of NASA's Project Independence, is able to generate power for 25 homes.

they have announced plans to do so. These nations include Brazil, India, Iran, Israel, Pakistan, People's Republic of China, Republic of China (Taiwan), and South Korea. Late in 1975, the announcement that the United States would assist Egypt with the construction of two nuclear power plants caused some domestic consternation and, as would be expected, concern in Israel as well. Assurances were given by the United States that the U. S. reactors supplied to Egypt would be operated under tight safeguards to prohibit diversion of fissionable materials for nuclear-weapons fabrication.

As more nations adopted the nuclear power option, the United States struggled with the question of how to assist such economic development while precluding the additional proliferation of nuclear weapons. One proposal was that world regional centers be constructed for handling fissionable material under international control.

Solar Energy

Much of the technology needed to build solar-heated and solar-cooled structures is well understood. However, until recently this knowledge was not put to practical use because the cost of solar collectors was much higher than that of traditional fuels. The situation is rapidly

Center section of Japan's Minato Bridge, is lifted into position. Connecting two parts of Osaka, the steel-truss cantilever span was completed in 1975.

HANSHIN EXPRESSWAY PUBLIC CORP.

ENGINEERING, CIVIL

Despite the fact that funds for civil engineering works, both public and private, were difficult to obtain in 1975, some noteworthy projects were being planned or were under construction in the United States and other countries.

BRIDGES

Significant bridges under construction or completed in 1975 included several in the United States, Pacific islands, and Japan.

United States. A type of bridge new to the United States will be built in Washington state over the Columbia River between Pasco and Kennewick. The 1,794-foot (547-meter) continuously prestressed concrete, stayed-girder structure consists of a 981-foot (299-meter) main span, flanked by 406.5-foot (124-meter) side spans. The main span is the world's second longest concrete stayed-girder. The cable-stayed design, never before constructed in the United States, will provide a vertical clearance of 58 feet (18 meters) and a horizontal navigational clearance of 950 feet (290 meters).

The Ohio River will be spanned at Wheeling, W. Va., with a 780-foot (238-meter) tied-arch steel bridge scheduled for completion in 1977. The $12 million vehicular structure will be 88 feet (27 meters) wide and will carry two 24-foot (7-meter) lanes of Interstate Highway 70.

Pacific. The world's longest prestressed concrete box-girder span will connect two islands in the Pacific Trust Territory east of the Philippines. The 790-foot (547-meter) main span over the channel is flanked by 176-foot (54-meter) side spans for a total length of 1,142 feet (601 meters). Its 30-foot (9-meter) wide deck will carry two lanes of traffic.

Japan. Japan's longest steel-truss cantilever bridge, the Minato Bridge, was opened to traffic in 1975. The $127 million vehicular bridge that links the Port of Osaka with Minato Ward of Osaka City is 3,214-foot (980-meter) long and 61.5-foot (19-meter) wide. The 1,673-foot (510-meter) main span ranks third in the world. Its double-deck construction has four lanes per deck. Four years in building, it incorporates 52,800 tons of steel and 2.5 million cubic feet (70,000 cu meters) of concrete.

Japan is scheduled to complete in 1976 the world's longest concrete box-girder span, which will connect Shimonoseki City on Japan's main island, Honshu, with the island of Hikoshima in the Sea of Japan. The 779-foot (237-meter) main span is flanked by a pair of 436-foot (130-meter) side spans. The two-lane bridge has a 31-foot (9-meter) wide deck.

CANALS

Canals in the United States were under construction or in the planning stages, and in Egypt the Suez Canal was reopened.

United States. In the South, work was under way on the 253-mile (407-km) Tennessee-Tombigbee ship canal. The Tenn-Tom project, expected to cost $703 million, is scheduled for completion in 1981. It will be 14 feet (4 meters) deep from Demopolis, Ala., north through Mississippi to the Tennessee River at Pickwick Reservoir in northeastern Mississippi. The waterway will have a 300-foot (91-meter) bottom width and a top width of 450 feet (137 meters). It will permit navigation from the central United States to Mobile, Ala., on the Gulf Coast.

California is planning to dig a 43-mile (69-km) canal to divert water from the Sacramento River around the delta formed by the Sacramento and San Joaquin rivers at the head of San Francisco Bay. The $286-million Peripheral Canal will form a vital link in the state water project to protect the ecology and supply water

Construction continued on Crystal Dam on Colorado's Gunnison River. The double-curvature, thin-arch structure, scheduled for completion in 1977, will provide hydroelectric power and will regulate the river's flow.

BUREAU OF RECLAMATION

to the southern part of the state. The canal will be 30 feet (9 meters) deep, 200 feet (61 meters) wide at the bottom, and 400 to 500 feet (122 to 152 meters) wide at the top. The project is scheduled for completion by 1980.

Egypt. In June 1975, Egypt reopened the Suez Canal to international shipping, eight years after the 103-mile (166-km) long canal was closed by the 1967 Israeli-Arab War.

DAMS

Major dam construction aimed at increasing hydroelectric capacity and irrigation supplies.

United States. The Bureau of Reclamation is constructing Auburn Dam on the American River, northeast of Sacramento, Calif. Auburn is a thin-arch, double-curvature concrete dam, 685 feet (209 meters) high, with a crest length of 4,150 feet (1,265 meters), making it one of the world's longest arch dams. It will back up a reservoir that will supply municipal, industrial, and irrigation water for several counties.

Scheduled for completion in 1977 is another Bureau of Reclamation project, Crystal Dam, on the Gunnison River near Montrose, Colo. The double-curvature, thin-arch concrete structure is 635 feet (194 meters) long, 323 feet (98 meters) high, 29 feet (9 meters) thick at the base, and 10 feet (3 meters) thick at the crest. Containing 154,000 cubic yards (117,741 cu meters) of concrete, Crystal will be the thinnest dam for its height in the world. The $22 million project will supply electric power and guarantee regular flows in the Gunnison River.

Also under construction is the Harry S. Truman Dam on the Osage River, about 1.5 miles (2.6 km) northwest of Warsaw, Mo., at the headwaters of the Lake of the Ozarks. The concrete and earth structure will control the flow of both the Osage and South Grand Rivers. The compacted earth and rockfill portion of the dam will be 5,000 feet (1,524 meters) long and 94 feet (29 meters) high. The embankment, with a dike section, will contain 8.5 million cubic yards (6.4 million cu meters) of material. When completed in 1980, at an estimated cost of $332 million, the dam will form a lake for recreation and power development.

Turkey. Karakaya Dam will be a 568-foot (173-meter) high, double-curvature concrete arch dam, 1,509 feet (460 meters) long. Located on the Euphrates River, 100 miles (161 km) south of Turkey's Keban Dam, the structure will contain 2.6 million cubic yards (2 million cu meters) of concrete. Construction on the $250 million project will begin in 1976 with completion scheduled for 1981. It will impound water for irrigation and power.

Workmen check the cutter head of a boring machine at Tonner No. 2 Tunnel, near Los Angeles. The tunnel is a key link in a program to give dry southern California northern water.

METROPOLITAN WATER DISTRICT OF SOUTHERN CALIFORNIA

USSR. Chirkey Dam on the Sulak River, upstream from the west shore of the Caspian Sea, is a 738-foot (231-meter) high, 1,165-foot (355-meter) long, double-curvature, concrete arch structure scheduled for completion in 1976. Highest of its type in the Soviet Union, it contains 1.7 million cubic yards (1.3 million cu meters) of concrete. Its impounded reservoir will produce hydroelectric power.

TUNNELS

New tunnels for highways and for water supplies were completed or were under construction in 1975.

United States. Scheduled for completion in 1976 is the 3.5-mile (5.6-km) Tonner No. 2 Tunnel, east of Los Angeles. The water supply tunnel is lined with a concrete pipe 8 feet (2.4 meters) in diameter and 6.5 inches (16.5 cm) thick. The tunnel is part of the Metropolitan Water District of Southern California's $1.3 billion program to distribute northern California water to the southern part of the state. About half completed in 1975, the system will include 300 miles (483 km) of tunnel and pipeline.

Construction was under way on the second bore of the two-lane Eisenhower Memorial Tunnel that carries Interstate Highway 70 through the Continental Divide 60 miles (97 km) west of Denver, Colo. It is the highest highway tunnel in the world and the longest in North America at 1.7 miles (3 km). The original two-lane tunnel was opened in 1973.

Japan. In 1975, Japan opened the two-lane, 5.3-mile (8.5-km) Mt. Ena Tunnel as part of the Chuo Expressway between Tokyo and Nagoya. At one point it is 3,300 feet (1,006 meters) beneath a peak of the Japanese Alps. The bore is 44.2 feet (13.5 meters) wide by 30 feet (9 meters) high and is lined with 2 feet (0.6 meter) of concrete. A paralleling pilot tunnel serves as a ventilation duct for the main tunnel. A second two-lane tunnel will be constructed to parallel the existing tunnel.

Finland. One of the longest continuous rock tunnels in the world is being driven 75 miles (120 km) to supply Helsinki and surrounding area with an adequate supply of potable water. The horseshoe-shaped tunnel, 18.5 square yards (15.5 sq meters) in area, stretches from Lake Paijanne, northeast of the Finnish capital, to a new 654-million cubic yard (500-million cu meter) capacity reservoir in Vantaa on the outskirts of Helsinki. Costing $70 million, the project is scheduled for completion in 1980.

WILLIAM H. QUIRK
North American Editor
"Construction Industry International" Magazine

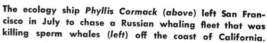

The ecology ship *Phyllis Cormack* (above) left San Francisco in July to chase a Russian whaling fleet that was killing sperm whales (*left*) off the coast of California.

ENVIRONMENT

Despite severe global recession and the onslaught of energy development, environmental issues proved surprisingly resilient as 1975 drew to a close.

WORLD ENVIRONMENT

The year was notable for the emergence of several trends.

UNEP Environment Fund. The Environment Fund of the United Nations Environmental Program (UNEP) has committed $102 million to nearly 200 global environmental projects. The largest sums went to fund the human settlements conference scheduled for 1976 in Vancouver, British Columbia ($1.5 million), environmental monitoring ($1.3 million), and the Mediterranean conventions ($1.7 million).

Smaller sums went to a host of diverse projects, ranging from film production to climate modeling, giving rise to charges by contributing nations that the fund was spread too thin. Slowness in allocating money led to a cutback in U. S. funding from $10 million in 1974 to $5 million in 1975.

Earthwatch Begins. After nearly three years of planning, two components of the Earthwatch program have begun operation. The International Referral Service for environmental information services opened in the United States at the Environmental Protection Agency. It was the first link in a projected computerized directory of information sources.

The Global Environmental Monitoring System (GEMS), a mosaic of existing and planned data collection systems, was still embroiled in defining standards. Significant accomplishments in 1975 included the start of Indian Ocean monitoring, African forest mapping, operation of baseline stations to record long-term atmospheric trends, and the establishment of an international monitoring center in London. Work also proceeded on the International Register of Toxic Chemicals, which is to serve as a clearinghouse on actions to take in case of accidents involving dangerous chemicals.

Cleanup of the Earth's Oceans. Probably the biggest UNEP accomplishment in 1975 was the negotiation of a treaty to protect the Mediterranean Sea. Of the 18 Mediterranean nations, 16 agreed to the legal basis for regional cleanup. The treaty has few real teeth, however. Monitoring activities, such as an oil spill control center in Malta, are its major provisions.

Progress in protecting the shallow Baltic, Caspian, and Caribbean seas was slower. Although a Baltic treaty was drafted, only one of the seven bordering nations signed it. Iran and the USSR have agreed on future Caspian cooperation, but it will start modestly, with a jointly-named research ship.

Twelve states have signed the 1972 Convention for the Prevention of Pollution from Ships, but three more signatures are needed for ratification. Under the provisions of the treaty, certain kinds of ocean dumping would require licensing or be prohibited entirely pending environmental impact studies.

Law of the Sea. Despite great hopes, the 1975 Geneva Conference again failed to produce a seabed treaty. While environmentalists wait, most nations are moving forward unilaterally with mining and drilling operations. It is feared that once such operations are established, nations will be loath to relinquish authority to the

proposed International Seabed Authority. Agreement on a 200-mile (360-km) economic zone for countries bordering on oceans seems close at hand, but will have to await still another conference in the spring of 1976 in New York City.

Endangered Species. Signed by 57 of 80 nations, the Endangered Species Treaty restricts, but does not ban, trade in products derived from endangered species. In addition, it prohibits the export of the most-threatened species unless approval is obtained from a designated national authority.

Endangered species received additional protection in 1975, when the USSR and Japan agreed to stop exterminating the sperm whale and to adhere to International Whaling Commission quotas. The Japanese are substituting sharks. Six Latin American nations bordering the Amazon agreed to protect that jungle through creation of a multinational park.

Developing Nations Turnabout. Developing nations, which had bristled at the concept of environmental controls in 1972, regarding them as colonialism in disguise, proved the strongest supporters of UNEP. Brazil, for example, had previously been apathetic about environmental issues, but in 1975 it drafted its first national environmental legislation. The legislation encouraged the rise of environmental action groups, mandated ecology courses in schools, and began enforcing conservation measures.

Colombia updated its 1863 environmental statute with strong safeguards, which will probably be tested by U. S. interests seeking to exploit the nation's rich coal fields. Venezuela strengthened its 1973 law and began moving heavy industry from its cities. Turkey began building refining plants to clean its coal supply. Pakistan, with financial aid from Iran, initiated water cleanup. China continued its secretive population control program. Capitalistic aspects of China's economy caused problems when managers faced with production quotas are reluctant to divert money to pollution control at the expense of production.

Industrial Nations. Regional and national environmental programs continued to advance in most industrialized nations, despite funding cutbacks. The Organization for Economic Cooperation and Development (OECD), which represents 24 of the heavily industrialized countries, continued its strong environmental program. The European Economic Community (EEC) initiated programs to protect its water supplies, control waste oils, and help clean up the Mediterranean. France passed a strong environmental law, limited building height in Paris, canceled the Left Bank expressway, and converted the former Les Halles area into a green space. Greece wrote environmental safeguards into its new constitution, and West Germany passed a law requiring disclosure of pollution control. Japan continued to spend heavily, earmarking $2.2 billion for environmental protection, with

UPI

Aluminum-can recycling, as at this East Rutherford, N. J., center, has increased rapidly.

16% of all capital allocated for environmental controls.

Nuclear Power. Spurred on by the fourfold increase in the price of fossil fuels, many nations plunged headlong into the race for nuclear power plants. In 1975, 38 nations increased their planned use of nuclear power by 34% from the previous year, according to Atomic Industrial Forum. World nuclear capacity rose from 16,300 megawatts in 1970 to 82,000 megawatts in 1975, and it is expected to reach 220,-000 megawatts in 1980, according to the International Atomic Energy Agency. EEC countries plan to increase their nuclear reliance to 17% of total energy by 1985, from its present 1.4% share. Individual states may exceed the average. France plans 20% reliance by 1985; West Germany, 40% by 1985; and Italy, where nuclear construction is entangled in political bickering, plans 90% reliance by 1990.

But opposition materialized as fast as the plans could be unveiled, accompanied by protests, demonstrations, and even sabotage. The Netherlands deferred its nuclear plans in the face of strong protest, and Sweden sharply curtailed plans that would have made it the biggest per capita consumer of nuclear energy. In Britain, the influential weekly, *The Economist*, marshaled public opinion with its special issue "The Case Against Nuclear Power." (See also EN-ERGY.)

Mankind at the Turning Point. The environmental problems of the year—ocean dumping, forest leveling, oil spills, fish killing, and the strong thrust to develop energy resources at the expense of the environment—were familiar to

environmentalists. But 1975 was also a year when the first real signs of world cooperation appeared.

Almost symbolic of this cooperation was the title of the second report from the Club of Rome, released at mid-year: "Mankind at the Turning Point." It considerably softened the doomsday projections of the controversial first study, "The Limits to Growth." Mankind can have economic growth without killing itself, concluded researchers Mihajlo Mesovic of Case Western Reserve University and Eduard Pestel of Hanover University in Germany. But the approach must be balanced and based on scientific planning. Echoing that opinion was another study by a Harvard/Brandeis group headed by Wassily Leontief, which concluded that although mankind will generate four times as many pollutants in the year 2000 as in 1970, pollution need not reach the environment.

As the year ended, the machinery that could provide the necessary planning and control had been established. The question that remained, however, was whether global politics and national self-interest would permit it to do its work.

U. S. ENVIRONMENT

In the United States, 1975 was a mixed year for environmental protection. On the one hand, the nation's cleanup program moved into high gear as $9 billion in impounded water pollution funds was released and as more effluent-standards and clean-air implementation plans were approved. On the other hand, it was also a year of somber realization that the United States would not meet the cleanup deadlines mandated by the various environmental acts passed since 1970. Automakers were given a two-year reprieve from the 1975 clean-air goals. The Environmental Protection Agency (EPA) had to

NASA Atmosphere Explorer E carried instruments to determine whether the ozone layer is affected by pollutants.

retreat from indirect control of air pollution sources. Finally, it was realized that the water quality standards set by the 1972 act could not be met without the expenditure of an additional $30 billion.

Government and the Environment. All three branches of the government seemed to cool distinctly toward environmental issues. President Ford urged relaxation of environmental controls in his State of the Union message, vetoed a mild strip-mining control bill, and opposed land use legislation. Congress failed to override the president's strip-mine veto, weakened the National Environmental Policy Act slightly, and despite the infusion of new liberal blood, failed to report land-use legislation from committee. The judicial branch, which had provided an almost unbroken string of environmental court victories since 1970, discouraged environmental litigation by denying recovery of court costs even in successful suits.

New Gains. In the context of the most severe economic setback since the 1930's, however, and in the midst of the intense conflict between environmental and energy interests, it was surprising that the environmental issue survived and even scored some new gains. An appeals court upheld the controversial "no growth" statute of Petaluma, Calif., which could become an important weapon in land use planning. Despite pressure from energy interests, the Clean Air Act was not substantially weakened, and offshore ports for supertankers were regulated by a new statute. The Atomic Energy Commission, long criticized by environmentalists, was phased out and replaced by two agencies, the Nuclear Reg-

A worker adjusts a skimmer as a boom stops oil from spreading after a spill off the Florida coast in July.

A convoy of more than 400 coal trucks paraded through Virginia to Washington, D. C., in April to protest strip-mining legislation, later vetoed by President Ford.

ulatory Commission and the Energy Research and Development Administration (ERDA). Two top pesticide targets of environmentalists, aldrin and dieldrin, had their registrations canceled by EPA.

National Interest. Although the administration acted as though public sentiment toward environmental causes had cooled, national polls and the membership rosters of environmental organizations seemed to indicate the opposite. The total issue of "environment" did not command the fervor it once had but splintered into its natural components—land use, energy, landmarks preservation, pesticide control, billboards, endangered species protection, and similar specific causes. A special poll, conducted by the Opinion Research Corporation in August revealed that 60% of the public favored paying higher prices to amortize environmental controls, with only 21% opposed. In addition, 86% felt the United States was paying dearly for lack of past controls, and an even greater percentage felt that further delays would cost more in the long run. The poll also found that 48% favored pollution control devices on cars, while 38%

were opposed, and that 43% favored stricter strip-mining controls, even at the expense of higher electric bills.

Since the issue of a better environment could attract support during the bottoming-out of the worst recession since the 1930's, environmentalists hoped they would be able to marshal even greater public support when the economy returned to normal.

JAMES G. KOLLEGGER
Environment Information Center, Inc.

ETHIOPIA

In 1975, Haile Selassie, 83, emperor of Ethiopia from 1930–74, died in his sleep. The Ethiopian military junta pressed for political and economic change, and fighting continued unabated in the Eritrea region.

Haile Selassie. An era came to an end Aug. 27, 1975, when Haile Selassie, the last emperor of the 3,000-year-old Ethiopian monarchy, died in his sleep due to the results of ill health. He was buried with little ceremony within 24 hours. Haile Selassie, who ruled Ethiopia as emperor

for 44 years, had been removed from power in 1974 by the Ethiopian military and had been kept under house arrest until his death. (See also OBITUARIES.)

Political and Economic Change. The 120-man provisional military administrative committee chaired by Brig. Gen. Tafari Banti, but controlled by 37-year-old Deputy Chairman Maj. Mengistu Haile Mariam, continued to push for the new socialist order proclaimed at the end of 1974. The feudal land system, in existence for centuries, was officially abolished on March 4, 1975. According to the new rulers, "All rural land shall be the collective property of the Ethiopian people." A limit of 25 acres (10 hectares) on private land holding was declared, and tenants and landlords were to share equally in cultivated land.

The government's proclamation officially ended the feudal land tenure system by which the old nobility had controlled the Ethiopian political system. The government did not make serious attempts to implement the nationalization decree, although it did send more than 25,000 college and high school students from Addis Ababa to rural communities to explain to peasants their rights under the decree. Students complained about the program because they felt they were being evicted from Addis Ababa for criticizing the new government.

In a further effort to gain control of the economy, the military nationalized all banks, mortgage companies, and insurance firms on Jan. 1, 1975. The government declared that, "Appropriate compensation will be paid in the future to the shareholders." This was followed on May 17 with the nationalization of all private aircraft companies, privately-owned planes, and foreign-owned supermarkets. Missionary aircraft were exempt from the order.

The military abolished the Ethiopian monarchy March 21 and annulled its 1974 appointment of Crown Prince Asfa Wossen as king-designate. All titles of nobility were also abolished.

Between March and July, 22 Ethiopians were executed after having been found guilty of opposing the new government. This brought the total number of official executions by the new government to 82. The International Commission of Jurists and the International League for the Rights of Man appealed to the Ethiopian junta to halt its executions, claiming that they violated the Universal Declaration of Human Rights.

For the first time Ethiopian Muslims were permitted to celebrate publicly the birth of Mohammed. The Ogaden region of Ethiopia was hit with a drought, and some 250,000 nomads sought aid in relief camps.

Eritrean-Ethiopian Violence. Savage fighting between Eritrean separatists and Ethiopia continued in 1975. The government's effort to put down the secessionist movement aimed at keeping Ethiopia intact and maintaining control of the Eritrean Red Sea ports of Assab and Massawa, Ethiopia's only outlets to the sea. Ethiopia attacked Eritrea with troops, bombers, artillery, and armored vehicles.

Half of Ethiopia's 40,000 troops were deployed in Eritrea, and many civilians were among the more than 3,000 people killed as a result of the fighting. Asmara, the capital of Eritrea, was persistently bombed from the air from January to July and was militarily sealed off in August.

Eritrean separatists failed in their attempt to prevent oil shipped to Assab from reaching Addis Ababa, but the government attempts to starve the Eritrean separatists failed too, as Arab states supported the secessionists. By the end of September strikes and student protests caused the government to declare a state of emergency in Addis Ababa and the surrounding area. The severe economic drain of attempting to snuff out the Eritrean separatists was clearly straining the nation's political and economic fabric.

The United States agreed on March 17, 1975, to supply Ethiopia with an emergency $7 million of ammunition, $18 million less than Ethiopia had requested. Sudan failed in its attempt to negotiate a peace settlement between opposing political forces.

Foreign Affairs. It was reported by the U. S. Department of Defense that the USSR had established a naval base at Berbera, Somalia, only a few hundred miles from Ethiopia's border. It was expected that Ethiopia would insist on additional arms from the United States for its own national security. In June, North Korea was recognized by Ethiopia. Ethiopia renounced its claim to the adjoining French territory of Afars and Issas on July 30 and proclaimed its support for the independence of this French colony.

Books. A number of important books on Ethiopia appeared in 1975. Among them were *Ethiopia, Anatomy of a Traditional Polity* by John Markakis, and *The Dying Lion, Feudalism and Modernization in Ethiopia* by Patrick Gilkes.

PETER SCHWAB
*State University of New
York at Purchase*

ETHIOPIA · Information Highlights

Official Name: Empire of Ethiopia.
Location: Eastern Africa.
Area: 471,777 square miles (1,221,900 sq km).
Population (1975 est.): 28,000,000.
Chief City (1971 est.): Addis Ababa, the capital, 881,400.
Government: Provisional military administrative committee.
Monetary Unit: Ethiopian dollar (2.09 E. dollars equal U. S.$1, July 1975).
Gross National Product (1972 est.): $2,265,000,000.
Manufacturing (major products): Processed foods, textiles, cement, leather and shoes.
Major Agricultural Products: Coffee, cotton, sugarcane, corn, millet and sorghum, oilseeds, pulses, cattle, sheep.
Foreign Trade (1974): *Exports,* $222,000,000; *imports,* $227,000,000.

Members of the American Indian movement leave the Fairchild semiconductor plant in Shiprock, N. M., in March after occupying it for a week.

ETHNIC GROUPS

Two issues that have long affected minority groups in the United States continued to be important in 1975. First, the safeguarding of equal rights in employment and the integration of racially segregated schools were not pursued as vigorously as many thought they should be. Second, American Indians actively sought to claim their rights and to bring their social conditions to public notice.

Integration in Employment. A number of criticisms were leveled at government agencies for failing to protect minority employment rights. The U. S. Commission on Civil Rights (CCR) charged the Office of Revenue Sharing with failing in its $32.2 billion program to enforce regulations prohibiting discrimination in spending revenue-sharing funds. The CCR said that discrimination in employment and delivery of benefits by state and local governments was "far-reaching" and urged Congress to appropriate $7.5 million to ensure proper monitoring of the program. Several private organizations made a similar charge, alleging that state and local governments receiving revenue-sharing funds were not allocating appropriate amounts for services to the poor and were making contracts with companies that discriminated against blacks and women. The Government Accounting Office averred that local governments receiving such funds were evading federal anti-discrimination rules by diverting their own funds into areas where difficulties in compliance might arise.

Other government agencies were accused of discriminating against minorities in their own hiring practices. Several previously unpublished studies of the Civil Service Commission came to light, showing that certain federal agencies paid little regard to anti-bias rules in hiring and promoting employees. The CCR singled out as especially guilty the Civil Service Commission and the Equal Employment Opportunities Commission (EEOC) itself.

However valid these charges may have been, government agencies did enforce many civil rights regulations in 1975. EEOC charged the nation's largest brokerage house, Merrill Lynch, Pierce, Fenner and Smith, Inc. with violating federal law by discriminating against black and other minorities in "recruiting, hiring, assignment, training, promotion, and other terms and conditions of employment." The company took measures to comply with EEOC demands. The EEOC also sued the Adolf Coors Co. for refusing to hire minority persons and won its case in a U. S. appellate court against the AFL-CIO International Longshoremen's Association. The association had been maintaining racially segregated local unions.

The Federal Communications Commission revised its equal-opportunities guidelines to compel radio and television stations to set up goals and timetables for correcting discrimination practices in hiring and promoting minority individuals. The Justice Department obtained a court order requiring the city of Tallahassee, Fla., to hire qualified blacks in proportion to the number of blacks in the city labor force. The Justice Department also sued Birmingham, Ala., and several neighboring towns for discriminating against blacks and women in government jobs. Several federal agencies cooperated to force American Telephone and Telegraph Co., the nation's largest employer, to hire and promote minority persons at a faster rate.

Judicial Decisions. The federal courts made several important decisions concerning discrimination against minorities in hiring and promoting employees. The Supreme Court ruled that victims of discrimination in employment and advancement need not prove their employers' bad faith in order to qualify for awards of compensation. A district court judge ordered the Amer-

ican Cast Iron Pipe Co. to pay $1 million of income previously denied to 833 black employees who had been discriminated against in promotion decisions. An appellate court ordered nine steel companies to cease discriminating against minorities and women and to create a fund of $31 million from which 61,000 blacks, Spanish-surnamed persons, and women were to be paid back salaries. Federal courts also ordered that federal revenue-sharing funds be cut off from the city of Chicago until racial and sexual bias in hiring police officers ceased.

Integration in Education. Estimates of the progress of racial and ethnic integration in U. S. schools were not optimistic. A report of the CCR indicated that the proportion of blacks in integrated schools had increased in the South but had not in the North. As of 1972, 71% of blacks in the North still attended mostly black schools. The report expressed the fear that the South would follow the Northern pattern of racial segregation by residential separation. Many concerned leaders in education worried that education for blacks was worse than it had been in 1954, when the landmark decision by the Supreme Court was handed down.

Federal Agencies Blamed. Federal agencies again came under fire for failing to enforce integration in public schools. The CCR accused the Department of Health, Education, and Welfare (HEW) of depending too heavily on voluntary compliance and neglecting the sanction of withdrawing government funds from uncooperative

President Ford (right) congratulates Lowell Perry, new chairman of the Equal Employment Opportunity Commission, after swearing-in ceremonies in May.

UPI

school systems. It also accused the Internal Revenue Service of neglecting to use its power to withdraw tax-exempt status from non-profit and private schools that had been created to avoid public-school integration.

Court-Ordered Busing. Federal courts continued to take the lead in obliging school systems to integrate, often requiring that children be bused to bring proper racial proportions into public schools. Rulings in Indianapolis, Ind., Omaha, Neb., and Stockton, Calif., ordered such busing.

In two major cities court-ordered programs for busing children encountered vigorous opposition. The most violent resistance arose in Boston. At the close of 1974 three members of the Boston School Committee were cited for civil contempt for refusing to approve a desegregation plan proposed by the federal district court. The Committee's reluctance, however, represented the sentiments of many Boston residents. Violent protests against busing occurred throughout the year. Conflict over school integration contributed to racial conflict in the summer. After six black Bible salesmen were attacked on a public beach in South Boston, black leaders called for a black "picnic" in the area to "reassert the rights of all Boston residents to use all public facilities." On the day of the "picnic" more than 800 policemen were used to keep hundreds of blacks and whites apart, eventually forcing them off the beach and away from each other.

Schools opened in the fall of 1975 under a court-devised plan for busing 21,000 students, 3,000 more than had been bused the previous year. To avoid violence more than 1,500 state and local policemen were on guard at schools and busing routes. For the first time federal officials, including 100 U. S. marshals and 50 agents of the Federal Bureau of Investigation, assisted them. When South Boston High School reopened in the fall of 1975, there were more police on guard than there were students. On December 9, Federal Judge W. Arthur Garrity, Jr., put South Boston High School in receivership. He declared that the School Committee was thwarting his desegregation order issued in June 1974.

Louisville, Ky., residents also resisted school integration orders of the federal courts. The courts found that both the city, which is mainly black, and its neighboring county school districts, which are mainly white, had been discriminatory. They ordered that the school districts merge and that 22,600 children be bused between the city and its suburbs. The order was greeted with public outrage. Shortly after the schools opened, 8–10,000 whites demonstrated around a high school, and damaged 39 school buses and a police car. In this and other related disturbances nearly 300 persons were arrested. After 800 national guardsmen were called up, the situation calmed and about 80% of the expected enrollment actually attended classes. The state of Ken-

The Festival of American Folklife in Washington, D. C., sponsored by the National Park Service and the Smithsonian Institution, featured a mariachi band.

SMITHSONIAN INSTITUTION

tucky sued the federal government for $3.5 million to pay for the busing program, hoping to initiate a constitutional amendment prohibiting busing for the purpose of school desegregation.

Other Methods. The courts also acted in other ways to desegregate the schools. A district court judge ordered HEW to enforce more swiftly desegregation guidelines for 125 school districts in 16 southern states and to act more firmly to desegregate 39 other school districts. The judge also established procedures for HEW to follow in applying pressures on school districts reluctant to comply with desegregation rulings.

Not all the court rulings directly favored racial integration of schools, however. An appellate court reversed the ruling of a lower court that 600,000 children in Los Angeles public schools should be bused to achieve racial integration, ruling that the Los Angeles school system had not "intentionally discriminated against minority students." In one case a federal court withdrew a previous busing order because the program had caused whites to flee the schools into which black children were bused. The schools receiving bused children had become as black as the ones from which they had been taken.

Indian Affairs. Activist issues dominated American Indian affairs in 1975. Marches and rallies staged by Navajos protesting the torture, murder, and mutilation of three Navajo men by teenagers prompted the CCR to conduct a study of Navajo conditions. The commission reported that in fact the Navajos were suffering "injustice and mistreatment." The CCR found that poverty was extensive, health care inadequate, and alcoholism rampant and that Indians were discriminated against in their contacts with local whites. Indians derided the U. S. Army's denial that the 1890 Wounded Knee battle was a massacre.

Menominee Action. On Jan. 1, 1975, 45 Menominee Indians seized an unused novitiate of the Roman Catholic Order of Alexian Brothers near Gresham, Wis. They occupied the novitiate

for 35 days until the Alexian Brothers agreed to grant the property, valued at $750,000, to a new Menominee government to be elected in a few weeks. The price was never stipulated. However, in July the Alexian Brothers withdrew their offer because, they said, nothing had transpired on the matter. The Menominee leaders had not pursued the offer further and, according to reports, the Indians were sharply divided on the issue. Five of the Indians who had originally seized the novitiate were charged with felonies.

Trouble at Pine Ridge. The Oglala Sioux were sharply divided over leadership of their tribe and especially over the militancy of the American Indian Movement (AIM). Responding to a complaint by Russel Means, a leader of AIM and an unsuccessful candidate for tribal council president of the Oglala in a 1974 election, the CCR discovered that the election had been highly irregular. "Almost one-third of all votes cast appear to have been in some manner improper," the commission reported. "The procedures for ensuring the security of the election were so inadequate that actual fraud or wrongdoing could easily have gone undetected."

Rivalries between supporters of the two candidates for tribal leader remained intense in 1975. Both the candidates were charged with violent crimes. In the first four months of 1975, 6 persons were killed and 67 assaulted on the Pine Ridge Reservation where the Sioux resided. Federal officials were taking stronger measures to quell the violence when a gunfight occurred in which one Indian and two FBI agents were killed.

The killings brought hundreds of FBI agents into the reservation to search for 16 Indians who allegedly had taken part in the shoot-out. The Indians protested that the FBI was searching many homes illegally and frightening their children. At year's end the dispute still had not been settled.

ROBERT L. CANFIELD
Washington University, Saint Louis

Heads of state at the Rambouillet economic summit in November include (*from left*) Aldo Moro of Italy, Harold Wilson of Britain, Gerald Ford of the United States, Giscard D'Estaing of France, Helmut Schmidt of West Germany, and Takeo Miki of Japan.

EUROPE

For Europe, the year 1975 was marked by political instability, economic recession, and in some areas by social disintegration.

Continuing Recession. Throughout 1975 the underpinnings of European society were gnawed at by recession and inflation, both of which were stimulated by the increasing cost of imported oil. The fivefold increase in the price of oil imposed in 1974 by the Organization of Petroleum Exporting Countries (OPEC), forced commodity prices up, caused large balance-of-payments deficits, and frightened governments into imposition of harsh deflationary programs. Credit was restricted, government spending curtailed, and imports discouraged.

World trade slowed, and for the first time since 1945, probably declined in 1975. The reduced markets for exports caused immediate cutbacks in employment in Great Britain and Italy. Even West Germany found it difficult to maintain export levels of such crucial items as automobiles and chemicals.

In 1975 most West European countries expected to register a decrease in the real gross national product. Britain expected a decline of 1%, while France's was about 2%, and Italy's and West Germany's 3%. Unemployment increased to levels that reminded many of the dangerous years of 1929–33, when similar distress had strengthened right-wing movements throughout Europe. In West Germany, where such parallels were most feared, unemployment was over 4% of the work force, or about 1.2 million workers. In France unemployment was almost 1 million, and in Britain it was 1.5 million.

Declines in production and increases in unemployment did little to cut inflation, except in West Germany, where draconian measures held the inflation rate to 5%. Britain, by contrast, where strikes led to wage increases of over 30%, suffered from an inflation rate of 28%. The most dramatic battle against inflation was won in Italy, though at a high price. As a result of devaluation, heavy taxes on such imports as oil and beef, and high interest rates, inflation was reduced from 35% to 9%. Unemployment, however, rose to over 1 million.

Prospects for Recovery. From midyear, there were some signs that the recession was coming to an end, and economists began to predict that there would be a slight increase of output in 1976. This change was attributed in part to moves by the major powers to stimulate their economies. The French and German governments agreed to spend $9 billion, largely in public investments. At the end of the year the Italian government felt that its economy could respond to $6 billion in new credits and investments without a renewal of serious inflation. The revival of the U. S. economy increased European export opportunities, while the strengthening of the dollar reduced the competitive advantage of the United States in overseas trade.

A slight improvement in relations with the oil exporting countries also helped prospects for recovery. The European powers were relieved when the OPEC members agreed in September to hold the price rise for oil to 10%. Further progress was made in paying for imported oil through barter arrangements. West European countries sold more than $16 billion worth of goods to the OPEC countries in 1975. Italy garnered orders for several massive construction projects, and German exports of finished goods almost doubled. France sold a subway system and a color television network to Iran. Finally, to recycle OPEC petrodollars, it was agreed that the International Monetary Fund should ad-

minister a $7 billion fund to aid oil-importing countries. A $25 billion contingency fund, covered by members of the Organization for Economic Cooperation and Development (OECD), was also established.

The European Economic Community (EEC) was able to do little to help its members out of the recession, since most recovery programs were applied on a national basis with little consultation with the EEC authorities. Three summit meetings of the nine heads of government were held, but these meetings achieved little. It was reported in April that the EEC probably would not achieve full monetary and economic union by 1980, as had been planned. In May, Jean Monnet disbanded his influential Action Committee for the United States of Europe. Nevertheless, Greece applied for full membership in the EEC in June, and a two-thirds majority of the British population voted to remain in EEC in June, after the British financial contribution to the EEC had been revised downward.

Northern European countries placed their hopes for greater economic and energy self-sufficiency on the exploitation of North Sea oil. Norway, assigned one of the richest sectors, found it necessary to slow production to avoid the inflationary impact of oil revenues of $2 billion a year. Britain, however, pressed exploration and exploitation in the important Argyll and Auk fields.

Slow Progress toward Detente. Concerned with economic problems, the European powers paid less attention than before to the progress of détente with the Communist bloc. Three parallel sets of negotiations took place—the Strategic Arms Limitation Talks (SALT) in Geneva, the Mutual and Balanced Force Reduction Talks (MBFR) in Vienna, and the Conference on Security and Cooperation in Europe (CSCE) in Helsinki. In spite of the Vladivostok agreement of November 1974 between U. S. President Gerald Ford and Soviet Communist party chief Leonid Brezhnev to complete in 1975 a 10-year treaty for mutual arms limitations, the SALT talks remained deadlocked, as did the MBFR talks on reduction of forces in Central Europe.

The Helsinki conference, however, proved more conclusive. Attended by government heads or representatives of 35 nations, the conference approved four "baskets" of agreements. The first recognized the inviolability of European frontiers. This was taken to be Western acceptance of the boundary changes in Eastern Europe that followed World War II. An agreement not to interfere in the internal affairs of other countries was interpreted by some experts as recognition of the communization of Eastern Europe. The third basket, of primary interest to the West, promised increased contact between the Western and Communist blocs through exchanges of information, easing of travel restrictions, and cooperation on cultural and educational programs. Finally, there was an agreement to have a follow-up conference. President Ford visited Poland on his way to Helsinki, and Rumania and Yugoslavia on his return, to emphasize U. S. interest in contacts with Eastern Europe.

Trade between the United States and the Soviet Union continued to increase despite a Soviet repudiation in January 1975 of a trade treaty as protest against a congressional amendment requiring greater freedom of emigration, especially of Jews, from Russia. Numerous agreements were concluded with U. S. companies for purchase of equipment, machine tools, and several complete factories. Faced with low harvests as a result of drought, the Soviet Union also stepped up its efforts to buy U. S. grain. To lessen the inflationary impact of these purchases, an agreement was reached in October to stabilize Soviet purchases for five years at a minimum of 6 million tons annually. However, U. S. negotiators failed to get a long-term agreement for purchase of Russian oil.

Cyprus. The West's defense position in the eastern Mediterranean was weakened by the enmity of Greece and Turkey over Cyprus, where the Turkish invasion force still held 40% of the island. Negotiations between Greek and Turkish Cypriot leaders under UN supervision made no progress, and 200,000 Greek Cypriot refugees were unable to return to their homes in the Turkish-held parts of Cyprus. U. S. forces in NATO became involved in the repercussions of the quarrel. U. S. bases in Turkey were taken over by Turkish forces after Congress refused in August to sanction continuance of arms sales to Turkey. The arms embargo was later eased by Congress. The Greek government began to close U. S. naval and air bases in retaliation for U. S. failure to dissuade Turkey from invading Cyprus.

Greece. The restoration of democracy continued in Greece. The monarchy was abolished by a majority vote of 69% in a referendum in December 1974, and a new constitution, which created a powerful presidency, was approved by parliament in June. The new president chosen by parliament was Constantine Tsatsos, the nominee of the New Democracy party of Premier Caramanlis.

Italy. In Italy and Portugal the Communist parties moved closer to power. The Italian Communists won 33.4% of the vote in regional elections in June. They gained control of Liguria and the important cities of Turin, Milan, Naples, and Venice, in addition to the "red belt" of Central Italy, which they already administered. Although the Christian Democrats were not prepared to welcome the Communists into the government in the "historic compromise" proposed by Communist party chief Enrico Berlinguer, they did oust their own vigorously anti-Communist party leader Amintore Fanfani in July. A major Communist drive for power was expected in the national elections of 1977.

Portugal. In Portugal, whose right-wing government was overthrown by an army revolt in

Conflict between supporters and opponents of British membership in the European Economic Community halts a London rally.

1974, April elections for a constituent assembly gave a large majority to the Socialists and Popular Democrats, while the Communists received only 13% of the vote. Nevertheless, Premier Vasco Gonçalves, backed by a majority in the Armed Forces Movement, continued to favor a left-wing policy. The Socialists left the government in protest in July, demanding the ouster of Gonçalves. Rioting spread through the strongly Roman Catholic north, and moderate forces in the army joined to compel the president to dismiss Gonçalves.

The government of moderate Adm. Pinheiro de Azevedo, appointed in September, put down a mismanaged attempt by radical paratroopers to seize power in November. A number of left-wing army officers were arrested, and the head of the security police, Gen. Otelo de Carvalho, was compelled to resign. Although the situation in Portugal was complicated by the arrival of some 300,000 refugees from Angola, which was given its independence in November, at year's end it appeared that the moderate forces in Portugal had finally taken command of the revolution.

Spain. For Spain, too, the problem of transition from the authoritarianism of Generalissimo Francisco Franco, who died in November, to the unknown strength of King Juan Carlos was complicated by the resurgence of minority and colonial problems. Urban guerrillas, composed of Basque separatists and Marxist revolutionaries, began a campaign of killing policemen, and in September, in spite of widespread protests in Western Europe, five separatists were executed. The executions provoked more terrorism, which slowed the restoration of political party organization begun by Premier Carlo Arias Navarro. Meanwhile, the demands of Morocco's King Hassan for annexation of the Spanish Sahara were dramatized by a massive march into

the area by Moroccans. A military clash was avoided, however, when Spain agreed to withdraw its forces by February 1976 and to share administration with Mauritania and Morocco until then.

Minority Problems. Demands by regional minorities disturbed many European governments and often led to terrorism. While Spain was attempting to control its Basque and Catalan separatists, the French in August brought police reinforcements into Corsica after riots in which four people were killed. Scottish and Welsh nationalists restricted their activities to seeking electoral support, while the Bretons in France demanded greater economic and educational autonomy. In Yugoslavia Croatian nationalists were convicted of treason and given prison sentences.

However, the greatest trouble spot was Northern Ireland. Both Roman Catholic and Protestant extremist groups continued to use violence against civilians. Two truces quickly broke down. A constitutional convention elected in May was deadlocked by the refusal of Protestant groups to share governmental power with Catholics. Terror was extended into England by the Provisional wing of the Irish Republican Army in a series of bombings.

F. ROY WILLIS
University of California, Davis

In May, Portugal's Mario Soares leads members of his Socialist party in a protest march in central Lisbon.

FA/HION

In 1975 the major fashion trends for women primarily evolved from and were influenced by denim and China. Men's wear leaned toward the casual, and denim was also a favorite.

WOMEN'S CLOTHES

The jean craze continued to mushroom at an unbelievable pace. The new jean, labeled the "cigarette," was narrow of leg and designed to be worn rolled up to mid-calf over boots. The better the figure was, the tighter the jean. Another jean modification was the two-zipper, a straight-leg jean that closed with two side front zippers instead of the usual fly front. The zippers were outlined in contrast stitching.

Denim in Demand. Denim, itself, was pre-washed, brushed, streaked, bleached, studded, and embroidered. Knits or wovens were dyed or printed to simulate denim. Jean stitching and styling on wrap-around or button-front skirts made them best-sellers. Blazers and shirt jackets, tenty jumpers, and chemises were made in denim to the profitable delight of retailers.

The acceptance of denim led to the quick exploitation and promotion of other "work" clothes, and soon olive drab and khaki chino fatigue uniforms, slate-blue gab mechanic suits, and railroad striped bib-front overalls became street fashion. It was an expression of the belief in the virtues of honest labor, even if the person wearing them was not engaged in it.

The Chinese Look. Politically, the effects of détente with China may not be known for years, but its influence was strong on fashion. Imports of Chinese goods and the negotiations for manufacturing of fashions and fabrics began in earnest now that Sino-American relations were better.

Pure Chinese silks in honan, shantung, and crash weaves began to appear in designer lines, and synthetics were produced for more modest budgets. A straw shoulder bag from mainland China was "the" summer accessory. Quilted "coolie" jackets and vests, frog closings, mandarin collars, and other classic oriental touches found their way into sportswear fashions. The brilliance of jade, chinese red, and cobalt mingled in stylized Oriental floral prints, and in loungewear, the pajama and the tunic were based on traditional cheongsams.

Ladylike Dressing. Legs long hidden by pants were stepping out. Skirts and dresses outsold pants for the first time in many years. The "Big Dress," a loosely fitted chemise or smock dress, and flared or gathered floral printed skirts with T-shirts became the summer uniform for smart

MONSANTO

The Chinese look, embracing designer lines, sportswear, and accessories, was a major trend in 1975.

women. Pants, of course, did not disappear. For evening, softly flared palazzo pants were a feminine way to dress up. In areas where winter weather made them a good investment, trim and tailored pantsuits, usually with blazers or vests, were popular.

With the return to skirts, the suit had a revival. The pulled-together look of what was, in fact, separates seemed to express the desire for ordered and coordinated dressing. Dramatic capes and soft coats, many unlined or double-faced to be reversible, often topped the suits or the multilayers of separates.

The Sporting Life. The jumper was back. A sportswear idea, it allowed women to move into dresses and still utilize sweaters and blouses collected as separates. Many jumpers were variations of the summer "Big Dress," but narrowed and usually with extended shoulders or three-quarter length wide kimono sleeves to accommodate sweaters and blouses.

Sweaters became an education in ethnic artistic expression. Mexican, Peruvian, Icelandic, and American Indian motifs colored and pat-

terned cardigans, wrap jackets, pullovers, and vests. Most were vividly-colored bulky knits. The flat knits, however, kept fashion pace with scenic motifs. Huge cowls replaced turtlenecks in basic pullovers in soft fabrications that combined wool and mohair or angora.

Use of Natural Fibers. Energy problems and ecological concerns made synthetics costlier and production undependable. Thus, the fabric emphasis switched to the natural fibers. Cotton, particularly in traditional corduroy, gingham, gauze, and chambray, was popular in sportswear. Wool flannels and gabardines, as well as mohair and angora, found a niche. In fact, natural materials of all types were used, not only in clothing, but in accessories. Straw, rope, stone, silver, jade, ivory, and raffia were a natural compliment to trend setting cotton, silk, and wool.

Accessories. The major accessories to emerge in 1975 were the espadrille and the scarf. Espadrilles began in the traditional way, as a canvas upper on a rope-soled wedge. It evolved as the

The craze for denim extended to yarns. This sweater combines denim with the fashionable layered-look.

year went on into suede, calf, or satin uppers trimmed, embroidered, open toed, or draped. The wedge took on matching fabrics or wood or raffia veneers.

Scarfs were used as head wrappings, done in simple peasant style, or elaborately as Arabian or African headdresses. The muffler draped the neck. It was a long, narrow, loosely knotted length of knit or crochet. Shawls were another important accessory look, replacing the sweater as the item one might toss on to ward off chills.

In jewelry, the Chinese inspiration was strong. Jade, ivory, and cinnabar, real or simulated, were used in bracelets, pins, and pendants. They were often carved with oriental motifs and hung from cords or had tassels as part of the necklace arrangement. Wood was painted in bright enamel colors and decorated with floral motifs. Handbags ranged from the sublime to the ridiculous. Small belt bags or clutches were one extreme, and the enormous tote, duffle, or huge, soft-leather pouch was the other.

The Feminine Foot. Shoes were delicate and feminine. T-straps, ankle straps, and sandals in soft calf and suede were the perfect way to accessorize the exposed leg. Heels were higher and more tapered, and even the conservative moccasin suit shoe had grace. Boots were still big. The crushed leg boot was worn with capes, coats, and skirts, and the new jean boot was westernized. It had a wide leg, low heel, and stitching trim of cowboy boots. Jeans were, in most cases, rolled to show them off.

Unisex Chic. Fads were not forgotten, and in 1975 they were unisex. T-shirts became fashion, especially when they were adorned with slogans, trademarks, cartoon figures, or portraits of personalities or movie stars. The earth or natural shoe designed to lower the heel and raise the sole of the foot for comfort, was a best-seller.

MEN'S WEAR

The news in menswear was the continuing adoption of mix and match coordinates. Groups consisting of two trouser styles, two jacket types, and several shirts in solids, prints, or patterns were merchandised to enable the customer to select one or more suits or casual looks from pieces coordinated for color, fit, style, and fabric. Purchase of all the pieces would constitute a total mini-wardrobe for a weekend or trip.

The Suit Fits. Leisure suits were still popular, but the three piece suit, which included a vest that was often reversible and tailored in fabrics such as pinstripes, herringbones, and flannels made a strong return. Suits had natural shoulder lines and a looser fit with clean, simple lines.

Casual Comfort. In casual clothing, comfort and function were the criteria for fashion. Shirts were less body conscious, and sweaters and jackets were loose and relaxed. Colors in casual clothes were a reflection of the khaki, olive drab, and denim trend. Contrasting these somber tones and the understated greys and camels for

MONSANTO

MONSANTO

(*Above left*) Long dresses, such as this cable knit with matching sweater, enjoyed a revival. Sportswear (*above*) matches stovepipe pants with a lanky tunic. (*Below*) In men's wear, the leisure suit, often in denim, underscored the popularity of casual clothing.

dress suits, bright hues appeared in shirtings and active sportswear items.

Denim, in its own way, is a traditional men's wear look. Worn with Shetland crewnecks, ethnically patterned sweaters, or western jackets, jeans were still the most popular "leisure" suit around.

Accessories. Shoes matched the tailored direction of ready-to-wear. The moccasin was favored, and wing-tips were becoming the newest shoe style. Toes were tapering, heels lowering, and far-out platforms had disappeared. Demi-boots and Western boots were worn with casual leisure suits or jeans, and the espadrille was the resort shoe.

Jewelry for men was big business. Silver and turquoise American Indian pendants, rings, and bracelets were in vogue, not to mention neck chains with ivory or silver sharks teeth, zodiac signs, or stone scarabs. Rings and bracelets in lover's knots or rigid bands of gold and sterling were cuffing wrists, and the digital watch was the businessman's macho accessory.

Bags for men became more acceptable. The shoulder tote that resembled a camera or travel bag was popular. Most males, however, still preferred a briefcase, but softer, less structured and thinner envelopes or underarm portfolios were the middle of the road fashion.

ANN ELKINS
Fashion Editor, "Good Housekeeping"

KENNEDY'S

FINLAND

Economic imbalance, new elections, and the largest summit conference in European history attracted major attention in Finland in 1975. In the opening speech to the parliament (Eduskunta), President Urho Kekkonen outlined the country's growing economic problems.

The Economy. A 17% annual inflation rate, rising unemployment, and a fourfold increase in the foreign trade deficit told the story of impending economic crisis. Because Finland relies heavily on foreign trade income, it was hard hit by the cutback in Western markets for its exports, mainly timber and pulp products. At the same time the country was shaken by the burgeoning cost of imports, especially the threefold increase in the price of oil from the USSR, which supplies two-thirds of Finland's oil needs. Although unemployment was at a low 2% in 1975, this figure was expected to double as orders from the West continued to shrink.

Despite these fears, the blanket agreement between the central organization of employers and the unions was successfully revised in 1975. It seemed that the country might have labor peace for at least a year.

Politics. The worsening economic situation plus disharmony in the cabinet of Premier Kalevi Sorsa led to the resignation of that 4-party coalition on June 4. President Kekkonen appointed Keijo Liinamaa, a Social Democrat and former undersecretary of labor, to head a caretaker cabinet until the elections were held on September 22.

The elections did not produce significant changes. The Social Democrats lost two seats, while the Center party increased its representation by four. Two seats were gained by the Conservatives, and the Communist-controlled Finnish People's Democratic League increased their seats by three. However, the non-socialist parties lost only one seat in the election and enjoy a majority of 12 in the 200-member Eduskunta.

On October 29, President Kekkonen asked Martti J. Miettunen of the Center party to form a new government. Miettunen, a former premier,

UPI

Finnish President Kekkonen welcomes USSR's Leonid Brezhnev to Helsinki prior to the European summit meeting.

agreed to try to form a majority government but said he would not lead a minority one. At the end of November he formed a five-party majority government.

While governments in Finland rise and fall rapidly, the political longevity of Urho Kekkonen seemed assured. Although his term in office was extended by the legislature to 1978, leaders of several parties asked that he run again when his term expires.

Summit Conference. The third and final stage of the Conference on Security and Cooperation in Europe was held in Helsinki, July 30–August 1, after nearly three years of lower-level preliminary planning. At its conclusion the 35 representatives signed a declaration which set forth general guidelines for human rights and relations in Europe and confirmed the inviolability of borders drawn at the end of World War II.

Beyond its political significance, the conference drew new attention to the Finnish role of neutrality. This attention brought to mind for many the term "Finlandization." Urho Kekkonen said that "Generally speaking, Finlandization should also be taken to refer to political conciliation with the Soviet Union, and I have noticed with satisfaction that there are many others who want to be Finlandized in this sense. In this sense it seems that only China and Albania do not want to be Finlandized."

Other Events. Hannu Salama, poet, novelist, and short-story writer, won the Literary Prize of the Nordic Council for 1975. In March, faced with protests from Brazil and Argentina, the government agreed not to dump poisonous wastes in the South Atlantic Ocean. In May the Soviet Communist party newspaper *Pravda* attacked the Finnish press for alleging Soviet involvement in Finnish Communist party affairs.

ERIK J. FRIIS
Editor, "The Scandinavian-American Bulletin"

FLORIDA

High unemployment, natural disasters, the penal system, and scandals held public attention in Florida during 1975.

Economy. Florida was unable to escape the effects of the national recession, which crippled two of the state's major industries, construction and tourism. Unemployment was higher than the national average. Unemployment and inflation were evidently contributing factors in the sharp decrease in the state's population growth rate. The exposure of a national land-securities fraud allegedly involving over 100 south Florida mortgage brokers may also have been a factor.

The legislature, anticipating the economic recession, approved reduced appropriations. Tax receipts were even lower than projected, but adequate to prevent a deficit. Some state officials, however, began predicting the need for higher or new taxes to meet state needs in 1976. The hope that offshore oil might bring new revenue seemed fruitless since 5 major companies ceased drilling after 15 "dry" holes.

Natural calamities added to the economic woes when summer floods inflicted $8.3 million in crop and property damage in eight panhandle counties. In September Hurricane Eloise struck the Gulf of Mexico resort areas around Panama City. Damage estimates in five panhandle counties ranged from $52 million to $150 million. In both cases federal aid was extended.

Freddie Pitts (left) and Albert Lee were pardoned and declared innocent of murder charges in September after spending 12 years in a Florida prison.

UPI

--- **FLORIDA · Information Highlights** ---

Area: 58,560 square miles (151,670 sq km).
Population (1974 est.): 8,090,000. *Density:* 138 per sq mi.
Chief Cities (1970 census): Tallahassee, the capital, 72,586; Jacksonville, 528,865; Miami, 334,859; Tampa, 277,767.
Government (1975): *Chief Officers*—governor, Reubin O'D. Askew (D); lt. gov., J. H. Williams (D). *Legislature*—Senate, 40 members; House of Representatives, 120.
Education (1974–75): *Enrollment*—public elementary schools, 809,271; public secondary schools, 747,783; nonpublic, 103,000; colleges and universities, 306,680 students. Public school expenditures, $1,271,297,000 ($928 per pupil).
State Finances (fiscal year 1974): *Revenues,* $4,326,520,000; *expenditures,* $4,084,511,000.
Personal Income (1974): $42,354,000,000; per capita, $5,235.
Labor Force (Aug. 1975): *Nonagricultural wage and salary earners,* 2,629,800; *insured unemployed,* 128,200.

Politics. One of the major political developments was Gov. Reubin Askew's announcement that he would not be a Democratic candidate for the presidential or vice-presidential nomination despite a national movement promoting his name. Other important events were related to the investigations of scandals in high political office. The state treasurer and two state supreme court justices resigned during impeachment proceedings against them. Former U. S. Sen. Edward Gurney, a Republican, was acquitted of campaign-contribution charges but was later indicted on other charges. A former fundraiser in the Gurney campaign was convicted and imprisoned. In the wake of the trial, a grand jury began investigating alleged campaign irregularities by U. S. Rep. L. A. "Skip" Bafalis, also a Republican.

Legislation and Welfare. Two convicted murderers were pardoned and pronounced innocent by the Florida cabinet, after 12 years imprisonment. This controversial case helped focus attention on the penal system, which became so overburdened that warehouses were converted to house inmates temporarily. New facilities under construction may be filled quickly since a 1975 law requires mandatory three-year sentences for crimes involving the use of firearms.

Reform was a major concern of the legislature, which enacted a bill of rights for the mentally retarded and reorganized the division of health and rehabilitative services. It also passed a stronger conflict-of-interest law. Consumer legislation included repeal of fair trade laws, creation of an agency to supervise condominiums, and a requirement that hospitals and nursing homes establish minimum standards for X rays and laboratory tests. In environmental affairs a law was passed requiring local governments to develop growth plans, and tighter controls were placed on dredge and fill operations. The state cabinet adopted restrictions on development of the Green Swamp, an important aquifer area.

J. LARRY DURRENCE
Florida Southern College

FOOD

In 1975, as in the past three years, food garnered headlines in terms of grain shortages, droughts, shipping boycotts, and waste. In November 1974, the World Food Conference in Rome outlined the many diverse problems relating to food availability, population, growth, cost, and waste. During 1975 implementation of the adopted resolutions progressed, but at a slow pace.

During the first nine months of 1975, crop shortages in certain areas of the world began to become evident and were verified when the USSR and other countries entered the grain-buying arena with large orders. During this same period, forecasts were made for larger than normal U. S. harvests in all grains (wheat, corn, oats, barley, and rye). These two facts—shortages and surpluses—pointed up the critical problem of feeding the world. (See also AGRICULTURE.)

WORLD FOOD SUPPLY

In 1972, when food scarcities and higher prices became evident, there was a dramatic reexamination of all aspects of the world food situation. During the period 1950–72, food production had increased, labor productivity had risen, and supplies of grain and other foods were ample. The result was lowered prices, movement of food and grain to needy areas, and a buildup of reserves. In 1972, world food production dropped by 1.6%, a relatively small drop, but one that had serious implications in certain geographical areas on specific commodities, trade patterns, prices, and consumption levels.

Sharp production declines occurred in South Asia, parts of drought-stricken Africa, and, more importantly, in Canada, Australia, and the USSR. The USSR, previously a grain exporter, became the world's largest importer of grain, buying 30 million tons in 1972–73. This was followed in 1973–74 by increased grain imports by the developing countries. In 1974, even though 1973 world grain production had risen, U. S. production had dropped, resulting in low stocks and higher prices. To further compound the picture, the USSR again entered the 1975 grain-buying market because of poor harvests.

Problem Areas. In this situation a number of problem areas needed to be emphasized. These included reduced grain stock levels that make prices more volatile, lack of provision for emergency disaster and famine relief, and rising costs of fertilizer needed to increase production in developing countries. Other areas of concern are national artificial price policies that maintain low consumer prices, lack of profit incentive to increase production, the need for free transfer of technological knowledge, the uncertainty of energy sources and costs, and the need to reduce waste.

Each of these areas at a given time or place can create problems that are, or could be, insurmountable. However, solutions need not require excessive amounts of time. Much can be achieved through concentrated action, cooperative coordination, and desire to achieve, but not until developed and developing nations recognize that food for the world extends beyond each nation's boundaries.

The Rome conference placed its main emphasis on long-range efforts to enhance agricultural production. Lesser emphasis was placed on population increase and economics, both of which are tied closely to the current world food situation and may be of more import than long-range planning. Borgstrom points out that the world's population is increasing at about 80 million people per year and will reach between 6 and 8 billion in the year 2000, which is 2 to 4 billion more than the world's current population. This projection, combined with the current economic picture, does not auger well for developing areas, since the purchasing power of developed countries is greater. The flow of food is toward the affluent rather than the needy.

UPI

Delegates from 36 countries to the UN Food Council met in Rome in June under the auspices of the UN's Food and Agriculture Organization. The council, formed as a result of the 1974 food conference in Rome, coordinates efforts to meet the world's food needs.

Food and Feed. The needs of the world—calories and protein—can be defined as food and feed. The hungry, the malnourished, and the starving are victims of poor distribution, lack of money, and waste. In 1975 food and feed supplies were considered sufficient for the world's population of humans and animals. Yet, when North American exports were examined, it was discovered that roughly 60% of the cereal grains went to the developed nations, with emphasis on livestock feeds, while wheat, rice, and soybeans were destined for the developing nations. The exception was the wheat purchases by the USSR.

However, since production increases tend to occur in developed nations, and population increases in developing nations, the two basic problems are money and distribution. Until political accord is reached, the solution to these problems will remain tenuous. However, a third factor—waste—is solvable on a national basis rather than an international one. Although there will always be a need to distribute needed nutrients throughout the world, elimination of waste could increase the available food supply within a given nation by 10% to 40%. Thus, many nations are overlooking a potential source of food and feed while negotiating for a faraway, and sometimes unavailable, source.

Grain Trade. The United States, Canada, and Australia are considered to be the world's largest grain producers and exporters. In 1972, when the Soviet wheat crop was poor, the grain trade began to change in a manner not previously noted.

The USSR, instead of reducing grain consumption by livestock, reduced grain shipments to Eastern Europe. In 1972–73 combined imports by Russia and Eastern Europe increased some 24 million tons over normal years. This amount reduced carryover stocks to a 20-year low and raised prices. The 1973–74 year saw a 10% increased grain acreage in the United States, Canada, and Australia, but poor weather caused a lower yield in the United States. Exports continued at the same level due to demand by Communist China, Japan, and Western Europe, further lowering stocks. In 1974, U. S. acreage rose, but adverse weather in growing areas, especially in the corn-growing areas, reduced the yield drastically, with resulting higher prices.

In 1975 the USSR, again due to poor harvests, purchased 10.2 million tons of wheat. At this point, trade ceased because President Ford intervened and because AFL-CIO members, at the behest of their president, George Meany, conducted a short grain-loading boycott. The impasse was resolved in October when the USSR concluded a five-year agreement with the United States to purchase at least 6 million tons of grain annually. This should help stabilize the world grain market.

Growers and Consumers. The Western granary (the United States, Canada, and Australia) and the Eastern granary (USSR) are the major producers of the world's grain. However, yields depend on the weather and climate. Developing or consuming nations, while striving to balance internal food supplies, are dependent on the crops of these two groups. Predictions by the Food and Agriculture Organization (FAO) based on current trends of imports by developing nations, plus population increases and growth income, show a need of an additional 85 million tons in these countries by 1985. Such an import increase would undoubtedly create foreign exchange money problems for some developing countries. Thus, until long-range plans for agricultural development and population control relieve the pressure, nutritional levels in many countries will vary widely with crop yields, money availability, inflation, and food aid.

Future Prospects. It is estimated that world grain production, now about 1.2 billion tons annually, will grow at a rate of 2.5% per year, with population rising at a 2% rate. Of the world's population growth 86% is in developing countries, and any drop in local supply can cause malnutrition or famine unless outside supplies are used to supplement the diet.

Dr. Sylvan Wittwer, director of the Michigan Agricultural Experiment Station, stated at an Institute of Food Technologists symposium, "There is enough food now produced to feed the world's hungry. We have more food per capita today than 20 years ago. That people are malnourished or starving is a question of food distribution, resources, and economics, not agricultural limits. The problem is putting food where the people are, and providing an income so they can buy it."

U. S. FOOD INDUSTRY

Consumers and the food industry faced similar problems in 1975. Concern over inflation, shortages, energy sources, substitutes, supplies, and costs were shared by both groups. The food industry was also occupied with governmental regulations designed to assure consumers of quality and to make certain that they were well informed.

Inflation and Rising Costs. With the cost of living rising at or near a double-digit inflation rate, industry was reexamining its primary role and future goals. The industry has been under attack by the various media for its role in rising food costs. While some of the "exposé" articles pointed up deficiencies, studies by the U. S. Department of Agriculture (USDA) and other agencies pointed out that the food industry did not make enormous profits in 1974–75.

A report issued by the Council on Wage and Price Stability on food prices indicated that big increases in the cost of food in recent years,

including a jump of 12.2% in 1974, resulted from rising costs in farming, higher transportation and fuel costs, and problems in world agriculture production. The report stated that 40% of the food dollar went to farmers and the remaining 60% to the food industry. It showed that profits of food distributors and manufacturers increased in 1974, yet were reasonable when compared with past levels. Other segments of the industry pointed out that physical distribution and packaging represented 30% of the retail cost of goods sold, while the National Restaurant Association revealed that over the two-year period between 1972 and 1974 food-at-home prices averaged 33.6% higher while food-away-from-home prices were up only 21.6%.

For anyone desiring further explanation of the food industry system, a bulletin entitled "The Food and Fiber System—How It Works" has been published by the Economic Research Service of the USDA. The bulletin is highly readable and informative and deals with the problem of why food bills have risen.

The Consumer. The consumer, confronting rising food prices daily, reacted in many different ways. Of paramount importance was the demand for additional information on all foods and a reaction to price. In a report released by the USDA, about two-thirds of consumers were always, or almost always, satisfied with nutrition labeling; 22% with manufacturers' advertisements; and 53% with ingredient labeling. Furthermore, food stores were rated higher than manufacturers. However, in expressing dissatisfaction, food stores or friends were named as primary outlets, with government (2.9%), manufacturers (6.6%), and boycotts (11%) named least.

Because of the consumer's growing power and desire for knowledge, the food industry faced many different legislative actions. On May 1, 1975, at the Consumer Advisory Council swearing-in ceremony, President Ford declared that there are "two very critical areas where the consumer needs help: (1) prices and (2) quality..." and that he considers it "very important, as we continue the efforts that have been made... to make sure... that the consumer is given the maximum protection by all agencies of the Federal Government."

Federal and State Actions. With the advance of consumerism and its many adherents, a great deal of legislation has been proposed, mostly at the federal level. One of the more encompassing bills would create an agency for consumer protection, whose purpose would be to represent the undefined "consumer interest" in the regulatory agencies' dealings with businessmen. Although passed by the Senate, the House version differs considerably; if that is passed a conference committee will be required to resolve details. Furthermore, President Ford has indicated he will veto the bill since the three-year cost is

President Ford (right) urges AFL-CIO President Meany to end boycott on loading grain for USSR.

estimated at $60 million, and existing agencies can perform the duties. Other proposed legislation included prevention of unreasonable or excessive costs to consumers from government programs, food surveillance bills requiring company-established safety systems, plus others dealing with the Consumer Product Safety Commission and food costs.

In other federal agency action, the Food and Drug Administration (FDA) indicated that it would propose manufacturing-practices regulations for the frozen food industry and other action on the use of polyvinyl chloride plastics that come in contact with food. The USDA delayed its revised standards for quality grades of beef until court rulings against the grades have been resolved, while an agreement between the FDA and the National Marine Fisheries Service clarified each agency's role in inspection and standardization activities for fish and fishery products.

Industry Progress. The food industry unveiled the results of its research and productivity in 1975. While not available by year's end, flexible pouches for heat-processed foods and the accompanying production system have been fully researched and should, in the near future, provide consumers with a new form of packaged, shelf-stable foods. Used in the Apollo space-feeding program and widely accepted in Europe and Japan, it was expected that the reheatable pouch would have a high sales potential.

In other areas industry was deeply involved in recycling of package materials; replacement of sucrose by corn-derived sweeteners; extraction of protein from vegetables, soy, leaves, and petroleum; greater use of byproducts; and better analytical techniques. The overall emphasis was placed on economy from field to consumer,

USDA

U. S. government chemist examines a new packaging material that could be used as a degradable mulch.

utilizing methods that conserve energy and materials and control costs.

NUTRITION

Key issues in the nutrition field were consumer oriented and involved food quality, both home and retail; nutritional content; and especially food costs.

Food Selection and Trends. The rise in inflation for all goods and services and the high cost of food have created a minor upheaval in consumer buying patterns. While price indicators showed a low point in the January-February 1975 period, the rise was steady thereafter. It was predicted that food prices would rise 10% between June 1975 and June 1976, with 3% attributed to Soviet grain purchases. In a trend that started in 1973, buyers (both home and institutional) continued to switch from the more convenient and higher priced forms of food to lower-cost and less-prepared foods. Sales of flour and other bulk items increased in this period.

Consumer Pressure. Both state and federal legislative proposals reflected the desire by consumer groups for more forthright information. In addition to the consumer protection agency legislation, a proposal by the FDA dealt with nutritional labeling for fresh fruits and vegetables whenever nutritional claims are made in stores and one by the Federal Trade Com-

mission (FTC) concerned false or misleading advertising.

A House agriculture subcommittee recommended governmental action "to protect consumers from retail food prices which are higher than is justified by raw farm commodity cost, and that FTC enforce antitrust laws so that competition among food processors and retailers will protect consumers against unfair widening of profit margins." On the state level, it has been proposed that restaurant menus show nutritional data, as well as whether the food served is frozen or fresh. As a result of these and other proposals, several conferences were held to determine the additional cost levied upon the consumer as a result of government actions.

Government Food Programs. Of the various government food aid programs, the Food Stamp program and the National School Lunch Act of 1975 caused the most controversy. The family food assistance programs aided 19.3 million people as of June 1975, an increase of 4.4 million participants in a year's time. Efforts were made to bring this rapid expansion under control. An amendment to the program required states to develop systems for monitoring and improving their administration of the food stamp program. Failure to take corrective action would result in federal withholding of funds for the program.

The School Lunch Act of 1975, which created controversy between the executive branch and Congress, was passed when Congress overrode a presidential veto. The crux of the bill centered around the recipients. President Ford wanted to limit the bill to those below the poverty level, while Congress wanted to include the unemployed. The cost of the act was estimated at $2.7 billion.

Home Canning. One of the results of rising food prices in 1975 was the turn by consumers to home food preservation. In an effort to provide more nutritious food at lower cost, homemakers turned to gardening and preserving. The U. S. Department of Agriculture estimated a new population of 6 million gardeners, many of whom planned to can (heat process) their bounty for the first time.

A massive campaign was initiated to ensure that consumers used safe and correct procedures in home canning. Improper methods, especially in canning vegetables, meats, poultry, and fish, can bring about serious illness or death from botulism, a toxin elaborated by a specific bacteria that produces a heat-resistant spore. Avoiding botulism requires canning under steam pressure to achieve temperatures of 240°F (116°C). Early in the year canning jars and lids were in short supply. While that shortage eased, it will be some time before the results of the educational campaign will be known.

KIRBY M. HAYES
University of Massachusetts

On Nov. 17, President Ford (*left*) addressed the joint press conference ending the six-nation economic summit at Rambouillet, France. Listening are French President Valéry Giscard d'-Estaing (*center*) and West German Chancellor Helmut Schmidt.

FRANCE

The year 1975 brought to France the usual complement of intractable problems. Prosperous but troubled, the French endured, like others, the deepening crisis of the West.

DOMESTIC AFFAIRS

President Valéry Giscard d'Estaing continued to work at projecting the image of a pragmatic, accessible chief of state, as ready to breakfast with garbage collectors as to lunch with emperors. "It was like being among friends," said the housewife who with her husband entertained the presidential couple at dinner Jan. 22, 1975. "He was *formidable*. He was very relaxed and told lots of amusing anecdotes." Guiding a television audience through his palace, Giscard played the piano, introduced his family, and talked of his "heavy and demanding duties." It was publicity for the grand design of "an advanced liberal society." Polled later, 83% of the French people approved of the style.

Giscard shifted cabinet ministers, replaced some, promoted others, and maintained control of his own Independent Republicans through the renewed party presidency of Michel Poniatowski, confidant and minister of the interior. Through Prime Minister Jacques Chirac he held the support of a majority of the Gaullist Union of Democrats for the Republic, the bitterly-divided and largest party in the National Assembly. A minority seemed to follow the former diplomat and foreign minister Michel Jobert, who announced the formation on March 16 of a new "assembly," the Movement of Democrats. Nationalist and conservative, the new party looked forward to the 1978 legislative elections.

At the center, Jean-Jacques Servan-Schreiber resigned the presidency of the Radical party on July 4, having failed to convince it of his reform program. His successor, Robert Fabre, the first opposition party leader to accept Giscard's offer of formal consultation, may thereby have helped make credible a "new style of democracy" in France.

Socialists and Communists, with much contention, kept the union of the left afloat. A strong left-wing Socialist minority sought closer ties with the Communists, but nearly 60% of Socialist voters was ready to participate in a national government without the Communists. Paradoxically, although François Mitterrand had rebuilt Socialist strength since 1971 with a Communist alliance, much of the new strength came from the anti-Communist left and center. Communist leader Georges Marchais, pressed by his radicals, publicly upbraided the Socialists for readiness to help run the capitalist system. Government legislation for proportional representation in municipal elections would deepen this quarrel. The Portuguese Communists' attempted coup sharpened Socialist suspicions. In the competition to dominate the left, the Socialists appeared to be ahead.

Foreseeing victory in the 1978 assembly elections, Mitterrand wished to quiet fears of governmental paralysis if he were prime minister and Giscard were president. But the constitution offered no assurance that Giscard would respond to such a majority. The Communists plainly predicted deadlock and crisis. Marchais said, "We do not see the future in terms of negotiation with Monsieur Giscard d'Estaing." Socialist fears were reinforced by the revelation of a secret speech Marchais made in 1972 suggesting a union-of-the-left victory as a mere prelude to a Communist takeover. Neither Marchais's criticism of the Communist Chinese on May 14 nor his later promise to ask for freedom of a dissident Soviet mathematician if detention was "unjustified" bolstered his claim to be independent of Moscow.

Reforms. President Giscard said that "reformist democracy" was "unbeatable." Legislation introduced and contemplated included regulation of municipal building, a capital gains tax, reform of education, and worker participation in industrial management. The divorce law was revised, abortion-on-demand became law, and French titles (save those of the Comte de Paris and Prince Napoléon) were declared obsolete.

Prostitutes still sought relief from police harassment. France had legalized the profession but outlawed solicitation. After demonstrations, occupation of churches, and formation of a national federation of prostitutes, the government established an investigative commission. Min-

In October unemployed French youth marched through Paris demonstrating against economic conditions.

ister of the Interior Poniatowski conceded that "the hypocritical and contradictory law" must be changed.

The censorship law was struck down, permitting films on such hitherto taboo subjects as World War I mutinies and the Dreyfus affair to be shown. A wave of pornographic films then swept into France, bringing opposition from Roman Catholics, led by the Archbishop of Paris, and Gaullists. By doubling taxes and by negotiating a "pornography charter" with the biggest movie chains, it was hoped the invasion could be curbed.

The government practice of wiretapping the opposition was not entirely reformed. A tap on the Trotskyite Revolutionary Communist League was uncovered in 1975.

Protest and Violence. Rapid increases in un-

On September 1, French leftists occupied Notre Dame Cathedral to protest Basque separatists' trial.

employment of the young brought demonstrations in Paris against "Saint Giscard, Patron Saint of the Jobless," on October 4. Government training plans and bonuses to employers of youth had little success.

This demonstration was mild, however, compared to other more violent protests seen during the year. On May 3, terrorists bombed a nuclear reactor site near Strasbourg. Two counter-intelligence agents were killed in Paris on June 27. A Lyons magistrate was killed on July 3. In general, the incidence of crimes of violence seemed to be on the rise. Vicious automobile banditry was practiced on roads south of Paris during the summer. Cars were rammed and their drivers robbed or killed.

French wine growers protested violently the importation of cheap Italian wines. Riots at Sète on March 26 brought temporary import suspension. Later, the growers threw up road, dock, and rail blocks, seized Montpellier airport, dumped 450,000 gallons (1.7 million liters) of Italian wine in Marseilles, and hurled gasoline bombs at tax offices. On September 11 the government imposed a tax on Italian wines in an attempt to aid the French growers. The French wine industry was not helped by the disclosure of still another Bordeaux adulteration scandal.

Strikes. Responding to Communist-Socialist rivalry, labor showed renewed militance. In February the largest labor organization, the CGT, unleashed "guerrilla" strikes against the Renault management over pay and job reclassification. Newspapers, hit by dwindling circulation and competition from television, were struck. Editorial staffs charged government pressure to obtain conformity. On June 13, the home of a newspaper union president was bombed. The same day the managing editor of *l'Agence France Presse* was fatally wounded in an attack intended for the identically-named editor of *Le Parisien Libéré*. A government report predicted the loss of 15,000 newspaper jobs in Paris alone following modernization of the industry.

General unemployment was estimated at well beyond the 1 million mark. On June 12 thousands marched in Paris to protest Interior Minister Poniatowski's violent police evictions of occupant strikers around the country. Giscard's "special field of operation is liberalism," commented *Le Monde*. "He leaves realism to his ministers."

Regional Autonomy. In Alsace, Brittany, and southwest France a reawakened sense of cultural distinctiveness demanded recognition from the central government. After 500 years of conflict with Breton culture, the government was formulating plans to subsidize it in 1975. At the same time, policemen were arresting and interrogating scores of suspected Breton separatists. The dual approach was intended to appease cultural historians and eradicate violent separatist movements before anyone was hurt.

Serious trouble did occur in Corsica. Strikes,

bombing, and fatal clashes with police disturbed the island in August and September. As a result, more separatist organizations were outlawed, and promises of economic aid were renewed. But little increase in cultural autonomy was gained. Regionalization and devolution of the central authority in France remained largely unfulfilled.

Economy. The government bent beneath the burden of a $7 billion balance-of-payments deficit, rising inflation, and increasing bankruptcies. The bank rate was lowered from 13% to 8%. Various schemes were announced in the spring and fall, including price controls, which angered shopkeepers; legislation against planned obsolescence; and public works. More than $7 billion was to be pumped into the economy, including direct grants to families and to the aged. Announcing this in September, and admitting it would put the 1975 deficit at $12 billion, the president stated, "We are going through the worst shock the world's economy has felt in nearly half a century." The costly attempt to build a national computer industry was abandoned. Fresh efforts to find oil in French territories were decreed.

While the fate of the Franco-British supersonic transport remained uncertain, a major aviation industry loss was suffered when the United States won the North Atlantic Treaty Organization (NATO) air forces fighter re-equipment competition. This blow was made more bitter by the revelation that, among others, Gen. Paul Stehlin, who had championed U. S. aircraft against French, had been on the payroll of the successful U. S. contractor.

Defense. In a television address on March 25, the president, answering Communist and Gaullist critics who charged he was taking France back to active cooperation with NATO, reaffirmed the need for independent nuclear strength. Underground testing was carried out on France's Pacific atolls.

The army, responding to internal demonstrations, began to reform itself. A top-secret report

French President Giscard d'Estaing *(left)* at the 31st International Paris Airshow on May 30.

UPI

leaked in December 1974 had revealed low morale and loss of confidence in the military hierarchy. In January 1975, Yves Bourges was named defense minister. The main problem he faced was that with nearly 500,000 men under arms, France spent less than 3% of its gross national product on the armed forces and much of that was for nuclear weaponry and equipment. Bourges' task was to put a large, ill-paid, conscript army into a meaningful relationship with modern warfare.

Community. In the French Community there were various protests and disturbances, but the year was largely without serious dissidence. Trouble erupted on the islands of St. Pierre and Miquelon in February. Complaining of low government wages and general neglect by Paris, the islanders collided with the governor. A general strike brought police reinforcements from France, but this action provoked such an uproar that after three months the islands were promised they would become an overseas department of France. After the fourth conference of the worldwide *Agence de Coopération Culturelle et Technique* in Mauritius on November 12–15, the organization seemed likely to become less France-oriented, but its accomplishments to date were minimal.

FOREIGN AFFAIRS

France's ambiguous relationship with NATO was not clarified by rapidly expanding cooperation with allied units in West Germany. Communist and Gaullist criticisms of France's nuclear armaments resulted in a nuclear-tipped surface-to-surface missile incapable of reaching the Communist countries. Nothing, however, prevented substantial loans and arms deliveries to Turkey and Greece.

Relations with Great Britain. Giscard suffered further Communist and Gaullist attacks by

---

FRANCE • Information Highlights

Official Name: French Republic.
Location: Western Europe.
Area: 211,207 square miles (547,026 sq km).
Population (1975 est.): 52,900,000.
Chief Cities (1975 est.): Paris, the capital, 8,500,000. (1968 census): Marseille, 889,029; Lyon, 527,800; Toulouse, 370,769.
Government: *Head of state,* Valéry Giscard d'Estaing, president (took office May 1974). *Chief minister,* Jacques Chirac, premier (took office May 1974). *Legislature*—Parliament: Senate and National Assembly.
Monetary Unit: Franc (4.400 francs equal U. S.$1, Aug. 1975).
Gross National Product (1974 est.): $270,800,000,000.
Manufacturing (major products): Steel, machinery, metals, chemicals, automobiles, airplanes, processed foods, beverages, clothing, textiles.
Major Agricultural Products: Wheat, barley, oats, sugar beets, vegetables, apples, grapes, cattle, fish.
Foreign Trade (1974): *Exports,* $39,487,000,000; *imports,* $45,483,000,000.

UPI

Rising behind a model of the Statue of Liberty, the first Japanese hotel outside Asia is being built in Paris.

agreeing in Dublin on March 11 to "just, realistic, and reasonable" new terms for maintaining Great Britain's membership in the European Economic Community (EEC). On May 23 he advocated "a political role" for the EEC, saying there was "a strong desire" in France for "some kind of political unity or unison."

Relations with West Germany. Relations with West Germany were good. President Walter Scheel made a five-day state visit on April 21–25. In announcing on May 8 that France was celebrating VE day, the day World War II ended in Europe, for the last time, Giscard unleashed a furor. Veterans', Resistance fighters', and deportees' groups attacked him. To them his statement sounded too much like collaboration with an old enemy. "Free men," said Michel Debré, former prime minister, "will always celebrate the anniversary of a date that opened the doors to the future." Five thousand Parisians marched to the tomb of the Unknown Soldier in protest. The mood of many in France had been characterized earlier when eight hooded former Resistance fighters held a Paris press conference on April 18. They promised death for major Nazi war criminals still at large unless West Germany guaranteed action by December 1.

Trouble Over Italian Wines. A wine glut in France and Italy caused suspension of Italian imports and threats of retaliation from Rome. An April accord produced demonstrations in France. In September a 12% tax was imposed on Italian wines. Defying a European Commission ultimatum to lift the tax, France was taken to the Court of Justice in Luxembourg in November, charged with infringement of the EEC free trade rules. The judgment went against France, but by year's end the tax expired.

Other Foreign Relations. During the June state visit of Portuguese President Francisco da Costa Gomes, Portugal was promised help to develop closer economic ties with the EEC. Relations with Spain, however, remained somewhat strained as a consequence of Basque separatist activity on French soil.

By agreeing to the declaration signed at the Conference on Security and Cooperation in Europe in Helsinki, France apparently improved its relations with the USSR. Prime Minister Chirac visited the USSR on March 19–24. President Giscard's five-day state visit to Moscow on October 14–18 was slightly marred by Soviet intransigence about continued ideological warfare. Having obtained the Helsinki summit agreement, the USSR no longer much troubled to cultivate a France turned more obviously toward the West.

The French and Israeli foreign ministers exchanged visits in an atmosphere Foreign Minister Jean Sauvagnargues characterized on April 29 as "disagreement in a friendly atmosphere." Relations with Egypt were cordial. During Egyptian President Sadat's state visit on Jan. 27–29, he was promised large-scale arms deliveries.

Giscard made a state visit on April 10–11 to Algeria, the first visit by a French president since Algeria became independent. He made a similar visit to Morocco on May 4–6. Relations with Chad deteriorated. France was suspected of acquiescing in the overthrow of President Tombalbaye on April 13 and condemned for meeting part of the ransom demands of rebels holding two French citizens in northern Chad. The new regime ordered withdrawal of French forces in the country. Visiting Zaire on August 7–9, Giscard announced support for African nationalism by denouncing apartheid and cutting off arms to South Africa, which, he said, could have "a continental use."

Relations with the United States remained friendly. A dispute about currency exchange rates was resolved at the Rambouillet economic summit conference on November 15–17. Giscard planned to visit the United States on May 17–20, 1976, for Bicentennial celebrations. Relations with Canada remained correct and cool.

JOHN C. CAIRNS
University of Toronto

AUSTIN POST—U. S. GEOLOGICAL SURVEY

Scientist observes crater of Washington's Mt. Baker, which first showed volcanic activity in March.

GEOLOGY

Geologists continued to make new advances and discoveries in 1975. Astrogeology contributed important information applicable to an understanding of the earth. Observations of Mercury obtained by the Mariner 10 spacecraft on flybys of the planet in March and September 1974 and March 1975 added greatly to comparative planetology.

Hundreds of excellent photographs were returned. These show a moonlike cratered surface as well as long, winding cliffs or scarps similar to certain fault traces on earth. The density is 5.45 times that of water (Earth, 5.5); thus, like Earth, the core must be relatively large and the outer shell thin. There has been little geologic activity since the period of major crater formation. The atmosphere is very thin, and there are no signs of surface water.

Exploration of the Oceans. The Deep Sea Drilling Project continued, with the research vessel *Glomar Challenger* adding basic data to an already impressive record. Showings of oil and gas were found off the shores of northern Norway, and evidence was documented for major changes in the North Atlantic during the middle Tertiary, some 30 million years ago. Six holes drilled in the western Atlantic and one in the eastern Atlantic revealed that the separation of South America and Africa had progressed to the point where free circulation between the North and South Atlantic was possible by middle Late Cretaceous time, 80 million years ago. The Amazon River began as a major stream in the Miocene, some 20 million years ago, as the Andes were uplifted.

Drilling of the basins and margins of the eastern South Atlantic close to the African coast and of the west coast of Africa north of the equator recorded an earlier time when South America and Africa were still in near proximity and oceanic circulation between them was highly restricted. Afterward, the *Glomar Challenger* returned to the Mediterranean Sea. Ten holes at 8 sites were drilled. Of chief interest are the meaning and origin of deposits of anhydrite, gypsum, and halite, which had been discovered in 1970 and again sampled in 1975. It is believed that these sediments were deposited in landlocked salt lakes and playas (the bottoms of desert basins) that were thousands of feet below sea level and not connected with the nearby Atlantic Ocean.

Land Drilling. A group of American geologists has proposed a program of deep, exploratory, noncommercial drilling across the continental United States. Holes up to 5.5 miles (8.8 km) deep would be drilled at sites selected chiefly for potential scientific value. Applications relevant to earthquake mechanisms and prediction, to the nature of the ancient "basement" that underlies most of the country, and to tapping geothermal energy would be expected. "Accidental" discovery of important mineral deposits would not be unexpected.

"Hot Spots." Attention focused on the well-known showplace Yellowstone Park, Wyo. This area displays some 10,000 manifestations of subterranean heat in the form of geysers, hot springs, and fumaroles. Earthquakes are common and there are numerous faults. A great volcanic event, dated about 600,000 years ago, culminated in the collapse of a large circular tract (caldera) within which the heat effects are chiefly localized.

For the first time geologists have been able to learn something about the heat source at Yellowstone. Using data from earthquake waves that pass through the area, scientists from the U. S. Geological Survey have outlined a mass of molten rock 95 miles (150 km) below the surface and about 30 miles (50 km) wide. Yellowstone is considered to be a "hot spot," which is

what geologists call a source of extreme heat lying deep in the lower crust (lithosphere) or upper mantle. A typical hot spot gives rise to an ascending plume of heated material that breaks the surface as an active volcano. The great volcanoes of Hawaii are the best current examples.

Hot-spot activity combines with the movement of the outer surficial shell of the earth with spectacular effects. As a lithospheric plate moves over a hot spot, a line or succession of volcanoes is created. Each of these is active only while it is above and connected with the rising plume of heated rock. As the plate moves on it carries a line of extinct volcanoes.

Some workers relate the Yellowstone activity to a southwestward movement of North America over a hot spot. This movement also created and left behind the Snake River Plain of Idaho, a lava-filled trench extending fingerlike from the large basalt fields of the Columbia Plateau.

Volcanic Ash and the Ice Age. Among the many theories as to the causes of ice ages is the idea that volcanic ash in the atmosphere cuts down solar radiation, with consequent cooling effects. Recently it has become possible to support this theory with facts. Scientists at the University of Rhode Island, utilizing information from the Deep Sea Drilling Project, have found positive evidence of heightened global increase in explosive volcanism during the last 2 million years. The total of about 270 layers of volcanic ash in the past 2 million years is four times the average number of layers of ash for the last 20 million years.

The effect is worldwide and suggests an underlying common cause, perhaps related in some way to plate movement. The relationship of increased volcanism and the onset of the great Pleistocene ice age seems to be more than coin-cidental. It has been shown, for example, that temperatures over the Greenland and Antarctic ice sheets have been inversely proportional to the amount of volcanic ash falling on them over a period of about 100,000 years.

Volcanoes and Earthquake Prediction. Modern volcanoes also made news. Guarded warnings were issued by the U. S. Geological Survey that Mt. St. Helens in southwestern Washington and Mt. Baker in northwestern Washington are showing signs of life. The past history of Mt. St. Helens, as shown by flanking deposits, has been one of intermittent powerful eruptions separated by quiet periods of a few centuries or less. Practically all the visible cone has been built since 500 B. C. Activity at Mt. Baker was first noticed in March 1975. Several eruptions of steam and debris have broken out and the temperature of a lake in one of the craters has risen to 77° F (25° C). These signs of heightened activity are being taken seriously, and resorts, campgrounds, and hiking trails in the Mt. Baker–Snoqualmie National Forest have been closed.

Earthquakes and their prediction are topics of growing concern. Additions to the list of possible warning signals include changes in the water level of nonflowing wells and faint "noises" from zones under stress.

Texas Pterosaur. In March it was announced that fossil bones found in sandstone outcroppings in the Big Bend National Park in west Texas had been determined to belong to an extinct winged reptile, or pterosaur. Discovered by Douglas Lawson, a graduate student in paleontology at the University of California, Berkeley, the fossils appear to represent a new species. Its estimated 51-foot (15.5-meter) wingspan makes it the largest flying animal known.

W. LEE STOKES
University of Utah

Douglas Lawson displays skeletal remains of the pterosaur that he found in Texas' Big Bend National Park. A winged reptile, the pterosaur lived about 60 million years ago and had a wingspan of about 51 feet (15.5 meters).

GEORGIA

Economic decline, presidential politics, overcrowded prisons, and natural disasters were in the news in Georgia in 1975. In Atlanta, the Peachtree Center Plaza Hotel, the South's tallest building, was topped out in October.

Economic Difficulties. As state revenues plummeted, a special budget-cutting session of the Georgia General Assembly was called in early summer. Legislators reduced expenditures in the original $2 billion budget by $125 million. Pay raises for state employees and school teachers as well as a $35 million property tax rebate plan were defeated. State departments and the state's colleges and universities also were forced to accept across-the-board budget cuts. In some cases services were curtailed or eliminated. The state department of natural resources, for example, closed some 35 state parks and historic sites.

Regular Session. In the regular session of the General Assembly earlier in the year, new revenue sources were approved for local governments, which were given the option of imposing local sales taxes and hotel-motel taxes. Imposition was to depend on local referenda. In other voting, the assembly defeated the federal Equal Rights Amendment.

Presidential Politics. Gov. George Busbee spearheaded an effort to get Southern states to establish presidential primaries on or near the same day in 1976 so that candidates would be forced to campaign in the South. May 4, 1976, was set as the date for Georgia's first presidential preference primary.

Busbee's efforts came even as former Georgia Gov. Jimmy Carter was stumping the country in his quest for the 1976 Democratic presidential nomination. Another Georgian, former Secretary of the Army Howard (Bo) Callaway, was serving as reelection campaign manager for President Gerald Ford. Georgia state senator Julian Bond, who was nominated for vice president from the floor of the Democratic national convention in 1968, announced he will not run for president in 1976 because of a lack of financial support.

Overcrowded Prisons. Whether caused by an increase in crime, improvements in law enforcement, or longer sentences dealt out by the courts, Georgia's prisons were bursting at the seams by late 1975. The Georgia sheriffs demanded that the state take charge of 1,000 prisoners crowded into their jails for lack of room in the state penal system. At the same time, the Georgia board of pardons and paroles unveiled a scheme to release at least 1,000 inmates from the prisons by cutting one year from the sentences of all nonviolent offenders.

Natural Disasters. Weather wreaked havoc on Georgia in the early months of 1975. On March 24 a tornado ripped the roof off the governor's mansion in Atlanta while the governor and his family huddled inside. Three people were killed, and 170 were injured, while damage estimates ran as high as $30 million. Another tornado leveled 80% of the business district in Ft. Valley, killing 2 and injuring 38. Storm-spawned flood waters brought the highest water in 30 years to the streets of Atlanta.

Medicine, Education, and Law. Scandal hit the Medicaid program in Georgia in 1975 as Governor Busbee initiated an investigation into charges of massive overcharging by some of the state's doctors. Later in the year, faced with an expected $65 million deficit in the Medicaid budget, the governor cut benefits to recipients and reduced payments to nursing homes. The latter measure brought threats by the homes to end their care of Medicaid patients.

The board of regents raised tuition to Georgia colleges and universities by an average of 15%.

In a landmark decision, expected to face U. S. Supreme Court scrutiny, the George supreme court ruled that zoning decisions by local governments are subject to court review, a decision many expected to open the way for protracted fights in zoning disputes. Earlier, Georgia's highest court issued another controversial ruling in holding that the state's "sunshine" law requiring open meetings of state agencies, did not apply to committee meetings of the Georgia house and senate.

Deaths. Two widely known Georgia political figures died in 1975. Richard B. Rich, founder of Rich's, Atlanta's largest department store, died at the age of 73. A civic leader for 50 years, Rich had headed the Metropolitan Atlanta Rapid Transit Authority board and was a prominent member of a leadership coalition credited with fostering Atlanta's fabulous successes in the 1960's.

James Lester ("Mr. Jim") Gillis of Soperton, a political power for more than 20 years as he presided over the state highway department, died at the age of 83. Gillis was credited by many as being the man behind successful gubernatorial candidates.

GENE STEPHENS
Georgia State University

GEORGIA · Information Highlights

Area: 58,876 square miles (152,489 sq km).
Population (1974 est.): 4,882,000. *Density:* 83 per sq mi.
Chief Cities (1970 census): Atlanta, the capital, 497,-421; Columbus, 155,028; Macon, 122,423.
Government (1975): *Chief Officers*—governor, George D. Busbee (D); lt. gov., Zell Miller (D); atty. gen., Arthur K. Bolton (D). *General Assembly*—Senate, 56 members; House of Representatives, 180 members.
Education (1974–75): *Enrollment*—public elementary schools, 673,205; public secondary, 408,280; nonpublic, 30,100; colleges and universities, 155,924 students. *Public school expenditures,* $864,369,000 ($873 per pupil).
State Finances (fiscal year 1974): *Revenues,* $2,748,308-000; *expenditures,* $2,618,445,000.
Personal Income (1974): $22,760,000,000; per capita, $4,662.
Labor Force (July 1975): *Nonagricultural wage and salary earners,* 1,815,500; *insured unemployed,* 63,-500 (4.3%).

West German Chancellor Helmut Schmidt and President Ford held a joint news conference in Bonn during Ford's European tour in July.

UPI

GERMANY

The geographical area of Germany consists of two separate states. The Federal Republic of Germany (West Germany) is a democratic, parliamentary republic and a member of such Western organizations as the North Atlantic Treaty Organization (NATO), the European Coal and Steel Community, and the European Economic Community (EEC). The German Democratic Republic (East Germany), also known as DDR from its German-language initials, is, in effect, a Communist one-party state. It is affiliated with the Warsaw Pact and the Council for Mutual Economic Assistance (COMECON), the Eastern counterparts of NATO and EEC.

Between these two states, West Berlin, a Western outpost within East Germany, maintains its precarious existence. Economically and culturally it is tied closely to West Germany, but politically and militarily it has a separate status.

FEDERAL REPUBLIC OF GERMANY
(West Germany)

The coalition government of Chancellor Helmut Schmidt, based on the Social Democratic party (SPD) and the Free Democratic party (FDP), functioned without serious difficulties throughout most of the year. Toward the end of the year, however, tensions developed over the means by which to fight the economic recession. The SPD called for more public-works projects and further social reforms. The party's left wing demanded a government-directed investment policy. The business-oriented FDP favored an end to social reforms, tax reductions as entrepreneurial incentives, wage restraints, and full freedom in investment decisions. Schmidt, a Social Democrat for pragmatic rather than ideological reasons, was sometimes closer to this latter position than to that of his own party.

Terrorism. Although West German authorities broke up a number of terrorist organizations, others carried on their activities. In April one group took over the West German embassy in Stockholm, Sweden, demanding the release of 26 imprisoned fellow terrorists. The request was denied, and the invaders soon surrendered. Earlier, a prominent West Berlin judge had been killed in retaliation against the death, after a hunger strike, of another imprisoned terrorist. West Berlin was also the scene of the kidnapping of Peter Lorenz, the city's opposition political leader. He was freed only after the release and flight to Aden of five jailed radicals. Even in isolated West Berlin it took many months before the kidnappers were captured.

In May, three years after their arrest, one terrorist group, whose leaders are the well-known Andreas Baader and Ulrike Meinhof, was finally brought to trial. The trial was held in a spe-

cially-built courtroom in Stuttgart, equipped with complex security devices to guard against raids and other disruptions by supporters of the defendants. The trial soon got entangled in legal issues, among them the question of the defendants' right to choose their defense attorneys. New problems arose when, due to a prolonged hunger strike and years of isolated imprisonment, the defendants proved physically and emotionally unable to comprehend the proceedings. The court decided to proceed without them. The decision was based on a law that permits such procedure if the incapacitation of the defendant is self-inflicted. As was pointed out by many observers on the basis of the medical testimony, this condition did not seem to apply in this case.

The continued presence of extremist radicalism focused attention again on governmental loyalty and security investigations. In both parliament and the press, the debate continued as to how to reconcile individual rights with the state's security needs. Public-opinion polls and legislative measures gave priority to the latter.

Economy. The West German economy remained stagnant throughout 1975. A plan launched in December 1974 and designed to spur the economy through tax reductions, investment allowances, low interest rates, and increased unemployment benefits did not produce the ex-

West Berlin police released Ettore Cannela from jail in March to fulfill demands by guerrillas who were holding a Berlin mayoral candidate.

UPI

pected results. One reason for the plan's failure was the continued decline of exports. The Bonn government was therefore greatly concerned about economic conditions in the United States, one of the country's main export markets. Chancellor Schmidt and others warned against Washington's preoccupation with inflation and its tight credit policies. They also worried about the effect on the U. S. economy of the possible default of New York City.

To reduce unemployment, which reached 1 million, or 4.4% of the labor force, hiring of foreign labor was stopped, except from EEC countries whose citizens enjoy equal treatment with West Germans. The contracts of many "guest workers" were canceled, with severance payments ranging from $1,800 to $3,000. Yet, as before, many West Germans were reluctant to take unattractive jobs in sanitation, mining, and agriculture, formerly held by foreigners. With unemployment benefits extended to a year, and yielding at least 68% of their last pay, they preferred to wait for more congenial work.

As part of the government's contingency planning, a $2 billion public works program was prepared. However, no final action was taken to implement it.

Social Conditions. As the economy declined, the relationship between capital and labor received increasing attention. In the face of the spreading recession, unions began to question the benefits of a free-market economy. The struggle for co-determination, that is, equal labor representation on the supervisory boards of corporations, was resumed. Labor demanded participation, not in daily management, but in the determination of overall policies and the supervision of the boards of directors. Unions joined other groups in the demand for governmental channeling of investments to assure an economic expansion that would also be beneficial socially. There were few calls, however, for the nationalization of large enterprises.

In February the constitutional court in Karlsruhe rejected as unconstitutional an abortion law passed by the West German parliament in June 1974. The law permitted abortions by request during the first three months of pregnancy. The court viewed such broad authorization as a violation of the constitutional guarantee of the right to life. It allowed, however, that abortions would be permissible in cases of rape, harm to the mother's health, possible deformity of the child, and other "grave hardships." A law was drafted to that effect.

Foreign Policy. West German foreign policy was dominated by the country's economic concerns. Bonn's one-time generosity in helping to fund EEC projects gave way to stringent retrenchments. West German vetoes blocked plans for additional food aid to poor nations and for extended insurance to less-developed countries against crop failures. When Minister of Agriculture Josef Ertl made some concessions on

—— WEST GERMANY · Information Highlights ——

Official Name: Federal Republic of Germany.
Location: North central Europe.
Area: 95,790 square miles (248,096 sq km). West Berlin, 186 square miles (481 sq km).
Population (1975 est.): 61,900,000.
Chief Cities (1974 est.): Bonn, the capital, 300,000; Hamburg, 1,900,000; Munich, 1,300,000.
Government: *Head of state,* Walter Scheel, president (took office July 1974). *Head of government,* Helmut Schmidt, federal chancellor (took office May 1974). *Legislature*—Parliament: Bundesrat and Bundestag.
Monetary Unit: Deutsche Mark (2.585 D. Marks equal U.S.$1, Aug. 1975).
Gross National Product (1973): $357,000,000,000.
Manufacturing (major products): Mechanical engineering products, automobiles, chemicals, iron and steel.
Major Agricultural Products: Rye, oats, wheat, barley, potatoes, sugar beets, hops, forest products, fish.
Foreign Trade (1974): *Exports,* $89,890,000,000; *imports,* $69,700,000,000.

farm prices at EEC negotiations in Brussels, he was at once disavowed by the government.

Relations with the United States were similarly affected. Bonn indicated its unwillingness to contribute any longer to the upkeep of U.S. forces on German soil, a stand made easier by the fact that U.S. calls for the withdrawal of their troops from Europe are rarely heard. Bonn's outspoken demands for a review of U.S. economic policies were another measure of its concerns. Tensions also arose over a West German-Brazilian agreement providing for the delivery of nuclear equipment to Brazil. U.S. protests that adequate safeguards against abuses for military purposes had not been taken were dismissed as expressions of jealousy by disappointed economic competitors.

In June, President Walter Scheel paid a state visit to the United States. President Gerald Ford welcomed him as the representative of a state that "in many respects could serve as a model for the development of the modern industrial state." Scheel, in an address before Congress, praised the "well tried partnership" between the United States and the Federal Republic and described West Germany as a good ally in the defense of Western democracy. He warned his audience, however, that democracy could not survive unless it kept adjusting to social needs. The speech reflected the self-confidence with which West Germany viewed its position in world affairs. A visit by President Ford to Bonn in July failed to reassure his hosts that the conservative U.S. economic policies would not impede either U.S. or European economic recovery.

Relations with the Soviet Union were again plagued by questions of the political and legal status of West Berlin. An agreement that West German firms would build a nuclear plant in Kaliningrad was held up by disputes. The main question was whether West Berlin, as well as West Germany, would be supplied with electricity from that plant. A new agreement with Poland provided for the resettlement of some 120,000 ethnic Germans in return for West German credits and Bonn's agreement to honor social-insurance claims of Poles who were formerly German citizens.

As relations with the USSR declined, those with China improved. When Schmidt visited China in November, he was the first Western

The West German economy sagged in 1975, and Volkswagen workers waited to hear decisions on layoffs.

In February supporters of a new abortion law protested a court ruling that the law was unconstitutional.

West German President Walter Scheel met with Israeli Prime Minister Rabin in July to discuss the Middle East.

leader to be taken on a tour of the border province of Sinkiang, one of the areas of Sino-Soviet confrontation.

GERMAN DEMOCRATIC REPUBLIC
(East Germany)

The 30th anniversary of the German surrender in World War II, barely noticed in the Federal Republic, was proclaimed an official holiday in the DDR. Celebrated as "Liberation Day," it was hailed as an early step toward socialist progress. At the same time, all speakers noted that only one part of Germany could take advantage of this opportunity since the Western powers blocked all progressive socialist developments in the areas under their control. The Russians, on the other hand, were praised for having helped the East Germans advance toward socialism. There were glowing reaffirmations of the close ties linking the USSR and the DDR.

Economy. In the course of the year the DDR was increasingly affected by the inflationary price rises that beset the Western world. Raw-material imports of oil, cotton, paper, and coffee from non-Communist countries rose in some cases four and fivefold between 1972 and 1975. Other increases were expected for 1976 at the expiration of trade agreements with the Soviet Union and other East European countries, from which the DDR obtains the bulk of its imports. The increases were, however, only partly reflected in higher consumer prices. Most old prices were maintained by subsidies through

1975. They were expected to remain stable also in 1976 when imports from the Soviet bloc became more expensive.

Meanwhile, savings were effected in various ways. Newspapers were published six rather than seven times a week. Car travel on official business was severely limited. Price increases for raw materials and energy were introduced at the production level to enforce greater efficiency and economy. For visiting foreigners, moreover, prices for hotel accommodations and many other services were raised, as were export prices in general. Special emphasis was placed on production for export in order to maintain a balance of payments.

Culture. Reading is one of the most widespread activities in the DDR. In 1974, 5,697 titles were published, with a total printing of 127 million copies. Given the rising price of paper, which is imported from Finland and Sweden, book production faced a serious financial problem. At the Leipzig book fair Deputy Minister of Culture Klaus Hoepcke noted that books were written, not for some individuals, but for everyone, and should therefore be read in public reading rooms or borrowed from public libraries rather than be owned individually.

The major publishing event of the year was the appearance of the first three volumes of a new edition of Marx's and Engels' collected works. This edition was expected to be printed in 100 volumes and to be completed in 20 years. All texts will be printed in their original languages, 60% in German, the rest in the 12 other languages the two men used. Their own letters, moreover, will be supplemented with those of their correspondents. The project is sponsored jointly by the Institutes for Marxism-Leninism in Moscow and East Berlin.

Foreign Policy. The friendship pact between the DDR and the USSR was renewed in October. It provided for close collaboration in all fields, especially in the economic area, where integration of productive capacities and planning was to continue. Special attention was to be

---

—— EAST GERMANY • Information Highlights ——

Official Name: German Democratic Republic.
Location: North central Europe.
Area: 41,768 square miles (108,178 sq km).
Population (1974 est.): 17,170,000.
Chief Cities (1971 census): East Berlin, the capital, 1,086,374; Leipzig, 583,885; Dresden, 502,432.
Government: *Head of state,* Willi Stoph, chairman of the Council of State (took office 1973). *Head of government,* Horst Sindermann, minister-president (took office in 1973). *First secretary of the Socialist Unity (Communist) party,* Erich Honecker (took office 1971). *Legislature* (unicameral)—Volkskammer (People's Chamber).
Monetary Unit: Ostmark (1.78 Ostmarks equal U. S.$1, Sept. 1974).
Gross National Product (1973 est.): $38,200,000,000.
Manufacturing (major products): Iron and steel, machinery, chemicals, transport equipment, electronics.
Major Agricultural Products: Rye, potatoes, sugar beets, wheat, oats, barley, livestock.
Foreign Trade (1974 est.): *Exports,* $8,000,000,000; *imports,* $9,500,000,000.

Ambassador John Sherman Cooper toasts East Germany's Communist Party leader Erich Honecker at the U. S. exhibit at the Leipzig Fair. The United States was officially represented at the fair for the first time in March.

UPI

paid to the preservation of West Berlin's separate status.

In implementation of the plans for closer economic cooperation, 5,800 East German workers went to the Soviet Union to help build pipelines through which the Eastern European countries are to be supplied with gas from the Soviet Union. Similar crews were sent by Poland, Hungary, Czechoslovakia, and Bulgaria.

A cultural exchange pact with the United States provided for the exchange of 10 East German and U. S. scholars during 1976–77.

In June, Archbishop Agostino Casaroli, the senior Vatican diplomat, visited East Berlin. He apparently explored further the question of the establishment of diplomatic relations between the Vatican and the DDR.

WEST BERLIN

West Berlin, too, was affected by the general economic decline, but unemployment was lower there than in West Germany. The city was forced to slash its expenditures and raise rates on most public services. However, its credit remained unimpaired since the city has the financial backing of the West German government. A gambling casino that was opened in September proved to be a useful new source of revenue.

In city elections in March the Christian Democratic Union emerged for the first time as the largest party. Its success was due partly to the kidnapping by an urban guerrilla group of the party's mayoral candidate, Peter Lorenz. Like West Germany, West Berlin was being governed by a Social Democratic-Free Democratic coalition, headed by the Social Democratic mayor, Klaus Schütz.

Legal Status. West Berlin's relationship to West Germany continued to be a source of recurrent disputes. Whether West German consuls could represent only West Berlin citizens in foreign countries, as the Soviet bloc countries maintained in a literal interpretation of the Four-Power Berlin Agreement of 1971, or whether their right of representation extended to West Berlin corporations and institutions remained an unsolved question.

Similarly, a visit by U. S. Secretary of State Henry Kissinger to the city with West German

Foreign Minister Hans-Dietrich Genscher gave rise to sharp protests from the Soviet Union. The USSR said that Genscher's presence suggested political ties with West Germany that were in clear violation of the Four-Power Agreement on West Berlin. There were also objections to the proposed establishment of an EEC-sponsored research institute of professional training.

EAST-WEST GERMAN RELATIONS

Contacts between the two Germanys continued to improve slowly. West German citizens were allowed to travel by car in the DDR. Visas were no longer issued for visits just to one East German district, but to the entire country. Train travel was expedited, and additional border crossings were opened. Negotiations began about the construction of a new Autobahn between Hamburg and West Berlin, to be financed largely by West Germany.

Trade. Commerce between the two states also kept increasing. In the course of 1975 expanded clearing and credit arrangements were made. Trade relations suffered a setback, however, when the DDR was charged with "dumping" some goods, particularly textiles, in West German markets. The Bonn government reduced quotas for textile imports from the DDR, and, by requesting special permits, closely supervised all such imports. There were reports of plans for joint chemical projects and for the construction of a steel plant by Krupp in Thuringia.

A kind of "human" trade has also been carried on for some time between the two states. The West German government has been buying freedom for prisoners held in East Germany in exchange for cash payments or industrial products. Many of those freed were persons who had been caught and imprisoned for trying to escape from the DDR. The exchanges continued in 1975.

Border Demarcation. A joint commission has been at work since 1973 marking the 450-mile (720-km) East-West German boundary line. Although Bonn denied that there were any agreements, this precise demarcation was further evidence of the permanence of that border.

ANDREAS DORPALEN, *The Ohio State University*

U. S. Ambassador Shirley Temple Black was honored in Cape Coast in September. Ghanaian citizens presented Ambassador Black with an "Afonfena" sword, symbol of a deputy Omanhena, or chief.

AP

GHANA

Faced by complex domestic, economic, and political issues, the government of Col. Ignatius K. Acheampong maintained generally conservative policies during 1975.

Economy. In its fourth year in power the Supreme Military Council (formerly the National Redemption Council), of which Acheampong is chairman, faced a growing budget gap. It resulted from escalating import costs, particularly of oil, and stagnant or declining export revenues, especially from cocoa, which accounted for 70% of foreign exchange earnings. Acheampong claimed Ghana lost close to $100 million due to a drop in world cocoa prices.

The brightest part of the economic picture came from "Operation Feed Yourself," through which rice farms were able to meet local needs, although transport inefficiencies impeded distribution. To bolster domestic industries, the government banned textile imports and announced that local mills would be required to use Ghanaian-grown cotton after 1977.

Politics. Col. Acheampong seemed reluctant to leave the country and attended neither the Commonwealth heads of government meeting in Jamaica nor the Organization of African Unity (OAU) summit meeting in Uganda, during which Gen. Yakubu Gowon, military leader of Nigeria, was deposed. He also spurned a suggestion in March that he become president, on the grounds that accepting such a title would be seen as a lust for power.

Secessionist claims on Ghana's eastern border were revived early in 1975. In February a large delegation of traditional chiefs from the Volta region asked for immediate negotiations between the government of Ghana and the so-called Western Togoland Liberation Movement, a secessionist group. The chiefs had presented a letter that threatened that Ghanaian and foreign diplomats would be taken hostage if their demands were not met. The controversy subsided, however, and in August, the government granted a three-month amnesty to members of the movement but warned that future subversive activities would be dealt with "severely."

Steps to honor Kwame Nkrumah, Ghana's first prime minister and president, were announced in August. Nkrumah was ousted in a 1966 military coup and died in exile in 1972. Two large-scale projects associated with his rule, the Accra-Tema motorway and the statehouse built for the 1965 OAU summit meeting, were renamed in his honor, and a mausoleum will be built in his native village.

Foreign Affairs. The government maintained active interest in the OAU. Ghana was selected as part of an eight-state delegation to settle disputes among the three contending liberation movements in Angola—a task never carried to fruition. Ghana took exception to a proposed OAU resolution recommending Israel's expulsion from the United Nations.

Ghana reestablished diplomatic relations with Zambia, which had been broken after the 1966 coup against Nkrumah, and established formal relations with Portugal. The new U. S. ambassador, Shirley Temple Black, presented her credentials in Accra in December 1974 and traveled widely in Ghana. The Organization of African Trade Union Unity, headquartered in Accra, held its inaugural general council meeting there in March. Ghana also signed the treaty establishing the Economic Community of West African States (ECOWAS).

CLAUDE E. WELCH, JR.
State University of New York at Buffalo

GHANA · Information Highlights

Official Name: Republic of Ghana.
Location: West Africa.
Area: 92,099 square miles (238,537 sq km).
Population (1975 est.): 10,300,000.
Chief Cities (1973 est.): Accra, the capital, 848,800; Kumasi, 249,000.
Government: *Head of state,* Col. I. K. Acheampong, chairman of National Redemption Council (took office Jan. 1972). *Legislature*—National Assembly (dissolved Jan. 1972).
Monetary Unit: New cedi (1.1538 new cedis equal U. S. $1, July 1975).
Gross National Product (1974 est.): $3,660,000,000.
Manufacturing (major products): processed agricultural products, wood products, cement.
Major Agricultural Products: Cocoa, corn, cassava, groundnuts, sweet potatoes, forest products.
Foreign Trade (1974): *Exports,* $755,000,000; *imports,* $822,000,000.

Prime Minister Harold Wilson addressed coal miners at their July convention in Scarborough and asked that they slash their wage-hike demands.

GREAT BRITAIN

Britain fought its way through another difficult year in 1975, continuing to face serious economic problems coupled with a new resurgence of Irish terrorism on the mainland. However, the people of Britain showed few signs of unrest, and there were even some omens of hope. The precious North Sea oil began to flow, the government's anti-inflation policy began successfully, and there were even faint signs of a settlement in the seven-year-old Northern Ireland crisis, which had continued as long as World War II.

Economy. The country's economic problems were stark enough to make any glimmers of hope cause optimism. The inflation rate touched 26%, the public-sector deficit reached toward £12 billion ($25 billion), unemployment moved up to about 1.3 million, and the pound sterling sank gently over the year to its lowest figure ever, just over twice the value of the U. S. dollar. In November, the government announced that it had obtained another huge loan, of nearly £1 billion ($2.1 billion) from the International Monetary Fund.

Nevertheless, there were signs of real hope, and perhaps the most important economic event of the year was the government's July plan for wage restraint. After 15 months of fruitless attempts to cajole the trade unions into accepting restraint, Prime Minister Harold Wilson was able to announce an agreement among labor, industry, and government, by which all wage increases for the following 12 months would be limited to £6 ($12.60) per week. He achieved this partly by the Labour government's pro-union policy and partly because the workers began to realize that inflation was creating a huge threat to employment.

The £6 figure, chosen at the suggestion of Jack Jones, Britain's most prominent union leader, represented roughly 10% of the average wage, and government ministers announced that they hoped to bring the inflation rate down to below 10% within a year. The limit was described as "voluntary," although it was made perfectly clear that compulsory legislation would be introduced if the £6 was ever breached.

By the end of the year, there had been no significant break in the limit, and the government was beginning to talk guardedly about some cautious reflation early in 1976.

There were also other signs of hope. Unemployment seemed certain to remain well below the dreaded 2 million figure, and the government introduced a "temporary employment subsidy," under which employers with too little work to offer could retain staff with the help of government funds. The plan started quietly but was scheduled to be expanded.

North Sea Oil. The high-quality oil extracted at great expense and with great difficulty from the storm-wracked North Sea began to flow in November, and for the first time British motorists were filling up with British gasoline. The oil, essential to paying the country's international debts and providing vital industrial investment, will account for almost all Britain's oil needs by the 1980's and may make the nation one of the world's largest producers. The Labour govern-

UPI

Air and sea patrols were assigned to regular surveillance duty of Britain's vast North Sea oil fields.

ment passed legislation giving the state a 51% share of all new fields and allowing it to take over a majority share in existing fields "by agreement." Oil companies argued strongly that this would restrict exploration.

Industry. Industrial investment, which had fallen throughout the early part of the year, also showed signs of having reached its bottom, with industrialists saying that they hoped to increase investment in 1976. The stock exchange, which started the year at a miserably low index of 161, had advanced to 375 by the end of the year, reflecting in exaggerated form the new confidence.

The government passed new legislation to increase public investment in industry but abandoned its earlier policy of shoring up ailing firms at almost limitless public expense. Instead, a policy was developed with the labor unions and industry by which the state would assist only firms that had bright future prospects. The plan was received with some skepticism by all sides, though with a general recognition that the public would have to make up for a general failure of private individuals to invest adequately in Britain's outdated industry. Shortly before the legislation was passed, the government pledged £1.5 billion ($3.2 billion) to the sickly British Leyland auto firm, assuming that it too would regain its health within a few years.

Politics. Politically, 1975 was also a turbulent year for Britain, with the first referendum ever held on a major constitutional question, the first woman leader of an important political party, and a growing debate on the whole future of the United Kingdom.

Britain's first female political leader is Margaret Thatcher, the daughter of a Lincolnshire storekeeper, who in February became leader of the Conservative party and of the parliamentary opposition. She replaced former prime minister Edward Heath through a brilliantly fought campaign, a strong appeal to her party's right-wing roots, and a striking display of political bravado.

Heath, who had lost two successive general elections, realized in January that he would have to offer himself for reelection by his party's members of parliament. Thatcher was the only substantial figure to oppose him on the first ballot, and her political nerve and acumen were enough to sweep her to victory even over the Heath heir-apparent, liberal William Whitelaw.

She rapidly celebrated her victory by dismissing from senior posts many of the most important liberals identified with the Heath regime. She pledged to return the party to its right-wing roots, stressing the need for inequality and her dislike of state intervention in industry and social affairs. She also swiftly scored a major success in a by-election in a London suburb, suggesting that the electorate did not feel any prejudice against a female political leader. The Conservatives' annual conference in October awarded her a massive and impressive standing ovation. Heath refused to take a post under her leadership and privately expressed deep dislike of her and her policies.

On December 29, two landmark measures came into effect that gave women equal legal protection. The Equal Pay Act mandated similar wages to men's for similar work, while the Sex Discrimination Act covered other areas.

Referendum. Britain's first referendum was held in order to give the public the choice of whether to remain within the European Economic Community (EEC). The referendum's intention was to defeat the anti-EEC wing of the governing Labour party, which was in a majority and was preventing the pro-EEC Prime Minister Wilson from giving Britain's wholehearted support to the EEC.

Wilson decided to appeal over the heads of his party and against the opposition of many of his cabinet, who were given the unique opportunity of attacking government policy in public as a means of preventing the cabinet from falling apart.

Only Labour left-wingers plus a few Conservative right-wingers led the anti-EEC campaign, and almost the entire weight of British political opinion fought strongly for continued membership in the EEC. In spite of the vexing issue of rising prices, many of which were blamed on the EEC, the electorate voted strongly in favor of membership. A total of 14.9 million voted for continued membership and 6.8 million against, a split of 69%–31%. It was an overwhelming victory.

Ironically, the other eight EEC nations, which had believed Britain would now play a more cooperative role in the EEC, found that the weight of the vote had had the opposite

Conservative party leader Margaret Thatcher joined the battle for England's continued membership in the European Economic Community. A national referendum was held in June and an overwhelming majority of the population voted for continued membership.

UPI

effect. Britain swiftly showed its independence by demanding a separate, non-EEC, place at the world conference on energy supplies, and gave no indication of accepting EEC decisions that appeared to work against British interests.

Nationalism. Significantly, both Scotland and Wales voted in favor of EEC membership, a severe blow to the nationalist, separatist parties in both regions. These parties, particularly in Scotland, were by the end of the year posing a serious threat to the unity of the United Kingdom.

Most of Britain's oil is off the Scottish shore, and this wealth has fueled the growth of Scottish desire for independence. The government, recognizing the danger to Britain's energy supplies, attempted to counter the threat by offering limited independence in the form of a Scottish assembly, with powers mainly over Scottish affairs.

Under increasing pressure from the nationalist parties, the government spent a year examining the problem and the major constitutional issues. By November it was forced to admit temporary defeat, and the "devolution" schemes were postponed for at least a year. There were furious charges of betrayal by the nationalists and expressions of relief from politicians, who feared that the process would end with the eventual destruction of the links among England, Scotland, and Wales.

Jubilant nationalists recognized that they were the victors in either case. The government

might finally grant their demands, which in turn could lead to a total split among the various parts of the United Kingdom, or it might renege on its own promises, in which case the nationalists believe they could count on sweeping electoral victories.

The House of Lords. The year also marked the reopening of the old problem of Britain's second chamber, the House of Lords. Unlike the U. S. Senate, this chamber is not elected, and since the beginning of the 20th century it has declined to exercise its powers, fearing its own abolition. But the heavily Conservative House of Lords in November rejected legislation from the elected House of Commons concerned with labor-union rights.

Although the unwritten British constitution allows the Commons ultimately to override the Lords, ministers were infuriated and began to consider the reform or abolition of the Lords. If this were to happen, it would strip the British aristocracy of its final constitutional rights, leaving the nation a democracy in the full and total sense of the word.

Terrorism. Britain's terrorist problem continued unabated throughout 1975, although there were some indications that politicians in Northern Ireland were beginning to edge toward a solution in that strife-torn province.

The Provisional Irish Republican Army (IRA), the main agents of violence in Northern Ireland, agreed to a truce with Britain in February. The IRA agreed not to continue their

bombing and terrorism campaign, and the British agreed to release most or all of the 400 people detained without trial. Britain also offered limited recognition to the IRA by giving its representatives "hot-line" telephone access to senior civil servants.

In Northern Ireland the truce worked moderately well, though many IRA cells ignored it and planted occasional bombs as well as killing a small number of policemen and soldiers. In Britain, it had almost no effect, as IRA cells, apparently working without the control of their Irish leadership, continued a vicious and indiscriminate bombing campaign.

No fewer than 27 bombs had been planted in England, chiefly in London, by November, killing eight people. In late November publisher Ross McWhirter, who had offered rewards for the capture of terrorists, was shot to death by gunmen at his home.

By the end of the year, the IRA had adopted the tactics of not giving warnings about bombs and of including in their devices metal objects designed to cause additional harm. In August, a bomb killed two people in the lobby of London's Hilton Hotel, and in October one person was killed in the Ritz Hotel. Three died in a series of explosions in expensive restaurants, in which bombs loaded with nails and ball-bearings were tossed through windows.

One of the most shocking incidents involved a bomb attached to the car of a Conservative member of parliament, Hugh Fraser. At the time he was the host of Caroline Kennedy, the

Sandbags barricade the windows of a London hotel to prevent terrorists from hurling bombs in the window.

UPI

daughter of the former U. S. president, and was about to drive her to work. Before they entered the car, the bomb exploded, killing Professor Gordon Hamilton Fairley, one of the world's leading experts on the treatment of cancer.

This bomb, and the many others, led to calls for the return of the death penalty. These were likely to be ignored by leaders in government and Parliament, but there was no indication that they would bring about any major change in British policy in Northern Ireland.

Meanwhile, the police had some success in catching the bombers, and more than 17 people were convicted of causing explosions in 1974 and 1975. The government introduced legislation that confirmed its powers to exclude suspected terrorists from the country, even if they have not been found guilty in a court of law.

Northern Ireland. In Northern Ireland, the fury of the terrorists turned instead to internecine feuds, in which Protestant terrorist gangs killed their Roman Catholic equivalents and vice versa. The main paramilitary organizations on each side of the religious divide tried to establish their supremacy by killing leading members of their rival organizations. Although few soldiers and police died, the total number of civilian dead after seven years of fighting rose to over 1,000.

The government attempted to find a political settlement by establishing a Northern Ireland Constitutional Convention. This was elected and began work in May, and the hope was that Protestants and Roman Catholics would finally agree on a compromise settlement.

With the British government taking a backseat role throughout its proceedings, the convention met for six months' debate. At one time a compromise did seem possible, when William Craig, a principal Protestant leader, suggested a temporary coalition government between his party and the main Roman Catholic party.

Craig's colleagues, however, fearing too much Roman Catholic participation in government, rejected his plan, and the convention ended with the two sides seemingly as far apart as ever. On the one hand the main Protestant parties demanded a Northern Ireland parliament linked to Britain, but giving the Protestant majority full powers over most Northern Irish life. On the other hand, the Roman Catholic parties insisted on a full share in government to protect the rights of their own people. In spite of this gap, however, politicians claimed privately that there was still hope for agreement, arguing that Britain would be able to use as its final sanction a threat to withdraw both troops and money from the province.

The British government continued to claim that it had no intention of withdrawing troops and was able to draw comfort from the fact that, in spite of the bombings in London, the British people did not raise any great cry for a complete withdrawal from Northern Ireland.

U. S. STATE DEPARTMENT

In July, Ambassador Elliot Richardson opened the U. S. embassy's "Young America" show of paintings from the Pennsylvania Academy for the Fine Arts.

Other Events. Police and government officials also congratulated themselves on the resolution of another delicate terrorist operation—the Spaghetti House siege. This was an aborted robbery attempt in which seven restauranteurs were held in a restaurant storeroom for a week after they had interrupted three armed robbers. The police adopted a policy of neither giving any concessions to the gunmen nor offering any violence to them or their hostages. This "wait and see" policy worked when, after a week, all the hostages were led out unharmed, and the gunmen surrendered. It was the first major test of British reaction to this form of terrorism and was agreed to be a substantial success.

SIMON HOGGART
The Manchester "Guardian"

—— **GREAT BRITAIN · Information Highlights** ——

Official Name: United Kingdom of Great Britain and Northern Ireland.
Area: 94,226 square miles (244,046 sq km).
Population (1975 est.): 56,400,000.
Chief Cities (1972 est.): London, the capital, 7,353,810; Birmingham, 1,006,760; Glasgow, 861,900; Liverpool, 588,600.
Government: *Head of state,* Elizabeth II, queen (acceded Feb. 1952). *Head of government,* Harold Wilson, prime minister (took office March 1974). *Legislature*—Parliament: House of Lords and House of Commons.
Monetary Unit: Pound (0.4737 pound equals U. S.$1, Aug. 1975).
Gross National Product (1974 est.): $188,000,000,000.
Manufacturing (major products): Iron and steel, motor vehicles, aircraft, textiles, chemicals.
Major Agricultural Products: Barley, oats, sugar beets, potatoes, wheat.
Foreign Trade (1974): *Exports,* $32,988,000,000; *imports,* $46,233,000,000.

GREECE

During 1975, Premier Constantine Caramanlis worked to strengthen democracy in Greece. His efforts were complicated by a continuing crisis in Greek-Turkish relations over the island of Cyprus.

The New Constitution. In January 1975 the Greek parliament began to debate the draft of a new constitution supported by Premier Caramanlis. Since the electorate had already voted the previous December not to restore the monarchy, the draft outlined a republican form of government with a strong presidency modeled on the present French system.

Caramanlis obviously hoped to give Greece a stable government that could prevent the reemergence of an authoritarian military regime like the one that had ruled the country from April 1967 to July 1974. The military regime ended only when its rulers became disastrously involved in a coup on Cyprus, which precipitated the invasion and occupation of about 40% of the island by the Turks.

Despite the Greek opposition's claims that a strong presidency was a threat to the republic, Caramanlis' New Democracy party had the strength needed to secure approval of the constitution in parliament on June 7. The 208 members of the New Democracy party present voted approval, and 8 absent party members also

Former dictator George Papadopoulos pleaded not guilty to high-treason charges as his trial began in July.

UPI

indicated their concurrence. The opposition groups in the 300-seat parliament did not appear. Following ratification of the document by the premier and by Greece's interim president, Michael Stassinopoulos, parliament chose a new president on June 19 by a vote of 210–65. He was Constantine Tsatsos, the candidate proposed by Caramanlis and one of the chief architects of the new constitution. The parliamentary opposition, though fragmented, called for a revision of the constitution to reduce the president's powers as a means of protecting civil liberties.

The Trials. Premier Caramanlis faced public clamor to see that justice prevailed against both those who had led the military regime in 1967–74 and those who had been involved in torture and other repressive acts. The premier moved cautiously to prevent the armed forces from thinking that the republican government was turning against them by bringing to trial formerly high military officials. This was a critical matter since the defection of the armed forces from the military regime over Cyprus in July 1974 was the chief means by which civilian rule had been reinstated in Greece.

In late July 1975, 20 leaders of the 1967 coup that had established the military dictatorship were brought to trial on charges of treason and insurrection. Among them were the former head of the government, George Papadopoulos, and two former deputy premiers, Stylianos Pattakos and Nicholas Makarezos. Dimitrios Ioannidis, former chief of the military police, who had masterminded the overthrow of Papadopoulos within the military regime in November 1973, was also brought to trial. On August 23, Papadopoulos, Pattakos, and Makarezos were sentenced to death, and Ioannidis was given life imprisonment. The government, however, commuted the three death sentences to life imprisonment. On September 12 a 36-day court martial ended with stern sentences imposed on 16 officers and enlisted men who were found guilty of torture and abuse of authority. Papadopoulos and Ioannidis went on trial again in October, along with 31 others, on charges stemming from the army's storming of Athens Polytechnic University in 1973. On December 30, Ioannides, Papadopoulos, and 19 others were convicted.

The Cyprus Issue. Greek-Turkish relations remained strained over the Cyprus issue since the Caramanlis government gave strong support to the president of Cyprus, Archbishop Makarios, in his stand against the Turkish occupation of part of the island. Caramanlis personally took a role in trying to find some solution to the problem and held meetings with French, U. S., Turkish, and British statesmen. A meeting in Brussels with Turkish Premier Süleyman Demirel resulted in a statement that their countries' disagreements should be settled peacefully. In October, Caramanlis visited England and Italy for consultations.

The unresolved Cyprus issue also affected Greece's relations with the United States. The strong efforts made by President Ford and Secretary of State Kissinger to persuade Congress to lift a ban against arms aid to Turkey gave anti-U. S. elements in Greece the opportunity to condemn U. S. policy as being pro-Turkish. The lifting of that ban in October caused further anti-U. S. agitation in Greece, and the Caramanlis government expressed regret at the decision.

GEORGE J. MARCOPOULOS
Tufts University

In June Christina Onassis, Aristotle Onassis' daughter, and Alexander Andreadis were married in Athens.

UPI

GREECE • Information Highlights

Official Name: Hellenic Republic.
Location: Southeastern Europe.
Area: 50,944 square miles (131,944 sq km).
Population (1975 est.): 8,900,000.
Chief Cities (1971 census): Athens, the capital, 867,023; Salonika, 345,799; Piraeus, 187,458.
Government: *Head of state,* Constantine Tsatsos, president (took office June 1975). *Head of government,* Constantine Caramanlis, premier (took office July 1974). *Legislature*—Parliament.
Monetary Unit: Drachma (30.08 drachmas equal U. S.$1, May 1975).
Gross National Product (1974 est.): $18,600,000,000.
Manufacturing (major products): Construction materials, textiles, chemicals, petroleum products, processed foods, metals, ships.
Major Agricultural Products: Tobacco, grapes, cotton, wheat, olives, citrus fruits, tomatoes, raisins.
Foreign Trade (1974): *Exports,* $2,038,000,000; *imports,* $4,385,000,000.

GUINEA-BISSAU

During its first full year of independence, Guinea-Bissau experienced some internal political difficulties and supported other former Portuguese colonies as they became independent.

Cape Verde Islands. The unresolved issue of the Cape Verde Islands continued to be a major preoccupation for the new government of Guinea-Bissau, and even, at one point, threatened its stability. The African Party for the Independence of Guinea and Cape Verde (PAIGC), Guinea-Bissau's leading party, was led by Cape Verdeans who were committed to liberate both the islands and Portuguese Guinea. Eventually the revolutionary leaders planned to unite the two territories. Portugal extended recognition of the Republic of Guinea-Bissau in 1974, but despite indications that the islanders strongly supported the PAIGC, Gen. António de Spinola's government insisted on postponing a decision on the status of the islands. At the end of March, a conspiracy to overthrow Guinea-Bissau's PAIGC government, and thereby block the seemingly inevitable extension of PAIGC control over the islands, was uncovered. All plotters had been associated with the former Portuguese administration, militia, or secret police. In the meantime, however, the new Portuguese government headed by Vasco Gonçalves had come to accept the PAIGC as the legitimate representative of the people of Cape Verde, and the islands became independent on June 5, 1975. Although legally separate, the governments of Guinea-Bissau and Cape Verde pledged to explore the possibility of linking the two territories into some sort of political union.

Domestic Developments. Following the attempted coup, and despite its earlier policy of not penalizing those who had sided with Portugal during the war of liberation, the government of Guinea-Bissau proceeded to arrest a number of persons. By early May the number of political detainees in the country was officially listed as 188. In economic developments, the banks were nationalized, and the government took majority control of the two major Portuguese commercial firms. The National Popular Assembly also nationalized major plantations and confiscated property belonging to "collaborators."

Foreign Affairs. The two major sources of aid for the government are Portugal and the USSR, which actively backed the liberation

---

─── **GUINEA-BISSAU · Information Highlights** ───

Official Name: Republic of Guinea-Bissau.
Location: West African Coast.
Area: 13,948 square miles (36,125 sq km).
Population (1975 est.): 500,000.
Chief City (1970 est.): Bissau, the capital, 62,101.
Government: *Head of state,* Luíz de Almeida Cabral, president (took office Sept. 1974). *Head of government,* Luíz Cabral.
Monetary Unit: Portuguese escudo (26.54 escudos equal U. S.$1, July 1975).
Major Agricultural Products: Groundnuts, rice, millet, coconuts, palm oil.

movement. Relations with Guinea, which gave the PAIGC unwavering support, were exceptionally cordial. Senegal, whose attitude toward the PAIGC was often more ambiguous, went out of its way to show goodwill toward the new government. The sense of solidarity that the PAIGC felt toward other liberation movements in the former Portuguese territories resulted in the development of close ties with the government of Mozambique and also led to Guinea-Bissau's prompt recognition of the MPLA government in Angola.

EDOUARD BUSTIN
Boston University

GUYANA

The regime of Prime Minister Lynden Forbes Burnham and his People's National Congress party tightened its control throughout the year. Burnham also continued his quest for international recognition and prestige for himself and his country.

Members of the principal opposition party, the pro-Soviet Communist People's Progressive party (PPP), headed by former premier Cheddi Jagan, continued to refuse to take their seats in parliament because they insisted that the last election had been stolen by the government. At the same time, there was a certain amount of persecution of the PPP and its leadership. Both Jagan's home and the headquarters of the PPP were raided by the police early in the year. In March, the Inter-American Press Association reported that freedom of the press was endangered in Guyana.

The government pushed forward its program of trying to put the economy of Guyana in Guyanese hands. To this end, the holdings of the Reynolds Bauxite Co. were purchased in January. Although the nominal price was $14.5 million, $6.9 million was deducted as a tax on the 1974 output of metal grade bauxite ore. With the purchase of the Reynolds property, the entire bauxite industry came under Guyanese government control.

The government also nationalized a small part of the sugar industry, the largest source of exports. In March it bought the holdings of the Demerara Company Ltd., which included two sugar factories and subsidiary operations.

In his efforts to widen his government's contacts and prestige, Prime Minister Burnham made a trip to Europe and Asia in March, visiting Rumania and China, where he was received by Premier Chou En-lai. In Cuba, in April, he talked extensively with Premier Fidel Castro. Burnham was impressed by what he saw in these countries, announcing that there was much that Guyana could learn from these "socialist" nations.

Guyana enjoyed added prestige during 1975 as a result of having been chosen as one of the nonpermanent members of the UN Security Council in December 1974.

——————— GUYANA · Information Highlights ———————

Official Name: Republic of Guyana.
Location: Northeast coast of South America.
Area: 83,000 square miles (214,970 sq km).
Population (1975 est.): 800,000.
Chief City (1970 census): Georgetown, the capital, 167,068 (metro. area).
Government: *Head of state,* Arthur Chung, president (took office March 1970). *Head of government,* Forbes Burnham, prime minister (Dec. 1964). *Legislature* (unicameral): National Assembly.
Monetary Unit: Guyana dollar (2.43 G. dollars equal U. S.$1, July 1975).
Gross National Product (1974 est.): $340,000,000.
Major Agricultural Products: Sugarcane, rice, corn.
Foreign Trade (1974): *Exports,* $216,000,000; *imports,* $210,000,000.

Economy. The economic picture in Guyana during the year was mixed. Inflation was serious, but government efforts to stimulate economic development continued. For the first time, Guyana could claim a merchant marine. In January the newly-established Guybulk Shipping Co. Ltd. took title to the motor vessel Arrocano, and in February it acquired a second ship. Both were designed principally to carry bauxite and were owned jointly by the Guyanese company and a Norwegian firm.

ROBERT J. ALEXANDER
Rutgers University

HAWAII

The year 1975 in Hawaii saw a growing consensus that islands limited in resources cannot indefinitely continue to support unlimited economic growth. From young Hawaiian activists to established industrialists, almost everyone agreed that the state must plan for its future and that political and social leaders must work to limit future development. Gov. George R. Ariyoshi's administration began preparing a state general plan to be finished by 1977. Major aims of the plan would include the expansion of Hawaii's agricultural self-sufficiency and the diversion of future population growth from Oahu, which has 80% of the state's people, to the outer islands.

A vital section of the plan would be a 10-year growth plan for the tourism industry. Two groups studying the future of Hawaii's economy —one public and one private—released results showing that tourism, not agriculture, would be the only viable way to provide sufficient jobs and capital during the next decade.

The conclusion did not entirely discourage those persons anxious to reduce Hawaii's dependence on tourism, a $1 billion industry subject to many factors beyond state control. However, the conclusion did underline the importance of keeping tourism from destroying Hawaii's fragile social and physical environment, which attracted almost 2.5 million visitors in 1975.

Efforts to boost agriculture were mixed. A $5.5 million state project to maintain agriculture on abandoned sugar lands teetered near failure. But during its five-year boundary review, the State Land Use Commission appeared more sensitive to farmers' demands to reclassify fewer agricultural lands as urban.

Ecological Efforts. The state legislature passed a shoreline protection bill designed to prohibit construction harmful to the coast. The Honolulu city council approved creation of special design districts around Diamond Head crater and Waikiki to prevent further deterioration of those already crowded areas.

To reduce Hawaii's increasing dependence on the automobile, planners completed work on a rapid transit design in Honolulu, and the state transportation director held the nation's first

State legislators and businessmen associated with Hawaii's tourist industry meet with Gov. George R. Ariyoshi (*second from left*) to discuss the industry's future.

HAWAII · Information Highlights

Area: 6,450 square miles (16,706 sq km).
Population (1974 est.): 847,000. *Density:* 129 per sq mi.
Chief Cities (1970 census): Honolulu, the capital, 324,-871; Kailua, 33,783; Kaneohe, 29,903; Hilo, 26,353.
Government (1975): *Chief Officers*—governor, George R. Ariyoshi (D); lt. gov., Nelson K. Doi (D). *Legislature*—Senate, 25 members; House of Representatives, 51 members.
Education (1974–75): *Enrollment*—public elementary schools, 94,609; public secondary schools, 82,421; nonpublic schools, 20,000; colleges and universities, 43,861 students. *Public school expenditures,* $181,-802,000 ($1,092 per pupil).
State Finances (fiscal year 1974): *Revenues,* $989,507,-000; *expenditures,* $990,859,000.
Personal Income (1974): $4,970,000,000; per capita, $5,882.
Labor Force (Aug. 1975): *Nonagricultural wage and salary earners,* 345,000; *insured unemployed,* 15,000.

state conference on ways to limit cars. The limitations would become part of the state general plan. Work also proceeded on plans to set up a state-owned, inter-island ferry system to improve communications. Several persons, including Lt. Gov. Nelson K. Doi, raised the idea of a U. S. constitutional amendment allowing Hawaii to limit in-migration.

Economy. The state's economy slowed down under recessionary pressures in 1975. Economists said Hawaii would probably never again experience the spectacular 20% annual personal-income gains of the 1960's. Tourism income equaled 1974 totals, and unemployment remained between 7% and 8%. Pineapple and sugar profits dipped from their high 1974 levels.

Political Developments. Politically, Democrats Gov. George Ariyoshi and Honolulu Mayor Frank F. Fasi, Ariyoshi's major primary opponent in 1974, continued to feud on a variety of issues. Fasi was expected to run for a third term as Honolulu's mayor and, if successful, to try for the governorship again in 1978.

Earthquake. On November 29 the islands were shaken by the area's strongest earthquakes in nearly 100 years. There were no deaths, but there was extensive property damage, and volcanic eruptions were triggered by the two earthquakes.

DAVID J. SMOLLAR
Honolulu "Advertiser"

HONG KONG

The economy of Hong Kong in 1975 was affected by the global economic recession, and many public projects were shelved. Queen Elizabeth made a four-day tour in May, marking the first visit to Hong Kong by a reigning British monarch.

Economy. In the first six months of 1975, exports dropped 14.5%, reexports 13%, and imports 17%, compared with the same period in 1974. Despite the economic slowdown, the number of registered companies rose from 32,609 in April 1974 to 36,552 in April 1975, and foreign companies from 843 to 878. U. S. investment in 136 companies amounted to $304 million. The

Hong Kong dollar was floated on Nov. 25, 1974, for an unlimited period of time. Travelers checks issued in Hong Kong dollars, and new coins for HK$2 and 20 cents were introduced in 1975.

The Tsimshatsui Cultural Complex, school building programs, and many other projects were postponed because of the lack of public funds. Despite the increase in taxes, there was still a deficit budgeted for 1975–76. The Loans Bill was passed to empower the government to borrow money and issue bonds. Hong Kong obtained from the Asian Development Bank a loan approval for $20 million annually for the next four or five years. The only loan from the bank to Hong Kong so far was $21.5 million for the Castle Peak desalinization plant, the world's largest, which began to produce drinking water in March.

The number of telephones reached 1 million in June. This gave an average of one telephone per four persons, the second highest rate in Asia after Japan.

Corruption. Since its establishment in February 1974, the Independent Commission Against Corruption has brought about the arrest of over 100 people. The conviction of several senior police officers highlighted the allegation of police corruption in Hong Kong.

Vietnamese Refugees. The government approached about 20 countries to give sanctuary to nearly 4,000 South Vietnamese refugees who arrived in Hong Kong in May 1975. By September, however, less than 1,000 had been accepted by the United States and some other countries.

Relationship with China. Under a secret agreement with Peking, the government began on Nov. 30, 1974, to return captured escapees to China. The number of captured illegal immigrants from China dropped from 690 in November 1974 to 52 in February 1975.

Hong Kong is still a major supplier of goods to China, and the Kowloon-Canton Railway carries an annual average of 1.2 million tons of freight and 14 million passengers. About 80 branches of the 12 pro-China banks in Hong Kong generate an annual average of $200 million in foreign exchange earnings for China.

CHUEN-YAN DAVID LAI
University of Victoria, B. C.

HONG KONG · Information Highlights

Location: Southeastern coast of China.
Area: 398 square miles (1,034 sq km).
Population (1975 est.): 4,200,000.
Chief City (1971): Victoria, the capital, 521,612.
Government: *Head of state,* Elizabeth II, queen (acceded Feb. 1952). *Head of government,* Sir Murray MacLehose, governor (took office 1971).
Monetary Unit: Hong Kong dollar (5.08 H. K. dollars equal U. S.$1, July 1974).
Gross National Product (1973 est.): $5,600,000,000.
Manufacturing (major products): Textiles, clothing, furniture, jewelry, electronic components.
Foreign Trade (1974): *Exports,* $5,060,000,000; *imports,* $5,686,000,000.

U. S. federal tax rebates of $2,000, which the government hoped would stimulate home buying, failed to generate much enthusiasm. The housing industry remained in a major slump throughout 1975.

HOUSING

The world's housing markets continued in the doldrums during 1975, particularly in those countries hardest hit by the energy crisis. The governments of many countries made attempts to overcome their housing slumps, and some new legislation was helpful to home builders and buyers, but governmental actions during the year were not sufficient to reverse the downward trends.

Housing in the United States

The housing industry is of fundamental importance to the health of the U. S. economy. A sharp rise in housing starts has led the recovery phase in all recessions but one since the end of World War II. Thus it is not surprising that the designers of U. S. economic policy for 1974–75 placed particular emphasis on the need to stimulate the declining housing market. It was generally feared that a failure of the housing market to turn upward would ruin all hopes for general economic recovery. As 1975 drew to a close, there was little evidence to convince most economists that new housing construction was on the upsurge or that the housing market would provide the needed spark for national economic recovery.

Expectations of a Banner Year in Housing. The year 1975 was widely forecast to be the year of recovery—in both the national economy and the housing market. Instead, the first quarter of 1975 saw an increase in the rate of decline in economic production and in housing production, providing little basis for optimism. The one glimmer of hope that did appear during this period

was a reduction in the rate of inflation. The double-digit rates seen in 1974 were reduced to below 7%, the lowest rate in nearly four years. In addition, savings and loan associations and mutual savings banks received record-high flows of new deposits during the first quarter of 1975, making home mortgages more readily available in most areas of the country.

Despite this early growth in savings, however, new private housing starts in 1975 were below the 1.3 million units of 1974, continuing the downward trend in total starts that began in 1973. During the first half of 1974, some 775,-000 unit starts were recorded, but during the same period in 1975 the number fell to 515,000 units. At mid-1975, some pointers indicated that the U. S. economy had turned from recession to recovery, but home building showed only sluggish signs of revival.

Housing Costs. The housing market was particularly affected by inflation during the early 1970's, and the median price of new homes sold rose from $23,900 in 1970 to $36,500 in 1975—an increase of nearly 53%. During this same period the Composite Constructions Cost Index of the Department of Commerce showed an increase of 56.9%. Housing rents rose significantly less than the cost of owner-occupied housing, with an increase of only 24.5% over the same five-year period. Nevertheless, housing rents received a great deal of attention during 1975 as various consumer groups pushed for some form of rent control.

Apartments. Multifamily housing construction fell throughout 1974 and continued to drop even further in 1975, with less than 200,000 starts for the entire year. Since rents increased at a rate less than the general price level for all

goods and services, there was little incentive for multifamily construction. In addition, mortgage funds for multifamily construction were in short supply and available only at relatively high rates.

The market for condominiums continued to suffer from the adverse publicity of 1974, as well as from the severe overbuilding of earlier years. In certain areas of the country, particularly in Florida and California, great numbers of condominium units remained unsold. For the nation as a whole, some 200,000 new condominiums were available for sale, and it should be some time before developers again become interested in this segment of the market.

Emergency Housing Act of 1975. At midyear, President Gerald Ford signed the Emergency Housing Act of 1975, which was designed both to support the sagging housing market and to provide assistance to economically pressed homeowners who were struggling to keep their homes. Specifically, the legislation increased the mortgage purchase authority of the Government National Mortgage Association (Ginnie Mae) by $10 billion, fixed the mortgage interest rate ceiling at 7.5%, and extended the program coverage to include condominium mortgages. In addition, the secretary of Housing and Urban Development was provided with standby authority to give temporary assistance to help defray mortgage payments on homes owned by persons temporarily unemployed or underemployed as a result of the recession. The special assistance was to take the form of co-insurance on loans or credits advanced by lending institutions and actual mortgage relief payments to lenders on behalf of eligible homeowners.

Real Estate Settlement Procedures Act of 1974. In December 1974 the Real Estate Settlement Procedures Act was signed into law, but it was not until June 1975 that the act was actually implemented. The legislation was enacted in response to the finding by Congress that many home buyers paid unnecessarily high settlement costs because of certain deceptive and fraudulent practices. The new law requires advance disclosure of all charges connected with transferring a real estate title and obtaining a mortgage loan used to finance the purchase of property. The purpose of the advance disclosure is to inform consumers of all closing costs at the time they apply for a mortgage loan to finance the purchase of a home and thus to make possible comparison shopping of settlement charges to enable the buyer to obtain competitive fees. By the year's end, Congress was taking action to modify the reporting requirements because of the claim that "red tape" caused unnecessary delays in processing home mortgages.

Tax Reduction Act of 1975. Another legislative action taken by Congress to aid home buyers and to attempt to stimulate the national housing market was the passage of the Tax Reduction Act of 1975, which was signed into law on March 30. The law authorizes a federal income tax credit of 5% of the purchase price of a new home that is bought or constructed by the taxpayer. The credit is applied against the actual tax owed by the home buyer and may not exceed $2,000. The law requires that the home must have been under construction before March 26, 1975, and the purchase made by the end of the year, but 1976 tax credits may be taken if the house was begun before March 26, 1975. The purchase must be made at the lowest price for which the home was ever offered for sale, preventing sellers from taking advantage of the tax credit. Furthermore, the new home must be the principal place of residence of the buyer, so the purchase of summer homes does not qualify under the act.

Congress estimated that the total tax credits allowable under the act could amount to $600 million, but by midyear, builders judged that the tax credit had stimulated very little additional home buying.

These congressional legislative actions represented significant moves to fight the national housing slump and aid home buyers in their quest for new and improved housing. However, the efforts seemed to have little real impact on improving the housing picture during 1975.

Housing in Canada

The pronounced downturns in Canadian housing starts that began during the latter half of 1974 continued through the early months of 1975. Another continuation of past trends was seen in housing prices. As were other countries during this period, Canada was plagued by inflation, but it was particularly rampant in the housing market. The long-recognized factor of the postwar "baby boom" was a dominant force in the increase in the demand for new housing. In addition, tax reform legislation in Canada has made home ownership about the only remaining type of investment from which tax-free capital gains can be realized. These factors played an important part in pushing housing prices even higher in 1975.

Rentals. In contrast to housing prices, rental costs increased by substantially less than general price levels, especially in the cities of Halifax, Montreal, Toronto, Vancouver, and Winnipeg. These "bargain" rentals were attributed to high levels of construction of rental housing during the past several years, with a total of over 440,-000 units built during 1971–74. In 1975, however, the number of apartment and row housing completions declined, resulting in an upward pressure on rents.

Housing in Other Countries

Western Europe. As in the United States, the Western European housing industry felt the general effects of economic recession throughout 1975. As governments reduced expenditures and raised the cost of borrowing to fight inflation, housing construction was a natural victim.

New York City's Galleria impressively incorporates shops, offices, and luxury apartments. The soaring central atrium is topped by a skylight.

DAVID K. SPECTER, AIA

Housing in West Germany, one of the world's strongest and most stable economies, went through its worst period in 30 years. Construction volume was down significantly in spite of the government's efforts to stimulate the home building industry through the funding of a variety of small projects.

The housing picture in France was similar, with the government creating an inflation-fighting budget for 1975 that cut back state-aided housing by nearly 10%. Inflation was one of the chief culprits in the French housing construction decline, with double-digit price increases that persisted for a large part of the year reducing construction volume. Soaring interest rates similarly dampened private housing starts, so that housing production in 1975 fell substantially from the level of the previous year.

The housing crisis in Italy reached drastic proportions in the early part of 1975, with 40,-000 Italians complaining of inadequate government action to supply low-income rental housing. An $83 million low-rent program has been delayed for more than three years, and if the 1975 rate of inflation continues, less than 3,000 of the planned 4,200 units can be constructed at current prices. New programs of apartment construction were announced to spur the languishing home-building industry, but Italy's shaky financial position cast doubt on the feasibility of many of these programs.

In Britain the construction industry had one of the nation's highest unemployment rates in 1975, and public expenditure cuts in the previous year, designed to combat inflation, created additional problems in the housing sector. At mid-year, the Labour government introduced a "buy-now-and-pay-later" plan to stimulate home building. The plan allows first-home buyers with annual incomes under $9,120 to defer part of their mortgage payments for up to 10 years on houses that cost less than $26,400. This plan was advanced in the hope of reversing the trend of declining housing starts in the nation. Much of Great Britain's housing is deteriorated, and new housing is needed.

Japan. In 1974, Japan experienced negative economic growth in real terms for the first time since the compilation of income statistics began in 1951. Private housing, however, ran counter to the decline in the general economy and continued a modest recovery during 1975. Government spending in the housing sector expanded by over 20%, but inflation eroded much of the benefit of this increase, so that the real increase in units constructed was far less.

Extreme land speculation both by major corporations and individuals continued to plague Japan's efforts to furnish housing at affordable prices for low and middle-income families. It is estimated, for example, that land prices in Tokyo increased an average of 4,000% from 1955 to 1975. Such increases in land cost make it nearly impossible to build housing near the center of Tokyo, within a commuting distance of an hour to an hour and a half.

STEPHEN D. MESSNER
University of Connecticut

HUNGARY

Domestic politics was of prime importance in Hungary in 1975, which saw the convening of the 11th Congress of the Hungarian Communist party and the election of a new National Assembly.

Domestic Affairs. On March 17–22, the 11th Congress of the Hungarian Communist party was attended by Leonid Brezhnev of the USSR and all the top leaders of the Warsaw Pact countries except Rumania's President Nicolae Ceauşescu. Various party and state reforms were recommended, and goals for the fifth five-year plan (1976–80) were formulated. The party's central committee was enlarged from 105 to 125 members. Nine members of the Politburo were reelected, and four were replaced.

On June 15 the new National Assembly was elected, and its tenure was extended to five years. Of 7,760,464 eligible voters, 7,527,169 deposited valid votes. The Communist-led Patriotic People's Front received 7,497,060 votes, approximately 99.6%. János Kádár, first secretary of the Hungarian Socialist Workers' (Communist) party, received 99.9% of the votes cast for his office, and Premier Gyorgy Lazar received 99.8%. The new assembly elected the highest officials in the executive and judicial branches of the government. Former Premier Jenö Fock, who resigned in May, was replaced by Lazar, an influential member of the Politburo.

A new law was passed reorganizing and improving social insurance for retirement; old age pensions; and widows' support; as well as disability, orphans', maternity, family, and funeral allowances. Party recommendations to increase agricultural output during the years 1976–80 by 16% to 18% and per capita real income by 23% to 25% were favorably discussed. The ministry of culture was reorganized.

Economy. According to the official data released in the spring of 1975, the national income increased in 1974 by 7%, industrial production by 8.2%, agricultural production by 3.7%, and real wages by 5.5%. Exports grew by 11.7% and imports by 34.4%, causing a trade deficit of over $600 million. The trade balance with the socialist countries was favorable, however. Tourism increased by 15%. About 8.3 million foreigners visited Hungary, 80% of them coming from the socialist countries. Over 3 million Hungarians went abroad, 92% of them to other socialist countries.

Contrary to expectations and in spite of official optimism, the economic situation worsened in 1975. Increased prices of imports from the West, deficiencies in planning, as well as decreasing productivity resulted in shortages of various consumer goods. Party and state officials called upon the population to face the difficulties with understanding and to exercise self-restraint.

In January wholesale prices increased by 8%.

UPI

Soviet leader Leonid Brezhnev speaks at the 11th Congress of the Hungarian Communist party in March.

In August the prices of gasoline and construction materials were increased by 20% to 49%. Most of the newspapers and several magazines reduced the frequency and size of their editions to balance the higher cost of print paper, mostly imported. Shortages of textiles and leather goods were reported in the press. The national bank severely curtailed its hard currency loan program, raised interest rates, and prohibited imports of nonessential western products, particularly automobiles and luxury goods.

In order to increase labor productivity several economic reforms were inaugurated; for example, restructuring relations between enterprises and government planning organs, and

─────── **HUNGARY · Information Highlights** ───────

Official Name: Hungarian Peoples Republic.
Location: Southeast central Europe.
Area: 35,919 square miles (93,030 sq km).
Population (1975): 10,500,000.
Chief Cities (1975 est.): Budapest, the capital, 2,039,000; Miskolc, 190,000; Debrecen, 173,000.
Government: *Head of state,* Pál Losonczi, chairman of the presidential council (took office 1967). *Head of government,* Gyorgy Lazar, premier (took office 1975). *First Secretary of the Hungarian Socialist Workers' (Communist) party,* János Kádár (took office 1956). *Legislature* (unicameral)—Parliament.
Monetary Unit: Forint (9.39 forints equal U. S.$1, Aug. 1975).
Gross National Product (1974 est.): $19,500,000,000.
Manufacturing (major products): Machinery and tools, vehicles, chemicals, pharmaceuticals.
Major Agricultural Products: Corn, wheat, potatoes.
Foreign Trade (1974): *Exports,* $4,991,000,000; *imports,* $5,426,000,000.

introducing "enterprise democracy" by which the workers would have a greater voice in management.

Foreign Policy and Trade. Government and party spokesmen as well as the mass media emphasized the advantages of détente and international cooperation. The Conference on Security and Cooperation in Europe, held in Helsinki, was widely praised, and the Soviet position was applauded.

In January an agreement was reached with the Soviet Union to increase trade between both countries by 8.3%, to about $2.8 billion annually. The Soviet Union also committed itself to deliver substantial quantities of oil and oil products at 1974 price levels.

In June the Council for Mutual Economic Assistance (COMECON) met in Budapest to analyze the results of the member countries' five-year plans ending in 1975. A greater economic integration through increased joint-capital investments was agreed upon, and several joint projects involving two or more countries were to be executed during 1976–80.

Although greater cooperation with the Soviet Union was considered a necessity, the usefulness of trade with the West was also conceded. The delegates agreed that greater efforts were needed to synchronize national plans within the COMECON community.

JAN KARSKI
Georgetown University

ICELAND

During 1975 Iceland extended its fishing limits in a controversial move aimed at curtailing foreign fishing.

Fisheries Limit. On October 15 Iceland's fisheries limit was extended to 200 nautical miles (370 km) and agreements that had permitted some foreign fishing inside the previous 50-nautical-mile (93-km) zone expired a month later. Although there had been some discussion, no new accord had been reached with nations claiming fishing interests in waters inside the extended fisheries zone.

Toward the end of November, however, an accommodation was made with West Germany, which had not recognized the 50-mile limit adopted in 1973 and continued trawler operations in defiance of Icelandic coast guard vessels. Of the nations contesting Iceland's new move to prevent overexploitation of fish stocks, Britain lodged the most vocal protests, breaking off talks and dispatching a small naval force to protect its trawlers from harassment and capture by Icelandic patrol boats. Acrimony increased after a ramming and shooting incident on December 11 between Icelandic and British vessels.

The 200-mile extension was the latest in a series of moves to gain full control of fisheries on the continental shelf, implementing a policy that Iceland set as far back as 1948. Prior

extensions took place in 1952, 1958, and 1973. Britain opposed all of these moves, invoking trade sanctions the first time and resorting to naval action on the latter two occasions, as it did for the third time to the dismay and anger of Icelanders.

All of Iceland's efforts to curtail foreign fishing in nearby waters were dictated by the fact that the economy is overwhelmingly dependent on exports derived from fisheries. Widespread support for the concept of 200-mile economic jurisdiction at the Caracas Conference on the Law of the Sea was cited as justification for extending the fishing limit, as were findings by Icelandic and British marine researchers, indicating that several species of demersal fish were endangered.

Iceland's fishing industry was ill prepared to compete with operations subsidized by other European nations where fisheries are of marginal economic importance, and Iceland has been hit hard by trade barriers against fish products exported to the European Economic Community.

Economy. Largely due to low prices for fish on international markets, the Icelandic economy declined in 1975. Its foreign trade position deteriorated during the year, as did real income, and further hardships loomed ahead if circumstances remained unchanged. Other economic woes stemmed from the soaring prices of imported oil, large amounts of which were needed for the fishing fleet and for ocean transport. However, determined efforts to harness domestic sources of energy—both hydroelectric and geothermal—for electricity and home heating continued at an accelerated rate.

With foreign exchange reserves dropping, the Icelandic currency (*króna*), already devalued in August 1974, was again devalued by 20% in February. Although there was little labor unrest except for a trawlermen's strike in the spring, government plans to control the galloping inflation of about 50%, the highest among the OECD (Organization for Economic Cooperation and Development) nations, were not successful.

HAUKUR BÖDVARSSON
"Icelandic Review"

——— ICELAND • Information Highlights ———
Official Name: Republic of Iceland.
Location: North Atlantic Ocean.
Area: 39,768 square miles (103,000 sq km).
Population (1975 est.): 200,000.
Chief City (1974 est.): Reykjavik, the capital, 90,000.
Government: *Head of state,* Kristján Eldjárn, president (took office for 2d 4-year term Aug. 1972). *Head of government,* Geir Hallgrímsson, prime minister (took office Aug. 1974). *Legislature*—Althing: Upper House and Lower House.
Monetary Unit: Króna (158 krónur equal U.S.$1, July 1975).
Gross National Product (1973 est.): $700,000,000.
Manufacturing (major products): Fish products, clothing, shoes, chemicals, fertilizers.
Major Agricultural Products: Potatoes, hay, dairy products, fish, sheep.
Foreign Trade (1974): *Exports,* $346,000,000; *imports,* $553,000,000.

IDAHO

In 1975, landlocked Idaho opened a "seaport" that linked it with the Pacific Ocean via the Snake and Columbia rivers. The legislature had an active session, and adverse weather hampered agriculture.

Legislation. The legislature increased general fund spending from $199.4 million in 1974 to $222.6 million in 1975. State legislators increased appropriations for public schools from $70.6 million to $86.3 million and those for higher education from $42 million to $49 million. They also instituted state support for kindergartens. After much resistance, the legislature appropriated nearly $6 million of the $23 million anticipated budget surplus to match federal highway funds.

In other legislative action, a small start in land-use planning was made. Bills were introduced requiring automobile liability insurance, prohibiting smoking in public places, and setting a $100,000 limit on medical malpractice suits. A district court later ruled that the malpractice act was unconstitutional. The legislature passed a tax relief bill favoring people with higher incomes, but Gov. Cecil Andrus vetoed it.

For the third consecutive year, opponents of the Equal Rights Amendment attempted, but failed, to withdraw the state's 1972 ratification. Other bills that failed included those to allow collective bargaining for public employees, to give cities new sources of tax revenues, and to change rape to sexual assault and to apply to both sexes.

Environment and Natural Resources. A very cold spring hampered crop growth, and unusual August rains further slowed growth and delayed harvesting. Fall rains made good fall pastures and gave the next year's crops an excellent start.

Lewiston dedicated its inland "seaport." The $344 million project links the Snake River with a widened Columbia River leading out to the Pacific Ocean. Barges started carrying grain to coastal areas and returning with heavy cargo.

North Idaho Indians asked for the return to them of Heyburn State Park. They alleged that leasing lakeside cottage sites violates the park's dedication for public purposes and voids the transfer of the former Indian territory to the state.

The state fish and game department initiated a "catch and release" steelhead program so that fishing will not deplete the resource further. A program to have sandhill cranes hatch and raise the almost-extinct whooping cranes seemed to have succeeded.

Other Events. A district court held that dependence by state school districts on unequal property valuations to finance public education violated the state constitution's equal protection clause. The state supreme court reversed that finding, saying any changes in the method of taxation should be made by the legislature, not the courts.

Rep. George Hansen of Pocatello became the first member of Congress to be sentenced to jail for violation of the 1971 Federal Election Campaign Act that requires the filing of campaign finances. The jail sentence was commuted in April. Teachers' strikes took place in six school districts in the fall. A poll taken in Boise revealed that 55% of the participants thought state employees to be dishonest.

CLIFFORD DOBLER
University of Idaho

ILLINOIS

Illinois agriculture experienced a record year, but the state's politicians found 1975 frustrating. The state's two top Democrats, Gov. Daniel Walker and Mayor Richard J. Daley of Chicago, continued a bitter feud with an eye on the 1976 elections.

Agriculture. Nearly $2 billion worth of grain and other products from Illinois farms were exported overseas in fiscal 1975. It represented 9% of the nation's farm exports according to federal government figures. An ideal growing season with spring rains and a warm summer brought in a record corn crop. Agricultural experts estimated a harvest of 1.2 billion bushels of corn and 286.6 million bushels of soybeans.

Politics. The Democratic party started the year in firm control of the Illinois General Assembly. The Democrats had a majority of 101 seats to 76 for the Republicans in the House and of 34 seats to 25 in the Senate. But the ideological dispute between Walker, an independent Democrat, and Daley, an organization Democrat, prevented the party from capitalizing on its majority in the legislature.

Clyde Choate, a downstate representative, made a bid for speaker of the House. He had Daley's support but was opposed by Walker. The Republican minority held together, while the Democrats split. After marathon balloting it became clear that Choate could not muster enough votes. Daley switched his organization support to William Redmond, a man also ac-

---

IDAHO • Information Highlights

Area: 83,557 square miles (216,413 sq km).
Population (1974 est.): 799,000. *Density:* 9 per sq mi.
Chief Cities (1970 census): Boise, the capital, 74,990; Pocatello, 40,036; Idaho Falls, 35,776.
Government (1975): *Chief Officers*—governor, Cecil D. Andrus (D); lt. gov., John V. Evans (D). *Legislature* —Senate, 35 members; House of Representatives, 70 members.
Education (1974–75): *Enrollment*—public elementary schools, 91,060; public secondary schools, 96,492; nonpublic schools, 5,700; colleges and universities, 35,714 students. *Public school expenditures,* $134,438,000 ($771 per pupil).
State Finances (fiscal year 1974): *Revenues* $535,975,000; *expenditures* $503,965,000.
Personal Income (1974): $3,943,000,000; per capita, $4,934.
Labor Force (Aug. 1975): *Nonagricultural wage and salary earners,* 275,200; *insured unemployed,* 9,400.

UPI

Part of a record corn crop is piled on a field in Illinois, which had a lack of grain-elevator space.

Bills on no-fault automobile insurance, tough gun controls, and collective bargaining rights for public employees and teachers failed. The legislature selected the monarch butterfly as the official state insect and decided to let schoolchildren select a state animal by referendum.

Toward the end of the legislative session, Governor Walker said the state was heading for a fiscal crisis, and he ordered a 6% across-the-board cut in the budget. This triggered strong reaction from special-interest organizations, but Walker was adamant. He said the alternative was an increase in taxes, which he refused to support. Even with the cuts, some fiscal experts warned that the state would have a deficit.

More pressure was added when public school teachers in Chicago got a favorable contract that required the city to seek more state funds. Daley mounted an intensive campaign in the legislature to get the needed money for the Chicago school system. After he won by one vote in the House of Representatives, a coalition of Republicans and independent Democrats defeated Daley's efforts in the Senate.

While the Democrats feuded, the Republicans attempted to reorganize after being badly defeated in the 1974 elections. James Thompson, U. S. Attorney in Chicago, resigned to bid for the Republican gubernatorial nomination. Richard Cooper, a businessman, also announced for the GOP nomination. Thompson had earned a strong reputation for convicting several powerful politicians, including former Gov. Otto Kerner and close associates of Mayor Daley.

Jobs. Unemployment in Illinois and the Chicago area was the highest since the Depression years. Statewide figures for September were 495,800 unemployed or 9.8% of the work force. Chicago area figures were higher with 326,900 or 10.2% of the work force unemployed. Some communities in the southern portion of the state reported higher unemployment rates, whereas others were relatively unaffected and had unemployment as low as 4%.

DAVID E. HALVORSEN
"Chicago Tribune"

ceptable to Walker. Redmond, with a long legislative career in the House ranks, admitted he was awed by the speakership but attempted to bring the Democrats together.

The split between Walker and Daley was too deep to allow party unity. Daley attempted to get a new congressional reapportionment plan through the legislature and failed. He tried to restrict the crossover voting permitted in the Illinois primaries, and failed. He sought to remove the Walker roadblock to construction of the crosstown expressway on Chicago's west side and failed. Walker, on the other hand, could not get legislative support for a $4.5 million bond program that he said would stimulate construction and create 60,000 jobs badly needed in the state because of the recession.

Legislative Action. Because of the political turmoil, the General Assembly did not have a productive session. The legislature did pass a bill giving tax breaks to the elderly and to farmers. Another major bill that became law set a limit of $500,000 on malpractice suits against doctors. The bill also established a review board consisting of a doctor, a lawyer, and a judge to screen all cases.

A controversial redlining bill was passed. Redlining is the practice by lending institutions of refusing mortgage or home improvement loans, primarily in deteriorated neighborhoods. The law requires lending institutions to disclose by geographical areas where they make loans and gives persons who believe they are victims of redlining the right to accuse the institutions.

ILLINOIS · Information Highlights

Area: 56,400 square miles (146,076 sq km).
Population (1974 est.): 11,131,000. *Density:* 200 per sq mi.
Chief Cities (1970 census): Springfield, the capital, 91,753; Chicago, 3,369,359; Rockford, 147,370.
Government (1975): *Chief Officers*—governor, Daniel Walker (D); lt. gov., Neil F. Hartigan (D). *General Assembly*—Senate 59 members; House of Representatives 177 members.
Education (1974–75): *Enrollment*—public elementary schools, 1,572,145 pupils; public secondary, 724,096; nonpublic, 407,000; colleges and universities, 533,388 students. *Public school expenditures,* $2,625,542,000 ($1,246 per pupil).
State Finances (fiscal year 1974): *Revenues,* $7,254,548,000; *expenditures,* $6,523,804,000.
Personal Income (1974): $70,534,000,000; per capita, $6,337.
Labor Force (July 1975): *Nonagricultural wage and salary earners,* 4,295,100; *insured unemployed,* 214,000 (5%).

Prime Minister Gandhi speaks to supporters outside her home in June as opposition to her mounted.

INDIA

With the proclamation of a national emergency on June 26, India was confronted with the most serious political crisis since independence, raising doubts about the future of the democratic experiment. Internally, the economic picture improved considerably, but imports, the balance of payments deficit, and debt service liabilities all increased alarmingly.

Opposition to Gandhi. The year began with a wave of violence. Among the victims was Railway Minister L. N. Mishra, who died as a result of a bomb explosion in Samastipur, Bihar, on Jan. 2, 1975. He was the first Indian cabinet minister to be assassinated. The growing agitation against the government of Prime Minister Gandhi by a variety of leftist and rightist groups led by Jayaprakash Narayan, known as J. P., created an atmosphere of uncertainty in the country. One of the largest demonstrations was staged in New Delhi on March 6, when J. P. led a "people's march" of over 100,000 persons and presented a number of demands to the parliament.

In April, shortly after the government announced its decision to extend president's rule (direct rule by the central government) in Gujarat another six months, Morarji Desai went on a "fast unto death" in support of the demand for an election in that state. After Desai, a former

deputy prime minister and a prominent leader of the Congress party, had fasted a week, Prime Minister Indira Gandhi yielded and promised elections in a few weeks. Following an intensive campaign, during which the major opposition parties formed a "Janata Front" and Gandhi campaigned vigorously in many parts of the state, the elections were held on June 8 and 11. The results were a surprising reverse for the Congress party, whose strength in the Gujarat Assembly fell from 140 to 75 seats. The Janata Front won 87 seats and on June 18 formed a government, led by Babubhai Patel as chief minister.

Shortly before the results of the Gujarat elections became known, Gandhi experienced an even more severe reverse when the judge of the High Court of Allahabad (Gandhi's home city) ruled that Gandhi had been guilty of corrupt election practices in her constituency in Uttar Pradesh during the general elections in 1971. If upheld, the decision would have disbarred Gandhi from political life for six years. Gandhi appealed this decision, and announced that she would remain as prime minister. Her legal right to remain in office, pending the decision of the Supreme Court on her appeal, was affirmed by a judge of the Supreme Court on June 24. On the following evening the main opposition groups staged a mammoth rally in New Delhi, at which J. P. appealed to the military, the police, and the civil servants to turn against the "corrupt" government and issued a call for a one-week national campaign of resistance, beginning on June 29.

Political Crisis and Aftermath. That night many opposition leaders, including J. P. and Morarji Desai, were arrested, and in the early morning of June 26 the president of India proclaimed a national emergency under Article 352 of the Indian constitution. He cited a threat to the security of the country due to "internal disturbances." It was the first time a national emergency had been proclaimed for this reason. In a broadcast to the nation on the same day, Gandhi said that the emergency was necessary because "forces of disintegration are in full play, and communal passions are being aroused, threatening our unity." She expressed confidence that "internal conditions will speedily improve to enable us to dispense with this proclamation as soon as possible."

Immediately after the proclamation of emergency, strict censorship was imposed on all Indian newspapers and all foreign correspondents. The restrictions were tightened in subsequent weeks, as reflected in the tough "guidelines for the press" issued on July 22. In the first four months of the emergency six foreign correspondents were expelled, and restrictions were placed on the facilities available to foreign broadcasters. Some Indian newspapers were suppressed, and a few editors were arrested. The best known Indian journalist to be arrested, Kuldip Nayar, editor of the *Indian Express,* the largest English language newspaper in India, was released on

September 12. Three days later his arrest was declared to be illegal by the New Delhi High Court. Political debate in India virtually ceased after the emergency was proclaimed.

The Indian Parliament began a special three-week session on July 21, with some 30 members under arrest and with most of the opposition members boycotting the sessions. It ratified the emergency proclamation and amended the constitution to make a declaration of national emergency "non-justiciable." It also amended the Maintenance of Internal Security Act of 1951 to take away natural law or common law rights for a person detained under the act and amended both the basic electoral law and the constitution to invalidate retroactively any court judgment declaring the election of a prime minister to be void. On November 7 a five-man bench of the Supreme Court, in a historic decision, ruled that Gandhi was not guilty because of the changes in the election laws made by Parliament in August.

Jayaprakash Narayan leads some 100,000 demonstrators opposing the policies of Indira Gandhi.

UPI

Although the proclamation of emergency and the draconian measures that followed were strongly criticized in other democratic countries, and to some extent in India itself, most Indians seemed to feel that the country needed the kind of shock treatment that Gandhi administered. They seemed to be particularly pleased by the promise of various economic and social reforms, the decline in prices of basic commodities, the crackdown on hoarders, black-marketers, and "undesirable elements," and the increased courtesy and efficiency in the bureaucracy.

Gandhi's long-term intentions remained unclear, but she insisted that she still believed in democracy and wished to restore normal democratic freedoms "as soon as possible," without the permissiveness and license of the past. She pointed out that she was using constitutional methods to meet an extra-constitutional challenge that no government could ignore, but she did not hesitate to resort to measures that gave her increasingly broad powers. These powers were seemingly made permanent in December. A presidential ordinance transferred some censorship regulations into permanent law and the Congress party, at its annual session, unanimously approved resolutions calling for major constitutional changes, the indefinite extension of the emergency, and the postponement of the 1976 general elections until 1977.

Other Political Developments. On November 30 several important changes in the central council of ministers were announced. Swaran Singh, who had been a cabinet member in various posts since 1952, was removed as minister of defense. G. S. Dhillon, speaker of the Lok Sabha, became minister of shipping and transport. Bansi Lal, chief minister of Haryana, was appointed defense minister on December 19.

Important developments in the Indian states in 1975, in addition to those in Gujarat, included an unexpected change in government in Maharashtra in late February, when S. B. Chavan replaced V. P. Naik as chief minister. Sheikh Abdullah was installed as chief minister of Jammu and Kashmir on February 25, a position from which he had been removed in 1953. In Nagaland, president's rule was proclaimed on March 22, and on November 11 the government reached an accord with leaders of the underground movement in Nagaland. A vote in Sikkim in April to abolish the post of Chogyal and to merge with India made possible the incorporation of Sikkim as the 22nd state in the Indian Union in May. On November 30 president's rule was proclaimed in Uttar Pradesh, India's most populous state and the home state of Gandhi.

The Economy. In spite of a number of adverse factors, the economic picture improved in 1975. After three bad years, the monsoon rains were good in most parts of the country, and a bumper grain crop was harvested. By mid-1975 inflation, which had risen to 31% in 1974, was almost completely halted. The emergency seemed

to have a healthy effect on the economy. On July 1, Gandhi announced a 20-point program of economic reforms, including land reforms, a ceiling on urban property, relief for rural debtors, and minimum wages for agricultural laborers. Later economic and social reforms included plans to set up a chain of rural banks, to assure equal pay for women, to end the custom of the dowry, and to institute a 12-point program leading to a policy of nationwide prohibition.

The annual report of the Reserve Bank of India for 1974–75, released on September 13, indicated that the outlook for growth in India in 1975–76 was quite bright. In spite of the semi-stagnation in the industrial sector and an overall growth rate of only about 2% in the economy in 1974–75, the report stated that a growth rate of 5%–6% in 1975–76 should be possible. It called attention to the halting of inflation—a major achievement—and to the strong prospect of increases in national income (which had fallen in 1974–75), in the allocations for development, and in external aid. Among the unfavorable factors listed in the report were the probable continuance of the foreign exchange gap at existing levels, an increase in the trade deficit, and budget deficits of both the central and the state governments.

A growth in the volume of exports in 1974–75 of about 29%, while impressive, was more than offset by a 49% increase in the cost of imports. The outlay for imports of oil alone amounted to $1.5 billion. Debt service obligations continued to rise sharply.

Foreign Relations. Domestic problems and developments overshadowed foreign policy in 1975. On Jan. 9, 1975, India became the first non-Arab country to extend official recognition to the Palestine Liberation Organization. It granted the PLO full diplomatic status and gave it permission to open an office in New Delhi. Also in January, Gandhi made official visits to the Maldive Republic and to Iraq. In late April and early May she participated in the Commonwealth Prime Ministers Conference in Kingston, Jamaica.

India-Pakistan relations, which seemed to be improving in 1972–74, remained stalemated in 1975, especially after the breakdown in May of talks on the resumption of air links. Indian reactions to the coup in Bangladesh in mid-August were quite muted. Gandhi and other Indian leaders deplored the assassination of Sheikh Mujibur Rahman and members of his family, but the government of India extended recognition to the new government in Bangladesh on August 27.

Indian relations with the United States remained cool. When Daniel P. Moynihan left India in early January, after serving as U. S. ambassador for two years, he expressed regret that the relations between the United States and India were so "thin" and "fragile." U. S. reactions to India's recognition of the PLO were quite critical. The most serious blow to Indo-U. S. relations in 1975 was the decision by the U. S. government, announced on February 24, to lift the 10-year-old embargo on arms sales to India and Pakistan, a

Prime Minister Gandhi meets with Mexican President Luis Echeverría in July. Echeverría visited during the furor over the prime minister's activities.

UPI

Indian laborers involved in a program sponsored by CARE earn food for their work on an earthen dam in Madhya Pradesh.

UPI

move welcomed in Pakistan but strongly criticized in India. The Indian government lodged an official protest, and Foreign Minister Y. B. Chavan canceled plans to go to Washington in March for the first meeting of the Indo-U. S. Joint Commission. This had been agreed on when Secretary of State Kissinger visited India in October 1974.

When William Saxbe presented his credentials as the new U. S. ambassador on March 8, the president of India departed somewhat from protocol to express his concern over "recent developments." Indians were upset by the widespread criticism in the United States of the proclamation of national emergency and Gandhi's emergency measures. They were further disturbed by President Ford's cancellation of plans to visit India in 1975 and by his expressions of regret at the turn of events in India. These feelings were somewhat assuaged in October, when Foreign Minister Chavan reconsidered his earlier refusal and joined Kissinger in presiding over the first meeting of the Indo-U. S. Joint Commission. At that time President Ford assured Chavan that he meant no offense to India and hoped to visit India at some later date.

In late September and early October, President Fakhruddin Ali Ahmed made an official nine-day visit to Hungary and Yugoslavia. Among the distinguished official visitors to India in 1975 were Adam Malik, foreign minister of Indonesia, and Dzemal Bijedic, prime minister of Yugoslavia.

General. India entered the space age on April 19 with the launching of its first earth satellite, named Aryabhata. It was built by Indian scientists with the assistance of Soviet scientists, and launched from a site in the Soviet Union.

On August 1, India's first Satellite Instructional Television Experiment (SITE) project became operational. On a one-year experimental basis, educational programs prepared in India were beamed to 2,400 villages in 6 Indian states. They were transmitted from a U. S.-built communications satellite, positioned over Africa and made available by the U. S. National Aeronautics and Space Administration.

On December 27, an explosion, followed by flooding, hit a coal mine in Bihar state, about 160 miles (255 km) northwest of Calcutta. About 400 miners were estimated to have died in the disaster.

Among the prominent Indians who died in 1975 were Sarvepalli Radhakrishnan, a world-famous philosopher and the second president of India, and Kumaraswami Kamaraj, a former "king-maker" in the undivided Congress party.

NORMAN D. PALMER
University of Pennsylvania

--------- **INDIA · Information Highlights** ---------

Official Name: Republic of India.
Location: South Asia.
Area: 1,266,598 square miles (3,280,483 sq km).
Population (1974 est.): 613,200,000.
Chief Cities (1973 est.): New Delhi, the capital, 3,600,-000; Bombay, 6,000,000; Madras, 2,500,000.
Government: *Head of state,* Fakhruddin Ali Ahmed, president (took office Aug. 1974). *Head of government,* Mrs. Indira Gandhi, prime minister (took office Jan. 1966). *Legislature*—Parliament: Rajya (Council of States) and Lok Sabha (House of the People).
Monetary Unit: Rupee (8.576 rupees equal U. S.$1, July 1975).
Gross National Product (1974 est.): $86,700,000,000.
Manufacturing (major products): Iron and steel, industrial machinery and equipment, chemicals.
Major Agricultural Products: Rice, wheat, groundnuts, barley, sesame, sugarcane, corn, rubber.
Foreign Trade (1974): *Exports,* $4,186,000,000; *imports,* $5,324,000,000.

INDIANA

Indiana's economy showed signs of an upswing in late 1975 as bumper corn crops were harvested, and unemployment declined. Politics and politicians also made news.

Legislation. The Indiana General Assembly enacted significant legislation during its long 61-day session, including a new provision for nomination of governor, lieutenant governor, and U. S. senators by direct primary rather than by state party convention. A bill limiting malpractice judgments against doctors and their insurers to a maximum of $500,000 was hotly debated but eventually passed.

Legislators also approved a new county court system to replace justice of the peace courts, except in Lake county, by 1976, and all town and city courts, except in Gary, Hammond, and East Chicago, by 1980. In a rare action the Indiana Supreme Court issued an opinion that declared unconstitutional a portion of the county court law that would allow laymen to serve as judges. No case contesting the law had been brought before the justices. Additional legislation gave judges the power to spare rape victims from having to testify about their past personal and sexual experiences unless the court determined beforehand that such testimony bore on the alleged crime. A campaign contribution law allowing unions and corporations to make limited political contributions in elections for nonfederal offices was also passed.

The General Assembly rejected measures that would have provided for no-fault insurance, instituted a state lottery, established minimum liquor and wine prices, and repealed the phosphate detergent ban. Also defeated were both the state and federal equal rights amendments. Gov. Otis R. Bowen vetoed bills intended to decriminalize public intoxication and to provide special noncriminal treatment for persons found drunk in public, and legislation that permitted county councils to authorize pari-mutuel betting at state-licensed horse race tracks.

Budget. The General Assembly, in a last-minute race to avoid a special session, put together a one-year budget of approximately $3 billion. Of this amount, $25 million in revenue-sharing funds was set aside for counties, cities, and towns, and $43.5 million was designated for highway maintenance. The principal beneficiaries under the new budget were the state's mental hospitals. In danger of closing altogether or severely curtailing their staff and services, mental institutions received sufficient state funding to enlarge their facilities and to hire 200 new employees.

Property tax relief was held to the statutory minimum of 20% for 1976. Governor Bowen vetoed budget measures raising the state adjusted gross income tax exemption for dependents from $500 to $1,000, and providing for a flat grant of $40 per pupil, based on average daily attendance, for each school corporation in the state.

Economy. More than 250,000 Hoosiers were jobless during the first six months of 1975, but Indiana's economy began a gradual upswing in July. Unemployment compensation claims peaked in April and then declined. The state's extensive automotive industry, however, improved less rapidly than other sectors of the economy. Because of a bumper corn crop and increased cattle sales, Indiana's farm income in 1975 exceeded the record gross cash receipts of $3.2 billion in 1974.

The Southwind Maritime Center near Evansville, a new port on the Ohio River, opened formally on October 8 with the arrival of the first commercial barge shipment. This facility provides the southern part of the state with year-round shipping facilities.

Elections. Democrats made numerical gains in municipal elections in Indiana on November 4, but their successes appeared to be the result of local issues and conditions rather than reflections of national politics. Significant Republican victories included the retention of the Indianapolis mayoralty, where former Rep. William G. Hudnut succeeded Mayor Richard G. Lugar.

Lugar was expected to announce his candidacy in 1976 for the U. S. Senate seat of Democrat R. Vance Hartke. Hartke was already challenged by former Republican Gov. Edgar D. Whitcomb. Republican Otis R. Bowen will seek his second consecutive term as governor of Indiana in 1976, and on October 21, at his farm near Shirkieville, Democratic Sen. Birch E. Bayh, Jr., announced his candidacy for the presidency of the United States.

Encephalitis. Indiana was one of the worst-hit states in the outbreak of viral encephalitis that swept through the United States in the fall of 1975. There were more than 40 confirmed cases, and at least 14 deaths were attributed to the disease. Marion, Allen, and Bartholomew counties were among the hardest hit.

LORNA LUTES SYLVESTER, *Indiana University*

INDIANA · Information Highlights

Area: 36,291 square miles (93,994 sq km).
Population (1974 est.): 5,330,000. *Density:* 147 per sq mi.
Chief Cities (1970 census): Indianapolis, the capital, 744,743; Fort Wayne, 178,021; Gary, 175,415; Evansville, 138,764.
Government (1975): *Chief Officers*—governor, Otis R. Bowen (R); lt. gov., Robert D. Orr (R). *General Assembly*—Senate, 50 members; House of Representatives, 100 members.
Education (1974–75): *Enrollment*—public elementary schools, 620,234 pupils; public secondary, 566,560; nonpublic, 98,300; colleges and universities, 203,833 students. *Public school expenditures,* $1,032,288,000 ($927 per pupil).
State Finances (fiscal year 1974): *Revenues,* $2,734,000,000; *expenditures,* $2,275,371,000.
Personal Income (1974): $28,053,000,000; per capita, $5,263.
Labor Force (Aug. 1975): *Nonagricultural wage and salary earners,* 1,955,800; *insured unemployed,* 62,400.

INDONESIA

The regime of President Suharto continued to play down politics and stress intense efforts to develop the economy. Though endowed with considerable natural resources, Indonesia was still among the world's lowest per-capita-income countries in 1975.

Economy. An international consortium of 13 countries, including Australia, France, Japan, the United Kingdom, and the United States, has given about $4 billion in aid to Indonesia since 1966. Galloping inflation has been checked, the budget surplus approaches $2 billion, foreign currency reserves of over $2.5 billion have been built up, and the annual growth rate runs at 7%–8%. Though Indonesia has not raised the price of oil as much as the other OPEC countries, its revenues from the export of oil were about $3 billion in 1975.

In spite of these national achievements, the huge state-owned oil company, Pertamina, ran into severe financial difficulties. It had diversified too broadly, had become overextended, and was caught in a tight money market. In May it was revealed that its short-term debts totaled about $3 billion. The government assumed Pertamina's foreign obligations and instituted closer control over its activities.

Foreign Relations. President Ferdinand E. Marcos of the Philippines stated on February 2 that he had asked President Suharto for help in his negotiations for peace with the Muslim rebels in the Philippines. A border patrol agreement was signed between the two countries on March 11.

President Suharto returned to Jakarta on July 8 from a 12-day world tour, visiting Iran, Yugoslavia, Canada, the United States, and Japan. With the leaders of these countries he discussed the situation in Southeast Asia after the conclusion of the war in Vietnam. President Ford assured the Indonesian president that, despite the withdrawal from Indochina, the United States remained committed to an active presence in Southeast Asia.

Timor. A revolt in the Portuguese half of Timor—a fragment of a once vast colonial empire—caused Indonesia deep concern in 1975. In the 17th century, when the Dutch drove the Portuguese out of the Indonesian archipelago, Portugal managed to retain control over the eastern half of Timor plus an enclave in the western half. Largest of the Lesser Sunda Islands, Timor is the closest of the Indonesian group to Australia. The area of the whole island is less than 14,000 square miles (36,260 sq km) with a population of about 1.5 million.

When the rightist Lisbon government was overthrown in April 1974, and the new government later declared that Timor could have its independence in 1978, the Indonesian government expressed concern about the future status of the Portuguese territory. Foreign Minister Adam Malik assured the Portuguese government that Indonesia had no ambitions for territorial expansion but indicated that he thought the best solution of the problem of Timor was integration of the territory into Indonesia. Other spokesmen let it be known that Indonesia could not tolerate having the territory fall under the control of radicals.

The Indonesian government apparently fears use of the territory as a base of operations by Indonesian Communists. When the revolt broke out on August 18, Malik declared that Indonesia would provide protection for the people of the territory if they wanted to join Indonesia. According to Jakarta, there are three parties in the Timor territory favoring merger with Indonesia.

The revolt soon turned into a bitter civil war between the leftist Timorese Revolutionary Front, more commonly known as Fretlin, which demanded independence, and the conservative Timor Democratic Union, which also desired independence but had the support of the Portuguese settlers in the territory.

Jakarta sought Lisbon's approval to intervene and bring peace to the distracted territory, but Lisbon refused the request. Jakarta proposed pacification of the territory by Indonesian military forces to be joined later by Australian and Malaysian units, but this proposal was also unacceptable to Portugal and was rejected by Australia. The Indonesian government repeatedly denied that any of its forces were fighting in Portuguese Timor, but such reports persisted. Fretlin, which seemed to have won over its opponents, declared that many Indonesians were among the troops killed by its forces.

Several thousand Portuguese Timorese have fled to Australia, and some 40,000 have taken refuge in Indonesia. The Indonesian Information Service stated on September 27 that President Suharto was considering a petition from the people of the Portuguese territory who wish to join Indonesia.

AMRY VANDENBOSCH
University of Kentucky

INDONESIA · Information Highlights

Official Name: Republic of Indonesia.
Location: Southeast Asia.
Area: 735,269 square miles (1,904,345 sq km).
Population (1975 est.): 136,000,000.
Chief Cities (1974 est.): Jakarta, the capital, 5,000,000; Surabaja, 2,000,000; Bandung, 2,000,000; Medan, 1,000,000.
Government: *Head of state and of government,* Suharto, president (took office for second 5-year term March 1973). *Legislature* (unicameral)—Dewan Perwakilan Rakyat (House of Representatives).
Monetary Unit: Rupiah (415 rupiahs equal U. S.$1, May 1975).
Gross National Product (1974 est.): $15,000,000,000.
Manufacturing (major products): Processed agricultural products, petroleum products, mineral products, cotton textiles, tires, cement.
Major Agricultural Products: Rice, rubber, sweet potatoes, cassava, copra, sugarcane, coffee.
Foreign Trade (1974): *Exports,* $7,420,800,000; *imports,* $3,835,500,000.

Elements of the trans-Alaska oil pipeline are displayed in a demonstration section built before actual work on the 798-mile (1,284-km) route began.

UPI

INDUSTRIAL REVIEW

World industrial production experienced in 1975 its worst crisis since the 1930's. Among the highly visible effects of the recession, which hit the developed world with little warning, were cutbacks in oil production and the disappearance of some old, well-known names in the automobile industry. Also worrisome to the recession-ridden industries of the developed world was the strong drive by developing countries to industrialize in order to escape dependence on a narrow resource base.

Steel was a case in point. In all developed countries the industry looked to governments for help. Japan, the biggest steel-exporting country, with almost 30% of its steel output shipped abroad, was the prime example. Japanese steel in 1974 undersold the metal from other producing countries by a wide margin. Aggressive competition at a time when heavy steel users—shipbuilders, automakers, and machinery producers—were cutting down on their purchases, drove home the point that the industry was headed toward chaos. While established steel industries lacked the financial resources for investment at home, developing countries received aid in their efforts to build the most advanced steelmaking facilities.

United States

U. S. industrial production dropped 6.7% in 1975 as the nation experienced its worst economic downturn since the end of World War II. Overall manufacturing activity dropped 10.5%, with durables down 13% and nondurables down 8.4%. Utilities showed a 2.7% gain, and mining declined by 2.2%, according to preliminary estimates by the Federal Reserve Board (FRB). The industrial production index, prepared by the board of governors of the Federal Reserve System, measures the physical volume of production of U. S. factories, mines, and utilities. It covers about 40% of the nation's total output of goods and services, and reflects current trends in the economy.

The decline in industrial production was aggravated by extremely high inventory accumulation. This was a result of inflation, price controls, and shortage scares of the 1972–1974 period.

Production advances were few in 1975. In durable goods, whatever stability there was stemmed from government orders for defense products. This was reflected in production increases of 2.6% for ships and boats.

Output lagged in nondurable goods as well. The only advances recorded were for soaps and toiletries, 8.2%; petroleum refining, 0.7%; and agricultural chemicals, about 1%.

Consumer Goods. Production of consumer goods dropped nearly 5%. Consumer durables declined 13%, with autos off 9% and home goods dropping 14%. The output of appliances and television and home audio products plummeted 14%. The usually steady consumer-nondurables sector also suffered a 1% decline. There was a small, although surprising, decline in foods and tobacco, about 1%. Clothing production was down 10%. Nonfood staples, consisting of chemical and paper products, fuel, and lighting, wound up the year with a 2% gain.

Among consumer products that suffered in 1975 were aerosol products, whose fluorocarbon propellants were under attack as potentially harmful. A surge in home gardening led to a

temporary shortage of canning-jar lids, putting manufacturers on three shifts, seven days a week, in order to meet demand. Production was boosted to over 2 billion lids, an 80% increase from 1974. The bicycle boom of recent years came upon hard times in 1975, with manufacturers' shipments cut in half. Consumer products that promised energy savings, such as microwave ovens, heat pumps, and freezers, were reported in good demand.

Metals. Domestic steel shipments fell 27%, to about 80 million tons in 1975. The tonnage of raw steel poured dropped about 20% from the 145.7 million tons the industry produced in 1974. Nonferrous metals had a 21% decline in production.

Transportation. Transportation equipment manufacturers saw their output decline by 9%. An especially sharp setback was suffered by the producers of mobile homes, with output down 40%. New car production dropped 8%, after a 24% decline in 1974. Production of trucks and buses declined almost 15%, despite a recovery toward year's end.

Energy. Total energy production registered a 1% gain on the FRB index in 1975. Oil and gas extraction actually declined, dropping to 105 (1967 = 100), as compared to 107.7 on the FRB production index for 1974. The Federal Power Commission warned industrial users at midyear that interstate natural gas pipelines might be unable to supply about 20% of their customers' requirements between April 1975 and March 1976 because of the increasing shortage of that fuel.

At a U.S. copper plant the flow of molten copper is channeled into molds.

ANACONDA

Coal was the bright spot in energy production in 1975, with production increasing 4% over the 638 million tons produced in 1974. The industry planned to double its capacity to 1.2 billion tons of production capacity by 1985.

Manufacturing. Manufacturing received little support from business on spending for new plant and equipment. Total capital spending by business was estimated at $113.5 billion in 1975, only 1% more than in 1974. The Bureau of Economic Analysis pointed out that if the higher 1975 prices were taken into account, real capital spending actually declined 11.5% in 1975.

Manufacturers increased expenditures for new plant and equipment by 5.3%, with nondurables producers hiking outlays by 12.1% and durables manufacturers cutting back by 1.8%. In nondurables, petroleum industries led with an increase of 31%, followed by papermakers with 15%. Among durables producers, capital-spending cutbacks by the motor vehicle and electrical machinery industries were partially offset by a 38% spending increase by the iron and steel industry.

Capital Spending. Capital spending by the nonmanufacturing industries dropped by 2%, reflecting cutbacks by airlines, electric utilities, and communication and commercial firms. Spending was increased 10% by mining and 29% by other transportation, reflecting the construction of the oil pipeline in Alaska.

Other Statistics. Manufacturing industries employed 20 million workers in 1973, 870,000 more than in 1972, according to the 1973 Annual Survey of Manufactures issued by the Bureau of the Census in October 1975. Manufacturing payrolls totaled $193 billion, an 11% gain from the previous year.

Value added by manufacture reached $404 billion in 1974, 14% higher than in 1972. "Value added" is the difference between the value of shipments and the value of materials, supplies, containers, and fuel consumed in the production process. It is the best measuring stick for determining an industry's relative economic importance. The five giants in U. S. manufacturing in 1973 in terms of value added were the following industries: transportation equipment, $45.7 billion; nonelectrical machinery, $44.6 billion; food and related products, $39.7 billion; chemicals and allied products, $36.2 billion; and electric and electronic equipment, $35 billion.

Capacity utilization in manufacturing dropped 14% in 1975 to its lowest rate since World War II. The FRB's preliminary estimates place 1975 capacity utilization in manufacturing at a meager 68% of the measure's base year of 1967. Among industries, capacity utilization was highest in petroleum, but even there it was well below that of 1974.

AGO AMBRE, *Current Business Analysis Division, Bureau of Economic Analysis, U. S. Department of Commerce*

In the restaurant of the Monticello (N. Y.) Raceway, designer Ted Asnis used clustered seating, TV screens, and neon tubes to appeal to young people.

INTERIOR DESIGN

Reflecting our present culture's preoccupation with escaping reality, interior design today, much like fashion, has ventured into the world of myth and fantasy.

"We are a lot less pure today about what we can accept as good design than in the past. Pop laxed us, at least, into seeing the humor of today's Tudor lounge with styrofoam oak beams and Elizabethan serving wenches on the 58th floor of a steel-and-concrete skyscraper . . . why is so much design out of touch with reality . . . ? Interior designers who were established in the 50's linger on (creating) 'the theatre' of hotel rooms, restaurants and other public spaces. They reflect an era of neoromantic sets by Jo Mielziner, Donald Onslager and others with their layerings of scrim and projections of flats. Like those settings, interior designers have gone off into realms of fantasy and status symbols" (C. Ray Smith, *Interiors*, October 1974).

Restaurants. "Restaurants ought to convey a feeling of fantasy and make-believe and satisfy people's desire for beauty and a special kind of warmth" (Warren Platner, *Interior Design*, August 1975). It is not surprising then that the distinguished contemporary designer George Nelson recreated for NYMM'S, a restaurant in New York City's Merchandise Mart, the circus atmosphere of P. T. Barnum. The decor is particularly appropriate since the Mart is on the old Barnum Hippodrome site. A veritable circus of lights, swinging acrobats, cutouts of ads, and other Barnum memorabilia fill every open space with a resulting festive atmosphere.

At the raceway in Monticello, N. Y., designer Ted Asnis fulfilled his client's desire for "something spacey, a little way out, and more like what young people are into today." A sense of unreality was created with neon tubes of various colors floating in a black void also punctuated with numerous suspended TV screens. Within the darkness, large clusters of cocktail seating (Vernor Panton's upholstered chairs) appear to float in space above disappearing bases of tiny bent metal rods.

Offices. In office design, image is all-important. Appearances must conform to a company's sense of itself, whether conservative, traditional, dynamic, contemporary, or avant-garde. The

image of success must be clearly defined by the designer and communicated in positive terms to the company's client.

"Reassurance and success with a conservative image" was the image a California shipping firm asked Environmental Planning and Research Inc. to create. Their solution was not so much in the handling of space as through refinement of detail and opulence of materials. The drama unfolds with the entry wall covered in silk and others done in red velvet. Custom furniture, subtly lit art, a profusion of living plants, and thick wool rugs set into parquet oak floors add to the general sense of dignified well being.

A personal affection for color and decoration (with paint) is foremost in the design of Michael Graves for the Fort Wayne Ear, Nose and Throat Association clinic and offices. Separate corridors of yellow, green, and orange cross and recross in dramatic interplay, delineating traffic patterns. In the manner of theatrical flats, enclosed offices are layered plane on plane, creating not a series of rooms but miniature buildings within an overall space, some cylindrical, some rectilinear. Each is colored to match its own corridor.

In Los Angeles, Banca Commerciale Italiana requested Milton I. Swimmer Planning & Design, Inc. to design an environment for its offices that reconciled American tastes with a strong sense of Italy. Dark Italian granite on floors and smoked glass partitions were used to create a somber backdrop for the stark white marble sculpture of Italy's Carmelo Capello. All furnishings and accessories were chosen for their Italianate qualities and rarity.

Schools. No longer functional factories for learning, schools are being designed for a sense of warmth and friendliness, such as the Demus Elementary School near St. Louis designed by architects Hoffman/Sauer and Associates. The plan is open, with interiors painted vivid yellow, orange, or green; floors thickly carpeted; and the few existing walls or partitions used as "art galleries." Plants and trees soften flat planes.

Residences. Nowhere is myth and fantasy as apparent as in the home. Here, permissiveness allows the designer's theatrical talent full bent. Michael diSantis, for example, camouflaged the functionalism of storage in a New Jersey kitchen with super graphics—geometrics—that race up walls and over cabinets, successfully hiding every surface on the way.

Gloria Vanderbilt, painter and designer, created for her family an eye-distracting display of her own work by layering pattern on pattern on sofa cushions, rugs, draperies, papered walls, and in large bright collages of her own making. "Of all the lunatic crazes to hit California, the current fascination with ancient Egypt would seem unpromising as a premise for contemporary decor" (*Interiors*, July 1975). Despite this admonition, designer Davis Doolin has recreated the murals of Abu Simbel on the walls of a Telegraph Hill flat.

JEANNE WEEKS
Associate, American Society of Interior Designers

The offices of the Fort Wayne Ear, Nose and Throat Association use a theatrical approach, including receptionist's office like a ticket booth.

BALTHAZAR KORAB

U. S. Treasury Secretary William E. Simon addresses opening session of International Monetary Fund meeting. His September 2 speech was made in Washington, D. C.

international finance

During 1975 the world economy tried to cope with the conflicting problems of inflation and recession while simultaneously suffering from the unequal distribution of international payments, which arose partially from higher oil prices. Current account deficits of oil-importing countries were financed by the investment of surpluses of oil-exporting countries in national and international financial markets together with the expansion of official financing.

BALANCE OF PAYMENTS

A broad picture of the balance of payments current accounts in 1975 showed a drop in the surplus of major oil-exporting countries from $70 billion in 1974 to about $50 billion, and a change by the industrial countries from a 1974 deficit of $12 billion to an approximate balance or slight surplus. For the more developed, primary producing countries the 1975 deficit was the same as in 1974, $12 billion. Less developed countries with no oil showed a deficit of about $35 billion. These current account balances were strongly influenced by the recession in the industrial world in the first half of the year, even though there was some upturn in the second half.

Industrial countries initiated important fiscal changes in the first half of 1975, including shifts in both tax and spending plans. In addition, there was relatively moderate relaxation of monetary policy. The Organization for Economic Cooperation and Development (OECD) predicted, in late July, rising unemployment for most western industrial economies for the rest of 1975. Unemployment in the 24 OECD countries was 15 million, which was well above historical standards.

CAPITAL FLOWS AND THE CURRENCY MARKET

Industrial countries in 1975 used capital inflows from the countries in the Organization of Petroleum Exporting Countries (OPEC) and elsewhere to help meet their import needs. Also, the situation in the European currency market improved during the year while the existence of floating rates of currency exchange increased the flexibility of adjustment in payments situations.

United States. In the United States there was an $8–$9 billion trade surplus in 1975. U. S. exports to oil-exporting nations and the Soviet Union were nearly twice those of 1974. U. S. oil imports in 1975 were $26–$27 billion. In spite of favorable trade reports, however, there was world-wide speculation against the dollar during the first half of the year. The United States reacted by taking such measures as reducing reserve requirements on European dollar borrowings by national banks, thus reducing U. S. dollars held abroad. Also, the Federal Reserve System intervened in foreign exchange markets, along with other central banks, to help stem the speculative tide.

In the latter part of the year the dollar had strengthened to the point where foreign currencies could be purchased and used to repay the costs of intervention, much of which had been financed by drawings on swap lines. Swap lines are short term, reciprocal lines of credit between the Federal Reserve System and 14 major foreign central banks and the Bank for International Settlements.

Capital Flows. Also, during the year the Soviet Union and its Eastern European allies borrowed heavily in international capital markets. Proceeds were used to help finance a sizable trade deficit with the West, part of which was the result of grain purchases from the United States and Canada. Capital inflows into the United States from the OPEC countries were down from the $11 billion of 1974 to an annual rate of about $4 billion.

At end of June oil producers owned $1.6 billion in U. S. government securities, up from $364 million at end of 1974. Stock holdings were up by $659 million during the first half of the year as compared with $367 million for all of 1974. Long-term bank deposits increased by $449 million for the first six months, after rising by only $40 million for all 1974. The big decline was in short-term deposit liabilities and

savings certificates, which accounted for 87% of the buildup in 1974, when $9.7 billion was pumped into such investments. By the end of June 1975, the amount that remained in such investments not only had not grown but had shrunk by over $1 billion.

OPEC. Twice during 1975 the OPEC countries met regarding the pricing policies of the cartel. In June the decision was to freeze the then current price until October 1. In late September the decision was to boost the oil price by 10% on October 1 and to freeze prices at that level for nine months until June 1, 1976. The October price could be extended until the end of 1976. If adopted by all members, this decision could have added about $9.3 billion to annual revenue. At the time of the announcement, however, some members were discounting on sales, and others were reducing premiums.

OPEC's production ran about 28 million barrels a day, as compared with the 33 million produced just before the 1973 embargo, with a concomitant slowing in the rate of increase in international reserves. Saudi Arabia produced little more than 50% of its capacity. Iran's output was down by nearly 20% and overall OPEC output was down by 14%. A few OPEC nations, such as Saudi Arabia and Kuwait, received more money than they could spend, but at least four members borrowed up to $2 billion in 1975.

Other OPEC activity included a Venezuelan law providing for complete nationalization of its petroleum industry on Jan. 1, 1976. Affected were 21 privately owned companies, mostly subsidiaries of U. S. companies. OPEC was also influential in bringing about a resumption in talks between developed and developing countries on energy and related problems, after an abortive spring meeting, by making a resumption of the dialogue a condition for moderation on prices at the September meeting.

GOLD AND THE EXCHANGE RATE

On Jan. 1, 1975, France revalued its gold reserves, which resulted in an instant accounting increase from $4.3 to $16.4 billion. As of that same date U. S. citizens were permitted for the first time in 41 years to own gold. Twice during the year, on January 6 and June 30, the U. S. Treasury held public auctions of gold.

The January auction did not elicit much interest; 2 million ounces were offered but bids for only 753,000 ounces were accepted at an average price of $165.67 an ounce. Interest was heavier in June when 500,000 ounces were offered, with the Treasury accepting about 10% of bids totaling 4 million ounces. The average price was $165.05 per ounce. Revenue from both auctions totaled about $207 million. The U. S. stockpile after both sales was 274.7 million ounces valued at approximately $11.5 billion at the official rate of $42.22 an ounce.

Also, during the year Iran, the Philippines, and the United Kingdom made major changes in the laws and regulations governing the holding and dealing in gold. In addition, South Africa, the world's leading gold producer, devalued its currency frequently during the year in relation to the dollar, the last change, in mid-September, being a devaluation of the rand by 17% against the dollar, the steepest devaluation since World War II.

South Africa's actions reflected the strength of the dollar during the latter part of the year. In addition, the international status of gold was significantly diminished by actions of the International Monetary Fund (IMF) at its annual meeting in Washington, D. C., in September. Both these pressures resulted in a drop in the price of gold from a high of $195.25 on Dec. 20, 1974, to as low as $129 an ounce in early fall 1975.

International Monetary Fund. The IMF gold-sales pact was contingent upon solving exchange rate problems and quota changes in January 1976. There was, however, agreement to sell one-sixth (25 million ounces) of the fund's gold at market prices with the profit, possibly as much as $2.5 billion, being used to aid poor nations, and the return of 25 million ounces to member nations that had originally provided them in meeting quota contributions. IMF members also voted to abolish the official price of gold and to eliminate requirements to use gold in transactions with IMF. In addition to the gold package, member countries of the IMF agreed to an increase in quotas that represented a 32.5% increase in its resources to 39 billion in Special Drawing Rights (SDR), in order to aid in settling payment imbalances. An SDR equals about $1.20. The U. S. share would be 20% rather than the approximate 21.5% at present.

The fund continued the oil facility started in 1974 to provide financing to members facing balance-of-payments problems caused by increases in the costs of petroleum. These resources were in addition to others available from the fund. During 1974 about SDR 2.5 billion were used, and a balance of approximately SDR 450 million carried forward for use in the 1975 oil facility. Borrowing arrangements were concluded with 12 lenders for a total of SDR 2.9 billion to complete the 1975 facility. During 1974, 40 members used the oil facility and by mid-August 1975, 11 members had used a total of SDR 1.05 billion of the 1975 facility.

Emerging Monetary System. Currency exchange rate systems existing since early 1973 have been generally viewed as being transitional. The quadrupling of oil prices, high inflation, and the widespread recession beginning in late 1974 and continuing well into 1975 virtually precluded the use of a fixed exchange rate system.

During the 1973–75 period the most noteworthy feature of exchange rate arrangements was the floating of currencies of major industrial countries, which accounted for the bulk of world trade. The only announced margins since

early 1973 were those set in the European narrow margins arrangement (the "snake"), with currencies of all other industrial countries floating independently of each other and the "snake" currencies. Under the "snake" arrangement Belgium, Denmark, France, Germany, Luxembourg, the Netherlands, Norway, Sweden, and Switzerland maintained a maximum margin of 2.25% for exchange rate fluctuations between participant currencies, while these currencies floated jointly against the currencies of nonparticipating countries.

All floating currencies were subject to varying degrees of official intervention. Changes in interest rate differentials were a frequent cause of capital movements under a fixed exchange rate and also gave rise to pressures on rates in the present floating system. A cause for concern about the present monetary system was that floating rates could potentially be a source of inflation and could quicken the transmission of inflation between countries.

SDR Standards. Inflation and floating exchange rates have been factors accelerating the movement toward a Special Drawing Right (SDR) Standard. The consensus that reduced the role of gold in the monetary system was necessary for the move toward the new standard of "paper gold." In July 1974 the IMF decided to value the SDR in terms of a "basket" of 16 currencies instead of exclusively the U. S. dollar. A number of countries decided early in 1975 to establish the value of their currency in terms of a basket of currencies, SDR included, rather than continue to peg on a single currency.

In January 1975, Burma advised the fund of a new central rate for its currency in terms of the SDR. Iran, Saudi Arabia, and Qatar gave notice in early spring of the decision to discontinue the fixed relationship between their currencies and the U. S. dollar and switched to SDR. Kuwait and Fiji fixed the rate for their currencies on the basis of a weighted basket of the currencies of their major trading partners. Malawi adopted a fixed relationship to the SDR in June 1975.

The use of SDR's has also spread to commercial transactions. By April 1, 1977, worldwide airline passenger fares, cargo rates, and other air transport transactions are to be quoted in SDR's instead of dollars or pounds sterling. The first Eurobonds denominated in SDR's have been issued and sold, and Suez Canal tolls have been quoted in SDR's instead of Egyptian pounds. OPEC nations considered the adoption of an SDR pricing system for oil.

At the close of 1975 the most important unsettled issue in monetary reform remained the currency rates. Some officials. of the European Economic Community, especially the French, argued for a return to a par value system while U. S. officials found floating rates acceptable. Discussions suggested that any new system would permit greater flexibility for changing exchange rates than the aborted par value system, with exchange rates becoming more a matter of international concern and subject to an agreed-upon code of behavior.

JOHN R. MATTHEWS, JR.
College of William and Mary

Representatives of industrialized, developing, or oil-producing countries met in Paris in October to begin discussions of world economic problems.

UPI

The Organization of Petroleum Exporting Countries (OPEC) met in Vienna in September to set a new oil price. The result was a 10% rise in crude petroleum prices.

INTERNATIONAL TRADE

The worldwide recession that began in the latter part of 1974 and continued in many countries through most of 1975 acted as a severe depressant to the international exchange of goods. Following two years of extremely buoyant trade, exports slowed perceptibly in 1975. From preliminary estimates it appeared that exports would rise by only 5% to 10% to a value ranging from $810 to $850 billion. Such an advance represented little, if any, increase in the volume of goods traded.

U. S. trade made a dramatic turnaround in the year, moving from a deficit in 1974 following the huge oil import price rise, to an enormous surplus. By year's end it was expected to be the largest in U. S. history.

TRADE TRENDS

Imports into most industrial countries dropped significantly in 1975 as the recession became deeper and more prolonged than any since the end of World War II. Exports were generally maintained or expanded through continued strong sales to the oil-producing and other developing countries. The oil-rich countries were able to continue spectacular increases in purchases to implement their expanded development plans as a result of their growing incomes from the fourfold oil price rise. To sustain any import growth, however, the non-oil-producing developing nations were forced to draw on past earnings, monetary reserves, and borrowings.

Prices of most foods and crude materials traded internationally decreased slightly in 1975, while those for nonferrous base metals, which had soared in 1973–74, fell sharply. Even the price of oil—which the Organization of Petroleum Exporting Countries (OPEC) did not officially change until October 1—was lowered slightly by certain producing countries when nations cut purchases of this high-priced product. Reduced demand resulted from the slowdown in economic activity and conservation measures instituted to save energy. At the beginning of the final quarter of the year, however, OPEC announced a 10% rise in the prices charged for crude petroleum.

United States. The deep recession in the United States ironically resulted in an abrupt favorable shift in the trade balance. From a deficit of $2.3 billion in 1974, trade through September 1975 moved to a surplus of $11.2 billion at a seasonally-adjusted annual rate. Since demand was reduced because of lower industrial production and sluggish consumer expenditures, imports declined in the first 9 months by 5.5% in value and about 14% in quantity to a total of $94.6 billion in annual rate. Exports expanded to $105.8 billion, 8% above the 1974 total. The quantity of U. S. goods shipped abroad was about 3% below that in 1974.

The U. S. balance improved with all major trading partners except Japan. The surplus with the European Economic Community doubled in value to over $6 billion at an annual rate, while that with the non-oil-producing developing countries rose to nearly $10 billion. Lower imports of consumer goods, food, and industrial supplies, coupled with further advances in exports, were responsible for these higher surpluses. The oil producers continued to expand their purchases of U. S. goods at an exceptionally fast rate for the second year. Thus, although oil imports from these countries rose in value, the U. S. deficit with them was cut by nearly a third to about $8.5 billion. Trade with Canada, long in a deficit position, was nearly in balance, but the imbalance with Japan increased slightly.

U. S. Exports. The expansion in exports in the first nine months of 1975 resulted entirely from growth in sales of nonagricultural products, which advanced by 15% over 1974. Despite the slump in capital investment abroad, sales of machinery continued to grow, in part because such equipment was being delivered to fill orders placed months earlier. A major source of

strength came from deliveries to the OPEC countries.

Strong growth also continued in sales of motor vehicles, notably passenger cars to Canada and trucks to Iran, where the internal transportation system was being modernized. Exports of a number of industrial materials dropped off, or leveled, as a result of the slump abroad. Coal, however, proved an exception. Large increases were recorded in export prices and moderate growth in quantity.

Agricultural shipments were marginally below their January–September 1974 value in the same months of 1975. Wheat exports were higher, but soybeans, animal feed, and cotton all registered declines. In October, President Gerald R. Ford announced a five-year trade agreement with the Soviet Union for the sale of U. S. grain, beginning with the 1976 harvest. Strong competition from Brazil and reduced demand for feed cut U. S. sales of soybeans and feed, while the worldwide textile recession cut cotton-import requirements.

U. S. Imports. Imports of most major products declined in value as the drop in economic activity cut deeply into domestic demand. Petroleum imports, which had been a major cause of

This Russian ship sat idle in Houston in August when longshoremen stopped loading grain for the USSR.

UPI

the deficit in 1974 trade, were only 3% higher in value and were 2% lower in volume. The value of other supplies for industry, however, fell by 4%. Imports of consumer items were nearly 10% below 1974 as a result of sluggish demand, particularly for cars and other durable goods. With the exception of sugar, almost all food imports were reduced, with the biggest drop in meat and fish.

U. S. Balance of Payments. U. S. international transactions, as measured by the basic balance (the balance on current account and long-term capital) moved to a surplus of $938 million in the first six months. This was a $1.5 billion shift from the deficit of the first half of 1974. Numerous major changes occurred in the principal transactions in these two periods. Trade, on an adjusted payments basis, changed by $6.8 billion from deficit to surplus. Outflows for government grants dropped by $2.6 billion from their high level in the first half of 1974, and net investment income fell by $2.4 billion because of lower net income from the petroleum industry. Government capital flows shifted by $2.7 billion from net inflow to outflow, while long-term private capital outflows rose by $3.6 billion.

The official reserve transactions balance, which includes short-term private capital flows and errors and omissions, rose from a deficit of $3.6 billion to a $4.9 billion deficit.

Canada. As imports rose strongly through August, Canadian trade moved into a deficit of Canadian (C) C$1.6 billion compared to a C$600 million surplus in the first 8 months of 1974. Purchases from abroad advanced by 13% to C$22.8 billion. The increases were heavily concentrated, with crude oil, automotive equipment, and machinery accounting for 75% of the rise.

Canadian exports rose by only 2% to C$21.2 billion. Larger values for sales of natural gas, automotive equipment, pulp, and newsprint were almost offset by sharp decreases in crude petroleum, nonferrous metal, and lumber sales.

Prices of goods traded by Canada continued to rise considerably in 1975. At midyear average import prices were 16% above those in 1974, while export prices advanced about 9%. Thus, it appeared that the volume of goods contracted, with the drop in export volume almost twice that for imports.

Canada's current account deficit, seasonally adjusted, totaled C$2.6 billion in the first half of 1975 compared to only C$143 million a year earlier. The shift from trade surplus to deficit was the major factor in the larger imbalance. Non-merchandise accounts continued at a loss, with travel expenditures abroad particularly large. Total net capital inflows, plus a fall in Canada's official reserves of around C$500 million, financed the deficit.

Western Europe. Exports from Western Europe continued to expand in the first half of

UPI

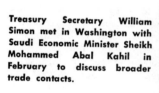

Treasury Secretary William Simon met in Washington with Saudi Economic Minister Sheikh Mohammed Abal Kahil in February to discuss broader trade contacts.

1975, but the 15% growth over the same period of 1974 represented a considerable slowing from the advances of the two preceding years. In fact, when price inflation was removed from these values, real growth appeared to be minimal. Imports into these countries rose at a more modest rate and represented a drop in volume compared to the first half of 1974. As in the United States, demand in West Europe was considerably reduced by the recession that followed the earlier boom and the oil crisis of early 1974. With production well below the levels of 1973–74, unemployment at its highest peak since the 1930's, and capital investment and profits sluggish, the European market was relatively unreceptive to imports.

As a result, several major countries reported an improvement in their trade balances compared with 1974 as imports slowed and exports to the oil producers and other developing countries sustained earnings. In both Italy and France, for example, there was a shift from a deficit to a surplus in trade. Through September of 1974, France had totaled a $2.8 billion deficit. This changed to a $2.0 billion surplus in the first 9 months of 1975. The Italian shift was equally dramatic, from a $5.9 billion deficit in January–August 1974 to a $500 million positive balance in the same 1975 period.

The United Kingdom cut its nine-month 1974 imbalance almost in half to $4.8 billion in 1975, as exports climbed by 17%, and imports rose by a mere 1%. The value of imported oil showed a large drop, due almost entirely to the lower quantity imported. The strong growth of British exports resulted in part from the increased price competitiveness of British goods resulting from the continued reduction through the year in the value of the pound sterling.

West Germany, in contrast to the other major countries in Europe, reported a considerable reduction in the large positive trade balance of January–September 1974. The 3% rise in exports was not enough to cover price rises and

was far below the 9% import growth. Nevertheless, the surplus of $14.9 billion was much larger than that of any of the other developed nations. West German shipments held up as well as they did because of a large backlog of export orders, and, along with many other countries, extraordinary shipments to the oil-producers. They were, however, hindered to some extent by the fact that the German mark was considered to be somewhat overvalued.

TARIFFS AND TRADE RESTRICTIONS

With the passage of the Trade Act of 1974 at the end of that year, the U. S. government was able to implement more fully its participation in the Multinational Trade Negotiations (MTN) in Geneva, Switzerland, which technically opened in September 1973. As the year progressed, six groups and several subgroups, established to consider various phases of the negotiations, held occasional meetings, supplemented by bilateral consultations between countries. The groups included agriculture, tariffs, non-tariff measures, tropical products, sectors, and safeguards. At the same time, in the United States, 27 industry, 6 labor, and several agriculture technical advisory committees, required by the act to advise government negotiators, met to consider the proposed U. S. offerings. They also presented reports on their findings to the special representative for trade negotiations, Frederick B. Dent, former secretary of commerce.

On August 3, a new U. S. trade agreement went into effect, granting "most-favored-nation" treatment to imports from Rumania. Such treatment, in effect lowering duties on Rumanian goods to those levied on imports from most other countries, was provided for in the 1974 trade act for imports from socialist nations, provided certain conditions were met regarding emigration.

FRANCES L. HALL
*Director, International Trade Analysis
Staff, U. S. Department of Commerce*

IOWA

The Democrats had control of the legislature for the first time in a decade but worked with the Republican governor without major difficulties. Excellent harvests kept Iowans, especially farmers, prosperous in 1975.

Legislature. Iowa's General Assembly was controlled for the first time in 10 years by the Democrats. In the Senate the majority could not be classed as a "working majority" since the Democrats held 26 seats while the Republicans held 24. In the House the majority was greater, with 60 Democrats to 40 Republicans. The Democrats thus organized both chambers and elected Dale Cochran of Fort Dodge speaker of the House and Sen. Minnette Doderer of Iowa City president pro tem of the Senate. Republican Lt. Gov. Arthur A. Neu was the presiding officer in the Senate under the Iowa Constitution but was stripped of many of his normal powers of committee appointments by the Democrats.

Republican Gov. Robert D. Ray, beginning an unprecedented fourth term, recommended a record budget of more than $1 billion for each year of the biennium. The Democratic controlled House and Senate, however, decided to switch to annual appropriations and passed appropriations for only the first year of the two year period. Totals approximated Governor Ray's recommendations although there were some minor variations.

No major new taxes were enacted by the 66th General Assembly, as the treasury surplus was estimated at more than $200 million. Increases in salaries for state employees of more than 10% were approved. The state's aid to Iowa cities was increased to more than $12 million. Other major legislation increased the retirement benefits to be received by retired employees of cities, counties, and school districts as well as by state employees covered by the Iowa Public Employees Retirement System.

Collective bargaining for all public employees went into effect on July 1, 1975, but would not begin for persons under the state board of regents until July 1, 1976. All state government departments were included in the operations of an administrative procedures act passed to ensure regular and uniform processes of administration, including public hearings and rule making.

Agriculture. Despite a severe drought that made July and August the driest in 30 years, the Iowa corn harvest went over the 1-billion-bushel mark. The soybean crop, which had also been expected to suffer, was the second largest in Iowa history. However, the per acre harvest was lower since a larger number of acres both of corn and soybeans had been planted than in previous years.

Employment. Unemployment in Iowa during 1975 continued higher than in the last 20 years, reaching 5.6% in August. It still remained below the national average.

Newsmaker. President Gerald Ford's visit to the Iowa state fair helped to boost the total attendance to more than 500,000 people. President Eisenhower was the only other president to have visited the Iowa fair.

Urban Affairs. Iowa City began operating under a new city charter, making it the first city in the state to draft such a document under the new home rule amendment to the Iowa constitution. Four special charter cities continued to operate under charters granted prior to 1857 by the legislature, while the other 950 incorporated municipalities operate under general statute law.

RUSSELL M. ROSS
University of Iowa

IRAN

Iran in 1975 held consistently to the course that Shah Mohammed Reza Pahlavi has mapped out for it in recent years. The nation continued a strenuous policy of economic development sustained by enormous oil revenues and a firm domestic policy that hopes to gain popular support but is ruthless with sedition. In addition, Iran continued a massive arms buildup to counter any threats to national independence and to support the growing role that it aims to play as a regional leader. Substantial progress was also made during the year in settling long-standing differences with neighboring Iraq. See also special feature on pages 36–45.

One-Party Government. The day-to-day work of carrying on government continued to be in the hands of the Shah's trusted prime minister, Amir Abbas Hoveida, who in January 1975 completed a decade in office. Experimentation with the structure of the parliamentary system, however, continued. A decree issued by the Shah on March 2 dissolved the existing two-party system and called on all Iranians to join the new Rastakhiz (National Resurrection) party, which would be Iran's only political party "for at least the next two years." The secretary-general of the new party was Hoveida, hitherto chief of the governing Iran Novin (New Iran)

─── **IOWA • Information Highlights** ───

Area: 56,290 square miles (145,791 sq km).

Population (1974 est.): 2,855,000. *Density:* 51 per sq mi.

Chief Cities (1970 census): *Chief Officers*—governor, Robert D. Ray (R); lt. gov., Arthur A. Neu (R). *General Assembly*—Senate, 50 members; House of Representatives, 100 members.

Education (1974–75): *Enrollment*—public elementary schools, 328,566 pupils; public secondary schools, 288,919; nonpublic schools, 65,400; colleges and universities, 113,714 students. *Public school expenditures,* $644,691,000 ($1,056 per pupil).

State Finances (fiscal year 1974): *Revenues,* $1,786,-136,000; *expenditures,* $1,627,392,000.

Personal Income (1974): $15,137,000,000; *per capita,* $5,302.

Labor Force (Aug. 1975): *Nonagricultural wage and salary earners,* 1,008,200; *insured unemployed,* 27,-000.

party, which was abolished along with the weak opposition Mardom (People's) party. The new party's constitution was adopted on May 2 by an assembly of delegates.

General Election. The first general election under the new single-party system was held on June 20. Elections were for the 268 seats in the Majlis (Chamber of Deputies) and for 30 seats in the Senate, to which a further 30 senators were nominated by the Shah. Voters were able to choose among the 750 candidates put forward by the Rastakhiz party. Of those elected about 80% were newcomers to the Majlis. The Majlis included more women and more representatives of professional and workers' groups than previous legislatures.

Worker Participation. Also on March 2 the Shah announced a far-reaching series of economic changes. In privately-owned industries, 49% of the shares was to be sold to the workers, or to the public if the workers did not buy them. In government-owned enterprises, except for oil, steel, copper, and transport, 99% of the shares was to be sold to their workers, or to the public, though management rights would remain with the state. A minimum national monthly wage of $184 was established.

Economic Matters. In 1975, as in the recent past, a large number of impressive trade agreements were concluded with developed and developing countries, the largest being that with the United States. The pace slackened, however, and several announced deals were quietly shelved, because of falling demands for oil and therefore decreased oil revenues. Before the Organization of Petroleum Exporting Countries (OPEC) meeting in September, the Shah had said that a 30%–35% rise in oil prices was necessary to offset inflation, but Iran later accepted agreement on 10%.

Foreign Affairs. The most important foreign policy change was the détente of March 6 with Iraq, under which the Shah ended his support of the rebel Kurds in Iraq and received Iraqi concessions on the disputed Shatt-al-Arab River frontier. Iran also established good relations during the year with Egypt. The Shah is pursuing aims of regional leadership that have made some progress.

ARTHUR CAMPBELL TURNER
University of California, Riverside

IRAQ

On balance the year 1975 was a satisfactory one for Iraq. The government was stable, and the long-standing domestic problem with the Kurdish minority seemed to have reached a fairly definitive solution. Iraqi foreign relations were being conducted with a novel flexibility that made some observers believe that Iraq's hard-line attitude toward the Arab-Israeli dispute might be undergoing some modification.

Iraq continued to be ruled, as it has been since July 1968, by the Baath Party. There have been no major changes in the nature of this authoritarian and radical regime in recent years. Communists have participated since 1973 in the "National Progressive Front," upon which the government's power is based.

Role of Vice President. The president and prime minister, in his eighth year of office in 1975, was Ahmed Hassan al-Bakr. The vice president, Saddam Hussein Takriti, seemed to be enjoying increased prestige and power. He was given much of the credit for the initiatives in foreign policy that eased Iraq's formerly hostile relations with its conservative neighbors.

Relations with Iran. The most significant event of the year for Iraq was the pact that quite surprisingly brought to an end the hostile relations with Iran. Iraq's monarchical and conservative neighbors—Iran, Saudi Arabia, Kuwait, and the Gulf emirates—have been distrustful since 1968 of the missionary zeal of the radicals running Iraq, the more so since the 1972 treaty of friendship between Moscow and Baghdad.

Iran had been able to pressure Iraq effectively by giving support to the chronic and troublesome Kurdish rebellion in Iraq. The Kurds are a non-Arab Muslim people without a state of their own but with a long history of resistance to various oppressors. They constitute about 20% of the population of Iraq and are also to be found in neighboring parts of Turkey and Iran. It is in Iraq, however, that they have found the greatest difficulty in maintaining their identity and traditions. Beginning in 1961, they conducted a guerrilla struggle against the government of Iraq, which Baghdad had not been able to suppress. The key factor was Iranian readiness to provide supplies and a sanctuary across the border.

The Algiers Agreement. The explosive Kurdish situation was abruptly defused in the spring of 1975. On March 6 in Algiers, at a meeting of the Organization of Petroleum Exporting Countries (OPEC), Saddam Hussein Takriti, Iraqi vice president, and the Shah of Iran announced that they had signed an agreement

---

IRAN · Information Highlights

Official Name: Empire of Iran.
Location: Southwest Asia.
Area: 636,294 square miles (1,648,000 sq km).
Population (1975 est.): 32,900,000.
Chief Cities (1973 est.): Teheran, the capital, 2,800,000; Isfahan, 540,000; Meshed, 530,090; Tabriz, 480,000.
Government: *Head of state,* Mohammed Reza Pahlavi, shah (acceded Sept. 1941; crowned Oct. 1967). *Head of government,* Amir Abbas Hoveida, premier (took office Jan. 1965). *Legislature*—Parliament: Senate and Majlis (Lower House).
Monetary Unit: Rial (67.88 rials equal U. S.$1, Aug. 1975).
Gross National Product (1974 est.): $35,600,000,000.
Manufacturing (major products): Petroleum products, iron, steel, textiles, carpets, food products.
Major Agricultural Products: Wheat, rice, barley, cotton, tobacco, almonds, fruits, fish (caviar).
Foreign Trade (1974 est.): *Exports,* $12,000,000,000; *imports,* $3,000,000,000.

UPI

In March, Kurdish rebels eat a meal after surrendering to the Iraqi army.
The Kurdish revolt collapsed when Iran withdrew its support of the rebellion.

eliminating all the matters in dispute between their countries. A formal "treaty of reconciliation" was signed at Baghdad on June 13. The Shah forthwith dropped his support of the Iraqi Kurds.

On the other hand, Iraq in the pact made substantial concessions on frontier questions that had long bedeviled Iraqi-Iranian relations. The most important was control of the Shatt-al-Arab River, the confluence of the Tigris and Euphrates, which forms the boundary between the two countries just north of the Persian Gulf. Iraq gave up claims to exclusive control of the waterway.

End of Kurdish Resistance. The Algiers Agreement isolated the Kurds and immediately deprived them of outside assistance. Their resistance quickly collapsed in the face of a new Iraqi army offensive. By early April the government was in control of all the Kurd-inhabited area. Of the 200,000 Kurds who fled into Iran about half soon returned to accept amnesty.

After the crushing of the rebellion, it was reported that many Kurds were being moved to the south of Iraq from their former homes and that a number of the rebels had been executed. In July the report from Damascus, Syria, of the founding of a new group, the Kurdistan National Movement, raised the question whether Kurdish resistance had been extinguished.

Agreements with Kuwait and Saudi Arabia. Iraq had for many years entertained territorial claims against its small but rich neighbor Kuwait, whose independent existence it reluctantly recognized in 1963. An impetus toward settlement was provided by the visit to Kuwait and Baghdad of President Sadat of Egypt on May 12–16. On June 25 it was reported that Iraq and Kuwait had reached an agreement settling their border dispute. Also, on July 2 an agreement with Saudi Arabia was concluded for partition of the "neutral zone" of desert lying between them. The dispute over the territory had a history going back to 1922.

Strained Relations with Syria. While Iraq was achieving better relations with Iran, Kuwait, and Saudi Arabia, it was paradoxically unable to do so with Syria's Baath regime. A bitter dispute persisted over the sharing of the Euphrates River water on which Iraqi agriculture depends. Syria had imposed a reduced flow since 1973, causing a substantial reduction in Iraqi crops. An agreement on the water dispute reached at Jiddah on May 1 might prove fragile, because it was followed by even more exacerbated feuding over other matters.

Iraq, the fourth-largest oil producer in the Middle East, was demonstrating resentment at the end of November at the failure of some OPEC countries to implement the 10% price rise. It had been decided upon at the OPEC meeting in Vienna in September.

ARTHER CAMPBELL TURNER
University of California, Riverside

--------- **IRAQ · Information Highlights** ---------

Official Name: Republic of Iraq.
Location: Southwest Asia.
Area: 167,925 square miles (434,924 sq km).
Population (1975 est.): 11,100,000.
Chief Cities (1970 est.): Baghdad, the capital, 2,183,800 (met. area); Basra, 370,900; Mosul, 293,100.
Government: *Head of state,* Ahmed Hassan al-Bakr, president (took office July 1968). *Head of government,* Ahmed Hassan al-Bakr.
Monetary Unit: Dinar (0.2961 dinar equals U. S.$1, July 1974).
Gross National Product (1974 est.): $5,600,000,000.
Manufacturing (major products): Petroleum products, processed foods, textiles, cigarettes, cement.
Major Agricultural Products: Barley, wheat, dates, rice, cotton, tobacco.
Foreign Trade (1973): *Exports,* $2,292,000,000; *imports,* $898,000,000.

IRELAND

The Irish republic lost its most famous political leader on August 29, when Eamon de Valera died. As a commander in the Easter rebellion of 1916, and as a powerful advocate of the Sinn Fein cause thereafter, "Dev," as he was called, remained a bitter opponent of the partition of Ireland.

De Valera was the major political force in Ireland from the end of civil war in 1924 until the 1960s. Devoted to the creation of a democratic and united Ireland, de Valera symbolized the nation's long and costly fight for freedom. An impressive state funeral preceded his burial in Glasnevin cemetery on September 2. (See also OBITUARIES.)

Economy. The Irish government fought a losing battle against inflation, which was reflected by a 24% increase in the cost of living during the first half of 1975. Faced with an unemployment rate of 8.5%, Finance Minister Richie Ryan introduced a special, anti-inflationary budget on June 26. The budget placed subsidies of 25% on essential foods and public transport and raised taxes of individuals in the higher income brackets.

The government emphasized that the war against inflation would be lost unless the trade unions restrained their demands for higher wages. The unions agreed to modify the national wage agreement by basing future wage claims on a cost-of-living index. The government also worked out terms for leasing the rights for exploring offshore oil and gas resources so that the state would receive some 80% of all revenues from the wells.

Conflict in Northern Ireland. During the year the coalition government of Fine Gael and Labour intensified its campaign against the Official and Provisional wings of the Irish Republican Army (IRA), and other "illegal" organizations sworn to overthrow the substate of Northern Ireland.

While British authorities convicted 12 Irish terrorists of bombings in England, the Irish government prosecuted two of the "most wanted" IRA suspects. On April 15 the Dublin special criminal court sentenced Kevin Mallon, deputy chief of staff of the Provisionals, to 10 years' imprisonment on charges of shooting at a policeman and escaping from prison. David O'Connell, deputy president of Sinn Fein and reputed architect of Provisional policy, was arrested in Dublin on July 9. He was sentenced by the same court on July 25 to one year in jail for belonging to the IRA.

In January, 16 prisoners with IRA affiliations went on a hunger strike in Portlaoise prison to protest their treatment as common criminals. Minister for Justice Patrick Cooney rejected their demand for privileges accorded to political prisoners. On March 10, 12 suspected IRA guerrillas, awaiting trial, escaped from the court house in Newry. Two of these men were recaptured immediately, and four more were caught later in Dublin, only to be released on bail. On March 17 prison guards at Portlaoise managed to foil another mass escape. In this case, after the prisoners had dynamited a door, the guards opened fire, killing one prisoner and wounding two others.

As part of a widespread effort to curb the flow of arms from "revolutionary" groups and regimes overseas into IRA arsenals, a delegation of members of the Dail (Irish parliament) visited Libya in April. These legislators tried in vain to persuade senior officials of the Libyan government to cut off the supply of weapons and ammunition to the IRA.

The continued animosities and violence of communal conflict in the six counties of the north spilled over into the Irish republic, as guerrillas used bullets and bombs to polarize opinion. On June 22 a trainload of 300 IRA supporters, on their annual pilgrimage to the grave of the revolutionary Theobald Wolfe Tone, narrowly escaped injury when a bomb blew up a bridge just after the train had passed over it.

During October, a Dutch businessman who lived near Limerick was kidnapped and held hostage by guerrillas who hoped to force the release from prison of two IRA leaders and an English revolutionary. The drama came to an end on November 7, when the terrorists surrendered to police.

With the collapse of efforts by moderates to create a constitutional convention acceptable to all parties and groups in Northern Ireland, Irishmen on both sides of the border had little to look forward to except more suffering and bloodshed.

Diplomatic Relations. During 1974–75 the Irish government established formal diplomatic ties with a number of Mediterranean countries, including Algeria, Egypt, Israel, and Lebanon. In May 1975, U. S. Ambassador to Ireland John D. J. Moore retired from his post after distinguished service to Irish-American relations.

L. PERRY CURTIS, JR.
Brown University

IRELAND · Information Highlights

Official Name: Ireland
Location: Island in the eastern North Atlantic Ocean.
Area: 27,136 square miles (70,283 sq km).
Population (1975 est.): 3,100,000.
Chief Cities (1973 est.): Dublin, the capital, 680,000; Cork, 224,000; Limerick, 140,000.
Government: *Head of state,* Cearbhall Ó Dálaigh, president (took office Dec. 19, 1974). *Head of government,* Liam Cosgrave, prime minister (taoiseach, took office March 1973). *Legislature*—Parliament; House of Representatives (Dáil Éireann) and Senate (Seanad Éireann).
Monetary Unit: Pound (0.4327 pound equals U. S.$1, May 1975).
Gross National Product (1974 est.): $6,300,000,000.
Manufacturing (major products): Processed foods, clothing, textiles, paper products.
Major Agricultural Products: Wheat, potatoes, sugar beets.
Foreign Trade (1974): *Exports,* $2,694,000,000; *imports,* $3,905,000,000.

ISRAEL

The year 1975 was one of continuing strain and anxiety for Israel. Israel, of course, has never known any time of assured tranquillity, but the tensions have been particularly great since the war of October 1973. That war ended the belief, generated by the easy victory in the Six-Day War of 1967, that Israel had an overwhelming military superiority over its Arab neighbors. And the Arabs' successful use of the oil weapon produced an international climate of increasing hostility toward Israel. (See also MIDDLE EAST; UNITED NATIONS.)

Unanswered Questions. Many fundamental questions remained unresolved. These included what concessions would have to be made to purchase peace and whether it could be obtained merely by limited concessions in the Sinai Desert or whether concessions would have to be made also on the much more sensitive matters of the Golan Heights and Jerusalem. The Palestinians remained a problem. Israel was also concerned about whether any concessions, however great, would elicit from the Arabs a genuine acceptance of the legitimacy of Israel's existence. If not, why yield strategic advantages that in a possible next war might make the difference between victory and defeat? But the making of concessions was not, in fact, a matter of free choice. Israel was under heavy pressure from the United States, and U. S. support was basic to Israel's existence.

Sinai Accords. These questions proved insoluble in the first round of diplomatic steps in March, but after a five-day visit to Washington in June by Premier Itzhak Rabin, and after further negotiations culminating in a period of strenuous "shuttle diplomacy" by U. S. Secretary of State Henry Kissinger at the end of August, a limited accord between Israel and Egypt was achieved. This was the outcome not of direct dealings with Egypt, which Israel would much prefer, but of Kissinger's mediation.

The Sinai pact, initialed by Israel at a September 1 ceremony in Jerusalem, amounted from Israel's point of view to giving up a great deal and getting little in return. By its terms Israel yielded to Egyptian demands that it withdraw from the Giddi and Mitla passes in the Sinai and return the Abu Rudeis oilfields to Egypt. The rather modest Egyptian concessions amounted to a general promise to relax the more rigorous aspects of its militant stance against Israel. The most specific point was the undertaking to permit nonmilitary Israeli cargoes to pass through the Suez Canal. This last point was put into effect in October. An accord on an Egyptian surveillance station was reached on December 29.

The Sinai agreement was described by Premier Rabin as no more than a chance to "buy time." It did not perceptibly lessen the chance of war with Syria over the Golan Heights, and it did not take into account the increasingly serious and central question of the Palestinians.

U. S. Secretary of State Henry Kissinger signs accord calling for U. S. civilians to man Sinai warning posts.

The Economy. Israeli difficulties did not concern only high-level diplomacy and strategy. There was a very grave economic problem, also a result of the 1973 war. Until that war, the Israeli economy was an example of striking success. Growing at an average annual rate of 9%, it had no balance of payments problem. But the cost of the war, continuing military expenses on a much higher level, and much higher prices of imported oil and food, totally changed the picture. Defense spending quadrupled within three years. In 1975 it was estimated at $3.5 billion. There was a steadily-increasing balance of payments deficit, reaching $3.5 billion in 1975 and expected to be about $4 billion in 1976. It was met only in part by U. S. aid. In introducing the draft budget for 1975–76 to the Knesset on February 24, Finance Minister Yehoshua Rabinowicz said that defense spending amounted to 40% of the budget, as compared with 17% before the 1973 war. The war itself had cost the equivalent of almost a year's gross national product. The London Institute for Strategic Studies reported in October that defense expenditures in Israel were running about $1,034 per person annually, or about two and a half times what the United States or the Soviet Union spends.

ISRAEL · Information Highlights

Official Name: State of Israel.
Location: Southwest Asia.
Area: 7,992 square miles (20,700 sq km).
Population (1975 est.): 3,400,000.
Chief Cities (1972 census): Jerusalem, the capital, 304,500; Tel Aviv-Jaffa, 362,200; Haifa, 217,400.
Government: *Head of state,* Ephraim Katzir, president (took office May 1973). *Head of government,* Itzhak Rabin, prime minister (took office June 1974). *Legislature* (unicameral)—Knesset.
Monetary Unit: Pound (6.12 pounds equal U. S.$1, July 1975).
Gross National Product (1974 est.): $11,700,000,000.
Manufacturing (major products): Polished diamonds, processed foods, chemicals, petroleum products, aircraft, electric and electronic equipment, textiles, clothing.
Major Agricultural Products: Citrus fruits, vegetables, cotton, eggs.
Foreign Trade (1973): *Exports,* $1,382,000,000; *imports,* $2,944,000,000.

The Israeli economy, instead of operating without waste in the crisis, was noted for its inefficiency. One in four employed Israelis was on the government payroll in 1975, while 28,000 industrial jobs could not be filled. Industrial productivity was poor—falling below the level of Italy. Night shifts were unacceptable to labor. Tax dodging was widespread, and in an attempt to cope with it, a simplified system of income tax was instituted by the government and came into force on August 1.

A widespread and complicated large-scale financial scandal involving diversion of state funds came to light in May. The national watchword, many observers say, had become hedonism rather than sacrifice. Foreign travel by Israelis increased 12.5% in 1975 over 1974. The Israeli government was aware of many of these weaknesses but felt impotent to deal with them resolutely in a country where trade unions are so strong.

Devaluations. The defects of the economy were inevitably reflected in the feebleness of the currency. The Israeli pound in 1975 was subject to a series of devaluations. The Israeli cabinet on June 17 decided on a 2% devaluation and also authorized a cabinet committee to make further devaluations, if needed, at a rate of 2% each month. In October, however, there was an additional 19% devaluation as well as new sales taxes.

Population. The strain of life in Israel is spelled out also in ominous demographic trends. Immigration to Israel from all sources was 55,-000 in 1973 and 32,000 in 1974, but the 1975 yearly total was estimated at only 16,000. The main reason was the decline in the number of Soviet Jews coming to Israel. Fewer were being allowed to leave the Soviet Union and of those who did leave, about 30% went to destinations other than Israel. Emigration increased, and in 1975 ran at an annual level of about 16,000, or approximately the same figure as immigration. The birthrate, however, rose significantly.

Internal Developments. Itzhak Rabin continued, with a slender Knesset majority, as premier, having held office since June 1974. He gave an impression of calm and stability in the face of great difficulties. On June 1 he appointed as his special adviser on military matters Maj. Gen. Ariel Sharon, the architect of the effective Israeli strike across the Suez Canal in the 1973 war. A new element was added to the complex array of political parties with the formation in May by Arieh Eliav of Yaad (Challenge), a new party comprising four members of the Knesset.

A major area of political differences in Israel was the question of whether to plant new settlements in the territories acquired in 1967. In fact some 60 new settlements have been created in certain of these areas, although some unauthorized settlements have also been broken up by government troops.

An Israeli-built jet fighter of advanced design was publicly shown for the first time on April 16. The crash of a military plane on November 25, which killed 20 men, was Israel's worst air disaster to date.

Terrorism and Reprisals. Israel was the target of a number of terrorist attacks. The worst of the year occurred on March 5 when 18 persons, including 6 non-Israelis, were slain after 8 Palestinian guerrillas seized a hotel in Tel Aviv. Israel also made a number of retaliatory attacks on guerrilla camps in Lebanon.

Soviet Contacts. Two Soviet envoys held talks in Jerusalem in early April with Premier Rabin and the defense and foreign ministers. These were the first high-level contacts since December 1973, but there was no resumption of normal diplomatic relations.

ARTHUR CAMPBELL TURNER
University of California, Riverside

The Israeli-built Kfir (Lion Cub) fighter-bomber was shown in April. It is a single-seated jet that flies at twice the speed of sound.

In Rome, jubilant Communists celebrate their June 15th victory in a regional election. The Communists are the main political force in north-central Italy.

ITALY

Italy's economy improved in some respects in 1975. The Communist party registered significant gains at the expense of the Christian Democrats in regional administrative elections.

ECONOMICS

Italy's gross national product (GNP) grew only 3.9% in 1974, compared to 5.9% in 1973. Estimates for 1975 suggested a further decline. On the other hand, the inflation rate, which was about 25% in 1974, declined in 1975, perhaps to 20%. The country's balance of payments deficit was also expected to be reduced to about $2 billion.

The International Monetary Fund awarded Italy a loan in August of $936 million, the largest that agency had made to any nation. Italy hoped to reduce its petroleum imports by $500–$600 million annually. It also arranged in 1975 to repay $500 million on the $2 billion loan received from West Germany in 1974.

Problems facing the Italian economy included slumping industrial production and domestic consumption, recurrent strikes, agrarian difficulties, and rising unemployment. Unemployment reached nearly 6%, a 20-year high, and was aggravated by the return of many workers from foreign countries.

The entire economic structure needed reexamination, according to the annual report issued in June by Guido Carli, the stern governor of the central Bank of Italy. He urged more efficient coordination of the public and private sectors of the economy and argued for more rigorous control over public expenditures. Defending his "moderate" monetary policy, Carli advised his countrymen to adjust to a less opulent way of life. He also criticized Italy's excessive reliance on the United States, which he accused of exporting its inflation.

When the government announced a $5.3 billion spending package on August 19, Carli resigned the post he had held for 15 years. He was succeeded by his deputy, Paoli Baffi, who will handle domestic economic problems, while Rinaldo Ossola will take charge of international monetary matters.

A government decision in August to adopt the West German PAL system of color television will require a $1 billion expenditure by the state TV monopoly, an action criticized by many as wasteful.

A blueprint for rescuing Venice from the ravages of floods, land subsidence, and pollution was approved by the government in April. About $480 million has been earmarked for this task under a bill passed in 1973.

POLITICS

Italy entered 1975 with a minority coalition government made up of Christian Democrats and the small Republican party. Premier Aldo Moro, a Christian Democrat, expected parliamentary support from the Socialists and Social Democrats.

At the Communist party's national congress in March, Enrico Berlinguer reaffirmed the desire for a "historic compromise" that would enable the Communists to share in decision-making with the Christian Democrats, although not necessarily entering into the government. He declared that the Communist party favored Italy's

remaining in both the European Economic Community (EEC) and the North Atlantic Treaty Organization (NATO). Most Christian Democratic leaders at the national level expressed very little interest in these Communist overtures.

Regional Administrative Elections. In anticipation of the administrative elections to be held in 15 of Italy's 20 regions on June 15, Parliament voted to lower the voting age from 21 to 18, thereby adding 3 million new voters to the electorate of 37 million.

The June elections inflicted the most serious setback the Christian Democrats had experienced in 30 years. Their faction-ridden party suffers from superannuated leadership, political immobility, and a chronic inability to cope satisfactorily with inflation, recession, and social inequities. It received only 35.3% of the vote, compared to 38.4% in the previous election. The Communists, on the other hand, increased their strength from 28.3% to 33.4%. Surveys indicated that perhaps 60% of the newly-enfranchised young voters cast their ballots for the Communists. The Socialists won 12.1%, compared to 9.8% before. The Social Democratic and Republican parties remained stable at 5.6% and 3.3% respectively. The neo-Fascist Social Movement-National Right Wing ticket lost strength, polling only 6.9%. The Liberals and other small parties dropped to 4.1% of the vote.

The election results established an entirely new game of politics. The left now controlled a solid belt of six regional governments in north-central Italy, extending from Piedmont through Liguria, Emilia-Romagna, Tuscany, and Umbria to the Marches. Communists have become the principal political force in 23 cities, including Turin, Genoa, Milan, Venice, Bologna, Florence, Perugia, Rome, Naples, and Cagliari. Declaring that the elections were of "extraordinary importance," Communist leader Berlinguer intensified his campaign to seek an accommodation with the Christian Democrats. At the same time he called for increased productivity and investments, elimination of waste in the public sector, tax reforms, an emergency construction program, an attack on crime and corruption, and debate on legalizing abortion.

Meanwhile Premier Moro tried to broaden his shaky government by seeking the addition of the Socialists and Social Democrats. Both these parties expressed reluctance to reestablish a center-left government until the Christian Democratic party seriously reexamined its own policies. They objected especially to Amintore Fanfani's continuation as secretary of that party. Fanfani had led the unsuccessful Vatican-supported fight against divorce in the referendum of May 1974. Fanfani's fate was settled on July 22 after four days of wrangling at the National Council of the Christian Democratic party where he was ousted by a vote of 103 to 69. Dr. Benigno

Zaccagnini, a little-known Resistance veteran from Faenza, was named interim secretary of the Christian Democratic party.

In the autumn Francesco De Martino, leader of the Socialist party, indicated that his followers opposed a "historic compromise" at this juncture but might consider a "left-wing alternative" of Socialists, Communists, and other parties after the 1977 parliamentary elections.

Family Law. After seven years of debate, Parliament passed a new family law in April that raised the minimum age for marriage to 18 and terminated the legal powers of the Italian husband to be a family despot. Equality within the marriage partnership is now guaranteed. The new legislation conflicts with Roman Catholic canon law, which still permits marriage at the earlier ages of 16 for boys and 14 for girls. Elimination of this legal anomaly will probably require revision of the Concordat of 1929, a move that the Moro government favors negotiating with the Holy See.

Abortion. The legalization of abortion gained increasing attention and was backed by most of the leftist parties. A major breakthrough occurred in February when the Constitutional Court ruled that some of the present penal code provisions covering abortion were "partly unconstitutional." Abortion is not a crime, the court held, if pregnancy endangers the physical or psychological health of the mother.

Violence. Violence, both political and nonpolitical, escalated in 1975. During the election campaign, hit-and-run raids by neo-Fascists and extreme leftists became almost daily occurrences. A prominent Christian Democratic member of parliament was kidnapped in Sardinia in November. He was the 49th person to be kidnapped during the year. That same month Pier

President Ford and Secretary of State Kissinger greet Pope Paul VI on June 3 visit to Vatican.

UPI

Paolo Pasolini, a well-known filmmaker, was bludgeoned to death in Rome.

Scandals. The U. S. Senate Foreign Relations subcommittee on multinational corporations revealed that various Italian officials of petroleum and other corporations had made substantial financial contributions to Italian political parties for favors. Over a nine-year period at least $46 million was paid out by one corporation's officials, mostly to parties in the governing coalition, but also including $86,000 to the Communist party. Such practices, known as the "strategy of lubrication," are not uncommon in Italy.

FOREIGN RELATIONS

U. S. President Ford and Secretary of State Kissinger were in Rome on June 3 to meet with Italian government leaders and Pope Paul VI. They hoped that their visit would strengthen the Christian Democrats in the forthcoming regional elections. Kissinger made it clear that the United States did not wish to see the Communists admitted to the Italian government or sharing a voice in NATO policymaking.

After the election he put pressure on the Christian Democratic party to "revitalize itself," and in a statement that brought back memories of U. S. involvement in Italian politics in 1948, he said, "We're giving Italy as much advice and as much encouragement as we can." Washington also announced a delay in plans to remove obsolete nuclear warheads from Italy, in case such an action be construed as a sign that the United States had decided that Italy was about to become Communist.

Leftist quarters in Italy were annoyed when the United States in October delayed issuing a visa to the head of the foreign section of the Italian Communist party so he could fulfill an invitation to speak at the Council on Foreign Relations in New York City. They were even angrier when they learned that Giorgio Almirante, leader of the neo-Fascist Social Movement, was being invited that same month to the White House for a discussion with members of President Ford's staff.

Relations with Other Nations. On October 1, Italy's friendly ties with Tito's Yugoslavia were strengthened by their joint announcement of final confirmation of the October 1954 agreements regarding Trieste and the boundary in Venezia Giulia.

Italy generally catered to Middle East oil producers in the hope of obtaining preferential treatment in the allotment of supplies and in the reinvestment in Italy of funds from the OPEC nations. Italy, however, did not support the resolution in the UN General Assembly that condemned Zionism as racist. The Italian Communist party also denounced this Soviet-backed resolution.

Premier Moro represented Italy at the European Security Conference in Helsinki in July. President Leone made a state visit to Moscow in November, the first by an Italian president since 1960.

Premier Moro was invited by President Giscard d'Estaing of France to a conference in Rambouillet in November of the heads of government of six major industrial powers. The conferees included the United States, Japan, West Germany, France, Britain, and Italy. They agreed to monitor international exchange rates and to facilitate faster action by their central banks in coping with fiscal crises.

CHARLES F. DELZELL
Vanderbilt University

Italian President Giovanni Leone (*center*), with Soviet President Nikolai Podgorny (*left*), on arrival in the USSR for a six-day visit in November.

UPI

--- **ITALY · Information Highlights** ---

Official Name: Italian Republic.
Location: Southern Europe.
Area: 116,303 square miles (301,225 sq km).
Population (1975 est.): 55,000,000.
Chief Cities (1971 census): Rome, the capital, 2,779,836; Milan, 1,724,173; Naples, 1,232,877; Turin, 1,177,939.
Government: *Head of state,* Giovanni Leone, president (took office Dec. 1971). *Head of government,* Aldo Moro, premier (took office Nov. 1974). *Legislature—* Parliament: Senate and Chamber of Deputies.
Monetary Unit: Lira (668.8 lire equal U. S.$1, Aug. 1975).
Gross National Product (1973 est.): $128,400,000,000.
Manufacturing (major products): Automobiles, petroleum products, machinery, processed foods, chemicals.
Major Agricultural Products: Wheat, grapes, tomatoes, citrus fruits, rice, vegetables, olives, nuts.
Foreign Trade (1974): *Exports,* $32,806,000,000; *imports,* $44,338,000,000.

Emperor Hirohito and Empress Nagako toured the Smithsonian Institution with President and Mrs. Ford during the Japanese leader's U. S. visit in October. The painting on the wall was executed by the empress.

UPI

JAPAN

On August 15 at the Nippon Budokan Hall in Tokyo, the Japanese government held a memorial service for over 3 million persons killed in World War II. Attended by Emperor Hirohito, Empress Nagako, and Premier Takeo Miki, the ceremony marked the 30th anniversary of the end of the conflict. According to the premier's office, the nation's population exceeded 111 million. About half of all these Japanese were born after Aug. 15, 1945, when Japan accepted surrender terms.

Japan's postwar generation faced the despair of defeat and experienced an unprecedented occupation, mainly by U. S. forces, between 1945 and 1952. After the peace treaty, the country moved from reconstruction to the headlong growth of the 1960's. Like any other post-industrial society, in the early 1970's Japan encountered the acute worldwide energy shortage and felt the impact of what the Japanese called stagflation. By 1975 there were signs that the Japanese economy had turned the corner toward controlled growth again. In any case, Japan boasted the second largest gross national product (GNP) in the non-Communist world.

Japan's status as a world power was demonstrated in 1975 by a series of visits to Japan by high-level leaders and by Japanese involvement in summit conferences abroad. The historic visit by the emperor and empress to the United States symbolized both the close postwar ties to the United States and the closing chapter of wartime memories.

INTERNATIONAL AFFAIRS

Although Japan's basic policy of cooperation with the United States, within the context of the Japanese-U. S. security treaty system, remained unchanged, a need to conduct a thorough review of Asian policy was recognized in May. The

UPI

Ties between Great Britain and Japan were strengthened by the May visit to Tokyo of Queen Elizabeth.

need arose from the collapse of the U. S. effort in Indochina, and South Vietnam's surrender to Communist-led forces. The foreign ministry's annual *Blue Book on Diplomacy,* published in September 1975, assigned priority to the promotion of good relations with neighboring nations in the East Asian region. Most significantly, Foreign Minister Kiichi Miyazawa referred to the need for stability on the Korean peninsula, considered necessary for the peace and security of Japan.

Relations with the United States. On Jan. 24, 1975, Foreign Minister Miyazawa, in a policy speech to the Diet, pledged maintenance of the relationship with the United States as the cornerstone of Japan's foreign policy. The nation would, however, develop a "diversified diplomacy" aimed to develop ties with other nations, including those with different political systems. On June 18, U. S. Secretary of State Henry Kissinger, in a speech to the Japan Society in New

York, promised that the United States would not turn away from Asia as a result of the setback in Indochina. Between these speeches, on April 10, Miyazawa consulted with Kissinger in Washington on security issues and the forthcoming summit meeting.

In November, 1974, U. S. President Ford was in Japan, the first incumbent U. S. president to visit the country. In the first meeting since the new Miki cabinet was formed, the premier consulted with the president in Washington on August 5–6. Celebrating an era of "no-problem" diplomacy, the communiqué stressed the importance of the U. S.-Japan security agreement. The United States promised to maintain its forces in South Korea. Premier Miki expressed Japan's intention to ratify the nuclear non-proliferation treaty "at the earliest possible opportunity."

On August 28, after his visit to Korea, U. S. Defense Secretary James R. Schlesinger in Tokyo reaffirmed the intention to maintain U. S. forces in South Korea. With Michita Sakata, director general of defense, he agreed to establish an annual ministerial meeting on defense to implement the security treaty.

Returning from a visit to Peking, Secretary Kissinger stopped over in Tokyo on October 23–24 to confer with Premier Miki. Their talks centered on the deadlocked Japan-China peace treaty negotiations and the summit conference of industrial nations in Paris on November 15–17.

The first official visit of a Japanese monarch to the continental United States was less important politically but nonetheless significant symbolically. On September 30, Emperor Hirohito and Empress Nagako left Tokyo, accompanied by Deputy Premier Takeo Fukuda and representatives of the imperial household agency. After a 2-day rest in Williamsburg, Va., the imperial couple were received at the White House on October 2. On October 3 the emperor and empress hosted an official dinner at the Smithsonian Institution. They toured New York City, including a stop at the United Nations on October 5–6; Chicago on October 7; and Los Angeles, San Diego, and San Francisco on October 8–10. They wound up their tour in Hawaii on October 11–13, and returned to Tokyo on October 14. In a speech in Washington, the emperor used the strongest phrase yet when he stated that he "deeply deplored" Japan's role in the Pacific war.

Interspersed with the ceremonial functions were a number of activities reflecting the couple's personal interests. The emperor, an avid marine biologist, inspected oceanographic institutes at Woods Hole, Mass., and La Jolla, Calif. The empress, an accomplished artist, visited the Freer Gallery in Washington. Both stopped at Disneyland.

Relations with Korea. The Korean peninsula, an object of Japanese and U. S. concern and the subject of conflicting UN resolutions, remained divided between the jurisdictions of the Demo-

UPI

Junko Tabei became the first woman to climb Mt. Everest, the world's highest peak, in June.

cratic People's Republic of (North) Korea and the Republic of (South) Korea. Late in October, Premier Miki told the Diet that recognition of North Korea was "not on the political or diplomatic list."

Japan had given South Korean representatives a similar assurance at the ministerial conference, held in Seoul on September 15. This long-delayed meeting was held after an exchange of oral agreements between Miyazawa and Foreign Minister Kim Dong-jo, in July. Seoul did not admit to complicity in the abduction from Tokyo of an opposition leader, Kim Dae-jung, in 1973, but privately agreed to dismiss one of its Tokyo embassy officials allegedly connected with the kidnapping. Tokyo in turn agreed to take steps to avert crimes by Koreans resident in Japan, such as the attempted plan to assassinate Korean President Park Chung Hee in 1974. Meanwhile, the foreign ministry announced that Japan would extend to South Korea economic assistance of $300 million annually, beginning in 1976.

Relations with China. Japan was walking a similar diplomatic tightrope in its relations with the People's Republic of China and the Republic of China (Taiwan). Tokyo had resumed normal relations with Peking in 1972, but talks toward a peace treaty were snagged on the Chinese desire to include a so-called anti-hegemony clause. On September 24, Miyazawa, in New York City for a meeting of the UN General Assembly, entered the first foreign-minister-level negotiations with Chiao Kuan-hua, his Chinese counterpart. The exchange led only to a difference of opinion. China wanted to use the anti-hegemony principle to thwart the USSR, while Japan insisted that it was a universal principle.

Meanwhile, on September 15, Tokyo reestablished civil aviation service on a private basis with Taipei. With no formal diplomatic tie to Taiwan, Japan thus revived contact by air. Contacts had been severed when Tokyo-Peking service was established in 1974.

Relations with the USSR. In talks .with the Soviet Union toward a settlement of wartime issues, progress was slow. Communist party chief Leonid Brezhnev proposed a treaty of peace and friendship, but in February Premier Miki turned the suggestion aside. A settlement awaited solution of the "northern territories" issue, the continued occupation of the southern Kuril Islands by the USSR. Meanwhile, in October the Hokkaido government asked the foreign ministry to protest seizures of and fines levied on Japanese fishing vessels that were operating in the area of the Kurils.

Relations with Great Britain. Japanese ties with Britain were symbolically strengthened by the visit on May 6–12 of Queen Elizabeth and the duke of Edinburgh to Japan. The emperor and empress had stopped in London on their European tour in 1971.

DOMESTIC AFFAIRS

In November 1974, shortly after President Ford's visit, Kakuei Tanaka had been forced out of the premiership because of "Japan's Watergate," an investigation of his interlocking financial and political power. Two of his own party faction chiefs, Takeo Miki and Takeo Fukuda, had resigned in protest against Tanaka's campaign practices. On December 9, the Diet selected Takeo Miki to be premier after his surprise election as president of the majority Liberal-Democratic party (LDP). With only a slim majority, Miki attempted a strategy of compromise with opposition parties, in order to lift Japan out of a sharp recession.

Party Politics and Elections. When Premier Miki first addressed the 75th session of the Diet in January, his LDP held 277 of 491 seats in the House of Representatives, with the remainder split among opposition parties including the Japan Socialists (JSP), the Japan Communists (JCP), Komeito (KMT), and the Democratic Socialists (DSP). In the House of Councillors the LDP occupied 128 of 252 seats.

From the majority LDP, Miki formed a cabinet composed of powerful faction leaders including Fukuda as deputy premier, Miyazawa as foreign minister, Masayoshi Ohira as finance minister, and Yasuhiro Nakasone as secretary general of the LDP. He chose a non-party intellectual, Michio Nagai, to be education minister.

In local elections held between January and the end of April, the "conservative" LDP and "progressive" opposition parties fought to a standoff. A conservative, Yoshiaki Nakaya won the gubernatorial race in Aichi, the prefecture that encompasses Nagoya, and the LDP placed 12 candidates in other governorships. The leftists

UPI

Prince Akihito and Princess Michiko narrowly escaped injury when bombs exploded during their Okinawa visit.

won urban strongholds in Tokyo, Kanagawa (including Yokohama), and Osaka. The popular Gov. Ryokichi Minobe of Tokyo, despite a rift in his JSP–JCP coalition, won a third term by a narrow margin. On April 27 conservatives won mayoralties in 121 of 165 contested cities.

The Economy. In all of these elections, inflation was identified as the priority problem on the domestic front. In October, the consumer price index (CPI) for the 23 Tokyo wards was still rising at a 1.7% monthly rate, representing a 10.2% rise over 1974, to a level of 177.6 (1970=100). On October 25, the House of Representatives passed three controversial bills designed to increase tobacco prices, liquor taxes, and postal rates. It was estimated that these would raise the CPI by an additional 0.9% per month.

Although unemployment remained relatively low (1.7% of the labor force), Japan faced complicated economic problems never experienced by Japan's postwar generation. In 1974, the GNP reached a nominal level of 131,880 billion yen ($438 billion), but in 1970 prices this netted only 89,190 billion yen ($297 billion). Thus the GNP actually fell by almost 2%, the first net annual decline since World War II. In a revised economic outlook published by the government in October, experts predicted that real GNP for the fiscal year 1975–76 would total about $300 billion, up 2.2% over fiscal 1974.

In January the LDP government proposed a balanced budget totaling 21,288 billion yen ($71 billion), an increase of about 25% over the previous year. On October 9 the Miki cabinet introduced a supplementary budget designed to lift the economy out of recession. Of total expenditures on public works, housing, anti-pollution projects, and trade, some 2,290 billion yen ($7.6 billion) was to be financed by so-called deficit

Prime Minister Takeo Miki and President Ford met at the White House in August to discuss mutual problems.

Mattresses are spread in a Tokyo plant to prepare for a railway strike that began Nov. 26 and lasted 10 days.

bonds. It was the first time in 10 years that the government issued such deficit-financing bonds. In the Diet on October 17, Finance Minister Ohira promised that the government would try to return to a balanced budget in 1976–77 without issuing additional deficit-financing bonds. Ohira promised relief to financially-troubled local governments.

In the 1960's the Japanese became used to an economy of growth, buttressed by a strong propensity to consume. In the 1975 White Paper on the People's Life, released by the cabinet in November, it was pointed out that the Japanese had rediscovered the traditional virtue of frugality. Conservative consumption, according to the paper, would be a useful instrument in realizing a smooth transition from a high growth to a low but stable growth pattern. Real-term consumer spending in fiscal 1974–75 had increased by only 1.1% over the previous year.

Social Problems. An echo of the growth period was heard, however, in Expo '75, the International Ocean Exposition opened July 19 on the Motobu Peninsula, Okinawa. This sea fair, scheduled to run for six months, was dedicated by Crown Prince Akihito. Its theme was environmental, "the sea we would like to see." Two days before the opening, the celebration was marred when radical students in Naha threw a fire bomb at the crown prince and Princess Michiko. The couple narrowly escaped injury. The protest symptomized some Okinawans' res-

In May, Japan hosted the 9th World Petroleum Congress, attended by Prince Akihito and Princess Michiko. More than 70 countries were represented at the six-day conference.

tiveness over the display of the main islands' wealth and power and the relative neglect of Okinawa and the Ryukyu Islands.

In rapid growth or stable growth, the Japanese life style continued to change at a geometric rate on the four main islands. In a preliminary 1975 census report, the agriculture-forestry ministry reported that the number of farming households had dropped below the 5 million level for the first time in modern history. This number was down 8.3% from that recorded in the 1970 survey, the sharpest 5-year decrease on record. The farming population declined by 12.8% to 23,195,000. Only one out of every eight Japanese families was engaged exclusively in agriculture. Nearly 90% of the farming households depended on additional income from other activities.

The remainder of the Japanese households was made up of city-dwellers. Of the total 1975 estimated population of 111 million, some 23 million lived in Japan's 10 largest cities. Tokyo's wards held 8.6 million people, and Osaka had a population of 2.8 million.

Death of Sato. Former Premier Eisaku Sato died of a cerebral hemorrhage in Tokyo on June 3, 1975. Premier from 1964 to 1972, Sato held the record for unbroken tenure as leader of the nation. He was awarded the Nobel Prize for Peace in 1974.

ARDATH W. BURKS
Rutgers University

The 25th anniversary of Japan's Self Defense Forces was celebrated at the Asaka Camp near Tokyo in November.

JAPAN · Information Highlights

Official Name: Japan.
Location: East Asia.
Area: 143,689 square miles (372,154 sq km).
Population (1975 est.): 111,100,000.
Chief Cities (1975): Tokyo, the capital, 11,500,000; Osaka, 2,800,000; Yokohama, 2,600,000; Nagoya, 2,-000,000.
Government: *Head of state,* Hirohito, emperor (acceded 1926). *Head of government,* Takeo Miki, premier (took office December 1974). *Legislature*—Diet: House of Councillors and House of Representatives.
Monetary Unit: Yen (297.4 yen equal U. S.$1, Aug. 1975).
Gross National Product (1974 est.): $457,000,000,000.
Manufacturing (major products): Ships, automobiles, electronic components, textiles, iron, steel, petrochemicals, machinery, electrical appliances, processed foods.
Major Agricultural Products: Rice, wheat, barley, potatoes, vegetables, fruits, tobacco, tea, fish.
Foreign Trade (1974): *Exports,* $55,580,000,000; *imports,* $62,061,000,000.

JORDAN

In 1975, Jordan's King Hussein regained some of the ground he lost at the October 1974 Arab summit conference in Rabat, Morocco. In 1974, Arab heads of state had agreed to name the Palestine Liberation Organization (PLO) in Hussein's place as the sole legitimate spokesman for Palestinians on the West Bank of the Jordan River. Developments in the U. S.-mediated negotiations between Israel and Egypt on the Sinai question, however, tended to make it impossible for Arab leaders to keep the Jordanian monarch isolated indefinitely. Simultaneously, Hussein's own quiet efforts and a controversial arms deal with the United States facilitated his return to a position of influence in Arab politics.

Inter-Arab Affairs. Although Hussein had strong doubts about the PLO's ability to negotiate an Israeli withdrawal from the West Bank in order to establish an independent Palestinian entity, he publicly endorsed the PLO's new role, adding on January 21 that he would be the first to recognize a Palestine provisional government-in-exile headed by PLO leader Yasir Arafat. He spoke of improved relations with the PLO but reiterated his refusal to allow guerrillas to operate from Jordan. It was this situation that caused the bloody Jordanian civil war of September 1970. Meanwhile, Hussein took steps to undermine the PLO's chances—which were already quite slim as Israel refused to recognize the guerrilla organization—of delivering the settlement he could not. In 1975, Jordan poured unprecedented amounts of development funds into the West Bank to give the population an alternative to total collaboration with the Israelis. To this end, Jordan budgeted $9 million for the West Bank in 1975, thus doubling its 1974 expenditures for the area.

At the same time, Hussein directed efforts toward improving his relations with Egypt and Syria. The cornerstones of his 1975 diplomatic campaign were communication and coordination with the rest of the Arab world. In addition, he successfully maintained a balance between the Syrians and the Egyptians, whose relations were strained by the Sinai negotiations. In May the king invited President Anwar Sadat on the first state visit ever by an Egyptian head of government. He also made a new approach to Syria's President Hafez al-Assad that led to top-level coordination of both countries' political, military, and economic strategies.

The new ties with Syria were facilitated by the Sinai disengagement talks; the negotiations appeared to be moving toward Egypt's giving up its military option. On April 3, Hussein visited Damascus for talks with President Assad on the possibility of coordinating political strategies. Following Assad's visit to Amman on June 10, marking the first visit of a Syrian president to Jordan since 1957, a ministerial joint supreme committee was formed to take responsibility for planning the coordination of political, military, economic, cultural, and educational matters. On August 18, King Hussein led a delegation of top Jordanian officials to Damascus for further talks. The formation of a joint political command, called the Supreme Syrian-Jordanian Command Council and headed by Assad and Hussein, was announced on August 22.

Although the joint command council fell short of being a true joint military command, it was announced that on issues of war and peace, Jordan and Syria would "adopt joint and coordinated decisions and positions." This was interpreted to warn Israel that if the new Sinai settlement did not permit the intervention of Egyptian military forces in a new war with Syria, Israel would still be faced with a two-front war.

With the strengthening of ties with Syria, Hussein's strategy for regaining his political stature led to success; rather than being considered an outcast, Hussein was again enjoying the status of a full-fledged member of the Arab world and being consulted on major decisions. In addition, the regained popularity resulted in military and economic aid to Jordan from the oil-rich Arab states that was estimated to reach $300 million by the end of the year.

U. S.-Jordanian Relations. Following Hussein's April 28–May 11 visit to the United States, a severe strain was placed on future relations when the U. S. Congress moved against a Ford administration proposal to sell Jordan $350 million in arms, including 14 mobile batteries of the sophisticated Hawk anti-aircraft missile system. Congress, doubting that the missiles would be used for defensive purposes only, tried to stop the deal, but, when Hussein threatened to buy Soviet weapons, offered a compromise in September whereby Jordan could buy the missiles if it agreed to place them on fixed sites.

On September 18, Hussein refused to accept the terms, calling them "insulting to Jordan's national dignity." The incident thus marked a new phase in what had been Jordan's long-friendly relations with the United States.

F. NICHOLAS WILLARD
Georgetown University

------ **JORDAN · Information Highlights** ------

Official Name: Hashemite Kingdom of Jordan.
Location: Southwest Asia.
Area: 37,738 square miles (97,740 sq km).
Population (1975 est.): 2,700,000.
Chief Cities (1972 est.): Amman, the capital, 520,700; Zarqa, 225,000; Irbid, 115,000.
Government: *Head of state,* Hussein ibn Talal, king (acceded Aug. 1952). *Head of government,* Zaid al-Rifai, premier (took office May 1973). *Legislature—* National Assembly: Senate and House of Representatives.
Monetary Unit: Dinar (0.3110 dinar equals U. S.$1, July 1974).
Gross National Product (1974 est.): $1,000,000,000.
Manufacturing (major products): Cement, petroleum products, cigarettes, vegetable oil, flour.
Major Agricultural Products: Wheat, tomatoes, barley, fruits, corn, olives, sorghum, grapes, tobacco.
Foreign Trade (1974): *Exports,* $115,000,000; *imports,* $487,000,000.

KANSAS

Kansas felt the same economic pinches as other areas of the United States in 1975, but the situation was less critical than in the more populous areas of the nation. The high cost of living brought more discussion about wages than ever before, particularly where public employment was concerned, and a number of cities were confronted by threats of strikes by teachers, police, and fire departments. In Kansas City the police struck for a brief time, but there were no serious consequences.

Agriculture. Wheat production in Kansas in 1975 stood at 345 million bushels, 26 million bushels above the 1974 crop. The corn crop was estimated at 137.28 million bushels, up 4%. The sorghum grain crop was estimated at 148.5 million bushels, up 12% over 1974, and soybean production, at 22.4 million bushels, was up also. Unfortunately for the farmer, crop prices were down in 1975. Some wheat men felt that federal politics and mixed reactions nationwide to another wheat deal with the Soviet Union eliminated much of their incentive for a strong 1976 market, but others disagreed.

The cattle industry, depressed since 1973, got a boost in 1975 as young cattle began to fill Kansas feedlots again. Feeder cattle placements in March 1975 were 131% greater than at the same time in 1974, and an upward trend continued although recovery to the high 1972 level was not envisioned at any time during the year.

Weather. Kansas experienced little severe storm weather, but the summer was one of the driest on record, especially in the eastern part of the state. After the drought was broken, another prolonged dry spell followed in September and October, which delayed the planting of winter wheat. There was some blowing dust in western Kansas in the spring and summer, and the entire state experienced the unusual temperature inversion in early July that brought haze and even smog to the Great Plains.

Legislation. The 1975 Legislature appropriated a record budget of almost $1.5 billion, some $10 million more than had been recommended by Gov. Robert Bennett. Of that, $23 million was allocated for state employee salary increases, which the governor had favored. Legislators got an increased expense allowance but no pay raise. Although there was some bitterness in the 1975 session, with charges made that too many major decisions were made by too few legislators, the session ended with positive action outweighing the negative. Nearly $39 million in additional state aid for local school districts and increased aid to public junior colleges was provided. Faculty salaries at state colleges and universities were increased, and some funds for new campus construction were allocated.

A new seven-member court of appeals was created to relieve some of the appellate load

AP

Kansas suffered severe dry spells in summer and in early fall, which left many farm ponds completely dry.

of the state supreme court, beginning in 1977. The politically-oriented highway commission was replaced by a department of transportation. Among other accomplishments were codification of banking laws, an improved commercial credit code, increased state aid for vocational education and for local mental health centers, and broadened powers for the department of health and environment.

ROBERT W. RICHMOND
Kansas State Historical Society

KANSAS · Information Highlights

Area: 82,264 square miles (213,064 sq km).
Population (1974 est.): 2,270,000. *Density:* 28 per sq mi.
Chief Cities (1970 census): Topeka, the capital, 125,011; Wichita, 276,554; Kansas City, 168,213; Overland Park, 79,034.
Government (1975): *Chief Officers*—governor, Robert F. Bennett (R); lt. gov., Shelby Smith (R). *Legislature*—Senate, 40 members; House of Representatives, 125 members.
Education (1974–75): *Enrollment*—public elementary schools, 243,296 pupils; public secondary schools, 206,268; nonpublic schools, 32,000; colleges and universities, 113,352 students. *Public school expenditures,* $445,890,000 ($990 per pupil).
State Finances (fiscal year 1974): *Revenues,* $1,234,-503,000; *expenditures,* $1,112,219,000.
Personal Income (1974): $12,272,000,000; per capita, $5,406.
Labor Force (Aug. 1975): *Nonagricultural wage and salary earners,* 777,800; *insured unemployed,* 17,500.

UPI

A National Guardsman stands watch in Louisville in September, when anti-busing demonstrations flared up.

KENTUCKY

The year 1975 was relatively quiet in Kentucky, although there was a gubernatorial election, spring and summer flash floods in some parts of the state, and protests in Louisville and Jefferson county against court ordered busing. Gov. Julian Carroll, a Democrat, won the November election. In the face of a declining birth rate nationwide, the population increased as Kentuckians returned home in large numbers from depressed industrial areas in the North and Middle West. College enrollments climbed, while at the same time the state's economic outlook became somewhat darker.

─────── KENTUCKY · Information Highlights ───────

Area: 40,395 square miles (104,623 sq km).
Population (1974 est.): 3,357,000. *Density:* 83 per sq mi.
Chief Cities (1970 census): Frankfort, the capital, 21,902; Louisville, 361,958; Lexington, 108,137; Covington, 52,535.
Government (1975): *Chief Officers*—governor, Julian M. Carroll (D); lt. gov., Thelma Stovall (D). *General Assembly*—Senate, 38 members; House of Representatives, 100 members.
Education (1974–75): *Enrollment*—public elementary schools, 436,144 pupils; public secondary, 265,229; nonpublic, 57,600; colleges and universities, 113,755 students. *Public school expenditures,* $476,798,000 ($722 per pupil).
State Finances (fiscal year 1974): *Revenues,* $2,075,580,-000; *expenditures,* $1,816,615,000.
Personal Income (1974): $15,007,000,000; per capita, $4,-470.
Labor Force (July 1975): *Nonagricultural wage and salary earners,* 1,071,800; *insured unemployed,* 46,-100 (4.2%).

Coal mining continued at a high level, but previous boom prices fell. Whisky production declined. Burley tobacco farmers were warned to expect a competitive market for their crop, expected to be larger than that of 1974. Allocations of natural gas for schools and industry were cut back drastically.

The Weather. Heavy rains in mid-March caused flooding in mountain valleys and river plains and led President Gerald R. Ford to declare 11 southern and western counties of the state disaster areas. Two months later, floods hit eastern Kentucky, where four additional counties were added to the disaster list. Waterlogged fields delayed the planting of crops in the western part of the state and, months later, fall rains in all areas damaged corn and tobacco as the harvest season approached.

Desegregation. In July the 6th U. S. circuit court of appeals instructed District Judge James F. Gordon to institute desegregation of public schools in Louisville and Jefferson county, where school boards had exhausted efforts to avoid compliance with a 1973 federal court ruling ordering the integration. Attempts to obtain further delays were rejected by federal judges, and on September 4, Judge Gordon's plan for busing between schools in Louisville and those in the surrounding suburbs of Jefferson county went into effect.

The protest, immediate and persistent, included marches, boycotts, violent confrontations with police, fires, and stoning of buses carrying children. In late October there was a demonstration, apparently organized by labor leaders, by some 3,000 white Louisvillians in Washington, D. C.

Politics. Voters remained apathetic most of the year, while political hopefuls in record numbers filed for the various state offices. Republican leaders settled on Robert E. Gable, a wealthy landowner. Julian M. Carroll, an incumbent and a former lieutenant governor, was the leading contender for the Democrats. Both Gable and Carroll easily won nominations in the May primaries, in which the only surprise was the victory of veteran politician Thelma Stovall over 10 opponents in the Democratic race for lieutenant governor.

The campaigns preceding the November elections brought out no major issues and stirred little excitement until eruption of the busing controversy in Jefferson county. Gable immediately announced his opposition to forced busing as Carroll followed in short order, and other candidates and office holders fell into line. Governor Carroll's majority was of record proportions, and Stovall became the first woman to win the lieutenant governorship. Two constitutional amendments won the electorate's approval; one of them requires a drastic overhaul of the state's judicial system.

JAMES F. HOPKINS
University of Kentucky

UPI

President Jomo Kenyatta (2nd from right) stands on the steps of the state house in Mombasa in March with rival leaders of the Angolan liberation movement.

KENYA

The assassination of Josiah Mwangi Kariuki, a major critic of the Kenyan government of President Jomo Kenyatta, made 1975 a tumultuous year in the nation's politics. The country's political institutions, established at independence in 1963, were severely shaken.

The Assassination. Kariuki had never risen higher than an assistant minister in Kenyatta's government. He had, however, become a major political figure because of his charges that the government did not do enough for Kenya's impoverished population, and he made large donations to various causes throughout the country from his own considerable wealth.

The events surrounding Kariuki's death in early March and the belated discovery of his body convinced many Kenyans that the government was involved in the plot against Kariuki. These suspicions sparked numerous protests and a parliamentary inquiry. A select committee of the National Assembly named the men it believed had killed Kariuki and implicated the government's general service unit, the special police. A vote of the National Assembly on June 11 to accept the committee's report was made possible by the pro-committee votes of Minister for Works Masinde Muliro and two assistant ministers, all of whom were immediately dismissed from their positions. Other government critics were jailed. On October 15 the crisis suddenly deepened when two members of parliament, Martin Shikuku and the deputy speaker, John Marie Seroney, were arrested and indefinitely detained. This followed Shikuku's warning that there were those who were trying to kill parliament as they had the Kenya African National Union (KANU),

Kenya's only political party. On October 16, Kenyatta told KANU that other members who did not support the government would receive the same treatment. "The hawk," said Kenyatta "is always in the sky and ready to swoop on the chickens."

East African Relations. In recent years, Kenya has tried to avoid involvement in the fight between Uganda and Tanzania, its partners in the East African Community (EAC). However, cooperation within the community continues to deteriorate because of disputes over finances and other EAC policies. In a June meeting of the National Assembly, Attorney General Charles Njonjo called for the dissolution of the community, but Finance Minister Mwai Kibaki later supported the EAC because of its financial benefits. A formal review of the 1967 EAC treaty, expected to be completed in 1976, was authorized by the three member states in August.

Kenya's relations with its neighbors were also affected adversely by an escalating arms race. In August Defense Minister James Gichuru announced plans to use a $5 million credit from the United States to purchase modern warplanes. Kenya's buildup will counter new planes, mainly Russian and Chinese, acquired by the bordering states of Uganda, Tanzania, Somalia, and Ethiopia. In the past Kenya has relied heavily on British arms and military training.

Economic Development. Economic growth in 1975 continued to be slowed by the increased expense of petroleum imports. To help correct the country's balance of payments deficit, the International Monetary Fund (IMF) loaned Kenya $84 million. The World Bank announced a loan of $63 million toward construction of the Gitaru hydroelectric power station on the upper Tana River. A 10-nation UN study released during the year argued that economists had been overestimating the income gap between Kenya and the United States, which was, however, substantial. Agricultural exports from Kenya to the United States rose 34% to $28.6 million in 1974. Major products exported included coffee, tea, and processed sugar.

JAY E. HAKES
University of New Orleans

KENYA · Information Highlights

Official Name: Republic of Kenya.
Location: East coast of Africa.
Area: 244,959 square miles (582,644 sq km).
Population (1975 est.): 13,300,000.
Chief Cities (1970 est.): Nairobi, the capital, 535,200; Mombasa, 255,400.
Government: *Head of state,* Jomo Kenyatta, president (took office Dec. 1964). *Head of government,* Jomo Kenyatta. *Legislature* (unicameral)—National Assembly.
Monetary Unit: Kenya shilling (8.16 shillings equal U. S. $1, Oct. 1975).
Gross National Product (1974 est.): $2,500,000,000.
Manufacturing (major products): Construction materials, processed agricultural products, petroleum products.
Major Agricultural Products: Coffee, tea, sugarcane, sisal, corn, cassava, pyrethrum, fruits, livestock.
Foreign Trade (1974 est.): *Exports,* $600,000,000; *imports,* $1,038,000,000.

Roman Catholic priest James Sinnott tearfully parts with supporters in South Korea in April after authorities refused to renew his visa.

KOREA

The two Koreas talked peace and warned of war, fueling mutual misperception and spiralling the arms race between them. Without parallel as garrison states, they were orthodox, rigid poles of antitheses: South Korea, the spearhead of anti-communism, and North Korea, the vanguard of anti-imperialism. In 1975, South Korea again failed to gain UN membership.

SOUTH KOREA

The heavily export-oriented economy, increasingly dependent on foreign sources for credit, capital, oil, and food grains, reeled from the effects of worldwide recession and inflated costs of imported raw materials. A $2.4 billion trade deficit in 1974 forced a 20% currency devaluation in December 1974. Even so, the GNP grew 8.2% in 1974, impressive but a sharp drop from the record 16.5% increase of 1973. The 1975 growth rate was estimated at 6.5%.

Improvements in living conditions lagged behind rising expectations. Uneven income distribution and unplanned urbanization accentuated sociopolitical tensions in cities. By mid-year the urban-rural population ratio reached 56%–44%, compared with 35%–65% in 1966. About 80% of urban workers earned less than $60 a month —half the minimum cost-of-living for a family.

Politics and Repression. President Park Chung Hee was determined to keep his autocratic constitution as long as North Korea clung to its vow to unify Korea "by force." Opposition leader Kim Young-sam criticized Park for exaggerating the threat from North Korea to justify repression. He called on Park to resign and change the nation's charter to pave the way for democratization. Results of a mid-February referendum showed 73.1% supporting Park, but the opposition argued that Park would have been defeated in a free balloting.

After the plebiscite, the government sought to soften criticism at home and abroad by releasing most of the 203 political prisoners convicted in secret military trials in 1974. Ignoring official warnings, some, like the renowned poet

Kim Chi-ha, stated after release that they had been subject to torture to extract confessions. Kim was rearrested on charges of aiding North Korea. Political crackdowns intensified. The leading independent daily *Dong-a Ilbo* was forced by a sudden advertising boycott to compromise its "free press" philosophy.

In April renewed student demonstrations were swiftly suppressed, and the presidents of Seoul's three leading universities were forced to resign. Eight persons convicted as members of the "People's Revolutionary party" were hanged. A U. S. Roman Catholic priest was expelled for protesting the executions and was the second priest to be deported since December 1974. In May, in the aftermath of the fall of Vietnam to the Communists, an emergency decree was issued outlawing all criticism of the constitution and prohibiting emigration by prominent individuals and the flight of capital. It was the ninth emergency decree issued since January 1974. Two new paramilitary groups—a defense corps of high school and college students and a civil defense corps of 3.5 million males—were created. A $400 million annual defense tax bill was enacted to make South Korea militarily independent by 1980.

Foreign Relations. In reaffirming support of South Korea against any North Korean attack, the United States disclosed in June a "9-day re-

——— SOUTH KOREA · Information Highlights ———

Official Name: Republic of Korea.
Location: Northeastern Asia.
Area: 38,022 square miles (98,477 sq km).
Population (1975 est.): 33,960,000.
Chief Cities (1970 census): Seoul, the capital, 5,536,377; Pusan, 1,880,710; Taegu, 1,082,750; Inchon, 646,013.
Government: *Head of state,* Park Chung Hee, president (took office Dec. 1963). *Head of government,* Kim Jong Pil, premier (took office June 1971). *Legislature* (unicameral)—National Assembly.
Monetary Unit: Won (484 won equal U. S.$1, March 1975).
Gross National Product (1974 est.): $12,144,000,000.
Manufacturing (major products): Textiles, electronic equipment, petrochemicals, clothing, plywood, hair products, processed foods, metal products, furniture, ships.
Major Agricultural Products: Rice, barley, wheat, soybeans, sweet potatoes and yams, fish.
Foreign Trade (1973): *Exports,* $3,221,000,000; *imports,* $4,218,000,000.

taliatory war plan" and in July left open the option of nuclear weapons as a last resort. In August it also promised "appropriate support and assistance" to help South Korea attain self-defense capability under the latter's new five-year military improvement program (1976–80).

August and September saw the failure of Seoul's bid to secure UN membership and to gain recognition as a "nonaligned" state. A pro-Seoul resolution calling for conditional termination of the UN Command (UNC) in January 1976 was approved by the First (Political) Committee of the United Nations, as was a conflicting pro-North Korea resolution. In other developments, the United States and Japan agreed in August that the security of South Korea was "necessary for peace and security in East Asia, including Japan." In September, South Korea expressed interest in exploring the USSR's 1969 proposal for an Asian collective security system that neither the People's Republic of China nor North Korea welcomed.

UPI

In October UN speech, Li Jong Mok of North Korea denounces U. S. colonial domination of South Korea.

NORTH KOREA

The North Korean government stated in March that 70% of required industrial raw materials was produced domestically and that the "self-reliant" economy was not affected by worldwide recession. Unconfirmed reports said that North Korea had a payments problem, partly due to a sharp drop in world prices for major metals exports. In time for the 30th anniversary of the Korean Workers party (KWP) on October 10, the six-year plan (1971–76) was declared completed by August, 16 months ahead of schedule. An annual industrial growth average of 18.4% and grain production of 7 million tons in 1974 were announced.

North Korea remained an austere society. There was still a gap in urban-rural living standards, but it was narrowing. Almost everyone was guaranteed the basic necessities of life, plus free medical care. Personal sacrifice was heavy, and if there were rising expectations, they were not as powerful a force as they were in South Korea. In March it was officially claimed that the per capita national income surpassed $1,000.

Political Developments. President Kim Il Sung was firmly in command, with no sign of internal opposition. He was reportedly grooming his son, Kim Chong Il as heir-apparent. The sixth congress of the KWP was called for 1976. President Kim again disclaimed any intention of invading South Korea, but found little credence in Seoul in the face of his oft-stated vow to "actively support and encourage" revolution in the south.

Foreign Relations. In foreign affairs, he rejected in January the "cross recognition" formula—the U. S. and Japanese recognition of the Pyongyang government in exchange for Soviet and Chinese recognition of Seoul—as a "two Koreas plot." Kim made a series of foreign visits, the first since 1961, to China in April; to

Rumania, Algeria, and Mauritania in May; and to Bulgaria and Yugoslavia in June. These trips were designed to project an image of peaceful intent, to promote economic cooperation, and to secure support for the forthcoming showdown with South Korea in the United Nations.

In August, North Korea was voted membership by nonaligned countries meeting in Lima, Peru. It also reportedly informed the United States, through Japan, of Kim's wish to have Washington send an envoy to Pyongyang to prepare an agenda for direct talks. North Korea pulled off a major diplomatic coup in October when the UN's First Committee adopted a pro-Pyongyang resolution for unconditional disbanding of the UNC, the withdrawal of all foreign troops under UN flags from the south, and the replacement of the 1953 armistice accord with a new peace agreement through direct Pyongyang-Washington negotiations.

North and South Korean Red Cross officials met intermittently at Panmunjom without result. Political dialogue remained dormant with the North-South Coordinating Committee unable to reconvene.

RINN-SUP SHINN
The American University

——— NORTH KOREA · Information Highlights ———

Official Name: Democratic People's Republic of Korea.
Location: Northeastern Asia.
Area: 46,540 square miles (120,538 sq km).
Population (1975 est.): 23,800,000.
Chief Cities (1972): P'yonggyang, the capital, 957,000; Hamhung, 484,000.
Government: *Head of state,* Kim Il Sung, president and secretary general of the Korean Workers' (Communist) party (took office Dec. 1972). *Head of government,* Kim Il Sung, premier (took office Dec. 1972). *Legislature* (unicameral)—Supreme People's Assembly.
Monetary Unit: Won (0.961 won equals U. S.$1, Aug. 1974).
Gross National Product (1972 est.): $3,500,000,000.
Manufacturing (major products): Cement, metallurgical coke, pig iron and ferroalloys, textiles.
Major Agricultural Products: Rice, sweet potatoes and yams, soybeans, livestock, fish.
Foreign Trade: *Chief exports*—metals, farm products; *chief imports*—machinery.

In February New York City construction workers protested the depressed state of the construction industry.

LABOR

For labor and the economy, 1975 saw a reversal of previous recessionary trends in the United States and in many other industrialized nations.

United States

In the United States, the twin ravages of inflation and recession moderated. Double-digit inflation, which plagued the nation through much of 1974, decreased to an annual rate of about 7% toward the end of 1975. Also, the recession eased as the economy turned upward, the gross national product (GNP) rose, and labor productivity mounted. In the third quarter, the GNP jumped by an annual rate of 11.2%, a 20-year record, after previous declines. Productivity in the private economic sector increased in the same quarter at a 9.5% annual rate, the highest since the first quarter of 1971, and unit labor costs dropped 2.4%.

However, the index of economic indicators fell by 0.9% in September, indicating a letup in the upturn. Also, the wholesale price index jumped 1.8% in October, but it held steady in November. Unemployment did not respond readily to the stimulative trend. The jobless rate edged down from 9.2% in May to 8.3% in November. The number of unemployed stood at 8 million in October, up 50% over the previous year. Those employed totaled 85.4 million, up 1.4 million from the low point in March.

Wages and Employment. Earnings of workers in the economy as a whole lagged behind inflation. The Labor Department estimated that real average weekly earnings in September were down 2.9% from September 1974. This purchasing power figure reflected a 7.8% rise in the Consumer Price Index from a year earlier and a 1.4% drop in average weekly hours, which a 6.2% increase in average hourly earnings failed to counterbalance.

However, real spendable earnings, arrived at by deducting Social Security and federal income taxes from gross earnings, were put at 1% higher than in 1974. This rise occurred because of the cut in federal income taxes.

Workers in plants with over 1,000 employees, covered by major collective bargaining settlements, did better. During the first nine months of 1975 these settlements provided for average wage increases of 7.8% annually over the life of the multi-year contracts, and averaged 10.3% in the first year. The 7.8% figure was up from an average of 7.3% in major contracts negotiated in 1974.

The AFL-CIO and some economists voiced fears that the economic upturn would be short-lived. The AFL-CIO clashed repeatedly with the administration of President Gerald R. Ford over proposed legislation and other actions to spur the economy. The AFL-CIO called for greater federal spending and other measures to "put America back to work" and denounced presidential vetoes of job-making projects voted by Congress.

Strikes. Workers in the public sector took center stage, spotlighted by a series of labor disputes. Strikes flared in large part because government at all levels, beset with budget problems that were intensified by the recession and inflation and facing concerned taxpayers, sought to hold down wages. Public sector employees, on the other hand, fought against bearing the brunt of the budgetary crises and often struck, even though such strikes were generally illegal.

Walkouts by teachers in the 1975–76 school year totaled over 160 by mid-October, more than the 121 strikes recorded in the entire previous school year. In the local public sector as a whole, strikes numbered over 500. These included some by police and firemen, a few of which were marked by violence. In some communities police and firemen reported in "sick," or they "resigned" instead of striking formally. Most disputes were settled for salary increases that totaled less than the rise in living costs.

Most federal employees received only a 5% salary increase, effective October 1, as proposed by President Ford, instead of the 8.66% to which they would have been entitled under a "comparability" formula gearing their pay to the trend in the private sector. Congress failed to muster a majority to override President Ford's 5% ceiling. However, unions representing 600,000 employees of the autonomous postal service, and government blue collar workers covered by separate regulations, negotiated raises substantially higher than 5%.

In the private sector strikes declined, partly because few major industrial contracts expired

in 1975. Also, the recession tended to induce acceptance of relatively moderate settlements. In some cases, particularly on several hard-hit airlines, unions waived wage increases in 1975.

During the first nine months of 1975 all measures of strike activity diminished, according to the Bureau of Labor Statistics. The number of strikes, the number of workers involved, and manufacturing shutdowns attributed to strikes declined below 1974 levels.

One of the major settlements reached without a strike came in the railroads. There unions representing over 500,000 employees negotiated agreements calling for wage increases, fringe benefits, and other adjustments estimated at over 40% over a three-year period.

Union Membership. Membership in labor unions and related public and professional associations with headquarters in the United States rose by 1.1 million, or 4.8% over a two-year period, to 24.2 million, the Bureau of Labor Statistics reported. It said that unions and professional associations represented 24.5% of the labor force, up 0.2% over a two-year period. Unions alone were listed as representing 21.6%, down 0.2% over 2 years.

The same study showed that the fastest growth since 1965 was among unions representing public sector employees. The most substantial gainers were the American Federation of Teachers, with a 344% rise; the State, County, and Municipal Employees Union, 176%; and the American Federation of Government Employees representing federal workers, 116%. Public health workers, including interns and doctors in hospitals, also turned to unionism in significant numbers, engaging in strikes in some instances.

Employee Ownership Developments. Much publicized during the year were several employee ownership developments. One of the first involved an asbestos mine and factory in Lowell, Vt., which the owners, the GAF Corp., planned to close rather than spend $1 million on government-mandated anti-pollution equipment. The 300 employees, with the help of loans from state and federal agencies, acquired the facility. They formed the Vermont Asbestos Group, Inc., to operate it, and named seven members of their union to the company's governing board.

A second case was the South Bend (Ind.) Lathe Co., which the parent firm, Amsted Industries, planned to liquidate. The 450 workers, backed by union leaders, local bankers, city officials, and federal agencies, arranged $10 million in financing to acquire the machine tool company through an employee stock ownership trust. Loans were to be repaid over 25 years out of pre-tax earnings, and the stock was to be allocated gradually to the employees.

A third example was a knitting mill in Saratoga Springs, N.Y., which made products for Cluett, Peabody & Co. Cluett had announced a planned sale of the plant and laid off the bulk of the employees. The 41 remaining employees

Labor leader Cesar Chavez complained in September that secret-ballot elections for farm workers were "tainted."

pooled their savings, borrowed on insurance, got a loan from the state, and bought the plant, which they renamed the Saratoga Knitting Mill. In all three cases a rise in productivity and efficiency was reported under employee ownership.

Soviet Grain. Organized labor won a drive against an uncontrolled purchase by the Soviet Union of grains on the U.S. market. A major feature of the drive was an August boycott against loading grain shipments to the USSR. President Ford suspended grain sales to the USSR early in September pending negotiation of a long-term grain agreement. In turn the unions suspended the boycott. An agreement was announced in October under which grain sales to the Soviet Union would be stabilized over a five-year period, with minimum and maximum purchases. The AFL-CIO hailed the pact, and maritime unions ended the boycott.

California Agriculture. One of the major worker representation battles of the year took place on California's big farms under terms of a new state law. As of early November, the United Farm Workers (UFW), headed by Cesar Chavez, and backed by the AFL-CIO, had won the right to represent nearly 16,000 workers in 150 elections, while the rival Teamsters Union had won the right to represent about 10,300 workers in 96 elections. Another 11,000 were involved in undecided and challenged contests, and more elections were to be held. Though the UFW came out on top it did so by smaller margins than it had anticipated. Chavez claimed UFW victories were hampered by grower and Teamster Union intimidation.

REUBEN LEVIN
Editor, "Labor" Newspaper

LAOS

Laos officially became a Communist country in 1975 when the six-century-old monarchy was abolished, and the coalition government of Communists and non-Communists was dissolved. It was announced on December 3 that the monarchy had been abolished on December 1, and the Kingdom of a Million Elephants was replaced by the Democratic People's Republic of Laos. Kapsone Phomvihan, a leader of the Communist Pathet Lao, became prime minister and Prince Souphanouvong, half-brother of deposed Prime Minister Prince Souvanna Phouma, became the first president of the new government. Phomvihan was also secretary-general of the Laos People's party, which controls the Pathet Lao forces that fought against the monarchy for years. He had not been seen in public since the late 1950's.

Communist control had been gained in effect if not in name, in a virtually bloodless takeover between May and August. This takeover had been expected for months and had been encouraged by the failure of the United States to prevent the overthrow of its South Vietnamese and Cambodian allies. Thousands of anti-Communist Laotians fled to Thailand during the year.

U. S. Deterrence Ends. The war between the Communists and the anti-Communists became a cold one after the cessation of fighting in 1973. The Pathet Lao and the non-Communists shared participation in a coalition government from April 1974. The Communists possessed the capability to take over the country militarily, or politically through the coalition, but did not do so for fear of provoking increased U. S. support of the conservative side. When the United States failed to act to save the falling South Vietnamese and Cambodian governments in April, however, the Pathet Lao decided that it could take over without intervention by the United States.

Politics. The Communists maneuvered the resignations of several right-wing cabinet ministers in May. These and key military leaders, including Defense Minister Sisoukna Champassak and U. S.-backed Gen. Vang Pao of the Meo tribe, fled the country. Between May and August the Pathet Lao, who directly administered 75% of Laos, "reunified" the land by taking over the 25% of the country previously controlled by the non-Communists and by setting up "people's councils" and "liberation committees." The "liberation" of the administrative capital of Vientiane in August completed the process of Communist takeover. There was practically no bloodshed.

The ease of the Communist takeover stemmed from the fact that many of the country's conservatives refused to resist and fled the land, while neutralists such as Souvanna Phouma seemingly acquiesced in the Pathet Lao capture of the government. Souvanna Phouma remained in Laos as an advisor to the new government as did former King Savang Vatthana.

Economy. Laos was virtually bankrupt in late 1975, the result of more than a decade of war that ended in 1973 and the failure to rehabilitate the country in the following two years. The flight of capital and goods following Vietnam's fall and the reaction to the Communist takeover there in the middle months of the year had their effect. Inflation was severe, rice was scarce, as were cooking oil and gasoline, and exports were negligible. About 20% of the country's 3 million inhabitants were refugees, requiring various kinds of support.

The Laotian currency, the kip, fell to its lowest level in years. Temporary relief was provided when the Foreign Exchange Operations Fund nations—the United States, Japan, Australia, France, and Britain—agreed in July to extend their support of the kip for an additional six months. Such backing previously had been at the level of $32 million a year, but it was questionable whether the United States would continue to support the Laotian currency, given the political changes in the country.

Foreign Relations. U. S.-Laotian relations rapidly deteriorated as the Pathet Lao takeover progressed. The United States, which gave a badly needed $33 million in economic assistance to Laos during 1974, was forced by the Communists to close out its aid mission at the end of June. By this time the size of the once-huge U. S. embassy staff had been cut to 22 persons. Washington, however, apparently wanted to retain an embassy in Vientiane despite persisting harassment, partly as a listening post in Indochina, where it no longer had any other diplomatic presence.

The Soviet Union moved into the political vacuum created by the reduced U. S. presence, having 700 or more technicians in the country by year's end. China kept a lower profile but supplied badly needed rice. North Vietnamese forces remained in eastern Laos and increased their presence in the south of the country.

RICHARD BUTWELL
*State University of New York
College at Fredonia*

LAOS · Information Highlights

Official Name: People's Democratic Republic of Laos.
Location: Southeast Asia.
Area: 91,429 square miles (236,800 sq km).
Population (1975 est.): 3,300,000.
Chief Cities (1970 est.): Vientiane, the capital, 150,000; Luang Prabang, the royal capital, 25,000.
Government: *Head of state*, Prince Souphanouvong, president. *Head of government*, Kaysone Phomvihan, prime minister. *Legislature* (unicameral)—National Assembly.
Monetary Unit: Kip (750 kips equal U. S.$1, April 1975).
Gross National Product (1972 est.): $202,000,000.
Manufacturing (major products): Cigarettes, textiles.
Major Agricultural Products: Rice, corn, coffee, cotton, tobacco, cardamom, vegetables, forest products.
Foreign Trade (1972): *Exports,* $3,000,000; *imports,* 44,-000,000.

LATIN AMERICA

The nations of Latin America welcomed Cuba back into the hemispheric fold in 1975 by formally lifting the economic and diplomatic sanctions imposed on the Communist island by the Organization of American States (OAS) 11 years earlier. Cuba was included, and the United State excluded, from a Western Hemisphere economic association that was set up by a treaty signed in 1975 by the representatives of 25 Latin American and Caribbean countries. The governments of two nations, Peru and Honduras, were overthrown by military coups during the year, while in Argentina, President Isabel Perón clung tenaciously to power, despite a deteriorating economy and increased guerrilla activity.

The OAS and Cuba. On July 29 the foreign ministers of the OAS countries, meeting in San José, Costa Rica, voted 16–3, with 2 abstentions, to allow member nations to deal with Cuba "in the form esteemed convenient by each state." Thus ended the supposedly binding, but largely disregarded, diplomatic ostracism and trade embargo imposed on Cuba by the OAS at the urging of the United States in 1964. An evolving liberal attitude by the United States on the Cuban question had been evident in 1974. At that time Washington's representative abstained from voting, instead of voting against, a similar motion, which failed to gain the necessary two-thirds majority. In 1975 the United States went

a step further and voted in favor of the repeal of collective sanctions. Only the right-wing governments of Chile, Paraguay, and Uruguay voted against repeal. Brazil and Nicaragua abstained.

While the United States in 1975 authorized foreign subsidiaries of U. S. companies to trade with Cuba, Washington still refused to resume direct commercial and diplomatic relations with the Havana regime, citing Cuba's confiscation of $2 billion in U. S. property, its support of Puerto Rican independence, and its military intervention in Angola. Of greater concern to most Latin American countries was the United States Trade Act, signed by President Gerald Ford on Jan. 3, 1975. It provided for generally lower tariffs on imports from underdeveloped countries, but excluded from preferential treatment imports both from countries that nationalize U. S. property without compensation and from member nations of the Organization of Petroleum Exporting Countries (OPEC) or similar cartels. OPEC member's Venezuela and Ecuador were quick to denounce the act, and were supported by most of their Latin American neighbors, including usually pro-U. S. Brazil and prospective OPEC member Mexico.

New Economic System. Mexico joined Venezuela in calling for the creation of an exclusive organization of Latin American and Caribbean nations to help them withstand outside economic pressure. While the sponsors of the project declared that it was "against nobody," its objectives seemed to conflict with the economic interests of the world's industrial powers, especially those of the United States.

In a meeting in Panama in August, the repre-

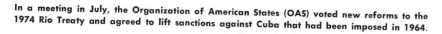

In a meeting in July, the Organization of American States (OAS) voted new reforms to the 1974 Rio Treaty and agreed to lift sanctions against Cuba that had been imposed in 1964.

UPI

moribund Central American Common Market (CACOM), whose members are Guatemala, El Salvador, Honduras, Nicaragua, and Costa Rica, seemed to improve during 1975, as their presidents met four times in amicable summit conferences. Still, no concrete steps were taken toward a formal peace treaty between the belligerents of the 1969 war, Honduras and El Salvador. Until this long-awaited settlement is reached, there can be no revival of CACOM.

Among members of the Andean Pact (Venezuela, Colombia, Ecuador, Peru, Bolivia, and Chile), squabbling continued about the best policy toward outside investment. Ecuador and Colombia joined Chile in expressing doubts about the wisdom of some of the restrictions placed on foreign development capital. Nevertheless, the spirit of cooperation within the group remained relatively strong. To speed progress toward an Andean common market, Colombia unilaterally reduced by 10% its tariffs on a wide range of manufactured imports from other pact nations. The six member nations held two conferences on arms limitations in 1975, with the delegates agreeing to recommend to their governments that highly sophisticated weaponry and offensive armaments be banned from the subregion. During the year there was also much discussion, but apparently little progress toward a solution, of the thorny problem of providing Bolivia with a corridor to the Pacific. If territorial contiguity is to be preserved, the corridor would have to lie across land occupied by Chile, but claimed by Peru.

Panama Canal Question. Negotiations between the United States and Panama over the future of the Panama Canal bogged down in 1975. The agreement signed in 1974 by U. S. Secretary of State Henry Kissinger and Panamanian strongman Omar Torrijos, which acknowledged that Panama would eventually gain full sovereignty over the canal, was roundly denounced in the U. S. Congress. In June 1975 the House of Representatives voted to cut off funds for further negotiations with Panama, despite Kissinger's protests that good relations between the United States and Latin America depended on continued negotiations with Panama. U. S. special negotiator Ellsworth Bunker warned that the canal was extremely vulnerable to sabotage and terrorist acts and that it would be difficult to keep in operation against all-out Panamanian opposition.

Nevertheless, with the canal question threatening to become an issue in the 1976 U. S. elections, Kissinger, in an apparent repudiation of the 1974 agreement, declared in September that "the United States must maintain the right, unilaterally, to defend the canal for an indefinite period." Nevertheless, the negotiations continued. General Torrijos, who had staked his reputation on securing a favorable treaty, probably decided against breaking off the talks for fear that this would be seen as an admission

UPI

Argentine President Isabel Perón tells top labor leaders in July that she will solve the country's severe labor crisis.

sentatives of 25 Latin American and Caribbean nations, including Cuba, voted to proceed with the formation of the Latin American Economic System (LAES). The aims of the new organization would include joint marketing of regional raw materials, formulation of a regional economic policy to discourage decisions by foreign nations or companies considered harmful to Latin America, regional financing of national development schemes, and the formation of multinational Latin American companies.

The nations that had agreed to the August declaration sent their representatives back to Panama to sign the treaty establishing LAES on October 18. The treaty specifically affirms the right of countries to choose their own political, social, and economic arrangements. Before the treaty can be fully implemented, it must be ratified by the signatory governments.

Other Economic Associations. Meanwhile, existing subregional economic associations were having certain difficulties. Plans of the Caribbean Common Market (CARICOM, made up of former British colonies in the Antilles) to build an aluminum smelter in Trinidad were shelved when Jamaica accepted financing from nonmembers Mexico and Venezuela to build a smelter in Jamaica. Prime Minister Eric Williams of Trinidad and Tobago accused the Jamaicans of selling out "a major Caribbean integration project for 30 ingots of aluminum."

Relations among the members of the

Gen. Francisco Morales Bermúdez, the new president of Peru, waves to crowds on his way to the Conference of Non-Aligned Nations in Lima on August 30.

of failure, which could lead to his overthrow. If he could hold on until after the U. S. elections, it was felt, Torrijos would get his treaty.

In the meantime, Torrijos continued to collect declarations of support from Latin American and Third World nations. In August the Conference of Non-Aligned Nations, meeting in Lima, Peru, announced its solidarity with Panama on the canal question, and accepted Panama as one of its four Latin American members, along with Cuba, Peru, and Argentina. In November the five Central American presidents, meeting in Guatemala City with Torrijos as their guest, declared their support for Panama in its dispute with the United States over the canal.

Venezuelan and Brazilian Oil. As expected, Venezuela took final steps in 1975 for the nationalization of its petroleum industry. The nationalization law, signed in August, created a government corporation, Petrovén, which was to have a monopoly of oil production in Venezuelan territory, effective Jan. 1, 1976. After that date, private foreign oil companies might engage in oil drilling in Venezuela only through mixed ventures with Petrovén, for a limited time and under strict conditions. The provision of the law allowing foreign participation was strongly condemned by nationalistic opponents of Venezuelan President Carlos Andrés Pérez. In Brazil a similar uproar was set off when President Ernesto Geisel's government announced, in October, that the government oil monopoly Petrobrás would award contracts to foreign companies to drill for petroleum in the national territory.

Political Developments. To the surprise of many, President Luis Echeverría of Mexico designated as his successor José López Portillo, the minister of finance, whose taxation policies have been unpopular with Mexican businessmen. López Portillo, whose election to the 1976–82 presidential term is virtually assured, is expected to follow Echeverría's mildly reformist line.

In Argentina, President Isabel Perón retained her position despite an alarming increase in rural and urban terrorism, unrest in the armed forces, charges of corruption, a deteriorating economy,

waning support within the Peronist labor movement, and periodic bouts with illness. In 1975 she was forced to abandon her wage and price stabilization policy, fire her trusted friend and advisor, José López Rega, and take two leaves of absence. In December she barely thwarted a coup by rightist air force officers.

Allegations that Honduran President Oswaldo López Arellano had received a $1 million bribe from United Brands, the giant U. S. banana corporation, led to his overthrow in a bloodless coup in April. The new Honduran leader, Col. Juan Alberto Melgar Castro, declared his support for agrarian reform and his opposition to "foreign monopolists."

In Peru, ailing President Juan Velasco Alvarado was quietly removed from power in August and replaced by Gen. Francisco Morales Bermúdez. While Morales proclaimed his firm devotion to Peru's leftist military revolution, the new president began steering a more moderate course than that of his militantly nationalistic predecessor.

The Peruvian coup seemed to trigger a move by conservative civilian and army elements to overthrow the military government of neighboring Ecuador. Troops loyal to Ecuadorian President Guillermo Rodríguez Lara crushed the revolt early in September. There was a revival of Marxist guerrilla activity in Colombia and some dissatisfaction within the Colombian army due to the firing of its popular commander, Gen. Alvaro Valencia Tovar, by President Adolfo López Michelsen in May.

Independence Movements. A new nation was born on November 25 when Surinam, formerly Dutch Guiana, received its independence from the Netherlands. Great Britain was eager to grant independence to Belize, formerly British Honduras, but was prevented from doing so by Guatemala's persistent claims to the territory. In November, British troop reinforcements were dispatched to Belize to forestall a threatened Guatemalan invasion.

NEILL MACAULAY
University of Florida

UPI

Associate Justice William O. Douglas retired from the U. S. Supreme Court in late November.

Law

The major events in law in 1975 included the retirement of Justice William O. Douglas from the U. S. Supreme Court and progress toward revising the law of the sea. Confrontations in the Spanish Sahara raised the issue of territorial sovereignty. Other legal developments are reviewed in the articles CIVIL LIBERTIES AND CIVIL RIGHTS; CRIME; DISARMAMENT; PRISONS; and UNITED NATIONS.

U. S. Supreme Court

The 1974–75 term of the U. S. Supreme Court was a comparatively quiet one. The court handed down fewer decisions than in preceding terms, and fewer were of major importance, thus moving toward Chief Justice Warren E. Burger's goal of reducing the court's policy making role. While decisions in the areas of labor, business, and antitrust regulation appeared conservative, some rulings on individual rights and freedom of speech and press were surprisingly liberal. Decision on what would have been the term's most controversial issue, capital punishment, was postponed to the following term.

Justice William O. Douglas, who had served the longest of any member in the court's history, suffered a stroke and missed a number of court sessions. On November 12 he announced his retirement, citing the "incessant and demanding pain which depletes my energy." Replying to Douglas's retirement letter, President Ford said, "Your distinguished years of service are unequaled in all the history of the Court." On November 28, Ford nominated Judge John Paul

Stevens of the U. S. Court of Appeals for the Seventh Circuit to replace Douglas. Stevens was considered a centrist, neither markedly conservative nor liberal.

The general opinion-alignment on the court remained much as in recent terms. The four Nixon appointees, Chief Justice Burger and Justices Harry A. Blackmun, Lewis F. Powell, and William H. Rehnquist, were joined by Byron White or Potter Stewart, or both, often enough to control the great majority of controversial cases. However, there were some signs of cleavage among the Nixon justices who voted together in only 69% of the cases, compared with 75% in the preceding term. The minority of Douglas, William J. Brennan, and Thurgood Marshall maintained the liberal traditions of the Warren Court.

The court handed down 123 signed opinions, of which 43 (33%) were unanimous. This compares with 140 signed opinions (31% unanimous) in the preceding term. The court also issued 21 per curiam opinions, 14 of them unanimous. In spite of the fact that Douglas did not participate in 22 cases, he had the most dissents, 54; followed by Brennan with 36; Marshall 30; Stewart and Rehnquist 23 each; Burger 16; White 14; Powell 13; and Blackmun 10.

GOVERNMENTAL POWERS

The presidency won one case and lost one. The court ruled that President Nixon had exceeded his authority when he impounded $9 billion that Congress had ordered spent for sewage treatment plants (*Train* v. *City of New York*). The presidential pardoning power was held to be virtually unlimited and unreviewable in *Schick* v. *Reed*. President Eisenhower, in commuting the death sentence of a soldier to life imprisonment, had attached the condition that he never be paroled, an action the court upheld.

The power of a Senate committee to subpoena the bank records of a group under investigation was held to be unquestionable because of the immunity granted to Congressmen by the "speech and debate" clause of the Constitution (*Eastland* v. *U. S. Servicemen's Fund*).

The court unanimously confirmed the title of the federal government to all oil and gas resources on the Atlantic Ocean's outer continental shelf beyond the 3-mile (4.8-km) limit (*United State* v. *Maine*). Ohio's contention that salaries of state employees were not subject to federal wage controls was rejected in *Fry* v. *United States*.

EQUAL PROTECTION

The court continued to deal with claims that differential treatment of the sexes is unconstitutional. This position was rejected in *Schlesinger* v. *Ballard* where the court held (5–4) that the Navy can retain female officers who are passed over for promotion for 13 years, while male

officers with no promotions after 9 years must be discharged.

Three other decisions, however, held that sexually-based distinctions violated equal protection. *Weinberger* v. *Wiesenfeld* struck down a provision of Social Security law that authorized survivors' benefits for the widow of a deceased worker with children but denied them to a widower in the same situation. A state requirement that divorced fathers must support their sons until their 21st birthday but allowed payments for daughters to stop at 18 was voided in *Stanton* v. *Stanton.*

Louisiana excluded women from jury service unless they went to the courthouse and volunteered. The court had upheld this law in 1961, but in *Taylor* v. *Louisiana* it now reversed that ruling as denying to criminal defendants their right to trial by a fair cross section of the community.

There were no school segregation cases. The principal case involving alleged racial discrimination was *Richmond* v. *United States,* which held it was not a violation of the 1965 Voting Rights Act for the city of Richmond, Va., to reduce its previously black majority to a minority by annexing predominantly white areas, as long as the black citizens were fairly represented as a proportion of the city's population in the new city council.

Exclusionary zoning, which seems likely to be a major issue in the future, was avoided by the court. A suit brought by various civil rights organizations and individuals, contending that zoning laws prevented poor and middle class citizens from living in a Rochester, N.Y., suburb, was rejected in *Warth* v. *Seldin* on the ground that the parties had not personally suffered harm from the restrictions and so had no standing to sue.

DUE PROCESS

With Justices White and Stewart joining the liberals, the court extended due process rights to school children in two cases. *Goss* v. *Lopez* ruled (5–4) that students could not be suspended from public school unless they had been notified of the charges against them and given a chance to defend themselves. *Wood* v. *Strickland* held that school officials who discipline students unfairly cannot defend themselves in civil rights suits by claiming ignorance of the pupils' due process rights.

In an important recognition of the rights of the mentally ill, *O'Connor* v. *Donaldson* ruled unanimously that mental patients cannot be confined in institutions against their will and without treatment if they are not dangerous and are capable of surviving on the outside.

FIRST AMENDMENT RIGHTS

The court was on balance sympathetic to First Amendment claims. *Cox Broadcasting Co.* v. *Cohn* reversed the conviction of a broadcaster who revealed the name of a rape victim, contrary to Georgia law. But a jury award of $60,000 for invasion of the privacy of a widow who was the subject of a newspaper article containing "knowing falsehoods" was upheld in *Cantrell* v. *Forest City Publishing Co.*

The action of a Virginia newspaper in printing an ad for a New York abortion service, contrary to state law prohibiting such advertising, was held to be protected by the First Amendment (*Bigelow* v. *Virginia*). But the court declined to review a lower court order under which a former Central Intelligence Agency (CIA) employee had to submit all his future writing about the CIA to the agency for prepublication censorship (*Knopf* v. *Colby*). Similarly, the court refused to pass on gag orders restricting press coverage of criminal trials (*Times-Picayune* v. *Schulingkamp*).

City officials in Chattanooga, Tenn., refused to rent a city auditorium for performance of the rock musical *Hair,* on the ground that it was obscene. The court reversed, holding that theatrical productions have the same constitutional protection against advance censorship enjoyed by newspapers and books and that only after a court hearing could a play be treated as obscene (*Southeastern Promotions Ltd.* v. *Conrad*). A city ordinance making drive-in theaters criminally liable for showing films including nudity that are visible from outside the theater grounds was struck down in *Erznoznik* v. *Jacksonville.*

Reading strictly the First Amendment ban on entanglement of church and state, the court in *Meek* v. *Pittinger* invalidated most of a Pennsylvania law intended to aid children attending nonpublic schools. The court approved loans of textbooks to private and parochial school students. However, it disapproved the lending of teaching materials and equipment and the provision of other services.

The Freedom of Information Act was narrowly interpreted to require rejection of an effort to secure reports on airline safety from the Federal Aviation Administration (FAA) because the airlines objected to public disclosure of the material (*Administrator, FAA* v. *Robertson*).

CRIMINAL PUNISHMENT

Following the court's holding in the 1972 case of *Furman* v. *Georgia* that capital punishment as now administered is so unpredictable as to constitute cruel and unusual punishment, many states revised their statutes to make the death penalty mandatory for certain crimes. In North Carolina this result was achieved by judicial interpretation of existing statutes. The court heard arguments in one of the resulting cases, *Fowler* v. *North Carolina* but then postponed decision to the following term.

The court decided in *Faretta* v. *California* that a competent person accused of crime has a constitutional right to refuse a state-provided

The Rights of Children

The question of whether minors in the United States have the same constitutional rights, enforceable by the federal courts, as adults came under severe scrutiny during 1975. The authority of parents and of parental surrogates such as teachers, social workers, police, hospital workers, and agents of juvenile courts to act in "the child's best interest" was being phased out. It was being replaced with a positive recognition of a child's right, as a Minnesota decision stated (*Herbstman* v. *Shiflan*), "to live in a suitable place free from neglect, cruelty, drunkenness, criminality or depravity on the part of parents." A child, under the law, is not an adult, but a child is a person.

School Discipline. The law relative to suspensions and expulsions of children from school had been in chaos for over a decade, with one court holding that all suspensions must be preceded by a hearing, while another upheld suspensions lasting up to 25 days without notice or hearing. The matter of student due process came to the attention of the Supreme Court in the 1975 cases of *Goss* v. *Lopez* and *Wood* v. *Strickland*.

In *Goss* v. *Lopez,* which concerned a group of Columbus, Ohio, pupils, the Supreme Court ruled (5–4) that public school students have a constitutional right to a hearing before they can be suspended from school. "Young people do not shed their constitutional right at the schoolhouse door," the court said. Unless a pupil's presence in school poses real danger to people or property, he must be informed of the charges against him and given an opportunity to defend himself before being suspended. It has still not been determined whether pupils will be entitled to be represented by counsel in formal hearings if faced with lengthy suspensions or outright expulsions, or whether they have the right to cross-examine the school authorities' witnesses.

In *Wood* v. *Strickland* the court ruled that students who believe they have been disciplined illegally can sue school officials for damages. The court held that school officials could not defend themselves against suits by claiming ignorance of the pupils' constitutional rights. In October 1975, however, the court affirmed that states may permit teachers to administer corporal punishment if there are safeguards.

Right to an Education. The Children's Defense Fund charged in 1975 that the U. S. public schools pushed out or systematically excluded more than 2 million children who should be enrolled in classes. These included youngsters who do not speak English, who are poor, or who are pregnant or married, and those who needed special help with seeing, hearing, walking, reading, learning, or adjusting.

Federal and state statutes and court decisions of the past few years have changed the permissive nature of public school services to handicapped children, including those handicapped by poverty, neglect, delinquency, and cultural or linguistic isolation. These have been changed to mandatory requirements for providing special education services for all children needing such services and to provide these services without unnecessary delay. With the exception of severely handicapped children, those needing special services are "mainstreamed," educated together with children who do not have exceptional needs.

Courts have found that school performance declined among children in special programs in part because of the label attached to those children.

It is conceivable that future courts will award monetary damages for educational negligence or malfeasance to those who are pushed through school without receiving an education or who are wrongfully deprived of promotion.

Right to Files. Congress passed in 1974 the Family Educational Rights and Privacy Act, which gave parents and students 18 years of age and over the right to inspect school records. In 1975 the Department of Health, Education, and Welfare detailed its rules on access to school files. School officials were apprehensive that, through timidity, teachers and guidance counselors would omit from their records essential critical information. Proponents of the legislation felt that material that could not survive challenge should be deleted from the files.

Juvenile Justice. The Supreme Court has said that "neither the Fourteenth Amendment nor the Bill of Rights is for adults alone." A debate in 1975 concerned whether so-called status offenses, which would not be considered crimes if committed by adults but which subject children to the jurisdiction of the juvenile courts, should be removed from the domain of the court system. These include truancy, running away, smoking, drinking, disobeying authority, and ungovernableness.

Other Issues. Children are winning the right to have their interests represented when their parents seek a divorce. Authorities have also held that children should be consulted regarding their medical needs and whether they should be freed for adoption and that they should have an opportunity to manage their own financial affairs.

MARTIN GRUBERG

lawyer and to conduct his own defense. *Bond* v. *Jones* ruled that the guarantee against double jeopardy applies to juveniles and bars their prosecution as adults for actions already found in juvenile court to violate the law.

Limiting the 1966 *Miranda* decision, *Oregon* v. *Hass* upheld the use for impeachment purposes of statements made to police by a suspect, after he had asked for a lawyer but before the lawyer had arrived. An illegal arrest was held not to have been remedied when police informed a suspect of his constitutional rights before questioning him (*Brown* v. *Illinois*). The court limited the use against a defendant of the fact that he had remained silent when he was first interrogated by the police (*United States* v. *Hale*).

Two unanimous opinions limited the powers of the U. S. Border Patrol to keep out illegal aliens. *United States* v. *Brignoni-Ponce* held that officers could not search cars at traffic points miles from the Mexican border without probable cause to believe that the cars contained illegal aliens. *United States* v. *Ortiz* ruled that cars could not be stopped for inquiries about citizenship of occupants if the only grounds for suspicion were that the passengers appeared to be of Mexican descent.

BUSINESS AND LABOR

In its most important ruling affecting business, the court upheld the 1973 railroad reorganization plan enacted by Congress to rescue the Penn Central and seven other failing railroads in the Northeast and Middle West and merge them in a single, self-sustaining, private system (*Regional Rail Reorganization Act Cases*).

In *Goldfarb* v. *Virginia State Bar* the court unanimously ruled that uniform minimum legal fees charged by lawyers in real estate transfers were a form of illegal price fixing. All the other antitrust cases during the term were decided favorably for business. A large city bank was permitted to acquire control of smaller suburban banks with which it had been in a close working relationship (*United States* v. *Citizens & Southern Nat. Bank*).

Mergers involving local companies doing business within a single state were held not to violate the Clayton Act (*United States* v. *American Bldg. Maintenance Industries*). *Gulf Oil Corp.* v. *Copp Paving Co.* held that the Robinson-Patman Act against price discrimination does not apply to companies whose activities do not cross state boundaries. Closed operations of the mutual fund industry and fixed commissions formerly charged by stockbrokers were both ruled exempt from price-fixing laws (*Gordon* v. *N. Y. Stock Exchange* and *United States* v. *National Association of Securities Dealers*).

The court split 4 to 4 in a case concerning the use of photocopying machines to reproduce copyrighted material, leaving standing a Court of Claims ruling that photocopying does not infringe copyright (*Williams & Wilkins Co.* v. *United States*).

The court cut back on the immunity from antitrust laws that labor unions have enjoyed for decades. A union that had sought to compel a contractor to boycott nonunion subcontractors was held liable for treble damages. This was instead of being charged only with an unfair labor practice under the Taft-Hartley Act (*Connell Construction Co.* v. *Plumbers & Steamfitters Union*).

Stockholders have no right to sue in federal court to halt illegal expenditure of corporate funds in political campaigns or to collect damages because of such spending (*Cort* v. *Ash*). The president of a national supermarket chain was held personally responsible under the federal food and drug laws for unsanitary conditions in a company warehouse (*United States* v. *Park*).

COURTS

In *Alyeska Pipeline* v. *Wilderness Society* the court rejected a judge's award of attorneys' fees to the environmentalists who had challenged construction of the Alaska pipeline. An Illinois judge could not jail 59 anti-Daley Democrats for contempt because they participated in the party's 1972 convention in violation of a court order (*Cousins* v. *Wigoda*).

Federal court jurisdiction was limited in *Hicks* v. *Miranda*. After police had seized an allegedly obscene film, the theater owner filed a civil rights suit in federal court seeking to have the California obscenity law declared unconstitutional. Local prosecutors then filed state criminal charges against the owner, and the Supreme Court ruled that the federal court should then have dismissed the civil suit in deference to the state proceeding. In *Johnson* v. *Mississippi* the court refused to allow the trial of black civil rights activists to be removed from state to federal court.

C. HERMAN PRITCHETT
University of California, Santa Barbara

INTERNATIONAL LAW

Significant developments in international law during 1975 concerned four important areas: law of the sea, arms control, use of force, and sovereignty.

The Law of the Sea. The UN Conference on the Law of the Sea met at Geneva in 1975. The Geneva session narrowed issues and framed them in an *Informal Single Negotiating Text*. This document was expected to form the basis for final discussions that may lead to a comprehensive sea law treaty in 1976.

Agreement was reached on two basic rights for coastal states. First, they would have full sovereignty over a 12-nautical mile (22-km) territorial sea adjacent to the coast, and, second, they would have exclusive rights to explore and exploit both fishing and mining resources out to

The Moroccan "peace march" into Spanish Sahara in November raised questions of territorial sovereignty.

UPI

a maximum of 200 nautical miles (370 km), an area to be called the coastal state's economic zone. Important rights retained by noncoastal states would include innocent passage in the territorial sea, unimpeded transit of straits used for international navigation, and full freedom of navigation and overflight outside the 12-mile territorial sea.

The major issues remaining to be decided include allocation of rights and duties relating to marine pollution and the precise contours of the institution that will control the deep seabed. Also, the structure of the machinery for the settlement of sea-law disputes must be agreed upon. Whether agreement is reached at the UN Conference in 1976 or not, it is likely the 200-mile limit will soon prevail throughout the Western Hemisphere.

Arms Control. On March 26 the major powers ratified the 1972 convention prohibiting the development, production, and stockpiling of bacteriological weapons. In addition, on April 29, the United States became a party to the 1925 Geneva Protocol prohibiting the use of gas and bacteriological weapons in warfare. In completing its ratification, however, the United States maintained that the protocol does not extend to riot control agents and chemical herbicides.

On August 21 the United States and the USSR tabled a draft convention on environmental warfare at the Geneva Conference of the Committee on Disarmament. The draft convention would oblige the parties "not to engage in military or any other hostile use of environmental modification techniques having widespread, long-lasting or severe effects."

Use of Force: The Mayaguez Affair. Three days in May saw swift military action by the United States and sharp controversy over the legal basis for this action. On May 12 the S. S. Mayaguez, a U. S.-flag merchant vessel carrying goods from Hong Kong to Thailand, was seized by Cambodian naval patrol boats as it passed near Poulo Wai Island, some 60 miles (97 km) off the Cambodian coast in the Gulf of Siam. The U. S. vessel was taken to neighboring Koh Tang Island on May 13, and the 39-man crew was removed to Sihanoukville on the mainland on May 14. Calling the seizure of the Mayaguez an "act of piracy," the United States demanded its immediate release on May 12 and airlifted 1,100 Marines to Thailand. Having received no response, on May 14 the United States attacked and sank three Cambodian gunboats near Koh Tang Island and landed 200 Marines there. At about the same time, Cambodia broadcast an offer to release the Mayaguez, and the crew was put aboard a Thai fishing boat to return to the Mayaguez. The crew was picked up by a U. S. destroyer, but the U. S. action continued, culminating in air strikes at an air base and a petroleum depot near Sihanoukville.

While there was general domestic praise for the "firmness" of the action taken to recover the Mayaguez, some questioned whether the United States had sufficiently utilized diplomacy before resorting to force. Pointing out that the Mayaguez had been seized in waters claimed to be Cambodian territorial sea and that Cambodia suspected the vessel of spying, critics said that the United States had failed to seek a solution of the dispute by negotiation as required by Article 33 of the UN Charter. Some also charged that even if the United States had justifiably acted in self-defense, the force used had been excessive.

Spanish Sahara. At year's end there appeared to be a grave danger of armed conflict over the future of the Spanish Sahara, an African territory that borders on Morocco, Algeria, and Mauritania. On October 16 the International Court gave an advisory opinion to the effect that neither Morocco nor Mauritania had sovereign rights in the territory. The way appeared open for self-determination by the territory's 70,000 residents, as Algeria and Spain had wanted. However, King Hassan of Morocco immediately mobilized 350,000 unarmed Moroccan volunteers for a peaceful "green march" into the territory.

Morocco, Mauritania, and Spain then negotiated a treaty providing for a transitional joint administration, Spanish withdrawal by February 1976, and respect for the views of the Saharans as expressed through their local assembly. Algeria denounced the agreement as denying the Saharans their right to self-determination. Supported by Algeria, a majority of the local assembly declared that body dissolved and pledged to fight for total independence. At year's end the Moroccan marchers had withdrawn, and the Spanish were reported to be prepared to leave to avoid involvement in fighting between Morocco and Algerian-backed Saharan nationalists. The UN General Assembly issued a call for self-determination.

DANIEL G. PARTAN
Boston University

LEBANON

An April attack on Palestinian commandos by conservative Falange party militiamen precipitated the polarization of Lebanon's Muslim majority and its Maronite Christian minority and plunged the country into civil war. The bitter sectarian battle, which left President Suleiman Franjieh powerless to intervene, left the republic with thousands dead and wounded and costs running higher than the equivalent of a year's gross national product. Although the fighting began between rightist Lebanese forces and Palestinian guerrillas, the issue that perpetuated the tragedy was the demand for reforms that would give Muslims a fairer share of power in Lebanon's political system.

April-June Cabinet Crises. The first round of fighting lasted from April 13–21 and left nearly 500 casualties. As the battle spread through the capital city of Beirut's suburbs, Palestinians were aided by Muslim leftists while Falangist forces were joined by units of Camille Chamoun's conservative National Liberal party. A cease-fire was effected with the arrest of the Falangists responsible for an April 13 attack. Subsequent sectarian recriminations led to a cabinet crisis that forced Premier Rashid Sohl to resign on May 15. The resignation touched off hostilities that raged until the end of the month near the Christian suburb of Dekwaneh. On May 23, Franjieh announced the formation of Lebanon's first military government in 32 years, selecting an officer of the predominantly Christian-led army, Noureddin Rifai, as premier. The choice of Rifai provoked strong criticism from Muslim groups, and, because he was unable to end the fighting, Rifai resigned on May 28.

On the same day, former premier Rashid Karami was asked to form a government. His efforts were stalled until June 30 when he announced the formation of a compromise six-man cabinet in which both Muslim and Christian interests were represented.

Army Intervention. The 16,000-member Lebanese army, which has Christian officers for its Muslim troops, did not enter the conflict until September when a battle broke out between the largely Muslim community of Tripoli, Karami's home, and the Christian community of Zgharta, Franjieh's mountain home. Within a week, Interior Minister Chamoun called upon the army to separate the two communities. However, fighting spread, without army intervention, to Beirut on September 16 and continued, despite four cease-fires, into October, with casualties estimated at 350 dead and 600 wounded. After mediation efforts by Palestinians and a Syrian delegation, Karami announced on September 24 the formation of a National Dialogue Committee, representing most political and religious groups, to discuss political reforms.

Urban Warfare. For no discernible cause, intense house-to-house warfare broke out in Beirut on October 8. During the month, eight cease-fires were called but to no avail. By November 1, the total number of businesses destroyed rose to 3,500, more than half of Beirut's foreign community had fled, and some 300,000 Lebanese had become refugees. Large portions of the resort city were destroyed and evacuated.

Fighting again broke out in mid-December and focused on the downtown resort area, with each side attempting to maintain strongholds in seaside hotels. Late in the month, Premier Karami announced political reforms that would strip the Christians of their legislative majority, and another truce was established.

F. NICHOLAS WILLARD, *Georgetown University*

A masked gunnman runs for cover in late June during the worst civil strife in Lebanon since 1958.

UPI

LEBANON • Information Highlights

Official Name: Republic of Lebanon.
Location: Southwest Asia.
Area: 4,015 square miles (10,400 sq km).
Population (1975 est.): 2,900,000.
Chief Cities (1974 est.): Beirut, the capital, 1,000,000; Tripoli, 128,000.
Government: *Head of state,* Suleiman Franjieh, president (took office Sept. 1970). *Head of government,* Rashid Karami, premier (took office May 1975). *Legislature* (unicameral)—Chamber of Deputies.
Monetary Unit: Lebanese Pound (2.23 pounds equal U. S.$1, July 1975).
Gross National Product (1974 est.): $3,700,000,000.
Manufacturing (major products): Processed foods, textiles, petroleum products, cement, tobacco products.
Major Agricultural Products: Cereals, fruits, vegetables, tobacco, wheat.
Foreign Trade (1974): *Exports,* $588,000,000; *imports,* $1,331,000,000.

Shown in an architectural model, the James Madison Memorial Building of the Library of Congress will be completed in late 1976 or early 1977. It will enable the Library to centralize many activities.

libraries

American librarianship was dominated by three decisive events during 1975. These included issuance in July of *Toward a National Program for Library and Information Services,* the final report of the National Commission on Libraries and Information Science. The other two were President Ford's nomination in June of Daniel J. Boorstin to be the twelfth Librarian of Congress and the U. S. Supreme Court's February deadlock decision in *Williams and Wilkins Co.* v. *United States.* Williams and Wilkins, a publisher of medical and scientific materials, had brought a violation-of-copyright suit against the National Library of Medicine and the National Institutes of Health.

National Commission Report. The final report of the National Commission on Libraries and Information Science was endorsed by the Council of the American Library Association (ALA) in July 1975.

Toward a National Program for Library and Information Services underwent numerous drafts between 1973 and 1975. Originally, the report placed almost exclusive emphasis on the development of a national information network. In its final form, the program more clearly recognizes the importance of adapting library and information service to local cultural and economic conditions. Outside library activities, service to independent learners and to those seeking to upgrade and develop occupational skills, and programs for special constituencies such as ethnic groups and the physically handicapped are no longer neglected.

Although the final report does not define a clear-cut division of labor between the public and private sectors in a national network, this crucial allocation of responsibility will undoubtedly occur when Congress and the administration decide to implement the national program. Getting that implementation underway will be the task of Alphonse F. Trezza, former director of the Illinois State Library, who became executive director of the commission on August 1.

There were objections to the report, however, from both librarians and that portion of the private sector directly concerned with information handling. At a commission hearing in Philadelphia on May 21, librarians complained about several features of the draft report. They objected to a provision about information services, with its apparent assignment of a central role to for-profit information processing and publishing interests at the expense of supporting library and other public activity in that area.

Other criticisms of the draft report centered on its failure to establish funding priorities, to pay attention to children's library service, to clarify the relationship within a national network of print and nonprint communication media, and to select a permanent federal agency to coordinate a national program. Finally, the report's failure to delineate clearly the responsibilities within a national network of federal, state, and local library agencies was criticized.

On the other hand, representatives of private concerns insisted that the document emphasized free access to information, thereby unfairly limiting the potential role within a national system of profit-seeking business firms. They also suggested that the private sector was prepared to provide greater speed and better cost-effectiveness in the distribution of information than were governmental agencies.

Library of Congress. President Ford's nomination of Daniel Boorstin, senior historian at the National Museum of History and Technology, for the post of Librarian of Congress provoked considerable opposition from the library community. Objections to the nomination revolved around Boorstin's status as a historian rather than a librarian, his lack of experience with library administration and technology, and his questionable acceptability to the staff of the Library. After considerable debate, he was confirmed by the Senate on September 26.

Earlier, the annual conference of the ALA had expressed its opposition to the nomination on July 4 and had concluded that Boorstin's career as a historian and an official at the Smithsonian Institution did not qualify him to meet the responsibilities confronting a Librarian of Congress. Urging that the appointee be a qualified professional librarian, the association demanded that it be given the privilege of review and rejection for cause in connection with presidential nominations for librarian of Congress. This type of prerogative is exercised by the American Bar Association over nominees for the Supreme Court.

In testimony before the Senate Committee on Rules and Administration on July 30, Robert Wedgeworth, executive director of the ALA, observed that it was just as unreasonable to expect a person who is unfamiliar with the administration of a large research library to become a successful Librarian of Congress as it would be to expect someone unfamiliar with the law to become a satisfactory attorney general. Similar opposition was voiced by the Special Libraries Association and by the American Society for Information Science. The Black Employees of the Library of Congress, a staff organization, contended that Boorstin, while director of the National Museum of History and Technology, had been unresponsive in matters such as equal opportunity and affirmative action.

The association's opposition to Boorstin's nomination may also be related to the issue of copyright. Authors and publishers generally supported his nomination because of their fear that a library partisan at the head of the Library of Congress would support legislation authorizing the kind of relatively unrestricted duplication of copyrighted material that would cut into their livelihoods.

Williams and Wilkins Case. A third event of significance to U. S. librarians had to do directly with copyright, specifically the case of *Williams and Wilkins* v. *United States*. The publisher accuses the federal government of systematically photocopying, for use by individuals and libraries, medical and scientific publications covered by copyright. On February 25, the Supreme Court, with Justice Harry A. Blackmun abstaining, split four-to-four on Williams and Wilkins' appeal of an earlier decision by the Court of Claims. The Court of Claims had found

The nomination of Daniel J. Boorstin as Librarian of Congress caused controversy, but it was approved.

in favor of the defendants, the National Library of Medicine and the National Institutes of Health. The action of the Supreme Court suggested that resolution of the copyright issue might more readily occur in the legislative than in the judicial branch of the federal government.

Copyright Revision. In May the House Committee on the Judiciary heard testimony on the General Copyright Revision Bill (HR 2223). This proposal resembles a bill that emerged from the Senate Judiciary Committee on July 3, 1974, and was passed by the full Senate on Sept. 9, 1974, only to die in December 1974, with the adjournment of Congress and without concurrent action by the House. Edmon Low, representing six national library associations, including the ALA, addressed the Committee. He stated that the proposed legislation's failure to define what constitutes systematic photocopying of copyrighted materials leaves libraries that do photocopying for purposes of interlibrary loan open to "harassing but unjustifiable suits" from publishers and authors.

While librarians sought assurance that any new copyright law would permit the making of single copies of copyrighted materials on behalf of the public good, the National Education Association argued for a more liberal bill permitting the making of multiple copies for classroom use. Conversely, the publishers said that both interlibrary photocopying and massive reproduction of materials for the classroom constituted "on-demand publishing" by what would in effect be reprint houses completely ignoring intellectual property rights. Because the proposed bill would permit "fair use" of copyrighted material and prohibit "systematic reproduction" of the same, but leaves both of these phrases essentially undefined, it is expected that the whole issue will eventually be tossed back to the courts.

In order to pass Congress, copyright legislation will need to be sufficiently vague and general as to beg immediate judicial interpretation.

Information Power was the theme of National Library Week in 1975. Sponsored by the American Library Association, the program stressed the resources of U. S. libraries.

In pictures, on film, in books, on tape, your library has all the answers.

National Library Week, 1975.

In the meantime, the 1909 law has been extended until Dec. 31, 1976, and a National Commission on New Technological Uses of Copyrighted Works has been created. It is composed of copyright owners, the users of copyrighted works, representatives of the public, and the Librarian of Congress, whose task it will be to study the problem of the uses of copyrighted material over the next three years.

Library Education. The number of graduate library schools accredited by the ALA increased to 65 in 1975. Master's degree programs were approved at the Graduate School of Library Service, University of Alabama; the School of Library Media, Alabama A and M University; the School of Library Science, North Carolina Central University; the College of Librarianship, University of South Carolina; and the Library Science/Audiovisual Program, University of South Florida.

The 1975 Beta Phi Mu Award for distinguished service to education for librarianship went to Kenneth R. Shaffer, formerly director of the School of Library Science at Simmons College in Boston.

National Library Week. The theme of National Library Week, April 13–19, was "Information Power." This event was sponsored by the ALA, the National Book Committee having decided to terminate its cosponsorship in late 1974. The ALA intends to make National Library Week integral to a year-round effort to promote libraries, their services, and communication materials, non-print as well as print.

ALA Conference. The 94th Annual Conference of the American Library Association was held in San Francisco, June 29–July 5. Over 1,400 sessions were attended by the 11,569 registrants. Allie Beth Martin became president of the ALA, and Clara S. Jones, director of the Detroit Public Library, was elected vice-president and president-elect.

Awards. The year's major library awards included the following:

The Joseph W. Lippincott Award for distinguished service in the library profession went to Leon Carnovsky, professor emeritus, Graduate Library School, University of Chicago. Professor Margaret W. Ayrault, of the Graduate School of Library Studies, University of Hawaii, received the Margaret Mann Citation for outstanding professional contribution in cataloging and classification. For distinguished contribution to reference librarianship, the Isadore Gilbert Mudge Citation went to Jean L. Conner, former director, division of library development, New York State Library. The Grolier Foundation Award, for stimulation and guidance of reading by young people, was given to Jane B. Williams for career service in Detroit and North Carolina.

International Library Activities. Oslo, Norway, was the site of the 41st general council meeting of the International Federation of Library Associations, August 11–18. The subject of the meeting was the organizational structure of the federation. There are now 604 members of the federation from 94 countries, 500 of which attended the Oslo sessions. In 1976 the federation will sponsor two meetings, one in Oslo and one in Seoul, South Korea. In the following year there will be a world conference celebrating the federation's 50th anniversary, and the 1978 meeting will be held in South America.

DAN BERGEN
University of Rhode Island, Kingston

LIBYA

Libya acted as a major spokesman for the Arab "rejectionist" approach to the Middle East problem in 1975. It worked against compromises with Israel and condemned Arab leaders, particularly Egypt's President Anwar Sadat, who took less radical positions.

The oil-rich nation also drew closer to the Soviet Union, which provided extensive military and economic assistance to Libya in several accords. This rapprochement also aggravated relations between Libya and Egypt.

The mistrust between Libya and Egypt dated from the latter's declining President Muammar el-Qaddafi's 1973 offer to unite the two states. An exchange of bitter personal denunciations between Sadat and Qaddafi began in the spring and continued all year in spite of efforts at mediation by other Arab politicians. Each accused the other of interfering in the internal affairs of the other, and Qaddafi blamed Egypt for an unsuccessful coup as well as an attempt on his life. A number of Libyan army officers also implicated in these plots were jailed.

Relations with USSR. One reason behind the renewed animosity was Soviet President Aleksei Kosygin's visit to Libya in May. During his trip he signed a treaty that provided Libya with substantial Soviet arms, particularly planes, tanks, and missiles valued at $1 billion. The contingent of some 500 Soviet technicians and advisors serving with the Libyan armed forces, many of them replacements for advisors withdrawn by Sadat after 1973, was also strengthened to help maintain the armaments and to train the Libyans in their use.

Egypt strongly protested the sale and exaggerated its dimensions. Egypt feared that these weapons might be used against it rather than the ostensible common enemy, Israel, and was offended that the USSR had sold equipment to Libya that had been denied to Egypt after Sadat had evicted his own Soviet advisors. The Egyptian claim that Libya had become little more than a Soviet satellite was belied, however, by Qaddafi's firm insistence that Soviet pressure to establish a naval base in Libya be withstood. He continued to adhere strictly to his previous policy of keeping the area free of all foreign bases.

Shortly after the military aid agreement a second Libyan-Soviet pact granted economic and technical assistance for the construction of a nuclear power plant in Libya. Qaddafi had earlier publicized his interest in such a project, announcing his intention to lure Arab scientists working abroad to Libya, where they would help develop atomic facilities. The agreement stressed the use of the plant for peaceful purposes. Use of atomic energy could solve a major problem of Libyan agriculture by providing the means to bring underground water to the surface for irrigation.

Stance Toward Israel. Appearing before the Organization of African Unity, the Islamic Foreign Ministers Conference, and the nonaligned nations bloc meeting in Peru, Libyan representatives spoke out vehemently against Israel, demanding its expulsion from the United Nations. Libya also boycotted a series of meetings between members of the Arab League and the European Economic Community (EEC) as a protest against the EEC's improved commercial relations with Israel.

Relations with Other Countries. Revolutionary movements throughout the world, especially Muslim dominated ones, received considerable Libyan support. The beneficiaries of military and economic aid included rebels in the Eritrea region of Ethiopia and the Philippines, the Palestine Liberation Organization, and Lebanese Muslim groups engaged in a civil war with their Christian countrymen. Libya spent millions of dollars supporting various Muslim factions in Lebanon alone.

Libya offered leadership in an African, as well as Arab, context, granting rapid diplomatic recognition to the military government in Chad in the spring, and initiating meetings with the new Nigerian government soon after it came to power in the summer.

Libya concluded foreign trade and aid agreements with Gabon, Malta, Argentina, Rumania, and Turkey, as well as a number of other nations. Generally, these countries received Libyan oil in return for agricultural and industrial commodities, political support, or, in the case of Turkey, badly needed workers for Libya's undermanned economy. The government was able to utilize petroleum as an effective economic lever again in 1975.

In order to heighten output, the Libyan National Oil Company undertook the construction of several new refineries, while the government continued the gradual nationalization of major foreign firms.

KENNETH J. PERKINS
University of South Carolina

------ **LIBYA · Information Highlights** ------

Official Name: Libyan Arab Republic.
Location: North Africa.
Area: 679,360 square miles (1,759,540 sq km).
Population (1975 est.): 2,300,000.
Chief Cities (1970 est.): Tripoli, joint capital, 264,000; Benghazi, joint capital, 170,000.
Government: *Head of state,* Muammar el-Qaddafi, president, Revolutionary Command Council (took office 1969). *Head of government,* Abdul Salam Jallud, premier (took office 1972).
Monetary Unit: Dinar (0.2959 dinar equals U. S.$1, July 1974).
Gross National Product (1974 est.): $5,900,000,000.
Manufacturing (major products): Petroleum products, processed foods.
Major Agricultural Products: Wheat, barley, tomatoes, dates, olives, peanuts, vegetables.
Foreign Trade (1973): *Exports,* $3,596,000,000; *imports,* $1,903,000,000.

LITERATURE

Rising costs in a recession economy affected publishers throughout the world. They were reluctant to risk major expenditures on new writers and concentrated their efforts on established authors. In October the Swedish Academy awarded the 1975 Nobel Prize in literature to Italian poet Eugenio Montale (see PRIZES AND AWARDS).

Reviews of the year's developments in the various major literatures follow.

American Literature

Many worthwhile books appeared in 1975, but only a few, like E. L. Doctorow's *Ragtime* and Saul Bellow's *Humboldt's Gift,* generated real excitement. The lack of new faces was likely due to rising costs, which make risk-taking unattractive for publishers. Book sales were high, but so were their prices.

Awards. The National Book Awards were made amid serious criticism. The expense of the ceremonies, the sharing of awards, and the proliferation of prizes put the continuation of the event in jeopardy.

The award for fiction was shared by Robert Stone's *The Dog Soldiers* and Thomas Williams' *The Hair of Harold Roux.* Marilyn Hacker's *Presentation Piece* won in poetry. The arts and letters prize was shared by Roger Shattuck's *Marcel Proust* and Thomas Lewis's *The Lives of a Cell.*

Richard B. Sewall was recognized for his biography, *The Life of Emily Dickinson,* and Bernard Bailyn was honored for his history, *The Ordeal of Thomas Hutchinson.* The contemporary affairs award went to Theodore Rosengarten's *All God's Dangers: The Life of Nate Shaw.* Robert Nozick's *Anarchy, State and Utopia* won in philosophy, and Silvano Arieti's *Interpretation of Schizophrenia* was the science winner. The translation award went to Anthony Kerrigan's *The Agony of Christianity* and *Essays of Faith* by Miguel D. Unamuno.

The Pulitzer Prize for fiction went to Michael Shaara's story of the battle of Gettysburg, *The Killer Angels.* Gary Snyder's *Turtle Island* won in poetry. In drama *Seascape* was honored, giving Edward Albee his second Pulitzer Prize. Annie Dillard's *Pilgrim at Tinker Creek* was the general nonfiction winner. The award for biography was shared by Robert A. Caro's *The Power Broker,* a study of Robert Moses, and Dumas Malone's first five volumes of *Jefferson and His Time,* his monumental study of Thomas Jefferson.

The National Institute of Arts and Letters and the Academy of Arts and Letters awarded the William Dean Howells medal for the best fiction of the last five years to Thomas Pynchon.

JILL KREMENTZ

Saul Bellow's *Humboldt's Gift* was one of the major U. S. literary events of 1975. A novel about a writer, it exposes various aspects of human frailty.

VIKING PRESS

The reclusive Pynchon acknowledged the honor but declined the medal.

Novels. Saul Bellow reaffirmed his importance to American literature with *Humboldt's Gift.* Bellow's Von Humboldt Fleisher, inspired by Delmore Schwartz, pays sympathetic tribute to the gifted poet who died in obscurity. Humboldt is seen through the eyes of Charles Citrine, a successful writer living in Chicago, who is hounded by his former wife's lawyers, harassed by his present mistress, and besieged by a small-

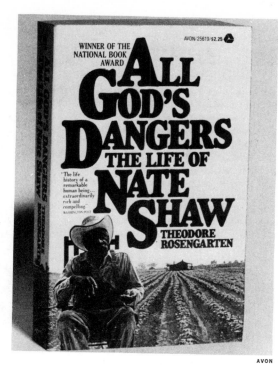

Theodore Rosengarten's *All God's Dangers: The Life of Nate Shaw* won a National Book Award in 1975.

on a man attempting to have his wife murdered proved paradoxically touching. Even more unlikely was Rosalyn Drexler's success with *The Cosmopolitan Girl,* in which the heroine takes a dog as her lover. Richard Brautigan's whimsical style however, did not seem appropriate to his violent mystery, *Willard and His Bowling Trophies.* William Burroughs continued his assault on the conventional novel in *The Last Words of Dutch Schultz,* a fiction in the form of a film script. Critics seemed unsure whether Frederick Exley's *Pages From a Cold Island* was novel or autobiography. Donald Barthelme's *The Dead Father* wittily explodes the conventions of storytelling to create its own fabulous fable.

Jerzy Kosinski's *Cockpit,* the drily told story of mindless revenges, and Joyce Carol Oates' *The Assassins* with its political violence, both reflected current anxieties in the United States. John Updike's *A Month of Sundays,* an account of a minister reviewing his life and many sins, did not receive much critical praise. Nor was George V. Higgins' interesting political novel, *A City on a Hill,* enthusiastically received.

James McCourt's ingenious first novel, *Mawrdew Czgowchwz,* was beautifully rendered. It is a realistically detailed fantasy about opera lovers in New York City who go mad for the divine lady of the title.

Two important posthumous works were Harvey Swados' *Celebration,* the inspiring journal of

The 1975 Pulitzer Prize for fiction went to Michael Shaara, author of *Killer Angels.*

time gangster, Rinaldo Cantabile, who admires Citrine. In taking what seems to be a marvelously ironic view of his own career, Bellow displays an affectionate understanding of human frailty.

E. L. Doctorow's *Ragtime* excited literary critics with its daring mixture of reality and fantasy, and stunned publishers with its record-breaking $1.8 million price for paperback rights. Told in a crisp but lyrical style that suggests the ragtime of the title, it evokes the spirit and the rhythms of the first decades of the 20th century. The main incident concerns a black piano player's violent revenge for the wanton destruction of his Model T Ford, but by intermingling his own characters with such people as Harry Houdini and Emma Goldman, Doctorow recreated a historical period as fiction truer than fact.

A long-awaited event was William Gaddis' second novel, *JR. The Recognitions,* published in 1955, gained a following despite its great length and difficulty. *JR,* with its endless pages of confused conversations and schoolboy plottings, stirred similar controversy.

The persistence of the traditional realist family story was demonstrated by Larry Woiwode's *Beyond the Bedroom Wall,* a convincing depiction of several generations of Midwesterners. Similarly, Reynolds Price avoided current fashion in his moving southern saga, *The Surface of the Earth.* Less successful was Larry McMurty's Texas novel, *Terms of Endearment.*

Bizarre subject matter proved fruitful for Thomas Berger, whose *Sneaky People,* centering

ATHENEUM

Edward Albee won his second Pulitzer Prize in 1975, with *Seascape* cited in the drama category.

an 89-year-old radical, and John Dos Passos' *Century's Ebb,* which continued up to Lee Harvey Oswald, President Kennedy's assassin, the pungent biographies Dos Passos developed in *U. S. A.*

Short Fiction. Leonard Michaels was widely praised for his second collection of short stories, *I Would Have Saved Them If I Could.* Despite the odd situations they depict, his works are often moving as well as clever. Vladimir Nabokov continued to move his life's work into English with *Tyrants Destroyed,* very early stories from his Russian emigré years. Isaac Bashevis Singer's *Passions* and Joyce Carol Oates' *The Seduction* attested to their authors' consistent ability and amazing energy.

The Collected Short Stories of Hortense Calisher demonstrated the achievement of this admired, but not widely known, writer whose talents are best revealed in these shorter works. Thirty years of haunting work were assembled in *The Collected Stories of William Goyen.*

Poetry. The diverse sources of inspiration for U. S. poets are well demonstrated by the way in which strong work appears from poets all over the United States on subjects intimate and remote and in styles private and public. Women poets with their striking self-revelations, like Erica Jong in *Loveroot,* Rosemary Daniell in *A Sexual Tour of the Deep South,* and Nikki Gio-

vanni in *The Women and the Men,* demonstrated welcome vitality. A narrative style is struck successfully in Audre Lord's *The New York Head Shop and Museum.* The political commitment in Denise Levertov's *The Freeing of the Dust,* the humor of Kenneth Koch's *The Art of Love,* and the rewarding difficulties of A. R. Ammon's *Diversifications* were also noteworthy.

George Oppen's *Collected Poems* brought together five volumes of the spare, crisp verse he has been writing for over 40 years. Galway Kinnell selected poems from 1946 to 1964 in *The Avenue Bearing the Initial of Christ into the New World.* Adrienne Rich's *Poems* were selected from her work since 1950. Robert Bly edited David Ignatow's *Selected Poems.*

The posthumous volume of W. H. Auden's last poems, *Thank You, Fog* showed him as wise and witty as ever. Anne Sexton's suicide preceded the publication of the ominously titled, *The Awful Rowing Toward God* in which she speaks again of her yearning for death.

Literary History and Criticism. It was an unusually rich year for criticism. Harold Bloom's *A Map of Misreading* imaginatively showed how each generation reinterprets its literary heritage. Hugh Kenner discussed U. S. modernist writers in *A Homemade World.* Frederick Crews continued his speculations on the relationship of psychoanalysis and literary criticism in *Out of My System.*

The eminent teacher and critic, Lionel Trilling, died on November 5. Exploiting a wide range of disciplines, including literature, history, philosophy, and psychology, he ordered and arranged the idea of an epoch into lucid, spacious, and thought-provoking essays. (See also OBITUARIES.)

Important poets and novelists published their essays. Allen Tate's *Memoirs and Opinions* was drawn from 50 years of work. Robert Penn Warren's *Democracy and Poetry* discussed the relationship of artists to government, and Philip Roth's *Reading Myself and Others* included many remarks on his own fiction. Walker Percy's *The Message in the Bottle* collected his philosophical speculations, while John Updike's *Picked-Up Pieces* assembled his careful book reviews, essays, and interviews.

Leon Edel edited the first two volumes of Henry James' *Letters* as well as *The Twenties,* the first in a series of the diaries and notebooks of Edmund Wilson. Casual writings and early essays were assembled in Lewis Mumford's *Findings and Keepings 1914–1936.* A vivid account of Henry Miller's disillusioning trip across the United States in 1940 was contained in *The Nightmare Notebook.* Tennessee Williams tells of his vicissitudes with incredible frankness in his *Memoirs.*

Brendan Gill's *Here at The New Yorker* is an affectionate account prompted by the 50th anniversary of the magazine. A more serious contribution to U. S. literary history is Hugh

Lionel Trilling, well known for his contributions to literary criticism, died on November 5.

Ford's *Published in Paris.* His story of the self-exiled British and American authors in Paris between 1920 and 1939 is both a realistic appraisal of the writers and a careful account of the contribution made by their printers and publishers.

Robert Coles' *William Carlos Williams: The Knack of Survival in America* sensitively discusses the poet's fiction. Williams' distinctive contribution to poetry is contrasted with T. S. Eliot's and Ezra Pound's in Louis Simpson's *Three on the Tower.*

History and Biography. Literary biographies were particularly interesting. R. W. B. Lewis' *Edith Wharton* revealed that the writer of those sharply ironic comedies and tragedies of manners was a strong and passionate person. Virginia Spencer Carr's biography of Carson McCullers, *The Lonely Hunter,* was shocking to some. The intimate revelations by the many people Carr interviewed made a fascinating portrait. Burton Bernstein's *Thurber* showed an unpleasant and petty man who was able to turn his exasperation into delightful fables and charming drawings. Reed Whittemore's *William Carlos Williams: Poet From Jersey,* was moving and effective. Darwin Payne's *The Man of Only Yesterday* was an interesting account of the life of the popular social historian, Frederick Lewis Allen. Frank R. Rossiter's *Charles Ives and His America* vivid-

ly shows the fierce individualism of the innovative composer.

Several books appeared that suggested the origins of problems that are yet unsolved. The distrust of a military establishment is clearly detailed in Richard H. Kohn's *Eagle and Sword,* which tells the story of the controversy between 1783 and 1802 over whether the United States should establish a standing army. The United States' simultaneous commitment ideologically to justice and politically to slavery and manifest destiny is illuminated in David Brion Davis' *The Problem of Slavery in the Age of Revolution 1770–1823.* Similarly, Michael Paul Rogin's *Fathers and Children* examines how Andrew Jackson's internal drives influenced his violent subjugation of Indians. In *Meeting at Potsdam,* Charles L. Mee strongly argues that the peace conference was deliberately subverted by the participants, each of whom had reasons for perpetuating discord.

A monumental contribution to intellectual history was H. Stuart Hughes' *The Sea Change.* Its publication completed his panoramic history of 20th-century European social thought.

Other Nonfiction. Buckminster Fuller, one of the original minds in the United States, published what he regarded as his great work. His *Synergetics* is a huge, idiosyncratic exploration into the geometry of thinking and the possibilities of technology and has enough thought-provoking ideas for many years of nourishment. Very different, but similarly valuable, is Edward O. Wilson's *Sociobiology,* a lucid synthesis on ethology.

In *The Philosophy of Andy Warhol,* one of the most inventive U. S. artists tried to explain himself. But his ideas on nothingness and boredom are better conveyed through his graphics than the printed word.

Psychoanalytic thinkers added to the understanding of society. Rollo May's *The Courage to Create* uses such notoriously difficult figures as Van Gogh and Dylan Thomas to argue for the healthiness of the creative act. Erik Erikson again demonstrated his vital humanism in *Life History and the Historical Moment.*

Watergate continued to precipitate books, but Theodore White's *Breach of Faith* was not judged a totally satisfactory account of the unmaking of a president. Neither were the more personal accounts like William Safire's *Before the Fall* or Jimmy Breslin's *How the Good Guys Finally Won.* On the other hand, Elizabeth Drew's *Washington Journal* was cited as a model of reporting.

Philip Agee, a Central Intelligence Agency operative disillusioned by his experiences in South America, not only told the stories but named the agents in his highly controversial, *Inside the Company.* Tom Wicker went deeper than investigative reporting in his personal, moving account of the Attica, N. Y., prison riots, *A Time To Die.* Wicker persuasively argues that

callousness and political ambition brought about the needless loss of many lives. The effects of such scandals are shown in Robert S. Gilmour and Robert B. Lamb's *Political Alienation in Contemporary America,* a disturbing report on the widespread disillusion with government.

Difficult subjects were seriously examined in Susan Brownmiller's *Against Our Will* and C. A. Tripp's *The Homosexual Matrix.* Brownmiller studies the psychosocial and political ramifications of rape, while Tripp makes a major contribution to the understanding of a complex social problem.

JEROME H. STERN
Florida State University

Children's Literature

Estimates of 1975's production of children's books placed the number of individual titles published at 1,600, a decrease of 200 from 1974. High production costs, a depressed economy, and the lack of federal funds formerly available to schools and libraries were cited as primary reasons for the decline. Generally, publishers placed less emphasis on color in picture books and produced fewer biographies, volumes of poetry, and revised editions than in prior years. Production totals of paperbacks remained steady, approximately 300 titles, but even in this area there were worries about higher production and distribution costs.

Virginia Hamilton won the American Library Association's Newbery Medal for *M. C. Higgins the Great.*

MACMILLAN

Awards. The major awards presented by the American Library Association (ALA) in 1975 for children's books published the previous year were given to Virginia Hamilton and Gerald McDermott. The ALA's John Newbery Medal for the most distinguished contribution to American literature for children went to Hamilton for her novel *M. C. Higgins, the Great.* It is the story of a young black coming to terms with his own identity and his family heritage in the Appalachian hill country. This same title also won the National Book Award for children's books. The ALA's Randolph Caldecott Medal for the most distinguished picture book was given to Gerald McDermott for his illustrations in *Arrow to the Sun,* an adaptation of a Pueblo Indian legend.

Eleanor Clymer received the 33d annual award of the Child Study Association of America/Wel-Met for dealing realistically with problems in the young people's world in *Luke Was There.* It is the story of a boy learning to trust adults amid fears and frustrations.

Popular Themes. Considerable emphasis was placed by publishers during the year on nonfiction accounts of birds, animals, insects, and reptiles. The affinity of young girls for horses was reflected in dozens of books. Sports books, fiction and fact, continued apace, with added attention placed on female accomplishments in athletics as well as in other fields of endeavor. Problems of divorce, adoption, and alcoholism and their effects on children were the substance of many novels. How-to books were again numerous as were volumes on witchcraft and the occult. Love, conception, and childbirth were graphically presented in several best-selling books.

Poetry. In poetry there were two books that stood out. X. J. Kennedy's *One Winter Night in August* contained a lively collection of nonsense jungles for readers 9 to 13 years old. *Cakes and Custard,* a handsomely illustrated collection of familiar and lesser known nursery rhymes chosen by Brian Alderson, was for children 5 years old and up.

Younger Readers. There were several excellent picture books for the four-year-old and up group. Mitsumasa Anno's *Anno's Alphabet* was a unique alphabet book with paradoxical illustrations, while Kay Saari's *The Kidnapping of the Coffee Pot* was about a lawn mower, a pair of old shoes, a lantern, and a coffee pot living in the city dump, with surreal illustrations by Henri Galeron. Faith Towle's retelling of a legend from India in *The Magic Cooking Pot* was distinguished by her exquisite batik illustrations, beautifully reproduced. Arnold Lobel's *Owl at Home* had four charming tales about a completely domesticated bird.

Elinor Lander Horwitz's *When the Sky Is Like Lace* was a whimsically imaginative book illustrated by Barbara Cooney. Verna Aardema retold an African folktale in *Why Mosquitoes*

The 1975 American Library Association Caldecott Award for the most distinguished picture book went to Gerald McDermott (*right*) for his illustrations in *Arrow to the Sun,* an adaptation of a Pueblo Indian tale that enjoyed great success.

Buzz in People's Ears, which had decorative art, based on African motifs, by Leo and Diane Dillon.

For ages 7 to 10 there were three outstanding titles. Remy Charlip's and Jerry Joyner's *Thirteen* featured 13 stories told graphically and simultaneously on each double page. Peter Spier traced the story of a Model-T in *Tin Lizzie,* while Jan Adkins' *Inside* had cross-section views of things common and complex.

Age Ten and Up. For ages 10 and up there were several noteworthy books. Felice Holman's and Nanine Valen's *The Drac* contained five tales from France of dragons and demons, while John Gardner's *Dragon, Dragon* had four original fairy tales told with tongue-in-cheek. In Mary Norton's *Are All the Giants Dead?* a modern boy travels to a land where the fairy tale characters of the past have grown old. Mordecai Richler's *Jacob Two-Two Meets the Hooded Fang* was a tall tale about a small boy who was rescued from a nightmarish child's prison by Child Power.

Sharon Bell Mathis' *The Hundred Penny Box,* about an old lady's memories, had warmly luminous illustrations by Leo and Diane Dillon. Natalie Babbitt's *Tuck Everlasting* was the story of a family that has eternal life.

For the teen-age audience the most distinguished works treated the struggle of working and growing up. *Bert Breen's Barn,* by Walter Edmonds, was about the labors and dreams of an upstate New York boy at the turn of the century, while Bill and Vera Cleaver's *Dust of the Earth* was a sensitive account of a girl and her family living in the harsh Dakotas of the 1920's. Crystal Thrasher's *The Dark Didn't Catch Me,* a first novel, portrayed life, work, and death in Indiana during the Depression.

Other volumes worthy of note for teen-agers included M. E. Kerr's *Is That You, Miss Blue?,* a funny, sharp, and unconventional novel about a girls' boarding school, and Eleanor Cameron's elegant *To the Green Mountains,* the evocation of a young girl's life in a small Ohio town during World War I. *Z for Zachariah,* by Robert C. O'Brien, was a novel about a 16-year-old girl trying to survive in a remote Pennsylvania valley after a nuclear war. Laurence Yep's *Dragonwings* was set in California at the time of the

Chinese immigration and concerned a boy's sacrifice for his father's dream to build an airplane.

GEORGE A. WOODS
*Editor, Children's Books,
"The New York Times"*

Canadian Literature in English

Canadian books in 1975 continued to demonstrate that Canadians are losing their traditional indifference to their own affairs and are showing growing interest in all aspects of their country.

Nonfiction. The first volume of Peter C. Newman's *The Canadian Establishment* is subtitled *The Great Dynasties.* It is a fascinating examination of Canada's ruling businessmen by a first-class reporter. Ivan Illich's *Medical Nemesis* attacks the effects of state-controlled medicine in Canada. In *The Failure of the Social Welfare System in Canada,* Andrew Armitage makes a careful study of welfare systems in Canada and points out inadequacies.

Lynne Gordon's *The Consumer's Handbook,* subtitled *99 Commercial Ripoffs and How to Spot Them,* is a practical guide for Canadian buyers. In *Hollywood's Canada,* prolific Pierre Berton shows how Hollywood's image of Canada has been consistently false since the one-reel silent movies of 1907. *The Great Canadian Beer Book,* edited by Gerald Donaldson and Gerald Lampert, is a pleasing draught of information about Canada's beers.

In *Campobello: The Outer Island,* poet Alden Nowlan gives an entertaining prose history of the island where Franklin Delano Roosevelt spent many of his summers. George Woodcock examines the causes of the decline of British imperialism in *Who Killed the British Empire?,* while John F. Kendle treats a segment of that subject in *The Round Table Movement and Imperial Unity.* Ivan Avakumovic's *Communism in Canada* is a scholarly history of the Communist party of Canada.

Poetry. *The Collected Poems of Earle Birney,* in two volumes, gathers together the best works of a dean of Canadian poetry. Forty years and 13 previous books of poems are represented in this collection. *The Darkening Fire* is a selection of Irving Layton's poetry from 1945 to 1968. It reinforced his position as one of Canada's best and most powerful poets. Alden Nowlan's ninth book of poetry, *I'm a Stranger Here Myself,* proved him once again to be a passionate and perceptive observer of both himself and other people.

Stanley Cooperman's *Greco's Book* is a fine poem in a splendid limited edition. George Bowering's *At War With the U. S.* added to his growing reputation. Florence McNeil's second book of poetry, *Ghost Towns,* deals with love, family, and childhood. *A Knight in Dried Plums* is another disarming volume by David McFadden.

Seymour Mayne produced his ninth volume of poetry, *Name.* Under the title *The Sad Truths: New Poems,* John Robert Colombo, explores an interesting selection of subjects. Helena Rosenthal's *Listen to the Old Mother* ranges from the erotic to the humorous. Joe Rosenblatt's *Virgins and Vampires* is a witty journey into the animal part of human nature. *The Poet's Record: Verses on Canadian History,* edited by Keith Wilson and Elva Motheral, shows the relationship between Canadian poetry and Canadian history.

Fiction. Robertson Davies' *World of Wonders* is the final novel in a trilogy that began with *Fifth Business* in 1970. Many view it as the best of the trilogy and the best of Davies' life. Sylvia Fraser's *The Candy Factory* is a finely written panoramic novel that fulfilled the promise of her earlier work. Leading novelist Ernest Buckler shows he is also a master of the short story in *The Rebellion of Young David and Other Stories.*

Sinclair Ross's *Sawbones Memorial* is a fine story about the only doctor in a little Saskatchewan town. Brian Moore's *The Great Victorian Collection* is a clever fantasy showing what happens to an assistant professor of history who dreams into existence a collection of treasures from the Victorian era.

Morley Callaghan's *A Fine and Private Place* is about a writer, Eugene Shore, who, like Callaghan himself, is lauded abroad and ignored at home. Callaghan demonstrates his power with words, but some critics found the book disappointing, especially in plot structure.

James Clavell, who wrote *King Rat,* produced his third novel, *Shogun,* a well-wrought story of Japan in 1600. Adele Wiseman's *Crackpot* is a sometimes sad, sometimes funny story of a remarkable Russian Jewish girl who emigrates to Canada and becomes a prostitute. Matt Cohen's *Wooden Hunters,* his third novel, is set in a British Columbia logging area. Ernest Perrault's second novel, *Spoil,* is an exciting tale about the search for oil in Canada's far north.

DAVID SAVAGE
Simon Fraser University

Canadian Literature in French

There were three major French Canadian literary events in 1975. The first was the death of the poet Alain Grandbois on March 18. Author of *Îles de la nuit* (1944) and *L'Étoile pourpre* (1958), Grandbois was regarded as the moving force behind modern French Canadian poetry. Second, the International Book Fair—the only one of its kind in North America—was held for the first time in Montreal in the spring. Finally, during the summer *Quinze* became the first cooperative publishing house to be established in Quebec.

No new authors published important works in 1975. The prominent figures remained young writers who had already established themselves by their earlier works.

Poetry. The fine collection by J. Brault entitled *Poèmes de quatre côtés* includes "nontrans-

lations" from the work of four English-speaking poets, interspersed with the author's own reflections on writing and poetry. In *Demain les dieux naîtront*, P. Chamberland characterizes the new cultural sensibility as mystical-erotic and anarchistic, while P. M. Lapointe in *Tableaux de l'amoureuse* offers a sequel to *Le réel absolu* (1971).

Novel. There were three new novels of particular significance. *Epidémie* by André Major is a continuation of the chronicle that began in 1974 and appeared in *Epouvantail. Neige noire* by J. Aquin, is a novel-scenario recalling the baroque quality of his earlier works, *Trou de mémoire* (1968) and *L'Antiphonaire* (1969). Finally, *Don Quichotte de la démanche* by V. L. Beaulieu earned the author the Prix du Gouverneur général.

Nonfiction. The best essay of the year was *Journal dénoué*, the "inner autobiography" of the poet F. Quellette and a humorous portrayal of one of the most authentic representatives of the Hexagon generation. In the field of literary criticism, L. Gauvin's *Le Parti pris littéraire* is an assessment of the ideological movement that most influenced literature and thought in Quebec during the 1960's. Also noteworthy are two works by J. Blais: *Présence d'Alain Grandbois* and a study of poetry in Quebec from 1934 to 1944.

FRANÇOIS RICARD
McGill University

English Literature

British readers and publishers have been accused of escapism through nostalgia for the past, especially for the Edwardian era. A strong interest in the earlier years of the 20th century was evident in British books published in 1975, although the Edwardian enthusiasm extends from the reign of Edward VII to that of Edward VIII. Whether it is a symptom of the times or only part of a natural cycle of interest in certain periods of history is uncertain. Memoirs dominated publishers' lists and reviewers' columns in 1975. Novelists and poets, however, were still active in Britain.

Nonfiction. *The Reith Diaries,* a selection from the daily journal of Lord Reith, general manager and then director-general of the British Broadcasting Corp. from its beginning until 1938, shocked many readers. This posthumous book, which displays the author's egomania, his admiration for Hitler and Mussolini in the 1930's, and his hatred of many of the great men of his day, damaged Reith's reputation, which had been high. *The Letters of J. R. Ackerley,* the correspondence of the late literary editor of the BBC journal *The Listener,* is a more pleasing book. It reflects literary life in London from the 1930's to the 1960's and Ackerley's witty personality.

Guy Chapman's *A Kind of Survivor* recounts the author's life as a publisher, historian, and husband of novelist Storm Jameson, but makes it clear that his service as an infantry officer from 1915 to 1918 was the most vivid experience of his life. Rosina Harrison's *Rose: My Life in Service,* like the television series *Upstairs, Downstairs,* appeals to the interest of a servantless society in the relationships between servants and their masters. It also provides a domestic portrait of the late Lady Astor, daughter of a Virginia family, who became the first woman member of Parliament and a famous hostess at her country home, Cliveden.

In *The Enchanted Places* Christopher Milne tells what it was like to be the model for Christopher Robin, hero of A. A. Milne's famous books for children. Helen Corke, the Helen of D. H. Lawrence's poems and the Helena of his novel *The Trespasser,* writes in *In Our Infancy* of her relationship with Lawrence. Dora Russell describes her marriage to and divorce from philosopher Bertrand Russell, in *The Tamarisk Tree,* and Kathleen Raine recounts her life as a poet in the second volume of her autobiography, *The Land Unknown.*

Among several biographies of Edward VIII, Frances Donaldson's is the best documented. Ryder Rowland's *Edith Cavell* is a careful study of the English nurse executed by the Germans in 1915. Michael Holroyd completed his biography of the painter Augustus John with the publication of *The Years of Experience.* Other important but less definitive studies included Robert Skidelsky's life of British fascist Oswald Mosley, Harold Acton's memoir of novelist and historian Nancy Mitford, Christopher Sykes' study of Evelyn Waugh, and Janet Hitchman's *Such a Strange Lady,* a life of Dorothy L. Sayers, translator of Dante and author of detective novels and *The Man Born to be King.*

Among notable biographical and critical studies of the lives and works of men and women of letters are two books on Charles Kingsley, who died in 1975. They are Brenda Colloms' *Charles Kingsley* and Susan Chitty's *The Beast and the Monk.* Branda Colloms' study is the more complete, but Susan Chitty has published new material from Kingsley's love letters and erotic drawings. In *The Glass, the Shadow, and the Fire,* Philip Mason illuminates Kipling's life and fiction, with the help of knowledge gained during his own service in India. Robert Gittings deals with Hardy's life until the death of his first wife in *Young Thomas Hardy,* and Philip Callow, in *Son and Lover,* examines the life of D. H. Lawrence until his departure from England in 1919. Both biographers drew upon new material for their studies.

Several books testify to a revival of interest in poets of the late 19th and early 20th centuries. Brocard Sewell writes of the life and poetry of Olive Custance, wife of Lord Alfred Douglas, himself a poet and a friend of Oscar Wilde. Jon Stallworthy explores the life and poems of Wilfred Owen, who was killed on the Western

Front in November 1918 at the age of 25. Desmond Graham, in *Keith Douglas, 1920–1944,* writes of another poet killed in a war.

Most remarkable is the revival of interest in Isaac Rosenberg. Three separate critical biographies, by Joseph Cohen, Jean Liddiard, and Jean Moorcroft Wilson, see Rosenberg, who died in 1918 at the age of 27, as one of most notable of the poets killed in World War I.

Poetry. Two senior poets, Robert Graves and John Betjeman, published collections of poems. Graves' *At the Gate* consists mainly of love poems that reflect a variety of moods and tone. John Betjeman's *A Nip in the Air* contains two poems that were written in his role as poet laureate, one on the investiture of the Prince of Wales and another on the wedding of Princess Anne. There are also topographical poems, typical of this poet, which describe both the landscape of the countryside and the architecture of the town. A narrative poem in blank verse, "Shattered Image," depicts the situation of a public relations man accused of making improper advances to a minor. The most poignant poems in the collection consider the approach of death.

Charles Causley's large volume, *Collected Poems 1951–1975,* contains musical, narrative poems, many of them ballads. The poems range from tales for children and biblical stories with a local and contemporary setting to incidents of war at sea. Bernard Gutteridge's *Old Damson-Face: Poems 1934–1974* displays sympathetic, ironic humor in economical lines that, particularly in recent poems, usually avoid rhyme and regular meter. The poems of Ruth Pitter's *End of Drought* depict gardens and countryside with visual clarity and with a wide range of style and feeling. Jenny Joseph's *Rose in the Afternoon* dramatizes moments of strong emotion, while Elizabeth Jenning's *Growing-Points* captures some of the poet's experiences in simple language.

Peter Scupham's new collection, *Pre-histories,* shows considerable technical skill and the ability to condense meaning in precise language. His chief concern is the relationship of the present to past and future. Alan Ross' *Open Sea* collects and adds to his war poetry. John Hewitt's *Out of My Time* observes sensitively the appearances, actions, and personalities of other people. The poems of Seamus Heaney, a fellow Ulsterman, in *North* illuminate the violent present in Northern Ireland by relating it to Ireland's troubled past.

Two newer poets, Hugo Williams and J. H. Prynne, published interesting collections. Some of Williams' poems in *Some Sweet Day* are like still-life paintings that capture the moods inanimate objects may evoke. Prynne uses his scientific knowledge to good effect in the poems of *Wound Response.*

Two novelists, Alan Sillitoe and John Wain, tried their hands at verse. Though Sillitoe's *Storms* may be of interest to admirers of his novels, Wain's *Feng,* a verse drama based on an early version of the Hamlet story, is the more successful of the two books.

Fiction. With the publication of *Hearing Secret Harmonies,* Anthony Powell's series of novels, *A Dance to the Music of Time,* concluded. The series began in 1951 with *A Question of Upbringing.* It compares in scope with Galsworthy's *Forsyte Saga* and Snow's *Strangers and Brothers* series. The narrator, Jenkins, brings the complex plot to a resolution and concludes the stories of the characters who have survived from earlier volumes.

Another series, more modest but still imposing, concluded in 1975 with a fourth novel. Paul Scott's *A Division of the Spoils* recreates life in India when it was part of the British Empire.

Iris Murdoch's *A Word Child* has been praised by reviewers as one of her best novels. The narrator, Hilary Burde, rises from an orphanage to an Oxford fellowship as a result of his gift for languages. However, burdened by guilt and the victim of repeated disaster, he falls to the rank of a minor civil servant. There is some hope at the end of the novel that he has reached wisdom through suffering.

Three novels that contain more direct moral lessons are given distant settings. The slightest of the three, Martin Amis' *Dead Babies,* depicts the speech and actions of spoiled, obscene teenagers of the future. Doris Lessing's *The Memoirs of a Survivor* describes a future in which there are such constant shortages and so few services that people must live by bartering and foraging. There is a hint that disaster may be transcended by the exercise of psychic powers. *Shardik,* by Richard Adams, author of *Watership Down* and apparent successor to J. R. R. Tolkien, is set in a distant past created in imaginative detail. The effect upon people of a great white bear they take to be a god is the subject of Adams' story.

Other notable novels are Margaret Drabble's *Realms of Gold,* Elaine Feinstein's *Children of the Rose,* Beryl Bainbridge's *Sweet William,* Rena Sally's *The Sea Road West,* Maurice Leitch's *Stamping Ground,* and Christopher Leach's *The Pheasant Shoot.* Interesting collections of short stories include Francis Wyndham's *Out of the War,* Ian McEwan's *First Love, Last Rites,* and Gwyn Williams' *Two Sketches of Womanhood.*

Obituary. P. G. Wodehouse, who had lived in the United States since 1947, died on Feb. 14, 1975, at the age of 93. His rift with his countrymen, caused by his broadcasts from Berlin as a German internee during World War II, was healed in January 1975, when he was knighted by the British. He continued to write about Jeeves and other imaginary Edwardians until his death.

J. K. Johnstone
University of Saskatchewan

Louisiana's Superdome, the largest arena-stadium in the world, opened in August as criticism continued about the cost of the structure and of the maintenance contract for it.

LOUISIANA SUPERDOME

LOUISIANA

Louisiana ended 1975 on a political note, with statewide elections that saw Gov. Edwin Edwards win reelection with an impressive first primary victory over five other candidates. Other issues of interest in the state included the completion of the controversial Louisiana Superdome and overcrowding in the prisons.

Elections. In the gubernatorial race, Edwards gathered 62% of the vote. With three exceptions, all other statewide officeholders were returned to their posts.

The exceptions were the office of secretary of state, which was vacated by veteran politician Wade O. Martin, Jr. in his unsuccessful gubernatorial campaign, and the posts of superintendent of education and commissioner of agriculture. In the latter, long-time incumbent Dave Pearce withdrew following the first primary after running behind political newcomer Gil Dozier of Baton Rouge. In the race for secretary of state, P. J. Mills of New Orleans was defeated by state Sen. Paul Hardy of St. Martinville in a runoff in December. Also defeated was incumbent Education Superintendent Louis Michot, who lost to Shreveport educator Kelly Nix.

Superdome. The $162 million Louisiana Superdome was finally completed in August, much behind schedule but in time for the New Orleans Saints' first preseason football game.

The controversy that has dogged the project from its inception continued. There was heavy criticism of Superdome Services Inc., a black-run company responsible for maintenance, cleanup, and security services for the dome. The criticism stemmed from alleged incompetence and the linking of Sherman Copelin, the group's president, to fraud scandals involving a private health services group. However, Copelin maintained that many of the charges were racially motivated.

Tidelands. In September, the United States presented Louisiana with a $136.2 million check in partial settlement of the 25-year-old tidelands royalties dispute. The state had claimed title to 258,000 acres (104,000 hectares) of offshore oil-rich lands, but the U. S. Supreme Court ruled that Louisiana was entitled to only 75,000 acres (30,350 hectares). The money was used to help retire the state debt.

Prisons. In early September, a U. S. district judge in Baton Rouge ordered that the state penitentiary at Angola could accept no more prisoners until overcrowding and other adverse conditions were corrected. At that time, the state prison contained more than 3,700 men. The judge ordered a reduction to 2,640, either by transferal or construction of new facilities at Angola. Meanwhile, local sheriffs' overcrowding problems increased.

JOSEPH W. DARBY III
"The Times-Picayune," New Orleans

LOUISIANA • Information Highlights

Area: 48,523 square miles (125,675 sq km).

Population (1974 est.): 3,764,000. *Density:* 83 per sq mi.

Chief Cities (1970 census): Baton Rouge, the capital, 165,963; New Orleans, 593,471; Shreveport, 182,064.

Government (1975): *Chief Officers*—governor, Edwin W. Edwards (D); lt. gov., James E. Fitzmorris, Jr. (D). *Legislature*—Senate, 39 members; House of Representatives, 105 members.

Education (1974–75): *Enrollment*—public elementary schools, 590,432 pupils; public secondary schools, 250,310; nonpublic schools, 129,500; colleges and universities, 140,565 students. *Public school expenditures*, $707,709,000 ($914 per pupil).

State Finances (fiscal year 1974): *Revenues*, $2,606,229,-000; *expenditures*, $2,401,410,000.

Personal Income (1974): $16,223,000,000; per capita, $4,310.

Labor Force (Aug. 1975): *Nonagricultural wage and salary earners*, 1,187,500; *insured unemployed*, 54,400.

LUXEMBOURG

Aside from the deepening economic depression, 1975 was a rather uneventful year for Luxembourg.

Economy. Iron and steel production dominates the economic life of the country, accounting for 40% of employment and contributing 25% to the gross national product. Despite a 45% drop in steel production, the rate of unemployment remained insignificant due to an emergency work plan instituted in cooperation with the strong labor unions. The workers remained on the payrolls of the steel companies but were loaned out to work on public projects such as repairing roads and clearing forests. The

—— **LUXEMBOURG · Information Highlights** ——

Official Name: Grand Duchy of Luxembourg.
Area: 999 square miles (2,586 sq km).
Population (1975 est.): 300,000.
Chief Cities (1975 est.): Luxembourg, the capital, 78,-800; Esch-sur-Alzette, 27,700; Differdange, 18,300.
Government: *Head of state,* Jean, grand duke (acceded 1964). *Head of government,* Gaston Thorn, premier (took office June 18, 1974). *Legislature* (unicameral) —Chamber of Deputies.
Monetary Unit: Franc (39.47 francs equal U. S.$1, Aug. 1975).
Gross National Product (1974): $1,900,000,000.
Manufacturing (major products): Iron and steel, chemicals, fertilizers, textiles, nonferrous metals.
Major Agricultural Products: Barley, wheat, oats, grapes, potatoes.
Foreign Trade (Luxembourg-Belgium, 1974): *Exports,* $28,130,000,000; *imports,* $29,600,000,000.

government reimbursed the employers. The cost of the program was estimated at about $3 million a month.

Luxembourg's rate of inflation in 1975 was about 11%, one of the lowest in the world. The government combated inflation with a complex of regulations, including the restriction of profit margins in the marketing of household electric articles and other appliances.

The economy of Luxembourg is not burdened with military expenditures. This small country enjoys one of the highest annual per capita incomes in the world and spends less than 1% of its gross national product on defense.

The remarkable growth of Luxembourg as a financial center has made banking an important factor in the economy. The number of banking institutions increased from 13 in 1955 to approximately 80 in 1975. The number of people employed by banks has risen from about 1,000 to more than 5,000. Banking activity accounts for 10% of the country's fiscal receipts.

Politics. Gaston Thorn, the premier and foreign minister, was elected president of the 1975 General Assembly of the United Nations. On invitation of the Presidium of the Supreme Soviet of the USSR, Grand Duke Jean and Grand Duchess Charlotte visited Moscow June 5 to 10.

AMRY VANDENBOSCH
University of Kentucky

MAINE

The year 1975 saw James B. Longley inaugurated as Maine's 57th governor. Longley was the nation's only independent governor and immediately set out to implement many of the cost-cutting and efficiency programs that he had advocated before his election.

Politics and Government. Though the state budget was actually increased by $120 million, most of the increase was allocated to towns and cities under the Educational Equalization Act of 1974 (as amended in 1975). This act calls for state aid up to 50% of local school costs. A number of coastal communities, such as Castine and Wiscasset, protested its impact on their property taxes and spearheaded an unsuccessful

effort to repeal the law, employing methods of civil disobedience.

Most state agencies found their budgets cut or left the same as in 1974. State employees were denied cost-of-living increases, which produced an unprecedented public display of unhappiness by many of them. Governor Longley called for the resignation of the board of trustees of the University of Maine for having allegedly mismanaged that institution. Their refusal earned them the coveted Alexander Mecklejohn Academic Freedom Award of the American Association of University Professors. In other educational matters, Patrick McCarthy was appointed the second chancellor of the University of Maine, and Dr. William Cole was installed as president of Nasson College.

On November 4, Maine voters accepted constitutional amendments calling for annual legislative sessions and elimination of the 155-year-old appointed executive council.

Economy. Unemployment in Maine rose to over 11% in 1975. Inflation spurred on by high fuel costs led to serious economic problems. In October the Maine Woodsmen's Association led a two-week work action against paper companies. Evergreen Valley, a state-guaranteed venture to develop a four-season recreational center in Stoneham, declared bankruptcy. Both the winter sport and the summer tourist seasons experienced great success, however, aided by especially favorable weather conditions.

Environment. The Environmental Protection Agency gave the Pittston Company approval to build an oil refinery—but not a dock—at Eastport. Canadian refusal to grant permission for tankers' passage through the waters of Passamaquoddy Bay, raised doubts about whether a refinery would ever be built.

Bicentennial. There were successful reenactments of the first naval battle of the American Revolution at Machias, of Arnold's march to Quebec, and of the burning of Falmouth. They were all part of Maine's effort to observe the nation's 200th birthday.

RONALD F. BANKS
University of Maine

———— **MAINE · Information Highlights** ————

Area: 33,215 square miles (86,027 sq km).
Population (1974 est.): 1,047,000. *Density:* 31 per sq mi.
Chief Cities (1970 census): Augusta, the capital, 21,945; Portland, 65,116; Lewiston, 41,779; Bangor, 33,168.
Government (1975): *Chief Officers*—governor, James B. Longley (I); sec. of state, Markham Gartley (R). *Legislature*—Senate, 33; House of Representatives, 151 members.
Education (1974–75): *Enrollment*—public elementary schools, 174,439 pupils; public secondary schools, 76,204; nonpublic schools, 18,100; colleges and universities, 36,634 students. *Public school expenditures,* $204,538,000 ($886 per pupil).
State Finances (fiscal year 1974): *Revenues,* $714,581,-000; *expenditures,* $659,273,000.
Personal Income (1974): $4,648,000,000; per capita, $4,-439.
Labor Force: *Nonagricultural wage and salary earners* (July 1975), 356,400; *insured unemployed* (Aug. 1975), 16,700.

MALAYSIA

For Malaysia, 1975 was a year lacking spectacular events. However, there were no major setbacks except in the area of internal security. On September 21, Sultan Tunku Lahya Petru al-Marhum was sworn in as head of state, with official installation scheduled for 1976.

Political Events. The principal development in domestic politics concerned Sabah, where the activities of the state's chief minister, Tun Mustapha, had become a source of increasing concern to Kuala Lumpur. Besides his authoritarianism, extravagance, and tolerance of corruption, Mustapha strained Malaysian-Philippine relations with his public espousal of the cause of Muslims in the Philippines rebelling against Manila's authority. He even suggested that Sabah might secede from Malaysia, presumably to join the predominantly Muslim areas of the southern Philippines in forming a new, independent Muslim nation. The defection of several supporters led to Mustapha's resignation as chief minister on October 31. However, he remained president of Sabah's largest political party and a figure of great political influence.

In West Malaysia (Malaya) the dominant political party, the United Malay National Organization (UMNO), held its triennial general assembly and elected three vice-presidents (and potential prime ministers). These men were Ghafar Baba, minister for agriculture and rural development; Tengku Razaleigh Hamzah, chairman of the national petroleum company; and Dr. Mahathir Mohamed, education minister. The elections assumed added significance due to a heart attack suffered earlier in the year by Hussein Onn, the UMNO deputy president and the nation's deputy prime minister.

Economy. Although buffeted by the recession and inflation troubling the industrialized nations that constitute Malaysia's overseas markets, the prospects for the economy remained guardedly optimistic. Government statistics indicated a 4% real growth in the gross national product for 1975, with a projected 6.5% rate for 1976. Other positive indicators included a favorable balance of payments, a moderation in the rate of inflation, and a leveling off of unemployment. Oil became a significant factor in the economy with production at 80,000 barrels-per-day and estimates of future production ranging from 300,000 to 1 million barrels-per-day. After a slump in 1974, world prices for natural rubber rebounded in 1975, and long-term prospects appeared bright as high petroleum prices eroded the competitive position of synthetic rubber. Malaysia, Thailand, and Indonesia, which produce 86% of the world's natural rubber, agreed to a "supply rationalization scheme" designed to prevent the large price fluctuations of the past.

Security. Increased Communist guerrilla activity in West Malaysia continued in 1975. This occurred despite an apparent schism of the Malayan Communist party (MCP) into three factions. The east-west highway under construction from Penang to Kota Bahru was the focus of several Communist clashes with security forces. However, the most spectacular incidents—the bombing of the National Monument and the headquarters of the paramilitary police—occurred in Kuala Lumpur. This reflected a new departure in Communist tactics—urban guerrilla warfare.

Foreign Affairs. Major foreign policy developments concerned China, Indochina, and the Malacca Strait. A congratulatory message from Peking to the Malayan Communist party was viewed in Kuala Lumpur as a violation of the agreement reached during Prime Minister Abdul Razak's 1974 visit to China. The defeat of the anti-Communist forces in Indochina posed the difficult question of how stable relations could be established with the new Communist governments in Cambodia, Laos, and South Vietnam. Moreover, it was feared that Malayan Communist insurgents would benefit not only psychologically but also in terms of surplus armaments from the Indochina conflict.

Malaysia's desire to control ship traffic in the Malacca Strait received dramatic reinforcement when an oil tanker ran aground off Singapore in January, spilling large quantities of crude oil. In February, Malaysia, Indonesia, and Singapore agreed to joint measures in the strait "for the safety of navigation and control of marine pollution." The nations continued to disagree on whether the waterway should be considered within the territorial sea of the littoral states, as Malaysia and Indonesia claimed, or whether it should remain part of the international high seas, as Singapore insisted.

Two other events thrust Malaysia briefly into the global limelight. Boxer Muhammad Ali defeated Joe Bugner in a heavyweight championship fight on July 1. In August, Japanese Red Army guerrillas forced their way into the U. S. consulate and took more than 50 hostages. All were later released unharmed.

MARVIN C. OTT
Mount Holyoke College

MALAYSIA · Information Highlights

Official Name: Malaysia.
Location: Southeast Asia.
Area: 127,316 square miles (329,749 sq km).
Population (1975 est.): 12,100,000.
Chief Cities (1970 census): Kuala Lumpur, the capital, 451,728; Pinang, 270,019; Ipoh, 247,689.
Government: *Head of state:* Sultan Tunku Abdul Halim Mu'adzam (took office 1971). *Head of government,* Tun Abdul Razak, prime minister (1970). *Legislature*—Parliament: Dewan Negara (Senate) and Dewan Ra'ayat (House of Representatives).
Monetary Unit: Malaysian dollar (2.40 M. dollars equal U. S.$1, Aug. 1974).
Gross National Product (1974 est.): $6,400,000,000.
Manufacturing (major products): Petroleum products, refined sugar, rubber goods, steel, lumber.
Major Agricultural Products: Rubber, rice, palm oil and kernels, tea, pepper, coconuts, spices.
Foreign Trade (1974): *Exports,* $4,546,800,000; *imports,* $4,440,900,000.

MANITOBA

Manitoba experienced a prosperous year, relatively well cushioned from the effects of economic recession and unemployment.

Inflation. The effects of inflation, however, were felt as Premier Edward Schreyer's April 24 deficit budget showed. Despite an estimated 20% increase in revenues, the projected deficit was $6.4 million. Schreyer has publicly advocated the imposition of wage and price controls for two years. His government's restraint policies were felt especially by the universities and the medical profession. The province's nurses received a 35.6% salary increase in March, but controversies between the province's doctors and Health Minister Larry Desjardins continued.

Politics. With Premier Schreyer's New Democratic party (NDP) government enjoying a secure majority in the Legislative Assembly and with no general election expected until 1977, both opposition parties took the opportunity to change their leaders. In February, I. H. Asper voluntarily resigned from the leadership of the Liberal party and was replaced by lawyer Charles Huband. After a bitter campaign Progressive Conservative leader Sidney Spivak was defeated at a party convention on December 6. Former Attorney General Sterling Lyon won the position by a substantial majority (264–207) and was expected to move the party significantly to the right. The Progressive Conservatives won two seats in June, dashing Liberal hopes of a comeback. Party standings in the Legislature are NDP, 31; Progressive-Conservative, 23; and Liberals, 3.

Government Industries. Financial concern and political controversy surrounded government-owned corporations. Flyer Industries, which builds buses, had a large back-log of orders but failed to meet delivery dates or to make a profit. Saunders Aircraft swallowed more than $38 million in subsidies and grants but failed to find sufficient buyers of its aircraft. The new Skywest Airlines, jointly owned by the NDP governments of Manitoba and Saskatchewan, was refused a license by the federal Air Transport

Board, which alleged that the company's application was inadequately documented.

Garrison Dam. Throughout the year concern mounted over the approaching completion of the Garrison Dam Diversion Project in North Dakota. When the International Joint Commission held public hearings in Winnipeg in November, both official and private Manitoban opinion was opposed to the project on the grounds that serious deterioration of the quality of water flowing into the Red and Souris rivers would result.

JOHN A. BOVEY
Provincial Archivist of Manitoba

MARIANA ISLANDS

On June 17, 1975, the people of the northern Mariana Islands in the western Pacific Ocean voted by a 4 to 1 margin to approve a covenant that would make the islands a commonwealth of the United States, similar to Puerto Rico.

Geography. The northern Marianas are a 400-mile (645-km) north-to-south chain of 14 small islands approximately 1,500 miles (2,400 km) east of the Philippines and 1,350 miles (2,160 km) south of Japan. Saipan, the main island, contains about 85% of the 14,000 inhabitants. Other important islands are Rota and Tinian, from which was launched the first atom bomb raid on Japan in 1945. Guam, the southernmost island of the Marianas, is a U. S. territory and was not included in the commonwealth. Since 1948, the northern Marianas have been administered by the United States as a district of the UN Trust Territory of the Pacific Islands.

Commonwealth Covenant. The Mariana Commonwealth Covenant was concluded in February by representatives of both the Mariana islanders and of U. S. President Gerald Ford. Voter ratification was only the first step in creating the commonwealth. The U. S. Congress must approve the covenant, the president must approve a constitution drafted by the people, and the UN Security Council must consent to the islands' separation from the trust territory. UN action is not expected until at least 1980.

As commonwealth residents, the people would enjoy full U. S. citizenship and be eligible for all federal programs and services. The United States would give about $14 million in aid annually for at least 7 years, and for 50 years would rent, for possible military use, two thirds of Tinian, part of Saipan's harbor, and a deserted island used as a bombing range.

Under U. S. control, the islands would be a vital strategic defense bastion because of their proximity to Asia. This geographical position proved valuable in the spring of 1975, when more than 30,000 refugees from South Vietnam were airlifted to Guam while awaiting resettlement in the United States.

RICHARD G. WEST
*Former Senior Editor
"Encyclopedia Americana"*

MANITOBA · Information Highlights

Area: 251,000 square miles (650,090 sq km).
Population (1975 est.): 1,020,000.
Chief Cities: Winnipeg, the capital (1974), 570,000; St. James-Assiniboia (1971), 71,431.
Government (1975): *Chief Officers*—lt. gov., W. J. McKeag; premier, Edward Schreyer (New Democratic party); atty. gen., Howard R. Pawley (NDP); min. of educ., Ben Hanuschak (NDP); chief justice, Samuel Freedman. *Legislature*—Legislative Assembly, 57 members.
Education (1975–76): *Enrollment:* public elementary and secondary schools, 227,240; private schools, 6,460; Indian (federal) schools, 7,410; colleges and universities, 16,350 students. *Public school expenditures,* $230,362,000.
Public Finance (fiscal year 1974–75 est.): *Revenues,* $1,012,000,000; *expenditures,* $1,133,000,000.
Personal Income (1972): $3,551,000,000; average annual income per person, $3,557.
(All monetary figures given in Canadian dollars.)

MARINE BIOLOGY

Many advances were made in marine biology during 1975 that hold promise of fruitful returns from sealife. A notable event of the year was the visit of a distinguished amateur marine biologist, Emperor Hirohito of Japan, to the laboratory at Woods Hole, Mass.

Sponge Toxin. Numerous scientists were working with toxins, antibiotics, and other substances from marine organisms that offer promise for the prevention or treatment of human diseases. A sponge from the Red Sea has been found to produce a substance that repels fish and thus prevents predation on the sponge. The substance is toxic to fish and also inhibits the growth of certain bacteria, apparently by interfering with the action of the important enzyme cholinesterase, found in man and many animals, including fish.

Immune Bacteria. Scientists investigating marine microorganisms have observed that intestinal bacteria exposed to various heavy metals and antibiotics become immune to their toxic effects. These bacteria are capable of surviving after being discharged with sewage wastes into estuaries and oceans. Some marine biologists believe that shellfish eaten raw or improperly cooked may be contaminated by these bacteria. There is thus a danger that these bacteria will cause infections that are resistant to presently available antibiotics.

Marine Food Chain. Many small multicellular marine animals and protozoa feed on bacteria. If bacteria can survive in environments polluted with industrial and sewage wastes containing toxic heavy metals, the metals may enter the bacteria and become incorporated into marine food webs.

Marine scientists at the Fisheries Radiobiological Laboratory, Lowestoft, England, are studying the movement of tracer radioactive metals through simple experimental food chains consisting of one species of algae and a snail. Their object is to determine whether metals can pass directly from seawater into an animal, or only indirectly by first being incorporated into plant material and then eaten. It is extremely important to understand how metals become involved in food chains, both because many metals are toxic and because other metals serve as micronutrients for certain metabolic functions in marine life.

Advances in Aquaculture. Increasing attention is being given to aquaculture projects in estuarine and marine waters. Initial efforts to rear such species as clams, oysters, and lobsters have met with some success, but further research is being done in such problems as disease and cannibalism in marine animals kept in crowded aquarium systems. Scientists rearing salmon, for instance, have developed vaccines that will prevent certain diseases troublesome in hatchery operations. Other scientists are studying the ge-

UPI

Japanese Emperor Hirohito, a skilled marine biologist, visited Woods Hole Oceanographic Institution in October.

netics of selected marine organisms to find strains that grow more rapidly and attain a larger size.

Some scientists are attempting to introduce new species or varieties of marine organisms into certain areas. For instance, some European scientists wish to culture large kelp such as the *Macrocystis* from California waters. Introduction of an exotic species, however, creates the danger that it will "escape" and affect the survival of indigenous species. Thus, studies of the reproduction of many species are being made in order to develop sterilization techniques or other ways of preventing the spread of introduced species.

Along these same lines, marine scientists gave considerable attention during 1975 to the spread of organisms into new, formerly uncolonized areas, through such passages as the Panama and Suez canals. While it was formerly thought that the freshwater lakes along the length of the Panama Canal would prevent mixing of Atlantic and Pacific fauna, it was recently reported that several species of finfish have moved from one ocean to another. Some are believed to have been carried in growth attached to vessel hulls or as eggs and larvae in bilge waters. In any case, little is presently known about the effect of these migrants on the marine ecosystems into which they have moved.

JOHN B. PEARCE
Sandy Hook Laboratory
National Oceanic and Atmospheric
Administration

MARYLAND

Major events in the state in 1975 centered around the state legislature, the governor, and politics. On November 24, Governor Mandel and five associates were indicted on charges that included "a pattern of racketeering activity" and bribery. The governor said he would prove his innocence at his trial, expected to take place in 1976.

Legislation. A special legislative session was convened to complete a $31 million tax package that included aid to local governments and to elderly property owners. Gov. Marvin Mandel authorized a county's temporary tax on apartment and commercial rents through late 1976, firmly stating he would authorize no similar taxes elsewhere.

Three new medical malpractice insurance laws were enacted that established the nation's first nonprofit insurance company administered by doctors. Legislation to encourage the housing market loosened regulations on home mortgages, created a home financing authority, and extended the 10% limit on home mortgage rates.

Other successful administration-backed bills included legislation establishing the mandatory death penalty for certain crimes, setting up a statewide prosecutor's office, and revising the state's juvenile-court-system laws. A constitutional amendment to have appellate court judges run for election on their records rather than against an opponent was signed but must be ratified by voters. The governor's bills to abolish legislatively-distributed state college scholarships and a proposed bond issue for baseball's Baltimore Orioles failed.

Reorganizations. The Rosenberg Commission completed its study of higher education systems in Maryland. It recommended that a super board of higher education be created to control the policy decisions of the board of regents of the University of Maryland, the state college board, and the community college board. It also proposed creation of a joint board for education that would coordinate the budgets of the higher education and of the secondary and elementary education boards. If adopted, the existing Maryland Council on Higher Education, a coordinating body appointed by the governor, would be abolished.

A three-year study of Maryland government, chaired by former Baltimore judge Joseph Sherbow, produced a 1,500-page report but recommended few major changes because it was believed that Marylanders wanted no drastic approaches. The Sherbow Commission recommended phasing out of the state property tax, a major debate topic of the legislature, but retaining property taxes for hard-pressed local governments. The commission also suggested a number of shifts to streamline state-government bureaucracy.

Investigations. George Beall, who directed the federal grand jury investigations of Spiro Agnew and other former Maryland county officials who were also convicted, resigned as U. S. attorney. He was replaced by Jervis Finney, a former Republican state senator. In November, Governor Mandel was indicted for profiting from favors to friends, also indicted, who benefited by state actions.

Political Prospects. Governor Mandel announced he was considering filing for the Democratic nomination to oppose Republican Sen. J. Glenn Beall in 1976. Rep. Paul Sarbanes and former Sen. Joseph Tydings are the primary competition for the Democratic nomination. Over 40 members of the House of Delegates formed a nonpartisan legislative study group, modeled after the Democratic study group in the U. S. Congress, to improve legislative handling of complex issues.

THOMAS P. MURPHY, *University of Maryland*

MARYLAND · Information Highlights

Area: 10,577 square miles (27,394 sq km).
Population (1974 est.): 4,094,000. *Density:* 390 per sq mi.
Chief Cities (1970 census): Annapolis, the capital, 30,-095; Baltimore, 905,759; Dundalk, 85,377; Towson, 77,799.
Government (1975): *Chief Officers*—governor, Marvin Mandel (D); lt. gov., Blair Lee III (D). *General Assembly*—Senate, 47 members; House of Delegates, 141 members.
Education (1974–75): *Enrollment*—public elementary schools, 474,537 pupils; public secondary, 419,672; nonpublic, 106,600; colleges and universities, 186,-915 students. *Public school expenditures,* $979,-354,000 ($1,213 per pupil).
State Finances (fiscal year 1974): *Revenues,* $2,782,498,-000; *expenditures,* $2,810,456,000.
Personal Income (1974): $24,077,000,000; per capita, $5,881.
Labor Force (Aug. 1975): *Nonagricultural wage and salary earners,* 1,432,000; *insured unemployed,* 54,-600.

MASSACHUSETTS

President Gerald R. Ford was the honored visitor at Massachusetts' bicentennial observances in April with stops in Boston, Lexington, and Concord. On April 19 he spoke at Concord Bridge, where one of the epic battles of the Revolutionary War occurred, and later laid a wreath at the statue of the Minuteman on the battle green in Lexington. Over 160,000 people jammed the historic sites for the ceremonies. The previous day, some 40,000 persons, mainly young people, held a "people's bicentennial" observance at Concord Bridge, focusing on social problems still facing the nation.

The presidential visit proved to be one highlight of a troubled year for Massachusetts.

State Fiscal Problems. Tax and revenue problems had been the source of storm and stress in the Revolution, and many of the same issues occupied the citizens of the Bay State two centuries later. Gov. Michael S. Dukakis, who began his first term in January, wrestled all year with rising costs for state services and increased demands for state assistance in a time of eco-

nomic hardship. The budget eventually passed by the legislature trimmed many state programs, including those at the 30 state-run colleges, welfare assistance, medical care, and other important state activities.

Along with the austerity in spending there was an increase in taxes, including a rise in the limited sales tax from 3% to 5%. The sales tax had not been increased since it went into effect in 1966. A proposal to broaden the tax to apply to clothing and other items was defeated.

The cuts in the budget and tax increases produced an unprecedented number of protest demonstrations by various citizens' groups at the State House on Boston's Beacon Hill. Passage of the budget put to the test relations between the new governor and Thomas W. McGee, newly-elected speaker of the House and Kevin Harrington, president of the state Senate. All three are members of the Democratic party.

Real Estate Taxes Changed. Another major financial issue was the product of a court decision requiring cities and towns to assess all taxable real estate at 100% of fair market value. The requirement would raise property taxes substantially in many communities, especially in cities where industrial properties have been assessed at rates higher than those for residential property. Most larger cities and towns assess at less than 100% of market value. A number of proposals, including a constitutional amendment, were introduced to reverse the decision.

Two other issues prompted considerable debate during 1975. Proposals to explore for offshore oil and gas deposits drew nearer to reality when test drillings off the coast were authorized in autumn. The issue was of major concern to New England, where there are no indigenous oil or natural gas deposits, and the drillings drew much criticism from environmental groups.

The year also saw discussion on the issue of the state assuming control of energy-producing utilities. The "public power" question, long dormant in industrial Massachusettts, where energy costs are high, was predicted to be heading for a showdown in the legislature in 1976. A petition on the issue, sponsored by U. S. Rep. Michael Harrington, obtained more than 90,000 signatures. The petition called for a state authority to be responsible for all future power generating plants. If the legislature defeats the proposal, it will appear on the ballot in the 1976 state elections.

School Teachers Strike. Strikes by public school teachers closed schools in three cities in September. Affected were Lynn and New Bedford, where strikes lasted several weeks, and Boston, where teachers stayed out for two weeks.

New Firearms Law. A 1975 law provided that owners of any handgun, rifle, or shotgun must obtain a firearms identification card, issued by local police officials. The law also required a mandatory one-year prison sentence for anyone convicted of carrying a firearm without proper

UPI

President Ford placed a wreath at the Minuteman statue in Lexington on April 19, the bicentennial of the battles of Lexington and Concord.

identification. The law, one of the strictest gun-control measures in the nation, was seen as a test of the feasibility of legal regulation in reducing the use of firearms in the commission of crimes as well as deaths and injuries resulting from gun accidents.

J. F. K. Library Site Disputed. Disagreement and uncertainty continued over the location of the John F. Kennedy Memorial Library and Museum, originally scheduled for construction near Harvard Square in Cambridge. The Kennedy Library Corporation, Harvard University, the city of Cambridge, and several Cambridge citizens' groups failed to reach agreement on a compromise plan that would have placed the library on the Harvard Square site, with the museum located elsewhere.

HARVEY BOULAY
Boston University

--- **MASSACHUSETTS** · Information Highlights ---

Area: 8,257 square miles (21,386 sq km).
Population (1974 est.): 5,800,000; *Density:* 740 per sq mi.
Chief Cities (1970 census): Boston, the capital, 641,-071; Worcester, 176,572; Springfield, 163,905.
Government (1975): *Chief Officers*—governor, Michael S. Dukakis (D); lt. gov., Thomas P. O'Neill III (D). *General Court*—Senate, 40 members; House of Representatives, 240 members.
Education (1974–75): *Enrollment*—public elementary schools, 836,500 pupils; public secondary, 323,600; nonpublic, 182,700; colleges and universities, 356,-239 students. *Public school expenditures,* $1,341,-195,000 ($1,180 per pupil).
State Finances (fiscal year 1974): *Revenues,* $3,967,637,-000; *expenditures,* $4,229,191,000.
Personal Income (1974): $33,242,000,000; per capita, $5,731.
Labor Force (Aug. 1975): *Nonagricultural wage and salary earners,* 2,338,400; *insured unemployed,* 142,-000.

Physicians met with leaders of the California state legislature in Sacramento in May to demand immediate relief from soaring medical malpractice rates.

UPI

MEDICINE

Medicine captured more than its usual share of the headlines in 1975, largely because of the malpractice-insurance crisis and the ethical and legal problems raised by the long-term use of life-sustaining equipment in patients who have no hope of recovery. Nonetheless, advances continued to be made in many areas of medicine.

Malpractice Insurance. One of the most dramatic events of 1975 was the withholding of all but emergency services for short periods of time by doctors in New York and California. This step was taken to publicize the predicament of doctors faced with astronomical increases in the cost of malpractice insurance, brought about by a sharp rise in malpractice claims. An estimated 26,500 physicians and other health-care providers were named as defendants in new claims recorded by the Insurance Commission in 1970. For 1975 the estimated figure was well over 40,000; at the present rate of increase, claims may run as high as 82,000 by 1980. In 1969, only 4.3% of all doctors were being sued, but in 1974 the figure was 10%. Surgeons are most likely to have suits brought against them, with the greatest percentage of claims filed against surgeons in the subspecialties, particularly cardiovascular disease, neurology, and orthopedics. Physicians least likely to be sued are internists, pediatricians, and general practitioners who do not perform surgery.

Claim Payments. The dollar amount paid in malpractice suits has also risen sharply. In 1969 the average payment was $6,700 per claim; by 1974 the figure had jumped to $12,535. In 1970 less than one payment in a thousand was for more than $1 million. But in 1975 several awards as high as $4 million each were made. The rise in total claims and in successful claims has great-

ly inflated the premiums doctors must pay for malpractice insurance. In New York state, for example, physicians paid 93.5% more for malpractice protection in 1974 than they had a year earlier.

There are several reasons for the increase in malpractice claims. Perhaps the most important one is that patients' expectations of medical science have risen. Widespread public knowledge about such medical miracles as heart transplants and lifesaving drugs has led many patients to expect more of their doctors than the doctors can realistically provide. According to many observers, this discontent is a major reason for malpractice suits.

Malpractice Legislation. Changes in the laws that govern malpractice suits are advocated by many. Indiana was the first state to pass comprehensive malpractice legislation since the crisis began. The Indiana law included provisions for mandatory nonbinding arbitration by a Medical Injury Liability Commission. The commission can set awards up to $100,000 against an insurance carrier and up to $400,000 additional to meet medical expenses from a special "catastrophic fund." The Indiana law set a limit on contingency fees that may be paid to lawyers from this fund and created a state-funded $1.5 million insurance authority to cover providers of medical care who have been denied insurance by two or more regular carriers. Another clause provided that a suit may not be instituted if more than two years have elapsed after an alleged malpractice incident.

Other states, including California, New York, and Maryland, have passed laws that provide for joint underwriting of malpractice policies by several insurance companies, or underwriting by insurance companies operated by the doctors themselves. Passage of such legislation is a ma-

jor step toward solving the problem of the rising cost of malpractice insurance, which is not only disastrous for physicians but also adds to the rising cost of medical care.

Quinlan Case. An issue directly related to the medical profession's preoccupation with malpractice suits continued to command public attention as 1975 neared its end. Despite parental pleas, two New Jersey physicians refused to turn off a respirator sustaining the life of Karen Ann Quinlan, a young woman who had suffered irreparable brain damage, and the distraught parents took the matter to the courts. A major reason for the physicians' refusal was said to be fear of a malpractice suit. However, the case had deeper implications, involving the question whether or not life should be sustained indefinitely by artificial means when there is no hope of the return of brain function. The court declined to accept responsibility for making a decision in the Quinlan case.

Childhood Diseases. Infectious diseases drew attention again in 1975 as the Center for Disease Control in Atlanta designated October as Immunization Action Month. Many children remain unprotected by immunization against the common childhood diseases. Only 63% of preschool children have been immunized against polio, 64% against measles, and 60% against rubella. So it was not surprising that the incidence of rubella in 1975 was almost double that of the year earlier. Similar increases were noted for measles and polio, but in none of these diseases was the incidence as high as it had been before the introduction of the vaccines.

Other Infectious Diseases. Venereal disease rates declined somewhat in 1975. Reported cases of syphilis were fewer than in 1974, and gonorrhea, though still on the rise, was increasing at a slower rate. Reports from the Public Health Service indicated that there were still about 80,-000 new cases of syphilis and 2.7 million new cases of gonorrhea reported each year.

Plague and encephalitis, uncommon but serious infectious diseases, were reported in significant numbers in the United States in 1975. Plague, known as the "black death" during the Middle Ages, when it killed more than 25 million people, was reported in recent years in the Far East and Middle East. In 1975 several cases were reported in Utah and New Mexico.

Bubonic plague is caused by a bacterium called *Pasteurella pestis* that lives in and infects such members of the rodent family as mice, rats, squirrels, and gerbils. Fleas and other insects take these bacteria into their bodies when they suck blood from the rodent hosts. The bacteria multiply in the digestive tract of the insects. When the infected insect again bites an animal or human, the bacteria enter the victim's bloodstream and are carried into the nearest lymph node. There they multiply and cause an enlarged, tender, swollen area called a "bubo," from which the bubonic plague takes its name.

UPI

Karen Quinlan's parents petitioned for legal permission to stop medical treatment of their brain-damaged daughter.

Plague can be passed from person to person in droplets with coughing or sneezing. Plague bacteria transmitted this way do not cause bubo formation; rather, they reproduce in the lungs and cause plague pneumonia, with cough, severe respiratory distress, and a rapidly progressive course. In both types of plague, the patient is seriously ill, with a high fever and signs of severe infection. If the disease is untreated, about 50% of the patients with plague will succumb.

Antibiotics are helpful in treating both bubonic plague and plague pneumonia, but treatment must be begun within the first 15 hours if the patient is to survive. Streptomycin, chloramphenicol, and tetracycline are all useful. The disease can be prevented by eliminating the insect vectors and their rodent hosts. Vaccines to protect against the disease have been developed, but their effectiveness has not been conclusively demonstrated.

More cases of insect-borne encephalitis were reported in 1975 than in recent years. This disease causes inflammation of the brain, which results in fever, headache, drowsiness, convulsions, and coma in terminal cases. Most serious is the fever, which can often rise so high as to cause permanent brain damage.

California virus was the cause of most of the reported encephalitis in 1975. This virus, like the plague bacterium, is transmitted to humans from animals by insect bite. California-virus encephalitis is sometimes called "farm encephalitis" because it is most likely to occur in farm communities where rodents abound. Most of its victims are children, usually under age 16 and most often between 5 and 7 years old. Nerve and brain damage with personality changes are common sequels to this type of encephalitis, but the death rate is less than 5%. There is no specific

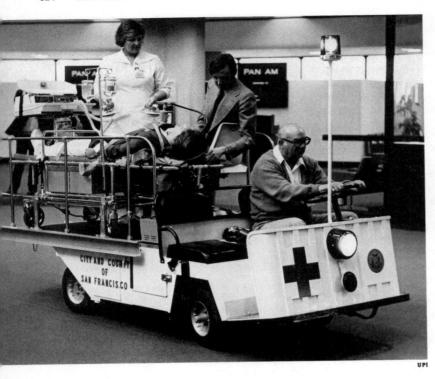

Medical personnel demonstrate a new electric mini-ambulance at San Francisco International Airport. It permits them to speed through long corridors to bring emergency aid, especially to victims of heart attack.

UPI

treatment; antibiotics are not useful since the disease is caused by a virus. Treatment is directed at controlling the fever, which seems to be the direct cause of most of the permanent brain damage.

California virus and several other types of viruses that cause encephalitis are called arthropod-borne or arboviruses because they are transmitted by insects and ticks (phylum Arthropoda). Prevention is aimed at controlling the insect vector. Despite the prevalence of "farm encephalitis" in 1975, another serious and similar virus illness, Venezuelan equine encephalomyelitis failed to appear in the United States for the fourth consecutive year. This disease, like Western equine encephalomyelitis, is somewhat more severe than farm encephalitis and is spread to humans by insects, in this case with horses acting as hosts.

Culture of Leprosy Bacterium. A medical milestone of 1975 was the successful culture of the organism *Mycobacterium leprae* by Dr. Olaf K. Skinsnes of the University of Hawaii Medical School. The success followed more than a century of futile attempts by other scientists. This organism is the causative agent of leprosy, or Hansen's disease, the dread affliction that affects over 11 million people around the world, according to the World Health Organization. Although drug treatment of leprosy has been successful, signs of bacterial resistance are appearing. Thus, Dr. Skinsnes hopes that the new culture technique will drastically shorten the time presently required for drug-resistance tests. Further, if other scientists validate Dr. Skinsnes' results,

there is a real possibility that a leprosy vaccine may ultimately be developed.

Vitamin C Studies. Evaluation of vitamin C (ascorbic acid) as a preventive or cure for the common cold continued. An exhaustive review published in the *Journal of the American Medical Association* suggested that there is no clear, reproducible pattern indicating the effectiveness of vitamin C on the common cold.

Some studies have indicated that kidney stones are prone to develop in certain people who are taking as much as 4 grams daily of vitamin C. There is evidence in experimental animals, but not in humans, that doses of vitamin C may adversely affect fertility and cause damage to the fetus. There is also a suggestion that diabetic-like increases occur in the blood sugar levels of experimental animals given high doses of ascorbic acid. However, some human diabetic patients seem to require smaller doses of insulin when taking vitamin C. It is accepted that a dose of a gram per day of ascorbic acid may cause diarrhea and sometimes nausea and abdominal pain in some patients. There is also some indication that large doses of vitamin C can lead to dependence on such doses, with the signs and symptoms of scurvy appearing when the large doses are withdrawn. Scurvy is the term used for the vitamin C deficiency state. So, while vitamin C intake in large dosage has not proved to be helpful in preventing or treating the common cold, there are indications that it may be harmful.

Hidden Dangers in Chinese Herbal Remedies. Self-medication in the form of over-the-counter

Chinese herbal medicines has become popular. The Chinese medicines are said to be helpful in curing such painful conditions as arthritis, rheumatism, and back pain and are also offered for the treatment of circulatory disorders and for sexual rejuvenation. The medicines are said to contain a wide variety of Chinese herbs and other organic substances such as scorpions, tiger bone, turtle shells, and male mouse droppings. But in many cases, along with the exotic material, the medicines contain the analgesics aminopyrine and phenylbutazone. Both of these drugs must be used with extreme caution because they are known to depress bone-marrow production of white blood cells, resulting in leukopenia. This is a serious condition that can lead to fulminating infection, septicemia, and death. Deaths have in fact been reported from use of these herbal remedies.

Advances in Allergy Research. A significant breakthrough in the conquest of allergic diseases was reported in 1975. This was the laboratory synthesis of a proteinlike substance that can be used to block the allergic reaction.

Allergic diseases include asthma, hay fever, and hives, a troublesome group of illnesses that are important causes of loss of time from school and work. Allergic diseases develop in patients who are sensitive to common substances such as ragweed or animal dander. When these substances enter the body of an allergic person, the white blood cells (lymphocytes) become sensitized. These cells produce antibodies in the form of small protein molecules called class E immunoglobulins (IgE). IgE molecules, in turn, can become attached to other blood cells called mast cells and basophils, causing these cells to become sensitive to the pollen or other protein that originally stimulated the body to produce IgE. Sensitized mast cells and basophils reacting to pollen produce histamine and other mediator chemicals that directly cause the allergy symptoms. The proteinlike substance that has been synthesized is a polypeptide very similar in structure to the site on the white blood cell where the IgE molecule becomes attached. By binding to the reactive site on the cell, the newly developed polypeptide blocks the attaching of the IgE molecule, preventing sensitization of the cell from taking place. This in turn eliminates the liberation of mediator substances from the white cell, thereby preventing the development of the allergy symptoms.

In 1975 the new polypeptide was used only experimentally. It is administered by injection into the skin to prevent skin-test reactions. Given by mouth or by systemic injection, the polypeptide is broken down by the normal processes of the body into ineffective fragments. Although the synthetic protein is not useful for treatment in its present form, it should prove to be a useful research tool.

A new drug for treating asthma was introduced in 1975. The medicine, beclomethasone

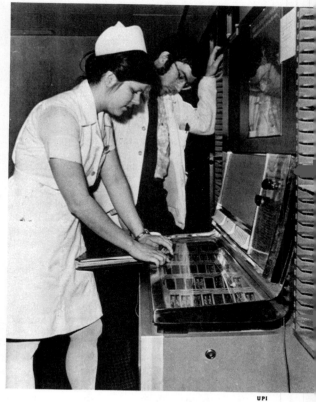

UPI

Students at Albany (NY) Medical Center can select from among 160 recordings on patient care and treatment contained in the center's "medical education jukebox."

diproprionate, prevents asthma when inhaled. Beclomethasone is a member of the group of drugs related to the corticosteroid hormones secreted by the adrenal cortex. All of these drugs are useful in the treatment of asthma and other allergic diseases, but all have serious side effects. However, since the new medication is inhaled directly into the lungs, it is believed that it is not absorbed into the body in sufficient dosage to produce the usual side effects of corticosteroid-related drugs. No adverse effects of the drug were reported in 1975. However, beclomethasone was not available through regular pharmaceutical channels for treatment of the routine case of asthma.

A drug long on the market has been approved by the Food and Drug Administration for a new use. On the prescription of a physician, diethylstilbestrol (DES), a synthetic female hormone, has been approved for limited use in birth control in certain emergency conditions. DES has been in use for many years. Between 1940 and 1960, many women were treated with DES to prevent miscarriage, but when better methods were developed, the use of the hormone for this purpose was discontinued. In recent years, cancer of the vagina or cervix has developed in

some daughters of women who had been treated with DES. Also, certain abnormalities were found in the reproductive and urinary tracts of these children. Furthermore, DES is one of a family of drugs used in birth control pills that have the possible side effects of causing blood clots in the legs, lungs, and brain, as well as hypertension and eye disease.

When used for contraception, DES seems to prevent implantation of the fertilized egg in the uterus. To prevent pregnancy, the drug must be taken in 25-milligram doses twice daily for five days. Because it affects implantation, DES can be used as a "morning after" contraceptive following unprotected intercourse.

New Technique of Cancer Cell Identification. A new method for identifying cancer cells by the way they scatter a laser beam has been developed by the biophysics and instrument group under Dr. Gary Salzman at the Los Alamos Scientific Laboratory in New Mexico. A low-power laser beam is directed at cells in a saline solution passing through a tube. A detector system converts the cell's light-scattering pattern into an electrical signal that can be compared with a computer-stored catalog of light patterns indicative of cancer cells. So far the technique has correctly detected cervical and vaginal cancer cells. It is faster and may prove to be more accurate than the "Pap" test in current use.

Cardiovascular Disease in Women. At the American Heart Association meeting in November, Dr. William B. Kannel, director of the Framingham Heart Disease and Epidemiology Study, reported that the lower incidence of cardiovascular disease in women as compared with men is not restricted to the premenopausal period. Among the 1,686 women who entered the study in 1948, 14 heart attacks or strokes had occurred in those who were still premenopausal and 55 in those who had reached the menopause. Although menopause increases the incidence of cardiovascular disease, it is still only a third of that in the men, and the disease is less severe. Comparison of men and women with identical risk factors, such as hypertension, diabetes, and high cholesterol levels, revealed that the women were still at lower risk. This finding suggests that there is a biologic sex difference in the way these risk factors are handled.

Cardiac Pacemakers. Cardiac pacemakers drew attention in 1975 when it became apparent that their functioning could be impaired by exposure to radiation leaked from a microwave oven. A cardiac pacemaker is an electronic device that can stimulate the heart to beat at a normal rate and rhythm. With illness, the heartbeat may become arrhythmic—either too slow, too fast, or irregular, depending on disease involved. Arrhythmias can cause diminished cardiac output, blood clots in the circulation that lodge in the lungs or other parts of the body, and sometimes death. Disturbances of heart rhythm are treated by drugs or by electronic cardiac pacemakers,

which can sense when the intrinsic, normal rate of the heart muscle becomes abnormal. The pacemaker can supplement the intrinsic rate or replace it completely.

Pacemakers are connected to the heart by wires passed into the heart either by threading them through a vein until they reach the inner surface of the heart or by open surgical techniques, whereby the wires are placed in contact with and sewn into the heart muscle itself. The pacemaker, about the size of a pocket watch, is implanted under the skin near the heart.

Pacemakers are usually powered by batteries and will work only as long as the battery continues to have power. The earliest batteries ran for a year or two, then had to be replaced. Since 1974 experimental models have been developed that can be recharged while still in use. Atomic-powered models have been implanted in animals which may run indefinitely. For the present, however, batteries still have to be replaced. A technique has been devised whereby the condition of the battery can be determined electronically and the information transmitted by telephone circuit to a medical center for evaluation, freeing the patient from the need to make frequent visits to the doctor for checks on the condition of the pacemaker. This method, combined with longer-lasting batteries and the possibility of recharging the units without removing them from the body, has increased the feasibility of more widespread use of cardiac pacemakers in the treatment of heart disease.

Heimlich Maneuver. A new technique of emergency treatment for patients who choke on food or other objects has been approved. Choking on food is estimated to cause 3,000 deaths each year in the United States, making it the sixth most common cause of accidental death. The lifesaving maneuver was conceived and publicized by Dr. Henry J. Heimlich, a surgeon at the Jewish Hospital in Cincinnati. It involves sudden intense pressure on the upper abdomen of a victim who is choking from food or other object lodged in the windpipe. The sudden exterior pressure tends to increase the pressure inside the lungs and windpipe, dislodging the foreign object. The Heimlich maneuver has been credited with saving more than 160 lives in the first nine months since it was described. Those rescued included 121 adults and 41 children, the youngest being 9 months of age. The maneuver was performed by lay persons in 75 cases and in 6 cases by the victim himself exerting the pressure on his abdomen. However, some are dubious that the Heimlich technique can be safely performed by nonphysicians, since there is a possibility that lay persons may inappropriately apply the maneuver to a patient who appears to be choking but is really experiencing a severe heart attack. (See also special feature on pages 60–64.)

IRWIN J. POLK, M. D.
St. Luke's Hospital, New York City

meteorology

In 1975 much attention focused on suspicions that man's activities may have brought about undesirable climatic alterations beyond the natural fluctuations. These are the target of an ambitious program sponsored by the National Science Foundation, called CLIMAP, which intends to map the climates of past ages with the help of cores from deep-sea drilling and from the Greenland ice cover. Sea cores indicate volcanic eruptions that spread dust around the globe. They show high volcanic activity on earth for the last 20 million years. The dust veil that shields the earth from solar radiation has been adduced as a cause of the Pleistocene glaciations.

Temperature Research. The Greenland ice cores hold clues about the more recent past, back to about 550 A.D. The amount of heavy oxygen (O^{18}) in the water forming the ice is a clue to the temperature prevalent at the time of deposit. The analysis clearly shows the warm era that existed around 1000 A.D., when the island was first settled, and the cold interval, starting around 1400, that doomed the Greenland colony. This "little ice age" dominated until the beginning of the 20th century, when a warming trend developed.

There have been dire predictions of another ice age for the northern hemisphere because of cooling that seemed prevalent in the 1960's, but so far the 1970's have shown a reversal to warming. In the southern hemisphere, New Zealand has warmed up by $1°$ C in the past three decades, showing that temperature evolution of the globe is hardly uniform.

Pollution Dangers. Man-made pollution also shows increased local effects. As much as 35% of the ultraviolet radiation reaching the surface of the earth is screened out over urban areas, such as Los Angeles and St. Louis. The U.S. Environmental Protection Agency claimed that photochemical smog plaguing cities is a consequence of chemical changes induced in exhaust gases of motor vehicles and that the smog has spread to rural areas. Some believe this blue haze is caused naturally by photochemical reaction with terpenes from vegetation.

Although the washout of pollutants by rain provides welcome relief for breathing, it is not an unmitigated blessing. Some effluents from fuels with high sulfur content make the rain acid, which detrimentally affects plant and aquatic life.

The major debate during 1975 regarding pollutants and climate centered around possible man-made effects on the stratospheric ozone layer. A study by the U.S. Department of Transportation, evaluated by a committee of the National Academy of Science, concluded that the oxides of nitrogen in the exhausts of supersonic transport aircraft will destroy ozone, and if large fleets of the current types operate at levels above 10 miles (16 km), substantial reductions in the ozone layer might occur. This would permit biologically harmful ultraviolet radiation to penetrate to the ground. There would also be a cooling in the stratosphere, but climatic consequences at the ground were judged to be minor. Reduction of the harmful exhaust gases by redesigning the engines of supersonic aircraft was suggested.

A further possible disturbing influence concerns chlorofluoro-methanes, usually designated Freons, diffusing from the surface to the stratosphere, where they release chlorine that might also destroy ozone. The Freons are released into the air from spray cans and escape from refrigeration systems. This issue is not completely resolved but may result in a ban of Freons as propellants. More detailed analysis of ozone observations has shown that there are considerable fluctuations in the stratospheric ozone, which increased until the beginning of the 1970's and declined afterward. Solar influences are present, and recent work has shown that oxides of nitrogen produced in the upper atmosphere by streams of energetic protons from solar flares may temporarily cause a considerable natural decrease of ozone.

Atmospheric Observations. The first results from 1974's great multi-nation experiment to watch the tropical atmosphere, Global Atmo-

Governor George Busbee surveys tornado damage to the Georgia governor's mansion in Atlanta on March 24.

UPI

September Storms Hit Hard

The weather in 1975 brought a deadly blizzard to the Midwest United States, record heat in Western Europe, and drought to the Soviet Union.

December 1974–February 1975. In the eastern United States winter was generally a mild season. Temperatures from the Great Lakes to New England and along the Atlantic seaboard were 4° F warmer than average. Most of this warmth occurred in December with fall weather lingering to Christmas. The southern Great Plains and the southern Rocky Mountain region were about 4° F colder than average. Precipitation was not far from average with storms in December bringing snow to the Midwest and floods in the middle Atlantic states. The northern prairie states and Arizona were quite dry. The worst blizzard in 35 years, causing 50 deaths, hit areas from the Dakotas to New York State. Early tornadoes in February caused devastation in Fort Valley, Ga.; Alten, Okla.; and Tuscaloosa, Ala. Floods in Nacogdoches, Tex.; Elba, Ala.; and in Kentucky, Ohio, and West Virginia caused casualties and required evacuations.

Landslides and avalanches killed many in the Philippines, Iceland, and Austria. Typhoons hit the central Philippines in December and January. A blizzard affected the Adriatic area of southern Italy and Yugoslavia.

The worst disaster of the season occurred in Australia when a rare tropical cyclone struck the northern city of Darwin on Christmas 1974 with 120-mph winds. It left 45 dead, destroyed 90% of the housing, and required the evacuation of 20,000 people, about half of the population. Another cyclone (Trixie) hit west Australia in February with high winds, causing flood and destruction.

At the end of February floods and landslides resulted in many deaths in Colombia and Ecuador. Floods killed 160 in Thailand and Burma and impaired the rice crops. Fall-sown crops in Europe were delayed. India's Punjab crops were promising. Yield prospects were off in Argentina.

March–May. Nearly the entire United States was cooler than average. The coldest spots were in Montana (4°–6° F colder than average) and parts of Colorado and Arizona (4° F colder). March was unusually wet, except in the southern and central Great Plains, but on the whole seasonal rains were not far from average. Wild weather in the middle of March caused heavy snow in Missouri and Arkansas and freezing rain along the Atlantic Seaboard. New Mexico cattle needed hay airlifted, and people had to be evacuated in West Virginia and Kentucky. On March 24 tornadoes struck Georgia, damaging the governor's mansion in Atlanta and killing 3, injuring 118, and leaving 1,000 homeless.

On April 5 a storm hit the Northeast. Snow paralyzed Chicago, and 42 deaths occurred. Gales blew from Pennsylvania to Maine, and northern New England had 33 inches of new snow. A tanker was lost at sea southeast of New York City. Floods occurred in the Ohio River; Chotawhatchee River, Ala.; Red Cedar and Bank Rivers, Mich.; Mississippi Delta; and the Red and Black Rivers in Mississippi. North Dakota and Kentucky were declared disaster areas from flooding.

There were also floods in west-central Argentina, Brazil, and northern Iran, but Haiti was drought-stricken and required food relief. Tropical cyclones hit southern Bangladesh on April 28 leaving 30 dead, 400 injured. In south Punjab and north Sind, Pakistan, four were killed, and much damage was done. On May 6–7 the Irrawaddy River in Burma flooded, leaving 253 dead, sinking 50 river craft, killing 6,000 cattle, and destroying many buildings.

June–August. June temperatures were close to the average in the United States, but those in July were considerably higher than average in the northern half of the nation. In August they were above average from the Dakotas to Oklahoma and eastward to the Atlantic coast, but the intermountain region was quite cool.

Rainfall was varied radically, with severe weather in eastern North Dakota and Montana causing extensive floods in June. The Southwest was dry, and in July there was incipient drought in Iowa and Illinois, detrimental to the corn crop. Wichita, Kan., had the driest July on record, while in Minneapolis, Minn., it was the driest since 1937 and in Des Moines, Iowa, the driest since 1947. However, August rains relieved the moisture stress on the crops. East of the Appalachians dryness prevailed in the latter part of the season.

Floods plagued east-central Europe, but crops and pastures suffered from drought in Scandinavia, England, and Ireland. In France the drought threatened the water supplies. Record heat also prevailed in western Europe. In the Soviet Union drought prevailed east of the Volga, with a major crop failure in Kazakhstan. In July heavy frosts in Brazil destroyed about 70% of the coffee crop. Rains were favorable in India and Australia.

Severe weather and tornadoes caused deaths and destruction in northeastern Illinois, southwestern Wisconsin, and eastern Iowa in the middle of June. Floods in the third week of June stopped train traffic between Philadelphia and New York City. In August the Florida panhandle was also flooded by 15 inches of rain from a tropical depression. In the third week of August heavy rainfall in the Great Lakes region left 6 feet of water in Cleveland. Hundreds were struck by lightning in that storm.

Floods hit Canada's British Columbia in July and also Pernambuco, Brazil, where 70 were killed and 150,000 rendered homeless by a rampage of the Chapiberibi River. Early in August, Iwaki, Japan, was struck by floods. An extremely rare flood hit Smara in the Sahara desert of Spanish Morocco. In the middle of August two typhoons, Phyllis and Rita, caused deaths and widespread damage. At the end of the month Hurricane Caroline struck severe blows at Cuba and Mexico.

September–November. The fall was a fairly warm season, especially east of the Mississippi River. Indian summer with record-breaking temperatures lingered into November. The Labor Day weekend was marred by tornadoes in Minnesota and floods in Michigan and West Virginia. Simultaneously, Hurricane Caroline struck northern Mexico. It relieved the drought there but drove thousands of people from their homes.

Eloise, which developed September 16 over the South Atlantic, swept with furious winds over Puerto Rico, the Dominican Republic, and Cuba leaving at least 50 dead and 30,000 homeless. Moving inland on September 23, it dumped 8–14 inches of rain locally through September 30, leading to 10 deaths and extensive property damage in Maryland, Pennsylvania, and New York. In the last week of October Pacific hurricane Olivia struck the Mexican coast near Mazatlan killing and injuring scores and rendering 30,000 homeless.

In the middle of November a violent storm sank an ore ship with 35 aboard in Lake Superior. At month's end Santa Ana gales fanned a fire in the Angeles National Forest, burning 70,000 acres and destroying many homes. A wild snow-storm on Thanksgiving paralyzed the Midwest with up to 18 inches of snow.

Weather adversities continued to plague the Soviet Union. In October mudslides caused devastation in the Turkmen Republic. Widespread torrential rains caused damage in the Ukraine and on the Black Sea coast. Moscow was paralyzed at the end of November by an early snowfall of 8–15 inches. This final harvest quarter also revealed the full extent of the Russian crop failure, illustrated by a 25% short-fall of the vital small-grain crop.

H. E. LANDSBERG

A week of rain caused by Hurricane Eloise in late September forced 20,000 people in Pennsylvania from their homes.

UPI

Extensive flooding in the Mid-Atlantic states in July disrupted transportation. In Trenton, N. J., Penn Central tracks were under water.

UPI

spheric Research Program (GARP), of which the Global Tropical Atlantic Experiment (GATE) was a part, began to materialize. A major objective was the study of convective systems, which produce much of the atmosphere's energy and sometimes turn into major tropical storms. It was found that extremely large cloud formations are long-lived. On the other hand, nocturnal satellite photographs showed that huge, violent thunderstorms often develop within two hours over the Atlantic and vanish equally quickly. These storms, dubbed "super novas," have been likened to some types of western hailstorms. The pictures responsible for the discovery were taken by the U. S. Synchronous Meteorological Satellite (SMS-1), which was launched just prior to GATE into a stationary orbit over the Atlantic.

In February 1975 SMS-1 was joined by SMS-2, which keeps watch to the west. Earlier, in November 1974, NOAA-4, a roving satellite, began circling in a sun-synchronous orbit at a 900-mile (1,440-km) altitude, gathering vertical atmospheric temperature data, measuring surface temperature, and monitoring solar protons. In June 1975, NASA launched a meteorological research satellite, Nimbus-F6, into a polar orbit, scanning the whole earth twice a day. It measures the portion of solar radiation reflected by surface and earth emissions and determines the ozone distribution in the stratosphere. In addition, Nimbus-F6 serves as a weather communications relay, picking up signals from weather balloons and sending the data to stations on the ground.

International Conference. The Seventh Congress of the World Meteorological Organization (WMO), a specialized agency of the United Nations, met in Geneva, Switzerland, in April–May 1975. Important actions were taken to initiate an international weather modification research program. Plans were made for a comprehensive First Global Experiment of World Wide Weather Observations, starting in 1978 with the aim of improving extended weather forecasts. An agricultural meteorological program designed to assist developing countries in raising more crops was also approved.

H. E. Landsberg
University of Maryland

UPI

President Echeverría proclaimed a 200-mile (320-km) territorial limit for Mexico in October UN speech.

MEXICO

The choice of the government party's 1976 presidential candidate emphasized Mexico's concern with economic problems in the years of recession and inflation. Efforts to stimulate the economy appeared to be working, and only minor political problems marked the year. President Echeverría continued his efforts to make Mexico a Third World leader. In June and July, one of the most important meetings of International Women's Year (IWY) was held in Mexico City.

Politics. Speculation as to the identity of the ruling *Partido Revolucionario Institucional*'s (PRI) 1976 presidential candidate ended in late September when word spread that the nominee would be Treasury Minister José López Portillo. Although the selection process was secret, the choice of an expert public administrator seemed to indicate that the government considered economic problems more serious than political problems. The usual source of PRI candidates (certain victors in elections) has been the government ministry. The nominee, a political moderate, seemed likely to continue many of the liberal reforms instituted by President Echeverría, a childhood friend.

The official nomination and adoption of the "basic plan of government" as the party's platform came in November. The National Action party, the major opposition, met in November

to debate electoral participation and select a nominee. As in past elections, the other parties were expected to support the PRI nominee.

Many of the other political events were attempts to influence the selection of the PRI nominee. The two new leftist parties did not receive the official recognition necessary to be on the ballot. The leftist minister of national patrimony was dismissed in January for advocating Mexican membership in OPEC (Organization of Petroleum Exporting Countries). The governors of Hidalgo and Guerrero were removed from office by Congress for violating their constitutional mandates. An attack on President Echeverría at the National University in March, although unprecedented, was not serious. Assertions that the U. S. Central Intelligence Agency was involved were discounted. Students blamed Echeverría for his involvement in the 1968 protests in which students were killed.

Education. In a continuing effort to increase educational opportunities, Mexico budgeted $2.4 billion for its 16 million students. New state universities were created in Ciudad Juárez, Chiapas state, and Coahuila state, as well as a tropical agriculture school and a southeastern ecological research institute. The federal government pays 50% of state university costs and has increased support for the national university and national polytechnic institute by 80% since 1970.

New government-issued textbooks in the social and natural sciences drew strong protests from the conservative National Parents Union, which asserted that the texts teach Marxist-Leninism and abnormal sexual practices. Echeverría defended the texts as being consistent with Mexican nationalism and democratic views.

Labor. Continuing the emphasis on the working classes as the heart of the Mexican Revolution, the government introduced a number of pro-labor measures. In August federal employees' salaries were raised by 16%, an increase usually followed by the private sector. New laws strengthened enforcement of minimum wages, fixed minimum professional salaries, increased profit-sharing funds, and created and expanded worker-protection and development

--- **MEXICO · Information Highlights** ---

Official Name: United Mexican States.
Location: Southern North America.
Area: 761,602 square miles (1,972,546 sq km).
Population (1975 est.): 59,200,000.
Chief Cities (1974): Mexico City, the capital, 7,000,000; Guadalajara, 1,200,000; Monterey, 1,000,000.
Government: *Head of state,* Luis Echeverría Álvarez, president (took office Dec. 1970). *Head of government,* Luis Echeverría Álvarez. *Legislature*—Congress: Senate and Chamber of Deputies.
Monetary Unit: Peso (12.5 pesos equal U. S.$1, March 1975).
Gross National Product (1974 est.): $59,000,000,000.
Manufacturing (major products): Petroleum products, iron, steel, chemicals, transport equipment, aluminum, pharmaceuticals, cement.
Major Agricultural Products: Corn, cotton, sugarcane, wheat, vegetables, citrus fruits, fish.
Foreign Trade (1974): *Exports,* $3,420,000,000; *imports,* $6,518,000,000.

agencies. A consumer protection measure, sent to Congress in the fall, was expected to pass with little opposition.

Agrarian Policy. Major changes in agrarian policy included the creation of the ministry of agrarian reform and the formation of the Ocampo Pact, which unified the four major farmer organizations. Both measures brought rural Mexico more firmly under government control. Some 19% of total public investment was designated for the rural sector. The government continued its policy of promoting increased agricultural production, rural industrialization, and collective approaches to agriculture. Existing agricultural credit institutions were consolidated into the National Rural Credit Bank, and a National Basic Food Grain Production Company was created.

Economy. Efforts to counter international inflationary and recessionary pressures showed signs of success by September. The central bank reported that the consumer price index rose only 8.3% and the wholesale price index 9.4% in the first eight months of 1975. Industrial production was up 2.2% over the 1974 average in the first six months of the year. However, by July production had risen 6.1% since December 1974. Leading the recovery were electricity (up 7.9%), manufacturing (up 7.4%), construction (up 6.7%), and petroleum (up 3.1%). Petrochemicals and mining had fallen 28.1% and 7.8%, respectively, since December.

Tourism and border transaction, important for earning foreign exchange as well as income, fell during the year, prompting the creation of the ministry of tourism and the exemption of tourists from the 15% hotel and restaurant tax. Although exports fell 7% in the first quarter, new export stimulation efforts and a simplified tariff schedule encouraged a trade revival by midyear.

The government adopted the policy of promoting employment, offsetting declining private investment with public monies, and maintaining a demand for goods and services. Through increased taxation and charges for services, government revenue increased 48% to represent 11% of the gross domestic product. Income for state participation and decentralized agencies increased 20%. The government planned to spend about $24 billion, an increase of 25%, during 1975. Of this, $7.3 billion was destined for public investment. Industry was given top priority with a 35% share.

New banking laws fostered the consolidation of numerous specialized credit institutions into single, multi-purpose banks in an effort to increase private investment and regulatory control. Mexico again resorted to international money markets, including Iran, but the Bank of Mexico reserves and drawing rights totaled $2.7 billion.

Energy. Mexican crude petroleum production was expected to reach 830,000 barrels a day by

UPI

José López Portillo waves to crowds in October as he begins his campaign for the presidency in 1976.

the end of the year, allowing the country to continue exports and earn foreign exchange. Mexico exported $176 million of petroleum products in the first six months of 1975. A new oil field was discovered in Chiapas state in August, and natural gas, which Mexico had been importing, was discovered in the northern part of the country. Energy policy called for self-financed increases in capacity while searching for diversified, new sources.

International Affairs. President Echeverría continued his policy of seeking Third World leadership as well as trade and loan agreements. In July and August, he made a 14-country, 41-day tour of 3 continents, the longest presidential trip in Mexican history. His support of Third World causes, including those of the Panamanians and the Palestinians, was interpreted as an effort to obtain the secretary generalship of the United Nations or a Nobel Peace Prize. On other fronts, Mexico planned to extend its offshore control to 200 miles (320 km), thus preserving the Gulf of California for Mexican exploitation. Diplomatic relations were extended to a number of nonaligned and socialist nations. The Pan American Games were staged in Mexico City in October.

Women's World Conference. Mexico hosted the UN-sponsored Commission on Women's Legal and Social Conditions from June 19 to July 2. Attended by prominent women from throughout the world, the conference was addressed by President Echeverría. (See also WOMEN.)

DONALD J. MABRY
Mississippi State University

GREENFIELD VILLAGE & HENRY FORD MUSEUM

Michigan's Bicentennial programs include an exhibit of early crafts that will tour 76 U.S. cities through 1976.

MICHIGAN

The disappearance of former Teamsters Union President James R. Hoffa, the resignation of state Supreme Court Justice John B. Swainson, and controversy over a court decision freeing the criminally insane claimed headlines in Michigan during 1975.

Hoffa Disappearance. An intensive investigation was started when James Hoffa, a powerful labor leader, disappeared on July 30 from a restaurant in a Detroit suburb. Despite the efforts of local, state, and federal authorities, the disappearance remained a mystery. Hoffa vanished shortly before he was to launch a bid for renewed involvement in Teamster affairs.

Swainson Resignation. Supreme Court Justice John B. Swainson was accused of accepting a bribe to influence the court to overturn the conviction of a burglar. In a trial that started on October 20 in federal district court in Detroit, Swainson was acquitted of the bribery charge but found guilty of perjury for lying to a grand jury about some aspects of the case. He resigned from the court pending an appeal of his conviction.

Criminally Insane. A Michigan Supreme Court ruling directed state health officials to release suspected criminals whom they believe are not mentally ill. The ruling applied to persons confined to mental institutions after being found innocent of a crime because of insanity. Two newly released hospital inmates, originally confined on murder charges, were accused of new slayings shortly after their release. This episode started a controversy that prompted the state legislature to write new laws to circumvent the court ruling.

Budget Deficit. Sharp reductions in state spending were ordered in an attempt to reduce a budget deficit expected to reach $300 million by the end of the 1975 fiscal year. The deficit was blamed on reduced revenue resulting from the economic recession. Cutbacks included lay-offs of teachers in state colleges and reductions in aid to welfare recipients.

Political Reform. A law regulating lobbyists, requiring financial disclosure by political candidates, and enacting safeguards against conflict of interest by public officials was approved by the state legislature. It was signed by Gov. William Milliken on August 27.

A single-business tax measure, designed to stimulate industrial expansion, create jobs, and stabilize state revenues, was enacted in August. The tax replaced eight previous tax levies with a single 2.35% tax on a base that included payrolls, profits, interest, and depreciation.

Oil Drilling. The plans of major oil companies to develop wells in the Pigeon River State Forest continued to encounter local opposition. The state leased mineral rights to the forest in Michigan's northern Lower Peninsula in 1968. However, environmentalists successfully blocked renewed efforts to expand operations beyond five existing wells operated by the Shell Oil Company.

Districting. Michigan's system of redrawing its legislative districts after each 10-year federal census to conform to the one-man, one-vote principle was approved in October by the U.S. Supreme Court. The state's method had been challenged by a group of minority party officials.

CHARLES W. THEISEN
The Detroit "News"

MICHIGAN • Information Highlights

Area: 58,216 square miles (150,779 sq km).
Population (1974 est.): 9,098,000. *Density:* 156 per sq mi.
Chief Cities (1970 census): Lansing, the capital, 131,546; Detroit, 1,513,601.
Government (1975): *Chief Officers*—governor, William G. Milliken (R); lt. gov., James J. Damman (R). *Legislature*—Senate, 38 members; House of Representatives, 110 members.
Education (1974–75): *Enrollment*—public elementary schools, 1,448,345 pupils; public secondary, 689,267; nonpublic, 244,300; colleges and universities, 457,-342 students. *Public school expenditures,* $2,413,-755,000 ($1,196 per pupil).
State Finances (fiscal year 1974): *Revenues,* $6,874,158,-000; *expenditures,* $6,434,408,000.
Personal Income (1974): $53,930,000,000; per capita, $5,928.
Labor Force (Aug. 1975): *Nonagricultural wage and salary earners,* 3,130,600; *insured unemployed,* 195,-000.

MICROBIOLOGY

Numerous activities in microbiology during 1975 drew worldwide attention.

Physiology and Genetics. Interesting research was done on various kinds of cellular membranes in microbes to determine their structure and function and how nutrients, waste products, and other substances enter and leave the cells. The unique membrane of one bacterium, *Halobacterium halobium,* for example, contains a pigment (bacteriorhodopsin) that converts light energy into metabolic energy. Other than the chlorophyll systems of plants, this is the only known system that converts light to life-sustaining energy. Bacteriorhodopsin is so similar to animal visual pigments that it serves as a model for the study of vision. Also, it may prompt the development of artificial methods of changing light into energy for life maintenance.

Great attention was given during the year to the manipulation of the genetic characteristics of microorganisms, the study of the resistance of microorganisms to antibiotics, and a proposed moratorium on certain types of experiments that alter the genetic composition of microorganisms. Some scientists fear that the transfer of chromosomal genes or microbial plasmids from one microorganism to another may accidentally create new diseases or even cause widespread dissemination of cancer-producing viruses.

Food. Because of the world shortage of protein, extensive research was done in 1975 on producing protein from the single-celled organisms yeast and bacteria. Two processes received the greatest attention. The first was a "village-level" technology for upgrading crop wastes into protein foods for pigs and poultry, and the second was a technique for using a simple carbon source such as methanol and inorganic salts to produce high-quality protein and amino acids.

Agriculture. One of the great discoveries in the history of agriculture occurred in 1975. For many years the fixation of gaseous nitrogen (N_2) from the air by the root-dwelling bacteria (rhizobia) of leguminous (N_2-fixating) plants has been a main source of plant protein, contributing many times more nitrogen to the soil each year than the total of the world's commercial fertilizer.

The many past attempts to grow rhizobia capable of N_2 fixation in the absence of living plant material were unsuccessful. It was assumed that plants themselves contributed the genetic material that enabled the rhizobia to convert N_2 to ammonia or the other nitrogen compounds important for plant growth. Scientists in Australia and Canada reported in 1975 successful cultivation of N_2-fixating rhizobia in the absence of plant material and found that only a pentose sugar, arabinose or xylose, and a dicarboxylic acid such as succinate are needed for N_2 fixation.

Thus, it is the genes of the rhizobia themselves that enable fixation of N_2, and the plant roots may possibly serve as little more than compartments for the bacteria. It is now important to determine how readily the new discoveries can be used to enable N_2 fixation by other plants and forage crops besides legumes.

Medicine. Certain bacterial diseases are still not under control in the world, and some (typhoid, dysentery, gonorrhea, and epidemic meningitis) appear to be on the increase. In Brazil in 1974 an epidemic of meningitis resulted in 40,000 cases and 4,000 deaths. Only a massive immunization program prevented the disease from spreading further.

Malaria was still a major problem, with outbreaks in Southeast Asia on the increase and with 4 million cases estimated in India alone in 1975. With the resistance of the malarial parasite to drugs and insecticides and with the reduced use of insecticides, future prospects for eradication of the disease by such methods are dim. Thus, research efforts have turned toward the development of a suitable vaccine against malaria.

The most promising vaccine so far was developed in 1975 and contained emulsified malaria organisms in the merozoite (highly infectious) stage taken from blood plasma. Rhesus monkeys were used as the experimental animal, and the vaccine is now being evaluated in the owl monkey.

Influenza virus has been suspected but never proved to be the cause of congenital central-nervous-system malformations in man. The major obstacle to proof of the malformation-producing potential of this and other viruses has been the lack of a primate model.

In 1975, it was shown that influenza virus can induce congenital hydrocephalus, which can lead to severe mental retardation, in the fetus of the rhesus monkey. Therefore, since the influenza virus can cross the human placenta and infect the fetus, caution is needed in the use of live viruses to vaccinate pregnant women against influenza.

An RNA virus that is closely associated with human acute myelogenous leukemia was demonstrated by a group of scientists at the National Cancer Institute. The virus passed all tests available to prove that it is a human virus, justifying the long search for a virus linked to human cancer.

Progress is being made toward producing an antiviral vaccine for certain human lymph gland cancers (lymphomas) through studies on experimental animals. A vaccine prepared in 1975 reduced the mortality from Marek's lymphoma by 94% in vaccinated chickens injected with the virulent virus. Animal tests of vaccines against lymphomas in which herpes viruses are implicated were also started.

J. R. PORTER
University of Iowa

MIDDLE EAST

The Middle East situation changed more in 1975 than it had in 1974. The most important change was the second interim Sinai agreement between Egypt and Israel, which was concluded early in September and in which the United States mediated. The agreement and its probable long-range results created much controversy. It did, however, move the most important bilateral relationship, that between Israel and Egypt, off dead center, and it created the possibility of further improvements. Whatever other developments of actual or potential importance occurred, the Sinai pact rightly commanded the primary focus of attention.

The disengagement agreement did not come early in the year, and it did not come easily. It came about only as a result of the indefatigable diplomacy of U. S. Secretary of State Henry Kissinger, who persisted in his endeavors in the face of prolonged lack of success. It has been obvious that the two initial disengagement agreements that had terminated the 1973 war and had been concluded on Israel's fronts with Egypt and Syria were merely armistices. They would have to be replaced as soon as possible by something more definitive if there were to be any hope of lasting peace. Kissinger's gambit was to postpone reconvening the Geneva conference, with its implausible mission of constructing a grand overall settlement of the Arab-Israeli strife, and to opt instead for a "step-by-step" approach. In this approach, one thing at a time would be tackled in the hope that, if this were done successfully, there would be a cumulative impetus that would make the next stage easier. The first objective chosen was the central one of a more definite separation of Egyptian and Israeli forces in the Sinai Peninsula.

On September 8, Secretary of State Kissinger explains Sinai accord to House International Relations Committee.

UPI

Deadlock in February and March. The negotiations of February and March were fruitless. Kissinger carried out two peace missions in those months—his eighth and ninth missions to the Middle East since the 1973 war. The Secretary visited Israel, Egypt, Syria, Jordan, Iran, and Saudi Arabia. The main elements of what he sought resembled in outline what was actually achieved six months later: a 30-mile (48-km) withdrawal of Israeli forces, uncovering the strategic Milta and Giddi passes and forfeiting the rich Abu Rudeis oilfield on the Gulf of Suez. In return the Egyptian government promised some actions in regard to peaceful intentions with Israel in the future. This set of negotiations broke down when President Anwar el-Sadat of Egypt refused the categorical declaration of nonbelligerency toward Israel that was Israeli Prime Minister Itzhak Rabin's irreducible demand in return for Israel's substantial and specific concessions.

Negotiations—Second Round. U. S. pressure for a negotiated interim settlement continued, and the diplomatic atmosphere became slightly more favorable. President Ford conferred amicably with Sadat in Salzburg June 2, and Rabin was in Washington from June 11 to 15. During the Ford-Sadat meeting, Israel, as a gesture of goodwill, ordered a partial withdrawal of its forces in the Sinai. The Suez Canal, closed to ship traffic for 8 years, reopened without event in June. On July 24 the UN Security Council, with Egypt's consent, approved a three-month extension of the mandate keeping UN forces in the Sinai. The mandate of the UN body on the Golan Heights at the Syrian front had been renewed for six months, until November. Throughout 1975 the military situation on these two fronts was relatively quiet, and only minor cease-fire violations were reported. This certainly marked an improvement over previous years.

A new round of shuttle diplomacy began on August 21 when Kissinger arrived in Israel. The hostile demonstrations that he encountered were evidence of the resentment and apprehension felt by many Israelis at the pressure that the United States had been exerting to procure an agreement. The second round of negotiations proved successful, and Egypt and Israel formally accepted the interim settlement at separate ceremonies on September 1 and together at Geneva three days later.

Terms of the Sinai Agreement. There were several basic features of the agreement. In accepting what was specifically described as "not a final peace agreement," Egypt and Israel both pledged themselves to work for a peaceful resolution of "the conflict between them and in the Middle East." They undertook "not to resort to the threat or use of force or military blockade against each other" and to observe scrupulously the existing cease-fire. Israeli forces were to be withdrawn behind the Giddi and Mitla passes, and Israel was to yield the

Egyptian oil workers and officials celebrate the return of Sinai oilfields in November. The Israeli withdrawal from the fields followed the signing of a new Middle East accord.

Abu Rudeis oilfield. The Shah of Iran had pledged in February to make available to Israel compensating supplies of oil.

The forward military position of each side was to become a "limited force zone," in which the types of weapons and the size of forces permissible were prescribed. Between these two limited force zones was the zone where the UN Emergency Force was to continue its functions. Its mandate was to be extended annually. This was a concession by Egypt. More important was the concession in Article VII, which stated that "nonmilitary cargoes destined for or coming from Israel shall be permitted through the Suez Canal." A joint commission was set up for the duration of the agreement to oversee its working.

The key feature of the agreement was the added U. S. proposal for an early-warning system to be established in the area of the passes "to perform the functions of visual and electronic surveillance." The system would diminish the likelihood of a surprise attack by either nation and would be manned in part by about 200 U. S. civilians. This provision, whose implementation needed approval by the U. S. Congress, was regarded by Israel as indispensable. On September 4, Israel symbolized this by merely initialing the documents. It did not sign them until October 10, after congressional approval had been obtained.

The agreement provided that details of the implementations should be worked out by representatives of the two parties in Geneva. This began later in September and proceeded with surprising smoothness. On October 22, Egypt and Israel agreed to the establishment of a joint military headquarters in the Sinai to facilitate the carrying out of the agreements. Israeli technicians hauled down their flag at the Abu Rudeis oilfield on November 30, and it was taken over by Egypt.

Controversy over the Agreement. Assessments of the Sinai disengagement varied widely. U. S. congressional opinion at first showed great wariness over the proposal to employ U. S. citizens in the area, but this aspect in the end won substantial majorities in both houses. There was also initial alarm at the revelation of the existence of three related documents that constituted moral commitments. In the most important document the United States pledged itself "on an on-going and long-term basis" to be fully responsive to Israel's military, energy, and economic needs. It is possible to argue, however, that this was not more than a formal statement of existing policy. The United States also committed itself to consult with Egypt if Israel should break the agreement.

Critics of the Sinai agreement have argued that the United States squandered an excessive amount of diplomatic capital to achieve a minor military adjustment and that the pact did nothing of substance to tackle the unsolved problems in the Middle East. On the other hand, it was argued that substantial progress was made, that the agreement bought time, and that it may well prove to be a step toward a more comprehensive peace. President Sadat showed courage and common sense in concluding the agreement and thus braving the inevitable barrage of criticism that ensued from the more radical Arab states.

Sadat's Egypt is entering on a new course of policy, both domestic and foreign. The estrangement between Egypt and the Soviet Union was very marked. But the Soviet Union still has an important influence in the Middle East and during the year made an enormous new arms deal with Libya. There were possibilities also that Jordan, disenchanted with the United States, may turn to the USSR for arms.

Terror and Counterstrikes. If the military situation on the Sinai and Golan fronts was quiet, the same could not be said of the ubiquitous Palestinian terrorist activity against Israel. In the course of 1975 about 50 Israelis died as a result of terrorist attacks of various kinds. In reprisals, Israeli warplanes on at least eight occasions attacked Palestinian camps in Lebanon. Israeli raids killed more Arabs than Arab terrorists killed Israelis, but there was reason to doubt the raids' political effectiveness. The major Israeli raid in December led straight

to UN decisions prejudicial to Israeli interests. Also, the renewal of the UN Golan force mandate for six months was linked, in practice, to the decision to let the Palestine Liberation Organization (PLO) be represented at the Security Council Middle East debate in January. Some signs also were seen of a waning of U. S. support for Israel.

The most dramatic terrorist attack in 1975 occurred on December 21, when a group of pro-Palestinian guerrillas stormed the headquarters of the Organization of Petroleum Exporting Countries (OPEC) in Vienna, taking 10 OPEC ministers hostage. After receiving an airplane, the group flew to various Middle East nations, dropping off hostages, with the last released in Algiers on December 23. Algeria granted the terrorists political asylum.

The growing strength of the Palestinian issue was significant. It was a nightmare for Israel, because the PLO has not so far indicated any willingness to accept Israel's existence. PLO influence was seen in the UN vote condemning Zionism as "racist."

Strife in Lebanon. It was the internal weakness of Lebanon that made it such a secure sanctuary for terrorists. Civil strife in Lebanon, especially in Beirut, between armed Muslims and Christian Falangists reached such a pitch in 1975 that the disintegration of the Lebanese state seemed

UPI

Israeli security forces search through wreckage of the Savoy Hotel in Tel Aviv, after commandoes forced out Arab guerrillas in March.

Gunmen man roof-top positions in Beirut, Lebanon, as fierce fighting between Muslims and Christian Falangists continues in the strife-torn city.

UPI

an imminent possibility. Fighting began in April and continued with an interminable series of cease-fires repeatedly broken throughout the rest of the year. (See also LEBANON.)

Turkey. The ending by Congress of U. S. military aid to Turkey led to Turkey's demand that the United States remove its military bases there. The Turkish government was beset by terrorist action against its ambassadors abroad. Two of them were murdered. The greatest death-toll of the year in the Middle East was the result of a natural disaster, the Turkish earthquake in September that killed about 2,500.

Increasing Stability. In some respects it could be said that there was increasing stability in the Middle East. Not only had Israel and Egypt mutually renounced the use of force, but relations among other states showed some improvements. Iraq and Iran ended their long-standing differences—at the expense of the Kurds. Iraq and Kuwait also ended their disputes, and Iraq and Syria at least made some gestures of goodwill. Iraq and Saudi Arabia also settled some outstanding issues. The radical threats to the established order in the Persian Gulf seemed to be lessening. The Organization of Petroleum Exporting Countries (OPEC) surprised observers in September by continuing to hold together and by agreeing to a 10% price increase, though in fact not all countries were observing the agreement with equal fidelity.

ARTHUR CAMPBELL TURNER
University of California, Riverside

President Ford (*left*) confers with Gen. Alexander Haig, NATO military commander, in March during a Washington stopover in Haig's tour of NATO countries.

MILITARY FORCES

With the termination of the conflict in Vietnam and with no new outbreak of major violence in the Middle East, 1975 was an unusually peaceful year in comparison to the recent past. The decrease in the use of military forces, however, was not reflected by any substantial reduction in military forces held in readiness.

World Developments

The military forces present in the world during 1975 could be classified into five broad groups. Each could be associated with a particular type of political confrontation that seemed to justify, in the minds of government decision makers, the need to acquire arms and to train men to use armaments. Heading this list, in terms of money spent and the destructive potential of the weapons, was the arms competition between the Soviet Union and the United States. Two other areas of major arms acquisition were the rivalry between the two giants of the Communist world, the Peoples Republic of China and the Soviet Union, and the confrontation between the Arab world and Israel.

A fourth area of arms activity involved a number of lesser nations and subnational groups in Africa, Latin America, and Asia. On those continents, old and new animosities combined with internal political struggles to fuel increased arms acquisition and use. In contrast to the other areas of arms competition, this type of activity generally involved much smaller, less expensive, and less sophisticated weaponry. A fifth area of armament, the proliferation of nuclear weapons, remained potentially significant. Many concerned with future arms developments were disturbed by the possibility that additional nations would acquire the kind of nuclear arsenals now possessed by the United States, the Soviet Union, Great Britain, France, and China.

The Superpowers. Two much-heralded efforts to slow the arms competition between the United States and the Soviet Union produced few results in 1975. Hopes were officially expressed at the year's end, however, for substantive agreements in the near future.

At the strategic level, the second round of the Strategic Arms Limitation Talks (SALT II) failed to produce agreements limiting the number of strategic offensive delivery vehicles permitted each nation. It was the hope of the United States that an agreement could be reached to limit both nations to 2,400 offensive-delivery vehicles, such as long range bombers and missiles, and to limit the number of missiles equipped with MIRV's (multiple individually-targeted re-entry vehicles) to 1,320. Negotiations on these matters were conducted amid allegations made by a few that the Soviets were evading some of the provisions of the first strategic arms limitation agreement. That 1972 accord limited the United States to 1,054 intercontinental ballistic missiles (ICBMs) and 656 medium-range missiles launched from submarines. The Soviet Union was restricted to 1,618 ICBM's and 710 submarine-launched missiles. Further, both nations were restricted to a small number of anti-ballistic defense missiles.

The administration of President Gerald R. Ford, like the one of Richard M. Nixon before it, defended the seeming numerical inequality of offensive delivery vehicles by noting two offsetting advantages possessed by the United States. These supporters contended that the United States operated 500 long range bombers compared to 160 for the Soviet Union, and that many of the U. S. missiles were equipped with MIRV's, while the Soviets were just beginning to place MIRV's on some of their missiles.

In an apparent effort to move the SALT II negotiations to a conclusion, President Ford warned late in 1975 that if no progress were forthcoming he would ask Congress to increase

the strategic weapons budget by $3 billion. This would put U. S. expenditures for strategic weapons at $12.8 billion.

New Weapons. Several strategic weapons systems are becoming available should the United States decide to increase and modernize its arsenal. One such system is the B-1 supersonic bomber. The Air Force has indicated it would like to deploy 244 of the new bombers. If the new B-1's are not built, the Air Force has a less dramatic option with the development of a nuclear armed ALCM (air-launched cruise missile), which could be carried aboard the current B-52 bomber force. Such a missile would substantially increase the effectiveness of the bombers because they could be released some distance from the target, thus permitting the aircraft to avoid flying over heavily defended target areas.

A major new strategic weapons system is the *Trident* submarine and its accompanying new missiles. If the arms competition with the Soviet Union warrants it, a new fleet of *Trident* submarines can be available during the late 1970's and early 1980's. A new ICBM is also under development. The missile, termed the MX ICBM, would be more powerful and more accurate than the presently deployed Minuteman missiles. In addition to being capable of replacing the Minuteman missiles in their current silos, the MX ICBM could be deployed in a land-mobile mode and also carried aboard aircraft. The interest in mobility was caused by the fear that rapidly improving Soviet missile capabilities could enable the Soviets to destroy a number of the immobile Minuteman missiles before they are launched.

A second major, and to date fruitless, effort was made in 1975 to reduce the arms deployed in Europe by the United States in association with its NATO allies and by the Soviet Union in conjunction with the Warsaw Pact members. The hope was that a mutual security conference could be held to agree upon military force reductions in Europe.

While in Helsinki, Finland, July 30–August 1, President Ford met with Soviet Communist party Chairman Leonid Brezhnev to discuss détente, but at year's end the forces maintained by the United States and the USSR in their respective zones of Europe remained constant.

ARMS COMPETITION

An area of growing U. S. and Soviet arms rivalry was the Indian Ocean. The U. S. has developed a naval base on the British-held island of Diego Garcia to service periodic deployments from the Pacific-based 7th Fleet. Soviet naval vessels were also seen in the area, and the Pentagon claimed that the Soviets were establishing basing rights and facilities along the horn of Africa. U. S. interest in the Indian Ocean was related to the belief that the ocean approaches to the oil-rich Persian Gulf states must be protected.

Chinese-Soviet Arms Competition. The Soviet Union maintained over 40 divisions, approximately 25% of their total divisional strength, and 900 tactical aircraft in Soviet Asia. The Chinese kept 90 divisions of their 210-division force to counter the Soviet armies across the border. The West has assumed that both nations have nuclear missiles targeted upon one another, although in this competition the Soviets retained a substantial advantage.

The Middle East Arms Race. Since the conclusion of the 1973 Israeli-Arab War, the nations of the Middle East have sought to replace weapons lost in that encounter and to obtain newer models as a hedge against another outbreak of hostilities. Among the various arming activities of the Middle East nations, the arms

UPI

A technician checks newly-developed cruise missile. Armed with nuclear or tactical warheads, they can be launched from ships, aircraft, or land.

deal that created the most consternation was the request by Israel to purchase U. S. Pershing missiles. These missiles have a range of approximately 500 miles (800 km) and can carry a nuclear warhead.

Spokesmen in the United States supporting the Israeli request argued that the Pershings would offset the numerically superior Arab forces and compensate for the possession by Egypt of similar missiles believed to have been previously supplied by the Soviet Union. The argument against the Pershing request was based on the fear that the Israelis would add secretly-developed nuclear warheads to the Pershings and thus trigger greater arms acquisition activity on the part of the Arab states.

A complicating factor in the Middle East arms race was the apparent agreement by the United States to consider supplying some military equipment to Egypt, the largest of the Arab states. The development was linked to the U. S. emphasis upon an "even-handed" policy toward both the Arabs and the Israelis.

In an unrelated development in the Middle East, the U. S. Congress partially rescinded an embargo placed upon arms shipments to Turkey after Turkish intervention in the civil war on Cyprus. It was generally expected that the lifting of the embargo would result in the Turks' rescinding their policy of closing down U. S. bases in Turkey, which are used for surveillance of the Soviet Union. The Turkish action had been taken as a retaliatory move after the U. S. embargo was announced.

Conventional Arms Traffic. While much of the attention by the world's press centered upon the arms competition among the larger nations and among countries in the Middle East, smaller nations and subnational organizations continued their acquisition of more modest armaments. In hard economic times the lucrative trade in smaller weapons tempted various nations either to enter the marketplace or to expand an existing trade. The United States headed the list of arms exporters in 1975, followed by the Soviet Union, France, Britain, Italy, and West Germany.

Proliferation of Nuclear Weapons. In 1975 those nations associated with the Nuclear Nonproliferation Treaty met to discuss ways of extending the prohibitions of the treaty to nations not adhering to it. One possibility, still not adopted by the end of 1975, would be to negotiate a new worldwide agreement to prohibit all underground tests of nuclear weapons. A treaty already existed banning nuclear weapons tests above ground, in water, or in space. A problem with this approach was that some nations, such as India, regarded the development of peaceful nuclear explosives as essential to their industrial progress. How to ban nuclear weapons tests but permit peaceful nuclear explosive research remained a difficult and unresolved problem.

At the end of the year a number of nations technically capable of developing nuclear weapons still had not ratified the Nuclear Nonproliferation Treaty. These included India, Brazil, Argentina, Japan, the Republic of South Africa, and Pakistan.

ROBERT M. LAWRENCE
Colorado State University

U. S. Developments

An amphibious force backed by five aircraft carriers completed the United States' withdrawal from Vietnam on April 30, 1975, ending the nation's longest war. Increased naval activity by the Soviet Union stimulated a military development on the British-owned island of Diego Garcia in the Indian Ocean. Inflation and the sharply increased costs of manpower and weap-

UPI

Sen. Edmund Muskie points at chart during U. S. defense budget hearings at which Secretary of Defense James Schlesinger defended the increased budget.

The U. S. S. *Nimitz*, shown during sea trials, is the largest aircraft carrier ever built. Nuclear-powered, it carries about 100 jets.

onry further aggravated problems of U. S. security.

The Cost of the Armed Forces. The armed forces' first peacetime budget in a decade reduced overall military force levels while seeking an $8 billion increase. The record-high budget of $92.8 billion reflected a steady increase in military spending and the marked effects of inflation on arms production costs. Military costs continued to decline as a percentage of the total federal budget and of the gross national product. Substantial pay raises to stimulate enlistments in the volunteer services increased personnel costs to 53% of the defense budget. Weapons costs, increasing at approximately 15% per year, were reflected in the budget as the United States continued to develop costly and sophisticated weapons.

Weapons and Technology. The critical question faced by defense planners in 1975 was the issue of quality versus quantity in weapons development. Experts argued over whether expenditures should emphasize relatively few, very expensive weapons or should be concentrated on larger numbers of cheaper, less sophisticated models. Technological advances have helped compensate for numbers but modern war has raised new questions about the continued use of sophisticated ships, aircraft, and tanks when matched against massive use of a wide variety of highly mobile, relatively inexpensive, surface and air launched missiles. The U. S. Navy, for example, had an acute problem in the cost of the nuclear-powered aircraft carrier. The 95,000 ton, $1 billion-plus USS *Nimitz,* which completed its maiden cruise to Europe in 1975, is the backbone of the fleet. It is able to project maximum power to trouble spots around the world without reliance on overseas bases. Plans for additional giant carriers were rejected by Secretary of Defense James R. Schlesinger on the basis that strong conventional forces are a better means of preventing local wars from escalating into nuclear wars. A lower-cost sea control ship proposed by the Navy was rejected by Congress. A compromise "midi-carrier" of about 50,000 tons, possibly nonnuclear, was estimated to cost close to $1 billion but could not handle the F-14, the Navy's top fighter plane. Congress also questioned Defense Department proposals for a nuclear-powered cruiser at $1.2 billion, new funds for the B-1 bomber, the air warning and control aircraft, and the *Trident* submarine.

Personnel. The nation's security, for the second year, depended upon a volunteer force. Overall quality showed little change from the best years of the draft. About 66% of the enlisted men were high school graduates compared with 68% in 1964, the last year of a peacetime draft. Black enlistees decreased from 21% to 20%, and women played an increasingly important role in all service occupations except combat positions, which were denied by law.

The decision to allow women to attend the Air Force, Army, Coast Guard, and Navy service academies, beginning in the summer of 1976, was historically significant. Facing the same admission, professional education, and development programs as men, women will compete in noncontact intercollegiate sports and train for future careers in noncombat fields. The Department of Defense Committee on Excellence in Education directed consolidation of the National War College and the Industrial College of the Armed Forces at Fort McNair, Washington, D. C., under a single University of National Defense.

Command. Gen. Lewis H. Wilson succeeded Gen. Robert H. Cushman as commandant of the U. S. Marine Corps on July 1, 1975. Martin R. Hoffman succeeded Howard H. Callaway as secretary of the Army on August 5. In November, Secretary of Defense James R. Schlesinger was replaced by former White House Chief of Staff Donald Rumsfeld.

PAUL R. SCHRATZ, *Captain, USN, Retired*
Advanced Research Programs,
U. S. Naval War College

Technician regulates ore loading at an Arizona open-pit copper mine through the use of remote control to move the train.

MINING

The performance of the world's mining and mineral industry in 1975 was influenced by worldwide cutbacks in industrial activity because of economic problems and by continuing short supplies and high prices for energy materials. Output of most mineral commodities (including fuels), if not down from 1974 levels, at least failed to grow at the rates that had prevailed in the late 1960's and early 1970's.

Preliminary estimates indicated that the total value of world crude mineral production (including fuels) in 1975 reached a level of about $120 billion (in terms of 1968 constant dollars), compared with approximately $115.4 billion in 1974. Comparable figures for other recent years are as follows (in billions): 1968, $88.0; 1969, $91.9; 1970, $97.8; 1971, $101.7; 1972, $104.6; and 1973, $111.5.

Production Changes. The bulk of the 1974 and 1975 increases was registered by nations with centrally planned economies—the USSR, China, Albania, Bulgaria, Czechoslovakia, East Germany, Hungary, Mongolia, North Korea, Poland, Rumania, and North Vietnam—and by the developing market economy nations of Africa, Asia, and Latin America. The industrialized market economy nations—the United States, Canada, Japan, Australia, and the countries of Western Europe—registered small increases or declines.

International and intranational political problems in such areas as Angola, Mozambique, Portugal, Cambodia, Vietnam, Cyprus, the Spanish Sahara, and the Middle East tended to retard production and facility development in those areas. On the brighter side, the reopening of the Suez Canal, which occurred in June, was expected to have a positive effect on mineral shipment, but the size of the effect and the possible reduction in shipping rates could not be assessed at the close of 1975.

Greater Production Control. The trend toward increased domestic control of mineral production facilities in the developing countries continued in 1975, as did the trend toward required increased processing of minerals in these areas. Both these trends reflected the desires of the developing nations to ensure that a greater portion of the profits resulting from mineral-industry activities be directed into their own economies rather than into the economies of the developed nations.

Methods employed to increase domestic control of mineral-industry activity took a variety of forms. These ranged from outright nationalization with the facilities to be operated by a government corporation, through requirements that a substantial share of any operating company be owned within the country (either by the government or by private firms), and to simple increases in taxation to provide more revenue for the government.

The relative success of the Organization of Petroleum Exporting Countries (OPEC) in achieving oil-price changes favorable to its member nations continued to provide stimulation for the development of other commodity-oriented international alliances. In addition to the long-established International Tin Council (ITC) and Intergovernmental Council of Copper Exporting Countries (CIPEC) and the recently established

WORLD PRODUCTION OF MAJOR MINERAL COMMODITIES

Aluminum, smelter
(thousand metric tons)

	1973	1974
United States	4,108	4,448
USSR[e]	1,360	1,430
Japan	1,102	1,124
Canada	942	1,007
West Germany	533	689
Norway	620	649
France	359	395
United Kingdom	252	293
Netherlands	190	252
Italy	184	223
Australia	207	219
Spain	162	189
Rumania	141	187
Ghana	151	157
China[e]	150	150
Other countries[a]	1,694	1,759
Total	12,155	13,171

Antimony, mine[b] (metric tons)

	1973	1974
South Africa	15,700	15,301
Bolivia	14,852	13,060
China[e]	12,000	12,000
USSR	7,100	7,300
Thailand	3,414	4,236
Turkey	3,353	e3,400
Mexico	2,388	2,407
Morocco	1,133	2,141
Yugoslavia	2,055	e2,034
Australia	1,486	e1,500
Italy	1,358	e1,270
Canada	859	e1,250
Guatemala	872	e900
Peru	770	e800
Other countries[a]	2,513	3,242
Total	69,853	70,841

Asbestos (thousand metric tons)

	1973	1974
Canada	1,690	1,655
USSR[e]	1,280	1,350
South Africa	333	335
China[e]	210	210
Italy	149	150
United States	136	102
Rhodesia[e]	80	80
Australia	41	e56
Brazil	47	45
Other countries[a]	129	122
Total	4,095	4,105

Barite (thousand metric tons)

	1973	1974
United States	1,002	1,003
USSR[e]	323	330
West Germany	327	298
Mexico	255	e250
Ireland[e]	250	250
Peru[e]	220	220
Thailand	112	201
China[e]	165	180
Italy	166	180
India	117	e120
North Korea[e]	120	120
Rumania[e]	116	116
Canada	92	e115
Iran	95	e115
Other countries[a]	866	864
Total	4,226	4,362

Bauxite[c] (thousand metric tons)

	1973	1974
Australia	17,596	20,057
Jamaica	13,600	15,328
Surinam	7,110	e7,112
Guinea[e]	3,050	6,600
USSR[e]	4,300	4,300
Guyana	3,276	e3,150
Greece	2,749	3,004
France	3,133	2,909
Hungary	2,600	2,751
Yugoslavia	2,167	2,370
United States	1,909	1,981
Dominican Republic	1,145	1,410
Indonesia	1,229	1,290
India	1,284	1,068
Malaysia	1,143	919
Other countries[a]	3,668	4,007
Total	69,959	78,256

Cement (million metric tons)

	1973	1974
USSR	109.5	115.0
United States	79.4	75.2
Japan	78.1	73.1
Italy	36.3	36.3
West Germany	41.0	36.0
France	30.7	32.5
China[e]	25.0	27.0
Spain	22.2	23.7
United Kingdom	20.0	17.8
Poland	15.5	16.8
Brazil	13.4	14.9
India	15.0	14.3
Rumania	9.8	11.1
Mexico	9.8	10.5
Canada	10.1	10.3

Cement (cont'd) (million metric tons)

	1973	1974
East Germany	9.5	10.1
Other countries[a]	176.0	179.6
Total	701.3	704.2

Chromite[c] (thousand metric tons)

	1973	1974
USSR	1,900	1,950
South Africa	1,650	1,877
Albania	611	e665
Rhodesia[e]	550	590
Philippines	580	529
Turkey[e]	450	500
India	288	363
Malagasy Republic	158	156
Finland	135	155
Iran	140	e145
Other countries[a]	261	267
Total	6,723	7,197

Coal, all grades[d] (million metric tons)

	1973	1974
USSR	667.6	678.6
United States	543.0	551.2
China[e]	430.0	445.0
East Germany	247.0	244.0
West Germany	216.0	220.9
Poland	195.8	201.8
Czechoslovakia	109.0	110.0
United Kingdom	135.4	109.0
Australia	85.3	91.9
India	80.3	86.3
South Africa	62.4	65.4
North Korea[e]	37.0	40.9
Yugoslavia	32.4	33.6
Rumania	24.9	26.9
Hungary	26.2	25.8
France	28.4	25.7
Bulgaria	26.8	24.3
Canada	20.5	21.4
Japan	22.5	20.4
Other countries[a]	116.9	106.6
Total	3,107.4	3,129.7

Copper, mine[b] (thousand metric tons)

	1973	1974
United States	1,558	1,446
Chile	735	906
Canada	824	842
USSR[e]	700	740
Zambia	707	698
Zaire	488	499
Australia	220	256
Philippines	221	225
Peru	219	223
Poland	155	190
Papua New Guinea	183	184
South Africa	176	179
Yugoslavia	112	e123
China[e]	100	100
Mexico	81	83
Japan	91	82
Indonesia	38	65
Other countries[a]	512	515
Total	7,120	7,356

Diamond (thousand carats)

	1973	1974
Zaire	12,940	e13,000
USSR[e]	9,500	9,800
South Africa	7,565	7,502
Botswana	2,416	2,718
Ghana	2,317	2,573
Angola	2,125	e2,100
Sierra Leone	1,404	e1,670
South West Africa	1,600	1,570
Venezuela	778	700
Liberia	817	636
Other countries[a]	1,678	1,816
Total	43,140	44,085

Fluorspar[f] (thousand metric tons)

	1973	1974
Mexico	1,086	1,112
USSR[e]	440	450
Spain	385	e421
Thailand	377	e390
France	260	270
China[e]	250	270
Italy	236	249
Mongolia[e]	240	240
United Kingdom	233	e235
South Africa	210	208
United States	226	182
Canada	137	e136
Other countries[a]	545	539
Total	4,625	4,702

Gas, natural (billion cubic feet)
Gross production:

	1973	1974
United States	24,067	22,850
USSR[e]	8,800	9,700
Canada	3,567	3,486
Netherlands	2,501	2,957
Iran	1,699	1,767
Venezuela	1,746	1,640
Saudi Arabia[e]	1,440	1,570
China[e]	1,100	1,200
United Kingdom	1,018	1,160
Rumania	1,033	1,063
Nigeria	736	1,018

Gas, natural (cont'd) (billion cubic feet)
Gross production:

	1973	1974
Mexico	677	745
West Germany	706	735
United Arab Emirates[e]	583	639
Other countries[a]	6,236	6,351
Total	55,909	56,881

Gold, mine[b] (thousand troy ounces)

	1973	1974
South Africa	27,495	24,363
USSR[e]	7,100	7,300
Canada	1,954	1,718
United States	1,176	1,127
Ghana	723	e760
Papua New Guinea	722	726
Philippines	572	536
Australia	554	520
Rhodesia[e]	500	500
Colombia	216	265
Brazil	203	e210
Yugoslavia	176	e177
North Korea[e]	160	160
Japan	188	140
Other countries[a]	1,259	1,778
Total	42,998	39,780

Graphite (thousand metric tons)

	1973	1974
USSR[e]	80.0	80.0
North Korea[e]	75.0	75.0
Mexico	65.4	e68.0
South Korea	43.6	e45.0
China[e]	30.0	30.0
Austria	17.2	24.7
Malagasy Republic	14.0	17.3
Sri Lanka	6.2	9.4
Other countries[a]	40.0	42.1
Total	371.4	391.5

Gypsum (thousand metric tons)

	1973	1974
United States	12,300	10,885
Canada	7,611	7,471
France	6,160	6,220
USSR[e]	4,700	4,700
Spain	4,471	e4,400
Italy[e]	3,500	3,500
West Germany	2,948	e3,200
United Kingdom	3,849	3,115
Iran[e]	2,400	2,400
Mexico	1,514	1,387
Australia	1,161	e1,200
India	884	1,050
Poland[e]	850	850
Austria	871	804
China[e]	630	650
Czechoslovakia	578	e600
Argentina	454	e454
Greece	420	e420
Other countries[a]	6,261	6,691
Total	61,562	59,997

Iron Ore (million metric tons)

	1973	1974
USSR	216.1	225.0
Australia	84.8	96.7
United States	89.1	85.7
Brazil	55.0	71.0
China[e]	66.0	70.0
France	54.2	54.3
Canada	48.9	50.0
Sweden	34.7	37.0
India	35.4	34.9
Venezuela	23.1	26.4
Mauritania	10.5	11.7
South Africa	11.0	10.8
Chile	9.4	10.3
Peru	9.0	9.5
North Korea[e]	8.9	9.4
Spain	7.3	8.6
Other countries[a]	96.5	92.2
Total	859.9	903.5

Iron, steel ingots (million metric tons)

	1973	1974
USSR	131.4	136.0
United States	136.8	132.2
Japan	119.3	117.1
West Germany	49.5	53.2
China[e]	27.0	27.0
France	25.3	27.0
Italy	21.0	23.8
United Kingdom	26.6	22.4
Belgium	15.5	16.2
Poland	14.1	14.6
Czechoslovakia	13.2	13.9
Canada	13.4	13.6
Rumania	8.2	8.9
Australia	7.7	7.8
Brazil	7.2	7.5
India	7.0	6.7
Luxembourg	5.9	6.4
East Germany	5.9	6.1
Sweden	5.7	6.0
Netherlands	5.6	5.8
South Africa	5.6	5.8
Mexico	4.8	5.1
Other countries[a]	40.5	43.7
Total	697.2	706.8

WORLD PRODUCTION OF MAJOR MINERAL COMMODITIES (Continued)

Lead, smelter (thousand metric tons)

	1973	1974
United States	624	621
USSR[e]	470	475
Australia	340	340
Mexico	173	200
Japan	189	179
France	167	160
Canada	187	125
Yugoslavia	113	125
West Germany	86	116
Bulgaria	100	108
China[e]	100	100
Belgium	103	100
North Korea[e]	80	95
Peru	83	81
Spain	87	79
Poland	65	66
South West Africa	64	64
Other countries[a]	410	426
Total	3,441	3,460

Magnesium (thousand metric tons)

	1973	1974
United States	111.1	[e]112.0
USSR[e]	57.0	60.0
Norway	37.5	38.2
Japan	11.2	8.9
Italy	8.9	7.4
France	8.6	6.5
Canada	6.2	5.9
China[e]	1.0	1.0
Total	241.5	239.9

Manganese Ore[c] (thousand metric tons)

	1973	1974
USSR	8,245	[e]8,500
South Africa	4,176	3,745
Gabon	1,919	2,138
Brazil	2,157	[e]1,800
Australia	1,522	1,522
India	1,535	1,447
China[e]	1,000	1,000
Mexico	364	403
Zaire	334	309
Ghana	318	[e]300
Morocco	146	175
Japan	189	167
Other countries[a]	329	372
Total	22,234	21,878

Mercury (76-pound flasks)

	1973	1974
Spain	60,076	[e]60,200
USSR[e]	52,000	54,000
China[e]	26,000	26,000
Italy	32,692	24,950
Mexico	21,640	[e]21,200
Yugoslavia	15,606	15,838
Canada[g]	12,500	14,000
Algeria	13,300	[e]13,300
Turkey	8,439	[e]8,400
Czechoslovakia	6,991	[e]7,100
Other countries[a]	19,021	17,298
Total	268,265	262,286

Molybdenum[b] (metric tons)

	1973	1974
United States	52,553	50,807
Canada	13,785	13,428
Chile	5,885	9,757
USSR[e]	8,500	8,800
China[e]	1,500	1,500
Other countries[a]	1,314	1,109
Total	83,537	85,401

Nickel, mine[b] (thousand metric tons)

	1973	1974
Canada	249.0	271.8
USSR[e]	115.0	125.0
New Caledonia	109.3	129.6
Australia	40.2	40.4
Cuba[e]	32.0	32.0
Dominican Republic	30.1	[e]30.0
Greece	26.3	25.0
Indonesia	19.4	[e]21.4
South Africa	20.8	[e]21.0
United States	16.6	15.1
Rhodesia	11.8	12.0
Other countries[a]	18.4	28.7
Total	688.9	752.0

Petroleum, crude (million barrels)

	1973	1974
USSR	3,094	3,374
United States	3,361	3,203
Saudi Arabia	2,773	3,096
Iran	2,139	2,211
Venezuela	1,229	1,086
Kuwait	1,102	930
Nigeria	750	823
Iraq	737	680
Canada	648	617
Libya	794	555
United Arab Emirates[h]	559	616

Petroleum, crude (cont'd) (million barrels)

	1973	1974
Indonesia	489	502
China[e]	365	475
Algeria	401	373
Mexico	191	238
Qatar	208	189
Argentina	154	151
Australia	142	141
Rumania	107	108
Oman	107	106
Other countries[a]	1,018	1,042
Total	20,368	20,516

Phosphate Rock (thousand metric tons)

	1973	1974
United States	38,226	41,446
USSR	21,250	22,540
Morocco	17,077	19,721
Tunisia	3,473	3,823
China[e]	3,000	3,000
Togo	2,292	2,572
Nauru	2,323	2,288
Senegal	1,752	1,877
Christmas Island	1,538	1,764
South Africa	1,365	1,352
Jordan	1,106	1,595
North Vietnam[e]	500	1,200
Israel	781	951
Other countries[a]	4,098	6,129
Total	98,781	110,258

Potash (thousand metric tons of K_2O equivalent)

	1973	1974
USSR	5,900	[e]6,100
Canada	4,454	5,508
East Germany	2,556	2,865
West Germany	2,548	2,620
United States	2,361	2,513
France	2,262	2,276
Other countries[a]	1,961	1,984
Total	22,042	23,866

Pyrite[c] (thousand metric tons)

	1973	1974
USSR[e]	8,200	8,500
Spain	2,401	2,600
China[e]	2,000	2,000
Japan	1,275	1,286
Italy	1,169	1,168
Rumania[e]	870	870
Finland	777	722
Norway	792	664
Portugal	532	511
South Africa	551	511
Morocco	407	509
North Korea[e]	500	500
Greece	430	500
Sweden	450	[e]450
United States	568	431
West Germany	428	[e]430
Other countries[a]	1,941	1,988
Total	23,291	23,640

Salt (million metric tons)

	1973	1974
United States	39.86	42.11
China[e]	18.00	18.00
USSR	12.20	12.50
West Germany	10.20	10.98
United Kingdom	8.37	[e]8.40
India	6.86	[e]6.34
France	5.78	6.00
Italy	4.87	[e]5.21
Canada	5.05	5.17
Australia	4.06	[e]4.80
Mexico	4.32	[e]4.30
Rumania	3.30	3.92
Netherlands	3.04	3.39
Poland	3.08	3.30
East Germany	2.29	[e]2.40
Other countries[a]	20.13	15.45
Total	151.41	152.27

Silver, mine (million troy ounces)

	1973	1974
Canada	47.49	43.76
USSR[e]	41.00	42.00
Peru	42.02	41.00
Mexico	38.79	37.55
United States	37.83	33.76
Australia	22.42	21.62
Japan	8.55	7.31
Chile	5.04	6.65
Poland[e]	4.80	6.00
Bolivia	5.80	5.38
Yugoslavia	4.30	4.70
Sweden	4.69	[e]4.50
Honduras	3.15	3.66
Spain	3.64	[e]3.60

Silver, mine (cont'd) (million troy ounces)

	1973	1974
France	4.18	[e]3.33
Other countries[a]	35.23	32.41
Total	308.93	297.23

Sulfur, all forms[i] (thousand metric tons)

	1973	1974
United States	10,397	11,602
USSR[e]	8,050	8,300
Canada	8,127	7,953
Poland[e]	3,540	4,310
Mexico	1,672	2,387
France	1,956	1,950
Japan	1,266	1,362
Spain	1,241	1,319
China[e]	1,150	1,150
Italy[e]	905	890
Iraq	535	[e]850
Finland	817	791
West Germany	642	725
Iran	568	[e]700
Other countries[a]	4,675	5,067
Total	45,541	49,356

Tin, mine[b] (thousand long tons)

	1973	1974
Malaysia	71.1	67.0
USSR[e]	29.0	29.5
Bolivia	29.8	29.0
Indonesia	21.9	24.6
Thailand	20.6	20.0
China[e]	20.0	20.0
Australia	10.1	10.0
Nigeria	5.7	5.4
Other countries[a]	24.2	22.1
Total	232.4	227.6

Titanium materials[c,i] (thousand metric tons)

Ilmenite	1973	1974
Norway	750	848
Australia	719	825
United States	721	670
Malaysia	185	[e]190
Finland	159	152
Other countries[a]	183	179
Total ilmenite	2,717	2,864
Rutile		
Australia	326	322
Other countries[a]	14	12
Total rutile	340	334
Titaniferous slag		
Canada	855	845
Japan	4	4
Total titaniferous slag	859	849

Tungsten, mine[b] (metric tons)

	1973	1974
China[e]	8,000	8,500
USSR[e]	7,400	7,600
United States	3,936	3,348
South Korea	2,252	3,078
Thailand	2,602	2,204
North Korea[e]	2,150	2,150
Bolivia	1,934	2,028
Portugal	1,513	1,488
Canada	1,669	1,275
Australia	1,298	[e]1,100
Brazil	995	[e]1,000
Other countries[a]	5,152	4,593
Total	38,901	38,364

Uranium Oxide (U_3O_8)[b,i] (metric tons)

	1973	1974
United States	12,007	10,458
Canada	4,317	4,265
South Africa	3,094	3,074
France	1,917	[e]2,000
Niger	949	1,118
Gabon	646	773
Other countries[a]	323	245
Total	23,253	21,933

Zinc, smelter (thousand metric tons)

	1973	1974
Japan	843	850
USSR[e]	670	680
United States	529	504
Canada	533	426
Belgium	281	294
Australia	297	277
France	259	277
West Germany	241	250
Poland	235	233
Italy	182	196
North Korea[e]	130	132
Spain	107	129
China	100	100
Finland	81	92
Yugoslavia	63	86
United Kingdom	84	84
Bulgaria	80	84
Other countries[a]	589	720
Total	5,304	5,414

[a] Estimated in part. [b] Content of ore. [c] Gross weight. [d] Includes anthracite, bituminous coal, and lignite. [e] Estimate. [f] Marketable. [g] Output of Cominco only, excludes production (if any) by minor producers. [h] Abu Dhabi and Dubai. [i] Includes (1) Frasch process sulfur, (2) elemental sulfur mined by conventional methods, (3) by-product-recovered elemental sulfur, and (4) recovered sulfur content of pyrite and other sulfide ores. [j] Excludes output (if any) by Albania, Bulgaria, China, Czechoslovakia, East Germany, Hungary, North Korea, Mongolia, Poland, Rumania, the USSR, and North Vietnam.

International Bauxite Association (IBA), there were proposals for the formation of groups for iron ore, mercury, silver, tungsten, and zinc. In the case of mercury, the effort went as far as the convening of the First International Mercury Congress in 1974 and subsequent follow-up meetings in 1975.

Ferrous Ores and Metals. Preliminary information available suggests that 1975 world iron-ore output was only slightly greater than the 903.5 million metric-ton level of 1974. Part-year 1975 returns for several major producers, including most notably the United States and Canada, suggested declines in output by these countries. Similarly, it was expected that final 1975 returns would show no substantial change in output levels over those of 1974 for ferro-alloying metals such as manganese, chromite, and tungsten. World steel output in 1975 was estimated at about 710 million metric tons, a very small increase over the 1974 total. Developed-market-economy countries registered a small decline as a group, while the centrally-planned-economy countries and developing-market-economy countries increased output sufficiently to raise the world total slightly.

Nonferrous Ores and Metals. As in the case of ferrous metals, world production of most nonferrous metals and ores distinctly slowed in the early months of 1975. Incomplete returns suggested that world totals for aluminum, copper, lead, tin, and zinc would be only marginally up from those registered for 1974, whether measured in terms of mine production or smelter output.

Detailed statistics on 1975 mercury output were not available, but the existence of substantial stocks in major producing nations such as Italy and Spain undoubtedly were a deterrent to increased production in the western nations. Another factor that contributed to unsatisfactory 1975 market conditions was the release in 1974 of significant quantities of mercury from the USSR on European, Japanese, and Western Hemisphere markets and the apparent existence of even more substantial quantities of this commodity for export from the USSR.

A fairly substantial increase in nickel output was expected for 1975. This was predicated upon the anticipated completion of some additional facilities and increased output from other recently completed installations.

Precious Metals. World output of both gold and silver registered declines in 1974 from 1973, despite high prices for these metals, and the outlook for significant output increases in 1975 seemed dim. In the case of gold, new mines were opening and under development, but it seemed unlikely that their output would be sufficient to compensate for production declines elsewhere. The chances of increased silver production were lessened, primarily because copper and lead production increased only slightly. Their ores are major sources of silver as a by-product.

World platinum production totaled about 5.7 million troy ounces in 1974, with the Republic of South Africa and the Soviet Union together accounting for over 90% of the total.

Fertilizer Materials. Despite optimistic forecasts by industry in the waning months of 1974 of expanding demand for nitrogen, phosphate, rock, and potash, market conditions for these materials were relatively poor through the first three quarters of 1975. New phosphate and potash mines under development seemed destined to contribute to a substantial surplus of stocks unless sales picked up or new developments were curtailed.

Miscellaneous. A lengthy strike in the Canadian asbestos industry sharply curtailed output of that commodity in the nation that led the world in asbestos production in 1974. Undoubtedly, 1975 output in the USSR, the second largest producer in 1974, topped that of Canada in 1975. The Canadian strike resulted in a very tight supply situation in developed-market-economy countries.

Part-year returns on cement output for 1975 suggested that output of this most important construction commodity declined in most developed-market-economy nations and that gains in other countries may not have been sufficient for the world total to top the 704.2 million metric-ton level of 1974. The lower output levels among the developed-market-economy nations presumably were the result of reduced construction that stemmed from recessionary economic trends. The cement industry situation was probably also reflected in reduced world gypsum output, but little firm 1975 production data were available.

World natural diamond output in 1975 probably closely approximated the 44.1 million carat level of 1974. This natural diamond supply was supplemented by the production of manufactured diamonds in several countries. In the United States alone, manufactured diamond output was estimated at 17 million carats in 1973 and presumably exceeded that level in both 1974 and 1975. Most of the natural diamond production and virtually all of the manufactured diamond output was destined for industrial use rather than for jewelry applications.

World sulfur output was expected to register growth again in 1975, although the amount of the increase over the 1974 level remained in doubt. Continued growth in by-product output was virtually assured, because increasing pressures in many nations for reduced atmospheric and water pollution led to increased sulfur recovery from coal, oil, and nonferrous metal operations. Growth in production was expected in Poland, where Frasch recovery has been under way for several years, and in Iraq, a relatively new major producer. (See also ENERGY.)

CHARLES L. KIMBELL
Office of Technical Data Services
U. S. Bureau of Mines

MINNESOTA

Once again in 1975 weather-caused disasters in Minnesota took a heavy toll in property damage. Strikes also marred the economic scene. The legislature took steps to ease the effects of the nationwide recession.

Weather. On January 10–12 a blizzard labeled by the National Weather Service as the state's worst winter storm of the century struck central Minnesota. It left in its wake 35 storm-related deaths and losses of more than $14 million in livestock and buildings. A windstorm that swept through the suburbs north of the Twin Cities of Minneapolis and St. Paul on May 19 caused property damage of $5.1 million.

On July 17, President Gerald R. Ford declared 10 counties and part of another, all in the Red River valley, a major disaster area following extensive flooding by rain storms that began on June 28. There was an estimated $300 million in damages to crops, especially sugar beets, and other property from the floods. An August drought in southwestern and west-central Minnesota was responsible for losses of some $57 million in corn crops.

Economy. As a result of poor growing conditions in 1974, together with lower crop prices, farm income in the state fell sharply for the period of January–May 1975, almost $261 million below the comparable period for 1974. A series of strikes in the basic building trades from May through July interrupted highway, heavy, and building construction in Minnesota, affecting more than 15,000 workers.

The fiscal position of the state remained strong, with a surplus in its treasury of over $400 million reported in July. Gov. Wendell Anderson, who traveled widely during the year, made visits to the USSR and China in an effort to encourage trade exchanges between these nations and Minnesota.

The Environment. Little progress was made in the course of the year in the dispute between the state and the Reserve Mining Company over the discharge of asbestos-laden wastes from taconite mining into Lake Superior at Silver Bay. The 8th Circuit Court of Appeals had set no timetable in 1974 when it ordered Reserve to take "reasonable" steps to remedy the threat to health posed by the dumping of tailings into Lake Superior and the emission of fibers into the air. The state therefore asked the U. S. Supreme Court to intervene, but on March 31 it refused. Proposals for on-land disposal of the wastes were under discussion between state environmental agencies and the company at the end of the year.

In other environmental matters the legislature acted to ban the sale of pop-top cans starting in 1977. It also added $40 million to the state's $55 million program of matching funds for the construction of municipal sewage treatment facilities.

Legislative Action. There were several major components of the state legislature's $5 billion budget for 1975–77. Appropriations for school aid were $1.59 billion (the largest single spending bill in the state's history); for health, welfare, and corrections, $586.2 million; for higher education and the state Department of Education, $537 million; and for other state departments, $352.5 million.

A $122 million spending program for highways and public transit was coupled to a rise in the state tax on gasoline from 7 to 9 cents a gallon. This was the only new general tax levied during the session. In addition, more than $200 million in property-tax relief was promised. The tax bill provided for credits to homeowners and renters under a formula linking property taxes to household income. The state also took over 90% of county welfare costs and increased state aid to local governments in order to reduce further the demands on property taxes.

Among other acts passed by the 1975 legislature were a weak hand-gun control law. Other legislation changed the designation of the seven state colleges to universities and appropriated $19.5 million for the purchase of parks and recreational land throughout the state.

The murder of two inmates by fellow prisoners, riots, and reports of drug traffic at Stillwater State Prison triggered a legislative inquiry into the operations of the Minnesota Corrections Department. At year's end a departmental reorganization was under way.

Indian Affairs. The Regional Native American Center of Minneapolis opened on May 7. The first of its kind in the United States, it combines under one roof social, recreational, and cultural services for Indians in Minnesota and surrounding states.

Election. On November 4 in Minneapolis former mayor Charles Stenvig, an Independent, narrowly defeated the incumbent mayor, Albert Hofstede of the Democratic-Farmer-Labor party. Stenvig had a conservative reputation, while Hofstede was generally considered liberal.

JEANNE SINNEN
University of Minnesota Press

MINNESOTA · Information Highlights

Area: 84,068 square miles (217,736 sq km).
Population (1974 est.): 3,917,000. *Density:* 47 per sq mi.
Chief Cities (1970 census): St. Paul, the capital, 309,828; Minneapolis, 434,400.
Government (1975): *Chief Officers*—governor, Wendell R. Anderson (D); lt. gov., Rudy Perpich (D). *Legislature*—Senate, 67 members; House of Representatives, 134 members.
Education (1974–75): *Enrollment*—public elementary schools, 437,618 pupils; public secondary, 451,917; nonpublic, 107,600; colleges and universities, 187,230 students. *Public school expenditures,* $1,045,612,-000 ($1,246 per pupil).
State Finances (fiscal year 1974): *Revenues,* $3,043,-538,000; *expenditures,* $2,780,101,000.
Personal Income (1974): $21,346,000,000; per capita, $5,450.
Labor Force (Aug. 1975): *Nonagricultural wage and salary earners,* 1,477,200; *insured unemployed,* 47,100.

Gov. William Waller made extensive efforts during 1975 to attract new industry to Mississippi, including leading trade missions to the Middle East.

MISSISSIPPI

The economy, the legislature, and the quadrennial state and local elections highlighted the news in Mississippi in 1975.

The Economy. For much of the year, the economy was characterized by decline. By summer's end, however, the unemployment rate had begun to drop, and there were other signs that a slow recovery was underway. Nevertheless, the dominant mood remained one of caution.

The Legislature. Despite downward economic trends, the election-year legislature approved a record-high budget for fiscal 1975–76. Balanced by taking funds from the state's declining surplus rather than by increasing taxes, the budget contained within its $61 million increase a $22 million pay hike for schoolteachers.

In other actions, the legislature established an open-meetings policy for public bodies, passed a bill calling for educational accountability, and enacted several election reforms.

Redistricting. In orders issued June 25 and July 11, a three-judge panel headed by J. P. Coleman of the Fifth U. S. Circuit Court of Appeals imposed a "temporary" seating plan for the 1975 legislative elections. Modifying a limited reapportionment scheme fashioned by the legislature earlier in the year, the panel ordered single-member districts for populous Harrison, Hinds, and Jackson counties; fractured some former districts; and straddled county lines for the first time. The legislature's plan had been challenged primarily on grounds that it diluted black voting strength.

Elections. Although Republicans made their strongest challenge since Reconstruction years, Democrats maintained their hold on all statewide offices in the November 4 elections and continued to dominate legislative and local posts. In the race for governor, Charles C. "Cliff" Finch received 52% of the almost 700,000 votes cast to defeat issue-oriented Republican Gil Carmichael (45%) and black independent Henry J. Kirksey (3%). Finch was a Batesville attorney and self-styled "workingman's candidate" who had overcome Lt. Gov. William Winter in the Democratic primary runoff. For the first time, race was not an issue in the contest, since both Finch and Carmichael actively courted black voters. Evelyn Gandy, state insurance commissioner and veteran officeholder, easily defeated her Republican opponent, becoming the first woman in the state to be elected lieutenant governor.

Republicans entered 40 legislative races but won only 5 seats, 4 of which were held by incumbents. At the local level, they captured 2 of 69 offices they sought. Blacks won 4 legislative posts including 1 held by an incumbent, gained political control of Claiborne and Jefferson counties, and elected a number of county and county-district officials.

Other Events. During the summer and fall, an outbreak of encephalitis claimed the lives of approximately 40 persons, most of whom were elderly and infirm. First detected in Greenville, in Washington county, the mosquito-transmitted disease spread to some 60% of the state's 82 counties.

In April and October Gov. William Waller led trade missions to Iran, Iraq, Kuwait, and Saudi Arabia. In August, a high-ranking delegation from Kuwait visited Mississippi.

DANA B. BRAMMER
University of Mississippi

--- **MISSISSIPPI · Information Highlights** ---

Area: 47,716 square miles (123,584 sq km).
Population (1974 est.): 2,324,000. *Density:* 48 per sq mi.
Chief Cities (1970 census): Jackson, the capital, 153,-968; Biloxi, 48,486; Meridian, 45,083.
Government (1975): *Chief Officers*—governor, William L. Waller (D); lt. gov., William F. Winter (D). *Legislature*—Senate, 52 members; House of Representatives, 122 members.
Education (1974–75): *Enrollment*—public elementary schools, 289,164 pupils; public secondary, 224,312; nonpublic, 62,200; colleges and universities, 87,167 students. *Public school expenditures,* $352,059,000 ($716 per pupil).
State Finances (fiscal year 1974): *Revenues,* $1,470,666,-000; *expenditures,* $1,395,240,000.
Personal Income (1974): $8,747,000,000; per capita, $3,764.
Labor Force (Aug. 1975): *Nonagricultural wage and salary earners,* 678,400; *insured unemployed,* 27,400.

MISSOURI

Investigations into political contributions made by private business marked a year dominated by government action and court decisions. A continuing investigation into the administration of former Gov. Warren E. Hearnes (1965–73) concentrated on the role of banks in political decision making. Three bank executives were indicted by a federal grand jury in Kansas City and two former bank presidents, Ray Evans and James Brown, both of Kansas City, subsequently pleaded guilty to misapplying bank funds for political purposes. The third, Donald Lasater, president of the state's largest bank, Mercantile Trust Co. of St. Louis, was acquitted following an indictment for perjury for testimony given before a grand jury investigating stock transactions and political contributions.

Two other potentially significant investigations were begun. One, by the Public Service Commission, concerned political contributions by Southwestern Bell Telephone Co., and one by the attorney general's office looked into the lack of competitive bidding in many municipal insurance purchases.

State Government. In legislative developments, laws were enacted to reinstate the death penalty and to continue a sales tax in St. Louis and Kansas City to finance mass transit. Laws were tightened regulating lobbyists, and doctors were allowed to form an association to provide malpractice insurance. The state Senate rejected ratification of the Equal Rights Amendment after state House approval.

The state supreme court upheld the state's senatorial districts, which had been found by a lower circuit court not to be as compact as possible. In politics, Sen. Stuart Symington and Rep. William Hungate announced they would retire from Congress at the end of their present terms.

Court Decisions. A challenge to the state's new abortion law was accepted for arguments by the U.S. Supreme Court. A federal district court had previously upheld some portions of it and overturned others.

WALKER—MISSOURI TOURISM

Historic keel boat nears Rocheport, which will stage an early 19th-century political convention in 1976 as part of Missouri's Bicentennial celebrations.

Environmentalists lost early court challenges seeking to halt construction of the $100,000,000 Meramec Basin project and a nuclear power plant by Union Electric. They did, however, succeed in delaying construction of a new dam and locks on the Mississippi River at Alton, Ill. Appeals were filed in higher courts in each of these cases. In the Meramec case, the Indiana bat, which hibernates in caves along the Meramec River and is protected by the Endangered Species Act, was being used as a tactic to stop construction of dams on the river.

The American Civil Liberties Union said in a federal suit that conditions at the state penitentiary constituted cruel and unusual punishment. Another jolt to the prison system came when Carolyn Atkins, superintendent of the Tipton Correction Center for Women, was stabbed and seriously wounded by an inmate.

Artists. Thomas Hart Benton, known nationally for his paintings, died. (See also OBITUARIES.) Interest in another Missouri artist, George Caleb Bingham, was resurrected, when the Mercantile Library of St. Louis announced that 117 of his sketches owned by the library would be put up for sale. A citizens' committee led by Gov. Christopher Bond was trying to raise $1,800,000 to keep the sketches in Missouri.

RONALD D. WILLNOW
St. Louis "Post-Dispatch"

MISSOURI · Information Highlights

Area: 69,686 square miles (180,487 sq km).

Population (1974 est.): 4,777,000. *Density:* 69 per sq mi.

Chief Cities (1970 census): Jefferson City, the capital, 32,407; St.Louis, 622,236.

Government (1975): *Chief Officers*—governor, Christopher S. Bond (R); lt. gov., William C. Phelps (R). *General Assembly*—Senate, 34 members; House of Representatives, 163 members.

Education (1974–75): *Enrollment*—public elementary schools, 541,709 pupils; public secondary, 459,996; nonpublic, 96,000; colleges and universities, 200,717 students, *Public school expenditures,* $859,486,000 ($942 per pupil).

State Finances (fiscal year 1974): *Revenues,* $2,261,942,-000; *expenditures,* $2,049,510,000.

Personal Income (1974): $24,152,000,000; per capita, $5,056.

Labor Force (July 1975): *Nonagricultural wage and salary earners,* 1,726,200; *insured unemployed,* 73,-600 (5.0%).

UPI

President Gerald Ford (*right*) and Canadian energy minister Donald Macdonald jointly pull a switch while dedicating Montana's Libby Dam on August 24.

MONTANA

The 44th Montana Legislative Assembly was unique in several ways. An amendment to the 1972 Constitution replaced the 60-day annual session with the traditional biennial sessions of 90 days. All members had been elected from single member districts for the first time, including 13 women. The Democrats were in control of both the executive and legislative branches.

Taxation. The session made record general fund appropriations of $376 million but also predicted record surplus funds. A new coal tax changed the base from a 34 cents-per-ton tax, yielding $20.2 million, to a 20% value tax on lignite and 30% on higher quality coal, which would yield $68.8 million. The tax on natural gas was also changed from a quantity tax to 2.65% of the wellhead value, matching a similar tax on crude oil. The state gasoline tax was raised three-fourths of a cent per gallon to 7.75 cents per gallon.

Legislation. County commissioners were authorized to establish small claims courts to handle claims under $1,500. All real estate sale prices are to be reported to the state department of revenue. Public intoxication is to be treated as an illness rather than a crime. An office of

special judge to rule on workmen's compensation claims disputes was created. Two political scandals produced legislative action. First, financial support was appropriated for continuing an inquiry by the Republican attorney general into corrupt practices in the Workmen's Compensation division; and second, the newly established and relatively unfunded state educational television broadcasting system was abolished when charges of illegal action by officers were sustained.

At year's end, judicial decisions were still pending in two controversies. In one, the board of regents asked continued freedom to manage its allocated funds without detailed supervision from the department of the budget. In the other, several counties have contested the methods being used by the department of revenue in carrying out its constitutional mandate to supervise the revaluation of property every five years.

Special Session. A special one-day session of the legislature was called on August 4. It corrected the failure of the regular session to levy a routine six-mill property tax to raise $15.8 million for the university system.

Environment and Economics. Environmental and energy matters were highlighted by the completion and dedication of the Libby Dam on August 24 with President Ford and Canadian officials present. The dam will generate 854,000 kilowatts of power and will provide added water storage for the Columbia River system. Two major coal-powered electrical plants are near completion at Colstrip, and grand jury proceedings continue on a request by the Montana Power Co. for two additional plants. The Montana Major Siting Act is a new law regulating the erection of electrical energy plants.

Record precipitation resulted in favorable crop and range production, in spite of an alarming grasshopper infestation. Moderately high agricultural prices and continued high tourist spending contributed to favorable economic conditions.

MERRILL G. BURLINGAME
Montana State University

MONTANA · Information Highlights

Area: 147,138 square miles (381,087 sq km).
Population (1974 est.): 735,000. *Density:* 5 per sq mi.
Chief Cities (1970 census): Helena, the capital, 22,557; Billings, 61,581; Great Falls, 60,091.
Government (1975): *Chief Officers*—governor, Thomas L. Judge (D); lt. gov., W. E. Christiansen (D). *Legislature*—Senate, 50 members; House of Representatives, 100 members.
Education (1974–75): *Enrollment*—public elementary schools, 115,142 pupils; public secondary, 57,016; nonpublic, 10,000; colleges and universities, 28,092 students. *Public school expenditures,* $162,515,000 ($1,023 per pupil).
State Finances (fiscal year 1974): *Revenues,* $545,045,000; *expenditures,* $476,150,000.
Personal Income (1974): $3,511,000,000; per capita, $4,776.
Labor Force (July 1975): *Nonagricultural wage and salary earners,* 250,000; *insured unemployed,* 6,000 (2.4%).

MOROCCO

Unity was the political keynote for Morocco in 1975, and nationalist fervor culminated in a dramatic march by unarmed Moroccans into neighboring Spanish Sahara to claim the territory for their nation and their king, Hassan II.

Spanish Sahara. The march ended a year of diplomatic offensives coupled with saber-rattling, aimed at gaining control of Spanish Sahara, the phosphate-rich Spanish colony to Morocco's south. A Spanish-Moroccan agreement, arrived at as Spain's Generalissimo Francisco Franco lay dying, called on Spain to leave the colony by Feb. 28, 1976. Spain's $625-million investment in Spanish Sahara's phosphate mines was guaranteed, and provisions were made for the joint operation of the phosphate industry. The eastern and southern portions of the territory were to be ceded to Mauritania, which had also laid claim to the Sahara.

As 1975 drew to a close, it was difficult to say if the dispute had been resolved. Throughout the year, Morocco's militant neighbor Algeria had urged a referendum to allow the inhabitants the right to self-determination. Algeria's point of view was echoed by the United Nations and, early on, by the Organization of African Unity, and it caused at least two ruptures in the Spanish-Moroccan talks. Despite a provision in the final agreement for a referendum, to be held after the Spanish withdrawal, Algeria threatened to step up small-scale warfare between Moroccan troops and an Algeria-backed liberation group, Polisario. At the end of the year, it remained to be seen whether promising Algeria an outlet to the Atlantic Ocean through Sahara, which would make it commercially feasible to exploit iron-ore reserves in Algeria's westernmost region, would quiet Algerian objections to the settlement.

Morocco's King Hassan had been leaning toward a diplomatic solution to his Spanish Saharan claim early in 1975, when Spain was making clear its intention to leave its colony. Both Morocco and Mauritania sought to head off a Spanish referendum in the colony by taking their claim of historical ties to the region to the International Court of Justice at The Hague for a nonbinding opinion. But the World Court found no legal ties, although it conceded that some of the tribes of the Western Sahara had owed allegiance to Morocco and what is now Mauritania at the time of colonization by the Spanish. With this avenue closed to him, King Hassan revealed plans for a march into the desert. The march had probably been planned for months as a last alternative to force a conclusion to the Spanish Sahara question.

Politics. If the clouds of dust raised by the 350,000 enthusiastic, flag-waving, slogan-shouting men and women who marched into the Sahara on November 6 obscured conditions that had existed in Morocco during the year, King Hassan's intent may well have been satisfied. Hassan may have been trying to unite his people against an outside enemy as a substitute for confronting divisions at home. In a sense, the Saharan march was King Hassan's gamble that he could offer action even bolder than that demanded by the traditional opposition party, Istiqlal. On November 9, King Hassan called off the march, saying that it had fulfilled its goal, but rivalry for control of Spanish Sahara continued.

There were other diplomatic triumphs for King Hassan in 1975. In May, French President Valéry Giscard d'Estaing became the first French head of state to visit Rabat since Moroccan independence from France in 1956. In the aftermath of this historical reconciliation, Morocco more than doubled the amount of capital that could be repatriated by French residents leaving the North African nation. Giscard d'Estaing's visit, marked enthusiastically by Moroccans, followed by less than a month his first visit to Algeria. Some observers interpreted this to mean that France did not favor one nation's position on Spanish Sahara over another.

Economy. Morocco's economic performance in 1975 did not live up to the promise of 1974. By midyear it was announced that there would be a 40% cut in the phosphate production that had been planned for 1975. Overall production was to be 15 million tons, down from 20 million tons in 1974. Some analysts attributed the drop to world reaction against the sixfold price increase imposed since 1973 by the Moroccan phosphate monopoly, which dominates the international market. Control of Saharan phosphates would raise Morocco's share of proven world phosphate-rock reserves from 56% to 66%. In addition to cutbacks in production, Morocco also began to cut published prices to compete with less expensive U. S. phosphates.

Agricultural production was down, with a sharply reduced summer grain harvest. The decline in production was caused by drought in the fall of 1974 and winter of 1975.

NANCY MCKEON
The African-American Institute

MOROCCO • Information Highlights

Official Name: Kingdom of Morocco.
Location: Northwest Africa.
Area: 172,413 square miles (446,550 sq km).
Population (1975 est.): 17,500,000.
Chief Cities (1973 est.): Rabat, the capital, 385,000; Casablanca, 2,000,000; Marrakesh, 330,000; Fez, 322,-000.
Government: *Head of state,* Hassan II, king (acceded 1961). *Head of government,* Ahmed Osman, premier (took office 1972).
Monetary Unit: Dirham (4.12 dirhams equal U. S.$1, Aug. 1975).
Gross National Product (1972 est.): $4,844,000,000.
Manufacturing (major products): Processed foods, metals, textiles, wine, cement, leather goods, chemicals and pharmaceuticals.
Major Agricultural Products: Barley, wheat, citrus fruits, vegetables, sugar beets, almonds, tomatoes, grapes, sheep, wool.
Foreign Trade (1974): *Exports,* $1,488,000,000; *imports,* $1,651,000,000.

Jaws, a thriller about the effects of a shark menace, became the top-grossing film in history and was one of the most costly to produce.

Motion Pictures

The biggest word in the Hollywood vocabulary for 1975 was *Jaws*. Within five months of its release in the United States and Canada, the thriller about a shark menace had realized $95 million at the box office to become the top grossing film in history. Distribution had not even begun in other countries. Even allowing for the rise in admission prices over the years, the record was impressive. Signs pointed to the phenomenon's having a profound effect on the course of the U. S. film industry.

Return to Big Budgets. Hollywood could be observed going back to its old habits. *Jaws* was dramatic proof that huge sums of money could be earned with blockbuster pictures. There had been similar indications with *The Exorcist, Earthquake,* and other films that had high-return potential on substantial budgets. The upheaval that had taken place earlier in the film industry had resulted in an almost miserly approach to picture making. Low budgets were in, expensive films out. When someone shouted "cut," he was more likely to be talking about budgets than about completing a scene before the cameras. But some producers began to take chances again, and the rich rewards of numerous triumphs, such as *The Godfather* and *The Godfather II,* have started the financial spiral upward again.

With this kind of thinking prevailing, the tendency was to make fewer pictures and to make them count. There was little inclination to make a small or daring film when a formula picture geared toward a mass audience could be successful. It was still too early to measure the ultimate effect of this trend. However, Hollywood loomed as tougher terrain than ever for the independent filmmaker with the specialized story and the serious or controversial subject.

Other Film Subjects. The film business has always been two-sided. While the above developments were taking place, the public was still being given a wide choice of viewing possibilities, particularly in the larger urban areas. Many of the major directors from the United States and other countries had pictures that opened in 1975. Robert Altman's sprawling, imaginative *Nashville* was one of the outstanding films of the year and quickly won accolades from critics. Stanley Kubrick, who works with the secrecy of national security when making a film, unveiled his latest, *Barry Lyndon,* in time for the holiday season. Michelangelo Antonioni's *The Passenger,* starring Jack Nicholson, was a favorite with buffs. Vittorio De Sica, one of the great modern directors, whose death left a void, came through glowingly with *A Brief Vacation,* dramatizing the problems of a woman. The belatedly released *Distant Thunder,* by Satyajit Ray of India, a unique, delicate film about the specter of famine, was hailed as a masterwork. Sidney Lumet's intensive *Dog Day Afternoon* had something to say about society's reactions to violent acts. John Huston's ambitious *The Man Who Would Be King,* based on the story by Rudyard Kipling, was another film for which he will be remembered.

Comedy. The need to laugh, even more pressing in times of mounting problems, was gratified with much excellent comedy. Woody Allen's *Love and Death,* imbued with sophisticated humor plus an insider's spoof of film genres, ranked high. *Smile,* Michael Ritchie's sharply satirical look at a Young American Miss beauty contest and the adults who run it, did honor to the tradition of entertaining social comment. The sublimely ridiculous *Monty Python and the Holy Grail* won advocates, as did *Hearts of the West,* a jaundiced glance at Hollywood in the 1930's. *Shampoo,* an audacious comedy starring Warren Beatty as a frantic Hollywood hairdresser, commented stylishly on the 1960's. Peter Sellers again demonstrated his drollery in *The Return of the Pink Panther.* Mike Nichols teamed with Warren Beatty and

Jack Nicholson in an odd period piece, *The Fortune,* but the picture was frail. Gene Wilder, director, actor, and screenwriter decided that Sherlock Holmes should have help, and filmed *The Adventure of Sherlock Holmes' Smarter Brother.*

Foreign Films. The sands shifted perceptibly on the foreign-language scene. Films from Germany, Switzerland, and other countries competed increasingly for attention with those from France and Italy. A renaissance is under way in Germany, as enthusiastic filmmakers try to pick up on the creative level that existed before the Hitler period. *The Mystery of Kasper Hauser* was a success at both the Cannes and New York Film Festivals. *The First Right of Freedom,* a homosexual drama, and *The Lost Honor of Katharina Blum,* an exposé of gutter journalism, were other outstanding films from Germany. *The Middle of the World, The Invitation,* and *The Wonderful Crook* were three striking examples of activity by Swiss filmmakers. *Xala,* a tale of changing patterns in emerging nations, reflects movement in Third World countries and was filmed in Senegal. Finland contributed *The Earth Is a Simple Song.*

France persisted as the major foreign source. François Truffaut's *The Story of Adele H.* vividly conveyed the obsessive love of Victor Hugo's daughter for a soldier who had rejected her. Louis Malle plunged into a world of fantasy with *Black Moon.* Costa-Gavras bared the story of French collaboration in illegal special courts during the Nazi occupation in *Special Section. Le Secret* hauntingly portrayed man's battle against the omnipotent forces of authority. All of these films were caught in the shrinking market for imports.

Nostalgia. No longer a special fad, nostalgia was well-entrenched as an ingredient for many films not relying primarily on that approach. In 1975, however, many filmmakers were using nostalgia as the major theme. *Hester Street* was most striking, waxing nostalgic over the turn-of-the century period of immigration. This low-budget, independent film made by Joan Micklin Silver starred a largely unknown cast. The most disastrous example of nostalgia was Peter Bogdanovich's 1930's-style musical *At Long Last Love,* venomously criticized and ill-fated at the box office. *Farewell, My Lovely* successfully revived the old Raymond Chandler mystery with Robert Mitchum as star. An attempt to re-create the 1930's in Los Angeles with the filming of F. Scott Fitzgerald's *The Day of the Locust* had only tepid results.

Documentaries. The most controversial documentary, *Hearts and Minds,* grappled with the meaning of the Vietnam War. Director Peter Davis probed U. S. involvement in search of effects on Vietnam and on life in the United States. The picture won an Oscar, but also evoked a torrent of protest when an acceptance speech by the producer aroused the ire of some

Motion Picture Academy spokesmen. Shirley MacLaine, who was invited to China, tried to capture the highpoints of what she found in her controversial documentary *The Other Half of the Sky: A China Memoir. Broken Treaty at Battle Mountain,* which Robert Redford took pains to support and promote, delved into resistance by Indians to takeovers of their land. The Depression years were recalled in *Brother Can You Spare a Dime?,* a jaunty collection of film clips that conveyed events and personalities of those traumatic years. Orson Welles created an off-beat documentary, *F for Fake,* intertwining the lives of literary hoaxer Clifford Irving with art forger Elmyr de Hory, and Welles playfully added a hoax of his own. Documentary filmmakers seemed willing to undertake subjects with potential for stirring arguments, but audience resistance to fact films continued.

Pornography. For the first time the New York Film Festival scheduled a hard-core sex film. *Exhibition,* a French import, was invited, and the step helped to legitimatize the genre. In France such films were being shown openly in commercial theaters for the first time. Would-be censors in the United States did not give up their battle to block film pornography, but despite a patchwork of pro and con court decisions, the manufacture, showing, and distribution of such pictures continued. *The New York Times* published accounts of alleged Mafia involvement in the lucrative industry. The legal questions remained a tangle that left room for years of litigation.

Violence. Anger grew at the proliferation of violence in films. Richard Heffner, director of the rating board of the Motion Picture Association of America, leaned toward more stringent ratings for violent content. The plethora of killing, maiming, and torture encompassed major films as well as the exploitation quickies. *Rollerball,* about a deadly futuristic sport, came in for its share of condemnation. Another type of criticism was heard from protesters against the killing or injuring of animals in the making of films. No sign of any letup in violence was discernible in a year of competition to make films more sensational. The success of *Jaws* was one measure of public response to violent death as a form of entertainment.

People. Jack Nicholson moved toward becoming one of the most charismatic of superstars with his tour de force in *One Flew Over the Cuckoo's Nest.* Ellen Burstyn emerged as a major star by winning an Oscar for *Alice Doesn't Live Here Anymore,* a much praised, and also much-criticized, film about a woman's struggle to find her way in life. Lina Wertmuller further solidified her place as the world's most acclaimed woman director with *Swept Away,* a political love story from Italy. Art Carney was a surprise winner of the Oscar for his 1974 performance in *Harry and Tonto.* Francis Ford Coppola became one of the most powerful

Jack Nicholson became a favorite among movie buffs in 1975 with his charismatic role in *The Passenger*, in which he played a newsman in Africa who switches identities with a dead man.

METRO-GOLDWYN-MAYER-INC.

Art Carney (*left*) won the Oscar for best actor in *Harry and Tonto*, and Francis Ford Coppola won a total of three Oscars for his *Godfather II* in 1975.

WARNER BROS. INC.   UPI

Kris Kristofferson co-starred with Ellen Burstyn in *Alice Doesn't Live Here Anymore*. Burstyn won an Oscar for her role as a woman trying to define her role in life.

NOTABLE MOTION PICTURES OF 1975

The following list of films released in the United States in 1975 presents a cross section of the most popular, most typical, or most widely discussed motion pictures of the year.

The Adventure of Sherlock Holmes' Smarter Brother. Director, Gene Wilder; screenplay, Wilder. With Wilder, Madeline Kahn.

Alice Doesn't Live Here Anymore. Director, Martin Scorsese; screenplay, Robert Getchell. With Ellen Burstyn, Kris Kristofferson, Diane Ladd.

At Long Last Love. Director, Peter Bogdanovich; screenplay, Peter Bogdanovich; music and lyrics, Cole Porter. With Burt Reynolds, Cybill Shepherd, Madeline Kahn.

Barry Lyndon. Director, Stanley Kubrick; screenplay, Kubrick, based on novel by William Makepeace Thackeray. With Ryan O'Neal, Marisa Berenson.

Bite the Bullet. Director, Richard Brooks; screenplay, Brooks. With Gene Hackman, Candice Bergen, James Coburn, Ben Johnson.

Black Moon. Director, Louis Malle; screenplay, Malle, Ghislain Uhry and Joyce Brunuel. With Carolyn Harrison, Theresa Giehse, Alexandra Stewart, Joe Dallesandro.

A Brief Vacation. Director, Vittorio De Sica; screenplay, Cesare Zavattini. With Florinda Bolkan, Daniel Quenaud, Adriana Asti, Renalto Salvatori.

Conduct Unbecoming. Director, Michael Anderson; screenplay, Robert Enders from the play by Barry England. With Michael York, Richard Attenborough, Trevor Howard, Stacy Keach.

Coonskin (animation). Director, Ralph Bakshi; screenplay, Bakshi. With Barry White, Charles Gordone, Scat Man Crothers, Philip Thomas.

The Day of the Locust. Director, John Schlesinger; screenplay, Waldo Salt from a novel by Nathanael West. With Karen Black, William Atherton, Donald Sutherland, Burgess Meredith.

Distant Thunder. Director, Satyajit Ray; screenplay, Ray. With Soumitra Chatterji, Babita, Sandhya Roy.

Dog Day Afternoon. Director, Sidney Lumet; screenplay, Frank Pierson from an article by P. F. Kluge and Thomas Moore. With Al Pacino, John Cazale, James Broderick, Charles Durning.

Farewell, My Lovely. Director, Dick Richards; screenplay, David Zelag Goodman from the novel by Raymond Chandler. With Robert Mitchum, Charlotte Rampling, John Ireland, Sylvia Miles.

F for Fake. Director, Orson Welles; screenplay, Welles. With Welles, Clifford Irving, Elmyr de Hory, Edith Irving, Joseph Cotten.

The Fortune. Director, Mike Nichols; screenplay, Adrien Joyce. With Stockard Channing, Warren Beatty, Jack Nicholson, Florence Stanley.

The Four Musketeers. Director, Richard Lester; screenplay, George MacDonald Fraser, suggested by *The Three Musketeers* by Alexandre Dumas. With Oliver Reed, Faye Dunaway, Raquel Welch, Michael York.

French Connection II. Director, John Frankenheimer; screenplay, Robert and Laurie Dillon and Alexander Jacobs. With Gene Hackman, Fernando Rey, Bernard Fresson, Jean-Pierre Castaldi.

Funny Lady. Director, Herbert Ross; screenplay, Arnold Shulman and Jay Presson Allen. With Barbra Streisand, James Caan, Omar Sharif.

Give 'Em Hell, Harry. Directors, Peter H. Hunt and Steve Binder; screenplay, Samuel Gallu. With James Whitmore.

The Great Waldo Pepper. Director, George Roy Hill; screenplay, William Goldman from the story by Hill. With Robert Redford, Bo Svenson, Bo Brundin, Susan Sarandon.

Hard Times. Director, Walter Hill; screenplay, Hill, Bryan Gindorff, Bruce Henstell from story by Gindorff, Henstell. With Charles Bronson, James Coburn, Jill Ireland, Strother Martin.

Hearts of the West. Director, Howard Zeiff; screenplay, Rob Thompson. With Jeff Bridges, Andy Griffith, Donald Pleasence, Alan Arkin.

Hester Street. Director, Joan Micklin Silver; screenplay, Silver adapted from *Yekl*, by Abraham Cahan. With Steve Keats, Carol Kane, Mel Howard, Dorrie Kavanaugh.

The Invitation. Director, Claude Goretta; screenplay, Claude Goretta and Michel Viala. With Jean Luc Bideau, François Simon, Cecile Vassort.

Jaws. Director, Steven Spielberg; screenplay by Peter Benchley and Carl Gottlieb from the novel by Benchley. With Roy Scheider, Robert Shaw.

Love and Death. Director, Woody Allen; screenplay, Allen. With Woody Allen, Diane Keaton, Olga Georges-Picot, James Tolkan, Jessica Harper.

The Magic Flute. Director, Ingmar Bergman; opera by Mozart. With Josef Kostlinger, Irma Urrila, Hakan Hagegard, Elisabeth Erikson.

The Man Who Would Be King. Director, John Huston; screenplay, Huston, Gladys Hill, based on story by Rudyard Kipling. With Michael Caine, Sean Connery, Christopher Plummer.

Milestones. Directors, Robert Kramer and John Douglas; screenplay, Kramer and Douglas. With Mary Chapelle, Douglas, Kalaho, Lou Ho.

Monty Python and the Holy Grail. Directors, Terry Gilliam and Terry Jones; screenplay, Gilliam, Jones, Graham Chapman, John Cleese, Eric Idle, Michael Palin. With Chapman, Cleese, Gilliam, Idle, Jones, Palin.

The Mystery of Kasper Hauser. Director, Werner Herzog; screenplay, Herzog. With Bruno S., Walter Ladengast, Brigitte Mira.

Nashville. Director, Robert Altman; screenplay, Joan Tewksbury. With Karen Black, Ronee Blakley, Keith Carradine, Henry Gibson.

Night Moves. Director, Arthur Penn; screenplay, Alan Sharp. With Gene Hackman, Susan Clark, Jennifer Warren, Edward Binns.

Once Is Not Enough. Director, Guy Green; screenplay by Julius J. Epstein from the novel by Jacqueline Susann. With Kirk Douglas, Alexis Smith, David Janssen, Deborah Raffin.

One Flew Over the Cuckoo's Nest. Director, Milos Forman; screenplay, Lawrence Hauben, Bo Goldman based on novel by Ken Kesey. With Jack Nicholson, Louise Fletcher, William Redfield.

The Other Half of the Sky: A China Documentary. Director, Shirley MacLaine; documentary.

The Passenger. Director, Michelangelo Antonioni; screenplay, Antonioni, Mark Peploe, and Peter Wollen, based on a story by Peploe. With Jack Nicholson, Maria Schneider, Jenny Runacre.

The Return of the Pink Panther. Director, Blake Edwards; screenplay, Frank Waldman and Blake Edwards. With Peter Sellers, Christopher Plummer, Catherine Schell, Herbert Lom.

Rooster Cogburn and the Lady. Director, Stuart Millar; screenplay, Martin Julien, suggested by a character in a novel by Charles Portis. With Katharine Hepburn, John Wayne, Anthony Zerbe, Richard Jordan.

Royal Flash. Director, Richard Lester; screenplay, George MacDonald Fraser from his own novel. With Malcolm McDowell, Alan Bates, Florinda Bolkan, Oliver Reed, Britt Ekland.

Shampoo. Director, Hal Ashby; screenplay, Robert Towne and Warren Beatty. With Warren Beatty, Julie Christie, Goldie Hawn, Jack Warden.

Smile. Director, Michael Ritchie; screenplay, Jerry Belson. With Bruce Dern, Barbara Feldon, Michael Kidd, Geoffrey Lewis.

Special Section. Director, Costa-Gavras; screenplay, Jorge Semprun, Costa-Gavras based on works by Herve Villere. With Claude Pieplu, Jacques Perrin.

The Stepford Wives. Director, Bryan Forbes; screenplay, William Goldman based on book by Ira Levin. With Katharine Ross, Paula Prentiss, Peter Masterson, Nanette Newman, Patrick O'Neal.

The Story of Adele H. Director, François Truffaut; screenplay, Truffaut, Jean Gruault, and Suzanne Schiffman from "The Diary of Adele Hugo," edited by Frances V. Guille. With Isabelle Adjani, Bruce Robinson, Sylvia Marriott, Reubin Dorey.

The Sunshine Boys. Director, Herbert Ross; screenplay, Neil Simon from his stage play. With Walter Matthau, George Burns, Richard Benjamin.

Swept Away. Director, Lina Wertmuller; screenplay, Lina Wertmuller. With Mariangela Melato, Giancarlo Giannini.

Three Days of the Condor. Director, Sydney Pollack; screenplay, Lorenzo Semple, Jr., and David Rayfiel from the novel by James Grady. With Robert Redford, Faye Dunaway, Cliff Robertson, Max Von Sydow.

Tommy. Director, Ken Russell; screenplay, Ken Russell based on rock opera by The Who. With Roger Daltrey, Ann-Margret, Oliver Reed, Elton John.

The Wind and the Lion. Director, John Milius; screenplay, Milius. With Sean Connery, Candice Bergen, Brian Keith, John Huston.

W. W. and the Dixie Dance Kings. Director, John G. Avildsen; screenplay, Thomas Richman. With Burt Reynolds, Art Carney, Conny Van Dyke, Jerry Reed.

The Great Waldo Pepper, starring Robert Redford as a barnstorming pilot, was one of the early successes in 1975.

French Connection II, an action-packed sequel to French Connection, starred Gene Hackman and was an enormous success at the box office in 1975.

among the relatively new crop of directors because of his two *Godfather* triumphs. Steven Spielberg was much in demand as the young man who hit the jackpot directing *Jaws*.

Diana Ross proved her star-power at the box office for her role as a fashion designer in *Mahogany*, even though most critics dismissed the film as trite. Faye Dunaway gained new popularity in the aftermath of her Academy nomination (but not victory) for *Chinatown* and ventured a prediction that there would soon be more good roles for women to offset the continuing male domination of the screen. George Burns, at 79, played his first film character role and was hilarious as one of the two battling vaudevillians of *The Sunshine Boys*. Walter Matthau, as the other, garnered his share of laughs in Neil Simon's adaptation of his Broadway play.

Developments. An institution that offered much hope for breaking some of the traditional obstacles to wider dissemination of cultural attractions ran into crushing problems. The American Film Theatre (AFT) had been offering movie versions of significant plays. In 1975 one of its best was *In Celebration,* a British family-life drama directed by Lindsay Anderson. The AFT had instituted a subscription sale of tickets, but it charged that entrenched distributors would not permit individual theaters to interrupt other showings for two days of AFT fare. The matter went into litigation. AFT, however, abandoned its plans to make more films, at least temporarily, and put into general release its first year of subscription pictures.

More viewers were watching comparatively new films on their television sets. Home Box Office, a pay television system, won enthusiasts for its uninterrupted cable TV showings of pictures only recently out of first-run situations. The development signaled vast potential for increased film entertainment at home.

WILLIAM WOLF, *Film Critic, "Cue" Magazine*

MOZAMBIQUE

The People's Republic of Mozambique joined the community of independent African nations on June 25, 1975, when it became fully independent from Portugal. Mozambique is a nation in East Africa with a population of more than 9.2 million, including over 200,000 whites and Asians. It pursued a cautious foreign-relations policy, maintaining close ties with the USSR and China but also refusing to antagonize South Africa, its neighbor.

Background. Following political upheaval in Portugal in April 1974, the Mozambique Liberation Front (FRELIMO) had dramatically expanded its operations. On Sept. 7, 1974, it had obtained an agreement from Portugal recognizing it as the sole representative of the people of Mozambique. The date of independence was set for June 25, 1975, to coincide with the 13th anniversary of the founding of FRELIMO. The announcement of this agreement triggered a brief uprising by right-wing white settlers in Lourenço Marques that was suppressed within three days by the combined action of loyal Portuguese troops and FRELIMO militants.

Transitional Government. Under the newly-appointed Portuguese high commissioner, Adm. Victor Crespo, a transitional government including six FRELIMO and three Portuguese members took office on Sept. 20, 1974. The new government was immediately faced with serious economic problems arising in part from the disruption of the economy during the liberation struggle and from the massive outflow of capital and of skilled Europeans. Disastrous floods in the lower Limpopo Valley and the threat of famine in central and northern districts further complicated the situation during the early months of 1975, necessitating an airlift of emergency supplies by UN agencies.

Political Problems. FRELIMO concentrated on the political mobilization of the population, especially in those areas that had remained under Portuguese control during the liberation struggle. A major party conference was held in February 1975 at Mocuba in the central province of Zambezia. The fate of those Mozambicans who had either sided with the Portuguese or tried to compete with FRELIMO by organizing rival political formations was particularly difficult to handle. Several of these individuals were "persuaded" to make a public confession of their sins. Nevertheless, FRELIMO President Samora Machel decided to spare the lives of these dissenters as a gesture of national reconciliation.

New Government. The constitution of Mozambique was adopted by the FRELIMO Central Committee on June 20, and on June 25 Mozambique became officially independent under the presidency of Samora Machel. Machel was one of the founding members of FRELIMO and its military leader from the first days of the liberation struggle. The new government immedi-

Mozambique president-designate Samora Machel (*right*) is greeted June 23 on return from 13-year exile.

ately nationalized all health services, took over all private schools, and banned private law practice as a first step toward the establishment of a new legal and judiciary system. It also announced its intention to set up rural collectives on the Tanzanian model. In November, Mozambique was among the first countries to recognize Angola's MPLA government. On December 19 the government said it had suppressed a revolt.

Foreign Relations. Only six Western countries, including Great Britain, were represented at the independence celebrations, while those who had supported Portugal's colonial war, including the United States, were not invited. Mozambique has good relations with the Soviet Union and China, both of which had actively supported its struggle, but carefully avoided giving preferred treatment to either. The realism of Mozambique's foreign policy was further demonstrated by the decision not to sever economic relations with South Africa. These economic ties provide Mozambique with a vital source of foreign exchange in the form of compensation paid for Mozambican laborers employed in South Africa, and in the form of handling charges for South African trade shipped through the port of Lourenço Marques. On the other hand, Mozambique announced its intention to block shipments to or from Rhodesia normally handled through the port of Beira.

EDOUARD BUSTIN
Boston University

—— **MOZAMBIQUE · Information Highlights** ——

Official Name: People's Republic of Mozambique.
Location: East Africa.
Area: 302,328 square miles (783,029 sq km).
Population (1975 est.): 9,200,000.
Chief City (1973 est.): Lourenço Marques, the capital, 383,775.
Government: *Head of state,* Samora Machel (took office June 1975).
Gross National Product (1972 est.): $2,000,000,000.
Major Agricultural Products: Cashews, cotton, sugar, copra, tea.

Music

Moscow's Bolshoi Opera brought six Russian operas to the United States in 1975, including (*above*) *Eugene Onegin*. The tour was the first appearance in the United States of the Bolshoi Opera. Russian composer Dmitri Shostakovich (*below*) died on August 9.

The economic recession influenced classical and popular music in 1975. It was an active year in both areas, with new performances and performers receiving attention.

Classical Music

Classical music's perennial twin problems—artistic direction and financial support—intensified in 1975, but the news of most enduring significance was personal—the death on August 9 of Dmitri Shostakovich, at the age of 69.

Shostakovich. Since Igor Stravinsky's death in 1971, no living composer had rivaled Shostakovich in stature, although his outward acceptance of Soviet cultural dictates led to widespread misunderstanding of his music in the West, where his work was too often viewed in political terms. The painfully introverted Shostakovich turned inward in the face of periodic government harassment and, in the last decade of his life, progressive physical debility, but he remained productive to the end, leaving behind some half-dozen finished works unperformed.

Britten, Copland. There was more pleasant news of the two composers closest to Shostakovich in stature, the Englishman Benjamin Britten and Aaron Copland of the United States.

Britten had seemed permanently incapacitated by a stroke and complications suffered in 1973, but the 1975 Aldeburgh Festival offered

evidence of partial recovery. The festival, an annual event that Britten and his longtime friend and collaborator, tenor Peter Pears, operate at their home on the English seacoast, featured the premiere of two works written since the illness. *Canticle V: The Death of Saint Narcissus* was for tenor and harp, and a suite on English folk tunes was called *A Time There Was*. *Saint Narcissus* reached New York City as early as November, via the Chamber Music Society of Lincoln Center.

Health seemed no problem for Copland, who celebrated his 75th birthday on November 14. "To tell the truth," he said in a *Musical America* interview, "there's a certain air of unreality about it. I don't feel my age." Copland credited his good health in part to his greatly increased conducting activity since 1960, including the extensive "Copland Conducts Copland" series for Columbia Records.

Premieres. A wide range of music was heard for the first time in 1975. Dominick Argento's *From the Diary of Virginia Woolf* (mezzo-soprano Janet Baker and pianist Martin Isepp) was performed in Minneapolis, Minn., on Jan. 5, 1975, and later won the 1975 Pulitzer Prize for Music. Among the many other premieres were: Pierre Boulez' *Rituel* (Berkshire Music Center Orchestra under Gunther Schuller, August 14), Elliott Carter's *Duo* for Violin and Piano (Paul Zukofsky and Gilbert Kalish, New York City, March 21), Michael Colgrass' *Concertmasters* (Detroit Symphony under Aldo Ceccato, October 9), and Antal Dorati's piano concerto (Ilse von Alpenheim with the National Symphony under Dorati, October 28). Additional premieres included Alberto Ginastera's *Turbae ad Passionem Gregioranam* (Philadelphia Orchestra under Eugene Ormandy, March 20), George Rochberg's violin concerto (Isaac Stern with the Pittsburgh Symphony under Donald Johanos, April 4), and Roger Sessions' *Three Choruses on Biblical Texts* (at Amherst College, February 8).

Money and the Met. Nearly all performing institutions felt the dual impact of skyrocketing costs and inadequate revenues. Labor contracts became increasingly difficult to negotiate, and strikes and curtailed seasons became normal.

New York City's Metropolitan Opera, the most visible symbol of music's economic crisis, survived 1975 without a strike because of an agreement by its unions to extend their expired contracts through December 31. The Met's financial peril played a key role in the reorganization of the company's management. With Anthony Bliss named to the new post of executive director, general manager Schuyler Chapin lost much of his authority. When it was subsequently announced that principal conductor James Levine would become music director with full artistic authority at the start of the 1976–77 season, no one was surprised that Chapin's contract was not renewed and his job abolished.

Opera Performances. Artistically, the Met's major success of 1975 was the new production of *Boris Godunov*, unveiled in December 1974. It used a combination of Mussorgsky's two basic versions, rather than that of Rimsky-Korsakov. Beverly Sills scored an expected personal triumph in her April debut at the Met, a new production of Rossini's *Siege of Corinth*. The opera itself was badly served, however, and when staged again as the 1975–76 season opener, the opera was greeted with near hostility. Rossini took the blame for the Met's failure. The new fall productions were Mozart's *Marriage of Figaro* (Steuart Bedford conducting) and Puccini's *Il Trittico* (Sixten Ehrling conducting).

The New York City Opera's spring season included new productions of Richard Strauss's *Salome* and Korngold's *Die tote Stadt*. In the fall came Donizetti's *Daughter of the Regiment* (with Sills) and Wagner's *Die Meistersinger*. The latter, in a new English translation by John Gutman, was the company's first Wagner in many years. Norman Bailey made his company debut as Hans Sachs.

The Juilliard School's American Opera Theater attempted to salvage Samuel Barber's *Antony and Cleopatra*, a lavish fiasco at its 1966 premiere, as the first performance in the new Metropolitan Opera House. Despite the composer's extensive revisions that included heavy cuts and some new music and a more intimate setting, the opera still fared poorly.

The San Francisco Opera's fall season featured new productions of Monteverdi's *Coronation of Poppea* (conducted by Raymond Leppard) and Wagner's *Flying Dutchman* (conducted by Kenneth Schermerhorn). There were also appearances by Montserrat Caballé (*Norma*), Heather Harper (*Werther*), and Joan Sutherland (*Il Trovatore*). Sutherland also sang the title role of Donizetti's *Lucia di Lammermoor* with

Beverly Sills (*second from left*) made a triumphant Metropolitan Opera debut in the *Siege of Corinth*.

UPI

the Chicago Lyric Opera, whose new productions included Gluck's *Orfeo ed Euridice* (with Ileana Cotrubas and Richard Stilwell, Jean Fournet conducting) and Verdi's *Otello* (Carlo Cossutta and Gilda Cruz-Romo, Bruno Bartoletti conducting).

The Dallas Civic Opera entered its second season without Lawrence Kelly, who started the company and directed it until his death in 1973. Former musical director Nicola Rescigno officially succeeded Kelly in the fall of 1975, and Rescigno himself conducted the new productions of Offenbach's *Tales of Hoffmann* (with Alfredo Kraus) and Wagner's *Tristan und Isolde* (with Roberta Knie and Jon Vickers). Fernando Previtali conducted Donizetti's *Anna Bolena* (with Renata Scotto and Tatiana Troyanos). The enterprising Houston Grand Opera Company's schedule included new productions of Richard Strauss's *Der Rosenkavalier*, Berg's *Lulu*, Joplin's *Treemonisha* (a production later transferred to Washington, D. C., and New York City), and Handel's *Rinaldo* (with Marilyn Horne). In Boston, Sarah Caldwell staged and conducted Berlioz' *Benvenuto Cellini* (with Jon Vickers).

Ambitious projects flourished in unexpected places—for example, Meyerbeer's *Les Huguenots* in New Orleans, Ernst Křenek's *Life of Orestes* in Portland, and Wagner's complete *Ring* cycle in Seattle. The *Ring* cycle was done once in German, once in English.

Festival Opera. The major events at Salzburg were Karl Böhm conducting Mozart's *Così fan tutte* and Richard Strauss's *Die Frau ohne Schatten* and Herbert von Karajan conducting Mozart's *Marriage of Figaro* and Verdi's *Don Carlos*. The Bayreuth Festival opened with Wolfgang Wagner's new staging of his grandfather's *Parsifal*, which eradicated all traces of Wolfgang's late brother Wieland at Beyreuth. Wolfgang's productions of *Die Meistersinger* and *Ring* cycle were revived for 1975, and the *Tristan und Isolde* was August Everding's 1974 staging. Horst Stein conducted *Parsifal* and the *Ring*, Carlos Kleiber *Tristan*, and Heinrich Hollreiser *Meistersinger*.

The highlight at Glyndebourne was a new production of Stravinsky's *Rake's Progress*, designed by David Hockney and staged by John Cox. Bernard Haitink's conducting won special praise, and the largely U. S. cast, notably Donald Gramm as Nick Shadow, proved impressive. At the Edinburgh Festival, Welsh baritone Geraint Evans directed and sang the title role in Mozart's *Marriage of Figaro*.

Year of the Russians. Moscow's Bolshoi Opera made its long-awaited U. S. debut, performing six operas by Tchaikovsky, Mussorgsky, Prokofiev, and company director Kiril Molchanov in New York City and Washington, D. C., during June and July.

Perhaps the most ubiquitous musician of 1975 was the expatriate cellist/conductor Mstislav Rostropovich, already named to succeed Antal Dorati as music director of Washington's National Symphony. Rostropovich could be heard—often with his wife, soprano Galina Vishnevskaya—playing or conducting opera, operetta, and concerts from Vienna to San Francisco.

Obituary. The list of distinguished musicians who died in 1975 included composers Leroy Anderson and Luigi Dallapiccola and conductors Helmut Koch and Jean Morel. Singers who died included sopranos Frida Leider and Toti dal Monte, tenors Max Lorenz and Richard Tucker, and bass-baritone Norman Treigle. Metropolitan Opera broadcast announcer Milton Cross also died.

KENNETH FURIE
Music Editor, "High Fidelity"

POPULAR MUSIC

It was a year for cautious experimenting with forms and formulas that had worked before, a time for cutting back on provocative poses and pronouncements, a time for dispassionate music. One apparent reason for caution was the economic recession, and another was concern of people about threats to their personal security, a concern that in different times can be devoted to relative abstractions, such as the state of the world. If the songwriters and performers sensed a need for music that soothed rather than incited, it was understandable that they looked to the past. Present-day models of such music were in short supply.

Rock had been the dominant theme in popular music since the early 1960's, and nominally it still was. Surveys indicated that record buyers and concert goers listed rock as their favorite kind of music. Single rock performers and various bands experimented with a quieter, jazz-oriented improvisation of rock.

A new rock star, Bruce Springsteen, arrived on the popular music scene and was widely acclaimed.

COLUMBIA

Rock became part of the establishment. The Rolling Stones' tour of America was heavily attended, but the concerts were not rallies of a dedicated counterculture, as in past years. They were part of show business, and these were celebrity events.

A taste for the old structure of rock remained, however; the Eagles, using less and less country flavoring in their rock sound, enjoyed increased popularity in 1975. The folk-based singing, writing, and acoustic instrumention of the early 1960's gained renewed popularity, as the continued success of Gordon Lightfoot, John Denver, and Joan Baez proved.

Bruce Springsteen emerged as a new rock star. Heavily promoted, he received generally good reviews from critics, although most found comparisons with superstars Bob Dylan and Elton John premature.

Several forces combined to decentralize popular music. The major capitals of pop music—New York City, California, and London—meant less to many listeners. Provincial centers, whether Nashville, Memphis, Detroit, Austin, or some other place whose name was identified with a certain style, were far more favored.

Reggae, salsa, and other Latin forms had their loyalists, the country music audience continued to grow, and jazz took on a somewhat looser definition and a larger audience. There was cross-talk among the provinces, however, and mergers and consolidations seemed to keep pace with decentralization. Joni Mitchell won public acceptance on the basis of her folk music, but as she toured with jazz reed player Tom Scott, she was singing, and apparently writing, to complement the complex instrumental colors and textures he devised.

Linda Ronstadt's success in concerts and albums seemed to indicate that the audience was ready for superior singing, a conclusion reinforced by Ella Fitzgerald's sold-out college concerts and the new attention paid to Waylon Jennings, Maria Muldaur, and Anne Murray. Although Ronstadt sang mostly country music, she was identified by her audience as a rock performer. It seemed politically prudent to call music rock, whether it was or not, and to avoid calling it country. However, it was evident that Latin styles were influencing jazz, jazz was influencing rock, rock and country were continuing to influence each other, and the past, or disaffection with the present, was influencing everything.

Discotheques made a roaring comeback in the cities. They created a demand for music that stimulated physical movement, not music designed to inspire thought about social injustice, alienation, or loneliness. The discotheques were an effect, not a cause, but they helped increase the general demand for songs with innocuous lyrics and performances emphasizing instrumentation and ornamentation. Protest songs were not suitable, and "glitter" rock, which pro-

ASYLUM

The Eagles had continued success in 1975 with their combination of rock and country sound.

duced performers like David Bowie and Alice Cooper, lost its appeal. Elton John's career remained active, but he had always worked as hard on the sound of it as he had on the sight of it.

There was little about popular music in 1975 that was startling or innovative, although there were refinements in the production and presentation of it. The performers were better musicians than the folk-poets of the past had been, and there was greater variety in their repertoires. It was a year for trying to do things well but not boldly, for form over content, for sharpening instrumental and vocal skills, and for softening rhetoric.

NOEL COPPAGE
Contributing Editor, "Stereo Review"

The Rolling Stones, featuring superstar Mick Jagger (*second from right*), made a U. S. tour in 1975.

NEBRASKA

Excellent crops, natural disasters, two legislative sessions, educational change, and football claimed the attention of Nebraskans in 1975.

Agriculture. In spite of drought, Nebraska produced more corn, grain sorghum, and soybeans than in 1974. Wheat production dropped slightly. Prices were good for grain and livestock. Drought damaged pastures and newly-seeded wheat in the fall, but aided the harvest.

Natural Disasters. The worst blizzard on record in the area struck eastern Nebraska on Jan. 10, 1975. It immobilized traffic, left 14 Nebraskans dead, and destroyed livestock. Western Omaha was devastated by a tornado on May 6. Damage was extensive but, miraculously, few were killed although hundreds were injured. Although cleanup, rebuilding, and repair began immediately, much remained to be done at year's end.

Legislature and Government. The regular session of Nebraska's legislature adjourned on May 23 after 89 days. It took the first steps to regulate groundwater for irrigation and to provide support for mass transportation. The legislature raised the maximum home-mortgage rate to 11% and authorized the building of reformatories at both Omaha and Lincoln as well as a $10 million science building at the University of Nebraska at Lincoln. It also increased workmen's compensation, veterans' assistance, aid to dependent children, and salaries of state employees. Budget and taxes were major concerns, and before the legislature adjourned Gov. J. J. Exon vetoed appropriations totaling 37.3 million.

The governor called a special session of the legislature on October 23 to consider cutting expenditures for the 1976 fiscal year by $7 million to avert what Exon called a penniless treasury and a dramatic tax increase the following year.

Education. The legislature approved measures to allow private school students to ride public school buses, and to permit election of the Omaha school board by districts. However, it failed to override the governor's veto of a bill that would have appropriated $15 million a year additional for public schools. The U. S. circuit court of appeals reversed the decision of a district court and ordered prompt integration of Omaha schools. Teachers were shifted for the 1975 opening, and students were to be integrated by the fall of 1976.

Short-lived John F. Kennedy College closed, but both Creighton University and the University of Nebraska at Lincoln had record fall enrollments. The state colleges, technical community colleges, and the University of Nebraska system consumed 30% of state tax funds in 1975, and a legislative committee was formed to study coordination of state higher education.

Miscellaneous. Other important events in 1975 included adoption of a lottery in Omaha and the bankruptcy of American Beef Packers. The University of Nebraska Cornhusker football team had another very successful season.

ORVILLE H. ZABEL
Creighton University

NEPAL

Nepal, a mountainous, impoverished nation of 12 million people, landlocked between India and China, celebrated the coronation of King Birendra Bir Bikram Shah Dev on Feb. 24, 1975. Birendra had ruled since the death of his father in 1972, but the coronation was delayed by astrological signs and other considerations. Biren-

Newly-crowned King Birendra Bir Bikram Shah Dev and Queen Aishwarya ride through Katmandu in February.

UPI

NEBRASKA · Information Highlights

Area: 77,227 square miles (200,018 sq km).
Population (1974 est.): 1,543,000. *Density:* 20 per sq mi.
Chief Cities (1970 census): Lincoln, the capital, 149,-518; Omaha, 346,929; Grand Island, 31,269; Hastings, 23,580.
Government (1975): *Chief Officers*—governor, J. James Exon (D); lt. gov., Gerald T. Whelan (D). *Legislature* (unicameral)—49 members (nonpartisan).
Education (1974–75): *Enrollment*—public elementary schools, 170,802 pupils; public secondary, 147,990; nonpublic, 41,000; colleges and universities, 67,292 students. *Public school expenditures,* $310,397,000 ($999 per pupil).
State Finances (fiscal year 1974): *Revenues* $754,832,-000; *expenditures* $698,260,000.
Personal Income (1974): $7,526,000,000; per capita, $4,-877.
Labor Force: *Nonagricultural wage and salary earners* (July 1975), 559,500; *insured unemployed* (Aug. 1975), 14,200.

dra is the first formally educated king in Nepal's history. He attended school in India, England, Japan, and the United States (Harvard). The coronation was the occasion for many foreign visitors to come to Nepal. Among them were Prince Charles of Great Britain and Crown Prince Akihito of Japan. In his coronation address the king spoke of a new bond between the people and himself and promised that he would dedicate himself to a "new age" of progress for his country and an end to the age-old poverty that continues to grip it.

The other major event during the year was the first ascent of the difficult southwest face of Mt. Everest by two British mountain climbers on September 24.

CARL LEIDEN
University of Texas at Austin

NEPAL • Information Highlights

Official Name: Kingdom of Nepal.
Location: Central Asia.
Area: 54,362 square miles (140,797 sq km).
Population (1975 est.): 12,600,000.
Chief City (1971 census): Katmandu, the capital, 195,-300.
Government: *Head of state,* Birendra Bir Bikram Shah Dev (acceded 1972).
Monetary Unit: Rupee (10.56 rupees equal U. S.$1, April 1975).
Major Agricultural Products: Rice, corn, millet, sugarcane, tobacco, jute.

NETHERLANDS

A worsening recession and problems arising from decolonization were the chief issues faced by the Netherlands in 1975.

Surinam. On November 25, Surinam, formerly known as Dutch Guiana, became independent. Surinamese in increasing numbers migrated to the Netherlands, the figure running at several thousand a week as the independence deadline approached. The number of Surinamese in the Netherlands neared the 100,000 mark. For Surinam, whose population was less than 400,000, the loss of so many of its better-educated citizens was a serious matter. For the Netherlands, the influx of so many people during a recession caused great strains.

The causes of the accelerated emigration from Surinam were chiefly poverty, racial tension, and the fear that after independence entry into the Netherlands would be restricted. For an economically underdeveloped country educational levels are high in Surinam, but education has outrun employment opportunities. The people of Surinam are racially mixed. Creoles constitute about 38% of the population; Asian Indians, called Hindustani, 32%; Indonesians, 14%; Bush Negroes (descendants of runaway slaves), 10%; and American Indians, Chinese, and Europeans about 1.5% each.

Fearing for their safety, the Hindustani urged postponement of independence and guarantees for fair treatment of the Indian community. On May 15 racial tensions erupted with demonstrations and the burning of buildings. The two gov-

UPI

In August, Dutch bargemen blockaded waterways to protest government cargo-distribution plans.

ernments discussed the terms of independence from March 17 to 27 but reached no agreement. Surinam wanted liberal entry rights into the Netherlands for its citizens and twice as much economic aid as the Dutch were prepared to give.

South Molucca Islands. The Dutch also had trouble with some former colonials from Southeast Asia. On Dec. 27, 1974, some 500 South Moluccans staged a demonstration at the Peace Palace in The Hague. They wanted independence for the South Molucca Islands from Indonesia, a former Dutch colony. In December, South Moluccan terrorists seized a Dutch train and Indonesia's embassy. They killed three train passengers, but the rest were released unharmed, as were the embassy hostages.

Economy. The recession deepened in 1975 and showed few signs of an upturn. At the end of July unemployment stood at 202,000 (5.2% of the work force), an increase of 8% over June. The rate of inflation for the year ending in July was 10.4%, the lowest in the European Economic Community and was 5.2% for the first 7 months of 1975. Foreign trade was stagnant and domestic demand weak. Government expenditures were expected to rise $1.2 billion due to a new public works program. Anticipated revenue was due to be nearly $1 billion below expenditures. On August 8 Parliament came to the aid of financially distressed KLM (the national Dutch airline) by approving the purchase

—— NETHERLANDS · Information Highlights ——
Official Name: Kingdom of the Netherlands.
Location: Northwestern Europe.
Area: 15,770 square miles (40,844 sq km).
Population (1975 est.): 13,600,000.
Chief Cities (1972 est.): Amsterdam, the capital, 807,-742; Rotterdam, 670,060; The Hague, 525,368.
Government: *Head of state,* Juliana, queen (acceded Sept. 1948). *Head of government,* Joop den Uyl, prime minister (took office May 1973). *Legislature* —Staten General: First Chamber and Second Chamber.
Monetary Unit: Guilder (2.395 guilders equal U. S.$1, March 1975).
Gross National Product (1974 est.): $70,100,000,000.
Manufacturing (major products): Metals, processed foods, petroleum products, chemicals, textiles, machinery, electrical appliances, clothing.
Major Agricultural Products: Sugar beets, potatoes, wheat, barley, rye, oats, flax.
Foreign Trade (1974): *Exports,* $32,810,000,000; *imports,* $32,631,000,000.

of $76 million of the airline's preferred stock. This act increased the government's share of the ownership of the company from 70% to 78%.

Politics. Independent barge owners won a victory over the government when the latter proposed to alter the system of sharing freight to the disadvantage of small operators, who were having difficulty competing with big companies. On August 25 the independent operators instituted a blockade of the Rhine River and major Dutch ports with some 800 barges. Three days later Parliament rejected the bill, and the barriers were removed.

Foreign Affairs. The Netherlands government is seeking to repair its strained relations with the Arab countries without compromising its position with respect to Israel, a position the Arabs regard as overly friendly. Foreign Minister Max van der Stoel was to make an official visit to Saudi Arabia, but when the Arab government refused to grant a visa to a Dutch Jewish journalist who was to accompany him, van der Stoel postponed the trip. However during van der Stoel's friendly visit to Egypt on May 16, Egypt and the Netherlands signed a broad technical and economic cooperation agreement.

AMRY VANDENBOSCH
University of Kentucky

NEVADA

Despite the national recession and an average state unemployment rate of 10%, tourism and the general economy flourished in Nevada throughout 1975. Finding the state's prosperity difficult to believe, the legislature carried over a $20 million surplus reserve into the 1975–77 biennium budget. However, the continuing increase in gambling activity appeared to reinforce the theory that Nevada's main industry is "recession-proof."

Legislation. The Democrats enjoyed the largest majorities in the legislature of any party in this century. Nevertheless, the biennial legislative session spent a record 122 days considering controversial legislation and problems with the drafting of bills.

The most emotionally-charged issue of the session was consideration of the proposed Equal Rights Amendment (ERA) to the U. S. Constitution. The Assembly approved the ERA by a vote of 27–13, only to have the Senate defeat the resolution by a 12–8 margin. The amendment's backers were encouraged by the four-vote increase over the 1973 Senate vote but vowed to campaign against those legislators who had opposed the amendments.

Major measures passed by the legislature included campaign finance and conflict of interest legislation, establishment of a state Ethics Commission, regulation of lobbying, and a state antitrust law. There was also legislation prohibiting smoking in many public places, changes in some existing laws to end sexual discrimination, and legislation improving the terms of medical malpractice insurance. With a very healthy surplus in the general fund, the legislature approved recommendations by Gov. Michael O'Callaghan to grant state employees a 15% pay raise retroactive to January 1 and to increase substantially state aid to the public schools.

One of the most complicated legislative acts provided for the consolidation of the city of Las Vegas and surrounding Clark county. However, in October portions of the Metropolitan Cities Incorporation Law were declared unconstitutional in an advisory opinion by state Atty. Gen. Robert List.

Economy. General fund revenues from gambling and sales taxes increased by 12% and 8%, respectively, over the previous fiscal year. The huge success of Metro-Goldwyn-Mayer's Grand Hotel in Las Vegas prompted MGM to plan to construct a 1,000-room hotel-casino in Reno.

Education. School teachers suffered a setback when the legislature narrowed the scope of issues that may be negotiated in contracts. The Clark county and Western Nevada community colleges had a combined 30% enrollment increase in the fall semester, and the universities in Las Vegas and Reno had increases of 8% and 4%, respectively.

DON W. DRIGGS
University of Nevada

—— NEVADA · Information Highlights ——
Area: 110,540 square miles (286,299 sq km).
Population (1974 est.): 573,000. *Density:* 5 per sq mi.
Chief Cities (1970 census): Carson City, the capital, 15,468; Las Vegas, 125,787; Reno, 72,863.
Government (1975): *Chief Officers*—governor, Michael O'Callaghan (D); lt. gov., Robert E. Rose (D). *Legislature*—Senate, 20 members; Assembly, 40 members.
Education (1974–75): *Enrollment*—public elementary schools, 73,162 pupils; public secondary, 63,889; nonpublic, 2,800; colleges and universities, 26,214 students. *Public school expenditures,* $118,791,000 ($979 per pupil).
State Finances (fiscal year 1974): *Revenues,* $502,240,-000; *expenditures,* $420,890,000.
Personal Income (1974): $3,480,000,000; per capita, $6,073.
Labor Force (July 1975): *Nonagricultural wage and salary earners,* 279,900; *insured unemployed,* 11,100.

NEW BRUNSWICK

Economic developments and measures to cope with inflation dominated the news in 1975. There were also noteworthy events in the fields of politics and social policy, industry, and jurisprudence.

Government and Economics. On March 21, Finance Minister A. E. Stairs submitted a $1.1 billion budget aimed at alleviating unemployment as well as inflation. A $63.7 million deficit was forecast. Expenditures included a record $159 million for capital projects designed to create employment. Measures aimed at fighting inflation, or easing its effects, included higher social-assistance payments, housing subsidies for low-income groups, and a 2% cut in personal income taxes.

When the budget was introduced, provincial unemployment was running at more than 13% of the labor force and as high as 30% in some depressed regions, such as the northeast. By October the rate had dipped to 10.4%. Inflation was at an annual rate of 10%–11% through most of the year.

In the legislative session that opened March 11 and closed in June, approval was given a program to provide free prescription drugs to persons over 65 and to a farm-income insurance program. Before adjourning, the legislators also voted themselves a 14.2% pay increase from $10,500 to $12,000 annually.

Dube Resigns. Jean-Eudes Dube resigned April 9 as the Liberal representative for Restigouche to fill a vacancy on the federal court. Dube was one of four cabinet ministers dumped by Prime Minister Trudeau following the 1974 federal election. He had been public works minister since 1972 and before that veterans affairs minister. Maurice Harquail, deputy mayor of Campbellton, kept the Restigouche seat for the Liberals in an October 15 by-election.

Nuclear Power. In Ottawa, federal Environment Minister Jeanne Sauve announced on May 2 that the federal government had approved construction of a $900 million nuclear generating station 20 miles (32 km) southwest of St. John. The federal government will pay 50% of the

cost of the 600-megawatt plant, expected to be ready by 1980.

Bricklin in Receivership. The trouble-plagued Bricklin Canada Ltd. car operation went into receivership in September after producing 2,875 cars. The receivership was granted by the New Brunswick Supreme Court after Bricklin began having trouble with its creditors. The provincial government, one of three secured creditors, had invested $20 million in the $30-million enterprise, which produced distinctive, gull-winged cars. Bricklin Canada employed 700 men in plants at St. John and Minto.

Newspapers. The New Brunswick Supreme Court overturned the 1974 monopoly convictions and $150,000 in fines against K. C. Irving Ltd. of St. John and three associated companies, which publish all five of New Brunswick's English-language newspapers. The court in an appeal judgment June 4 found that the five papers operate independently of one another and enjoy "complete autonomy."

Justice. On April 1 a Supreme Court jury in Moncton found James Hutchinson and Richard Ambrose guilty of slaying two city policemen on Dec. 12, 1974. The two were sentenced to be hanged June 13, but a series of stays of execution kept them from the gallows.

JOHN BEST
Chief, Canada World News, Ottawa

NEW HAMPSHIRE

The dispute over the contested 1974 election to fill the U. S. Senate seat vacated by retiring Republican Norris Cotton dominated New Hampshire affairs in 1975. The controversy left the state with only one senator for eight months.

Senate Election. In November 1974, Republican Louis C. Wyman, a five-term congressman, apparently defeated Democrat John A. Durkin, seeking his first elective office, by 355 votes of 121,000 cast. A recount then gave Durkin the victory by 10 votes, but further check by the State Ballot Law Commission brought in a 2-vote margin for Wyman. Durkin asked the U. S. Senate, as the sole judge of its members' credentials, to rule on the contest.

The Senate Rules Committee finally put the issue to the whole Senate. After 100 hours of debate, 30 days, and 35 inconclusive roll call votes along party lines, on July 30 the Senate declared the seat vacant and referred the matter back to the state. A day earlier, Durkin had agreed to a special election.

A warm campaign preceded the vote on September 16. President Ford and former Gov. Ronald Reagan of California came to speak for Wyman. The total vote was larger than it had been in November. Durkin won, with 140,273 (53.5%) to Wyman's 113,004 (43.1%). Carmen Chimento of the American party polled 8,853 votes. Durkin was sworn in as a senator on September 18.

NEW BRUNSWICK · Information Highlights

Area: 28,354 square miles (73,437 sq km).

Population (1975 est.): 676,000.

Chief Cities (1973 est.): Fredericton, the capital, 25,000; St. John, 110,000; Moncton, 50,000.

Government (1975): *Chief Officers*—lt. gov., Hedard Robichaud; premier, Richard B. Hatfield (Progressive Conservative); prov. secy., Marie Hanifan; min. of justice, John Baxter. *Legislature*—Legislative Assembly, 58 members.

Education (1975–76): *Enrollment*—public elementary and secondary schools, 162,900 pupils; private schools, 480; Indian (federal) schools, 720; colleges and universities, 10,100 students. *Public school expenditures,* $145,067,000.

Public Finance (fiscal year 1974–75 est.): *Revenues,* $742,000,000; *expenditures,* $791,000,000.

Personal Income (1972): $1,793,000,000; average annual income per person, $2,810.

(All monetary figures are in Canadian dollars.)

In September, John Durkin won the New Hampshire senatorial election nearly a year after the original contest between Durkin and Republican Louis Wyman was called a tie.

UPI

Legislature. The work of the 1975 session of the 424-member general court benefited from improved relationships with Gov. Meldrim Thomson. A welfare reform bill, backed by the governor, which expanded the duties and powers of the commissioner of health and welfare, became law. Another important measure banned strikes by public employees, including teachers, and provided for collective bargaining.

New criminal laws fixed more severe sentences for habitual offenders and established procedures for reviewing sentences in criminal cases. They also confirmed conservation officers as peace officers, raised jurors' pay, and revised the probation code.

Finances. A general fund appropriation of $324.5 million, 25% above the "thrift" budget that Thomson had sought, was approved. One $12 million revenue item closed loopholes in the business profits tax, raised taxes on beer and tobacco, and doubled the corporate franchise tax. State employees received a $5-a-week raise.

On March 19 the U. S. Supreme Court ruled that New Hampshire's income tax on commuters from other states was unconstitutional because no comparable tax was imposed on its residents. New Hampshire remains the only state with no general income or sales tax.

National Politics. As the state whose February 24 presidential primary is traditionally earliest in the nation, New Hampshire felt preliminary stirrings in 1975 of the 1976 campaign, intensified by the Ford and Reagan visits. Governor Thomson indicated that he would promote a challenge of Ford by Reagan in the primary and said that if Reagan did not run, Thomson would run himself. Thomson was active during the year as chairman of the Conservative Caucus, a national organization based in Virginia, that is dedicated to conservative principles.

RICHARD G. WEST
Former Senior Editor "Encyclopedia Americana"

NEW JERSEY

Fiscal problems of critical proportions dominated the political atmosphere of the state throughout 1975. Money had to be raised in order to cover expanding social services and to finance the state public school system, which by court order must be supported by means other than local property taxes. The situation was complicated by the state constitutional stipulation of a balanced budget and by a reduction in sales tax revenues.

Governor Byrne's Budget. In January Gov. Brendan T. Byrne warned the legislature that there could be a budget deficit as high as $600 million and recommended new taxes to offset it. The estimated deficit did not cover the $300 million thought necessary to finance education, however, so a total of $900 million would have to be raised, almost one-third of the $2.7 billion fiscal 1975 budget.

The fiscal 1976 budget, submitted February 4, amounted to $2.82 billion. In spite of $300 million in spending cutbacks there was a deficit of $487 million. Once again Byrne pushed for a state income tax that would raise $1 billion, enough to offset the deficit as well as pay for the state's educational needs. The size of the deficit, together with overwhelming Democratic majorities in both houses of the Legislature,

---

— NEW HAMPSHIRE · Information Highlights —

Area: 9,304 square miles (24,097 sq km).
Population (1974 est.): 808,000. *Density:* 87 per sq mi.
Chief Cities (1970 census): Concord, the capital, 30,-022; Manchester, 87,754; Nashua, 55,820; Portsmouth, 25,717.
Government (1975): *Chief Officers*—governor, Meldrim Thomson, Jr. (R); secy. of state, Robert L. Stark (R). *General Court*—Senate, 24 members; House of Representatives, 400 members.
Education (1974–75): *Enrollment*—public elementary schools, 102,760 pupils; public secondary, 69,357; nonpublic, 25,400; colleges and universities, 34,365. *Public school expenditures,* $147,781,000 ($936 per pupil).
State Finances (fiscal year 1974): *Revenues,* $467,491,-000; *expenditures,* $452,159,000.
Personal Income (1974): $4,156,000,000; per capita, $5,143.
Labor Force (July 1975): *Nonagricultural wage and salary earners,* 311,800; *insured unemployed,* 15,000.

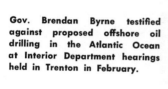

Gov. Brendan Byrne testified against proposed offshore oil drilling in the Atlantic Ocean at Interior Department hearings held in Trenton in February.

UPI

gave him hope that the long string of income tax defeats would be reversed.

By spring no positive tax action had been taken, mainly due to some skepticism among Republican assemblymen and among senators of both parties concerning the seriousness of the crisis. In the opinion of some the deficit was made larger than necessary for political reasons. In June the Senate rejected a plan for a state surcharge on federal income tax payments, and there had been no legislative approval of the budget.

The Emergency Session. On June 19, Byrne called the legislature into emergency session with an admonishment that the budget must be approved within 12 days or else the state would start a new fiscal year with no financial means to carry on the government. He described the situation as the worst fiscal crisis in the state's history. Four days later, Assembly Democrats approved Byrne's projected strategy of vetoing the budget conditionally on the grounds that the Senate had not passed an income tax to raise supporting revenue. The Assembly, by a vote of 42–26, passed a $2.8 billion budget with a $412 million deficit, presumably forcing the Senate either to approve an income tax or to face responsibility for massive spending cutbacks involving state aid to schools, higher education, and mass transportation.

After some hesitation the Senate, by a vote of 21–17, turned down an income tax for the fifth time in 11 months, thus bringing the crisis to an acute stage. Byrne vetoed the budget, which combined with $384 million in spending cuts, would have thrown out of work as many as 28,000 state and public employees.

Summer Developments. Throughout July there was an atmosphere of general bitterness among the governor, legislators, state and public employees, and municipal officials. From Byrne's point of view the Senate's action in June meant the most crushing defeat of his term in office, and he recognized reluctantly that the income

tax issue was dead. His opponents in the legislature refused to believe that his invocation of crisis was genuine and not politically motivated, and even among his supporters there was criticism of his leadership. The shakiness of New Jersey's fiscal affairs was seen when Moody's Investors' Service lowered its ratings of state general obligation bonds from a top AAA to a lower AA and threatened to reduce municipal bond ratings as well.

By early August a stopgap solution to the budgetary problem was put into effect. Governor Byrne reluctantly signed a $257 million "nuisance" tax bill, involving an increase in the sales tax; a state property tax; and an unearned income tax on capital gains, dividends, and interest. In addition, bond issues totaling $922 million were placed on the ballot for voter approval in November. These would have financed mass transit and highway construction, sewers and water systems, state institutions and agencies, and low and middle income housing. The proposed bonds were decisively rejected by the voters, and Governor Byrne again warned that a fiscal crisis was imminent.

HERMANN K. PLATT
St. Peter's College, Jersey City

——— **NEW JERSEY** · **Information Highlights** ———

Area: 7,836 square miles (20,295 sq km).
Population (1974 est.): 7,330,000. *Density:* 980 per sq mi.
Chief Cities (1970 census): Trenton, the capital, 104,638; Newark, 382,288; Jersey City, 260,545.
Government (1975): *Chief Officers*—governor, Brendan T. Byrne (D); secy. of state, J. Edward Crabiel (D). *Legislature*—Senate, 40 members; General Assembly, 80 members.
Education (1973–74): *Enrollment*—public elementary schools, 967,200 pupils; public secondary, 520,800. (1974–75): nonpublic, 239,800; colleges and universities, 275,864 students. *Public school expenditures,* $1,945,222,000 ($1,440 per pupil).
State Finances (fiscal year 1974): *Revenues,* $4,607,734,-000; *expenditures,* $4,389,803,000.
Personal Income (1974): $46,798,000,000; per capita, $6,384.
Labor Force (Aug. 1975): *Nonagricultural wage and salary earners,* 2,649,600; *insured unemployed,* 152,-000.

NEW MEXICO

In 1975, New Mexicans grew increasingly concerned that swift development of the state's vast energy resources for export to other parts of the country would lead to serious social, political, and environmental problems. Construction of the nation's first coal gasification plants, strip mining of coal on the Navajo reservation, development of geothermal well fields, expansion of uranium mining, and increased production of gas and oil all proceeded in the state. New Mexico had an unemployment rate of 8–9% in 1975 and was 49th among the 50 states in personal income.

Indians. Armed members of the American Indian Movement (AIM) seized and occupied the Fairchild Camera and Instrument Co. in Shiprock for eight days, beginning February 24. Their intention was to force the rehiring of 140 Navajo employees dismissed by the company. The disturbance caused Fairchild to close its plant permanently. In June, AIM held its national convention in Farmington and called for a cultural revolution among the nation's Indians.

In Albuquerque the All Pueblo Council began work on a multimillion dollar Indian cultural center. The facility, designed in a horseshoe shape similar to the ancient ruin of Pueblo Bonito at Chaco Canyon, is scheduled for completion in 1976.

Health. An outbreak of rabies in the Mesilla Valley surrounding Las Cruces and a record number of cases of bubonic plague in the north-ern part of the state led public health officials to adopt strict control measures. By the end of October, 16 persons had been stricken with plague, the largest number of cases reported in any state in 30 years. The health and social services department took steps to acquaint the public with the dangers of the disease, set up special clinics, and began a program to trap wild rodents, hosts for the plague-carrying fleas.

Energy and Environment. New Mexico State University in Las Cruces dedicated a new solar-heated and solar-cooled building, the largest such structure in the world. It will serve as a solar energy research model for the Energy Research and Development Institute at the school. Officials declared that the project will demonstrate to the nation New Mexico's commitment to this new field of research.

Scientists at Los Alamos Scientific Laboratory announced results of experiments to produce energy from algae. Using laser beams to study photosynthesis and to grow algae many times faster than normal, they noted that 1 acre (.4 hectare) of land can be made to yield 1,400 tons of high protein algae for food each year. The algae can then be used to produce large amounts of hydrogen for fuel and methane gas for fertilizer.

Leaders of the new 10-state Western Governors Regional Energy Policy Office (WGREPO) met in Santa Fe in mid-June to plan a common strategy for energy development and conservation. New Mexico's Gov. Jerry Apodaca is chairman of the group. In late October, Albuquerque hosted a national energy conference attended by prominent political leaders and representatives from banking interests and utilities.

Under pressure by concerned citizens, the U. S. Bureau of Land Management began developing requirements for environmental impact statements to accompany the granting of new leases on federal lands in the potash district near Carlsbad. The requirements are intended to regulate the effect of the potash industry on air, water, and land in the area.

MARC SIMMONS
Author, "Spanish Government in New Mexico"

Gov. Jerry Apodaca of New Mexico hosted a Western states meeting to plan energy and conservation moves.

------ **NEW MEXICO · Information Highlights** ------

Area: 121,666 square miles (315,115 sq km).
Population (1974 est.): 1,122,000. *Density:* 9 per sq mi.
Chief Cities (1970 census): Santa Fe, the capital, 41,-167; Albuquerque, 243,751; Las Cruces, 37,857; Roswell, 33,908.
Government (1975): *Chief Officers*—governor, Jerry Apodaca (D); lt. gov., Robert F. Ferguson (D). *Legislature*—Senate, 42 members; House of Representatives, 70 members.
Education (1974–75): *Enrollment*—public elementary schools, 188,073 pupils; public secondary schools, 94,309; nonpublic schools, 12,700; colleges and universities, 50,666 students. *Public school expenditures,* $237,417,000 ($923 per pupil).
State Finances (fiscal year 1974): *Revenues,* $906,143,-000; *expenditures,* $795,143,000.
Personal Income (1974): $4,642,000,000; per capita, $4,137.
Labor Force (Aug. 1975): *Nonagricultural wage and salary earners,* 374,500; *insured unemployed,* 14,300.

NEW YORK

A grim picture greeted the new administration of Democratic Gov. Hugh L. Carey in 1975. Delivering his initial State of the State message to the 198th Legislature, Carey warned that there would be an end to using the state as a "horn of plenty" for local subsidies and payrolls and an end to a "lavish" style of government. Finances had a special meaning for New York in 1975.

Fiscal Problems. Carey proposed the raising of $800 million in new taxes, including a 10-cent per gallon tax levy on gasoline. New Yorkers were already paying $170 in taxes for each $1,000 earned, the highest in the nation. A $10.4 billion budget was eventually passed without the taxes proposed by Carey, but only after major trade-offs between Democrats and Republicans. The state, however, ended its fiscal year with an $18.5 million defeat.

In May, Carey asked the U. S. Congress to provide $4 billion in aid for the state, of which $100 million would be for New York City. At the same time, he proposed new cuts in the state budget to meet what he believed would be a $500 million deficit. As a result of a growing fiscal crisis, the governor proposed cuts at state park facilities and the firing of 1,000 state employees. Five hundred were actually dismissed, mostly from the executive department after the governor rejected a 6% pay rise for state employees. Purchasing of new equipment was curtailed or halted.

The crisis in New York City became increasingly tied to that of the state, and by the end of the year the municipal loan market was either closed or increasingly expensive. Governor Carey wore out a path to Washington, D. C., bringing his message of the necessity of federal loan guarantees, especially to the city, to prevent fiscal disaster for the entire state.

Legislation. While money was the crucial issue, it was not the only one that faced a harried Legislature. A number of bills were passed reforming the criminal process. The state legislators passed, and the governor vetoed, legislation that sharply reduced penalties under the state's controversial drug law.

Other bills passed included repeal of the fair trade law that had been on the books for 35 years. It was considered a triumph for the consumer advocates. Residents were allowed to register to vote by mail in an attempt to increase registration in poor areas. A total of $250 million was allotted for improved railroad service. The Municipal Assistance Corporation (Big MAC), a state agency designed to meet New York City's financial woes, was created after a good deal of bitter debate.

Nursing Homes. Widespread abuses in nursing homes were investigated, including charges of over-billing, poor care, and stealing welfare checks from elderly patients. Assemblyman

UPI

Gov. Hugh Carey (left) and Comptroller Arthur Levitt testify in Washington for federal help for New York.

Andrew Stein, chairman of the Temporary State Commission on Living Costs, began an investigation that implicated Bernard Bergman, owner of many such homes. Stein also alleged that the state was bilked of at least $400 million on improper Medicaid payments, but the assembly refused to extend the term of the committee, which expired on March 31.

Urban Development Corporations. Another scandal that also attracted attention concerned the Urban Development Corporation, a public authority created in 1968 to provide low- and middle-income housing in the state. A shortage in agency funds resulted in a $178 million appropriation by the legislature in February. Governor Carey estimated another $500 to $600 million would be necessary to fulfill the corporation's long-term obligations. A new Project Finance Agency was created to rescue the insolvent corporation, and state and private banks were committed to a program to purchase bonds. The whole project, however, bogged down in charges of poor financial operations.

Doctors. Another crisis occurred when in-

NEW YORK • Information Highlights

Area: 49,576 square miles (128,402 sq km).
Population (1974 est.): 18,111,000. *Density:* 381 per sq mi.
Chief Cities (1970 census): Albany, the capital, 115,-781; New York, 7,895,563; Buffalo, 462,768; Rochester, 296,233.
Government (1975): *Chief Officers*—governor, Hugh L. Carey (D); lt. gov., Mary Anne Krupsak (D). *Legislature*—Senate, 60 members; Assembly, 150 members.
Education (1974–75): *Enrollment*—public elementary schools, 1,789,763 pupils; public secondary schools, 1,646,084; nonpublic schools, 684,800; colleges and universities, 947,299 students. *Public school expenditures,* $5,721,221,000 ($1,851 per pupil).
State Finances (fiscal year 1974): *Revenues,* $16,010,-816,000; *expenditures,* $15,453,285,000.
Personal Income (1974): $113,094,000,000; per capita, $6,244.
Labor Force (July 1975): *Nonagricultural wage and salary earners,* 6,878,000; *insured unemployed,* 349,300.

surers of doctors and hospitals announced early in the year that they would not continue to cover their clients due to increased litigation and high jury awards in malpractice suits. Governor Carey and the legislature agreed to set up a Medical Malpractice Underwriting Association offering liability insurance, but rates were also increased by 15% to 80%. The New York State Medical Society opposed the malpractice law because of its increased costs and its failure to define clearly the term "malpractice," even though the legislation was designed to protect doctors from such suits. A doctors' strike and slowdown in various hospitals was instituted. After several days, doctors resumed their duties while awaiting the report of the governor's commission on suggested changes in the law.

Floods. Nature also added to New York's problems. In late September heavy rains inundated parts of New York City, Westchester, and nine counties in north-central New York. The region was declared a disaster area, enabling citizens and communities to receive federal loans.

Election. The major election issues in 1975, an off-year, were the state Equal Rights Amendment (ERA) and a housing bond issue, both of which failed.

LEO HERSHKOWITZ
Queens College, City University of New York

NEW ZEALAND

In the November general election, the National party regained office in a dramatic, landslide victory. Provisional results gave the National party 53 seats to the Labour party's 34. In the overall swing in votes to the National party of 8.4%, Labour lost 21 seats, including those of three cabinet ministers.

The election campaign was not as bitter and tough as had been forecast and centered on inflation, the economy, and industrial relations. Minor parties once again failed to win representation. The new cabinet is very experienced and the prime minister, Robert Muldoon, will retain the finance portfolio himself.

The Economy. With the very adverse balance of trade continuing, the government arranged a further series of international loans. Overseas borrowing for 1974–75 totaled $634.5 million.

Inflation in 1974 reached 12.6%, and in August 1975 the New Zealand dollar was devalued by 15%. The purpose was to curb the external deficit and to provide a more equitable income for farmers, who, despite earlier measures such as stabilization schemes for lamb and wool and higher fertilizer subsidies, were suffering from greatly reduced yields. Though not alarming in terms of absolute figures, unemployment climbed steadily, reaching 10,000 in August.

The May budget foresaw little or no growth in the economy, and the government aimed to buy time by borrowing in the hope that the downward trend in overseas trade would be re-

versed. There was no attempt to balance the budget, and much of the expected $500 million deficit was accounted for by a broad tax concession that was equivalent to a salary rise of 3% to 4%. In addition, a general wage increase of 11 cents an hour was announced, but this was offset by higher sales taxes and a rise in the price of gasoline to $1 per gallon. Basic welfare benefits received a modest adjustment.

Government. Prime Minister W. E. Rowling made two major overseas visits. In February, during the course of his tour of six European states, discussions centered on New Zealand's trade outlets. He attended the Commonwealth conference in Jamaica in May and later called on President Gerald Ford and Secretary of State Henry Kissinger in Washington. They expressed interest in the concept of a nuclear-free zone in the South Pacific. In February, Hugh Watt, formerly deputy prime minister, was appointed New Zealand high commissioner to Great Britain, with cabinet rank.

Much important legislation was passed or came into effect during the year. In April the New Zealand Broadcasting Corporation was broken up and was replaced by three separate radio and television organizations, and the revolutionary Superannuation Act came into operation. In September a controversial piece of legislation was passed that forbids the publication of the name of the accused in a trial, unless the court orders otherwise or at the defendant's request, until a guilty verdict has been returned.

Domestic Affairs. In February, Dr. W. B. Sutch, a former secretary of industries and commerce, was acquitted of a charge of spying under the Official Secrets Act. He died six months later, aged 68. A royal commission of enquiry into contraception, sterilization, and abortion was announced in June. John Walker, of Auckland, broke the world mile record in August when he ran the distance at Göteborg, Sweden, in 3 minutes 49.4 seconds. During a storm in August, a small freighter, the *Capitaine Bougainville,* caught fire off the Northland coast, and 16 crew members and passengers perished.

G. W. A. BUSH, *The University of Auckland*

NEW ZEALAND · Information Highlights

Official Name: New Zealand.
Location: South Pacific Ocean.
Area: 103,736 square miles (268,675 sq km).
Population (1974 est.): 3,030,000.
Chief Cities (1975 est.): Wellington, the capital, 346,900; Auckland, 775,460; Christchurch, 320,530.
Government: *Head of state,* Elizabeth II, queen, represented by Sir Denis Blundell, governor-general (took office Sept. 1972). *Head of government,* Robert Muldoon, prime minister (took office Nov. 1975). *Legislature* (unicameral)—House of Representatives.
Monetary Unit: New Zealand dollar (0.7883 N. Z. dollar equals U. S.$1, July 1975).
Gross National Product (1974): $11,700,000,000.
Manufacturing (major products): Processed foods, meat, wood products, cement, fertilizers.
Major Agricultural Products: Wheat, potatoes, dairy products, sheep wool, forest products.
Foreign Trade (1974): *Exports,* $2,040,000,000; *imports,* $3,010,000,000.

NEWFOUNDLAND

An attempted return to power by a former premier of Newfoundland and a strike in the fishing industry highlighted the year.

Politics and Government. Defeated in the 1972 election, Joseph Smallwood found being out of public office uncongenial. His first step was to attempt to regain the leadership of his old Liberal party. But in October 1974 at a leadership convention, Smallwood lost to Ed Roberts. His next step was to form his own Reform Liberal party in August 1975. Conveniently the current premier, F. D. Moores, called a provincial election for September 16. Both the Progressive Conservative (PC) government and the Liberals fielded 51 candidates for the newly enlarged House of Assembly, the Reform Liberals fielded 28, and the New Democratic party (NDP) trailed with 17 candidates The results produced a victory for the PC's with 30 seats and 46% of the vote. Sixteen seats went to the Liberals (38% of the vote) and 4 to the Reform Liberals (11% of the vote), while the NDP elected none. One former Liberal ran and won as an Independent. It was a noteworthy election for another reason. Women candidates totaled four, and one woman Liberal won, the first woman elected since 1927.

Finances and Economy. The year opened with a bitter strike in one of the most important sectors of the economy—the fishing industry. From January until August the trawlermen of the island's south coast fought to end their traditional status as "co-adventurers," which tied their wages to the size of the catch. Their point was finally won. Generally fishing was not good in 1975, and demands were made that the government of Canada declare, unilaterally if need be, a 200-mile (320-km) "zone of management." Some relief from over-fishing was achieved in October when the USSR agreed that a reduced quota would be introduced. In March the government produced the first $1 billion budget in the province's history. No major tax changes were announced. Federal authorities agreed to share 50-50 in the costs (up to $343 million) of building a transmission line from the Labrador site of a planned power development to the

island of Newfoundland. Many of the hopes of the province for economic betterment lie in Labrador, which has oil and gas off the coast and relatively cheap power from its rivers.

SUSAN McCORQUODALE
Memorial University of Newfoundland

NIGERIA

Inadequate distribution of the increasing petroleum wealth, government inefficiency, and belief in widespread high level graft convinced a large segment of the military to stage an overthrow of their superiors. In a bloodless coup, General Yakubu Gowon was replaced as head of state by Brig. Gen. Muritala Ramat Mohammed.

Economic Development. Nigeria's petroleum industry in 1974 earned about $8.9 billion on exports. The total produced was a modest 1% more than the previous year, but due to OPEC price increases petroleum income was almost three times as large. Even though cocoa and timber exports remained high, Nigeria's dependence upon petroleum revenues increased, and petroleum accounted for 92% of all Nigerian exports. The overall strength of the economy was shown by its $5.2 billion external reserves.

Much of Nigeria's new-found wealth was used to finance much-needed federal and state development projects. However, the mass of urban and rural workers were benefited only marginally by the petroleum bonanza. The consumer price index, which in 1974 had risen only 16%, increased in 1975 by over 34%. The military government, recognizing the need for comprehensive wage increases in the public sector, had in 1972 appointed an investigative commission headed by Chief Joseph Udoji. The central government accepted most of the commission's recommendations for higher wages, which was made public in December 1974. Instead of calming worker dissatisfaction, the ensuing large wage increases for public workers touched off further demands from nongovernment workers. A series of strikes by doctors, electrical workers, bus drivers, and teachers in January and February produced the worst economic crisis since the general strike of 1964 and paralyzed the major cities. Settlements of a maximum of 30% increase, backdated to April 1974, were finally granted by the government. The cost of all the awards resulted in outlays of $610 million in the first year.

The wage increases immediately triggered a price rise in all consumer items, thus wiping out much of the workers' benefits. The Gowon government's credibility with the trade unions, university teachers, students, and even civil servants was damaged by its handling of the wage awards. Charges of government corruption and inefficiency increased in all sectors. Vital services were paralyzed by an increasing and unresponsive bureaucracy, as illustrated by the backlog of

— NEWFOUNDLAND · Information Highlights —

Area: 156,185 square miles (404,520 sq km).

Population (1975): 550,000.

Chief Cities (1974): St. John's, the capital, 132,000; Corner Brook (1971), 26,309.

Government (1975): *Chief Officers*—lt. gov., Gordon Winter; premier, F. D. Moores (Progressive Conservative); min. of justice, T. A. Hickman (PC); min. of educ., G. R. Ottenheimer (PC); chief justice, Robert S. Furlong. *Legislature*—Legislative Assembly, 43 members.

Education (1975–76): *Enrollment*—public elementary and secondary schools, 154,600; private schools, 910; colleges and universities, 5,450 students. *Public school expenditures* (1972), $94,660,000.

Public Finance (fiscal year 1974–75 est.): *Revenues,* $661,000,000; *expenditures,* $750,000,000.

Personal Income (1972): $1,310,000,000; average annual income per person, $2,477.

(All monetary figures are in Canadian dollars.)

Brig. Gen. Muritala Ramat Moham-med who became the new Nigerian head-of-state on July 29 after over-throwing Gen. Yakubu Gowon in a bloodless coup.

UPI

over 300 ships waiting to be unloaded at Lagos.

Foreign Affairs. During his tenure, President Gowon continued as one of the major moderate spokesmen for the continent. He continued to voice his opposition to détente with the Republic of South Africa and to support plans for greater cooperation among African states. Nigeria participated actively in the negotiations leading to the Lome Convention, which gave Africa and the Pacific and Caribbean territories easy access to the markets of the European Economic Community. Gowon's government was a key factor in the creation of the 15-member Economic Community of West African States (ECOWAS). Gowon was expected to be one of the major cohesive forces at the Organization of African Unity (OAU) summit meeting in Kampala, Uganda. He was there when the news of the overthrow of his government reached him.

The July Coup. On the morning of Tuesday, July 29, exactly nine years after the second military coup, Col. Joseph Garba announced to the nation that junior officers of the armed forces had deposed General Gowon. There was no active opposition and no bloodshed. Except for a brief period of mandatory curfew, there was no dislocation of normal services. General Gowon in Kampala pledged his loyalty to the new government and then flew to London to join his family.

The new leader appointed as head of the Supreme Military Council was a 37-year-old Hausa, Brig. Gen. Muritala Mohammed, who had distinguished himself by leading the second infantry division during Nigeria's civil war. In his first address to the nation, Mohammed gave

as the main reason for the takeover the continued inaction of the Gowon government when faced with the fact of want in the midst of plenty. Because of general allegations of graft and misuse of public funds, Mohammed replaced all heads of government services, forced the retirement of all senior military officers, and appointed new governors for all the states. By his reorganization, governors would no longer be members of the Supreme Military Council, but would be subordinate to the chief of the defense staff.

Mohammed appointed more civilians as federal ministers, and proposed the creation of a National Council of States, to be composed of representative civilians to deal specifically with states' problems. The coup and the new government's actions and statements have revived such questions as a return to civilian rule, moving the capital, and the creation of more states.

HARRY A. GAILEY, *San Jose State University*

--- **NIGERIA · Information Highlights** ---

Official Name: Federal Republic of Nigeria.
Location: West Africa.
Area: 356,668 square miles (923,768 sq km).
Population (1973 census): 79,760,000.
Chief Cities (1971 est.): Lagos, the capital, 901,000; Ibadan, 758,000; Ogbomosho, 387,000; Kano, 357,000.
Government: *Head of state and government,* Brig. Gen. Murtala Ramat Muhammad (assumed power Aug. 1975).
Monetary Unit: Naira (0.6078 naira equals U. S.$1, June 1975).
Gross National Product (1972 est.): $8,650,000,000.
Manufacturing (major products): Processed foods, cotton textiles, cement, petroleum products.
Major Agricultural Products: Groundnuts, palm kernels, cacao, rubber, cotton, sweet potatoes and yams, forest products, fish.
Foreign Trade (1973): *Exports,* $3,385,000,000; *imports,* $1,877,000,000.

NORTH CAROLINA

Inflation, unemployment, shortage of natural gas, growing dissatisfaction with the quality of public education, and the crisis over medical malpractice insurance were leading stories in North Carolina in 1975. The trial of Joan Little received national attention.

The Economy. Unemployment rose to over 10% in January, dropping slightly later in the year. Prices, however, continued at record levels. The business decline was accompanied by a slower growth rate in state revenues, and general fund income rose only 6.84% during the fiscal year. It was, however, a good year for tourism.

The Budget. Faced with a condition unprecedented since the Great Depression, the General Assembly cut nearly $300 million from the proposed budget. Still, a record $6.6 billion budget, up $500 million, was approved. The controversy over whether to build a second state medical school was settled by the appropriation of $32 million for the conversion of East Carolina University's one-year program into a full degree-granting program. Funds were also provided for upgrading the law school at predominantly-black North Carolina Central University and for the planning of a school of veterinary science at North Carolina State University. Tuition assistance to students in private colleges was doubled to $400.

Other Legislation. The Equal Rights Amendment was rejected; and environmental, consumer, and labor legislation fared badly. State primaries were moved from May to August, and the state's fair trade law was repealed. Disagreements between the Democratic legislature and the Republican governor were reflected in the transfer of some appointive power to the presiding officers of the two houses and the granting of virtual autonomy to the State Ports Authority.

Insurance and Natural Gas. Age was eliminated as a factor in setting automobile insurance rates. Despite legislation on medical malpractice insurance, a crisis developed when the largest underwriter discontinued writing policies in the state. Another crisis arose over the anticipated 29% shortage in the supply of natural gas for the 1975–76 winter.

Education. Disagreements between Dallas Herring, the board of education chairman who advocated "basic education," and Craig Phillips, the superintendent of public instruction who endorsed experimental and social programs, sparked a growing debate over the quality of education in the state's public schools. Budgets for several of Phillips' priority programs were cut by the legislature.

People in the News. Susie M. Sharp, the first woman to be popularly elected as a state supreme court chief justice, took office in January. Labor commissioner Billy Creel died August 29, and the new Republican commissioner, Avery Nye, Jr., promptly swept leading Democrats

from the department. Gov. James Holshouser endorsed the reelection of President Ford, but Republican Sen. Jesse Helms endorsed Ronald Reagan. Former governor Terry Sanford began an underdog campaign for the Democratic presidential nomination.

Joan Little Trial. The trial of Joan Little, a black prison inmate charged in the murder of a white jailer, ended in acquittal on August 15. The trial received national publicity and the intense interest of black, women's, civil rights, and prison reform groups.

H. G. JONES
University of North Carolina

NORTH DAKOTA

The major events of 1975 were the hardships of extreme weather conditions, passage of the Equal Rights Amendment, and the appointment of Thomas Kleppe as interior secretary.

Weather. Torrential rains in late June flooded portions of 12 counties in North Dakota's fertile Red River valley, wiped out about 1.5 million acres (600,000 hectares) of crops worth $176.5 million and caused major damage to farm property and numerous communities. Earlier, a January blizzard called "the storm of the century" left 13 persons dead. It was followed in March by three storms that dropped up to 26 inches (660 mm) of snow on some parts of the state. The heavy snow accumulation combined with a late spring runoff flooded the Red River and its tributaries and the Mouse River near the Canadian border. The January and March storms killed 20,000 head of livestock in pastures, feedlots, and lambing pens.

Despite the hot, dry weather during the growing season, North Dakota farmers harvested their second largest wheat crop and a record yield of sugarbeets. Overall 1975 was an average year for other farm products, but prices were down from 1974 levels.

Legislature. The state Legislative Assembly passed the Equal Rights Amendment (ERA). It also passed the nation's toughest drunk driving law, calling for vehicle impoundment, and a

—— NORTH DAKOTA · Information Highlights ——

Area: 70,665 square miles (183,022 sq km).
Population (1974 est.): 637,000. *Density:* 9 per sq mi.
Chief Cities (1970 census): Bismarck, the capital, 34,-703; Fargo, 53,365; Grand Forks, 39,008; Minot, 32,-290.
Government (1975): *Chief Officers*—governor, Arthur A. Link (D); lt. gov., Wayne G. Sanstead (D). *Legislative Assembly*—Senate, 51 members; House of Representatives, 102 members.
Education (1974–75): *Enrollment*—public elementary schools, 66,797 pupils; public secondary schools, 66,444; nonpublic schools, 11,000; colleges and universities, 28,544 students. *Public school expenditures,* $123,595,000 ($904 per pupil).
State Finances (fiscal year 1974): *Revenues,* $508,728,-000; *expenditures,* $435,020,000.
Personal Income (1974): $3,534,000,000; per capita, $5,-547.
Labor Force (July 1975): *Nonagricultural wage and salary earners,* 199,600; *insured unemployed,* 2,800.

modified no-fault insurance law. A per-ton coal severance tax helped to fund a coal-mining impact office, and there was a new mining reclamation act. Other measures included state college tuition reciprocity with Minnesota, and a reapportionment plan with single-senator districts.

The legislature failed to approve a state department of natural resources and revenue sharing. It also denied funds for a statewide educational television network and for public kindergartens. Efforts to refer the vote on the ERA, as well as the biennial appropriation for the University of North Dakota, to the electorate were blocked by state supreme court decisions.

Apportionment. The legislature's reapportionment plan was upset by a federal district court panel because of its population disparities between legislative districts. The plan had supplanted a court-supervised multi-senate-districts plan that was voided by the U. S. Supreme Court because it violated the one-man one-vote principle. A new proposal being considered by the district court, drawn by a different court appointee, reduced the senate to 50 members, all to be elected in 1976. It ignored traditional political boundaries, and if adopted by the court, will radically change the makeup of the 1977 assembly. Individuals and groups submitted substitute plans and numerous amendments.

Environment. Canada's concern that the $500 million Garrison Diversion irrigation project in North Dakota might pollute water flowing into Manitoba prompted the International Joint Commission to investigate the giant project formally while construction continues. The position of the U. S. State Department is that there are both beneficial and adverse effects on waters crossing the international boundary.

President Gerald Ford nominated North Dakotan Thomas Kleppe as secretary of the interior. A former congressman, Kleppe was head of the Small Business Administration. His appointment as the state's first cabinet member received bipartisan support in North Dakota and Congress, and he was confirmed.

STAN CANN
"The Forum," Fargo

NORTHWEST TERRITORIES

In March 1975 the residents of the Northwest Territories went to the polls to select their first fully-elected territorial council. Fifteen members were elected from across the 1.3 million square miles (3.4 million sq km) that compose Canada's Northwest Territories. In previous years the council had consisted of a combination of elected members and members appointed by the federal government.

The new council selected its own speaker—the commissioner had previously presided—and for the first time placed two of its members on the territories' executive committee. They had responsibilities for the departments of education and social development. These are considered significant steps in the evolution toward responsible government.

Legislation. The council passed a budget of $164 million for 1975, an increase of about 10% over 1974. Other legislation passed included insurance-ordinance amendments designed to protect consumers. The council also passed an ordinance to establish a board to advise the council on scientific, engineering, and technological resources.

Mackenzie Valley Pipeline. Undoubtedly the major event to occur during 1975 was the pipeline inquiry being held by Justice Thomas Berger. It was investigating the social, environmental, and economic aspects of applications to build a multi-billion-dollar pipeline through the Mackenzie Valley to carry gas to southern markets.

In addition to the main hearings in Yellowknife, Justice Berger held meetings in communities along the proposed route and also visited Alaska to study actual pipeline problems. At the same time as the Berger inquiry was being held, hearings also began in Ottawa before the National Energy Board. The final decision as to whether the Mackenzie Valley pipeline will be built, and what regulatory conditions will apply if it is built, rested with the government of Canada.

ROSS M. HARVEY
*Assistant Director of Information
Government of the Northwest Territories*

—— NORTHWEST TERRITORIES · Information ——
Highlights

Area: 1,304,903 square miles (3,379,699 sq km).
Population (1975 est.): 39,000.
Chief City (1975 est.): Yellowknife, the capital, 8,500.
Government (1974): *Chief Officer*—commissioner, Stuart M. Hodgson. *Legislature*—Territorial Council, 15 elected members.
Education (Sept. 1975): *Enrollment*—elementary and secondary schools, 13,794 pupils. *Public school expenditures* (1974–75), $32,227,200.
Public Finance (fiscal year 1975–76 est.): *Revenues,* $164,219,100; *expenditures,* $164,201,700.
Mining (1974 est.): Production value, $223,047,000.
(All monetary figures are in Canadian dollars.)

NORWAY

The world recession began to affect Norway's economy in 1975, although its effects came later than in most western industrial nations, and were not as drastic. Prime Minister Trygve Bratteli took steps to retire from the political scene. King Olav V visited the United States in October.

Economy. Shipping, particularly tanker shipping, was hard hit, and industries producing primarily for export experienced a steep fall in orders. These included the metals smelting, forest products, and fish canning and freezing industries. Shipbuilders that had specialized in producing large tankers suffered indirectly from the slump in the tanker market, which led several shipowners to cancel orders. The Labor government of Prime Minister Bratteli gave high priority to countering recessionary trends. The budget for 1975, drawn up in the fall of 1974, was designed to stimulate domestic demand by raising real, disposable incomes through tax cuts and increases in subsidies and social security payments. The budget for 1976, presented in October 1975, promised further tax concessions and other benefits aimed at raising consumer spending power.

Early in 1975, the government started a series of moves to help industries hit by the recession. These included easier credit facilities, to allow companies to produce for stock. The large Aker shipbuilding group, faced with liquidity problems following a wave of cancellations on tanker orders, received a direct loan from the State Fund for Aid to Industry, plus the guarantee of a large foreign loan. In addition, the government agreed to provide state loan guarantees.

The shipping industry also received government aid. A large tanker owner hit by the slump, Hilmar Reksten, was able to raise cash by selling shipping and industrial shares to the government. The Storting (parliament) approved the deal because Reksten needed money to pay contract-cancellation fees to Norwegian shipyards, where he had ordered tankers. Many non-Socialist Storting members were worried by the fact that the sale increased the state's shareholdings in several key Norwegian industries. It led to state control of the Norwegian coal mines on Spitsbergen.

The non-Socialists urged that the shares should be resold to private interests as soon as possible. It appeared doubtful whether this would happen. The two socialist parties, Labor and the extremist Socialist Left Party (SV), together had a majority of one over the non-Socialist parties and were expected to defeat any proposal to sell shares that the government wanted to keep.

The extensive government spending to sustain the economy, coupled with falling earnings by exporters and the merchant fleet, led to a

UPI

Oil-drilling and production platform was assembled in Stavanger and towed to a North Sea site.

sharp rise in the balance-of-payments deficit. In October, it was officially estimated that the deficit for the whole of 1975 would reach nearly $2.7 billion, almost twice as high as originally estimated. To help finance the deficit, the government borrowed abroad. In addition, it provided state guarantees for borrowing abroad by private industry. Foreign lenders readily provided the money, because Norway was regarded as a good credit risk, in view of its future revenues from offshore oil and gas. The government, for its part, believed it was worth spending some of these revenues in advance, in order to protect Norwegians from the full impact of the world recession.

Oil Industry. Offshore oil development continued at the "moderate" pace prescribed by government policy, which aimed at avoiding distortions in the economy. Late in 1974, the government had allocated a handful of new oil concessions in Norway's sector of the North Sea. Only 8 blocks were allocated, out of 32. The modest allocation was a disappointment to many Norwegian companies with interests in platform building and oil-base operation.

Politics. Among the year's major political events were the local government elections in

September. The Labor party secured 38.2% of the vote and the Conservative party 21.4%. Extremist parties on both left and right did poorly. Voter support for the smaller parties of the center was little changed from the previous local elections, four years earlier. The result was an increase in the number of municipal councils dominated by the non-Socialist parties.

Prime Minister Bratteli stepped down in April as chairman of the Labor party, and was replaced by Reiulf Steen, the party's deputy chairman. Late in September, Bratteli announced that in January he would also retire as prime minister. The party announced that its new prime minister would be Odvar Nordli, Labor's parliamentary leader. Nordli was widely regarded as a moderate, pragmatic politician.

King Olav. King Olav V visited the United States in October, in connection with the 150th anniversary of the first Norwegian emigration to the United States. He was enthusiastically received, particularly by Norwegian-American groups.

THOR GJESTER, *"Norwegian Journal of Commerce and Shipping,"* Oslo

——— **NORWAY · Information Highlights** ———

Official Name: Kingdom of Norway.
Location: Northern Europe.
Area: 125,181 square miles (324,219 sq km).
Population (1975 est.): 4,000,000.
Chief Cities (1974 est.): Oslo, the capital, 477,500; Bergen, 212,000; Trondheim, 129,200.
Government: *Head of state,* Olav V, king (acceded Sept. 1957). *Head of government,* Trygve Bratteli, prime minister (took office Oct. 1973). *Legislature*— Storting: Lagting and Odelsting.
Monetary Unit: Krone (4.94 kroner equal U. S.$1, May 1975).
Gross National Product (1974 est.): $18,400,000,000.
Manufacturing (major products): Metals, pulp and paper, chemicals, ships, fish products.
Major Agricultural Products: Potatoes, barley, apples, pears, dairy products, livestock.
Foreign Trade (1974): *Exports,* $6,274,000,000; *imports,* $8,414,000,000.

NOVA SCOTIA

Nova Scotians during 1975 were preoccupied with the problem of rising food and fuel prices, prolonged labor market disputes, the observance of International Women's Year, and the enactment of some significant legislative measures.

Legislature and Government. The Liberal government during its second term in office enacted 112 bills of 157 proposed. These included the Collection Agencies Act, the Consumer Protection Act, the Licensing and Regulation of Direct Sellers Act, and acts related to the establishment of the Cansteel and the Nova Scotia Research Foundation corporations.

The Collection Agencies Act was designed to protect the interests of debtors against the malpractices of various collection agencies. The Consumer Protection Act and the Licensing and Regulation of Direct Sellers Act protected the interests of provincial consumers.

The provincial government, under the Nova Scotia Research Foundation Corporation Act, for the first time established an independent crown agency to undertake research for encouraging the use of modern technology by industry and government. Another crown agency, Cansteel Corp., was created to promote the concept of a new steel complex in Cape Breton, to review the role of Sydney Steel Corp., and to undertake preliminary studies before finally establishing a new steel complex.

International Women's Year. As part of the celebration of International Women's Year, the provincial government appointed a task force to report on all matters pertaining to the improvement of the status of women in Nova Scotia. The task force was chaired by Dr. Mairi Macdonald and held hearings across the province.

Economy. The provincial economy reflected a strong inflationary bias in 1975. During the first five months of the year, the cost of living index shot up by 10%. This absorbed a greater part of a 16.4% increase in the average weekly wages and salaries of the residents, whose economic position relative to the rest of the country deteriorated further. The national gain in real income was around 18% as compared to the 6% gain netted by Nova Scotians. More serious than that was the continuous deterioration in the provincial unemployment rate during the year. The investment level was down. Labor unrest further dampened the growth of the economy. Both the Maritime Telephone and Telegraph and the Nova Scotia Power Corp., together employing more than 3,000 workers, were affected by legal strikes lasting for nearly two months.

However, the upturn was apparently underway in Nova Scotia by the end of 1975, and signs of revival in the construction sector indicated that the provincial economy might soon expand again. Moreover, the future development of a steel complex in Sydney, and the launching of a $120 million Wreck Cove hydroelectric project, scheduled for completion in 1977, provided grounds for optimism in the growth potential of the provincial economy.

R. P. SETH
Mount Saint Vincent University, Halifax

——— **NOVA SCOTIA · Information Highlights** ———

Area: 21,425 square miles (55,490 sq km).
Chief Cities (1971 census): Halifax, the capital, 122,-035; Dartmouth, 64,770; Sydney, 33,230.
Government (1975): *Chief Officers*—lt. gov., Dr. Clarence Gosse; premier, Gerald A. Regan (Liberal); atty. gen., Allan E. Sullivan (L); min. of educ., J. William Gilles (L); chief justice, Ian M. McKeigan. *Legislature*— Legislative Assembly, 46 members (31 Liberal; 12 Progressive Conservative, 3 New Democratic).
Education (1974–75): *Enrollment:* public elementary and secondary schools, 203,890 pupils; private schools, 1,220; colleges and universities, 17,410 students. *Public school expenditures* (1973–74), $212,481,000.
Public Finance (fiscal year 1975–76 est.): *Revenues,* $728,293,400; *expenditures,* $876,094,200.
Personal Income (1974): $3,244,000,000.
(All monetary figures are in Canadian dollars.)

CHINESE INFORMATION SERVICE

CHIANG KAI-SHEK (1887–1975)
Leader of Nationalist China

CHIANG KAI-SHEK

President of the Republic of China: b. Chekiang, China, Oct. 31, 1887; d. Taiwan, April 5, 1975.

Chiang Kai-shek, revolutionary general and ruler of Nationalist China from 1927 until his death, was the last survivor of World War II's Big Four of Franklin Roosevelt, Winston Churchill, Joseph Stalin, and Chiang. His effect on history, while unquestionably great, will no doubt be decided by future historians.

Early Life. Born on Oct. 31, 1887, in Fenghua, Chekiang, the son of a salt merchant, Chiang lost his father when he was nine. He was brought up by his devout Buddhist mother whose "kindness and perseverance" saved the family from "utter ruin," according to Chiang.

Military Career. In 1907, Chiang was sent to Tokyo for two years of advanced military instruction. During these years he met Dr. Sun Yat-sen and joined Tung Meng Hui, a secret organization and forerunner of the Kuomintang or Nationalist party. When revolt against the Manchu dynasty flared in 1911, Chiang resigned from the Japanese army, returned to China, and participated in the overthrow of the Manchus and the inauguration of the Republic of China on Jan. 1, 1912.

From 1913 to 1921, Chiang was in the brokerage business in Shanghai. In 1921, he became chief of staff of Sun's Canton-based regime. In September 1923, Sun sent him to Moscow to help organize Soviet military assistance against the rival, Peking-based government of the warlords. Upon his return, Chiang warned Sun that the Soviet Union was intent on taking over China's revolutionary movement. In 1924, Chiang organized and became the first superintendent of the Whampoa Military Academy. When Sun died in 1925, Chiang led the major elements of the Kuomintang in a bloody struggle against the Communists and the warlords. After the Northern Expedition against rebellious warlords, Chiang became the leader of a unified China in 1928.

Marriage and Christian Faith. In 1927, Chiang married Soong Mei-ling, the youngest sister of the powerful banker, T. V. Soong. A dedicated Christian and graduate of Wellesley College, Madame Chiang proved to be an invaluable partner to Chiang, who now became a devout Christian.

National Tragedies. Chiang's efforts at nation building were obstructed both by domestic and foreign forces. After Mao Tse-tung's Communists broke down the coalition with Kuomintang in 1927, Chiang first purged his adversaries and then by 1934 drove them to Shensi province in China's northwest. But Japan's 1931 invasion of Manchuria worried the northern warlords, who wanted Chiang to use his armies against the invaders rather than the Communists.

In 1936, after secret negotiations between the government and the Communists to form a united front against Japan were successfully concluded, Chiang went to Sian, where he was captured by the warlords and, after a bizarre period of debate, released. Then the Japanese launched a full-scale invasion on July 7, 1937. On August 21, China signed a non-aggression treaty with the USSR, which then offered military aid.

After Japan's attack on Pearl Harbor in December 1941, U. S. strategists recognized Chiang as the most effective force against the Japanese. Chiang became the supreme commander of Allied forces in the China theater, but sharp differences between Chiang and Gen. Joseph W. Stilwell over the policy toward the Chinese Communists developed. Chiang asked for and got Stilwell's recall. In 1945, Gen. George C. Marshall was sent in a final effort to keep civil war from breaking out, but it proved to be fruitless. From 1945 to 1949 the United States supported Chiang in his unsuccessful bid to defeat the Communists and, after he had retreated to Taiwan, supported his regime there.

Nationalist President. Chiang became the first elected constitutional president of the Republic of China on March 29, 1948. Retiring temporarily on Jan. 21, 1949, he was recalled on March 1, 1950, by popular demand. Reelected four times, he served as president until his death. Chiang's leadership and U. S. support have given Taiwan a rapidly growing economy.

T. H. TSUAN, *The Royal Asiatic Society of Great Britain and Ireland*

UPI

FAISAL (1906?–1975)
Assassinated at the height of power

FAISAL

King of Saudi Arabia: b. Riyadh, Saudi Arabia, probably in 1906; d. Riyadh, March 25, 1975.

King Faisal held the throne of Saudi Arabia during a crucial decade in which the world's need for petroleum gave Saudi Arabia, the largest oil exporter, a position of increasing importance. Conscious of his influence, Faisal used his power to further the goals of Saudi Arabia and the Islamic world. He was assassinated in his capital, Riyadh, on March 25 by a nephew, Prince Faisal ibn Musaid, who was later executed publicly for the slaying.

Early Years. King Faisal ibn Abd al-Aziz al-Saud was born in Riyadh, probably in 1906. He was raised in the home of his maternal grandfather, al-Shaikh of the distinguished Wahhabi family. He learned early the ways of the desert raider, riding bareback, eating sparingly, rising two hours before dawn, and becoming a crack shot. His education was in the hands of the local *ulema* (religious scholars). In the great influenza epidemic of 1918 several sons of Ibn Saud died, leaving Faisal the second in line of succession.

In 1919, Great Britain invited Ibn Saud to send a member of his family to England, and Faisal was chosen. He had an audience with King George V and visited Wales and Ireland.

Rise to Power. At the age of 20, Faisal led with distinction an army to quell a rebellion in Asir on the western coast of Arabia. In 1924–25 he helped his father conquer the Hejaz, and they entered the holy city of Mecca together in 1926 as conquerors. Faisal became viceroy of the Hejaz and his father's foreign minister. In 1926 he visited England and France, and he made another tour of Europe, including the USSR, in 1931. In 1931, he was appointed president of the newly-created Council of Deputies, and all key government departments reported to him. He carried out his duties with great skill.

During World War II, Prince Faisal visited the United States and met important government officials. In 1953, Ibn Saud died and Faisal's older brother, Saud, became king. Faisal was named crown prince and prime minister. Under King Saud affairs were mismanaged to the extent that the unofficial council of royal princes insisted that Prince Faisal assume active leadership of the government. He curbed spending and began to restore solvency to the state. Many chafed under his economic stringency, and in 1960, King Saud reasserted his power and forced Prince Faisal to resign. A reconciliation took place, and Faisal became foreign minister again in 1962. Government affairs, however, continued to deteriorate until Mar. 28, 1964, when Faisal took full power, naming himself viceroy, prime minister, and commander in chief. Finally, on Nov. 2, 1964, Faisal became king when Saud was deposed and left the country.

Leadership. As king, Faisal steered a middle course between conservative members of the royal family, who wished to return to the austere ways of Saud, and the younger members, who stressed modernization. He supported the Arab League but opposed Soviet influence in Iraq and Egypt and tried to prevent radical movements in Yemen and Aden. After the Israeli-Arab War in June 1967, Faisal came to the financial aid of Egypt, Jordan, and Syria.

Following the death of Egypt's President Nasser in 1970, King Faisal became the dominant figure in the Arab world. An avowed enemy of Communism and Zionism, he was happy when Egypt expelled Soviet advisers in 1972. He strongly supported the Organization of Petroleum Exporting Countries (OPEC) in its oil policies and in July 1973 warned that he would use his oil and monetary power if the United States did not modify its policy toward Israel. After the Israeli-Arab War in October 1973, Faisal enforced the oil embargo with caution.

King Faisal was a moderate in his policies and actions. He kept a tight rein on all areas of government but preferred to speak through his ministers and aides. During his last 20 years he was not well, and in 1957 he underwent three stomach operations in the United States. He had three wives, at least eight sons, and many daughters. Most of the sons were educated in the United States, and several held high government positions in Saudi Arabia at the time of their father's death.

SYDNEY NETTLETON FISHER
The Ohio State University

FRANCO, Francisco

Head of state of Spain: b. El Ferrol, Galicia, Spain, Dec. 4, 1892; d. Madrid, Nov. 20, 1975.

Francisco Franco was the dictator and the head of state of Spain from April 1939 until shortly before his death. Ultraconservative, authoritarian, capable of using cruelty and terror as political weapons, he was the last living member of the Fascist triumvirate that included Adolf Hitler and Benito Mussolini.

Physically unprepossessing and lacking outward charm and oratorical ability, Franco kept his undisputed power as chief of state by carefully balancing the forces that supported him—landowners, industrialists, bankers, the military, and the Roman Catholic Church. All decisions, large and petty, were referred to Franco, who kept his own counsel. "Not even his collar knows what he is thinking," associates said of him. Although repression was the lot of Spaniards for 36 years, Franco brought the economy from poverty levels to moderate prosperity. Per capita income quadrupled between 1962 and 1975. Diplomatically, Franco helped Spain by cementing a military alliance with the United States in 1953. This helped to keep Spain stable, despite recurring internal tensions and external democratic pressures.

Life and Work. Francisco Paulino Hermenegildo Teodúla Franco Bahamonde was the son of Nicolás Franco, a naval officer, and Pilar Bahamonde, a woman of good family. He was raised to join the navy but went to an army school instead, from which he was commissioned a second lieutenant in 1910. Sent to North Africa in 1912, he fought rebel tribesmen and became, in rapid succession, the Army's youngest captain, major, colonel, and general. He was praised for valor, exacting discipline, and organizational ability. He rose to be head of the Spanish Foreign Legion and was credited with the defeat of Adb-el-Krim, the Riff chieftain.

After the monarchy fell in 1931, the republic moved toward the right, and Franco was named chief of the army general staff. In 1936, the republic veered left (but not Communist), and a generals' group plotted to overthrow it. When the uprising began on July 18, Franco was not in its lead, but owing to the deaths of others, he was invested as the Nationalist leader in October 1936. The Civil War lasted until April 1939, when Madrid fell. Hitler and Mussolini aided Franco with arms, troops, and money. The exceptionally bloody conflict left Spain devastated. With victory, Franco executed thousands of Republican sympathizers. Memory of the Civil War influenced Franco's foes until his death.

In World War II, Franco supported the Axis without joining it. His regime was banned from the United Nations as a Fascist power until 1955, but its ostracism was effectively ended in

UPI

FRANCISCO FRANCO (1892–1975)
Authoritarian leader of Spain.

1950 with a U. S. decision to acquire bases in Spain as a Cold War move against the Soviet Union. Franco cannily used his U. S. connection to lure foreign investments and to develop inexpensive tourism. He offered tax concessions, cheap labor, and high profits. Meantime, a corps of technocrats emerged, and these, carefully supervised, reigned in industry and commerce. The press, however, was kept in check, and democratic rights were suppressed. The ensuing stability was often ruptured by acts of terrorism, including the assassination of the premier, Adm. Luis Carrero Blanco, in 1973.

In 1969, Franco designated Prince Juan Carlos de Borbón as his successor, to become king and chief of state, on Franco's death. In Franco's final illness, the prince was vested with temporary power, and he became king upon Franco's death.

Personal Life. Franco worked and lived in El Pardo Palace. His home life was simple. He and his wife, Carmen, married in 1923 and had one daughter. He relaxed by hunting and playing with his grandchildren. He also enjoyed ceremonies—openings of everything from theaters to industrial exhibits. At these, he waved in a stiff, almost formal manner, and forced an occasional smile. He came to be regarded more as an institution than as a person. He had long prepared for his death by building a Pharaonic tomb carved out of living rock near Madrid. It is surmounted by a cross 500 feet (152 meters) tall. As his last illness grew prolonged, the Roman Catholic Church, once a staunch supporter, moved away from him. He was left chiefly with the backing of the military.

ALDEN WHITMAN
"The New York Times"

HAILE SELASSIE

Emperor of Ethiopia: b. Hararar, Ethiopia, July 23, 1892; d. Addis Ababa, Aug. 27, 1975.

Haile Selassie was one of the 20th century's best-known leaders. He ruled Ethiopia as emperor for 44 years, leading it into the first stages of modernization, before his methods were rejected by young Ethiopian activists, and he was toppled from power. From the mid-1930's he received world acclaim as a gallant leader, and in the 1950's and 1960's he was a spokesman for the emerging nations of Africa.

Early Life. Born Lij Tafari Makonnen, he was the only son of Ras Makonnen, cousin and adviser to Emperor Menelik II. Tafari was educated at the court and gained administrative experience as a provincial governor. In 1912, he married Wayzero Menen, Menelik's great-granddaughter, by whom he had six children.

Regent and Heir. Menelik died in 1913, and was succeeded by his grandson Lij Yasu, whose conversion to Islam alienated him from the Christian majority in Ethiopia. Tafari brought about his downfall in 1916. Menelik's daughter Zauditu was crowned empress, and Tafari became regent and heir to the throne. From 1916 to 1928, Tafari extended his power and built up his own military force. He established schools throughout the country and began a program of sending Ethiopians abroad for study. In 1923, he succeeded in having Ethiopia admitted to the League of Nations.

Emperor. Tafari assumed the title of king (*negus*) in 1928. When Empress Zauditu died in 1930, Tafari was crowned emperor and took the name Haile Selassie ("Power of the Holy Trinity"). In 1931, Haile Selassie granted Ethiopia a constitution (its first), providing for a parliament. All formal power, however, remained with the emperor.

Ethiopia was invaded by Italy in 1935, and in 1936, Haile Selassie was forced into exile. In a memorable speech before the League of Nations on June 30, 1936, he appealed, in vain, for the imposition of military sanctions on Italy, warning the members that "God and history will remember your judgment." After four years in exile, in England, Haile Selassie helped lead a British military expedition that defeated Italian forces in Ethiopia. The emperor returned to Addis Ababa in May 1941.

After the restoration, Haile Selassie attempted to consolidate his power and create political and economic stability. Major land-reform programs were initiated in 1942 and 1944. The emperor's heroic stance during the Italian invasion and his appearance before the League of Nations made him a world figure.

In 1955, a revised constitution was promulgated, introducing universal adult suffrage and giving added powers to the parliament. A coup d'etat was quickly suppressed in 1960. Haile

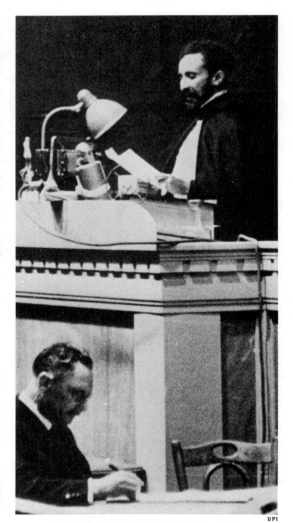

HAILE SELASSIE (1892–1975)
Eloquence at the League of Nations

Selassie played a key role in the formation of the Organization of African Unity, created in 1963 in Addis Ababa, still its headquarters. Also in 1963, he twice visited the United States, the second time to attend the funeral of President John F. Kennedy, where his dignity created great sympathy for him and his country.

In 1967, Haile Selassie signed a land reform bill meant to limit some of the feudal land abuses existing in Ethiopia. The law, however, was never adequately carried out, and tenants remained at the mercy of their landlords.

Decline of Influence. From 1967 student unrest, peasant rebellions in Gojam and Tigre provinces, a secessionist movement in Eritrea, and periodic famines led to the weakening of Haile Selassie's authority. On Sept. 12, 1974, he was ousted from power by a military coup and placed under arrest. He remained in detention until he died in his sleep, Aug. 27, 1975.

PETER SCHWAB
State University of New York at Purchase

MINDSZENTY, Jozsef Cardinal

Roman Catholic Cardinal, former Primate of Hungary; b. Csehimindszent, Hungary, Mar. 29, 1892; d. Vienna, Austria, May 9, 1975.

Jozsef Cardinal Mindszenty, next only to the popes of the mid-20th-century, was possibly the most celebrated Roman Catholic prelate of the period. For more than three decades he was looked upon as a symbol of loyalty to the church and a heroic symbol of defiance to Nazi and Communist tyranny. Ironically, at the time of his death he was in exile from his native land and lay stripped of his titles of Archbishop of Esztergom and Primate of Hungary.

Early Life. Described by some as a "martyr" for humanity and by others as a "relic" of the Cold War, Cardinal Mindszenty was born Jozsef Pehm in a small Hungarian village, the son of its mayor, Janos Pehm, and his wife. The Pehms were of German origin, but for 300 years the family had lived in Hungary and farmed its small plot of land. The cardinal was to show his great love for his native land—and his contempt for invading armies—years later when, during the German occupation, he assumed the name of his native village as his own while others of German ancestry were dropping their Hungarian names for their former German ones.

Young Jozsef grew up on his father's land, helping with the chores until leaving for the seminary in nearby Szomathely. Ordained in 1915, Pehm immediately won attention, through his writings and preaching, as an outspoken advocate of the masses. One of the first results of this advocacy, after being named pastor in Zalaegerszeg four years later, was imprisonment at the hands of Bela Kuhn, when the Communists set up their short-lived regime in 1919.

Man of Controversy. He was named bishop of Veszprem on Mar. 3, 1944, shortly before the Nazis took over complete control of Hungary. His sharply-worded pastoral letters and sermons denouncing Nazism as the "new paganism," and his condemnation of Nazi persecution of the Jews, made him and his chancery the focal point of Hungarian resistance efforts. It also earned him imprisonment again.

He played no favorites, however. He was just as tough when the Communists took over after the war. The sting of his voice became louder when, on Oct. 2, 1945, he was named archbishop of Esztergom and primate of Hungary by Pope Pius XII and when, on Feb. 18, 1946, he was named a cardinal.

Finally, on Dec. 26, 1948, following three years of verbal combat, he was jailed by the Communists on charges of espionage, treason, and illicit dealing in currency. Anticipating his arrest, he had left a statement saying that if he were seized, any "confession" he might make would only be the consequence of "human frailty" and would, therefore, be null and void.

UPI

Cardinal Mindszenty (*left*) is greeted by Pope Paul VI upon his arrival in Rome in September 1971.

Early in 1949 he was brought to trial before what U. S. President Harry S. Truman called a "kangaroo court" and on Feb. 8, 1949, despite protests from throughout the world, was found guilty of all charges and was sentenced to life in prison. Later the cardinal was to say that he had been tortured through long hours of interrogation and days without sleep, and that during ensuing years he suffered "the worst kind of imprisonment, the very worst kind." In July 1955, he was moved from prison to house arrest and for four days during the uprising of the Hungarian Freedom Fighters in October 1956, was free to resume his offices in Budapest.

Refuge and Exile. With the onslaught of Soviet tanks, however, and the crushing of the revolt, the cardinal sought refuge in the U. S. legation in Budapest. He remained there until ordered to the Vatican by Pope Paul VI on Sept. 28, 1971, as part of an accord to ease church-state relations in Hungary. Leaving his homeland, the cardinal said, was "perhaps the heaviest cross of my life."

Received warmly in Rome, Mindszenty remained there only four weeks before seeking permanent residence at the Pazmaneum in Vienna, the house of studies for Hungarian seminarians. It is 45 miles (72 km) from the border of the two countries, and he lived there until his death. Following surgery, he died in Vienna from a blood clot.

Stripped of his titles as head of the primatial see 15 months earlier (Feb. 5, 1974), the prelate was hailed by Pope Paul upon his death as "a singular priest and pastor . . . zealous in the faith, fierce in sentiment and immovable in what seemed to him to be his duty and right."

OWEN J. MURPHY, JR.
Editor, "The Catholic Free Press"

ARISTOTLE ONASSIS (1900–1975)
"The Golden Greek"

ONASSIS, Aristotle Socrates

Greek shipping magnate: b. Izmir, Turkey, Sept. 21, 1900; d. Paris, Mar. 15, 1975.

Known to friend and foe alike as "the Golden Greek," Aristotle Socrates Onassis was a shipping tycoon, multimillionaire dealer in real estate and high finance, and a political intriguer who knew and made use of power. He amassed a $500 million-plus fortune after beginning with a $60 stake.

Although he professed to hate publicity, Onassis drew it to himself like a magnet by his choice of friends, whom he entertained lavishly and publicly, and by his taste in women. He was married first to Athina Livanos, the daughter of a Greek shipping tycoon even richer than Onassis. Then, for almost a decade he carried on an internationally-headlined affair with Maria Callas, the famed soprano. Finally, in 1968 he married the most glamorous and famous widow of her time, Jacqueline Bouvier Kennedy, wife of the assassinated President John F. Kennedy. She was 29 years his junior.

Onassis' financial dealings, serpentine in their complexity, included controlling interests in more than 100 companies involved in oil transport; baby food manufacturing; real estate, including office and apartment buildings on four continents; and an airline. At one time he even owned—without breaking the bank—the Monte Carlo casino.

Early Years. Born in the Turkish city of Smyrna, now Izmir, in the large Greek colony there, he was the son of Socrates Onassis, a tobacco seller, and the former Penelope Dologou. In 1922, Kemal Ataturk's troops ruthlessly took over the area for Turkey and herded males of Greek heritage into concentration camps. Onassis escaped with his family and wound up alone in 1923 in Buenos Aires, with $60.

Business Career. After working for a local telephone company, Onassis got into tobacco importing, and by 1930 was a millionaire. On the then depressed shipping market, he bought six freighters at $20,000 each. "You could pick up a ship for the same price as a Rolls Royce," he said. He added to his fleet for a decade, and when World War II came, his fleet, mostly in precious oil tankers, was the world's fifth largest in tonnage.

Onassis was one of the first shippers to order supertankers, helping make the Suez Canal, closed by war in 1956, almost obsolete. (The 150,000-ton tankers simply went around the Cape of Good Hope, at enormous financial benefits to their owners.) Onassis' ships were registered in "flag of convenience" countries with low tax rates, like Panama and Liberia. "My favorite country," Onassis said, "is the one that grants maximum immunity from taxes, trade restrictions, and unreasonable regulations."

Love and Death. It was on one of his famous cruises on the yacht *Christina,* a floating palace served by 50 crewmen and featuring a $200,000 El Greco in the lounge, that in 1959 a romance bloomed between Onassis and Maria Callas. Her Italian husband and the Winston Churchills were also aboard at the time. Onassis divorced his wife, and Callas separated legally from her husband. The couple were inseparable for years, until shortly before Onassis shocked the world by marrying Jacqueline Kennedy on his private Ionian Sea island of Skorpios.

By 1973, when he had developed myasthenia gravis, a debilitating neurological disease, Onassis had become a saddened man. His investment in Olympic Airways, which he had acquired from the Greek government, had declined enormously because of unsettling political conditions and the drop in tourism. Though ill, he personally campaigned in a New Hampshire town to win permission to build an oil refinery there, and was turned down.

But most important, as he grew more ill, he had to face the fact of the death of his only son, Alexander, in an airplane crash in Athens. His daughter Christina embarked on a brief, disastrous marriage with a real estate man in California, and he felt that his own marriage was shaky. Onassis left the bulk of his huge estate to his daughter, but provided a comfortable lifetime stipend for his wife and each of her two children by President Kennedy.

ALBIN KREBS, *"The New York Times"*

obituaries · 1975

The following is a selected list of over 200 prominent persons who died in 1975. Separate articles on major figures appear on the preceding pages.

Adderley, Julian (Cannonball) (46), U. S. jazz musician; known for his talent on the soprano, tenor, and alto saxophones; d. Gary, Ind., Aug. 9.

Anderson, Clinton P. (80), U. S. politician and cabinet member; representative and senator from New Mexico; served in Truman cabinet as secretary of agriculture; chairman of Senate Aeronautical and Space Sciences Committee (1963–72): d. Albuquerque, N. M., Nov. 11.

Anderson, Leroy (66), U. S. composer and conductor: b. Cambridge, Mass., June 29, 1908; d. Woodbury, Conn., May 18, 1975. He was known in particular for works featuring sounds of familiar objects, such as *The Syncopated Clock* and *The Typewriter*. His *Blue Tango* (1952) became the first instrumental composition to reach the top of the Hit Parade. The son of Swedish immigrants, he studied music at Harvard University (B. A., 1929, M. A., 1930). Anderson guest-conducted a number of leading orchestras, including Arthur Fiedler's Boston Pops. Among his popular hits are *Sleigh Ride, China Doll*; and *Promenade*; and he also wrote such symphonic works as *Irish Suite*.

Andric, Ivo (82), Yugoslav novelist and Nobel Prize-winning author (1961) of *The Bridge on the Drina*; his works were translated into 24 languages; served in the diplomatic service and as a member of the national assembly: d. Belgrade, March 13.

Baker, Josephine (68), U. S.-born French singer and dancer: b. St. Louis, Mo., June 3, 1906; d. Paris, France, April 12, 1975. An expatriate from the black ghetto of St. Louis, she became an internationally renowned cabaret entertainer after making her Paris debut in *La Revue Nègre* in 1925. Noted for her sultry soprano voice, her graceful figure, and her electrifying personality, she epitomized black talent and beauty to French audiences, to whom she introduced "le jazz hot" and the Charleston. A citizen of France since 1937, she was awarded the Legion of Honor for her work with the Resistance during World War II. Over the years, she adopted a dozen orphans of various nationalities, whom she called her "rainbow tribe."

Bech, Joseph (88), Luxembourg statesman and former premier (1926–41) and foreign minister; participated in the founding of the United Nations and the European Common Market; a signer of the North Atlantic Treaty (1949): d. Luxembourg, March 8.

Benton, Thomas Hart (85), U. S. painter: b. Neosho, Mo., April 15, 1889; d. Kansas City, Mo., Jan. 19, 1975. Once described by Harry S. Truman as "the best damned painter in America," he was noted for his colorful, earthy canvases and murals, which depicted vigorously and realistically scenes of homespun America and its regional characters from history and folklore. The son

"Cannonball" Adderley

Leroy Anderson

Josephine Baker

Anslinger, Harry J. (83); U. S. civil servant; headed the Treasury Department's Bureau of Narcotics for 32 years (ending 1962); fought for uniform drug laws in all states and for the proper use of all drugs; U. S. representative to the United Nations Narcotics Commission: d. Hollidaysburg, Pa., Nov. 14.

Arendt, Hannah (69), German-born U. S. political scientist and philosopher; escaped Hitler's Germany and later left Nazi-occupied France for the United States. She was a lecturer at many leading colleges and universities and an expert on 20th century nazism and communism. She was also the author of eight major works, including *The Origins of Totalitarianism* (1951), *Eichmann in Jerusalem, A Report* (1963), and *On Revolution* (1963); first U. S. citizen to receive Denmark's Sonning Prize for contributions to European civilization: d. New York, N. Y., Dec. 4.

Bailey, John M(oran) (70), U. S. political party official and lawyer: b. Hartford, Conn., Nov. 23, 1904; d. there, Apr. 10, 1975. As Democratic state chairman in Connecticut (1946–75) and chairman of the Democratic National Committee (1961–68) he was a powerful behind-the-scenes political figure. After studying at Catholic University (B. A., 1926) and Harvard Law School (LL. B., 1929), he served in appointive posts on the state and local level. Bailey played a key role in the successful gubernatorial campaigns of Chester Bowles in 1948, Abraham A. Ribicoff in 1954, and Ella T. Grasso in 1974. He organized a Kennedy-for-vice-president campaign in 1956 and was appointed Democratic national chairman after John F. Kennedy's inauguration as president in 1961.

Baker, George (59), U. S. artist and cartoonist; a former Walt Disney artist, who created the cartoon *Sad Sack* during World War II while serving in the Army: d. San Gabriel, Calif., May 7.

of a congressman, he was named after his grand-uncle, who was Missouri's first U. S. senator. After dropping out of high school at 17, he went to work as a caricaturist for the Joplin *American*. Later he studied at the Chicago Art Institute, lived in Paris for three years, saw World War I naval service, and taught at the Art Students League in New York and at the Kansas City Art Institute. Although his disdain for modern art and European aestheticism often brought him into conflict with the art establishment, he attained great popularity in the 1930's with such regional paintings as *The Jealous Lover of Lone Green Valley*. His monumental mural *America Today* at the New School for Social Research in New York City is considered his masterpiece.

Black, Eli M. (53), U. S. executive and chairman of troubled United Brands Co.; an ordained rabbi, he was a trustee of Lincoln Center for the Performing Arts and several Jewish philanthropies: d. New York, N. Y., Feb. 3.

Blue, Ben (73), Canadian-born, U. S. comedian; sad-faced star of stage, film, radio, television, and nightclubs; began his career at 15 as chorus boy in *Irene*; films include *Panama Hattie* (1942), *My Wild Irish Rose* (1947), *The Russians are Coming, the Russians are Coming, It's a Mad, Mad, Mad, Mad World*: d. Hollywood, Calif., March 7.

Booth, Charles Brandon (87), U. S. social welfare leader and retired head of Volunteers of America (1949–58); grandson of Salvation Army's founder Gen. William Booth; active in Big Brother and Big Sister organizations: d. La Mesa, Calif., April 14.

Braden, Carl (60), U. S. civil rights activist; former executive director of Southern Conference Education Fund; leader of Training Institute for Propaganda Organizing in Louisville, Ky.; served a prison term for refusing to testify before the House Committee on UnAmerican Activities: d. Louisville, Ky., Feb. 18.

Bronk, Dr. Detlev (78), U.S. scientist and educator; formulated theory of biophysics; president of Johns Hopkins University (1949–53); first president and later president emeritus of Rockefeller Institute (from 1953); headed National Academy of Sciences (1950–62): d. New York, N. Y., Nov. 17.

Brundage, Avery (87), U.S. and international athletic association official: b. Detroit, Mich., Sept. 28, 1887; d. Garmisch-Partenkirchen, West Germany, May 8, 1975. From 1925–53 he presided over the U.S. Olympic Association and Committee, and served as vice president of the International Olympic Committee from 1945–52 and as its president from 1952–72. He zealously defended amateurism in athletic competition, often reaping unpopularity because of his controversial decisions. He graduated from the University of Illinois in 1909 and took part in the pentathlon and decathlon events at the 1912 Olympics in Stockholm.

Bulganin, Nikolai A(leksandrovich) (79), Soviet statesman: b. Nizhni Novgorod, Russia, June 11, 1895; d. Moscow, USSR, Feb. 24, 1975. A member of the ruling elite of the USSR for over a decade, he served as chairman of the council of ministers, or premier, from 1955–58, sharing power with Communist party first secretary Nikita S. Khrushchev. Known as the "B and K team," he and Khrushchev traveled to world capitals to relax East-West tensions. He joined the Bolshevik party in 1917, and as a protege of Stalin rose rapidly in government and party ranks. Named defense minister in 1953, he was a member of the Presidium from 1952–58 until he was ousted by Krushchev after siding against him in an "antiparty" group.

Burns, John A. (66), former U.S. governor of Hawaii; during World War II he defended the loyalty of Japanese citizens and helped to found two military units comprised largely of Japanese volunteers; instrumental in achieving Hawaiian statehood; Democratic governor of Hawaii (1962–75): d. Kaiwi, Oahu, April 5.

Bushnell, Asa S. (75), U.S. sports administrator; Commissioner of the Eastern College Athletic Conference (1938–1970); secretary of the United States Olympic Committee: d. Princeton, N. J., March 22.

Camp, Charles (82), U.S. paleontologist; professor emeritus at the University of California at Berkeley; discovered rich fossil field in New Mexico with bones dating back 75 million years: d. Berkeley, Calif., August 14.

Cantacuzene, Princess Julia Grant (99), granddaughter of President Ulysses S. Grant; Washington society figure: d. Washington, D. C., Oct. 5.

Carpentier, Georges (81), French boxer, best known for his losing bout with Jack Dempsey in 1921, which was boxing's first $1 million gate in the United States: d. Paris, Oct. 28.

Charles, Ezzard (53), U.S. boxer: b. Lawrenceville, Ga., July 7, 1921; d. Chicago, Ill., May 28, 1975. Known as one of the most skilled tacticians of the ring, he defeated Jersey Joe Walcott in June 1949 for the world heavyweight championship vacated by the retirement of Joe Louis but lost the title to Walcott in July 1951. He began to box as an amateur at 16 and turned professional in 1940. In 1950 he ended a comeback bid by Joe Louis by outpointing the former champion. Charles tried to regain the heavyweight crown but was twice defeated by Rocky Marciano. Of the 122 bouts he fought between 1940 and 1959 he won 96, including 58 by knockouts.

Ezzard Charles

UPI

Bob Considine

UPI

After his retirement he was active in community projects on Chicago's south side. He was elected to boxing's Hall of Fame in 1970.

Chiang Kai-shek. See separate article preceding this section.

Considine, Robert B. (Bob) (68), U.S. journalist; syndicated columnist for 105 Hearst newspapers; made regular appearances as a radio and television commentator; author or co-author of 25 books; his *On the Line* column began in 1933: d. New York, N. Y., Sept. 25.

Conte, Richard (59), U.S. stage and screen actor; known for his character roles; appeared in films *Thieves' Highway* (1949), *Guadalcanal Diary* (1943), *I'll Cry Tomorrow* (1956), and on Broadway: d. Los Angeles, Calif., April 15.

Coolidge, William D. (101), U.S. inventor; developed a method of working hot tungsten that led to improved light bulbs; invented (1913) the X-ray tube that is the model of tubes still in use; vice president and director of research for General Electric Co.; associated with the development of the atomic bomb; recipient of many awards and member of the National Inventors Hall of Fame: d. Schenectady, N. Y., Feb. 3.

Cordier, Andrew W(ellington) (74), U.S. educator and UN official: b. Canton, Ohio, March 3, 1901; d. Manhasset, N. Y., July 11, 1975. A skilled troubleshooter and conciliator, he began his career as chairman of the history department of Manchester College in Indiana, after graduating from there in 1922 and receiving his Ph.D. from the University of Chicago in 1927. Working for the U.S. State Department to organize the United Nations, Cordier served from 1946–62 as executive assistant to the UN secretary general. From 1962–68 and from 1970–72, he was dean of the School of International Affairs at Columbia University. As acting president of Columbia in 1968–69 and president in 1969–70, he restored harmony to its troubled campus following student riots.

Dallapiccola, Luigi (71), Italian composer; a musical theorist who followed the 12-tone mode; pioneer of modern music; his works include operas *Volo di Notte, Ulisse,* and *Cinque Canti:* d. Florence, Feb. 19.

De Valera, Eamon (92), Irish statesman: b. New York, N. Y., Oct. 14, 1882; d. Dublin, Ireland, Aug. 29, 1975. One of Ireland's most revered political figures, he played a key role in his country's struggle for independence from Great Britain. Of Spanish-Irish parentage, he was raised in Ireland and graduated from the National University in Dublin in 1904. After several years as a teacher he joined the nationalist Sinn Fein party. During the 1916 Easter Rebellion he served as a commandant with the Irish Volunteers and narrowly escaped execution by the British. In 1917 he was elected president of the Sinn Fein and the Volunteers. After founding the Fianna Fáil party in 1926, he became opposition leader in the parliament of the Irish Free State. As prime minister and foreign minister from 1932 to 1948 he introduced a new constitution in 1937 and maintained Ireland's neutrality in World War II. After the establishment of the Republic of Ireland in 1949 he again served as prime minister, from 1951 to 1954 and from 1957 to 1959, and then as president, a largely ceremonial post, from 1959 until his retirement in 1973.

Dobzhansky, Theodosius (75), world famous geneticist, noted for his research and writing on evolution; professor of genetics at the University of California from 1971–75: d. Davis, Calif., Dec. 18.

Donohue, Mark (38), U.S. racing car driver; won three national sports car championships as an amateur; winner (1972) of the Indianapolis 500; retired (1974) but returned the same year: d. in an accident, Graz, Austria, Aug. 19.

Doxiadis, Constantinos Apostolos (62), Bulgarian-born Greek architect and urban planner; Minister of Development and Coordination following World War II; helped plan Greece's reconstruction; developed ekistics, the science of human settlement; among his projects are urban and rural renewal for Iraq, the new Pakistani capital of Islamabad, and Eastwick in Philadelphia: d. Athens, June 28.

Duclos, Jacques (78), French Communist party leader; worked vigorously for the Resistance during World War II; served as vice president of the Consultative Assembly, which reestablished republican government after the war; in the National Assembly and Senate; ran for president (1969): d. Paris, April 25.

Dunning, John R. (67), U.S. physicist and educator; led in discovery of the method of isolation of uranium-235 during World War II; dean of Columbia University School of Engineering (1950–69); early expert on the neutron: d. Key Biscayne, Fla., Aug. 25.

Escrivá de Balaguer, Monsignor Josemaria (73), Spanish-born Roman Catholic clergyman; founder (1928) and president general of Opus Dei (the works of God), a secular organization emphasizing Christian virtue and professionalism in work; author of *Camino (The Way)*, which summed up his teachings: d. Rome, June 26.

Evans, Walker (71), U. S. photographer: b. St. Louis, Mo., Nov. 3, 1903; d. New Haven, Conn., April 10, 1975. Capturing the "deep beauty in things as they are," he presented bleak, unadorned, and starkly realistic views of Depression-era sharecroppers, subway passengers, ghost towns, and junk yards. Originally attracted by writing, he turned to photography in 1928 after leaving Williams College to study in Paris. As a member of the Farm Security Administration 1935–37 he took photographs documenting rural poverty in the South, 31 of which were in James Agee's *Let Us Now Praise Famous Men* (1941). Evans was a contributing editor of *Time* from 1943–45 and associate editor of *Fortune* from 1945–65. He joined the faculty of Yale University as a professor of graphic design in 1965.

Faisal. See separate article preceding this section.

Fine, Larry (73), U. S. comedian and member of the Three Stooges comedy team from 1925; made over 200 movies beginning with *Soup to Nuts* (1930) and ending with *Snow White and the Three Stooges* (1961): d. Woodland Hills, Calif., June 24.

Fox, Jacob Nelson (Nellie) (47), U. S. baseball player; second baseman for the Chicago White Sox (1950–64); named American League's Most Valuable Player (1959): d. St. Thomas, Pa., Dec. 1.

Franco, Francisco. See separate article preceding this section.

Fresnay, Pierre (77), French stage and film actor; his stage roles included *La Grande Illusion*, Pagnol's trilogy *Maurius, Fanny*, and *Cesar*, and *Conversation Piece* in London; resigned his membership in the Comédie Française for political reasons; appeared in 70 movies: d. Paris, Jan. 9.

Fuller, Ida (100), recipient of the first social security check in 1940, when her payment of $22 matched her total investment: d. Brattleboro, Vt., Jan. 27.

Gibbons, Euell (64), U. S. author, noted for his books on natural foods, including *Stalking the Wild Asparagus* (1962). He also made many television appearances, often on commercials to promote eating foods grown in the wilds. d. Sunbury, Pa., Dec. 29.

Gilchrist, Huntington (83), U. S. authority on international relations; director of the industry division of the Marshall Plan for Europe; technical representative for the United Nations; founded the International Schools Service; retired executive of American Cynamid Co.: d. Ridgefield, Conn., Jan. 13.

Richard Conte

Eamon de Valera

UPI

Green, Constance McLaughlin (78), U. S. historian, writer; won the Pulitzer Prize in history in 1963 for *Washington, Village and Capital, 1800–1878*. After receiving her doctorate from Yale in 1936, she went to work as an instructor of history at Smith College, where she was named head of the Smith College Council of Industrial Relations. In the years that followed she held important posts with the American Red Cross, the University of London, the Defense Department, and the Rockefeller Foundation: d. Annapolis, Md., Dec. 5.

Green, Martyn (75), British actor; appeared in many dramas and musicals but best known for his interpretation of Gilbert and Sullivan roles; member of D'Oyly Carte Opera Co. in London (1922–51); Broadway roles include *Black Comedy* and *Visit to a Small Planet*: d. Hollywood, Calif., Feb. 8.

Grove, Robert Moses ("Lefty") (75), U. S. baseball player: b. Lonaconing, Md., March 6, 1900; d. Norwalk, Ohio, May 22, 1975. During his 17-year major league career as a star pitcher with the Philadelphia Athletics and the Boston Red Sox he recorded 2,266 strikeouts, a lifetime earned run average of 3.06, and a winning percentage of .682. He joined Connie Mack's Philadelphia A's in 1925. During the three seasons from 1929–31, in which he helped the A's win the pennant, he scored 79 wins and only 15 losses. He was sold to the Boston Red Sox in 1934 for $125,000. In 1941 he ended his career with 300 major league wins and 141 losses. Grove was elected to baseball's Hall of Fame in 1947.

Haile Selassie. See separate article preceding this section.

Halsted, Anna Roosevelt (69), daughter of U. S. President Franklin D. Roosevelt; active in public affairs; women's page editor of the Seattle *Post-Intelligencer* (1936–43); assistant to her father at the Yalta Conference (1945): d. New York, N. Y., Dec. 1.

Hansen, Alvin H. (87), U. S. economist and advocate of Keynesian principles; influenced U. S. economic policy during the New Deal and during and following World War II; professor at Harvard and the University of Minnesota; instrumental in the creation of the Social Security system (1935) and the drafting of the Full Employment Act (1946); author of 15 books on economics: d. Alexandria, Va., June 6.

Hayward, Susan (55?), U. S. actress: b. Brooklyn, N. Y., June 30, 1919 (?); d. Beverly Hills, Calif., March 14, 1975. A pert, attractive redhead, noted for her portrayals of ill-fated women, she appeared in over 50 films during a career spanning more than three decades. She won the 1958 best actress Academy Award for her portrayal of the doomed B-girl Barbara Graham in *I Want to Live* and received Oscar nominations for *Smash-Up* (1947), *My Foolish Heart* (1950), *With a Song in My Heart* (1952), and *I'll Cry Tomorrow* (1957). Born Edythe Marrener in Brooklyn, she made her screen debut in *Beau Geste* (1939). Among her last films were *Valley of the Dolls* (1967), *The Revengers* (1971), and two television movies.

Heald, Henry (71), U. S. educator and administrator; president of Illinois Institute of Technology (1940–52), New York University (1952–56), and the Ford Foundation (1956–63): d. Winter Park, Fla., Nov. 23.

Hepworth, Dame Barbara (72), British sculptor: b. Wakefield, Yorkshire, England, Jan. 10, 1903; d. St. Ives, Cornwall, England, May 20, 1975. She was noted for her monumental abstract geometric forms executed in wood, metal, and stone and influenced by the art of ancient Egypt and by the rugged land and seascapes of Cornwall. She studied at the Leeds School of Art, at the London Royal College of Art, and in Italy. Beginning with her *Pierced Form* (1931), she perforated virtually all of her sculptures with holes—her artistic signature. Among her more than 500 works are *Single Form* (1963), a memorial to Dag Hammarskjold at the UN headquarters; and *Figure*, at the John F. Kennedy Center in Washington, D. C. She was created a commander of the British Empire in 1958 and a dame in 1965.

Hibbs, Ben (73), U. S. magazine editor; joined the *Saturday Evening Post* (1942), and later went to *Reader's Digest*; worked on the writings of his friend, Dwight D. Eisenhower; appointed (1951) to U. S. Advisory Committee of Information: d. Penn Valley, Pa., March 29.

Hill, Graham (46), British racing driver; winner of Monaco Grand Prix an unprecedented five times and the U.S. Grand Prix three times; only driver to acquire the "triple crown" by winning the World Formula One (1962, 1968), the Indianapolis 500 (1966), and Le Mans (1972): d. in a plane crash, near London, Nov. 29.

Hogg, Ima (93), U. S. philanthropist; founded Houston Symphony; donated land and antiques to the state of Texas: d. London, Aug. 20.

Howard, Moe (78), U. S. comedian and last surviving member of Three Stooges team; made *Soup to Nuts*, the first of over 200 movies, in 1930; appeared on Broadway in *Scandals* (1939): d. Hollywood, Calif., May 4.

Huxley, Sir Julian (Sorell) (87), British biologist, humanist, and author: b. London, England, June 22, 1887; d. London, Feb. 14, 1975. He promoted a theory of "evolution-

UPI

UPI

Graham Hill   **Sir Julian Huxley**

ary humanism" that placed ultimate faith in human poten-
tialities with stress on population control and genetic
breeding. Among his activities, he taught at Oxford and
at London's King's College, supervised biological movies,
and from 1946–48 was the first director general of
UNESCO. A grandson of the Darwinian scientist Thomas
H. Huxley, and a brother of the late novelist Aldous
Huxley, he was educated at Eton and Oxford. He wrote
48 books, including poetry, philosophy, and religion, as
well as the natural sciences. His autobiography, *Memories,*
was published in 1970. He was knighted in 1958.

Ittleson, Blanche Frank (99), mental health pioneer and
philanthropist; began her work with maladjusted girls in
1919; founded the Henry Ittleson Center for Child Research (1953) to care for emotionally disturbed children;
director of the National Association for Mental Health:
d. Palm Beach, Fla., Aug. 16.

Jenckes, Virginia E. (97), first congresswoman from Indiana;
served three terms (1933–39) in Congress; an outspoken
anti-Communist who gave assistance to refugees from the
Communist-suppressed Hungarian revolt (1956); served
three terms in Congress (1932–37): d. Terre Haute, Ind.,
Jan. 9.

Josi, Enrico (90), Italian archaeologist; specialist in Christian archaeology; discovered the tomb of Saint Peter
under the Basilica (1949): d. Rome, Sept. 1.

Judson, Arthur (93), leading U. S. concert manager; founded
with two partners what was to become the Columbia
Broadcasting System (1926); formed Columbia Concerts
Corporation, a coalition of independent managers, which
had a virtual monopoly on orchestral conductors in the
1930's; managed simultaneously the New York Philhar-
monic-Symphony and the Philadelphia Orchestra (1930–
35): d. Rye, N. Y., Jan. 28.

Julian, Dr. Percy L. (76), U. S. research chemist and civil
rights leader; early synthecizer of cortisone drugs; his
work on soybeans led to the isolation of soya protein;
raised money for NAACP legal fees to enforce civil rights
legislation: d. Waukegan, Ill., April 19.

Kay, Marshall (70), U. S. geologist; an originator of the
continental drift theory of enlarging continents; associated
with Columbia University (from 1929) where he was New-
berry Professor Emeritus of Geology: d. Englewood, N. J.,
Sept. 2.

Keating, Kenneth B(arnard) (74), U. S. public official and
diplomat: b. Lima, N. Y., May 18, 1900; d. New York,
N. Y., May 5, 1975. He served as U. S. ambassador to
India from 1969–72 and as ambassador to Israel from 1972
until his death. After his degree from Harvard Law
School (LL. B., 1923) he practiced in Rochester. A moderate Republican, he was elected in 1946 to the House of
Representatives, where he established a reputation as a
liberal on civil rights but a staunch anti-Communist and
"law and order" advocate. In 1958 he was elected to the
Senate, where he became the first to call attention to the
Soviet missile buildup in Cuba in 1962. Defeated for reelection by Robert F. Kennedy in 1964, he served from
1965–69 as judge of the New York state court of appeals.

Keres, Paul (59), Estonian chess player and grand master;
champion of the Soviet Union (1947, 1950, 1951); winner
of four world chess Olympiads; author of several books
on chess: d. Helsinki, Finland, June 5.

Kober, Arthur (74), U. S. humorist and playwright; known
for his popularization of Bronx dialect and creator of
character Bella Gross who appeared in his works, *Thunder*

Over the Bronx (1935) and in series in the *New Yorker:*
d. New York, N. Y., June 12.

Kuts, Vladimir (48), USSR long distance runner; broke two
Olympic records and won gold medals at the 1956 Olympics in Melbourne: d. Moscow, Aug. 16.

Ladejinsky, Wolf (76), Russian-born U. S. agricultural technician, who was prominent in agrarian reform following
World War II in Japan, Formosa, Vietnam, Korea, Indonesia, and recently India; involved in a controversy during
the Eisenhower administration when mistakenly termed a
security risk: d. Washington, D. C., July 1.

Lamont, Helen Lamb (69), U. S. economist, author, and
educator; during World War II worked on plans for the
occupation of Japan and later studied the economy of India; her books include *Economic Development of India*
(1972); with husband Corliss Lamont opposed U. S. involvement in Vietnam: d. New York, N. Y., July 21.

Levi, Carlo (72), Italian writer and painter; best known for
his book, *Christ Stopped in Eboli* (1947); a man of many
talents who served in the Italian Senate (1963–72): d.
Rome, Jan. 4.

Lincoln, Brig. Gen. George A. (67), U. S. military officer;
known as a top strategist during World War II; was involved in the postwar structure in Korea; administered the
90-day wage-price freeze (1971) during the Nixon administration; consultant to several military and government
agencies, and professor at Denver University: d. Colorado
Springs, Colo., May 24.

Lopez, Vincent (80), U. S. pianist and bandleader; popular
on radio, television, and in nightclubs; associated with the
song "Nola," which became his trademark: d. North
Miami, Fla., Sept. 20.

Lund, DeWayne (Tiny) (43), U. S. stock car racer; winner of
three Grand National races, including the Daytona 500
(1963); held record of 41 victories on the Grand American circuit: d. in a crash, Talladega, Ala., Aug. 17.

Maas, Aubrey Gellen (40), U. S. television and film producer
and writer; co-producer of film *Alice Doesn't Live Here
Anymore* (1974) and television play *Crown Matrimonial*
(1974); wrote adaptations of many classics for television;
author of the novel *Wait Till the Sun Shines Nellie*
(1966): d. New York, N. Y., July 1.

Mabley, Jackie "Moms" (78?), U. S. comedienne: b. Bre-
vard, N. C., 1897 (?); d. White Plains, N. Y., May 23,
1975. A popular performer on the black vaudeville and
nightclub circuit for half a century before attaining general popularity in the 1960's, she was best known for her
standup act as the raunchy, ragged, gravel-voiced old lady,
always attracted to young men. Born Loretta May Aiken,
she began her showbusiness career in her teens, eventually
becoming a regular at such spots as Harlem's Cotton Club
and Apollo Theatre. Her first recording for Chess Records, *Moms Mabley—The Funniest Woman in the World*
(1960), sold over 1 million copies. She made her television debut in the all-black special *A Time for Laughter*
(1967). In 1974 she starred in the film *Amazing Grace.*

MacPhail, Leland Stanford (Larry) (85), U. S. baseball executive of the 1930's and 1940's; introduced night baseball
to the National League; associated with the Cincinnati
Reds, Brooklyn Dodgers, and New York Yankees: d.
Miami, Fla., Oct. 1.

Main, Marjorie (85), U. S. actress; triumphed on Broadway
in *Dead End* (1935); other stage performances include
The Women (1936) and *Salvation* (1928); in films known
for her role as Ma Kettle, which began in *The Egg and I*
(1947) and became a series of pictures: d. Los Angeles,
Calif., April 10.

March, Fredric (77), U. S. actor: b. Racine, Wis., Aug. 31,
1897; d. Los Angeles, Calif., April 14, 1975. A versatile
actor of stage and screen, he won Academy Awards as
best actor for his performances in the dual title role in
Dr. Jekyll and Mr. Hyde (1932) and as a returning veteran in *The Best Years of Our Lives* (1946). He was
nominated for an Oscar for his Willy Loman in *Death of
a Salesman* (1951). He and his wife, Florence Eldridge,
whom he married in 1927, often co-starred in films and
plays, notably in the Broadway production of *Long Day's
Journey into Night* (1956–57), which won him a Tony
award. Born Frederick McIntyre Bickel, he went to New
York in 1919 to be a banker but turned to acting. Beginning with *The Dummy* (1929), he appeared in 69 motion
pictures; his last movie was *The Iceman Cometh* (1973).

Maserati, Ernesto (77), Italian automobile manufacturer;
built and drove racing cars in the 1920's and 1930's, which
won many victories; founder of the company that produced the Maserati luxury car: d. Bologna, Italy, Dec. 1.

McAuliffe, Anthony C(lement) (77), U. S. army officer: b.
Washington, D. C., July 2, 1898; d. there, Aug. 11, 1975.

As commander of the 101st Airborne Division, at Bastogne, Belgium, during the Battle of the Bulge in December 1944, he won renown for replying "Nuts!" to a German ultimatum that he surrender his greatly outnumbered forces. Later he commanded the 103rd Infantry Division, which captured Innsbruck and the Brenner Pass. The son of a civil servant, he graduated from the U. S. Military Academy in 1918. In the postwar years he held staff and command posts in the United States, the Pacific, and Europe, and in 1955–56 he was commander in chief of U. S. forces in Europe. Retiring from the army in 1956 as a general, he was vice president of the American Cyanamid Company from 1957–63.

McCormack, Maj. Gen. James (64), U. S. military officer; assigned to the Atomic Energy Commission following World War II (1947–55); headed Institute for Defense Analysis following retirement (1955–58); chairman of the Communications Satellite Corp. (Comsat) (1965–70): d. Hilton Head, S. C., Jan. 3.

Medwick, Joe (Ducky) (63), U. S. baseball player; joined the St. Louis Cardinals (1932), and went to the Brooklyn Dodgers (1940); named to Baseball Hall of Fame (1968): d. St. Petersburg, Fla., March 21.

Meouchi, Paul Cardinal (80), Lebanese clergyman; patriarch of the Maronite Church from 1955; became the first Maronite to be named a cardinal (1955); an important political figure who strove to maintain a balance between Muslims and Christians in Lebanon: d. Bkerke, Lebanon, Jan. 11.

Mesta, Perle (85?), U. S. society hostess: b. Sturgis, Mich., 1890?; d. Oklahoma City, Okla., March 16, 1975. She was the reigning society hostess of Washington, D. C., for three decades, beginning in 1941, and was known for her lavish parties, especially during the Truman and Eisenhower years. From 1949–53 she served as U. S. ambassador to the Grand Duchy of Luxembourg. Her life and career as "hostess with the mostes'" inspired the Irving Berlin musical *Call Me Madam*, starring Ethel Merman. Born Pearl Fried Skirvin, she inherited a fortune from her father, oilman William B. Skirvin, and from her husband, Pittsburgh industrialist George Mesta, to whom she was married from 1917 until his death in 1925. Her autobiography, *Perle: My Story*, was published in 1960.

Mindszenty, Jozsef Cardinal. See separate article preceding this section.

Moley, Raymond (Charles) (88), U. S. presidential advisor and political scientist: b. Berea, Ohio, Sept. 27, 1886; d. Phoenix, Ariz., Feb. 18, 1975. The most influential of President Franklin D. Roosevelt's early advisors, he organized and headed Roosevelt's original "brain trust" and coined the term "New Deal." Educated at Oberlin College (M. A., 1913) and Columbia University (Ph. D., 1918), he was a professor of government at Columbia from 1923–54. Essentially a conservative, he supported Republican candidates from 1940. He was editor of *Today* from 1934–37 and contributing editor of *Newsweek* from 1937–68, and he also wrote a syndicated newspaper column. His books include *After Seven Years* (1939) and *The First New Deal* (1966). In 1970 he was awarded the presidential Medal of Freedom.

Mollet, Guy (69), French political figure; Socialist leader (1949–69); premier (1956–57); responsible for sending draftees to fight in Algeria (1956); ordered French intervention in the Suez crisis (1956): d. Paris, Oct. 3.

Montana, Bob (54), U. S. cartoonist; created (1942) the *Archie* comic strip: d. Meredith, N. H., Jan. 4.

Muhammad, Elijah (77), U. S. religious leader: b. Sandersville, Ga., Oct. 7, 1897; d. Chicago, Ill., Feb. 25, 1975. Under his guidance, the Nation of Islam or Black Muslim movement became a major religious movement, with 82 temples throughout the United States and a multimillion-dollar empire of business firms, banks, publishing enterprises, farms, and educational institutions. He preached black supremacy, self-respect, and economic independence to its tens of thousands of adherents, drawn largely from urban blacks. Born Elijah Poole, the son of a sharecropper and Baptist preacher, he moved to Detroit and became a disciple of W. D. Fard, who founded the Nation of Islam in 1930. After Fard's disappearance in 1934 he assumed its leadership, later moving its headquarters to Chicago.

Mujibur Rahman, Sheikh (55), president of Bangladesh: b. Tungipara, East Pakistan (later Bangladesh), March 17, 1920; d. Dacca, Aug. 15, 1975. Known as Sheikh Mujib, he led the independence movement in Bangladesh from its inception in the 1960's, heading the Awami League and being imprisoned for his activities. He became a national legend and returned from prison in 1972 after the successful battle to separate East Pakistan from West Pakistan and to create a new nation of Bangladesh. As prime min-

UPI

Elijah Muhammad

ister he grew increasingly autocratic but was unable to solve the country's overwhelming population, food, and economic problems. He assumed the office of president in January 1975 and tried unsuccessfully to tighten his control of the country. His government was overthrown, and he was killed in a coup by dissident military officers.

Nelson, Ozzie (68), U. S. entertainer; b. Jersey City, N. J., March 20, 1907; d. Hollywood, Calif., June 3, 1975. As the all-American husband in the situation comedy series *The Adventures of Ozzie and Harriet,* which he also produced and directed, he was a familiar fixture on radio from 1944–54 and television from 1952–66. A law student and football star at Rutgers University, he turned to bandleading in the 1930's, and in 1935 he married his vocalist, Harriet Hilliard. Their family comedy show eventually included their sons, David and Ricky. The Nelsons made a television comeback in the short-lived comedy series *Ozzie's Girls* in 1973. In addition, Nelson directed episodes of *Adam 12* and other television programs.

Norfolk, Duke of (66), British nobleman; Bernard Marmaduke Fitzalan-Howard became the 16th duke of Norfolk (1917); had the hereditary duty of organizing great pageants of state such as coronations, royal weddings, and funerals; Britain's leading Roman Catholic layman: d. London, Jan. 30.

Novotny, Antonin (70), Czechoslovakian Communist party leader; named first secretary of the Central Committee (1951); and general secretary (1953); maintained iron control over the party and was virtual ruler of Czechoslovakia (1953–68); assumed the title of president in 1957; stripped of power and presidency (1968): d. Prague, Jan. 28.

Onassis, Aristotle. See separate article preceding this section.

Parks, Larry (60), U. S. actor; known for his performance in the film, *The Jolson Story* (1946); became the first actor to admit past membership in the Communist party before the House UnAmerican Activities Committee (1951): d. Studio City, Calif., April 13.

Pasolini, Pier Paolo (53), Italian film director; poet and novelist; films include *The Gospel According to St. Matthew* (1964), *The Canterbury Tales* (1970), and *A Thousand and One Nights* (1974): murdered in Ostia, Italy, Nov. 2.

Payson, Joan Whitney (72), principal owner of the New York Mets, head of Greentree Stables, and trustee of both the Museum of Modern Art and the Metropolitan Museum of Art: d. New York City, Oct. 4.

Perse, St.-John (Alexis Saint-Leger Leger) (88), French poet and diplomat; secretary-general of the ministry of foreign affairs (1932–40); works include *Chronique* (1959) and *Oiseaux* (1962); won the Nobel Prize for Literature (1960): d. Giens, France, Sept. 20.

Prefontaine, Steve (24), U. S. distance runner; holder of every U. S. outdoor distance record above 2,000 meters; placed fourth in the 5,000 meter race at the 1972 Olympics: d. in automobile accident in Eugene, Ore., May 30.

Priest, Ivy Baker (69), former U. S. treasurer; served as treasurer for eight years, beginning in 1953; was elected treasurer of California (1966–74); as a Republican committeewoman, she was the first woman to nominate a presidential candidate (1968): d. Santa Monica, Calif., June 23.

Radhakrishnan, Sir Sarvepalli (86), Indian philosopher and statesman: b. Tiruttani, India, Sept. 5, 1888; d. Madras, India, April 16, 1975. Among his services to India was his membership in its constituent assembly. In 1949 he was chairman of UNESCO. From 1949–52 he was ambassador to the USSR; from 1952–62 he was vice president, and from 1962–67 he was honored with the ceremonial office of president. A member of the Telugu Brahmin caste and educated at Madras Christian College, he taught philosophy at Calcutta University from 1921–31, and from 1936–39 he was the first Indian to hold a chair at Oxford. His works include *Indian Philosophy* (1923–26), *East and West in Religion* (1933), and *Religion in a Changing World* (1967). He was knighted in 1931.

Revson, Charles (68), U. S. businessman; one of the founders of Revlon, Inc. (1932) and president and leading force of the cosmetics empire: d. New York, N. Y., Aug. 24.

Robinson, Sir Robert (88), British organic chemist; Waynflete Professor of Chemistry at Oxford University for 25 years; knighted (1939); won the Nobel Prize (1947) for his research into plant biology, including alkaloids; member of the Royal Society and Soviet Union's Academy of Sciences: d. Great Missenden, England, Feb. 8.

Sapir, Pinhas (68), Israeli political leader and public official: b. Suwalki, Poland, Oct. 15, 1907; d. Beersheba, Israel, Aug. 12, 1975. An influential figure in Israel's dominant Mapai party, he served as its secretary general for several years and helped Golda Meir and Yitzhak Rabin attain the premiership. As minister of commerce or finance in various cabinets from 1955–74 he played a key role in promoting capital investment in Israel. He immigrated to Palestine in 1929 and during the 1948–49 war for independence he raised funds and purchased weapons. He favored the return of occupied lands acquired in the 1967 war in exchange for a political settlement with the Arabs. In 1974 he became chairman of the World Zionist Organization and of the executive board of the Jewish Agency.

Sato, Eisaku (74), Japanese statesman; b. Tabuse, Yamaguchi prefecture, Japan, March 27, 1901; d. Tokyo, June 2, 1975. As premier from 1964–72 he developed Japan into a major economic and industrial nation, while fostering international cooperation and friendship with the United States. In 1974 he shared the Nobel Peace Prize for "stabilization of conditions in the Pacific area" such as Japan's signing of the 1970 nuclear nonproliferation treaty and the 1971 agreement with the United States restoring Japanese sovereignty over Okinawa and the Bonin Islands. The son of a sake brewer and a descendant of samurai warriors, he graduated from Tokyo Imperial University with a law degree in 1924. After World War II he served in the government and was finance minister from 1958–60.

Serling, Rod (50), U. S. television writer and producer: b. Syracuse, N. Y., Dec. 25, 1924; d. Rochester, N. Y., June 28, 1975. He earned five Emmy awards, as well as the Peabody, Sylvania, and Christopher awards for his taut, topical, and socially critical dramas, including *Patterns* (1955), *Requiem for a Heavyweight* (1956), *A Town Has Turned to Dust* (1958), *Rank and File* (1959), and *In the Presence of Mine Enemies* (1960). He was perhaps best known as the creator of the fantasy-science fiction series *Twilight Zone* (1959), and as host of the *Night Gallery* series. He also wrote screenplays for films, including *Planet of the Apes* (1968). At his death he was teaching dramatic writing at Ithaca College, N. Y.

Sheean, Vincent (75), U. S. journalist and author; as correspondent for several papers reported on many history-making events, including Mussolini's march on Rome, the revolution in China, the Spanish Civil War, and the assassination of Gandhi; wrote over 20 works of nonfiction and several novels; best known works include *Personal History* (1935), *Not Peace But a Sword* (1939), and *Dorothy and Red* (1963); known for his sincere, reflective style of reporting: d. Arolo, Italy, March 16.

Short, Luke (Frederick D. Glidden) (67), U. S. author; known for his stories of Western adventure, some of which appeared in magazine serials and were adapted into movies: d. Aspen, Colo., Aug. 18.

Shostakovich, Dmitri (68), Soviet composer: b. St. Petersburg, Russia, Sept. 25, 1906; d. Moscow, USSR, Aug. 9, 1975. Internationally recognized as the outstanding contemporary Soviet composer, he wrote hundreds of compositions, including 15 symphonies, as well as chamber music, oratorios, operas, ballets, musical comedies, motion picture scores, and works for piano, violin, and cello. His serious symphonic works are distinguished by their dramatic intensity and melodic brilliance. The son of a chemist, he studied piano as a child, began to compose at 11, and graduated from the Leningrad Conservatory in 1925. The premiere of his First Symphony in 1926 brought him international acclaim. Soviet authorities alternately castigated him for lack of ideological purity and proclaimed him a Hero of Socialist Labor, finally awarding him the Order of Lenin.

Stengel, Casey (85), former U. S. baseball player and manager: b. Kansas City, Mo., July 30, 1890; d. Glendale, Calif., Sept. 29, 1975. One of baseball's most colorful and popular personalities, noted for his salty "Stengelese" jargon, he was associated with the game for more than 50 years. The son of a German immigrant, he was born Charles Dillon Stengel. Abandoning the ambition to become a dentist, he became a professional baseball player in the minor leagues in 1910, joining the majors as an outfielder two years later. During 14 seasons with the National League teams of Brooklyn, Pittsburgh, Philadelphia, New York, and Boston, he had a batting average of .284. He managed the Brooklyn Dodgers from 1934 to 1936 and the Boston Braves from 1938 to 1943. He reached the peak of his career as manager of the New York Yankees from 1949 to 1960. During his first five years with the Yankees he led the team to a record five consecutive World Series victories. He became the first manager of the New York Mets in 1962, and remained associated with the team as titular vice president after his retirement in 1965. Stengel was elected to baseball's Hall of Fame in 1966.

Stevens, George (Cooper) (70), U. S. motion picture director: b. Oakland, Calif., Dec. 8, 1904; d. Lancaster, Calif., March 8, 1975. He directed 25 feature films, ranging from light comedy to serious drama. He won Academy Awards for *A Place in the Sun* (1951) and *Giant* (1956) and received the Motion Picture Academy's Irving Thalberg award for "high quality of production" in 1953. He began his career as a cameraman, writer, and director of Hal Roach two-reel comedies. Among his early films were *Alice Adams* (1935), *Swing Time* (1936), and *Gunga Din* (1939). During World War II he filmed the D-Day landings and documented Dachau death camp scenes for the Nuremberg trials. His later films included *Shane* (1953), *The Diary of Anne Frank* (1959), *The Greatest Story Ever Told* (1965), and his last, *The Only Game in Town* (1970).

Stillman, Irving M. (79), U. S. physician; author of four diet books, including *The Doctor's Quick Weight Loss Diet* (1967): d. North Miami, Fla., Aug. 26.

Stout, Rex (Todhunter) (88), b. Nobleville, Ind., Dec. 1, 1886; d. Danbury, Conn., Oct. 27, 1975. The dean of U. S. mystery writers, he was noted for his cerebral whodunits featuring the corpulent, gourmandizing, orchid-growing armchair detective Nero Wolfe and his legman Archie Goodwin. A member of a Quaker family, Stout grew up in rural Kansas and achieved local fame as a mathematical prodigy. In the 1920's he devised the Educational Thrift System, a scheme for recruiting school children as bank depositors, which brought him enough income to enable him to devote his full time to writing. His 46 Wolfe novels, beginning with *Fer-de-Lance* (1934) and including *Too Many Cooks* (1938), *The Silent Speaker* (1946), *The Golden Spiders* (1953), *The Mother Hunt* (1963), *A Doorbell Rang* (1965), and *A Family Affair* (1975), sold 45 million copies in 22 languages. During World War II Stout was active in anti-Nazi causes and served as chairman of the War Writers Board.

Tertis, Lionel (98), British violist, internationally known as a soloist; played chamber music with Pablo Casals; designed Tertis viola, violin, and cello; wrote autobiography *Cinderella No More:* d. London, Feb. 22.

Eisaku Sato

UPI

Casey Stengel

UPI

Tolson, Clyde A. (74), U. S. former official of the Federal Bureau of Investigation; long-time associate of J. Edgar Hoover; joined FBI in 1928; became Hoover's assistant (1938); named associate director (1947): d. Washington, D. C., April 14.

Tombalbaye, Ngarta (56), president of Chad, killed in a military coup; had ruled Chad since it gained independence in 1960; entered politics in 1946 and helped found Chad Progressive party, which later became the nation's only political party: d. N'Djemena, Chad, April 13.

Toynbee, Arnold J(oseph) (86), British historian: b. London, April 14, 1889; d. York, England, Oct. 22, 1975. In his monumental 12-volume synthesis, *A Study of History* (1934–61), he chronicled and analyzed the rise and decline of 26 civilizations from ancient to modern times. Taking a panoramic view of world history, he stressed the significance of spiritual forces in civilization and concluded that a society's health and survival depends on its ability to meet the challenges of its environment. The son of a social worker, he was educated at Oxford University, later studied in Greece, and worked for the British foreign office during World Wars I and II. In 1955 he retired after some 30 years as research professor of international history at the University of London and as director of studies at the Royal Institute of International Affairs. Among his numerous other published works are *Greek Historical Thought* (1924), *The World and the West* (1953), *Hannibal's Legacy* (1965), and *Constantine Porphyrogenitus and His World* (1973).

Treacher, Arthur (81), British born actor and television personality, known for his characterization of the crusty butler; his films include *Anything Goes* (1936); *Star Spangled Rhythm* (1942); *National Velvet* (1944); *Mary Poppins* (1964); stage roles in *That School For Scandal* (1931) and *Panama Hattie* (1940); appeared frequently on the Merv Griffin show: d. Manhasset, N. Y., Dec. 14.

Trilling, Lionel (70), U. S. writer and critic: b. New York, N. Y., July 4, 1905: d. New York, N. Y., Nov. 5, 1975. Best known for lucid and imaginative literary criticism, he viewed literature within the context of the history of ideas, subjecting it to psychological analysis and emphasizing its moral aspects. The son of a businessman, he was educated at Columbia University (B. A., 1925; Ph. D., 1938), and served on its faculty from 1931 until his retirement in 1974. He was also a visiting professor at Oxford and Harvard universities. Among his works are studies of Matthew Arnold, E. M. Forster, and Sigmund Freud, and several volumes of essays, including *The Liberal Imagination* (1950), *The Opposing Self* (1955), and *Beyond Culture* (1965). He also wrote short stories and a novel, *The Middle of the Journey* (1947), whose protagonist was modeled in part on the ex-Communist government witness Whittaker Chambers. Trilling was active in liberal causes but resisted radical ideas and considered himself "a great skeptic on the question of social truth."

Tucker, Richard (60), U. S. opera singer: b. Brooklyn, N. Y., Aug. 28, 1914; d. Kalamazoo, Mich., Jan. 8, 1975. For 30 years a member of the Metropolitan Opera, he was considered one of the greatest operatic tenors of his time. His voice was noted for its strength and durability. Born Reuben Ticker, the son of Rumanian Jewish immigrants, he began to sing in synagogues as a boy, eventually becoming an ordained cantor. After his marriage, he decided to emulate his brother-in-law, operatic tenor Jan Peerce, and make a career as a singer. He made his debut at the Metropolitan Opera in January 1945 as Enzo in *La Gioconda*. Other roles included Don José in *Carmen*, Radames in *Aida*, Canio in *Pagliacci*, Rodolfo in *La Boheme*, and Eleazar in *La Juive*.

Tung Pi-wu (89), Chinese leader; a revolutionary and one of the founders of the Chinese Communist party (1921); a delegate to the San Francisco Conference that established the United Nations (1945); Chinese chief of state (1969–75): d. Peking, April 2.

Tunis, John R. (85), U. S. author; wrote numerous magazine articles and a series of books about young readers; best known novel was *The Iron Duke* (1938): d. Essex, Conn., Feb. 4.

Tunnell, Emlen (50), U. S. football star; one of football's greatest defensive backs; played 11 seasons for the New York Giants; first black elected to the Pro Football Hall of Fame (1967): d. Pleasantville, N. Y., July 23.

Um, Kalthoum (77), Egyptian singer; sang in the classical Islamic tradition; gained popularity through her broadcasts, recordings, and films: d. Cairo, Feb. 3.

Ure, Mary (42), British actress; starred in *Look Back in Anger* (1957) on Broadway and *Old Times* (1971) in London; received Academy Award nomination (1961) for *Sons and Lovers*: d. London, April 3.

Van Acker, Achille H. (77), Belgian leader; Socialist member of the Belgian Chamber of Deputies since 1927 and elected president (1961); served as premier and as cabinet minister: d. Bruges, July 10.

Van Dusen, Henry (77), U. S. clergyman and educator; president of Union Theological Seminary (1945–63); participated in the founding of the World Council of Churches (1948); worked to promote ecumenism and world Christianity; author and editor of numerous works: d. Belle Meade, N. J., Feb. 13.

Vionnet, Madeleine (98), French couturier; inventor of the bias cut that revolutionized women's fashions; at her peak of influence in the 1930's: d. Paris, March 2.

Waddington, C. H. (69), British geneticist and philosopher; known for developing a method of growing embryos of mammals in an artificial environment and for his study into genetic material later known as DNA: d. Edinburgh, Sept. 26.

Wahloo, Per (48), Swedish author; creator, with his wife Maj Sjowall, of a series of detective novels about Martin Beck of the Stockholm police, including *The Man on the Balcony* and *The Laughing Policeman*: d. Malmo, June 23.

Wellman, William A. (82), U. S. motion picture director; best known films include *Wings* (1929), *Public Enemy* (1932), *Beau Geste* (1939), *The Light That Failed* (1939), *The Ox-Bow Incident* (1943): d. Los Angeles, Calif., Dec. 9.

Wheeler, Burton K(endall) (92), U. S. senator; b. Hudson, Mass., Feb. 27, 1881; d. Washington, D. C., Jan. 6, 1975. A Democratic U. S. senator from Montana from 1923–47, he was an early supporter of Roosevelt's New Deal but emerged as an isolationist before World War II, charging that the Lend-Lease program of early 1941 would "plow under every fourth American boy." He also opposed F. D. R.'s "court packing" scheme in 1937. The son of a Quaker farmer, he graduated from University of Michigan Law School in 1905 and served as U. S. attorney for Montana, 1913–20. In 1924 he launched a vigorous Senate investigation of the Teapot Dome oil-lease scandal. From 1946 he practiced corporate law in Washington, D. C.

Wheeler, Earle (67), U. S. general, served as Army chief of staff from 1962–64 and as chairman of the joint chiefs of staff until he retired in 1970. In 1973 he gained nationwide publicity when he confirmed that Richard Nixon had personally ordered secret air attacks over Cambodia in 1969. He received many decorations during his 38-year career in the Army, among them the Bronze Star with Oak Leaf Cluster, the Legion of Merit, the French Legion of Honor, and the French Croix de Guerre with Palm: d. Frederick, Md., Dec. 18.

Whitton, Charlotte (78), Canadian women's rights activist; mayor of Ottawa (1950–56, 1960–64); alderman (1966–72): d. Ottawa, Jan. 25.

Wilder, Thornton (78), U. S. playwright and novelist; known for his simple, elegant prose and his treatment of universal truths in human nature; received three Pulitzer Prizes, for the novel *The Bridge of San Luis Rey* (1928), and the dramas *Our Town* (1938), and *The Skin of Our Teeth* (1943); his last novel, *The Eighth Day*, won the National Book Award (1968); his play, *The Matchmaker*, was adapted in the popular musical *Hello, Dolly!*; lectured at Harvard and the University of Chicago; after 1957 he lived a life of seclusion in Connecticut; awarded (1965) the National Medal for Literature of the National Book Committee, presented by President Lyndon Johnson: d. New Haven, Conn., Dec. 7.

Williams, David M. (Carbine) (74), U. S. weapons designer; designed the M-1 carbine used in World War II while serving a prison term: d. Raleigh, N. C., Jan. 8.

Wodehouse, P(elham) G(renville) (93), British humorist: b. Guildford, England, Oct. 15, 1881; d. Southampton, N. Y., Feb. 14, 1975. A master of lighthearted, gently satirical prose about the British upper classes, he wrote 97 books and hundreds of articles and stories, as well as plays, movie scripts, and lyrics for musicals. The son of a Hong Kong civil servant, he studied at Dulwich College. He published his first novel, *The Pothunters*, in 1902 and the first of his "Jeeves" books in 1919 featuring the worldly-wise, impeccably-English butler, Jeeves, and his amiable, scatterbrained young master, Bertie Wooster. Oxford conferred a doctorate of letters on him in 1939, and in 1975 he was made a knight by Queen Elizabeth. Living in the United States since World War II, he became a citizen in 1956.

Yergan, Max (82), U. S. educator and civil rights figure; leader of Council on African Affairs and National Negro Congress; worked for civil rights of black Africans: d. Mount Kisco, N. Y., April 11.

OCEANIA

Independence for Papua New Guinea and the ending of international tensions that had arisen from France's atmospheric nuclear testing over the South Pacific were highlights of 1975. During the year political developments in Oceania overshadowed social and economic change. The matters of major concern were continued inflationary pressures and the end of the "tourism boom" that began in the late 1960's.

Independence. The formal independence of Papua New Guinea (PNG) came on September 16. An announcement by Gov. Gen. Sir John Guise of the country's independence from Australia was heard by about 1.5 million of PNG's 2.6 million people. Celebrations in Port Moresby were attended by representatives of 37 nations. The principal guest was Britain's Prince Charles, who opened the national parliament. Prime Minister Michael Somare made it clear that PNG shared the hopes and problems of the South Pacific and intended to develop its strong links there. Independence came after a turbulent year in which Somare held together a fragile coalition government, only part of which initially shared his aim of rapid disengagement from Australia.

On Bougainville, an outlying island, two days of violent rioting by more than 1,000 miners resulted in a temporary closing of the major copper mine. In August, Bougainville secessionists renamed their island a republic, but the PNG government's large shareholdings in that island's important copper industry precluded any chance of recognition of separatist aims.

Among issues concerning Australia-PNG relations that were unresolved at independence were Australia's military-assistance involvement, the future of Australian investment, and agreement on the use of Torres Strait. Sir Maori Kiki, minister for defense, foreign relations, and trade, visited Peking in February. He returned with hopes for developing trade relations with China.

French Territories. Following visits to New Caledonia, French Polynesia, and New Hebrides, French Overseas Territories Minister Olivier Stirn ruled out independence as a goal for these territories. He promised instead that there would be moves toward greater autonomy in which French responsibility remained. In June, underground nuclear tests were begun at Fangataufa Atoll in French Polynesia. Later in the year, during talks in Australia and New Zealand, Stirn found what he described as "a new rapport" following the end of France's atmospheric nuclear testing in the area. Meanwhile, moves were begun by Fiji and other nations to have the Pacific made a "nuclear free" zone.

Stirn's talks on revision of New Caledonia's status indicated enhanced autonomy would be given to a similar council and to the municipalities. In the Condominium of New Hebrides, political leaders generally expressed satisfaction with the cautious progress toward greater participation in affairs through the advisory council approved in Franco-British discussions.

Economic and Political Change. In the trust territory of Micronesia, a new law authorized each district legislature to "create or designate a legal entity within its jurisdiction to hold title to public lands." The move damaged the Congress of Micronesia's hope of securing control of public lands in order to preclude any individual district land holding arrangement with U. S. military authorities. The Mariana Islands moved toward a permanent political relationship with the United States through the Mariana Commonwealth Covenant, signed on Saipan in February. (See also MARIANA ISLANDS.)

The Gilbert and Ellice Islands House of Assembly met in May for the last time with Ellice Islands members. From October 1, taking the name of Tuvalu, the Ellice Islands launched a new government with the good wishes of Gilbertese legislators. A delegation from the British Solomon Islands Protectorate visited London for talks and an agreement was reached for self-government by mid-1977. In June the territory was officially renamed Solomon Islands. The 3,700 people of Niue voted for the first time, electing legislators. Initial legislation provided a $2-a-week pension for all persons over 65.

Western Samoa's Prime Minister Fiame Mataafa died after a long illness. He had been in office since 1973, following his initial term from 1959 to 1970. Western Samoa's five-year economic development plan began with the creation of an industrial zone that encouraged foreign businesses. This was seen as a sign of closer involvement with the outside world.

Nauru, with buoyant revenues from the island's phosphate deposit, completed work on a $4 million civic center, including a theater, library, space for a large supermarket, and the offices of the Australian High Commission. Also financed from phosphate bounties, the 50-story Nauru House neared completion in Melbourne as the city's largest building.

Three French oil companies initiated exploration of the seabed off New Caledonia, but the territory's nickel output declined. Early hopes in Cook Islands for a manganese industry faded when tests showed seabed nodules held insufficient ore to warrant extraction.

Support for Indigenous Cultures. A conference in Nouméa established a South Pacific Art Festival Council and agreed to sponsor the second South Pacific Arts Festival in February 1976. Initial payments from a $1.3 million Australian grant to assist in preserving and developing South Pacific cultures went to 11 groups sponsoring various local projects from the creative arts to archives. The money was intended to encourage and support growing interest among islanders in indigenous cultures.

R. M. YOUNGER
Author, "Australia and the Australians"

Research vessel *Glomar Challenger* (*above*) took Deep Sea Drilling Project cores in the Indian Ocean that yielded fossilized skeletons (*below*) of deep-sea organisms.

OCEANOGRAPHY

International cooperation dominated oceanographic research in 1975. Foremost of these efforts was the International Decade of Ocean Exploration (IDOE), which was proposed for the 1970's and which has been supported with U. S. funds since 1972. This effort to accelerate understanding of the oceans' influence on man and of man's impact on the marine environment has begun to show significant achievements.

One major effort of IDOE has been directed toward the study of areas of upwelling, which are the most productive ocean areas in fish. The project known as CUEA (Coastal Upwellings and Ecosystems Analysis) has involved surveys off West Africa, the Peru coast, and the western coast of the United States. Fisheries production in the region off West Africa may be limited by the absence of a major coastal current, reducing the volume of water movement parallel to the shore. In addition, the areas of highest plankton growth occur far offshore in this vicinity.

With data accumulated from several cruises in the Peruvian upwelling, mathematical modeling was used to explore the seasonal and spatial changes in the food-chain relationships. Results suggested that the system shows changes throughout the entire year. The present computer model raised questions about carbon and nitrogen recycling, interaction of phytoplankton species, protein yield, and other aspects of the total ecosystem. This will assist in designing additional field studies during the program.

Observations in the central North Pacific area suggested that a strengthening of the sub-

tropical westerly winds may precede by some eight months the onset of unusual oceanic conditions in nearshore areas, such as the appearance of the *El Niño* current off the west coast of South America. This sporadic seasonal alteration of the circulation causes a cessation of the cold water upwelling, a decrease in the nutrient supply to surface waters, and, consequently, the disappearance of the Peruvian anchovy fishery. Another indication of an oncoming *El Niño* is a change in the Equatorial Countercurrent passing several remote islands. Indications from 1975 cruises will be used to develop a predictive ability that could lead toward a more sustained fishery.

International Cooperation. In 1973 the Soviet Union and the United States signed an agreement on cooperation in studies of the world ocean that included some aspects of IDOE. The continuing examination of large-scale ocean/atmosphere interaction has been carried on by the Global Atmospheric Research Project (GARP) and the Global Atmospheric Tropical Experiment (GATE).

GATE involved 40 research ships from 10 nations, including the United States, Canada, Britain, Japan, and the USSR, working in coordination with research aircraft based at Dakar, Senegal, in western Africa in the summer of 1974. Weather satellite photographs and computer forecasts were correlated with direct observation in the equatorial Atlantic in order to evaluate the heat energy disseminated from tropical cloud formations. Such efforts have improved the long-range predictive ability for meteorological conditions in all parts of the world.

The United States Committee for GARP has planned for the first GARP Global Experiment (FGGE) in 1978, which will include periods of intensive observation of monsoon and polar weather systems. In addition, international climate research cooperation was planned for the next decade.

Deep-Sea Circulation. A major study of ocean currents and circulation, initiated under the Mid Ocean Dynamics Experiment (MODE), continued as POLYMODE. It combined previously separate U.S. and Soviet programs into the study of eddy phenomena in the deep circulation. Results from the MODE program include the establishment of the existence and importance of the mid-ocean eddies and the development of new instruments and techniques. In addition, the project aided in the reinterpretation of other existing data.

Studies of the variability of the major currents that appear at the ocean boundaries defined the scale of meandering in the Gulf Stream and showed meandering also to occur in the Japan (Kuroshio) Current. Seasonal variability in the Florida Current was also confirmed. The increased refinement of instrumentation and sensing devices led to an awareness of small-scale variability and microstructure in oceans. Internal gravity waves, which have their origin in the combined effects of density stratification, wind, currents, and roughness of the sea bed, also attracted much notice.

The design for POLYMODE will involve a longer, more intensively instrumented program, covering a larger swath of the Atlantic Ocean. The 1976–1978 field program will feature an intensive survey throughout 1977. As in the case of upwelling systems, variations in ocean currents caused by eddies can have major effects on weather patterns, fishing, dispersal of pollutants, and coastal recreation. Related studies of oceanic chemistry have been advanced through the GEOSECS project (Geochemical Ocean Sections Study), which seeks to examine the abyssal circulation of the world ocean through the distribution of chemical tracers.

Deep Sea Drilling Program. The Deep Sea Drilling Program (DSDP) continued to amass data about the history of the earth. By early 1975, 525 holes had been drilled in the earth's crust at 359 sites in the major ocean basins and the marginal seas of the world, with the exception of the ice-bound Arctic. Cores were recovered from as much as 22,198 feet (6,766 meters) beneath sea level and in water up to 20,500-feet (6,250-meters) deep, with maximum penetration of 4,311 feet (1,314 meters) achieved in the southeast Atlantic.

Cores have come primarily from the oceanic sedimentary layers in which the historical record of the ocean basins is preserved, but recently emphasis has been placed on drilling into igneous layers beneath the sediment. Results of DSDP were influential in establishing wide acceptance of sea-floor spreading, determining ages and stages for a growing ocean such as the Atlantic, and assessing the age and prior conditions for compressed areas of the Pacific plate.

In 1975 the drilling vessel *Glomar Challenger* surveyed areas of the Atlantic Ocean and the Mediterranean Sea. Detailed explanations of the ancient circulation patterns and of the early rifting of the Atlantic Ocean will be developed from these latest cores. In the 1975 drilling in the eastern Mediterranean further evidence was obtained for Pleistocene crustal upheavals that dammed the outlet to the Atlantic Ocean and caused formation of a dry lake bed for long time periods.

DSDP ended in August 1975 and was succeeded by an International Phase of Ocean Drilling initially scheduled to last until 1978. This new program puts major emphasis on deeper crustal penetrations. The expanded international group for scientific planning and funding included representatives from the Soviet Union, France, and West Germany, in addition to several American institutions.

Other Investigations. Other geological and geophysical investigations included determinations of marine gravity, heat flow, and marine magnetism. All these areas contribute to the continuing development of plate tectonic theory. Perhaps the most dramatic data was supplied by Project FAMOUS (French-American Mid-Ocean Undersea Study) in 1974, in which manned submersibles completed 47 dives to the inner rift valley floor of the mid-Ocean ridge in the North Atlantic, southwest of the Azores. For the first time, the volcanic activity that is believed to be responsible for sea-floor spreading was directly observed and samples obtained. (See also GEOLOGY)

DAVID A. McGILL
U. S. Coast Guard Academy

Jury members in the Kent State civil damages suits trial tour the university grounds where the shootings took place. In August the court ruled that no compensation would be awarded.

UPI

OHIO

Legislation and constitutional issues interested Ohioans in 1975.

Politics. In November 1974, Republican James A. Rhodes had won a narrow victory over Gov. John J. Gilligan. The disappointed Democrats controlled the legislature, however, with a 54–15 majority in the House and a 21–12 majority in the Senate. They then quickly passed six partisan bills, hoping Gilligan would sign them into law before he left office on Jan. 13, 1975. One proposed boundary changes of several congressional districts to Democratic advantage, while another extended unemployment benefits for Ohioans. A third provided for the removal of Ohio's consumer protection enforcement authority from the department of commerce to the Democratic attorney general's office.

Democrats feared that the Republican lieutenant governor would delay signing the bills until Gilligan left office. Democrats sought to have the bills signed by the president pro tempore of the senate, but court action halted this procedure. Gilligan signed the bills, but further litigation developed because they were not signed by the lieutenant governor and were transmitted to the secretary of state only after Gilligan left office. In September the Franklin county court of appeals upheld a lower court ruling that the measures were invalid.

Constitutional Amendments. Rhodes was inaugurated on Jan. 14, 1975. Eventually he secured voters' signatures in order to submit four proposed constitutional amendments to the voters in November. One sought to create and preserve jobs by tax incentives to industries that would expand or locate in Ohio. A second authorized the issuance of $1.75 billion in bonds and notes for the development of highways and other transportation facilities. A third would have established assistance for public housing, with special attention to nursing, extended care, and other health facilities. A fourth authorized the issuance of $2.75 billion in bonds and notes for capital improvements for governmental subdivisions, including energy, heart, and cancer facilities.

In the November vote all of Rhodes' proposals were defeated. The bond issues were rejected by 80% of the electorate, a margin attributed by some observers to general reluctance by voters to assume additional financial burdens at a time of economic uncertainty.

Legislation. Enacted into law were a moderate malpractice measure and a drug bill, lenient on the casual user. The legislature also passed a measure repealing the Ferguson Act, which had prohibited strikes by public employees. Under the new law they would have had the right to bargain collectively for wages, hours, and conditions of employment with a limited right to strike, except for policemen, firemen, and guards at prisons and mental institutions. Rhodes vetoed the measure.

Kent State Trial. In 1974 a federal jury agreed that National Guard troops and others concerned in the killing of students at Kent State University during a 1970 campus uprising were not liable for criminal action. Another long trial involving large claims for pecuniary damages ended in August 1975 with a verdict denying such compensation. In September the federal district judge refused a motion for a new trial.

World Series. The Cincinnati Reds defeated the Boston Red Sox in seven games to win the 1975 World Series. The victory brought the title home to the "birthplace of professional baseball" for the first time in 35 years.

FRANCIS P. WEISENBURGER
The Ohio State University

──────── **OHIO • Information Highlights** ────────

Area: 41,222 square miles (106,765 sq km).
Population (1974 est.): 10,737,000. *Density:* 263 per sq mi.
Chief Cities (1970 census): Columbus, the capital, 540,025; Cleveland, 750,879; Cincinnati, 452,524.
Government (1975): *Chief Officers*—governor, James A. Rhodes (R); lt. gov., Richard F. Celeste (D). *General Assembly*—Senate, 33 members; House of Representatives, 99 members.
Education (1974–75): *Enrollment*—public elementary schools, 1,401,040 pupils; public secondary, 920,110; nonpublic, 293,900; colleges and universities, 408,836 students. *Public school expenditures*, $2,135,247,000 ($963 per pupil).
State Finances (fiscal year 1974): *Revenues*, $6,109,499,000; *expenditures*, $5,620,383,000.
Personal Income (1974): $59,580,000,000; per capita, $5,549.
Labor Force (July 1975): *Nonagricultural wage and salary earners*, 4,073,200; *insured unemployed*, 156,900 (3.8%).

AMERICAN REVOLUTION BICENTENNIAL AUTHORITY OF OKLAHOMA

The 1975 Oklahoma State Fair, held September 19–28 in Oklahoma City, was recognized as an official bicentennial project. The fair chose "Spirit of America Exposition" as its theme, and exhibitors were encouraged to follow the theme in their displays.

OKLAHOMA

The state's leading stories in 1975 centered on political scandals and reforms.

Scandals. Charges and impeachment proceedings hovered around various state officials. Even before his defeat for reelection, Gov. David Hall faced federal and state probes into his troubled administration. In early March, Hall became the first former Oklahoma governor to be convicted of a felony. He was later freed pending appeals. Immediately after the Hall conviction, the state legislature turned its attention to Secretary of State John Rogers. Allegations from the Hall trial led on June 5 to the impeachment of Rogers, who stopped the proceedings by resigning in late June. Former State Treasurer Leo Winters, one year after his acquittal on extortion charges, was acquitted of remaining charges of mail fraud in May 1975, ending three years of federal investigations and trials.

Reforms. The new governor, David Boren, elected in 1974 on a slate of open and honest government, continued his shake-up of state departments to obtain greater efficiency. The youngest chief executive in the nation, Boren enjoyed an excellent working relationship with the legislature. The first session became the busiest in state history, with the greatest number of bills introduced and the largest appropria-

tions. Legislative action was more open after the governor's reforms. In July, Oklahoma voters approved eight state questions that shortened election ballots for state offices, abolished certain elective offices, and strengthened the state's budgetary process.

Prisons. The state's corrections situation continued to plague officials. Corrections Director Russell Lash resigned in February 1975, denouncing political interference. Convicts seized 11 hostages at the Granite State Reformatory on June 5, but later released them unharmed. In August, Warren Benton was named head of the state's penal system. Benton, a correctional planner, had authored the model for Oklahoma's master corrections plan.

Education. Under the governor's program, the legislature gave record amounts of money to public schools and higher education, increasing teachers' benefits at the same time. Oklahoma City and Tulsa public schools faced continued enrollment declines in the aftermath of desegregation attempts, one court-ordered, the other voluntary. The Justice Department dropped its desegregation suit against Tulsa's school system, but the National Association for the Advancement of Colored People continued the action.

Natural Disasters. Storm damage in February 1975 was $12 million after tornadoes and high winds struck Altus and Duncan, leaving 4 dead and 112 injured. In May a tornado struck Stillwater. Damage from this storm and others, affecting 20 counties, was $21 million.

Nationally prominent Oklahomans in 1975 included former U. S. Sen. Fred Harris, running for the 1976 Democratic party presidential nomination on his "new populist" platform, and the nation's youngest general, astronaut Tom Stafford, commander of the Apollo-Soyuz flight. Others included the University of Oklahoma's Barry Switzer, in his third year as coach of the highly successful Sooners football team, and Carl Albert, speaker of the U. S. House of Representatives.

C. B. CLARKE
University of Oklahoma

--- **OKLAHOMA · Information Highlights** ---

Area: 69,919 square miles (181,090 sq km).
Population (1974 est.): 2,709,000. *Density:* 39 per sq mi.
Chief Cities (1970 census): Oklahoma City, the capital, 368,856; Tulsa, 330,350; Lawton, 74,470; Norman, 52,117.
Government (1975): *Chief Officers*—governor, David L. Boren (D); lt. gov., George Nigh (D). *Legislature*—Senate, 48 members; House of Representatives, 101 members.
Education (1974–75): *Enrollment*—public elementary schools, 327,253 pupils; public secondary, 274,127; nonpublic, 11,500; colleges and universities, 132,825 students. *Public school expenditures,* $445,020,000 ($784 per pupil).
State Finances (fiscal year 1974): *Revenues,* $1,566,069,-000; *expenditures,* $1,479,637,000.
Personal Income (1974): $12,371,000,000; per capita, $4,566.
Labor Force (July 1975): *Nonagricultural wage and salary earners,* 860,000; *insured unemployed,* 15,000 (1.7%).

OLDER POPULATION

Although they still faced more problems than those in other age groups, the 31 million U. S. citizens over 60 years of age saw 1975 bring them broader consideration than in the past. The Tax Reduction Act of 1975 provided a special $50 payment to recipients of social security (SSA), railroad retirement, and supplemental security income (SSI) benefits; refunds on a portion of 1974 income taxes; and liberalized computation of 1975 taxes for low-income people. Beginning with their July checks, SSA and SSI beneficiaries received an 8% cost-of-living increase. In August, the Congress increased compensation for veterans with service-connected disabilities, their widows and dependents, including parents. (See SOCIAL WELFARE—*Social Security*.)

Extension of the Comprehensive Employment and Training Act and the Older Americans Community Service Employment Act afforded employment to sizable numbers of older persons. An appropriation of $16.4 million was made for winterization of homes of elderly people. The House of Representatives created a Select Committee on Aging, a counterpart to the Senate Special Committee on Aging.

Nutrition. By the fall of 1975, the National Nutrition Program for the Elderly was serving 240,000 meals 5 days a week at 4,200 sites throughout the country. The Administration on Aging (AOA) expected this total to reach 300,000 meals in 1976 at a new funding level of $150 million. Of the 705,000 people eating one or more meals per week under the program, 473,000 had incomes below the poverty level, and 169,000 were minority group members. Nutrition, education, and opportunity for socialization are important elements of the program.

Coordination. The AOA and 525 state and area agencies coordinated programs at several levels of government. A major 1975 activity of the AOA was the negotiation of 15 agreements involving 18 federal departments and agencies aimed at improving services to older people. The purpose, stressed by Commissioner on Aging Arthur S. Flemming, was to coordinate all such activities and programs, avoid possible duplication, and provide the best services to older citizens. By year's end, similar agreements had been signed by service agencies at state and community levels.

Particularly notable was the agreement between the Department of Health, Education, and Welfare's (HEW) Social and Rehabilitation Service and the AOA for joint action in implementing the new Title XX of the Social Security Act. Title XX was designed to give older people their share of the $2.5 billion annual appropriation for services to low income families and persons.

Housing. Although housing is one of the greatest needs of older people, additional fund-

ADMINISTRATION ON AGING

The St. Louis Nutrition Project is funded under Title VII of the Older Americans Act.

ing for elderly housing was largely stalemated during the year. In spite of pressure from Congress, the Department of Housing and Urban Development (HUD) continued the virtual moratorium on loans and interest subsidies for such housing in favor of rent allowances paid directly to older people.

The International Center for Social Gerontology, aided by grants from HUD and HEW, and the Senate Special Committee on Aging promoted the development of specially designed congregate housing. This type of housing affords ready access to health, social, and recreational services for impaired but not ill older people. Congregate housing is part of the growing effort to make services available to 3 million impaired older people in their own homes in order to enable them to continue to live independently in the community instead of having to seek refuge in long-term-care medical facilities, which are expensive and provide more services than most persons need.

Research and Training. A new National Institute on Aging, created by Congress, became operative. The AOA awarded 342 grants and contracts, amounting to $22.5 million, for training, research, and demonstration projects during the year. In a national competition, 50 awards totaling $3.7 million were made to 47 colleges and universities in 34 states. These included 5 awards to consortia representing 16 cooperating institutions. The prime purpose was to establish

Nursing Homes

The nursing home industry in the United States found itself the target of numerous investigations on the local, state, and federal levels in 1975. Hearings revealed widespread abuse of patients, complex financial irregularities, and questionable political influence. As a result, new legislation was introduced to protect both the patient and the taxpayer from unscrupulous nursing home operators.

Background. More than 1.2 million aged persons—5% of the older population—were patients in 22,000 U.S. nursing homes, homes for the aged, and other long-term care facilities in 1975. It is estimated that two out of every five older persons will require such care for varying lengths of time.

The majority of patients are about 75 years of age, poor, white, and female. In 1974, the average cost of care was $500 per month, but often more than twice that amount in luxury facilities and in those providing high-quality care. The aggregate cost in that year reached $7.5 billion—$3.9 paid from public funds and $3.6 billion from private sources.

In recent decades, a sharp increase in the older population and the number of persons requiring long-term medical and nursing care overwhelmed public and private nonprofit facilities. When Medicare and Medicaid bene-fits were extended to nursing homes in 1965, the number of nursing homes doubled.

The federal government was concerned with the nursing home problem as early as the 1940's when it subsidized construction of long-term-care facilities and attempted to raise levels of care through licensing, inspection, and standard-setting. Legislation regulating environmental safety, fire prevention, sanitation, and quality of food and care was enacted but has largely gone unenforced.

Scandal. One of the most wide-ranging investigations of the nursing home industry took place in New York state under the Temporary State Commission on Living Costs and the Economy, chaired by Assemblyman Andrew Stein, and the Moreland Act Commission on Nursing Homes, chaired by Morris Abram. The investigations revealed an incredible web of hidden ownership, patient neglect, overbilling, payment for no-show jobs, and political influence. At the same time, in Washington, the U.S. Senate Subcommittee on Long-Term Care uncovered many of the same abuses.

One result of the investigations of the nursing home industry was the handing down of indictments on both the state and federal levels against two owners of chains of nursing homes. Each of the owners was charged with stealing the amount of $1.2 million in Medicaid and Medicare funds.

Ombudsman Program. A new approach to improvement of care is being made through the establishment of a nationwide ombudsman program under the direction of the Administration on Aging (AOA), a branch of the U.S. Department of Health, Education, and Welfare.

The program will work toward the establishment of local mechanisms for receiving complaints made by patients, their families, and friends and resolving them with the aid of government agencies, citizens' organizations, and nursing home associations. Additionally, ombudsmen will be required to call to the attention of appropriate administrative agencies and legislative bodies any policies, regulations, and practices that may be obstacles to the provision of good care. The AOA's regulation prohibits state agencies on aging from locating an ombudsman program within any agency that licenses, certifies, surveys, regulates, or provides services to long-term care facilities.

CERNORIA D. JOHNSON
Administration on Aging, U.S. Department of Health, Education, and Welfare

N.Y. Assemblyman Andrew Stein (*left*) with U.S. Sen. Frank Moss conducts a public hearing on nursing home abuses in New York City in January 1975.

UPI

and develop higher education programs to prepare students to serve the elderly.

Grants totaling $1 million each were made to legal service agencies and to state agencies in support of nursing-home ombudsman activities. The legal service grants were for research, curriculum development, and demonstration projects. The ombudsman grants were to enable state agencies on aging to monitor the quality of nursing home care throughout the United States.

International Developments. The 10th triennial International Congress of Gerontology took place in Jerusalem at midyear. Some 2,200 participants from 40 countries joined 800 Israelis in exchanging information from research and program experience.

Federal Council on the Aging. The Federal Council on the Aging, a new advisory group created by the Congress, organized and submitted its first report during 1975. President Gerald R. Ford publicly took exception to the council's plea for raising the level of funding for programs to assist older people. He said that "I sympathize with this concern, but I am determined to reduce the burden of inflation on our older citizens and that effort demands that government spending be limited . . . The report does not reflect the administration's policies which must respect a broader range of responsibilities and priorities."

CLARK TIBBITTS
Director, National Clearinghouse on Aging Administration on Aging, U. S. Department of Health, Education, and Welfare

ONTARIO

Ontario felt the strain of inflation and recession during 1975, experienced growing friction between the provincial and federal governments, and saw the near defeat of the Progressive Conservative government, in power since 1943.

Economic Policy. To stimulate the economy and revive the government's flagging political support, the April budget promised expenditures of about $10.2 billion, an increase of 16.8% and a record deficit of $1.6 billion. To relieve high unemployment in industries producing automobiles, furniture, and appliances, the sales tax was cut from 7% to 5%. The provincial income tax was reduced for pensioners and low-income families. A welfare package raised the minimum guaranteed income to $240 a month and provided free prescription drugs for the aged. To encourage house construction, grants of $1,500 were given to first-time home buyers. Grants to municipalities totaled 30% of provincial expenditure, while health care accounted for a further 28%.

Worried about the inflationary effect of increased fuel costs, Premier William G. Davis imposed in July a 90-day freeze on gasoline and heating-oil prices. The price freeze was extended later during the election campaign. The failure of the provincial economy to respond as anticipated led Treasurer Darcy McKeough to introduce a "mini-budget" in July. The treasurer was highly critical of the June federal budget as inadequate to stimulate new jobs or housing.

A controversial measure introduced a sales-tax rebate on all new North American cars below a certain capacity. The measure was intended to stimulate purchases of Canadian cars and to relieve unemployment in the national automobile industry, which is concentrated in the province. The federal government objected, and the province was forced to extend the sales tax rebate to imported cars as well. Because of escalating costs, Ontario also gave the federal government notice that it intended to enter no further cost-sharing programs.

Environmental Concerns. Federal schemes to build a new international airport at Pickering, near Toronto, aroused strong opposition, and the province attempted to delay the project. In late September, it refused completely to cooperate, and the federal government postponed the project indefinitely.

The Election. The tax reductions and price freezes were widely interpreted as preludes to the election finally called by Premier Davis for September 17. In an often bitter campaign, the Liberals attacked the government for its education policy, runaway spending, and scandals. The New Democratic party (NDP) concentrated on housing, high rents, and the disappearance of good farm land. During the campaign, Premier Davis yielded to NDP pressure and introduced a policy aimed at rent control. Election day saw the government reduced to a minority position, from 78 seats to 51. The Liberal party, although increasing its representation from 20 seats to 36, lost its status as official opposition to the NDP, which doubled its seats to 38. Stephen Lewis, the NDP leader, replaced Robert Nixon as leader of the opposition. Nixon resigned as Liberal leader.

PETER J. KING, *Carlton University*

ONTARIO • Information Highlights

Area: 412,582 square miles (1,068,587 sq km).
Population (1975): 8,273,000.
Chief Cities (1974): Toronto, the provincial capital, 2,-741,000; Hamilton, 520,000; Ottawa, the federal capital, 626,000.
Government (1975): *Chief Officers*—lt. gov. Pauline McGibbon; premier, William G. Davis (Progressive Conservative); atty. gen., Robert Welch; Min. of educ., Thomas Wells; Chief justice, Dalton Wells. *Legislature*—Legislative Assembly, 117 members.
Education (1975–76): *Enrollment*—public elementary and secondary schools, 1,983,900 pupils; private schools, 48,820; Indian (federal) schools, 8,020; colleges and universities, 138,650 students. *Public school expenditures,* $2,147,188,000.
Public Finance (fiscal year 1974–75 est.): *Revenues,* $8,376,000,000; *expenditures,* $8,341,000,000.
Personal Income (1972): $33,835,000,000; average annual income per person, 4,366.
(All monetary figures given in Canadian dollars.)

UPI

Crater Lake National Park was closed for three weeks in 1975 because of contamination from a broken sewage line.

OREGON

Oregon's biennial legislature met in 1975 in a long, rather lackluster, session with minimal leadership from any source. Although some significant measures were enacted, the main issues were resolved anticlimactically. The so-called "Christmas tree" omnibus tax measure purported to lower the tax liabilities of most citizens except those in the higher income brackets.

Legislation. A threatened doctor's strike due to the soaring cost and potential cancellation of malpractice insurance was avoided. The legislature established an excess-liability fund, to be financed by the doctors and administered by the state insurance commissioner, to cover claims beyond prescribed limits. The legislation also set limits on attorneys' fees in such cases. The constitutionality of the measure was expected to be challenged.

Following strong lobbying by grass seed growers, a major agricultural interest, the legislature repealed the 1975 ban on field burning of the stubble, much to the distress of Gov. Robert W. Straub and the Environmental Quality Commission. Following repeal of the ban, the legislature placed a three-year phase-out plan on field burning.

The environmentalists scored a victory when, again pioneering in pollution control, Oregon enacted a ban on the sale of aerosol cans employing fluorocarbon as a propellant. It is the first such bill in the nation and will take effect in 1977. Environmentalists failed to gain a moratorium on nuclear power plants, but a ban on the storage of nuclear wastes was enacted.

In September a one-day special session of the legislature repealed the criminal records law, which had been hastily passed in the closing days of the regular session without full realization of its implications. The law forbade the release to the public or to the media of any police or court actions and part of the law was held to be unconstitutional.

Employment. Perhaps the most dramatic news of the year was the threat of a strike by state employees, excluding college teachers, which was permissible under the 1973 bargaining act. Following months of very tense bargaining and an affirmative strike vote by the Oregon State Employees Association, a strike was finally avoided.

Oregon continued to be among the hardest-hit states in the nation in unemployment. Steadily rising unemployment figures reached 11.2% in July, the highest since the depression of the 1930's. The legislature's early enactment of Governor Straub's emergency job plan package did not deter the rise. The lumber and wood products markets continued to be depressed and were not buoyed by President Gerald R. Ford's veto of the first national housing bill. It was not possible to determine whether or not a slight autumn drop in the jobless figures indicated a lasting reversal of the trend.

A three week shutdown of Crater Lake National Park in July followed reports of illness among employees and visitors. The cause was a contaminated water supply, and this led to much criticism of the National Park Service. U. S. Sen. Mark Hatfield conducted hearings on the matter in the state. Several suits and finally a class action suit were filed against Crater Lake Lodge, Inc., alleging gastrointestinal illness and disabilities suffered from consuming contaminated water.

JOANNE AMSPOKER
Oregon College of Education

─────── **OREGON • Information Highlights** ───────

Area, 96,981 square miles (251,181 sq km).
Population (1974 est.): 2,226,000. *Density:* 23 per sq mi.
Chief Cities (1970 census): Salem, the capital, 68,856; Portland, 380,555; Eugene, 78,389.
Government (1975): *Chief Officers*—governor, Robert W. Straub (D); secy. of state, Clay Myers (R). *Legislative Assembly*—Senate, 30 members; House of Representatives, 60 members.
Education (1974–75): *Enrollment*—public elementary schools, 277,278 pupils; public secondary schools, 204,305; nonpublic schools, 23,600; colleges and universities, 139,055 students. *Public schools expenditures,* $526,958,000 ($1,223 per pupil).
State Finances (fiscal year 1974): *Revenues,* $1,666,854,-000; *expenditures,* $1,504,609,000.
Personal Income (1974): $11,941,000,000; per capita, $5,270.
Labor Force (July 1975): *Nonagricultural wage and salary earners,* 827,600; *insured unemployed,* 41,100 (5.4%).

Ottawa high school students operated a limited number of classes in their self-instruction program during the teachers' strike that lasted from late February until April.

OTTAWA

During 1975, Ottawa, Canada's national capital, continued its policy of discouraging conventional urban development. New area redevelopment programs were introduced. Limitations on building heights in the center of town were extended to discourage high-rise office development. The preservation of heritage areas was encouraged. The aim is to make the center of the city a good place for people to live.

Government. The shape of urban government in the Ottawa region again came under consideration. Criticism was expressed that Ottawa was grossly over-governed, with federal, provincial, regional, and municipal levels of government jostling each other. Following recommendations made by Douglas Fullerton, former chairman of the National Capital Commission, a joint committee of the federal Senate and House of Commons investigated the whole structure of the capital area. The province also commissioned a study. The federal government made no secret of its desire to see Hull, on the Quebec side of the Ottawa River, considered as part of the national capital. It has already transferred many government departments and is constructing new office complexes there. It also proposes to move the National Gallery of Canada and the national Museum of Science and Technology into Quebec.

Municipal Finance. The city of Ottawa was forced to raise taxes by 14% in 1975. It estimated an operating budget of $83.3 million for the year, some $30 million of which was to come from federal and provincial grants. Physical environment and community development were major items (20% and 30% respectively) of a capital budget of $45.8 million. The regional government estimated expenditures of $93.7 million, a sharp increase over the $65.6 million of 1974. The greatest increase was for a transportation system that would expand services in an era of rapidly rising costs. The regional transport commission's deficit was expected to jump by 220%. The large tax increase, necessitated by high regional expenditures, drew strong opposition from the component municipalities, especially the city of Ottawa, which have to collect the revenue.

Education. City of Ottawa high schools were closed by a teachers' strike from late February until April. The major issues were pay and working conditions. A contract granting a 31% pay increase ended the strike. High schools in the suburban areas remained open, however. The teachers and the Carleton school board agreed to a new contract without a strike.

PETER J. KING
Carleton University

PAKISTAN

The year 1975 was not an untypical one in Pakistan's brief history. It had its usual problems with India and unearthed old ones with Afghanistan. Despite a touch of domestic turbulence, its government remained stable. The economy continued to improve.

Foreign Affairs. Prime Minister Zulfikar Ali Bhutto said in January that he viewed India's "expansionism" with great concern. He was particularly distressed by the Indian development of nuclear weapons. At the time Bhutto's chief interest was having the U. S. ban on arms shipment to Pakistan lifted. This ban was ended in late February but only after much public soul-searching by U. S. officials. These officials not only found Congressional opinion mixed

Pakistan's Prime Minister Zulfikar Ali Bhutto met at the White House in February with President Ford to ask for further military assistance and food aid from the United States.

UPI

but, as expected, received considerable vilification from the Indian government for their efforts. Bhutto himself had journeyed to Washington in early February to press his nation's case. Whatever ultimate military value these weapons would have, the promise of them not only bolstered Bhutto in domestic politics but also added immeasurably to Pakistani feelings of security. Predictably, India assailed the United States for the decision, but the turmoil did not last.

In June, when Indian domestic politics took an authoritarian turn, Bhutto chose to avoid direct comment. By late summer the Pakistani press began to criticize the Indian government with such headlines as "Life and Liberty Snuffed Out [in India]" and "Indira [Gandhi] Turns the Screw." Privately Pakistani officials expressed their fear that the Indians would resort to some "diversionary" action against the Pakistanis. However, only talk characterized the relations between the two countries during the year. In May, India and Pakistan failed to work out a program of overflight and air connections.

As early as February, Bhutto accused Afghanistan of fomenting trouble in Pakistan's Northwest Frontier Province (NWFP). The issue—the political fate of Pushtu-speaking Pathan tribesmen in the NWFP—was a very old one, going back to Pakistan's founding in 1947. Afghanistan has consistently supported autonomy for these tribesmen. Such autonomy would mean the further breakup of Pakistan, already troubled by language and religious separatism. In February, after the assassination of a close political aide, Bhutto took over the direct administration of the NWFP and outlawed the National Awami party, which had followed a friendly policy toward Afghanistan. By August

there was a great deal of small-scale violence and terrorism in the NWFP and a few major incidents, but at year's end the situation remained static.

Relations with Bangladesh—the old eastern wing of Pakistan—warmed over the year. The August coup against President Sheikh Mujibur Rahman that resulted in his death produced a government friendlier to Pakistan, a trend that continued during further political turmoil in Bangladesh. Diplomatic relations between the two countries were finally resumed.

Pakistan's relations with other Muslim countries were generally quite good. By June over $500 million in aid had been contributed since June 1974 by about 30 Muslim countries. The largest contributor was Iran, with more than $250 million. Pakistan stressed its Muslim character and has supported these states in its own foreign relations policies. United States-Pakistan relations were good, as indeed they have been throughout most of the nearly 30 years of Pakistani history.

─────── **PAKISTAN · Information Highlights** ───────
Official Name: Islamic Republic of Pakistan.
Location: South Asia.
Area: 310,403 square miles (803,943 sq km).
Population (1975 est.): 70,600,000.
Chief Cities (1974): Islamabad, the capital, 250,000; Karachi, 3,500,000; Lahor, 2,100,000.
Government: *Head of state,* Chaudhri Fazal Elahi, president (took office Aug. 1973). *Head of government,* Zulfikar Ali Bhutto, prime minister (took office Aug. 1973). *Legislature*—Parliament: Senate and National Assembly.
Monetary Unit: Rupee (9.931 rupees equal U. S.$1, March 1975).
Gross National Product (1974): $7,600,000,000.
Manufacturing (major products): Textiles, processed foods, cement, petroleum products.
Major Agricultural Products: Wheat, cotton, rice, sugarcane, corn, millet, chickpeas, rapeseed, livestock.
Foreign Trade (1974): *Exports,* $1,105,000,000; *imports,* $1,738,000,000.

Domestic Affairs. The major earthquake that struck in late December 1974 in the Karakoram mountains north of Rawalpindi killed about 5,000 people and injured 15,000. The world quickly rallied with aid, with King Faisal of Saudi Arabia alone contributing $10 million.

The Pakistani economy was remarkably healthy during 1975; one newspaper called it "the most buoyant on the Asian subcontinent." Problems of poverty, overpopulation, and health care remained, but the Bhutto government could be proud of its solid economic achievements.

Domestic political troubles remained as well. The NWFP was a troubled spot. In February a close political aide of Bhutto, Hyat Mohammad Khan Sherpao, was assassinated at Peshawar University. It was this act that triggered Bhutto's determination to outlaw the troublesome National Awami party. In late February, Pakistani security police raided universities throughout the country and confiscated "considerable" arms and ammunition.

In the fall, a major political demonstration in Lahore was broken up by police, leaving many dead and wounded. Yet, violence is not unusual in Pakistani history. The fact remains that the country is remarkably stable under Bhutto, with a developing economy and a sense of national purpose.

CARL LEIDEN
University of Texas at Austin

PANAMA

It became increasingly difficult for the administration of Gen. Omar Torrijos Herrera to rule the isthmus in 1975. Panama Canal treaty talks slowed markedly, and the government became more involved in the national economy.

Unrest and Repression. A truce reached in July with 300 student leaders was broken in September, when unruly student activists stoned the U. S. Embassy in a violent demonstration. In March the government closed down an opposition newspaper, *La Opinión Pública,* and canceled its printing license before its first issue had appeared. Conservatives backing the paper pleaded for public discussion of treaty issues. After pro-government forces raided a radio station in the capital, the regime forced a more rigorous censorship on news media. A May decree obligated radio and television stations to obtain official clearance for reports on canal negotiations and student activities. A dissident businessman was jailed for 22 days for attacking Torrijos' policies.

Treaty Talks. Great differences between the Panamanian and U. S. positions on a new canal pact were made public when Panamanian students released a detailed document on the negotiations. After 11 years of intermittent negotiations, crucial unresolved points included the duration of a new treaty and the defense of the waterway. Panama insisted on termination of the treaty within 25 years, while the United States asked that it be maintained for 50 to 80 years, contingent upon expansion of the interoceanic canal. Panama was willing to allow the United States to retain 3 military bases for defense of the waterway, not the 13 requested.

Ever larger numbers of Panamanians resigned themselves to a stalemate in the negotiations until after the 1976 general election in the United States. However, Torrijos continued to gain support for his position in the negotiations in his travels in Central and South America in 1975. As a result of hard campaigning, Panama won a two-year term on the UN Security Council.

Economic Development. Panama selected Texasgulf, Inc. to operate its $800-million Cerro Colorado copper project. Plans were for the foreign operating company to hold about a 15% interest in the undertaking, with the Panamanian government retaining the remainder. For its exploration and technical studies of the 2.2-billion-ton ore deposit, Panama awarded Canadian Javelin a settlement of $23.6 million when the two parties failed to reach an agreement on exploitation rights.

In September the government-owned Bananera del Pacífico began to assume control of banana production for export. By the end of 1977, Panama will have assumed all assets of the Chiriquí Land Company, a subsidiary of United Brands and producer of the bananas exported from Panama. A takeover of export banana production will cost Panama some $40 million, and payment will be in bananas for foreign markets. United Brands will continue to market all bananas exported from Panama.

The Torrijos government moved ahead on a $100 million transisthmian oil pipeline, with a capacity for 1 million barrels daily. The Inter-American Development Bank awarded Panama a $30 million loan in September for the construction of rural roads. The licensing of 10 additional banks, including the Bankers Trust Company and the Royal Bank of Canada, augmented Panama's role as a regional banking center

LARRY L. PIPPIN, *Elbert Covell College University of the Pacific*

─────── **PANAMA · Information Highlights** ───────

Official Name: Republic of Panama.
Location: On the isthmus of Panama, which links Central America and South America.
Area: 29,209 square miles (75,650 sq km).
Population (1975 est.): 1,700,000.
Chief City (1974): Panama, the capital, 455,027.
Government: *Military junta,* led by Gen. Omar Torrijos Herrera (took power Oct. 1972). *Head of state,* Demetrio Lakas Bahas, president (took office Dec. 1969). *Legislature:* unicameral—Peoples Assembly.
Monetary Unit: Balboa (1 balboa equals U. S.$1, July 1974).
Gross National Product (1973 est.): 1,360,000,000.
Manufacturing (major products): Processed foods, petroleum products, textiles, wood products.
Major Agricultural Products: Bananas, vegetables, rice, forest products, fish.
Foreign Trade (1974): *Exports,* $200,520,000; *imports,* $794,960,000.

PARAGUAY

A growing schism between the Roman Catholic Church and the government, repression of political dissent, and continued economic growth were the major developments in 1975.

Political Unrest. Following the discovery of a plot to kill President Alfredo Stroessner in November 1974, one terrorist was killed and six others, some of whom were from the president's Colorado party, were arrested. By March 1975 an additional 1,000 people had been detained. Further party dissent surfaced when 500 young members called for a new president when Stroessner ends his fifth term in 1978. The weak opposition Radical Liberal party (PRL) ended its cooperation with the government, charging it with harassment of PRL leaders, violation of human rights, and peasant repression.

The national council of bishops denounced the government for its raid on a church-sponsored village in which eight people were killed. The government responded by calling the church an institution "contaminated with Communism," deporting several priests and inviting the Catholic Relief Service to leave the country. It was in this tense environment that municipal elections were held in October. As expected, the dominant Colorado party triumphed over the three minor parties.

Economic Developments. Although July frosts caused considerable crop damage, and farmers were discontented with the crop prices, the economic picture was generally good. The 1974 growth rate of 8% was expected to continue during 1975. The first step toward the construction of the joint Brazilian-Paraguayan Itaipú Dam, which will provide hydroelectric power, began in September when work started on re-channeling the Parana River. Also begun was a joint steel mill with an anticipated annual capacity of 100,000 tons. The influx of Brazilian money and settlers caused concern among some Paraguayans about Paraguay's sovereignty.

South African Prime Minister B. J. Vorster visited in September and extended loans of $31 million for housing and agricultural projects.

LEO B. LOTT, *University of Montana*

------ **PARAGUAY · Information Highlights** ------

Official Name: Republic of Paraguay.
Location: Central South America.
Area: 157,047 square miles (406,752 sq km).
Population (1975 est.): 2,600,000.
Chief City (1974 est.): Asunción, the capital, 400,000.
Government: *Head of state and government,* Gen. Alfredo Stroessner, president (took office Aug. 1954). *Legislature*—Congress: Senate and Chamber of Deputies.
Monetary Unit: Guarani (126 guaranies equal U. S.$1, May 1975).
Gross National Product (1973 est.): $798,000,000.
Manufacturing (major products): Meats, leather, wood products, quebracho extract, vegetable oil.
Major Agricultural Products: Cassava, bananas, tobacco, cotton, soybeans, oilseeds, citrus fruits, cattle, forest products.
Foreign Trade (1974): *Exports,* $169,800,000; *imports,* $151,400,000.

PENNSYLVANIA

In a year meant to celebrate the start of the nation's Bicentennial, the state was faced with political battles, inflation, and natural disasters. In addition state employees, seeking higher pay, walked off their jobs for four days in July. Democratic Governor Shapp declared his candidacy for the presidency, and Democratic mayors were reelected in Philadelphia and Pittsburgh.

The Governor. In September 1975, Pennsylvania's Gov. Milton J. Shapp announced his intention to campaign vigorously for the Democratic party presidential nomination. Shapp, who is in his second term as governor, is a former engineer. He is one of the few Jewish contenders for the national nomination.

Shapp's national campaign may be clouded by allegations in Pennsylvania that he personally accepted two cash contributions amounting to $20,000 in his 1970 gubernatorial campaign. These funds allegedly were given to Shapp by an engineer whose firm had several million dollars worth of Commonwealth of Pennsylvania contracts. The governor testified before a federal grand jury investigating the matter. Shapp reputedly said that he could not trace the disposition of the funds and that no formal accounting of the funds was made.

The Legislature. On Oct. 16, 1975, the state legislature adjourned for a month without passing a proposed new code of legislative ethics. The legislature rejected a stricter code in 1974. The 1975 bill, which passed the state Senate but received an initially unenthusiastic response in the House, called for public identification of all sources of income above $2,500, excluding real estate holdings, stock traded on recognized markets, and secured loans. No penalty section was included in the legislation, but it is stricter than the present code of ethics, which was adopted in 1958.

Employment. In August 1975, Pennsylvania's unemployment reached its highest level in 17 months. The seasonally-adjusted rate of 9.8% was more than double the seasonally adjusted rate of August 1974. Commonwealth Secretary of Labor and Industry Paul Smith said that the state's unemployment compensation fund was nearly bankrupt and that the chances of a significant economic upturn in the future were slim.

A study of equal employment policies of Pennsylvania governmental agencies showed that little progress had been made during the year. No state agency had implemented an affirmative action plan for employment of minorities as of spring 1975. Governor Shapp, who disbanded his Equal Rights Task Force in 1972, dismantled the Governor's Affirmative Action Council in May 1975 and set up an Affirmative Action Bureau under the jurisdiction of the state secretary of administration. The governor felt that placing the unit within an operating governmental agency would facilitate prompt action.

Area: 45,333 square miles (117,412 sq km).
Population (1974 est.): 11,835,000. *Density:* 261 per sq mi.
Chief Cities (1970 census): Harrisburg, the capital, 68,-061; Philadelphia, 1,950,098; Pittsburgh, 520,117.
Government (1975): *Chief Officers*—governor, Milton J. Shapp (D); lt. gov., Ernest P. Kline (D). *General Assembly*—Senate, 50 members; House of Representatives, 203 members.
Education (1974–75): *Enrollment*—public elementary schools, 1,148,817 pupils; public secondary, 1,128,-030; nonpublic, 459,300; colleges and universities, 439,055 students. *Public school expenditures,* $2,-733,067,000 ($1,263 per pupil).
State Finances (fiscal year 1974): *Revenues,* $8,286,099,-000; *expenditures,* $8,056,510,000.
Personal Income (1974): $64,976,000,000; per capita, $5,490.
Labor Force (July 1975): *Nonagricultural wage and salary earners,* 4,359,800; *insured unemployed,* 263,-000 (6%).

A month later, the highest ranking black officer in the Pennsylvania air national guard, Col. Harold Pierce, resigned. He alleged that the guard's leadership and Governor Shapp blocked the rise of blacks to key posts. Pierce, a physician, pointed out that only 6 of the 570 Pennsylvania Air National Guard officers were black. Of 4,200 guardsmen, only 162 were blacks. Colonel Pierce questioned the commonwealth's commitment to equal opportunity for all Pennsylvanians.

Crime. The governor's criminal justice commission approved $1 million to underwrite the continued investigation by Walter M. Phillips, Jr., of alleged government corruption in Philadelphia, the state's major city. The state legislature, led by Sen. Henry H. Cranfrani, a Democrat of Philadelphia, attempted to halt Phillips' work. The commission, with only one dissenting vote, decided to continue Phillips' investigation for one more year. Phillips wanted to bring to trial most of the 42 people indicted by the grand jury as a result of his previous work. Included in this group were policemen, city officials, and others accused of serious offenses.

Flooding of the Susquehanna River. In June 1972 a tropical storm caused the Susquehanna River to flood, nearly destroying Wilkes-Barre. In September 1975, the storm-swollen Susquehanna roared safely past the sandbagged city. However, Harrisburg, the state's capital city, was flooded again as it had been in 1972. Governor Shapp called out about 3,000 national guardsmen to help in the emergency, which left about 20,000 people homeless and caused extensive property damage.

Elections. In the November elections the Democrats retained control of Philadelphia and Pittsburgh, with the positions of Mayor Frank Rizzo and Mayor Peter Flaherty, respectively, enhanced by the Democratic victories. Republicans, however, maintained their majorities in suburban Philadelphia counties of Bucks, Chester, Delaware, and Montgomery.

MIRIAM ERSHKOWITZ
Temple University

PERU

Peru's most significant events in 1975 were the ouster of President Juan Velasco Alvarado August 29, financing of the world's largest open pit copper mine, and the withdrawal of foreign oil companies from the Amazon region.

Coup Installs Morales Bermúdez. In a coup on August 29, President Juan Velasco Alvarado was replaced by Gen. Francisco Morales Bermúdez, formerly prime minister and minister of war. One goal of the coup was elimination of the increasing arbitrariness of Velasco. Morales Bermúdez assumed the presidency on August 30 and named new military commanders.

In September many political and trade union leaders returned from exile. Several magazines banned by Velasco's regime resumed publication.

Police Strike. On February 5–6, 86 persons were killed, 162 were wounded, and at least 1,012 were arrested in Lima as the army crushed a strike by police for higher wages. Angry civilians set fire to or looted government-controlled newspaper offices, hotels, and the army officers' club before order was restored. The government claimed that the strike and riots were organized by the opposition APRA party and the U. S. Central Intelligence Agency. Both groups denied the charges.

Economic Developments. The Southern Peru Copper Corp. announced on Jan. 5, 1975, the completion of financing for a $620 million open-pit copper mining project in Cuajone. The estimated reserves of 468 million tons would make it the world's largest open-pit copper mine. After four years of exploration, only Occidental Petroleum of 29 foreign oil companies and the government's Petroperu had struck refinable oil in the swampy Amazon region.

On June 30 the government announced a series of decrees to curb inflation. In addition, the measures attempted to make Peru more attractive to foreign creditors and to overcome the first trade deficit in several years. The deficit, due principally to lower international copper prices and the increased costs of imported capital goods, raw materials, and food, was expected to reach $985 million in 1975.

NEALE J. PEARSON, *Texas Tech University*

Official Name: Republic of Peru.
Location: West coast of South America.
Area: 496,223 square miles (1,285,216 sq km).
Population (1975 est.): 15,300,000.
Chief City (1972 census): Lima, the capital, 3,350,000 (met. area).
Government: *Head of state,* Gen. Francisco Morales Bermúdez (took office August 1975).
Monetary Unit: Sol (38.70 soles equal U. S.$1, May 1975).
Gross National Product (1974 est.): $9,500,000.
Manufacturing (major products): Processed foods, textiles, chemicals, metal products, automobiles, fish meal, fish, oil.
Major Agricultural Products: Cotton, sugar, rice, coffee, sheep, potatoes, fish.
Foreign Trade: *Exports* (1973), $1,050,000,000; *imports* (1974), $1,270,000,000.

PHILIPPINES

There was increasing political uneasiness in the Philippines both before and after the third anniversary of President Ferdinand E. Marcos' 1972 declaration of martial law, but there were no signs of an early ending to the "emergency" rule. There were changes, however, in foreign policy, stemming in part from the fall of the anti-Communist regimes in South Vietnam and Cambodia.

Politics. About 90% of the eligible voters participated in a February referendum that supported Marcos' martial law, but they were given no opportunity to endorse any alternative. Reflective of presidential indecision and the country's growing opposition to martial law, the date of the vote was twice postponed and the referendum questions changed.

A symbol of the opposition to Marcos' dictatorship was provided by former Senator Benigno S. Aquino, who was jailed after the 1972 takeover. Aquino, accused of treason by the government, embarked on a protest-fast, which he ended on its 40th day. He and 13 others also filed petitions in the Philippine supreme court, contending that Marcos held office illegally. They lost the case.

The passage of the 3rd anniversary of martial law was followed by a series of demands for a return to elected government. These were advanced by the Civil Liberties Union (led by highly-respected former senators José W. Diokno and Jovito Salonga, and by Jesuit intellectual Father Horacio de la Costa), and by former foreign secretary and influential author-educator Salvador P. Lopez. The outpouring of opposition to the Marcos regime was the strongest in more than two years.

Muslim Insurrection. The Muslim rebellion, which broke out in 1968 and intensified in 1972 after the Marcos takeover, continued despite a reported "truce" arranged by the government in August. Some 70% of the Philippine army, about 50,000 men, was employed against the Muslim insurgents, who sought separation for those areas of Mindanao, Sulu, and Jolo in which followers of the Islamic faith predominated.

More than 1.5 million people had been displaced by the insurrection through 1975. Military dead may have reached 3,000 since the fighting started, with no reliable estimate of the number of rebels killed. According to the government, 7,000 Muslim insurgents had surrendered, but rebel leaders claimed that these were not hard-core participants in the fighting. Government estimates placed the number of insurrectionists at about 8,000, but the figure was probably in the 20–30,000 range.

Muslims comprise a 5% minority, mainly located in the southern islands, in a country where Christians overwhelmingly predominate. Libya and some other Mediterranean Islamic countries provided military and financial aid to

---

PHILIPPINES · Information Highlights

Official Name: Republic of the Philippines.
Location: Southeast Asia.
Area: 115,830 square miles (300,000 sq km).
Population (1975 est.): 44,400,000.
Chief Cities (1974 est.): Quezon City, the capital, 848,-000; Manila, 1,500,000; Cebu, 375,000.
Government: *Head of state,* Ferdinand E. Marcos, president (took office for 2d term Dec. 1969). *Head of government,* Marcos, prime minister (took office under new constitution Jan. 1973). *Legislature* (unicameral)—National Assembly.
Monetary Unit: Peso (7.02 pesos equal U.S.$1, May 1975).
Gross National Product (1974 est.): $8,800,000,000.
Manufacturing (major products): Petroleum products, processed foods, tobacco products, plywood and veneers, paper.
Major Agricultural Products: Rice, corn, coconuts, sugarcane, abaca, sweet potatoes, lumber.
Foreign Trade (1973): *Exports,* $1,798,000,000; *imports,* $1,773,000,000.

---

the rebels. Part of this aid was channelled through the friendly leadership of the nearby eastern Malaysian state of Sabah.

Economy. There was a slowdown in the Philippine rate of inflation during the year, but there was also a downturn in the country's balance of payments situation and an increase in its external debt. Trade with the United States, its onetime colonial ruler, fell off 36% in the first half of 1975, while trade with Japan grew 18% during the same period. U.S. corporations, which held land in the country in violation of the terms of the Philippine constitution, gave up their efforts to retain such property. Their possession of this land had been authorized by a 1946 agreement between Manila and Washington. The successor treaty expired in 1974.

Foreign Relations. The fall of the Indochinese lands of South Vietnam and Cambodia, which the Philippines generally saw as a result of withdrawn U.S. support, was followed by several important foreign policy actions.

Informal talks were begun with the United States and were designed to increase Philippine control over strategic U.S. air and naval bases in the country. President Marcos stated that he wished to place the bases under complete Philippine sovereignty and turn them into "economically productive facilities" as well as military installations.

In June, President Marcos visited Peking and agreed to exchange diplomatic representatives with China. He also established diplomatic ties with North Vietnam, North Korea, and Cuba. A scheduled trip to the Soviet Union was postponed, however, ostensibly because of "cold weather" in Moscow but quite possibly as a result of mounting domestic political opposition.

The Philippines did not abandon traditional ties with such non-Communist countries as the United States, but it expanded its network of international connections. It also sought improved relations with Middle Eastern Islamic lands, whose favor and vital oil it almost lost in 1974 because of the Muslim rebellion.

RICHARD BUTWELL
State University of New York at Fredonia

GEOFFREY CLEMENTS/WHITNEY MUSEUM OF AMERICAN ART

The Whitney Museum of American Art held its first survey of photography in the United States in January 1975. The exhibition was considered influential in the acceptance of photography as an art form.

photography

In 1975, photography achieved new status as an art form. Many art galleries exhibited photographs for the first time, and a new museum of photography completed its first year of operation. Collectors paid higher prices for prints and equipment. U. S. amateurs were snapping 2 billion images a year. Manufacturers of photographic equipment, recognizing a popularity that even recession and inflation could not quell, offered increasingly sophisticated equipment for professionals and amateurs.

NEW EQUIPMENT

The Contax RTS, product of the new Yashica/Zeiss collaboration, led the growing group of systems cameras. Miranda, with its dx-3 system, made its first entry in a field already occupied by Canon, Minolta, Nikon, and Olympus. These companies offer a basic camera body that can be fitted with an array of lenses, close-up devices, motor drive, and other features. Olympus, whose OM-1 system was introduced in 1973, was scheduled to release its OM-2, a fully automatic version, in 1976.

110 Pocket Cameras. Kodak added flash to the pocket 110 Instamatic camera, its 1972 innovation whose size, weight, and automatic exposure system appealed to the amateur. The five new 110's—four Trimlites and a Tele-Instamatic 608—made use of General Electric's new "Flip-flash" flashbulbs. These are activated by a piezoelectric generator built into the camera, eliminating the need for batteries or other striker devices. Canon, Minolta, and Rollei also introduced compact 110's, and Sedic produced a 110 with a motor.

The most advanced of Kodak's Trimlites, the 48, contains a "feeler" in its film chamber and flash socket to provide correct exposure for ASA 400 color negative film, which had not been released by the end of 1975. The new film is said to be much "faster" and more sensitive to low light conditions than the ASA 80 film used in 110's. The emulsion would create a high, single exposure-index for color and black and white images.

Instant Print Cameras. Polaroid introduced the third model of its SX-70 system at half the consumer cost of its first model. More than 2 million units of the instant print SX-70 were sold between 1973 and 1975. Polaroid also revamped its color emulsion, introducing a more deeply color-saturated Polacolor 2 instant film, and brought suit against a company whose camera uses SX-70 film.

Other New Products. Among the top quality lenses introduced in 1975 were many zooms and ultra-wide focal lengths. Light in weight, their compact design was made possible by incorporating lenses varying slightly from sphericity (aspherics) in the Canon lenses and solid cata-

The new Kodak Tele-Instamatic 608 camera features a normal lens (25 mm) and a telephoto lens (43 mm).

dioptric design (combining lenses and mirrors) in the Vivitar series 1.

A new Kodak Ektasound 150 movie camera and two new Kodak Ektasound movie projectors were announced by Eastman Kodak. The Ektasound 150 movie camera provides one-step sound movies with automatic lip-synchronization. The Ektasound 235B and 245B share such features as increased illumination and an automatic stop feature, which operates if the film has been secured to the supply reel. The Ektasound 245B movie projector adds sound-recording capability.

Other developments in new equipment included Honeywell's automatic focusing device, which can be used in still, motion, or television cameras. Xerox developed an accessory for the Model 6500 color copier that prints enlargements of 35-mm slides on plain paper. Finally, many companies joined the competition to produce developing kits for home color processing.

PHOTOGRAPHY AS ART

By whatever standards success is measured, shows, media coverage, or sales, the activity in all spheres provided proof of a widespread acceptance of the photographic image as art.

In New York City, considered by many the photographic capital of the world, the Whitney Museum of American Art held its first survey of photography in the United States. Although much controversy surrounded the choice of the 85 photographers represented, the retrospective exhibit of 260 images was widely hailed as a significant step in the acceptance of photography as art. A totally photographic museum, the International Center of Photography (ICP) held classes and shows during its first year of operation. And, while the Museum of Modern Art in New York City and the George Eastman House in Rochester, N.Y., have always maintained large photography archives, university art galleries and libraries have begun to establish or add extensively to their photography collections.

The influential "Arts and Leisure" section of the Sunday New York Times replaced its more locally-oriented treatment of photography with more prominent coverage on the art page and reviews of major shows by art critic Hilton Kramer. Art Forum, a prestigious U.S. art journal, featured a number of articles on photography in 1975.

"Suddenly photography is the great event in art, and painting is standing aside," Richard Avedon said in a Newsweek review of his show at Marlborough Gallery in New York. For the first time, the prestigious Marlborough Gallery, until then dealers only in painting and sculpture, opened its doors to photography and hired a

In 1975, Eastman Kodak introduced the Kodak Ektasound 150 movie camera (foreground) with automatic lip-synchronization and the Ektasound 235B and 245B movie projectors that boasted increased illumination and sound-recording capability.

photography director. A limited-edition portfolio of Avedon's prints went on sale, and more shows of top living photographers were slated.

At the Museum of Modern Art in New York City, Edward Weston received a major retrospective, and Irving Penn's platinum prints of cigarette butts were shown. The fact that Avedon and Penn, well-known commercial fashion photographers, had shows of noncommercial work indicated the overall gallery trend toward showing photography as a personal art. Melissa Shook's daily self-portraits appeared at Foto, a new gallery devoted to the work of lesser-known photographers. Duane Michels' archetypes and photos-with-rhyme were shown at the Light Gallery.

Personal projects by young photographers appeared in increasing numbers of photography books, such as Charles Gatewood's *Sidetripping,* which featured images of the freakier side of U. S. society, and Jill Freedman's *Circus Days.* Other photographers, especially established masters, presented their work for sale in portfolios and individual prints. Minor White offered his 12-print Jupiter Portfolio at $1,600, and Ansel Adams, who announced he would not fill private print orders after 1975, set his per-print price at $800.

The top entry in photojournalism was *Minamata,* W. Eugene and Aileen Smith's essay on the mercury poisoning from industrial wastes of a small Japanese town. Also notable was the first publication of *A Victorian Album,* by Julia Margaret Cameron and Her Circle. A famous photographic collection, it was auctioned in London in 1974 for almost $100,000, a record. The work of contemporary women photographers appeared in a half-dozen group shows in New York, and a historical survey of the Women of Photography opened in San Francisco. Less traditional forms of visual imagery appeared, including a survey of Polaroid photography at the International Center of Photography and holography exhibits in established art galleries. Many shows, books, and symposia focused on the revived interest in photo history, and book distribution boomed as Laurel opened a warehouse and published a 70-page catalogue solely for photographic books.

Newspaper articles headed "Photo Market Goes Bullish" and "Blow Up—The Story of Photography in Today's Art Market" told the story of the incredible surge to buy images, especially those of earlier photographers. Two auctions of photographs in New York City's Sotheby-Park Bernet auction rooms brought in receipts totaling $135,000 and $185,000, respectively. A symposium in Lincoln Center sponsored by *Art in America* magazine was held—at an expensive $50 a head—to provide collecting information.

Walker Evans. Walker Evans, who had a major influence on modern photography, died in April. Photography, he believed, was the art of

UPI

Ansel Adams held a nature photography course at Yosemite National Park in which Susan Ford was a student.

seeing unblinkingly. Without compromise or overstatement he recorded the poverty, waste, and broken promises of U. S. society from the 1930's to the mid-1970's. From 1935 to 1938 he was a roving social historian with the photographic unit of the New Deal's Farm Security Administration. Evans' stature was assured in 1941 with the publication of his 31 photographs that accompanied James Agee's *Let Us Now Praise Famous Men.* In 1971, New York City's Museum of Modern Art had a retrospective exhibit of Evans' social chronicle.

BARBARA L. LOBRON
Journalist, Editor, Photographer

Noted photographer Walker Evans, who chronicled U. S. poverty in the 1930's, died in April at the age of 71.

JERRY L. THOMPSON

PHYSICS

Physics had an exceptional year in 1975. A fundamental magnetic particle known as the magnetic monopole may have been detected. The unexpected discovery and confirmation of two new elementary particles, called psi particles, was a landmark advance in high-energy physics. Significant steps forward were achieved in the unification of the forces between matter, laser separation of isotopes, and controlled thermonuclear fusion. And during 1975, the Atomic Energy Commission went out of existence.

Magnetic Monopole. In 1931, P. A. M. Dirac showed theoretically that the existence of a fundamental magnetic particle carrying a single magnetic charge (like a magnet with one pole) is possible. Since then, experimenters have searched fruitlessly for this magnetic monopole in particle accelerators, cosmic rays, iron ores, ocean sediments, meteorites, and lunar rocks.

In August, a group of four cosmic-ray researchers from the University of California at Berkeley and the University of Houston announced the discovery of a track they interpreted as that of a magnetic monopole in a particle detector made up of a stack of films and plastic sheets. The detector was carried by a balloon to 130,000 feet (39,625 meters) above Sioux City, Ia., to search out heavy cosmic-ray particles. On etching the sheets, the investigators found them completely penetrated by one unusual track, made, they believed, by the magnetic monopole. The track indicated a particle of at least 600 proton masses with a charge 137 times stronger than the electric charge of an electron. However, other physicists suggest that a platinum nucleus may have made

the track. At the year's end, the issue was still unsettled.

New Elementary Particles. The discovery of two new elementary particles was the most sensational news in years for particle physics, perhaps indicating a whole new family of particles. Late in 1974, a group of researchers at Brookhaven National Laboratory, led by S. C. C. Ting of M. I. T., and another group at the Stanford Linear Accelerator Center (SLAC), while carrying on colliding-beam experiments, discovered a new particle with anomalous properties. The particle was called J by the former group, psi by the latter. Almost immediately, the discovery was confirmed by a group at Frascati, Italy. Then 10 days after the first discovery, the research group at Stanford found another unusual particle, called psi prime.

Many theoretical explanations have been put forth for these new particles, but the situation is still very cloudy. The new particles have a very large mass, but last an anomalously long time. New properties called "color" and "charm" had been proposed earlier for quarks, theoretical subparticles of elementary particles. Some of these same properties may be involved in the new particles.

Another anomaly observed in these SLAC colliding-beam experiments remains to be explained. It was noted that on occasion an electron and positron collided to produce an electron, a muon, and some missing energy. This anomalous production of particles might be explained by a pair of new particles, called U (or unknown) particles, which then yield the electron or a muon and one or two neutrinos. But whether the U particle is a heavy lepton, a heavy meson, or an elementary boson, or some

UPI

Physicists from the University of California at Berkeley and the University of Houston gather around detector that helped them discover what is believed to be a magnetic monopole. Scientists have searched for this fundamental magnetic particle for decades.

other explanation is in order, has not as yet been clarified.

These results illustrated the value of colliding-beam experiments. Two colliding particles produce an effective energy many times greater than one particle of the same bombarding energy striking a stationary target. To obtain sufficient intensity, the beams are trapped (or stored). Such a facility was used at SLAC in the experiments in which the new particles were discovered.

Unification of Forces. Until the discovery of the new particles, the hottest topic in particle physics involved neutrino experiments at Fermi National Accelerator Laboratory in Illinois (Fermilab) and elsewhere. The massless, chargeless neutrinos rarely interact with matter, and then only through the weak interaction. The four known forces between matter are the weak force (between such lighter particles as electrons), the strong nuclear force gluing nucleons together in the atomic nucleus, and the familiar electromagnetic and gravitational forces. Until recently, no one has been able to connect any of these forces, although physicists have hoped to unite them under one universal law. Neutrino experiments at Fermilab during the past year have continued to support a common origin for weak and electromagnetic forces, as predicted by the unified field theories. Thus the first step in the unification of these forces may be the connection between the weak and electromagnetic interactions.

Isotope Separation. The separation of isotopes is of practical importance in modern industry. The most famous is the separation of uranium 235 (which splits by fission readily and is the fuel of most fission reactors) from uranium 238, which makes up 99.3% of natural uranium. Since both these isotopes have almost identical chemical properties, chemical processes alone cannot be used to separate them. Gaseous diffusion or centrifuge methods are the standard techniques used. Development of the gaseous diffusion method was perhaps the greatest difficulty faced in the Manhattan (atomic bomb) Project. The method involves repeating diffusion many thousands of times to separate the isotopes. The energy expenditure involved is extremely large.

Recently, a new way to obtain separation of isotopes has been developed using the very precise frequencies of lasers to excite specific isotopes. Once they are excited, they can be separated by chemical and physical reactions. In principle, the energy requirements are drastically reduced, and so are the capital investments, since the cycle is not repeated thousands of times as in the diffusion process. So far, isotopes of boron, sulfur, chlorine, and bromine have been separated by this method. The production of isotopes is important for medical, industrial, and research applications, but the major application is clearly to uranium. Much of this research is classified, but what is known about the results suggests that laser separation has promise as an inexpensive method of separating uranium isotopes.

Controlled Thermonuclear Fusion. One basic world problem is the development of new energy sources. The ultimate alternative to the fission processes employed in present-day reactors is controlled thermonuclear fusion, but the practical problems in controlled fusion are monumental: the materials must be heated sufficiently for the fusion reaction to occur, and the reaction must be contained. The temperatures involved are in the range from 10 million to 100 million degrees Kelvin. At such extremely high temperatures, the fusion materials form a plasma (ionized gas). Since no solid wall can contain plasma at such high temperatures, researchers have used magnetic fields as a container.

A new version of a magnetic mirror device for plasma confinement has enabled a team at the Lawrence Livermore Laboratory to produce plasma temperatures more than four times higher than those yielded by the old device, with ten times longer plasma confinement time. However, this is still not adequate for practical use in a fusion reactor, and mirror machines are more likely to be used to test materials under reactor-like conditions.

A major fusion test reactor is proposed for construction at Princeton. This machine would be the largest magnetic containment device of the Tokamak design (named after the original Russian design of the 1960's). It would incorporate the most recent ideas, including the injection of neutral ions to provide the conditions for fusion. Neutral ions enter plasma freely, are ionized, and thus add energy and particles to it.

In one typical laser alternative to such designs, several laser beams striking a target might yield nuclear fusion by creating an implosion. In another scheme, a laser-induced implosion might be combined with magnetic containment for controlled fusion.

The massive federal support of controlled-fusion research reflects both optimism that the technological difficulties can be overcome and increased concern over long-range sources of energy.

ERDA. The Atomic Energy Commission is now defunct, replaced in 1975 by the Nuclear Regulatory Commission (which now performs the AEC's regulatory and licensing functions) and the Energy Research and Development Administration (with broad energy research and development responsibility). Since the old AEC was the largest supporter of physics research and development in the United States, particularly of high energy physics, the physics community's hopes are now centered on ERDA.

GARY MITCHELL
North Carolina State University

POLAND

The domestic political situation in Poland continued relatively stable, with no major changes in the leadership of the ruling Communist Polish United Workers' party or in the government. Nevertheless, the regime sought to tighten control over its own organization and the country as a whole. A reorganization of the party apparatus was announced in May, transferring control of a number of major party media to the central party authorities in Warsaw. The reform also increased the number of regional secretaries and provincial administrators from 17 to 49, thus reducing the power base of each regional party leader.

Increased censorship of the press and dismissals of independent-minded editors, such as Gustaw Gottesman of the weekly *Literatura* and Krzysztof Toeplitz of the satirical magazine *Szpilki,* characterized the new policy. In April a senior party secretary declared that it was high time for Polish writers and intellectuals to start taking advice from the party instead of giving it. Freedom of debate in parliament, particularly by the five independent Roman Catholic deputies, was more circumscribed than in the past four years. A cultural chill, or "recompression," was felt throughout the country.

Economy. Polish industrial production continued to expand at a brisk pace. Estimates of an 11% annual increase in 1975 placed Poland among the industrial leaders of Europe and the world. Inflation was contained at a level of about 3 or 4%, and real incomes continued to rise, perhaps as much as 8% in the first half of 1975. However, shortages of various consumer goods, particularly meats and poultry, continued to be acute throughout the year. Housing, automobiles, and appliances also remained in short supply.

The Polish balance of trade grew increasingly adverse. The regime's efforts to sell more Polish goods lagged behind massive imports designed to shore up long-neglected domestic consumption. Despite appreciable improvements in living standards, there were continuing reports from the industrial and port cities of intermittent worker restlessness and discontent. Expansion of Polish exports, increased labor productivity, and improvements in the performance of agriculture appeared particularly crucial in heading off popular discontent.

Church-State Relations. Despite some unresolved differences, church-state relations were relatively amicable. The regime's spokesman on religious affairs, Kazimierz Kąkol, declared in midyear that as long as Polish citizens wanted the Roman Catholic Church to serve them, the regime would safeguard its existence. Kąkol denied any attempt by the regime to exclude Polish bishops from government negotiations with the Vatican. In practical terms, the regime agreed to reduce tax burdens on various church properties, granted more church building permits, and reduced bureaucratic red tape involving the church's educational activities.

A major source of conflict was the appointment of new bishops. The important Wroclaw See, left vacant by the death of Cardinal Kominek early in 1974, remained unfilled. Several nominees put forward by the church were blocked by the regime.

Foreign Affairs. In late July, U. S. President Gerald Ford visited Poland and was warmly welcomed by hundreds of thousands of people in Warsaw. The visit was largely symbolic for both sides, with emphasis on furthering détente and mutual cooperation.

Edward Gierek, the Polish party leader, and President Ford endorsed the principle of mutual, balanced-arms reduction in Europe, but no agreement was reached on how East-West differences might be resolved.

More substantive U. S.-Polish negotiations took place in Washington, D. C., in September, with prospects of large Polish grain purchases from the United States.

The most significant development of the year was a Polish-West German agreement in August, terminating two years of conflict between the countries on the issues of free emigration for Germans still resident in Poland and credits and reparations from West Germany demanded by Poland. A summit meeting in Helsinki between Gierek and West German Chancellor Helmut Schmidt produced a $500 million grant and $400 million in low-interest credit for Poland in exchange for the repatriation of some 125,000 Germans to be carried out over a period of 4 years. The agreement restored Polish-West German relations to a level of harmony not experienced since 1970.

Within the Communist world, Polish foreign policy continued to emphasize close cooperation with and support of the Soviet Union. In addition, there were especially close links with East Germany and Czechoslovakia.

ALEXANDER J. GROTH
University of California, Davis

POLAND · Information Highlights

Official Name: Polish People's Republic.
Location: Eastern Europe.
Area: 120,724 square miles (312,677 sq km).
Population (1975 est.): 33,800,000.
Chief Cities (1974 est.): Warsaw, the capital, 1,300,000; Łodz, 774,000; Cracow, 610,000.
Government: *President of Council of State,* Henryk Jablonski (1972). *Premier,* Piotr Jaroszewicz (1970). *First Secretary United Polish Workers' party,* Edward Gierek (took office 1970). *Legislature* (unicameral)—Sejm.
Monetary Unit: Zloty (3.20 zlotys equal U. S.$1, July 1974).
Gross National Product (1974 est.): $60,800,000,000.
Manufacturing (major products): Petroleum products, transport equipment, chemicals, machinery.
Major Agricultural Products: Rye, oats, potatoes, sugar beets, wheat, tobacco, livestock.
Foreign Trade (1974): *Exports,* $8,632,000,000; *imports,* $10,880,000,000.

POLAR RESEARCH

Polar research activity by the United States was highlighted by the dedication of a new research station at the South Pole on Jan. 9, 1975. Research in the Arctic concentrated on Alaska and Greenland.

Antarctic. The station, consisting of a large geodesic dome and other structures, replaces a complex first used in the 1957–58 International Geophysical Year. It is expected to last 15 to 20 years until it, like its predecessor, is drifted over and crushed by snow and ice.

Investigators from universities and government agencies are collecting data and performing experiments at the new station to assess Antarctica's effect on world weather and climate and to monitor background levels of pollution and other atmospheric constituents. Other work includes study of the effects of cold, isolation, and other stresses on persons at the station.

Seventeen researchers and support technicians wintered at the new facility in 1975. The station is isolated from February to October because the intense cold prevents airplane flights, which are the only available means of reaching the site.

The South Pole work is just one facet of research programs fielded by 10 nations in Antarctica. About 900 miles (1,440 km) from the Pole, University of Maine geologists obtained firm evidence in the 1974–75 austral summer that an extensive ice sheet filled much of the Ross Sea as recently as 5,300 years ago. The ice essentially was an expansion of West Antarctic ice. This finding has significance for studies of past world climates, because ice variations are both a cause and an indicator of climate variations.

Two research ships of the U. S. academic fleet joined an Argentine-operated research ship for two months in early 1975 to perform an integrated oceanographic study of waters in the Scotia Arc and the Drake Passage. Through this constricted, 600 mile-wide (960 km) passage between Antarctica and South America flows the Circumantarctic current, the world's largest, which influences currents and other oceanic conditions in wide areas of the world.

In all, some 3,000 researchers and support personnel deployed to Antarctica in the 1974–75 austral summer, and approximately 500 remained to continue their projects in the 1975 winter. Eighty-eight of the winterers were at the four year-round antarctic stations operated by the United States.

Representatives of the 12 Antarctic Treaty signatory nations met at Oslo, Norway, June 9–20, 1975, the eighth such meeting since the treaty's 1961 ratification. The thorny question of possible exploitation of antarctic minerals was discussed at length. The discussions resulted in a recommendation that the treaty nations' governments develop an approach toward exploitation that would be internationally acceptable. A

U. S. NAVY

The Amundsen–Scott South Pole Station, dedicated in 1975, has year-round living and research quarters.

special meeting will be held at Paris in 1976 to study the issue further.

Arctic. In March 1975, U. S. and Canadian researchers established a large array of experimental stations on the Arctic Ocean pack ice about 400 miles (640 km) north of Barrow, Alaska. In addition to a main station and three manned satellite stations, a series of automatic data-collection stations was emplaced for satellite interrogation. This Arctic Ice Dynamics Joint Experiment, or AIDJEX, begun in 1971, is aimed at understanding interactions among ocean, ice, and atmosphere so that ice-movement forecasts can be improved. At construction sites along the route of the trans-Alaska pipeline, researchers evaluated environmental changes and performed archaeological investigations.

Forty investigators from Denmark, Switzerland, and the United States worked in central Greenland in the 1975 summer to investigate characteristics of the ice sheet. Surface strain was measured, and snow-ice samples were taken with a wireline drill to depths of 100 meters (328 feet). Temperature profiles were made of the boreholes, and entrapped gases were extracted from the bottom of a 95-meter (312-foot) hole in order to date the ice and determine atmospheric conditions when the ice was deposited there thousands of years ago. Other glaciological work, including retrieval of a 60-meter (197-foot) core for dating annual layers of ice, was done on the Hans Tausen Ice Cap in northern Greenland.

GUY G. GUTHRIDGE AND JERRY R. STRINGER
Office of Polar Programs
National Science Foundation

POPULATION

During 1975 the world's population passed the 4 billion mark. If the current rate of increase continues, the world's population will double again by about the year 2010. Such rapid population growth has affected the quality of life everywhere, especially in the developing nations.

The problem has been most acute in the poorer nations where, according to the Agency for International Development (AID), food availability per person rose only 4% in the 20 years preceding 1975. In 1975 some 800 million people suffered from malnutrition, illiteracy remained at nearly 60%, and more than 85% of the people had no access to basic health and family planning services.

Family Planning. By 1975 almost all developing nations with populations of 10 million or more had policies supporting family planning either for health and welfare reasons, or specifically to reduce the birth rate. As of August 1975, the only exceptions were Burma, Ethiopia, Peru, and North Korea.

One indication of the growing commitment by governments to take action was the increase in contributions made by nations other than the United States to international family planning programs. Although the U. S. contribution to the UN Fund for Population Activities nearly doubled between 1970 and 1975, for example, its share declined to less than 30% compared with 55% in the late 1960's.

UNITED STATES POPULATION TRENDS

In July 1975, the total population of the United States was estimated to be 213.1 million. The crude birth rate, the number of births per 1,000 persons, was 15.0 for the 12-month period ending in July 1975. This was about 1% higher than the rate for the corresponding period ending in 1974. The increase in 1975 marked a reversal in the decline in national fertility, which brought the crude birth rate down from 17.7 for the 12 months ending in August 1971 to 14.8 for the corresponding period ending in 1974.

The upturn in 1975 may have been the beginning of a rise in the national birth rate. Researchers June Sklar, of the University of California, and Beth Berkov, of the California State Department of Health, have shown that the low level of legitimate fertility that persisted through the late 1960's and early 1970's was caused in large part by the postponement of childbearing by young women just coming into the childbearing age. During the latter part of the 1970's, numbers of women born during the peak baby boom years of the middle and late 1950's will be entering their 20's. If reproductive patterns continue at the previous rate, by 1980 the increased numbers of potential new mothers would raise the crude birth rate by about 9%.

If they do not postpone childbearing, fertility could rise even higher.

Coinciding with the trend toward postponement of the start of childbearing has been the increasing postponement of marriage itself. The proportion single among women aged 20 to 24, for example, increased from 28% to 40% between 1960 and 1974.

Paul C. Glick, of the U. S. Bureau of the Census, specified several factors responsible for the delay in marriage. There were nearly three times as many women enrolled in college in 1972 as in 1960. Young women today are victims of the "marriage squeeze"—the excess of young women born during the baby boom after World War II who reach their most marriageable age range two or three years before men born in the same year. Another factor has been the greater employment of women outside the home. Insofar as the revival of the women's movement has been a factor, Dr. Glick suggested that "the excess of marriageable women in the last few years may have contributed as much to the development of that movement, as the ideology of the movement has contributed to the increase in singleness."

Refugees. The resettlement of 131,000 Vietnamese refugees in 1975 illustrated an important aspect of U. S. immigration policy in recent years. Since 1956, refugees from Hungary, Cuba, and Vietnam have accounted for about 15% of all immigrants to the United States. Given the decline in national fertility since the early 1960's, the amount of total population growth due to immigration increased from just over 9% at that time to about 20% during the years 1970–75.

Illegal immigration into the United States is a growing problem, and, according to the Population Reference Bureau, the number of illegal immigrants each year far exceeds the number of immigrants officially admitted.

CANADIAN POPULATION TRENDS

During the 12-month period ending April 1, 1975, the population of Canada increased by 353,000 to reach a total of 22.7 million. The 1974 birth rate remained unchanged from 1973 at 15.5 per 1,000 population.

An unusually large influx of immigrants came to Canada in 1974. This was a contributing factor in the announcement in October 1974 of new rules designed to restrict the inflow to Canada of less-well-skilled immigrants. About three-fourths of the increase in Canadian immigration between 1973 and 1974 was accounted for by persons coming from four areas: the United Kingdom and Ireland, the West Indies, Portugal, and Asia. Immigration from the United Kingdom and Ireland, for example, increased by 41% from 28,102 in 1973 to 39,748 in 1974.

ROBERT E. KENNEDY, JR.
University of Minnesota

VITAL STATISTICS OF SELECTED COUNTRIES

	Estimated population mid-1975	Birthrate per 1000 population	Death rate per 1000 population	Rate (%) of population growth	Years to double population	Population % under 15 years	Population projection to 2000
World...............	3,967,000,000	31.5	12.8	1.9	36	36	6,253,000,000
North America							
Canada................	22,800,000	18.6	7.7	1.3	53	27	31,600,000
Cuba.................	9,500,000	29.1	6.6	2.0	35	38	15,300,000
Dominican Republic.....	5,100,000	45.8	11.0	3.3	21	48	11,800,000
El Salvador..	4,100,000	42.2	11.1	3.1	22	46	8,800,000
Guatemala............	6,100,000	42.8	13.7	2.9	24	44	12,400,000
Haiti................	4,600,000	35.8	16.5	1.4	50	40	7,000,000
Honduras.............	3,000,000	49.3	14.6	3.5	20	47	6,900,000
Mexico..............	59,200,000	42.0	8.6	3.2	22	46	132,200,000
Nicaragua............	2,300,000	48.3	13.9	3.3	21	48	5,200,000
Puerto Rico..........	2,900,000	22.6	6.8	1.1	63	34	3,700,000
United States.........	213,900,000	16.2	9.4	0.9	77	25	264,400,000
South America							
Argentina............	25,400,000	21.8	8.8	1.3	53	28	32,900,000
Bolivia..............	5,400,000	43.7	18.0	2.5	28	43	10,300,000
Brazil...............	109,700,000	37.1	8.8	2.8	25	42	212,500,000
Chile................	10,300,000	27.9	9.2	1.8	38	36	15,400,000
Colombia.............	25,900,000	40.6	8.8	3.2	22	46	51,500,000
Ecuador..............	7,100,000	41.8	9.5	3.2	22	46	14,800,000
Paraguay.............	2,600,000	39.8	8.9	2.8	25	45	5,300,000
Peru.................	15,300,000	41.0	11.9	2.9	24	44	30,600,000
Uruguay..............	3,100,000	20.4	9.3	1.0	69	28	3,900,000
Venezuela............	12,200,000	36.1	7.1	2.9	24	44	23,600,000
Europe							
Austria..............	7,500,000	14.7	12.2	0.2	347	24	8,100,000
Belgium..............	9,800,000	14.8	11.2	0.4	173	23	10,800,000
Bulgaria.............	8,800,000	16.2	9.2	0.7	99	22	10,000,000
Czechoslovakia........	14,800,000	17.0	11.2	0.6	116	23	16,800,000
Denmark..............	5,000,000	14.0	10.1	0.4	173	22	5,400,000
Finland..............	4,700,000	13.2	9.3	0.2	347	22	4,700,000
France...............	52,900,000	17.0	10.6	0.9	77	24	62,100,000
Germany, East........	17,200,000	13.9	12.4	0.2	347	22	18,200,000
Germany, West........	61,900,000	12.0	12.1	0.3	231	22	66,200,000
Greece...............	8,900,000	15.4	9.4	0.3	231	23	9,600,000
Hungary..............	10,500,000	15.3	11.5	0.4	173	20	11,100,000
Ireland..............	3,100,000	22.1	10.4	1.2	58	30	4,000,000
Italy................	55,000,000	16.0	9.8	0.5	139	24	60,900,000
Netherlands..........	13,600,000	16.8	8.7	0.8	87	26	16,000,000
Norway...............	4,000,000	16.7	10.1	0.7	99	24	4,500,000
Poland...............	33,800,000	16.8	8.6	0.8	87	24	39,800,000
Portugal.............	8,800,000	18.4	10.1	0.3	231	27	9,900,000
Rumania..............	21,200,000	19.3	10.3	0.9	77	25	25,800,000
Spain................	35,400,000	19.5	8.3	1.0	69	27	44,900,000
Sweden...............	8,300,000	14.2	10.5	0.6	116	21	9,400,000
Switzerland..........	6,500,000	14.7	10.0	0.8	87	23	7,400,000
United Kingdom........	56,400,000	16.1	11.7	0.3	231	24	62,800,000
USSR.................	255,000,000	17.8	7.9	1.0	69	36	315,000,000
Yugoslavia...........	21,300,000	18.2	9.2	0.9	77	26	25,700,000
Africa							
Algeria..............	16,800,000	48.7	15.4	3.2	22	48	36,700,000
Egypt................	37,500,000	37.8	14.0	2.4	29	41	64,600,000
Ethiopia.............	28,000,000	49.4	25.8	2.4	29	44	53,700,000
Kenya................	13,300,000	48.7	16.0	3.3	21	46	31,000,000
Morocco..............	17,500,000	46.2	15.7	2.9	24	47	35,900,000
Nigeria..............	62,900,000	49.3	22.7	2.7	26	45	134,900,000
South Africa.........	24,700,000	42.9	15.5	2.7	26	41	50,000,000
Sudan................	18,300,000	47.8	17.5	3.0	23	45	39,000,000
Tanzania.............	15,400,000	50.2	20.1	3.0	23	47	34,000,000
Zaïre................	24,500,000	45.2	20.5	2.5	28	44	49,400,000
Asia							
Afghanistan..........	19,300,000	49.2	23.8	2.5	28	44	36,700,000
Bangladesh...........	73,700,000	49.5	28.1	1.7	41	46	144,300,000
Burma................	31,200,000	39.5	15.8	2.4	29	41	54,900,000
China (Mainland)......	822,800,000	26.9	10.3	1.7	41	33	1,126,200,000
China (Taiwan)........	16,000,000	24.0	5.0	1.9	36	39	21,800,000
India................	613,200,000	39.9	15.7	2.4	29	42	1,059,400,000
Indonesia............	136,000,000	42.9	16.9	2.6	27	44	237,500,000
Iran.................	32,900,000	45.3	15.6	3.0	23	46	66,600,000
Japan................	111,100,000	19.2	6.6	1.3	53	24	132,900,000
Korea, North.........	15,900,000	35.7	9.4	2.6	27	42	27,500,000
Korea, South.........	33,900,000	28.7	8.8	2.0	35	37	52,000,000
Malaysia.............	12,100,000	38.7	9.9	2.9	24	44	22,100,000
Nepal................	12,600,000	42.9	20.3	2.2	32	42	23,200,000
Pakistan.............	70,600,000	47.4	16.5	3.1	22	46	146,900,000
Philippines..........	44,400,000	43.8	10.5	3.3	21	46	89,700,000
Sri Lanka............	14,000,000	28.6	6.4	2.2	32	39	21,300,000
Thailand.............	42,100,000	43.4	10.8	3.3	21	46	85,600,000
Turkey...............	39,900,000	39.4	12.5	2.5	28	42	72,600,000
Vietnam, North........	23,800,000	41.4	17.9	2.4	29	41	43,100,000
Vietnam, South........	19,700,000	41.7	23.6	1.8	38	41	32,700,000
Oceania							
Australia............	13,800,000	21.0	8.1	1.9	36	28	20,200,000
New Zealand..........	3,000,000	22.3	8.3	1.4	50	30	4,300,000

Figures are from the United Nations and the U.S. Bureau of the Census
as compiled by the Population Reference Bureau, Washington, D.C.

UPI

In August, amid rising political violence, demonstrators destroy a Communist party member's car near Oporto.

PORTUGAL

During 1975 Portugal had a series of unstable leftist governments and a sinking economy. Its international position steadily worsened, and the Azores Islands threatened secession.

Politics. Portugal held an election on April 25, the anniversary of Premier Marcello Caetano's overthrow, to choose members of a constituent assembly. The two moderate left-wing parties, Socialists and Popular Democrats, polled 38% and 24% of the vote respectively. The Communists received 12.7% and the right-wing Center Democrats 7.3%; the remaining 18% was divided among splinter groups. Alvaro Cunhal, the Communist leader and hard-line Stalinist, soon said that his party would not abide by the outcome of elections.

The Armed Forces Movement, which had overthrown the rightist dictatorship in 1974, made clear its determination to govern the country indefinitely. Mario Soares, leader of the Socialists, the largest Portuguese political party, joined a military-dominated coalition cabinet as minister without portfolio, only to find himself shunted aside as the Communist or Communist-oriented officers steered Portugal toward Marxism. Effective power was ostensibly wielded by a military Supreme Revolutionary Council numbering 29 officers of diverse leftist views. They frequently disagreed and issued self-contradictory bulletins. In order to halt growing chaos, in late July the Armed Forces Movement gave supreme power to a triumvirate composed of provisional President Francisco da Costa Gomes, a moderate; Premier Vasco Gonçalves, a radical; and Brig. Gen. Otelo de Carvalho, of uncertain leftist ideology.

The change brought no improvement, and meanwhile anti-Communist outbreaks began, centering around conservative Oporto in north Portugal. Communist headquarters were raided and burned, and the police, mostly intimidated holdovers from Caetano's regime, generally avoided confrontations with political demonstrators.

Premier Gonçalves, almost, if not quite, a Communist himself, found his authority dwindling and chaos spreading, and in late August President Costa Gomes removed him and appointed him chief of the armed forces instead. Moderate officers, notably former foreign minister Maj. Ernesto Melo Antunes, objected to Gonçalves' new assignment but temporarily acquiesced. The premiership meanwhile went to Vice Admiral José Pinheiro de Azevedo, naval chief of staff, who, after much negotiation, formed a cabinet according to party strength shown in the April election. The Socialists obtained four seats, the Popular Democrats two, and the Communists one. Antunes, firmly committed to Portuguese ties with Western Europe, returned as foreign minister.

Pinheiro pledged to "preserve the gains made by the revolution" and to continue building a socialist Portugal, but also promised "democratic pluralism," meaning representation in government by all political parties. Some Communist military units refused to accept the Pinheiro compromise, and in October they rebelled and seized installations in both Lisbon and Oporto. The troops were finally persuaded to call off the mutinies and submit to the authorities.

In mid-October, Pinheiro addressed a radio plea to Portuguese laborers, urging them to talk less and work more. He cited falling production, a growing budget deficit, and rising inflation. Saying that workers' excessive demands made survival of industry hard, Pinheiro added that

---

——— PORTUGAL · Information Highlights ———

Official Name: Portuguese Republic.
Location: Southwestern Europe.
Area: 35,553 square miles (92,082 sq km).
Population (1975 est.): 8,800,000.
Chief Cities (1970 census): Lisbon, the capital, 782,266; Oporto, 310,437.
Government: *Head of state,* Francisco da Costa Gomes, provisional president. *Head of government,* José Batista Pinheiro de Azevedo (took office August 1975). *Legislature* (unicameral)—National Assembly.
Monetary Unit: Escudo (24.41 escudos equal U.S.$1, May 1975).
Gross National Product (1974 est.): $12,200,000,000.
Manufacturing (major products): Wine, canned fish, processed foods, textiles, ships.
Major Agricultural Products: Grapes, tomatoes, potatoes, wheat, figs, olives, fish, forest products.
Foreign Trade (1974): *Exports,* $2,320,000,000; *imports,* $4,590,000,000.

firms nationalized under Communist pressure were running deficits, and that Portugal could not yet dispense with private enterprise.

Economy. The Portuguese economic outlook steadily darkened. Foreign earnings decreased as remittances home from Portuguese workers abroad declined and tourism fell by $100 million a month. Unemployment rose to 300,000, or 10% of the work force, and skilled technicians and professional men left when possible for Brazil, Spain, and North America. The gross national product, which rose by 8.1% in 1973, fell about 6% in 1975. Portugal's foreign currency reserves were nearly expended by year's end and though the government could then draw on its large gold stocks estimated to be as high as $5 billion, there would be nothing to fall back on once these were exhausted.

Workers' councils, which were allowed to share in the running of large and small businesses, severely hamstrung output by strikes and by causing managers either to be fired or to abandon their companies. Foreign holdings were thus far exempted, but the widespread nationalization of banks, industries, and insurance companies halted foreign investment, and some foreign-owned firms simply turned their premises over to the workers. The middle classes were pressed to the wall by a 30% inflation, but laborers escaped its worst effects because their legally-increased pay continued even from factories not operating. Money to provide such pay came chiefly from the busy government printing presses.

Small farmers in northern Portugal began to cut production. They were discouraged by the failure of Lisbon's leftist bureaucrats to understand agriculture; by rising costs of fertilizers, pesticides, and animal fodder; and by the paper work now required of farmers. *Latifúndios* (large estates) were being seized in the south, where crop yields were sure to decrease because of vandalism and the ignorance and inexperience of those taking over. A food shortage, which was already evident for some items, threatened to be severe in 1976.

All this nullified efforts to obtain needed capital abroad. In July, Portugal applied for a $1 billion loan from the European Economic Community (EEC), while Socialist leader Mario Soares urged the EEC to withhold financial aid unless democracy were guaranteed. The EEC postponed a decision, keeping the door open but declaring that it would not finance a Portuguese military dictatorship. The USSR seemed willing to pour in large sums to create a Communist Portugal, but they presumably would draw the line at bailing out a bankrupt economy and then propping it up indefinitely.

The Azores and Madeira. These island groups, governed as integral parts of Portugal, each cast less than a 2% Communist vote in April. The conservative islanders felt their interests neglected as they paid higher taxes and prices than mainland Portugal and their agricultural econ-

UPI

Portuguese Premier José Pinheiro de Azevedo acknowledges the cheers of supporters as he appeals for national unity.

omies suffered from government-enforced low prices. Central to Azorean dissatisfaction was the fear that Lisbon would not renew the lease on the U. S.-operated base at Lajes on Terceira, which gave high-wage employment to thousands of islanders.

Many Azoreans seriously considered establishing a breakaway nation called the Atlantic Republic of the Azores and Madeira, confident that the Madeirans would join them. The United States, still hoping to reach agreement with Portugal over Lajes, steered clear of any involvement or commitment.

Foreign Affairs. Portugal's standing in the North Atlantic Treaty Organization (NATO) became precarious as fear grew that its leftist military officials would hand over to the USSR any important secrets they learned. Premier Gonçalves visited NATO Brussels headquarters in June and denied that his country was slipping into Communist hands, but he failed to convince NATO leaders. Important military information was withheld from the Portuguese, though their country was not expelled from NATO for fear of driving it further to the left.

The former Portuguese colonies of Cape Verde, Angola, and Mozambique became independent in 1975. In the Pacific there was unrest in Portuguese Timor, with some groups committed to overthrowing Portuguese rule.

CHARLES E. NOWELL
University of Illinois

U. S. POSTAL SERVICE

POSTAL SERVICE

Benjamin F. Bailar became the new postmaster general of the United States in February 1975. Bailar, a former deputy postmaster general, had been an executive with American Can Company, as was his predecessor Elmer K. Klassen. He is the third head of the U. S. Postal Service since it began operations as an independent establishment in the executive branch of the government on July 1, 1971.

Also new in 1975 were a three-year contract with some 700,000 postal workers, an increase in the rates for first class mail and special services, and the elimination of domestic air mail as a separate category. In addition, the local postmark, eliminated in 1971, is being returned by popular demand but on a gradual basis.

Strike Averted. A strike was narrowly averted when a collective bargaining agreement with postal workers was reached on July 21. The agreement included an increase in basic wages of $1,500 over the three-year period, representing a cost of $1.8 billion to the postal service. In addition, postal workers will continue to receive semiannual cost-of-living increases and be protected from layoffs.

Economy Measures. Notwithstanding efforts to reduce both labor and fuel costs, the Postal Service continued to operate at a deficit and to depend on federal subsidies. Although less than 50% of the mail was processed by hand (as opposed to 90% in 1970), labor costs accounted for 85% of the Postal Service budget.

With over 218,897 vehicles, the Postal Service is one of the nation's largest consumers of gasoline. However, it has been successful in reducing the use of gasoline by 1% from 1973 to 1975, even though the number of postal vehicles increased by 18.5%. In response to the energy crisis, it has been experimenting with more economical, less polluting alternatives, including hydrogen gas and electricity. Los Angeles and Charleston, S. C., are among the eight cities where electric vehicles were used.

Elimination of Air Mail Classification. Effective in October 1975, first class mail service was upgraded to domestic air mail status, thereby eliminating the necessity for the air mail classification. Following this action, it was announced that the price for a first class stamp would increase from 10 cents to 13 cents on Dec. 28, 1975. The 10-cent rate had been in effect since March 1974.

Rate Dispute. The scheduled rate increases for first class mail and other categories ran into legal hurdles in mid-December. On December 16, Federal District Court Judge John J. Sirica issued an injunction against the increases, saying that the Postal Service could not legally "put into effect temporary increases in postal rates." On December 29 the U. S. Court of Appeals lifted the injunction, which had been appealed by the Postal Service. The service argued that it had complied with the law and that the increases were needed to prevent a rise in deficits. Supreme Court Chief Justice Warren Burger denied a last-minute appeal to block the increases, which went into effect on December 31.

Innovations. As one of several efforts to improve mail delivery, "Operation Mail Track" was introduced in 1975. This was an undercover test of the mail delivery system, which used cooperating businesses in 76 cities to record the time mail was received, the date of the postmark, and the condition of the mail. "Early Alert" is a different type of operation, designed to provide security for New York City's senior citizens. A red sticker placed inside the mailbox of an older person alerts the carrier to keep a special watch for personal problems. If mail is not collected by the addressee within a reasonable time, the carrier notifies the Office of Aging, which takes further steps to make certain that the person is not ill. This service represents a practice that postal carriers had been providing on an informal basis for many years.

A philatelic advertising campaign aimed at the 16 million stamp collectors in the United States successfully yielded revenues in excess of costs. In fiscal year 1975 the campaign yielded a return of approximately $52 million. However, other vital statistics were not so encouraging. In the fiscal year ending June 30, 1975, the Postal Service suffered a net loss of $988,758,000 from a total income of $11,585,447,000. The outstanding question that remains is whether the reorganized Postal Service can ever become a self-sustaining enterprise as well as an efficient public service.

DAVID R. BLOODSWORTH
University of Massachusetts

PRINCE EDWARD ISLAND

Measures were taken in 1975 to stimulate Prince Edward Island's primarily agrarian economy and to secure the province's electricity supply. In the political arena, stiff new regulations were proposed to deal with conflict-of-interest situations.

Economy. An announcement in Ottawa March 27 said potato farmers on Prince Edward Island would have most of their production losses covered by the federal government beginning April 1. The losses to potato farmers resulted from overproduction in a generally depressed market. The federal subsidy still left income from potato sales slightly below production costs.

The speech from the throne opening the 53d legislature April 3 talked about the need for an effective potato marketing system. "This province and its potato producers can no longer afford disorderly marketing mechanisms which . . . reduce our competitive position and disrupt our provincial economy." Further government assistance was pledged to the province's two other major industries, fishing and tourism.

Finance Minister T. Earle Hickey budgeted for a $2.9 million deficit on government operations for fiscal year 1975–76. Total expenditures were forecast at $185.2 million and revenues at $182.3 million.

Politics. On May 27 a special committee of the legislature said a declaration of financial interests and dealings should be required of all members of the legislature. Members and their families should report all gifts worth more than $500. A standing committee consisting of the premier, opposition leader, and a speaker should judge whether there had been conflict of interest. Conservative candidate David Lee defeated Liberal David McLane by 63 votes in Queen's 5th, a district that had been held by the ruling Liberals.

Electricity. The federal government agreed to pay half the cost of a $36 million underwater electrical cable across the 9-mile (14-km) Northumberland Strait between Prince Edward Island and New Brunswick. The province earmarked $10 million for the project.

JOHN BEST, *Chief, Canada World News*

PRINCE EDWARD ISLAND · Information Highlights

Area: 2,184 square miles (5,656 sq km).
Population (1975): 119,000.
Chief Cities (1971 census): Charlottetown, the capital, 19,133; Summerside, 9,439.
Government (1975): *Chief Officers*—lt. gov., Gordon L. Bennett; premier, Alexander B. Campbell (Liberal); min. of justice and prov. secy., Alexander Campbell; min. of educ., Bennett Campbell; chief justice, R. R. Bell. *Legislature*—Legislative Assembly, 32 members.
Education (1975–76): *Enrollment:* public elementary and secondary schools, 28,515 pupils; Indian (federal) schools, 75; colleges and universities, 1,430. *Public school expenditures,* $22,829,000.
Public Finance (fiscal year 1974–75 est.): *Revenues,* $159,000,000; *expenditures,* $150,000,000.
Personal Income (1972): $276,000,000; average annual income per person, $2,478.
(All monetary figures are in Canadian dollars.)

PRISONS

In January 1975, Gov. Edmund G. Brown, Jr., of California publicly noted that prisons do not rehabilitate, punish, or protect. Nevertheless, although the cost of keeping an individual imprisoned continued to rise during 1975, and the public showed no signs of supporting larger allocations for prison facilities, the inmate population across the country increased alarmingly, in some cases even spilling beyond prison walls. Sporadic violence erupted in prisons throughout the nation, and the Attica trials, receiving little publicity, stretched on throughout the year.

Overcrowding. Severely crowded conditions in the prisons of many states continued to build up over the year, in some cases reaching crisis proportions. The sharp rise in the prison population was most evident in Florida, although it was by no means limited to that state. Florida began the year with a state prison population of 11,420, but within 10 months it had risen to over 15,000, an increase of more than 30%. The condition existed in spite of the fact that large numbers of prisoners regarded by authorities as "least dangerous" were simply released to make room for the newer convicts. In many prisons a cell designed for four prisoners contained eight to ten. In other facilities, tents surrounded by makeshift fences were serving as prisons.

Longer Sentences and Higher Costs. Public pressures and new laws in several states resulted in generally longer sentences and fewer paroles being given out by judges. In Florida, a new law mandated a minimum of 25 years' imprisonment without parole for all capital crimes. One result was that as those convicted under the new laws reached prison, the length of the average sentence for all prisoners increased dramatically. One Florida prison, the Sumpter Correctional Institution, housed about 800 prisoners in January 1973. The number of inmates serving life sentences rose from 117 at that time to 177 in January 1975. During the same period, the average sentence for those not serving life terms rose from 12 to 17.4 years. The costs of maintaining a prisoner at Sumpter were about $5,000 a year in 1975. Adding 5.4 years of average prison time for 800 prisoners would represent a minimum additional outlay of $22 million. No legislature had begun to consider seriously that additional costs of this magnitude may result from imposition of longer sentences.

A nationwide study released in September reported that in a two-year period the yearly cost of keeping a juvenile delinquent in jail had risen about 40% to nearly $10,000. Operating expenses for the nation's juvenile prisons alone were estimated at $500 million in 1975.

A cell block at New York City's Rikers Island men's detention center was wrecked in prisoner takeover on November 23–24.

Under a New York state law passed in 1973, sellers of even small amounts of drugs receive mandatory life sentences. The resulting backlog in the courts was only beginning to be felt in 1975, but initial indications suggested that prison facilities would become increasingly strained. With more than 1,500 Class A felony arraignments remaining to be disposed, available prison facilities were already virtually filled to capacity. Most of those arraigned will go to trial under existing laws, and a large percentage of those convicted will receive substantial jail sentences.

Prison Violence. Increasing tensions and their release in violence were manifested in a number of the nation's prisons. In September a riot in the Tennessee State Penitentiary left 39 injured. The facility, which authorities say should only have 1,200 prisoners, contained 2,100. Meanwhile, construction on a half-completed, $4.5 million prison at Morristown, Tenn., was at least temporarily halted by angry local residents who dynamited the site and in other ways prevented construction workers from reaching the project.

In many prisons throughout the country, homosexual rape and the fear of it are major problems that are aggravated by prison tensions. As direct control of prisoners by authorities becomes more difficult, other forms of governance by the prisoners themselves emerge. In some cases this has led to fierce conflict among rival gangs seeking power or between the gangs and officials. In April, Warden Frank Finkbeiner of the Joliet Correctional Center in Illinois announced the transfer of three gang leaders to another state penitentiary because of the trouble they had been causing. In protest, 200 inmates took 12 hostages and seized control of a wing of the prison. Eight persons were injured, and one inmate was stabbed to death by other prisoners as he attempted to act as peacemaker during the uprising.

Attica. The Attica uprising of 1971, frequently described as the bloodiest episode in U.S. prison history, was covered by hundreds of reporters. Following the episode, in which 43 persons were killed, a grand jury eventually handed down 1,400 separate indictments naming 62 persons, all inmates or former inmates. Although 39 of the 43 men killed died from the gun fire of state forces retaking the prison, it was not until October 1975 that an indictment named a law enforcement officer.

In April, some three-and-a-half years after the event, the first trial was concluded. Two former inmates were found guilty for their role in the death of a prison guard. In June, a Buffalo jury found three others innocent of charges stemming from an alleged attack on three guards. As the year progressed, 8 of the 62 men named had pleaded guilty to reduced charges. Most other charges were dismissed for various legal reasons. By year's end, only 7 indictments involving 25 inmates and 1 indictment against the state trooper remained to go on trial.

DONALD GOODMAN
John Jay College of Criminal Justice,
City University of New York

In April, 1,000 marchers in Albany, N. Y., demanded amnesty for prisoners charged in 1971 Attica Prison riot.

Danish professor Aage Bohr, son of 1922 Nobel Prize winner Niels Bohr, won the 1975 prize in physics.

PRIZES AND AWARDS

The National Institute of Arts and Letters announced in August that it had taken over the sponsorship of two long-established literary awards—the National Book Awards and the National Medal for Literature. The programs were previously sponsored by the National Book Committee, which declared in 1975 that it was no longer able to obtain the financing necessary to continue those activities. A major change also occurred within the Rockefeller Foundation, which announced a new program for 1976. Under a new grant, the Rockefeller Public Service Awards will now honor individuals both in and out of government service. The program was previously limited to members of the federal career services.

School desegregation and the nursing home controversy figured importantly in several 1975 awards. The Boston *Globe* won a Pulitzer Prize for its handling of the Boston school desegregation crisis and John Hess of *The New York Times* received several awards for his coverage of the nursing home controversy in New York City.

A selected list of the most important and newsworthy prizes announced in 1975 follows.

NOBEL PRIZES

Nobel Prizes were awarded in 1975 in peace, economics, literature, physics, chemistry, or physiology or medicine.

The prizes (valued at about $143,000 each) were presented on December 10. The peace prize was presented in Oslo, Norway; the others in Stockholm by King Carl XVI Gustav of Sweden. Mrs. Andrei D. Sakharov accepted the 1975 Nobel Peace Prize for her husband, who was refused a visa from the USSR to attend the ceremonies.

Peace. The 1975 Nobel Peace Prize went to Andrei D. Sakharov of the Soviet Union. Sakharov, a physicist who played a key role in the development of the Soviet Union's hydrogen bomb, was refused a visa to attend the ceremonies in Stockholm because of "security reasons," according to authorities. Sakharov was honored for his dedication to the cause of human rights.

Economics. The 1975 Nobel Prize in economics was shared by Tjalling C. Koopmans of Yale University and Leonid V. Kantorovich of the Soviet Union. They were cited "for their contributions to the theory of optimum allocation of resources."

Literature. The 1975 Nobel Prize in literature went to Eugenio Montale, a 79-year-old Italian poet, for his interpretation of human values under "an outlook on life with no illusions." The Swedish Academy acclaimed him "one of the most important poets of the contemporary West."

Physics. The 1975 Nobel Prize in physics was shared by James Rainwater, 57, of Columbia University, and two Danes, Aage N. Bohr, 53, and Ben R. Mottelson, 49. In announcing the award, the Swedish Academy of Sciences cited the three scientists' contributions to the field of nuclear physics, particularly to "the development of the theory of the structure of the atomic nucleus."

Chemistry. The 1975 Nobel Prize in chemistry was shared by John W. Cornforth, 58, of the University of Sussex, England, and Yugoslav-born Vladimir Prelog, 69, a professor at the Federal Technical University at Zurich, Switzerland. Dr. Cornforth was honored for his study of enzymes, and Dr. Prelog was cited for developing systematic rules concerning atomic structure.

Physiology or Medicine. The 1975 Nobel Prize in physiology or medicine was shared by Dr. David Baltimore, 37, professor of microbiology at the Massachusetts Institute of Technology; Dr. Renatto Dulbecco, 61, of the Imperial Cancer Research Laboratory in London; and Dr. Howard Temin, 41, professor of oncology at the McArdle Memorial Laboratory of the University of Wisconsin. The three were cited for "discoveries concerning the interaction between tumor viruses and the genetic material of the cell."

PULITZER PRIZES

Winners of the Pulitzer Prizes were announced by the trustees of Columbia University on May 6, 1975.

Journalism. Investigative local reporting—Indianapolis *Star* for "disclosure of local police corruption and dilatory law enforcement." Local general reporting—Xenia (Ohio) *Daily Gazette* for coverage of the Xenia tornado. Editorial writing—John Daniel Maurice, Charleston (W. Va.) *Daily Mail,* for editorials on the textbook controversy in Kanawha county schools. International reporting—William Mullen and Ovie Carter, Chicago *Tribune,* for series on famine in Africa and India. National reporting—Donald Bartlett and James Steele, Philadelphia *Inquirer,* for series on the Internal Revenue Service exposing "unequal application of federal tax laws." Spot news photography—Gerald Gay, Seattle *Times,* for a photo of four firemen resting after an early morning home fire. Feature photography—Matthew Lewis, Washington *Post,* first color photos to win a Pulitzer (*Potomac Sunday News* supplement). Commentary—Mary McGrory, Washington *Star,* for discussion of public affairs. Criticism—Robert Ebert, film critic for the Chicago *Sun-Tmes.* Editorial cartooning—Garry Trudeau, for "Doonesbury." Public service—Boston *Globe,* for coverage of the Boston school desegregation crisis.

Letters. Poetry—Gary Snyder, for *Turtle Island.* Biography—Robert A. Caro, for *The Power Broker: Robert Moses and the Fall of New York.* History—Dumas Malone, for *Jefferson and his Times.* General nonfiction—Annie Dillard, for *Pilgrim at Tinker Creek.* Fiction—Michael Shaara, for *The Killer Angels.*

Music. Dominic Argento, for *From the Diary of Virginia Woolf.*

Drama. Edward Albee, for *Seascape.*

ARTS

American Institute of Architects awards: George Hoover of Muchow Associates for Park Central urban renewal project in Denver; Fred Foote of Mitchell/Giurgola for Columbus East High School in Columbus, Ind.; Ralph Rapson for Cedar Square West in Minneapolis; Michael Graves for Hanselmann

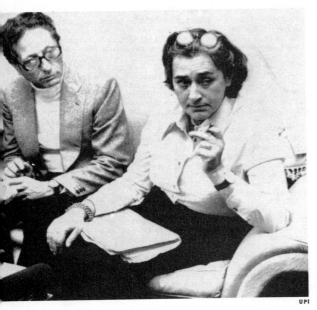

UPI

Mrs. Andrei Sakharov went to Oslo to accept her husband's Nobel Prize after he was refused a Soviet visa.

House in Fort Wayne, Ind.; I. M. Pei and Partners for Herbert F. Johnson Museum at Cornell University.

Art Dealers Association of America Award for "outstanding achievements in art history" ($3,000)—Jakob Rosenberg, Harvard University.

Dance Magazine Awards—Alvin Ailey, Arthur Mitchell, Cynthia Gregory.

National Academy of Recording Arts and Sciences, Grammy Awards for excellence in phonograph records: record of the year—*I Honestly Love You,* sung by Olivia Newton-John; song of the year—*The Way We Were,* Marvin Hamlisch and Marilyn and Alan Bergman, writers; album of the year—Stevie Wonder for *Fulfillingness' First Finale;* male vocal performance—Stevie Wonder for *Fulfillingness' First Finale;* female vocal performance—Olivia Newton-John for *I Honestly Love You;* group vocal performance—Paul McCartney and Wings for *Band on the Run;* new artist—Marvin Hamlisch for Best Jazz Performances; male country vocal—Ronnie Milsap for *Please Don't Tell Me How the Story Ends;* female country vocal—Ann Murray for *Love Song;* country music song—*A Very Special Long Love,* Norris Wilson and Billy Sherill, writers; male rhythm and blues vocal performance—Stevie Wonder for *Boogie on Reggae Woman;* female rhythm and blues vocal performance—Aretha Franklin for *Ain't Nothin' Like the Real Thing;* rhythm and blues song—*Livin' for the City* by Stevie Wonder; best instrumental composition—*Tubular Bells;* best Broadway score—*Raisin,* Judd Woldin and Robert Britton, writers; classical album of the year—*Symphonie Fantastique* by Berlioz (Solti); best classical vocal—*Leontyne Price Sings Richard Strauss;* best comedy recording—*That Nigger's Crazy* by Richard Pryor.

Don Kirshner's National Rock Music Awards; outstanding rock personality—Elton John; best male vocalist—Stevie Wonder; best female vocalist—Joni Mitchell; best album—*Blood on the Tracks* by Bob Dylan; best single—*You're No Good* by Linda Ronstadt; best group—Eagles; best new male vocalist—Dan Fogelberg; best new female vocalist—Phoebe Snow; best new group—Bad Company; best rhythm and blues single—*Lady Marmelade,* by LaBelle; best rhythm and blues album—*That's The Way of the World,* by Earth, Wind, and Fire; Rock Music Hall of Fame—Chuck Berry; best rock movie or theatrical production—*Tommy;* best song composer—D. Henley, G. Frey, J. D. Souther for *Best of Love;* best producer—George Martin; public service award—Joan Baez.

Arthur Rubenstein International Piano Competition award: first prize ($5,000)—Emmanuel Ax for works of Chopin, Schubert, and Liszt.

International League for the Rights of Man Human Rights Award: Mstislav Rostropovich and Galina Vishnevskaya.

National Institute of Arts and Letters Awards: award for distinguished service to the arts—George Balanchine; Arnold

W. Brunner Memorial Prize in architecture ($1,000)—Lewis Davis and Samuel Brody; Charles Ives Award ($10,000)—Charles Ives Society and Music Library, Yale University; Richard and Hinda Rosenthal Foundation Award ($2,000)—Richard Merkin and Ishmael Reed; Marjorie Peabody Waite Award ($1,500)—Charles Newman.

JOURNALISM

Maria Moors Cabot Gold Medals for "distinguished journalistic contributions to the advancement of inter-American understanding" ($1,000)—Sam Summerlin, Associated Press; Enrique Gobson, *Caretas* (Peru); special citations—David Kraislburd, *El Dia* (La Plata, Argentina); Walter Everett, American Press Institute, Norman Ingrey, Buenos Aires *Herald,* and the Associated Press.

Long Island University, George Polk Memorial Awards: foreign reporting—Donald Kirk, Chicago *Tribune;* national reporting—Seymour Hersh, New York *Times;* metropolitan reporting—Richard Severo, New York *Times;* community service—William Anderson, Harley Bierce, and Richard Cady, Indianapolis *Star;* magazine reporting—Edward Brecher and Robert Harris, *Consumer Reports;* television documentary—NBC News; news photography—Werner Braum, Gorman Press Agency; book—Mary Adelaide Mendelson for *Tender Loving Greed;* special award—Sydney Schanberg, New York *Times.*

Newspaper Guild of New York Page One Awards: John Hess, New York *Times,* for coverage of nursing-home controversy.

Press Award of Merit of the Women's Press Club: John Hess, New York *Times.*

Press Award of Merit of the Golden Ring Council: John Hess, New York *Times.*

Society of Professional Journalists' Award: Chicago *Defender.*

Sidney Hillman Foundation Award: Seymour Hersh, New York *Times.*

Alfred I. DuPont-Columbia University Awards: Fred Fredd and NBC News, A. V. West and ABC News, Don Hewitt and CBS News, National Public Affairs Center for Television, KFWB (Los Angeles), KNXT-TV (Los Angeles), WKY-TV (Oklahoma City), TVTV and WNET/13 (New York), WBVI-TV (New York).

Lincoln University Unity Awards in Media for programming: Chicago *Daily News,* Chicago *Sun-Times,* Philadelphia *Evening Bulletin,* Kansas City *Star;* economic reporting—*Time* magazine.

Sevellon Brown Memorial Award: Boston *Globe.*

Mike Berger Award: Diedre Carmody, New York *Times,* and Peter Coutros, New York *Daily News.*

Nieman Fellowships: Peter Behr, Gannett; Dale Burke, *The Missoulian;* Eugene Carlson, UPI; Cornelia Carrier, *Times-Picayune,* New Orleans; Foster Davis, CBS News (Los Angeles); Robert Gilette, *Science* magazine; Jim Henderson, Tulsa *Daily World;* Ronald Javers, Philadelphia *Daily News;* Arnold Markowitz, Miami *Herald;* David McNeely, Dallas *Morning News;* James Rubin, AP; Margaret Scarf, freelance; Lester Sloane, *Newsweek;* Raymond White, WTOP-TV (Washington).

Deadline Club Awards: public service reporting on TV—John Stossel, WCBS-TV; James Wright Brown Award—James Tuite, New York *Times;* public service reporting on radio—John and Christine Lyons, WNEW; financial news writing—John Parker, *Business Week;* news photography—Dennis Cook, UPI; science writing—Edward Edelson, New York *Daily News.*

Newswomen's Club Front Page Awards: Deidre Carmody, New York *Times;* Jane Brody, New York *Times;* Rita Delfiner, New York *Post;* Joyce Purnick, New York *Post;* Aloa Alvarez, New York *Post;* Annie Dillard, *Harper's;* Meg Greenfield, *Newsweek;* Naomi Lasdon, *Newsday;* Barbara Walters, NBC-TV; Joan Konner, NBC News; Irene Cornell, WCBS Radio.

Overseas Press Club Awards: OPC President's Award—Lowell Thomas; best daily newspaper or wire service from abroad—Robert Kaiser, Washington *Post;* best daily newspaper or wire service interpretation of foreign affairs—Donald Bartlett and James Steele, Philadelphia *Inquirer;* best daily newspaper or wire service photographic reporting from abroad—Ovie Carter, Chicago *Tribune;* best photographic reporting from abroad in a book or magazine—Eddie Adams, *Time;* best radio spot news reporting from abroad—ABC Radio news team; best radio interpretation of foreign affairs—John Chancellor, NBC; best radio documentary on foreign affairs—Ted Koppel, ABC; best TV spot news reporting from abroad—Lou Cioffi, ABC; best TV interpretation of foreign affairs—John Palmer, Phil Brady, Liz Trotta, Tom Streithorst, NBC; best TV documentary on foreign affairs—Bill McLaughlin, CBS; best magazine reporting from abroad—Frances Fitzgerald, *Harper's;* best magazine interpretation of foreign affairs—Robert Shaplen, The *New Yorker;* best book on foreign affairs—Cornelius Ryan for *A Bridge Too Far;* best

cartoon on foreign affairs—Tony Auth, Philadelphia *Inquirer;* best business news reporting from abroad—Philip Whitcomb, *Christian Science Monitor;* best article or report on Latin America in any medium—William Waters, Arizona *Daily Star;* best article or report on Asia in any medium—H. Edward Kim, *National Geographic;* Madeline Dana Ross Award—K. Kenneth Paik, Kansas City *Times;* Harry Jones, Jr., Kansas City *Star;* Robert Capa Gold Medal—W. Eugene Smith, *Camera 35.*

LITERATURE

Academy of American Poets awards: Fellowship Award ($10,000)—Robert Hayden, University of Michigan; Copernicus Award—Kenneth Rexroth; Edgar Allen Poe Award—Charles Simic; Lamont Poetry Prize—Lisel Mueller for *The Private Life;* Walt Whitman Award—Reg Saner for *Climbing into the Roots.*

American Library Association (ALA) Awards: Newbery Medal—Virginia Hamilton for *M. C. Higgins the Great;* Caldecott Medal—Gerald McDermott, illustrator, for *Arrow to the Sun;* Clarence Day Award—Margaret Craig McNamara for *Reading is FUNdamental;* Grolier Award—Jane B. Wilson; Margaret Mann Citation—Margaret Ayrault, University of Hawaii; J. W. Lippincott Award—Leon Carnovsky, University of Chicago.

Bancroft Prizes of Columbia University for distinguished writing in U. S. history and international relations ($4,000 each): Stanley Engerman and Robert Fogel for *Time on the Cross;* Eugene Genovese for *Roll, Jordan, Roll;* Alexander George and Richard Smoke for *Deterrence in American Foreign Policy: Theory and Practice.*

Bollingen Prize: A. R. Ammons for *Sphere.*

Governor General's Awards (Canadian): Charles Ritchie, Ralph Gustafson, Margaret Laurence, Victor-Levy Beaulieu, Nicole Brossard, Louise Dechêne.

National Book Awards ($1,000 each): fiction—Robert Stone for *Dog Soldiers* and Thomas Williams for *The Hair of Harold Roux;* arts and letters—Roger Shattuck for *Marcel Proust* and Thomas Lewis for *The Lives of a Cell;* philosophy and religion—Robert Nozick for *Anarchy, State and Utopia;* biography—Richard B. Sewall for *The Life of Emily Dickinson;* poetry—Marilyn Hacker for *Presentation Piece;* contemporary affairs—Theodore Rosengarten for *All God's Dangers: The Life of Nate Shaw;* sciences—Silvano Arieti for *Interpretation of Schizophrenia;* history—Bernard Bailyn for *The Ordeal of Thomas Hutchinson;* translation—Anthony Kerrigan for *The Agony of Christianity and Essays of Faith* by Miguel Unomuno; children's—Virginia Hamilton for *M. C. Higgins the Great.*

National Institute of Arts and Letters awards in literature: Howells Medal—Thomas Pynchon for *Gravity's Rainbow;* Gold Medal for Belle Letters and Criticism—Kenneth Burke; merit for poetry—Galway Kinnell; E. M. Foster Award ($5,000)—Seamus Heaney; Arts and Letters awards ($3,000)—Albert Calvin, Harry Bertola, Barbara Falk, Claus Hole, William Talbot, William Burroughs, J. P. Donleavy, John Gardner, William Gass, Terrence McNally, Tillie Olsen, John Pack, Mark Strand, Colin Turnbull, Helen Vendler, Marc Antonio Consoli, Charles Dodge, Daniel Perlongo, Christian Wolff.

PUBLIC SERVICE

American Institute of Public Service Awards for distinguished public service ($5,000 each): Katherine Graham (Washington *Post*), Rep. Peter Rodino, R. Emmett Tyrell, Jr., Rev. Leon Howard Sullivan.

Society for the Family of Man Award, sponsored by the Council of Churches of the City of New York—President Gerald R. Ford.

Southern Christian Leadership Conference (SCLC) Martin Luther King Award—Rep. Peter Rodino. Audubon Medal: Maurice Strong.

SCIENCE & TECHNOLOGY

Lewis S. Rosenstein Award: Dr. Arth Pardee, Princeton University; Dr. H. Umbarger, Purdue University.

Harvey Prize: Dr. Edward Teller, Dr. George Klein.

Louisa Gross Horowitz Prize in Medicine: Dr. Sune Bergstrom, Dr. Bengt Samuelsson.

National Medal of Science: Linus C. Pauling.

Albert Lasker Medical Research Awards: clinical research ($10,000)—Godfrey Houndsfield, British engineer, and William Oldendorf, neurologist, University of California; Roger Guillemin, Salk Institute and Andrew Schally, Veteran's Administration; basic research ($5,000)—Frank Dixon, Scripps Clinic, and Henry Kunkel, Rockefeller University; special award ($10,000)—Karl Beyer, Jr., James Sprague, John Baer, Frederick Novello, Merck, Sharp & Dohme Research Laboratories; public service ($10,000)—Yves Stein, Research to Prevent Blindness, Inc.

American Chemical Society Awards: Irving Langmuir Award in chemical analysis ($5,000)—Robert H. Cole; Nuclear Applications Award ($2,000)—John R. Huizenga.

American Physical Society awards: Oliver E. Buckley Solid State Physics Prize ($1,000)—George Feher; High Polymer Physics Prize ($1,000)—John P. Schiffer; Tom W. Bonner Prize in nuclear physics ($1,000)—Richard S. Stein.

National Aeronautics and Space Administration (NASA) Distinguished Service Awards: Robert Curtin, Donald Hearth, Chester M. Lee, Joseph Mahon, William Nordberg, David Williamson.

TELEVISION AND RADIO

Academy of Television Arts and Sciences ("Emmy") Awards: best variety special—*An Evening with John Denver* (ABC); best dramatic series—*Upstairs, Downstairs* (PBS); best variety series—*The Carol Burnett Show* (CBS); best comedy series—*The Mary Tyler Moore Show* (CBS); best actor in a special—Laurence Olivier in *Love Among the Ruins;* best actress in a special—Katherine Hepburn in *Love Among the Ruins;* best actor in a comedy—Tony Randall in *The Odd Couple;* best actress in a comedy—Valerie Harper in *Rhoda;* best actor in a drama—Robert Blake in *Baretta;* best actress in a drama—Jean Marsh in *Upstairs, Downstairs;* best supporting actress in a comedy—Cloris Leachman in *The Mary Tyler Moore Show;* best supporting actress in a drama—Zohra Lampert in *Kojak.*

THEATER AND MOTION PICTURES

Academy of Motion Pictures Arts and Sciences ("Oscar") Awards: best film—*The Godfather II;* best foreign language film—*Amarcord;* best actor—Art Carney in *Harry and Tonto;* best actress—Ellen Burstyn in *Alice Doesn't Live Here Anymore;* best supporting actor—Robert DeNiro in *Godfather II;* best supporting actress—Ingrid Bergman in *Murder on the Orient Express;* best director—Francis Ford Coppola for *Godfather II;* best screenplay based on material from another medium—Francis Ford Coppola for *Godfather II;* best original screenplay—Robert Towne for *Chinatown;* best original dramatic score—*Godfather II;* best song—Al Kash and Joel Hirschorn for *We May Never Love Like This Again;* best art direction—*Godfather II;* best set direction—*Godfather II;* best costume design—*The Great Gatsby;* best cinematography—*The Towering Inferno;* best short subject (live)—*One-Eyed Men Are Kings;* best animated short subject—*Closed Mondays;* best documentary feature film—*Hearts and Minds;* best documentary short subject—*Don't;* best film editing—*The Towering Inferno;* best achievement in sound—Ronald Pierce and Melvin Metcalfe for *Earthquake;* Jean Hersholt Humanitarian Award—Arthur B. Krim; special citations—Howard Hawks and Jean Renoir; visual effects award—*Earthquake.*

American Theater Wing, Antoinette Perry ("Tony") Awards: best musical—*The Wiz;* best actor (musical)—John Cullum in *Shenandoah;* best actress (musical)—Angela Lansbury in *Gypsy;* best actor (drama)—John Kani and Winston Ntshona in *Sizwe Banzi is Dead* and *The Island;* best actress (drama)—Ellen Burstyn in *Same Time, Next Year;* best dramatic supporting actor—Frank Langella in *Seascape;* best dramatic supporting actress—Rita Moreno in *The Ritz;* best musical supporting actor—Ted Ross in *The Wiz;* best musical supporting actress—DeeDee Bridgewater in *The Wiz;* best director for drama—John Dexter for *Equus;* best director for a musical—Geoffrey Holder for *The Wiz;* best costume design—Geoffrey Holder for *The Wiz;* best set design—Carl Toms for *Sherlock Holmes;* lighting—Neil Peter Jampolis for *Sherlock Holmes;* best score—Charlie Small for *The Wiz;* best choreography—George Faison for *The Wiz;* best dramatic author—Peter Shaffer for *Equus;* best dramatic producer—Kermit Bloomgarden and Doris Cole Abrams for *Equus;* best musical producer—Ken Harper for *The Wiz;* best book of a musical—James Lee Barrett, Peter Udell, Philip Rose for *Shenandoah;* special award to Neil Simon for outstanding theatrical achievement.

Cannes International Film Festival Awards: grand prize—*A Chronicle of the Years of Heat* (Algerian); best actor—Vittorio Gassman in *A Woman's Perfume* (Italian); best actress—Valerie Perrine in *Lenny* (American).

New York Drama Critics' Circle Theater Awards: best drama—*Equus* by Peter Shaffer; American drama—*The Taking of Miss Janie* by Ed Bullins; musical—*A Chorus Line,* conceived by Michael Bennett.

New York Film Critics' Circle Awards: best actor—Jack Nicholson in *One Flew Over the Cuckoo's Nest;* best actress—Isabelle Adjani in *The Story of Adele H.;* best director—Robert Altman in *Nashville;* best film—*Nashville;* best screenplay—François Truffaut, Jean Gruault, and Suzanne Schiffman for *The Story of Adele H.;* best supporting actor—Alan Arkin in *Hearts of the West;* best supporting actress—Lily Tomlin in *Nashville.*

Pressman at Fredericksburg newspaper checks copy of the *Washington Post* printed at his plant. October strike damage forced the *Post* to use other presses.

PUBLISHING

In 1975 book, magazine, and newspaper publishers were beset by economic worries as costs of paper, printing, and mailing continued to rise sharply. To combat the "postal nightmare" *Time* and *Reader's Digest* both tested the feasibility of using newspaper carriers. A Washington newsletter, *Postal World,* was planned to assist mail users. The cost of newsprint showed a 44% increase in two years. In response, daily papers sold for 15 cents and up, while many magazines were $1 or more. Cost-cutting led some newspapers to cut their page width, some magazines to turn to lighter-weight paper. Throughout the industry, manpower-saving technology was adopted, sparking personnel layoffs and labor disputes.

The copyright situation remained confused after a 4–4 Supreme Court decision in the *Williams and Wilkins Co.* v. *United States* case. (See also Law—*Supreme Court.*) Publishers and authors remained alarmed over extensive photocopying of their products.

Books

Increased publishing costs as well as added expenses in all operations placed a tighter squeeze on libraries in 1975. The American Library Association called for higher funding, but President Gerald Ford threatened a cutback in Library Services and Construction Act money. Congress did override his veto of the Educational Appropriation Bill. Local efforts to hike tax levies faced an uncertain future.

Publishers Weekly reported 14,998 new books during first half of 1975, up 223 over 1974. Prices were up, with hardcover books averaging $15.89, up 16%, and paperbacks $5, up 19%, over 1974. Exports were up 25%.

The Association of American Publishers reported 1974 sales up 10.5% to $3,532,500,000. Increases were primarily in trade and textbook areas, with only slight hikes in Bibles and mass-market paperbacks. Larger publishers recorded pretax profits of 8%, while smaller publishers and university presses faced deficits. The *Wall Street Journal* in late 1975 predicted a more favorable outlook for textbook publishers, especially "the old-line, independent publisher." However, while dollar sales were up, actual copies sold were not. More books appeared, with fewer sales per book, thus increasing marketing costs. Publishers viewed 1975 as a year of "leveling off" in the industry. Members were urged to adopt the newest publishing technologies, to gain and to achieve a faster turnover in sales. Cutbacks in personnel did occur.

Notable Nonfiction. In the aftermath of the Watergate case there were more books with a political or governmental base. Theodore H. White's *Breach of Faith,* summarizing President Nixon's rise and fall, reached the top of the bestseller list. Others dealt with the Central Intelligence Agency, the Federal Bureau of Investigation, and the Kennedy family.

People were concerned with their minds, bodies, and pocketbooks. Debates over transcendental meditation continued, with Harold M. Bloomfield's *T.M.: Discovering Energy and Overcoming Stress* among the bestsellers. *Total Fitness in 30 Minutes a Week* by Laurence E. Morehouse and Leonard Gross attracted thousands of weight-conscious Americans. Sylvia Porter's *Money Book* reached the top of the list with its layman's interpretations of a complex topic.

Mystery fans turned to the *Bermuda Triangle* by Charles Berlitz with J. Manson Valentine and made it a bestseller. *Bermuda Triangle Mystery —Solved* later appeared. *Jaws,* a 1974 hardcover bestseller, sold millions in paperback in 1975. Television personality Edwin Newman became the English teacher for millions as his *Strictly Speaking* informed people about what was wrong with their grammar.

Other leaders in nonfiction included Brendan Gill's recollections, *Here at The New Yorker,* which appeared during the magazine's 50th anniversary. Washington newsman Benjamin Brad-

lee revealed his *Conversations with Kennedy*. Others high on the list included Jacob Bronowski's *The Ascent of Man*, and *Helter Skelter*, by Vincent Bugliosi, with Curt Gentry, a history of the Charles Manson family. The latter's sales increased after attempts on President Ford's life.

The "worrisome times" were credited with continued high sales of Bibles. More than 15 million were sold in 1975 with another 25 million distributed by Bible societies. After a decade in print, *Good News for Modern Man* approached the 50 million circulation figure. Singer Johnny Cash appeared before the Christian Booksellers Association convention in 1975 to promote his *Man in Black* book about his Christian experience.

Notable Fiction. Only a handful of books maintained high positions on the *Publishers Weekly* best-seller list. *Centennial* by James A. Michener led the fiction category for four months, and remained on the list most of the year. Joseph Heller's *Something Happened* and *The Seven-Per-Cent Solution* by John H. Watson, edited by Nicholas Meyer, were early leaders. Arthur Hailey's *Moneychangers* took over in April, with John D. MacDonald's *The Dreadful Lemon Sky* near the top. Judith Rossner's *Looking for Mister Goodbar* arrived in midyear, and in July, E. L. Doctorow's *Ragtime* began its long hold on top place.

On the lighter side, "Peanuts" reached its 25th anniversary as creator Charles M. Schulz put together *Peanuts Jubilee, My Life and Art*. More than 100 million copies of other Peanuts books had already been sold. Walt Disney's books found a steady market. C. G. Trudeau collected 500 of his adventures in cartoons for the *Doonesbury Chronicles*, promoted with tongue-in-cheek as "the perfect gift for President Ford."

Magazines

Magazines reported slight declines in circulation and advertising for the first half of 1975. The Magazine Publishers Association reported ad revenue down 2% to $643,423,754, while ad pages were down 9%.

Only slight changes occurred among the top 10 magazines in circulation. *TV Guide* remained first with 19,684,429, followed by *Reader's Digest* at 18,487,284. *National Geographic*, a heavy gainer, reached 8,990,341. Others included *Family Circle, Woman's Day, Better Homes and Gardens, McCall's, Ladies' Home Journal, Playboy*, and *Good Housekeeping*.

TV Guide also remained ahead in advertising income, with $61,612,175 for the first half of 1975, compared with $59,993,131 for *Time*. *Newsweek* was third with $41 million, followed by *Reader's Digest, Sports Illustrated, Business Week, Better Homes and Gardens*, and *Family Circle*. *Parade* and *Family Weekly*, magazine supplements included with newspapers, were among the top 10.

Business Week replaced the traditional leader, *The New Yorker*, in consumer ad pages. *The New York Times Magazine, TV Guide, Newsweek, Time, Sports Illustrated, Yachting, New York*, and *Popular Photography* followed.

Travel Agent continued to lead specialized business publications in ad pages, followed by *Oil & Gas Journal, Machine Design, Medical Economics, Engineering News-Record, Plant Engineering, Iron Age, Chemical Engineering, Design News*, and *Telephony*.

Hugh Hefner's *Playboy* empire ran into difficulties, with his outside enterprises losing money, and his magazine circulation down because of higher per-copy costs and increased competition. Rebates went to advertisers when *Playboy*'s circulation dropped below 6 million. *Playgirl* also lost circulation, from 1,350,000 to 1,100,000. Some newsstand distributors and advertisers were offended by the trend toward greater explicitness among adult magazines.

The Johnson Publishing Co. continued to dominate the black magazine field, with sales of $34 million in 1974, led by *Ebony*. *Essence*, begun in 1969 by four black men, survived some "incredibly tough years" to turn a profit in 1975, with circulation guarantee of 500,000 for 1976. Readership studies indicated blacks had turned more toward their own publications, deserting some traditional magazines. *Ebony* was read by 60% of black women and *Essence* by 27%, with only 10%–12% reading *McCall's, Ladies' Home Journal*, and *Good Housekeeping*. *Ebony* and *Jet* attracted more black men, while *Sports Illustrated* barely edged out *Black Sports*.

New Magazines. More new magazines appeared. The success of *People*, which reached a circulation of 1.6 million by the end of 1975, inspired the founding of *In the Know*, a pictorial and feature monthly.

World, a spin-off from the *National Geographic School Bulletin*, began with an 800,000 press run. Seeking to tap the youth market, *World* competed with *Highlights for Children* and *Ranger Rick's Nature Magazine*. Its parent, *National Geographic*, continued to expand.

High Times, an unusual publication that claimed a 300,000 circulation, discussed drugs and their effects, a roundup on drug busts, prices in the United States and around the world, and similar topics.

Francis Ford Coppola, a well-known film maker, entered the magazine business, taking over the *City of San Francisco* in mid-1975. Sales more than doubled, while its bold articles created "outraged talk" among city readers.

Other specialized publications continued to seek markets, such as *Condominium Living, Paddle World, American Film, Popular Gardening Indoors, Communications Retailing, Marquee*, and others. *Artemis*, a newsletter for enterprising women, also got underway.

Youth Beat, for the 12–17 age group, began in daily newspapers as a weekly insert late in

RANDOM HOUSE

E. L. Doctorow's *Ragtime* dominated the fiction best-seller list in 1975.

1975, with 41 markets signed for early 1976, and a circulation of 12.7 million. Raymond Mason, termed "a new and major force in the media field" by Gallagher Reports, and his Charter Publishing Co. were active. He purchased *Redbook* and the Dayton printing division of *McCall's* and took over Billie Jean King's young *WomenSports*. *True* was also sold, with the new owners planning to make it a "girlie-adventure" publication.

Ladies' Home Journal, American Home, McCall's, Good Housekeeping, and *Redbook* cut their unprofitable circulation to attract more advertisers. *Ladies' Home Journal* voiced hopes that by 1980 circulation would produce 80% of the magazine's revenues.

Newspapers

Readers tired of Watergate, Vietnam, Patty Hearst, and other long-running stories, so many newspapers shifted their emphasis to local coverage, with more articles on people and services.

Technological advances continued, with a computer-based system making it possible to provide instant changes in content. Reporters may soon have portable video display terminals (VDT) with which they can change copy. Papers such as the *Wall Street Journal* that print in numerous widely-separated plants will be able to utilize laser and other facsimile transmission systems.

Newspaper Statistics. *Editor & Publisher's* daily circulation figures for U. S. newspapers were down 2% for early 1975. In 1974, the 340 morning papers reported 26,144,966 copies sold; the 1,449 evening papers, 35,752,231. The total

of 61,897,197 was down 1,300,000 from 1973. There were 21 all-day papers. Sunday papers totaled 641, maintaining a steady circulation that reached 51,678,726.

U. S. readers paid $3.6 billion and Canadians $289 million to buy papers, providing approximately 30% of the dailies' revenue. Advertising revenues were up. Publishers continued to switch to offset with the laser facsimile system coming into wider use. The Los Angeles *Times*, for example, used the system to maintain contacts with its satellite plant 40 miles (64 km) away.

Strikes and Jobs. Strikes hit some newspapers, with the *Washington Post* heavily damaged by pressmen in October. The Newspaper Guild and the International Typographical Union, alarmed at economic dismissals and mandatory retirements, viewed a merger as their only choice.

Nevertheless, journalism schools reported increased enrollments, especially among the minorities. The "postgraduate blues" reflected the tight job market. Editors deplored "a spelling and grammar crisis," and a feeling of ignorance or hostility to the profit motive.

Women and minorities gained more equality. The Journalism Council reported more jobs for them in advertising, broadcasting, newspapers, and periodicals, but not in motion pictures. Another study indicated that "black newspaper readers voiced an increasing desire and need for their own community newspapers."

Editorial Debates. Freedom of the press debates continued. Media groups opposed the proposed Criminal Information Control and Protection of Privacy Act of 1975, charging it would "make the operation of the criminal justice systems virtually unaccountable to the public." The American Bar Association wanted to "bring about an accommodation between the courts and the news media on the issue of 'gag' rules."

Criticism of newspapers also continued. Former Sen. Sam Ervin noted that "most of the press is fair," although at times he feared a failure to tell both sides. Others were upset by the coverage given the Patricia Hearst case and assassination attempts on President Ford. Editors viewed it as the traditional "You're cursed if you do, and cursed if you don't" situation.

Miscellaneous. The Toledo *Times* died in its 126th year because of "insufficient reader and advertiser interest." *Newsday* celebrated its 35th birthday. The Cincinnati *Enquirer* was sold for $55 million to Combined Communications Corp., and the Gannett chain added two Ohio papers to bring its total dailies to 53. Meanwhile, the Washington *Star*, and its new publisher, Joe L. Allbritton, feuded with the Federal Communications Commission to retain control over broadcast facilities in the capital city. New York City still awaited the long-promised *Press*, and Spanish-speaking residents of Los Angeles had a new paper, the *Express*.

WILLIAM HOWARD TAFT
University of Missouri

In September, Hurricane Eloise caused the worst flooding in a decade in Puerto Rico. Thirty-four people died and property loss was estimated at over $100 million.

UPI

PUERTO RICO

Preoccupation with a worsening economic situation monopolized the island's attention during 1975. Even politics took a back seat while unemployment, inflation, industrial strife, and an alarming growth in indebtedness presented a bleak prospect for the future.

Economy. In August 1975, the official estimate of unemployment reached a high of 19.9% of the total labor force of 896,000 persons. The unofficial estimate of real unemployment, which includes all those of working age, is 40%. The largest decline in employment, 23%, occurred in the construction industry.

At the end of fiscal year 1975, the manufacturing sector registered a decline of 15%. The tourist industry also declined with the closing of several luxury hotels, reducing available facilities by about 600 hotel rooms.

The only sector of the economy that showed slight improvement was agriculture, which registered an increase of 14.7%. However, this improvement had little overall effect since the sector contributes only about 11% of the gross national product (GNP). Sugar prices held firm, and 1975 production rose to 300,000 tons of sugar from some 3.4 million tons of cane. Drought and heavy rains at harvest time prevented similar increases in coffee and tobacco production.

The gross national product rose from $6.8 billion to $7.4 billion in fiscal 1975, but once an adjustment was made for inflation this actually amounted to a decrease in the GNP of about 3.5%. The island's attempt to deal with this economic reversal was hampered greatly by its already overextended borrowing. Short-term indebtedness grew to over $1 billion, $400 million more than in 1974.

The only relief from this adverse economic situation came from U. S. federal government grants, particularly the food stamp program, which pumped about $40 million a month into the island economy and affected some 450,000 families. About 1.6 million people, over half the population, received support through this federal program. As a result, both food and department stores enjoyed increased economic activity during 1975.

Hurricane. In September 1975, Puerto Rico was brushed by tropical storm Eloise, which dumped torrential rains on the island, particularly on its southern and western coasts, causing the worst flooding the island had experienced in 10 years. Thirty-four lives were lost, and both public and private property damage was estimated at over $100 million. The federal government declared the island a disaster area, making it eligible to receive financial aid from the Federal Disaster Assistance Administration.

Politics. The government of Puerto Rico, in cooperation with all of the principal political parties on the island, carried out the first registration of voters in over 50 years. The registration process was patterned after a Canadian model and involved the registration of the potential voter in his home. The resulting voting lists produced the names of over 1.6 million persons eligible to vote in the 1976 elections.

Committee on Puerto Rico. The joint United States-Puerto Rico Ad Hoc Commission completed its work. The final report on the suggested changes in the relationship between Puerto Rico and the United States was turned over to President Ford and Gov. Rafael Hernández Colón.

THOMAS G. MATHEWS
University of Puerto Rico

------ **PUERTO RICO • Information Highlights** ------

Area: 3,435 square miles (8,897 sq km).
Population (1975 est.): 2,900,000. *Density:* 790 per sq mi.
Chief Cities (1970 census): San Juan, the capital, 452,-749; Bayamon, 147,552; Ponce, 128,233; Carolina, 94,271.
Government (1975): *Chief Officers*—governor, Rafael Hernández Colón (Popular Democratic party); secretary of state, Victor M. Pons, Jr.; attorney general, Francisco de Jésus Schuck. *Legislature*—Senate, 29 members; House of Representatives, 54 members.
Education (1973–74): *Enrollment*—public elementary schools, 432,277 pupils; public secondary schools, 280,183. (1974–75): nonpublic schools, 56,000; colleges and universities, 89,671 students. *Public school expenditures*, $353,734 ($536 per pupil).
Gross National Product (fiscal year 1975): $7,400,000,-000.
Labor Force (August 1975): 896,000; unemployed (est.), 19.9%.

The Canadian government's plans to place four of its unions under trusteeship provoked this closed-door meeting of the Quebec Federation of Labour in May. The session was called to decide how to combat the government's actions.

UPI

QUEBEC

In 1975 three issues galvanized the citizens of Quebec. These were the investigation into organized crime, the royal commission of inquiry into conditions in the construction industry, and the continuing battle over the Official Language Act (Bill 22).

Investigation into Organized Crime. The commission, instituted some years ago by the government of Quebec as part of a campaign to rid Quebec of organized crime, spent most of 1975 investigating criminal activity in the preparation and sale of processed meat. The commission revealed that large quantities of meat used in processed foods were contaminated and did not meet the standards set by law and regulation.

It was alleged that sick animals were sold to processing plants through the contacts of organized crime and the complicity of provincial health inspectors and plant officials. Further, the commission found the Quebec government guilty of negligence. The report stated that the government's indifference could be described as criminal in certain instances and that its delay in instituting powerful instruments of control constituted complicity.

Inquiry of the Construction Industry. A royal commission of inquiry had been appointed in May 1974 after rioting construction workers at the Baie James project caused millions of dollars of damage.

After months of investigation, the commission, led by Judge Robert Cliche, found that the management of the labor unions concerned was corrupt and that the workers were not receiving the services to which they were entitled. The commission also discovered massive corruption among the executives of the contracting companies involved, whose activities appeared to have been sanctioned by the highest authorities in the province. The government acted quickly to repair the situation. A new minister of labor was appointed, and new agencies of control and supervision were instituted.

Official Languages Act. The controversy which surrounded the passing of the Official Languages Act (Bill 22) in July 1974 continued during 1975. Doubting its constitutional validity, the Montreal Protestant school board in February petitioned the federal cabinet to void the legislation, or to refer the question of its validity to the Supreme Court of Canada. Prime Minister Pierre Trudeau and his cabinet refused to intervene. In September the school board of Lakeshore launched action in the Quebec superior court to challenge the act's constitutionality.

Greater controversy arose from the application of the act. Major concern focused on the section of the act that requires students without "sufficient" knowledge of English to attend French-speaking schools. Quebec's large immigrant population has seen, in this section of the act, a barrier to education in English for their children and a resultant loss of economic well-being.

Many parents whose native language is neither English nor French labored hard to prepare their children for English aptitude tests. They then discovered during the summer that although their children passed the tests they could not be admitted to English-speaking schools. Government officials had limited the number of places available in those schools. Protests, including street demonstrations, and radio and television campaigns, followed. The minister of education resigned because of his disagreement with the government's language policy.

LAURIER L. LaPIERRE
McGill University

——— **QUEBEC · Information Highlights** ———

Area: 594,860 square miles (1,540,687 sq km).
Population (1975 est.): 6,193,000.
Chief Cities (1974 est.): Quebec, the capital, 190,000; Montreal, 1,215,000; Laval, 230,000.
Government (1975): *Chief Officers*—lt. gov., Hughes Lapointe; premier, Robert Bourassa (Liberal); min. of justice, Jérôme Choquette (L); min. of educ., Francis Cloutier (L); chief justice, Lucien Tremblay. *Legislature*—Legislative Assembly, 110 members.
and secondary schools, 1,360,700 pupils; private
Education (1975–76): *Enrollment*—public elementary and secondary schools, 1,360,700 pupils; private schools, 82,120; Indian (federal) schools, 3,980; colleges and universities, 66,100 students. *Public school expenditures*, $1,522,226,000.
Public Finance (fiscal year 1974–75 est.): *Revenues,* $7,684,000,000; *expenditures,* $7,388,000,000.
Personal Income (1972): $20,350,000,000; average annual income per person, $3,003.
(All monetary figures are in Canadian dollars.)

RCA RECORDS

Antal Dorati completed his cycle of Haydn symphonies with the release of Volume Nine (*above*) in 1975. Pianist Vladimir Horowitz (*right*) smiled as he signed a new recording contract with RCA.

recordings

Record companies in 1975 felt the recession, ever so slightly. Classical sales and recordings increased, and popular artists were headed up by female vocalists. Jazz continued on the upswing, recruiting more and more young rock followers. The audio-equipment industry successfully responded to the recession with larger and more expensive equipment.

CLASSICAL RECORDS

The record companies learned in 1975 that records are not recession-proof after all. However, the classical release lists, more ambitious than ever, showed no signs of hard times.

In fact, there were more U. S. orchestras recording on classical discs than ever. With European musicians' fees rising rapidly, U. S. union scales no longer seemed so preposterous. Ironically, much of this activity was by European-based companies: Decca/London (recording in Chicago, Cleveland, Los Angeles, Washington); Deutsche Grammophon, or DG (Boston, Chicago); and for the first time Philips (Boston, San Francisco). Columbia and RCA continued to record in New York and Philadelphia, respectively. Vox recorded in Utah, St. Louis, Minnesota, and Baltimore. In fact, two American operas were recorded by European companies, Gershwin's *Porgy and Bess* (London) and Joplin's *Treemonisha* (DG).

The Ravel centennial produced a spate of releases, including orchestral works by Jean Martinon (Angel), Stanislaw Skrowaczewski (Vox), Pierre Boulez (Columbia), and Seiji Ozawa (DG), and piano works by Abbey Simon (Vox), Pascal Rogé (London), Philippe Entremont (Columbia), and Martha Argerich (DG). The aftermath of 1974's Schoenberg centennial brought two recordings each of the *Gurre-Lieder* (Pierre Boulez

for Columbia, János Ferencsik for EMI), *Moses und Aron* (Michael Gielen for Philips, Boulez for Columbia), and the piano works (Paul Jacobs for Nonesuch, Maurizio Pollini for DG). Columbia also taped the Juilliard Quartet in the five string quartets and *Transfigured Night*. Other 20th-century "old masters" received special attention, including the complete orchestral works of Debussy (Jean Martinon for Angel) and Kodály (Antal Dorati for London), and more Mahler.

Perhaps the most fashionable of "in" composers are Haydn and Verdi. Noteworthy on the Haydn front were the conclusion of Antal Dorati's 48-disc symphony cycle (London) and the start of his series of the operas with *La Fedeltà premiata* (Philips). On the Verdi front there were new versions of *Aida* and *A Masked Ball* conducted by the fast-rising Riccardo Muti from Angel and the stereo premiere of *Un Giorno di regno* and the first *I Masnadieri* from Philips. Other operas recorded for the first time

NOTABLE CLASSICAL RELEASES OF 1975

BEETHOVEN: *Symphony No. 5.* Vienna Philharmonic, Carlos Kleiber, conductor (DG)
BERLIOZ: *The Damnation of Faust.* Edith Mathis, Stuart Burrows, Donald McIntyre; Seiji Ozawa, conductor (DG)
DVOŘÁK: *String Quartet, Op. 106.* Prague Quartet (DG)
HAYDN: *String Quartets, Op. 74, No. 3, and Op. 76, No. 3.* Alban Berg Quartet (Telefunken)
MASSENET: *La Navarraise.* Lucia Popp, Alain Vanzo; Antonio de Almeida, conductor (Columbia)
MOZART: *The Abduction from the Seraglio; The Impresario.* Arleen Auger, Peter Schreier, Kurt Moll; Karl Böhm, conductor (DG)
SCHOENBERG: *Moses and Aron.* Louis Devos, Günter Reich; Michael Gielen, conductor (Philips)
SCHOENBERG: *Piano Works.* Paul Jacobs (Nonesuch)
SCHUBERT: *Piano Trios.* Henryk Szeryng, violin; Pierre Fournier, cello; Artur Rubinstein, piano (RCA)
VERDI: *I Masnadieri.* Montserrat Caballé, Carlo Bergonzi; Lamberto Gardelli, conductor (Philips)

Linda Ronstadt grew rapidly in popularity in 1975 and received enthusiastic reviews for two discs.

included Rossini's *Siege of Corinth* (Angel), Weber's *Euryanthe* (Angel), Massenet's *La Navarraise* (both Columbia and RCA), Korngold's *Die tote Stadt* (RCA), Vaughan Williams' *Sir John in Love* (Angel), and Dallapiccola's *Il Prigioniero* (London).

The musical press conference of 1975 featured pianist Vladimir Horowitz signing a new RCA contract, returning to the Red Seal fold after recording for Columbia since 1962. RCA also signed the 89-year-old Artur Rubinstein for another five years. Columbia succeeded Angel as the U. S. licensee for the Russian Melodiya catalog, and, in an unprecedented agreement, Melodiya began issuing Columbia records in the USSR. RCA made news when it issued six four-disc sets devoted to violinist Jascha Heifetz. The farewell of the year concerned Goddard Lieberson, longtime Columbia Records boss, who retired.

KENNETH FURIE
Music Editor, "High Fidelity"

POPULAR RECORDS

Talk of a "depression psychology" could be heard in some alcoves of the popular recording industry in 1975. There were indications that the record companies, while not appearing very worried about their own economics, were taking into account the audience's anxiety concerning finances. Some of the music recorded was patently escapist in nature compared to the "relevancy" politics played by popular music in past years. This, and the frenzied dancing that went with it, could be roughly parallel to the last-fling-in-Florida syndrome that temporarily pumped up tourism. Considerable diversity remained, however, and recordings did not surge headlong into deintellectualization, fast action, and nostalgia as movies and television did.

Many of the changes were subtle and, according to critics, not all bad. Lyrics were less dominating, and records were more carefully produced, with more attention paid to the blend of voices and instruments. Execution received the kind of recognition that conception had been given, and the singer seemed to be gaining on the song. For pop records it was a year of professionalism and refinement.

John Prine and Steve Goodman, known for their writing, recorded *Common Sense* and *Jessie's Jig & Other Favorites*, respectively, two of the year's better albums that put a premium on musicianship and production. Two male singers whose voices are mightier than their pens, Waylon Jennings and Jesse Colin Young, turned out exceptional albums in 1975, Jennings' *Dreaming My Dreams* and Young's *Songbird*.

Outstanding female voices made 1975's "International Women's Year" designation seem apt. There were such celebrated albums as Linda Ronstadt's *Heart Like a Wheel* and *Prisoner in Disguise*, Maria Muldaur's delicate *Waitress in a Donut Shop*, Janis Ian's *Between the Lines*, Emmylou Harris' *Pieces of the Sky*, and Joan Baez' *Diamonds and Rust*, besides her work with other singers in the first volume of Earl Scruggs' *Anniversary Special*.

Discotheques, all but dormant for a decade, made a noisy reprise in cities, creating an interesting, if regressive, demand for bass-boosted music, vaguely influenced by rock, soul, Latin, and jazz beats. Consumer Rapport, a group of studio musicians, recorded *Ease on Down the Road*, which was introduced at a New York discotheque and sold 100,000 copies in two weeks with no radio play. Soul singer, Barry White and Gloria Gaynor became discotheque stars with the Hustle (New York and Los Angeles versions) and the Bump becoming popular dances.

Hard rock grew stale, although Bruce Springsteen's *Born to Run* was received with great success. Critics praised Springsteen lavishly and compared him to Bob Dylan and Mick Jagger. The Rolling Stones' newest recording, *Metamorphosis*, also received widespread attention. The folk connection with rock remained healthy. Gordon Lightfoot's *Cold on the Shoulder* advanced his reputation, and Bob Dylan generated excitement with a new album, *Blood on the*

NOTABLE POPULAR RELEASES OF 1975

JOAN BAEZ: *Diamonds and Rust* (A&M)
BOB DYLAN: *Blood on the Tracks* (Columbia)
EMMYLOU HARRIS: *Pieces of the Sky* (Reprise)
JANIS IAN: *Between the Lines* (Columbia)
WAYLON JENNINGS: *Dreaming My Dreams* (RCA)
GORDON LIGHTFOOT: *Cold on the Shoulder* (Reprise)
MARIA MULDAUR: *Waitress in a Donut Shop* (Reprise)
THE ROLLING STONES: *Metamorphosis* (London)
LINDA RONSTADT: *Prisoner in Disguise* (Asylum), *Heart Like a Wheel* (Capitol)
BRUCE SPRINGSTEEN: *Born to Run* (Columbia)
JESSE COLIN YOUNG: *Songbird* (Warner Brothers)

Tracks, and an "old" one, Columbia's remastered release of his home-recorded effort with The Band in 1967, called *The Basement Tapes.*

NOEL COPPAGE
Contributing Editor, "Stereo Review"

JAZZ RECORDS

Jazz continued to show signs in 1975 of return from limbo in which it has wandered since the 1960's. One positive sign was the emergence of several top jazz-rock attractions luring young rock followers into a curiosity about jazz. The most successful of these groups, which blend jazz and rock harmoniously, were led by musicians who had previously played with Miles Davis. The most prominent were drummer Billy Cobham (*Shabazz,* Atlantic), pianist Chick Corea (*No Mystery,* Polydor), and pianist Herbie Hancock (*Treasure Chest,* Warner Bros.).

At the same time, Norman Granz, who had been one of the most prolific producers of jazz recordings when jazz was at a peak of popularity in the 1950's, returned with a new label, Pablo. He promptly released a remarkable 13-disc set of piano solos recorded by Art Tatum in the early 1950's. With new recordings by Duke Ellington, Count Basie, Dizzy Gillespie, and Ella Fitzgerald also on the label, it was evident that Granz was picking up where he had left off.

RCA launched a promising reissue series covering pre-World War II pop music, country music, and blues, as well as jazz. RCA's first releases included volume one in what will be a complete chronological set of all recordings made by Benny Goodman for RCA-Victor.

Another milestone in recording was a five-disc set of *The Complete Works for Piano of Scott Joplin* (RCA), played by Dick Hyman. Hyman also conducted the New York Jazz Repertory Company in his own successfully evocative arrangements of music associated with Louis Armstrong (*Satchmo Remembered,* Atlantic).

The memorable farewell jazz concert of the disbanded Modern Jazz Quartet, became an equally memorable record, *Last Concert* (Atlantic). Other notable jazz records of 1975 included Duke Ellington's *Eastbourne Performance* (RCA), Keith Jarret's *Facing You* (ECM-Polydor), Marian McPartland's *Solo Concert at Haverford* (Halcyon), Walter Norris' *Drifting* (Enja), Jess Stacy's *Stacy Still Swings* (Chiaroscuro), Joe Venuti's *Blue Four* (Chiaroscuro), and Lester Young's *Newly Discovered Performances, Vol. I* (ESP).

JOHN S. WILSON
"The New York Times" and
"High Fidelity" Magazine

AUDIO EQUIPMENT AND TECHNIQUES

As economic contractions persisted throughout 1975, the U. S. high-fidelity industry experienced a loss of consumer support for the medium priced equipment that had made up the bulk of its income in 1973 and 1974. Many buyers

The Rolling Stones made a triumphant U. S. tour and saw *Metamorphosis* rise on the popularity charts.

were clearly gravitating toward the lower price ranges in which complete systems cost $400 or less. Others joined a hard core of hobby enthusiasts that maintained, and even increased, the demand for products in the deluxe category, in which complete systems cost $1,000 and more.

In response, large, relatively expensive new speaker systems appeared on the market during the year, and tape equipment grew still more elaborate. Most significantly, Fisher, JVC, Pioneer, and Sansui introduced basic stereo power amplifiers with output capabilities well in excess of 100 watts per channel.

Four-Channel Stereo. In early autumn, quadraphonic sound seemed destined to have another disappointing year, with sales slow and industry promotion correspondingly inactive. However, the year brought forth the most sophisticated matrix decoders and CD-4 demodulators yet. Sansui introduced the QSD-1, a QS decoder and synthesizer with Vario-Matrix logic operating independently in three frequency bands. JVC's Model 1000 CD-4 demodulator approached the flexibility and performance of studio CD-4 equipment. A new SQ decoder shown in prototype form by Audionics marked the first move by an exclusively audiophile-oriented company into matrix technology.

HPF Speaker. In 1974, Pioneer announced the development of a high-polymer material that could be fabricated conveniently as a thin, sturdy film, exhibiting a piezoelectric effect. This presaged some promising developments in electro-acoustic transducers, and in 1975 the first speaker system employing high-polymer-film (HPF) tweeters appeared as the Pioneer Model HPM-200.

RALPH W. HODGES
Associate Technical Editor, "Stereo Review"

UPI

Portrait by Joseph Dawley of Mother Elizabeth Seton, the first U. S.-born citizen to be canonized. She was declared a saint on September 14.

RELIGION

During 1975, Mother Elizabeth Seton was canonized and became the first saint from the United States. Plans were announced to recognize Father John Veniaminoff (1822–79), a Siberian missionary priest, as a saint of the Orthodox Eastern church. Political unrest contributed to religious turmoil in Lebanon, Ethiopia, Turkey, Greece, and South Africa. The sixth annual Islamic Foreign Ministers Conference was held in July in Jidda, Saudi Arabia. These and other developments are covered under the following headings: (1) General Survey; (2) Protestantism; (3) Roman Catholicism; (4) Judaism; (5) Orthodox Eastern Church; (6) Islam; and (7) Far Eastern Religions in the United States.

General Survey

The year 1975 was one in which general interest in personal ecstasy and transcendentalism combined with a continued concern for cultural identity to form the dominant trends in religion.

African Religion. The revival of native religious traditions on the African continent gained momentum. Associated with the search for values to undergird nationalistic developments, tribal religions offered the opportunity for a sense of personal identity and participation. In Chad the revival of initiation rites was accompanied by reprisals against clergy and laity of the 5% Christian minority. President Mobuto's "authenticity" program in Zaire barred public observance of Christmas. The apartheid policy of the government of South Africa led to the seizure of the ecumenical and interracially-staffed Federal Theological Seminary in Alice. In East Africa, however, Roman Catholics reported growth.

Islam. Sufism, the Islamic mysticism leading to the goal of communion with the deity through contemplation and ecstasy, continued to be an important aspect of the Muslim world. In Libya, a stiffening of Islamic law sought to preserve Islamic tradition in the face of outside influences. Arab-world Muslims met with Third-World Christians in Cairo to present a united front against Zionism and Israel. In the United States, the Nation of Islam sect faced the death of their leader Elijah Muhammad and relaxed their race-hatred theme.

Judaism. Jewish theological seminaries in the United States began to meet the demand for rabbis, but the lack of interest in traditional religious professions continued to concern the Jewish community. Hasidic Judaism extended its influence beyond the literary world in an apparent missionary thrust. In opposition to the desired zero population growth of the rest of the world, some Orthodox and Conservative Jews supported larger families as a necessity for Jewish survival.

Christianity. An unofficial gathering of American theologians issued an appeal for theological affirmation and condemned 13 "heresies" that were the prime fare of avant garde secular theologians in the 1960's. Theological interest in dying and death became more sophisticated as theologians began to be critical of some of the very naturalistic ideology previously accepted.

According to a variety of polls and surveys, there was a decline in membership in U. S. religious bodies, most of which represented an erosion within mainline churches. Evangelical and fundamentalist groups continued to grow. According to the Gallup Poll, the church, the public schools, and the Supreme Court (in that order) are the institutions in which people express the greatest confidence.

The charismatic movement began to level off in intensity, to achieve greater acceptance, and to face problems of internal regulation. Evan-

gelicals moved closer to worldwide identity and strength with the selection of a Nairobi Baptist as executive secretary. Billy Graham retained symbolic power as honorary chairman of what is frequently called the Lausanne movement.

RICHARD E. WENTZ, *Arizona State University*

Protestantism

During 1975, Protestants instituted massive programs to help resettle some 130,000 South Vietnamese refugees in the United States. The churches also undertook massive campaigns to battle world hunger.

For the first time, the total membership of religious bodies in the United States showed a slight loss, according to the *Yearbook of American and Canadian Churches 1975,* with a large majority of Protestant denominations losing members.

The Southern Baptist Convention, largest U. S. Protestant church, was the sole exception, showing a gain of almost 2% to reach a total of 12,517,648. The United Methodist Church dropped below the 10-million membership mark. Fastest growing church bodies included conservatively-oriented, smaller denominations, such as the Church of the Nazarene and Seventh Day Adventists.

Protestant leaders were also concerned about the decline of Sunday school. Since 1959, United Methodist School attendance declined 22.7%, with 77% of all schools in the church having less than 100 active students. However, monetary contributions to the church increased as membership dipped. Forty Protestant denominations received $4,840,314,858, an increase of 7.7% over 1974. Both the National and World Council of Churches suffered from decreased funding from their constituent bodies, thus necessitating reductions in programming and staffs.

Controversies. Two major items held the attention of Protestantism during the year: controversy and a trend toward theological conservatism. The Lutheran Church-Missouri Synod, second largest U. S. Lutheran body, continued to be torn apart by a bitter struggle that began in 1968 with the election of Jacob A. O. Preus as president. At its 1975 convention, the synod voted to oust any professor, minister, or congregation not subscribing to a confession of faith written by its president. At least eight district presidents (bishops) defied the synod and threatened to withdraw. At year's end the controversy still continued.

An equally bitter controversy racked the Episcopal Church. Eleven women deacons were ordained into the priesthood in 1974 in a Philadelphia ceremony later declared invalid by the House of Bishops. The four bishops who presided at the ordination were censured in 1975. There were calls for a split in the church, but the final decision on the ordination of women priests will not be made until the church's General Convention in 1976. The church is also

UPI

Services held by women ordained as priests in the Episcopal Church stirred controversy in 1975.

heatedly debating a drastic revision of the *1928 Book of Common Prayer.*

Conservatism. The trend toward a more conservative theology in Protestantism and Roman Catholicism received national attention when 18 Protestant, Roman Catholic, and Orthodox Eastern theologians met at Connecticut's Hartford Seminary and issued an ecumenical "Appeal for Theological Affirmation," which identified and rejected 13 "pervasive" themes in modern Christianity. The document affirmed traditional Christian beliefs and attempted to refocus modern theology on Christian affirmations. The central issue of the conference was to reaffirm the idea of God as an all-powerful creator who exists beyond the world.

The ecumenical movement suffered several setbacks. In Canada, the Anglican bishops rejected the *Plan for Union* for their church with the United Church of Canada and the Christian Church (Disciples of Christ). The merger had first been proposed in 1944. A joint committee will prepare a revised *Plan for Union* for consideration in 1979.

ALFRED P. KLAUSLER, *The Christian Century*

Roman Catholicism

Mother Elizabeth Ann Bayley Seton, the first U. S.-born citizen to be canonized, was declared a saint in St. Peter's Square in the Vatican in September before a crowd of 100,000 people. The special mass marked the culmination of nearly 100 years of effort by many American Roman Catholics to have Mother Seton declared a saint. The mass marked an eventful year in Roman Catholic life.

World Message. Pope Paul VI set the tone for 1975 as a Holy Year dedicated to "renewal and

reconciliation." At a Mass on Christmas 1974, he asked the world to "come united in heart and soul to celebrate together the jubilee." He also celebrated midnight Mass on Christmas 1975, asking the wide circles of non-Christian mankind to join with all Christendom in a spirit of love and forgiveness.

The themes of love and forgiveness, concern, and reconciliation and renewal were keystones of other papal addresses in Rome in 1975. They were echoed in all parts of the world by other bishops, priests, sisters, brothers, and laity as they looked at a world still in turmoil 10 years after the close of the Second Vatican Council. Natural disaster and civil strife throughout the world were a preoccupation of Pope Paul during the year. He repeatedly called for aid for the world's needy and pleaded for an end to war.

Ecumenical Renewal. A major preoccupation of prelates, priests, and laity during 1975, however, was an assessment of the progress—or not —toward the internal renewal of the Roman Catholic Church. It had been promised by the Ecumenical Council that closed a decade earlier, on Dec. 8, 1965.

Stimulated by the observance of International Women's Year, which was applauded by most Church leaders, considerable discussion during 1975 centered on the role of women in the Church, particularly concerning the prohibition of women priests. Despite pronouncements by Pope Paul VI and Archbishop Joseph L. Bernardin of Cincinnati, president of the U. S. Conference of Bishops, reaffirming that prohibition, the chorus grew louder as the year continued for a change in that law.

Approaches toward Christian unity and reform of religious communities within the Church were dramatized by Catholic participation at the end of 1974 in the installation of an Anglican Archbishop of Canterbury, Dr. Frederick D. Coggan. There was also the publication by the Vatican of new guidelines for ecumenical activity, which stress that "local needs and problems" should determine ecumenical actions.

Priests' Council. Other concerns capturing the attention of Catholics during 1975 were on the agenda of a national meeting of the National Federation of Priests' Councils in the United States. It discussed (1) divorced and remarried Catholics, (2) distribution of the world's resources, (3) alienated youth, (4) liberal and conservative Catholics, and (5) resigned priests.

Nowhere, perhaps, was the promise of the Ecumenical Council or the hope of the Holy Year more pronounced than in the United States where the Church inaugurated a celebration of the nation's Bicentennial under the theme: "Liberty and Justice For All." The celebration began with six public hearings on the national level to discuss injustices in all areas of life: ecclesial, civil, social, economic, and familial. The hearings were to be complemented by discussions on the parish, archdiocesan, and regional levels. All were aimed at providing input for a national bicentennial convocation in Detroit in October 1976. A five-year "pastoral plan" of action was to be developed for the U. S. Church to fight injustice and to assure freedom for all.

The urgency of such an effort had been dramatized in February 1975 by 25 archbishops from 13 states in the Appalachian Region, which stretches from upstate New York to Alabama. In a pastoral letter, written in blank verse, they issued a call for action "which will right the wrongs that bring suffering to people." The "cries of powerlessness from the region called Appalachia," they wrote, are also echoed "across the land, across the earth, in the sufferings of too many peoples. Together these sufferings form a single cry."

Cardinal Mindszenty. Jozsef Cardinal Mindszenty, former primate of Hungary, died in May. (See also OBITUARIES.)

OWEN J. MURPHY, JR., *The Catholic Free Press*

Judaism

The traumatic impact of the Yom Kippur War of 1973 turned into a positive force in 1975. Its political reverberations made press headlines, and its religious impact upon world Judaism was manifested in several significant developments. In the United States a search for Jewish religious-cultural values and demonstrations of Jewish solidarity among youth reaffirmed a growing pride in Jewish identity.

Continued Arab hostility and terrorist acts against Israel, and the harassment of Jews in the Soviet Union contributed to this upsurge of Jewish awareness. It was reflected in a growing popularity of Judaic studies, religious discussion groups, and the establishment of kosher kitchens on college campuses, and in continued nationwide demonstrations by youth on behalf of Israel. Mobile vans or "Mitzvah Tanks" of Lubavitch Hasidim promoted ritual observance by accommodating men for prayer with phylacteries and distributing to women candlesticks for Sabbath lights.

The 30th anniversary of the end of the Holocaust—the mass persecution and destruction of European Jewry (1933–45)—observed by various programs on radio and television and by seminars at educational institutions enhanced a sense of common Jewish destiny and identification. The Jewish identity search was not reflected in synagogue affiliation. Rabbinical leaders expressed concern over the lowered Jewish birthrate threatening the survival of Judaism. Conservative rabbis resolved to promote bigger families. The Reform rabbinical conference authorized a study of the issue.

Israel. Demonstrations against yielding territorial parts of Biblical Israel to the Arabs drew increasing support from the populace. Such public appeal groups as Gush Emunim, composed mainly of younger members of the National Religious party, led the demonstrations.

In July, Greek Orthodox Archbishop Seraphim (*seated*) of Athens attended the annual council meeting of the archdiocese of Archbishop Iakovos of North and South America in Athens. Stability returned to church life in Greece in 1975.

UPI

Army chaplains reported a new eagerness among soldiers for a closer knowledge of Judaism and its practices. However, criticism was leveled in the Knesset (legislature) against the religious establishment for its failure to assume spiritual leadership. Simultaneously, the role of the religious courts was challenged by the introduction of a civil marriage bill.

Soviet Jewry. The Soviet government announced a raise in the emigration tax and stepped up its campaign of harassment and arrest of Jews wishing to emigrate to Israel. This action came despite the signing by President Ford of a U. S.-USSR trade bill that made easing of Soviet emigration restrictions a contingency.

LIVIA E. BITTON, *Herbert H. Lehman College, City University of New York*

Orthodox Eastern Church

The Orthodox Patriarchate of Constantinople continued to maintain its precarious existence in Istanbul in spite of hostilities between the Turks and the Greeks. On Cyprus, Archbishop Makarios III returned at the end of 1974 as president and ecclesiastical primate for the Greek parts of the island. Opposition to his return from many Cypriote bishops for his uncanonical political activity proved ineffectual.

In Greece, the return of democracy brought a certain stability to church life, with Archbishop Seraphim continuing as archbishop of Athens. Ieronymos, the former primate of the Church of Greece, was indicted for illegal actions, together with other bishops installed in office under the dictatorship. Weak attempts to legislate the separation of church and state in Greece failed. Orthodoxy remained the established religion of the nation with any proselytizing by other religious groups forbidden by law.

In the USSR, religious interest, particularly among the youth, continued to grow. However, the Soviet government failed to recognize any religious sect. Orthodox churchmen from the USSR were permitted to visit the United States in February as part of a delegation of church hierarchy invited by the National Council of Churches.

During his U. S. visit in 1975, Aleksandr Solzhenitsyn, the exiled Soviet writer, called on the Orthodox Church in the free world to support the believing members of the church in Russia and to foster Christian principles as the antidote to repressive totalitarianism.

Plans were announced to recognize John Veniaminoff (1822–79) as a saint of the church. Father Veniaminoff was a famous Siberian and Alaskan missionary priest who later became Metropolitan Innocent of Moscow. He is known for his translations of numerous biblical and ecclesiastical writings into many languages, including Aleut and Tlingit Indian.

Conferences of Orthodox theologians were held on an international scale to formulate church policy. Orthodox leaders in Britain and North America were unanimous in their objection to the ordination of women to the presbyterial and episcopal offices of the church. Strong warnings were issued that the decision to have women in the hierarchy of the Anglican and Episcopalian churches would gravely harm their relationship with the Orthodox.

THOMAS HOPKO
St. Vladimir's Orthodox Theological Seminary

Islam

Politics and religion were closely intertwined for Muslims in many parts of the world in 1975, amid calls for Islamic solidarity. The interrelationship of politics and religion sometimes proved an asset for Islam, but it sometimes caused the Muslim community great suffering.

The most serious problem Muslims faced was the fighting that erupted in Lebanon early in 1975. While ostensibly a political conflict between Palestinian refugees and Lebanese citizens protesting the virtual autonomy of Palestinian organizations in their country, the hostilities rapidly took on religious overtones. Nearly all the Palestinians involved were Muslims, while the Lebanese protestors belonged to paramilitary wings of Christian political parties. By the end of the year fighting had disrupted the country and claimed thousands of lives. The sectarian animosity threatened to destroy the nation's delicate political balance, which is predicated on religious groups sharing power. (See also LEBANON.)

In Ethiopia, where roughly half the population is Muslim and half Christian, Muslim festivals were celebrated as national holidays for the first time in many years. This was a result of the overthrow of Emperor Haile Selassie, whose regime had looked down on Islam. The new military government, however, in a bid for national unity, emphasized the need for religious freedom. Similarly, India's largest Muslim political party welcomed Prime Minister Indira Gandhi's restrictive legislation of the summer, claiming it would protect Muslim rights as a minority and prevent discrimination by the Hindu majority.

Islamic solidarity was the theme of the sixth annual Islamic Foreign Ministers Conference which met in Jidda, Saudi Arabia, in July. Representatives of 39 countries and the Palestine Liberation Organization discussed issues affecting Muslims throughout the world. With regard to the Middle East, the conference created a permanent commission of 13 members to conduct a worldwide campaign for Muslim rights in the holy city of Jerusalem. At the conference it was also learned that the Philippine government would grant greater autonomy to its Muslim minority, whose status had been a major concern of past conferences.

KENNETH J. PERKINS
University of South Carolina

Far Eastern Religions in the U. S.

Since the early 1970's, Asian religious traditions have begun to permeate, in a subtle manner, U. S. society at large as well as affecting Judaism and Christianity. These traditions include attitudes toward self-realization, disciplined life-style, and techniques of transformation. According to a Gallup Poll, however, the proportion of those people in the United States who describe themselves as Buddhist, Hindu, or Muslim is less than 1%.

One of the oldest Asian religions in the United States is the Jodo Shinshu sect of Japanese Buddhism. Emphasis is placed on salvation by faith in the wisdom and compassion of the Amida Buddha. The sect has become a denomination known as Buddhist Churches of America, with close to 150,000 members. Nichiren Shoshu, another Buddhist movement of Japanese parentage, experienced a 19% growth, claiming a membership of 220,591. An aggressively evangelistic society that seeks to subdue the world, the movement traces its origin to the 13th century.

The Divine Light Mission, Hindu in origin, was slightly demoralized when the mother of its youthful guru, Maharaj Ji, ousted him for "falling from the path." A spiritual technique, called the Knowledge, combined with a secret rite known as "blissing out," commanded the interest of youth.

Chanting is a phenomenon common to most of the Asian movements that have attracted Americans. Perhaps the best-known of chanters are the followers of the International Society for Krishna Consciousness (Hare Krishna). The group is dedicated to an ascetic life-style and a form of worship yoga related to Lord Krishna, a classic Hindu manifestation of God.

The Unification Church of Sun Myung Moon continued to make headlines. The church was frequently accused of brainwashing its youthful adherents with a curious blend of fundamentalist Christianity and Asian religiosity represented by its Korean leader.

The significance of Eastern religions is a mark of pluralism in the United States, a symptom of change in the country's cultural integrity, and a measure of the ineffectiveness of its traditional religions.

RICHARD E. WENTZ, *Arizona State University*

In September, some 30,000 adherents of the Buddhist Nicheren Shoshu movement crowded Honolulu's Waikiki Beach for a convention centered on a man-made island.

UPI

RHODE ISLAND

If Rhode Islanders thought they had seen the worst of their economic problems during 1974, they found out in 1975 they were wrong. Unemployment soared to over 16%, the highest of any state. The year began with predictions of a serious state budget crunch. To avert a tax increase or deficit, Gov. Philip W. Noel proposed 5% pay cuts for all state employees and other economies including holding the line on state appropriations for education. The General Assembly managed to avoid both the pay cut and an income tax increase by raising tobacco and gasoline taxes. By fall, however, shortfalls in tax collections threatened to upset the budget's precarious balance.

The Economy. Some progress was made in replacing the jobs lost through the closings of naval bases. One company began building submarine components at Quonset Point using labor that had completed a state-sponsored job training program. Plans were made to locate yacht building and marina facilities at Newport, and state officials began promoting Narragansett Bay as a base for possible impending offshore oil exploration. Tourism, particularly in Newport, showed an encouraging increase. Discussion of possibly locating a nuclear generating plant on Navy land at Charlestown continued. Labor unrest mounted as the year wore on. In October, Brown and Sharpe, a machine tool manufacturer and one of the state's largest employers, went on strike, joining other struck plants.

Politics. The political pot continued to bubble long after the 1974 election. Vincent Cianci, the new Republican mayor of Providence, began a very active administration and a long-running battle with the deeply split Democratic contingent on the city council. Appointments, the budget, and the size of a tax increase figured in the struggle.

In the early fall, the state's senior U.S. senator, John O. Pastore, announced that he would not seek reelection in 1976. He was first elected to the Senate in 1950. Speculation began immediately, not only regarding his possible

UPI

Gov. Philip Noel of Rhode Island faced a 16% unemployment rate and other economic problems in 1975.

successor, but about all the other changes in the political lineup that would result. Governor Noel seemed likely to seek the Senate seat, Lt. Gov. J. Joseph Garrahy indicated interest in the governorship if Noel should move to the Senate, and a growing number of other politicians began maneuvering to fill other prospective vacancies on the Democratic party slate. Both former Gov. John Chafee and Mayor Cianci were mentioned as Republican senatorial prospects. Whatever happened in the 1976 elections, the "political map" of the state would be profoundly altered.

Education. The depressed economic situation heightened education's difficulties. Communities tried to hold down school costs, and the state attempted to do the same for public higher education. An unprecedented wave of teacher strikes resulted. Teachers were on picket lines in three of the larger cities, Cranston, Pawtucket, and Woonsocket, and in several towns. The faculty of the state's junior college also struck, and similar action was narrowly averted at the University of Rhode Island and Rhode Island College. Eventually all strikes were settled, but not before judges had sent many teacher union leaders to jail. The new state Commissioner of Education, Thomas C. Schmidt, had a very trying first year in office.

ELMER E. CORNWELL, JR.
Brown University

------ **RHODE ISLAND · Information Highlights** ------

Area: 1,214 square miles (3,144 sq km).
Population (1974 est.): 937,000. *Density:* 772 per sq mi.
Chief Cities (1970 census): Providence, the capital, 179,116; Warwick, 83,694; Pawtucket, 76,984.
Government (1975): *Chief Officers*—governor, Philip W. Noel (D); lt. gov., J. Joseph Garrahy (D). *General Assembly*—Senate, 50 members; House of Representatives, 100 members.
Education (1974–75): *Enrollment*—public elementary schools, 105,000 pupils; public secondary, 73,662; nonpublic, 34,000; **colleges and universities,** 59,436 students. *Public school expenditures,* $201,570,000 ($1,211 per pupil).
State Finances (fiscal year 1974): *Revenues,* $689,548,-000; *expenditures,* $658,751,000.
Personal Income (1974): $5,038,000,000; per capita, $5,-376.
Labor Force (July 1975): *Nonagricultural wage and salary earners,* 352,600; *insured unemployed,* 26,700 (7.5%).

RHODESIA

The breakdown of talks about Rhodesia's future, a split among black African nationalists, and continued guerrilla activities were the main events in Rhodesia in 1975.

Talks Collapse. Talks held at Victoria Falls between white and black Rhodesians on August 25–26 to resolve Rhodesia's political future failed. Prime Minister Ian D. Smith, who led the 275,000 white Rhodesians in breaking away from Britain in 1965, charged African National Council (ANC) leaders, representing Rhodesia's 5.7 million black Africans, with the talks' breakdown. Bishop Abel T. Muzorewa, ANC president, said Smith's refusal to grant amnesty to exiled ANC leaders caused the failure.

Preparation for the constitution revision talks had been made August 9–10 when Smith, South African Prime Minister B. J. Vorster, and a representative from neighboring Zambia met in Pretoria, South Africa. Vorster pressed Smith into the talks because he wanted détente with blacks in southern Africa. Vorster and Zambia's President Kenneth D. Kaunda attended the Victoria Falls talks, which were held in a South African railroad car on the Zambezi River Bridge on the Rhodesia-Zambia border. Smith's October 12 remark that South Africa's interference had delayed settlement evoked Vorster's resentment.

Nkomo Elected. Joshua Nkomo was elected ANC president at a controversial Salisbury congress September 27–28. Nkomo, a moderate and former head of the banned Zimbabwe African People's Union (ZAPU), has been criticized by previous ANC president Muzorewa and by the Rev. Ndabaningi Sithole, militant former head of the banned Zimbabwe African National Union (ZANU). Both Muzorewa and Sithole are self-exiled in Zambia, fearing arrest in Rhodesia. Nkomo thus heads a divided ANC. Smith met October 31 and November 1 with Nkomo for constitutional talks. But the ANC split still divided Africans. About 35,000 attended a rally for Muzorewa October 26.

Resignation. Cabinet Information Minister Wickus de Kock resigned in late October. He allegedly wanted one white and two black states. Smith rejected separate development, wishing to bring blacks into his government gradually, including his cabinet, leading to parity and eventual black majority rule.

RHODESIA · Information Highlights

Area: 150,803 square miles (390,580 sq km).
Population (1975 est.): 6,300,000.
Chief Cities (1969 census, met. areas): Salisbury, the capital, 386,040; Bulawayo, 245,040.
Government: *Head of state,* John Wrathall, president (took office Dec. 1975). *Head of government,* Ian Smith, prime minister (took office 1964).
Monetary Unit: Rhodesian dollar (0.5348 R. dollar equals U. S.$1, Oct. 1974).
Major Agricultural Products: Tobacco, sugar, tea, groundnuts, cotton, corn, millet, and sorghum.
Foreign Trade (1972): *Exports,* $499,000,000; *imports,* $417,000,000.

South African Forces Leave. On August 1, South Africa withdrew 200 police, who had been aiding Rhodesia against guerrilla attacks. South African police, 18 of whom have been killed in Rhodesia since December 1972, once totaled 2,000 in Rhodesia. Guerrilla attacks continued throughout 1975 along the eastern border with Mozambique, where there were dawn-to-dusk curfews. Rhodesia recruited foreign mercenaries, reportedly including 60 from the United States, to fight guerrillas.

U. S. Buys Rhodesian Chrome. On September 25 the U. S. House of Representatives voted 209–187 to continue the importation of Rhodesian chrome ore, an essential defense material. Black Africans resented U. S. purchases, which violated UN sanctions and aided Rhodesia's white government. But U. S. conservatives did not want the United States to have to rely on the higher-priced chrome ore of the USSR, the only other major source. U. S. liberals said that the United States has huge stockpiles of chrome ore and should not violate UN rules nor provoke black African anger.

FRANKLIN PARKER
West Virginia University

RUMANIA

In 1975 the main lines of Rumanian development, both at home and abroad, remained unchanged.

Domestic Affairs. Domestic political changes continued to strengthen the personal power of Nicolae Ceauşescu, secretary general of the Rumanian Communist party and president of the republic. On March 9, elections were held for a new five-year term of the Rumanian parliament, the Grand National Assembly. In preelection speeches, Ceauşescu, illustrating his country's precarious position within the Soviet sphere, promised cooperation with the Council for Mutual Economic Assistance (COMECON) as well as "great attention to strengthening defense capabilities." The new Assembly immediately reelected Ceauşescu as head of state and approved various changes in the government of Premier Manea Manescu recommended by the Rumanian Communist party.

Foreign Affairs. Rumania continued its complicated, multifaceted policy designed to guarantee and improve its own security. This included wary cooperation with the Soviet Union and the other countries of the Warsaw Pact, mediation between the Soviet Union and Communist China, and special collaboration with the developing nations and the Third World states (including both the Arab states and Israel). In fact, Rumania pursued good relations with all countries of the world, including the capitalist ones.

Rumania immediately established diplomatic relations with the People's Republic of Mozambique when that country gained independence in June and responded favorably to a communica-

RUMANIA • Information Highlights

Official Name: Socialist Republic of Rumania.
Location: Southeastern Europe.
Area: 91,700 square miles (237,500 sq km).
Population (1975 est.): 21,200,000.
Chief Cities (1971 est.): Bucharest, the capital, 1,488,-300; Cluj, 205,400; Timisoara, 195,500; Iaşi, 188,000.
Government: *Head of state,* Nicolae Ceauşescu, president and secretary general of the Communist party (took office 1965). *Head of government,* Manea Manescu, premier (took office March 1974). *Legislature* (unicameral)—Grand National Assembly.
Monetary Unit: Leu (4.97 lei equal U.S.$1, 1975).
Gross National Product (1973 est.): $31,000,000,000.
Manufacturing (major products): Construction materials, metals, chemicals, machinery, processed foods, textiles, petroleum products.
Major Agricultural Products: Corn, sugar beets, potatoes, wheat, rye, sunflower seeds.
Foreign Trade (1973): *Exports,* $3,675,000,000; *imports,* $3,447,000,000.

tion from Greece expressing the desire for closer relations between the two countries. Rumania also expanded its ties with the newly-leftist and fellow Latin nation of Portugal. In late October, Ceauşescu paid an official four-day visit to Portugal, becoming the first Communist head of state and the first president of any European country to visit Portugal since the ousting of the rightist regime in April 1974. It was speculated that Ceauşescu may have counseled the new regime to reduce its involvement in the North Atlantic Treaty Organization (NATO) and broaden its ties with Eastern Europe. In return he may have offered Rumanian mediation between the warring factions backed by Moscow and Peking in Angola.

Rumanian relations with the United States continued to prosper. In April, a U.S.-Rumanian trade agreement was signed, granting Rumania most-favored-nation status. Rumania thus became the third Communist country to gain such status, qualifying for it because of its agreement to remove barriers to Jewish emigration. The agreement was cemented by a brief stopover in the United States by Ceauşescu on June 11, during his trip to Latin America. It was formally implemented during President Ford's visit to Bucharest on August 2–3. The two statesmen agreed to accelerate the implementation of the treaty's economic, industrial, technological, and agricultural provisions. They also pledged their mutual efforts to achieve world disarmament and expressed their support for the inviolable sovereignty of all countries, "regardless of their size or political, economic, and social systems."

JOSEPH F. ZACEK
State University of New York at Albany

SÃO TOMÉ and PRÍNCIPE

São Tomé and Príncipe, two islands off the west coast of Africa, in the Gulf of Guinea, became the smallest independent African state on July 12, 1975. Portugal transferred sovereignty to the only local political formation of any significance, the São Tomé and Príncipe Liberation Movement (MLSTP). On Aug. 4, 1974, the Portuguese government recognized the islands'

UPI

President Ford and Rumanian President Ceauşescu wave to cheering crowds in Sinaia during Ford's European tour.

right to independence, and on November 26 it concluded an agreement with the MLSTP in Algiers. Under the terms of the agreement, a transitional government headed by José d'Alva, assistant secretary general of the MLSTP, took over in December 1974. Manuel Pinto da Costa, secretary general of the MLSTP, became the new republic's first president in July 1975. Miguel Trovoada, formerly in charge of external relations for the party, became the prime minister and minister of foreign affairs and defense in the new administration. José d'Alva was in charge of economic coordination.

São Tomé and Príncipe were discovered by Portuguese navigators in 1471. Over the years, they acquired a racially mixed population made up of various Mediterranean, Jewish, and African elements. They have a total area of 372 square miles (963 sq km) and a population of 76,000. São Tomé and Príncipe have a plantation economy based on coconuts, cocoa, and coffee, which together account for two-thirds of their exports.

EDOUARD BUSTIN
Boston University

SÃO TOMÉ AND PRÍNCIPE • Information Highlights

Official Name: Democratic Republic of São Tomé e Príncipe.
Location: Islands off the west coast of Africa in the Gulf of Guinea.
Area: 372 square miles (963 sq km).
Population (1975 est.): 76,000.
Chief City: São Tomé, the capital.
Government: *Head of state,* Manuel Pinto da Costa, president (took office July 1975). *Head of government,* Miguel Trovoada, prime minister (took office July 1975).
Major Agricultural Products: Coconuts, cocoa, coffee.

Dressed in 19th-century western costumes, participants parade during Buffalo Days, a popular annual event in Regina.

SASKATCHEWAN

Saskatchewan continued its strong economic growth both in agriculture and in extractive industries in 1975. Unemployment remained the lowest in Canada.

Elections. A June election returned Premier Allan Blakeney's socialist New Democratic party government to power with a reduction from 44 to 39 seats in the legislature. A revitalized Conservative party, in the words of its new leader, Dick Colver, "fooled the political scientists and the pundits" by capturing 7 seats and 27% of the popular vote, having held no seats in the legislature since 1967. The Liberals held 15 seats.

Strikes. Saskatchewan government services ground to a halt in August when 5,000 blue collar workers stopped up to 90% of civil servants from crossing picket lines for several days. In January the government used legislative power for the first time since its election in 1971 to force Saskatchewan Power workers back to their jobs. Withdrawal of teacher services was common throughout the province. High wage demands continued despite federal government appeals for voluntary restraints.

Economy. The economy remained healthy, with the unemployment rate the lowest in Canada and the cost of living well below the national average. Yields for cereal crops were above average; grades were lowered by heavy rains and frost during harvest. Demands for Saskatchewan's natural resources remained excellent. The government acted strongly to ensure that substantial amounts of resource income stayed in the province in spite of opposition from the private sector and a continuing battle with the federal government over resource control. The province's enormous deposits of potash, a fer-

tilizer urgently needed to grow food for a hungry world, were one of the focal points of this lively debate.

Health and Social Services. The Saskatchewan Prescription Drug Plan, which went into effect September 1, ensured that residents would pay only $2 to have their prescription filled at the pharmacy of their choice provided the drug falls within a formulary of some 1,200 drugs. The first provincial gerontologist, Dr. Louis Skoll, was appointed to develop and promote the well-being of the elderly.

Regina City Hall. Construction of an $8.8 million city hall complex in Regina proceeded over the summer despite opposition by a citizens' group that circulated a petition to force a plebiscite on the need for a new hall. The citizens' committee presented the 7,500-name petition to the city council in February 1975, but the council voted to disregard it. Having taken their cause to the Saskatchewan Court of Appeal, which declared their petition invalid, the petitioners appealed to the Supreme Court of Canada. The Supreme Court overturned the provincial court decision and ordered Regina to conduct a plebiscite. Burgesses voted overwhelmingly to proceed with construction of the new complex.

Sports. The Western Canada Summer Games, held in Regina August 10–17, were part of a "national game plan" to develop better athletes for Canada. It was the first time the four western provinces had undertaken athletic competition on such a large scale. British Columbia swept most of the events, amassing 113 gold medals out of the 178 awarded. Regina's legacy of the Games is Lawson Aquatic Centre.

DOROTHY HAYDEN
Regina Public Library

— SASKATCHEWAN · Information Highlights —

Area: 251,700 square miles (651,900 sq km).
Population (1975 est.): 920,000.
Chief Cities (1974 est.): Regina, the capital, 151,000; Saskatoon, 130,000; Moose Jaw, 32,000.
Government (1975): *Chief Officers*—lt. gov., Stephen Worobetz; premier, Allan Blakeney (New Democratic party); atty. gen., Roy Romanow (NDP); min. of educ., Gordon MacMurchy (NDP); chief justice, E. M. Culliton. *Legislature*—Legislative Assembly, 60 members.
Education (1975–76): *Enrollment*—public elementary and secondary schools, 216,810 pupils; private schools, 1,400 Indian (federal) schools, 6,810; colleges and universities, 12,870 students. *Public school expenditures,* $200,916,000.
Public Finance (fiscal year 1974–75 est.): *Revenues,* $901,000,000; *expenditures,* $983,000,000.
Personal Income (1972): $2,719,000,000; average annual income per person, $2,991.
(All monetary figures are in Canadian dollars.)

U. S. Vice President Rockefeller delivers a personal note from President Ford to King Khalid conveying condolences over the death of King Faisal.

SAUDI ARABIA

Despite the assassination of King Faisal, 1975 was a year of solid advances for oil-rich Saudi Arabia.

Faisal and Khalid. On March 25, 1975, King Faisal was assassinated in the royal palace by his nephew Prince Faisal ibn Musaid. No conspiracy was discovered and the prince was found guilty by a court of justice and was beheaded on June 18th. Within hours of King Faisal's death, the royal council of princes elevated his half-brother, Crown Prince Khalid, to the throne. King Khalid retained the posts of prime minister and foreign minister and named his half-brother Prince Fahd as crown prince, deputy prime minister, and minister of the interior. King Khalid also proclaimed amnesty for all political prisoners in Saudi Arabia.

Another half-brother, Prince Abdallah, was named second deputy prime minister and commander of the National Guard. Prince Nayif (Prince Fahd's brother) was made minister of state for the interior, and Prince Faisal (King Faisal's son) became minister of state for foreign affairs. The other cabinet members under King Faisal retained their posts, and King Khalid announced that governmental policies would remain as formerly. Other royal princes held important positions in the cabinet, such as Prince Sultan (full brother of Fahd and Nayif) as minister of defense and air minister; and half-brothers Prince Mitaib as minister of public works and housing, and Prince Majid as minister of municipal and rural affairs. In this way King Khalid tried to unify his more than 30 brothers around him.

In May 1975, King Khalid gave Prince Fahd power to handle the daily affairs of government under Khalid's broad direction. On August 12 it was announced that an appointed consultative council would be set up to act as a kind of parliament. Furthermore, administrative centers would be established in each of the 11 provinces with local administrators and councils.

Finance and the Economy. Before King Faisal was killed, he appointed Abdul Aziz al-Kurishi as the new head of the Saudi Arabian Monetary Agency, the central bank. He found the reserves at over $14 billion and growing rapidly. On March 14 he severed the tie between the riyal and the dollar ($1=3.55 riyals) and tied the riyal to the special drawing rights of the International Monetary Fund (the so-called paper gold) so that the effective rate became $1=3.47 riyals. It was estimated that Saudi Arabia invested about $8 billion in the United States during 1974 and large sums in Great Britain and Western Europe. In August, $273 million was loaned to Yemen for road construction, grain silos and mills, and relief on the condition that all Soviet military advisers leave by October 1.

A second 5-year plan was announced on May 18 by the Council of Ministers in the amount of $150 billion to be administered by Hisham Nazir, planning minister. This called for $25 billion for industrialization, agricultural expansion, 200,000 housing units, and 8,500 miles (13,600 km) of paved roads. One aim was to secure western capital participation to ensure the soundness of the projects and export markets.

--- **SAUDI ARABIA · Information Highlights** ---

Official Name: Kingdom of Saudi Arabia.
Location: Arabian Peninsula in southwest Asia.
Area: 830,000 square miles (2,149,690 sq km).
Population (1975 est.): 9,000,000.
Chief Cities (1975 est.): Riyadh, the capital, 450,000; Jidda, 500,000; Mecca, 250,000.
Government: *Head of state,* Khalid ibn Abd al-Aziz al-Saud, king (acceded March 1975). *Head of government,* Khalid ibn Abd al-Aziz al-Saud.
Monetary Unit: Riyal (3.53 riyals equal U. S.$1, Aug. 1975).
Gross National Product (1972 est.): $5,250,000,000.
Manufacturing (major products): Petroleum products, cement, fertilizers, iron and steel.
Major Agricultural Products: Dates, vegetables, wheat.
Foreign Trade (1974 est.): *Exports,* $33,500,000,000; *imports,* $4,000,000,000.

Oil remained the source of 90% of the 1975–76 budget. Expenditures for the year were posted at $32 billion, and income was estimated at $27.6 billion, the difference being made up from state reserves. Oil capacity is 11.2 million barrels per day but by the middle of 1975 production was running at 5.6 million barrels per day. At the Organization of Petroleum Exporting Countries (OPEC) meetings in Vienna in September, Oil Minister Sheikh Ahmed Yamani urged against any increase in oil prices and was able to hold the advance to 10%. In 1975, Saudi Arabia negotiated with Aramco for the sale of Aramco's remaining 40% of the petroleum company to Saudi Arabia for $800 million.

Foreign Affairs. The new regime set out a more vigorous policy for peace and Arab solidarity. In addition to sanctioning financial support for Egypt, Syria, Jordan, and the Palestinians, Prince Fahd visited Iraq in June 1975, the first time since 1960 a member of the royal family had gone to Baghdad. A border agreement was signed on July 2, dividing the neutral zone equally between the two countries. Also in June, Saudi Arabia mediated the Euphrates water dispute between Syria and Iraq. Prince Fahd visited Damascus in connection with the water plan and granted Syria $150 million in aid.

Presidents Sadat of Egypt and Assad of Syria came to Riyadh to confer with King Khalid in April to strengthen Arab relations, and in July the king went to Cairo to show his support of President Sadat. The Shah of Iran came to Riyadh in April to discuss common interests in the Persian Gulf region. In September, U. S. Secretary of State Kissinger visited Saudi Arabia and received support for his efforts toward an interim agreement between Egypt and Israel. In July the 6th Islamic Conference was held at Jiddah, where the 40-nation group seated the representative from the Palestine Liberation Organization (PLO) and passed a unanimous resolution calling for Israel's UN ouster.

In September, Prince Fahd was in London where he met with Queen Elizabeth and Prime Minister Wilson. He advanced $1 billion to England against arms shipments and industrial development assistance. In France, Prince Fahd advanced another $1-billion loan as an investment in the French arms industry.

Military. Saudi Arabia held repeated discussions with Iraq and Iran about the defenses of the Persian Gulf region and suggested a joint naval defense agreement with Iraq. Mediation of problems between Iraq and Kuwait were initiated. An agreement to purchase for $750 million some 60 F-5 jet fighters, parts, and trainers from the United States was made, and it was estimated that $1–2 billion would be spent in the United States for arms in 1975. Saudi Arabia also purchased large amounts of arms in England and France.

SYDNEY NETTLETON FISHER
The Ohio State University

SINGAPORE

Singapore marked the completion of its first decade as an independent republic in 1975.

Political Events. Singapore continued to exhibit its usual political stability, and Prime Minister Lee Kuan Yew's position remained secure. Controls over potential sources of opposition were tightened by a newspaper and printing presses act restricting the ownership of newspaper management shares to people approved by the minister of culture. Having created a one-party state, the government tends to rest its legitimacy on its reputation for efficiency and incorruptibility. Hence, the trial for corruption of Minister of State for the Environment Wee Toon Boon, was significant. The first minister in Lee Kuan Yew's government to be tried on such charges, he was convicted and sentenced to 4.5 years in prison and a $3,000 fine.

In an effort to alleviate traffic congestion, the government instituted a controversial area licensing scheme. It limited vehicle access to the central business district to those willing to pay a $3 per day fee. Others must use an expanded bus service.

Economy. After an average annual growth in the gross national product of 13% from 1968 to 1973, the rate of economic expansion slackened to 6.8% in 1974. To counteract recessionary pressures, the 1975 budget called for a 60% rise in development expenditure, aimed at stimulating the economy through new industrial projects and increased construction activity. In addition, steps were planned to spur exports and to attract more foreign investment through tax incentives. The government continued to pursue policies designed to develop Singapore as a center of tourism, finance, and sophisticated technical skills.

Foreign Affairs. In a major foreign policy initiative, Foreign Minister Rajaratnam led a Singapore delegation to Peking. Although the two countries stopped short of establishing formal diplomatic relations, they agreed to strengthen ties in trade and cultural fields.

MARVIN C. OTT
Mount Holyoke College

────── **SINGAPORE • Information Highlights** ──────

Official Name: Republic of Singapore.
Location: Southeast Asia.
Area: 244 square miles (581 sq km).
Population (1975 est.): 2,200,000.
Chief City (1970 census): Singapore, the capital, 2,122,-466.
Government: *Head of state,* Benjamin H. Sheares, president (took office 1971). *Head of government,* Lee Kuan Yew, prime minister (took office 1959). *Legislature* (unicameral)—Parliament.
Monetary Unit: Singapore dollar (2.48 S. dollars equal U. S.$1, July 1975).
Gross National Product (1974): $5,300,000,000.
Manufacturing (major products): Petroleum products, steel, textiles, tires, wood products, processed foods, electronics, ships, assembled automobiles, electrical appliances, precision instruments.
Foreign Trade (1974): *Exports,* $5,897,000,000; *imports,* $8,502,000,000.

SOCIAL WELFARE

New developments in the field of social welfare during 1975 are reviewed in this article under the following headings: (1) General Survey; (2) Health Care; (3) Child Welfare; and (4) U. S. Social Security.

General Survey

Continued high unemployment in the United States during 1975 forced record numbers of people into public assistance and related programs. More than 11 million children and adults received Aid to Families with Dependent Children (AFDC), and additional millions obtained food stamps. To the "man in the street," this often seemed evidence of the recipients' willful laziness and of connivance by the government staffs. With the administration of President Ford proclaiming its disapproval of social programs, media concentration on allegations of welfare fraud and wastefulness led one observer to assert that the bureaucracy was more concerned with avoiding accusations of loose administration than with carrying out the mandates of the programs.

New Social Service Provisions. In January 1975, after two years of heated debate, a new Title XX of the Social Security Act was signed. This established new ground rules for financing and administrating federally-assisted, state social-service programs. Unlike former rigid federal mandates, states are now free to establish their own arrays of programs, within broad limits, provided that full opportunity is given for citizen participation in the selection. Services must fall under one or another of five categories: self-support; self-sufficiency; prevention of abuse, neglect, or exploitation; prevention of inappropriate institutionalization; and arrangement for appropriate institutional care.

In general, services are to be without charge to persons with incomes below 80% of the state median income. When the services are offered to others, increasing fees are to be charged, up to payment of full cost for those with incomes above 115% of the state median. Federal matching funds up to fixed limits are available for each state. Greater citizen participation in state planning is demanded under this law. Services under the new ground rules were planned between April and September, and the plans went into effect October 1.

Confrontations. No other major federal social legislation was enacted except in the health field. However, a contest of wills continued between a majority in Congress seeking to strengthen and extend various social programs and President Ford, who sought to reduce them as detrimental to sound fiscal policy. In spite of a few overridden vetoes, Ford fared well in most confrontations. Furthermore, through administrative regulations, penalties, and threats of penalties, constant pressure was placed on states to bring their policies and practices into conformity with standards set by the president's appointees. Among the notable pressures were demands, backed by threats to withhold federal funds, that the states improve their investigatory and administrative controls over AFDC caseloads to achieve greater levels of accuracy.

Late in 1975, a New York state audit of welfare families previously labeled ineligible found that 32% of these families were actually eligible for some form of assistance. The audit report indicated that the proportion of totally ineligible AFDC families had been reduced to a new low of 5.8% and attacked federal "bureaucratic requirements and complex regulations," "arbitrary and unrealistic short-range targets," and failure to face "the need for welfare reform."

Ironically, it was the Social Security Administration, known for decades for its administrative efficiency, which admitted to computer errors of nearly $500 million in the Supplemental Security Income (SSI) program. The administration, in turn, was trying to collect this sum from the states. Health, Education, and Welfare (HEW) Secretary Caspar Weinberger and Social Security Commissioner James Cardwell, leading spokesmen for business methods in welfare, both resigned about the time the public was informed about the computer errors.

As the year ended, the most vigorous administration and congressional efforts were directed toward revision of the food stamp program. Participants in this program to supplement the food budgets of the poor had increased from about 14 million in the fall of 1974 to 19.5 million in May .1975 and then dropped to 18.8 million in the fall. Under this program a family of four with a net income of $300 a month pays about $83 a month for $162 worth of food stamps.

Throughout the year criticism was directed against high income eligibility limits, the eligibility of college students and strikers, and alleged fraudulent use of the stamps. It seemed likely that some modifications would be enacted.

Renewed Proposals. Proposals were renewed for transfer of the AFDC to federal administration. The AFDC is the only major public assistance program still under state jurisdiction. This would be a natural complement to the SSI program, and fiscally-beleaguered New York City would be saved millions of dollars. However, since its elimination from the 1972 welfare package, this proposal has not received much active support. With more than twice as many recipients as those presently under SSI, it is seen as too large and too costly a program. When it is seriously debated, the income floor to be provided for nearly all U. S. citizens will become a crucial consideration, and the balancing of individual need, fiscal policy, and federal-state relations in providing for the poor will be extremely complex.

Another group of proposals was for establishment of a major public-employment program

to accomplish much-needed work in schools, hospitals, and other public activities, while reducing the drain on unemployment funds and public assistance. A limited, short-term program was established in 1974, but the prospects for a substantial long-term program are unclear.

Review of Old Programs. New programs are exciting, but old ones are in constant need of review. The problems associated with starting the SSI program in 1974 had appeared to be subsiding until the massive computerized overpayments came to light in mid-1975. Legislation authorizing revenue sharing, upon which many cities have relied to pay their bills, must be renewed, and many people demanded that in any extension of revenue sharing Congress require greater attention to human services.

One of the more bizarre episodes of the year came when schoolteachers found that the unemployment compensation law had been revised in such a way that they were eligible for benefits during their summer vacations. When thousands of teachers began applying, Congress hastily deleted this provision. Meanwhile, private pension plans were having to conform to much stricter regulations to protect the interests of long-term employees. In too many instances in the past, such employees found themselves excluded from pensions when the time came for retirement.

Worldwide Problems. Plans for the establishment of "new towns" to relieve some of the problems of older urban centers in the United States were not progressing as fast as the promoters of the idea had anticipated. Lack of financial support from the federal government was given as a main reason. But whatever the block, the problem is real and is a worldwide phenomenon. In Norway, for instance, the energy crisis has stimulated oil drilling and production in the North Sea, with the result that people with generations-old roots in rural communities are being drawn to mushrooming small communities elsewhere, with consequent strains for both the old residents and the newcomers. Even more disturbing in these expanding Norwegian communities is an influx of workmen from as far away as Asia, with different languages, customs, religions, and appearance. Such economically-essential migrant workers are sources of irritation in many countries, and they create new demands for social services.

Problems of chronic poverty and malnutrition in many countries, compounded in 1974 by drought and other natural disasters, were slightly eased in 1975. Drought in Africa was not quite so severe, and U. S. participation in worldwide food-aid efforts was increased. Yet, basic problems of maldistribution of wealth and resources among the nations remained. Some agreements between the industrialized and the developing nations were reached at the United Nations in September. They were designed to permit more equitable access to food as well as other goods in the future.

UPI

Doctors and interns at Cook County Hospital in Chicago demonstrate for better hospital conditions in October.

Health Care

Prime public attention during 1975 was centered on the right to be born, the right to die, and "malpractice" on the part of doctors at all stages of the life cycle. Less publicized, but of at least equal significance for the right of all persons to the delivery of health care, was the enactment and preliminary implementation of a new network of "health systems agencies."

Right to be Born. Since the Supreme Court decision of January 1973 legalized abortion at the request of the mother during the first three months of a pregnancy, legal abortions in New York and elsewhere increased phenomenally. According to a study of the Planned Parenthood Federation, U. S. legal abortions increased by 27% in 1973 over 1972, when many states still followed antiabortion laws. Abortions increased again in 1974 by 53% over 1972, reaching a 1974 total of 900,000.

Although by no means limited to any one geographical area or segment of the population, resistance to legalized abortion centered in the Roman Catholic church, guided by unequivocal pronouncements from the Vatican that, since life begins at conception, termination of pregnancy at any stage is murder. Abortion services

were picketed, and strenuous efforts were made to prevent the establishment of abortion services in public facilities. In the U. S. Congress, a proposed constitutional amendment to prohibit most abortions was defeated in committee, but the effort will undoubtedly continue.

Supporters of abortion accept the judicial decision that the fetus cannot be considered alive until it can survive outside the mother's body. It is argued on the personal side that a woman has the right to control what happens to and in her body, and, as long as the fetus is not viable, she has the right to abort it. On the societal side, it is asserted that it is no kindness to the child, the mother, or to the community to bring an unwanted child into the world to face the prospect of economic and social deprivation. Advocates of women's rights and leaders of some of the more liberal religious groups are among the supporters of abortion as a choice for women.

Right to Die. Euthanasia has been the subject of legal and moral controversy for some time. Positive actions that cut short the natural life of a person, even in the terminal stage of a fatal illness, have generally been judged murder. The increasing number of therapeutic and life-support machines that can add years to life complicate this judgment. Medicare has been amended to provide dialysis to sufferers from kidney disease, for example. The use of such machines is not compulsory; Sen. Wayne Morse of Oregon chose to die rather than live dependent on a dialysis machine. Other signs of life may disappear, however, and a person's physiological processes may still be maintained artificially. During 1975 several cases were initiated requesting permission to disconnect life-support machines in such circumstances, with prospect of long court battles to determine what constitutes death and who, if any one, should make such decisions.

Malpractice Insurance Crisis. In each of these situations, the possibility of both civil and criminal actions against the physicians involved has helped precipitate the drive for legal determinations. This is only one facet of the malpractice insurance crisis that came to the fore during 1975. Overburdened by rapid and astronomical increases in premiums for malpractice insurance, large segments of the medical profession struck, demanding protection against these burdens. Legislative action in several states eased the crisis, but the medical profession was wary that it might be renewed at any time. The causes of the crisis were unclear, but to the general public the strikes and increases in doctors' fees and hospital charges raised the issue of the right of all persons to obtain adequate health care services within their means.

Health Service Agencies. The unpredictable cost of health care for the individual has been one of the traditional arguments in favor of national health insurance. Experience under Medi-

care and Medicaid has indicated that unanticipated costs make it extremely difficult to formulate plans for a comprehensive insurance program that will function adequately in an industry as loosely organized and regulated as the health industry. Although pressure for health-insurance legislation seemed quiescent, even the American Medical Association came out in favor of one plan. Anticipating the ultimate passage of such legislation, Congress moved to establish controls that are expected to make the cost of insurance programs more predictable.

A major step in this direction was taken in January 1975 with enactment of the National Health Planning and Resource Development Act, which becomes operative throughout the United States in 1976. Several previously created types of health planning agencies are being phased out and replaced by "health systems agencies" that will have complete health-planning responsibilities within their geographical areas. The several health system agencies in each state will be under the jurisdiction of a state health-planning agency. It, in turn, will be responsible to the federal government through HEW's National Institutes of Health.

The new agencies will have unprecedented power to enforce their planning decisions. Failure to observe the mandates may result in financial penalties that would make it difficult, if not impossible, for an individual health-care unit such as a hospital to survive. Such failure could result in termination of all federal payments to an institution, including payments for Medicare patients. With these controls, it is anticipated that by the time national health insurance is enacted, many past cost uncertainties will have been reduced. Perhaps in anticipation of such future limitations on their expansion, numerous hospitals moved into building programs in 1975.

Child Welfare

Child abuse and child support received attention during a year when adjustments in programs were being made. Planning for and implementation of the new Title XX of the Social Security Act gave community groups opportunities to work out cooperative relations with state agencies on programs of special interest.

Child Abuse. There has been increasing awareness of the large number of children who suffer injuries inflicted by parents or caretakers. Physicians, hospitals, and schools have been alerted to watch for signs of injury, and many state laws require reporting of suspected cases. More rapid investigations and more careful medical diagnoses are bringing more cases of child abuse to official attention. This is one of the five basic types of service authorized under Title XX and one that is to be given free without income restrictions, which will probably encourage further activity in this area.

Title XX funds may also be used for a variety of other child-welfare services ranging

from adoptions and day-care services to pre-school education, special services for juvenile offenders, and special services for the develop-mentally disabled. Many of these are services that states themselves may not wish to under-take but that may be contracted for with either governmental or voluntary agencies.

Support from Deserting Fathers. Child sup-port from deserting fathers has been sought for decades. Recurrently, measures to find and col-lect from runaway fathers have foundered on interstate legal complications, the irregularity of payments (resulting in difficulties in public as-sistance budgeting), and the ease with which a man, once found, could disappear again. An amendment to Title IV of the Social Security Act atttempts to deal with these problems by using social security records to locate parents, by requiring payments to be made to a court, rather than the spouse, and by having the court transmit the payment to the state for credit against the AFDC grant.

There are difficulties, however. Civil liber-tarians are disturbed over the breach in the con-fidentiality of social security earnings records, seeing this as a potential part of a computerized network of information that could eliminate all privacy in the United States. From the stand-point of the mother, the requirement to initiate this kind of a search may mean forfeiting all chance of family reconciliation. Also, in many states where mothers have been permitted to use support payments to augment admittedly inade-quate assistance grants, it means a reduction in the meager funds on which the mother and her family must live.

RALPH E. PUMPHREY
Washington University, St. Louis

U. S. Social Security

No legislation amending the social security programs was enacted during 1975. The Tax Reduction Act of 1975 provided for a one-time bonus payment of $50 to beneficiaries in March 1975. The Supreme Court on March 19 ruled against a part of the Social Security Act that provided benefits to widows with children but denied them to widowers with dependents.

Financing. In 1975 social security contribu-tions were 5.85% for employees and employers and 7.9% for the self-employed on earnings up to $14,100. The first automatic cost-of-living in-crease (8%) in monthly benefits was effective in June 1975 for all beneficiaries enrolled in May, except those with the special minimum. Federal supplemental security income (SSI) pay-ments were raised by the same amount effective in July. Other automatic adjustments made for 1976 were an increase in the maximum taxable and creditable earnings base to $15,300 and a $20 increase in the amount a beneficiary may earn to $230 per month, without benefit loss.

A required review of hospital costs under the Medicare program led to increases in the

Stephen Wiesenfeld won a U. S. Supreme Court case in March that allows widowers Social Security benefits.

hospital insurance deductible amount to $104 and in patient cost-sharing for days above the 60 covered by law to $26 for the 61st–90th day of hospital care. Beyond the 90th day a benefi-ciary pays $52 for each reserve day used of his 60-day lifetime reserve. After 20 days in a skilled-nursing facility, he pays $13 daily to the 100th day.

Benefits. For the fiscal year ending June 30, 1975, nearly $62.5 billion was paid in monthly cash benefits and lump-sum payments. Total as-sets in the Old Age Survivors Insurance trust fund were $34.9 billion, while the Disability In-surance trust fund had $8.1 billion. In August 1975, 30,850,000 persons were receiving bene-fits at a monthly rate of $5 billion. The average check to a retired worker was $205.60, while the average disabled worker received $224.60.

About $10.4 billion was withdrawn from the hospital insurance trust fund. As of July 1974, almost 23.5 million persons were enrolled in the program. Average amounts reimbursed from July 1974 to April 1975 were $1,053 per in-patient hospital bill and $474 per skilled-nursing facility bill. In short-stay hospitals, the average number of covered days was 10.7. In the 12 months ending July 1975, $3.8 billion was with-drawn from the medical insurance trust fund as reimbursement for about 74.3 million bills, 80% of which were for physicians' services.

In January 1974 the Federal SSI program paid from general revenues for the aged, blind, and disabled replaced the state-federal programs. States may supplement it for all recipients and must supplement it for those adversely affected by the change. At a state's request, the Social Security Administration administers the supple-mentary payment. Federally administered SSI payments totaling $457 million went to 4,188,-500 persons in June 1975.

JAMES B. CARDWELL
formerly, Commissioner of Social Security

SOUTH AFRICA

For South Africa as for southern Africa in general, 1975 was a momentous year. Domestic affairs were overshadowed by external events, as might be expected following the collapse of Portuguese rule in Mozambique and Angola and the efforts of Prime Minister B. J. Vorster toward détente in southern Africa. Yet hardly less dramatic in some respects were a number of internal developments in South Africa's politics, economic policies, and apartheid practices.

Foreign Affairs. The escalation of violence in southern Africa and Prime Minister Vorster's efforts toward détente continued to occupy public and government attention. In the year since his dramatic "crossroads" speech in the Senate, Vorster sought, with some real success, to open new contacts with African states based on common interests in peace and economic progress.

President William Tolbert of Liberia helped to arrange some meetings between South African and black African leaders. By October 23, the first anniversary of the détente speech, Vorster was able to say that South Africa was "only standing on the threshold" of its détente policy with black Africa and had gone further than "I thought possible at the time I spoke."

On Feb. 18, 1975, Vorster revealed that there had been 15 meetings since late 1974 between representatives of South Africa and Zambia. It was the close understanding that Vorster forged with President Kaunda of Zambia that, in spite of the breakdown of the Victoria Falls talks, forced Ian Smith's government in Rhodesia to return to the conference table.

The key to détente, notwithstanding the widening conflict in Angola, was perceived to be the peaceful resolution of the Rhodesian question. In addition to talks with other African leaders, Vorster applied other pressures on Prime Minister Smith's government to maintain communications with Rhodesia's black majority. In February the sizable force of South African combat policemen that had helped fight black guerrillas in Rhodesia for many years was withdrawn.

In the fall, when Smith appeared to suggest in a television interview that Vorster's policy of détente had frustrated rather than facilitated a peaceful settlement, he was summoned to Pretoria and a four-hour meeting in Vorster's office. On October 20 they issued a joint statement in which Smith apologized for any misunderstanding, expressed his high appreciation of Vorster's efforts, and promised to do all he could to inaugurate constitutional talks aimed at a settlement.

The other area of major concern to South Africa was the widening conflict in Angola, where fighting raged after the Portuguese withdrew November 11. South African troops were dispatched over the border to defend the Cunene hydroelectric project, built jointly by South Africa and Angola. The government was increasingly concerned not only with the possible spill-

over of the civil war but also with the growing Soviet involvement in Angola.

The UN and Namibia/South West Africa. Settlement of the 30-year dispute with the United Nations over Namibia/South West Africa became imperative in 1975 when the Security Council gave South Africa until May 30 to demonstrate its compliance with UN resolutions to respect the unity and integrity of the territory and to withdraw totally from it. On May 20, Vorster stated that while self-determination and independence were the government's goals for the territory, he rejected both UN supervision and South West Africa Peoples Organization (SWAPO) dominance. However, he stressed his willingness to continue negotiations with the United Nations on the constitutional development of the region. At the same time, he referred to the imminence of the conference of tribal leaders there to discuss the future.

The UN deadline came and went. On June 6, Britain, France, and the United States vetoed a resolution in the Security Council that would have invoked the "threat to international peace" language, and decreed mandatory action against the republic for failure to comply.

The constitutional conference met September 1 in Windhoek with representatives of 11 tribal and ethnic groups. Leaders of black nationalist groups were not invited. Twelve days later the conference issued a declaration of intent that set a period of three years for the achievement of its goals. Emphasis was placed on the right of each ethnic group to have the greatest possible say in its own affairs. The conference met again in November to set up committees to review discriminatory legislation, and then adjourned until March 1976.

Domestic Affairs. The Vorster government made it clear that its diplomatic overtures to black Africa were not meant to signal the end of apartheid in South Africa. At the same time, it initiated a cautious program to reduce the "petty irritations" of segregation. The Nico Malan national theater complex was opened to all races in January. Visiting French and British rugby

—— SOUTH AFRICA · Information Highlights ——

Official Name: Republic of South Africa.
Location: Southern tip of Africa.
Area: 471,444 square miles (1,221,037 sq km).
Population (1975 est.): 24,700,000.
Chief Cities (1970 census): Pretoria, the administrative capital, 543,950; Cape Town, the legislative capital, 691,296; Johannesburg, 642,967; Durban, 495,458.
Government: *Head of state,* Jacobus Johannes Fouché, president (took office 1968). *Head of government,* Balthazar John Vorster, prime minister (took office 1966). *Legislature*—Parliament: Senate and House of Assembly.
Monetary Unit: Rand (0.7143 rand equals U. S.$1, Aug. 1975).
Gross National Product (1974 est.): $32,500,000,000.
Manufacturing (major products): Textiles, iron and steel, chemicals, fertilizers, assembled automobiles, metals, machinery and equipment.
Major Agricultural Products: Sugarcane, tobacco, corn, fruits, wheat, dairy products, sheep, wool.
Foreign Trade (1974): *Exports,* $5,635,000,000; *imports,* $7,030,000,000.

teams were permitted to play with specially selected multiracial South African teams. In May
the navy promoted a group of nonwhite seamen
to the rank of lieutenant. The government
drafted legislation to desegregate certain hotels
and restaurants, a move aimed at eliminating
embarrassing incidents involving black foreign
diplomats and visitors.

Interracial constitutional links were taken a
step further in January when Vorster held a series of meetings with homeland leaders and the
Coloured and Indian councils. The Coloured
Council continued to press for direct parliamentary representation and rejected the government's
proposed cabinet council scheme. Its chairman
was dismissed on November 11 for refusing to
pass the Coloured budget. The deadlock forced
the government to appoint a chairman to pass it.

In February, five United party members of
parliament broke away to found the Reform
party. Later this group merged with the Progressive party, which had seven members in Parliament, to form the Progressive Reform party.
The new party, whose policy is unequivocally
against apartheid, won the Bryanston by-election
on November 13.

On September 21 the rand was devalued
17.9% against the dollar. The minister of finance said the devaluation was designed to protect the balance of payments. The economy was
also hard hit by a slump in the price of gold. In
October the government declared price and wage
restraint provisions and opened more jobs to
blacks in an effort to increase production and to
counter the 17% inflation rate.

R. B. BALLINGER, *Rhode Island College*

SOUTH CAROLINA

South Carolina inaugurated a new governor
in 1975 and dealt with the problems of recession.

Government and Politics. The state government, faced with a poor economy, ordered an
8% reduction in 1975–76 expenditures but exempted employee salaries and some institutions
giving personal services. The reduction came at
a time when the state prison system was overflowing, mental institutions were strained to
maintain adequate staff for the continuation of
accreditation, and additional physical facilities
were needed by many departments.

The first Republican governor in 100 years,
James Edwards, was inaugurated in January.
Governor Edwards did not seriously challenge
the legislature, which was chiefly Democratic
and the more influential branch of government.
Numerous public issues were debated, including
the control of the Department of Social Services, preservation of virgin timber in the Con-
garee Swamp, the decentralization of mental
health institutions, water pollution, police brutality, and the control exercised by the Higher Education Commission over various institutions.
Other issues discussed included the housing of

prisoners, the freedom of information as applied
to public agencies, judicial reform under a unified court, the regulation of milk prices, and the
control of public utilities. No long-range progress was made in solving any of these issues.

The General Assembly had a long but fruitful session. It enacted a set of local-government
laws, which restructured and revitalized municipal and county government, removed many of
the loopholes in the gun law, and provided an
ethics law for governmental officials who earn
$20,000 or more. It also strengthened and ex-
panded the public kindergarten program, classified property according to use and established
assessing ratios, enacted the first statewide personnel act, and authorized a medical malpractice
insurance system. Judicial reform and reapportionment of the state senate into single-member
districts were still under consideration.

Education and Health. Public education continued to be upgraded, especially by significant
reductions in high-school dropouts and first-
grade failures. The kindergarten program was
expanded to cover 65% of the state. Students
enrolled in vocational, adult, and technical education reached an all time high. Despite opposition, the number of public-schoolteachers unions
increased to five. Significant new programs were
begun at the University of South Carolina, including a medical school and schools of criminal justice and public health. A major new library was completed. Many new programs were
initiated to improve health delivery services, to
reduce infant mortality, and to serve those ad-
dicted to alcohol or drugs.

Economy and Agriculture. In October the
economic indexes began to show major improvement, and the employment picture brightened.
The recession seriously hampered industrial expansion, and the natural gas shortage threatened
production in the Piedmont section of the state.
Housing development was hampered when the
state supreme court declared the proposed plan
for financing unconstitutional. Farm production
was good, but inflation greatly reduced profits.

ROBERT H. STOUDEMIRE
University of South Carolina

SMITHSONIAN INSTITUTION

South Dakota's exhibit of the Bicentennial festival of American Folklife, held in Washington, D. C., early in summer, was a demonstration on breaking workhorses.

SOUTH DAKOTA

During 1975, South Dakotans debated about the possible effects of plans by federal agencies to develop the Missouri River valley and to pump water from the river for an irrigation project in the northeastern counties. Tensions between Indians and non-Indians existed throughout the year.

Missouri Valley Development. Public interest was aroused by the plans of two federal agencies for the development of Lake Oahe, one of four lakes that were created through the construction of Missouri River dams. On three occasions groups voiced concerns at public hearings regarding the management of the lake and of a narrow strip of land along its shore, by the U. S. Army Corps of Engineers.

A statewide controversy of even more serious proportions erupted because of the U. S. Bureau of Reclamation plans to pump water from Lake Oahe to irrigate about 500,000 acres (200,000 hectares) of farmland in the northeastern counties. After work on the construction of pumping stations had begun, the opponents led a movement to force the suspension of the bureau's activity until important questions could be answered about possible future effects of the project. Most arguments about the plans of the two federal agencies evolved from conflicting ecological and economic development views. Many observers believed that the latter would prevail because of the economic recession precipitated by inflation and drought.

American Indians. Several developments caused ethnic tension during the year. In the spring, American Indian Movement (AIM) leader Russell Means was arrested, accused of involvement in the fatal shooting of Martin

Montileaux at the town of Scenic, and released on $50,000 bond. At about the same time groups of armed Indians took over a pork plant owned by the Yankton Sioux tribe and forced it to shut down.

In June a group of Indians assembled at a remote house on Pine Ridge Reservation and allegedly shot and killed Federal Bureau of Investigation agents Jack R. Coler and Ronald A. Williams, as the two men tried to serve warrants. Subsequently, buildings occupied by officials of the Bureau of Indian Affairs on Pine Ridge Reservation were bombed and suffered damage estimated at about $20,000.

Some efforts to alleviate tensions between Indians and non-Indians were significant. Gov. Richard F. Kneip worked with a task force, headed by Thomas Short Bull, to solve jurisdictional disputes between the state and tribal governments. A report issued by the task force offered hope that problems could be solved in the future.

Politics and Legislation. Partisan debates in the state legislature, where Democrats controlled the Senate and Republicans dominated the House of Representatives, led to the failure of several controversial bills. Governor Kneip's request for personal and corporate income taxes was rejected, and his plan to provide economic assistance for rural industries was spurned because it called for public funds to support private enterprise. Proposals for no-fault automobile insurance, for public control over land use planning in vital areas, and for reimbursement for innocent victims of violent crimes were defeated. The most important laws passed raised minimum wages for persons 18 years of age and under to $2 an hour, revised political campaign regulations, and provided $148.8 million to run the state government and its programs.

Economy. It was a lean year for many South Dakotans. Crop yields were poor in many parts of the state due to a drought from midsummer to harvest time. Unemployment rose to as high as 6%. Retail sales, construction activity, and tourism were all disappointing.

HERBERT T. HOOVER
University of South Dakota

U. S. astronauts Slayton, Stafford, and Brand pose with Soviet cosmonauts Leonov (*right, rear*) and Kubasov. The five men were the primary crew for the Apollo/Soyuz mission.

NASA

space exploration

The historic and highly successful rendezvous in space of the U. S. and the Soviet spacecraft, Apollo/Soyuz, was the highlight of space activities in 1975. When cosmonauts in Soyuz 18 spent over 63 days in space, they established a record for Soviet manned spacecraft. Exploration of the planets continued with the receipt and retransmission to earth of the first photographs of the surface of Venus by Venera 9 and 10 and with the launching of Vikings 1 and 2 for a rendezvous with Mars in the summer of 1976.

MANNED SPACE FLIGHT

The USSR launched a 20-ton space station, Salyut 4, into earth orbit on Dec. 26, 1974, to await the arrival of the Soyuz 17 and Soyuz 18 cosmonauts. The purpose of Salyut 4, which carried over 5,500 pounds (2,495 kg) of scientific equipment, was to provide a laboratory for cosmonauts to conduct scientific studies in the fields of astrophysics and geophysics and to survey earth's resources.

Soyuz 17. On January 11, the Soviets launched Soyuz 17 for a rendezvous with Salyut 4. The rendezvous was completed on January 12 by cosmonauts Aleksei Gubarev and Georgi Grechko. Activation of the Salyut's systems oc-

cupied much of the crew's time for the first few days, after which work directed at achieving the mission objectives was begun.

During the mission the cosmonauts conducted a number of investigations of the sun and other celestial bodies. These included collecting spectroscopic data on solar ultraviolet radiation and measuring the flux of X-ray radiation from sources deep in space. In a second group of investigations, the performance of man in space and his reactions to the zero-gravity environment were measured. These included studies of human vestibular and cardiovascular functions. The third class of studies included observation of the earth's atmosphere to measure the characteristics of neutral gas and plasma and to examine the earth's infrared radiation.

After transferring the results of scientific research into the Soyuz 17 spacecraft, the cosmonauts reentered the atmosphere in it on February 9 and landed 68 miles (110 km) northeast of Tselinograd, Kazakhstan, after spending 30 days in space.

Soyuz 18. An attempt to launch Soyuz 18 into an orbit for a second visit with the Salyut 4 space station failed on April 5. The mission was aborted because an improper staging sequence prevented separation of the upper stage from the lower stage. The two cosmonauts aboard, Vasily Lazarev and Oleg Makarov, landed safely in western Siberia near the Chinese border, a great distance from the normal Soyuz recovery area in Kazakhstan.

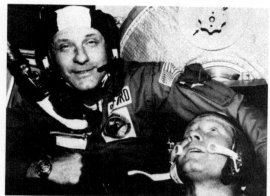

For the first time in history, space crews from two different countries, the United States and the Soviet Union, joined together for a space venture. Astronaut Stafford and Cosmonaut Leonov (*above, right*) meet in space. Apollo (*above*) is launched for the rendezvous with Soyuz (*right*). Soviet Ambassador Dobrynin (*below, foreground*) watches liftoff from NASA headquarters.

(ALL PHOTOS): NASA

On the second attempt, Soyuz 18 was successfully launched on May 24 with cosmonauts Pyotr Klimuk and Vitaly Sevastyanov. After three or four attempts the Soyuz 18 spacecraft docked with Salyut 4, and the crew activated the space station and prepared for scientific experiments. During their stay in space the cosmonauts conducted experiments in the fields of astrophysics, biology, and atmospheric science and surveyed earth resources. With a mirror X-ray telescope, they studied X-ray sources in the star systems of Scorpius, Virgo, and Cygnus, and with a camera system they conducted photographic surveys of the earth.

The Soyuz 18 cosmonauts returned to earth on July 26 after 63 days in space and more than 2 months aboard the Salyut 4 orbital station. The Soyuz 18 landed in almost the same place as Soyuz 19 and Soyuz 16, about 35 miles (56 km) northeast of Arkalyk, Kazakhstan. The flights of Soyuz 17 and 18 heightened the confidence of the Soviets in their stated goal of continually expanding the duration of their space station systems.

Apollo/Soyuz: Initial Phases. In the summer of 1975, for the first time in man's history of the exploration of space, manned spacecraft built and launched by two different nations rendezvoused in space and made joint scientific investigations. The Apollo/Soyuz mission performed by the United States and the Soviet Union was a historic event that was followed by millions of people around the world.

The mission began when the Soyuz 19 spacecraft with cosmonauts Aleksei Leonov and Valery Kubasov was launched on July 15 from the Baikonur Cosmodrome and inserted into earth orbit. During the second orbit, the Soyuz crew opened the hatch between the descent vehicle and the orbital module, removed their spacesuits, and checked out the attitude control system in both the automatic and manned modes. The first of two maneuvers to circularize the orbit was initiated near the end of the fourth orbit of the earth.

Meanwhile, the Apollo spacecraft, with astronauts Thomas Stafford, Vance Brand, and Donald Slayton aboard, was launched from the Kennedy Space Center on July 15, 7.5 hours after the launch of Soyuz. The U. S. lift-off and journey into space was broadcast live by an onboard television camera, a first in space travel. The live TV coverage of the Soyuz launch was also the first permitted by the Soviet Union.

After insertion into orbit and completion of the circularization maneuver, the Apollo crew performed the transposition, docking, and extraction of their docking module to place the spacecraft into the configuration for docking with Soyuz. The crew then had a rest period before proceeding with the final preparation for rendezvous and docking. Meanwhile, the Soyuz crew completed the circularization of their orbit and checkout of all their systems.

Apollo/Soyuz: Rendezvous and Return. The rendezvous and docking of Apollo and Soyuz took place on July 17, on schedule and viewed by millions by means of television cameras on board the Apollo spacecraft. Approximately three hours later, the hatch between the spacecraft was opened, and Astronaut Stafford and Cosmonaut Leonov shook hands.

Soviet Party Chairman Leonid Brezhnev relayed a message to the crews complimenting them on their achievements, and U. S. President Gerald Ford then conversed with the Apollo and Soyuz crew members. National flags were exchanged, and the international certificates in the Soyuz spacecraft were signed by all crew members.

After a rest period of several hours, the crew was awakened and began making earth observations over the Himalaya mountains, Africa, and the Arabian peninsula. With the completion of these experiments, preparations were made for transferring crews between the spacecraft. During the next 12 hours, three more transfers of crews took place. Major crew activity during this period included joint experiments, TV tours of each spacecraft, a joint press conference, and various activities symbolic of this first international space flight.

On July 19 the crews began preparations for the first undocking of Soyuz and Apollo. Following undocking, a simulated solar eclipse was performed, with the Apollo spacecraft blocking the sun from the Soyuz spacecraft. At the completion of this experiment, the two spacecraft docked once again to give the Soviet crew their second docking test. Several hours later, the final undocking took place after the Soyuz crew obtained photographs of the Apollo spacecraft.

After the two spacecraft separated, the Soyuz spacecraft performed a deorbit maneuver and reentered the earth's atmosphere, landing safely in Kazakhstan, 34 miles (54 km) northeast of Arkalyk on July 21. For the first time the landing of a Soviet spacecraft was televised live worldwide, and the Soyuz descent module was seen landing under a large orange and white parachute. The Soyuz crew had safely completed over 142 hours in space and almost 2 days of docked flight with the Apollo spacecraft.

Meanwhile, the Apollo spacecraft continued its mission in orbit. The Apollo crew conducted an ultraviolet absorption experiment to measure the concentration of atomic oxygen and nitrogen in space. Also, a Doppler tracking experiment was performed to detect and measure localized anomalies of the earth's magnetic field.

One day prior to the deorbit maneuver, the Apollo descent vehicle was separated from the docking module. On July 24 the Apollo spacecraft conducted deorbit maneuvers and reentered the earth's atmosphere. Landing occurred safely in the Pacific Ocean, 310 miles (500 km) northwest of Honolulu.

After recovery of the crew, crew interviews

and medical examinations indicated that they were experiencing eye and lung discomfort as a result of breathing combustion products during the latter portions of the descent. However, their general health was good, and after several days of rest they returned to Houston.

Apollo/Soyuz: Evaluation. Thus ended the historic joint mission of the Soyuz and Apollo spacecraft. Its success demonstrated that spacecraft built by different nations can rendezvous and dock in space and perform important scientific experiments. The importance of this capability will become more evident in the 1980's, when the space shuttle becomes operational, and many nations will be conducting manned experiments in space.

EARTH SATELLITES AND EARTH PROBES

Venus Probes. Two Soviet spacecraft, Venera 9 and 10, were launched on a 4-month journey to Venus on June 8 and June 14. Venera 9 went into orbit about Venus and launched a capsule that landed on the cloud-shrouded planet on October 22. During its 53-minute life on the surface, the capsule returned pictures of the surface showing piles of rocks typical of a young mountainscape. On October 25 the Venera 10 capsule also landed successfully and performed 65 minutes of work before failing because of the intense temperatures and an atmospheric pressure 90 times that on earth. The Venera 10 capsule, landing about 1,375 miles (2,210 km) from the spot where the Venera 9 capsule touched down, also took pictures of old mountain formations. In the second location the rocks were not as sharp and resembled huge pancakes between which were smaller weathered rocks of what were believed to be cooled lava or debris. The pictures taken by Venera 9 and 10 were the first ever taken of the surface of Venus, which is perpetually covered by clouds.

Mars Probe. On August 20 and September 9, the United States launched what were believed to be the most sophisticated spacecraft ever launched for the exploration of Mars, Viking 1 and Viking 2. Early in November, a battery charger aboard Viking 2 failed to work, but a backup charger performed successfully to keep the craft in sound shape for its landing on Mars.

After an 11-month journey, the 4-ton Viking 1 was scheduled to reach the vicinity of Mars on June 19, 1976, ready to go into orbit to check out the planned landing site. After orbiting the planet for some 18 days, the lander will be detached for a soft landing on the Martian surface. The lander will collect samples of the soil and rock and analyze them for chemical traces of animal or plant organisms. The information will be sent to the earth via a relay in the orbiting section of the spacecraft. The Viking will also send weather reports and seismic readings from the planet's surface as well as both black-and-white and color photographs of the surrounding Martian terrain.

UPI

Commander Klimuk (*left*) and Engineer Sevastyanov wave before boarding Soviet spaceship Soyuz 18 in May.

A successful Viking mission will give mankind its first detailed knowledge of the Martian environment and tell scientists whether the surface of Mars is capable of supporting some form of life. Viking 2, which will land about a month and a half after Viking 1, is on an identical mission but will be programmed to land at a different latitude. The orbiters are designed to operate for a total of 144 days in Mars orbit while the landers will operate for a total of 128 days on the surface.

Earth Resources and Weather Satellites. The United States launched LANDSAT-2 on January 22 to continue the collection of multispectral data to aid in the inventory and management of the earth's natural resouces. LANDSAT-2 joined LANDSAT-1, which had been collecting useful data since its launch on July 23, 1972.

On February 9 and October 16, the United States launched SMS-2 and GOES-A into synchronous orbit to provide continuous pictures of cloud cover between the western Pacific and eastern Atlantic oceans. These satellites are also used for locating, tracking, and predicting severe storms, such as hurricanes. On June 12, the United States launched an experimental weather satellite, Nimbus-6, to test new sensors and techniques for measuring characteristics of the atmosphere.

The USSR launched three meteorological satellites in its Meteor series in 1975. Meteors 21 and 22 were launched on April 1 and September 10, while the first of a new series, Meteor 2-1, was launched on July 11.

NASA

NASA

Viking Lander is sterilized in preparation for its 11-month trip to Mars with Viking 2, which began in September. At right is an artist's conception of a lander as it descends to the surface of Mars.

Communications Satellites. INTELSAT IVF-1 was launched on May 22 by the United States for the International Telecommunications Satellites Consortium and placed in a synchronous orbit over the Indian Ocean. This was the seventh and last of the INTELSAT IV series, which provides up to 9,000 two-way voice channels and up to 12 TV channels. The first of a new series, INTELSAT IV-A was launched September 25 and placed over the South Atlantic. It has a communication capacity two-thirds greater than one of the IVF-1 series.

The RCA Corporation domestic commercial communication satellite, RCA-Globcom Satcom (RCA-A), was launched in mid-December. The satellite can handle up to 24,000 one-way voice circuits or 24 simultaneous television circuits.

ANIK III (TELESAT-C), the third of a series of Canadian domestic communication satellites, was launched by the United States on May 7. This satellite, with a capacity of 10 TV channels or 9,600 telephone circuits, was stationed at 119° W longitude.

Symphonie B, the second French/Federal Republic of Germany satellite, was launched by the United States on August 27. This experimental satellite will test communications equipment and data transmission among South America, Europe, and Africa.

During 1975 the United States Applications Technology Satellite, ATS-6, launched on May 30, 1974, moved into position over India for a one-year experiment beginning August 1 to transmit instructional television programs to a thousand isolated villages throughout India.

The USSR launched eight domestic communication satellites in 1975. Three were in the Molniya 2 class (Molniya 2-12, 2-13, and 2-14; on February 6, July 8, and September 9); three were in the Molniya 1 class (Molniya 1-29, 1-30, and 1-31; on April 29, June 5, and September 2); and two were of the Molniya 3 class (Molniya 3-2 and 3-3 on April 14 and November 14).

Earth Orbiting Scientific Satellites. On March 27, the USSR launched Intercosmos 13, a joint USSR and Czechoslovakian satellite, to study the upper atmosphere. The United States launched GEOS-C on April 8 to measure precisely the topography of the ocean surface and the sea state and to evaluate the capability of several geophysical measuring systems.

The Soviet Union launched India's first satellite on April 19. Named for Aryabhata, a 5th century astronomer and mathematician, the 794-pound (360 kg) satellite carried instruments for measuring X rays, high-energy neutrons, gamma-rays, electrons, and ultraviolet radiation. On May 7, the United States launched Explorer 53 from the San Marco platform off the coast of Kenya for studying X-ray sources. Explorers 54 and 55 were launched in October and November to investigate the chemical processes and energy transfer mechanisms that control the earth's atmosphere.

The eighth in a series of satellites to study the sun, OSO-8, was launched on June 21 by the

United States to obtain information about the energy transfer in the sun's atmosphere, to continue investigations of the sun's 11-year sun-spot cycle, and to attempt to locate "black holes" in space.

The United States launched the European Space Agency's satellite, COS-B, on August 9 to make observations of cosmic rays.

ADVANCES IN SPACE TECHNOLOGY

Japan, France, and China launched new vehicles in 1975, and work continued on the U. S. Space Shuttle and the Spacelab.

Japanese Launch Vehicle. The Japanese successfully launched their new launch vehicle, N-1, on September 9 from the Tanegashima Space Center south of Kyushu. The N-1 launch vehicle is a 7.9-foot (2.4-meter) diameter rocket using a Thor-Delta first and third stage and an LE-3 second stage developed by the Japanese National Space Development Center. With the success of the N-1, Japan has the capability to launch a 1,325-pound (600-kg) payload into a 620-mile (1,000-km) earth orbit and a 285-pound (130-kg) payload into geostationary orbit. On the first test flight Japan also launched an experimental test satellite, ETS-1, to measure the vibration during the launch phase and satellite temperatures during its three-month life in space.

Other Satellite Launches. The French continued their space technology development with the second in a series of launches of the MAS-2 (SRET-2) satellite, which was launched on June 5 by the USSR in conjunction with its Molniya 1-30 launch. This satellite is designed to test structural materials, thermal insulating cooling, and a radiation system for cooling spacecraft. The French launched two other small experimental satellites, Castor and Pollux, carrying an ultrasensitive micron accelerometer and a new hydrazine-powered microrocket respectively.

The People's Republic of China's third developmental satellite was launched into a low orbit on July 26. The satellite, which reentered the atmosphere on September 14, obtained cloud pictures during its brief mission.

Space Shuttle. The development by the United States of the new Space Shuttle, which will permit more routine access to space with a reusable vehicle, made excellent progress during 1975. The main purpose of the Space Shuttle is to reduce the cost of delivering a great variety of large payloads to earth orbit. The Space Shuttle will also be able to service and retrieve earth-orbiting satellites.

During 1975 the first orbiter (the orbiting part of the Space Shuttle) was being fabricated and assembled in preparation for developmental landing tests in late 1977. The second orbiter, which will be used for the first manned orbiting flights in 1979, entered the fabrication phase in late 1975. The orbiter is launched by the Space-Shuttle booster system, which consists of two

UPI

NASA's Space Shuttle orbiter takes shape at the final assembly facility in Palmdale, Calif. It is the first attempt at a totally reusable space vehicle.

solid rocket boosters attached in parallel to an external tank. In 1975 the design phase of this system was completed, and its fabrication was initiated. The construction of the launch and landing facilities at the Kennedy Space Center in Florida also proceeded on schedule during 1975.

Spacelab. The development of the Spacelab by the European Space Agency (ESA) also proceeded on schedule during 1975. The Spacelab is being designed for placement in the cargo bay of the Space Shuttle and will be used for relatively short-duration, man-tended payloads. It is a manned space laboratory in which as many as three persons at a time can work in a shirt-sleeve environment on 7- to 30-day missions in earth orbit. Potential Spacelab users are designing experimental payloads for research in such areas as astronomy, the life sciences, atmospheric physics, and material sciences. The first orbital flight of the Spacelab is scheduled for 1980.

PITT G. THOME
*National Aeronautics
and Space Administration*

Juan Carlos was sworn in as Spain's new king on November 22, after the death of Francisco Franco.

SPAIN

Great changes marked the year 1975 in Spain as Generalissimo Francisco Franco died in November. (See also OBITUARIES.) He was succeeded by his chosen successor, Prince Juan Carlos. (See also BIOGRAPHY.) As King Juan Carlos I the new ruler faced a difficult task in governing a nation that had been troubled during the year by political violence, a widening church-state rift, radical Portugal as a neighbor, and by deteriorating diplomatic relations with Western Europe.

Change of Power. The most pressing Spanish political problem was that of the succession to Generalissimo Franco. Staunch supporters of the regime, including relatives of the dictator, said publicly that the time had come for him to withdraw and to transfer power to his chosen successor, Juan Carlos. Spanish sentiment favored enthronement of Juan Carlos while Franco still controlled Spain and could back the changeover with his great prestige, but the old dictator showed no signs of relinquishing the reins, evidently feeling that no one else could handle them.

Several factors stood in the way of Franco's deposition. Juan Carlos appeared to possess only moderate ability. His exiled father, Prince Juan, reiterated his own claim to the throne, dividing and confusing Spanish monarchists. Premier Carlos Arias Navarro vacillated, but seemed unwilling to risk a break with Franco. And as the Portuguese armed forces revolution took a leftward and more violent turn, most Spaniards had no wish to expose themselves to a similar prospect.

The problem provided its own solution late in October when a series of heart attacks made Franco's death seem imminent. On October 30, power as head of state, though not yet as king, was transferred to Juan Carlos by Premier Arias and Rodrigues de Valcarcel, president of the Cortes, or parliament.

On November 20, Franco died, and he was buried in the vast crypt he had had built in the Valley of the Fallen, the Civil War memorial near Madrid. Prince Juan Carlos became king as Juan Carlos I on November 22. While upholding the principles of Franco's rule, the new head of state also promised substantial improvements. He started his regime with a partial amnesty for Spanish prisoners.

Domestic Affairs. Spanish political violence increased as the year progressed. Centers of disaffection were the four Basque provinces of Navarra, Alava, Guipúzcoa, and Vizcaya, where Basques number about 600,000 of the total 2.5 million inhabitants. These provinces, which generally opposed Franco in the civil war of the 1930's, make up the most highly industrialized section of Spain and have an above-average per-capita income. Most Basques favored remaining within Spain, but desired complete cultural and partial political autonomy. However, Basque National Freedom (ETA), a Basque separatist organization committed to violence, so intensified attacks on Franco's security forces that on April 25 the government placed Guipúzcoa and Vizcaya provinces under a "state of emergency" order, meaning unlimited police control. Shortly before this, the Madrid authorities closed *Cambio-16*, the fastest-growing Spanish news weekly, for publishing articles on the sensitive Basque problem and censored or confiscated copies of other papers.

The Basque terrorists were not alone in violently opposing the government. A Maoist Marxist organization practiced assassination in other parts of Spain. Two Basque separatists and three Marxist terrorists were executed on September 27 for the murder of security policemen, and this reprisal caused a wave of indignation against Spain in Europe. Sixteen countries withdrew their ambassadors from Madrid. The United States, engaged in negotiations with Spain over military base rights and considering this a Spanish domestic matter, did not follow suit. The executions sparked new efforts by the terrorists, and the death toll of policemen rose quickly.

Economy. Spain's diplomatic estrangement from the rest of Europe following the ambassadors' recall placed the national economy in a delicate and vulnerable position. During the first six months of 1975, 58% of Spanish exports went to Western Europe, and 41% of the imports came from there. As Spanish policy had

President and Mrs. Ford met with Generalissimo Francisco Franco and his wife Carmen on May 31 during an official visit to Spain.

UPI

been to strengthen ties with Europe, the isolation was both economically and politically dangerous.

Yet, despite reversals, the Spanish economy grew during the first half of 1975. Annual percapita income reached an all-time high of $1,850. Spain engaged in the building of supertankers, steel plants and oil refineries were built, the chemical industry expanded, and three nuclear power stations were in operation. The life style of the Spanish middle class approached that of West Germany and France. Investments in Spain by the U. S. private sector amounted to $4.6 billion, with heavy commitments by other foreign sources of capital. By 1975, Spain had moved in 15 years from a backward agricultural society to the fifth largest European industrial economy. Spanish optimists believed that their country's greatly increased wealth would prevent its people from following the example of Portugal, debilitated by years of colonial wars.

The darker side of the economic picture was one of inflation, labor trouble with wildcat strikes, and a decrease in remittances from Spanish laborers abroad. Many of the emigrants seemed likely to return home, owing to the depression and growing unemployment in the European countries in which they worked.

The Church. The Roman Catholic Church could no longer be called a close associate of the Spanish government. A Catholic conference scheduled for late May in the poverty-stricken Vallecas district of Madrid under the presidency of Cardinal-Archbishop Enrique 'y Tarancón of Madrid-Alcalá was called off at the last moment by political authorities on the ground that outside radical elements might infiltrate the affair. A generation gap had clearly developed between the Spanish hierarchy and younger priests and nuns, some of whom were affiliated with an underground group called Christians for Marxism, favoring the aims but not the ideology of communism. Before the execution of the five terrorists in September, Pope Paul VI sent a plea for clemency, which the Spanish government ignored. After the accession of Juan Carlos, the church stated clearly that it would be ideologically independent from the state.

Foreign Affairs. Negotiations continued for renewal of U. S. base rights at Rota, Torrejón, Zaragoza, and Morón de la Frontera. President Gerald Ford visited Madrid May 31 and conferred with Franco in the hope of speeding the conclusion of the agreement. Spain wanted one of two things from the transaction that Ford lacked authority to grant: full membership in NATO or a broader security agreement with the United States. After protracted negotiations, an announcement from Washington on October 4 stated that Secretary of State Henry Kissinger and Spanish Foreign Minister Pedro Cortina Mauri had reached a new framework agreement. Few details were furnished, but apparently the United States would continue operating the bases with reduced personnel.

Spain prepared to relinquish possession of its Spanish Sahara colony as demanded by Morocco, though both Algeria and Mauritania claimed interests in the territory. Late in the year King Hassan II of Morocco announced a "peace march" by 350,000 of his subjects for the purpose of taking peaceful possession of the territory. Spain withdrew most civilians from the area though leaving military forces there temporarily. Although Hassan's followers crossed the border in November, they did not proceed far, and Hassan called off the march.

CHARLES E. NOWELL
University of Illinois

──── **SPAIN · Information Highlights** ────

Official Name: Spanish State.
Location: Iberian Peninsula in southwestern Europe.
Area: 194,897 square miles (504,782 sq km).
Population (1975 est.): 35,400,000.
Chief Cities (1975): Madrid, the capital, 3,500,000; Barcelona, 2,000,000; Valencia, 700,000.
Government: *Head of state,* King Juan Carlos I (took office Nov. 1975). *Head of government,* Carlos Arias Navarro, premier (took office Jan. 1975). *Legislature* (unicameral)—Las Cortes Españolas.
Monetary Unit: Peseta (58.35 pesetas equal U. S.$1, July 1975).
Gross National Product (1974 est.): $74,600,000,000.
Manufacturing (major products): Iron and steel, electrical machinery, automobiles, textiles, chemicals, ships, processed foods, leather.
Major Agricultural Products: Wheat, rye, barley, corn, citrus fruits, vegetables, almonds, olives, potatoes, fish, forest products, sheep.
Foreign Trade (1974): *Exports,* $7,157,000,000; *imports,* $15,502,000,000.

UPI

SPORTS

By Bill Braddock
"The New York Times"

Money, or the lack of it, was the root of most off-the-field problems in sports in 1975. Owners of many franchises were more concerned with finding financial backers than with the acquisition of players. With the recession economy in the United States, substantial help was not forthcoming. One football league died, a basketball league tottered, a hockey league shook, and even major league baseball became concerned over the future of some of its clubs as the year ended.

The predicted collapse of the World Football League came in October. When the league finished a disastrous first season, there had been some doubt of its trying again. New financial planning got it underway, but lack of attendance and television backing put it out of business on October 23.

Meanwhile, the American Basketball Association (ABA) made a continual and losing effort to keep all of its clubs alive, and there was speculation that the league would fold completely. Some said that the only salvation lay in a merger with the National Basketball Association (NBA). This was not a new idea. It had

already been blocked by the players' association, which had obtained a court ruling against the merger as an antitrust violation. There was no real reason for the NBA to merge. Through its own draft the NBA teams had rights to most of the ABA players.

The ABA started the season by moving the shaky Memphis Sounds to Baltimore, but the new club collapsed before play began. A few weeks later the San Diego Sails folded, and only last-minute efforts kept the Virginia Squires temporarily in business. By December, despite talk of merging with the Spirits of St. Louis, the Utah Stars had been dissolved. The St. Louis owner had considered moving to Cincinnati because of low attendance. Instead, St. Louis bought some of the Stars' players and hoped to lure new fans.

The NBA revealed that the average salary of its players was $109,781. Even with revenues from television, which amounted to at least $500,-000 for each team, there were money problems. However, the NBA was bolstered by a 15%–20% rise in attendance at the start of the 1975–76 season. One of the top NBA players did not have too much compassion for the owners' financial problems. "They made the contracts," he said. The average ABA salary was just under $100,000, and there was no overall income from television. The league had what it considered to be sound franchises in Louisville, Ky.; Indian-

apolis, Ind.; Long Island; San Antonio, Tex.; Denver, Colo.; and, if attendance improved, St. Louis.

The chief concern in hockey, especially in the National Hockey League (NHL), was a drop in attendance, the main source of income. Both leagues lost TV agreements. There were some clubs in the World Hockey Association (WHA) that appeared to be in serious trouble. During the off-season the Chicago and Baltimore franchises were dissolved, and the Vancouver franchise was moved to Calgary. The Minnesota Fighting Saints were battling with the North Stars of the NHL for the Twin Cities fans. The North Stars' attendance was down, probably because the team was worse. Two new WHA clubs had varying fortunes. The Cincinnati Stingers were thriving, but the Denver Spurs were unsuccessful and were moved to Ottawa, Ontario, as the year ended.

Baseball owners in December had to deal with the problems of two financially-disturbed teams, the Chicago White Sox and the San Francisco Giants. Bill Veeck, a former owner, finally came through with enough money to buy the White Sox and to keep the American League club in Chicago. The difficulties that faced Horace Stoneham and his Giants were unsettled at year's end.

Meanwhile, players' salaries in the big leagues had risen to a $50,000 average. An excellent World Series, watched on TV by record numbers of viewers, kept the owners satisfied with everything except their managers. They replaced about half of them. The players, however, were still making war on the reserve clause and demanding revised pension agreements. There was

Arthur Ashe beat Jimmy Connors in four sets to win the tennis championship at Wimbledon.

an ominous aura of a strike or a lockout before the start of the 1976 season.

Owners in the National Football League (NFL) also faced action by the players over pensions. The players wanted pay for exhibition games and what they called "freedom" issues. These had to do with contract options and the Rozelle Rule, by which the commissioner decided the terms on which a player who had played out his option could be signed by another team. The players wanted an arbitrator to decide the cases. The New England Patriots actually struck just before the start of the season. They were joined by some other teams, but the dispute was settled before it became a major issue. The players' position was supported on December 30, when a U. S. district court in Minneapolis ruled that the Rozelle Rule violated antitrust laws.

College Athletics. Most colleges had serious trouble maintaining complete athletic programs because of the general budget cutbacks in colleges. They were also disturbed by Title IX, the U. S. law that mandated equal rights for women's athletics, and a debate ensued over whether equal rights meant equal expenditures.

The National Collegiate Athletic Association (NCAA), trying to aid the colleges, ordered slashes in coaching staffs, banned the $15-per-month expense money for scholarship grants, and limited the size of traveling squads. The NCAA estimated that these moves cut total costs for schools in Divisions I and II, the larger institutions, by $15 million. Bear Bryant, the Alabama football coach, and Bobby Knight, the Indiana basketball coach, went to court over the order cutting their traveling squads.

Ohio State's Archie Griffin became the first player to win the coveted Heisman Trophy twice.

AUTO RACING

A. J. Foyt and Richard Petty raced different types of cars at different tracks, but they wound up with similar honors. Foyt took the United States Auto Club (USAC) championship for the sixth time, while Petty won the Nascar Grand National championship for the sixth time. Niki Lauda won the world championship, capturing five races.

Foyt won $355,662 on the USAC Championship Trail, and Petty won $378,865 in the Nascar Grand National Winston Cup competition. One big difference between their honors was that Foyt won his purses in 12 races, but Petty needed 30 contests, in which he finished first 13 times.

Foyt took the California 500 and $110,058. He finished third to Bobby Unser in the Indianapolis 500 and earned $74,667 and then won the Pocono-Schaefer 500 and $84,050. The 40-year-

Auto Racing Highlights

World Championship Grand Prix Races

Argentina (Buenos Aires, Jan. 12)—Emerson Fittipaldi, Brazil, driving a McLaren-Ford; distance 200 miles; time: 1 hour, 39 minutes, 26.29 seconds; average speed: 118.657 miles per hour

Brazil (São Paulo, Jan. 26)—Carlos Pace, Brazil; Brabham; 208 miles; 1:44:41.17; 113.316 mph

South Africa (Johannesburg, March 1)—Jody Scheckter, South Africa; Tyrrell-Ford; 200 miles; 1:43:16.90; 115.516 mph

Spain (Barcelona, April 27)—Jochen Mass, West Germany; McLaren-Ford; race cut to 64.4 miles because of accident that killed 4 spectators; points to leaders cut in half; 95.33 mph

Monaco (Monte Carlo, May 11)—Niki Lauda, Austria; Ferrari; 152.775 miles; 2:01:23.1; 75.53 mph

Belgium (Zolder, May 25)—Lauda; 184.6 miles; 1:43:53.98; 107.6 mph

Sweden (Anderstorp, June 8)—Lauda; 200 miles; 1:59:18; 100.5 mph

Netherlands (Zandvoort, June 22)—Jame Hunt, England; Hesketh-Ford; 197 miles; 1:46:57.40; 110.51 mph

France (Paul Ricard, July 6)—Lauda; 195 miles; 1:40:18.-84; 116.612 mph

Britain (Silverstone, July 19)—Fittipaldi; cut to 164 miles by rain; 1:22:00.5; 120.01 mph

Germany (Neuerburgring, Aug. 3)—Carlos Reutemann; Argentina; Brabham; 198.8 miles; 1:41:14.1; 117.66 mph

Austria (Zeltweg, Aug. 17)—Vittorio Brambilla, Italy; March-Ford; 57:59.6; cut to 108 miles by rain; 111.6 mph

Italy (Monza, Sept. 7)—Clay Regazzoni, Switzerland; Ferrari; 187 miles; 1:22:42.6; 136 mph

United States (Watkins Glen, Oct. 5)—Lauda; 199.243 miles; 1:42:58.175; 116.1 mph

United States Auto Club Championship Trail

Indianapolis 500 (Indianapolis Motor Speedway, May 25; cut to 435 miles by rain)—Bobby Unser, Albuquerque, N. M., driving Eagle-Offy; 174 laps; 2 hours, 54 minutes, 55.08 seconds; average speed 149.213 mph; winner's purse: $214,031

California 500 (Ontario, Calif., Motor Speedway, March 9)—A. J. Foyt, Houston, Tex.; Coyote-Ford; 200 laps; 3:14:22.28; 154.344 mph; $110,058

Schaefer 500 (Pocono International Speedway, June 29—cut to 425 miles by rain)—Foyt; 170 laps; 3:01:-13.30; 140.712 mph; $84,050

Bricklin 150 (Phoenix, Ariz., March 16)—Johnny Rutherford, Fort Worth, Tex.; McLaren-Offy; 150 laps; 1:21:06.12; 110.971 mph; $9,542

Trentonian 200 (Trenton, N. J., March 16)—Foyt; 134 laps; 1:17:59.07; 154.625 mph; $11,937

Rex Mays 150 (Milwaukee, June 8)—Foyt; 150 laps; 1:18:55.08; 114.042 mph; $17,039

Norton 200 (Brooklyn, Mich., July 20)—Foyt; 100 laps; 1:15:30.95; 158.907 mph; $15,562

Bettenhausen 200 (Milwaukee, Aug. 17)—Mike Mosley, Clermont, Ind.; Eagle-Offy; 200 laps; 1:44:54.07; 114.393 mph; $14,974

Michigan Grand Prix (Brooklyn, Mich., Sept. 13)—Tom Sneva, Spokane, Wash.; Penske-McLaren; 150 miles; 51:05:39; 176.160 mph; $11,821

Trenton 150 (Trenton, N. J., Sept. 21)—Gordon Johncock, Brownsville, Ind.; Wildcat; 1:12:52.07; 123.511 mph; $10,870

Phoenix 150 (Phoenix, Ariz., Nov. 9)—Foyt; 150 laps; 1:21:3; 111.055; $15,340

National Association for Stock Car Auto Racing
(Races of 400 or more miles)

Winston Western 500 (Riverside, Calif., Jan. 26)—Bobby Allison, Hueytown, Ala.; Matador; 5 hours, 4 minutes, 26 seconds; average speed: 98.627 mph; winner's purse: $12,035

Daytona 500 (Daytona Beach, Fla., Feb. 16)—Benny Parsons, Ellerbe, N. C.; Chevrolet; 3:15:15; 153.649 mph; $40,900

Carolina 500 (Rockingham, N. C., March 2)—Cale Yarborough, Timmonsville, S. C.; Chevrolet; 4:15:18; 117.588 mph; $14,200

Atlanta 500 (Hampton, Ga., March 23)—Richard Petty, Randleman, N. C., Dodge; 3:44:06; 133.496 mph; $16,500

Rebel 500 (Darlington, S. C., April 13)—Allison; 4:15:41; 117.597; $15,080

Winston 500 (Talladega, Ala., May 4)—Buddy Baker, Charlotte, N. C.; Ford; 3:26:59; 144.948 mph; $25,725

Mason Dixon 500 (Dover, Del., May 18–19; race halted after 140 laps by rain and resumed next day)—David Pearson, Spartanburg, S. C.; Mercury; 4:57:32; $14,-925

World 600 (Charlotte, N. C., May 25)—Petty; 4:07:42; 145.327 mph; $27,290

Tuborg 400 (Riverside, Calif., June 8)—Petty; 3:58:04; 101.028 mph; $15,135

Motor State 400 (Brooklyn, Mich., June 15)—Pearson; 3:02:39; 131.398 mph; $14,405

Firecracker 400 (Daytona Beach, Fla., July 4)—Petty; 2:31:32; 158.381 mph; $16,935

Purolator 500 (Pocono, Long Pond, Pa., Aug. 3)—Pearson; 3:29:10; 111.179 mph; $15,225

Talladega 500 (Talladega, Ala., Aug. 17)—Baker; 130.892 mph; $23,390

Champion Spark Plug 400 (Brooklyn, Mich., Aug. 24)—Petty; 3:43:05; 107.583 mph; $15,140

Southern 500 (Darlington, S. C., Sept. 1)—Allison; 4:21:-29; 116.828 mph; $22,150

Delaware 500 (Dover, Sept. 14)—Petty; 4:29:22; 111.372 mph; $15,250

National 500 (Charlotte, N. C., Oct. 5)—Petty; 3:47:22; 132.209 mph; $27,970

American 500 (Rockingham, N. C., Oct. 19)—Yarborough; 4:09:54; 120.129 mph; $16,930

Dixie 500 (Atlanta, Ga., Nov. 9)—Baker; 3:48:40; 130.90 mph; $15,550

Times 500 (Ontario, Calif., Nov. 23)—Baker; 3:33:12; 140.712 mph; $32,300

Other Major Sports Car Events

24 Hours of Daytona (Daytona, Fla., Feb. 1–2)—Peter Gregg and Hurley Haywood, Jacksonville, Fla.; Porsche Carrera; 2,606.04 miles; average speed: 108.531

Monza 1,000 Kilometers (Monza, Italy, 621 miles, April 20)—Jacques LaFitte, France, and Arturo Merzario, Italy; Alfa Romeo; 4:43:21.8; 131.802 mph

1,000 Kilometers of Spa (Francorchamps, Belgium; cut to 750 kilometers by rain, May 4)—Henri Pescarolo, France, and Derek Bell, England; Alfa Romeo; 3:32:58

Coppa Florio (Pergusa, Sicily, May 18)—Merzario and Jochen Mass, West Germany; Alfa Romeo; 5:25

24 Hours of Le Mans (Le Mans, France, June 14–15)—Jacky Ickx, Belgium, and Derek Bell, England; Gulf-Mirage-Ford; 2,850.55 miles; 118.98 mph

1,000 Kilometers of Austria (Zeltwegd, June 29; cut to 600 kilometers by rain; June 29)—Pecarolo and Bell; 3:34:50.8; 105 mph

Six Hours of Watkins Glen (Watkins Glen, N. Y.; cut to 4 hours, 49 minutes by rain; July 12)—Pescarolo and Bell; 506.55 miles

Individual Champions

World Grand Prix—Niki Lauda, Austria (64½ pts)

United States Auto Club—Championship Trail: A. J. Foyt, Houston, Tex. (4,920 pts; $355,662); stock car: Ramo Stott, Keokuk, Iowa; Plymouth (2,360 pts); dirt track: Jimmy Caruthers, Anaheim, Calif. (700 pts); sprint car: Larry Dickson, Marietta, Ohio (831 pts); midget: Ron (Sleepy) Tripp, Costa Mesa, Calif. (828 pts); Formula 5000 (run in conjunction with Sports Car Club of America); Brian Redman, England; Lola (227 pts)

Nascar—Grand National: Richard Petty, Randleman, N. C. (record sixth title): Dodge (4,783 pts; $378,865; Late Model Sportsman: L. D. Ottinger, Newport, Tenn. (9,417 pts); Modified: Jerry Cook, Rome, N. Y. (4,805 pts)

International Motor Sports Association—Camel GT Challenge Series (17 races): Peter Gregg, Jacksonville, Fla. (149½ pts; $44,175); leading money winner, Al Holbert, Warrington, Pa.; $46,025; Goodrich 250; Nick Craw, Washington (138 pts; $10,900); Bosch Gold Cup: Eddie Miller, Lakewood, Colo. (118 pts)

UPI

World champion Niki Lauda of Austria won the U.S. Grand Prix in October at Watkins Glen, N.Y.

old driver from Houston also won four of the shorter USAC races, the last on November 9 at Phoenix. It was his 54th Championship Trail victory.

Petty, 38, who drives a Dodge, posted his first victory on March 23 in the Atlanta 500 but received only $16,500. He took the Nascar title for the second year in a row and won more than $300,000 for the second time.

Bobby Unser's victory at Indianapolis was his second in the nation's most glamorous race. But this time a cloudburst ended the race after 435 miles. Driving an Eagle-Offy prepared by Dan Gurney, he beat Johnny Rutherford, the 1974 victor by 54 seconds. Foyt, in a Coyote-Ford of his own design, was driving with an ailing hip. Unser won $214,031.

In grand prix racing, Niki Lauda of Austria won the world title with 64½ points. He was first in 5 of the 14 races. Emerson Fittipaldi of Brazil, the 1974 champion, was second.

In pre-race practice for the Austrian Grand Prix, Mark Donohue, 38, one of the United States' most popular drivers, was critically injured. He died during brain surgery. Donohue had returned to racing after an eight-month retirement. Others killed during the season were Tiny Lund, a Nascar driver, Graham Hill, a former grand prix winner, and Tony Brise. Hill and Brise were killed in a plane crash on November 30.

BASEBALL

Baseball fans became so enchanted by the World Series battle between the Boston Red Sox and Cincinnati Reds that a record 75.9 million people watched the television broadcast of the final game on October 22. Cincinnati won that seventh game 4–3 with a run in the ninth inning, and took the championship, 4 games to 3. The sixth game, which the Red Sox won 7–6 on Carlton Fisk's homer in the 12th inning, was still being acclaimed as one of the greatest games in series history when the teams lined up again in Boston's Fenway Park for the conclusion.

The championship was the third for Cincinnati, but its first since 1940. Boston was playing in its eighth series and seeking its sixth triumph. The Red Sox, who won the first series in 1903, had not been champions since 1918. There was a strong opinion in New England that Boston would have been the champion in 1975 if the plate umpire had ruled interference on a sacrifice play in the 10th inning of the third game. Ed Armbrister bunted to the right of the plate and collided with Fisk, the Boston catcher. Fisk's wild throw to second allowed the runner from first to go to third, and he scored on a following hit. Boston claimed interference, but plate umpire Larry Barnett said no, and he was upheld by the other umpires.

The two league champions moved into the playoffs by diverse routes. Cincinnati's Big Red Machine won the Western Division with 108 victories, the most in the National League (NL) since Chicago's 116 in 1906. In the playoffs, the Reds routed Pittsburgh in three straight games. The Red Sox gained first place on June 29, but had to survive a late surge by Baltimore before clinching the American League (AL) Eastern Division title the day before the season ended.

The loss of Jim (Catfish) Hunter from their fine pitching staff did not keep the Oakland A's from taking the AL Western Division honors for the fifth straight year. It may have had some effect in the playoffs, where the A's bid for a fourth straight world championship was sabotaged by Boston in three games. Hunter, declared a free agent by an arbitrator in December 1974 after a contract dispute with Oakland, was signed to a $2.85 million pact by the New York Yankees. He won 23 games for New York.

The Red Sox, who had faded in the stretch in 1974, turned up with some amazing young players. Fred Lynn, a centerfielder, batted .331, knocked in 105 runs, and led the league in runs with 103. He was voted the AL most valuable player as well as rookie of the year and became the first player to win both awards in one season. Jim Rice, another rookie, served as left fielder and designated hitter. His left hand was broken by a pitch on September 21, ending his season. He batted .309, hit 22 homers, and drove in 102 runs. In June, Boston acquired Denny Doyle from California to play second base. He

UPI

Pirate Manny Sanguillen waits to tag Cincinnati's Cesar Geronimo in the National League playoffs.

solidified the infield. Carl Yastrzemski, Rico Petrocelli, and Fisk were the team's seasoned veterans. The pitchers were led by Rick Wise, Bill Lee, Reggie Cleveland, and Luis Tiant, a 34-year-old Cuban with varied deliveries who won two games in the series.

The Reds had strength at all positions. They were sparked by Johnny Bench, a catcher who was the NL's most valuable player in 1970 and 1972; Pete Rose, the 1973 NL player of the year; and 31-year-old Joe Morgan at second base. Morgan set the pace for the Reds' speedy baserunners. He hit .327, batted in 94 runs, and was voted most valuable in the NL. Rose moved to third base to give George Foster a chance to play left field next to Cesar Geronimo, an outstanding centerfielder. Tony Perez was at first and Dave Concepcion at short. The pitchers were led by Don Gullett, Gary Nolan, and Jack

Baseball Highlights

Professional—Major Leagues

AMERICAN LEAGUE
(Final Standings, 1975)

EASTERN DIVISION	W	L	Pct.	WESTERN DIVISION	W	L	Pct.
Boston	95	65	.594	Oakland	98	64	.605
Baltimore	90	69	.566	Kansas City	91	71	.562
New York	83	77	.519	Texas	79	83	.488
Cleveland	79	80	.497	Minnesota	76	86	.478
Milwaukee	68	94	.420	Chicago	75	86	.466
Detroit	57	102	.358	California	72	89	.447

NATIONAL LEAGUE
(Final Standings, 1975)

EASTERN DIVISION	W	L	Pct.	WESTERN DIVISION	W	L	Pct.
Pittsburgh	92	69	.571	Cincinnati	108	54	.667
Philadelphia	86	76	.531	Los Angeles	88	74	.543
New York	82	80	.506	San Francisco	80	81	.497
St. Louis	82	80	.506	San Diego	71	91	.438
Chicago	75	87	.463	Atlanta	67	94	.416
Montreal	75	87	.463	Houston	64	97	.398

Playoffs—American League: Boston defeated Oakland, 3 games to 0; National League: Cincinnati defeated Pittsburgh, 3 games to 0

World Series—Cincinnati defeated Boston, 4 games to 3; paid attendance, 7 games, 308,272; total receipts, $3,380,580; commissioner's office share, $507,087; share for each club and each league, $464,533; players' share of playoffs and series, $1,826,264 ($1,015,361 from first four games of series and $810,-903 from playoffs); including full shares of $19,060 for each Cincinnati player and $13,326 for each Boston player

First Game (Fenway Park, Boston, Oct. 11): Boston 6, Cincinnati 0; second game (Boston, Oct. 12): Cincinnati 3, Boston 2; third game (Riverfront Stadium, Cincinnati, Oct. 14): Cincinnati 6, Boston 5; fourth game (Cincinnati, Oct. 15): Boston 5, Cincinnati 4; fifth game (Cincinnati, Oct. 16): Cincinnati 6, Boston 2; sixth game (Boston, Oct. 21): rain and flooded grounds delayed series for three days: Boston 7, Cincinnati 6 (12 innings); seventh game (Boston, Oct. 22): Cincinnati 4, Boston 3

All-Star Game (Milwaukee, July 15)—National League 6, American League 3

Most Valuable Players—American League: Fred Lynn, Boston outfielder; National League: Joe Morgan, Cincinnati second baseman

Cy Young Memorial Awards (outstanding pitchers)—American League: Jim Palmer, Baltimore; National League: Tom Seaver, New York

Rookie of the Year—American League: Fred Lynn, Boston; National League: John Montefusco, San Francisco pitcher

Leading Batters—Percentage: American: Rod Carew, Minnesota, .359; National: Bill Madlock, Chicago, .354. Runs Batted In: American: George Scott, Milwaukee, 109; National: Greg Luzinski, Philadelphia, 121. Home Runs: American: Reggie Jackson, Oakland, and Scott, 36; National: Mike Schmidt, Philadelphia, 38

Leading Pitchers—Earned Run Average: American: Jim Palmer, Baltimore, 2.09; National: Randy Jones, San Diego, 2.23. Victories: American: Jim (Catfish) Hun-

ter, New York and Palmer, 23; National: Tom Seaver, New York, 22. Strikeouts: American: Frank Tanana, California, 268; National: Seaver, 243.

No-Hit Games Pitched—Nolan Ryan, California (AL) vs. Baltimore, 1–0; Ed Halicki, San Francisco (NL) vs. New York, 6–0; Vida Blue (5 innings), Glenn Abbott (1), Paul Lindblad (1), Rollie Fingers (2), Oakland (AL) vs. Calif., 5–0

Hall of Fame Inductees—Howard Earl Averill; Stanley Raymond Harris; William Jennings (Billy) Herman; Ralph McPherran Kiner; William Julius Johnson

Professional—Minor Leagues

American Association (AAA)—Evansville, East Division and playoff; Denver, West Division

International League (AAA)—Tidewater, regular season and playoffs

Pacific Coast League (AAA)—Salt Lake City, East Division; Hawaii, West Division and playoffs

Mexican League (AAA)—Tampico, Northeastern Division and playoffs; Saltillo, Northwestern Division; Cordoba, Southeastern Division, Puebla, Southwestern Division

Little World Series (American Association vs. International League)—Evansville defeated Tidewater, 4 games to 1

Eastern League (AA)—Reading, first half; Bristol, second half and championship

Southern League (AA)—Montgomery, Western Division and championship; Orlando, Eastern Division

Texas League (AA)—Lafayette, Eastern Division; Midland, Western Division; declared co-champions when rain cancelled fifth game with teams tied in games, 2–2

California League (A)—Reno

Carolina League (A)—Rocky Mount

Florida State League (A)—St. Petersburg, Northern Division and playoffs; Southern Division, Miami

Midwest League (A)—Waterloo, Northern Division and playoffs; Quad Cities, Southern Division

New York-Pennsylvania League (A)—Newark

Northwest League (A)—Eugene, Southern Division and playoffs; Portland, Northern Division

Western Carolina League (A)—Spartanburg

Intercollegiate Champions

NCAA—Division 1: Texas (defeated South Carolina, 5–1, in final); Division II: Florida Southern (defeated Marietta, 10–7, in final)

NAIA—Lewis University (defeated Sam Houston, 2–1, in final)

Amateur Champions

American Legion—Yakima, Wash.

Babe Ruth League (16–18)—Kirkland, Wash.

Big League World Series—Taiwan

Bronco League—San Pedro, Calif.

Colt League—Santa Clara, Calif.

Connie Mack League—Long Beach (Calif.) Cardinals

Dixie Youth World Series—Hattiesburg, Miss.

Little League—Lakewood Township, Ocean County, N. J. (defeated Tampa All-Stars, 4–3, in final)

Little League Senior—Mei-ho Club, Ping Tung, Taiwan

Mickey Mantle League—Putty Hill Optimists, Baltimore

National Baseball Congress—Boulder, Colo.

Pee Wee Reese League—Dallas (Tex.) Scorpions

Pony League—Covina, Calif.

Sandy Koufax League—Bayamon, Puerto Rico

Stan Musial League—Bishop Contractors, Flint, Mich.

Thorobred League—San Jose, Calif.

Billingham. They were aided by Rawly East-wick, who had 44 saves. The rookie was credited with one victory in the playoffs and two in the series.

The Cy Young pitching awards went to Jim Palmer of the Orioles, who led the AL in earned run average with 2.09 and tied Hunter for victories at 23; and to Tom Seaver of the Mets, who led the NL with 22 victories. Seaver struck out over 200 batters for the eighth season in a row, bettering the record shared by Walter Johnson and Rube Waddell. John (The Count) Montefusco, a San Francisco pitcher, was the NL rookie of the year. Rod Carew, with an average of .359, led AL hitters for the fourth straight season, while Bill Madlock of the Cubs was tops in the NL with .354.

Professional Basketball Highlights

National Basketball Association
(Final Standings, 1974–75)

Eastern Conference
Atlantic Division

	W	L	Pct.	For	Agst
Boston Celtics	60	22	.732	106.5	100.8
Buffalo Braves	49	33	.598	107.8	105.6
New York Knicks	40	42	.488	100.4	101.7
Philadelphia 76ers	34	48	.415	99.8	102.8

Central Division

	W	L	Pct.	For	Agst
Washington Bullets	60	22	.732	104.7	97.5
Houston Rockets	41	41	.500	103.9	102.9
Cleveland Cavaliers	40	42	.488	99.0	99.4
Atlanta Hawks	31	51	.378	105.1	106.5
New Orleans Jazz	23	59	.280	101.5	109.3

Western Conference
Midwest Division

	W	L	Pct.	For	Agst
Chicago Bulls	47	35	.573	98.1	95.0
Kansas City–Omaha Kings	44	38	.537	101.4	101.6
Detroit Pistons	40	42	.488	98.9	100.3
Milwaukee Bucks	38	44	.463	100.7	100.5

Pacific Division

	W	L	Pct.	For	Agst
Golden State Warriors	48	34	.585	108.5	105.2
Seattle SuperSonics	43	39	.524	103.1	104.1
Portland Trail Blazers	38	44	.463	103.8	103.3
Phoenix Suns	32	50	.390	101.2	103.6
Los Angeles Lakers	30	52	.366	103.2	107.2

Eastern Conference Playoffs—final: Washington defeated Boston, 4 games to 2; Western Conference: Golden State defeated Chicago, 4 games to 3; NBA championship: Golden State defeated Washington, 4 games to 0
Most Valuable Player—Bob McAdoo, Buffalo
Rookie of the Year—Keith Wilkes, Golden State
Leading Scorer—McAdoo, 2,831 points; 34.5 average per game

American Basketball Association
(Final Standings, 1974–75)

Eastern Division

	W	L	Pct.	Scoring Avg. For	Agst
Kentucky Colonels*	58	26	.690	108.9	101.7
New York Nets	58	26	.690	111.0	103.4
St. Louis, Spirits of	32	52	.381	109.0	113.4
Memphis Sounds	27	57	.321	103.6	108.9
Virginia Squires	15	69	.179	99.0	109.5

* Won playoff for first place

Western Division

	W	L	Pct.	For	Agst
Denver Nuggets	65	19	.774	118.7	111.4
San Antonio Spurs	51	33	.607	113.4	109.2
Indiana Pacers	45	39	.536	112.7	111.9
Utah Stars	38	46	.452	101.3	102.9
San Diego Conquistadors	31	53	.369	109.9	115.5

Eastern Division Playoffs—Final: Kentucky defeated St. Louis, 4 games to 1. Western Division: final: Indiana defeated Denver, 4 games to 3. ABA championship: Kentucky defeated Indiana, 4 games to 1
Most Valuable Player—Tie between Julius Erving, New York, and George McGinnis, Indiana
Rookie of the Year—Marvin Barnes, St. Louis
Leading Scorer—McGinnis, 2,353 points, 29.8 average per game

BASKETBALL

Professional

The playoffs in the National Basketball Association (NBA) were missing two of the usual ingredients—the perennially very strong Los Angeles Lakers and the Milwaukee Bucks. The playoffs took a still stranger turn when the Golden State Warriors won the championship, routing the favored Washington Bullets in four games. It was only the third time that a team had swept the final series.

Rick Barry paced the Warriors to their surprising victory, but it was their sounder all-round play that was the key to their success. The Bullets appeared to have cleared their biggest obstacle in the East Conference final by stopping the Boston Celtics, the only one of the usual powers to get into the playoffs. Washington and Boston had identical season won-lost records of 60–22, the best in the league. The fading of the Lakers, Knicks, and Bucks indicated a wide shift in the balance of power and brought about a large exchange of players during the summer.

The Knicks, needing a center, sought Kareem Abdul-Jabbar, who was unhappy in Milwaukee, but he went to Los Angeles. New York then got George McGinnis to leave Indiana of the American Basketball Association (ABA). However, Philadelphia held the NBA rights to the star center and received the player. New York was fined its first draft pick in 1976 for violating league rules.

In the American Basketball Association, 29 players were exchanged in efforts to bolster the line-ups. The Kentucky Colonels had finally won the championship by beating Indiana. Ten clubs were to begin the 1975–76 season, but Baltimore (the former Memphis franchise) gave up before play started, and San Diego folded two weeks after it began.

College

For most of the season Indiana was rated the top team. The Hoosiers rolled through the Big Ten competition with a perfect record of 18 victories, and on into the semifinals of the NCAA playoffs with an unbeaten string of 34 games. However, the Kentucky Wildcats then edged Indiana, 92–90. That made the Wildcats the favorites of the four teams left—Kentucky, Syracuse, Louisville, and the University of California, Los Angeles (UCLA).

In the semifinals, Kentucky routed Syracuse, 95–79, after UCLA had beaten Louisville, 75–74, on Rich Washington's shot with 4 seconds left in overtime. That brought together Kentucky, a tournament veteran that had won the title 4 times, and the UCLA Bruins, a 9-time winner.

Drama was added to the final in San Diego by the announcement by UCLA coach John Wooden that he was retiring. The championship game was a battle between big, bruising Ken-

UPI

tucky and fast-breaking and resourceful UCLA. The Bruins, who led 43–40 at the half, gradually pulled away and won 92–85.

It was the 10th championship in 12 years for UCLA, which had lost in the semifinals in 1974 after winning 7 straight titles. North Carolina State, the 1974 national champions, did not reach the playoffs in 1975.

Old Dominion defeated New Orleans, 76–74, for the Division II NCAA title, and LeMoyne-Owen of Memphis took Division III honors, defeating Glassboro State (N. J.), 57–54. The NAIA championship went to Grand Canyon of Arizona on a 65–64 victory over Midwestern of Texas. Delta State of Mississippi ended Immaculata of Philadelphia's three-year reign in women's college competition with a 90–81 victory in the final.

Rick Barry (*above*) paced the Golden State Warriors to the NBA championship. UCLA (*below*) continued to dazzle the fans, winning its 10th NCAA title.

UPI

Amateur Basketball Highlights

Major Tournaments

NCAA—Division I (San Diego, March 31)—UCLA 92, Kentucky 85; Division II (Evansville, Ind., March 15)—Old Dominion 76, New Orleans 74; Division III (Reading, Pa., March 15): LeMoyne-Owen 84, Glassboro State 54

National Intercollegiate (NAIA, Kansas City, March 15)—Grand Canyon 65, Midwestern 54

National Invitation Tournament (New York, March 23)—Princeton 80, Providence 69

Association for Intercollegiate Athletics for Women (AIAW, Harrisonburg, Va., March 22)—Delta State 90, Immaculata 81

Men's AAU (New Orleans, March 22)—Capitol Insulation, Los Angeles 105, California Junior College All-Stars 91

Women's AAU (Gallup, N. M., April 5)—Wayland Baptist College 68, Fullerton, Calif. 45

National Junior College (Hutchinson, Kan., March 22)—Western Texas 65, Southern Idaho 57

College Conference Champions

(Figures in parentheses indicate victories and losses in conference games only.)

Atlantic Coast—North Carolina (8–4); won championship tourney

Big Eight—Kansas (11–3)

Big Sky—Montana (13–1)

Big Ten—Indiana (18–0)

East Coast—East Section: La Salle (5–1) and American University (5–1). West Section: Lafayette (7–1) Lafayette won playoffs

Ivy League—Pennsylvania (13–1)

Mid-American—Central Michigan (10–4)

Missouri Valley—Louisville (12–2)

Ohio Valley—Middle Tennessee (14–2)

Pacific 8—University of California, Los Angeles (12–2)

Pacific Coast Athletic—Long Beach State (8–2)

Southeastern—Alabama (15–3) and Kentucky (15–3); Kentucky gained tournament berth because of record against Alabama

Southern—Furman (12–0); won championship tournament

Southwest—Texas A&M (12–2)

West Coast Athletic—Nevada–Las Vegas (13–1)

Western Athletic—Arizona State (12–2)

Yankee—Massachusetts (10–2)

BOXING

Muhammad Ali, who once said that boxing would die when he retired, carried out a big program to keep the sport alive in 1975. He defended the title four times in his second reign as heavyweight champion. Two of his bouts were fought in Asia, where heavyweights had previously been legends. In the fourth and most important of his bouts, Ali beat Joe Frazier in the third and rubber match of their series. That triumph, coming less than a year after he had demolished George Foreman and regained the title, convinced the most stubborn that Ali was

World heavyweight champion Muhammed Ali (*right*) pounds Joe Frazier during October bout in Manila. In a grueling fight Ali retained his title with a technical knockout after 14 rounds.

UPI

the best of the big fighters. Three other well-established leaders in their classes retained titles, but there were 11 new names on the championship lists of either the World Boxing Association or the World Boxing Council.

Ali knocked out Chuck Wepner, the pride of New Jersey, in his first defense in the 15th round at Richfield, Ohio, on March 24. He stopped Ron Lyle in the 11th round at Las Vegas, Nev., on May 16, and then outpointed Joe Bugner, the British and European champion, in the tropical heat of Kuala Lumpur, Malaysia, on July 1.

In what was described as a classic battle, Ali outlasted Frazier in Manila on October 1. Ali had the better of the fight in the early rounds, Frazier in the middle. Ali rallied at the close, and Frazier's manager tossed in the towel before the start of the 15th round to keep the former champion, whose eyes were almost closed, from serious injury. It went into the records as a knockout in the 14th round, the 34th by Ali in 49 bouts. He had lost only twice, once to Frazier and once to Ken Norton.

The longest reigning champion, Carlos Monzon of Argentina, successfully defended for the 12th time the WBA middleweight title that he won in 1970. He knocked out Gratien Tonna of France in the 5th round in Paris on December 14. It was his 80th consecutive victory. Roberto Duran of Panama kept the WBA lightweight crown. He knocked out Leoncío Ortiz of Mexico in December at San Juan, Puerto Rico. It was Duran's seventh defense since becoming champion in 1972. Antonio Cervantes of Colombia retained the WBA junior welterweight title by outpointing Esteban de Jesus of Panama, and stopping Hector Thompson of Australia in eight rounds.

A bad cut over his right eye ended the long tenure of Jose (Mantequilla) Napoles of Mexico as WBC welterweight champion. The bout was stopped in the sixth round at Mexico City on December 6, and the title was awarded to John Stracey of England. Napoles, champion since 1971, had twice beaten Armando Muniz of Los Angeles earlier in the year. Between those bouts the WBA stripped him of its title because he did not fight an approved challenger. Angel Espada of Puerto Rico won the vacated title by beating Clyde Gray of Toronto, on June 28. On October 11 he retained the title in a bout against Johnny Gant of Washington.

After Napoles had lost in Mexico City, Alfonso Zamora knocked out Socrates Batoto of the Philippines in the second round and retained the WBA bantamweight title.

Boxing Highlights

World Professional Champions

Junior Flyweight—Luís Estaba, Venezuela, World Boxing Council; new class not recognized by World Boxing Association

Flyweight—Erbito Salavarria, Philippines, WBA; Miguel Canto, Mexico, WBC

Bantamweight—Alfonso Zamora, Mexico, WBA; Rodolfo Martinez, Mexico, WBC

Featherweight—Alexis Arguello, Nicaragua, WBA; David Kotey, Ghana, WBC

Junior Lightweight—Ben Villaflor, Philippines, WBA; Alfredo Escalera, Puerto Rico, WBC

Lightweight—Roberto Duran, Panama, WBA; Guts Ishimatsu (Ishimatsu Suzuki), Japan, WBC

Junior Welterweight—Antonio Cervantes, Colombia, WBA; Saensak Muargsurin, Thailand, WBC

Welterweight—Angel Espada, Puerto Rico, WBA; John Stracey, England, WBC

Junior Middleweight—Elisha O'Bed, Bahamas, WBC; Yu Jae Do, South Korea, WBA

Middleweight—Carlos Monzon, Argentina, WBA; Rodrigo Valdez, Colombia, WBC

Light Heavyweight—Victor Galindez, Argentina, WBA; John Conteh, England, WBC

Heavyweight—Muhammad Ali, Cherry Hill, N. J.

National AAU Champions
(Shreveport, La., June 10-14)

106 Pounds—Claudell Atkins, St. Louis, Mo.
112 Pounds—Richard Rozelle, Columbus, Ohio
119 Pounds—Eichi Jumaway, Hawaii
125 Pounds—Dave Armstrong, Puyallup, Wash.
132 Pounds—Hilmer Kenty, Columbus, Ohio
139 Pounds—Ray Leonard, Palmer Park, Md.
147 Pounds—Clinton Jackson, Nashville, Tenn.
156 Pounds—Charles Walker, Mesa, Ariz.
165 Pounds—Tom Brooks, U. S. Air Force
178 Pounds—Leon Spinks, U. S. Marine Corps
Heavyweight—Michael Dokes, Akron, Ohio

FOOTBALL

Professional

Pittsburgh advanced to the Super Bowl for the second straight year and met the Dallas Cowboys in Super Bowl X on Jan. 18, 1976. The Steelers won 21-17.

UCLA's Wendell Tyler vaults over Ohio State defenders for a five-yard gain in the third quarter of the 1976 Rose Bowl. UCLA upset the highly-favored Buckeyes, 23–10.

In the first rounds of the playoffs, Pittsburgh had crushed the Baltimore Colts, 28–10, and then had defeated the Oakland Raiders, 16–10. The surprising Cowboys had won the NFC crown by upsetting the Los Angeles Rams, 37–7.

The Minnesota Vikings had a superior regular-season record, winning their first 10 games. With Fran Tarkenton setting career records for passing, and George Foreman leading the National Conference in receiving, rushing, and scoring, the Vikings had no trouble until Washington beat them in the closing seconds, 31–30. The Minnesota pace was equaled by that of the champion Pittsburgh Steelers, who lost their second game to Buffalo, then won 11 straight games.

With Cincinnati and Houston winning, the Steelers could not clinch division honors early as did the Vikings, the Oakland Raiders, and the Los Angeles Rams. The Raiders lost their fourth and fifth games but had no strong rivals in the division. After losing their opening game they rolled along toward a showdown in the playoffs.

The tough struggle was in the Eastern Division of the National Conference among St. Louis, Dallas, and Washington. The Cardinals had an exciting scoring team with Terry Metcalf rivaling O. J. Simpson of Buffalo as the outstanding runner and Jim Hart combining with Mel Gray in a high-scoring pass combination.

Tarkenton, in his 15th season without missing a game because of injury, overtook Johnny Unitas in two career scoring statistics—most completions and most touchdown passes. His 25 touchdown passes broke the single-season record. Simpson, running brilliantly as usual, set a record for season touchdowns with 23. The Bills weak defense, however, kept him from realizing his ambition of playing in the Super Bowl.

It was a rough season for quarterbacks. Jim Plunkett of New England, Steve Bartkowski of Atlanta, Bob Griese of Miami and his replacement, Earl Morrall, and Archie Manning of New Orleans were all sidelined by injuries. Joe Namath, who got a new $450,000 2-year pact, was benched at one point by the New York Jets for ineffectiveness.

College

Missouri and Kansas, who share one of college football's oldest rivalries, each had one splendid, upsetting game. Missouri opened the season with a stunning 20–7 triumph over Alabama, which knocked the Crimson Tide out of its accustomed place near the top of the rankings. Kansas took advantage of seven consecutive Oklahoma turnovers and triumphed, 23–3, for its first victory over the Sooners since 1964. That upset ended Oklahoma's 28-game winning streak and an unbeaten string of 37 games, the longest in the nation.

The preceding Saturday, California had come up with a milder surprise by downing Southern California, 28–14, and snapping the Trojans' unbeaten string of 18 games. Ohio State had stopped Penn State in October, and Pittsburgh, the East's other top team, had been trounced by Oklahoma, 46–10. These results left only Ohio State, Nebraska, Texas A&M, and Arizona State with perfect records. Michigan was unbeaten but tied twice.

A record NCAA crowd of 105,543 at Ann Arbor, Mich., on November 22, saw Ohio State score twice in the closing minutes and beat Michigan, 21–14. Ohio State thus clinched a Rose Bowl berth for the fourth straight year. Pete Johnson scored three touchdowns, but Archie Griffin was held to 46 yards, ending a series of 31 games in which he gained over 100 yards. Michigan beaten at home for the first time in 42 games, accepted an Orange Bowl bid.

In Norman the same day Oklahoma, which had squeaked through, 21–20, over Colorado and, 28–27, over Missouri, jolted Nebraska, 35–10. The Sooners went to the Orange Bowl and defeated Michigan, 14–6. Nebraska accepted a spot in the Fiesta Bowl, where it was toppled, 17–14, by Arizona State, which finished the season with a perfect 12–0 mark.

Two other major bowl spots were involved in "if" clauses. UCLA, which had lost one conference game to Washington, captured the Pacific-8 berth in the Rose Bowl by beating Southern California, 25–22, despite poor play. The Bruins tied for the title with California and were

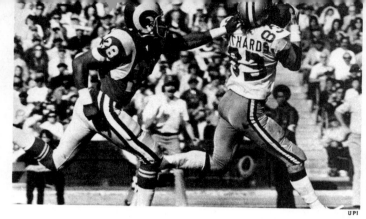

Dallas' Golden Richards catches a pass from Roger Staubach in the NFC championship game against the Los Angeles Rams. The underdog Cowboys trounced the Rams, 37–7.

UPI

chosen because they had beaten California, 28–14. UCLA had lost to Ohio State, 41–20, earlier in the season, but in the Rose Bowl the Bruins romped over Ohio State, 23–10. Texas A&M was still unbeaten after meeting Texas, but on December 6 Arkansas routed the Aggies, 31–6, tying them and Texas for the Southwest title. The Razorbacks got the Cotton Bowl assignment because the Texas teams had played in it more recently and crushed Georgia, 31–10.

Archie Griffin won the Heisman Trophy for the second straight year and became the first player to win the coveted award twice. His total rushing yardage of 5,177 yards for four seasons bettered the NCAA mark of 4,715 set by Ed Marinaro of Cornell in three years. Tony Dorsett of Pittsburgh had two sensational games with 268 yards against Army and 303 yards against Notre Dame. He ended the year with a 1,544 total. However, Ricky Bell of Southern California led with 1,875 yards. Johnson led the scorers with 25 touchdowns for 150 points.

Pro Football Highlights
NATIONAL FOOTBALL LEAGUE
Final Standing of the Teams

American Conference
Eastern Division

	W	L	T	Pct.	Pts.	OP
Baltimore	10	4	0	.714	395	269
Miami	10	4	0	.714	357	222
Buffalo	8	6	0	.571	420	355
New England	3	11	0	.214	258	358
New York Jets	3	11	0	.214	258	433

Central Division

	W	L	T	Pct.	Pts.	OP
Pittsburgh	12	2	0	.857	373	162
Cincinnati*	11	3	0	.786	340	246
Houston	10	4	0	.714	293	226
Cleveland	3	11	0	.214	218	372

Western Division

	W	L	T	Pct.	Pts.	OP
Oakland	11	3	0	.786	375	255
Denver	6	8	0	.429	254	307
Kansas City	5	9	0	.357	282	341
San Diego	2	12	0	.143	189	345

* Won fourth playoff berth

Playoffs—Pittsburgh defeated Baltimore, 28–10, Dec. 27; Oakland defeated Cincinnati, 31–28, Dec. 28
Conference Champion—Pittsburgh (defeated Oakland, 16–10, at Pittsburgh, Jan. 4, 1976)
League Champion (Super Bowl)—Pittsburgh (defeated Dallas, 21–17, at Miami, Jan. 18, 1976)

National Conference
Eastern Division

	W	L	T	Pct.	Pts.	OP
St. Louis	11	3	0	.786	356	276
Dallas*	10	4	0	.714	350	268
Washington	8	6	0	.571	325	276
New York Giants	5	9	0	.357	216	306
Philadelphia	4	10	0	.286	225	302

Central Division

	W	L	T	Pct.	Pts.	OP
Minnesota	12	2	0	.857	377	180
Detroit	7	7	0	.500	245	262
Chicago	4	10	0	.286	191	379
Green Bay	4	10	0	.286	226	285

Western Division

	W	L	T	Pct.	Pts.	OP
Los Angeles	12	2	0	.857	312	135
San Francisco	5	9	0	.357	255	286
Atlanta	4	10	0	.286	240	289
New Orleans	2	12	0	.143	165	360

* Won fourth playoff berth

Playoffs—Los Angeles defeated St. Louis, 35–23; Dallas defeated Minnesota, 17–14
Conference Champion—Dallas (defeated Los Angeles, 37–7, at Los Angeles, Jan. 4, 1976)

National Football League Leaders

American Conference

Scoring—O. J. Simpson, Buffalo (138 pts.)
Scoring (kickers)—Jan Stenerud, Kansas City (22 field goals, 30 extra points, 96 pts.)
Passing—Ken Anderson, Cincinnati (228 of 377 for 3,169 yards and 21 touchdowns; 60.5% completions)
Receiving—Tie between Reggie Rucker, Cleveland (60 for 770 yards) and Lydell Mitchell, Baltimore (60 for 544 yards)
Interceptions—Mel Blount, Pittsburgh (11)
Rushing—O. J. Simpson, Buffalo (329 for 1,817 yards)
Punting—Ray Guy, Oakland (43.8-yard average)
Punt Returns—Billy Johnson, Houston (15.3 average)

National Conference

Scoring—Chuck Foreman, Minnesota (132 pts)
Scoring (kickers)—Toni Frisch, Dallas (22 field goals, 38 extra points, 104 pts.)
Passing—Fran Tarkenton, Minnesota (273 of 425 for 2,994 yards and 25 touchdowns; 64.2% completions)
Receiving—Chuck Foreman, Minnesota (73 for 691 yards)
Interceptions—Paul Krause, Minnesota (10)
Rushing—Jim Otis, St. Louis (269 for 1,076 yards)
Punting—Herman Weaver, Detroit (42-yard average)
Punt Returns—Terry Metcalf, St. Louis (12.4-yards avg.)

CANADIAN FOOTBALL LEAGUE
Final Standing—1975

Eastern Conference

	W	L	T	For	Agst.	Pts.
Ottawa	10	5	1	394	280	21
Montreal	9	7	0	353	345	18
Hamilton	5	10	1	284	395	11
Toronto	5	10	1	261	324	11

Western Conference

	W	L	T	For	Agst.	Pts
Edmonton	12	4	0	432	370	24
Saskatchewan	10	5	1	373	309	21
Winnipeg	6	8	2	340	383	14
Calgary	6	10	0	387	363	12
British Columbia	6	10	0	276	331	12

Playoffs—Division Finals: Eastern: Montreal 20, Ottawa 10; Western: Edmonton 30, Saskatchewan 18. League Championship (Grey Cup): Edmonton 9, Montreal 8.

College Football Highlights

Intercollegiate and Conference Champions

National Press Polls—AP (writers and broadcasters): Oklahoma; UPI (coaches): Oklahoma
National Football Foundation Award (MacArthur Bowl): Oklahoma
Heisman Trophy—Archie Griffin, Ohio State back
Eastern (Lambert Trophy)—Penn State
Eastern Small College—Lambert Bowl: Ithaca; Lambert Cup: Lehigh
Atlantic Coast—Maryland (5–0)
Big Eight—Tie between Nebraska and Oklahoma (6–1)
Big Sky—Boise State (5–0–1)
Big Ten—Ohio State (8–0)
Ivy League—Harvard (6–1)
Mid-American—Miami (6–0)
Missouri Valley—Tulsa (4–0)
Ohio Valley—Tie between Tennessee Tech and Western Kentucky (6–1)
Pacific-8—Tie between California and UCLA (6–1)
Pacific Coast A. A.—San Jose State (5–0)
Southeastern—Alabama (6–0)
Southern—Richmond (5–1)
Southwest—Tie between Arkansas, Texas, and Texas A&M (6–1)
Western Athletic—Arizona State (7–0)
Yankee—New Hampshire (5–0)

Leading Independents

East—Penn State (9–2), Rutgers (9–2), Boston College (7–4), Navy (7–4), Pittsburgh (7–4)
Midwest—Notre Dame (8–3)
South—Virginia Tech (8–3), Georgia Tech (7–4), Memphis State (7–4), South Carolina (7–4), Southern Mississippi (7–4)
Southwest—North Texas State (7–4)
Far West—Hawaii (5–4), Utah State (6–5)

NCAA Playoff Bowls

Division III Final
Camellia Bowl (Sacramenta, Calif., Dec. 13)—Northern Michigan 16, Western Kentucky 14

Division III Final
Stagg Bowl (Phenix, Ala., Dec. 6)—Wittenberg 28, Ithaca 0

NAIA Championships

Champion Bowl, Division I (Kingsville, Tex., Dec. 13)—Texas A&I 37, Salem 0
Division II final (Thousand Oaks, Calif., Dec. 6)—Texas Lutheran 34, California Lutheran 8

Major Bowl Games

(December 1975 and Jan. 1, 1976)
Tangerine Bowl (Orlando, Fla., Dec. 20)—Miami (Ohio) 20, South Carolina 7
Liberty Bowl (Memphis, Tenn., Dec. 22)—Southern California 20, Texas A&M 0
Sun Bowl (El Paso, Tex., Dec. 26)—Pittsburgh 33, Kansas 19
Fiesta Bowl (Tempe, Ariz., Dec. 26)—Arizona State 17, Nebraska 14
Pelican Bowl (New Orleans, Dec. 26)—Southern University 15, South Carolina State 12
Astro-Bluebonnet Bowl (Houston, Dec. 27)—Texas 38, Colorado 21
Gator Bowl (Jacksonville, Fla., Dec. 29)—Maryland 13, Florida 0
Peach Bowl (Atlanta, Dec. 31)—West Virginia 13, North Carolina State 10
Sugar Bowl (New Orleans, Dec. 31)—Alabama 13, Penn State 6
Cotton Bowl (Dallas, Jan. 1)—Arkansas 31, Georgia 10
Orange Bowl (Miami, Jan. 1)—Oklahoma 14, Michigan 6
Rose Bowl (Pasadena, Calif., Jan. 1)—UCLA 23, Ohio State 10

UPI

Jack Nicklaus blasts out of a trap en route to a record-breaking fifth Masters title in April.

GOLF

Jack Nicklaus set a goal for 1975, failed to achieve it, and then said he was happy he hadn't. He had announced that he would try to win the pro golf grand slam—the Masters, the U. S. Open, the British Open, and the Professional Golf Association (PGA) championships. He triumphed in the first and last, but missed the U. S. Open by two shots and the British Open by one. After winning the PGA by two shots he said of the grand slam, "I'm almost glad I didn't win it. If I had, I'd be getting out of golf. But I'm enjoying the game too much, and I don't ever want to leave it. I want to win as many majors as I can."

His allusion to the majors was due to the fact that he had just won his 16th major championship—two U. S. amateurs, three U. S. Opens, two British Opens, five Masters, and four PGA's. His total was three more than Bobby Jones, the former record holder, had won.

Nicklaus also was the biggest winner on the Professional Golfers' Association tour. He won five tournaments, $298,149, and was named player of the year. Johnny Miller, the winner of the first two events, was the runner-up with four victories and $226,118. Two others, Tom Weiskopf and Hale Irwin, earned over $200,000.

When the Masters rolled around in early April, Nicklaus had already won two events. In the final round at Augusta he sank a long putt on the 16th hole for a birdie that beat Miller and Weiskopf by a stroke.

Nicklaus shot a bad 75 in the third round of the U. S. Open, which put him out of contention. Lou Graham and John Mahaffey, lesser-known tour golfers, tied at the end of four rounds at 287, and Graham won the 18-hole playoff. A playoff also decided the British Open with Tom Watson, a 25-year-old Missourian, defeating Jack Newton of Australia by a stroke.

Sandra Palmer, the women's player of the year, captured the U. S. Women's Open by four strokes, and with the $32,000 she had won in the Colgate-Dinah Shore tourney, led the LPGA tour with winnings of $76,375. JoAnne Carner was next, and Carol Mann, who had won only three tourneys since 1971, was third in a comeback that gained her four triumphs. Kathy Whitworth, the all-time leading money winner, won the LPGA title tourney and one other event,

adding $36,423 to her previous career earnings of $540,344.

Fred Ridley, a law student at Stetson University, won the U. S. Amateur title, beating Keith Fergus of Houston, 2-up in 36 holes. Beth Daniel of Charleston, S. C., defeated Donna Horton of Jacksonville, Fla., 3 and 2, for the U. S. Women's Amateur title. U. S. golfers took both British Amateur championships. Vinny Giles of Richmond, Va., the 1972 U. S. champion, won the men's title, and Nancy Roth Syms of Colorado Springs took the women's event. U. S. amateurs beat Britain-Ireland, 15½–8½, in Walker Cup matches, and the U. S. professionals defeated Britain-Ireland, 21–11, to retain the Ryder Cup.

———————— HOCKEY ————————

It was no surprise that the championships were retained by the Philadelphia Flyers in the National League and the Houston Aeros in the World Association. But the fine performance of the New York Islanders, totally unexpected, drew the most praise at the close of the season. The "other" New York team from Long Island knocked the prestigious Rangers out of the play-offs in the first round. The Islanders, a 3-year-old club, had won only 19 games in 1973–74. See also special feature on pages 46–53.

The Islanders dropped the first three games to the Pittsburgh Penguins in the next round. However, the team coached by Al Arbour tied a

Golf Highlights

Men's Individual Champions
U. S. Open—Lou Graham, Nashville, Tenn. (287)
British Open—Tom Watson, Kansas City, Mo. (279)
Masters—Jack Nicklaus, North Palm Beach, Fla. (276)
PGA Tourney—Jack Nicklaus (276)
Canadian Open—Tom Weiskopf (274)
Tournament of Champions—Al Geiberger (277)
PGA Senior—Charlie Sifford, Los Angeles (280); won play-off
Vardon Trophy—Bruce Crampton
World Senior Pro—Kel Nagle, Australia
World Series of Golf—Tom Watson (140)

Pro Team
PGA National—Jim Colbert, Dean Refram (252)
Ryder Cup—United States 21, Britain-Ireland 11
World Cup—United States (554); individual, Johnny Miller (275)

PGA Tournament Winners
Phoenix Open—Johnny Miller (260)
Tucson Open—Johnny Miller (263)
Bing Crosby Pro-Am—Gene Littler (280)
Hawaiian Open—Gary Groh (274)
Bob Hope Desert Classic—Johnny Miller (339)
San Diego Open—J. C. Snead (279); won playoff
Los Angeles Open—Pat Fitzsimons (275)
Gleason Inverrary Classic—Bob Murphy (273)
Citrus Open—Lee Trevino (276)
Doral-Eastern—Jack Nicklaus (276)
Jacksonville Open—Larry Ziegler (276)
Heritage Classic—Jack Nicklaus (271)
Greensboro Open—Tom Weiskopf (275)
Pensacola Open—Jerry McGee (271)
Tallahassee Open—Rik Massengale (274)
Houston Open—Bruce Crampton (273)
Nelson Classic—Tom Watson (269)
NBC New Orleans—Billy Casper (271)
Memphis Classic—Gene Littler (270)
Atlantic Classic—Hale Irwin (271)
Kemper Open—Ray Floyd (278)
IVB-Philadelphia—Tom Jenkins (275)
Western Open—Hale Irwin (283)
Milwaukee Open—Art Wall (271)
Quad Cities Open—Roger Maltbie (275)
Pleasant Valley—Roger Maltbie (276)
Westchester Classic—Gene Littler (271); won playoff
Hartford Open—Don Bies (267); won playoff
Tournament Players Championship—Al Geiberger (270)
B. C. Open—Don Iverson (274)
Southern Open—Hubert Green (264)
World Open—Jack Nicklaus (280); won playoff
Sahara Invitational—Dave Hill (270); won playoff
Kaiser International—Johnny Miller (272)
San Antonio Open—Don January (275); won playoff

Men's Individual Amateur Champions
U. S. Amateur—Fred Ridley, Cypress Gardens, Fla. (defeated Keith Fergus, 2-up, in final)
British Amateur—Vinny Giles, Richmond, Va. (defeated Mark James, 8 and 7, in final)
Canadian Amateur—Jim Nelford, Vancouver, B. C. (280)
U. S. Public Links—Randy Barenaba, Laie, Hawaii
U. S. Junior—Brett Mullin, Riverside, Calif.
National Collegiate (NCAA)—Division I: Jay Haas, Wake Forest (282); Division II: Jerry Wisz, California-Irvine (211); Division III: Charles Baskervill, Hampden-Sydney (223)
National Intercollegiate (NAIA)—Dan Gray, Texas Wesleyan (288)
Junior College—Bill Britton, Miami-Dade North (287)
USGA Senior—Bill Colm, Pebble Beach, Calif.
U. S. Senior G. A.—Dale Morey, High Point, N. C. (144)

Amateur Team Champions
Walker Cup—United States 15½, Britain-Ireland 8½
Derby Cup (Seniors)—U. S. 27, Britain 16½, Canada 10½
NCAA—Division I: Wake Forest (1,156); Division II: California-Irvine (886); Division III: Wooster (226)
NAIA—Texas Wesleyan (1,192)
Junior College—Miami-Dade North (1,182)

Women's Individual Pro Champions
U. S. Open—Sandra Palmer, Dallas, Tex. (295)
LPGA Tourney—Kathy Whitworth, Richardson, Tex. (288)
Vare Trophy—JoAnne Carner
Player of the Year—Sandra Palmer

Other LPGA Tour Winners
Burdine's Invitational—Donna Young (208)
Naples-Lely Classic—Sandra Haynie (211)
Orange Blossom—Amy Alcott (207)
San Isidro—Sue Roberts (214)
Karsten-Ping Open—Jane Blalock (209)
Colgate-Dinah Shore—Sandra Palmer (283)
Charity Classic—Sandra Haynie (212); won playoff
Birmingham Classic—Maria Astrologes (210); won playoff
Lady Tara—Donn Young (214)
American Defender—JoAnne Carner (206); won playoff
Girl Talk Classic—JoAnne Carner (213)
Lawson's Classic—Carol Mann (217)
Hoosier Classic—Betsy Cullen (211)
Peter Jackson—JoAnne Carner (214); won playoff
Wheeling Classic—Susie McAllister (212)
Borden's Classic—Carol Mann (209)
George Washington Classic—Carol Mann (206)
Patty Berg Classic—JoAnn Washam (206)
Jewish Hospital Open—Judy Rankin (207)
Dallas Civitan Open—Carol Mann (208)
Southgate Open—Kathy Whitworth (213)

Women's Individual Amateur Champions
U. S. Amateur—Beth Daniel, Charleston, S. C. (defeated Donna Horton, 3 and 2, in final)
British Amateur—Nancy Roth Syms, Colorado Springs (defeated Suzanne Cadden, 3 and 2, in final)
USGA Girls—Dayne Benson, Anaheim, Calif.
Canadian Amateur—Debbie Massie, Bethlehem, Pa. (293)
Intercollegiate—Barbara Barrow, San Diego State (300); won playoff
World Junior—Debbie Spencer, Honolulu (311)
USGA Senior—Mrs. Albert Bower, Pelham, N. Y. (234)

Women's Amateur Team Champions
Intercollegiate—Arizona State (1,246)

Leading Money Winners in 1975

Men's PGA

Jack Nicklaus	$298,149	Bob Murphy	127,471
Johnny Miller	226,118	Hubert Green	113,569
Tom Weiskopf	219,140	Ray Floyd	103,627
Hale Irwin	205,380	Billy Casper	102,275
Gene Littler	182,883	Lou Graham	96,425
Al Geiberger	175,693	Jerry McGee	93,569
Tom Watson	153,795	J. C. Snead	91,822
John Mahaffey	141,471	Tom Kite	87,045
Lee Trevino	134,206	Charles Coody	86,812
Bruce Crampton	132,532	Pat Fitzsimons	86,181

Women's PGA

Sandra Palmer	$76,375	Kathy McMullen	$39,766
JoAnne Carner	64,843	Kathy Whitworth	36,423
Carol Mann	64,727	Sandra Post	34,841
Sandra Haynie	61,614	Susie McAllister	31,437
Judy Rankin	50,175	JoAnn Washam	30,951
Jane Blalock	45,478	Carole Jo Skala	29,494
Donna C. Young	43,294	Pat Bradley	28,294

Philadelphia's Bobby Clarke (16) scores the winning goal against the Buffalo Sabres in the second game of the Stanley Cup finals. The Philadelphia Flyers won the cup for the second consecutive year.

UPI

league record by winning the next four and taking the series. Goalie Glenn Resch allowed only four tallies in those four games. He was aided by a staunch defense headed by Denis Potvin and Bert Marshall. Ed Westfall, the team captain, scored the seventh game's winning goal.

In the semifinals the Islanders again lost three games in a row, this time to the Flyers. The Flyers played the first two games without Bernie Parent, the winner of the Vezina Trophy as the best goalie in the league, who had a knee injury. The Islanders, now labeled the "Cinderella team," then came back with fine defensive play and evened the series. The champions, threatened with elimination, called in their good luck symbol, Kate Smith. After she had sung "God Bless America," the Flyers triumphed, 4–1.

With Parent back in top form, the Flyers won the Stanley Cup for the second season in a row by beating the Buffalo Sabres, 4 games to 2. Led by Bobby Clarke, the league's most valuable player, they took the first two games at home, lost two in Buffalo, then won the next two. Parent received the most valuable player award for the second straight year. In the final game at Buffalo the fans chanted in unison in the closing minutes, "Thank you, Sabres" in appreciation of the team's record. The Sabres had gained the final round by beating the Chicago Black Hawks, surprise winners over the Boston Bruins, and the Montreal Canadiens.

In regular season play, Buffalo, another of the newer teams, had won its division with 113 points, the same total run up by the Flyers and Canadiens in winning their sections. Montreal came within 2 games of the record by going unbeaten through 21 games. The fourth division was won by the Vancouver Canucks, who entered the league with Buffalo in 1970, with 86 points.

Houston dominated the WHA play during the season, in which the Quebec Nordiques and the New England Whalers also won division titles. In the playoffs, Houston reached the final by defeating Cleveland and San Diego, and Quebec advanced by ousting Phoenix and Minnesota. Houston routed Quebec in four straight games for the championship. The Houston

goalie, Ron Grahame, allowed 26 goals in 13 games as the team posted 10 consecutive victories. He was voted the outstanding player award named for Gordie Howe, the 47-year-old star of the Aeros. Bobby Hull, another NFL veteran and the Winnipeg Jets leader, won the WHA most valuable player award.

Hockey Highlights

National Hockey League
(Final Standings, 1974–75)

Prince of Wales Conference
James Norris Division

	W	L	T	Goals For	Goals Agst.	Pts.
Montreal Canadiens	47	14	19	374	225	113
Los Angeles Kings	42	17	21	269	185	105
Pittsburgh Penguins	37	28	15	326	289	89
Detroit Red Wings	23	45	12	259	335	58
Washington Capitals	8	67	5	181	446	21

Charles F. Adams Division

	W	L	T	For	Agst.	Pts.
Buffalo Sabres	49	16	15	354	240	113
Boston Bruins	40	26	14	345	245	94
Toronto Maple Leafs	31	33	16	280	309	78
California Golden Seals	19	48	13	212	316	51

Clarence Campbell Conference
Lester Patrick Division

	W	L	T	For	Agst.	Pts.
Philadelphia Flyers	51	18	11	293	181	113
New York Rangers	37	29	14	319	276	88
New York Islanders	33	25	22	264	221	88
Atlanta Flames	34	31	15	243	233	83

Conn Smythe Division

	W	L	T	For	Agst.	Pts.
Vancouver Canucks	38	32	10	271	254	86
St. Louis Blues	35	31	14	269	267	84
Chicago Black Hawks	37	35	8	268	241	82
Minnesota North Stars	23	50	7	221	341	53
Kansas City Scouts	15	54	11	184	328	41

Stanley Cup Playoffs

First Round—Toronto defeated Los Angeles, 2 games to 1; Chicago defeated Boston, 2 games to 1; Pittsburgh defeated St. Louis, 2 games to 0; New York Islanders defeated New York Rangers, 2 games to 1.
Quarterfinals—Philadelphia defeated Toronto, 4 games to 0; Buffalo defeated Chicago, 4 games to 1; Montreal defeated Vancouver, 4 games to 1; New York Islanders defeated Pittsburgh, 4 games to 3.
Semifinals—Buffalo defeated Montreal, 4 games to 2; Philadelphia defeated New York Islanders, 4 games to 3.
Final—Philadelphia defeated Buffalo, 4 games to 2.

Individual National Hockey League Awards
(Trophy winners receive $2,000 each from League)
Hart Trophy (most valuable)—Bobby Clarke, Philadelphia
Ross Trophy (leading scorer)—Bobby Orr, Boston
Norris Trophy (best defenseman)—Bobby Orr
Lady Byng Trophy (sportsmanship)—Marcel Dionne, Detroit
Vezina Trophy (goalie)—Bernie Parent, Philadelphia
Calder Trophy (rookie of year)—Eric Vail, Atlanta
Masterton Trophy (courage)—Don Luce, Buffalo
Conn Smythe Trophy (most valuable in playoff)—Bernie Parent

Hockey Highlights (continued)

World Hockey Association
(Final Standings, 1974–75)

Canadian Division

	W	L	T	Goals For	Agst.	Pts.
Quebec Nordiques	46	32	0	331	299	92
Toronto Toros	43	33	2	349	304	88
Winnipeg Jets	38	35	5	322	293	81
Vancouver Blazers	37	39	2	256	270	76
Edmonton Oilers	36	38	4	279	279	76

Eastern Division

	W	L	T	Goals For	Agst.	Pts.
New England Whalers	43	30	5	274	279	91
Cleveland Crusaders	35	40	3	236	258	73
Chicago Cougars	30	47	1	261	312	61
Indianapolis Racers	18	57	3	216	338	39

Western Division

	W	L	T	Goals For	Agst.	Pts.
Houston Aeros	53	25	0	369	247	106
San Diego Mariners	43	31	4	326	268	90
Minnesota Fighting Saints	42	33	3	308	279	87
Phoenix Roadrunners	39	31	8	300	265	86
Baltimore Blades*	21	53	4	205	341	46

*Started season in Detroit as Michigan Stags; moved to Baltimore, Jan. 23

Avco World Cup Playoffs

First Round—Houston defeated Cleveland, 4 games to 1; Quebec defeated Phoenix, 4 games to 1; Minnesota defeated New England, 4 games to 2; San Diego defeated Toronto, 4 games to 2
Semifinals—Houston defeated San Diego, 4 games to 0; Quebec defeated Minnesota, 4 games to 2
Final—Houston defeated Quebec, 4 games to 0

Individual World Hockey Association Awards

Most Valuable Player—Bobby Hull, Winnipeg
Defenseman of the Year—J. C. Tremblay, Quebec
Most Sportsmanlike—Mike Rogers, Edmonton
Rookie of the Year—Anders Hedberg, Winnipeg
Gordie Howe Award (most valuable in playoffs)—Ron Grahame, Houston goalie

Other Professional Champions

American League—North: Providence Reds; South: Virginia Wings; playoffs: Springfield Kings defeated New Haven Nighthawks, 4 games to 1
Central League—North: Salt Lake Golden Eagles; South: Dallas Black Hawks; playoffs: Salt Lake defeated Dallas, 4 games to 3

Amateur Champions

International League—North: Muskegon; South: Dayton; playoffs: Toledo
North American League—Regular season: Syracuse; playoffs: Johnstown
Southern League—Regular season and playoffs: Charlotte
United States League—Northern Division: Green Bay; Southern Division: Waterloo; playoffs: Thunder Bay
World—USSR; Class B: East Germany
Memorial Cup (Canadian junior)—Toronto Marlboros
Allan Cup (Canadian senior)—Thunder Bay
Amateur Hockey Association of the United States—Squirt: Warwick, R. I.; PeeWee: Grosse Pointe, Mich.; Bantam: Detroit; Midget: Detroit; Junior: (A) Detroit Junior Wings; (B) Ecorse, Mich.; Intermediate: St. Paul Park, Minn.

Intercollegiate Champions

NCAA—Michigan Tech (defeated Minnesota, 6–1, in final)
NAIA—St. Scholastica, Duluth (defeated Gustavus Adolphus, 7–1, in final)
ECAC—Division I: Boston University; Division II: Bowdoin; Division III: Bryant
WCHA—Minnesota
Canadian—Alberta (defeated Toronto in final)

——— HORSE RACING ———

A misstep in a match race with Foolish Pleasure at Belmont Park on July 6 cost Ruffian, an unbeaten 3-year-old filly, her life. Ruffian, in the lead after about a half-mile of the 1¼-mile race, broke her right ankle. She was pulled up by her jockey, Jacinto Vasquez, while Braulio Baeza guided Foolish Pleasure, the winner of the Kentucky Derby, to the finish and a prize of $350,000.

UPI

Wajima (*left*) edges Forego, the 1975 horse of the year, in the Marlboro Cup.

Horse Racing Highlights

Champions of the Year

Eclipse Awards

(Consolidation of polls of the Thoroughbred Racing Association, the Daily Racing Form, and the National Turf Writers Association.)
Horse of the Year—Forego
2-Year-Old Colt—Honest Pleasure
2-Year-Old Filly—Dearly Precious
3-Year-Old Colt—Wajima
3-Year-Old Filly—Ruffian
Older Colt or Gelding—Forego
Older Filly or Mare—Susan's Girl
Sprinter—Gallant Bob
Grass Horse—Snow Knight
Steeplechase—Life's Illusion

Major Stakes Winners

Arlington-Washington Park Futurity—Honest Pleasure
Belmont Stakes—Avatar
Brooklyn Handicap—Forego
California Derby (Golden Gate)—Diablo
Coaching Club American Oaks—Ruffian
Delaware Handicap—Susan's Girl
Flamingo (Hialeah)—Foolish Pleasure
Florida Derby (Gulfstream)—Prince Thou Art
Futurity (Belmont)—Soy Numero Uno
Hawthorne Gold Cup—Royal Glint
Hollywood Derby—Intrepid Hero
Hollywood Gold Cup—Ancient Title
Jockey Club Gold Cup (Aqueduct)—Group Plan
Kentucky Derby (Churchill Downs)—Foolish Pleasure
Louisiana Derby (Fair Grounds)—Master Derby
Marlboro Cup (Belmont)—Wajima
Monmouth Invitational—Wajima
National Thoroughbred Championship (Santa Anita)—Dulcia
Pan-American Turf Handicap (Gulfstream)—Buffalo Lark
Preakness (Pimlico)—Master Derby
Santa Anita Derby—Avatar
Sorority (Monmouth)—Dearly Precious
Suburban Handicap (Aqueduct)—Forego
Travers (Saratoga)—Wajima
United Nations Handicap (Atlantic City)—Royal Glint
Washington D. C. International (Laurel)—Nobiliary (France)
Widener (Hialeah)—Forego
Wood Memorial (Aqueduct)—Foolish Pleasure
Woodward Stakes (Belmont)—Forego

Quarter Horse

(Ruidoso Downs, N. M., Sept. 1)
All-American Futurity (purse $1 million)—Bugs Alive in 75 (Jerry Burgess, jockey; winner's purse $330,000)

Other Races

Ascot Gold Cup (England)—Sagara
Canadian Derby (Northlands)—Pampas Host
Canadian International (Woodbine)—Snow Knight
Epsom Derby (England)—Grundy
Epsom Oaks (England)—Juliette Marny
Grand National Steeplechase (England)—L'Escargot
Grand Prix de Paris—Matahawk

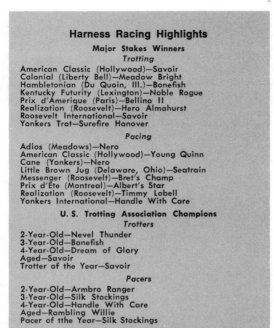

Harness Racing Highlights

Major Stakes Winners

Trotting

American Classic (Hollywood)—Savoir
Colonial (Liberty Bell)—Meadow Bright
Hambletonian (Du Quoin, Ill.)—Bonefish
Kentucky Futurity (Lexington)—Noble Rogue
Prix d'Amerique (Paris)—Bellino II
Realization (Roosevelt)—Hero Almahurst
Roosevelt International—Savoir
Yonkers Trot—Surefire Hanover

Pacing

Adios (Meadows)—Nero
American Classic (Hollywood)—Young Quinn
Cane (Yonkers)—Nero
Little Brown Jug (Delaware, Ohio)—Seatrain
Messenger (Roosevelt)—Bret's Champ
Prix d'Ete (Montreal)—Albert's Star
Realization (Roosevelt)—Timmy Lobell
Yonkers International—Handle With Care

U. S. Trotting Association Champions

Trotters

2-Year-Old—Nevel Thunder
3-Year-Old—Bonefish
4-Year-Old—Dream of Glory
Aged—Savoir
Trotter of the Year—Savoir

Pacers

2-Year-Old—Armbro Ranger
3-Year-Old—Silk Stockings
4-Year-Old—Handle With Care
Aged—Rambling Willie
Pacer of tthe Year—Silk Stockings

Harness Horse of the Year

Savoir (52 votes), Silk Stockings (48 votes)

UPI

The U. S. pursuit cycling team won the gold medal at the Pan American Games, upsetting the Colombians.

Surgery was performed to save the filly, but her excited movements after coming out of anesthesia undid the work, and she had to be destroyed the morning following the race. The big coal-black filly had won all of her 10 races over 2 years and $438,429. She took the triple crown for fillies and set track records in most of her races.

Foolish Pleasure's bid for the Triple Crown after winning the Kentucky Derby ahead of Avatar ended in the Preakness, which was won by Master Derby. Foolish Pleasure was second and was also the runner-up to Avatar in the Belmont Stakes. Forego again was named horse of the year. After 1975 his lifetime earnings totaled $1,163,516. Susan's Girl, the top-winning U. S. mare, finished her career with $1,251,668.

In harness racing, Savoir, a 7-year-old trotter who led in earnings with $351,385, was voted horse of the year. The pacers were led by Silk Stockings, a 3-year-old filly. She bettered two racing records and set a mark for female standardbreds with earnings of $336,312 for the season. Bonefish won the Hambletonian, while Seatrain won the Little Brown Jug.

——— PAN-AMERICAN GAMES ———

Long before their opening on October 13 in Mexico City, the Pan-American Games had run into difficulties. Chile had to give them up because of political problems; Brazil took over, but could not come up with enough money to stage them as scheduled in São Paolo. Also, it was doubtful that a meningitis epidemic in the Brazilian city could be controlled by the April 26 date set for the opening. Mexico City became the site because it had the facilities left from the 1968 Olympics. However, to give the Mexicans time to prepare properly, the games were rescheduled for October. The late date then became a problem for many U. S. athletes because it conflicted with college sessions.

Thirty-three nations sent over 3,000 athletes to the 15-day quadrennial sports festival. The competition in many events was intense but not outstanding. There was only one world record eclipsed in the major competitions, possibly because performances were affected by Mexico City's high altitude, but mainly because of the caliber of the performers.

The world record was posted by Joao Oliveiro of Brazil in the triple jump, with 58 feet 8¼ inches. Many Pan-Am marks were broken, especially by U. S. swimmers, who won 27 of the 29 events.

There had been much concern about the showing of the United States, because many of the top athletes in track and swimming did not compete. There was a further disconcerting note. The U. S. competitors were greeted with boos and whistling from the time they appeared in the opening-day parade. This upset many of the younger squad members, who had expected sportsmanlike treatment. Apparently the treatment led to greater U. S. efforts, and the United States won more medals than had been expected. Outside the arenas the U. S. athletes were well-received by the public.

Cuban athletes, applauded by the fans, performed well, especially in weight lifting. They put in an early bid to dominate the games, but

Pan-American Games

Medal Standing

	Gold	Silver	Bronze	Total
United States	117	85	46	248
Cuba	56	46	30	132
Canada	18	35	39	92
Mexico	9	13	37	59
Brazil	8	12	22	42
Argentina	3	5	7	15
Venezuela	0	1	11	12
Colombia	2	4	4	10
Puerto Rico	0	3	7	10
Dominican Republic	0	1	7	8
Panama	0	2	4	6
Jamaica	0	1	3	4
Ecuador	1	1	1	3
Guyana	1	1	0	2
Peru	1	1	0	2
Bahamas	0	1	1	2
Chile	0	0	2	2
Uruguay	0	0	2	2
Trinidad-Tobago	0	1	0	1
Netherlands Antilles	0	1	0	1
Guatemala	0	0	1	1
Barbados	0	0	1	1
Nicaragua	0	0	1	1
El Salvador	0	0	1	1

the overall depth of the U. S. squad soon became apparent. The U. S. team took 19 track titles, 14 of 18 shooting events, 12 of 20 wrestling titles, and 7 of 8 rowing events. They swept the honors in tennis, synchronized swimming, and woman's gymnastics.

Altogether the United States won 248 medals —117 gold for first place, 85 silver for second, and 46 bronze for third. The next best showing was by Cuba with 132 overall, 56 of them gold. Canada was third with 92 and Mexico fourth with 59.

The United States took the men's and women's basketball championships. Cuba won the baseball title with the U. S. team second. Brazil and Mexico shared the soccer title when the final game was halted with the score tied after the lights in the stadium went out. Ann Carr won five gold medals in gymnastics, while Kim Peyton and Kathy Heddy each won four gold medals in swimming.

——— SOCCER ———

Efforts to interest the U. S. sporting public in soccer were rewarded with some encouraging signs in 1975. Much of it, however, came from high schools and colleges, a source that will not produce its full effect on spectator interest for several years. The North American Soccer League (NASL), which had expanded to 20 teams, played to a total attendance of 1,730,000 for its regular season games, and to single-game playoff crowds of over 30,000. Much of the new enthusiasm was on the West Coast, which drew 42% of the attendance. The Tampa Bay Rowdies, also a good drawing team, won the league title, beating Portland, 2–0.

At midseason the New York Cosmos persuaded Pelé, the most famous of soccer players, to come out of retirement and sign with them. Wherever the Brazilian played, there were large crowds (35,620 in Washington, a NASL record). In Boston he was actually injured by an admiring crowd. However, the general rise in interest in the game was not because of Pelé's presence.

More encouraging signs came from the high schools and colleges, where soccer participation continued to grow. There were 650 colleges playing the game in 1975, compared with 45 when the NCAA began its soccer program in 1959. It appeared that even more interest was being generated in youngsters below the age of 10. The Athletic Youth Soccer Organization, similar to baseball's little leagues, had 4,112 teams operating on the West Coast alone. This developing group of fans won't reach its full potential for another 10 to 15 years, long after Pelé has quit.

The University of San Francisco Dons romped over Southern Illinois University at

Soccer Highlights

Northern American Soccer League

Northern Division

	W	L	Goals For	Agst.	BP*	Pts.
Boston Minutemen	13	9	41	29	38	116
Toronto Metros	13	9	39	28	36	114
New York Cosmos	10	12	39	38	31	91
Rochester Lancers	6	16	29	49	28	64
Hartford Bicentennials	6	16	27	51	25	61

Eastern Division

	W	L	Goals For	Agst.	BP*	Pts.
Tampa Bay Rowdies	16	6	46	27	39	135
Miami Toros	14	8	47	30	39	123
Washington Diplomats	12	10	42	47	40	112
Philadelphia Atoms	10	12	33	42	30	90
Baltimore Comets	9	13	34	52	33	87

Central Division

	W	L	Goals For	Agst.	BP*	Pts.
St. Louis Stars	13	9	38	34	37	115
Chicago Sting	12	10	39	33	34	106
Denver Dynamos	9	13	37	42	31	85
Dallas Tornado	9	13	33	38	29	83
San Antonio Thunder	6	16	24	46	23	59

Western Division

	W	L	Goals For	Agst.	BP*	Pts.
Portland Timbers	16	6	43	27	42	138
Seattle Sounders	15	7	42	28	39	129
Los Angeles Aztecs	12	10	42	33	35	107
Vancouver Whitecaps	11	11	38	28	33	99
San Jose Earthquakes	8	14	37	48	35	83

*BP—Bonus points awarded for each goal to a maximum of three per team per game; teams receive six points for victory, none for loss.

Playoffs—Miami defeated Boston, 2–1; St. Louis defeated Los Angeles, 1–0; Portland defeated Seattle, 2–1; Tampa Bay defeated Toronto, 1–0; Semifinals: Tampa Bay defeated Miami, 3–0; Portland defeated St. Louis, 2–1

Championships (San Jose, Calif. Aug. 24)—Tampa Bay defeated Portland, 2–0

League Awards—Most valuable player: Steve David, Miami Toros; Leading scorer: David (23 goals); Rookie of the year: Chris Bahr, Philadelphia Atoms

United States Champions

Challenge Cup—Maccabee, Los Angeles (defeated Inter-Giuliana, New York, 1–0, in final)

Amateur Cup—Chicago Kickers

Junior—Timo's Pizza, St. Louis

European Champions

English Association Cup: West Ham United; English League Cup: Aston Villa; Scottish League Cup: Glasgow Celtic; European Cup: Bayern Munich

Collegiate Champions

NCAA—Division I; Semifinals: University of San Francisco 2, Brown 1; Southern Illinois University at Edwardsville 3, Howard 1; Final: San Francisco 4, S. I. U.-Edwardsville 0. Third place: Brown defeated Howard, 2–0; Division II; Final: Baltimore defeated Seattle Pacific, 3–1; third place: Adelphi 9, Wisconsin-Green Bay 1; Division III: Final: Babson defeated Brockport, 1–0; third place: Ohio Wesleyan defeated Johns Hopkins, 1–0

NAIA—Semifinals: Quincy defeated Western New England, 3–0; Simon Fraser defeated Rockhurst (Mo.); Final: Quincy defeated Simon Fraser, 1–0; third place: Rockhurst defeated Western New England, 2–0

New York Cosmos' Pelé (left) battles for the ball during game with the Washington Diplomats in June.

Edwardsville, 4–0, and took the NCAA championship. The Dons had beaten Brown in the semifinals, 2–1 on the Edwardsville field. S. I. U. eliminated Howard, the 1974 champion, in the semifinals, 3–1. Baltimore won the NCAA Division II title, and Babson took the Division III crown. Quincy College won the NAIA title for the third year in a row, beating Simon Fraser, 1–0, in the final.

—————— SWIMMING ——————

Everybody who was somebody jumped into the pool at Cali, Colombia, for the world swimming championships, and the results were convincing if not startling. They showed again that other nations have not caught up with the U. S. men swimmers and that the East German women have strengthened their already excellent group. The swimming competition was combined with diving, water polo, and synchronized swimming in a 10-day July water carnival. There were 685 competitors from 39 countries, 380 of them swimmers and 68 divers.

When the United States and East Germany finished collecting gold medals for first place there were few left for the others. The U. S. men took eight championships and the women one. The East German men won three events, while the women raced off with ten. In total medals, including silver for second and bronze for third place, the United States won 31 (men 18, women 13) and East Germany 23 (men 4 and women 19). In addition, the United States won two of the diving championships and all three titles in synchronized swimming. The water polo title went to the Soviet Union, with Hungary second and Italy third. The other diving titles were taken by an Italian man and a Russian woman.

There were five world records bettered in the Cali meet and five more in the U. S. nationals at Kansas City, Kans., in August. In those two meets 19 records went under. In the world event, Kornelia Ender of East Germany swam the 100-meter butterfly in a record 1:01.24 and then sped through the 100-meter freestyle at 0:56.22 in the first leg of the 400-meter relay. In the relay she helped the East Germans cut the mark to 3:49.37. Her teammate, Birgit Treiber, set a record of 2:15.46 in the 200-meter backstroke. The fifth mark was bettered by the U. S. men's freestyle relay team, which swam the 400-meter event in 3:24.85.

Tim Shaw, 17, celebrated his graduation from a Long Beach, Calif., high school by breaking freestyle world records for 400 meters (3:53.95), 800 meters (8:13.68), and 1,500 meters (15:20.91) in the trials for the U. S. team in June. He went on to win the world titles for 200, 400, and 1,500-meter events. He again set the record for the 400 in 3:53.31 in the AAU national meet. The other world marks set in Kansas City were by Jim Montgomery in the 100-meter freestyle (50.59), Bruce Furniss in the 200-meter freestyle (1:50.32) and the 200-meter individual medley (2:06.08), and the Long Beach Swim Club in the 800-meter men's freestyle relay (7:30.54).

Shirley Babashoff, the world's best woman freestyler, took the world titles for 200 and 400 meters, after setting a world mark of 4:14.76 for the 400-meter event in the June trials. She captured the national titles in the 100, 200, and 400-meter events and anchored the Mission Viejo (Calif.) Nadadores in three winning relays. Babashoff took three titles at the AAU national short-course (indoor) meet in April, as the women broke 11 U. S. records and the men 4.

Janet Ely (left) congratulates Canada's Janet Nutter, platform diving winner at the Pan American Games.

Swimming Highlights

World Championships
(Cali, Colombia, July 22–27)

Men

100-Meter Freestyle—Andy Coan, Ft. Lauderdale, Fla. (0:51.25)
200-Meter Freestyle—Tim Shaw, Long Beach, Calif. (1:51.04)
400-Meter Freestyle—Shaw (3:54.88)
1,500-Meter Freestyle—Shaw (15:28.92)
100-Meter Backstroke—Roland Matthes, East Germany (0:58.15)
200-Meter Backstroke—Zoltan Verraszto, Hungary (2:05.05)
100-Meter Breaststroke—David Wilkie, Britain (1:04.26)
200-Meter Breaststroke—Wilkie (2:18.23)
100-Meter Butterfly—Greg Jagenburg, West Chester, Pa. (0:55.63)
200-Meter Butterfly—Bill Forrester, Jacksonville, Fla. (2:01.95)
200-Meter Ind. Medley—Andras Hargitay, Hungary (2:07.72)
400-Meter Ind. Medley—Hargitay (4:32.57)
400-Meter Freestyle Relay—United States (Bruce Furniss, Jim Montgomery, Andy Coan, John Murphy, *3:24.85)
400-Meter Medley Relay—United States (John Murphy, Rick Colella, Greg Jagenburg, Andy Coan, 3:49)
800-Meter Freestyle Relay—West Germany (Klaus Steinbach, Werner Lampe, Hajo Geissler, Peter Nocke, 7:39.44) United States finished first but was disqualified for leaving start of 4th leg before touch)

Women

100-Meter Freestyle—Kornelia Ender, East Germany (0:56.50)
200-Meter Freestyle—Shirley Babashoff, Fountain Valley, Calif. (2:02.5)
400-Meter Freestyle—Shirley Babashoff (4:16.87)
800-Meter Freestyle—Jenny Turrall, Australia (8:44.75)
100-Meter Backstroke—Ulrike Richter, East Germany (1:03.30)
200-Meter Backstroke—Birgit Treiber, East Germany (*2:15.46)
100-Meter Breaststroke—Hannelore Anke, East Germany (1:12.72)
200-Meter Breaststroke—Hannelore Anke (2:37.25)
100-Meter Butterfly—Kornelia Ender (*1:01.24)
200-Meter Butterfly—Rosemarie Kother, East Germany (2:13.82)
200-Meter Ind. Medley—Kathy Heddy, Summit, N. J. (2:19.80)
400-Meter Ind. Medley—Ulrike Tauber, East Germany (4:52.76)
400-Meter Freestyle Relay—East Germany (Kornelia Ender, Barbara Krause, Claudia Hempel, Ute Bruckner, *3:49.37)
400-Meter Medley Relay—East Germany (Ulrike Richter, Hannelore Anke, Rosemarie Kother, Kornelia Ender, 4:14.74)
* Bettered listed world record

National AAU Outdoor Championships
(Kansas City, Kan., Aug. 20–23)

Men

100-Meter Freestyle—Jim Montgomery, Madison, Wis. (0:51.04) (Montgomery bettered world record in trials with 0:50.59)
200-Meter Freestyle—Bruce Furniss, Long Beach, Calif. (*1:50.32)
400-Meter Freestyle—Tim Shaw, Long Beach, Calif. (*3:53.31)
1,500-Meter Freestyle—Bobby Hackett, Yonkers, N. Y. (15:32)
100-Meter Backstroke—John Naber, Menlo Park, Calif. (†0:57.35)
200-Meter Backstroke—Naber (†2:02.52)
100-Meter Breaststroke—Rick Colella, Seattle, Wash. (1:05.95)
200-Meter Breaststroke—Colella (2:21.32)
100-Meter Butterfly—Steve Baxter, Santa Clara, Calif. (0:55.29)
200-Meter Butterfly—Greg Jagenburg, West Chester, Pa. (2:00.73)
200-Meter Ind. Medley—Bruce Furniss (*2:06.08)
400-Meter Ind. Medley—Dave Hannula, Tacoma, Wash. (4:31.35)
400-Meter Freestyle Relay—Badger Dolphins, Madison, Wis. (Brad Horner, Scott Findorff, Jim Montgomery, Neil Rogers, 3:28.52)
400-Meter Medley Relay—Long Beach (Calif.) S. C. (Mike McIntyre, Kevin Williams, Ken Wills, Bruce Furniss, 3:51.55)
800-Meter Freestyle Relay—Long Beach S. C. (Rex Favero, Tim Shaw, Steve Furniss, Bruce Furniss, *7:30.54)

Women

100-Meter Freestyle—Shirley Babashoff, Fountain Valley, Calif. (†0:57.48)
200-Meter Freestyle—Shirley Babashoff (†2:02.39)
400-Meter Freestyle—Shirley Babashoff (4:15.63)
1,500-Meter Freestyle—Heather Greenwood, Fresno, Calif. (16:47.11)
100-Meter Backstroke—Linda Jezek, Santa Clara, Calif. (1:04.70)
200-Meter Backstroke—Melissa Belote, Springfield, Va. (†2:18.16)
100-Meter Breaststroke—Marcia Morey, Decatur, Ill. (†1:13.55)
200-Meter Breaststroke—Marcia Morey (†2:38.43)
100-Meter Butterfly—Camille Wright, New Albany, Ind. (1:02.90)
200-Meter Butterfly—Valerie Lee, Mission Viejo, Calif. (†2:15.07)
200-Meter Ind. Medley—Kathy Heddy, Summit, N. J. (†2:19.93)
400-Meter Ind. Medley—Jenni Franks, Wilmington, Del. (†4:53.86)
400-Meter Freestyle Relay—Mission Viejo (Calif.) Nadadores (Peggy Tosdal, Barb Hudson, Valerie Lee, Shirley Babashoff, 3:55.815)
400-Meter Medley Relay—Mission Viejo Nadadores (Lisa Hilger, Michelle Mercer, Peggy Tosdal, Shirley Babashoff, 4:24.07)
800-Meter Freestyle Relay—Mission Viejo Nadadores (Peggy Tosdal, Kelly Hammill, Valerie Lee, Shirley Babashoff, 8:25.61)
* Bettered listed world record; † bettered listed American record.

Diving

World Championships
(Cali, Colombia, July 18–22)

Men

Springboard—Lt. Phil Boggs, U. S. Air Force (597.12 pts)
Platform—Klaus DiBiasi, Italy (547.98)

Women

Springboard—Irinna Kalina, U. S. S. R. (489.81)
Platform—Janet Ely, Dallas, Tex. (403.89)

National AAU Outdoor
(Houston, Tex., Aug. 12–16)

Men

1-Meter—Tom Moore, Westerville, Ohio (529.95)
3-Meter—Lt. Phil Boggs, Air Force Academy (619.89)
Platform—Kent Vosler, Eaton, Ohio (545.34)

Women

1-Meter—Cynthia P. McIngvale, Dallas, Texas (483.78)
3-Meter—Cynthia McIngvale (465.2)
Platform—Janet Ely, Dallas (384.81)

National AAU Indoor Championships
(Cincinnati, April 9–12)

Men

100-Yard Freestyle—Andy Coan, Ft. Lauderdale, Fla. (0:44.50)
200-Yard Freestyle—Tim Shaw, Long Beach, Calif. (1:38.357)
500-Yard Freestyle—Shaw (4:22.57)
1,650-yard Freestyle—John Naber, So. Calif. (†15:09.51)
100-Yard Backstroke—Naber (0:50.368)
200-Yard Backstroke—Naber (1:48.135)
100-yard Breaststroke—John Hencken, Santa Clara, Calif. (0:56.166)
200-Yard Breaststroke—Hencken (2:00.894)
100-Yard Butterfly—Gary Hall, Cincinnati, Ohio (0:48.863)
200-Yard Butterfly—Greg Jagenburg, West Chester, Pa. (1:47.283)
200-Yard Medley—Lee Engstrand, Tennessee (†1:50.317)
400-Yard Medley—Andras Hargitay, Hungary (†3:54.916)
400-Yard Freestyle Relay—Indiana (Tom Hickcox, Ken Knox, Jim Montgomery, John Murphy, 2:59.340)
400-Yard Medley Relay—So. California (John Naber, Mark Chatfield, Joe Bottom, Scott Findorff, 3:19.722)
800-Yard Freestyle Relay—So. California (Rod Strachan, Scott Findorff, Mark Greenwood, John Naber, †6:35.613)
Team—University of Southern California (474 pts)

Women

100-Yard Freestyle—Shirley Babashoff, Mission Viejo Nadadores (Calif.) (0:50.974)
200-Yard Freestyle—Shirley Babashoff (1:49.528)
500-Yard Freestyle—Shirley Babashoff (4:50.950)
1,650-Yard Freestyle—Jo Harshbarger, Bellevue, Wash. (†16:27.114)
100-Yard Backstroke—Tauna Vandeweghe, Los Angeles (0:58.128)
200-Yard Backstroke—Nancy Garapick, Halifax, Nova Scotia (†2:02.843)
100-Yard Breaststroke—Kim Dunson, Dallas, Texas (†1:05.254)
200-Yard Breaststroke—Marcia Morey, Decatur, Ill. (†2:18.775)
100-Yard Butterfly—Deana Deardurff, Cincinnati, Ohio (†0:55.708)
200-Yard Butterfly—Valerie Lee, Mission Viejo (†2:00.702)
200-Yard Medley—Jenni Franks, Wilmington, Del. (†2:04.747)
400-Yard Medley—Jenni Franks (†4:24.516)
400-Yard Freestyle Relay—Mission Viejo Nadadores (Peggy Tosdal, Barb Hudson, Valerie Lee, Shirley Babashoff, †3:27.249)
400-Yard Medley Relay—Santa Clara (Calif.) S. C. (Linda Jesek, Mary Mirch, Meg Gerken, Kelly Rowell, †3:53.709)
800-Yard Freestyle Relay—Mission Viejo (Peggy Tosdal, Barb Hudson, Valerie Lee, Shirley Babashoff, †7:28.779)
Team—Mission Viejo (Calif.) Nadadores (283 pts.)
† Bettered listed American record

UPI

Manuel Orantes upset Jimmy Connors in straight sets to win the U. S. Open at Forest Hills.

Swimming Highlights (continued)
National AAU Indoor Diving
(Cleveland, April 2–5)

Men

1-Meter—Tim Moore, Columbus, Ohio (553.68 pts)
3-Meter—Phil Boggs, U. S. Air Force (596.82)
10-Meter Platform—Moore (522.99)

Women

1-Meter—Jenni Chandler, Lincoln, Ala. (446.49)
3-Meter—Carrie Irish, New Canaan, Conn. (511.41)
10-Meter Platform—Carrie Irish (346.83)

National Collegiate (NCAA) Championships
(Division I, Cleveland, March 26–29)

50-Yard Freestyle—Joe Bottom, So. California (0:20.11)
100-Yard Freestyle—Jonty Skinner, Alabama (0:43.92)
200-Yard Freestyle—George McDonnell, UCLA (1:38.04)
500-Yard Freestyle—John Naber, So. California (4:20.45)
1,650-Yard Freestyle—Mike Bruner, Stanford (15:16.54)
100-Yard Backstroke—Naber (0:49.947)
200-Yard Backstroke—Naber (1:46.82)
100-Yard Breaststroke—John Hencken, Stanford (0:55.59)
200-Yard Breaststroke—Hencken (2:00.83)
100-Yard Butterfly—Jeff Rolan, Utah (0:48.95)
200-Yard Butterfly—Robin Backhaus, Washington (1:47.16)
200-Yard Ind. Medley—Fred Tyler, Indiana (1:50.268)
400-Yard Ind. Medley—Lee Engstrand, Tennessee (3:57.80)
400-Yard Freestyle Relay—Indiana (Ken Knox, Jim Montgomery, John Murphy, Tom Hickcox, 2:58.41)
400-Yard Medley Relay—So. California (John Naber, Mark Chatfield, Joe Bottom, Scott Findorff, 3:19.22)
800-Yard Freestyle Relay—Indiana (Rick Thomas, John Murphy, Jim Montgomery, Fred Tyler, 6:36.293)
1-Meter Dive—Tim Moore, Ohio State (502.71 pts.)
3-Meter Dive—Moore (590.61)
Team—University of Southern California (344 pts.)

TENNIS

In early summer there was little to indicate that Jimmy Connors would not dominate the major tournament season as he had in 1974. The fact that he had already relinquished the Australian title in January was dismissed as an off-season lapse for the top-ranked player in the world. On April 26 in a challenge match televised worldwide from Las Vegas, Nev., Connors trounced John Newcombe, his conqueror in the Aussie final, in four sets. This match and an earlier challenge match with Rod Laver restored the aura of invincibility to the 22-year-old U. S. player. In the February match with Laver, Connors also won in four sets.

There were two startling upsets, however, the first by Arthur Ashe at Wimbledon, and the second by Manuel Orantes at Forest Hills. Ashe stunned the Wimbledon fans by taking the first two sets holding off Connors' frantic recovery efforts, and winning, 6–1, 6–1, 5–7, 6–4. Orantes, saying he learned much from Ashe's handling of Connors, drubbed the defender, 6–4, 6–3, 6–3, in the final of the U. S. Open. Thus Connors, the winner of three top tourneys in 1974, was the runner-up in each in 1975. He did not compete in the fourth top tournament, the French championship, which was won by Bjorn Borg, the 19-year-old Swedish star.

Except for one championship, Chris Evert dominated the women's division. Unbeatable on clay courts, the 20-year-old Florida star broke all records for women's earnings for a year with $362,227. The shift to a clay-type surface at

UPI

Chris Evert continued her domination of women's tennis in 1975, breaking all records for yearly earnings and winning numerous championships.

Tennis Highlights

Major Tournaments

Davis Cup—Semifinals: Czechoslovakia defeated Australia, 4–1; Sweden defeated Chile, 4–1. Final (Stockholm, Dec. 19–21): Sweden defeated Czechoslovakia, 3–2.

Wightman Cup (women, Cleveland, Sept. 13–14)—Britain defeated United States, 5–2.

Federation Cup (women, Aix-en-Provence, France, May 6–11)—Czechoslovakia defeated Australia, 3–0 in final.

Stevens Cup (senior men, Lake Kiamesha, N. Y., Aug. 25–27)—United States defeated Australia, 2–1, in final.

U. S. Open (Forest Hills, N. Y., Aug. 27–Sept. 7)—Men's singles: Manuel Orantes, Spain; women's singles: Chris Evert, Fort Lauderdale, Fla.; men's doubles: Jimmy Connors, Belleville, Ill., and Ilie Nastase, Rumania; women's doubles: Margaret Court, Australia, and Virginia Wade, England; mixed doubles: Rosemary Casals, San Francisco, and Dick Stockton, Dallas, Texas; junior men's singles: Howard Schoenfield, Beverly Hills, Calif.; junior women's singles: Natasha Chmyreva, USSR; men's 45 doubles: Bob Howe, South Africa, and Fred Kovaleski.

National Men's Indoor Open (Salisbury, Md., Feb. 9–16)—Singles: Jimmy Connors, Belleville, Ill.; doubles: Connors and Ilie Nastase, Rumania

National Women's Indoor (Boston, March 5–8)—Singles: Martina Navratilova, Czechoslovakia; doubles: Billie Jean King, San Mateo, Calif., and Rosemary Casals, San Francisco, Calif.

National Clay Court (Indianapolis, Aug. 5–11)—Men's singles: Manuel Orantes; women's singles: Chris Evert; men's doubles: Orantes and Juan Gisbert, Spain; women's doubles: Fiorella Bonicelli, Uruguay, and Isabel Fernandez, Colombia

National Amateur Grass Court (Newport, R. I., July 16–20)—Men's singles: Gonzalo Nunez, Austin, Tex.; women's singles: Lele Forood, Fort Lauderdale, Fla.; men's doubles: Steve Morris and Chris Gunning; women's doubles: JoAnn Russell, San Angelo, Tex., and Lele Forood; mixed doubles: Bill Scanlon, Dallas, and Mary Hamm, Mt. Pulaski, Ill.

National Amateur Clay Courts (Pittsburgh, June 23–29)—Men's singles: Victor Amaya, Holland, Mich.; women's singles: JoAnne Russell, Naples, Fla.; men's doubles: Butch Walts, Los Angeles, Calif., and Bill Maze, Emeryville, Calif.; women's doubles: Mary Hamm, Mt. Pulaski, Ill., and Diane Desfor, Long Beach, Calif.

National Men's 35 (Manhasset, N. Y., July 25–Aug. 3)—Singles: Gene Scott, New York; doubles: Scott and Fred Stolle, Australia

National Senior Clay Court (Charlottesville, Va.)—Singles: Del Sylvia, Knoxville, Tenn.; doubles: Tom Falkenburg, Stuart, Fla., and Tom Barlett, Tampa, Fla.

National Women's Senior Clay Court—Singles (40 and over): Nancy Reed, McLean, Va.; doubles: Nancy Reed and Nancy Neeld, Albuquerque, N. M.; singles (over 50): Betty Pratt, Winter Park, Fla.; (over 60): Sallie Lang, Winter Park, Fla.

National Junior (Kalamazoo, Mich.)—Singles: Howard Schoenfield, Beverly Hills, Calif.; doubles: Tony Giammalva, Houston, Tex., and Bill Scanlon, Dallas, Tex.

National Girls 18 (Philadelphia)—Singles: Beth Norton, Fairfield, Conn.; doubles: Lea Antonopolis, Glendora, Calif., and Berta McCallum, Pittsburgh, Pa.

Other U. S. Championships

NCAA, Division I—Singles: Billy Martin, UCLA; doubles: Butch Walts–Bruce Manson, So. California; team: UCLA. Division II—singles: Andy Rae, University of San Diego; doubles: Scott Carnahan–Bob Wright, California-Irvine; team: tie between San Diego and California-Irvine

NAIA—Singles: Dave Petersen, Gustavus-Adolphus; doubles: Benny Sims–Glenn Moolchan, Texas Southern; team: University of Redlands

Women's Intercollegiate—Singles: Stephanie Tolleson, Trinity (Texas); doubles: JoAnn Russell-Donna Stockton, Trinity; team: Trinity

Junior College –Singles: Perfecto Alina, Odessa; doubles: Paul Fineman–Virgilio Sison, Odessa; team: Odessa

National Interscholastic—Singles: Pem Guerry, Baylor Prep; doubles: Guerry–Wesley Cash, Baylor Prep

Other Countries

Wimbledon (Wimbledon, England, June 23–July 5)—Men's singles: Arthur Ashe, Miami, Fla.; women's singles: Billie Jean King, San Mateo, Calif.; men's doubles: Vito Gerulaitis, New York, and Sandy Mayer, Mendham, N. J.; women's doubles: Ann Kiyomura, San Mateo, Calif., and Kazuko Sawamatsu, Japan; mixed doubles: Margaret Court, Australia, and Marty Riessen, Amelia Island, Fla.; junior men: C. J. Lewis, New Zealand; junior women: Natasha Chmyreva, USSR

Australian Open (Melbourne, finals Jan. 1)—Men's singles: John Newcombe, Australia; women's singles: Evonne Goolagong, Australia; men's doubles: John Alexander and Phil Dent, Australia; women's doubles: Evonne Goolagong and Peggy Michel, Pacific Palisades, Calif.

French Open (Paris, June 4–15)—Men's singles: Bjorn Borg, Sweden; women's singles: Chris Evert; men's doubles: Brian Gottfried, Fort Lauderdale, Fla., and Raul Ramirez, Mexico; women's doubles: Chris Evert and Martina Navratilova; mixed doubles: Tom Koch, Brazil, and Fiorella Bonicelli, Uruguay

Italian Open (Rome, May 26–June 1)—Men's singles: Raul Ramirez, Mexico; women's singles: Chris Evert; men's doubles: Raul Ramirez and Brian Gottfried, Fort Lauderdale, Fla.; women's doubles: Chris Evert and Martina Navratilova; mixed doubles: Tom Koch, Brazil, and Fiorella Bonicelli, Uruguay

Canadian Open (Toronto, Aug. 11–17)—Men's singles: Manuel Orantes, Spain; women's singles: Marcie Louie, San Francisco, Calif.; men's doubles: Cliff Drysdale and Ray Moore, South Africa; women's doubles: Margaret Court and Julie Anthony, Santa Monica, Calif.

Professional Champions

U. S. Championship (Chestnut Hill, Mass., Aug. 26)—Bjorn Borg

World Championship Tennis tour final (Dallas, May 6–11)—Singles: Arthur Ashe, Miami, Fla.; doubles (Mexico City, May 1–4): Raul Ramirez, Mexico–Brian Gottfried, Fort Lauderdale, Fla. (Ramirez-Gottfried won challenge match in Dallas on May 12, from Frew McMillan and Bob Howe, South Africa)

Virginia Slims tour final (Los Angeles, April 1–5)—Chris Evert defeated Martina Navratilova, 6–4, 6–2

Team Tennis Championship—Pittsburgh Triangles defeated San Francisco Golden Gaters

LEADING MONEY WINNERS IN 1975
World Championship Tennis Tour

Arthur Ashe	$177,161	Mark Cox	$75,822
Rod Laver	109,731	Brian Gottfried	68,300
John Alexander	94,075	Roscoe Tanner	60,462
Raul Ramirez	86,680	Dick Stockton	60,275
Bjorn Borg	78,140	Harold Solomon	46,950

Virginia Slims

Chris Evert	$121,450	Billie Jean King	$35,200
Martina Navratilova	96,763	Olga Morozova	31,288
Virginia Wade	69,563	Francois Durr	29,200
Margaret Court	52,613	Julie Heldman	27,100
Evonne Goolagong	52,350	Betty Stove	21,325

Men's Overall Season Earnings
(Includes Commercial Union Grand Prix)

Arthur Ashe	$325,550	Brian Gottfried	$167,950
Manuel Orantes	265,835	Harold Solomon	161,300
Guillermo Vilas	246,675	Jimmy Connors*	159,172
Bjorn Borg	220,851	Roscoe Tanner	150,459
Raul Ramirez	205,560	John Alexander	138,050
Ilie Nastase	179,124	Rod Laver	120,416

* Not including challenge matches

Forest Hills helped her to win the U. S. Open for the first time. In the final two matches she disposed of the two young players who might dispute her ranking as the world's best woman player. In semifinal play she beat Martina Navratilova, a Czechoslovakian who defected the following week and was granted asylum in the United States. In the final she routed Evonne Goolagong Cawley, 6–0, 6–1.

However, Billie Jean King spoiled the year somewhat for Evert in the semifinals on the grass courts at Wimbledon. King rallied in the final set and defeated Evert, the defending champion, 2–6, 6–2, 6–3. It was a glorious effort for King, who captured her sixth title at Wimbledon in what she said would be her last major singles tournament.

Bjorn Borg and 23-year-old Guillermo Vilas of Argentina continued their fine play and their promise of being the top stars of the future. In December, Borg led Sweden to a 3–2 victory over Czechoslovakia in the Davis Cup. Vilas was the runner-up to Borg in Paris, and won the overall $100,000 prize as the leader in the Grand Prix competition. His earnings, and those of Ashe, however, were far overshadowed by Connors who won a total of $350,000 in his matches with Rod Laver and John Newcombe.

TRACK AND FIELD

After being overshadowed by field events for a long period, the one-mile run was reestablished as the glamour event of track. The world record for the mile was broken twice, and each of the new champions, Filbert Bayi of Tanzania and John Walker of New Zealand, promised that the mark would be lowered again before long. Bayi, 21, who learned to run by chasing antelopes, broke the record first on May 17 in the Freedom Games at Kingston, Jamaica, where the organizers had promised a Dream Mile. He bettered the eight-year-old mark of Jim Ryun by a tenth of a second, running the mile in 3:51. Five others in the eight-man field also finished under 4 minutes.

Bayi's record lasted only until August 12, when John Walker raced to a mark of 3:49.4 at Goteborg, Sweden. Walker had had a previous personal mark of 3:52.2 and had run a close second when Bayi bettered Ryun's world mark for 1,500 meters with 3:32.2 in the Commonwealth Games in February 1974.

Records in other running events, from sprints to relays, fell or were equaled during a season in which the athletes were thinking about the 1976 Olympics. Houston McTear, an 18-year-old Florida schoolboy, tied Ivory Crockett's world mark of 9 seconds for 100 yards. Two other dashmen, Silvio Leonard of Cuba and Steve Williams of San Diego, tied the often-equaled mark of 9.9 seconds for 100 meters.

Don Quarrie, a Jamaican, lowered the time for 220 yards and 200 meters to 19.8 seconds. Steve Williams was so close behind that he was credited with the same time at Eugene, Ore., on June 7. Guy Drut of France ran the 110-meter hurdles in 13 seconds at West Berlin on August 22. Anders Garderud of Sweden set a mark of 8:09.8 in the 3,000-meter steeplechase at Stockholm, July 1. A U. S. relay team stopped the clock at 3:02.4 for the mile at Durham, N. C., in an international meet on July 19.

There also were notable feats in the field events. Dave Roberts raised the pole vault mark ¾ of an inch to 18 feet 6½ inches in the Florida Relays on March 28. John Powell, a San Jose, Calif., policeman, threw the discus 226 feet 8 inches, 2 feet farther than John Van Reenan's March record. In an international decathlon meet, Bruce Jenner of San Diego set a record with 8,524 points. Joao Oliveira of Brazil broke the triple jump mark at the Pan-American Games in October with 58 feet 8¼ inches.

Jos Hermens of the Netherlands broke the record for 10 miles with 45:57.6 on September 13. In one effort on September 28 he set world marks for 20,000 meters (57:31.9) and one hour (12 miles, 1,759 yards).

Seven women's world records were broken, all by European athletes. Irina Szewinska of Poland raced the 440-yard event in 51.3 seconds in London on August 31. West Germans set relay records for 440 yards and the mile of 44.07 seconds and 3:30.3 respectively at the Durham meet.

Kathy Weston won the 800-meter race at the first U S A– People's Republic of China meet in Canton.

UPI

Track and Field Highlights
National AAU Indoor Championships
(Madison Square Garden, N. Y., Feb. 28)

Men

60 Yards—Hasely Crawford, Eastern Michigan (0:06)
60-Yard Hurdles—Charles Foster, N. C. Central (0:07.1)
600 Yards—Wesley Williams Jr., Mickey's Missiles, San Diego (1:11.2)
1,000 Yards—Rick Wohlhuter, U. of Chicago T. C. (2:06.4)
Mile—Filbert Bayi, Tanzania (4:02.1)
3 Miles—Miruts Yifter, Ethiopia (13:07.6)
2-Mile Walk—Ron Daniel, New York A. C. (13:36.8)
Sprint Medley Relay—Penn State (Mike Sands, Steve Hackman, Jack Davis, Mike Shine, 2:04.9)
Mile Relay—Seton Hall (Al Daley, Charles Joseph, Orlando Greene, Howard Brock, 3:15.1)
2-Mile Relay—U. of Chicago T. C. (Tom Bach, Ken Sparks, Lowell Paul, Rick Wohlhuter, 7:31.2)
Shot Put—Al Feuerbach, Pacific Coast Club, Long Beach, Calif. (67 ft 10 in)
35-Pound Weight—George Frenn, Hawaiian Gardens, Calif. (69 ft 4 in)
Pole Vault—Roland Carter, Gulf Coast T. C., Houston (17 ft 6 in)
High Jump—Dwight Stones, Pacific Coast Club, Long Beach (7 ft 3 in)
Long Jump—Arnie Robinson, Mickey's Missiles, San Diego (26 ft 3½ in)
Triple Jump—Tommy Haynes, U. S. Army (53 ft 8¾ in)
Team—New York A. C. (16 pts)

Women

60 Yards—Alice Annum, Sports Int., Washington (0:06.6)
60-Yard Hurdles—Modupe Oshikoya, Sports Int. (0:07.6)
220 Yards—Rosalyn Bryant, Mayor Daley Y. F., Chicago (0:23.6)
440 Yards—Robin Campbell, Sports International (0:55.1)
880 Yards—Kathy Weston, Will's Spikettes, Sacramento, Calif. (2:07.6)

Mile—Francie Larrieu, Pacific Coast Club, Long Beach, Calif. (4:42.8)
2 Miles—Brenda Webb, Kettering (Ohio) Striders (10:22)
Mile Walk—Susan Brodock, Rialto (Calif.) Road Runners (7:22.5)
640-Yard Relay—Sports International, Washington (Alice Annum, Rose Allwood, Gwen Norman, Debbie Armstrong, 1:10.4)
880-Yard Medley Relay—Atoms T. C., Brooklyn, N. Y. (Cheryl Toussaint, Pat Collins, Linda Cordy, Lorna Forde, 1:43.2)
Mile Relay—Atoms T. C. (Michele McMillan, Renee DeSandies, Renee Evans, Brenda Nichols, 3:51.2)
Long Jump—Marta Watson, Lakewood (Calif.) Int. 21 ft 2 in
High Jump—Joni Huntley, Oregon T. C., Eugene (6 ft)
Shot Put—Faina Melnick, U. S. S. R. (55 ft 7 in)
Team—Sports International, Washington (29 pts)

National AAU Outdoor Championships

Men

(Eugene, Ore., June 19–21)

100 Meters—Don Quarrie, Beverly Hills (Calif.) Striders (0:10.16)
200 Meters—Quarrie (0:20.12)
400 Meters—David Jenkins, Britain (0:44.93)
800 Meters—Mark Enyeart, Utah State (1:44.9)
1,500 Meters—Len Hilton, Pacific Coast Club, Long Beach, Calif. (3:38.3)
5,000 Meters—Marty Liquori, New York A. C. (13:29)
10,000 Meters—Frank Shorter, Florida T. C. Gainesville (28:02.6)
3,000-Meter Steeplechase—Randy Smith, Wichita State (8:28.2)
5,000-Meter Walk—Ron Laird, New York A. C. (22:08.6)
110-Meter Hurdles—Gerald Wilson, Beverly Hills Striders (0:13.38)
400-Meter Hurdles—Ralph Mann, Beverly Hills Striders (0:48.74)
Discus—John Powell, Pacific Coast Club (208 ft 10 in)
Hammer—Boris Djerassi, New York A. C. (222 ft 10 in)
High Jump—Tom Woods, Pacific Coast Club (7 ft 5½ in)
Long Jump—Arnie Robinson, San Diego (26 ft 5 in)
Triple Jump—Anthony Terry, West Valley T. C., San Mateo, Calif. (54 ft 9¾ in)
Pole Vault—Dan Baird, Maccabi T. C. (17 ft 6 in)
Javelin—Richard George, Brigham Young (272 ft 11 in)
Shot Put—Al Feuerbach, Pacific Coast Club (68 ft 10¾ in)

Women

(White Plains, N. Y., June 27–28)

100 Meters—Rosalyn Bryant, Mayor Daley Y. F., Chicago (0:11.6)
200 Meters—Debra Armstrong, Sports International, Washington (0:23)
400 Meters—Debra Sapenter, Prairie View (Tex.) T. C. (0:51.6)
800 Meters—Madeline Jackson, Cleveland T. C. (2:00.5)
1,500 Meters—Julie Brown, Los Angeles T. C. (4:13.5)
3,000 Meters—Lynn Bjorklund, Duke City Dashers, Albuquerque, N. M. (9:10.6)
100-Meter Hurdles—Jane Frederick, Los Angeles T. C. (0:13.8)
400-Meter Hurdles—Debbie Esser, Woodbine, Iowa (0:57.3)
1,500-Meter Walk—Lisa Metheny, Rialto (Calif.) Road Runners (6:46.6)
400-Meter Relay—Tennessee State (Deborah Clay, Theresa Baugh, Brenda Morehead, Chandra Cheeseborough, 0.45.8)
880-Yard Sprint Medley Relay—Sports International (Rose Allwood, Gwen Norman, Debra Armstrong, Robin Campbell, 1:40)
Mile Relay—Atoms T. C., Brooklyn (Brenda Nichols, Robin Blaine, Lorna Forde, Cheryl Toussaint, 3:37.9)
2-Mile Relay—Blue Ribbon T. C., Wyckliff, Ohio (Diane Vetter, Julie Stibbs, Janis Vetter, Debbie Vetter, 8:46.4)
Discus—Jean Roberts, Delaware S. C. Newark (159 ft 7 in)
Long Jump—Marta Watson, Lakewood (Calif.) Int. (21 ft 3 in)
Shot Put—Maren Seidler, Mayor Daley Y. F. (53 ft 2½ in)
Javelin—Kathy Schmidt, Los Angeles T. C. (209 ft 7 in)
High Jump—Joni Huntley, Oregon T. C. (6 ft)
Team—Los Angeles Track Club (55 pts.)

Decathlons

AAU—Fred Samara, New York A. C. (8,061 pts)
NCAA—Ramo Phil, Brigham Young (8,070)
USTFF—Bruce Jenner, San Jose, Calif. (8,138)
NAIA—James Herron, Cameron State (7,086)
AAU Junior—Tony Hale, Fisk Univ. (6,856)
U. S.–Poland–USSR Triple Meet—Jenner (*8,524)
* Betters listed world record

Pentathlons

AAU Women—Jane Frederick, Los Angeles T. C. (4,676)
AIAW—Mitzi McMillin, Colorado T. C., Boulder (3,717)

Marathons

Boston (2,041 starters, April 21)—William H. Rodgers, Boston (2:09.55); first woman to finish: Lisne Winter, Wolfsburg, Germany (2:42:33)
USTFF—John Bramley, Colorado State (2:21:15)
NAIA—Roger Vann, John Brown Univ. (2:29.14)
AAU Women (New York, Sept. 25)—Kim Merritt, Kenosha, Wis. (2:46:14)

Other Team Champions

NAIA—Southeastern Louisiana (68 pts)
NCAA, Division II—California State–Northridge (57 pts)
NCAA, Division III—Southern U.-New Orleans (66 pts)
Women's Collegiate (AIAW)—UCLA (89 pts)

National Collegiate (NCAA) Indoor Championships

(Detroit, March 13–15)

60 Yards—Hasely Crawford, Eastern Michigan (0:06)
60-Yard Hurdles—Danny Smith, Florida State (0:07)
440 Yards—Mike Sands, Penn State (0:48.5)
600 Yards—Stan Vinson, Eastern Michigan (1:10.2)
880 Yards—Mark Enyeart, Utah State (1:52.4)
1,000 Yards—Keith Francis, Boston College (2:08.4)
Mile—Eamonn Coghlan, Villanova (4:02)
2 Miles—Nick Rose, Western Kentucky (8:44)
3 Miles—John Ngeno, Washington State (13:14.4)
Mile Relay—Florida (Beaufort Brown, Horace Tuitt, Noel Gray, Wimpy Alexander, 3:15.8)
2-Mile Relay—Princeton (Charles Norelli, Rich Aneser, Charles Hedrick, Craig Masback, 7:35)
Distance Medley Relay—Kansas State (Jim Hinchliffe, Lennie Harrison, Ted Settle, Jeff Schemmel, 9:48.2)
High Jump—Greg Joy, Texas–El Paso (7 ft 2 in)
Pole Vault—Earl Bell, Arkansas State (17 ft 2 in)
Long Jump—Theo Hamilton, Kansas (26 ft 7¼ in)
Triple Jump—Arnold Grimes, Texas–El Paso (55 ft 4 in)
Shot Put—Hans Hoglund, Texas–El Paso (67 ft 9¾ in)
35-Pound Weight—Peter Farmer, Texas–El Paso (69 ft 1½ in)
Team—Texas–El Paso (36 pts)

National Collegiate (NCAA) Outdoor Championships

(Provo, Utah, June 6–8)

100 Yards—Hasely Crawford, Eastern Michigan (0:09.35)
220 Yards—Reggie Jones, Tennessee (0:20.6)
440 Yards—Benny Brown, UCLA (0:45.34)
880 Yards—Mark Enyeart, Utah State (1:47.01)
Mile—Eamonn Coghlan, Villanova (4:00.06)
3 Miles—John Ngeno, Washington State (13:22.79)
6 Miles—Ngeno (28:20.66)
3,000-Meter Steeplechase—James Munyala, Texas–El Paso (8:47.93)
120-Yard Hurdles—Larry Shinn, Louisiana State (0:13.91)
440-Yard Hurdles—Craig Caudill, Indiana (0:50.44)
440-Yard Relay—So. California (Randy Williams, Mike Simmons, Ken Randle, James Gilkes, 0:39.09)
Mile Relay—Washington (Keith Tinner, Jerry Belur, Pablo Franco, Billy Hicks, 3:05.1)
Triple Jump—Ron Livers, San Jose State (55 ft 1¾ in)
Long Jump—Charlton Ehizuelen, Illinois (26 ft 11 in)
High Jump—Warren Shanklin, NE Louisiana (7 ft 1 in)
Shot Put—Hans Hoglund, Texas–El Paso (70 ft)
Discus—Jim McGoldrick, Texas (190 ft 1 in)
Hammer—Boris Djerassi, Northeastern (225 ft 8 in)
Javelin—Keith Goldie, Long Beach State (250 ft 2 in)
Pole Vault—Earl Bell, Arkansas State (18 ft 1 in)
Team—Texas–El Paso (55 pts)

U. S. Track and Field Federation Outdoor Championships

(Wichita, Kan., May 30–31)

Men

100 Yards—Robert Taylor, Gulf Coast T. C., Houston (0:09.52)
220 Yards—George Daniels, U. of Chicago T. C. (0:20.9)
440 Yards—Mark Collins, Baylor (0:46.46)
880 Yards—Randy Veltkamp, Oklahoma (1:49.51)
Mile—Rick Wohlhuter, U. of Chicago T. C. (3:53.3)
3 Miles—John Halberstadt, Pacific Coast Club, Long Beach, Calif. (13:17.56)
6 Miles—John Jones, Ohio T. C. (28:08.6)
3,000-Meter Steeplechase—Randy Smith, Wichita State (8:36.4)
120-Yard Hurdles—Vance Roland, Kansas State (0:13.7)
440-Yard Hurdles—Jim Bolding, Pacific Coast Club (0:48.95)
440-Yard Relay—Texas Christian (Glen Morris, Sam McKinney, Phil Delancy, Bill Collins, 0:40)
Mile Relay—Pacific Coast Club (Rob Cassleman, Mark Lutz, Dennis Schultz, Jim Bolding, 3:05.14)
Discus—John Powell, Pacific Coast Club (210 ft 9 in)
Javelin—Glenn Derwin, Gulf Coast T. C. (234 ft)
High Jump—Dwight Stones, Pacific Coast Club (7 ft 2 in)
Long Jump—Danny Seay, Kansas (26 ft 4¾ in)
Triple Jump—Ken Lorraway, So. Illinois (52 ft 3½ in)
Pole Vault—Earl Bell, Arkansas State (17 ft 8 in)
Hammer—Dave Morrison, Holy Cross (197 ft 4 in)
Shot Put—Bishop Dolegiewicz, Montreal (66 ft 2¼ in)

Women

100 Yards—Carol Cummings, Prairie View (Tex.) T. C. (0:10.81)
220 Yards—Carol Cummings (0:24.47)
440 Yards—Shirley Williams, Prairie View (0:55.61)
880 Yards—Cindy Bremser, Wisconsin (2:10.55)
Mile—Francie Larrieu, Pacific Coast Club (4:31.69)
440-Yard Hurdles—Debbie Esser, Woodbine (Iowa) (1:00.19)
Long Jump—Andrea Bruce, Prairie View (21 ft 1 in)
High Jump—Andrea Bruce (5 ft 8 in)

MISCELLANEOUS
SPORTS SUMMARIES

ARCHERY—World: *Men:* Darrell Pace, Reading, Ohio; *women:* Zebiniso Rustamova, USSR; *men's team:* United States; *women's team:* USSR; **National Archery Association:** *Men:* Darrell Pace; *women:* Irene Lorensen, Phoenix, Ariz. **National Field Archery Association:** *Freestyle: men's open:* Terry Ragsdale, White Oak, Texas; *amateur:* John Ashburn, Jr., Barrington, Ill.; *women's open:* Barbara Morris, Frankfort, Ky.; *amateur:* Michelle Sanderson, Hastings, Minn.; *Barebow: men's open:* Al Tuller, Platte City, Mo.; *amateur:* Don Morehead, Wheaton, Ill.; *women's open:* Gloria Shelley, Waterbury, Conn.; *amateur:* Eunice Schewe, Roscoe, Ill.

BADMINTON—U. S. Championships: *Men's singles:* Mike Adams, Flint, Mich.; *women's singles:* Judianne Kelly, Norwalk, Calif.; *men's doubles:* Don Paup, Washington, and Jim Poole, Westminster, Calif.; *women's doubles:* Diane Halles, Claremont, Calif.; and Carlene Starkey, LaMesa, Calif.; *mixed doubles:* Judianne Kelly and Mike Walker, Manhattan Beach, Calif.

BOATING—MOTORBOAT: *World offshore:* Wally Franz, Brazil; *U. S. offshore:* Sandy Saltullo, Fairview Park, Ohio; *unlimited hydroplanes:* Pride of Pay 'N Pak, George Henley, driver. *Distance races: Sam Griffith Memorial:* Bob Nordskog, Van Nuys, Calif.; *Bahamas 500:* Hal Sahlman, Boca Raton, Fla.; *Benihana Grand Prix:* Jon Varese, Fort Lauderdale, Fla.; *Marine City Classic:* Saltullo. **YACHTING: U. S. Yacht Racing Union Champions:** *Mallory Cup (Men):* Chris Pollock, Cedar Point, Conn.; *Adams Cup (women):* Cindy Batchelor, Pettipaug, Conn.; *Sears Cup (junior):* Mike Alexander, Coconut Grove, Fla.; *O'Day Trophy (single-handed):* Sam Altrueter, Fair Haven, N. J.; *Smythe Trophy (junior single-handed):* Shawn Kempton, Ocean Gate, N. J.; *Prince of Wales Trophy (club):* California Y. C., Los Angeles; *women's double-handed:* Nell Taylor and Sally Lindsay, Branford, Conn.; *junior double-handed:* Dan Hathaway and Scott Young, Dallas, Texas; *National Sea Explorer:* South Central Region. **Canada's Cup:** Golden Dazy, U. S. (Don Driner, skipper) defeated Marauder, Canada (David Howard, skipper). **College Champions:** *Single-handed (Foster Trophy):* Sam Altrueter, Tufts; *dinghies (Morss):* Yale; *sloops (Shields):* So. California; *overall (Fowle):* Tufts; *outstanding sailor (Morris):* Altrueter, Tufts; *women's dinghies:* Princeton. *Distance races: Annapolis to Newport (473 miles):* Salty Goose, Robert Derecktor, Mamaroneck, N. Y.; *Trans-Atlantic (Newport, R. I. to England, 3,160 miles):* Robin, Ted Hood, Marblehead, Mass. (sailed by Lee Van Gemert); *Trans-Pacific (Los Angeles to Honolulu, 2,225 miles):* Chutzpah, Stuart Cowan, Honolulu.

BOWLING—American Bowling Congress: *Regular Division: singles:* Jim Setser, Dayton, Ohio (756); *doubles:* Bob Metz and Steve Partlow, Dayton, Ohio (1,360); *all-events:* Bobby Meadows, Dallas, Tex. (2,033); *team:* Roy Black Chrysler, Cleveland (3,234). *Classic Division: singles:* Les Zikes, Chicago (710); *doubles:* Bill Bunetta, Fresno, Calif., and Marty Piraino, Syracuse, N.Y. (1,392); *all-events:* Bill Beach, Sharon, Pa. (1,993); *team:* Munsingwear No. 2, Minneapolis (2,980). *Booster Division: team:* Leisure Lanes, Kankakee, Ill. (2,929). *Masters:* Ed Ressler, Allentown, Pa. **Bowling Proprietors Association of America Open Championship:** Steve Neff, Sarasota, Fla. (defeated Paul Colwell, Tucson, Ariz., in final): *women:* Paula Sperber, Miami, Fla. **Women's International Bowling Congress:** *Open Division: singles:* Barbara Leicht, Albany, N. Y. (689); *doubles:* Jennette James, Oyster Bay, N. Y., and Dawn Raddatz, East Northport, N. Y. (1,234); *all-events:* Virginia Park, Whittier, Calif. (1,821); *team:* Atlanta Bowling Center, Buffalo, N. Y. (2,836). *Queens:* Cindy Powell, Navarre, Ohio (defeated Pat Costellos, Midwest City, Ohio, in final)

BRIDGE—World Team (Bermuda Bowl): Italy defeated North America by 26 points in final. (North American team: Alfred Sheinwold, Los Angeles, captain; Bob Wolff and Bob Hamman, Dallas, Tex; Eddie Kantar, Bill Eisenberg, John Swanson, Paul Soloway, Los Angeles).

CHESS—World competition: Anatoly Karpov, USSR, became champion when Bobby Fischer relinquished title in dispute over conditions for championship tourney. Karpov had won candidate's competition late in 1974. **U. S. Championship:** Walter Browne, Berkeley, Calif. **Open:** tie between Pal Benko, Jersey City, N. J. and William Lombardy, Ridgefield, N. J. **Women:** Diane Savereid, Santa Monica, Calif. *Men's amateur:* Tie between Frank Metz, Riverside, Calif., and Tom Nelson, Minnesota; *women's amateur:* Christine Hendrickson, Denver.

CROSS-COUNTRY—NCAA: *Division I (6 miles):* Craig Virgin, Illinois (28:23); *team:* Texas-El Paso (88 pts) *Division II (5 miles):* Ralph Serna, California-Irvine (23:40.6); California-Irvine (59); *Division III:* Vin Fleming, Lowell (24:27); North Central Illinois (91). **NAIA** *(5 miles):* Mike Boit, Eastern New Mexico (24:23); Edinboro State (97). **AAU** *(10,000 meters):* Greg Fredericks, Philadelphia Pioneers (28:57); Colorado Track Club (31). **WOMEN:** *Collegiate (AIAW, 3 miles):* Peg Neppel, Iowa State (16:31); Iowa State (96); *AAU (3 miles):* Lynn Bjorklund, Albuquerque (16:32.6); *team:* Los Angeles T. C. (87)

CURLING—World: Switzerland (defeated United States 7–3, in final). **U. S. Championships:** *men:* Seattle Granite Club, skipped by Ed Risling; *women:* Wilmette, Ill., skipped by Betty Duguid; *mixed:* Wausau, Wis., skipped by Neil Collins.

CYCLING—World championships: *Men's sprint:* Daniel Morelon, France; *women's sprint:* Sue Novarra, Flint, Mich.; *men's pursuit:* Thomas Huschke, East Germany; *women's pursuit:* Cornelia Van Hoosten-Hage, Netherlands; *road race (113 miles):* Adrianus Gevers, Netherlands (4:18:01). **U. S. championships:** *Road: senior (123 miles):* John Howard, Houston, Texas (5:05:27); *women (35 miles):* Linda Stein, Los Angeles; *junior (48 miles):* Larry Shields, Goleta, Calif.; *veterans (44 miles):* Nikola Farac-Ban, San Francisco. *Track: sprint:* Steve Woznick, Ridgefield Parks, N. J.; *pursuit:* Ron Skarin, Van Nuys, Calif. *10 miles:* Leroy Gatto, San Jose, Calif.; *team pursuit:* Southern California. *Women: sprint:* Sue Novarra, Flint, Mich.; *pursuit:* Mary Jane Reoch, Philadelphia. *Time trials (all 25 miles): men:* Wayne Stetina, Indianapolis (56:06.65); *women:* Mary Jane Reoch (1:02:04.4); *junior:* Paul Deem, San Pedro, Calif. (57:11.06); *veterans:* Larry Reade, Buffalo B. C. (1:00:08.8)

DOG SHOWS—Westminster (New York): *Best:* Ch. Sir Lancelot of Barvan, Old English sheepdog, owned by Mr. and Mrs. Ronald Vanword, of Newmarket, Ontario (3,035 dogs entered). **International** (Chicago): *Best:* Ch. Cummings Gold Rush Charlie, golden retriever, owned by Mrs. Robert V. Clark, Jr., of Middleburg, Va., and Dr. L. V. Johnson, Princeton, N. J.

FENCING—World championships: *foil:* Christian Noel, France; *team:* France; *épée:* Alexander Pusch, West Germany; *team:* Sweden; *saber:* Vladimir Nalimov, USSR; *team:* USSR; *women's foil:* Katalin Jencski-Stahl, Rumania; *team:* USSR. **U. S. championships:** *foil:* Ed Ballinger, New York; *team:* Fencers Club of New York; *épée:* Scott Bozek, Tanner City, Mass.; *team:* New York A. C.; *saber:* Peter Westbrook, Fencers Club of New York; *team:* Fencers Club of New York; *women's foil:* Nikki Tomlinson, New York; *team:* Halberstadt F. C., San Francisco; *overall team:* Fencers Club of New York. **NCAA:** *foil:* Greg Benko, Wayne State; *épée:* Risto Hurme, New York University; *saber:* Yuri Rabinovich, Wayne State; *team:* Wayne State. **Women's collegiate:** *all-round:* Miss Vincent Hurley, San Jose State; *team:* San Jose State.

GYMNASTICS—AAU: *all-round:* Mike Carter, Louisiana State University; *floor exercise:* Ron Gallimore, Tallahassee, Fla.; *rings:* Pete Studenski, Lincoln, Neb.; *horizontal bar:* Tim Shaw, California Gym Club; *parallel bars:* Shinsuke Shoji, Memphis, Tenn.; *vaulting:* Shoji; *pommel horse:* Russell Hoffman, West Chicago, Ill. *Women: all-round:* Roxanne Pierce, Philadelphia; *uneven bars:* Ann Carr; *balance beam:* Roxanne Pierce; *vault:* Ann Carr. **NCAA:** *Division I: all-round:* Wayne Young, Brigham Young; *floor exercise:* Kent Brown, Arizona State; *pommel horse:* Ted Marcy, Stanford; *rings:* Keith Heaver, Iowa State; *parallel bars:* Yoichi Tomita, Long Beach State; *vault:* Tom Beach, California; *horizontal bar:* Rick Larson, Iowa State; *team:* University of California. **Women's collegiate:** *all-round:* Cole Dowaliby, Southern Connecticut; *floor exercise:* Karen Schuckman, Penn State; *uneven parallel bars:* Diane Sepke, Illinois-Chicago Circle; *balance beam:* Cole Dowaliby; *vault:* tie among Karen Brezack, Clarion State; Laurel Anderson, Seattle Pacific; and Karen Schuckman.

HANDBALL—United States Handball Association champions: *4-wall: singles:* Jay Bilyeu, Fresno, Calif.; *doubles:* Marty Decatur and Steve Lott, New York; *masters singles:* Jack Scrivens, Portland, Ore.; *masters doubles:* Arnold Aguilar and Gabe Enriquez, Los Angeles; *golden masters doubles:* Ken Schneider, Chicago, and Irv Simon, Los Angeles. *3-wall: singles:* Lou Russo, New York; *doubles:* Joel Wisotsky and Wally Ulbrich, New York; *golden masters singles:* Larry Brown, Detroit; *masters doubles:* Jim Golden

and Frank Palazzolo, Detroit; *golden masters doubles:* Vic Hershkowitz and Harold Hanft, Fort Lauderdale, Fla. **AAU:** *one-wall: singles:* Ruby Obert, New York; *doubles:* Joel Wisotsky and Wally Ulbrich, New York; *masters doubles:* Artie Reyer and Joe Danilczyk, New York.

HORSE SHOWS—American Horse Shows Association Medals: *hunter seat:* Cynthia Hankins, Furlong, Pa.; *saddle seat:* Kate William, Tulsa, Okla.; *stock seat:* Melinda Robb, Rancho Santa Fe, Calif. **National Horse Show equitation championships:** ASPCA (Maclay) Katherine Burdsall, Glastonbury, Conn.; *saddle seat (Good Hands):* Kate Williams.

ICE SKATING, FIGURE—World: *Men:* Sergei Yolkov, USSR; *women:* Dianne de Leeuw, Netherlands; *pairs:* Irina Rodnina and Alexander Zaitsev, USSR; *dance:* Irina Moiseeva and Andrei Minenkov, USSR. **U. S. champions:** *men:* Gordon McKellen, Lake Placid, N.Y.; *women:* Dorothy Hamill, Riverside, Conn.; *pairs:* Melissa Militano, Dix Hills, N. Y., and Johnny Johns, Bloomfield Hill, Mich.; *dance:* Colleen O'Conner and Jim Millns, Colorado Springs.

ICE SKATING, SPEED—World champions: *Men: all-round:* Harm Kuipers, Netherlands; *women:* Karin Kessow, East Germany; *sprints: all-round: men:* Alexander Safranov, USSR; *women:* Shiela Young, Detroit. **U. S. champions:** *National Outdoor: men: all-round:* Rich Wurster, Grafton, Wis.; *women: all-round:* Nancy Swider, Park Ridge, Ill.; **National Indoor:** *men: all-round:* Bud Campbell, Paramount, Calif.; *women:* Michele Conroy, St. Paul. **North American Outdoor:** *men: all-round:* Wurster; *women:* Mary Moore, Syracuse, N. Y.; **North American Indoor:** *all-round: men:* Jim Lynch, Australia; *women:* Peggy Hartrich, St. Louis.

LACROSSE—NCAA champions: *Division I:* Maryland (defeated Navy, 20–13, in final); *Division II:* Cortland State (defeated Hobart, 12–11, in final); **Club:** Mount Washington Lacrosse Club.

PARACHUTING—U. S. champions: *Overall: men:* Jimmy Davis, Charlotte, N. C.; *women:* Debbie Schmidt, Joliet, Ill.

POLO—U. S. champions: *Open:* Milwaukee (defeated Tulsa-Dallas, 16–6, in final); *Gold Cup (18–22 goals):* Tulsa-Dallas; *Silver Cup (20 goals):* Dallas; 18 goals: Tulsa; 16 goals: Tulsa; *Continental Cup (11–14 goals):* Milwaukee; *Collegiate:* University of California, Davis (defeated Yale, 15–12, in final).

RODEO—World: *all-round:* Leo Camarillo, Oakdale, Calif.; *saddle bronc riding:* Monty Henson, Mesquite, Tex.; *bareback bronc:* Joe Alexander, Cora, Wyo.; *calf roping:* Jeff Copenhaver, Spokane, Wash.; *steer wrestling:* Frank Shepperson, Midwest, Wyo.; *bull riding:* Don Gay, Mesquite, Tex.; *team roping:* Camarillo; *barrel racing:* Jimmie Gibbs, Valley Mills, Tex.

ROWING—World: *Singles:* Peter-Michael Kolbe, West Germany; *eights:* East Germany; *double sculls:* Frank and Alf Hansen, Norway; *women: singles:* Christine Scheiblich, East Germany; *eights:* East Germany. **U. S. champions:** *singles:* Sean Drea, Ireland; *dash:* Jim Dietz, New York A. C.; *doubles:* Dietz and Larry Klecatsky, New York A. C.; *pairs with coxswains:* John Mathews, Darryl Vreugdenhil, and Ken Dreyfuss, coxswain, Vesper B. C. Philadelphia; *fours:* Vesper; *quads:* New York A. C.; *eights:* U. S. National Team. *Lightweight: singles:* Bill Belden, Undine Barge Club, Philadelphia; *doubles:* Klecatsky and Mike Verlin, New York A. C.; *pairs:* Frank Pisani and Ted Bonanno, New York A. C.; *senior: singles:* Guy Iverson, Undine; *eights:* Detroit. **Intercollegiate champions: I. R. A.:** *Varsity:* Wisconsin; *junior varsity:* Massachusetts Institute of Technology; *freshmen:* Penn; *pairs:* Penn; *pairs with coxswain:* Southern California; *fours:* Wisconsin; *fours without coxswain:* Oregon State; *team (Jim Ten Eyck Trophy):* Wisconsin. *Dad Vail Trophy: eights and overall:* Coast Guard Academy. *Eastern Sprints: varsity:* Harvard; *second varsity:* Harvard; *freshmen:* Penn; *team (Rowe Cup):* Harvard; *lightweight team (Jope Cup):* Harvard. *Mid-America Regatta:* Marietta. *Western Sprints: varsity and junior varsity:* Washington; *freshmen:* California; *team (Ebright Trophy):* Washington. *Dual regattas:* Harvard defeated Yale; Harvard defeated Washington; Cambridge defeated Oxford. **British Royal Henley:** *Diamond sculls:* Sean Drea, Ireland; *double sculls:* M. J. Hart and C. I. Baillieu, Britain; *Stewards' Cup (fours):* Potomac Boat Club, Washington; *Princess Elizabeth Challenge Cup (schoolboy eights):* Ridley College, St. Catharines, Ontario. *Grand Challenge Cup (eights):* Leander Club-Thames Trademen, England. *Women: U. S.: singles:* Wiki Royden, Cambridge, Mass.; *dash:* Gail Pierson, Cambridge; *pairs:* Ann and Marie Jonik, Philadelphia; *eights:* Wisconsin University; *lightweights: singles:* Karin Constant, Philadelphia

SHOOTING—Trapshooting: Grand American, Vandalia, Ohio: *Handicap: men:* Wayne Hegwood, Jackson, Miss. (20 yds, 99); *women:* Ann Kisner, Muscatine, Iowa (19 yds, 97); *junior:* David Keefe, Tiptonville, Tenn. (24 yds, 96); *veterans:* Walter Swogger, Walcotville, Ind. (22 yds, 96). **Skeet**—National Skeet Shooting Association champions: *Men:* Robert Paxton, San Antonio, Tex. (549); *women:* Jackie Ramsey, Dallas (540); *junior:* Steven Pyles, Temple Hill, Md. (538); *senior:* M. E. Kidd, Monroe, La. (536);

veterans: Tom Sanfilipo, Fairfield, Calif. (533); *collegiate:* Paxton; *junior women:* Catherine Forbush, Hamburg, N. Y. (358).

SKIING—World Cup: *men:* Gustavo Thoeni, Italy; *women:* Annemarie Moser-Proell, Austria. **U. S. champions:** *Alpine: men: downhill:* Andy Mill, Aspen, Colo.; *slalom:* Steve Mahre, White Pass, Wash.; *combined:* Greg Jones, South Lake Tahoe, Calif.; *giant slalom:* Phil Mahre, White Pass, Wash. *Women: downhill:* Gail Blackburne, Brunswick, Me.; *slalom:* Cindy Nelson, Lutsen, Minn.; *combined:* Becky Dorsey, Wenham, Mass.; *giant slalom:* Becky Dorsey; *Nordic: jumping:* Jerry Martin, Minneapolis (246 and 238 ft); *veteran:* Glen Kotlarek, Duluth, Minn.; *junior:* Roy Weaver, Iron Mountain, Mich.; *combined:* Mike Devecka, Bend, Ore.; *cross-country: men: 15-kilometers:* Bill Koch, Guilford, Vt.; *30 and 50 kilometers:* Tim Caldwell, Putney, Vt.; *women: 5, 10, and 20-kilometers:* Martha Rockwell, West Lebanon, N. H.; *freestyle: overall:* Bruce Bolesky, Melrose, N. Y.; *women:* Karen Colburn, Bangor, Me.; *Can-Am Trophy series: overall: men:* Peter Dodge, St. Johnsbury, Vt.; *women:* Leslie Leete Smith, Killington, Vt.

SOFTBALL—U. S. Amateur Softball Association: *Men: fast pitch:* Rising Sun Hotel, Reading, Pa.; *open slow pitch:* Pyramid Cafe, Lakewood, Ohio; *industrial slow pitch:* Nassau County (N. Y.) Police Dept.; *16-inch:* Josef's Restaurant, Chicago; *women: fast pitch:* Raybestos Brakettes, Stratford, Conn. (fifth straight); *open slow pitch:* Mark's Brothers Dots, North Miami, Fla.; *modified pitch:* Silvestri's, Staten Island, N. Y. **Girls Little League:** Medford, Ore., defeated Dix Hills, N. Y., 1–0, in final.

SQUASH RACQUETS—*Singles:* Victor Niederhoffer, New York; *doubles:* Michael J. Pierce and Maurice Hecksher 2d, Philadelphia; *veterans:* Pete Bostwick, Jr., New York; *seniors:* Bob Stuckert, Milwaukee; *team:* New York; *veterans doubles:* Don Leggat, Hamilton, Ont., and Charles Wright, Toronto; *senior doubles:* Eugene O'Conor and Tom Schweizer, Baltimore. *Women: singles:* Virginia Akabane, Rochester, N. Y.; *doubles:* Carol Thesieres and Jane Stauffer, Philadelphia. *Collegiate:* Wendy Zaharko, Princeton.

TABLE TENNIS—World: *singles:* Istvan Jonyer, Hungary; *women: singles:* Yung Sun Kim, North Korea; *doubles:* Jonyer and Gabor Gergely, Hungary; *women's doubles:* Maria Alexandru, Rumania, and Shoko Takahashi, Japan; *mixed doubles:* Stanislav Gomozkov and Tatjana Ferdman, USSR; *team: men (Swaything Cup):* China; *women (Corbillon Cup):* China. **U. S. champions:** *singles:* Kjell Johansson, Sweden; *women's singles:* Chung Hyun Sook, South Korea; *doubles:* Dragutin Surbek and Anton Stipancic, Yugoslavia; *women's doubles:* Ann-Christin Hellman and Eva Stroemvall, Sweden; *mixed doubles:* Choi Sung Kuk and Sung Hak So, South Korea

VOLLEYBALL—U. S. Volleyball Assn. champions: *men:* Charthouse, San Diego, Calif.; *women:* Adidas Volleyball Club, Anaheim, Calif.; *senior:* Captain Jack, Long Beach, Calif.; *collegiate:* Pepperdine. **AAU champions:** *men:* Outriggers Canoe Club, Honolulu; *women:* Chimo Volleyball Club, Vancouver, B. C. **Collegiate:** *NCAA:* UCLA; *NAIA:* California-Dominguez Hills; *women:* AIAW: UCLA; *junior college:* Kellogg Community College, Battle Creek, Mich.; *small college:* Texas Lutheran

WATER POLO—World: *U. S.: men:* Concord (Calif.) Aquatics; *women:* North Miami Beach, Fla.

WATER SKIING—World: *men: overall:* Carlos Suarez, Venezuela; *slalom:* Roby Zucchi, Italy; *tricks:* Suarez; *jumping:* Wayne Grimditch, Hillsboro Beach, Fla. *Women: overall:* Liz Allan Shetter, Groveland, Fla.; *tricks:* Maria Carrasco, Venezuela; *tricks and slalom:* Liz Shetter. *Team:* U. S. (12,226 pts). **U. S. champions:** *men: overall:* Ricky McCormick, Hialeah, Fla.; *slalom:* Kris La Point, Castro Valley, Calif.; *tricks:* Tony Krupa, Jackson, Mich.; *jumping:* Wayne Grimditch, Hillsboro Beach, Fla. *Women: overall: tricks and jumping:* Liz Allan Shetter, Groveland, Fla.; *slalom:* Cindy Todd, Pierson, Fla. *Seniors: overall: men:* Ken White, Honolulu; *women:* Barbara Cleveland, Hawthorne, Fla.

WEIGHT LIFTING—U. S. champions: *114 pounds:* Forrest Felton, Savannah, Ga.; *123:* John Yamauchi, Honolulu; *132:* Dave Hussey, St. Louis; *148:* Dan Cantore, San Francisco; *165:* Fred Lowe, Lansing, Mich.; *181:* Peter Rawluk, Los Angeles; *198:* Michael Karchut, Calumet City, Ill.; *242:* Mark Cameron, Middletown, R. I.; *super heavyweight:* Bruce Wilhelm, Phoenix, Ariz.

WRESTLING—AAU: *Freestyle: 105.5 pounds:* David Range, Cleveland; *114.5:* John Morley, New York A. C.; *125.5:* Mark Massery, Chicago; *136.5:* Doug Moses, Waterloo, Iowa; *149.5:* Gene Davis, Long Beach, Calif.; *163:* Carl Adams, Brentwood, N. Y.; *180.5:* John Peterson, Lancaster, Pa.; *198:* Russ Hellickson, Madison, Wis.; *220:* Greg Wojciechowski, Toledo, Ohio; *heavyweight:* Mike McCready, Dubuque, Iowa; *team:* Athletes in Action. **NCAA:** *118 pounds:* Shawn Garel, Oklahoma; *126:* John Fritz, Penn State; *134:* Mike Frick, Lehigh; *142:* Jim Bennett, Yale; *150:* Chuck Yagla, Iowa; *158:* Dan Holm, Iowa; *167:* Ron Ray, Oklahoma State; *177:* Mike Lieberman, Lehigh; *190:* Al Nacin, Iowa State; *heavyweight:* Larry Bielenberg, Oregon State; *team:* Iowa

SRI LANKA (Ceylon)

The most important political event of 1975 in Sri Lanka was the breakup of the United Front coalition that had been in power for 5 years. Economic difficulties, which had plagued the country for many years, multiplied.

Politics. There were growing difficulties between the two major parties in the United Front (UF) government, the Sri Lanka Freedom party (SLFP), led by Prime Minister Sirimavo Bandaranaike, and the Trotskyite Lanka Sama Samaj party (LSSP). The differences culminated in divergent positions on the question of compensation for tea plantations to be taken over by the government and led to the ouster of the LSSP members of the UF cabinet in September. Dr. N. M. Perera was replaced as finance minister by Felix Dias Bandaranaike, Dr. Colvin R. de Silva as minister of plantation industries by Hector Kobbekadduwa, and Leslie Goonewardene as transport minister by P. S. G. Kalugalle. Shortly afterward the remaining non-SLFP member, Peter Keuneman, minister of housing, a leader of the Communist party of Ceylon (CPC), also left the cabinet when the CPC decided to withdraw its support from the government. Mrs. Bandaranaike still retained a clear majority in the parliament.

The Economy. In 1975 the trade and balance of payments deficits reached new highs. Although the prices of traditional exports were the highest in more than a decade, the production of tea and rubber fell appreciably, and expenditures for essential food and raw-material (mostly oil) imports were even greater than anticipated. The economic situation was further affected by the continuing high level of inflation, a severe food shortage due to unprecedented drought, and growing external debt. In July, Sri Lanka signed a commercial cooperation agreement with the European Economic Community. In October the national assembly passed a bill nationalizing tea, rubber, and coconut plantations. The budget for fiscal 1976, introduced in the national assembly on November 5, envisioned a deficit of nearly $300 million. In his budget speech the finance minister announced what amounted to a nationalization of foreign banking in Sri Lanka.

--------- **SRI LANKA · Information Highlights** ---------
Official Name: Republic of Sri Lanka.
Location: Island off the southeastern coast of India.
Area: 25,332 square miles (65,610 sq km).
Population (1975 est.): 14,000,000.
Chief City (1973 est.): Colombo, the capital, 890,000.
Government: *Head of state,* William Gopallawa, president (took office May 1972). *Head of government,* Mrs. Sirimavo Bandaranaike, prime minister (May 1972).
Monetary Unit: Rupee (6.557 rupees equal U. S.$1, April 1975).
Gross National Product (1974 est.): $2,000,000,000.
Manufacturing (major products): Milled rice, chemicals, cement, petroleum products, paper.
Major Agricultural Products: Tea, rubber, coconuts.
Foreign Trade (1974): *Exports,* $510,000,000; *imports,* $680,000,000.

Foreign Relations. Bandaranaike attended the Commonwealth Heads of Government meetings in Kingston, Jamaica, in late April and early May. On the way she made an official visit to Iraq, and after the conference she visited Guyana. Among the prominent foreign leaders who made official visits to Sri Lanka in 1975 were President Kaunda of Zambia, President Echeverria of Mexico, and Prime Minister Bijedic of Yugoslavia. An especially warm reception was accorded a trade delegation from the People's Republic of China.

NORMAN D. PALMER
University of Pennsylvania

SELECTED U. S. COMMEMORATIVE STAMPS OF 1975		
Subject	Denomination	Date of Issue
Benjamin West	10¢	Feb. 10
Pioneer Space Mission	10¢	Feb. 28
Collective Bargaining	10¢	March 13
Mariner Space Mission	10¢	April 4
Lexington-Concord	10¢	April 19
Paul Laurence Dunbar	10¢	May 1
D. W. Griffith	10¢	May 27
Bunker Hill	10¢	June 17
Revolutionary War Uniforms	4x10¢	July 4
Apollo-Soyuz Mission	2x10¢	July 15
International Women's Year	10¢	Aug. 26
Postal Service Bicentennial	4x10¢	Sept. 3
Charles Thomson Postal Card	7¢	Sept. 14
Banking and Commerce	2x10¢	Oct. 6
Seafaring Envelope	10¢	Oct. 13
Christmas Mail Stamps	None	Oct. 14
Liberty Bell (booklets)	13¢	Oct. 31
Francis Parkman (coils)	3¢	Nov. 4
Liberty Tree (envelopes)	13¢	Nov. 8
Freedom of Press	11¢	Nov. 13
Old North Church	24¢	Nov. 14
American Flag	13¢	Nov. 15
American Eagle	13¢	Dec. 1

STAMP COLLECTING

To produce 2 billion stamps for the 1975 Christmas mail, the U. S. Postal Service started printing them before the increased postal rates were determined in August. Therefore, the two full-color designs, a Madonna and Child and a cherub and bell, had no indication of face values. They were sold at 10 cents, the first-class postal rate when they were issued on October 14. The action was a violation of Universal Postal Union regulations, but it provided an expedient solution to a perplexing problem.

Commemorative Issues. Another novelty came in the form of a joint U. S.-USSR commemorative issue that marked the linkup between the Apollo and Soyuz spacecraft on July 15. Both U. S. and Soviet artists made designs and then used one of each for super-size stamps, printed checkerboard fashion in panes of 24.

Because of its wide popular appeal, this accomplishment was similarly commemorated by numerous other postal administrations, notably those that capitalize on any headline event to produce and sell gaudy pictorial stickers for the stamp market rather than for any genuine postal need. Other universally recognized stamp subjects are those issued for International Women's Year and the Holy Year.

U. S. Christmas stamps were released in August without any indication of face value. Uncertainty over the timing of postal increases forced the Postal Service to adopt this policy.

Ghirlandaio: National Gallery
Christmas US postage

Merry Christmas!

US Postage 1975

Early Card by Louis Prang

UPI

President Gerald Ford surprised and pleased stamp collectors on March 13 when, during ceremonies of the "Collective Bargaining" stamp release, he admitted that he had been a collector since boyhood and had brought his album along when he moved into the White House.

International Philatelics. On the international scene, there was record activity in every area. During 1975 there were a number of international exhibitions. The first, staged in Madrid for the 125th anniversary of the first Spanish stamps, was the largest and most lavish. During the ten-day show, there were more than 500,000 visitors. Smaller ones were held in Finland, Belgium, and Austria. In addition, one was devoted exclusively to the finest aerophilatelic material, at the Swiss Transportation and Communications Museum in Lucerne. An exhibition in Manila marked the 40th anniversary of the first regular trans-Pacific air mail service in November 1935.

The market was extremely active in sales of classic issues by regular dealers and auctioneers, at ever increasing prices. A record was set in May, when Corinphila of Zurich put 8,000 Swiss, European, U. S. and other great stamp rarities under the hammer. Conservatively estimated to bring about $3.2 million when the catalogue was distributed, this collection actually brought just under $5 million a month later. The surprising success was attributed to the world-wide faith connoisseurs have in the future of fine stamps and the desire of some investors to use philatelic property as a defense against inflationary trends in the money market.

ERNEST A. KEHR, *Stamp News Bureau*

STOCKS AND BONDS

The stock market finally found its footing in 1975 and staged a rally that ranked as one of the sharpest in modern history. Investors had been waiting quite a while for the rebound because the market had just been through a devastating two-year decline. The decline had taken stock prices, as measured by the broad-based Standard & Poor's 500-stock index, to a 12-year low.

When viewed in this context, it is not surprising that when the rally came it was as breathtaking as the decline. In six months, the market rose over 36% from its early-January low. From midsummer until the end of the year, stock prices backed and filled within a broad range, attempting to consolidate the gains that the market had made during the first half of the year.

What made the market rally even more interesting was that it occurred during a period when the economy was still on shaky ground. It has been said that the market's performance reflects to a large extent investor expectations of events before they occur, and in 1975 investors were looking and hoping for a turnaround in the economy. It was not unusual, then, that the market marked time during the slow recovery in the latter part of the year, rising and falling as each new set of economic statistics was unveiled. The New York City financial crisis added another element of uncertainty, an element that was resolved only on a short-term basis as the year drew to a close.

Stock Prices. The stock market entered 1975 on an optimistic note. A rally that had gotten under way in late December 1974 began to gather momentum, fueled in part by seasonal reinvestment demand, but also by moves to stimulate the economy and an easing monetary stance. These factors more than offset the impact of adverse developments, including rising unemployment, a high level of interest rates, and the increasing financial difficulties of many

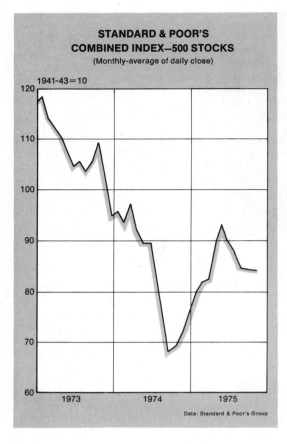

**STANDARD & POOR'S
COMBINED INDEX—500 STOCKS**
(Monthly-average of daily close)

1941-43=10

Data: Standard & Poor's Group

ruptcy of New York's Urban Development Corp., prompted some profit-taking.

Nevertheless, stock prices, on balance, pushed higher. Each stage of the advance seemed to attract a broadening circle of investors, both institutional (banks, mutual funds, insurance companies, and similar organizations) and individual. The leadership of the rally started with blue chip stocks and subsequently widened to include other sectors. Even such events as chaotic conditions in the credit market, or the assassination of King Faisal of Saudi Arabia, did no more than provide a brief interruption. The beginnings of the New York City financial crisis caused little more than a tremor in mid-May. In all, the longest period of hesitancy during the six and one-half month surge was less than a month. Each pause was long enough for demand to chew through the available supply and then propel stocks higher.

During June, however, it became increasingly difficult for stock prices to rise. Concerns over interest-rate levels and some fears over an apparent tightening of the Federal Reserve Bank's monetary policy began to surface.

The rally reached its high on July 15. Subsequently, stock prices began to back and fill. In less than a week, however, the falloff became more readily apparent. In seven trading sessions, Standard & Poor's 500-stock index gave up around 20% of its December-July surge. The abrupt reversal could be traced to three factors: (1) the magnitude of the first-half rebound, when stock-price valuations ran ahead of what was actually developing in the economy; (2) deliberate moves by the Federal Reserve to raise interest rates; and (3) an increasing realization that inflation had not been contained at that point.

The market retreated throughout the late summer, and among individual stocks the erosion was more pronounced than the decline in the popular averages. In late August, the list shook off its melancholy following Federal Reserve Chairman Arthur Burns's assertion that the monetary authorities would take steps to re-

real estate investment trusts (REIT's). The list continued to make progress, showing a stronger upward trend punctuated by brief and shallow setbacks. These pauses occurred when, for example, the administration's economic and energy program was unveiled. The combination of tax relief and a move toward domestic self-sufficiency in energy was viewed as too little, too late. Some weakness also occurred when General Motors, one of the bellwethers of the economy, cut its dividend. The threatened bank-

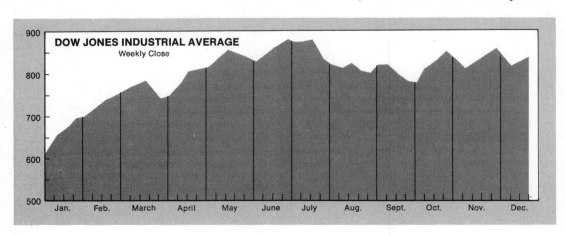

DOW JONES INDUSTRIAL AVERAGE
Weekly Close

Jan. Feb. March April May June July Aug. Sept. Oct. Nov. Dec.

lieve pressures on long-term interest rates. Investors moved back to the sidelines in early September—and stock prices slipped—as the specter of a possible default by New York City loomed large.

From September until the end of the year, the market moved back and forth within a fairly broad trading range. The sawtooth pattern developed as a result of the New York City affair. The ebb and flow of news from Washington; Albany, N. Y.; and New York City by and large dictated whether the market would be up or down. There were also indications that the economic recovery was not progressing as rapidly as might originally have been anticipated. In October, November, and December, the market had both peaks and troughs. But at year's end, stock prices were firming.

Earnings and Dividends. For most companies, earnings slipped in 1975. In terms of Standard & Poor's industrial-stock price index, net income (partly estimated) declined to $8.11 a share, down from $9.69 in 1974. Dividends, on the other hand, moved higher, averaging $3.83 (indicated) a share on Standard & Poor's 425-stock index, as against $3.72 in 1974. These stocks sold at an average price of 11.4 times partly-estimated earnings and had an average return of 4.2% in 1975, compared with a 1974 multiple of 10.2 and a yield of 4.4%.

Volume. Trading on the New York Stock Exchange in 1975 totaled 4.693 billion shares, up from 3.518 billion in 1974.

Bond Prices. Although the bond market in 1975 felt the same influences as the stock market, the overall reaction was contained in a much narrower channel. Yields on highest-grade industrials were at a low of 8.31% in mid-June and reached a high of 8.62% in early October. This compares with a 7.51% low and an 8.50% high in 1974.

In March and early April concern over the prospects of massive U.S. Treasury financing as well as anticipatory corporate bond financing caused bond yields to rise. The Federal Reserve, however, moved into the long-term bond market by making sizable purchases of Treasury maturities beyond 1980, and in a few weeks the markets stabilized. The New York City financial crisis had a significant impact on prices of municipal bonds, and this segment of the bond market was in disarray through the end of the year.

CAROLYN J. COLE
Paine, Webber, Jackson & Curtis, Inc.

SUDAN

Sudan, the largest country in Africa, rose to sudden international prominence in 1975 as the proposed site of a new "world breadbasket," to be developed by Arab oil money. While announcements of oil and natural gas discoveries further raised hopes for economic progress, Su-

─────── **SUDAN · Information Highlights** ───────

Official Name: Democratic Republic of Sudan.
Location: Northeast Africa.
Area: 967,497 square miles (2,505,813 sq km).
Population (1975 est.): 18,300,000.
Chief Cities (1970 est.): Khartoum, the capital, 261,840; Omdurman, 258,532.
Government: *Head of state,* Gen. Jaafar Mohammed al-Numeiry, president (took office Oct. 1971). *Legislature* (unicameral)—People's Assembly.
Monetary Unit: Pound (0.3482 pound equals U. S.$1, Aug. 1975).
Gross National Product (1972 est.): $1,875,000,000.
Manufacturing (major products): Vegetable oil, processed foods, textiles, shoes, pharmaceuticals.
Major Agricultural Products: Cotton, oilseeds, gum arabic, sorghum, sesame seeds, groundnuts, wheat, livestock.
Foreign Trade (1974): *Exports,* $406,000,000; *imports,* $745,000,000.

dan's political stability was called into question by a quickly thwarted coup d'etat and rumors of civil unrest in the country's southern area.

Coup Attempt. The coup attempt on September 5, crushed within hours by troops loyal to the government of Gen. Jaafer al-Numeiry, was laid to Communists and the Muslim Brotherhood, an extremist religious group with Libyan ties. The rebels had seized a radio station and had announced the overthrow of the government, but a tank assault quickly retook the station. Other government changes were milder. A cabinet reshuffle in January 1975 replaced at least 10 senior government ministers.

Civil Unrest. There were sporadic outbursts of violence in the south during 1975, some blamed on political misunderstandings, others on economic progress that was deemed too slow in coming. Largely, however, north-south unity was maintained for a third year, following a 17-year civil war.

Economy. On the economic front, Numeiry revealed at midyear that oil had been found in central Sudan and along the Red Sea coast. Discoveries of natural gas deposits were also announced in 1975.

But Sudan's big economic hope in 1975 lay in another resource—its cultivable virgin soil. Only about 10% of Sudan's arable land was under cultivation in 1975, but soil experts were predicting that satellite pictures taken by the U. S. National Aeronautics and Space Administration would reveal between 100 million and 200 million acres (40–81 million hectares) fit for farming.

Sudan's agricultural potential was noted by the Arab Fund for Economic and Social Development, which estimated that Sudan could provide as much as 35% to 40% of the Middle East's food imports by 1985. The fund reportedly set up a company to use Arab oil money and Western technology to develop Sudan into the first "food power" in Africa or the Middle East.

NANCY MCKEON
The African-American Institute

SURINAM. See LATIN AMERICA.

UPI

Police in Stockholm rescue a victim of terrorist gunmen who invaded, and later destroyed, the West German Embassy. The gunmen then surrendered.

SWEDEN

Sweden's young king, Carl XVI Gustaf, made a number of official visits abroad during the year and was warmly received everywhere. From April 10–12 he paid a state visit to Denmark, followed by a one-day private visit with his cousin, Queen Margrethe. In June he made a state visit to Iceland, and from July 8–11 he was the guest of Great Britain's Queen Elizabeth II and Prince Philip in Scotland, London, and Cambridge. On April 24, West German leftist gunmen attacked the West German embassy in Stockholm. When West Germany refused to release fellow terrorists, the gunmen set off explosions in the embassy and then surrendered.

Politics. Social Democratic leaders from 11 nations met in Stockholm on August 2 to discuss matters of common interest. The meeting, held on the initiative of Sweden's Prime Minister Olof Palme, followed the Helsinki conference on European security. The party leaders established a committee in support of democratic socialism in Portugal and against the expulsion of Israel from the United Nations.

On August 19, Gunnar Helén, the leader of Sweden's Liberal party, announced that he would resign from his post for reasons of health. His successor was Per Ahlmark, a member of Parliament since 1967 and a member of the Liberal party executive committee.

Economic democracy was the main feature of the new program adopted by the Social Democratic party at its 26th party congress held in Stockholm September 27–October 5. According to Prime Minister Palme, this program embodied the third phase in the strategy to transform society, the first two being the safeguarding of political democracy and the consolidation of social democracy. The program states that neither private capitalism nor state capitalism can establish security or justice within nations or solve the economic and political problems of the world. The program's position is that democratic socialism is the only viable means to achieve the emancipation of mankind. Work is put at the forefront of the party's policy, because working conditions determine the relationships of people and dominate society.

Swedish Academy Appointments. The prestigious Swedish Academy elected three new members to fill vacancies. The three are Per-Olof Sundman, a novelist and member of the Swedish legislature; Östen Sjöstrand, a poet and translator; and Professor Torgny Segerstedt, a former dean of Uppsala University.

Economy. It was reported that Sweden spent about 1% of its gross national product on aid to developing nations in 1975. Sweden was the first nation to reach the 1% goal in foreign aid set by Third World nations. For 1976–77 the Swedish International Development Authority requested appropriations totaling about $810 million. Since the authority was founded in 1965, Swedish development aid has increased tenfold.

After lengthy negotiations a two-year wage agreement for some 300,000 white-collar workers was signed on June 12 between the private employees' cartel and the Swedish employers' federation. Wages were to be increased by 13.9% in 1975 and by 7.9% in 1976. Additionally, a 3.2% "wage drift" was to be added to this amount in 1976.

Foreign Visitors. Edward Gierek, head of the Polish United Workers' party, visited Sweden in June. Among the results of his visit was a long-term cooperation agreement in the economic, technical, and scientific fields.

ERIK J. FRIIS
Editor, "The Scandinavian-American Bulletin"

--- **SWEDEN · Information Highlights** ---

Official Name: Kingdom of Sweden.
Location: Northern Europe.
Area: 173,649 square miles (449,750 sq km).
Population (1975 est.): 8,300,000.
Chief Cities (1971 est.): Stockholm, the capital, 723,680; Göteborg, 450,420; Malmö, 263,830.
Government: *Head of state,* Carl XVI Gustaf, king (acceded Sept. 19, 1973). *Head of government,* Olof Palme, prime minister (took office Oct. 1969). *Legislature* (unicameral)—Riksdag.
Monetary Unit: Krona (3.935 kronor equal U. S.$1, May 1975).
Gross National Product (1974 est.): $56,200,000,000.
Manufacturing (major products): Pulp and paper, iron and steel, machinery and equipment, ships.
Major Agricultural Products: Oats, sugar beets, potatoes, wheat, livestock, forest products.
Foreign Trade (1974): *Exports,* $14,084,000,000; *imports,* $14,560,000,000.

SWITZERLAND

Economic problems took priority in Switzerland during 1975, though perennial issues regarding alien workers, abortion, and the Jura region continued to arouse national interest.

Economic Recession. Along with continued consumer price inflation (9.5% in 1974), Switzerland in 1975 was adversely affected by the general economic recession that gripped the world's industrialized nations. On March 2, Swiss voters rejected a constitutional amendment that would have given the government greater power over economic and monetary policy. However, on June 19 the government obtained parliamentary approval of several emergency decrees aimed at stimulating the economy. These called for government investment of $400 million in the private construction industry, an increase in government risk guarantees of Swiss exports, and extensive improvements in federal unemployment insurance.

Earlier, on May 1, the government had removed the 7% restriction on expansion of commercial credit and had liberalized regulations on consumer loans and installment purchases. A series of voluntary control techniques enabled the Swiss Banking Commission to monitor foreign exchange transactions more closely, while the Swiss National Bank joined West Germany on August 22 in offering 4% bank lending rates, the lowest of any non-Communist industrial nation.

On June 8 voters approved sharp increases in wholesale and retail sales taxes and the gasoline tax. Also, taxes were increased from 10.45% to 11.5% on incomes over $100,000.

Compared to the same period in 1974, exports during the first six months of 1975 rose 14% while imports declined .3%. This served to reduce the dollar value of imports over exports from about $1.4 billion in 1974 to $585 million in 1975.

Unemployment. In May, 6,527 people registered as unemployed, compared with 64 a year earlier. Though minuscule compared to that of other nations, unemployment prompted mass demonstrations by Swiss trade union members on March 1, the first such activity in 20 years.

The registered unemployed did not include the many foreign workers who had lost jobs during the year and left the country. On August 1 the federal government issued new regulations aimed at further reducing a foreign seasonal work force that had already been cut 21.6% to 152,000 during the preceding 12 months.

Abortion Laws. On March 6 a coalition of extreme pro- and anti-abortion forces in the National Council defeated a government-sponsored moderate abortion bill. It would have extended legalized abortions to include certain well-defined, nonmedical reasons.

Jura Independence. On March 16 the three French-speaking districts that had originally voted in June 1974 against creating an independent Jurassian canton voted to remain with Berne canton rather than join the three districts that had voted favorably. On June 28, however, eight communes from these districts did opt to join it.

Elections. Results of parliamentary elections in October left the strength of the ruling four-party coalition unchanged.

During 1975, Switzerland joined in creating the European Space Agency and aided in airlifting thousands of refugees from Angola to Lisbon. Of great interest to the international literary community was the opening on August 12 in Zurich of the personal papers of Thomas Mann, revealing extensive diaries covering the years 1918–21, and 1933–55.

PAUL C. HELMREICH
Wheaton College, Mass.

SWITZERLAND · Information Highlights

Official Name: Swiss Confederation.
Location: Central Europe.
Area: 15,941 square miles (41,288 sq km).
Population (1975 est.): 6,500,000.
Chief Cities (1973): Bern, the capital, 166,000; Zurich, 432,400.
Government: *Head of state,* Pierre Graber, president (took office Jan. 1975). *Legislature*—Federal Assembly: Council of States and National Council.
Monetary Unit: Franc (2.714 francs equal U. S.$1, Aug. 1975).
Gross National Product (1973 est.): $38,800,000,000.
Manufacturing (major products): Machinery, chemicals, textiles, watches, clocks, clock parts.
Major Agricultural Products: Potatoes, sugar beets, wheat, barley, dairy products, forest products.
Foreign Trade (1974): *Exports,* $8,124,000,000; *imports,* $9,960,000,000.

SYRIA

In 1975, Syrian President Hafez al-Assad's foreign policy was threatened by his inability to forge a unified Arab front in negotiations with Israel and complicated by the instability of wartorn Lebanon. However, in other spheres, Assad was more successful. He maintained Syria's important ties with the Soviet Union, reestablished solid relations with Jordan's King Hussein, and obtained huge amounts of foreign aid, which helped to offset production drops in the agricultural sector and to underwrite substantial capital investments in Syrian industry.

Arab-Israeli Dilemma. Throughout 1975, President Assad maintained that a lasting Middle East peace could only be achieved in the context of an overall settlement requiring Israel's return to its pre-1967 boundaries and the recognition of the Palestine Liberation Organization (PLO) as the sole legitimate spokesman for restoring the rights of the Palestinian people. Assad supported the comprehensive approach of the internationally backed Geneva Peace Conference and opposed the U. S.-mediated, step-by-step formula for peace, particularly when Israel announced on January 27 that a second-stage agreement with Syria on the Golan Heights was impossible.

A shepherd guides his flock along the banks of the Euphrates River in Syria where a huge hydroelectric dam is being constructed with Soviet assistance.

UPI

Accordingly, Assad strongly criticized the Israeli-Egyptian negotiations that led to a second Sinai disengagement agreement in September. Nevertheless, Syria continued to maintain contact with the United States. U. S. Secretary of State Henry Kissinger visited Damascus several times, while Syrian Foreign Minister Abdel Halim Khaddam, during a visit to Washington on June 19–22, conceded that a gradual withdrawal by Israel would be acceptable if it were a part of a plan for total withdrawal. Syria appeared at times to be conciliatory to an incrementalist approach, but when the Sinai pact was announced, Assad tried to sabotage it. Echoing earlier declarations, Damascus called the agreement a policy of "dividing the solution," which could "only benefit Israel."

On September 18, Khaddam declared that Syria would have no relations with Egypt until the pact was renounced. In an effort to embarrass Egypt's President Anwar el-Sadat, Syria published the last series of telegrams between Sadat and Assad during the 1973 war to show that Egypt had initiated the cease-fire despite Syrian protests. In spite of earlier threats, relations with Egypt were not broken when the Sinai pact was ratified.

While the Israeli-Egyptian talks developed, Assad took steps to maintain a military option consistent with his February 3 statement that Syria had a "legitimate right to use every effective means to liberate its occupied territory." On April 3, a series of talks began with Jordan's King Hussein, which led to the August 22 announcement of the formation of a Supreme Syrian-Jordanian Command Council to coordinate both countries' political and military strat-

egies. The negotiations were highlighted by Assad's June trip to Amman, the first time in 19 years that a Syrian president had visited Jordan.

The Command Council, headed by Assad and King Hussein, was established so Syria and Jordan could "adopt joint and coordinated positions and decisions" on issues of war and peace. This declaration served as a warning to Israel that it would still have to fight on two fronts in another war, even if Egypt was precluded from military intervention as a result of the new Sinai disengagement pact.

A crisis on the Golan front was averted on November 30 when Assad, in exchange for a U. N. Security Council invitation for PLO participation in a Security Council debate on the Middle East, agreed to a six-month extension of the mandate of the U. N. Disengagement Observation Force.

Lebanese Crisis. During the bloody sectarian violence that threatened Lebanon's stability

---

SYRIA · Information Highlights

Official Name: Syrian Arab Republic.
Location: Southeast Asia.
Area: 71,498 square miles (185,180 sq km).
Population (1975 est.): 7,300,000.
Chief Cities (1974): Damascus, the capital, 835,000; Aleppo, 500,000; Homs, 164,000.
Government: *Head of state,* Lt. Gen. Hafez al-Assad, president (took office March 1971). *Head of government,* Mahmoud al-Ayubi, premier (took office Nov. 1972). *Legislature* (unicameral)—People's Council.
Monetary Unit: Pound (3.70 pounds equal U. S.$1, May 1975).
Gross National Product (1972 est.): $2,244,000,000.
Manufacturing (major products): Petroleum products, textiles, cement, glass, soap.
Major Agricultural Products: Wheat, barley, sugar beets.
Foreign Trade (1974): *Exports,* $728,000,000; *imports,* $1,202,900,000.

throughout most of 1975, Syria played an instrumental, if only partially successful, role in helping to bring about critical cease-fires in May, September, and October. Foreign Minister Khaddam's role as mediator was seen by most observers as a reflection of Assad's fear that if Lebanon's factional fighting led to total anarchy, Syria would be forced to intervene militarily to restore order and stability to its western flank. Assad was quite aware that if Syria were dragged into the fighting, Israel would also intervene. On September 23, the Israeli government said that Syrian intervention in the Lebanese conflict would be seen as constituting a threat to Israel's security. This threat was reiterated in October.

As a result, Assad summoned PLO leader Yasir Arafat and Lebanese Premier Rashid Karami to Damascus in mid-October and curtly informed them that the Christian-Muslim bloodshed must stop for the well-being of the Middle East. This last initiative was partially successful, and a confrontation with Israel was avoided.

Economy. Syria's industrial economy received a massive shot in the arm with the influx of some $910 million in foreign aid and the prospect of several hundred million dollars more. The aid, combined with hard currency reserves that reached $750 million, compared to $50 million in 1973, empowered the ministry of industry to commit almost $1.1 billion to industrial projects in 1975. Nearly all industries were the recipients of large capital investments, particularly phosphates, textiles, oil, steel, and tourism.

Oil production reached nearly 10 million tons, a 30% increase over 1974 levels, which were valued at $400 million. Cotton production, Syria's largest source of foreign exchange, dropped in 1975 because of a 10% decrease in the land under cultivation.

F. NICHOLAS WILLARD
Georgetown University

TANZANIA

International economic conditions continued to threaten Tanzania's financial position in 1975, but the country's third one-party election since independence was held as scheduled on October 26. The political union of the island of Zanzibar and mainland Tanzania (formerly Tanganyika) remained tenuous.

Political Developments. President Julius Nyerere was reelected unopposed in the October balloting, but voters in most constituencies chose from two candidates of the ruling Tanganyika African National Union (TANU). At TANU's biennial conference in September, President Nyerere reaffirmed the party's commitment to *ujamaa* (socialism). He reported that as of mid-year, 9.1 million people, about 65% of the mainland's rural population, were living in *ujamaa* villages, a dramatic increase from 1974's 15%. The entire rural population is scheduled for settlement in such villages by the end of 1976.

UPI

Two of four students kidnapped from the Gombe Research Station in Tanzania hold a press conference after their release in August. They had been held hostage for five weeks by Zaire-based guerrillas.

Economic Conditions. Tanzania was one of the countries in Africa most disastrously affected by the worldwide rise in commodity prices in 1974 and 1975. A satisfactory balance of payments position in 1973 has been destroyed by increased costs in imports such as petroleum, grain, milk products, and sugar. The government doubled the domestic price of sugar, thereby cutting consumption in half.

International Relations. Tanzania, along with Botswana and Zambia, boycotted the 12th heads of state conference of the Organization of African Unity (OAU). Tanzania expressed strong objections to the holding of the conference in Kampala, Uganda, which meant that the president of the host country, Idi Amin, assumed the OAU chairmanship.

JAY E. HAKES
University of New Orleans

——— **TANZANIA · Information Highlights** ———

Official Name: United Republic of Tanzania.
Location: East Africa.
Area: 364,899 square miles (945,087 sq km).
Population (1975 est.): 15,400,000.
Chief City (1974 est.): Dar es Salaam, the capital, 300,-000.
Government: *Head of state,* Julius K. Nyerere, president (took office 1964). *Chief minister,* Rashidi Kawawa, premier (took office 1972). *Legislature* (unicameral) —National Assembly.
Monetary Unit: Shilling (8.16 shillings equal U. S.$1, Oct. 1975).
Gross National Product (1972 est.): $1,583,000,000.
Manufacturing (major products): Textiles, cement, petroleum products, refined sugar, aluminum.
Major Agricultural Products: Cloves, sisal, cotton, coffee, oilseeds, groundnuts, tea, tobacco, sugarcane.
Foreign Trade (1973): *Exports,* $321,000,000; *imports,* $448,000,000.

TAXATION

High rates of both unemployment and inflation pose serious policy problems for any government. Although tax reductions or expenditure increases will reduce unemployment, they are also likely to add to inflationary pressures. In this situation governments must choose to emphasize either a reduction in the rate of inflation or a reduction in the rate of unemployment. This dilemma leads to the kind of serious controversy that characterized the U. S. federal government's tax and expenditure policy in 1975.

Congressional Action. In the fiscal 1976 budget, President Ford requested temporary tax reductions of $16 billion, with about 75% of the reduction benefiting individuals and 25% benefiting business firms. This reduction was proposed to be offset by increases in import duties and domestic excises on petroleum and by an excess-profits tax on companies producing petroleum.

The Congress greatly modified these proposals in the Tax Reduction Act of 1975, adopted in March. The act provided for about $20 billion in reductions, with 85% of the relief directed to individuals and with no offsetting petroleum excises. The tax reductions for individuals provided substantially-greater benefits to low-income brackets than had been requested by the President. The major provisions included a 10% rebate on 1974 personal income tax liabilities up to a maximum of $200 per family, an increase in the standard deduction, a $30 exemption credit, and an earned-income credit for certain low-income families, all applicable to 1975 tax liabilities. The investment credit for business firms was raised from 7% to 10%, and utilities were included.

In October, President Ford proposed that the 1975 tax cuts be made permanent and that the tax law be modified by raising the personal tax exemption from $750 to $1,000, with a standard deduction for married couples of $2,500. He also proposed an increase in the investment tax credit and a 2% cut in the corporation tax rate. The tax reductions would total $28 billion and would be paired with a corresponding reduction in federal spending. President Ford threatened to veto any tax reduction measures that did not establish a spending ceiling of $395 billion for the fiscal year starting October 1976.

The majority of the House Ways and Means Committee expressed opposition to the spending ceiling on the grounds that the President's budget proposals would not be submitted until late January 1976, and an early ceiling would greatly complicate the new Congressional budget procedures for 1976. In the meantime, the Ways and Means Committee completed a proposal to extend the 1975 tax reduction with a large number of other tax reform proposals. The most important of these provides additional deductions for child care, liberalizes the capital-loss carry-back, extends the 10% investment credit until 1980, and limits some tax shelters.

Congress eventually worked out a compromise with the President to continue the tax reductions into 1976, with a pledge to seek further expenditure reductions. Tax reforms were to be reconsidered in the next session.

State and Local Revenue. At all levels of government costs increase with inflation. Revenues will likewise increase, but the extent of increase is dependent on the nature of the tax system. Revenue from sales taxes and individual income taxes, for example, will increase more than revenue from the local property tax. Thus, in 1975 many states and local governments were in a serious fiscal crisis with costs rising more rapidly than revenue.

For fiscal 1975, ending June 30, total state-local tax revenue increased to $141.5 billion, 8.7% above 1974 revenue. General sales taxes, gross receipts taxes, and individual income taxes registered the sharpest gains. Gasoline tax revenues increased by only 1% and property tax revenues by 6.1%.

The years 1973 and 1974 were marked by relatively modest increases in state tax rates. In 1975, however, 20 states voted increased levies amounting to about $1 billion with actions pending in state legislatures at the end of the year that would add yet another $1 billion. The increases that were enacted typically took the form of higher excise tax rates, taxes on natural resources, and other miscellaneous revenue sources, rather than major increases in income and sales taxes. In a great many states local governments were empowered to levy additional taxes.

In addition to New York state and New York City, whose fiscal problems were far from resolved at the end of 1975, the states of Michigan, Massachusetts, New Jersey, and Connecticut appear to have had the most severe fiscal crises in 1975. In each case the crisis was at least partially alleviated by a combination of expenditure reductions and tax increases.

Supreme Court Decisions. The important tax decisions in 1975 did not concern tax liabilities specifically, but they did concern the power of the Internal Revenue Service to obtain information about taxpayers. In *U. S.* v. *Bisceglia*, the U. S. Supreme Court ruled that a bank must release the identity of a depositor when subpoenaed by the Internal Revenue Service (IRS). In this case, an unknown depositor had made a large transaction at a bank with very old and worn $100 bills. The IRS demanded that the bank identify the depositor. The power of the IRS to obtain financial records was also upheld in its efforts to obtain information about offshore oil leases from Humble Oil and Refining Co.

The Supreme Court affirmed a ruling of a district court that sustained a Tennessee tax on railroad property. The state had classified the property as a public utility rather than as com-

mercial and industrial property, thus subjecting it to a higher rate. A New Hampshire income tax on non-residents was annulled on the ground that the state did not apply a similar tax to its own residents.

Canada. Canadian taxpayers will benefit again in 1976 from the indexing of personal income tax exemptions to the cost of living. With an 11.3% inflation rate for the period ending September 20, exemptions were increased on 1976 income from $1,878 to $2,091. The national government anticipated a revenue loss of approximately $1 billion.

Other Countries. Western European countries continued to grapple with double-digit inflation and high unemployment during 1975. The most dramatic tax changes occurred in the United Kingdom where inflation rates have been 25%. Corporate and individual income taxes were increased, a special tax on automobiles was levied, a capital transfer tax was enacted, the Value Added Tax (VAT) for consumer durables was increased, and duties on alcoholic beverages and tobacco were also increased. In addition, a Petroleum Revenue Tax Act placed an unusually heavy retroactive levy on offshore oil company revenues. In September, the Chancellor of the Exchequer proposed an annual wealth tax on all net property holdings above £100,000 (about $210,000) at rates from 1%–5%, effective in 1977. If adopted, this levy will add a very heavy tax burden to upper-income brackets.

In West Germany a projected budget deficit prompted three tax changes. German industries will make higher contributions to unemployment compensation. The German VAT was increased from 11% to 13% effective Jan. 1, 1977. Tobacco and liquor excise tax rates were also increased.

Corporate, individual income, and sales taxes were sharply increased in Switzerland. In the Netherlands a large number of tax increases were adopted that amounted to a 3% increase in the burden on the average taxpayer. In Austria all taxpayer classifications were abolished in favor of a single taxpayer category. In Denmark depreciation allowances were increased to 45%, and previous business losses were allowed to be credited to future tax payments.

In Belgium, facing both inflation and the highest rate of unemployment in 20 years, an unusual levy was adopted. To encourage the employment of younger workers, older workers may retire three years earlier. The retirees' benefits are to be financed by a 10% excess profits tax based on company earnings above their 1973–74 average.

JESSE BURKHEAD
Syracuse University

TELECOMMUNICATIONS

Despite the overall sluggishness of the U. S. economy, telecommunications equipment and services markets grew steadily during 1975, and the outlook continues to be bright both in the United States and other countries.

Long-Term Market Growth. Data communications suppliers expect their segment of the telecommunications market to grow steadily, at least through 1985. Frost & Sullivan Co., a New York City-based research firm, estimated that the present $3.36 billion market for data communications equipment and services in the United States will increase at a real rate (discounting inflation) of 22.5% during the next three years, then taper off for an overall 10-year compounded growth rate of 15%.

Meanwhile, telephone-exchange equipment has become the major single hardware investment in telephone systems throughout the world. Robert Chapuis, a consultant to the International Telecommunications Union's Coordinating Committee for Telephone and Telegraph, pegged spending for plant in 1975 at some $25 billion total, with $10 billion allocated to switching equipment. Although conventional electromechanical switching is expected to dominate the market for years to come, computer-controlled exchanges are beginning to make headway in world markets. However, Bjorn Lundvall, president of Sweden's L. M. Ericsson, predicted that the late 1980's will be the earliest that the number of computer-controlled lines installed in a year will equal the number of electromechanical lines in systems outside the United States and Japan. By then, the Ericsson executive believes,

TELEPHONES IN MAJOR COUNTRIES			
Country	Telephones Jan. 1, 1974	% increase over 1973	No. per 100 population
Argentina	2,065,273	5.8	8.30
Australia	4,659,182	5.9	35.36
Austria	1,841,234	8.7	24.55
Belgium	2,503,036	8.6	25.72
Brazil	2,415,082	10.3	2.34
Bulgaria	640,842	10.2	7.37
Canada	11,668,292	6.2	52.31
China, Rep. of	742,304	24.4	4.77
Colombia, Rep. of	1,079,645	6.9	4.65
Czechoslovakia	2,354,313	5.5	16.09
Denmark	2,047,497	7.1	39.99
Finland	1,535,406	8.7	32.91
France	11,337,000	9.7	21.66
Germany, East	2,326,143	4.2	13.67
Germany, West	17,802,646	7.8	28.73
Greece	1,670,132	16.2	18.67
Hong Kong	913,411	14.9	21.65
Hungary	968,459	4.8	9.27
India	1,590,000	7.5	0.27
Iran	552,500	23.6	1.74
Israel	685,382	10.6	20.73
Italy	12,611,653	11.2	22.86
Japan	38,697,901	13.7	35.40
Korea, Rep. of	1,014,016	16.1	3.09
Mexico	2,222,654	13.5	4.20
Netherlands, The	4,317,006	7.7	32.00
New Zealand	1,410,532	6.3	46.35
Norway	1,308,420	3.7	32.93
Poland	2,237,603	7.2	6.68
Portugal	948,003	8.5	10.02
Rumania	886,166	—	4.25
South Africa, Republic of	1,816,291	6.4	7.54
Spain	6,331,474	10.8	18.13
Sweden	4,984,370	3.2	61.20
Switzerland	3,604,034	5.9	55.44
Turkey	807,294	10.8	2.09
United Kingdom	19,095,317	8.7	34.06
U.S.S.R.	14,260,700	8.0	5.68
United States	138,286,000	5.1	65.47
Venezuela, Rep. of	504,000	7.1	4.38
Yugoslavia	1,003,550	10.2	4.77

the annual total number of lines for these systems will be about 25 million.

Domestic Communications Satellites. After more than a decade of use in international communications, satellites are about to become an important part of the communications network of the United States. Westar, owned and operated by the Western Union Corp., became operational in the spring of 1975. It was the nation's first domestic satellite system. The Westar satellite is in a stationary orbit high above the equator. Its antenna can relay voice, video, or data transmissions. A second communications satellite, produced by RCA Global Communications, was scheduled to be launched, and a third system, to be operated by American Telephone & Telegraph Co. (AT&T), should be in orbit by mid-1976.

According to the Federal Communications Commission (FCC), there has been a steady increase in the number of requests for permission to construct and operate ground stations for receiving and transmitting signals to and from the satellite systems. Actually, 68 applications were filed with the FCC in fiscal 1975, up from 14 in fiscal 1974. The applications came from satellite companies as well as from businesses like Cities Service, which is erecting an antenna on an oil rig in the Gulf of Mexico.

The FCC has hired additional staff personnel and streamlined its regulatory procedures to handle the increased domestic satellites activity more efficiently and to help speed the processing of applications for earth stations. One move was to eliminate the requirement that two permits had to be obtained: one to purchase ground-station equipment and another to construct a station. The two steps were consolidated into one.

International Carriers. In August nine international communications carriers signed agreements totaling $137 million to construct and operate three submarine cable systems. One is to be between the Virgin Islands and the United States, one between Brazil and Venezuela, and one to expand the microwave system between the Virgin Islands and Puerto Rico. The three proposed cable systems are scheduled to be operational by 1977. The agreements involved three International Telephone & Telegraph Corp. (ITT) subsidiaries: ITT World Communications; All America Cables & Radio; and ITT Communications, Virgin Islands. The other carriers included AT&T, RCA Global Communications, Western Union International, TRT Telecommunications, the Brazilian Telecommunications Authority, and the National Telephone Co. of Venezuela.

Hi/Lo Case Reopened. The FCC decided in September to reopen the controversial "hi/lo" rates case of AT&T. The new rate structure charges business customers in large cities less than they would pay under traditional rates. Customers in smaller, so-called low-density, areas are charged more than they would pay

COURTESY WESTERN UNION TELEGRAPH

Western Union's Westar satellite, which became operational in the spring, blasts off from launching site.

under the traditional rate schedule. AT&T has been collecting revenues based on its hi/lo rate schedule since June 1974, subject to refund. The company claims that the new rate structure more closely reflects the cost of providing the services in different parts of the nation. The traditional method of charging for long-distance interstate calls is based on averaging nationwide costs.

Rather than issue a formal decision on hi/lo, the FCC found that evidence presented in the case was insufficient to draw a conclusion on the merits of AT&T's new rate structure. AT&T claims that without the hi/lo rates, it would lose about $100 million annually.

New Telecom Bureau Proposed. The chairman of the U. S. House Commerce Committee, Rep. Harley Staggers, introduced legislation to establish a Bureau of Telecommunications within the Commerce Department. Under Staggers's proposed bill, the bureau would be responsible for centralizing and directing all department telecommunications activities. These activities would be upgraded from the department's present Office of Telecommunications to the bureau level, placing the telecommunications effort on a par with the Bureau of Census, the National Bureau of Standards, the Patent Office, and other major Commerce Department functions.

The White House's Office of Telecommunications Policy (OTP) announced plans to study the technological burden now being placed on the electromagnetic spectrum. "Like air and water," said acting OTP director John Eger, the radio spectrum "is susceptible to oversubscription and pollution if not managed properly."

RONALD A. SCHNEIDERMAN
Electronics Magazine

Lawrence E. Spivak (*left*) closed his last *Meet the Press* show on November 9 with President Ford as the guest. Spivak was the news program's moderator for 28 years.

television and radio

Sex and violence, the "family hour," a viewers' revolt, and problems with Canada were features of a television year in the United States that was widely considered to be the worst in industry history, despite overall financial success for the networks.

TELEVISION

Television, Sex, and Violence. Late in 1974, Federal Communications Commission (FCC) Chairman Richard E. Wiley began exhorting the broadcasting industry to regulate the contents of its programs before the government decided to take over the task. Wiley's concern was in response to waves of protest over sexually-suggestive material in prime-time programs, protests expressed in what may well have been organized letter-writing campaigns addressed to the networks, the FCC, and Congress. The violence in TV programs had long been a target of social scientists and parents. CBS proposed, in reply to the FCC chairman, that the period from 8 to 9 P.M. be considered as the "family hour" and programmed only with material suitable for viewing by the whole family. The proposal was promptly endorsed by Sen. John O. Pastore, the chairman of the Senate Communications Subcommittee and a vociferous critic of TV "sex and violence." In January the three networks agreed to the suggestion, starting in September with the "new season." The concept became official when it was adopted in April by the National Association of Broadcasters (NAB) and added to the Television Code. There were mixed sociological, aesthetic, and critical reactions to the "family hour." In October the writers Guild of America, the Directors Guild, the Screen Actors Guild, and several prominent

writers, directors, and producers filed suit against the networks, the FCC, and the NAB, claiming censorship. They also charged governmental interference with their first amendment rights.

Ratings. There was shock for the networks in the Nielsen ratings for the first six weeks of the 1975–76 season (the new fall programs), and in some quarters of the industry the blandness of the "family hour" was held to be at least partially responsible. Nielsen found that, in the September 8 to October 19 viewing period, household viewing was down by 6%, although there remained the possibility that the total number of viewers had increased slightly. Equally disheartening to the networks and advertisers was the likelihood that the number of women in the 18–49 age bracket, the prime consuming group, was off by about 2%.

Entertainment. Critical and audience reaction to 1975's new programs was largely negative. In the "second season," beginning in January 1975, the networks offered 14 new programs. Only six survived into the fall, and only one of the six, *The Jeffersons,* was a real hit. With the "new season," in September, the networks served up 27 new programs. Within the first six weeks 8 had been cancelled, and 11 more were in serious danger. From all the new shows only *Phyllis,* starring the redoubtable Cloris Leachman, emerged as a clear hit. Preceded by *Rhoda* and followed by *All in The Family* (both in new time slots), *Phyllis* immediately became a Top Ten contender for CBS. NBC's *Joe Forrester,* ABC's *Starsky & Hutch,* and CBS's *Switch* also looked like winners. Replacements for the cancellations were expected to feature variety shows, few and far between during the beginning of the season.

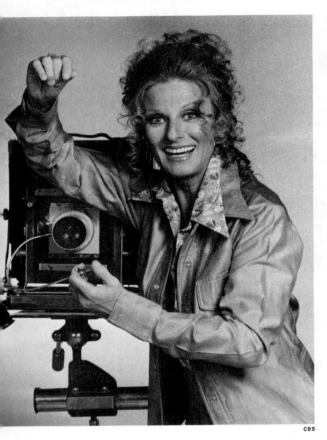

CBS

Cloris Leachman played a creative assistant in *Phyllis*, CBS television's successful fall series.

Daytime programming was marked by a new phenomenon, the successful extension of some programs, chiefly soap operas, to a full hour. NBC led the way with *Another World*, then lengthened *Days of Our Lives*, and gained impressively in share of audience. CBS countered by extending the game show, *The Price Is Right*, to an hour, and followed with an hour-long *As the World Turns*.

Whatever the disasters in primetime programs and whatever the losses in total viewing homes, commercial television did excellent business. Despite recession elsewhere, 1974 was a record-setting year, and 1975 gave promise of being even better.

Public Affairs. After the furor over NBC's 1972 documentary, *Pensions: The Broken Promise*, the networks seemed less inclined to deal with topics that might cause controversy. But on September 5, CBS televised the 90-minute documentary, *The Guns of Autumn*. The shooting started well before the broadcast. Alerted by the magazine of the National Rifle Association, gun and hunting groups brought such pressure on the program's advertisers that six cancelled their commercials. Only one advertiser

remained, with two 30-second spots. CBS fired a second blast by presenting on September 28 a 60-minute *Echoes of the Guns of August* (planned before the original broadcast) in which CBS defended itself but gave time to the expression of opposing views. One curious upshot of the two broadcasts was the filing by the Michigan United Conservation Clubs of a $300 million slander and libel suit against CBS, charging that the two documentaries had held about 1 million Michigan hunters up to ridicule.

The President and Television. President Gerald Ford made frequent use of prime TV time during the year, with the apparent assent of the networks. Then, with little warning, the President asked for time on Monday, October 6, for a hastily prepared speech on new tax proposals. ABC carried the speech, while CBS and NBC turned it down in favor of their scheduled programs. The White House then announced a press conference for Thursday of that same week. NBC and CBS carried it, and ABC refused it. This was the first time that the presidential "right" of unlimited access to the three networks had been denied.

The incidents brought into public view long-simmering questions about the "equal time" provisions of Section 315 of the Communications

Lloyd Bridges returned to prime-time television as the star of NBC's *Joe Forrester*.

NBC PHOTO

FORRESTER

The documentary *The Guns of Autumn*, shown in September, was criticized by hunting and gun groups for alleged prejudice against hunters.

CBS

Act. CBS and NBC turned down the President's speech on the ground that they might be unable to refuse equal time demands, because the President is a candidate for the Republican nomination. Earlier in the year the FCC had reversed previous decisions, ruling that it now considered press conferences and debates to be exempt from equal-time requirements. The Thursday press conference, therefore, offered no problems to the networks. In turning it down ABC merely made the journalistic judgment that it would not offer much of news value. It is likely that Section 315 will one day be repealed or drastically modified, and bills to this end have been introduced in both Senate and House.

Canada. Many Canadians have long felt that their own television was being "overwhelmed" by U. S. TV. Canadians see a great deal of it, through broadcasts from stations in cities near the border, through the purchase of U. S. programs by Canada's two networks, and especially through cable TV. Cable TV is more highly developed in Canada than in any other country in the world and serves about 40% of Canadian homes.

Early in 1975 a bill was proposed in Parliament to eliminate as a tax deduction those business expenses incurred by Canadian advertisers in using U. S. border stations to reach Canadian audiences. Shortly after, the Canadian Radio-Television Commission (CRTC) roiled both Canadian and U. S. waters by requiring of its cable systems, as a condition of their license renewals, that they delete from the U. S. programs they transmit a substantial number of U. S. commercials, substituting Canadian commercials and public service spots. The policy was instituted, according to the CRTC, primarily to return to Canada an estimated $20 million of advertising

revenue now going to the U. S. border stations. Even as three Buffalo, N. Y., stations petitioned the FCC for permission to "jam" Canadian reception of their signals, the whole problem landed in the State Department, as a question for diplomatic negotiation.

Cable Television. In all the confusion between cable TV and on-air broadcasting, one important agreement was reached during the year between American Telephone and Telegraph (AT&T) and the National Cable Television Association over pole attachment rates. FCC Chairman Wiley negotiated the compromise in order to resolve the question of FCC jurisdiction. Pay cable, offering regular cable subscribers movie-and-sports packages at a special figure, grew at a comfortable rate during the year, despite persistent charges of interference by on-air broadcasting interests. Although pay cable was still a small part of the total cable picture, NCTA reported that by July there were 98 pay cable companies operating in 18 states, with New York, California, Florida, and Pennsylvania accounting for 76 of the total.

Congress and TV Coverage. Increased openness in conducting government affairs was evident in several ways. In November the Senate unanimously adopted a resolution to open all its deliberations, whether on the floor or in committee, to public view and to require an open vote if need were felt for a closed meeting. A month earlier the Joint Committee on Congressional Operations had reaffirmed its recommendation of a year before that live broadcasting of Congressional proceedings be undertaken, and the House Rules Committee reported such broadcasting technically feasible. Plans were virtually completed for a new Congressional hearings room, designed to permit live broadcasting with

Daytime television placed increased emphasis on game shows in 1975. *The Money Maze* gave successful players the opportunity to win $10,000 in cash.

UPI

a minimum of "noise" from cameras and lights —in other words, a TV studio.

Federal Communications Commission. President Ford's reappointment of Abbott Washburn to a full term on the FCC was widely regarded as an indication that the President planned no change in the direction or composition of the commission. Some members of Congress, however, were more restive. Rep. Torbert Macdonald, chairman of the House Communications Subcommittee, introduced a bill entitled The FCC Reorganization and Reform Act. It was designed to free the FCC of domination both by the industry it is mandated to regulate and by the executive branch. Among many changes, the bill called for cutting the number of commissioners from 7 to 5, limiting the amount of staff, lengthening the term of office from 7 years to 10, and broadening the FCC constituency.

Under increasing pressure from Congress the FCC drafted legislation that would modernize existing restraints over the broadcasting of obscene, indecent, or profane material. The legislation would establish more stringent standards than those the U. S. Supreme Court had set in the *Miller* v. *California* case. The proposed bill had not been presented to Congress by year's end.

In another significant move, the FCC found unsatisfactory an agreement signed between Los

NOTABLE U. S. TELEVISION PROGRAMS OF 1975

Antonio and the Mayor—Howard Rodman's story of a young boy in a remote Mexican village, featuring Diego Gonzalves and Gregory Sierra. CBS, Jan. 8.

Antony and Cleopatra—The Royal Shakespeare Company's production of the Shakespeare play, directed by Jon Scofield and starring Richard Johnson, Janet Suzman, and Corin Redgrave. ABC, Jan. 4.

The Ascent of Man—Humanist-scientist Jacob Bronowski's view of intellectual evolution, in 13 weekly episodes. PBS, starting on Jan. 7.

Candide—A British Broadcasting Company adaptation of Voltaire's work, produced by Cedric Messina. PBS, Oct. 30.

The Chicago Conspiracy Trial—A recreation of the "Chicago Seven" trial, made by BBC in 1970. PBS, July 10.

Country Matters—Dramatizations of four short stories: "The Higgler," "The Black Dog," and "The Watercress Girl" by A. E. Coppard and "The Mill" by H. E. Bates. PBS, beginning Feb. 2.

Danny Kaye's Look-in at the Metropolitan Opera (Festival of lively arts for young people)—with opera stars Beverly Sills, Judith Blegen, and Robert Merrill. CBS, May 10.

A Girl Named Sooner—Adaptation by Suzanne Clauser of her 1972 novel, with a cast including Cloris Leachman, Susan Deer, Lee Remick, Richard Crenna, Ann Francis, Don Murray. NBC, June 18.

The Guns of Autumn—Controversial documentary about hunting, narrated by Dan Rather and produced by Irv Drasnin. CBS, Sept. 5.

The Incredible Machine—National Geographic Special, a study of the human body, using microphotographic techniques; narrated by E. G. Marshall. PBS, Oct. 28.

In This House of Brede—Adaptation by James Costigan of the Rumer Godden novel about life in an Anglican convent, with Diana Rigg, Judy Bowker, Gwen Watford, and Pamela Brown. CBS, Feb. 27.

The Legend of Lizzie Borden—TV-movie about the murders and the trial; with Elizabeth Montgomery, Fritz Weaver, and Ed Flanders. ABC, Feb. 10.

Life—First of three bicentennial documentaries written and narrated by David Brinkley on the meaning of Jefferson's words "life, liberty, and the pursuit of happiness." NBC, Oct. 28.

A Moon for the Misbegotten—Production of the Eugene O'Neill play, directed by José Quintero and Gordon Rigsby, and featuring Jason Robards, Colleen Dewhurst, and Ed Flanders. ABC, May 27.

Mr. Rooney Goes To Washington—A report by writer-narrator Andrew Rooney of his search for information through Washington officialdom. CBS, Jan. 26.

The Rebel and The Statesman—The third and fourth of four dramas on the life of Benjamin Franklin. In *The Rebel* Richard Widmark is a vigorous Franklin in England. CBS, Jan. 7. In *The Statesman*, Melvyn Douglas is Franklin full of years and wisdom. CBS, Jan. 26.

Sandburg's Lincoln—A six-part series based on the Pulitzer Prize-winning biography, written by Jerome Lawrence and Robert E. Lee, with Hal Holbrook as Lincoln, Sada Thompson, Elizabeth Ashley, Lloyd Nolan; part four, Lincoln as commander-in-chief. NBC, Sept. 3.

She Stoops To Conquer—British production of Goldsmith's 1773 comedy, featuring Tom Courtenay, Juliet Mills, and Ralph Richardson. PBS, Oct. 23.

Three by Balanchine—The New York City Ballet celebrating its master choreographer with three of his works; "Serenade," "Tarantella," and "Duo Concertant." PBS, May 21.

Welfare—Frederick Wiseman's cinema-verité tour through a New York City welfare center. PBS, Sept. 24.

What's Happened Since . . .—An update of 10 ABC News Closeup investigative reports since 1973; produced by Marlene Sanders. ABC, July 5.

The World Series—Baseball's fall classic, the best in many years. NBC, Oct. 11, 12, 14, 16, 21, and 22.

SUMMARY OF WORLD TELEVISION STATIONS AND SETS
(As of March 1975)

Country	Stations	Number of TV sets	Country	Stations	Number of TV sets	Country	Stations	Number of TV sets
Albania	1	3,000	Honduras	7	47,000	Paraguay	1	50,000
Algeria	7	410,000	Hong Kong	5	826,000	Peru	18	450,000
Angola	1		Hungary	18	2,540,000	Philippines	23	650,000
Antigua	1	15,000	Iceland	7	50,400	Poland	36	5,684,000
Argentina	34	4,300,000	India	5	250,000	Portugal	12	669,000
Australia	127	4,250,000	Indonesia	18	370,000	Puerto Rico	1	655,000
Austria	241	1,915,000	Iran	16	750,000	Qatar	2	28,000
Bangladesh	1	20,000	Iraq	6	500,000	Rhodesia	2	67,600
Barbados	1	35,000	Ireland	23	630,000	Rumania	20	2,500,000
Belgium	16	2,475,500	Israel	11	460,000	Samoa (American)	6	5,000
Bermuda	2	25,900	Italy	93	12,805,000	Saudi Arabia	8	300,000
Bolivia	1	24,000	Ivory Coast	6	85,500	Singapore	2	250,000
Brazil	52	8,700,000	Jamaica	10	100,000	Spain	35	6,125,000
Bulgaria	11	1,467,000	Japan	212	25,500,000	Sudan	2	85,000
Cambodia	2	30,000	Jordan	3	171,000	Surinam	1	33,000
Canada	546	9,800,000	Kenya	4	36,000	Sweden	266	4,115,000
Chile	38	1,500,000	Korea (South)	12	1,610,000	Switzerland	233	1,800,000
China (Mainland)	36	300,000	Kuwait	3	130,000	Syria	5	224,000
Colombia	18	1,200,000	Lebanon	9	410,000	Thailand	9	720,000
Costa Rica	4	154,000	Liberia	1	9,000	Trinidad & Tobago	3	100,000
Cuba	25	555,000	Libya	10	5,000	Tunisia	9	166,000
Cyprus	2	82,000	Luxembourg	3	88,500	Turkey	28	452,000
Czechoslovakia	28	3,610,000	Malaysia	32	737,500	Uganda	6	48,000
Denmark	30	1,739,000	Malta	1	75,000	United Arab Emirates	3	18,000
Dominican Republic	8	180,000	Martinique	1	15,000	United Kingdom	270	17,725,000
Ecuador	10	250,000	Mauritius	1	45,000	United States[2]	954	121,100,000
Egypt	30	600,000	Mexico	80	5,480,000	Upper Volta	1	7,700
El Salvador	5	109,300	Monaco	3	17,000	Uruguay	18	350,000
Ethiopia	4	28,000	Morocco	15	367,000	USSR	167	50,000,000
Finland	83	1,375,300	Netherlands	20	3,545,000	Venezuela	31	1,145,000
France	197	13,712,000	Netherlands Antilles	3	38,100	Vietnam (South)	1	500,000
Germany (East)	28	5,077,000	New Zealand	27	771,650	Virgin Islands	1	36,000
Germany (West)	184	17,600,000	Nicaragua	2	72,200	Yemen	3	30,000
Ghana	4	30,000	Nigeria	6	1,000,000	Yugoslavia	47	2,818,000
Greece	17	950,000	Norway	92	1,117,600	Zaire	2	7,500
Guadeloupe	2	12,000	Okinawa	2	230,000	Zambia	3	21,000
Guam	1	42,000	Pakistan	9	255,000			
Guatemala	3	145,000	Panama	11	209,000	Total[3]	19,870	363,769,812
Haiti	3	12,000						

[1] Stations included in U. S. count. [2] Preliminary estimate. [3] Includes 14,913 satellites and repeaters, and some small places not listed (Source: Television Factbook, 1975–76).

Angeles station KTTV(TV) and a citizen group, the National Association for Better Broadcasting. The commission disallowed the agreement largely on the ground that the station had given up control over its programming, thus avoiding responsibility for its broadcasting.

Public Broadcasting. Public Broadcasting's search for some agreement with Congress and the White House on long-term financing continued for still another year. By year's end it seemed as though there might emerge from Congress a plan for three-year funding (rather than the desired five-year term), providing matching funds of $88 million in 1976 and rising by steps to $160 million in 1980.

Black Ownership. The first black-owned television station in the continental United States, WGPR-TV, channel 62, Detroit, went on the air on Monday, September 29. The station planned to emphasize programming of local and black interest, and hoped, if successful, eventually to expand to a seven-station network.

JOHN M. GUNN
State University of New York at Albany

RADIO

Deregulation. Deregulation, the process of freeing radio stations from rules that no longer applied to, or seemed necessary to, their operation, took several forward steps during 1975. In 1974 the Federal Communications Commission (FCC) had eased some technical requirements for small station operations. In June 1975 it announced a liberalization of rules governing AM operations of any size. Recognizing

that rules it had adopted in 1964 and 1973 were unnecessarily restrictive (they were meant to slow down the growth of AM radio), the FCC eased requirements for frequency changes and for increases in power. The action on frequency changes resulted in better service for daytime-only stations desiring to expand service into nighttime. In addition, the FCC added a new power classification to those power steps at which a station is licensed to operate, filling the

Robert Blake, for *Baretta*, and Jean Marsh, for *Upstairs, Downstairs*, won Emmys for best actor and actress.

UPI

gap between 1 kilowatt and 5 kilowatts with a new 2.5 kilowatt step.

In October the White House Office of Telecommunications Policy announced that it was preparing a bill authorizing the FCC to conduct a 5-year test of radio deregulation in the 10 major markets. The experiment would do away with FCC oversight of fairness doctrine situations, program formats and percentages, and the amount of time given to commercials.

Radio News. As studies have made it clear that many listeners were finding radio rather than television their primary news source, radio has increasingly fed the need. All-news stations are a success, and at year's end there were 20, all in major cities. Many other stations, while committed to music formats, have larded their morning and afternoon "drive" times, the period in which people are on their way to and from work, with substantial amounts of news and features. National news services have helped this phenomenon. Beginning in June NBC offered an all-news News and Information Service (NIS) supplying approximately 50 minutes of news and features per hour, 7 days a week.

Radio Pioneer. Ernst F. W. Alexanderson died on May 14 in Schenectady, N. Y., at the age of 97. Dr. Alexanderson invented the high-frequency alternator that made voice broadcasting, and therefore radio, feasible. Throughout his life he worked for both General Electric and Radio Corporation of America, beginning his career with GE in 1902. Highly productive, he received 322 patents in radio and television.

JOHN M. GUNN
State University of New York at Albany

TELEVISION AND RADIO ENGINEERING

TV growth in the United States in 1975 was confined almost exclusively to public stations. TV broadcasting continued to expand outside the United States, and cable TV expanded worldwide. The first use was made of an earth-orbiting satellite to relay programs for U. S. pay-cable TV distribution. The sale of TV receivers slumped sharply again during the year.

TV Broadcasting. The number of TV broadcasting stations on the air in the United States at the end of 1975 was 961, compared with 947 at the end of 1974. New stations going on the air were almost exclusively public (noncommercial) stations, as the number of commercial stations actually remained constant at 709. Of the 961 stations, 610 operated in the VHF band (channels 2–13) and 351 in the UHF band (channels 16–69). TV broadcasting outside the United States continued a steady growth, reflected in the accompanying table. South Africa, the only developed nation without TV service, made plans to inaugurate service on Jan. 1, 1976. Cable TV also continued to expand abroad, especially in Canada.

Cable TV. According to the National Cable Television Association (NCTA), the number of cable TV (CATV) subscribers in the United States increased from 9.25 million to 10.25 million in 1975. This represented approximately 14.5% of the nation's 70.6 million TV homes.

Cable TV continued to lag in the large metropolitan areas as cable system operators continued efforts to provide popular programming. An ambitious start in this direction was made on Sept. 30, 1975, when the Muhammad Ali-Joe Frazier heavyweight championship fight, originating in the Philippines, was transmitted by a series of earth satellites to cable systems near Vero Beach, Fla., and Jackson, Miss. The bout was distributed as a "pay-cable" program for which subscribers to the Vero Beach and Jackson cable systems paid an extra charge.

Plans were under way for the expansion of pay-cable program distribution to large cities. By the end of 1975 at least 20 satellite receiving stations for pay-cable distribution were under construction.

TV Receivers. The decline in sales of both black-and-white and color TV receivers continued into 1975. Total U. S. sales during the year were approximately 11 million sets, of which approximately 6 million were color sets. TV receiver manufacturers continued to introduce innovations into their new product lines. Large screen projection sets appeared on the market, and an increasing number of new models featured pushbutton tuning employing varactor diodes.

Two competing systems of video discs were readied for home testing, and home video tape recorders appeared in some of the more expensive models. The industry concentrated on designs featuring reduced electrical power consumption in response to the national energy crisis.

AM and FM Radio. Both AM and FM radio broadcasting continued a steady although modest expansion in the United States. The number of AM stations increased during 1975 from 4,427 to 4,459, and the number of FM stations from 3,350 to 3,458 (including 760 noncommercial educational stations).

The National Quadraphonic Radio Committee (NQRC) reported to the FCC in December 1975 on the results of tests to permit the commission to standardize on a system of quadraphonic sound for FM broadcasting. A new committee was established to study the possibility of standardizing stereophonic broadcasting on AM radio.

The White House Office of Telecommunications Policy standardized an emergency alerting system to be operated by the National Weather Service (NWS). Battery-powered sets to receive the NWS transmissions appeared on the market. A virtual explosion occurred during 1975 in citizens band (CB) radio, a low-power, short-range, two-way communications system for use in private communications.

HOWARD T. HEAD
A. D. Ring & Associates

TENNESSEE

The General Assembly held the longest session in the state's history and turned attention primarily to fiscal responsibility, as the state's money problems became increasingly acute. Also during the year, education enrollments continued to climb, and crime remained a prime concern.

Legislative Action. Although Gov. Ray Blanton proposed a "bare bones" budget of $2.1 billion, some $73 million less than 1974's, the legislature cut $48.6 million from it. A proposed teachers' pay raise of $400 a year was cut to $150, and salary increases of all state employees were limited to a maximum of 2.5%. The salary issue brought protests from across the state, and some teacher groups threatened to strike. Judges, who had expected an 11% increase, alleged that the law limiting salary increases was unconstitutional and threatened suit.

In other legislative action, the lawmakers rejected bills calling for a constitutional convention that could have resulted in an amendment to include a personal income tax. Price-fixing statutes on liquors were repealed and abuses in the pension law were corrected. Candidates for public office were required to report all contributions and campaign expenditures.

Economy. Gains in labor and farm income have somewhat brightened the economic picture, but the rate of growth in personal income remained well below the national median. Durable goods manufacture suffered cutbacks in the first quarter of 1975, and the home building industry continued to decline. Although agriculture is a main source of employment in Tennessee, sagging dairy and beef-cattle prices have been primarily responsible for a decrease of 22,000 farms since 1965. A severe midsummer drought damaged corn and other grain crops and seriously curtailed major pasture crops.

Education. Record enrollments were reported across the state in schools and colleges. The University of Tennessee announced an enrollment of 48,636, a 6% increase over 1974. The board of trustees also announced plans for a $43 million building at Knoxville and a $5.4 million fine arts building at Chattanooga. Low salaries for teachers occasioned warnings of unrest from Tennessee Education Association (TEA) officials. Dr. Don Sahli, longtime TEA executive director, pledged legal aid to any TEA unit considering a strike.

Politics and the Cities. Richard Fulton resigned his fifth district (Nashville) congressional seat to become mayor of Nashville. Pledging economy in all urban operations, Fulton was elected overwhelmingly over four challengers. While most eastern cities were experiencing population stabilization, those in Tennessee continued to grow, fed largely by nearby suburban counties. The only major political contest was that held to fill Fulton's congressional seat.

Clifford Allen, a 63-year-old lawyer and tax assessor, was elected to the fifth district seat by an overwhelming majority.

Crime. Crime continued to grow in the urban and rural areas alike. Complaints of unhealthy and crowded conditions at the state penitentiary led to an inmate strike and violence that left 1 dead and 39 injured. The National Guard occupied the prison grounds.

ROBERT E. CORLEW
Middle Tennessee State University

------- **TENNESSEE • Information Highlights** -------
Area: 42,244 square miles (109,412 sq km).
Population (1974 est.): 4,129,000. *Density:* 98 per sq mi.
Chief Cities (1970 census): Nashville, the capital, 447,-877; Memphis, 623,530; Knoxville, 174,587.
Government (1975): *Chief Officers*—governor, Ray Blanton (D); lt. gov., John S. Wilder (D). *General Assembly*—Senate, 33 members; House of Representatives, 99 members.
Education (1974–75): *Enrollment*—public elementary schools, 535,256 pupils; public secondary, 337,563; nonpublic, 32,000; colleges and universities, 164,420 students. *Public school expenditures,* $616,711,000 ($741 per pupil).
State Finances (fiscal year 1974): *Revenues,* $2,036,-318,000; *expenditures,* $1,910,117,000.
Personal Income (1974): $18,516,000,000; per capita, $4,484.
Labor Force (Aug. 1975): *Nonagricultural wage and salary earners,* 1,540,800; *insured unemployed,* 64,-400.

TEXAS

Statewide voter rejection of all eight proposals for constitutional revision, the establishment by the 64th Legislature of a state utilities commission, and the end of one-man political rule in South Texas were the dominant events in Texas in 1975.

Constitution. On November 4, Texans overwhelmingly defeated an eight-part revision of the 99-year-old, much-amended state constitution. State leaders were split on the issue, but most voters, apparently confused by the issue, decided against any changes. Thus, after several years' work by state lawmakers and the expenditure of several million dollars in an effort to update the state's constitution, revision appeared unlikely for the foreseeable future.

The Legislature. One of the major accomplishments of the spring 1975 legislature was the creation of a state utilities commission. It was given authority to regulate local and long-distance telephone calls, and electric, water, and sewer rates in unincorporated areas. Cities will have the option in 1977 of whether to relinquish their regulatory authority over private electric, water, and sewer companies within their jurisdiction.

In the field of health care, lawmakers approved a bill to centralize the planning and development of health-care facilities. The bill also established a certification program in which a three-member commission must certify need before new facilities can be developed or old ones expanded.

UPI

The appointment of Dr. Lorene Rogers as president of the University of Texas at Austin caused controversy.

Legislators also authorized the establishment of health maintenance organizations (HMO's), designed to provide a prepaid alternative to conventional fee-for-service health care and to conventional health insurance. The bill allows anyone to establish an HMO after obtaining a certificate of authority from the state insurance commissioner.

The legislature also enacted a measure providing for a presidential primary election in 1976. This controversial election code revision was opposed by many who thought the measure was designed primarily to benefit the presidential candidacy of Democratic Sen. Lloyd Bentsen. The act expires after the 1976 national nominating conventions.

In another area, the legislature voted to improve financing of public schools to encourage equalization of educational opportunities between rich and poor districts. Lawmakers also approved a bill to keep Texas natural gas produced on future leases of state land from leaving the state. A bill regulating strip mining of uranium and coal was also passed.

A record $12.1 billion, two-year budget passed, as did a feeble start on state aid for mass transit. With a $1.4 billion surplus from natural gas and oil taxes, the state's finances were in excellent shape.

End of an Era. George Parr, the so-called "duke of Duval" county, deeply embroiled in a political feud and facing a prison term for income tax evasion, committed suicide April 1 on his South Texas ranch. With Parr's death, one-man political rule in South Texas apparently came to an end.

After Parr's death, some of his political foes were indicted on charges of filing false income tax reports. O. P. Carrillo, the leader of the Parr opposition and a state district judge, was convicted on tax charges and was impeached by the House on 10 counts of official wrongdoing. His case was set for trial by the Senate after his sentencing on the tax conviction on November 17.

University Controversy. The University of Texas board of regents, headed by newly named chairman Allan Shivers, former Texas governor, appointed Dr. Lorene Rogers as president of the University of Texas at Austin on September 17. Her appointment drew fire from students and faculty because they felt they were not given a voice in the selection of the new president. The appointment of Rogers followed by several months an order from the U. S. Department of Health, Education, and Welfare that the university must change its admission policies to bring in more minority students or face the loss of federal funds.

Other Issues. Unemployment and inflation rates rose throughout Texas in 1975, but at levels below the national average. The jobs provided by the state's oil and gas industries reduced the effects of the recession.

The Texas court of criminal appeals on April 16 upheld the 1973 death penalty law. A three-judge federal panel, however, ruled that the Texas obscenity law was unconstitutional. Texas Attorney General John Hill ruled in October that school districts may not legally charge students for supplies needed in class or for extracurricular activities.

MICHAEL LONSFORD
"The Houston Chronicle"

--------- **TEXAS · Information Highlights** ---------

Area: 267,338 square miles (692,405 sq km).
Population (1974 est.): 12,050,000. *Density:* 45 per sq mi.
Chief Cities (1970 census): Austin, the capital, 251,808; Houston, 1,232,802; Dallas, 844,401; San Antonio, 654,153.
Government (1975): *Chief Officers*—governor, Dolph Briscoe (D); lt. gov., William P. Hobby (D). *Legislature*—Senate, 31 members; House of Representatives, 150 members.
Education (1974–75): *Enrollment*—public elementary schools, 1,516,829 pupils; public secondary, 1,268,-467; nonpublic, 112,500; colleges and universities, 547,142 students. *Public school expenditures,* $2,-135,636,000 ($855 per pupil).
State Finances (fiscal year 1974): *Revenues,* $5,916,788,-000; *expenditures,* $5,027,016,000.
Personal Income (1974): $57,715,000,000; per capita $4,790.
Labor Force (Aug. 1975): *Nonagricultural wage and salary earners,* 4,427,000; *insured unemployed,* 77,-300.

On October 23, U. S. (*right*) and Thai military officers conduct ceremonies marking the closing of Nakhon Phanom Royal Thai Air Force Base, which had been used by the United States since 1963.

UPI

THAILAND

The year 1975 witnessed a major election and a quick succession of two coalition governments in Thailand. The government of Kukrit Pramoj survived the trauma of the U. S. exit from Vietnam and the resulting ripples of political uncertainty. At year's end it had achieved a remarkable quality of stability amid major national problems.

Domestic Affairs. In late January a parliamentary election was held, perhaps the freest election in Thai history. This could be attributed to the moderate policies of Premier Sanya Dharmasakti. More than 40 parties of every ideological hue contested the election. Twenty-two of them won at least one seat. No party was expected to win a majority of seats, and none did. The moderate Democratic party, led by Seni Pramoj, won 72 of a total 269 seats. After a month's negotiations Seni was able to form a government (the first elected government in a quarter-century) with the support of the Social Agrarian party. Together they had only 90 seats, far less than a majority.

In a major step the United States reassigned controversial ambassador William R. Kintner. Premier Seni was strongly pro-United States, but

--------- **THAILAND · Information Highlights** ---------

Official Name: Kingdom of Thailand.
Location: Southeast Asia.
Area: 198,456 square miles (514,000 sq km).
Population (1975 est.): 42,100,000.
Chief Cities (1975 est.): Bangkok, the capital, 4,000,-000; Chiang Mai, 100,000.
Government: *Head of state,* Bhumibol Aduladej, king (acceded June 1946). *Head of government,* Kukrit Pramoj, premier (took office March 1975). *Legislature*—National Assembly—Senate and House of Representatives.
Monetary Unit: Baht (20.38 baht equal U. S.$1, July 1975).
Gross National Product (1974 est.): $12,200,000,000.
Manufacturing (major products): Processed foods, textiles, clothing.
Major Agricultural Products: Rice, rubber, tapioca, corn, tobacco, fruits, sugarcane, kenaf and jute, forest products, fish.
Foreign Trade (1974): *Exports,* $2,400,000,000; *imports,* $3,100,000,000.

anti-U. S. feeling not only against Kintner and his alleged ties to the Central Intelligence Agency (CIA) in Thailand was very strong. Seni's government not unpredictably ran into difficulties, particularly with military-based right-wing parties. It fell in early March, to be replaced by a new coalition led by Kukrit Pramoj, leader of the moderate Social Action party, and brother of Seni. Kukrit, among other things, previously had been a motion picture star years before. He was known to U. S. audiences as the southeast Asian premier in *The Ugly American.* Kukrit's government faced not only the uncertainties of parliamentary instability, but also student unrest, concern about the U. S. presence, and the rapidly changing political situation in Indochina. However, he and his government survived the year.

Foreign Affairs. Thai-U. S. relations have been close for a long time; the nature of those relations seems crucial to both Thailand and to U. S. influence in East Asia. For months, however, there had been unrest in Thailand because U. S. military forces were still stationed there. This was noticeably exacerbated by the *Mayaguez* incident in May, in which U. S. marines from a staging point in Thailand freed the U. S. merchant ship *Mayaguez* from Cambodian hands. The immediate result was the recalling of the Thai ambassador from Washington. The U. S. withdrawal from Vietnam also produced problems for Thailand, including a reevaluation of relations with Laos, Cambodia, and North Vietnam. There were refugees as well.

In June a joint Thai-U. S. announcement scheduled the withdrawal of the last B-52 bombers from Thailand. In July the Thais declared military agreements with the United States no longer valid and gave March 20, 1976, as the deadline for the final removal of U. S. forces. Those forces were estimated at 17,000. In July Thailand and China established normal diplomatic relations.

CARL LEIDEN
The University of Texas, Austin

MARTHA SWOPE

theater

A *Chorus Line*, produced by Joseph Papp, was the biggest Broadway hit musical in 1975 and won the Drama Critics' Circle Award.

To a remarkable degree, the New York theater was dominated in 1975 by the activities of Joseph Papp, head of the New York Shakespeare Festival and the Vivian Beaumont Theater of Lincoln Center. In one year Papp was responsible for the hit musical *A Chorus Line,* which won the Drama Critics Circle "best musical" award; the Beaumont production of Ibsen's *A Doll's House,* with Liv Ullmann, a theatrical occasion that somehow became a national event; and Ed Bullins' *The Taking of Miss Janie* at Lincoln Center's Mitzi E. Newhouse Theater, winner of the Critics Circle Award for "best American play." Even when Papp was reversing himself and making obvious mistakes, he was still creating more excitement than anyone else in the United States.

Naturally, other prominent patterns were discernible, but Papp somehow managed to figure in all of them. Producers continued to import British plays and productions. Papp, who had formerly resisted the importation of foreign personnel, drew more headlines than his rivals by bringing Liv Ullmann to New York City from Norway. Broadway restored its own and its public's wavering faith in the most authentic U. S. theatrical creation, the big Broadway musical, with such hits as *The Wiz, Chicago,* and *A Chorus Line,* of which the last, Papp's production, was the biggest hit of all. In the summer the leadership of Actors Equity tried to stifle the off-off-Broadway movement by demanding a share of future profits in any play that used Equity members. The leadership was overruled by its own members, with Papp leading the fight to save off-off-Broadway. Early in the fall, a strike by the musicians' union closed all the Broadway musicals for several weeks.

Papp, who had been counting on profits from *A Chorus Line* to finance his other projects, was one of those who suffered most from the musicians' strike.

Activities of Joseph Papp. In the course of the year, Papp made some abrupt changes in policy, which later had to be modified. After two years of constant quarrels with critics and subscribers at the Vivian Beaumont Theater, Papp finally abandoned his policy of presenting new plays there and resolved to give the subscribers what they apparently wanted—"classical" plays. New plays that came to Papp's attention would be presented instead in a season on Broadway at the Booth Theater. Papp scheduled five plays by young writers whose previous work had been seen at his Public Theater. This policy was suddenly changed when financial problems forced the new plays back to their old home, the Public. The only one of these plays to reach the Booth was Dennis J. Reardon's *The Leaf People.* This occasionally interesting study of a primitive people resisting discovery by "civilization" was buried in a distracting, excessively elaborate production by Tom O'Horgan. It ran for only a week.

The glowing Liv Ullmann won universal admiration in *A Doll's House,* for which a Norwegian director was imported. It was agreed almost as universally, however, that her supporting cast, including Sam Waterston in the role of her husband, was far too weak. The last new plays at the Beaumont were not remarkable. In Bill Gunn's *Black Picture Show* a black writer examines his past and concludes, rather improbably, that he has sold out. Anthony Scully's *Little Black Sheep* showed the effect of Robert Kennedy's assassination on some extremely liber-

Director Bob Fosse's *Chicago* was one of the most popular musicals on Broadway in 1975. The show, starring Gwen Verdon (*right*) and Chita Rivera, was adapted from the 1920 play by Maurice Watkins.

MARTHA SWOPE

ated priests. It achieved distinction as possibly the most generally disliked play in the history of Lincoln Center.

The new schedule for Lincoln Center's next season did not go very far back into the past for its "classics." The only exception was a new version of the *Hamlet,* with Waterston in the lead, which had been staged during the summer in Central Park. The other plays were Pinero's *Trelawny of the "Wells,"* Shaw's *Mrs. Warren's Profession,* and Ibsen's *Peer Gynt,* which was to be acted by an all-black cast but was canceled in favor of Brecht's *Threepenny Opera.* The delicate charm of *Trelawny* suffered from being moved to a U.S. setting and from a heavy-handed approach to its comedy.

At Papp's Public Theater two visiting companies, the Manhattan Project and the Shaliko, demonstrated in the course of extended visits that they were really at their best only with the productions that had first put them on the map—*Alice in Wonderland* and Ibsen's *Ghosts* respectively. Papp's own productions fared better. *Kid Champion* was Thomas Babe's rough-hewn but promising drama of a rock singer's career. Michael Weller's *Fishing,* in somewhat the same vein as the same author's *Moonchildren,* observed the college generation of the 1960's in pursuit of a more simple existence in the Pacific Northwest.

Chorus Line. In the musical *A Chorus Line,* 17 dancers tell their life stories as they compete for 8 places in the chorus of a new show. Papp had previously shown his flair for musicals when he produced the original *Hair* and *Two Gentlemen of Verona.*

With *A Chorus Line* Papp ventured into the new genre of the "concept" musical, which subordinates every element to a general plan but steers clear of a conventional plot. Hal Prince was the pioneer of the "concept" play, with such shows as *Company* and *Follies. A Chorus Line*

succeeded as a musical and also as a moving self-portrait of show business. It immediately became the most popular show in town and quickly moved to Broadway.

Other Papp Productions. At the Mitzi E. Newhouse Theater (formerly the Forum) of Lincoln Center, Papp presented a pleasant but undistinguished version of *A Midsummer Night's Dream* and Ed Bullins' *The Taking of Miss Janie,* a play of black life that had originated at the New Federal Theater. Interpreting relations between blacks and whites in the 1960's, this play offers the rape of a white girl by a black man as a symbol of the interracial chaos. Individual scenes were colorful enough, but it seemed strange that yet another black dramatist had communicated to Papp the importance of offering yet another play on the impossibility of meaningful communication between blacks and whites. Such immediate issues were left far behind at Papp's Central Park Festival, where *Hamlet* was followed by *The Comedy of Errors,* set in Mussolini's Italy and played by a cast that spoke in heavy Italian accents and gestured furiously.

English Imports. On Broadway the unending tide of British importations continued, mainly because producers were reluctant to risk their money on the unknown, unpredictable shows that they might put together themselves. Only Papp was in the enviable position of having financial support from philanthropists and foundations as well as several off-Broadway auditoriums (in the Public Theater) where he could experiment.

Two British imports directed by John Gielgud were W. Somerset Maugham's *The Constant Wife* with Ingrid Bergman and Noel Coward's *Private Lives* with Maggie Smith. Coward's elegant nonsense survived better than Maugham's practical cynicism.

More elegant even than *Private Lives* was

Ellen Burstyn won a Tony for best actress in *Same Time Next Year* (*above left*), and *The Wiz* (*above right*) won best musical and several other awards. *Habeus Corpus* (*below*), a British play by Alan Bennett, was a popular farce.

NOTABLE BROADWAY
OPENINGS IN 1975

PLAYS

Ah, Wilderness!, by Eugene O'Neill; directed by Arvin Brown; with Geraldine Fitzgerald and Teresa Wright; September 18–November 23.

All God's Chillun Got Wings, by Eugene O'Neill; directed by George S. Scott; March 20–May 4.

Black Picture Show, by Bill Gunn, music and lyrics by Sam Waymon; directed by Gunn; January 6–February 9.

Clarence Darrow, by David W. Rintels; directed by John Houseman; with Henry Fonda; March 3–22.

The Constant Wife, by W. Somerset Maugham; directed by John Gielgud; with Ingrid Bergman; April 14–May 10.

Death of a Salesman, by Arthur Miller; directed by George C. Scott; with Scott, Teresa Wright, and James Farentino; June 26–August 24.

A Doll's House, by Henrik Ibsen, translated by Christopher Hampton; directed by Tormod Skagestad; with Liv Ullmann and Sam Waterston; March 5–April 20.

Don't Call Back, by Russell O'Neill; directed by Len Cariou; with Arlene Francis; March 18.

The First Breeze of Summer, by Leslie Lee; directed by Douglas Turner Ward; with Ward and Moses Gunn; June 10–July 20.

Habeas Corpus, by Alan Bennett; directed by Frank Dunlop; with Donald Sinden, Rachel Roberts, Jean Marsh; November 25–.

The Hashish Club, by Lance Larsen; directed by Jerome Guardino; January 3–11.

Hughie, by Eugene O'Neill, and *Duet,* by David Scott Milton; directed by Martin Fried; with Ben Gazzara; February 11–March 8.

Kennedy's Children, by Robert Patrick; directed by Clive Donner; with Shirley Knight; November 3–.

Lamppost Reunion, by Louis LaRusso II; directed by Tom Signorelli; with Gabriel Dell; October 16–December 21.

The Leaf People, by Dennis J. Reardon; directed by Tom O'Horgan; October 20–26.

A Letter for Queen Victoria, by Robert Wilson, music by Alan Lloyd and Michael Galasso; directed by Wilson; March 22–April 6.

Little Black Sheep, by Anthony Scully; directed by Edward Payson Call; May 7–June 1.

The Misanthrope, by Molière, adapted by Tony Harrison; directed by John Dexter; with Diana Rigg and Alec McCowen; March 12–May 31.

The Norman Conquests (three plays: *Table Manners, Living Together, Round and Round the Garden*), by Alan Ayckbourn; directed by Eric Thompson; with Richard Benjamin, Paula Prentiss, and Estelle Parsons; December 7–.

Private Lives, by Noel Coward; directed by John Gielgud; with Maggie Smith and John Standing; February 6–April 26.

P. S., Your Cat Is Dead!, by James Kirkwood; directed by Vivian Matalon; with Keir Dullea; April 7–April 20.

The Ritz, by Terrence McNally; directed by Robert Drivas; with Jack Weston and Rita Moreno; January 20–.

Same Time, Next Year, by Bernard Slade; directed by Gene Saks; with Ellen Burstyn and Charles Grodin; March 13–.

Seascape, by Edward Albee; directed by Albee; with Deborah Kerr and Barry Nelson; January 26–March 22.

The Skin of Our Teeth, by Thornton Wilder; directed by José Quintero; with Elizabeth Ashley; September 9–13.

Summer Brave, by William Inge; directed by Michael Montel; with Alexis Smith; October 26–November 8.

Travesties, by Tom Stoppard; directed by Peter Wood; with John Wood; October 30–.

Trelawny of the "Wells," by Arthur Wing Pinero; directed by A. J. Antoon; October 15–November 23.

Yentl, by Leah Napolin and Isaac Bashevis Singer; directed by Robert Kalfin; with Tovah Feldshuh; October 23–.

MUSICALS

Bette Midler's Clams on the Half Shell Revue, directed and choreographed by Joe Layton; with Midler; April 17–June 21.

Boccaccio, by Kenneth Cavander, music by Richard Peaslee; directed by Warren Enters; November 24–30.

Chicago, book by Fred Ebb and Bob Fosse, lyrics by Ebb, music by John Kander; directed and choreographed by Fosse; with Gwen Verdon, Jerry Orbach, and Chita Rivera; June 3–.

A Chorus Line, conceived by Michael Bennett, book by James Kirkwood and Nicholas Dante, lyrics by Edward Kleban, music by Marvin Hamlisch; directed and choreographed by Bennett; with Donna McKechnie; July 25–.

Dance with Me, by Greg Antonacci; directed and choreographed by Joel Zwick; January 23–.

Doctor Jazz, book, music, and lyrics by Buster Davis; directed and choreographed by Donald McKayle; with Bobby Van and Lola Falana; March 19–22.

Goodtime Charley, book by Sidney Michaels, lyrics by Hal Hackady, music by Larry Grossman; directed by Peter H. Hunt; with Joel Grey and Ann Reinking; March 3–May 31.

Hello, Dolly!, book by Michael Stewart, lyrics and music by Jerry Herman; directed by Lucia Victor; with Pearl Bailey; November 6–December 21.

The Lieutenant, book, music, and lyrics by Gene Curty, Nitra Scharfman, and Chuck Strand; directed by William Martin; March 9–16.

Man on the Moon, book, music, and lyrics by John Phillips; directed by Paul Morrissey; January 29–February 1.

Me and Bessie, conceived and written by Will Holt and Linda Hopkins; directed by Robert Greenwald; with Linda Hopkins; October 22–.

A Musical Jubilee, devised by Marilyn Clark and Charles Burr, continuity by Max Wilk; directed by Morton Da Costa; with Patrice Munsel and Lillian Gish; November 13–.

The Night That Made America Famous, music and lyrics by Harry Chapin; directed by Gene Frankel; with Chapin; February 27–April 6.

The Rocky Horror Show, book, music, and lyrics by Richard O'Brien; directed by Jim Sharman; March 10–April 6.

Rodgers & Hart, music by Richard Rodgers, lyrics by Lorenz Hart, concept by Richard Lewine and John Fearnley; directed by Burt Shevelove; May 13–August 16.

Shenandoah, book by James Lee Barrett, Peter Udell, and Philip Rose, lyrics by Udell, music by Gary Geld; directed by Rose; with John Cullum; January 7–.

Treemonisha, libretto and score by Scott Joplin; directed by Frank Corsaro; October 21–December 14.

We Interrupt This Program . . . , by Norman Krasna; directed by Jerry Adler; April 1–5.

The Wiz, based on L. Frank Baum's *The Wonderful Wizard of Oz,* book by William F. Brown, music and lyrics by Charlie Smalls; directed by Geoffrey Holder; January 5–.

the British National Theater's version of Molière's *The Misanthrope,* set by the adapter, Tony Harrison, in Charles DeGaulle's France and dominated by the *soignée* Diana Rigg as Célimène. From the Royal Shakespeare came Tom Stoppard's *Travesties,* an ingenious speculation on the simultaneous presence in Zurich in 1917 of James Joyce, V. I. Lenin, and Tristan Tzara, misremembered by an aging British consular official who was played with great skill by John Wood.

Other British vehicles were acted by mixed casts, including Alan Bennett's arch farcical exercise on sexual subjects, *Habeas Corpus,* and Alan Ayckbourn's *The Norman Conquests.* Ayckbourn's play was made up of three separate plays, each of them recording from a different area of the same house the marital and extramarital adventures of three couples during a single weekend. Described as the British Neil Simon, Ayckbourn actually resembles Simon only in his extraordinary success as a comic dramatist. Unlike Simon, who is a master of the one-line joke, Ayckbourn gets most of his laughs from characters and situations.

New Broadway Plays. *Kennedy's Children,* by Robert Patrick, might almost be called another British import. This U. S. play has had a strange history. The original off-off-Broadway production won little attention, but it became a hit in London, and its British director restaged it for Broadway. Its five speakers address their eloquent, often pathetic monologues directly to the audience, telling their own stories in such a way as to interpret the despair that has settled over the United States since the assassination of President Kennedy. If this peculiar technique works, it is because each character is a genuine, distinctive individual. The cast was strong, and Shirley Knight was particularly memorable as an actress who aspires to be the next generation's Marilyn Monroe.

The commercial hit among the straight plays was *Same Time, Next Year* by Bernard Slade, a Canadian living in the United States. This is a sex comedy in the tradition of *The Moon Is Blue* and *Any Wednesday.* Its two characters are a husband and wife (married to other people, of course) who meet for an annual assignation over a period of 25 years. Over the years their characters and even their vocations change, and they sometimes take note of historical events. All that remains constant is their annual need for each other. Slade writes with finesse and wit. Ellen Burstyn's verve in the feminine role won her a Tony Award as best actress in a straight play.

Broadway's only other interesting new U. S. play was *Yentl,* adapted from a story by Isaac Bashevis Singer and originally performed by the Chelsea Theater Center in 1974. This is the drama of an East European Jewish girl who masquerades as a boy in order to study the rabbinical lore normally forbidden to her. An engaging performance by Tovah Feldshuh helped audiences to feel at home in the unfamiliar world she presented.

Another U. S. play on Broadway that deserves notice is *The Ritz* by Terrence McNally. This single-minded farce was derived from a more interesting play called *The Tubs* that was acted at Yale and concerns a heterosexual trapped in a bathhouse patronized by homosexuals. Its only virtue was Rita Moreno's lively performance as a Puerto Rican singer who has more ambition than talent. Edward Albee's *Seascape* (which won the Pulitzer Prize) concerns a human couple welcoming two English-speaking lizards bent on improving their evolutionary standing. Louis LaRusso III's *Lamppost Reunion* is based on a hardboiled barroom dialogue in which one of the participants is intended to resemble Frank Sinatra. In James Kirkwood's *P. S. Your Cat Is Dead,* a burglar endeavors to persuade his captor of the virtues of homosexuality. Leslie Lee's *The First Breeze of Summer* is a ˋensitive dramatic record of several generations of black life in the United States, a play that moved from off-Broadway to a theater too large for its potential audience.

Musicals. The most successful musicals, in addition to *A Chorus Line,* were *The Wiz* and *Chicago.* Unfortunately, the charm of *The Wiz,* a marvelously energetic all-black adaptation of *The Wonderful Wizard of Oz,* eluded many critics dedicated to the view that the Judy Garland film was the last word on the subject. *Chicago,* an abrasive Brechtian adaptation of Maurice Watkins' 1920's play about a sensational murder trial, benefited greatly from direction by Bob Fosse and dancing by Gwen Verdon. Among the year's musical curiosities were *Treemonisha,* an opera written early in the century by ragtime composer Scott Joplin, and *Shenandoah,* a homey, liberal treatment of the Civil War, which survived an unfriendly press. There may be a question as to whether Robert Wilson's *A Letter to Queen Victoria* belongs among the musicals, despite its musical score. Wilson is an experimental director who achieves his best effects by the use of images. In *A Letter* he seemed betrayed by words, a medium he distrusts. He was more at home in *The $ Value of Man* at the Brooklyn Academy of Music.

Revivals. At a time when producers hesitated to invest in new U. S. dramatists, the older U. S. writers flourished in revivals. Among the revivals, Eugene O'Neill's *Ah, Wilderness!* in a production that traveled from New Haven's Long Wharf Theater to Broadway's Circle in the Square, Arthur Miller's *Death of a Salesman,* with George C. Scott admirably bitter in the lead, and Tennessee Williams' *Sweet Bird of Youth,* which went from the Kennedy Center to the Brooklyn Academy of Music, with Irene Worth playing her part to the hilt, fared well. Critics were not so happy with O'Neill's *All*

UPI

Ticket seekers line up to see *Chicago* on October 13, the day after the settlement of the musicians' strike.

God's Chillun Got Wings and *Hughie,* Thornton Wilder's *The Skin of Our Teeth,* and William Inge's *Summer Brave* (a later version of *Picnic*).

Off-Broadway. Most of the best of off-Broadway was presented through permanent institutions such as Joseph Papp's Shakespeare Festival. Robert Kalfin's Chelsea Theater Center provided two notable musicals. John Gay's *Polly,* a sequel to *The Beggar's Opera,* was adapted and directed by Kalfin himself at the Brooklyn Academy of Music. *Diamond Studs,* a concert-style musical dealing with Jesse James, was performed by two country-music groups "and friends," at Chelsea's Manhattan outpost. The American Place Theater offered Jonathan Reynolds' hilarious double bill, *Rubbers,* about an aggressive woman legislator in the state house, and *Yanks 3 Detroit 0 Top of the Seventh,* exploring a baseball pitcher's dilemmas. Marshall W. Mason's off-off-Broadway Circle Repertory Theater furnished three fascinating offbeat plays, Lanford Wilson's *The Mound Builders,* Julie Bovasso's *Down by the River Where the Waterlilies Are Disfigured Every Day,* and Corinne Jacker's *Harry Outside.*

Regional Theater. The highlight of the year in regional theater was probably *The Ascent of Mount Fuji* by Chingiz Aitmatov and Kaltai Mukhamedzhanov. The first Soviet play seen in the United States under the new international copyright agreement, *Ascent* was directed by Zelda Fichandler at her Arena Stage in Washington. This drama commented with commendable frankness on problems of guilt inherited from the Stalin era. In his first season at Stratford, Ontario, Robin Phillips directed an exceedingly impressive and cynical *Measure for Measure.*

International Theater. In England the greatest impact was made by the subsidized theaters. Peter Hall's National Theater won praise for *No Man's Land,* one of Harold Pinter's more difficult plays, in which John Gielgud and Ralph Richardson played two authors who may or may not be old acquaintances. Other notable productions were Shaw's *Heartbreak House; Phaedra Britannica,* with Diana Rigg playing Racine's *Phaedra* in the setting of 19th-century British India; and Trevor Griffiths' *Comedians,* a new play resembling *A Chorus Line* in its focus on auditioning comedians. The Royal Shakespeare fitted classics to its stars, presenting Glenda Jackson in Ibsen's *Hedda Gabler* and Nicol Williamson as Malvolio in *Twelfth Night.* The Royal Shakespeare made a favorable impression in its visit to the Brooklyn Academy of Music, especially with two of its non-stellar productions, Gorky's *Summerfolk* and *Love's Labor's Lost.* Otherwise, the best British efforts went into comedy, with Alan Ayckbourn and Simon Gray refining their familiar techniques in *Absent Friends* and *Otherwise Engaged* respectively, and Michael Frayn taking a satirical look at the library of a dying newspaper in *Alphabetical Order.*

The most important event in the Paris theater was *The Golden Age,* collectively created by Ariane Mnouchkine and her company. A critical glance at the world of today from the standpoint of the future, it contrasted the hard lot of a working-class Algerian with the wasteful life of the middle class. The most impressive creation of the German theater was Samuel Beckett's sensitive staging of his own *Waiting for Godot* in West Berlin. It was hard to find anything to match it in West Berlin's annual theater festival, where, as usual, the dominant company was Peter Stein's West Berlin Schaubühne, this time presenting a richly detailed naturalistic adaptation of Gorky's *Summerfolk.*

The Theater of the Nations, which had long made Paris its home, was revived in 1975 in Warsaw. The highlights of a brief but intense festival period included Ingmar Bergman's sexually oriented *Twelfth Night* from Stockholm, Giorgio Strehler's delicately wrought production of Goldoni's *Il Campiello,* and Besso Besson's bold use of masks in his East Berlin version of Brecht's *The Good Woman of Setzuan.* The presence of two of Peter Stein's older productions gave further confirmation of the director's preeminence in the European theater. Visiting productions from Japan and Uganda conveyed an impression of yet greater diversity in the theatrical world.

HENRY POPKIN
State University of New York at Buffalo;
Drama Critic, Westchester-Rockland Newspapers

In May the public had its first chance to compare the new 747-SP (special performance) jet with its big brother, the original 747. The SP is 47 feet (14.3 meters) shorter than the standard 747 and carries up to 288 passengers compared to the standard's 360.

transportation

The most significant transportation news of 1975 is reported in the following surveys. Additional developments are discussed under the headings AUTOMOBILES; ENGINEERING, CIVIL.

General Survey

The push for conservation of energy resulted in many cross-related improvements in the field of transportation in 1975.

Highway Travel. Both the highway-safety and fuel-consumption figures were helped by the 3% decrease in highway travel during the year—the first decrease since the end of World War II. Fourteen states together accounted for 60% of all travel in the United States.

Average Speed. Fuel consumption figures and safety have both been improved by the drop in average highway speeds resulting from efforts to enforce 55 miles-per-hour (mph) speed limits (1 mile = 1.6093 km). On main rural highways average speeds have dropped from 60.3 mph to 54.8 mph. On the interstate system, average speeds have dropped from 65 mph to 57 mph.

Highway Safety. Less driving and lower speeds led to fewer highway fatalities: 45,534 lives were lost as compared with 55,114 lives in 1974. The traffic fatality rate was by far the lowest in the industrialized world.

Fuel Consumption. Energy conservation measures were effective, for only 106.7 billion gallons (405.3 billion liters) of fuel were consumed in 1974, 4.3 billion gallons (16.3 billion liters) fewer than in 1973. California was the largest user, consuming 10.5 billion gallons (39.7 billion liters). The ten top states, which included California, Texas, New York, Ohio, Pennsylvania, Illinois, Michigan, Florida, New Jersey, and Georgia, accounted for 51% of the motor fuel used.

Motor Vehicle Registrations. Motor vehicle registrations continued to rise to a new level of 129,943,087 vehicles, up 4,273,095 from 1974. The total included 104,898,256 automobiles, 446,547 buses, and 24,598,284 trucks. California led the nation with 13.7 million vehicles; Texas, New York, Pennsylvania, Ohio, Illinois, Florida, and Michigan all registered more than 5 million vehicles.

Air Travel. Commuter airlines are the fastest growing branch of the commercial airline industry. In 1975 there were 190 carriers flying 1,042 aircraft, seating from 4 to 10 passengers, serving small and medium-sized cities. During 1974 they carried over 6 million passengers, which is more than the local service airlines carried in 1960 and more than the trunk carriers transported in 1944. In the same period, the local service airlines carried 39.9 million passengers.

Fatal air accidents increased sharply in 1974. The 467 fatalities in 9 fatal accidents by the certificated route and supplemental airlines made the death toll the highest since the record of 499 in 1960. For the fourth consecutive year and for 8 of the past 11 years, supplemental carriers conducting civil and military contract operations had no fatal accidents.

The number of airports in the United States rose to 13,602; 4,575 were publicly owned and 8,487 were privately owned. Lighted runways were provided at 3,999 locations and paved runways at 4,716. Airport activity was at a record level, with a total of 57,687,516 operations. Chicago's O'Hare International was the nation's busiest airport, with 665,331 operations.

Railroads. In spite of inflation, 1974 was a good year for the railroads. Total revenues of $17 billion represented an all-time high. The return on investment rose to 4%, the best since 1955, and employment rose to 525,000, the first increase since 1951. New-car orders reached 106,000, the highest level since 1955; and traffic was the highest ever.

However, 1975 did not start off as well, with 30 of the 64 Class I railroads reporting deficits in the first half of the year. The entire industry had a deficit of $115.7 million on revenues of $7.8 billion, down 4.8% from the first half of 1974.

JAMES R. ROMAN, JR.
The George Washington University

Air Transportation

Commercial aviation's worst fears came true in 1975 as fuel costs continued to soar, pushing almost all parts of the industry into a deficit. Airlines in many nations were able to cover some of the losses through increased fares, but U. S. firms were denied such relief by the Civil Aeronautics Board (CAB). Fears of a marked drop in passenger levels failed to materialize, but the slightly increased revenues over 1974 levels were not enough to ease the burden.

Profits and Losses. The Air Transport Association of America reported that U. S. airlines lost more than $250 million while carrying a near-record number of passengers. In 1974, the U. S. scheduled airline industry had earnings of $322 million on $14.7 billion in revenues. Even United, the largest airline in the West, was unable to stand the strain imposed by fuel prices. In 1974, it posted profits of $86.4 million, but in the first seven months of 1975 profits plummeted to $6.1 million. The U. S. federal government offered little assistance. On one hand, the Congress showed its willingness to consider favorably a $670 million, 10-year research and development program aimed at producing 40% to 50% fuel savings by current conventional transports. At the same time, the Ford administration fought for deregulation of petroleum prices, which would further increase fuel costs. These costs climbed an average of 18.1% in the 12 months ending September 30. On October 1, an additional 10% increase in the cost of crude oil was put into effect by the Organization of Petroleum Exporting Countries (OPEC).

The CAB denied requests by major U. S. airlines for fare increases ranging from 3.5% to 5%, allowing them only to make permanent a temporary 4% fare hike permitted in November 1974. Stunned carriers, their budgets already pared to the limit, immediately reapplied for slightly smaller rate boosts, and some joined together to seek a judicial review of the original denial. International Air Transport Association members, in contrast, agreed during their August meeting to raise fares between 3% and 5%.

Passenger Traffic. For the first half of 1975, passengers seemed to desert the airlines. Passenger traffic on the critical North Atlantic route dropped sharply during the first five months. The bottom in this major market was reached in April, when the decline exceeded 17%. By May, U. S. trunk carriers in scheduled domestic service experienced only a 1.9% decline. Increases were recorded the next month,

and by the year's end, it appeared that the passenger total would almost match previous records.

No-Frill Fares. Much of the year was used for an experiment with "no-frills" air fares, and the test got only mixed reviews. The system permitted sharply-reduced rates in exchange for elimination of reservations, meals, and films or other entertainment. National Airlines was the first to get CAB approval for a no-frills rate, 35% below conventional fares. Delta and Eastern followed with similar cuts, but other airlines held back. Despite encouragement from several government agencies, the CAB found that 95% of passengers on the no-frills flights were regular passengers who had switched to the flights because of the lower fares. Thus the plan led to a revenue loss.

SST. The year 1975 saw the British and French governments putting the final touches on their joint supersonic jet transport project, the Concorde. Both governments agreed to launch commercial Concorde service simultaneously early in 1976, with Air France operating from Paris to Rio de Janeiro, and British Airways flying from London to Bahrain in the Persian Gulf.

The French found no problems with the Concorde and certified it for service despite questions concerning the reliability of the auto-pilot system. After a series of landing tests the British government ordered a new investigation into the possibility of sound suppression when takeoff and landing noise at London's Heathrow Airport caused considerable concern. Although it appeared that there was no immediate threat to plans for the start of regular Concorde flights, studies were ordered to determine whether or not noise from engines could be reduced. The report revealed that the Concorde is more than twice as loud on takeoff as the noisiest aircraft now using Heathrow and up to six times as loud as the new generation of wide-body aircraft. It was estimated that the Concorde would exceed Heathrow noise limits on 80% of its flights and would require a special dispensation with regard to noise limits if it is to be permitted to operate from Heathrow.

Strong debate continued throughout 1975 in the United States over whether Concorde would be cleared for scheduled flights to U. S. cities. A final decision was to be made by Secretary of Transportation William Coleman. In their initial application, Concorde backers sought six flights daily to U. S. airports, with landings at Dulles airport outside Washington, D. C., and John F. Kennedy airport on Long Island, N. Y. Later in the year, an additional application was made for nonstop flights from Europe to Dallas-Fort Worth, Tex. The Federal Aviation Administration provided Coleman with a statement concluding that Concorde was dirtier and noisier than subsonic jets but making no recommendation for granting or denying approval.

Trans World Airlines (TWA) and Pan Ameri-

can Airways appealed to the president's Council on Wage and Price Stability to oppose giving landing rights to Concorde on the ground that it would "severely endanger the already fragile economic condition of our intercontinental domestic jet fleets." The council found, however, that at worst Pan Am and TWA might lose $30 million in revenues, or approximately a 1% decline in their total passenger revenues. Real losses would probably be considerably lower.

New Aircraft. The age of wide-body aircraft became even more an established fact with the growing use of the Lockheed 1-1011 Tri-Star, McDonnell-Douglas DC-10, and Airbus Industrie A-300b, which competes with the original Boeing 747. Both modified and all-new entries were being prepared to compete for orders from the carriers. One of these, the 747-SP, a shortened version of the 747, received its FAA air worthiness certification in December. This "special performance" offspring of the original jumbo jet was found to fly higher, farther, and faster than any other jumbo jet in the world. It marked its certification with the first nonstop flight from New York to Tokyo. This was a record nonstop distance for a jetliner loaded with passengers and took 14 hours.

Also late in the year, the Soviet YAK-42, a 100–120 passenger, three-engine transport, entered the flight-test stage just a few months after the Soviet Union began testing the Ilyushin IL-76, an all-cargo, wide-body transport. The two planes brought to completion a family of commercial aircraft with which the USSR hopes to penetrate the international market. The bulk of Russian aviation exports, now ranging from short-haul craft to the SST, has in the past been sold primarily to East European nations.

In 1975 there were attempts to renew U. S. interest in lighter-than-air (LTA) technology. Blimps and dirigibles, although slower than airplanes, require less fuel to move cargo. The exponent of LTA in the Congress was Arizona's Sen. Barry Goldwater, a member of the Senate Committee on Space and Aeronautics. He was responsible for prodding the National Aeronautics and Space Administration into granting Goodyear Aerospace Corp. $132,000 to examine the applicability of LTA technology to a system of feeding passengers from urban centers to major airfields, and as a method of transporting heavy and bulky machinery. Among the critics of the grant was Vice Adm. Charles E. Rosendahl, chief proponent of using LTA for military purposes. Rosendahl confessed that he found many of the commercial uses that LTA enthusiasts envisioned for blimps and dirigibles "enchanting . . . but unwise." Moreover, he found that all of them would "require very unusual cooperation from Mother Nature."

Hijacking. The number of firearms and other dangerous articles detected at airport passenger screening stations doubled during 1975. There were five attempts to hijack U. S. airliners dur-

ing the year, but none was successful. The last successful hijacking of a U. S. airliner was on Nov. 10, 1972. The screening program remained in effect throughout 1975. While the number of passengers screened remained approximately the same, more than 60,000 firearms and other dangerous articles, including ammunition and fireworks, were discovered. The increased rate of detection was attributed to improved screening procedures and to an increase in the use of X-ray machines.

JAMES R. WARGO
Correspondent, McGraw-Hill World News

Highways

Despite national attempts to discourage highway travel in view of the energy crisis, most aspects of highway development continued to expand. This is necessary because a viable highway structure is essential to the economic well-being of the nation.

General Highway Status. There are 3,806,883 miles (1 mile = 1.6093 km) of roads and streets in the United States. This includes 631,129 miles of municipal roads and streets, and 3,175,754 miles of rural road.

The federal government has jurisdiction only over roads of the national forests, parks, and so on, but federal aid highway funds, obtained through federal highway user taxes, provide aid for about 24% of the total roads and street mileage, including 27% of the rural mileage and 18% of the urban mileage.

About 765,000 miles of all roads and streets are unsurfaced. Granular material such as gravel or crushed stone surface 1.3 million miles, while the balance of over 1.7 million miles is paved.

Interstate Highway System. Of the 42,500-mile interstate system, 36,905 miles are open to traffic. During 1975, 1,084 miles were put into service, 2,631 miles were under improvement, and only 328 miles had not advanced to public hearings on location. The system consists of 33,901 miles of rural roads and 8,599 miles of urban highways.

Since work began on the system on July 1, 1956, a total of $59.31 billion has been spent or authorized for the system. However, because of inflation, it is estimated that 30.4% of the total cost of the system remains to be funded.

Appalachian Highway Program. The Appalachian Development Highway System authorized by Congress in 1965 provided for up to 2,700 miles of development highways and up to 1,600 miles of rural access roads in the 13-state Appalachian region.

Since that time, $2,547 billion in federal and state funds has been spent or obligated, resulting in 1,892 miles of highway and access roads completed or under construction. Engineering and right-of-way acquisition were underway on an additional 414 miles; designs have been approved or hearings held on 59 miles; and locations have been approved on 298 miles.

Rural and Secondary Programs.
Under the Federal Aid Rural Primary and Secondary Highway System and its urban extensions, since 1956, $41.65 billion worth of work involving 290,138 miles of construction contracts have been completed or are underway including $2.7 billion in 1975.

JAMES R. ROMAN, JR.
The George Washington University

Mass Transit

Several solid improvements were made in mass transportation during 1975, although no dramatic developments occurred. The Urban Mass Transportation Administration (UMTA) continued its grants, and new equipment for mass transportation was developed.

UMTA Grants. UMTA grants serve many purposes. For example, in May, out of grants totaling $195 million, $20,000 went to Utah's department of highways to support state government involvement in urban public transit planning, and $17 million went to Milwaukee, Wis., to aid in the acquisition of a private transportation company.

Other UMTA grants were for such projects as supporting bus-feeder operations to Bay Area Rapid Transit (BART) rail stations in San Francisco's east bay area. Another $8 million went to Washington, D. C., for construction of the National Visitors Center, which is designed to integrate intercity and commuter rail services with local transportation modes. Such facilities are needed to coordinate public transportation at a time when urban dependency on the automobile must decline.

A $274,000 grant was made to assist West Virginia's Transportation Remuneration Incentive Program (TRIP), which is a statewide and local program to improve transportation service generally, with a particular focus on the transportation needs of low-income groups, the elderly, and the handicapped.

Transit Equipment. The U. S. Department of Transportation's State of the Art Cars (SOAC), which are experimental urban transit rail cars representing the best in current technology, began extended public service on the Philadelphia Lindenwold High Speed Line. In previous revenue demonstrations in New York, Chicago, Boston, Cleveland, and Philadelphia, they met with enthusiasm from both riders and operators. The cars carry up to 300 riders at 80 mph with a noise level no higher than that of a modern office.

"Transbus," another UMTA-financed design, began operations in New York City. The low floors, wide doors, and improved lighting aid all transit riders but are particularly helpful to the elderly and to the handicapped. It is so designed that a person in a wheelchair can enter the vehicle easily.

Because of the push to reduce noise and air pollution, electric buses are becoming more pop-

UPI

In Germany, an experimental magnetic suspension train zips along special tracks at 120 mph (192 kph).

ular in high-density traffic areas, where they can operate at low average speeds. The city of Long Beach, Calif., is operating 21-passenger minibuses in the downtown area that can run from 10 A. M. to 4:30 P. M. without recharging their 2-ton batteries. Cars are banned from the new town of Roosevelt Island in New York City's East River, with free public transportation offered in the form of electric buses. Rochester, N. Y., tried battery-powered buses in the city's dial-a-bus system, since the vehicles must enter residential neighborhoods.

JAMES R. ROMAN, JR.
The George Washington University

Railroads

Late in 1975, a reorganization plan for many bankrupt railroads in the northeastern and midwestern United States was accepted by Congress. Railroad traffic and revenues suffered from the economic recession in 1975, the first year in which the railroad industry as a whole failed to make a profit.

ConRail Established. Overshadowing all other railroad developments in the United States in 1975 was the acceptance by Congress, in November, of a massive, federally financed reorganization of bankrupt railroads in the Northeast and Midwest. Out of this reorganization came a new common carrier, the Consolidated Railroad Corporation (ConRail), consisting of 15,000 miles (24,000 km) of line taken over from the Penn Central, the Central of New Jersey, the Lehigh Valley, and the Pennsylvania-Reading Seashore Lines, plus a small portion of the Ann Arbor and several light-density lines of the Erie Lackawanna and the Reading railroads. Most of the Erie Lackawanna and Reading lines went to a neighboring solvent system, the Chesapeake and Ohio (Chessie) for a cash payment of $54 million. Not affected by the ConRail reorganization was the Chicago, Rock Island & Pacific, which went into bankruptcy in the spring of 1975.

The reorganization plan, which was not to be-

come fully effective until well into 1976, contemplated the abandonment of about 5,700 miles (9,120 km) of lightly-patronized branch lines, although provision was made to continue certain of these lines for two years under federal and local subsidies. Private investors affected by the reorganization were unhappy with the compensation formula reached by the U. S. Railway Association (USRA), which prepared the plan under mandate of the Regional Rail Reorganization Act of 1973. To the Penn Central Railroad properties, for example, USRA affixed a "net liquidation value" of $471 million. Penn Central trustees claimed a "fair value" of more than $7 billion. A Supreme Court decision in December 1974 held that creditors dissatisfied with the compensation arrangements could sue the federal government under the Tucker Act, and it seemed likely that lawsuits deriving from the reorganization plan would be in the courts for decades to come.

The reorganization plan called for the investment of about $1.85 billion in federal money in ConRail. Control of the company will be vested in a government-dominated board as long as federal debt comprises more than half of ConRail's total debt. While many doubted, late in 1975, that ConRail would ever revert to private operation—some went so far as to call it de facto nationalization—there was wide agreement that this was "the only game in town," and it would have to be played.

Traffic and Revenues. In a year of deepening recession, all railroads suffered from attrition of traffic and revenues. In the first half of 1975, the railroad industry as a whole operated at a loss for the first time in history. For most of the year, freight carloadings were down 12%–14% from 1974 levels, and a series of rate increases amounting to a cumulative 40% in a period of just over 24 months was not sufficient to compensate for the loss. With fewer trains to operate, railroads furloughed thousands of employees and cut back on equipment and track-maintenance programs. Deliveries of new freight cars and locomotives remained high, due to substantial orders placed during the prior year, but orders for new cars dropped to a near record low and were expected to amount to only about one-fourth of the nearly 100,000 ordered in 1974.

No major railroad strikes occurred during the year. There was no important merger activity beyond the federally sponsored ConRail reorganization of bankrupt lines.

Passengers. The only Class I railroad that suffered relatively little financially from the recession was the National Railroad Passenger Corporation (Amtrak), whose losses are picked up and whose capital needs are met by the federal government. For the 1977 fiscal year, Congress authorized $350 million for Amtrak operating subsidies and more than $100 million for capital acquisitions. In addition, the federal government proposed a $1.4 billion program for re-

UPI

A computer monitors stress in experimental concrete ties installed on the Santa Fe line near Streator, Ill.

habilitating the Northeast Corridor line between Boston and Washington. Under the ConRail reorganization plan, this line will be devoted exclusively to passenger trains.

Late in 1975, Amtrak had 727 new passenger cars on order or in the process of delivery. These are conventional cars already familiar to most travelers. Amtrak planned to go to Europe for its next generation of high-speed trains.

LUTHER S. MILLER
Editor, "Railway Age"

Shipping

Oil Tankers. Much of the free world shipping industry was in crisis during 1975 because of a worldwide recession, increased oil prices, and reduced oil shipments. Super tankers were idle for extended periods. The average tonnage for 1975 was 4.4 million barrels of oil per day, 11.5% below 1974 averages. The low point came in April when tankers carried no more than 3.2 million barrels per day. As oil-consuming nations struggled to relieve their dependency on the Middle East reserves, there was a shift away from the Persian Gulf to other loading areas, particularly the Mediterranean. By the end of July, 649 Persian Gulf cargoes had been reported for a total of 58,843,000 tons. This was 214 fewer cargoes and 40 million fewer tons than for the first seven months of 1974.

No relief for imperiled tanker fleets was envisioned for 1976, and various nations sought drastic solutions. The government of Norway, for example, where 37% of the tankers registered under its flag were idle for the entire year, began consideration of a plan for a state-owned shipping company. Under this plan, the government would buy ships from Norwegian owners

who might otherwise have to sell them abroad at sharply reduced prices. Elsewhere, speculators were collecting oil tankers at bargain rates. Purchase prices averaged only a third of construction costs.

Satellite Communications. The tantalizing promise of satellite communications for maritime operations failed to materialize on schedule in 1975 when the international telecommunications consortium COMSAT General was forced to postpone the launch of the first in its series of MARISAT satellites. However, an eight-month test using an existing satellite and the Exxon-owned *Esso Bahamas* proved that ship communications had moved to the brink of the space age.

Until the series of satellites is put into operation, ship-to-ship and ship-to-shore communications will continue to rely primarily on Morse code to land-based communications centers—a procedure that, depending on atmospheric conditions, can take hours. By contrast, COMSAT is offering shippers instantaneous message delivery via voice, teletype, or facsimile presentation. With MARISAT, open sea navigation will be reduced from a presumed accuracy range of a few miles to immediate positioning with an accuracy range of plus or minus 1.25 miles (2 km). A shipping company will be able to track a vessel's progress on an hourly basis.

Prospective buyers learned from COMSAT that the cost of such efficiency would be high. Cost for TELEX service alone was pegged at $800 per ship per month, plus $4 per minute over 200 minutes. Telephone service rates were put at $10 per minute. These costs must be added to terminal equipment costs of $52,545 per ship. Orders were coming in slowly.

Grain Shipment Halted. The International Longshoremen's Association threatened to hold up shipments of grain to the Soviet Union and actually refused to load some freighters at west coast docks in July. The problem arose after the USSR negotiated the purchase of a minimum of 15 million tons of wheat and corn to supplement its poor harvests.

The U. S. Department of Agriculture and U. S. farming groups condemned the dock workers, but the union refused to budge for several weeks. They claimed that previous U. S. grain sales to the USSR had led to shortages in U. S. stocks and were significant if not principal contributors to successive waves of inflation. The issue was resolved in October when the USSR agreed to spread its purchases over an extended term and to pay higher shipping rates. Early reports of bumper U. S. grain harvests helped set the stage for the settlement. (See also INTERNATIONAL TRADE.)

Control of Panama Canal. Shipping interests in the United States became alarmed over growing enthusiasm in the government to turn full control of the Panama Canal over to Panama. The fear was that if U. S. control waned, Panama

UPI

The 1,100-foot (335-meter) oil tanker *Massachusetts* is the largest ship ever built in the United States.

would demand steep hikes in tolls, and the canal would become susceptible to politically-inspired closings as well as selective passage. At year's end, key forces in Congress and the State Department were still believed to be favorably disposed to turning control over to Panama.

During the year, six big passenger liners were withdrawn from active service or were declared redundant by their owners. These were Pacific & Orient's *Oronsay*, Shaw Savill's *Ocean Monarch*, Union Castle's *Reina del Mar*, French Line's *France*, and Italia's *Michelangelo* and *Raffaello*. The fate of these ships was uncertain. As ocean-borne passenger travel rates have declined, dozens of liners have been retired. There were no active bids for those ships retired in 1975.

JAMES R. WARGO
Correspondent, McGraw-Hill World News

The six berths at New York City's Passenger Ship Terminal were all occupied in July, for the second time in 1975, but sea travel declined overall during the year.

TRAVEL

Despite the worldwide combination of inflation, recession, and currency fluctuation, domestic and international travel continued to be both a popular leisure time activity and a business necessity in 1975. Gloomy predictions that soaring costs would send the pleasure traveler the way of the dodo and the passenger pigeon were proven false. Domestic travel was up by 10% over 1974 figures, with train and bus companies reporting the largest increases. Automobile travel rose by 15%. Domestic airlines, however, hurt by recession and soaring fuel costs, reported losses of $250 million in 1975. Middle income U. S. travelers shunned the airlines, which raised fares sharply. However, a decision by the Civil Aeronautics Board made public September 13 had begun to reverse this trend by year's end.

O. T. C. The Civil Aeronautics Board authorized "one stop inclusive tour charters," dubbed O. T. C. The new plan, by offering the individual a bargain formerly available only to members of "affinity groups," makes low cost travel and accommodations available to millions. Often, the total cost of an O. T. C. package, including air fare, accommodation, meals, sightseeing, and tips, is less than the lowest possible on a regularly-scheduled air fare.

O. T. C. is a U. S. version of a plan that has long been available to Europeans. Although O. T. C.'s are usually sold to the public through retail travel agents, it is the tour operator who is responsible for getting the tour off the ground.

He charters the plane, makes arrangements with hotels, and predicts the price of the package. Prices for an O. T. C. package are computed on the basis of charter air fare rates, which vary depending on the destination and the load factor of the plane, and a minimum of $15 a day for ground accommodations ($7.50 for a child under 12).

The CAB requires that O. T. C. organizers post performance bonds and keep most of the tour proceeds in an escrow account until after the tour group returns. This safeguard is intended to prevent travelers from being cheated or stranded, a frequent problem in the past with charter operations.

There are some limitations on O. T. C.'s. Domestic tours, including those to Canada, Mexico, and the Caribbean, require a four-day minimum stay, while all others must be at least seven days. Tickets for domestic O. T. C.'s had to be bought at least 15 days in advance in 1975, with a reduction to 7 days scheduled for 1976. International tickets must be secured no less than 30 days ahead of time.

Also, the destinations of O. T. C. tours are limited since they must be the site of many hotel rooms, rooms that have not always been easy to fill. The most popular destination for the first O. T. C. groups was Las Vegas, with Hawaii and Mexico close behind. The Caribbean islands are not yet readily available to tourists in search of an O. T. C. fare. To maintain high room rates during the peak season and to protect local airlines, many island hoteliers have rejected the new concept. Many European destinations were

not available to O. T. C. travelers. Prices in many European cities were so high that even an O. T. C. fare did not offer much enticement. However, tours were being offered to London, Paris, Rome, Amsterdam, Zurich, and Athens.

Effect of European Inflation. For the first time in several years the rate of inflation was higher in many European countries in 1975 than in the United States. Consequently many foreign travelers came to North America in 1975. During the first quarter of the year the United States experienced a favorable balance of tourist dollars. The $57 million surplus was the first of its kind for 14 years and was concrete evidence that tourism between the United States and the rest of the world was a two-way street.

An estimated 3.2 million U. S. citizens visited Europe in 1974, compared with 3.8 million in 1973. The decline was less than had been expected, probably because the U. S. dollar strengthened. By midsummer the number of U. S. visitors to Europe was about the same as it had been in 1974, although still far less than in the boom years of the late 1960's.

National Parks. Partly because of the uncertainty of the economic future and partly because of Bicentennial features, many vacationers traveled within the United States in 1975. More than 227 million persons visited the national parks and other park service facilities, ranging from the Statue of Liberty to Gold Rush ghost towns in California. Most of these visitors were unaware of the controversy that simmered within the National Park Service during the year. The basic disagreement was between those who wanted to add facilities and attractions to the parks, ranging from golf courses to rock music concerts, and those who thought such "improvements" were destroying the natural values the parks were established to preserve. Policy studies commissioned in 1972 suggested that the trend toward commercial services and entertainment within the parks had gone too far and suggested a return to more natural values.

The park service moved carefully in this direction. Concessions have been eased out, trailer-camping restricted, road building curtailed, and private vehicles barred from areas where they formerly were allowed. Although the changes triggered protests, National Parks Director Gary Everhardt planned to continue. "We've got to give preservation and protection of park values and resources the highest priority and the most of our attention for the next five or ten years, and hopefully beyond that," he said.

Bicentennial Celebrations. The first major event of the U. S. Bicentennial, a reenactment of Paul Revere's ride, took place in Middlesex county, Mass., on April 19. More than 150,000 tourists lined Revere's route, and stayed to watch British Redcoats rout Minutemen on the Lexington Green. The U. S. Travel Service expected these and myriad similar events across the country to draw 30 million foreign visitors and untold numbers of U. S. residents. Washington, D. C., alone expects 300,000 overnight visitors daily during the summer of 1976.

Other U. S. cities, large and small, were doing their best to reenact their part in the nation's birth, remind their citizens of the values cherished then, and, less idealistically, attract the tourist dollar. For example, Philadelphia's anniversary celebration was scheduled to include 200 events costing $200 million and 58 public works projects whose bill was expected to reach $172.4 million. The city expected 60 million persons to visit before the party is over.

For those unable to travel far to see Bicentennial attractions the Freedom Train visited 80 cities in 1975. Funded with $5.6 million in corporate donations, the train began its 21-month cross-country trip in April. Pulled by a restored steam engine, the red, white, and blue cars constitute a traveling museum of Americana, featuring everything from George Washington's copy of the Declaration of Independence to Judy Garland's dress from "The Wizard of Oz."

WILLIAM DAVIS
The "Boston Globe"

UPI

French and English officials met in March to discuss the Concorde's date of entry into public service.

Tunisian President Habib Bourguiba (*left*) greets Col. Muammar el-Qaddafi, leader of Libya's Revolutionary Command Council, in Tunis.

UPI

TUNISIA

Tunisia's economic boom—a carry-over from 1974—faded somewhat in 1975, and political opposition at home and in exile was rekindled. President Habib Bourguiba's leadership was not seriously challenged, however, although the question of his successor remained a favorite topic of speculation.

Economy. By mid-1975, the economic outlook for the North African nation was disenchanting for those who saw the success story of 1974 as a role-model for the economic future. The slight augmentation in oil production could not make up for the reduction in oil prices for Tunisian crude, which sold for $15.00 a barrel in 1974 and brought only $11.00 a barrel in 1975. Phosphate exports were cut by Tunisia, and by producers Morocco and Togo as well, in an effort to stifle attempts by consumer countries to cut the soaring price of phosphate. Sales of olive oil, of which Tunisia is the world's leading exporter, were cut by Italy's pressure on the European Economic Community (EEC) to halt EEC importation of the Tunisian product. While waiting for an amelioration of this problem, Tunisia put the brake on EEC imports. Despite this action, Tunisia's balance of payments with EEC countries showed a first-quarter deficit of $50 million.

However, Tunisian economic planners remained confident of their commodities' viability in the long run. The nation hopes to produce almost 8 million tons of phosphates by 1980. In 1975, 35% of the mined product was processed locally; by 1980 Tunisians intend to process 50% in the industrial plants at Sfax and Gabès.

Trial of Dissidents. Domestic tension centered around a series of state security trials, the last of which, in October, saw 89 young students and workers sentenced to prison terms ranging from several months to seven years. Generally, the students were suspected of plotting against the state. The specific charges included membership in an illegal Marxist-Leninist organization, spreading of false rumors, and disrespect for the presidency and government.

External Threat. The young people had complained of neo-colonialism in Tunisia, especially of foreign control of the economy. The same charge came from outside the country, too. Ahmed Ben Salah, a former minister of economy and planning, in exile in Europe since 1973, issued a "Manifesto for a New Tunisia" in June, calling for complete decolonization of Tunisia. With his radical economic ideas and his ties to Algeria's President Houari Boumédienne, Ben Salah is the key figure in the People's Unity Movement, which sees itself as a serious alternative to the ruling Destourien Socialist party in Tunisia.

Ben Salah and his group may become more important when succession to septuagenarian Bourguiba's leadership becomes imminent. In 1975, however, Prime Minister Hedi Nouira remained the logical successor, due to a constitutional reform that makes the prime minister president upon the president's death.

Conflict with Ethiopia. Tunisia found itself entangled in another African conflict when it recommended to the Organization of African Unity (OAU) that an observer from the Eritrean Liberation Front, a separatist movement in Ethiopia, be present at the OAU's annual meeting of the heads of state. As a result, Ethiopia broke relations with Tunisia, a move the latter termed "excessive."

NANCY McKEON
The African-American Institute

TUNISIA · Information Highlights

Official Name: Republic of Tunisia.
Location: North Africa.
Area: 63,170 square miles (164,150 sq km).
Population (1975 est.): 5,700,000.
Chief City (1966 est.): Tunis, the capital, 468,997.
Government: *Head of state,* Habib Bourguiba, president (took office 1957). *Chief minister,* Hedi Nouira, premier (took office Nov. 1970). *Legislature* (unicameral) —National Assembly.
Monetary Unit: Dinar (0.412 dinar equals U. S.$1, July 1975).
Gross National Product (1974 est.): $3,600,000,000.
Manufacturing (major products): Processed foods, wines, petroleum products, olive oil, pulp and wood products.
Major Agricultural Products: Wheat, olives, vegetables, grapes, citrus fruits, forest products.
Foreign Trade (1974): *Exports,* $795,000,000; *imports,* $977,000,000.

TURKEY

Turkey was faced with a number of grave problems during 1974–75, which were partly reflected in its inability to form a stable government. The problems on Cyprus, which Turkey invaded in 1974, remained critical. Student and labor unrest persisted, and martial law prevailed in a number of provinces. The rate of inflation during the year was about 30%. Some 2 million Turks were out of jobs and, because of recession in Western Europe, where some 1 million Turks were working, there was a threat that many might have to return home. Labor remittances, which had totaled some $900 million in 1973, were down 25% during 1975.

Politics. The political situation was turbulent in late 1974, with Bulent Ecevit resigning as prime minister and the successor government of Sadi Irmak falling on November 29, after 12 days in office. Political maneuvering followed. Chief of Staff Samih Sancar announced on Jan. 1, 1975, that the army could not remain aloof from the nation's problems and was distressed that measures to solve Turkey's problems had not been taken.

When Irmak failed to form a broad coalition government, President Fahri Korutürk then summoned Süleyman Demirel, former Justice party prime minister, to form a coalition government, with Ihsan Sabri Caglayangil as foreign minister. Demirel presented his program on April 6, calling for a bizonal federal solution of the Cyprus problem, opposing Greece's extension of territorial waters to 12 miles (19 km), supporting Turkey's membership in the North Atlantic Treaty Organization (NATO), promising development of the eastern provinces of Turkey, and extending health and unemployment benefits.

The Demirel government was barely sustained in the parliamentary election on October 12. The Justice party won 27 of 54 Senate seats at stake, a loss of 5 seats, and 4 of the 6 contested seats in the Assembly. The Republican People's party (RPP) captured 25 Senate seats and one Assembly seat. The National Sal-

UPI

Turkish Premier Demirel (center) and Greek Premier Caramanlis (left) and Foreign Minister Bitsios discuss the Cyprus issue in Brussels, Belgium, in May.

vation party gained 1 Senate seat, and other small parties were shut out. Bulent Ecevit called for Demirel's resignation, since his RPP received 44% of the vote and the Demirel coalition only 41%. But Demirel declared that the government would continue as long as economic and political stability existed. Regular elections were not scheduled until 1977.

Social and Economic Problems. The roots of the persistent crisis in the Turkish economy can be traced to the 1950's and 1960's when there was heavy expenditure on defense, virtual exemption of farmers from taxation, and irresponsible extravagance by the dominant Democrat party. No government since has been able to take the necessary corrective steps. The rate of inflation in 1975 stood at 30%, and the lira had to be devalued three times. Turkey's trade deficit in the first half of 1975 totaled more than $1 billion, an increase of 130% over the same period in 1974.

Foreign Affairs. Turkey continued to seek normalization of relations with Iran, its Arab and Balkan neighbors, and the USSR, but it had serious problems with Greece and the United States. Turkish-Greek problems arose over two major issues—the dispatching of some 40,000 Turkish troops to Cyprus in July 1974 when it appeared that *enosis* (union) with Greece was about to take place, and the Greek extension of territorial waters to 12 miles (19 km). While there was much discussion involving the Greek, Turkish, and Cypriot governments and while the Turkish government withdrew some troops, there was no resolution of this complicated problem. The Turkish government, whose troops occupied about 40% of Cyprus, with some 18% of the population of Turkish ethnic origin, consistently held to a bizonal division of Cyprus. Both the Greek and Cypriot governments rejected this plan. Meanwhile, the U. S. Congress, despite the opposition of the Ford administration, voted to cut off military aid to Turkey on Feb. 5, 1975, unless progress toward a solution of the Cyprus problem could be shown. U. S. aid had run to

---

——— TURKEY · Information Highlights ———

Official Name: Republic of Turkey.
Location: Southeastern Europe and southwestern Asia.
Area: 301,381 square miles (780,576 sq km).
Population (1975 est.): 39,900,000.
Chief Cities (1970 census): Ankara, the capital, 1,208,-791; Istanbul, 2,247,630; Izmir, 520,686.
Government: *Head of state,* Fahri Korutürk, president (took office April 1973). *Head of government,* Süleyman Demirel, premier (took office March 1975). *Legislature*—Grand National Assembly: Senate and National Assembly.
Monetary Unit: Lira (13.99 liras equal U. S.$1, April 1975).
Gross National Product (1974 est.): $19,000,000,000.
Manufacturing (major products): Textiles, petroleum products, cement, iron and steel, fertilizers, processed foods.
Major Agricultural Products: Raisins, wheat, cotton, rye, sugar beets, barley, fruit, tobacco, hazelnuts, sheep, cattle.
Foreign Trade (1974): *Exports,* $1,413,000,000; *imports,* $3,487,000,000.

more than $3 billion over the years. (See also CYPRUS.)

Turkey then announced it would have to reconsider its NATO membership, although no basic changes were expected. Turkish troops began to occupy U. S. bases, some of which were important intelligence centers, early in July 1975. The situation eased somewhat when, under pressure from the Ford administration, the House of Representatives allowed Turkey to buy $185 million worth of military equipment, including 24 F-5E jet fighters, for which contracts had been made before February 5. However, new purchases would depend on steps toward a solution of the Cyprus question.

By the end of the year, the atmosphere in U. S.-Turkish relations had improved slightly. Although Turkey had removed the 1971 ban on poppy growing, it appeared willing to cooperate with the United States in eliminating opium traffic.

Five major agreements were signed with Libya on Jan. 7, 1975, for cooperation and trade in oil, industrial, and military projects. A joint Libyan-Turkish statement on August 16 called for the establishment of a Turkish-Arab bank in Istanbul and full cooperation in the field of civil aviation. It was also reported that Turkey was buying 60 helicopters from the USSR, while an economic agreement concluded between the two countries in July was estimated to involve $600–$700 million.

HARRY N. HOWARD
The American University

UGANDA

The Organization of African Unity (OAU) summit conference in Kampala and the elevation of Ugandan President Idi Amin to the presidency of the OAU brought Uganda and its unorthodox leader increased attention in 1975.

OAU Summit. The meeting of African heads of state and prime ministers in late July and early August was the 12th annual summit conference of the OAU. Tanzania, Zambia, and Botswana staged the group's first boycott, and newly-independent Mozambique sent only a deputy foreign minister. In an explanation of its position, Tanzania criticized the OAU for giving respectability to the Amin regime, which it called "one of the most murderous administrations in Africa."

The choice of Amin as the new chairman of the OAU was in keeping with the traditional selection of the host country's head of state for the position. Amin's position as spokesman for the OAU became a matter of considerable controversy when he addressed the United Nations in October. Although the OAU had failed to agree on a resolution calling for the expulsion of Israel from the United Nations, Amin, in a speech before the General Assembly, advocated the "extinction" of Israel.

UPI

Uganda President Idi Amin and UN Secretary General Kurt Waldheim arrive at United Nations in October.

Amin's Critics. Even before the OAU summit, Amin's policies drew frequent criticism. Emmanuel Wakhweya, Uganda's finance minister, sought exile in London on January 18 and immediately cabled his resignation. He declared that "economic forces will compel Amin to change his policies or there will be an explosion in the country." Wakhweya also complained that the government was a "one-man show" and that there was a "lack of value of human life."

In June Denis Hills, a British university lecturer residing in Uganda, was sentenced to death for treason because he called Amin a "village tyrant" in an unpublished book he had written. Amin demanded that British Foreign Secretary James Callaghan come to Uganda to discuss political differences between the two countries or Hills would be executed. Callaghan initially refused. After weeks of negotiations and the intercession of numerous governments, Amin finally released Hills in July.

JAY E. HAKES
University of New Orleans

--- UGANDA · Information Highlights ---

Official Name: Republic of Uganda.
Location: East Africa.
Area: 91,134 square miles (236,036 sq km).
Population (1975 est.): 11,400,000.
Chief City (1969 census): Kampala, the capital, 330,700.
Government: *Head of state,* Gen. Idi Amin, president (took office Feb. 1971). *Head of government,* Gen. Idi Amin. *Legislature* (unicameral)—National Assembly (dissolved Feb. 1971).
Monetary Unit: Shilling (8.16 shillings equal U. S.$1, Oct. 1975).
Gross National Product (1973 est.): $1,500,000,000.
Manufacturing (major products): Processed agricultural products, steel, textiles.
Major Agricultural Products: Coffee, tea, millet, cotton, sisal, tobacco, sweet potatoes, cassava.
Foreign Trade (1974): *Exports,* $316,000,000; *imports,* $132,000,000.

Soviet Chairman Leonid Brezhnev (*right*) confers with President Ford about U. S.-Soviet relations during Ford's visit to Helsinki in August.

USSR

In contrast to the previous three years of détente, no new arms limitation agreements were signed by the two superpowers during 1975, and no chief leader from either side visited the other's country. Mutual distrust was indicated by Soviet cancellation of the 1972 U. S.-USSR trade agreement, U. S. refusal to grant most-favored-nation status to the Soviet Union, and a number of minor incidents. However, the two governments cooperated in a spectacular space docking of a U. S. and a Soviet spaceship, with the two crews working together in space.

Elsewhere the USSR had difficulties with Canada, Cambodia, China, Egypt, Japan, and Uganda. Its position improved in Southeast Asia, and in Africa the USSR played an active role in Angola. Domestically, the Soviet government continued to imprison dissident intellectuals and executed two state officials for major embezzlement.

The 9th USSR Five-Year Plan ended in 1975, with the Soviet Union outproducing the United States in coal, oil, steel, cement, chemical fertilizer, and timber. Because of almost continual bad weather, the cereal harvest slumped to 75% of the planned level, necessitating Soviet purchase of more than $2.5 billion worth of grains from non-Communist countries.

FOREIGN AFFAIRS

United States. On Jan. 10, 1975, the USSR renounced the 1972 U. S.-Soviet trade agreement because of alleged U. S. interference in USSR internal affairs. This resulted from action by the U. S. Congress in late 1974, which limited U. S. Export-Import bank credits to the USSR to $300 million for four years and stipulated that the Soviet government must liberalize emigration to obtain most-favored-nation status for Soviet im-

ports into the United States. In response to the renunciation, the U. S. government refused on January 14 to grant most-favored-nation status to the USSR.

In mid-January an unknown rifleman fired shots into the Soviet Mission to the United Nations, causing no injuries. The USSR government complained to the U. S. government that Soviet diplomats and offices in the United States were not properly protected by U. S. police.

On June 27 two Armenian immigrants were arrested in the United States as Soviet spies. U. S. authorities named three Soviet diplomats as co-conspirators—a former USSR delegate to the UN Human Rights Conference, a former secretary of the Soviet Mission to the United Nations, and a present secretary. In the same month, a U. S. congressional investigation revealed that both the United States and the USSR monitor each other's telephone calls, which are transmitted by satellite.

On August 17 the U. S. Coast Guard seized the Soviet fishing trawler *Zakaysk* 84 miles (134 km) off Cape May, N. J., for violating a 1974 U. S. law forbidding foreign fishing for lobsters and crabs on the U. S. continental shelf. In November the U. S. government forbade a U. S. corporation, IBM, from selling a computer system worth $11 million to Intourist, the Soviet tourist agency, on the grounds that the system could be used for military purposes.

After the USSR purchased more than 10 million tons of U. S. grain during July, a refusal by U. S. unions to load the grain and a fear that the purchases would inflate U. S. cereal prices led to an embargo on further sales. This grain sales moratorium resulted in a U. S.-USSR commercial treaty on October 20, requiring the Soviet purchase of 6–8 million metric tons of U. S. wheat and corn per year for five years, beginning on Oct. 1, 1976. Having thus protected the United States by putting Soviet grain purchases on a regular basis, President Ford lifted the moratorium, and the USSR bought an additional

1.6 million tons of U. S. grain in the fall of 1975. (See also INTERNATIONAL TRADE.)

Europe. In 1975, Soviet relations with Europe were marked by many new cooperation agreements. Trade treaties and pacts of scientific cooperation were concluded with France, Great Britain, Italy, Belgium, Luxembourg, and Yugoslavia. The USSR also signed cultural exchange pacts with Iceland and Portugal and rendered technical aid to both countries. Loans of $2.2 billion were obtained from Britain, and $900 million from Italy, in order to finance Soviet purchases from these countries.

The USSR government regarded as a victory the agreement concluded on August 1 in Helsinki by the Conference on Security and Cooperation in Europe, which recognized all frontiers of all signatory countries as inviolable. Thus, all Soviet territorial gains in both Europe and Asia from World War II were legitimized. In accord with provisions for freer international exchange of information, the Soviet government eased restrictions on some foreign newspapermen stationed in Moscow. However when the 1975 Nobel Peace Prize was awarded to the Soviet dissident scientist, Andrei D. Sakharov, the USSR press immediately accused him of opposing Soviet foreign policy. He was forbidden to travel to Norway to receive his Nobel Prize, on the grounds that as a former designer of hydrogen bombs he knew state secrets.

Early in 1975 the USSR doubled the price of the oil it supplies to its East European satellites, which depend mainly on the Soviet Union to satisfy their petroleum requirements. However,

Nobel Peace Prize winner Andrei Sakharov was denied a visa to attend the award ceremonies in Norway.

UPI

the new price was still one-third lower than the price paid for Soviet oil by West European countries. In June a meeting of the Council of Mutual Economic Assistance (CMEA—the USSR-East European-Cuban-Mongolian common market) agreed that for the next five years the East European satellites would help the USSR construct a gas pipeline, a cellulose plant, and an asbestos mine. The satellites would be repaid with long-term rights to purchase the products from these economic projects cheaply.

On October 7 the USSR and East Germany renewed their military alliance for 25 years, rewording the treaty so that each side will now defend the other not only in Europe but in any defensive war anywhere.

Middle East. Although the USSR continued to arm Syria against Israel, Soviet Middle Eastern policy was more active in the economic rather than the political sphere. In April an agreement among the USSR, West Germany, and Iran provided that, starting in 1981, Iranian natural gas would be shipped to West Germany via a pipeline to be constructed through the USSR. Almost simultaneously, the Soviet Union agreed to assist Iraq in the development of peaceful uses of atomic energy. During July the USSR granted a credit of $700 million to Turkey for the purchase of Soviet machinery to aid Turkish industrialization. The credit made Turkey one of the largest Third World recipients of Soviet technical aid.

Throughout 1975 the Soviet press criticized U. S. efforts to arrange an Israeli-Egyptian peace as only a partial solution to tension in the Middle East. In November the USSR formally asked the United States to reconvene the Geneva Peace Conference on the Middle East, with participants to include representatives of the Palestine Liberation Organization. In an article in a fall issue of the Soviet magazine *Communist*, Soviet Foreign Minister Gromyko warned that Israel might cease to exist if it continued its alleged aggressiveness.

USSR-Egyptian relations deteriorated during 1975, when the Soviet government refused to reschedule Egyptian repayment of its debt to the USSR, amounting to at least $4 billion. Egypt's seaports sometimes refused to repair or refuel Soviet naval ships, and the USSR was forced to withdraw several Soviet reconnaissance planes from Egyptian airports.

India. On April 19 the first Indian space satellite was launched on a Soviet rocket from a Soviet rocket base. The two countries agreed that the USSR would later launch a second Indian space vehicle.

Far East. Soviet leaders assumed a low-key attitude when Communist forces conquered Cambodia and South Vietnam in the spring of 1975 and peaceably assumed power in Laos. During the summer 1,500 Soviet advisors began rendering technical aid in Laos, replacing U. S. advisors who departed in June. In October the USSR

concluded two new technical aid pacts with North Vietnam, granting the latter a long-term Soviet loan for 1976–80. In contrast, the Cambodian Communists did not seek Soviet aid and forced the Soviet embassy to close after the Communist capture of the Cambodian capital.

Soviet-Chinese relations remained hostile throughout 1975, and the two most powerful Communist nations did not conclude their annual trade treaty until late July. A month earlier the USSR warned Japan not to sign a proposed Chinese-Japanese friendship pact, because the pact contained a clause that could be interpreted as anti-Soviet. During 1975 the USSR and Australia signed their first cultural exchange agreement, and during September, Thailand accepted a Soviet offer of technical aid for its oil industry.

Africa. The USSR continued to befriend African countries by concluding trade, technical aid, and cultural exchange pacts with Guinea-Bissau, an economic aid agreement with the Congo, a fisheries pact with Gambia, and a cultural exchange treaty with Tunisia. As a result of a visit by Soviet Premier Kosygin during May, Libya also concluded a cultural exchange pact and agreed to purchase $1 billion worth of Soviet armaments.

When the former Portuguese colony of Angola gained independence in November, the USSR immediately recognized the Popular Movement for the Liberation of Angola (MPLA) as the legal government of the new African state. In addition Soviet arms shipments aided the MPLA in its civil war against rival factions.

Shortly before Angolan independence, the Soviet government pressured Uganda to support the MPLA. Uganda refused and demanded an apology from the USSR. Instead of apologizing the USSR temporarily broke diplomatic relations with Uganda, from November 11 to 17.

Latin America. The USSR concluded trade and technical aid treaties with Argentina and Mexico and offered technical aid to Trinidad and Tobago. Along with its other massive assistance to Cuba, the USSR agreed to help increase Cuban output of nickel and cobalt, with part of the production to be shipped to the Soviet Union.

UPI

A Uganda-bound convoy carrying Soviet equipment was delayed by Kenyan officials in June but released later.

The Soviet press urged Latin American Communists to ally with other parties against U. S. influence in Latin America.

Canada. Benefiting from the poor Soviet grain harvest, Canada sold 4.3 million metric tons of cereals to the USSR. A minor crisis began in July, when the Canadian government closed its Atlantic ports to Soviet fishing ships because the USSR had not paid for damages by Soviet vessels to Canadian lobster traps and had greatly exceeded legal limits for fish catch near Newfoundland and Nova Scotia. On August 28, Canada and the USSR established a joint fisheries consultative commission for fishing problems. The ports reopened to Soviet fishing boats on September 29, after the USSR agreed to reduce its fishing off Canada's east coast.

SPACE AND DEFENSE

Space Program. Soviet rocketry achieved several great successes in 1975. Three times during the year a single rocket launched eight unmanned satellites, displaying Soviet progress in the development of multiple individually targeted reentry vehicles (MIRV's). Soviet rocket tests were conducted in June from Central Asia into the north Pacific Ocean and in September from north European USSR into an area of the Barents Sea claimed by both the USSR and Norway. During June two Soviet rockets were launched toward Venus, and in October both rockets soft-landed research capsules on the planet.

Manned flights commenced in January 1975 when the Soyuz 17 rocket with a two-man crew docked with the Salyut 4 orbital scientific station. The Soyuz crew boarded the Salyut and remained in space 30 days before returning to

---

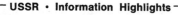

USSR • Information Highlights

Official Name: Union of Soviet Socialist Republics.
Area: 8,649,412 square miles (22,402,000 sq km).
Population (1975 est.): 255,060,000.
Chief Cities (1974 est.): Moscow, the capital, 7,500,000; Leningrad, 3,600,000; Kiev, 1,827,000.
Government: *Head of state*, Nikolai V. Podgorny, president (took office Dec. 1965). *Head of government*, Aleksei N. Kosygin, premier (took office Oct. 1964). *Secretary general of the Communist party*, Leonid I. Brezhnev (took office 1964). *Legislature*—Supreme Soviet: Soviet of the Union, Soviet of Nationalities.
Monetary Unit: Ruble (0.690 ruble equals U. S.$1, Aug. 1975).
Gross National Product (1974): $710,000,000,000.
Manufacturing (major products): Steel, cement, chemical fertilizer, machine tools, electric power.
Major Agricultural Products: Grain, sugar beets, sunflower seeds, potatoes, cotton.
Foreign Trade (1974): *Exports*, $27,400,000,000; *imports*, $24,900,000,000.

UPI

Soviet cosmonauts Leonov and Kubosov wave before boarding Soyuz for the joint U. S.-USSR space mission.

earth. An attempt to duplicate this feat in April failed, when a Soyuz craft suffered an equipment breakdown but managed to return safely to earth. In May the Soyuz 18 repeated the Soyuz 17 feat, this time with the two-man crew staying 63 days in space.

Soyuz-Apollo Flight. These flights were a rehearsal for the launching of the Soyuz 19, manned by Col. Alekse A. Leonov and Valery N. Kubasov, on July 15. Two days later this rocket docked with a U. S. Apollo spaceship, and the U. S. and Soviet crews visited each others' space vehicles. The two spacecraft parted on July 19, and the Soyuz 19 landed safely in Central Asia on July 21. In honor of this unprecedented international space feat, the Soviet government held an art exhibition, issued two commemorative stamps, and produced 500 million packs of cigarettes named Apollo-Soyuz. (See also SPACE EXPLORATION.)

Armed Forces. In 1975 the Soviet armed forces totaled about 3 million men. Their equipment included 36,000 tanks, 1,200 naval planes and helicopters, 2 aircraft carriers, 2 helicopter carriers, 44 nuclear submarines, and at least 60 MIRV intercontinental ballistic missiles (ICBM's). In April, for the first time in Soviet history, surface vessels, warplanes, and submarines of the USSR Northern, Baltic, Black Sea, Mediterranean, and Pacific fleets conducted simultaneous worldwide naval maneuvers.

GOVERNMENT AND POLITICS

One of the youngest Soviet leaders, Aleksandr N. Shelepin, resigned from the Politburo of the Soviet Communist party on April 16, allegedly at his own request. On May 22 he also resigned as head of the USSR trade unions, and during June he was appointed a vice-minister of a Soviet education ministry. Apparently he was removed from high office because he was regarded as a possible rival to Communist party leader Leonid Brezhnev.

Bulganin. On Feb. 24, 1975, Marshal Nikolai A. Bulganin, a member of the Politburo from 1948–58 and USSR premier from 1955–58, died in Moscow at the age of 79. He was not given a state funeral, possibly because he was removed from power in 1958 for opposing the then top Soviet leader, Nikita Khrushchev.

Minority Problems. During 1975 the Soviet press complained about widespread instances of anti-Russian nationalism in the Armenian Soviet Republic, whose party leader retired abruptly in July. There were also press complaints that the outlawed customs of bride purchase and bride abduction still existed in some localities of Muslim Central Asia.

Amnesty. In honor of the 30th anniversary of the Soviet victory over Nazi Germany, and also in recognition of International Women's Year, a limited amnesty released from Soviet prisons and prison camps disabled war veterans, men over 60 years of age, and women in numerous age and physical categories. Prison sentences were reduced for war veterans, veterans with war medals, women under 18, and women prisoners in general. Amnesty International still estimated that at least 10,000 people remained imprisoned in the USSR for political or religious reasons.

Crime. Two Soviet officials were executed for economic crimes. Mikhail Y. Leviyev, the manager of a Moscow state store and a Jew, had embezzled $2.7 million worth of goods, while Yuri S. Sosnovski, the director of a division of the Timber and Wood Processing Ministry, had accepted bribes of $140,000 from a Swiss businessman.

Dissidents. Many dissident intellectuals were arrested and imprisoned in 1975. Among them were author Anatoly Marchenko, for violating parole; physicist Andrei N. Tverdokhlebov and writer Mikola Rudenko, members of Amnesty International, for disseminating anti-Soviet propaganda; editor Vladimir Osipov, for anti-Soviet activities; and Edward Zelenin, for applying for an exit visa to display his paintings in Paris.

While performing in the United States in March, the world-famous Soviet cellist, Mstislav Rostropovich and his wife, opera singer Galina Vishnevskaya, decided not to return to the USSR. Their decision was based on the Soviet government's restrictions on artistic freedom.

Emigration. The number of Soviet Jews permitted to emigrate from the USSR in 1975 was about 10,500, half the number that left in 1974. Jews seeking to emigrate often were dismissed from their jobs, interrogated by the police, occasionally arrested, and sometimes sentenced to prison for 2 to 3 years.

Ecology. In 1975 the USSR was second only to Japan in the commercial killing of whales. To appease adverse world opinion, the Soviet government announced in June that it was disbanding one of its three Antarctic whaling fleets.

CULTURE

Obituary. Dmitri D. Shostakovich, world-famous Soviet composer, died of a heart ailment on August 9 at the age of 68. His state funeral was attended by two Politburo members.

Science. On October 14, Leonid V. Kantorovich, a Soviet mathematician, was named co-winner of the 1975 Nobel Prize in Economic Science. He was cited for his theory of optimum allocation of resources.

ECONOMY

Industry. Soviet industrial growth was about 7.7% in 1975, which was well above the 6.7% planned for the year but below the 8% achieved in 1974. During 1975 the largest Soviet blast furnace and biggest steel-rolling mill were completed in the Ukraine, both having annual capacities of several million tons. Two vast mineral deposits were discovered—apatite in East Siberia and salt in the Turkmen desert.

Although the USSR contains 20% of the world's industry, there is much industrial inefficiency. The Soviet press complained that factories suffered from shortages of oil, gas, metal, glass, paper, automation, and construction machinery.

Agriculture. Because of spring and summer droughts and early fall frosts, the 1975 grain harvest totaled only about 160 million metric tons in 1975. This was far below both the 1975 plan of 215.7 million tons and the 1974 harvest of 195.6 million tons. As a result, Soviet peasants were given prison sentences of from 2 to 3 years for stealing grain, stores urged bread conservation, and the USSR had to purchase more than 20 million tons of grains from the United States, Canada, Australia, and other capitalist countries.

Transport. The Soviet merchant marine was the fifth largest in the world in 1975, and the USSR fishing fleet was ranked first. Aeroflot, the official Soviet airline, opened new routes to Switzerland, Luxembourg, and Portugal. The 400-mile (640-km) Tyumen-Surgut railway was completed in August, linking the Trans-Siberian railway with the West Siberian oil fields.

Trade. Soviet foreign trade was planned to increase by 13% in 1975, but actually increased about 26%, with much of the increase being with Western industrial countries. The USSR's financial position in foreign trade deteriorated because of the $2 to $3 billion spent for vast grain imports. Nevertheless, the USSR rendered economic aid to 49 Third World countries, mostly in the Middle East and Africa.

ELLSWORTH RAYMOND
New York University

UPI

Marking the 30th anniversary of the end of World War II in Europe in May, Leonid Brezhnev (*lower right*) said that the Vietnam War's end should help détente.

Pipeline sections are swung into place in western Siberia, which has the USSR's largest oil deposit.

UPI

In September the Security Council refused to discuss the request for South Korea's UN admission, and, as a result, U. S. Ambassador Moynihan vetoed the admission of North and South Vietnam a few days later.

U. S. MISSION TO THE UN

UNITED NATIONS

The changing pattern of world political and economic relationships began to emerge clearly at the United Nations in 1975. The 82 members of the nonaligned group, which had appeared to be a solid bloc at the 1974 session of the General Assembly, were found to have divergent interests, which they followed increasingly as the year progressed.

The attitudes of the developed countries began to show signs of change, too. On both sides there was an increasing willingness to reach accommodation, evidenced most clearly in the special session of the assembly in September, which produced a plan to help narrow the gap between rich and poor nations. The initial inspiration for this plan stemmed from U. S. Secretary of State Henry Kissinger's proposals, presented to the assembly on September 1.

The old conflicts appeared again, however, in the regular assembly session in such resolutions as the one that declared Zionism a form of racism. This resolution was condemned by both houses of the U. S. Congress on November 11, when they called for reassessment of the U. S. role in the United Nations. In what was inevitably viewed as a countermove, the United States submitted a draft resolution demanding an unconditional amnesty for persons detained because of peaceful dissent with the policies of their governments. The resolution was withdrawn, however, on November 21.

Suggestions for the restructuring of the United Nations appeared from time to time during the year. The most notable among them was a report compiled by a group of high-level experts, submitted to UN Secretary General Kurt Waldheim on May 20. Entitled "A New United Nations Structure for Global Economic Cooperation," its chief recommendation was the creation of a new post of Director General for Development and International Economic Cooperation, to be second in rank only to the secretary general. A small step in the same general direction was taken at the Lima conference of the UN Industrial Development Organization (UNIDO), which recommended that UNIDO should be set up as a specialized agency on its own.

The principal activities of the United Nations in its 30th year are summarized below under the following headings: (1) General Assembly; (2) Security Council; (3) Economic and Social Council; (4) Trusteeship and Decolonization; and (5) Legal Activities.

GENERAL ASSEMBLY

The seventh special session of the General Assembly opened in New York on September 1, and was prolonged until September 16, the opening date for the regular assembly session, before unanimous agreement was reached on a resolution embodying measures to narrow the gap between rich and poor nations.

The wide-ranging recommendations contained in the resolution covered such major issues as industrialization, food and agriculture, science and technology, international trade, and the transfer of resources from developed to developing countries. They visualized steps to guarantee the purchasing power of developing countries by stabilizing their earnings. They also recommended easier Third World access to the science and technology and to the capital markets of the developed countries. Changes in the world monetary system and a redistribution of global wealth were advocated. Finally, the resolution advised the streamlining of the UN socioeconomic structure to enhance the role of developing countries in the organization.

When the 30th regular session of the assembly opened on September 16, Gaston Thorn, premier of Luxembourg, was elected president. The general debate, during which 121 representatives outlined their governments' views on world problems, lasted 24 days, from September 16 to October 9.

The session followed its usual lines, but it was also notable for the controversy among U. S., African, and Arab spokesmen triggered by the remarks on October 1 of Gen. Idi Amin, president of Uganda. Amin charged that Zionism controlled the United States and urged the extinction of Israel as a state. His remarks provoked a retort from Daniel P. Moynihan, chief U. S. delegate, in an address to an AFL-CIO convention in San Francisco on October 3. There Moynihan referred to an article describing Amin as a "racist murderer." Equally sharp reactions to Moynihan's speech from Arab and African spokesmen followed in the next few days.

Zionism. Further controversy was aroused when the assembly's Social Committee adopted a draft resolution on October 17 declaring that "Zionism is a form of racism and racial discrimination." The U. S. delegate on the committee, Leonard Garment, in his protest at the passage of the resolution, described it as "obscene" and "one of the most grievous errors in the 30-year life" of the United Nations. Garment added that the resolution "places the work of the UN in jeopardy." This controversy reached a peak on November 10 when the assembly itself adopted the resolution by a vote of 72–35, with 32 abstentions.

Palestinian Statehood. On October 10, the same day as the Zionism resolution, two resolutions designed to speed achievement of Palestinian statehood were passed by the assembly. The first, adopted by a vote of 93–18, with 27 abstentions, provided for a committee to draft a plan to carry out the 1974 assembly's assertion of the Palestinians' right to sovereign independence. The other resolution requested Security Council action to enable the Palestinians to exercise their rights in accordance with the 1974 assembly decision. It called for Palestine Liberation Organization (PLO) participation in all UN efforts for a Middle East settlement and asked that the PLO be invited to the Geneva conference. The vote on this resolution was 101 in favor, 8 against, and 25 abstentions. The United States was among the 8 countries in opposition.

Miscellaneous. Among the other subjects discussed by the assembly were the Cyprus problem, Southern Africa, Korea, disarmament, and human rights.

SECURITY COUNCIL

The Security Council was concerned in 1975 with problems similar to those it faced in 1974. Chief among them were Cyprus and the Middle East.

Cyprus. The council met five times between February 20 and 27 in response to a letter from the Cyprus government stating that Turkey had violated the assembly resolution of Nov. 5, 1974 and the Council's own resolution of Dec. 13, 1974. It adjourned, however, without taking any action in order to permit consultations among its members. With the council's consent, representatives of Cyprus, Greece, Turkey, Bulgaria, Rumania, and Saudi Arabia took part in the discussions without the right to vote. A resolution was adopted on March 12, without a vote, requesting the secretary general to assist in the resumption of talks between Greek and Turkish Cypriots. As a result of the mission, Secretary General Waldheim announced that negotiations would begin in Vienna in April. The talks took place from April 18 to May 3 under the secretary general's chairmanship. An expert committee was appointed to examine proposals on the powers and functions of a central government in Cyprus. A refugee transfer plan was finally agreed to on August 2.

Middle East. The council renewed the mandate of the UN Emergency Force for three-month periods in April and July, and then, on October 24, extended its life for a year. Similarly, the UN Disengagement Observer Force on the Syrian-Israeli border was renewed on May 28 for a six-month period. At each renewal the parties involved were called on to implement the various resolutions calling for the establishment of a just and durable peace in the Middle East.

UN Membership. Six new members—the Republic of Cape Verde, the Republic of São Tomé and Príncipe, the People's Republic of Mozambique, Papua-New Guinea, the Comoros, and Surinam—were recommended for UN membership by the Security Council during the year and were admitted during the General Assembly. A U. S. veto on September 30 blocked the admission of the Republic of Vietnam (South) and the Democratic Republic of Vietnam. This action followed the September 26 refusal of the council to take up the request for admission of the Republic of Korea. The vote on Korea was 7–7, with Cameroon abstaining. In casting its veto, the United States took the view that the Republic of Korea was as well qualified for membership as the two Vietnams, and that all three applications should be treated equally.

Western Sahara. After Spain's decision to grant independence to the Western Sahara, also called Spanish Sahara, the increasingly complicated situation there came before the council on November 2, when it urged all concerned to avoid any action that might increase tension in the area. A visit to the Sahara by a UN mission resulted in a recommendation of assembly action to enable Saharans to decide their future. A visit to Morocco, Mauritania, Algeria, and Spain by Secretary General Waldheim followed. In resolutions on November 6, the council deplored Morocco's march into Western Sahara, called for an immediate withdrawal, and requested that

ORGANIZATION OF THE UNITED NATIONS

THE SECRETARIAT

Secretary General: Kurt Waldheim (until Dec. 31, 1976)

THE GENERAL ASSEMBLY (1975)

President: Gaston Thorn (Luxembourg). The 144 member nations were as follows:

Afghanistan	Germany, Federal	Niger
Albania	Republic of	Nigeria
Algeria	Ghana	Norway
Argentina	Greece	Oman
Australia	Grenada	Pakistan
Austria	Guatemala	Panama
Bahamas	Guinea	Papua-New Guinea
Bahrain	Guinea-Bissau	Paraguay
Bangladesh	Guyana	Peru
Barbados	Haiti	Philippines
Belgium	Honduras	Poland
Belorussian SSR	Hungary	Portugal
Benin	Iceland	Qatar
Bhutan	India	Rumania
Bolivia	Indonesia	Rwanda
Botswana	Iran	São Tomé and
Brazil	Iraq	Príncipe
Bulgaria	Ireland	Saudi Arabia
Burma	Israel	Senegal
Burundi	Italy	Sierra Leone
Cambodia	Ivory Coast	Singapore
Cameroon	Jamaica	Somalia
Canada	Japan	South Africa
Cape Verde	Jordan	Spain
Central African	Kenya	Sri Lanka (Ceylon)
Republic	Kuwait	Sudan
Chad	Laos	Surinam
Chile	Lebanon	Swaziland
China, People's	Lesotho	Sweden
Republic of	Liberia	Syrian Arab Republic
Colombia	Libyan Arab	Tanzania, United
Comoros	Republic	Republic of
Congo	Luxembourg	Thailand
Costa Rica	Madagascar	Togo
Cuba	(Malagasy	Trinidad and Tobago
Cyprus	Republic)	Tunisia
Czechoslovakia	Malawi	Turkey
Denmark	Malaysia	Uganda
Dominican Republic	Maldives	Ukrainian SSR
Ecuador	Mali	USSR
Egypt	Malta	United Arab Emirates
El Salvador	Mauritania	United Kingdom
Equatorial Guinea	Mauritius	United States
Ethiopia	Mexico	Upper Volta
Fiji	Mongolia	Uruguay
Finland	Morocco	Venezuela
France	Mozambique	Yemen
Gabon	Nepal	Yemen, Democratic
Gambia	Netherlands	Yugoslavia
German Democratic	New Zealand	Zaire
Republic	Nicaragua	Zambia

COMMITTEES

General: Composed of 25 members as follows: The General Assembly president; the 17 General Assembly vice presidents (heads of delegations or their deputies of Bahrain, Bangladesh, Barbados, Bulgaria, China, Cuba, France, Mongolia, Mozambique, Norway, Peru, Senegal, Tunisia, USSR, United States, United Kingdom, Zaire); and the chairmen of the following main committees, which are composed of all 144 member countries:

First (Political and Security): Edouard Ghorra (Lebanon)

Special Political: Roberto Martinez Ordonez (Honduras)

Second (Economic and Financial): Olof Rydbeck (Sweden)

Third (Social, Humanitarian and Cultural): Ladislav Smid (Czechoslovakia)

Fourth (Trust and Non-Self-Governing Territories): Famah Joka-Bangura (Sierra Leone)

Fifth (Administrative and Budgetary): Christopher R. Thomas (Trinidad and Tobago)

Sixth (Legal): Frank X. J. C. Njenga (Kenya)

THE SECURITY COUNCIL (1976)

*(Membership ends on December 31 of the year noted; asterisks indicate permanent membership.)

Benin (1977)	Japan (1976)	Sweden (1976)
China*	Libya (1977)	Tanzania (1976)
France*	Pakistan (1977)	USSR*
Guyana (1976)	Panama (1977)	United Kingdom*
Italy (1976)	Rumania (1977)	United States*

Military Staff Committee: Representatives of chief of staffs of permanent members.

Disarmament Commission: Representatives of all UN members.

THE ECONOMIC AND SOCIAL COUNCIL (1976)

President: Iqbal Alchund (Pakistan), 58th and 59th sessions (1975). Membership ends on December 31 of the year noted.

Membership of ECONOMIC AND SOCIAL COUNCIL (1976)

Afghanistan (1978)	Ecuador (1977)	Nigeria (1978)
Algeria (1978)	Egypt (1976)	Norway (1977)
Argentina (1977)	Ethiopia (1977)	Pakistan (1977)
Australia (1976)	France (1978)	Peru (1977)
Austria (1978)	Gabon (1977)	Portugal (1978)
Bangladesh (1978)	Federal Republic	Rumania (1976)
Belgium (1976)	of Germany (1978)	Thailand (1976)
Bolivia (1978)	German Democratic	Togo (1978)
Brazil (1978)	Republic (1976)	Tunisia (1978)
Bulgaria (1977)	Greece (1978)	Uganda (1978)
Canada (1977)	Iran (1976)	USSR (1977)
China (1977)	Italy (1976)	United Kingdom
Colombia (1976)	Ivory Coast (1976)	(1977)
Congo (1976)	Jamaica (1976)	United States
Cuba (1978)	Japan (1977)	(1976)
Czechoslovakia	Jordan (1976)	Venezuela (1978)
(1977)	Kenya (1977)	Yemen (1977)
Democratic Yemen	Liberia (1976)	Yugoslavia (1978)
(1976)	Malaysia (1978)	Zaire (1977)
Denmark (1977)	Mexico (1976)	Zambia (1976)

THE TRUSTEESHIP COUNCIL (1975–76)

President: James Murray (United Kingdom), 42nd session (1975).

Australia[1]	France[2]	United Kingdom[2]
China[2]	USSR[2]	United States[1]

[1] Administers Trust Territory. [2] Permanent member of Security Council not administering Trust Territory.

THE INTERNATIONAL COURT OF JUSTICE

(Membership ends on February 5 of the year noted)
President: Manfred Lachs (Poland, 1985)
Vice President: Fouad Ammoun (Lebanon, 1976)

Isaac Forster (Senegal, 1982)	Federico de Castro (Spain, 1979)
André Gros (France, 1982)	Platon Morozov (USSR, 1979)
Taslim Olawale Elias (Nigeria, 1985)	Eduardo Jiménez da Aréchaga (Uruguay, 1979)
Herman Mosler (Federal Republic of Germany, 1985)	Sir Humphrey Waldock (United Kingdom, 1982)
Shigeru Oda (Japan, 1985)	Nagendra Singh (India, 1982)
Salah El Dine Taraza (Syrian Arab Republic, 1985)	José María Ruda (Argentina, 1982)
Hardy C. Dillard (U. S., 1979)	
Louis Ignacio-Pinto (Benin, 1979)	

SPECIALIZED AGENCIES

Food and Agriculture Organization (FAO); Intergovernmental Maritime Consultative Organization (IMCO); International Atomic Energy Agency (IAEA); International Bank for Reconstruction and Development (World Bank, IBRD); International Civil Aviation Organization (ICAO); International Development Association (IDA); International Finance Corporation (IFC); International Labor Organization (ILO); International Monetary Fund (IMF); International Telecommunication Union (ITU); United Nations Educational, Scientific and Cultural Organization (UNESCO); Universal Postal Union (UPU); United Nations International Children's Emergency Fund (UNICEF); World Health Organization (WHO); World Meteorological Organization (WMO).

---

all parties to the dispute cooperate with the secretary general's efforts to defuse the crisis. Acceding to the council's request, Morocco's King Hassan decided on November 9 to call back the march, and consultations between Waldheim and the interested parties continued, looking toward a solution under UN auspices. (See INTERNATIONAL COURT OF JUSTICE, below.)

Other Issues. Other matters that came before the council included a resolution proposing that the illegal occupation of Namibia (South West Africa) by South Africa was a threat to international peace. This resolution was defeated on June 6. On September 29, Mexico requested the suspension of Spain on the grounds of serious and repeated violations of human rights by the Franco regime. The council president, Moulaye El Hassan of Mauritania, after private discussions

with the council's membership, informed Mexico that the council was not the appropriate forum before which to bring such matters.

ECONOMIC AND SOCIAL COUNCIL

The annual organizational session of the Economic and Social Council was held on Jan. 13–28, 1975. Iqbal A. Akhund of Pakistan was elected president for the year. Agendas for the 58th session of the council in New York from April 8 to May 8, for the 59th session in Geneva from July 2 to August 1, and a work program for the entire year were approved.

The main results of the 58th session in April were an appeal to all states to assist the peoples of Indochina in reconstruction and the adoption of measures to combat the drought in the Sahelian zone in Africa. In July, the 59th session devoted most of its attention to preparations for the special session of the General Assembly, which was designed to deal with the economic differences between rich and poor nations. Apart from agreeing on an agenda, the session did little to promote agreement between the two groups.

The 27-member Population Commission held its 18th session on February 18–28 and considered the impact of the World Population Conference on UN population policies. It recommended the endorsement of UN programs as planned but felt that increased funding was required to carry them out.

The adoption of a "Declaration and Plan of Action on Industrial Development and Cooperation" resulted from the 2d General Conference of UNIDO, which met in Lima, Peru, on March 12–27. The plan urged that the share of developing countries in total world production should be increased from the existing level of 7% to at least 25% by the end of the 20th century.

The conference also recommended that UNIDO should be converted to a specialized agency and that an industrial development fund, financed by voluntary contributions, should be established.

Mexico City was the site of the World Conference of the International Women's Year on June 19–July 20. The conference adopted a "World Plan of Action," recommending, among other things, increased employment opportunities for women and the recognition of the economic value of women's work in the home, in domestic food production, and in voluntary activities. (See also WOMEN.)

TRUSTEESHIP AND DECOLONIZATION

The Trusteeship Council, meeting May 27–June 7, decided to send a visiting mission to Micronesia to observe the June 17 plebiscite in the Northern Marianas District. The purpose of the plebiscite was to determine whether the people approved a covenant establishing a commonwealth of the Northern Marianas in political union with the United States.

A draft resolution seeking majority rule in Southern Rhodesia was approved by the assembly's Committee on Non-Self-Governing Territories without objection. The committee also approved a resolution demanding South Africa's withdrawal from Namibia so that the people of the territory could achieve independence on November 13.

The Special Committee with Regard to the Implementation of the Declaration on the Granting of Independence to Colonial Countries and Peoples (the Committee of 24) met three times during the year. Its June meeting, held in Lisbon, marked the first time it had met in Europe. The committee completed its work for 1975 on August 21, after adopting a resolution reaffirming its recognition of the legitimacy of the struggles of peoples under colonial and alien domination to exercise their right to self-determination and independence.

LEGAL ACTIVITIES

The third session of the Conference on the Law of the Sea took place in Geneva from March 17 to May 9. Drafts were prepared by its three main committees to serve as a basis for future negotiations. It was proposed that Jamaica should be the location of the International Sea Bed Authority; that innocent passage in territorial seas should not be prejudicial to the peace, good order, and security of the coastal state; and that laws should be established to prevent pollution of the marine environment by the dumping of wastes. The Working Group on International Legislation on Shipping, after four years' work, produced a draft Convention on the Carriage of Goods by Sea at its 8th session, held February 10–21.

International Court of Justice. The major question before the International Court in 1975 was the determination of the legal position of the Western Sahara. The court's opinion was requested by the General Assembly in December 1974. After holding hearings on the possible appointment of a judge ad hoc, the court authorized Morocco by an order issued on May 22 to choose such a judge. Spain was then given until May 26 to submit its views on the Moroccan choice, Alphonse Boni, president of the supreme court of the Ivory Coast. The court's unanimous opinion, given on October 16, was that "the Western Sahara was not a territory belonging to no one (terra nullius)" at the time of its colonization by Spain. It felt that there were certain legal ties with Morocco and Mauritania at that time, but not ties of territorial sovereignty, and that these ties were not such as might affect the application of the principle of self-determination in the decolonization of Western Sahara. (See also LAW—*International Law.*)

RICHARD E. WEBB
Former Director, Reference and Library Division, British Information Services New York

UPI

Vice Premier Teng Hsiao-ping greets President and Mrs. Ford on their December 1 arrival in China.

UNITED STATES

The United States had an unsettling year domestically in 1975, while experiencing both success and failure in foreign relations. Domestically, the main issues were economic, but there was also concern about the 1976 elections and the probes into U. S. intelligence-gathering activities. (See special report in this article.) In foreign affairs, successes in the Middle East and in European relations were balanced by setbacks in Southeast Asia.

Domestic Affairs

The year 1975 found the United States in political and economic disarray. The nation had not yet recovered from the multiple shocks of war, scandal, and domestic violence that had marked the 1960's and early 1970's. In addition, it still had to contend with the energy shortage and the combined hardships of high prices and high unemployment. However, if there was considerable disenchantment, there was also evidence that the nation's institutions were fundamentally sturdy and still could meet the country's needs.

The Administration. President Ford's personal traits of candor and decency won him the admiration of many. He was handicapped, however, by the fact that he had been appointed to office rather than chosen in a national election and had inherited a number of vexing problems from the tenure of Richard Nixon, notably the energy crisis and the declining economy.

The President bluntly acknowledged these difficulties in his State of the Union address on Jan. 15, 1975. "I must say to you that the state of the union is not good," he declared. To boost the sagging economy he proposed a $16 billion tax cut for 1975, which Congress ultimately raised to $22.8 billion. When he reluctantly signed this compromise measure on March 29, the President warned of the need for reductions in federal spending to avoid "runaway double-digit inflation, which could well choke off any economic recovery."

The President also announced a program of energy conservation and increased production that relied heavily on raising prices of foreign and domestic oil. He proposed to cut oil consumption by 1 million barrels a day. Ford said he would use his presidential authority to raise the duty on crude oil imports in stages by $3 a barrel, but after a series of skirmishes and compromises with Congress, he settled for a $2-a-barrel increase.

The President sought to give his administration its own identity by replacing holdovers from the Nixon administration. For the cabinet he picked Edward H. Levi, president of the University of Chicago, as attorney general; William T. Coleman, the second black to be named to a cabinet post, as secretary of transportation; and John T. Dunlop, former head of the Cost of Living Council, as labor secretary. Carla Hills, a former assistant attorney general, was named secretary of Housing and Urban Development, and F. David Mathews, president of the University of Alabama, was Ford's choice for secretary of Health, Education, and Welfare.

All of these nominations were confirmed with little opposition. However, Ford's choice in April of former Wyoming Gov. Stanley K. Hathaway as interior secretary drew sharp criticism from conservationists, who charged that Hathaway was more concerned with economic development than with protection of natural resources. Hathaway was confirmed in June, but he resigned six weeks later because of "moderate depression" and physical exhaustion, which associates blamed in part on the bitter struggle to win Senate approval.

On November 3 the president announced sweeping changes in the ranks of his top advisers. James R. Schlesinger was removed as defense secretary and replaced by former White House Chief of Staff Donald Rumsfeld. William E. Colby was removed as head of the Central Intelligence Agency, and Rogers B. Morton quit as Commerce secretary. Ford designated George Bush, U. S. envoy to Communist China, to re-

place Colby, and Elliot L. Richardson, ambassador to Britain, to replace Morton. Secretary of State Henry Kissinger relinquished his position as National Security Council director to his deputy, Lt. Gen. Brent Scowcroft.

At the same time, Vice President Nelson Rockefeller announced his withdrawal from consideration as a possible running mate for Ford in 1976. Rockefeller declared that "party squabbles," which he blamed on conservative Republicans, had prompted his decision. He said he would support Ford for the Republican presidential nomination, but he would not rule out the possibility of seeking the presidency himself.

Although Ford at first maintained that the cabinet changes resulted solely from his desire to install his "own team" in the cabinet, he later conceded that "a growing tension" in his administration had led to the removal of Schlesinger, who reportedly wanted to take a harder line toward the Soviet Union than did Kissinger.

The President's supporters contended that Ford had strengthened his hold on the country by asserting decisive control over his administration. Critics argued that he had been less than candid in his early explanation of the shake-up. Ford faced the added danger that Schlesinger's removal would intensify opposition from conservatives who were suspicious of his policy of détente toward the Soviet Union.

In striving to lead the country, Ford was handicapped by the legacy of public distrust toward government leaders resulting from the scandals that had forced President Nixon and Vice President Agnew to resign in disgrace. Public suspicion and cynicism was intensified in 1975 as a result of sweeping investigations of government intelligence activities. Led by Vice President Rockefeller's commission and by committees of the House and Senate, these inquiries turned up many examples of abuse of power, notably by the Central Intelligence Agency, the Federal Bureau of Investigation, and the Internal Revenue Service. These activities, if not outright violations of the law, were certainly shocking and disturbing to many. The disclosures compounded the credibility problem for Ford and other political leaders.

The Congress. Democratic majorities in the 94th Congress assured that the inter-party warfare between Capitol Hill and the White House, which had marked the Nixon administration, would continue. The Democrats held 61 of the 100 Senate seats as the year began and increased the number to 62 after a special election in New Hampshire in September. In the House they controlled 290 of the 436 seats.

The Democratic majority in the House included 75 freshman congressmen who helped to produce some striking changes in the old order. They removed three senior committee chairmen: Wright Patman of Texas from Banking and

RICARDO THOMAS, THE WHITE HOUSE

Vice President Rockefeller journeyed to Saudi Arabia in March after death of King Faisal.

Currency; W. R. Poage of Texas from Agriculture; and F. Edward Hébert of Louisiana from Armed Services. A fourth veteran chairman, Wilbur Mills of Arkansas, resigned his post as head of the Ways and Means Committee after being touched by personal scandal. Not since 1925 had a majority party unseated more than one chairman.

The major change in the Senate concerned the rules governing cloture to stop a filibuster. Formerly a majority vote of two-thirds of those present was required for cloture, but on March 27 the Senate voted 56–27 to amend this rule to three-fifths of the Senate membership. The

President Ford inspects troops with Donald Rumsfeld (right), the newly-appointed secretary of defense.

UPI

two-thirds requirement had stood for 59 years, despite repeated attempts to change it, usually by liberal senators striving to aid passage of civil rights legislation.

When these internal problems had been resolved, the Congress began a series of struggles with the President. The Democratic-controlled legislature and the Republican chief executive held basically opposed views on two fundamental areas of public policy, energy and the economy. Ford's policy of cutting energy consumption and stimulating production by raising domestic oil prices ran counter to Democratic belief that such measures would damage the economy. The Democrats advocated cutting consumption more gradually by forcing reduced use of petroleum in new cars and restricting use of energy by industry.

Ultimately, the House and Senate passed a compromise bill, which rolled back oil prices by 12% and provided for phased decontrol of domestic oil prices over a 40-month period, instead of the immediate decontrol Ford had wanted. Despite his disagreement with some points, President Ford signed the bill on December 22.

In dealing with the economy, the President was concerned with keeping the already substantial budget deficit from growing even larger and with the threat of new rises in inflation. He advocated a $28 billion tax cut for 1976, asking that it be coupled with a $28 billion cut in government spending to begin in the next fiscal year. Democrats contended that such a cut in spending would hurt groups dependent on help from government programs. They preferred a plan to continue both the tax cuts passed earlier in the year and the government programs designed to boost the economy and reduce unemployment. Eventually Congress passed and President Ford signed a compromise six-month extension of the tax cuts.

The sharp political and philosophical differences between the President and the Congress produced a series of presidential vetoes, most of which the Congress was unable to override. By September 10 the President had vetoed 10 pieces of legislation and had been overridden only twice. Bills on which his vetoes were sustained included measures to suspend his power to boost oil import tariffs; to provide emergency farm support prices; to control strip mining; to spend $5.3 billion to create more than 1 million jobs; to spend $1.2 billion in emergency aid to homeowners; and to continue domestic oil price controls for six months. Congress managed to override vetoes of a $7.9 billion education appropriations bill and a $2 billion appropriations bill for public health and family planning.

On September 13, in a speech to a partisan Republican audience in Dallas, the President won a standing ovation when he pledged to use his veto power "again and again and again" to end what he called "25 years of reckless

UPI

The desire for work was dramatized in January 1975 by over 2,000 Chicago public-service job applicants.

Democratic spending." For their part, the Democrats contended hopefully that the presidential vetoes would provide them with a valuable issue in the 1976 campaign for the White House, particularly if the unemployment rate in the nation was still high.

Outside the controversial economic and energy areas, the 94th Congress enacted a number of major proposals with the President's signature. It extended the 1965 Voting Rights Act for seven years, with expansion of coverage to Spanish-speaking and other groups defined as language minorities. And it authorized $405 million for the relocation and resettlement of Vietnamese and Cambodian refugees who had fled to the United States after the collapse of military resistance to Communist forces in Indochina.

The Economy. The nation started off 1975 in the midst of a recession, and conditions worsened steadily in the early months of the year. In January unemployment stood at 8.2%, a 33-

year high. By March it had reached 8.7%, the worst since 1941. In May it climbed to 9.2%. The number of persons out of work for more than 15 weeks was estimated at 2.6 million. For the first time in 17 years the number of persons looking for jobs for a period of at least six months exceeded 1 million.

In June, however, unemployment dropped sharply to 8.6%. This decline turned out to be a harbinger of a third quarter that furnished economists with many signs of a general recovery. By September unemployment had dropped to 8.3%. Production of goods and services during July, August, and September increased at an annual rate of 13.2%, a figure that compared favorably with the average long-term economic growth rate of 3.5%.

Although a general upswing seemed well underway by year's end, the recovery was still spotty and offered some cause for concern. In October unemployment climbed again to 8.6%, but in November it declined to 8.3%. The consumer price index in October rose at an annual rate of 8.7%, up from 6.2% in September. Some observers found this figure uncomfortably close to the double-digit rate of inflation that had prevailed through 1974. (See also ECONOMY OF THE U. S.)

New York City. Economic problems struck hard at state and local governments, which were caught in a squeeze between rising costs and expanded welfare rolls, on the one hand, and declining revenues on the other. Probably hardest hit was New York, the nation's largest city. The same problems that beset other municipalities were compounded in New York City by a long period of financial mismanagement and by the strain of the expensive social problems instituted by the city's traditionally liberal administrations.

The seriousness of New York's problems was signaled on April 2, when the Standard & Poor credit rating service suspended its "good investment" rating for New York City bonds. The credit firm cited the possible "inability or unwillingness of the major underwriting banks to continue to purchase the city's notes and bonds."

—— **UNITED STATES · Information Highlights** ——

Official Name: United States of America.
Area: 3,615,123 square miles (9,363,169 sq km).
Population (Jan. 1, 1976 est.): 215,007,063.
Chief Cities (1970 census): Washington, D. C., the capital, 756,510; New York, 7,895,563; Chicago, 3,369,359; Los Angeles, 2,816,061; Philadelphia, 1,950,098.
Government: *Head of state and government,* Gerald R. Ford, president (took office Aug. 1974). *Legislature* —Congress: Senate and House of Representatives.
Monetary Unit: Dollar.
Gross National Product (3d quarter 1975 est.): $1,497,-800,000,000.
Manufacturing (major products): Motor vehicles, aircraft, ships and railroad equipment, industrial machinery, processed foods, chemicals, electrical equipment and supplies, fabricated metals.
Major Agricultural Products: Wheat, rye, corn, barley, oats, soybeans, tobacco, cotton, sorghum.
Foreign Trade (1974): *Exports,* $97,144,000,000; *imports,* $107,112,000,000.

UNITED STATES CABINET MEMBERS
(as of Dec. 31, 1975)

Secretary of State—Henry A. Kissinger
Secretary of the Treasury—William E. Simon
Secretary of Defense—Donald H. Rumsfeld
Attorney General—Edward H. Levi
Secretary of the Interior—Thomas S. Kleppe
Secretary of Agriculture—Earl L. Butz
Secretary of Commerce—Elliot L. Richardson
Secretary of Labor—John T. Dunlop
Secretary of Health, Education, and Welfare— F. David Mathews
Secretary of Housing and Urban Development —Carla A. Hills
Secretary of Transportation—William T. Coleman, Jr.

The state government loaned the city $400 million from state revenue-sharing funds so that the city could pay welfare benefits.

It soon became clear, however, that such stop-gap measures would not suffice. On September 9 the state legislature passed a $2.3 billion aid bill, which set strict financial controls on the city, and entrusted stewardship of city revenues to a state-appointed board of fiscal managers. Called the Municipal Assistance Corp., this board was dubbed "Big Mac" by New York Gov. Hugh Carey.

The city's financial situation was so dismal and complex that the new agency encountered difficulty selling its own bonds. Governor Carey and New York Mayor Abraham Beame sought help from the federal government in the form of guarantees for the bonds. On October 17 the city escaped default by less than an hour when the city teacher's union finally agreed to use $150 million in pension funds to purchase bonds.

Mayor Beame, testifying the next day before a Senate subcommittee, said that unless the city was given some federal aid, it would be forced into bankruptcy no later than December 1. Beame was supported by a number of the nation's leading bankers, who were concerned about the city's plight because of their municipal bond holdings and who warned that default could have dire consequences for the overall economy.

At first President Ford rejected the idea of any federal assistance to New York. In a speech October 29 he said the solution offered by legislative proposals requiring federal guarantees of New York bonds was nothing but "a mirage." He asserted that for the federal government to "bail out" the city would set a dangerous precedent.

State and city officials then launched a series of emergency measures to put the city's financial house in order and, hopefully, to persuade the President to shift his position. These were climaxed by the passage November 25 by a

94th CONGRESS OF THE U.S.

SENATE MEMBERSHIP

(As of January 1976: 62 Democrats, 38 Republicans)

Letters after senators' names refer to party affiliation—D for Democrat, R for Republican. Single asterisk (*) denotes term expiring in January 1977; double asterisk (**), term expiring in January 1979; triple asterisk (***), term expiring in January 1981.

ALABAMA
**J. Sparkman, D
***J. B. Allen, D

ALASKA
**T. Stevens, R
***M. Gravel, D

ARIZONA
*P. J. Fannin, R
***B. Goldwater, R

ARKANSAS
**J. L. McClellan, D
***Dale Bumpers, D

CALIFORNIA
***A. Cranston, D
*J. V. Tunney, D

COLORADO
**F. K. Haskell, D
***Gary Hart, D

CONNECTICUT
***A. A. Ribicoff, D
*L. P. Weicker, Jr., R

DELAWARE
*W. V. Roth, Jr., R
**J. R. Biden, Jr., D

FLORIDA
*L. Chiles, D
***Richard Stone, D

GEORGIA
***H. E. Talmadge, D
**S. A. Nunn, D

HAWAII
*H. L. Fong, R
***D. K. Inouye, D

IDAHO
***F. Church, D
**J. A. McClure, R

ILLINOIS
**C. H. Percy, R
***A. E. Stevenson III, D

INDIANA
*V. Hartke, D
***B. Bayh, D

IOWA
**R. Clark, D
***J. C. Culver, D

KANSAS
**J. B. Pearson, R
***R. Dole, R

KENTUCKY
**W. Huddleston, D
***W. H. Ford, D

LOUISIANA
***R. B. Long, D
**J. B. Johnston, Jr., D

MAINE
*E. S. Muskie, D
**W. D. Hathaway, D

MARYLAND
***C. McC. Mathias, Jr., R
*J. G. Beall, Jr., R

MASSACHUSETTS
*E. M. Kennedy, D
**E. W. Brooke, R

MICHIGAN
*P. A. Hart, D
**R. P. Griffin, R

MINNESOTA
**W. F. Mondale, D
*H. H. Humphrey, D

MISSISSIPPI
*J. O. Eastland, D
*J. C. Stennis, D

MISSOURI
*S. Symington, D
***T. F. Eagleton, D

MONTANA
*M. Mansfield, D
**L. Metcalf, D

NEBRASKA
*R. L. Hruska, R
**C. T. Curtis, R

NEVADA
*H. W. Cannon, D
***Paul Laxalt, R

NEW HAMPSHIRE
**T. J. McIntyre, D
***J. Durkin, D

NEW JERSEY
**C. P. Case, Jr., R
*H. A. Williams, Jr., D

NEW MEXICO
*J. M. Montoya, D
**P. V. Domenici, R

NEW YORK
***J. K. Javits, R
*J. L. Buckley, R[1]

NORTH CAROLINA
**J. Helms, R
***Robert Morgan, D

NORTH DAKOTA
***M. R. Young, R
*Q. N. Burdick, D

OHIO
*R. Taft, Jr., R
***J. H. Glenn, Jr., D

OKLAHOMA
***H. Bellmon, R
**D. F. Bartlett, R

OREGON
**M. O. Hatfield, R
***B. Packwood, R

PENNSYLVANIA
*H. Scott, R
***R. S. Schweiker, R

RHODE ISLAND
*J. O. Pastore, D
**C. Pell, D

SOUTH CAROLINA
**S. Thurmond, R
***E. F. Hollings, D

SOUTH DAKOTA
***G. S. McGovern, D
**J. G. Abourezk, D

TENNESSEE
**H. H. Baker, Jr., R
*W. E. Brock 3d, R

TEXAS
**J. G. Tower, R
*L. M. Bentsen, D

UTAH
*F. E. Moss, D
***Jake Garn, R

VERMONT
*R. T. Stafford, R
***P. J. Leahy, D

VIRGINIA
*H. F. Byrd, Jr., D[2]
**W. L. Scott, R

WASHINGTON
***W. G. Magnuson, D
*H. M. Jackson, D

WEST VIRGINIA
*J. Randolph, D
*R. C. Byrd, D

WISCONSIN
*W. Proxmire, D
***G. Nelson, D

WYOMING
*G. W. McGee, D
**C. P. Hansen, R

[1] Ran as a Conservative. [2] Ran as an Independent.

HOUSE MEMBERSHIP

(As of January 1976: 290 Democrats, 145 Republicans)

"At-L." in place of congressional district number means "representative at large." Asterisk (*) before name indicates elected Nov. 5, 1974; all others were reelected.

ALABAMA
1. J. Edwards, R
2. W. L. Dickinson, R
3. W. Nichols, D
4. T. Bevill, D
5. R. E. Jones, D
6. J. H. Buchanan, Jr., R
7. W. Flowers, D

ALASKA
At-L. D. Young, R

ARIZONA
1. J. J. Rhodes, R
2. M. K. Udall, D
3. S. Steiger, R
4. J. B. Conlan, R

ARKANSAS
1. W. V. Alexander, Jr., D
2. W. D. Mills, D
3. J. P. Hammerschmidt, R
4. R. H. Thornton, Jr., D

CALIFORNIA
1. H. T. Johnson, D
2. D. H. Clausen, R
3. J. E. Moss, D
4. R. L. Leggett, D
5. J. Burton, D
6. P. Burton, D
7. *George Miller, D
8. R. V. Dellums, D
9. F. H. Stark, D
10. D. Edwards, D
11. L. J. Ryan, D
12. P. N. McCloskey, Jr., R
13. *N. Y. Mineta, D
14. J. J. McFall, D
15. B. F. Sisk, D
16. B. L. Talcott, R
17. J. Krebs, D
18. W. M. Ketchum, R
19. R. J. Lagomarsino, R
20. B. M. Goldwater, Jr., R
21. J. C. Corman, D
22. C. J. Moorhead, R
23. T. M. Rees, D
24. *H. A. Waxman, D
25. E. R. Roybal, D
26. J. H. Rousselot, R
27. A. Bell, R
28. Y. B. Burke, D
29. A. F. Hawkins, D
30. G. E. Danielson, D
31. C. H. Wilson, D
32. G. M. Anderson, D
33. Del Clawson, R
34. *M. W. Hannaford, D
35. *J. Lloyd, D
36. G. E. Brown, Jr., D
37. J. L. Pettis, R
38. *J. M. Patterson, D
39. C. E. Wiggins, R
40. A. J. Hinshaw, R
41. B. Wilson, R
42. L. Van Deerlin, D
43. C. W. Burgener, R

COLORADO
1. P. Schroeder, D
2. *T. E. Wirth, D
3. F. E. Evans, D
4. J. P. Johnson, R
5. W. L. Armstrong, R

CONNECTICUT
1. W. R. Cotter, D
2. *C. J. Dodd, D
3. R. N. Giaimo, D
4. S. B. McKinney, R
5. R. A. Sarasin, R
6. *A. T. Moffett, D

DELAWARE
At-L. P. S. duPont 4th, R

FLORIDA
1. R. L. F. Sikes, D
2. Don Fuqua, D
3. C. E. Bennett, D
4. W. V. Chappell, Jr., D
5. *R. Kelly, R
6. C. W. Young, R
7. S. M. Gibbons, D
8. J. A. Haley, D
9. L. Frey, Jr., R
10. L. A. Bafalis, R
11. P. G. Rogers, D
12. J. H. Burke, R
13. W. Lehman, D
14. Claude Pepper, D
15. Dante B. Fascell, D

GEORGIA
1. R. B. Ginn, D
2. M. D. Mathis, D
3. J. Brinkley, D
4. *E. H. Levitas, D
5. A. Young, D
6. J. J. Flynt, Jr., D
7. *L. McDonald, D
8. W. S. Stuckey, Jr., D
9. P. M. Landrum, D
10. R. G. Stephens, Jr., D

HAWAII
1. S. M. Matsunaga, D
2. P. T. Mink, D

IDAHO
1. S. D. Symms, R
2. *G. Hansen, R

ILLINOIS
1. R. H. Metcalfe, D
2. M. F. Murphy, D
3. *M. A. Russo, D
4. E. J. Derwinski, R
5. J. C. Kluczynski, D
6. *H. J. Hyde, D
7. C. Collins, D
8. D. Rostenkowski, D
9. S. R. Yates, D
10. *A. J. Mikva, D
11. F. Annunzio, D
12. P. M. Crane, R
13. R. McClory, R
14. J. N. Erlenborn, R
15. *T. L. Hall, D
16. J. B. Anderson, R
17. G. M. O'Brien, R
18. R. H. Michel, R
19. T. Railsback, R
20. P. Findley, R
21. E. R. Madigan, R
22. G. E. Shipley, D
23. C. M. Price, D
24. *P. Simon, D

INDIANA
1. R. J. Madden, D
2. *F. J. Fithian, D
3. J. Brademas, D
4. J. E. Roush, D
5. E. H. Hillis, R
6. *D. W. Evans, D
7. J. T. Myers, R
8. *P. H. Hayes, D
9. L. H. Hamilton, D
10. *P. R. Sharp, D
11. *A. Jacobs, Jr., D

IOWA
1. E. Mezvinsky, D
2. *M. T. Blouin, D
3. *C. E. Grassley, R
4. N. Smith, D
5. *T. Harkin, D
6. *B. Bedell, D

KANSAS
1. K. G. Sebelius, R
2. *M. Keys, D
3. L. Winn, Jr., R
4. G. E. Shriver, R
5. J. Skubitz, R

KENTUCKY
1. *C. Hubbard, Jr., D
2. W. H. Natcher, D
3. R. L. Mazzoli, D
4. M. G. Snyder, R
5. T. L. Carter, R
6. J. B. Breckinridge, D
7. C. D. Perkins, D

LOUISIANA
1. F. E. Hébert, D
2. C. C. Boggs, D
3. D. C. Treen, R
4. J. D. Waggonner, Jr., D
5. O. E. Passman, D
6. Henson Moore, R[1]
7. J. B. Breaux, D
8. G. W. Long, D

MAINE
1. *D. F. Emery, R
2. W. S. Cohen, R

MARYLAND
1. R. E. Bauman, R
2. C. D. Long, D
3. P. S. Sarbanes, D
4. M. S. Holt, R
5. G. N. Spellman, D
6. G. E. Byron, D
7. P. J. Mitchell, D
8. G. Gude, R

MASSACHUSETTS
1. S. O. Conte, R
2. E. P. Boland, D
3. *J. D. Early, D
4. R. F. Drinan, D
5. *P. E. Tsongas, D
6. M. J. Harrington, D
7. T. H. Macdonald, D
8. T. P. O'Neill, Jr., D
9. J. J. Moakley, D
10. M. M. Heckler, R
11. J. A. Burke, D
12. G. E. Studds, D

MICHIGAN
1. J. Conyers, Jr., D
2. M. L. Esch, R
3. G. Brown, R
4. E. Hutchinson, R
5. R. F. Vander Veen, D
6. *B. Carr, D
7. D. W. Riegle, Jr., D
8. B. Traxler, D
9. G. A. Vander Jagt, R
10. E. A. Cederberg, R
11. P. E. Ruppe, R
12. J. G. O'Hara, D
13. C. C. Diggs, Jr., D
14. L. N. Nedzi, D
15. W. D. Ford, D
16. J. D. Dingell, D
17. *W. M. Brodhead, D
18. *J. J. Blanchard, D
19. W. S. Broomfield, R

MINNESOTA
1. A. H. Quie, R
2. *T. Hagedorn, R
3. B. Frenzel, R
4. J. E. Karth, D
5. D. M. Fraser, D
6. *R. Nolan, D
7. B. S. Bergland, D
8. *J. L. Oberstar, D

MISSISSIPPI
1. J. L. Whitten, D
2. D. R. Bowen, D
3. G. V. Montgomery, D
4. W. T. Cochran, R
5. T. Lott, R

MISSOURI
1. W. L. Clay, D
2. J. W. Symington, D
3. L. K. Sullivan, D
4. W. J. Randall, D
5. R. Bolling, D
6. J. L. Litton, D
7. G. Taylor, R
8. R. H. Ichord, D
9. W. L. Hungate, D
10. B. D. Burlison, D

MONTANA
1. *M. S. Baucus, D
2. J. Melcher, D

NEBRASKA
1. C. Thone, R
2. J. Y. McCollister, R
3. *V. Smith, R

NEVADA
At-L. *J. Santini, D

NEW HAMPSHIRE
1. *N. E. D'Amours, D
2. J. C. Cleveland, R

NEW JERSEY
1. *J. J. Florio, D
2. *W. J. Hughes, D
3. J. J. Howard, D
4. F. Thompson, Jr., D
5. *M. Fenwick, R
6. E. B. Forsythe, R
7. *A. Maguire, D
8. R. A. Roe, D
9. H. Helstoski, D
10. P. W. Rodino, D
11. J. G. Minish, D
12. M. J. Rinaldo, R
13. *H. S. Meyner, D
14. D. V. Daniels, D
15. E. J. Patten, D

NEW MEXICO
1. M. Lujan, Jr., R
2. H. Runnels, D

NEW YORK
1. O. G. Pike, D
2. *T. J. Downey, D
3. *J. Ambro, Jr., D
4. N. F. Lent, R
5. J. W. Wydler, R
6. L. L. Wolff, D
7. J. P. Addabbo, D
8. B. S. Rosenthal, D
9. J. J. Delaney, D
10. M. Biaggi, D
11. *J. H. Scheuer, D
12. S. A. Chisholm, D
13. *S. J. Solarz, D
14. *F. W. Richmond, D
15. *L. C. Zeferetti, D
16. E. Holtzman, D
17. J. M. Murphy, D
18. E. I. Koch, D
19. C. B. Rangel, D
20. B. S. Abzug, D
21. H. Badillo, D
22. J. B. Bingham, D
23. P. A. Peyser, R
24. *R. L. Ottinger, D
25. H. Fish, Jr., R
26. B. A. Gilman, R
27. *M. F. McHugh, D
28. S. S. Stratton, D
29. E. W. Pattison, D
30. R. C. McEwen, R
31. D. J. Mitchell, R
32. J. M. Hanley, D
33. W. F. Walsh, R
34. F. Horton, R
35. B. B. Conable, Jr., R
36. *J. J. LaFalce, D
37. *H. J. Nowak, D
38. J. F. Kemp, R
39. J. F. Hastings, R

NORTH CAROLINA
1. W. B. Jones, D
2. L. H. Fountain, D
3. D. N. Henderson, D
4. I. F. Andrews, D
5. *S. L. Neal, D
6. L. R. Preyer, D
7. C. G. Rose, D
8. *W. G. Hefner, D
9. J. G. Martin, R
10. J. T. Broyhill, R
11. R. A. Taylor, D

NORTH DAKOTA
At-L. M. Andrews, R

OHIO
1. *W. D. Gradison, Jr., R
2. D. D. Clancy, R
3. C. W. Whalen, Jr., R
4. T. Guyer, R
5. D. L. Latta, R
6. W. H. Harsha, R
7. C. J. Brown, R
8. *T. N. Kindness, R
9. T. L. Ashley, D
10. C. E. Miller, R
11. J. W. Stanton, R
12. S. L. Devine, R
13. C. A. Mosher, R
14. J. F. Seiberling, D
15. C. P. Wylie, R
16. R. S. Regula, R
17. J. M. Ashbrook, R
18. W. L. Hays, D
19. C. J. Carney, D
20. J. V. Stanton, D
21. L. Stokes, D
22. C. A. Vanik, D
23. *R. M. Mottl, D

OKLAHOMA
1. J. R. Jones, D
2. *T. M. Risenhoover, D
3. C. B. Albert, D
4. T. Steed, D
5. J. Jarman, R
6. *G. English, D

OREGON
1. *Les AuCoin, D
2. A. Ullman, D
3. *R. Duncan, D
4. *J. Weaver, D

PENNSYLVANIA
1. W. A. Barrett, D
2. R. N. C. Nix, D
3. W. J. Green, D
4. J. Eilberg, D
5. *R. T. Schulze, R
6. G. Yatron, D
7. *R. W. Edgar, D
8. E. G. Biester, Jr., R
9. E. G. Shuster, R
10. J. M. McDade, R
11. D. J. Flood, D
12. J. P. Murtha, D
13. L. Coughlin, R
14. W. S. Moorhead, D
15. F. B. Rooney, D
16. E. D. Eshleman, R
17. H. T. Schneebeli, R
18. H. J. Heinz III, R
19. *W. F. Goodling, R
20. J. M. Gaydos, D
21. J. H. Dent, D
22. T. E. Morgan, D
23. A. W. Johnson, R
24. J. P. Vigorito, D
25. *G. A. Myers, R

RHODE ISLAND
1. F. J. St Germain, D
2. *E. P. Beard, D

SOUTH CAROLINA
1. M. J. Davis, D
2. F. D. Spence, R
3. *B. Derrick, Jr., D
4. J. R. Mann, D
5. *K. L. Holland, D
6. *J. W. Jenrette, Jr., D

SOUTH DAKOTA
1. *L. Pressler, R
2. J. Abdnor, R

TENNESSEE
1. J. H. Quillen, R
2. J. J. Duncan, R
3. *M. Lloyd, D
4. J. L. Evins, D
5. C. R. Allen, D[1]
6. R. L. Beard, Jr., R
7. E. Jones, D
8. *H. E. Ford, D

TEXAS
1. W. Patman, D
2. C. Wilson, D
3. J. M. Collins, R
4. R. Roberts, D
5. A. W. Steelman, R
6. O. E. Teague, D
7. B. Archer, R
8. B. Eckhardt, D
9. J. Brooks, D
10. J. J. Pickle, D
11. W. R. Poage, D
12. J. C. Wright, Jr., D
13. *J. Hightower, D
14. J. Young, D
15. E. de la Garza, D
16. R. C. White, D
17. O. Burleson, D
18. B. C. Jordan, D
19. G. H. Mahon, D
20. H. B. Gonzalez, D
21. *R. Krueger, D
22. R. R. Casey, D
23. A. Kazen, Jr., D
24. D. Milford, D

UTAH
1. G. McKay, D
2. *A. T. Howe, D

VERMONT
At-L. *J. M. Jeffords, R

VIRGINIA
1. T. N. Downing, D
2. G. W. Whitehurst, R
3. D. E. Satterfield III, D
4. R. W. Daniel, Jr., R
5. W. C. Daniel, D
6. M. C. Butler, R
7. J. K. Robinson, R
8. *H. E. Harris II, D
9. W. C. Wampler, R
10. *J. L. Fisher, D

WASHINGTON
1. J. M. Pritchard, R
2. L. Meeds, D
3. *D. Bunker, D
4. M. McCormack, D
5. T. S. Foley, D
6. F. V. Hicks, D
7. B. Adams, D

WEST VIRGINIA
1. R. H. Mollohan, D
2. H. O. Staggers, D
3. J. Slack, D
4. K. Hechler, D

WISCONSIN
1. L. Aspin, D
2. R. W. Kastenmeier, D
3. *A. Baldus, D
4. C. J. Zablocki, D
5. H. S. Reuss, D
6. W. A. Steiger, R
7. D. R. Obey, D
8. *R. J. Cornell, D
9. *R. W. Kasten, Jr., R

WYOMING
At-L. T. Roncalio, D

PUERTO RICO
Resident Commissioner
J. Benitez

DISTRICT OF COLUMBIA
Delegate
W. E. Fauntroy, D

[1] Elected 1975 to fill vacancy

After two assassination attempts in September, security tightened up around the President.

UPI

special session of the state legislature of a $20-million New York City tax package, including a 25% income tax increase for city residents. This action, following earlier tax increases and drastic spending cutbacks by the city, prompted the President to relent.

On November 26, dropping his opposition to federal aid, the President proposed $2.3 billion in short-term federal loans. These, city officials said, would enable the city to avoid default. "New York City, by what they have done in conjunction with New York State, in conjunction with the noteholders, pension fund people, they have bailed themselves out," the President said. Although Ford's proposal would not end the crisis in New York, it was expected to ease, at least temporarily, the pressure on the city.

Politics. The traditional pre-campaign maneuvering among presidential hopefuls began earlier than usual. New reforms in campaign financing induced candidates to begin fundraising efforts sooner than in the past because they could no longer rely on a few large contributors. (See also ELECTIONS AND POLITICAL PARTIES.)

Ten Democrats officially declared their candidacies for their party's nomination. They were Indiana Sen. Birch Bayh, Texas Sen. Lloyd Bentsen, former Georgia Gov. Jimmy Carter, former Oklahoma Sen. Fred Harris, Washington Sen. Henry Jackson, former North Carolina Gov. Terry Sanford, Pennsylvania Gov. Milton Shapp, former Peace Corps director R. Sargent Shriver, Arizona Rep. Morris Udall, and Alabama Gov. George Wallace. In addition, Minnesota Sen. Hubert Humphrey said he would be available for a draft. In January 1976, West Virginia's Sen. Robert Byrd became the 11th Democratic candidate.

On the Republican side, former California Gov. Ronald Reagan said he would challenge president Ford for the GOP presidential nomination. Conservatives applauded Reagan's decision to campaign.

Presidential Security. The political scene was marred by unfortunate reminders of past tragedies. On two trips to California, on September 5 and September 22, President Ford escaped injury from apparent assassination attempts. The suspected would-be assassins were both women. One attempt was foiled by the Secret Service and the other by an alert bystander.

The Secret Service tightened security around the President, and agents were posted to guard most of the other candidates. The limitations of any security system were demonstrated on November 20 when a young man brandished a toy pistol at Ronald Reagan at point blank range. It seemed certain that the fear of possible violence would hang over the forthcoming campaign for the White House.

ROBERT SHOGAN
Washington Bureau, "Los Angeles Times"

Foreign Affairs

The year 1975 produced few important foreign relations consummations or significant new starts. It was primarily a year of transition and of continuation of policies and negotiations. U. S. relations underwent major review as a consequence of the Communist takeovers in Indochina and were affected by significant shifts of political leadership in South Vietnam and other countries.

For discussion of U. S. policy in Southeast Asia, see special feature on pages 22–31.

With the emergence of 8 new countries, the community of nations increased to 156 members. The United States maintained regular diplomatic relations with 135 of them and promoted its interests through more than 250 consular establishments. More than 20 foreign heads of state and government came to the United States on official visits, and President Ford ventured abroad on 4 summit trips. These included a Brussels North Atlantic Treaty Organization (NATO) council meeting in May and the Conference on Security and Cooperation in Europe at Helsinki at the end of July. In addition, he attended the six-nation Paris summit conclave on economic cooperation in November and held bilateral talks in Peking in December. Secretary of State Henry Kissinger continued his peripatetic diplomacy, undertaking more than a dozen trips abroad. The United States also sent representatives to approximately 775 international conferences and sessions of international organizations and signed nearly 275 treaties and agreements.

Early in November, President Ford announced the reorganization of his top-level foreign relations team. Although Kissinger continued as secretary of state, new appointees filled the positions of secretary of defense, national security advisor, and director of the Central Intelligence Agency.

Middle East. The United States maintained a low profile in the civil strife between Christians and Muslims in Lebanon but continued its mediatory diplomacy in the Arab-Israeli conflict. Despite two trips to the Mideast in February and March, Secretary Kissinger returned empty-handed and intimated that U. S. policy warranted reappraisal. The only alternatives in the Middle East appeared to be reconvening the multinational Geneva conference, which promised little likelihood of success, or war.

However, Secretary Kissinger set out in August on another Middle East mission, making 13 flights between Cairo and Jerusalem in two weeks. He succeeded in forging a new Sinai agreement. Israel and Egypt agreed not to use force or the threat of it to resolve their problems; Israel agreed to withdraw its troops from the Giddi and Mitla passes and to return the Abu Rudeis oil field; and Egypt authorized Israeli non-military cargoes to pass through the

UPI

In late April an Air America helicopter picks up U. S. and Vietnamese refugees escaping from Saigon.

Suez Canal. The United States agreed to provide multibillion dollar aid programs and about 200 U. S. civilian technicians to monitor the new truce electronically. Issues that remained unsettled included the Israeli-Syrian Golan Heights problem, Arab recognition of Israel, the status of Jerusalem, and the future of Palestinian refugees.

Cyprus and Turkey. The role played by the United States in the Cyprus crisis of 1974 did not satisfy Greece, Turkey, or the Congress. The last condemned the Turkish invasion and

Turks demonstrate before U. S. consulate in Istanbul over murder of two Turkish diplomats in the fall.

UPI

President Ford and Secretary of State Kissinger chat at the July 30 opening ceremony of the Conference on Security and Cooperation in Europe at Helsinki.

occupation of the northern part of the island with the use of U. S.-supplied arms in violation of U. S. law. In February, over White House objections, Congress voted to impose an arms embargo on Turkey until substantial progress was achieved in reaching a settlement, which Secretary Kissinger was unable to guarantee.

The President and the secretary of state then turned to urging Congress to rescind its action. In July, when the House of Representatives voted to reject such a reversal, Turkey retaliated by ordering a halt to U. S. military operations within its territory. Turkish officers took over two dozen U. S. installations, and Ankara threatened to close them down completely and permanently.

Fulfillment of this threat by Turkey would have blinded one of the most sophisticated and strategically located U. S. surveillance systems. Before events moved beyond retrieval, however, Congress was persuaded in October to lift its embargo partially to enable Turkey to fulfill its NATO obligations.

Detente. The principal issues involved in U. S.-Soviet relations in 1975 included the geopolitical balance in Europe, the Middle East, the Indian Ocean basin, and other areas; nuclear arms management; and trade expansion. No critical threats to European equilibrium occurred, and negotiations for mutual and balanced

force reduction (MBFR) produced little measurable progress. Although SALT talks on a new 10-year pact continued, a stalemate was reached in which Washington and Moscow waited for the other to compromise on critical issues. The summit meeting of President Ford and Chairman Leonid Brezhnev, planned for Washington to formalize the next step in Soviet-U. S. nuclear agreement, was postponed until 1976.

After more than two years of negotiation, a 35-nation summit Conference on Security and Cooperation in Europe (CSCE) convened at Helsinki. President Ford met the Soviet premier and other European leaders and signed a "declaration of policy intent." Not a formal treaty, it "committed" the signatories to accept the territorial status quo in Europe, respect sovereignty and the sanctity of borders, and ease the flow of people, ideas, information, publications, and commerce across national frontiers and the Iron Curtain. (See also EUROPE.)

Developing U. S. trade relations were linked by Congress to Soviet emigration policy. A trade agreement was signed that provided for the reduction of tariff rates based on the most-favored-nation principle, a $300 million Export-Import Bank trade credit for the Soviet Union, and repayment of more than $700 million of World War II Lend-Lease debts to the United

States. In January 1975 the USSR repudiated this agreement on the grounds that under the Trade Reform Act Congress not only fixed U. S. commercial policy for the Soviet government but also intervened in Soviet internal affairs by requiring set quotas for Soviet emigration, principally to Israel. Consequently, trade relations reverted to an item-by-item basis, although later in the year the USSR agreed in general to long-term grain arrangements to avoid emergency purchases that might disrupt the U. S. grain market.

Inter-American Affairs. For some years, Latin America has forged an ideology of independence from Washington, and the spirit of inter-Americanism has waned. The United States has shifted, therefore, from large meetings of multilateral forums to more direct country-to-country negotiation, and the dialogues engaged in by Secretary of State Kissinger with Latin American foreign ministers in 1973 and 1974 were discontinued.

The two thorniest specific issues to surface in 1975 concerned Cuba and Panama. In July another attempt, the third, was made to lift the 11-year inter-American diplomatic and trade embargo of Cuba. At a meeting at San José, Costa Rica, the United States switched from abstention to voting in favor of termination, and the necessary two-thirds vote was achieved. This vote left the revival of diplomatic and trade matters to individual governments. When Cuba evidenced willingness to move toward the revival of relations, the United States announced in August the partial lifting of its trade embargo. The following month it also intimated a readiness to begin normalizing contacts through discussions with Cuban representatives. Late in the year, however, Cuban intervention in Angola, particularly the sending of troops, created a new strain on U. S.-Cuban relations.

The canal treaty impasse with Panama constituted the most explosive immediate inter-American problem. Although negotiations to replace the 1903 treaty had been under way for years, change was opposed by Congress and other interests. Panama and the department of state agreed in principle to replace the existing unlimited treaty with one of fixed duration that would recognize Panama's sovereignty and lead to its phased assumption of responsibility for the Canal Zone. U. S. shipping rights and the security of the waterway would be guaranteed. However, in mid-1975 the House of Representatives voted to withhold appropriations for further negotiations. While similar action was narrowly defeated in the Senate, one-third of its members endorsed a resolution opposing changes in the existing treaty, and the issue remained unsettled.

Third World and the United Nations. The developing countries of the Third World mounted a challenge to the industrial nations, demanding a "new international economic order" to procure fundamental redistribution of wealth. Over the

UPI

On June 5, President Ford greets Indonesian President Suharto at Camp David, Md.

objections of the industrialized nations, in January 1975 they voted a "Charter of Economic Rights and Duties of States" in the UN General Assembly, and they brought their case before its seventh special session in September.

Seeking to avert ideological deadlock, the United States presented a comprehensive program, to be funded cooperatively by the oil-rich nations as well as the industrial states. The main thrust of the program was to buttress the economic security of the developing countries by insulating their export earnings from the shock of natural and man-made disasters. The proposal also called for creation of an international trust fund to spur capital investment, provide food and financial assistance to the poorest nations, and improve markets and commodity export outlets. The United States sought thereby to persuade delegates to face real issues, distinguish the truly poor nations from prosperous Third World oil producers, and defer detailed negotiation to more manageable forums.

A second problem in the ideological confrontation of Third World and other states developed from the Arab-led campaign to isolate Israel diplomatically. In 1974 the United Nations restricted Israel's debating rights and decided to permit the Palestine Liberation Organization (PLO) to participate in negotiations on the Palestine issue. In June 1975, the United States warned that it would oppose attempts to

President Ford and Secretary of State Kissinger lunch with Egyptian Foreign Minister Fahmy (*left*) and President Sadat (*second from right*) in Jacksonville, Fla., during Sadat's U.S. visit at the end of October.

UPI

unseat Israel in the United Nations. Nevertheless, in November a coalition of Arab, Communist, and Third World states voted in the General Assembly to declare Zionism a form of racism and invite the PLO to participate in the Geneva peace talks on the Middle East. The coalition also voted to establish a UN committee to promote the creation of a Palestinian homeland. These actions were denounced by U. S. leaders and evoked debate on future U. S. cooperation with the United Nations and Third World countries.

Global Policy Issues. The third UN conference on the law of the sea, launched in 1973, was continued at a second substantive 140-nation session in Geneva, March–May 1975, where an informal single negotiating treaty text was devised. Many contentious problems remained unresolved. Coastal and riparian problems included the extent of the territorial sea, guaranteed transit through international straits, and the degree of control of coastal states in offshore economic areas.

Another large problem was to define the nature of the international regime to exploit deep seabed resources, including its authority, voting procedures, and revenue management and revenue distribution. (See also LAW—INTERNATIONAL LAW.)

Crowning the UN International Women's Year a massive conference, consisting of 1,000 delegates and some 5,000 feminist leaders and spectators, convened in Mexico City in late June. Its goal was a 10-year plan of action to improve health care, education, and political and social participation of women. (See also WOMEN.)

The severity of the petroleum producers-consumers confrontation following the Arab-Israeli war of October 1973 abated somewhat in 1975, although the world's energy problem remained acute.

Through the International Energy Agency the industrialized states sought to negotiate arrangements to protect themselves against petroleum emergencies. They planned to unite in advance of meeting with the oil-producing nations to negotiate on prices, markets, guaranteed deliveries, and other matters.

The United States favored a varied international program of energy conservation, development of alternative resources, long-term purchase-price arrangements, and agreed consumer policy in advance of a general meeting with producers and Third World powers. Some governments insisted that discussions be broadened to include other resources as well. In October it was agreed to convene a foreign ministers' conference at Paris in mid-December in order to launch broad-range deliberations through several continuing panels—on oil-energy, raw materials, and Third World poverty and development.

At the end of the year most of the major global issues—food, population, the seas, petroleum, poverty, and resources management—remained unsettled. They were exacerbated not only by the continuance of regional crises, terrorism, and widespread weapons proliferation, but also by politicization of policy positions, bloc aggregations, and ideological factions. Although the year 1975 introduced no cataclysmic crises and produced some positive results, the agenda of problems confronting the United States and other powers tended to increase rather than to diminish.

ELMER PLISCHKE
University of Maryland

UPI

In January, Vice President Rockefeller convened the eight-member administration panel to investigate charges of illegal CIA spying on U. S. citizens. The panel report (*right*) appeared in June.

SPECIAL REPORT:

U.S. Intelligence Activities

The first full scale U. S. congressional inquiry into the Central Intelligence Agency (CIA) and other components of the nation's intelligence community was launched by a *New York Times* report of Dec. 22, 1974. Seymour Hersh, an investigative reporter in the newspaper's Washington bureau, wrote that the CIA, in direct violation of its charter, had conducted a massive, illegal domestic intelligence operation during the years of the Richard Nixon administration. Targets of the operation included members of the antiwar movement and other dissident groups.

In early January 1975 it was revealed that four top officials of the CIA unit linked to the alleged domestic spying had left the agency. Spokesmen for the CIA said that the four were taking advantage of retirement benefits available to employees who left government before the end of 1974.

Investigations. On Jan. 4, 1975, President Gerald R. Ford established a commission to investigate CIA activities within the United States. The eight-member group was headed by Vice President Nelson A. Rockefeller. Ford also announced that the Justice Department would

investigate to determine whether any CIA officials might be subject to prosecution for their alleged activities. The commission report initially was due to be completed April 4, but the deadline subsequently was extended to June.

Early evidence that the controversy was having an impact outside the United States came on Jan. 5, 1975, when *Pravda,* the Soviet Communist party newspaper, said "the much hailed bourgeois democracy in practice turns out to be a system of total surveillance and espionage."

After several congressional committees indicated that they wanted to examine the increasing number of charges, the Senate Democratic caucus voted 45–7 in favor of creating a bipartisan select committee to investigate CIA operations and those of other government intelligence units. Sen. Frank Church, a Democrat from Idaho, was chosen to head the new committee. The vote was a significant setback to Sen. John C. Stennis of Mississippi, who as chairman of the Senate Armed Services Committee traditionally presided over military matters, including the Senate's limited control over the CIA.

On February 19, the House followed suit by creating a select committee to look into illegal

In April former CIA Director Helms denounced charges of CIA-sponsored assassinations of foreign leaders.

or improper activities of federal intelligence agencies in the United States and overseas. Unlike the Senate, however, the House named the representative chiefly responsible for overseeing the CIA, Lucien Nedzi of Michigan, to serve as chairman of the new panel. Political infighting quickly developed in the House committee, sparked by the revelation that Nedzi had learned of CIA involvement in assassination plans and domestic law violations more than a year earlier and had not called for a congressional investigation. After months of wrangling and little progress in the investigation, a new committee was created in mid-July with a different chairman, Rep. Otis G. Pike of New York.

Secret Activities. Major elements of the *New York Time*'s account had been confirmed before the Senate and House committees were

fully operating. CIA Director William E. Colby acknowledged that the CIA had spied on U. S. political dissenters, opened mail of private citizens, planted informers inside domestic protest groups, and assembled its own files on some 10,000 U. S. citizens. Also, Ray S. Cline, former deputy director of the agency, told of the CIA's infiltration of the U. S. antiwar movement in an effort to get its agents, masquerading as radicals, recruited by Soviet intelligence. According to Cline, former presidents Lyndon B. Johnson and Richard M. Nixon had been "absolutely obsessed" with the belief that the Soviets were manipulating the Vietnam War protests.

In the midst of the wave of unfavorable publicity about the CIA, it was disclosed that the agency had scored something of an intelligence master stroke. The CIA had conducted a supersecret, six-year intelligence effort that recovered part of a sunken Soviet submarine and related equipment from deep in the Pacific Ocean.

The partial salvage, although it reportedly failed to recover hydrogen warhead missiles and codes, did reveal that the United States operates a highly sophisticated undersea listening system that allowed it to pinpoint the location of the submarine, a feat that the Soviets had been unable to accomplish since the submarine sank in 1968.

However, the relief from the storm of critical revelations was brief. It was disclosed in House testimony that the CIA for nearly 20 years had conducted an illegal mail-interception program. It was abandoned in 1973 only after the chief U. S. postal inspector demanded that the CIA either obtain higher approval or halt the operation. The program began in 1953 as a "mail cover," limited to monitoring information on the envelopes of letters. But two years later the CIA began opening and copying letters.

Assassination Plots. Shortly before the Rockefeller Commission issued its report, the vice

U. S. intelligence sources revealed in March that the *Glomar Explorer*, owned by Howard Hughes, was used by the CIA to raise a Soviet nuclear submarine that had exploded and sunk in the Pacific in 1968.

president announced that it would exclude information on charges that the CIA was involved in plots to assassinate foreign leaders, an area that became the focus of public interest. A spokesman for the commission said the panel had begun to examine the allegations only midway in its investigation and thus did not have time for a full examination. President Ford turned the commission's classified summary of the assassination plots, along with the publicly released report, over to the Justice Department for possible prosecutions.

In November, when the Senate Intelligence Committee issued its report on the United States involvement in assassination plots, over the strenuous objection of the White House, the reason for the claims of political sensitivity was apparent. The committee concluded that the CIA had initiated plots to assassinate Congolese Premier Patrice Lumumba and Cuban Premier Fidel Castro and had been involved in planning coups that resulted in the deaths of three other foreign leaders.

Under Presidents Dwight D. Eisenhower, John F. Kennedy, and Johnson, the committee found that assassinations of foreign leaders had become a deliberate policy of the CIA. The report did not, however, trace a specific plot or the broad assassination capability to a presidential order or approval. Such a link would have been extremely difficult to establish because of the pattern of resorting to euphemisms, circumlocutions, and the tactic of plausible denial whenever political murder was discussed. In its conclusion about presidential involvement in a coup attempt, the committee said that President Nixon had ordered CIA operatives to prevent the accession to power of Chilean Premier Salvador Allende in 1970. In the unsuccessful attempt to block Allende, the Chilean chief of staff, Gen. René Schneider, was killed in an abortive kidnapping.

Reports. The Rockefeller Commission, while side-stepping the assassination questions, concluded that the CIA had engaged in "plainly unlawful" conduct over its 28-year history, ranging from burglary through electronic bugging to testing the drug LSD on unsuspecting subjects. But the commission defended the CIA's overall record and said that no fundamental changes were needed in the agency's basic legislative charter, the National Security Act of 1947.

In subsequent House testimony, Comptroller General Elmer G. Staats demonstrated the lack of control that existed over elements of the intelligence community. He said that the General Accounting Office, Congress' accounting watchdog, had no idea how much money was being spent each year by the approximately one dozen agencies that make up the intelligence community. He said estimates of a $6 billion annual outlay were only a "guess."

The House Intelligence Committee, pursuing

Sen. Frank Church, the chairman, holds up a CIA dart gun at September intelligence hearing.

a course different from that of its Senate counterpart, concentrated on the risks, costs, and effectiveness of the U.S. intelligence effort. A former CIA intelligence analyst testified at one of the House committee's sessions that "corruption in the intelligence process" caused the United States to be taken by surprise in the 1968 Tet offensive in Vietnam.

The FBI. Although the CIA was the major focus of the controversy over the U.S. intelligence effort, other agencies drew fire also. The Federal Bureau of Investigation (FBI) was the target of substantial criticism, and such agencies as the Internal Revenue Service (IRS) and the National Security Agency (NSA) became involved as well.

Senate investigators disclosed that FBI agents had conducted at least 238 house and office break-ins, or "black bag jobs," over a 26-year period against "domestic subversive targets." Documents gathered by the Senate Intelligence Committee showed that the FBI regarded the break-ins as "clearly illegal" and took steps to hide and later destroy records of the illegal activities. In the first audit of the FBI's domestic intelligence operations, the General Accounting Office raised sweeping questions about the program, including the legal basis on which it had been conducted.

In November, FBI officials disclosed before the Senate Intelligence Committee that the agency had conducted an extensive campaign to discredit Nobel Peace Prize recipient Martin Luther King, Jr., as a civil rights leader. The disclosure triggered demands that the investigation of King's death be reopened.

By the end of 1975, there were mounting indications that the series of disclosures would produce the first congressional efforts since World War II to write legislation regulating the intelligence community.

RONALD J. OSTROW
Washington Bureau, "Los Angeles Times"

URUGUAY

Throughout the year, Uruguay remained under the thinly-disguised, armed-forces dictatorship headed by President Juan María Bordaberry. However, in May the regime was imperiled by a clash between Bordaberry, a civilian, and his military backers.

Political Developments. The crisis began May 21, when the president dismissed Eduardo Peile as head of the National Meat Institute (INAC), because Peile had ordered slaughterhouses to give priority to cattle from smaller ranches. The large ranchers protested, leading to Peile's dismissal. The military backed Peile, and during the controversy Bordaberry threatened to resign. A compromise upheld Peile's dismissal, but he remained a member of INAC's board, while Bordaberry nominee José María Rocca became head of the institute. At the same time, Peile's order to favor small ranchers was kept in force.

On Jan. 1, 1975, President Bordaberry outlawed the Communist and all other Marxist parties. At the same time he proclaimed a "new institutionality," with the "invaluable support" of the armed forces. However, on January 8, Rodney Arismendi, secretary general of the Communist party, who had been jailed since May 1974, was released and left for Moscow.

Other prominent political prisoners were also released during the year. These included the former dean of the architecture school, Carlos Reverditto, exiled early in January, and former Col. Carlos Zufriategui, associated with the left-wing Frente Amplio coalition, released on February 21.

New political arrests, however, continued during the year. On February 27, Communist leader Jaime Pérez was sentenced to 18 months in prison. The secretary general of the University Students Federation and a number of railroad union leaders were also jailed. On April 5, Carlos Borche, former director of the Uruguayan Press Association, was imprisoned.

Several foreign protests against the dictatorship were registered during the year. On July 29, Amnesty International accused the government of systematic arrest and torture of political opponents.

Economy. The country's economic situation continued to be serious. Inflation soared. Early in February the National Economic and Social Council adopted a number of measures to counteract the situation. These included a 6% devaluation of the peso, a 15% increase of private workers' wages as of February 1, a similar increase for government workers as of March 1, and increased prices of milk, water, electricity, fuel, meat, sugar, and liquor. Imports of capital goods were freed from controls. By the end of April the peso had been devalued by 19.69% since the beginning of the year. On April 25 the government decreed a drastic decrease in fuel use, because of the oil crisis.

Some foreign economic aid was forthcoming during the year. In June the Inter-American Development Bank extended a loan of $7 million to expand water supplies in small towns, and the International Monetary Fund gave Uruguay a loan of $27 million. Other Inter-American Development Bank loans included one for $14.4 million for expansion of cement production, and another for $28.4 million for telecommunications.

Perhaps the most important economic event of the year, however, was the signing in March of 30-year contracts with Gulf, Texaco, Chevron, and Exxon for offshore oil exploration. Each company agreed to pay $200,000 to use technical studies prepared for the government by a French company.

ROBERT J. ALEXANDER
Rutgers University

—————— URUGUAY · Information Highlights ——————

Official Name: Eastern Republic of Uruguay.
Location: Southeastern coast of South America.
Area: 68,536 square miles (177,508 sq km).
Population (1975 est.): 3,100,000.
Chief City (1967 est.): Montevideo, the capital, 1,280,-000.
Government: *Head of state,* Juan M. Bordaberry, president (took office March 1972). *Head of government,* Juan M. Bordaberry. *Legislature*—General Assembly (suspended June 1973).
Monetary Unit: Peso (2.37 pesos equal U. S.$1, April 1975).
Gross National Product (1973 est.): $1,848,000,000.
Manufacturing (major products): Meat products, textiles, construction and building materials, beverages, chemicals.
Major Agricultural Products: Wheat, corn, rice, livestock, wool.
Foreign Trade (1974): *Exports,* $382,000,000; *imports,* $487,000,000.

UTAH

Taxation and inflation were the major concerns in Utah in 1975.

Taxation. Utah taxpayers became subject to a substantial state-income-tax increase based on four main factors. These were the increase in rates authorized by the 1975 Utah Legislature, the inflation-induced increase as individuals moved into higher tax brackets, the inability of individuals to take advantage of more liberal 1975 federal provisions on their state returns, and higher state taxes resulting from smaller deductions for federal taxes.

The state income tax burden increases as income levels rise, because of Utah's tax brackets and rate structure. Further, business is often required to pay taxes on inventory "profits," even though such profits are needed to replace lower-cost goods sold with higher-priced merchandise or materials purchased. These and other tax "inequities" are plaguing the Utah citizen. Although considerable data have been published by the Utah Foundation, a non-profit agency established for the study of such problems, there was little evidence of public concern

──────── **UTAH • Information Highlights** ────────
Area: 84,916 square miles (219,932 sq km).
Population (1974 est.): 1,173,000. *Density:* 14 per sq mi.
Chief Cities (1970 census): Salt Lake City, the capital, 175,885; Ogden, 69,478; Provo, 53,131.
Government (1975): *Chief Officers*—governor, Calvin L. Rampton (D); secy. of state, Clyde L. Miller (D). *Legislature*—Senate, 29 members; House of Representatives, 75 members.
Education (1974–75): *Enrollment*—public elementary schools, 160,785 pupils; public secondary schools, 145,603; nonpublic schools, 4,400; colleges and universities, 82,036 students. *Public school expenditures,* $233,028,000 ($836 per pupil).
State Finances (fiscal year 1974): *Revenues,* $812,580,000; *expenditures,* $745,963,000.
Personal Income (1974): $5,222,000,000; per capita, $4,452.
Labor Force (Aug. 1975): *Nonagricultural wage and salary earners,* 446,700,000; *insured unemployed,* 13,700.

reflected in the political issues that were debated in the 1975 elections.

Politics. Elections in 1975 for local office were more concerned with personalities than issues. In the race for mayor of Salt Lake City, voters elected a newcomer, Ted Wilson, who is Utah's youngest mayor since the inception of the city commission form of government in 1912. The 36-year-old social services director rather handily defeated the incumbent, 64-year-old Conrad B. Harrison. The voter turnout was only moderate, representing no more than half the number of registered voters. One winner in the Salt Lake City commissioner race, Jess A. Agraz, had campaigned solely on the issue that his engineering experience made him the best qualified person to assume the streets commissioner position. Agraz became the first Salt Lake City commissioner of Mexican-American heritage.

Education. The teachers of the Granite Education Association voted overwhelmingly on Oct. 8, 1975, to strike against the Granite School District, the largest in the state. The dispute, primarily over salary increases, had been going on during most of 1975. As the school year began, the teachers agreed to meet classes without contracts, pending the report of a negotiation factfinder. The factfinder proposed that the impasse in the district's negotiations with the teachers could be resolved primarily through the application of a 10% across-the-board salary increase.

The district officials judged that the cost of the salary change would be prohibitive and that funds to accommodate the change were unavailable. The teachers claimed that the district officers had agreed to accept the factfinder's report, arguing that "Granite teachers have gone through the negotiations, mediation, and factfinding process, and we accepted the process. The board rejected the process which it initiated."

The strike was voted, another impasse developed, and students remained at home. After closed-door meetings between district officials and officers of the Granite Education Association throughout the week of October 13–17, an amicable settlement was concluded, and the teachers returned to the classroom.

Energy and Conservation. As is increasingly true throughout the West, Utah has sharp battles between advocates of energy development and conservationists. The possible construction of a 3,000-megawatt coal-fired electric plant on the Kaiparowits Plateau in southern Utah sparked a bitter controversy over the environmental and economic impact during the proposed plant's first round of federal hearings in Salt Lake City. The site is 100 miles (160 km) from Bryce Canyon, Zion, Grand Canyon, and Reef national parks.

LORENZO K. KIMBALL
University of Utah

VENEZUELA

The nationalizing of foreign industries, continuing political stability, and growing continental and international influence marked 1975 in Venezuela.

Political Affairs. President Carlos Andrés Pérez, head of one of the two democracies in South America, entered his second year with no serious threat to his government. His party, Democratic Action (AD), had an absolute majority in the Congress. The leading opposition party, the Christian Democrats, had virtually no independent program of its own since AD adopted most of the same viewpoints. The Movement to Socialism (MAS), a splinter of the Communist party, provided vigorous opposition, however, calling itself the "third electoral force of Venezuela." Former president Romulo Betancourt attended the annual convention of AD and took an active role for the first time since he left office. The principal political dis-

Venezuelan President Carlos Andrés Pérez addressed a special joint session of the Mexican Congress in March.

UPI

In February demonstrators protested the appointment of Harry Shlaudeman as U. S. ambassador to Venezuela.

pute centered around provisions of the oil-nationalization bill.

Budget. The 1975–76 budget called for an expenditure of about $7.7 billion, almost 20% below the 1974–75 budget. The lion's share went to education and social services.

Education. The president announced in his annual message that his administration had been able to include 80,000 4–6-year-old children into the educational system and that the education allotment in the budget had been increased 60%. He also announced the creation of scholarship and specialist-training programs.

Labor. Iron industry workers struck after the government takeover of U. S. companies to ensure that social benefits would continue under Venezuelan ownership. On April 30 the government decreed that all employers with 10 or more employees had to hire an additional 5% and train them, thus creating 100,000 additional jobs. To carry out all its policies and objectives, the government issued a great many decree laws, earning it the title of "decretocracia."

Oil. Sixty-one years of foreign domination of the oil industry ended on Jan. 1, 1976, when the properties of 20 foreign companies reverted to the nation. Although nationalization was a very popular issue in all sectors of society, the most prolonged political dispute of the year centered around a single clause of the nationalization bill. In Clause 5 the government proposed to allow Petroven, the state corporation set up to take over the oil industry, to contract with foreign companies for assistance in marketing, producing, and developing its holdings. The opposition held that to do so would compromise Venezuela's economic independence.

The government used its majority in Congress to push through its version of the bill. Petroven was funded with an initial capital of $1.8 billion and was to receive an additional $5 billion more during the following five years. In 1976 its domain will include 20,000 operating wells, a work force of 23,000 persons, 5 million acres (2 million hectares) of land, and some $5 billion in installations and equipment. Foreign companies are to be compensated in the amount of $1 billion, the approximate book value of their holdings. With the nationalization of the iron ore reserves on Jan. 1, 1975, the government gained control of 92% of its foreign exchange sources.

Venezuela's great oil wealth has brought much power and responsibility. In 1974 the petroleum industry grossed $10.8 billion. The country planned to invest 50% of its oil revenues in the Fondo de Inversiones de Venezuela, a government corporation that expected to use the revenue for agriculture, electricity, water, housing, transportation, and social services.

Oil politics also figured prominently in international relations. President Pérez attended the March meeting of the heads of state of the Organization of Petroleum Exporting Countries (OPEC). In September, OPEC adopted Venezuela's proposal to raise oil prices 10% for nine months beginning Oct. 1, 1975. For this and other reasons, both U. S. President Gerald R. Ford and Secretary of State Henry Kissinger criticized Venezuela and warned that the United States would not allow itself to "be exposed to the whim of others" in the matter of oil. Venezuela rejected the criticism but assured the United States that it still considered it to be its primary market.

Latin American countries with little or no oil expressed open criticism of Venezuela, in some cases labeling it imperialistic. Such criticism grew despite Venezuela's pledge of subsidies to Central American countries to hold up prices of their commodities in the world market. Venezuela agreed to use some of its wealth to finance statistical studies of Latin American food resources, hydrocarbon supplies, and demographic growth.

Diplomacy. Venezuela reestablished relations with Cuba after a 14-year break. It also recognized North Korea, China, Albania, and Bulgaria.

LEO B. LOTT, *University of Montana*

VENEZUELA · Information Highlights

Official Name: Republic of Venezuela.
Location: Northwestern South America.
Area: 352,143 square miles (912,050 sq km).
Population (1975 est.): 12,200,000.
Chief Cities (1974): Caracas, the capital, 2,400,000; Maracaibo, 900,000; Barquisimeto, 350,000.
Government: *Head of state,* Carlos Andrés Pérez, president (took office March 1974). *Head of government,* Carlos Andrés Pérez. *Legislature*—Congress: Senate and Chamber of Deputies.
Monetary Unit: Bolívar (4.28 bolívares equal U. S.$1, Aug. 1975).
Gross National Product (1975): $12,400,000,000.
Manufacturing (major products): Processed foods, paper and paperboard, petroleum products, beverages, metal products, furniture, clothing.
Major Agricultural Products: Coffee, cacao, bananas, sugarcane, cotton, rice, corn, dairy products.
Foreign Trade (1973): *Exports,* $5,440,000,000; *imports,* $2,570,000,000.

VERMONT

The state faced increased unemployment, a growing recession, and budget battles in 1975.

Government. The legislature convened in January 1975 with a reduced Republican majority in the Senate and no clear-cut majority in the House of Representatives. Timothy O'Connor became the first Democrat elected speaker of the House since before the Civil War. The leading candidates from the previous November's races for lieutenant governor, attorney general, auditor, and treaturer, all Democrats except the auditor, had failed to receive the required absolute majority in the popular election. Under a constitutional provision unused since 1913, they were elected by a joint session of the legislature.

Legislation. Among the principal actions of the 1975 legislature were the creation of an agency of transportation that absorbed the highway department, a ban on non-returnable beverage bottles, and the enactment of legislative control over future construction of nuclear power plants. In other controversial areas, a presidential primary bill was passed by the Senate and awaited final action in the House. Both houses failed to act on a proposed land use plan. A prolonged legislative struggle over Gov. Thomas P. Salmon's budget and tax-increase proposals ended with few cuts and no tax increases, the budget being balanced by one-time accounting adjustments.

Faced with an apparent shortage in revenue due to recession conditions and unemployment, the governor called a special session of the legislature in September to approve a one-cent increase in the state's 3% sales tax. The proposal was meant to offset an impending $8–$10 million dollar deficit that Salmon's fiscal analysts predicted. The legislature balked at this recommendation and refused to authorize any immediate tax increase. The lawmakers also imposed legal restrictions on Salmon's ability to implement some $6 million in budget cuts he had threatened to make if the legislature refused a tax hike. The legislature's only affirmative action was to approve some $3 million in preliminary budget cuts sought by Salmon.

Economy. Vermont suffered severely from the national recession, with unemployment above the national average, and per capita real income falling. Rising fuel and power costs contributed acutely to the state's difficulties. Despite a relatively mild winter, snowfall was sufficient for a successful skiing season, which kept state income from falling more precipitously.

A dry summer and rising feed prices created difficulties for agriculture, mainly dairying. Dairymen were also affected by the worst outbreak of brucellosis among their cattle in a decade.

Education. Faced with level state funding despite inflation, the University of Vermont and

Vermont Governor Salmon faced much legislative opposition in 1975 over his budget proposals.

the Vermont state colleges were forced to raise tuition and to curtail programs and salary increases. The union movement among teachers in public schools and the Vermont state colleges made considerable progress, and Governor Salmon successfully arbitrated to avert a faculty strike in the state colleges.

Other Events. In July the Windsor State Prison, built in 1809 and the oldest state prison complex in the United States, was formally closed. In August, after the spectacular grounding of a ferry in Lake Champlain, all 115 passengers and the crew were rescued without injury, and all 45 automobiles aboard were recovered.

SAMUEL B. HAND AND ROBERT V. DANIELS
University of Vermont

VERMONT · Information Highlights

Area: 9,609 square miles (24,887 sq km).

Population (1974 est.): 470,000. *Density:* 50 per sq mi.

Chief Cities (1970 census): Montpelier, the capital, 8,609; Burlington, 38,633; Rutland, 19,293; Bennington, 14,586.

Government (1975): *Chief Officers*—governor, Thomas P. Salmon (D); lt. gov., Brian D. Burns (D). *General Assembly*—Senate, 30 members; House of Representatives, 150 members.

Education (1974–75): *Enrollment*—public elementary schools, 63,783 pupils; public secondary schools, 41,588; nonpublic schools, 11,300; colleges and universities, 28,289 students. *Public school expenditures,* $111,839,000 ($1,088 per pupil).

State Finances (fiscal year 1974): *Revenues,* $424,305,-000; *expenditures,* $416,923,000.

Personal Income (1974): $2,157,000,000; per capita, $4,588.

Labor Force (Aug. 1975): *Nonagricultural wage and salary earners,* 160,500; *insured unemployed,* 9,300.

UPI
Refugees from Pleiku, their truck overflowing, flee in late
March from advancing Communist forces.

VIETNAM

Events in Vietnam occurred at a much faster
rate than even their Communist political and
military architects anticipated in 1975. The year
began with the Saigon government of President
Nguyen Van Thieu controlling most of the same
South Vietnamese territory as it had ruled at the
time of the January 1973 "cease-fire." Within
four months, however, Communist soldiers had
swept to an unexpectedly-swift victory over the
anti-Communist South Vietnamese regime, which
fell on April 30. The conquering Communists
initially indicated that reunification of the two
Vietnams would take "at least five years," and
both Hanoi and Saigon unsuccessfully sought
separate United Nations membership in July.
By year's end, however, steps had been taken to
unite the two territories, possibly as soon as the
first anniversary of the defeat of the Thieu regime. See also special feature on pages 22–31.

THE WAR AND ITS END

The offensive that toppled the Thieu government began in January, when the Communists

took the northern province of Phouc Long. In
March they successfully attacked Ban Me Thout,
capital of Dar Lac province and southern anchor
of the strategic Central Highlands. The Saigon
anti-Communist regime made no effort to retake
this important city. Instead, President Thieu
ordered his forces to retreat from the Central
Highlands altogether, terming the region "inde-
fensible." What was intended to be an orderly
tactical pullback turned into a rout, however,
and millions of dollars of U. S. arms, ammunition, and equipment were abandoned. Within
three weeks of the first assault on Ban Me Thout,
the northern three-quarters of South Vietnam
had fallen to the Communists. At April's start,
the Communists were within 40 miles (64 km)
of Saigon, and on April 30 the South Vietnamese
capital fell to them without a major battle in its
defense.

Thieu stepped down as leader of the South
Vietnamese government on April 21. He attacked the United States for allegedly abandoning the anti-Communist Saigon regime and left
the country himself five days later. Vice President Tran Van Huong, who took over from
Thieu, was himself replaced April 28 by Gen.
Duong Van Minh, a leading figure in the "third
force" political movement. It was Minh, acceptable to the Communists as transition leader, who
surrendered Saigon on April 30.

War Losses. An estimated 1.3 million North
and South Vietnamese lost their lives in the war
that ended on April 30, as well as 56,717 U. S.
citizens. Another 900 U. S. servicemen were
missing in action, and more than 300,000 U. S.
military personnel were wounded. The financial
cost of the war to the United States was $141
billion. Formal U. S. military aid to South Vietnam between 1950 and 1975 totaled $15.2 bil-
lion (28% of all U. S. arms aid). An arsenal
worth approximately $5 billion was abandoned
by the Thieu government in the last eight weeks
of the war. Thieu claimed that the United States
did not provide him with sufficient arms and
ammunition from 1974 on, but he abandoned at
least half the equipment he had in March.

U. S. Role and Response. The U. S. Congress
cut aid to South Vietnam by $700 million in
September 1974, while the USSR increased its
military and economic assistance to North Vietnam by a similar amount for 1975. U. S. President Gerald Ford asked Congress for nearly $1
billion in military and other aid in 1975, but the
legislators did not appear to take him seriously.
South Vietnamese leader Thieu called the United
States "irresponsible" and "inhumane" and
charged that Washington failed to honor an
earlier written pledge of former President Nixon
to increase aid in the event of large-scale Communist violation of the 1973 "cease-fire."

Congress did vote $405 million for resettle-
ment of 130,000 Vietnamese refugees who fled
their country after Saigon's fall. More than
5,500 Vietnamese were evacuated by the United

States together with 1,373 U. S. personnel. The other Vietnamese escapees fled in small boats.

NORTH VIETNAM

Although its agents were clearly in the ascendancy in the south, North Vietnam retained its separate identity throughout the year. Although some of the signs of bombing raids from the 1960's and early 1970's remained, the country and its capital assumed surprisingly quickly the appearance of a land at peace. Much progress was made toward recovery, with large-scale aid from the USSR.

Politics. The North Vietnamese took advantage of the approaching and actual end of the war to reassert the claim to leadership of the political elite that had guided the country through the conflict. Elections for a new National Assembly were held April 1, even as Communist forces were making their way toward Saigon. These elections were the fifth since the first such body was chosen in January 1946 after Ho Chi Minh had declared the country independent. The size of the assembly was enlarged to 425 members.

On June 7 a new cabinet was chosen by the resulting assembly. Almost all of the major leaders of the government retained the positions they previously held. Pham Van Dong continued as prime minister, while all nine deputy premiers, including military leader Gen. Vo Nguyen Giap, were also re-endorsed.

Economy. There was a food shortage in North Vietnam as the war ended, and the situation did not improve markedly during the year. A black market apparently flourished, despite government efforts to eradicate it. Housing conditions were below those of any of the non-Indochinese countries of Southeast Asia, water was not easily available, and living conditions remained harsh for the overwhelming majority of the population. At year's end, Hanoi's standard of living was much below that of Saigon's.

Mismanagement and worker apathy were officially declared to have hampered fulfillment of 1975 state plan quotas, which were high. A 28% increase in industrial output and a 39% expansion of coal production were expected. Progress was registered, however, as coal pro-

duction continued to rise to an annual total of 5 million tons (compared with 1.5 million in 1957), and most bridges were rebuilt.

Plans were announced to move 300,000 people to wastelands and the mountains to expand food output and plant forests.

Foreign Relations. With the war behind it, North Vietnam clearly cast its international lot with the Soviet Union, to the obvious political displeasure of neighboring China. In October, Party Secretary Le Duan visited Moscow, where he signed two aid agreements and a political declaration upholding Soviet views on détente with the United States. Earlier, the same leader had been a guest in Peking and had stated publicly to the Chinese that Hanoi intended to continue to have good relations with the USSR. He left China abruptly shortly thereafter without a joint statement and apparently without a new aid agreement. Historically, China has been Vietnam's enemy. Hanoi appeared to be using Moscow to keep Peking at bay and to be picking up maximum Soviet rehabilitation aid as a bonus.

In July both North and South Vietnam applied for UN membership, but the United States vetoed the applications. Earlier, South Korea had been denied entry into the world body. The U. S. representatives could not find the eligibility of the two Vietnams superior to that of South Korea and so vetoed their entry.

Premier Pham Van Dong, in the wake of Saigon's fall, called for the "normalization of relations" with the United States, stating, however, that U. S. reconstruction aid was a prerequisite. Washington, smarting with defeat, replied negatively, accusing Hanoi of "wholesale violations" of the 1973 "cease-fire." Both sides seemed to have softened their positions markedly

The war all but lost, South Vietnamese Rangers wait anxiously for evacuation planes.

UPI

── NORTH VIETNAM · Information Highlights ──

Official Name: Democratic Republic of Vietnam.
Location: Southeast Asia.
Area: 61,294 square miles (158,750 sq km).
Population (1975 est.): 23,800,000.
Chief City (1974): Hanoi, the capital, 643,000.
Government: *Head of state,* Ton Duc Thang, president (took office 1969). *Head of government,* Pham Van Dong, premier (took office 1954). *First secretary of Vietnam Workers' (Communist) party,* Le Duan. *Legislature* (unicameral)—National Assembly.
Monetary Unit: Dong (2.35 dong equal U. S.$1, July 1974).
Gross National Product (1972 est.): $1,800,000,000.
Manufacturing (major products): Processed foods, cement.
Major Agricultural Products: Rice, sugarcane, tea, sweet potatoes.

by the year's end, much more quickly than had been expected.

SOUTH VIETNAM

The U. S.-aided "Republic of Vietnam" gave way to the Hanoi-controlled "Revolutionary Government," a self-proclaimed "free and independent" state, after the April 30 fall of Saigon. The new regime declared "peaceful reunification" of the two Vietnams to be its eventual goal. Trade, travel, and communications between the two territories were almost immediately inaugurated, however, and non-military movement between north and south took place for the first time in 21 years. Although the government in Saigon and elsewhere in the country changed dramatically between May and December, other alterations took place slowly.

Politics. The new South Vietnamese government took the form of a military administrative committee, headed by North Vietnamese Gen. Tran Van Tra. The leaders of the "Provisional Revolutionary Government" took over in their own right, at least formally, on June 6. This followed the late May visit to Saigon of the three top North Vietnamese political leaders, Le Duan, Truong Chinh, and Pham Van Dong. Among other matters, the northern and southern Communists apparently agreed that reunification was at least five years off and that South Vietnam should elect a new National Assembly of its own as soon as possible, a decision that was altered in December.

The political organization under the new Communist leadership included division of the country into districts, which in turn were further subdivided into hamlets and neighborhoods, each with "union committees." Cells of about a dozen families within such neighborhoods were the basic organizational units of the country.

There was no large-scale, politically inspired "bloodbath" following the fall, as had been predicted, but civilian and military supporters of the former regime were required to take "re-education courses." Some were required to attend "re-education camps," from which, reportedly, not all participants returned. In addition, large numbers of civil servants were sent south, and many northern soldiers were encouraged to remain and establish their homes in the south.

Economy. The biggest problems, according to President Nguyen Huu Tho, were unemployment and the hunger of millions of people. Two of every seven urban dwellers were said to lack jobs. Other reports indicated that rice supplies were adequate, and prices remained stable (unlike previous years of rampant inflation). The rice harvest was one of the best in years, and there was even official talk of renewed export of the grain in 1976.

The new government indicated its intention to combat urban unemployment by moving 1.5 million people in Saigon and other cities to farm areas by 1977. The government apparently did not intend to copy the "forced-march" model of Cambodia's Communist rulers. Economic conditions, very difficult in the last weeks of the war, hardly improved overnight with the Communist victory, but the situation seemed very much in hand and steadily improving by year's end.

Foreign Relations. The new government proclaimed its foreign policy to be one of "peace and nonalignment." The USSR denied a Peking-inspired report that Moscow had asked for use of the former U. S. naval facility at Cam Ranh Bay. Partiality towards the Soviet Union was evident, however, in the press, which included very few references to the Chinese.

The prospect for some kind of resumed

At a May 7 victory celebration, thousands of Saigon citizens rally before the presidential palace in support of the new Provisional Revolutionary Government.

UPI

relations with the United States brightened at the year's end, as U. S. Secretary of State Henry Kissinger spoke positively respecting such normalization. This shift came after Saigon had indicated an interest in doing business with U. S. oil companies and other firms; 1,600 Vietnamese refugees had returned home; and Hanoi had clearly modified its posture toward contacts with Washington.

Toward Reunification? The goal of the Communist struggle against various Saigon regimes after 1954 had been reunification of the country as a single Communist nation. All evidence suggests that the Hanoi leadership did not expect to be able to overthrow the Thieu government as easily and quickly as it did and to take control of Saigon as early as April 30. This explains why the two Communist governments, in Hanoi and Saigon, initially spoke in terms of at least five years before reunification could take place. In July they even applied for separate UN membership.

Planned Elections. In late November, however, the two Vietnams announced plans to hold joint elections in the first half of 1976 to choose a National Assembly that would take a major step toward the reunification of the country. Both Hanoi and Saigon reportedly feared that a delay in reunification might tempt some new foreign intervention, possibly by one of the major Communist powers.

On December 28, speculation about reunification was confirmed by an announcement on Hanoi radio, which said that the election would be held in early April and that a joint assembly of North and South Vietnam would meet on April 30, the first anniversary of the fall of Saigon. The joint assembly would convene in Hanoi, and it was assumed that the northern city would be the capital of the reunified Vietnam. According to Hanoi, the resolutions on reunification were approved during a People's Representative Congress, held December 20–23 in Saigon. The resolutions were subsequently ratified by North Vietnam's national assembly, which underscored the dominant role of the north in the new political structure in Vietnam. Following the elections, which are to be on the basis of universal suffrage and direct secret

ballot, the single national assembly will have the responsibility of defining "state institutions," according to Hanoi. The assembly will also appoint leading state bodies and will pass a new constitution that will apply to the reunified Vietnam.

RICHARD BUTWELL
State University of New York
College at Fredonia

VIRGIN ISLANDS, U. S.

In 1975 in a microcosmic way, the Virgin Islands reflected some of the political and economic problems found in the United States. These included a politically divided government, inflation, unemployment, suspicion of political corruption, and a stagnate economy.

Political Friction. During his first year as governor, Cyril E. King, a former Democrat who broke away in 1969 to establish the Independent Citizens Movement, could count only on the votes of five members of his party in the 15-member legislature. Thus, political friction marked the relationship between the governor and the legislature. There was also strife between King and the resident commissioner for the Virgin Islands in the U. S. Congress, Ron DeLugo, a Democrat.

Federal Aid. The heavy rains in the final months of 1974 prompted the federal government to declare the Virgin Islands a disaster area thus making it eligible for federal relief. The Federal Disaster Assistance Administration allocated $3 million for relief. To deal with the high level of unemployment caused by the collapse of the construction industry and the closing of a number of labor-intensive industries, over $600,000 was granted in 1975 to the islands under the Emergency Jobs and Unemployment Assistance Act of 1974. Greater assistance was expected as a result of a move to incorporate Puerto Rico and the Virgin Islands into a Caribbean Regional Commission. Such a move would make the islands eligible for financial support for a regional economic development program sponsored by the Department of Commerce.

The highly-automatic heavy industries such as the petrochemical and aluminum complexes on the island of St. Croix continued to grow but at a much slower pace than in previous years. In mid-1975 a grand jury was convened to investigate charges made during the 1974 electoral campaign that bribery was used to secure legislative approval of a new oil refinery on St. Croix. By the end of 1975 no formal charges had been filed, and the result of the inquiry had not been made public. The new oil refinery, now under construction, was not expected to be producing oil before 1978. Its expected capacity will be 200,000 barrels a day.

THOMAS G. MATHEWS
University of Puerto Rico

— SOUTH VIETNAM • Information Highlights —

Official Name: Republic of Vietnam.
Location: Southeast Asia.
Area: 67,108 square miles (173,809 sq km).
Population (1975 est.): 19,700,000.
Chief Cities (1974 est.): Saigon, the capital, 3,500,000; Da Nang, 500,000; Hue, 200,000.
Government: *Head of state,* Nguyen Huu Tho, president.
Monetary Unit: Piastre (755 piastres equal U. S.$1, April 1975).
Gross National Product (1973): $3,100,000,000.
Manufacturing (major products): Processed foods, textiles, chemicals, rubber products.
Major Agricultural Products: Rice, rubber, corn, sweet potatoes, fruits, poultry, fish.
Foreign Trade (1973 est.): *Exports,* $60,600,000; *imports,* $716,000,000.

VIRGINIA

In 1975 as in 1974, the dominant economic and political mood in Virginia was one of conservatism and retrenchment. Gov. Mills Godwin authorized budget cutbacks, and the General Assembly rejected short-term borrowing as a solution to financial needs.

Legislature. When the assembly met early in the year, the major controversy developed over lagging revenues. A bloc of liberal Democrats advocated short-term borrowing of $25 million to cover any budget deficit. Republican Governor Godwin opposed the idea, and a combination of moderate and conservative Democrats plus Republicans defeated it.

In non-financial matters, the assembly also presented a conservative image by again failing to act on the Equal Rights Amendment, by rejecting all forms of collective bargaining or union representation of public employees, and by defeating proposals for a state lottery and a no-fault automobile insurance bill. The death penalty was restored for murders committed by hired slayers, prison inmates, or kidnappers. In a more liberal vein, the assembly changed divorce laws to reduce the waiting period and passed a bill requiring the treatment of alcoholism as a disease, not a crime. The assembly defeated a "death with dignity" bill that would have permitted a terminally ill patient to refuse extreme emergency treatment.

Japanese Emperor Hirohito, on extended U. S. trip, visits Colonial Williamsburg, where on Sept. 30 he was greeted by an honor guard of Virginia militiamen.

UPI

In higher education, the assembly passed several bills designed to help struggling private colleges through grants to students. Later in the year, however, when Sullins College, a private institution in Bristol, asked the state to assume ownership, the request was declined on the grounds of financial inability.

Governor Godwin acted to preserve a balanced budget, as required by the Virginia constitution. In August he directed that 5% be pared from the 1975–76 budget, and in September he directed a 5% reduction in state aid to local public education.

Elections. Money issues and collective bargaining provided the main issues in the fall elections for the General Assembly. The entire membership was up for election, but the Republican party, reflecting its continuing failure to establish a broad base in local politics, fielded candidates in fewer than half the races. Godwin campaigned strenuously for Republican candidates, strongly attacking Democratic incumbents who had favored short-term borrowing or collective bargaining. In western Virginia, however, candidates of both parties generally opposed both positions. The election results produced little change in the makeup of the legislature. Republicans retained their total of 5 seats in the 40-member state Senate and elected only 17 in the 100-member House, a decrease of 2.

Prisons. Overcrowding in Virginia prisons reached chronic proportions during 1975. Some convicts spent months in county and city jails waiting for transfers to state units, and sheriffs blamed several jailbreaks on the resulting idleness and congestion.

Law. The U. S. Supreme Court delivered three opinions in 1975 of direct interest to Virginia. In one it ruled that offshore oil lands belong to the nation, not the states. In another it struck down the practice of the Virginia bar in setting uniform legal fees. In the third, involving Richmond, the court ruled that southern cities can annex predominantly white suburbs and in so doing alter the city's racial balance.

WILLIAM LARSEN, *Radford College*

——— **VIRGINIA · Information Highlights** ———

Area: 40,817 square miles (105,716 sq km).
Population (1974 est.): 4,908,000. *Density:* 120 per sq mi.
Chief Cities (1970 census): Richmond, the capital, 249,-430; Norfolk, 307,951; Virginia Beach, 172,106.
Government (1975): *Chief Officers*—governor, Mills E. Godwin, Jr. (R); lt. gov., John N. Dalton (R). *General Assembly*—Senate, 40 members; House of Delegates, 100 members.
Education (1974–75): *Enrollment*—public elementary schools, 661,661 pupils; public secondary schools, 431,648; nonpublic schools, 60,500; colleges and universities, 215,851 students. *Public school expenditures,* $942,565,000 ($956 per pupil).
State Finances (fiscal year 1974): *Revenues,* $2,860,-088,000; *expenditures,* $2,849,198,000.
Personal Income (1974): $25,842,000,000; per capita, $5,265.
Labor Force (Aug. 1975): *Nonagricultural wage and salary earners,* 1,773,000; *insured unemployed,* 45,-800.

WASHINGTON

The longest legislative session in Washington history—148 days—produced little significant legislation and owed its unprecedented length to voter rejections of special education taxes in many school districts across the state. This forced upon the legislature the burden of solving local school district financing problems. Thousands of people marched and demonstrated at Olympia, and an impasse developed between the Senate and the House over the desirable level of school relief.

Legislation. Other than the school funding issue, perhaps the most critical issue of the legislative session was reform of the public-employee retirement and pension system. The legislature recognized that, as a result of piecemeal legislation in the past, the state retirement and pension system had developed unfunded liabilities in excess of $1.5 billion. A Senate pension reform bill was not acted upon by the House, and the matter was carried over to a future session.

The legislature, after much arguing by three-term Gov. Daniel J. Evans, passed a department of transportation bill. The final bill combined a departmental structure and a method of financing that were completely unacceptable to the governor, and he felt compelled to veto the entire measure.

Prompted by proposals from Seattle Mayor Wesley C. Uhlman and city Budget Director Walter Hundley to reduce the budget of the fire department, the Seattle Firefighters Union collected enough petition signatures to force a recall election of Mayor Uhlman. Specific charges contended that the mayor had knowingly appointed an incompetent budget director, had falsely reported to the city council about the vigor of pursuing arson-prevention programs, and had proposed fire department budget cuts, which would jeopardize life and property. Mayor Uhlman countered by saying the real issue was one of who was responsible for governing the city—the mayor and other city officials or city employees. In the recall campaign, the Firefight-

UPI

Sen. Jackson of Washington, a 1976 presidential hopeful, led the fight to block President Ford's energy program.

ers Union had the encouragement and support of employees of Seattle City Light. On July 1, by a vote of 78,204 to 45,344, Seattle voters rejected the recall attempt.

The employees of City Light had fought with the mayor earlier over his support of the superintendent of City Light. The superintendent had suspended and dismissed several employees who, he claimed, had habitually cheated on their lunch and coffee breaks. City Light employees had demanded the dismissal of the superintendent and made an abortive attempt to recall the mayor when he refused to do so.

Elections. Propositions more than personalities resulted in one of the largest off-year general election voter turnouts in years. Of principal interest were initiatives to place a tax of 12% on the profits of corporations to help fund public schools and to make the death penalty mandatory for certain types of murders. A referendum limiting the appointment to a vacancy in the U. S. Senate to a person from the same political party as the person being replaced was also on the ballot. Voters, by very wide majorities, defeated the corporate profits tax proposal and approved the death penalty proposal. Voters rejected the attempt to limit the governor in his power to make appointments to the U. S. Senate.

Of slightly less general interest, but no less decisive by voter response, were proposals for judicial reform, a constitutional change to allow state assistance of students in private schools, and a new charter for the city of Seattle. Each of these proposals was overwhelmingly rejected by the voters.

WARREN W. ETCHESON
University of Washington

——— **WASHINGTON • Information Highlights** ———

Area: 68,192 square miles (176,617 sq km).
Population (1974 est.): 3,476,000. *Density:* 52 per sq mi.
Chief Cities (1970 census): Olympia, the capital, 23,111; Seattle, 530,831; Spokane, 170,516; Tacoma, 154,581.
Government (1975): *Chief Officers*—governor, Daniel J. Evans (R); lt. gov., John A. Cherberg (D). *Legislature*—Senate, 49 members; House of Representatives, 98 members.
Education (1974–75): *Enrollment*—public elementary schools, 400,548 pupils; public secondary, 384,909; nonpublic, 42,300; colleges and universities, 210,018 students. *Public school expenditures,* $837,426,000 ($1,147 per pupil).
State Finances (fiscal year 1974): *Revenues,* $2,849,870,000; *expenditures,* $2,671,746,000.
Personal Income (1974): $19,642,000,000; per capita, $5,651.
Labor Force (Aug. 1975): *Nonagricultural wage and salary earners,* 1,211,000; *insured unemployed,* 76,500.

On January 2, Justice Thurgood Marshall (*left*) swears in Mayor Walter Washington as the first elected mayor of the District of Columbia in over 100 years.

WASHINGTON, D. C.

The year 1975 began with the inauguration ceremonies and festivities celebrating the city's first elected mayor, Walter E. Washington, and council in over 100 years. During this first year of home rule, the members of the city council introduced over 200 bills, passed more than 100 resolutions, and staffed the 10 standing and 2 special committees that held several hundred public hearings and wrote scores of committee reports. The district's residents displayed keen interest in their new government.

The federal government demonstrated a willingness to support the city's right to self-government. President Gerald Ford placed the district on equal footing with other cities by abolishing the special White House staff office that was responsible for supervising city affairs. Congress, which has the power to repeal legislation passed by the city council and retains authority over the city's budget, chose not to interfere with decisions made by the local government.

Federal Government. Congressional subcommittees held hearings on a constitutional amendment to give the district full voting representation in the House and Senate. The J. Edgar Hoover FBI Building, a new two block long headquarters for 7,400 Federal Bureau of Investigation employees, opened. The structure, which took 12 years and $126 million to complete, houses a gymnasium, film laboratory, printing plant, and sophisticated scientific crime-detection equipment. There are tourist facilities around a central, open-landscaped courtyard with fountains and sitting areas.

Education. The district's elected school board voted 7–4 on Oct. 9, 1975, to fire School Superintendent Barbara A. Sizemore, ending a two-year, problem-laden relationship and seven months of trying to obtain her removal. Sizemore, the $41,700-a-year head of the 170-school system, had been charged with administrative negligence and failure to follow board policy and direction.

Attempts to dismiss the school superin-

tendent, 14 months prior to the expiration of her 3-year contract, by a negotiated settlement rather than through lengthy and costly public hearings failed because both the board and superintendent rejected settlement proposals. Administrative hearings, required by the terms of her contract, began after Sizemore was unsuccessful in obtaining a court injunction to halt dismissal proceedings.

After two months of slow, tedious, and often uninteresting hearings, presiding judge Herbert Reid, Sr., decided that 13 of the 17 board charges had been proven and had met legal grounds on which the board may dismiss a superintendent. Vincent A. Reed was named acting superintendent, pending the selection of a permanent superintendent by the school board.

Transportation. Numerous problems delayed the anticipated 1975 opening of the first 4.5-mile (7.2-km) section of Washington's proposed 98-mile (157-km) subway system. The ultimate expansion of the system beyond the 43 miles (69 km) already under construction was in doubt. The problems included strikes, defective subway cars, local political arguments over routing and station locations, U. S. district court orders prohibiting use of stations without elevators for the handicapped, and inflationary cost overruns that increased the subway system's price to $4.5 billion. A supplemental appropriation from Congress and the federal government's release of funds once earmarked for the district's freeways permitted work to continue and renewed hope that the first trains would be running by early 1976.

Bicentennial. Three district bicentennial groups struggled to raise funds to finance special events for the millions of tourists expected during 1976. Lack of federal funds caused the scrapping of lofty proposals to make the city a model of clean, safe, and healthy living. Instead, plans were started to provide visitors to popular tourist sites with shorter and more entertaining waiting periods.

ELEANOR G. FELDBAUM
University of Maryland

Schoolteachers in West Virginia held a mass rally in support of a pay raise at the Charleston capitol building in November.

WEST VIRGINIA

The state was rocked December 18 by the indictment of Governor Moore for allegedly extorting $25,000 from a businessman seeking a state bank charter. Moore immediately denied that he had accepted the payments in 1972. Coal remained dominant in the state's economic picture, with high demand helping to keep West Virginia's unemployment below the national average.

Politics and Legislation. The political picture was little changed from recent years. Republican Gov. Arch A. Moore, Jr., and a heavily Democratic legislature squabbled throughout the year over vetoes, override votes, and budget and fiscal priorities. The regular session, and then a special one—by now a familiar aspect of the Moore years—went into recesses and then into continuations. Lawmakers gathered in Charleston in late October, still faced with such diverse issues as legalized dog racing, abortion-law reform, and additional pay raises for schoolteachers. The latter issue was sharpened by widespread threats of a teacher strike. On July 1 the state supreme court ruled against the governor's attempt to kill a legislative budget that had been liberally sprinkled with special items in what even members of the majority termed a pork-barrel operation.

The major accomplishments of the session included a higher severance tax on coal, with a major percentage of the increased revenue earmarked for the coal-producing counties. There was also an "open-meeting" law for all levels of government and authorization for road-building bonds, with an emphasis on critical, secondary mountain highways. Many observers felt, however, that the tone of the session was more accurately reflected in the pay raise for all members of the legislature, which was the first major bill passed.

The governor won a major battle when he interpreted an across-the-board pay raise for state employees as applying only to "deserving" ones. Although legislative leaders insisted the interpretation was contrary to their intent, no action was taken to override the chief executive. The confrontation continued into the fall session as the governor threatened the layoff of employees unless the legislature authorized additional highway bonds.

Newsmakers. John Kelly, state treasurer since 1960, resigned in July after he, an assistant, and four former bank officers were indicted for extortion and fraud. Kelly pleaded guilty and was imprisoned in the fall. He was succeeded by Ronald Pearson.

Textbook Dispute. The Kanawha county school textbook dispute moved from violence to the courts in 1975. Parents and fundamentalist ministers had protested that certain books were "unchristian" and "immoral." In January 1975, six persons were indicted on charges that they had conspired to destroy two county schools, and in April two of the six were convicted. Also in January, a federal judge ruled that the disputed books did not violate the First Amendment's guarantee of the separation of church and state.

Strikes. A one-month wildcat strike in August and early September idled 43,000 of the state's 50,000 miners. They were protesting "footdragging" in arbitration procedures.

W. REYNOLDS MCLEOD
West Virginia University

—— **WEST VIRGINIA · Information Highlights** ——

Area: 24,181 square miles (62,629 sq km).
Population (1974 est.): 1,791,000. *Density:* 74 per sq mi.
Chief Cities (1970 census): Charleston, the capital, 71,-505; Huntington, 74,315; Wheeling, 48,188.
Government (1975): *Chief Officers*—governor, Arch A. Moore, Jr. (R); secy. of state, Edgar F. Heiskell III (R). *Legislature*—Senate, 34 members; House of Delegates, 100 members.
Education (1974–75): *Enrollment*—public elementary schools, 228,656 pupils; public secondary, 175,785; nonpublic, 10,800; colleges and universities, 71,250 students. *Public school expenditures,* $320,802,000 ($838 per pupil).
State Finances (fiscal year 1974): *Revenues,* $1,355,-948,000; *expenditures,* $1,293,777,000.
Personal Income (1974): $7,862,000,000; per capita, $4,-390.
Labor Force (Aug. 1975): *Nonagricultural wage and salary earners,* 564,500; *insured unemployed,* 20,500.

Police guard Shawano county sheriff's office near Gresham while Indian demonstrators picket. During January Indians occupied a vacant Roman Catholic abbey that they wanted for use as a hospital.

UPI

WISCONSIN

Legislative action and a continuing saga of Indian occupation of a former school for Roman Catholic priests dominated the concerns of Wisconsin residents during 1975. Population losses slowed and the Wisconsin economy held up well.

Taxes. While there was no general tax increase in the budget adopted by the state legislature, the strain of rising costs was evident. The budget attempted to force local communities to hold the line on spending by placing limits on their annual property tax increases. Municipalities immediately started a campaign to repeal the provision but had to wait for another legislature's consideration. By year's end, Gov. Patrick Lucey had appointed a task force to study state-local relations and tax policies, particularly inequities in the property tax.

Legislative Action. While the budget consumed much of the lawmakers' time, some notable legislation that had been pending for several sessions was enacted. In 1974 a bill to remove most sex distinctions from state laws was defeated on the last day of the session. In 1975 after emotional debate over how the bill would affect the status of women, it passed both houses of the legislature.

In another area, five years of efforts to regulate the location of power plants ended with passage of a compromise bill that gave citizens, local governments, and the state a greater voice in the selection process. Another major bill sought to encourage new voters. It allowed them to register by postcard and to vote without prior registration. Republicans unsuccessfully argued that Democrats wanted the bill enacted because many of the new voters probably would vote Democratic.

Population. Estimates made by the state showed a surprising population trend in the first half of the 1970's. Population losses in the sparsely settled northern and western parts of Wisconsin during the 1960's were reversed and only four counties—including the most populous, Milwaukee—lost population in the first half of the 1970's. In contrast, 20 of the 72 counties lost population between 1960 and 1970.

The total state population was estimated at 4,581,701, up 3.7% from 1970.

Novitiate. An abandoned novitiate owned by the Alexian Brothers, a Roman Catholic order, was the setting for a drama that continued throughout the year. On January 1 the novitiate, near Gresham, was captured by a group of armed Indians from the nearby Menominee reservation who said they wanted to use it to benefit Indians. In the 34 days they held the property, the situation remained tense as the Indians' forces were increased and gunfire was exchanged. A tribal feud worsened and whites threatened to take things into their own hands. National Guard troops then ringed the area. Finally, the Alexians agreed to turn the property over to the tribe. Tribal leaders, however, said they did not want it, and the Alexians considered other proposals. Then, on October 12, a fire of undetermined origin gutted one of the two main buildings. While all this was taking place the tribe struggled to regain federal protection, having found that self-government brought only poverty and more problems.

Economy. The Wisconsin economy held up well in 1975. Unemployment of about 7% was below the national average. There was a loss of jobs in manufacturing, but strengths in such other areas as mining equipment helped offset the decline.

PAUL SALSINI, *The Milwaukee "Journal"*

——— **WISCONSIN • Information Highlights** ———

Area: 56,154 square miles (145,439 sq km).
Population (1975 est.): 4,581,701. *Density:* 82 per sq mi.
Chief Cities (1970 census): Madison, the capital, 172,-007; Milwaukee, 717,372; Racine, 95,162.
Government (1975): *Chief Officers*—governor, Patrick J. Lucey (D): lt. gov., Martin J. Schreiber (D). *Legislature*—Senate, 33 members; Assembly, 99 members.
Education (1974–75): *Enrollment*—public elementary schools, 553,962 pupils; public secondary schools, 420,371; nonpublic schools, 174,200; colleges and universities, 226,575 students. *Public school expenditures,* $1,025,593,000 ($1,135 per pupil).
State Finances (fiscal year 1974): *Revenues,* $3,347,687,-000; *expenditures,* $3,223,795,000.
Personal Income (1974): $23,790,000,000; per capita, $5,210.
Labor Force (July 1975): *Nonagricultural wage and salary earners,* 1,698,300; *insured unemployed,* 70,-700 (4.5%).

WOMEN

Women continued their gains for equality on many fronts in 1975. Significantly, Carla Anderson Hills was appointed secretary of Housing and Urban Development by President Gerald R. Ford. Hills, a lawyer and former assistant attorney general, is the first woman to hold the post and only the third woman cabinet member in U. S. history. Carol C. Laise, a State Department veteran, became the first woman to serve as director general of the Foreign Service.

Betty S. Murphy, previously a labor lawyer for both unions and management, was named to chair the National Labor Relations Board. Alice Mitchell Rivlin, a Brookings Institution economist, became the $40,000-a-year director of the new Congressional Budget Office. President Ford appointed Margita White his deputy press secretary and by executive order continued the Citizens' Advisory Council on the Status of Women for 1975–76.

Equal Rights Amendment. North Dakota, which in 1973 had rejected the Equal Rights Amendment (ERA), became the 34th state to ratify the measure. Despite the endorsement of President Ford, personal messages of support from Mrs. Ford, and the backing of virtually all women's organizations, the legislatures of Oklahoma, Arizona, Nevada, Georgia, and Utah rejected the amendment. The legislatures of Virginia and Louisiana refused to bring it to a vote.

Proponents of ERA redoubled efforts to obtain the required total of 38 approving states needed by 1979 to make it law. The National Federation of Business and Professional Women's Clubs voted $250,000 a year to support the amendment. The National Women's Political Caucus made defeat of candidates opposing it a 1976 goal.

Audrey Rowe Colom of Washington, D. C., a black woman who headed the Children's Defense Fund, was elected president of the National Women's Political Caucus at its second biennial convention. Colom, a Republican, defeated two opponents to succeed Frances (Sissy) Farenthold, Texas Democratic leader, in the post.

Banking and Credit. The First Women's Bank, a full service bank organized by women and with

UPI

Audrey Rowe Colom (*above, left*) was elected to succeed Frances Farenthold as president of the National Women's Political Caucus. (*Below*) New York's Lt. Gov. Mary Anne Krupsak opens an account at The First Women's Bank.

UPI

International Women's Year

Most of the world officially observed 1975 as International Women's Year (IWY). By vote, resolution, or proclamation, officials of public and private organizations and institutions promised new efforts to make a reality "the equal rights of men and women" pledged by member nations at the organization of the United Nations 30 years earlier.

A stylized peace dove, bearing the female symbol and equality sign, was designed by Valerie Pettis, a U. S. artist, and adopted by the UN as the official IWY emblem. It appeared on jewelry and posters. Achievements and aspirations of women were celebrated in many countries by exhibits, conferences, and issuance of commemorative postage stamps.

World Conference. The high point of the IWY observance was the UN World Conference, the first global meeting devoted to the women's movement. Held in Mexico City, this conference resulted largely from the planning and fund-raising of Helvi Sipila, a Finnish lawyer. A former president of the International Federation of Women Lawyers and Zonta International, she became the first woman named to a top UN job when she was appointed assistant secretary general for social development and humanitarian affairs in 1972.

As secretary general for IWY, she presided at the conference held from June 19–July 2, and attended by 1,300 delegates and advisers from 133 nations. These included Prime Minister Sirimavo Bandaranaike of Sri Lanka; Valentina V. Nikolayeva-Tereshkova of the Soviet Union, the world's first woman astronaut; and Françoise Giroud, France's secretary of state for women's affairs.

Across the Mexican city, meanwhile, Mildred Persinger of Dobbs Ferry, N. Y., a representative of the World Y. W. C. A. Council, presided over the Tribune, a nongovernmental forum. This was attended by 6,000 people, nearly all of them women, representing 91 countries, 8 liberation movements, and 114 organizations old and new.

Tribune speakers included Betty Friedan, founder of the National Organization for Women, as well as members of the Congress of Racial Equality, League of Women Voters, American Association of University Women, the American Association for the Advancement of Science, and many other groups. The Tribune reported both meetings in a lively daily paper, the *Xilonen,* named after the Aztec goddess of tender corn, who symbolized women's concern with health and nutrition. It was edited by Marjorie Paxson of the *Philadelphia Bulletin.*

U. S. Representatives. With 37 women and 6 men, the U. S. delegation was the largest at the conference. Japan was next with 33 people. Heading the U. S. group was Patricia Hutar, U. S. representative to the UN Commission on the Status of Women. Cohead for the first three days was Daniel Parker, administrator, Agency for International Development.

Other official U. S. representatives were Jewel LaFontant, former deputy solicitor general, Department of Justice; and Jill E. Ruckelshaus, an executive of the National Center for Voluntary Action. Ruckelshaus also chaired the National Commission on the Observance of IWY, a group appointed by President Gerald R. Ford. The group also included Patricia Carbine, publisher of *Ms.* magazine, Gov. Ella T. Grasso of Connecticut, Patricia Hutar, Anne L. Armstrong, Helen Copley, Lenore Hershey, Clare Boothe Luce, Barbara Walters and other well-known women.

A 10-Year Plan of Action. In advance of the Mexico City conference, UN committees drafted a 10-year plan of action with target dates for elimination of discrimination against women in education and all other phases of life. There were specific suggestions for placement of more women in higher levels at the UN. At the IWY meeting delegates proposed 894 changes in the world plan of action; more were received from the Tribune.

Third World nations demanded amendments seeking solutions to social and economic problems and for the elimination of Zionism, colonialism, and apartheid. Both major amendments passed, the latter by a vote of 89 to 2 with 18 abstentions. The negative votes were recorded by the United States and Israel.

Delegates unanimously adopted most of the proposals and took them home for presentation to their governments. One said "while sovereign states have a right to determine their own . . . population policies, individuals and couples should have access . . . to the information and means . . . to determine the number and spacing of their children."

IWY in the United States. IWY observances in the United States included the issuance of a commemorative stamp designed by Miriam Schottland of New York. The first UN stamp designed by a man-woman team, Asher Calderon and Ms. E. Kurti of Israel, marked IWY with male and female figures linked by an equals sign. While some were critical of the IWY conference, many believed it worthwhile. "The women's movement for the first time has a global focus," said Congresswoman Bella Abzug. The UN has proposed another world-wide conference, probably in Teheran in 1980 or 1985.

CAROLINE BIRD

President Luis Echeverría of Mexico is applauded after his address to the delegates to the World Conference of the International Women's Year, which was held in Mexico City in June.

UPI

80% of its $3 million capital from women, opened in New York City on Oct. 16, 1975.

The bank president is Madeline McWhinney, who had been the Federal Reserve Bank of New York's first woman assistant vice president. Mary Anne Krupsak, New York's lieutenant governor, and feminist movement leaders were among the first to open accounts. The bank's 7,000 stockholders include such women's colleges as Smith, Mt. Holyoke, Simmons, and Wellesley. Similar banks are planned in Los Angeles, San Diego and San Francisco, Calif.; Seattle, Wash.; Chicago, Ill.; Washington, D. C.; and Greenwich, Conn.

The Wells Fargo Bank of San Francisco announced that it expects 40% of its officers to be women by 1979. In a class-action-suit settlement approved by a federal court judge, the Ranier National Bank, Wash., agreed to spend $300,000 training women employees for better jobs.

Stiffer rules outlawing sex discrimination in the granting of credit were put in effect by the Federal Reserve Board. The stricter regulations implemented congressional action and heeded many suggestions of the National Organization for Women, Women's Equity Action League, and other women's organizations. Creditors may no longer cancel a woman's credit simply because she becomes separated or divorced. A married woman may have charge accounts in her maiden name. Interviewers cannot ask a woman credit applicant about her child-bearing intentions.

Education. The U. S. Air Force, Army, Coast Guard, and Naval academies were opened to women by an amendment attached to a Department of Defense appropriations bill passed by Congress. The corps of cadets at West Point expected to add 80 women in the fall of 1976.

College women in Reserve Officer Training Corps programs increased from 212 in 1972 to more than 6,000 in 1975. Congress defeated efforts to weaken Department of Health, Education, and Welfare rules prohibiting sex discrimination in federally-aided education programs.

Women are eligible for Rhodes scholarships for the first time in 1976. A woman, Dr. Lorene L. Rogers, was named president of the University of Texas, despite some student and faculty protests. Enrollment in women's colleges increased by 3% in the fall of 1975 over fall of 1974. Medical school freshmen classes had enrollments of 22% women in 1975 compared to 18% a year earlier.

Miscellaneous. In fiscal 1975, the Department of Labor ruled that $26,484,860 was owed to 31,843 workers by employers who had violated the Equal Pay Act, compared with $20,-623,830 found owed to 32,792 workers in 1974. A U. S. Supreme Court decision ruled a woman's Social Security taxes should benefit her surviving spouse as well as vice versa. The court also decided that the age for adulthood in state laws must be the same for both men and women. A U. S. court of appeals ruled that the General Electric Company's employee medical plan should cover pregnancy. A Pentagon ruling allowed pregnant women to remain in military service.

A California supreme court decision overturned a long-standing law requiring judges to tell juries that rape is easily charged and difficult to defend. Congress authorized a National Center for the Prevention and Control of Rape. Susan Brownmiller's book on rape, *Against Our Will,* received widespread attention.

CAROLINE BIRD, *Author of "Born Female" and "Enterprising Women"*

WYOMING

In 1975 Wyoming struggled to find the best way to use its various natural resources. Former Gov. Stanley K. Hathaway was confirmed as secretary of the interior in June but resigned the post in July.

Energy Development. Several problems in resources development were evident during 1975. Small Wyoming towns located near resources experienced a variety of community problems due to the rapid population growth accompanying development. Certain new coal-development plans in the Powder River Basin were halted by a suit in federal courts instituted by the Sierra Club and others against the secretary of the interior. The suit requires the federal government to file a regional impact statement before development can continue. A federal appeals court issued an injunction against the approval of new mining plans before the impact study is completed. The lifting of a federal moratorium on coal leasing also depends on the Sierra Club suit. The Wyoming state treasurer estimated that the state would lose nearly $28 million in coal severance taxes in 1975–77 while the study is completed, but this claim was disputed by the Sierra Club.

In another energy-development problem, a proposed coal-slurry pipeline was snagged in several ways. The proposed pipeline would carry some 25 million tons of coal a year from Wyoming to Arkansas. The project had been approved by the legislature, and the state engineer issued the necessary permits to use water from the deep Madison formation. However, the water was potable and not brackish, as originally claimed. South Dakota threatened a lawsuit over the use of the water underlying portions of both states, and railroads balked at providing rights-of-way to a slurry line they estimated might cost them $150 million a year in coal-hauling fees.

Pipeline backers attempted to persuade the U. S. Congress to permit the company to exercise eminent domain if necessary to acquire easements across railroads and other private property. In late October the company that would build the line was accused of pressuring a federal researcher to attach a disclaimer on his report that reflected unfavorably on certain aspects of the slurry method as compared to railroads. Earlier, there had been criticism of the issuance of a study grant to the company by a federal agency without competitive bidding.

Legislature. The legislature met in regular session with the smallest Republican majority in recent years and the first Democratic governor since 1959. Gov. Ed Herschler's charge to the legislature centered around the external pressures on Wyoming's resources because of the energy squeeze. The legislature responded with several important pieces of legislation including a plant-siting act, a land-use planning law, a community development authority, a coal-impact

——— WYOMING · Information Highlights ———

Area: 97,914 square miles (253,597 sq km).
Population (1974 est.): 359,000. *Density:* 4 per sq mi.
Chief Cities (1970 census): Cheyenne, the capital, 40,-914; Casper, 39,361; Laramie, 23,143; Rock Springs, 11,657.
Government (1975): *Chief Officers*—governor, Ed Herschler (D); secy. of state, Thyra Thomson (R). *Legislature*—Senate, 30 members; House of Representatives, 62 members.
Education (1974–75): *Enrollment*—public elementary schools, 45,768; public secondary schools, 40,816; nonpublic schools, 2,100; colleges and universities, 19,447 students. *Public school expenditures*, $93,-073,000 ($1,165 per pupil).
State Finances (fiscal year 1974): *Revenues*, $309,700,-000; *expenditures*, $270,990,000.
Personal Income (1974): $1,851,000,000; per capita, $5,-156.
Labor Force (Aug. 1975): *Nonagricultural wage and salary earners*, 145,500; *insured unemployed*, 1,600.

tax, and an optional 1% sales tax to meet impact problems. There were certain additional air-, land-, and water-quality protection acts.

Agriculture. Wyoming still ranked high as an agricultural state despite the impact of energy development. The state was 2nd in the United States in numbers of sheep and lambs, 20th in beef cattle, and among the top 10 in sugar beet and dry bean production. The trend toward fewer owners and larger spreads continued, with the average farm size reaching 4,338 acres (1,775 hectares).

JOHN B. RICHARD
University of Wyoming

YUGOSLAVIA

Domestic political stability was maintained in 1975 although measures to stifle critics and opponents were taken to insure against post-Tito disturbances. On February 28, a federal council for the defense of the constitutional order was established, composed of the eight highest state and party officials under the chairmanship of Vladimir Bakarić, vice president of Yugoslavia.

Eight dissident members of the University of Belgrade's philosophy department were suspended on January 28 by the Assembly of the Republic of Serbia. On February 21, the Zagreb-based philosophical journal *Praxis* was forced to cease publication. A week later, writer Mihajlo Mihajlov was sentenced to seven years imprisonment for spreading hostile propaganda. On Jan. 14, 1975, five Yugoslavs of Albanian nationality were jailed for subversive activities in the autonomous province of Kosovo. On February 17, 15 members of a so-called Croatian Liberation Army received severe prison terms.

By the year's end, key party leaders strongly attacked domestic Stalinist influences and attempts to set up illegal organizations. Internal security organs arrested several groups of allegedly pro-Moscow Communists.

Economy. Unfavorable international and domestic factors contributed to an overall negative performance by the national economy. Industrial production during the first eight months of 1975

was 6.3% over the same period in 1974. Labor productivity in particular reflected slow growth. The inflation rate was one of the highest in Europe, over 30%, and real personal income during the first eight months of 1975 was 2% lower than during the same period in 1974. The wheat harvest in 1975 was 33% below the bumper harvest in 1974; however, the corn harvest maintained the 1974 level. Reduced export possibilities and soaring inflation during the first six months of 1975 contributed to a heavy trade deficit, which increased 18% over the first half of 1974. Remittances from emigrant workers and from foreign tourists were also below expectations. Tens of thousands of Yugoslav citizens returning from employment abroad, as a result of the West European recession, had difficulties finding jobs. There were 500,000 persons seeking work in April, up 20% from the previous year.

Foreign Relations. Yugoslav-Soviet relations continued to be close formally, but there were underlying tensions. During Premier Džemal Bijedić's official visit to the Soviet Union on April 9–15, agreements on cooperation in nuclear energy and trade were signed. In May, however, Yugoslav sources indicated reluctance to follow Moscow's line for the planned meeting of European Communist parties.

The Yugoslav-Chinese rapprochement was heralded by both sides during Premier Bijedić's October visit to the People's Republic of China, where he met with Chairman Mao Tse-tung. On his Asian tour, Bijedić also visited North Vietnam and India. North Korean President Kim Il Sung visited Yugoslavia on June 5–9 and received Tito's endorsement of his foreign policy.

Yugoslav-U. S. relations also fluctuated. The Yugoslav press often strongly criticized U. S. foreign and domestic policies. Premier Bijedić's official visit to Washington, March 19–21, resulted in an agreement to further economic and financial cooperation. On March 31, the U. S. Export-Import Bank granted Yugoslavia a $9.1 million credit for industrial equipment. At the same time, Yugoslavia was one of the few Communist-ruled states to receive special U. S. tariff concessions extended to developing countries. On

UPI

Presidents Ford (*left*) and Tito (*right*) discuss economic problems during Ford's visit to Yugoslavia.

August 3–4, President Ford visited Yugoslavia and conferred at length with Tito. The problem of the U. S. embargo on arms supplies to Yugoslavia was on the agenda. In a speech at a banquet for President Ford, Tito stated that Israel had to evacuate Arab territories to ensure its own independence.

Relations between Yugoslavia and the European Economic Community were strengthened by a trade pact concluded on July 24. On November 10, Yugoslavia and Italy signed an agreement ending their 30-year frontier dispute over Trieste. Italy renounced claims to the area on the Istrian Peninsula south of Trieste known as Zone B, and Yugoslavia recognized Italian sovereignty over a strip north of Trieste, known as Zone A.

Greek Premier Constantine Caramanlis visited Belgrade on June 3, but his purpose of advancing Balkan cooperation was thwarted by the continuing Yugoslav-Bulgarian disputes over Macedonia. Yugoslav-Rumanian relations, however, remained close. In April the two countries successfully tested a jointly-produced military aircraft. In July and August, Tito headed the Yugoslav delegation to the Helsinki summit conference.

MILORAD M. DRACHKOVITCH
Stanford University

YUGOSLAVIA · Information Highlights

Official Name: Socialist Federal Republic of Yugoslavia.
Location: Southeastern Europe.
Area: 98,766 square miles (255,804 sq km).
Population (1975 est.): 21,300,000.
Chief Cities (1974 est.): Belgrade, the capital, 845,000; Zagreb, 602,000; Skopje, 389,000.
Government: *Head of state,* Tito (Josip Broz), president (took office 1953). *Head of government,* Džemal Bijedić, prime minister (took office 1971). *Legislature*—Federal Assembly: Federal Chamber and Chamber of Republics and Provinces.
Monetary Unit: Dinar (17 dinars equal U. S.$1, May 1975).
Gross National Product (1973 est.): $18,400,000,000.
Manufacturing (major products): Iron and steel, processed foods, chemicals, machinery, textiles.
Major Agricultural Products: Corn, wheat, fruits, potatoes, sugar beets, forest products, fish, livestock.
Foreign Trade (1974 est.): *Exports,* $3,700,000,000; *imports,* $7,500,000,000.

YUKON TERRITORY

Issues and events surrounding native land-claims negotiations, hydroelectric power development, and the possible route and impact of a pipeline dominated the headlines in 1975.

Government and Politics. Yukon attained a measure of fiscal autonomy when the federal government promised to share resource revenues. The Council of Yukon Indians accepted the federal government's settlement proposal as a working paper and Mar. 31, 1976, was estab-

Area: 207,076 square miles (536,327 sq km).
Population (1975 est.): 21,000.
Chief City (1971 census): Whitehorse, the capital, 11,-600.
Government (1975): *Chief Officers*—commissioner, James Smith; asst. commissioner, J. B. Fingland. *Legislature*—Territorial Council, 12 members.
Education (1975–76): *Enrollment:* public elementary and secondary schools, 5,660 pupils. *Public school expenditures* (1972), $6,742,000.
Public Finance (fiscal year 1974–75 est.): *Revenues,* $44,000,000; *expenditures,* $55,000,000.

lished as the deadline for agreement in principle on the crucial land-claims question. Two by-elections were held, one after a territorial councillor resigned over alleged voting irregularities.

Economy and Development. The Northern Canada power commission completed its controversial 32-megawatt hydroelectric power installation at Aishihik Lake. Throughout 1975, the Berger Inquiry continued to hear testimony about alternative routes, construction, and the social and environmental effects of a pipeline across Yukon. Expenditure on mineral exploration in 1975 was $18 million, a 50% increase over 1974.

W. BRIAN SPEIRS, *Territorial Archivist*

ZAIRE

The regime of President Mobutu Sese Seko celebrated its tenth anniversary on Nov. 24, 1975, in an atmosphere marred by financial difficulties, domestic unrest, and a deepening embroilment in the problems of Angola.

Economy. With the price of copper dropping from $3,000 a ton in 1973 to $1,000 in 1975, and with the price of imports rising sharply, Zaire's economic position became increasingly precarious. The servicing and repayment of the numerous loans incurred by Zaire to finance its ambitious development projects weighed heavily on the national budget. From $58 million in

1973, this burden grew to $315 million in 1975 (28.3% of the budget), creating what was euphemistically described as "a cash flow problem" for the country.

The economic downturn led to a general retrenchment of development projects and to attempts to cushion the effects of a massive inflation on the wage-earning population. Plans to boost the country's copper-producing capacity to 600,000 tons were still being implemented, however. The government planned to take control of the marketing of its mineral products and to initiate the construction of a copper-refining plant on its own territory.

Politics. Through the end of 1974, Mobutu attempted to restore his damaged credibility and to defuse domestic discontent by a number of spectacular moves. These included repeated denunciations of the self-serving "national bourgeoisie," which had been the mainstay of his regime, and the announcement of a "revolution within the revolution." After a year-end trip to China and North Korea, he prompted the political bureau of Zaire's single party to launch a massive campaign of agricultural development and ideological indoctrination along Chinese lines. The executive council (cabinet) was thoroughly reshuffled, and one of its senior members was charged with corruption. On that occasion, Mobutu also assumed direct control over the department of defense in an apparent attempt to tighten his hold of the military, whose lack of involvement in the developmental task had been criticized. Finally, the government decided to dispense with the legislative elections scheduled for the fall of 1975, although this involved only the ratification of a single list of candidates selected by the party. Instead, the new members of the legislature were declared "elected by acclamation" after their names had been publicly read off in all towns and villages.

People's Revolutionary Party. On May 19, 1975, a party of Zairese rebels claiming membership in the People's Revolutionary party (PRP) kidnapped three U. S. and one Dutch student from a zoological research center on the Tanzanian side of Lake Tanganyika and ferried them back to their stronghold in eastern Zaire. The embarrassed Mobutu government, reluctant to admit that the rebel movement that it had officially crushed in 1965 had never been fully eradicated, refused to negotiate with the kidnappers. The Zaire government even failed to aid in the release of the four hostages which had been arranged by private U. S. citizens and the U. S. ambassador to Tanzania.

Attempted Coup. A far more serious threat to the regime emerged in Kinshasa in the form of an attempted coup involving 11 generals, Mobutu's personal assistant in charge of security intelligence, a cabinet minister, and several other prominent personalities. Seven of the alleged conspirators were sentenced to death and 27 to various prison terms. However, the trial pro-

Zaire's President Mobutu welcomed France's President Giscard d'Estaing in Kinshasa in August.

UPI

ZAIRE · Information Highlights

Official Name: Republic of Zaire.
Location: Central equatorial Africa.
Area: 905,565 square miles (2,345,409 sq km).
Population (1975 est.): 24,500,000.
Chief Cities (1972 est.): Kinshasa, the capital, 1,623,760; Luluabourg, 506,000.
Government: *Head of state,* Mobutu Sese Seko, president (took office Nov. 1965). *Head of government,* Mobutu Sese Seko. *Legislature* (unicameral)—National Legislative Council.
Monetary Unit: Zaire (0.50 zaire equals U. S.$1, July 1975).
Gross National Product (1974 est.): $3,500,000,000.
Manufacturing (major products): Processed foods, clothing, textiles, soap.
Major Agricultural Products: Palm oil and kernels, coffee, rubber, tea, cacao, groundnuts, bananas, cassava.
Foreign Trade (1973): *Exports,* $805,000,000; *imports,* $605,000,000.

cedure was so irregular that the chief justice refused to be associated with it, a gesture for which he was deported to his native village. A thorough purge of the army also followed the abortive coup.

Relations with the United States. Charges by the government that the U. S. Central Intelligence Agency had been involved in the projected coup came as an even greater surprise than the attempt itself, given the consistent support extended by the United States to Mobutu since 1960. The Mobutu government demanded the recall of U. S. ambassador Deane Hinton, whose name had earlier been linked with the "destabilization" of the Allende government in Chile, but former U. S. ambassador to Kinshasa Sheldon Vance was quickly dispatched to Zaire and soon restored normal relations between the two countries. By the end of the year, the Ford administration was asking a reluctant Congress to approve an $80 million aid package to Zaire.

Angola. Overlapping U. S. and Zairese interests in neighboring Angola probably accounted for the eagerness with which both countries patched up their momentary differences. For years, Zaire actively supported the U. S.-backed Angolan National Liberation Front (FNLA) led by Mobutu's brother-in-law, Holden Roberto. As the rival nationalist movements in Angola edged toward open civil war, the FNLA's military capability was vastly enhanced by assistance received from Kinshasa. U. S. Senate investigations confirmed that Washington was backing Mobutu's intervention in Angola, as well as in the Cabinda enclave, whose extensive oil resources are being exploited by the Gulf Oil Corp. By the end of the year, it was still unclear how deeply the Mobutu regime could involve itself in the Angola situation without jeopardizing its own domestic stability.

EDOUARD BUSTIN
Boston University

ZOOLOGY

Although marine biology and animal behavior were probably the fields of greatest interest to zoologists in 1975, various environmental problems, especially those of rare and endangered species, continued to be featured in the popular press.

Pesticides. David W. Johnson of the University of Florida reported a decline of DDT in migratory songbirds since it was outlawed in the United States in 1972. However, a report in *Science* (April 25, 1975) indicated that the pesticide Toxaphene, hailed as a "safe" replacement for DDT, is an environmental contaminant. Among other "bad effects," Toxaphene in ponds and streams results in stunted growth and weak bones in fish, even in the minute amounts reaching watercourses in farm areas.

Evolution. Charles Darwin's theory of natural selection, of interest since the mid-19th century, received new attention. The publication, in 1975, of Darwin's *Natural Selection: Being the Second Part of His Big Species Book Written from 1856 to 1858,* edited by R. C. Stauffer (Cambridge University Press), was hailed as a major zoology landmark. Until it appeared, few had ever seen the material from which the famous *The Origin of Species* was abstracted, and most did not even know that it was an abstract.

Paleontology. Douglas A. Lawson of the University of California, Berkeley, reported a spectacular fossil, a pterosaur from the late Cretaceous of west Texas. This flying reptile, with probable vulture-like food habits, had a wingspread of almost 51 feet (15.5 meters), making it the largest known flying creature.

Thousands of tiny fossils, 0.1–0.2 inches (5–10 mm) in diameter, have been collected in four different Iowa counties since they were first reported in 1902. Richard A. Davis of the University of Cincinnati and Holmes A. Semken, Jr., of the University of Iowa finally de-

A six-gilled shark, which could grow to be the largest in captivity, is exercised to restore proper breathing at the Vancouver (British Columbia) Aquarium.

UPI

The first whooping crane (*left*) ever bred in captivity was hatched in Maryland in May by the U.S. Fish and Wildlife Service. (*Below*) Dozens of enthusiasts view a small bird believed to be a Ross's Gull (the smaller of the two at left), a Siberian bird rarely seen in North America. It was spotted in Massachusetts in March.

scribed these "horse-collars" (so-called because of their shape) as a new genus and species of unknown affinities. By year's end, paleontologists still could not agree whether these fossils were plants or animals, let alone what parts were represented.

Behavior. Colonial nesting birds, such as bank swallows, all produce their young at about the same time. Often this has been attributed to a similar response to some environmental "trigger." Stephen T. Emlen and Natalie J. Demong of Cornell University showed that synchronous breeding has great survival value to the species. Demands for food are high when nestlings must be fed. However, areas of concentration of food sources (airborne insects) constantly shift, influenced by winds and other factors, and these birds appear to use a "pooling of information" about such sources. The information pooling may be inadvertently achieved when individuals returning to nest sites after an unsuccessful hunt follow other birds to food sources. The end result is better-fed young with a higher survival rate.

Mutualism is a biological state in which two organisms live in an association beneficial to both and without which neither can survive. A classic example is the relationship between the termite, which cannot digest the cellulose in its food, and the protozoon that lives in the termite's digestive tract and cannot survive outside. The protozoon digests enough cellulose for its own needs and the termite's. In contrast, a parasite survives at the expense of, and contributes nothing to, its host.

Daniel H. Janzen of the University of Michigan discovered a species that is parasitic on the mutualism between certain Central American ants and certain swollen-thorn acacias. The acacias produce food and nesting structures for the ants. In return, the ants patrol the acacia's leaves and stems, protecting it from herbivores and vines. The ants cannot survive elsewhere, and the acacia rarely survives to maturity without the ants' services. The parasite on this relationship is another ant species that uses the acacia's food and nesting sites but does nothing to protect the plant.

E. LENDELL COCKRUM
University of Arizona

contributors

Following is a complete list of the distinguished authorities who contributed articles to this edition of the annual. Their professional affiliations are shown, together with the titles of their articles.

ADAMS, GEORGE, Legislative Reference Librarian, Connecticut State Library: BIOGRAPHY—*Ella Grasso:* CONNECTICUT

ADRIAN, CHARLES R., Professor of Political Science, University of California, Riverside: BIOGRAPHY—*Edmund G. Brown;* CALIFORNIA

ALEXANDER, ROBERT J., Professor of Economics and Political Science, Rutgers Univ.: ECUADOR; GUYANA; URUGUAY

ALLER, LAWRENCE H., Professor of Astronomy, University of California, Los Angeles: ASTRONOMY

ALVEY, EDWARD, JR., Professor Emeritus of Education, Mary Washington College: EDUCATION

AMBRE, AGO, Economist, Bureau of Economic Analysis, U. S. Department of Commerce: INDUSTRIAL REVIEW

AMSPOKER, JOANNE, Professor of History, Oregon College of Education: OREGON

BALLINGER, RONALD B., Professor and Chairman, Department of History, Rhode Island College: SOUTH AFRICA

BANKS, RONALD F., Associate Professor of History, University of Maine: MAINE

BENDIG, WILLIAM C., Publisher and Editor-in-Chief, *The Art Gallery Magazine:* ART

BERGEN, DANIEL P., Professor, Graduate Library School, University of Rhode Island: LIBRARIES

BEST, JOHN, Chief, *Canada World News,* Ottawa: CITIES AND URBAN AFFAIRS—*Vancouver;* NEW BRUNSWICK; PRINCE EDWARD ISLAND

BIRD, CAROLINE, Author, *Born Female, Everything a Woman Needs to Know to Get Paid What She's Worth,* and *Enterprising Women:* WOMEN—*Special Report: International Women's Year*

BITTON, LIVIA E., Assistant Professor of Classical and Oriental Languages, Herbert H. Lehman College, City University of New York: RELIGION—*Judaism*

BLOODSWORTH, DAVID R., Assistant Director, Labor Relations and Research Center, University of Massachusetts: POSTAL SERVICE

BÖDVARSSON, HAUKUR, Editorial Staff, *Iceland Review:* ICELAND

BOULAY, HARVEY, Assistant Professor of Political Science, Boston University: MASSACHUSETTS

BOVEY, JOHN A., Provincial Archivist of Manitoba: MANITOBA

BOWERS, Q. DAVID, Columnist, *Coin World;* Author, *Coins and Collectors, High Profits from Rare Coin Investment,* and *Coin Collecting for Profit:* COIN COLLECTING

BRADDOCK, BILL, Sports Department, *The New York Times:* BIOGRAPHY—*Arthur Ashe, Chris Evert;* SPORTS

BRAMMER, DANA B., Assistant Director, Bureau of Governmental Research, University of Mississippi: MISSISSIPPI

BURKHEAD, JESSE, Professor of Economics, Syracuse University: TAXATION

BURKS, ARDATH W., Professor of Political Science and Associate Vice President for Academic Affairs, Rutgers University: JAPAN; BIOGRAPHY—*Takeo Miki*

BURLINGAME, MERRILL G., Professor of History, Montana State University: MONTANA

BUSH, G. W. A., Senior Lecturer in Political Science, University of Auckland: NEW ZEALAND

BUSTIN, EDOUARD, Professor of Political Science, Boston University; Author, *Luanda Under British Rule, The Politics of Ethnicity:* ANGOLA; CAPE VERDE; GUINEA-BISSAU; MOZAMBIQUE; SÃO TOMÉ AND PRÍNCIPE; ZAIRE

BUTWELL, RICHARD, Dean of Arts and Sciences, State University of New York College at Fredonia; Author, *Southeast Asia: A Political Introduction, Southeast Asia—Today and Tomorrow,* and *U Nu of Burma:* SOUTHEAST ASIA—*The New Era;* BURMA; CAMBODIA; LAOS; PHILIPPINES; VIETNAM

CAIRNS, JOHN C., Professor of History, University of Toronto: FRANCE

CANFIELD, ROBERT L., Associate Professor of Anthropology, Washington University, St. Louis: ETHNIC GROUPS

CANN, STAN, State Editor, *The Forum:* NORTH DAKOTA

CARDWELL, JAMES B., formerly, Commissioner of Social Security: SOCIAL WELFARE—*Social Security*

CHALMERS, J. W., Faculty of Education, University of Alberta: ALBERTA

CHEVRETTE, FRANÇOIS, Associate Professor, Faculty of Law, University of Montreal: CITIES AND URBAN AFFAIRS—*Montreal*

CLARK, C. B., Graduate Assistant in History, University of Oklahoma: OKLAHOMA

COCKRUM, E. LENDELL, Professor of Biological Sciences, University of Arizona: ZOOLOGY

COHEN, SIDNEY, Professor of Psychiatry, University of California, Los Angeles: DRUG ADDICTION AND ABUSE

COLE, CAROLYN J., Paine, Webber, Jackson & Curtis Inc.: STOCKS AND BONDS

COPPAGE, NOEL, Contributing Editor, *Stereo Review:* MUSIC—*Popular Music;* RECORDINGS—*Popular Records*

CORLEW, ROBERT E., Chairman, Department of History, Middle Tennessee State University: TENNESSEE

CORNWELL, ELMER E., JR., Professor of Political Science, Brown University: RHODE ISLAND

CURTIS, L. PERRY, JR., Professor of History, Brown University: IRELAND

DARBY, JOSEPH W., III, Assistant City Editor, *The Times-Picayune,* New Orleans: LOUISIANA

DAVIS, WILLIAM A., Travel Editor, *Boston Globe:* TRAVEL

DeBUSK, A. GIB, Department of Biological Sciences, The Florida State University: BIOCHEMISTRY

DELZELL, CHARLES F., Professor of History, Vanderbilt University: ITALY

DOBLER, CLIFFORD, Professor, College of Business Law, University of Idaho: IDAHO

DOLAN, PAUL, Professor of Political Science, University of Delaware: DELAWARE

DORPALEN, ANDREAS, Professor of History, The Ohio State University: GERMANY

DRACHKOVITCH, MILORAD M., Senior Fellow, The Hoover Institution, Stanford University: YUGOSLAVIA

DRIGGS, DON W., Chairperson, Department of Political Science, University of Nevada, Reno: NEVADA

DUFF, ERNEST A., Professor of Political Science, Randolph-Macon Woman's College: COLOMBIA

DURRENCE, J. LARRY, Department of History, Florida Southern College: FLORIDA

ELKINS, ANN, Fashion Director, *Good Housekeeping Magazine:* FASHION

ERSHKOWITZ, MIRIAM, Temple University; Coauthor, *Black Politics in Philadelphia:* PENNSYLVANIA

ESKENAZI, GERALD, Sports Reporter, *The New York Times;* Author, *A Thinking Man's Guide To Pro Hockey, Year on Ice:* HOCKEY FEVER—*Professional Hockey*

ETCHESON, WARREN W., Associate Dean, School of Business Administration, University of Washington: WASHINGTON

EWEGEN, BOB, Staff Writer, The Denver *Post:* COLORADO

FANNING, JAMES, Landscape Architect and contributor to garden magazines: THE BOOM IN HOUSEPLANTS

FELDBAUM, ELEANOR G., Research Associate, Bureau of Governmental Research, University of Maryland: WASHINGTON, D. C.

FISHER, SIDNEY NETTLETON, Emeritus Professor of History, The Ohio State University: BIOGRAPHY—*Khalid;* OBITUARIES—*Faisal;* SAUDI ARABIA

FRIIS, ERIK J., Editor and Publisher, *The Scandinavian-American Bulletin:* DENMARK; FINLAND; SWEDEN

FURIE, KENNETH, Music Editor, *High Fidelity Magazine:* MUSIC—*Classical Music;* RECORDINGS—*Classical Records*

GAILEY, HARRY A., Professor of History, San Jose State University: NIGERIA

GEIS, GILBERT, Professor, Program in Social Ecology, University of California, Irvine; Author, *Man, Crime, and Society:* CRIME

GJESTER, THOR, City Editor, *Norwegian Journal of Commerce and Shipping,* Oslo: NORWAY

GOODMAN, DONALD, John Jay College of Criminal Justice, City University of New York: PRISONS

GORDON, MAYNARD M., Editor, *Motor News Analysis* and *The Imported Car Reports:* AUTOMOBILES

GROTH, ALEXANDER J., Professor of Political Science, University of California, Davis: POLAND

GRUBER, MARTIN, Professor of Political Science, University of Wisconsin, Oshkosh: CIVIL LIBERTIES AND RIGHTS; LAW—*Special Report: Rights of Children*

GUNN, JOHN M., Professor of Radio-TV-Film, State University of New York at Albany: TELEVISION AND RADIO

GUTHERIDGE, GUY G., Director, Polar Information Service, Office of Polar Programs, National Science Foundation: POLAR RESEARCH

HAINES, WALTER W., Professor of Economics, New York University; Author, *Money, Prices and Policy:* BANKING

HAKES, JAY E., Associate Professor of Political Science, University of New Orleans: KENYA; TANZANIA; UGANDA

HALL, FRANCES L., Director, International Trade Analysis Division, Bureau of International Commerce, U. S. Department of Commerce: INTERNATIONAL TRADE

HALVORSEN, DAVID E., Assistant to the Editor, *Chicago Tribune:* ILLINOIS

HAND, SAM, Professor of History, University of Vermont: VERMONT

HARVEY, ROSS M., Chief of Publications, Department of Information, Government of Northwest Territories: NORTHWEST TERRITORIES

HAYDEN, DOROTHY, Prairie History Room, Regina Public Library, Sask.: SASKATCHEWAN

HAYES, KIRBY M., Professor of Food Science and Nutrition, University of Massachusetts: FOOD

HEAD, HOWARD T., Partner, A. D. Ring & Associates, Consulting Radio Engineers: TELEVISION AND RADIO—*Television and Radio Engineering*

HELMREICH, E. C., Thomas B. Reed Professor of History and Political Science,· Bowdoin College: AUSTRIA

HELMREICH, PAUL C., Professor of History, Wheaton College, Norton, Mass.: SWITZERLAND

HELMS, ANDREA R. C., Associate Professor of Political Science, University of Alaska, Fairbanks: ALASKA

HERBERT, WALTER B., Consultant on Canadian Cultural Matters; Fellow of the Royal Society of Arts: CANADA—*Cultural Affairs*

HERSHKOWITZ, LEO, Professor of History, Queens College, City University of New York: NEW YORK STATE

HODGES, RALPH W., Associate Technical Editor, *Stereo Review;* Contributing Editor, *Popular Electronics:* RECORDINGS—*Audio Equipment and Techniques*

HOGGART, SIMON, Parliamentary Correspondent, The Manchester *Guardian:* GREAT BRITAIN

HOOVER, HERBERT T., Professor of History, The University of South Dakota: SOUTH DAKOTA

HOPKINS, JAMES F., Professor Emeritus, Department of History, University of Kentucky: KENTUCKY

HOPKO, THOMAS, St. Vladimir's Orthodox Theological Seminary: RELIGION—*Orthodox Eastern Church*

HOWARD, HARRY N., Former Professor of Middle East Studies, The American University; Board of Governors, Middle East Institute: TURKEY

HUCKSHORN, ROBERT J., Professor and Chairman, Department of Political Science, Florida Atlantic University: BIOGRAPHY—*Gerald R. Ford*

JACKSON, JANE F., Medical Writer and Editor: PREVENTIVE HEALTH CARE—*Early Diagnosis*

JACOBS, WALTER DARNELL, Professor of Government and Politics, University of Maryland: BIOGRAPHY—*Henry Kissinger; Edward Levi; Nelson A. Rockefeller*

JAFFE, HERMAN, Department of Anthropology, Brooklyn College, City University of New York: ANTHROPOLOGY

JARVIS, ERIC, Department of History, University of Western Ontario: CITIES AND URBAN AFFAIRS—*Toronto*

JOHNSON, CERNORIA, Administration on Aging, Department of Health, Education, and Welfare: OLDER POPULATION—*Special Report: Nursing Homes*

JOHNSTONE, JOHN K., Professor and Chairman, Department of English, Univ. of Saskatchewan: LITERATURE—*English Literature*

JONES, H. G., Curator, North Carolina Collection, University of North Carolina Library: NORTH CAROLINA

KARSKI, JAN, Department of Government, Georgetown University: BULGARIA; HUNGARY

KEE, HERBERT W., Executive Director, Research and Analysis, Department of Economic Development, British Columbia: BRITISH COLUMBIA

KEHR, ERNEST A., Director, Stamp News Bureau: STAMP COLLECTING

KELLER, EUGENIA, Managing Editor, *Chemistry* Magazine: CHEMISTRY

KENNEDY, ROBERT E., JR., Associate Professor, Department of Sociology, University of Minnesota: POPULATION

KIMBALL, LORENZO K., Associate Professor of Political Science, University of Utah: UTAH

KIMBELL, CHARLES L., Physical Scientist, Office of Technical Data Services, United States Bureau of Mines: MINING

KING, PETER J., Associate Professor of History, Carleton University: OTTAWA

KLAUSLER, ALFRED P., Editor at Large, *Christian Century;* RELIGION—*Protestantism*

KOLLEGGER, JAMES G., President and Publisher, Environment Information Center, Inc.: ENVIRONMENT

KREBS, ALBIN, *The New York Times:* OBITUARIES—*Aristotle Onassis*

LAI, CHUEN-YAN DAVID, Associate Professor of Geography, University of Victoria, B. C.: HONG KONG

LANDSBERG, H. E., Professor, Institute for Fluid Dynamics and Applied Mathematics, University of Maryland: METEOROLOGY

LaPIERRE, LAURIER L., Professor of History, McGill University, Montreal: QUEBEC

LARSEN, WILLIAM, Professor of History, Radford College: VIRGINIA

LARSON, T. A., Professor of History, University of Wyoming; Author, *History of Wyoming:* WYOMING

LAWRENCE, ROBERT M., Department of Political Science, Colorado State University: ENERGY; MILITARY FORCES—*World Developments*

LEFEVER, ERNEST W., Senior Fellow, Foreign Policy Studies Program, The Brookings Institution: DISARMAMENT AND ARMS CONTROL

LEIDEN, CARL, Professor of Government, University of Texas at Austin: BANGLADESH; BIOGRAPHY—*Itzhak Rabin, Anwar el-Sadat;* EGYPT; NEPAL; PAKISTAN; THAILAND

LEVIN, RUBEN, Editor, *Labor* Newspaper: LABOR

LEVINE, EDWARD L., Professor of Government, Skidmore College: ELECTIONS AND POLITICAL PARTIES

LEWIS, OSCAR, *San Francisco: Mission to Metropolis, The Big Four,* and other books: CITIES AND URBAN AFFAIRS—*San Francisco*

LLOYD, ROBERT M., Director, Research and Management Services, South Carolina Appalachian Council of Governments: CITIES AND URBAN AFFAIRS

LOBRON, BARBARA, Writer, Editor, Photographer: PHOTOGRAPHY

LONSFORD, MIKE, *Houston Chronicle:* TEXAS

LOTT, LEO B., Professor and Chairman, Department of Political Science, University of Montana: PARAGUAY; VENEZUELA

MABRY, DONALD J., Associate Professor of History, Mississippi State University: MEXICO

MACAULAY, NEILL, Professor of History, University of Florida; Author, *The Prestes Column:* BRAZIL; LATIN AMERICA

McCORQUODALE, SUSAN, Associate Professor of Political Science, Memorial University of Newfoundland: NEWFOUNDLAND

McGILL, DAVID, Professor of Ocean Science, U. S. Coast Guard Academy: OCEANOGRAPHY

McKEON, NANCY, Editor, *African Update,* The African-American Institute: ALGERIA; MOROCCO; SUDAN; TUNISIA

McLEOD, W. REYNOLDS, Assistant Professor of History, West Virginia University: WEST VIRGINIA

MALCOLM, ANDREW, National Correspondent, *The New York Times;* Author, *Unknown Award:* SOUTHEAST ASIA —*Refugees*

MARCOPOULOS, GEORGE J., Associate Professor of History, Tufts University: CYPRUS; GREECE

MATHEWS, THOMAS G., Research Professor, Institute of Caribbean Studies, University of Puerto Rico: CARIBBEAN; PUERTO RICO; VIRGIN ISLANDS, U. S.

MATTHEWS, JOHN R., JR., Professor of Economics, College of William and Mary: THE NEW POWER IN THE MIDDLE EAST—*Iranian Petroleum Industry;* INTERNATIONAL FINANCE

MEMOLO, MARCELLA M., Public Information Officer, U. S. Agricultural Research Service: AGRICULTURE—*U. S. Agricultural Research*

MESSNER, STEPHEN D., Head, Department of Finance, School of Business Administration, University of Connecticut: HOUSING

METZEN, EDWARD, Department of Family Economics and Management, University of Missouri, Coauthor, *You Are A Consumer:* CONSUMERISM

MEYER, EDWARD H., Chairman of the Board and President, Grey Advertising Inc.: ADVERTISING

MEYER, RALPH C., Associate Professor of Political Science, Fordham University at Lincoln Center: ASIA

MILLER, LUTHER S., Editor, *Railway Age:* TRANSPORTATION —*Railroads*

MILLINGTON, THOMAS M., Chairman, Department of Political Science, Hobart and William Smith Colleges: BOLIVIA

MITCHELL, GARY, Professor of Physics, North Carolina State University at Raleigh: PHYSICS

MOORE, CHARLES W., Professor of Architecture, University of California, Los Angeles: ARCHITECTURE

MURPHY, OWEN J., JR., Editor, *The Catholic Free Press,* Worcester, Massachusetts: RELIGION—*Roman Catholicism;* OBITUARIES—*Cardinal Mindszenty*

MURPHY, THOMAS, Institute for Urban Studies, University of Maryland; Author, *Universities in the Urban Crisis:* MARYLAND

NEILL, R. F., Associate Professor of Economics, St. Patrick's College, Carleton University: BIOGRAPHY—*Pierre Trudeau;* CANADA; CANADA—*Special Report: Olympic Montreal*

NOLAN, WILLIAM C., Associate Professor of Political Science, Southern State College: ARKANSAS

NOWELL, CHARLES E., Professor of History, Emeritus, University of Illinois: PORTUGAL; SPAIN

OSTROW, RONALD J., Washington Correspondent, *Los Angeles Times:* UNITED STATES—*Special Report: Intelligence*

OTT, MARVIN C., Assistant Professor of Political Science, Mount Holyoke College: MALAYSIA; SINGAPORE

PALMER, NORMAN D., Professor of Political Science and South Asian Studies, University of Pennsylvania: BIOGRAPHY—*Indira Gandhi;* INDIA; SRI LANKA

PANO, NICHOLAS C., Assistant Professor of History, Western Illinois University: ALBANIA

PARKER, FRANKLIN, Benedum Professor of Education, West Virginia University: AFRICA; RHODESIA

PARTAN, DANIEL G., Professor of Law, Boston University: LAW—*International Law*

PEARCE, JOHN B., Officer-in-Charge, Sandy Hook Marine Laboratory, N. J., NOAA: MARINE BIOLOGY

PEARSON, NEALE J., Associate Professor of Government, Texas Tech University: CHILE; PERU

PERKINS, KENNETH J., Assistant Professor of History, University of South Carolina: LIBYA; RELIGION—*Islam*

PHEBUS, GEORGE E., JR., Supervisor, Processing Laboratory, Department of Anthropology, National Museum of Natural History, Smithsonian Institution: ARCHAEOLOGY—*Western Hemisphere*

PHILLIPS, JACKSON, Senior Vice President, Moody's Investors Service, Inc.: ECONOMY OF THE U. S.; ECONOMY OF THE U. S.—*Special Report: Unemployment*

PIPPIN, LARRY L., Professor of Political Science, Elbert Covell College, University of the Pacific: ARGENTINA; PANAMA

PLATT, HERMANN K., Associate Professor of History, St. Peter's College, Jersey City: NEW JERSEY

PLISCHKE, ELMER, Professor of Government and Politics, University of Maryland: SOUTHEAST ASIA—*American Foreign Policy and the Far East;* UNITED STATES—*Foreign Affairs*

POLK, IRWIN J., Director of Children's Allergy Service, St. Luke's Hospital, New York City: MEDICINE; PREVENTIVE HEALTH CARE—*Prenatal Diagnosis*

POPKIN, HENRY, Professor of English, State University of New York at Buffalo; Drama Critic, Westchester-Rockland Newspapers: THEATER

PORTER, J. R., Professor and Chairman, Department of Microbiology, College of Medicine, University of Iowa: MICROBIOLOGY

POULLADA, LEON, Northern Arizona University; Author, *Reform and Rebellion in Afghanistan:* AFGHANISTAN

PRITCHETT, C. HERMAN, Professor of Political Science, University of California, Santa Barbara: LAW—*Supreme Court*

PUMPHREY, RALPH E., Professor of Social Work, Washington University, St. Louis: SOCIAL WELFARE—*Survey, Child Welfare, Health Care*

QUIRK, WILLIAM H., North American Editor, *Construction Industry International* Magazine: ENGINEERING, CIVIL

RAYMOND, ELLSWORTH, Professor of Politics, New York University; Author, *The Soviet State* and *A Picture History of Eastern Europe:* BIOGRAPHY—*Leonid Brezhnev;* UNION OF SOVIET SOCIALIST REPUBLICS

RICARD, FRANÇOIS, Assistant Professor, Department of French Language and Literature, McGill University: LITERATURE—*Canadian Literature in French*

RICHARD, JOHN B., Department of Political Science, University of Wyoming: WYOMING

RICHMOND, ROBERT W., State Archivist, Kansas State Historical Society: KANSAS

ROMAN, JAMES R., JR., President, Lynn Machine and Tool Co.: TRANSPORTATION—*General Survey, Highways, Mass Transit*

ROSS, RUSSELL M., Professor of Political Science, University of Iowa: IOWA

ROWLETT, RALPH M., Associate Professor of Anthropology, University of Missouri—Columbia: ARCHAEOLOGY—*Eastern Hemisphere*

SADLER, LOUIS R., Associate Professor of History, New Mexico State University: CENTRAL AMERICA; CUBA

SALSINI, PAUL, State Editor, the Milwaukee *Journal:* WISCONSIN

SAVAGE, DAVID, Lecturer, Department of English, Simon Fraser University: LITERATURE—*Canadian Literature in English*

SAVORY, ROGER M., Professor of Islamic Studies, University of Toronto: THE NEW POWER IN THE MIDDLE EAST—*Persian Heritage*

SCHNEIDERMAN, RONALD A., New York Bureau Manager, *Electronics* Magazine (McGraw-Hill Publications Co.): TELECOMMUNICATIONS

SCHRATZ, PAUL R., Captain, USN (Ret.); Naval War College: MILITARY FORCES—*U. S. Developments*

SCHWAB, PETER, Associate Professor of Political Science, State University of New York at Purchase: ETHIOPIA; OBITUARIES—*Haile Selassie*

SETH, R. P., Chairman, Department of Economics, Mount Saint Vincent University, Halifax: NOVA SCOTIA

SEYMOUR, CHARLES, JR., Professor of the History of Art, Yale University: THE LEGACY OF MICHELANGELO

SHINN, RINN-SUP, Senior Research Scientist, The American University, Washington, D. C.: KOREA

SHOGAN, ROBERT, National Political Correspondent, Washington Bureau, *Los Angeles Times;* Author, *A Question of Judgment: The Fortas Case and the Struggle for the Supreme Court:* UNITED STATES—*Domestic Affairs*

SIMMONS, MARC, Author, *Spanish Government in New Mexico* and *The Little Lion of the Southwest:* NEW MEXICO

SIMS, JOHN F., Dance and Theater Critic, United Press International: DANCE

SINNEN, JEANNE, Senior Editor, University of Minnesota Press: MINNESOTA

SLOAN, HENRY S., Associate Editor, *Current Biography:* BIOGRAPHY (in part); OBITUARIES (in part)

SMOLLAR, DAVID, Staff Writer, The *Honolulu Advertiser:* HAWAII

SPEIRS, W. BRIAN, Territorial Archivist, Yukon Territory: YUKON TERRITORY

STEPHENS, GENE, Assistant to the Dean, School of Urban Life, Georgia State University: GEORGIA

STERN, JEROME H., Associate Professor of English, Florida State University: LITERATURE—*American Literature*

STOKES, W. LEE, Professor of Geology, University of Utah: GEOLOGY

STOUDEMIRE, ROBERT H., Director, Bureau of Governmental Research, University of South Carolina: SOUTH CAROLINA

SYLVESTER, LORNA LUTES, Associate Editor, *Indiana Magazine of History,* Indiana University: INDIANA

TABORSKY, EDWARD, Professor of Government, University of Texas at Austin: CZECHOSLOVAKIA

TAN, CHESTER C., Professor of History, New York University; Author, *The Boxer Catastrophe* and *Chinese Political Thought in the Twentieth Century:* CHINA

TAFT, WILLIAM HOWARD, Professor of Journalism, University of Missouri: PUBLISHING

THEISEN, CHARLES W., Staff Writer, The Detroit *News:* MICHIGAN

THOMAS, JAMES D., Professor of Political Science, Bureau of Public Administration, University of Alabama: ALABAMA

THOME, PITT G., Deputy Director for Earth Observations Flight Program, National Aeronautics and Space Administration: SPACE EXPLORATION

TIBBITTS, CLARK, Director, National Clearinghouse on Aging, Office of Human Development, Administration on Aging, Department of Health, Education, and Welfare: OLDER POPULATION

TRUMBLE, HAL, Executive Director, Amateur Hockey Association of the United States: HOCKEY FEVER—*The Boom on Ice, Kids on Skates*

TSUAN, T. H., The Royal Asiatic Society of Great Britain and Ireland, London: OBITUARIES—*Chiang Kai-shek*

TURNER, ARTHUR CAMPBELL, Professor of Political Science, University of California, Riverside: THE NEW POWER IN THE MIDDLE EAST—*Iran Today, The Shah and His Family;* IRAN; IRAQ; ISRAEL; MIDDLE EAST

VANDENBOSCH, AMRY, Professor Emeritus of Political Science, University of Kentucky: BELGIUM; INDONESIA; LUXEMBOURG; NETHERLANDS

WARGO, JAMES, Correspondent, McGraw-Hill *World News:* TRANSPORTATION—*Air Transportation, Shipping*

WEBB, RICHARD E., Former Director, Reference and Library Division, British Information Services, New York: UNITED NATIONS

WEEKS, JEANNE G., Associate, American Society of Interior Designers: INTERIOR DESIGN

WEISENBURGER, FRANCIS P., Professor Emeritus of History, The Ohio State University: OHIO

WELCH, CLAUDE E., JR., Professor of Political Science, State University of New York at Buffalo: GHANA

WENTZ, RICHARD E., Professor of Humanities, Coordinator of Religious Studies, Arizona State University: RELIGION—*General Survey, Far Eastern Religions in the U. S.*

WEST, RICHARD G., Former Senior Editor, *Encyclopedia Americana:* BIOGRAPHY—*Carla Hills;* MARIANA ISLANDS; NEW HAMPSHIRE

WESTERN, JOE, Senior Editor, *The National Observer:* AGRICULTURE—*World Agriculture, U. S. Agriculture*

WHITE, JOHN P., Professor of Political Science, Arizona State University: ARIZONA

WHITMAN, ALDEN, Chief Obituary Writer, *The New York Times:* OBITUARIES—*Francisco Franco*

WILLARD, F. NICHOLAS, Department of History, Georgetown University: JORDAN; LEBANON; SYRIA

WILLIS, F. ROY, Professor of History, University of California, Davis: EUROPE

WILLNOW, RONALD D., News Editor, St. Louis *Post-Dispatch:* MISSOURI

WILSON, JOHN S., Jazz Critic, *The New York Times* and *High Fidelity* Magazine; Author, *Jazz: The Transition Years—1940–1960:* RECORDINGS—*Jazz*

WOLF, WILLIAM, Film Critic, *Cue* Magazine; Former Chairman, New York Film Critics; Lecturer, New York University and St. John's University: MOTION PICTURES

WOODS, GEORGE A., Children's Books Editor, *The New York Times:* LITERATURE—*Children's Literature*

WOODWARD, WARREN S., Executive Secretary, National Society of the Sons of the American Revolution: THE BICENTENNIAL OF THE UNITED STATES

YOUNGER, R. M., Author, *The Changing World of Australia; Australia and the Australians:* AUSTRALIA; OCEANIA

ZABEL, ORVILLE H., Professor of History, Creighton University: BIOGRAPHY—*Ronald Reagan, George C. Wallace:* NEBRASKA

ZACEK, JOSEPH F., Professor and Chairman of History, State University of New York at Albany: RUMANIA

A

Main article headings appear in this index as bold-faced capitals; subjects within articles appear as lower-case entries. Main article page numbers and general references are listed first under each entry; the subentries which follow them on separate lines direct the reader to related topics appearing elsewhere. Both the general references and the subentries should be consulted for maximum usefulness of this index. Illustrations are indexed herein. Cross references are to the entries in this index.